ECONOMICS FOR BUSINESS

Pearson

At Pearson, we have a simple mission: to help people make more of their lives through learning.

We combine innovative learning technology with trusted content and educational expertise to provide engaging and effective learning experiences that serve people wherever and whenever they are learning.

From classroom to boardroom, our curriculum materials, digital learning tools and testing programmes help to educate millions of people worldwide – more than any other private enterprise.

Every day our work helps learning flourish, and wherever learning flourishes, so do people.

To learn more, please visit us at **www.pearson.com/uk**

ECONOMICS FOR BUSINESS

Eighth edition

John Sloman

The Economics Network, University of Bristol
Visiting Professor, University of the West of England

Dean Garratt

Aston Business School

Jon Guest

Aston Business School

Elizabeth Jones

University of Warwick

Pearson

Harlow, England • London • New York • Boston • San Francisco • Toronto • Sydney
Dubai • Singapore • Hong Kong • Tokyo • Seoul • Taipei • New Delhi
Cape Town • São Paulo • Mexico City • Madrid • Amsterdam • Munich • Paris • Milan

PEARSON EDUCATION LIMITED
KAO Two
KAO Park
Harlow CM17 9NA
United Kingdom
Tel: +44 (0)1279 623623
Web: www.pearson.com/uk

First published by Prentice Hall 1998 (print)
Second edition published 2001 (print)
Third edition published 2004 (print)
Fourth edition published 2007 (print)
Fifth edition published 2010 (print)
Sixth edition published 2013 (print and electronic)
Seventh edition published 2016 (print and electronic)
Eighth edition published 2019 (print and electronic)

ISBN: 978–1–292–23927–9 (print)
       978–1–292–23929–3 (PDF)
       978–1–292–23932–3 (ePub)

British Library Cataloguing-in-Publication Data
A catalogue record for the print edition is available from the British Library

Library of Congress Cataloguing-in-Publication Data
Names: Sloman, John, 1947- author.
Title: Economics for business / John Sloman, the Economics Network,
   University of Bristol, Visiting Professor, University of the West of
   England, Dean Garratt, Aston Business School, Jon Guest, Aston
   Business School, Elizabeth Jones, University of Warwick.
Description: Eighth edition. | Harlow, England ; London ; New York : Pearson,
   2019.
Identifiers: LCCN 2018051734| ISBN 9781292239279 (print) | ISBN 9781292239293
   (pdf) | ISBN 9781292239323 (epub)
Subjects: LCSH: Economics. | Business. | Managerial economics.
Classification: LCC HB171.5 .S6353 2019 | DDC 330—dc23
LC record available at https://urldefense.proofpoint.com/v2/url?u=https-3A__lccn.loc.
gov_2018051734&d=DwIFAg&c=0YLnzTkWOdJlub_y7qAx8Q&r=UgkiZZrrEyeXQ5q2nOZp4K37
ruImTqfxO7fR5jNxstQ&m=WpoVvGJn0nMdqbFFwlYOuaCtwksREiI_E49k7EFMnGA&s=
SPwdI3N9RkU3iMYLURWiKrxdkDg6K1n5OhTfYlYdzNE&e=

10 9 8 7 6 5 4 3 2 1
23 22 21 20 19

All Part and Chapter opener images © John Sloman

Print edition typeset in 8/12pt Stone Serif ITC Pro by Pearson CSC
Print edition printed and bound by L.E.G.O. S.p.A., Italy

NOTE THAT ANY PAGE CROSS REFERENCES REFER TO THE PRINT EDITION

About the authors

John Sloman was Director of the Economics Network (www.economicsnetwork.ac.uk) from 1999 to 2012. The Economics Network is a UK-wide organisation based at the University of Bristol and provides a range of services designed to promote and share good practice in learning and teaching Economics. John is now a Visiting Fellow at Bristol and a Senior Associate with the Economics Network.

John is also Visiting Professor at the University of the West of England (UWE), Bristol, where, from 1992 to 1999, he was Head of School of Economics. He taught at UWE until 2007. John has taught a range of courses, including economic principles on social science and business studies degrees, development economics, comparative economic systems, intermediate macroeconomics and managerial economics. He has also taught economics on various professional courses.

He is also the co-author with Alison Wride and Dean Garratt of *Economics* (Pearson Education, 10th edition 2018), with Dean Garratt of *Essentials of Economics* (Pearson Education, 8th edition 2019) and with Elizabeth Jones of *Essential Economics for Business* (5th edition 2017). Translations or editions of the various books are available for a number of different countries with the help of co-authors around the world.

John is very interested in promoting new methods of teaching economics, including group exercises, experiments, role playing, computer-aided learning and the use of audience response systems and podcasting in teaching. He has organised and spoken at conferences for both lecturers and students of economics throughout the UK and in many other countries.

As part of his work with the Economics Network he has contributed to its two sites for students and prospective students of economics: Studying Economics (www.studyingeconomics.ac.uk) and Why Study Economics? (www.whystudyeconomics.ac.uk)

From March to June 1997, John was a visiting lecturer at the University of Western Australia. In July and August 2000, he was again a visiting lecturer at the University of Western Australia and also at Murdoch University in Perth. In 2007, John received a Lifetime Achievement Award as 'outstanding teacher and ambassador of economics' presented jointly by the Higher Education Academy, the Government Economic Service and the Scottish Economic Society.

Dr Dean Garratt is a Senior Teaching Fellow at Aston Business School. He joined Aston University in September 2018 having previously been a Principal Lecturer at Nottingham Business School. Dean teaches economics at a variety of levels, including modules in macroeconomics and economic principles for business and management students. He is passionate about encouraging students to communicate economics more intuitively, to deepen their interest in economics and to apply economics to a range of issues.

Earlier in his career Dean worked as an economic assistant at both HM Treasury and at the Council of Mortgage Lenders. While at these institutions he was researching and briefing on a variety of issues relating to the household sector and to the housing and mortgage markets.

Dean is a Senior Fellow of the Higher Education Academy and an Associate of the Economics Network which aims to promote high-quality teaching practice. He has been involved in several projects promoting a problem-based learning (PBL) approach in the teaching of economics. In 2006, Dean was awarded the Outstanding Teaching Prize by the Economics Network. The award recognises exemplary teaching practice that deepens and inspires interest in economics. In 2013, he won the student-nominated Nottingham Business School teacher of the year award.

Dean is an academic assessor for the Government Economic Service (GES) helping to assess candidates at Economic Assessment Centres (EACs). In this role he assesses candidates looking to join the GES, the UK's largest employer of professional economists.

Dean runs sessions on HM Treasury's Graduate Development Programme (GDP). These sessions cover principles in policy making, applying economics principles and ideas to analyse policy issues and contemporary developments in macroeconomics.

Outside of work, Dean is an avid watcher of many sports. Having been born in Leicester, he is a season ticket holder at both Leicester City Football Club and Leicestershire County Cricket Club.

Jon Guest

Jon is a Senior Teaching Fellow at Aston Business School and a Teaching Associate at Warwick Business School. He joined Aston University in September 2017 having previously been a Senior Lecturer at Nottingham Business School, a Principal Teaching Fellow at Warwick Business School and a Senior Lecturer Coventry University.

Jon has taught on a range of courses including Principles of Microeconomics, Intermediate Microeconomics, Economic Issues and Behavioural Economics. He has also taught economics on various professional courses for the Government Economic Service and HM-Treasury.

Jon has worked on developing teaching methods that promote a more active learning environment in the classroom. In particular, he has published journal articles and carried out a number of funded research projects on the impact of games and experiments on student learning. These include an on-line version of the TV show 'Deal or No Deal' and games that involve students acting as buyers and sellers in the classroom. He has also recently included a series of short videos on economics topics and implemented elements of the flipped classroom into his teaching.

Jon is also interested in innovative ways of providing students with feedback on their work.

Through his work as an Associate of the Economics Network, Jon has run sessions on innovative pedagogic practices at a number of universities and major national events. He is also an academic assessor for the Economics Assessment Centres run by the Government Economic Service. This involves interviewing candidates and evaluating their ability to apply economic reasoning to a range of policy issues. He has also acted as an External Examiner for a number of UK universities.

The quality of his teaching was formally recognised when he became the first Government Economic Service Approved Tutor in 2005 and won the student nominated award from the Economics Network in the same year. Jon was awarded the prestigious National Teaching Fellowship by the Higher Education Academy in 2011.

Jon is a regular contributor and editor of the Economic Review and is a co-author of the 10th edition of the textbook, Economics. He has published chapters in books on the Economics of Sport and regularly writes cases for the 'Sloman in the News' website. He has also published research on the self-evaluation skills of undergraduate students.

Outside of work Jon is a keen runner and has completed the London Marathon. However, he now has to accept that he is slower than both of his teenage sons – Dan and Tom. He is also a long suffering supporter of Portsmouth Football Club.

Elizabeth Jones is a Professor in the Department of Economics at the University of Warwick. She joined the University of Warwick in 2012 and was the Deputy Director of Undergraduate Studies for 2 years. Since 2014, she has been the Director of Undergraduate Studies, with overall responsibility for all Undergraduate Degree programmes within the Economics Department. She is a Founding and now Alumni Fellow of the Warwick International Higher Education Academy and through this, she has been involved in developing and sharing best practice in teaching and learning within Higher Education. She was the external panellist for the curriculum review at the London School of Economics, advising on content, delivery and assessment.

She has previously co-ordinated and taught at the Warwick Economics Summer School and has also been involved in delivering the Warwick Economics Summer School in New Delhi, India. Within this, Elizabeth was delivering introductory courses in Economics to 16-18 year olds and has also delivered taster events to schools in Asia about studying Economics at University.

Prior to being at Warwick, Elizabeth was a Lecturer at the University of Exeter within the Business School and was in this position for 5 years, following the completion of her MSc in Economics. She also taught A level Economics and Business

Studies at Exeter Tutorial College and continues to work as an Examiner in Economics for AQA. She is also a member of the OCR Consultative Forum and has previously been involved in reviewing A level syllabi for the main Examining bodies.

Elizabeth has taught a range of courses including Principles of Economics; Economics for Business; Intermediate Microeconomics; Economics of Social Policy; Economics of Education and Applied Economics. She has won multiple student-nominated awards for teaching at Warwick and Exeter University, winning the Best Lecturer prize at the 2017 Warwick Awards for Teaching Excellence. , where she used her prize money to invest in her development as a teacher at a conference in Boston. She has a passion for teaching Economics and particularly enjoys teaching Economics to non-economists and loves interacting with students both inside and outside of the classroom.

Elizabeth has taught on a number of professional courses, with EML Learning Ltd, where she teaches Economics for Non-economists and Intermediate Microeconomics to the public sector. She has delivered courses across all government Departments, including BIS, Department for Transport, HM-Treasury and the Department for Health. She is involved in teaching on the Graduate Development Programme for the new intake of HM Treasury employees twice each year, where she delivers sessions on economics, the role of policy and its implementation.

Outside of work, Elizabeth loves any and all sports. She is an avid fan of Formula 1 and tennis and provides ongoing support to her father's beloved Kilmarnock FC.

Brief contents

Detailed contents

Part K MACROECONOMIC POLICY

Preface

TO THE STUDENT

If you are studying economics on a business degree or diploma, then this book is written for you. Although we cover all the major principles of economics, the focus throughout is on the world of business. For this reason, we also cover several topics that do not appear in traditional economics textbooks.

As well as making considerable use of business examples throughout the text, we have included many case studies (in boxes). These illustrate how economics can be used to understand particular business problems or aspects of the business environment. Many of these case studies cover issues that you are likely to read about in the newspapers. Some cover general business issues; others look at specific companies. Nearly all of them cover topical issues, including the rise of online business, the video gaming market, entrepreneurship, the social responsibility of business, the effects of business activity on the environment, competition and growth strategy, mergers and takeovers, executive pay, the banking crisis of the late 2000s, the sluggish recovery from recession, quantitative easing, the role of global trade, increased competition from newly industrialised countries and the effects of Brexit.

The style of writing is direct and straightforward, with short paragraphs to aid rapid comprehension. There are also questions interspersed throughout the text in 'Pause for thought' panels. These encourage you to reflect on what you are learning and to see how the various ideas and theories relate to different issues. Definitions of all key terms are given in definition boxes, with defined terms appearing in bold. Also, we have highlighted 44 'Key ideas', which are fundamental to 'thinking like an economist'. We refer back to these every time they recur in the book. This helps you to see how the subject ties together, and also helps you to develop a toolkit of concepts that can be used in a host of different contexts.

Summaries are given at the end of each chapter, with points numbered according to the section in which they appear. These summaries should help you in reviewing the material you have covered and in revising for exams. Each chapter finishes with a series of questions. These can be used to check your understanding of the chapter and help you to see how its material can be applied to various business problems. References to various useful websites are listed at the end of each Part of the book.

The book also has a blog, *The Sloman Economics News Site,* with frequent postings by the authors. The blog discusses topical issues, links to relevant articles, videos and data and asks questions for you to think about.

There is also an open-access student website. This companion website contains 154 additional case studies, answers to 'Pause for thought' questions, animations of key models in the book with audio explanations suitable for playing on a smart phone, tablet or computer, a set of videoed interviews with business people about decision making and the relevance of economics to their businesses, hotlinks to 285 websites, plus other materials to improve your understanding of concepts and techniques used in economics.

We hope that, in using this book, you will share some of our fascination for economics. It is a subject that is highly relevant to the world in which we live. And it is a world where many of our needs are served by business – whether as employers or as producers of the goods and services we buy. After graduating, you will probably take up employment in business. A thorough grounding in economic principles should prove invaluable in the business decisions you may well have to make.

TO LECTURERS AND TUTORS

The aim of this book is to provide a course in economic principles as they apply to the business environment. It is designed to be used by first-year undergraduates on business studies degrees and diplomas where economics is taught from the business perspective. It is also suitable for students studying economics on postgraduate courses in management, including the MBA, and various professional courses.

Being essentially a book on economics, we cover all the major topics found in standard economics texts – indeed, some of the material in the principle sections is drawn directly from *Economics* (10th edition). But, in addition, there are several specialist business chapters and sections to build upon and enliven the subject for business studies students. These have been fully updated and revised for this new edition. The following are some examples of these additional topics:

- The business environment
- Business organisations
- Characteristics theory
- Consumer behaviour and behavioural economics
- Advertising and marketing of products
- Business strategy
- Alternative aims of firms
- Behavioural analysis of firms
- Growth strategy
- Strategic alliances and various other forms of co-operation between firms
- The small-firm sector
- Pricing in practice, including topics such as mark-up pricing, an extended analysis of first-, second- and third-degree price discrimination in various contexts, multiple product pricing, transfer pricing and pricing over the product life cycle
- Government and the firm, including policies towards research and development (R&D) and policies towards training
- Government and the market, including environmental policy and transport policy
- Financial markets and the funding of business investment
- The financial well-being of firms, households and governments and its impact on the business environment
- The multinational corporation
- Globalisation and business
- Trading blocs and their development
- Monetary union, the future of the Eurozone and implications for business
- The impact of Brexit on business

The text is split into 32 chapters. Each chapter is kept relatively short to enable the material to be covered in a single lecture or class. Each chapter finishes with a summary and review questions, which can be used for seminars or discussion sessions.

The chapters are grouped into 11 Parts:

- Part A Business and economics (Chapters 1–3) establishes the place of business within the economy and the relevance of economics to business decision making.
- Part B Business and markets (Chapters 4 and 5) looks at the operation of markets. It covers supply and demand analysis and examines the importance of the concept of elasticity for business decisions.
- Part C Background to demand (Chapters 6–8) considers the consumer – how consumer behaviour can be predicted and how, via advertising and marketing, consumer demand can be influenced.
- Part D Background to supply (Chapters 9 and 10) focuses on the relationship between the quantity that businesses produce and their costs, revenue and profits.
- Part E Supply: short-run decision making by firms (Chapters 11–13) presents the traditional analysis of market structures and the implications that such structures have for business conduct and performance. Part E finishes (Chapter 13) by considering various alternative theories of the firm to that of short-run profit maximisation.
- Part F Supply: alternative strategies (Chapters 14–17) starts by looking at business strategy. It also examines how businesses attempt to grow and how size can influence business actions. It finishes by considering why pricing strategies differ from one firm to another and how these strategies are influenced by the market conditions in which firms operate.
- Part G The firm in the factor market (Chapters 18 and 19) focuses on the market for labour and the market for capital. It examines what determines the factor proportions that firms use and how factor prices are determined.
- Part H The relationship between government and business (Chapters 20–22) establishes the theoretical rationale behind government intervention in the economy, and then assesses the relationship between the government and the individual firm and the government and the market.
- Part I Business in the international environment (Chapters 23–25) starts by examining the process of globalisation and the growth of the multinational business. It then turns to international trade and the benefits that accrue from it. It also examines the issue of protection and international moves to advance free trade. Finally, it examines the expansion of regional trading agreements.
- Part J The macroeconomic environment (Chapters 26–29) considers the macroeconomic framework in which

firms operate. We focus on the principal macroeconomic variables, investigate the role of money in the economy, and briefly outline the theoretical models underpinning the relationships between these variables.

- Part K Macroeconomic policy (Chapters 30–32) examines the mechanics of government intervention at a macro level as well as its impact on business and its potential benefits and drawbacks. Demand-side and supply-side policy and economic policy co-ordination between countries are all considered.

Extensive revision

As with previous editions, the eighth edition of *Economics for Business* contains a great deal of applied material. Consequently, there have been considerable revisions from the previous editions to reflect contemporary issues, debates and policy interventions. Specifically, you will find that:

- many of the boxes are new or extensively revised;
- there are many new examples given in the text;
- all tables and charts have been updated, as have factual references in the text;

- economic analysis and debate has been strengthened and revised at various points in the book in the light of economic events and developments in economic thinking;
- building on the revisions in previous editions, we have enhanced further our discussion around behavioural economics. In particular, we have expanded our treatment of consumer demand in a new chapter (Chapter 7). This has allowed us to explore in more detail the traditional economics treatment of the 'rational consumer' alongside insights from behavioural economics;
- we have extended the analysis throughout the book on the issues of globalisation and financialisation;
- the text provides extensive coverage of the recent developments in money and banking and their impact on the economy;
- all policy sections have been thoroughly revised to reflect the changes that have taken place since the last edition. This includes an analysis of the implications of the Brexit vote and also of the Trump administration's policies in several parts of the book;
- most importantly, every part of the book has been carefully considered and, if necessary, redrafted, to ensure both maximum clarity and contemporary relevance.

SPECIAL FEATURES

The book contains the following special features:

- A direct and straightforward written style, with short paragraphs to aid rapid comprehension. The constant aim is to provide maximum clarity.
- Attractive full-colour design. The careful and consistent use of colour and shading makes the text more attractive to students and easier to use by giving clear signals as to the book's structure.
- Double-page opening spreads for each of the 11 Parts of the book. These contain an introduction to the material covered and an article from the *Financial Times* on one of the topics.
- Key ideas highlighted and explained where they first appear. There are 44 of these ideas, which are fundamental to the study of economics. Students can see them recurring throughout the book, and an icon appears in the margin to refer back to the page where the idea first appears. Showing how ideas can be used in a variety of contexts helps students to 'think like an economist' and to relate the different parts of the subject. All 44 Key ideas are defined in a special section at the end of the book.
- 'Pause for thought' questions integrated throughout the text. These encourage students to reflect on what they have just read and make the learning process a more

active one. Answers to these questions appear on the student website.

- Highlighted technical terms, all of which are clearly defined in definition panels on the page on which they appear. This feature has proved very popular in previous editions and is especially useful for students when revising.
- A comprehensive glossary of all technical terms.
- Additional applied material can be found in the boxes within each chapter. The extensive use of applied material makes learning much more interesting for students and helps to bring the subject alive. This is particularly important for business students who need to relate economic theory to their other subjects and to the world of business generally. The boxes are current and include discussion of a range of companies and business topics. They are ideal for use as case studies in class. Answers to the questions in boxes can be found on the lecturer website, which lecturers can make available to students, if they choose.
- Boxes containing questions allowing students to assess their own understanding. New to this edition, each box contains an activity designed to develop important skills around research, data analysis and the communication of economic ideas and principles. These skills are not

only of use to students while at university but also in the world of work. They are frequently identified by employers as being especially valuable. Hence, undertaking the activities in the boxes helps students to increase their employability.

■ Additional case studies with questions appearing on the student website are referred to at the end of each Part. Again, they can be used for class, with answers available on the lecturer website, which can be distributed to students, if lecturers choose to do so.

■ Detailed summaries appear at the end of each chapter with the points numbered by the chapter section in which they are made. These allow students not only to check their comprehension of the chapter's contents, but also to get a clear overview of the material they have been studying.

■ A series of review questions concluding each chapter to test students' understanding of the chapter's salient points. These questions can be used for seminars or as set work to be completed in the students' own time. Again, answers are available on the lecturer website.

■ References at the end of each Part to a list of relevant websites, details of which can be found in the Web appendix at the end of the book. You can access any of these sites easily from the book's own website (at www.pearsonblog.campaignserver.co.uk/). When you enter the site, click on 'Hotlinks'. You will find all the sites from the Web appendix listed. Click on the one you want and the 'hotlink' will take you straight to it.

■ A comprehensive index, including reference to all defined terms. This enables students to look up a definition as required and to see it used in context.

SUPPLEMENTS

Blog

Visit the book's blog, The *Sloman Economics News Site,* at www.pearsonblog.campaignserver.co.uk/. This refers to topical issues in economics and relates them to particular chapters in the book. There are frequent postings by the authors, with each one providing an introduction to the topic, and then links to relevant articles, videos, podcasts, data and official documents, and then questions which students and lecturers will find relevant for homework or class discussion.

Student website

There is an open-access companion website for students with a large range of other resources, including:

■ animations of key models with audio explanations. These 'audio animations' can be watched online or downloaded to a computer, MP4 player, smart phone, etc;

■ links to the *Sloman Economics News Site* blog, chapter by chapter, with news items added several times each month, with introductions, links to newspaper and other articles and to relevant data, questions for use in class or for private study, and references to chapters in the book. You can search the extensive archive by chapter or keyword;

■ 154 case studies with questions for self-study, ordered Part-by-Part and referred to in the text;

■ updated list of 285 hotlinks to sites of use for economics;

■ answers to all in-chapter (Pause for thought) questions;

■ videoed interviews with a number of business people, where they discuss business decision making and the relevance of economic concepts to them.

Additional resources for lecturers and tutors

There are many additional resources for lecturers and tutors that can be downloaded from the Lecturer Resources section of the book's website at www.pearsoned.co.uk/sloman. These have been thoroughly revised for the eighth edition. These include:

■ PowerPoint® slide shows in full colour for use with a data projector in lectures and classes. These can also be made available to students by loading them on to a local network. There are several types of slideshows:
  – *All figures from the book and most of the tables.* Each figure is built up in a logical sequence, thereby allowing lecturers to show them in lectures in an animated form. There is also a non-animated version suitable for printing or for display on an OHP or visualiser.
  – *Customisable lecture slideshows.* There is one for each chapter of the book. Each one can be easily edited, with points added, deleted or moved, so as to suit particular lectures. A consistent use of colour is made to show how the points tie together. It is not intended that all the material is covered in a single lecture; you can break at any point. It is just convenient to organise them by chapter. They come in various versions:
    • Lecture slideshows with integrated diagrams. These include animated diagrams, charts and tables at the appropriate points.
    • Lecture slideshows with integrated diagrams and questions. These are like the above but also include multiple-choice questions, allowing lectures to become more interactive. They can be used with or without an audience response system (ARS).

A special ARS version is available for TurningPoint® and is ready to use with appropriate 'clickers' or with smartphones, tablets or laptops.

- Lecture plans without the diagrams. These allow you to construct your own diagrams on the blackboard, whiteboard or visualiser or to use pre-prepared ones on a visualiser or OHP.

■ Case studies. These, also available on the student companion website, can be reproduced and used for classroom exercises or for student assignments. Answers are also provided (not available on the student site).

■ Workshops. There are 24 of these, each one covering one or more chapters. They are in Word® and can be reproduced for use with large groups (up to 200 students) in a lecture theatre or large classroom. Suggestions for use are given in an accompanying file. Answers to all workshops are given in separate Word® files.

■ Teaching/learning case studies. There are 20 of these. They examine various approaches to teaching introductory economics and ways to improve student learning of introductory economics.

■ Answers to all end-of-chapter questions, Pause for thought questions, questions in boxes, questions in the case studies on the student website and to the 24 workshops. They have been completely revised with new hyperlinks where appropriate.

The following two pages show in diagrammatic form all the student and lecturer resources.

ACKNOWLEDGEMENTS

As with previous editions, we've had great support from the team at Pearson, including Catherine Yates, Carole Drummond and Natalia Jaszczuk. We'd like to thank all of them for their hard work and encouragement. Thanks, too, to the many users of the book who have given us feedback. We always value their comments. Please continue to send us your views.

Kevin Hinde and Mark Sutcliffe, co-authors with John on previous editions, have moved on to new ventures. However, many of their wise words and ideas are still embedded in this eighth edition and, for that, we once more offer a huge thank you.

Our families have also been remarkably tolerant and supportive throughout the writing of this new edition. Thanks especially to Alison, Pat, Helen, Elizabeth, Douglas and Harriet, who all seem to have perfected a subtle blend of encouragement, humour, patience and tolerance.

John, Dean, Elizabeth and Jon

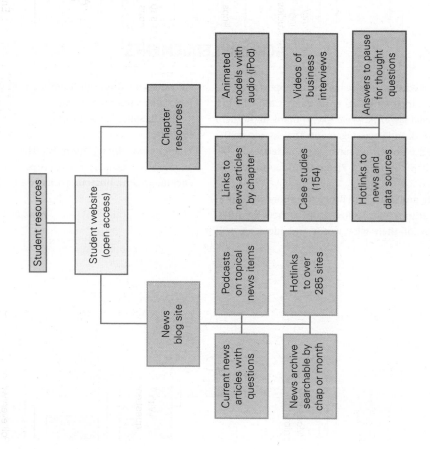

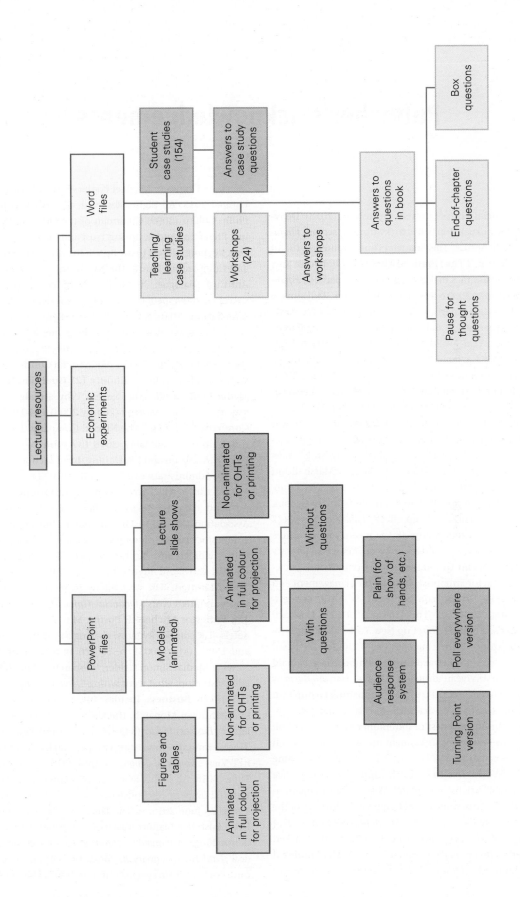

Publisher's acknowledgements

Text

2 The Financial Times Limited: Cornish, C. (2018) 'Deliveroo's speedy expansion belies tricky time for sector', *Financial Times,* 30 April. © The Financial Times Limited 2018. All Rights Reserved. **3 The Financial Times Limited:** John Kay, 'Everyday economics makes for good fun at parties', *Financial Times,* 2 May 2006 **6 BBC:** Jamie Robertson, 'Lidl aims to shake off budget image with London stores'; BBC News (10 September 2015) **6 Lidl:** https://www.lidl.co.uk/en/Grocer-of-the-Year-Award-3488.htm **9 Independent Digital News & Media:** James Thompson, 'Lidl and Aldi see sales soar amid economic downturn', *Independent* (24 June 2008) **34 The Financial Times Limited:** How paying chief executives less can help corporate performance Feb 12, 2017 © The Financial Times Limited. **34 Independent Digital News & Media:** Zlata Rodionova, 'Link between high executive pay and performance "negligible", study finds'; *Independent* (28 December 2016) **35 MSCI Inc.:** Ric Marshall and Linda-Eling Lee, Are CEOs paid for performance, MSCI (July 2016) **35 The Financial Times Limited:** Brian Groom, 'Executive pay: The trickle-up effect', *Financial Times* (27 July 2011) **35 Reuters:** Many UK CEOs earn more in three days than a typical worker does in a year', Reuters (3 January 2018) **38 European Union:** European Commission, Directorate-General for Enterprise, Innovation Management and the Knowledge-Driven Economy (ECSC-EC-EAEC Brussels-Luxembourg, 2004). **42 The Financial Times Limited:** 'Computerised trading drives up New York cocoa price' By Emiko Terazono © The Financial Times Limited 2018. All Rights Reserved. **43 Harvard Business Publishing:** Donald Sull, 'How to survive in turbulent markets', *Harvard Business Review,* February 2009, p. 80 **61 BMJ Publishing Group Ltd:** Sadie Boniface, Jack W. Scannell and Sally Marlow, 'Evidence for the effectiveness of minimum pricing of alcohol: a systematic review and assessment using the Bradford Hill Criteria for causality, *BMJ Journal,* Volume 7, Issue 5 (6 June 2017) **71 World Health Organization:** Estimating Price and Income Elasticity of Demand, World Health Organisation (2015) **80 Investopedia, LLC:** Elvis Picardo, 'Five of the largest asset bubbles in history'; *Investopedia* (23 June 2015) **81 Telegraph Media Group Limited :** 'Bitcoin price tracker: live chart'; *The Telegraph* (6 March 2018) **86 The Financial Times Limited :** 'Online shopping boom leads to record increase in vans' By Michael Pooler © The Financial Times Limited 2015. All Rights Reserved. **87 Crown copyright:** Philip Collins (2009) Chairman of the Office of Fair Trading, Preserving and Restoring Trust and Confidence in Markets. Keynote address to the British Institute of International and Comparative Law at the Ninth Annual Trans-Atlantic Antitrust Dialogue, 30 April, www.oft.gov.uk/shared_oft/speeches/2009/spe0809.pdf **117 American Marketing Association:** Brian Wasink, Robert J. Kent and Stephen J. Hoch, 'An anchoring and adjustment model of purchase quantity decisions', *Journal of Marketing Research,* vol. 35 (February 1998), pp. 71–81 **119 Financial Conduct Authority:** Financial Conduct Authority **122 Guardian News and Media Limited:** Richard Reeves, 'Why a nudge from the state beats a slap', *Observer* (20 July 2008) **134 The Nielsen Company (US), LLC.:** The Nilesen Company, The rise and rise again of private label, 2018 **137 John Wiley & Sons:** From H.A. Lipson and J.R. Darling, Introduction to Marketing: An Administrative Approach (John Wiley & Sons, Inc., 1971). **138 WARC/Advertising Association:** Based on Adspend database takeaway tables (WARC/Advertising Association, 2018) **144 The Financial Times Limited:** 'US airline stocks tumble after warnings of higher fuel costs' By Patti Waldmeir and Pan Kwan Yuk © The Financial Times Limited 2018. All Rights Reserved. **145 The Financial Times Limited:** 'UK steel hit by perfect storm of falling prices and high costs', *Financial Times,* 29 September 2015 **158 Professor Michael E Porter:** M.E. Porter and C.H.M. Ketels, 'UK competitiveness: moving to the next stage, DTI and ESRC' (May 2003), p. 5. **176 Independent Digital News & Media:** Simon Calder, 'Monarch airlines goes into administration: what went wrong?', *Independent* (1 October 2017) **176 Business Insider Inc.:** Will Martin, 'What brought down Monarch, the UK's biggest ever airline collapse?', *Business Insider* (3 October 2017) **180 The Financial Times Limited:** 'Eliminating competition in order to protect itFT View', *Financial Times,* 30 April 2018, © The Financial Times 2018. All Rights Reserved. **181 The Financial Times Limited:** 'Supermarket price war moves upmarket', *Financial Times,* 25 June 2015. © The Financial Times Limited. **186 Latin Post:** K. J. Mariño, 'Fast food competition intensifies as Burger King, McDonald's, Wendy's fight for cheapest meal deal', *Latin Post* (5 January 2016) **187 BBC:** Bryan Lufkin, 'How can a fast food chain ever make money from a $1 burger?', BBC

Capital (23 February 2018) **187 BBC:** Bryan Lufkin, 'How can a fast food chain ever make money from a $1 burger?', BBC Capital (23 February 2018) **198 The Financial Times Limited:** Murad Ahmed, 'Camelot overhauls Lottery as ticket sales fall', *Financial Times,* 21 November 2017 **6 Organization of the Petroleum Exporting Countries:** OPEC **212 Ofgem:** 'Ofgem refers the energy market for a full competition investigation', *Press Release,* Ofgem (26 June 2014) **212 Crown copyright:** Energy Market Investigation: Summary of Final Report, Competition and Markets Authority (24 June 2016, updated 27 February 2018) **213 Crown copyright:** Energy Market Investigation: Summary of Final Report, op. cit. **214 BBC:** https://www.bbc.com/news/business-35408064 **219 Cengage Learning:** Thomas J. Nechyba, Microeconomics: an Intuitive Approach with Calculus, Cengage (2010) **240 The Financial Times Limited:** 'Industrial giants caught in LED headlights' By Chris Bryant, 2015 © The Financial Times Limited 2015. All Rights Reserved. **272 Operations Buzz:** Ram Ganeshan, 'The iPhone 4 Supply Chain' Operations Buzz (28 November 2010) **274 Telegraph Media Group Limited:** 'Why Northern Rock was doomed to fail', *Daily Telegraph* (17 September 2007) **297 University of Pennsylvania:** J.Turow, L. Feldman and K Meltzer, 'Open to exploitation: America's shoppers on-line and off-line', Departmental Papers, Annenberg Public Policy Center of the University of Pennsylvania (June 2005) **312 The Financial Times Limited:** German employers forced to reveal gender pay gap By Tobias Buck © The Financial Times Limited 2018. All Rights Reserved. **313 The Financial Times Limited:** 'Zero-hours contracts hold their place in UK labour market', *Financial Times,* 2 September 2015 **331 Crown copyright:** Universal Credit: Welfare that works, DWP **325 Guardian News and Media Limited:** Sally Weale, 'Students demand compensation from universities over lecturer strikes', *Guardian,* 7 February 2018 **337 Chartered Institute of Personnel and Development:** 'Selection methods', CIPD Factsheet, Chartered Institute of Personnel and Development (2018) **355 Offshore Wind Journal:** David Foxwell , 'UK offshore wind on track to 2020 target', *Offshore Wind Journal* (17 April 2018) **362 The Financial Times Limited:** 'Global fines for price-fixing hit $5.3bn record high' By Caroline Binham, Legal Correspondent © The Financial Times Limited 2015. **363 European Union:** Neelie Kroes, European Commission Competition Commissioner, 'Competition, the crisis and the road to recovery', Address at the Economic Club of Toronto, 30 March 2009 **375 The Economist Newspaper Limited:** 'Commons Sense', *The Economist,* 31 July 2008. **375 The Economist Newspaper Limited:** 'Commons Sense', *The Economist,* 31 July 2008. **375 The Economist Newspaper Limited:** 'Commons Sense', *The Economist,* 31 July 2008. **375 Australian Indigenous cultural heritage:** Australian Indigenous cultural heritage (https://www.australia.gov.au/information-and-services/culture-and-arts/indigenous-culture-and-history) **383 Microsoft:** Brad Smith, 'Greener datacenters for a brighter future: Microsoft's commitment to renewable energy', Microsoft on the Issues blog (19/5/2016) **387 Startups:** Anita Roddick interview, Startups.co.uk **387 Guardian News and Media Limited:** L'Oréal to sell Body Shop to Brazil's Natura in €1bn deal **404 Crown copyright:** David Sainsbury et al., Report of the Independent Panel on Technical Education, GOV.UK (April 2016) **412 Världsnaturfonden WWF:** Stern Review on the Economics of Climate Change, Executive Summary, HM Treasury (2006). **413 United Nations:** IPCC Report: 'severe and pervasive' impacts of climate change will be felt everywhere' UN and Climate Change, United Nations (31 March 2014) **440 The Financial Times Limited:** The G7 consists of Canada, France, Germany, Italy, Japan, the United Kingdom, and the United States© The Financial Times Limited 2018. All Rights Reserved. **441 Holtzbrinck Publishing Group:** Torsten Riecke and Jens Münchrath, 'It's time to rewind', Handelsblatt Global, 19 August 2016, **444 Lagardère Group:** P. Legrain, Open World: The Truth about Globalisation (Abacus, 2003). **444 Organisation for Economic Co-operation and Development:** A. Gurria, Managing globalisation and the role of the OECD (OECD, 2006). **444 International Monetary Fund:** IMF staff, Globalization: A Brief Overview (OECD, 2008). **445 G. Yip:** G. Yip, Total Global Strategy (Prentice Hall, 1995) **460 Guardian News and Media Limited:** Prem Sikka, 'Shifting profits across borders', *The Guardian,* 12 February 2009 **463 Bloomberg:** 'Tesco stumbles with Wal-Mart as China shoppers buy local', Bloomberg (19 October 2012) (available at http://www.bloomberg.com/news/articles/2012-10-18/tesco-stumbles-with-wal-mart-as-china-shoppers-buy-local) **463 Bloomberg:** 'Tesco stumbles with Wal-Mart as China shoppers buy local', Bloomberg (19 October 2012) (available at http://www.bloomberg.com/news/articles/2012-10-18/tesco-stumbles-with-wal-mart-as-china-shoppers-buy-local) **478 European Union:** 'Global policy without democracy' (speech by Pascal Lamy, EU Trade Commissioner, given in 2001). **489 European Union:** Single Market Scoreboard (Performance per governance tool): Transposition, 07/2017 edition (for reporting period 12/2015-12/2016), (European Commission) **492 Organisation for Economic Co-operation and Development:** The economic consequences of Brexit: a taxing decision, OECD (25 April 2016) **496 The Financial Times Limited:** Consumer spending continues to decline despite UK wage pick-up, Delphine Strauss in London © The Financial Times Limited 2018 **497 Bank for International Settlements:** Mervyn King, Former Governor of the Bank of England, 'Finance: a return from risk', speech to the Worshipful Company of International Bankers, at the Mansion House, 17 March 2009 **528 Organisation for Economic Co-operation and Development:** The well-being of nations: the role of human and social capital,OECD,2001 **579 Crown Copyright:** Statistical Interactive Database, Bank of England, series LPQVWNV and LPQVWNQ (data published 29 March 2018) and series YBHA, Office for National Statistics **624 The Financial Times Limited:** *The Financial Times,* 24 May 2018 ECB to maintain 'steady hand' in face of eurozone growth slowdown By Claire Jones **625 Alistair Darling:** Alistair Darling, Chancellor of the Exchequer, Budget speech, 21 April 2009 **644 Federal Reserve System:** Press release, Board of Governors of the Federal Reserve System (16 December 2008).

Photographs

v, v, vi, vi, 2, 3, 4, 16, 27, 42, 43, 44, 64, 86, 87, 88, 111, 125, 144, 145, 146, 167, 180, 181, 182, 202, 225, 240, 241, 242, 257, 277, 290, 312, 313, 314, 340, 362, 363, 364, 390, 410, 440, 441, 443, 465, 482, 496, 497, 499, 537, 555, 590, 624, 625, 626, 651, 671 **John Sloman:** Photo Courtesy of John Sloman

Business and economics

The FT Reports . . .

Financial Times, 30 April 2018.

Deliveroo's speedy expansion belies tricky time for sector

By Chloe Cornish

Had its driver assessment system been operational when Deliveroo's co-founder and chief executive delivered its first ever order, he would not have scored highly.

William Shu, a former banker, motor-scooted a calzone from an Italian restaurant through London streets to a friend, only to eat the folded pizza himself – as he was hungry.

Deliveroo, which he says he started simply "to solve a personal problem", has topped this year's FT 1000 list of Europe's fastest growing companies. Between 2013, when Mr Shu and co-founder Greg Orlowski started the enterprise, and 2016, its revenues grew by a staggering compound annual growth rate of 924 per cent.

Deliveroo's platform provides 10 000 UK restaurants with delivery drivers on a combination of bicycles, scooters and cars.

"I kind of knew it would work in central London," says Mr Shu. But it was demand outside the capital that encouraged the company's breakneck growth: "That makes you more ambitious and want to go to more places." Since launch, Deliveroo has raised $957m in venture capital, according to company figures.

As Deliveroo has expanded into other UK cities, Europe and Asia, critics have questioned the profitability of its business model.

This is against the backdrop of a proliferation of competing app-based services, such as UberEats, part of the US ride-hailing company, and Just Eat, another FT 1000 business.

In 2016 . . . Deliveroo made losses of £129.1m on revenues of £128.6m. Mr Shu argues that this did not reflect performance in the cities Deliveroo has been operating in longest. "That year we expanded into 11 new countries, so there's an upfront investment required to do that," he says.

"I can assure you that the mature markets are much more profitable than newer markets," he adds, citing greater efficiencies and lower marketing costs.

Labour groups and Deliveroo riders have attacked the company over the flexible working arrangements it has with drivers. Mr Shu says this flexibility is the reason 92 per cent of Deliveroo's casual workforce choose to work for it. The company has 1000 people applying to do so each week in the UK, he says.

It now operates so-called "dark kitchens", which restaurants can use to produce food off-site. It offers restaurants help with branding and is even extending its consulting services to advise them on adding more marketable dishes to their menus.

It is all a matter of riders, restaurants and customers, he says. Without any one of these "the whole triangle breaks down".

I dread admitting I am an economist. The cab driver quizzes you on what is going to happen to the economy, the dinner companion turns to talk to the person on the other side and the immigration officer says, with heavy sarcasm, that his country needs people like you.

John Kay, 'Everyday economics makes for good fun at parties', *Financial Times,* 2 May 2006

Businesses play a key role in all our lives. Whatever their size, and whatever the goods or services they provide, they depend on us as consumers to buy their products.

But just as businesses rely on us for their income, many of us also rely on them for our income. The wages we earn depend on our employer's success, and that success in turn depends on us as suppliers of labour.

And it is not just as customers and workers that we are affected by business. The success of business in general affects the health of the whole economy and thus the lives of us all.

The extract from the *Financial Times* takes the case of Deliveroo. To be successful, firms must be capable of responding to changes in the market environment in which they operate. This requires a thorough understanding of economics. Developing a business strategy that simultaneously responds to technological changes, changes in consumer tastes and the activities of rival companies is not an easy task. Fortunately, economics provides frameworks for thinking about these issues, and many more.

In Part A of this text, we consider the relationship between business and economics.

In Chapter 1 we look at the structure of industry and its importance in determining firms' behaviour. We also look at a range of other factors that may affect business decisions and how we can analyse the environment in which a firm operates in order to help it devise an appropriate business strategy.

Then, in Chapter 2 we ask what it is that economists do and, in particular, how economists set about analysing the world of business and the things businesses do. In particular, we focus on rational decision making – how to get the best outcome from limited resources.

Finally, in Chapter 3 we look at the different ways in which firms are organised: at their legal structure, at their internal organisation and at their goals.

Key terms

The business environment
PEST and STEEPLE analysis
Production
Firms
Industries
Industrial sectors
Standard Industrial Classification (SIC)
Industrial concentration
Structure–conduct–performance
Scarcity
Factors of production
Macroeconomics
Microeconomics
Opportunity cost
Marginal costs
Marginal benefits
Rational choices
Circular flow of income
Transaction costs
Principal and agent
Business organisation
Price taker
Perfectly competitive market
Price mechanism
Demand
Supply

1 Chapter

The business environment and business economics

Business issues covered in this chapter

- What do business economists do?
- What is meant by the 'business environment'?
- How are businesses influenced by their national and global market environment?
- How are different types of industry classified in the official statistics?
- What things influence a firm's behaviour and performance?

What is business economics?

What is the role of *business economics*? What will you study in this text?

The world economy has experienced many changes in recent decades, including the 2008/09 financial crisis and subsequent recession, the political changes in the USA, the vote to leave the EU in Britain, ongoing terrorist attacks, a growing environmental agenda, political tensions with Russia and changes in key emerging economies, such as China and India, to name a few. All of these events have had profound effects on businesses across the world and many have created an uncertain business environment, making it increasingly challenging for firms to operate.

Business economists examine *firms*: the changing environment in which they operate, the decisions they make, and the effects of these decisions – on themselves, on their customers, on their employees, on their business rivals, on the public at large and on the domestic and international economy.

All firms are different but, in one way or another, they are all involved in the production of goods and services. They use inputs, which cost money, to make output that earns money. The difference between the revenue earned and the costs incurred constitutes the firm's profit. Although firms may pursue a range of objectives, we assume that firms normally will want to make as much profit as possible or, at the very least, avoid a decline in profits.

In order to meet these and other objectives, managers will need to make effective choices: what to produce, how much to produce and at what price; what techniques of production to use, how many workers to employ and of what type, what suppliers to use for raw materials, equipment, etc. Business economists study these choices. They study economic decision making by firms.

The study of decision making can be broken down into three stages:

The external influences on the firm (the 'business environment'). Here we are referring to the various factors that affect the firm that are largely outside its direct control. Examples are the competition it faces, the prices its suppliers charge, the state of the economy (e.g. whether growing or in recession) and the level of interest rates. Businesses need a clear understanding of their environment before they can set about making the right decisions.

Internal decisions of the firm. Given a firm's knowledge of these external factors, how will it then decide on prices, output, inputs, marketing, investment, etc.? Here the business economist can play a major role in helping firms achieve their business objectives.

The external effects of business decision making. When the firm has made its decisions and acted on them, how do the results affect the firm's rivals, its customers and the wider public? In other words, what is the impact of a firm's decision making on people outside the firm? Are firms' actions in the public interest or is there a case for government intervention?

What do business economists do?

Our study of business will involve three types of activity:

- *Description.* We will describe the objectives of businesses (e.g. making profit or increasing market share), the types of market in which firms operate (e.g. competitive or non-competitive) and the constraints on decision making (e.g. the costs of production, the level of consumer demand and the state of the economy).
- *Analysis.* We will analyse how a firm's costs might vary with the amount of output it produces and how its revenues will be affected by a change in consumer demand or a change in the price charged by rivals. We will also analyse the upswings and downswings in the economy: something that will have a crucial bearing on the profitability of many companies.
- *Recommendations.* Given the objectives of a firm, the business economist can help to show how those objectives can best be met. For example, if a firm wants to maximise its profits, the business economist can advise on what prices to charge, how much to invest, how much to advertise, etc. Of course, any such recommendations will only be as good as the data on which they are based. In an uncertain environment, recommendations will necessarily be more tentative.

In this chapter, as an introduction to the subject of business economics, we shall consider the place of the firm within its business environment, and assess how these external influences are likely to shape and determine its actions. In order to discuss the relationship between a business's actions and its environment, first we need to define what the business environment is.

1.1 THE BUSINESS ENVIRONMENT

Traditionally, we identify four dimensions to the business environment: political, economic, social/cultural and technological.

Political factors. Firms are directly affected by the actions of government and other political events. These might be major events affecting the whole of the business community, such as the problems in Syria and Iraq, the tensions between Russia and the USA, Britain leaving the EU or a change of government. Alternatively, they may be actions affecting just one part of the economy. For example, the charge on plastic carrier bags affects the retail sector and the ban on smoking in public places affects the tobacco industry.

Economic factors. Businesses are affected by a range of economic factors, including the changing costs of raw materials, the entry of a new rival into the market, the current availability of investment funds, the economic performance of the

domestic and world economy, and changes in domestic and foreign economic policy.

It is normal to divide the economic environment in which the firm operates into two levels:

- *The microeconomic environment.* This includes all the economic factors that are *specific* to a particular firm operating in its own particular market. Thus one firm may be operating in a highly competitive market, whereas another may not; one firm may be faced with rapidly changing consumer tastes (e.g. a designer clothing manufacturer), while another may be faced with a virtually constant consumer demand (e.g. a potato merchant); one firm may face rapidly rising costs, whereas another may find that costs are constant or falling.
- *The macroeconomic environment.* This is the *national* and *international* economic situation in which business as a whole operates. Business in general will fare much better when the economy is growing, as opposed to when

BOX 1.1	A LIDL SUCCESS STORY

Making the best of your business environment

Lidl's history dates back to the 1930s, when Josef Schwarz, a partner in a German fruit wholesaler, developed the firm into a general food wholesaler. His son, Dieter, continued the development of the Schwarz-Gruppe and began to create the basis of the Lidl that we recognise today: a firm focusing on the discount end of the market. He changed the name of the supermarket from Schwarzmarkt ('black market') to Lidl, despite facing some legal issues relating to the surname 'Lidl'.

In 1973, the first Lidl store was opened in Germany. It had 3 employees and 500 product lines. Keeping costs down was a key aspect of the business, with unsold stock being removed quickly from shelves, products being left in original packaging and store size kept small. This was an approach already established by the other famous German discounter, Aldi. The strategy proved a success and, by the end of the decade, 30 Lidl stores were open in Germany and this number continued to grow, reaching 300 by the 1980s.[1]

It was the following decade when Lidl's presence outside of Germany began, with stores first opening in France and then in the UK in 1994. Over the next 10 years, it recorded consistent growth in the UK and quickly added to its stores, opening its 700th in the UK in 2018, where it now sells over 2000 products. The Lidl group now has over 10 000 stores worldwide, 150 distribution centres and operates in 28 countries globally.

It has retained its focus on low-cost products, which has proved to be a successful strategy to break the dominance of the big supermarket chains in the UK. According to Statista,[2] Lidl's market share in August 2012 was just 2.8 per cent; by 2017, it had increased to 5.2 per cent. So, although it still remains a fairly small player in the UK supermarket industry, Lidl's growth is significant. In the three months to May 2017, the whole UK market grew by 3.7 per cent, the fastest growth in over three and a half years. Yet Lidl recorded growth of 17.8 per cent, second only behind Aldi with 18.3 per cent growth.[3] According to Kantar, Lidl's UK sales continued to rise in 2017, with the retailer earning revenue of £5.8 billion.

How has Lidl broken into such a competitive market and recorded such high growth? What lessons are there for other businesses? How has its performance been affected by its business environment – by consumer tastes, by the actions of its rivals, by the state of the national and world economies and by government policy?

In particular, how would an economist analyse Lidl's performance so as to advise it on its best strategy for the future? This is the sort of thing that business economists do and the sort of thing we will be doing throughout this text. We will also look at the impact of the behaviour of businesses on their customers, on employees, on competitors and on society in

general. So let's take a closer look at Lidl and relate its business in general to the topics covered in this text.

The market environment

To be successful, it is important for Lidl to get its product and strategy right. This means understanding the markets in which it operates and how consumer demand responds to changes in prices and to the other services being offered.

The supermarket industry in the UK is very competitive and is dominated by the big four: Tesco, Sainsbury's, Asda and Morrisons. In addition, there are other retailers, focused more on the high-end market, including Waitrose and Marks & Spencer. Aldi and Lidl, by contrast, focus on the opposite end of the market: no frills, low cost, budget products. However, few households viewed Lidl as the place where you would go to to do your weekly shop. Instead, Lidl seemed to be more about stocking up on products.

While Lidl's low prices are crucial for its success, the quality of the products is equally important. Consumers will not be willing to pay a price, however low, if the food is of poor quality and if similar products can be purchased from other stores. With Lidl's rise to a legitimate competitor, the big four supermarkets in the UK were forced to respond and we have seen an increasingly competitive food industry, with many pressures being placed on suppliers, creating its own range of ethical issues. When setting prices and designing/sourcing products, consideration must be given to what rival companies are doing. Lidl's prices and product quality must be competitive to maintain its sales, profitability and increase its position in the global market and Lidl recognised the importance of this aspect.

While Lidl had always been an attractive place to shop for lower-income households, it wanted to expand its appeal. During and after the financial crisis, especially when food prices in the UK were rising faster than incomes, many middle- and even higher-income households began to be swayed into shopping at the budget retailer, keen on finding cheaper products. With its drive to become more upmarket, this meant that it was increasingly important for Lidl to focus on the quality of its products and change the perception that low cost meant low quality. In 2015, Lidl started to focus on changing its image as a budget retailer, opening stores in London, adapting its marketing, while still maintaining the low-cost nature of its products. David Gray from Planet Retail said:

> This is part of an ongoing strategy, with Lidl putting in more premium ranges, more fresh bakery products, more brands, to make it more like a mainstream supermarket.[4]

The strategy appears to have worked. In 2016, six of Lidl's products won their categories in the Quality Food Awards and, for the first time, Lidl was named Grocer of the Year at the 2015 Grover Gold Awards, beating Waitrose, Asda and Aldi. Lidl's UK CEO at the time, Ronny Gottschlich, reflected on the award and the changes introduced within Lidl commenting that:

> This is an incredible achievement . . . More and more people are coming to Lidl for their full supermarket shop,

[1] www.lidl.co.uk/en/About-Us.htm.

[2] www.statista.com/statistics/280208/grocery-market-share-in-the-united-kingdom-uk/.

[3] Sarah Butler and Julia Kollewe 'Lidl on course to surpass Waitrose and enter UK supermarket top seven'; *The Guardian* (3 May 2017).

[4] Jamie Robertson 'Lidl aims to shake off budget image with London stores'; BBC News (10 September 2015).

with old preconceptions continuing to change all the time . . . We are committed to investing in our own brand ranges so that we can offer our customers premium products and ingredients at the lowest possible prices, helping them to shop a little smarter and save as much money as possible, every single day.[5]

We look at how markets work in general in Chapters 4 and 5 and at different market structures and competition between firms in Chapters 11 to 13.

Products, employment and sustainability

Lidl's product range.

One of the key factors behind Lidl is its local sourcing of products, with around 70 per cent of products in UK stores sourced from UK farmers and producers. It has also recognised the increasing importance that customers place on sustainability and environmental issues, producing a Sustainability Report for the first time in 2016/17. Part of the aim here was to tackle the perception that low cost meant low quality and in this sustainability report, the UK CEO of Lidl noted that, 'We hope to challenge these misconceptions and increase our transparency by outlining our sustainability achievements to date and setting out our priorities and commitments for the future.'[6]

Lidl has launched four 'Big Steps': 'Buying British', 'Sourcing Responsibly', 'Tackling Food Waste' and 'Supporting Active & Healthy Lifestyles'. It is increasingly focused on these issues, for example through its sourcing of Fairtrade cocoa and sustainable fish. It is focusing an increasing number of resources on making positive changes in these areas and advertising them to consumers. Given the global nature of the business, it sources products from over 700 suppliers in 60 different countries and hence its supply chain is complex, requiring constant monitoring to ensure that quality is maintained at each stage.

Another of Lidl's key features is the development of its own-brand products, which offer cheaper alternatives to many everyday products. This development was, in part, a response to changing consumer demands as finances became tighter for many households. Lidl has had much success in this area, picking up numerous awards for its own-brand products. In 2016, Lidl was dominant at the Grocer Own Label Awards, picking up 63 medals and, in 2017, it was in second place, behind Aldi in terms of the number of Awards.

We look specifically at consumer demand and methods of stimulating it in Chapters 6 to 8 and a range of environmental issues and corporate social responsibility in Chapters 20 and 22.

Employees.

Lidl has 20 000 employees in stores across the UK and aims to become the UK's most attractive employer. In 2015, Lidl became the first UK supermarket to pay its workers the national living wage, aiming to 'share its success' with the staff, though controversy did arise when it emerged that this would be applied in England, Wales and Scotland, but not in Northern Ireland.

Lidl has experienced issues with its employees, including conflict with trade unions and issues of spying (more below), but its Sustainability Report does address human rights and working conditions, particularly focusing on the importance of low prices in its stores and how this links to pay and working conditions, especially within its complex supply chain.

Growth strategy.

Lidl has expanded considerably from its initial stores in Germany and now has stores in almost every country in Europe. In June 2017, it became Croatia's second largest supermarket and then broke into the US market, initially taking 2.6 per cent of the share of supermarket visits. Demand did then drop off, but personnel changes in the USA made a difference and sales rebounded towards the end of the year. Lidl plans to continue its expansion in the USA and in the UK, where a £1.45 billion investment programme is planned by 2019, with 60 new stores opening each year and significant growth in its logistics network. This includes new distribution centres in Wednesbury, in Southampton and plans for more in various other locations, creating 1500 new jobs. We are also seeing Lidl diversifying into clothing. This includes the introduction of an affordable but high-end 'Heidi Klum' range in its stores. Only time will tell whether this is a good fit for the budget retailer, despite its recent image change.

Employment issues are considered in Chapter 18, while strategic decisions such as growth by expansion in the domestic and global economy are examined in Chapters 14, 15 and 23.

Dealing with controversy

Despite Lidl's remarkable success, it hasn't all been straightforward and an important element for any business is how it deals with controversy and any issues that affect its public image.

One challenge came in 2008, when it emerged that Lidl was, essentially, spying on its employees, keeping records of toilet breaks, health concerns, finances and even relationships, with details learnt from private phone calls. Further, such information was being used by managers when making decisions about employees. Lidl confirmed that it knew about this and even condoned the policy, which was aimed to stop any staff issues before they became a problem and protect the company's financial position. Lidl did not have any staff devoted to press and public relations but, after confirming that the company would make employees more aware of the monitoring, Lidl bounced back.[7]

The same year, controversy emerged in Sweden, first when buying alcohol was required to enter a competition and second when Lidl staff poured cleaning products and detergents over food that was past its expiration date and placed in Lidl bins. Lidl was accused of poisoning the homeless who took the food, despite the warning that it had been poisoned. Lidl apologised for these actions and its rise continued.

In 2014, Lidl UK stopped its employees from speaking any language other than English, including Welsh in its Wales stores to ensure a 'comfortable environment' for all customers and employees.[8] This sparked controversy,

---

[5] www.lidl.co.uk/en/Grocer-of-the-Year-Award-3488.htm.

[6] www.lidl.co.uk/en/sustainability.htm.

[7] Debra Kelly, 'The untold truth of Lidl'; *Mashed*.

[8] '"English only" rule at Lidl shops sparks Welsh row' BBC News, (7 November 2014).

but Lidl hit back noting that, 'Employees could speak any language customers addressed them in – including Welsh.'

A deadly spider and its babies were found in a bunch of Lidl's bananas in the UK in August 2016 and similar issues have occurred in other countries, including Germany. In 2017, Lidl UK faced a social media backlash as customers criticised its decision to airbrush Christian symbols from its packaging and this controversy spilled over to Germany, Belgium and other European countries, where customers were also angry at the move.

Lidl has developed its press and media relations, in part to deal with responses to such issues. Its marketing strategy will continue to be crucial as it tries to shake off the image of a budget retailer. Despite ongoing issues in many countries, the retailer has proved resilient.

The economy

So do the fortunes of Lidl and other companies depend solely on their policies and those of their competitors? The answer is no.

One important element of a company's business environment is largely beyond its control: the state of the national economy and, for internationally trading companies, of the global economy. When the world economy is booming, sales and profits are likely to grow without too much effort by the company. However, when the global economy declines, as we saw in the economic downturn from 2008, trading conditions will become much tougher.

In the years after the financial crisis, the global economy remained in a vulnerable position and this led to many companies entering administration. These included Woolworths, Jessops, HMV, Comet, Blockbuster and Peacocks. However, it also presented opportunities for companies like Aldi and Lidl, which were able to take advantage of households who were looking for cheaper prices. In the 12 weeks to June 2008, Aldi saw its sales increase by 20.7 per cent, while Lidl's sales grew by 12.8 per cent, both well above the growth rates of the dominant supermarkets. Steve Gotham, a project director at Allegra Strategies, said:

> Clearly the economic circumstances in the UK are playing into the hands of the discounters. They are appealing to new customers and those new customers are coming from more middle-class backgrounds.[9]

---

[9] James Thompson, 'Lidl and Aldi see sales soar amid economic downturn', *Independent* (24 June 2008).

Aldi's and Lidl's competitors continued to face difficulties with their financial performance as the economy struggled to recover. In 2015, sales at Tesco declined by 2 per cent from the previous year, with Morrisons falling by 1.7 per cent and Asda's sales falling 3.5 per cent in the last quarter of 2015 relative to the same time the previous year. Lidl took the opportunity to increase its market share and, together with Aldi, saw their combined share of the market move from 5 per cent in 2012 to 12 per cent by 2017. Previously, it had taken them nine years for their collective market share to double from 2.5 per cent to 5 per cent.[10]

According to Barclays Research, Lidl's international sales have increased from €28 billion in 2012 to €41.5 billion in 2016, and the UK performance mirrors its international success. This success is more reflective to the success of its low-cost strategy, rather than the trends of the global or UK economy. Although this might seem unusual, it is the very nature of Lidl's strategy that means it is the perfect retailer to take advantage of an economic downturn. At the other end of the UK retailers, Waitrose was also more insulated against the financial crisis than the 'Big Four' (Asda, Tesco, Sainsbury's and Morrisons) due to the nature of the products it sells.

The 2017 Christmas trading period saw the German retailer's UK sales rise by 16 per cent and 22 December saw Lidl UK's highest ever trading day. However, Lidl's expansion plans have proved to be costly. While its operational margin has fallen to 4.3 per cent, its lowest since 2012, this is still a healthy figure relative to the industry, once again indicating the success of this retailer. Whether such positive trading can be sustained will be determined by Lidl's strategy in the coming years.

We examine the national and international business environment in Chapters 23 to 29. We also examine the impact on business of government policies to affect the economy – policies such as changes in taxation, interest rates, exchange rates and customs duties in Chapters 30 to 32.

 What challenges is Lidl likely to face in the coming years?

 Choose a well-known company that trades globally and do a Web search to find out how well it has performed in recent years and how it has been influenced by various aspects of its business environment.

---

[10] Kantar World Panel.

---

it is in recession, as we saw after the 2008 financial crisis. In examining the macroeconomic environment, we will also be looking at the policies that governments adopt in their attempt to steer the economy, since these policies, by affecting things such as taxation, interest rates and exchange rates, will have a major impact on firms.

Social/cultural factors. This aspect concerns social attitudes and values. These include attitudes towards working conditions and the length of the working day, equal opportunities for different groups of people (whether by ethnicity, gender, physical attributes, etc.), the nature and purity of products, the use and abuse of animals, and images portrayed in advertising.

The social/cultural environment also includes social trends, such as an increase in the average age of the population, or changes in attitudes towards seeking paid employment while bringing up small children. Various ethical issues, especially concerning the protection of the environment, are

BOX 1.2 THE BIOTECHNOLOGY INDUSTRY

Its business environment

There are few areas of business that cause such controversy as biotechnology. It has generated new medicines, created pest-resistant crops, developed eco-friendly industrial processes and, through genetic mapping, is providing incalculable advances in gene therapy. These developments, however, have raised profound ethical issues. Many areas of biotechnology are uncontentious, but genetic modification and cloning have met with considerable public hostility, colouring many people's views of biotechnology in general.

Biotechnology refers to the application of knowledge about living organisms and their components to make new products and develop new industrial processes. For many it is seen as the next wave in the development of the knowledge-based economy. The sector has grown significantly over the past 15 years, making significant contributions to global growth and job creation. In 2015, the global biotechnology industry was worth $500 billion and, although 2016 and 2017 presented many issues for the industry in terms of financing and of strategic and policy uncertainty, the industry is bouncing back and, according to a report by Grand View Research Inc., it will be valued at $727 billion by 2025.[1]

The global structure of the industry

The biotechnology sector is becoming increasingly global, with many new competitors emerging in Asia, but it is still the USA that dominates this sector. According to the Biotechnology Report from Ernst & Young (EY),[2] the USA has many more private and public companies than Europe, employing 135 750 workers in its public companies, while less than half this number are employed in comparable companies across Europe. Revenue growth for biotech companies in the USA fell for a second year in 2016, rising by only 4 per cent to reach $112.2 billion. However, in Europe, revenue growth increased from 4 per cent in 2015 to 19 per cent in 2016, reaching $27.2 billion, but only thanks to the acquisition of Baxalta by Shire, without which revenue growth would actually have been negative.

Mergers and acquisitions (M&As).

The biotechnology industry in Europe has outperformed other market sectors over the past few years, but this is largely down to merger and acquisition (M&A) activity, which in 2016 was Europe's strongest M&A year in a decade. However, it was 2015 that was a record year for global M&A activity in the biotechnology sector, with 79 deals taking place. Even though biotech M&A activity in 2016 was 12 per cent lower, there were still five significant deals (worth over $5 billion each), which accounted for 75 per cent of the sector's M&A activity[3] and 2016 did record the second highest aggregate M&A value and volume. There was also a significant amount of M&A activity in China, worth $6.8 billion, according to the Chinese investment bank, China Renaissance. This included deals where Chinese biotech and pharma companies purchased US or European companies, indicating China's intentions in the sector.

Countries' share of the global biotech sector.

Although US biotech companies have seen their worldwide share of patent applications decline from 44 per cent in the early 2000s to around 34 per cent in 2015, it is still the dominant country, according to the OECD. The EU28 accounted for 24 per cent of worldwide biotech patent applications in 2015 – little change from its 25 per cent figure in 2000. The big mover according to this metric is South Korea, with its share rising from 1.7 per cent in 2000 to 10 per cent in 2014.[4]

The Asian biotech sector is growing and the whole industry has seen a shift, with more capital flows coming from China, which is another of the Asian countries looking to make a global mark in this sector. However, until recently, government regulations meant that many of the most effective medicines were not available in China, despite its place as the second biggest market for pharmaceuticals. Now that these regulations are being relaxed, Chinese biotech companies will certainly join the race to develop drugs and investment into the sector will only rise.

Research and Development (R&D)

Although revenue growth in both the US and European biotechnology sector slowed to 7 per cent in 2016, following 2 years of double digit growth, a larger share of biotech company revenues went into R&D. According to the latest data from the OECD, R&D expenditure by biotech firms in the USA totalled $38.6 billion and this represented growth of over 40 per cent since 2012. When compared to Europe as a whole, the US biotechnology sector spends over twice as much on R&D and, although the industry is dominated by small and medium-sized businesses, it is the larger firms that dominate in terms of R&D. In most countries, biotech firms are geographically clustered, forming industry networks around key universities and research institutes. We will see the benefits of this in terms of costs in Chapter 9.

One of the big issues facing the biotech industry is the return on investment (ROI) in R&D. With medical and technological advances, as well as an ageing population, we are seeing more chronic diseases and the need to develop new drugs. However, this is a costly business, with estimates ranging from $1 billion to $2.5 billion per drug. Biotech companies are, therefore, under significant pressure to continue to invest in expensive new drug development, while facing increasing pressure to reduce prices.

Cutting the costs associated with drug development will be crucial, particularly the costs of clinical trials. Technology will be important in streamlining processes and making trials and testing more efficient and Artificial Intelligence is also likely to play a significant role. Some companies have already taken steps to address poor R&D productivity, including focusing on developing those drugs that have the greatest revenue potential, such as oncology and immunotherapy, and looking into developing personalised medicines. The big biotech companies, in particular, will need to continue to address poor R&D productivity if they and the wider sector are to remain feasible.

---

[1] 'Biotechnology Market Analysis: By Application (Health, Food & Agriculture, Natural Resources & Environment, Industrial Processing Bioinformatics); By Technology, And Segment Forecasts, 2014 – 2025', Grand View Research (August 2017).

[2] *Beyond Borders: Biotechnology Report 2017*, Ernst & Young (16 June 2017).

▶

Funding and the future

The costs of drug development have seen little change and it can still take a decade for new drugs to make it to market. This means that there can be a very long delay between biotech companies incurring the costs and generating the revenues; hence funding is essential. Most countries provide significant financial support to their biotech firms and encourage firms to form collaborative agreements and partnerships.

For example, the EUREKA programme was launched in 1985 as an intergovernmental network to promote innovation and provide easier access to finance. Now consisting of 41 members, including the EU itself, it provides support for collaborative ventures through a series of National Project Co-ordinators who help to secure national or EU funding. Successful projects are awarded the internationally recognised Eureka label.[5]

Although government funding is important, the majority of funding for the industry comes from 'venture capital' (investment by individuals and firms in new and possibly risky sectors). Such funding is extremely volatile. For example, biotech companies saw their share prices rise in 1999 and 2000 and then collapse, before seeing growth until 2007. The financial crisis then had an adverse impact on investment in both the EU (−79 per cent) and the US (−62 per cent) biotechnology industries and this had a serious impact on the viability of some businesses in the sector. However, the sector as a whole weathered the downturn relatively well and, from 2012 to 2015, investment recovered and biotech shares soared, with many tripling in value. Then in 2016, with economic and political uncertainty, there was a 27 per cent fall in investment into the industry, though early-stage capital financing remained buoyant.

With continuing economic and political risk, the biotech sector faces a number of challenges going forwards.

In 2016, 'the UK enjoyed the most financings of any European market (78), as well as the highest total innovation capital financing (US$1.3 billion, 25 per cent of the total) and highest total venture financing (US$590 million, 30 per cent of all European venture capital)'.[6] However, in 2019, the UK is due to leave the European Union and this will pose significant challenges, above and beyond the relocation of the European Medicines Agency from London.

Asian biotech companies will provide increasing competition to a sector that has undergone significant consolidation over the past decade. Furthermore, the uncertainty of health care reform in the USA, together with possible tax reforms, hiring freezes and funding cuts, will only add to the pressures on the biotechnology industry, as it faces the ongoing issues of poor R&D productivity and the costs of drug development.

 From the brief outline above, identify the political, economic, social and technological dimensions shaping the biotechnology industry's business environment.

---

[3] *Beyond Borders: Biotechnology Report 2017*, Ernst & Young (16 June 2017).
[4] *Key biotechnology indicators*, OECD (November 2017).
[5] www.eurekanetwork.org/.
[6] *Key biotechnology indicators* (op. cit.).

---

also having a growing impact on the actions of business and the image that many firms seek to present.

Technological factors. Over the past 30 years there has been significant technological change, which has had a huge impact on how firms produce, advertise and sell their products. Online shopping has continued to grow, creating a global market place for firms, while causing problems for high street retailers. It has also changed how business is organised, providing more opportunities for smaller online retailers and changing the structure of many markets.

The use of robots and other forms of computer-controlled production has changed the nature of work for many workers. The information-technology revolution has enabled much more rapid communication and has made it possible for firms across the world to work together more effectively. The working environment has become more flexible and efficient, with many workers able to do their job from home, while travelling or from another country.

The division of the factors affecting a firm into political, economic, social and technological is commonly known as a *PEST analysis*. However, we can add a further three factors to create *STEEPLE analysis*. The additional elements are:

Environmental (ecological) factors. This has become an increasingly important issue in politics and business, with many firms aiming, and even being forced by government policy changes, to take a greener approach to business. Consumers are more environmentally aware and a green image can be useful in generating finance from investors and government. Business attitudes towards the environment are examined in sections 20.5 and 22.1.

Legal factors. Businesses are affected by the legal framework in which they operate. Examples include industrial relations

Definitions

PEST analysis Where the political, economic, social and technological factors shaping a business environment are assessed by a business so as to devise future business strategy.

STEEPLE analysis Where the social, technological, economic, environmental, political, legal and ethical factors shaping a business environment are assessed by a business so as to devise future business strategy.

legislation, product safety standards, regulations governing pricing in the privatised industries and laws preventing collusion between firms. We examine some of these laws in Chapter 21.

Ethical factors. Firms are increasingly under pressure to adopt a more socially responsible attitude towards business, with concerns over working conditions, product safety and quality and truthful advertising. With various companies finding themselves in difficulties over suspect business practices and with consumers' increasing awareness of these issues, many firms have been forced to adapt their business practices. Examples include Volkswagen and its 'defeat device', which gave more favourable emissions readings under test conditions; sexual harassment allegations affecting Weinstein Co. and a whole host of scandals affecting Uber. Business ethics and corporate responsibility are examined in section 20.5.

This framework is used widely by organisations to audit their business environment and to help them establish a strategic approach to their business activities. It is, nevertheless, important to recognise that there is a great overlap and interaction among these sets of factors. Laws and government policies reflect social attitudes; technological factors determine economic ones, such as costs and productivity; technological progress often reflects the desire of researchers to meet social or environmental needs; and so on.

As well as such interaction, we must also be aware of the fact that the business environment is constantly changing. Some of these changes are gradual, some are revolutionary. To be successful, a business will need to adapt to these changes and, wherever possible, take advantage of them. Ultimately, the better business managers understand the environment in which they operate, the more likely they are to be successful, either in exploiting ever-changing opportunities or in avoiding potential disasters.

Although we shall be touching on political, social and technological factors, it is economic factors that will be our main focus of concern when examining the business environment.

> ### Pause for thought
>
> *Under which heading of a PEST or STEEPLE analysis would you locate training and education? What about a tax on plastic bottles?*

> **KEY IDEA 1**
>
> ***The behaviour and performance of firms is affected by the business environment.*** **The business environment includes economic, political/legal, social/cultural and technological factors, as well as environmental, legal and ethical ones.**

1.2 THE STRUCTURE OF INDUSTRY

One of the most important and influential elements of the business environment is the *structure of industry*. How a firm performs depends on the state of its particular industry and the amount of competition it faces. Knowledge of the structure of an industry is therefore crucial if we are to understand business behaviour and its likely outcomes.

In this section we will consider how the production of different types of goods and services is classified and how firms are located in different industrial groups.

Classifying production

When analysing production it is common to distinguish three broad categories:

- *Primary production.* This refers to the production and extraction of natural resources such as minerals and sources of energy. It also includes output from agriculture.
- *Secondary production.* This refers to the output of the manufacturing and construction sectors of the economy.

- *Tertiary production.* This refers to the production of services, and includes a wide range of sectors such as finance, the leisure industry, retailing and transport.

Figures 1.1 and 1.2 show the share of output (or ***gross domestic product (GDP)***) and employment of these three sectors in 1974 and 2016. They illustrate how the tertiary

> ### Definitions
>
> **Primary production** The production and extraction of natural resources, plus agriculture.
>
> **Secondary production** The production from manufacturing and construction sectors of the economy.
>
> **Tertiary production** The production from the service sector of the economy.
>
> **Gross domestic product (GDP)** The value of output produced within the country typically over a 12-month period.

Figure 1.1	Output of industrial sectors (as a percentage of GDP)

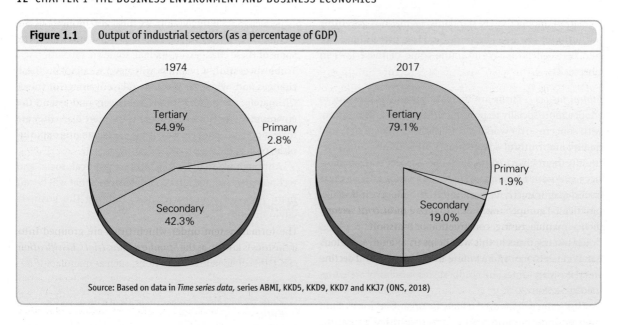

Source: Based on data in *Time series data,* series ABMI, KKD5, KKD9, KKD7 and KKJ7 (ONS, 2018)

Figure 1.2	Employment by industrial sector (percentage of total employees)

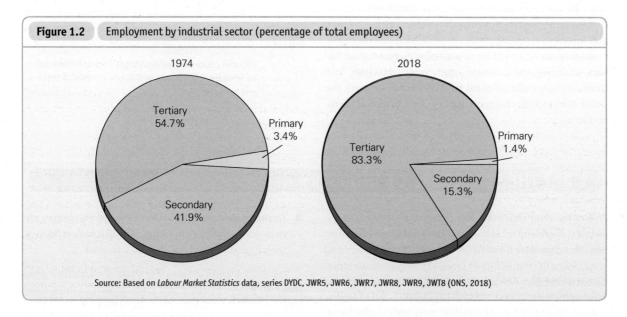

Source: Based on *Labour Market Statistics* data, series DYDC, JWR5, JWR6, JWR7, JWR8, JWR9, JWT8 (ONS, 2018)

sector has expanded rapidly. In 2016, it contributed some 78.3 per cent to total output and employed 83.1 per cent of all workers. By contrast, the share of output and employment of the secondary sector has declined. In 2016, it accounted for only 21.1 per cent of output and 15.7 per cent of employment.

This trend is symptomatic of a process known as *deindustrialisation* – a decline in the share of manufacturing in GDP. Many commentators argue that this process of deindustrialisation is inevitable and that the existence of a large and growing tertiary sector in the UK economy reflects its maturity. Similar trends can also be observed in many other countries.

Definition

Deindustrialisation The decline in the contribution to production of the manufacturing sector of the economy.

Furthermore, it is possible to identify part of the tertiary sector as a fourth or 'quaternary' sector. This refers to the knowledge-based part of the economy and includes services such as education, information generation and sharing, research and development, consultation, culture and parts of government. This sector has been growing as a proportion of the tertiary sector.

The classification of production into primary, secondary and tertiary, and even quaternary, allows us to consider broad changes in the economy. However, if we require a more comprehensive analysis of the structure of industry and its changes over time, we need to classify firms into *particular* industries. The following section outlines the classification process used in the UK and the EU.

Classifying firms into industries

An *industry* refers to a group of firms that produce a particular category of product, such as the electrical goods industry, the holiday industry or the insurance industry. Industries can then be grouped together into broad *industrial sectors*, such as manufacturing, construction or transport.

Classifying firms in this way helps us to analyse various trends in the economy, including areas of growth and decline and those parts of the economy with specific needs, such as training or transport infrastructure. Perhaps, most importantly, it helps economists and business people to understand and predict the behaviour of firms that are in direct competition with each other. In such cases, however, it may be necessary to draw the boundaries of an industry quite narrowly.

To illustrate this, take the case of the vehicle industry. The vehicle industry produces cars, lorries, vans and coaches. The common characteristic of these vehicles is that they are self-propelled road transport vehicles. In other words, we could draw the boundaries of an industry in terms of the broad physical or technical characteristics of the products it produces. The problem with this type of categorisation, however, is that these products may not be substitutes in an *economic* sense. If I am thinking of buying a new vehicle to replace my car, I am hardly likely to consider buying a coach or a lorry! If we are to group together products that are genuine competitors for each other, we will want to divide industries into more narrow categories, e.g. family cars, sports cars, etc.

On the other hand, if we draw the boundaries of an industry too narrowly, we may end up ignoring the effects of competition from another closely related industry. For example, if we are to understand the pricing strategies of electricity supply companies in the household market, it might be better to focus on the whole domestic fuel industry.

Thus how narrowly or broadly we draw the boundaries of an industry depends on the purposes of our analysis. You should note that the definition of an industry is based on the *supply* characteristics of firms, not on the qualities that consumers might attribute to products. For example, we classify cars into several groups according to size, price, engine capacity, design, model (e.g. luxury, saloon, seven-seater and sports), etc. These are demand-side characteristics of motor cars determined by consumers' tastes. The government, on the other hand, will categorise a company such as Nissan as belonging to the 'motor car' industry because making cars is its principal activity, and it does this even though Nissan produces a variety of models each with numerous features to suit individual consumer needs.

Both demand- and supply-side measures are equally valid ways of analysing the competitive behaviour of firms, and governments will look at both when there is a particular issue of economic importance, such as a merger between car companies. However, the supply-side measure is more simply calculated and is less susceptible to change, thereby making it preferable for general use.

Standard Industrial Classification

The formal system under which firms are grouped into industries is known as the *Standard Industrial Classification (SIC)*. It is divided into 21 sections, such as manufacturing, transport and storage, real estate activities and education and each section has its own divisions, such as manufacturing being divided into manufacture of food products, of textiles or basic metals. These divisions are then divided into groups, then into classes and even subclasses (as you can see in Case Study A2 on the student website). The case study also shows how the different sectors have grown over time.

Over the past 70 years, revisions have been made to the SIC in order to reflect changes in the UK's industrial structure, such as the emergence of new products and industries and to bring the UK and EU systems of industry classification into alignment.

Changes in the structure of the UK economy

We can use the SIC to consider how UK industry has changed over time, in terms of output and employment. Often, it can be very important to look at changes in output and employment within the sub-divisions of the SIC in order to identify whether whole sectors are experiencing changes or if changes are affecting specific parts of a sector.

For example, in the UK there has been significant growth in the output of the services industries, including financial services, though some parts of the retail banking sector have seen a decline in employment due to technological change (fewer counter staff are required in high street banks, given the

---

Definitions

Industry A group of firms producing a particular product or service.

Industrial sector A grouping of industries producing similar products or services.

Standard Industrial Classification (SIC) The name given to the formal classification of firms into industries used by the government in order to collect data on business and industry trends.

growth in cash machines, credit cards, etc.). Figure 1.2 shows that manufacturing has seen a general decline in employment, as the UK has moved towards the tertiary sector, though some sub-divisions within manufacturing have seen growth, such as instruments and electrical engineering.

We can also use the SIC to consider which sectors of the economy are particularly susceptible to the strength of the economy. For example, construction and real estate tend to experience significant growth in employment during periods of economic growth and falls in employment during periods of economic decline.

The SIC also allows us to consider wider issues, such as *industrial concentration*. This provides business economists with information about the structure of an industry, in terms of whether it is dominated by a few large firms (those employing 250 or more people), such as the electricity, gas and mining sectors, or if an industry is comprised of lots of small and medium-sized enterprises (SMEs). As we will see in

the next section and at many other points throughout this book, the structure of an industry is an important determinant of firm behaviour and market outcomes.

Pause for thought

Give some examples of things we might learn about the likely behaviour and performance of businesses in an industry by knowing something about the industrial concentration of that industry.

Definition

Industrial concentration The degree to which an industry is dominated by large business enterprises.

1.3 THE DETERMINANTS OF BUSINESS PERFORMANCE

Structure–conduct–performance

KI 1
p 11

It should be apparent from our analysis thus far that business performance is strongly influenced by the market structure within which the firm operates. This is known as the *structure–conduct–performance paradigm*.

The structure of an industry depends on many factors. Some concern consumer demand, such as consumer tastes and whether there are close substitute products. Others concern production (supply), such as technology and the availability of resources.

These factors determine the competitiveness of an industry and influence firms' behaviour, as a business operating in a highly competitive market structure will conduct its activities differently from a business in a market with relatively few competitors. For example, the more competitive the market, the more aggressive the business may have to be in order to sell its product and remain competitive. The less competitive the market, the greater the power that a firm may have to increase prices and the greater is the chance that collusion between producers might be the preferred strategy, as a means of reducing the uncertainty and costs of any degree of competition.

Such conduct will, in turn, influence how well businesses perform. Performance can be measured by several different indicators, such as profitability, market share or growth in market share, and changes in share prices, especially relative to those of other firms in the industry, to name some of the most commonly used.

Throughout the text, we will see how market structure affects business conduct, and how business conduct affects business performance. Chapters 11, 12 and 21 are particularly relevant here.

It would be wrong, however, to argue that business performance is totally shaped by external factors such as market structure. In fact, the internal aims and organisation of business may be very influential in determining success.

Internal aims and organisation

Economists traditionally have assumed that businesses aim to maximise their profits. This traditional 'theory of the firm' shows the output that a firm should sell and at what price, if its objective is to make as much profit as possible.

Although this is still the case for many firms, as businesses have grown and become increasingly complex, more specialist managers have been employed to make the day-to-day decisions. This complexity of organisation makes the assumption of profit maximisation too simplistic in many cases.

With complex products and production lines, we have seen the emergence of increasingly distinct groups within firms, including the owners (shareholders) and the managers who are employed for their specialist knowledge. The problem is that the objectives of managers and owners may well differ and are often in conflict.

KI 7
p 30

The owners of a business may want to maximise profits to increase their dividends. This could involve a relatively high price and low sales. However, the managers may want to maximise sales and reduce prices to achieve this goal, or may have different goals entirely, especially if they do not receive any share of the profit. Their actions may reduce profits, creating a conflict between objectives.

Understanding these possible conflicts is crucial when trying to establish the objectives of a business. Whose objectives are being pursued? We will look at these conflicts and solutions in Chapters 3 and 13.

It is not only the aims of a business that affect its performance. Performance also depends on the following:

■ *Internal structure.* The way in which the firm is organised (e.g. into departments or specialised units) will affect its costs, its aggressiveness in the market, its willingness to innovate, etc.

■ *Information.* The better informed a business is about its markets, about its costs of production, about alternative techniques and about alternative products it could make, the better will it be able to fulfil its goals.

■ *The competence of management.* The performance of a business will depend on the skills, experience, motivation, dedication and sensitivity of its managers.

■ *The quality of the workforce.* The more skilled and the better motivated is a company's workforce, the better will be its results.

■ *Systems.* The functioning of any organisation will depend on the systems in place: information systems, systems for motivation (rewards, penalties, team spirit, etc.), technical systems (for sequencing production, for quality control, for setting specifications), distributional systems (transport, ordering and supply), financial systems (for accounting and auditing), and so on.

We shall be examining many of these features of internal organisation in subsequent chapters.

> ## Pause for thought
>
> *Other than profit and sales, what other objectives might managers have and how would you expect this to affect the price charged and output sold?*

SUMMARY

1a Business economics is about the study of economic decisions made by business and the influences upon this. It is also concerned with the effects that this decision making has upon other businesses and the performance of the economy in general.

1b The business environment refers to the environment within which business decision making takes place. When analysing a business's environment it has been traditional to divide it into four dimensions: political, economic, social and technological (PEST). It is common practice nowadays, however, to add a further three dimensions: environmental, ethical and legal (STEEPLE).

1c The economic dimension of the business environment is divided into two: the microeconomic environment and the macroeconomic environment. The microenvironment concerns factors specific to a particular firm in a particular market. The macroenvironment concerns how national and international economic circumstances affect all business, although to different degrees.

2a Production is divided into primary, secondary, tertiary or quaternary. In most advanced countries, the tertiary and quaternary sectors have grown relative to the secondary sector.

2b Firms are classified into industries and industries into sectors. Such classification enables us to chart changes in industrial structure over time and to assess changing patterns of industrial concentration, its causes and effects.

3 The performance of a business is determined by a wide range of both internal and external factors, such as business organisation, the aims of owners and managers, and market structure.

REVIEW QUESTIONS

1 Assume you are a Japanese car manufacturer with a plant located in the UK and are seeking to devise a business strategy for the twenty-first century. Conduct a STEEPLE analysis on the UK car industry and evaluate the various strategies that the business might pursue.

2 What is the Standard Industrial Classification (SIC)? In what ways might such a classification system be useful? Can you think of any limitations or problems such a system might have over time?

3 Into which of the three sectors would you put (a) the fertiliser industry; (b) a marketing agency serving the electronics industry?

4 Consider a country other than the UK and investigate the changes in its industrial structure. Are the changes similar to or different from those in the UK?

5 Outline the main determinants of business performance. Distinguish whether these are micro- or macroeconomic.

Economics and the world of business

Business issues covered in this chapter

- How do economists set about analysing business decision making?
- What are the core economic concepts that are necessary to understand the economic choices that businesses have to make, such as what to produce, what inputs and what technology to use, where to locate their production and how best to compete with other firms?
- What is meant by 'opportunity cost'? How is it relevant when people make economic choices?
- What is the difference between microeconomics and macroeconomics?

2.1 WHAT DO ECONOMISTS STUDY?

You may never have studied economics before and, yet, as individuals, we are constantly facing economic problems and making economic decisions. What should I buy in the supermarket? Should I save up for a summer holiday, or spend more on day-to-day living? Should I go to university, or should I try to find a job now?

Traditional and social media are full of stories relating to the economy and to particular economic issues, such as price changes, new products, the effects of globalisation, changes in interest rates, government policy, the state of public finances, fluctuations in exchange rates and changes in the performance of the economy. All of these events and more are relevant to our lives and directly impact businesses of all sizes.

Furthermore, with recent events, such as the financial crisis, the UK's vote to leave the EU, changes in US politics, calls for greater protectionism, growing environmental concerns and questions of inequality, interest in economics has grown.

Therefore, anybody studying economics is doing so at incredibly interesting, if not turbulent, times. In addition, there continues to be a lively debate among economists about the discipline: a debate fuelled initially by the financial crisis. This text aims to give you a better understanding of the economic influences on business in a dynamic world.

Tackling the problem of scarcity

In the previous chapter we looked at various aspects of the business environment and the influences on firms. We also looked at some of the economic problems that businesses face. But what contribution can economists make to the analysis of these problems and to recommending solutions?

To answer this question we need to go one stage back and ask what it is that economists study in general. What is it that makes a problem an *economic* problem? The answer is that there is one central problem faced by all individuals, firms, governments and in all societies, no matter how rich they are. From this one problem stem all the other economic problems we will be looking at throughout this book. This is the problem of *scarcity*.

Would you like more money? Your answer is probably yes, as this will mean you can buy more goods and services. And it does not matter how wealthy you are: almost everyone will answer yes! Consumer wants are virtually unlimited.

The production of goods and services involves the use of inputs, or *factors of production* as they are often called. There are three broad types of inputs:

- Human resources: *labour*. The labour force is limited both in number and in skills.
- Natural resources: *land and raw materials*. The world's land area is limited, as are its raw materials.
- Manufactured resources: *capital*. Capital consists of all those inputs that themselves have had to be produced in the first place. The world has a limited stock of capital: a limited supply of factories, machines, transportation and other equipment. The productivity of capital is limited by the state of technology.

As all of these resources are limited, this means that, at any one time, the world can produce only a limited amount of goods and services.

So here is the reason for scarcity: human wants are virtually unlimited, whereas the resources available to satisfy these wants are limited. We can thus define *scarcity* as follows:

 Scarcity is the excess of human wants over what can actually be produced. Because of scarcity, various choices have to be made between alternatives.

Of course, we do not all face the problem of scarcity to the same degree. A poor person unable to afford enough to eat or a decent place to live will hardly see it as a 'problem' that a rich person cannot afford a second Ferrari. But economists do not claim that we all face an *equal* problem of scarcity. The point is that people, both rich and poor, want more than they can have and this will cause them to behave in certain ways. Economics studies that behaviour.

Pause for thought

If we would all like more money, why doesn't the government or central bank print a lot more? Could this solve the problem of scarcity 'at a stroke'?

Two of the key elements in satisfying wants are, therefore, *consumption* and *production*. As far as consumption is concerned, economics studies how much the population spends; what the pattern of consumption is in the economy; and how much people buy of particular items. The business economist, in particular, studies consumer behaviour; how sensitive consumer demand is to changes in prices, advertising, fashion and other factors; and how the firm can seek to persuade the consumer to buy its products.

As far as production is concerned, economics studies how much the economy produces in total; what influences the rate of growth of production; and why the production of some goods increases and the production of others falls. The business economist tends to focus on the role of the firm in this process: what determines the output of individual businesses and the range of products they produce; what techniques firms use and why; and what determines their investment decisions and how many workers they employ.

We will be studying the way in which firms use their resources to produce goods and services and how consumers make their choices given the constraints they face. Economics therefore studies choices and behaviour which, in one way or another, are related to consumption and production.

Definitions

Scarcity The excess of human wants over what can actually be produced to fulfil these wants.

Factors of production (or resources) The inputs into the production of goods and services: labour, land and raw materials, and capital.

Labour All forms of human input, both physical and mental, into current production.

Land (and raw materials) Inputs into production that are provided by nature, e.g. unimproved land and mineral deposits in the ground.

Capital All inputs into production that have themselves been produced, e.g. factories, machines and tools.

Consumption The act of using goods and services to satisfy wants. This will normally involve purchasing the goods and services.

Production The transformation of inputs into outputs by firms in order to earn profit (or meet some other objective).

Demand and supply

We said that economics is concerned with consumption and production. Another way of looking at this is in terms of *demand* and *supply*. In fact, demand and supply and the relationship between them lie at the very centre of economics. But what do we mean by the terms, and what is their relationship with the problem of scarcity?

Demand is related to wants. If goods and services were free, people simply would demand and consume whatever they wanted. Such wants are virtually boundless: perhaps only limited by people's imagination.

Supply, on the other hand, is limited. The amount that firms can supply depends on the resources and technology available .

Given the problem of scarcity, given that human wants exceed what can actually be produced, *potential* demands will exceed *potential* supplies. Society therefore has to find some way of dealing with this problem. Somehow it has to try to match demand and supply. This applies at the level of the economy overall: *aggregate* demand will need to be balanced against *aggregate* supply. In other words, total spending in the economy must balance total production. It also applies at the level of individual goods and services. The demand and supply of cabbages must balance, as must the demand and supply of TVs, cars, houses and bus journeys.

But if potential demand exceeds potential supply, how are *actual* demand and supply to be made equal? Either demand has to be curtailed or supply has to be increased, or a combination of the two. Economics studies this process. It studies how demand adjusts to available supplies, and how supply adjusts to consumer demands.

Dividing up the subject

Economics traditionally is divided into two main branches – *microeconomics* and *macroeconomics,* where 'micro' means small and 'macro' means big.

- *Microeconomics* examines the individual parts of the economy. It is concerned with the factors that determine the demand and supply of particular goods and services and resources: cars, butter, clothes and haircuts; electricians, shop assistants, blast furnaces, computers and oil. It explores issues in competition between firms and the rationale for trade.

- *Macroeconomics* examines the economy as a whole. It is thus concerned with **aggregate demand** and **aggregate supply**. By 'aggregate demand' we mean the total amount of spending in the economy, whether by consumers, by overseas customers for our exports, by the government, or by firms when they buy capital equipment or stock up on raw materials. By 'aggregate supply' we mean the total national output of goods and services.

Business economics, because it studies firms, is concerned largely with microeconomic issues. Nevertheless, given that businesses are affected by what is going on in the economy as a whole, it is still important for the business economist to study the macroeconomic environment and its effects on individual firms.

> ### Definitions
>
> **Microeconomics** The branch of economics that studies individual units (e.g. households, firms and industries). It studies the interrelationships between these units in determining the pattern of production and distribution of goods and services.
>
> **Macroeconomics** The branch of economics that studies economic aggregates (grand totals), for example the overall level of prices, output and employment in the economy.
>
> **Aggregate demand (*AD*)** Total spending on goods and services made in the economy. It consists of four elements: consumer spending (*C*), investment (*I*), government spending (*G*) and the expenditure on exports (*X*), less any expenditure on foreign goods and services (*M*): $AD = C + I + G + X - M$.
>
> **Aggregate supply** The total amount that firms plan to supply at any given level of prices.

2.2 BUSINESS ECONOMICS: MICROECONOMIC CHOICES

Microeconomics and choice

Scarce resources mean that choices have to be made. There are three main categories of choice that must be made in any society:

- *What* goods and services are going to be produced and in what quantities, given that there are not enough resources to produce all the things that people desire? How many cars, how much wheat, how much insurance, how many rock concerts, etc. will be produced?

- *How* are things going to be produced, given that there is normally more than one way of producing things? What resources are going to be used and in what quantities? What techniques of production are going to be adopted? Will cars be produced by robots or by assembly-line workers? Will electricity be produced from coal, oil, gas, nuclear fission, renewable resources or a mixture of these?

- *For whom* are things going to be produced? In other words, how is the nation's income going to be distributed? After all, the higher your income, the more you can consume of the nation's output. What will be the wages of farm workers, printers, cleaners and accountants? How much will pensioners receive? How much profit will owners of private companies receive or will state-owned industries make? How will goods and services be allocated?

All societies have to make these choices, whether they be made by individuals, by groups or by the government. These choices can be seen as *micro*economic choices, since they are concerned not with the *total* amount of national output, but with the *individual* goods and services that make it up: what they are, how they are made and who gets the incomes to buy them.

Choice and opportunity cost

Choice involves sacrifice. The more food you choose to buy, the less money you will have to spend on other goods. The more food a nation produces, the fewer resources there will be for producing other goods. In other words, the production or consumption of one thing involves the sacrifice of alternatives. This sacrifice of alternatives in the production (or consumption) of a good is known as its **opportunity cost**.

 KEY IDEA 3 *The opportunity cost of something is what you give up to get it/do it.* In other words, it is cost measured in terms of the best alternative forgone.

If the workers on a farm can produce either 1000 tonnes of wheat or 2000 tonnes of barley, then the opportunity cost of producing 1 tonne of wheat is the 2 tonnes of barley forgone. The opportunity cost of buying a textbook is the new pair of jeans you also wanted that you have had to go without. The opportunity cost of working overtime is the leisure you have sacrificed.

Rational choices

Economists often refer to **rational choices**. This simply means the weighing up of the *costs* and *benefits* of any activity, whether it be firms choosing what and how much to produce, workers choosing whether to take a particular job or to work extra hours, or consumers choosing what to buy.

Imagine you are shopping and you want to buy a loaf of bread. Do you spend a lot of money and buy a high-quality, organic hand-crafted loaf, or do you buy a cheap factory-produced loaf? To make a rational (i.e. sensible) decision, you will need to weigh up the costs and benefits of each alternative. The hand-crafted loaf may give you a lot of enjoyment, but it has a high opportunity cost: because it is expensive, you will need to sacrifice quite a lot of consumption of other goods if you decide to buy it. If you buy the cheap one, however, although you will not enjoy it so much, you will have more money left over to buy other things: it has a lower opportunity cost.

Pause for thought

Assume that you are looking for a job and are offered two. One is more pleasant to do, but pays less. How would you make a rational choice between the two jobs?

Thus rational decision making, as far as consumers are concerned, involves choosing those items that give you the best value for money: i.e. the *greatest benefit relative to cost*.

The same principles apply to firms when deciding what to produce. For example, should a car firm open up another production line? A rational decision will, again, involve weighing up the benefits and costs. The benefits are the revenues that the firm will earn from selling the extra cars. The costs will include the extra labour costs, raw material costs, costs of component parts, etc. It will be profitable to open up the new production line only if the revenues earned exceed the costs entailed: in other words, if it earns a profit.

 KEY IDEA 4 *Rational decision making involves weighing up the marginal benefit and marginal cost of any activity.* If the marginal benefit exceeds the marginal cost, it is rational to do the activity (or to do more of it). If the marginal cost exceeds the marginal benefit, it is rational not to do it (or to do less of it).

In the more complex situation of deciding which model of car to produce, or how many of each model, the firm must weigh up the relative benefits and costs of each: i.e. it will want to produce the most profitable product mix.

Marginal costs and benefits

In economics we argue that rational choices involve weighing up **marginal costs** and **marginal benefits**. These are the costs and benefits of doing a little bit more or a little bit less

KI 4 p19

Definitions

Opportunity cost The cost of any activity measured in terms of the best alternative forgone.

Rational choices Choices that involve weighing up the benefit of any activity against its opportunity cost.

Marginal costs The additional cost of doing a little bit more (or 1 *unit* more if a unit can be measured) of an activity.

Marginal benefits The additional benefits of doing a little bit more (or 1 *unit* more if a unit can be measured) of an activity.

BOX 2.1	WHAT, HOW AND FOR WHOM

Who answers these questions?

As we have seen, in microeconomics there are three key questions: what to produce; how to produce; for whom to produce. These questions have to be answered because of the problem of scarcity. However, the scarcity problem does not tell us anything about who answers these questions and how the problems are addressed.

In some economies, it is the government or some central planning authority that answers these questions. This is known as a *planned* or *command economy*. At the other end of the spectrum is a *free-market* or *laissez-faire economy*, where there is no government intervention and it is individuals and firms who answer the questions above.

In practice, all economies are *mixed economies*, where decisions are taken by government, individuals and firms. It is the degree of government intervention that distinguishes different economic systems and determines how far towards each end of the spectrum an economy lies.

In countries such as North Korea, China or Cuba, the government has a large role, whereas in the USA, Ireland, Switzerland and various other Western economies, the government plays a much smaller role. Furthermore, governments differ in the type of intervention, such as regulation, taxation and public ownership, so any comparisons between countries and the amount of intervention should be made with caution.

Over the past 30 years, there has been a general shift towards the free-market end of the spectrum, as more and more countries have moved away from central planning. So, why are more countries increasingly relying on the free market to answer the questions of what, how and for whom to produce?

The command economy

In a command economy, it is the role of the state to allocate resources. It will decide how much should be invested and in what industries. It may tell each industry and individual firms which goods to produce, how much to produce and how they should be producing: e.g. the technology to use and labour requirements.

The state will also have a role in deciding how output should be distributed between consumers and the payments received for resources, such as labour, i.e. the 'for whom' question. Government may distribute goods based on its judgement of its people's needs; it could distribute goods and services directly through rationing or could determine the distribution of income and perhaps prices to influence consumer expenditure.

Although countries have moved more towards the free-market, there are advantages of this type of economic system. Governments can achieve high rates of growth through its allocation of resources to investment and also avoid unemployment by dictating the allocation of labour. Goods and services such as education, policing and national defence would be provided and governments could take account of 'bad' things, such as pollution, which is unlikely to happen in an economy where there is no government intervention. However, there is likely to be a significant amount of bureaucracy and the administrative costs of a command economy are prohibitive, as modern economies are very complex, meaning that planning would require a huge amount of complex information.

Furthermore, incentives may be very limited. For example, if income is distributed relatively equally between individuals,

---

Definitions

Planned or **command economy** An economy where all economic decisions are taken by the central (or local) authorities.

Free-market or **laissez-faire economy** An economy where all economic decisions are taken by individual households and firms, with no government intervention.

Mixed economy An economy where economic decisions are made partly through the market and partly by the government.

---

of a specific activity. They can be contrasted with the *total* costs and benefits of the activity.

Take a familiar example. What time will you set the alarm clock to go off tomorrow morning? Let us say that you have to leave home at 8.30. Perhaps you will set the alarm for 7.00. That will give you plenty of time to get up and get ready, but it will mean a relatively short night's sleep. Perhaps, then, you will decide to set it for 7.30 or even 8.00. That will give you a longer night's sleep, but much more of a rush in the morning to get ready.

So how do you make a rational decision about when the alarm should go off? What you have to do is to weigh up the costs and benefits of *additional* sleep. Each extra minute in

bed gives you more sleep (the marginal benefit), but gives you more of a rush when you get up (the marginal cost). The decision is, therefore, based on the costs and benefits of *extra* sleep, not on the *total* costs and benefits of a whole night's sleep.

This same principle applies to rational decisions made by consumers, workers and firms. For example, the car firm we were considering just now will weigh up the marginal costs and benefits of producing cars: in other words, it will compare the costs and revenue of producing *additional* cars. If additional cars add more to the firm's revenue than to its costs, it will be profitable to produce them.

this could reduce the incentive to work harder or to train. Or if firms are rewarded by meeting targets for output, they may reduce the quality of goods in order to meet the targets.

Consumers and producers may lack individual liberty, being told what to produce and consume and this, in turn, could create shortages and surpluses. Government may dictate what is produced, but what happens if consumers don't want the goods that the government requires firms to produce? A shortage will emerge and, with the state setting prices, the price cannot adjust to eliminate the shortage. Conversely, too much of some goods may be produced, given consumer tastes, and, once again, the price cannot adjust to eliminate the surplus. In both cases, there is an inefficient use and allocation of resources.

Most of these problems were experienced in the former Soviet Union and the other Eastern bloc countries, and were part of the reason for the overthrow of their communist regimes.

The free-market economy

In a free-market economy, it is the firms who decide what to produce and they will respond to consumer tastes.
As consumer demand or supply conditions change, prices can adjust. A shortage will push prices up and a surplus will push them down. And so, unlike in a command economy, shortages and surpluses can be eliminated.

This is one of the main advantages of a free-market economy. Resources will be used more efficiently, as firms and consumers have an incentive to act in their own self-interest. And these incentives can help to minimise the economic problem of scarcity. It also has the advantage of allowing individuals to have their liberty and make their own decisions and, because planning is not required, the bureaucracy and administrative costs are lower.

Despite the movement towards this type of economic system, it does still have its disadvantages. Without any government, some goods and services may not be produced, such as

national defence and street lights. Others may be under- or overproduced, including education and those goods whose manufacture creates pollution respectively. Unemployment may be high and society could be very unequal, perhaps through some firms dominating the market and earning substantial profits, and those people with power and influence exploiting those without.

The mixed economy

Given that there are disadvantages to both a free-market and a command economy, it is hardly surprising that all economies are mixed. Some goods/services are left entirely to the free market, where producers respond to signals from consumers when deciding what to produce and how much to charge. Other goods and services have some light-touch intervention, perhaps through regulation of price, quality or information – we often see this in utilities, such as energy or water. However, as we saw in the section above, a free-market economy may not produce some goods and services at all and it is in these cases where there may be a much larger role for the government to ensure an efficient allocation of resources, for example through the provision of health care or defence. But it is worth bearing in mind that while markets can fail, so can governments. We consider various forms of government intervention in Chapters 20, 21 and 22.

1. Draw a spectrum of economic systems ranging from command economy to free-market economy. Pick some countries and decide where you think they lie. Think about the role of government in each country and in which areas the government intervenes.
2. How would the positioning of countries along the spectrum of economic systems change if you were considering the 1980s?

Research the structure of the Chinese economy. What is the balance between planning and private decision making by companies?

Microeconomic choices and the firm

All economic decisions made by firms involve choices. The business economist studies these choices and their results.

We will look at the choices of how much to produce, what price to charge the customer, how many inputs to use, what types of input to use and in what combination. Firms will also need to make choices that have a much longer-term effect, such as whether to expand the scale of its operations, whether to invest in new plants, engage in research and development, whether to merge with or take over another company, diversify into other markets, or increase the amount it exports.

The right choices (in terms of best meeting the firm's objectives) will vary according to the type of market in which the firm operates, its predictions about future demand, its degree of power in the market, the actions and reactions of competitors, the degree and type of government intervention, the current tax regime, the availability of finance, and so on. In short, we will be studying the whole range of economic choices made by firms and how they may change in different scenarios.

In all these cases, the owners of firms will want the best possible choices to be made: i.e. those choices that best meet the objectives of the firm. Making the best choices, as we have seen, will involve weighing up the marginal benefits against the marginal opportunity costs of each decision.

KI 3
p 19

BOX 2.2 THE OPPORTUNITY COSTS OF STUDYING ECONOMICS

What are you sacrificing?

You may not have realised it, but you probably consider opportunity costs many times a day. The reason is that we are constantly making choices: what to buy, what to eat, what to wear, whether to go out, how much to study, and so on. Each time we make a choice to do something, we are, in effect, rejecting doing some alternative – after all, we can't do everything. This alternative forgone is the opportunity cost of our action.

Sometimes the opportunity costs of our actions are the direct monetary costs we incur. Sometimes it is more complicated.

Take the opportunity costs of your choices as a student of economics.

Buying a textbook costing £44.49

This does involve a direct money payment. What you have to consider is the alternatives you could have bought with the £44.49. You then have to weigh up the benefit from the best alternative against the benefit of the textbook.

1. *What might prevent you from making the best decision?*

Coming to classes

You may or may not be paying course fees. Even if you are, there is no extra (marginal) monetary cost in coming to classes once the fees have been paid. You will not get a refund by skipping classes!

So are the opportunity costs zero? No: by coming to classes you are not working in the library; you are not having an extra hour in bed; you are not sitting drinking coffee with friends, and so on. If you are making a rational decision to come to classes, then you will consider such possible alternatives.

2. *If there are several other things you could have done, is the opportunity cost the sum of all of them?*

Choosing to study at university or college

What are the opportunity costs of being a student in higher education?

At first, it might seem that the costs would include the following:

- tuition fees;
- books, stationery, etc.;
- accommodation expenses;
- transport;
- food, entertainment and other living expenses.

But adding these up does not give the opportunity cost. The opportunity cost is the sacrifice entailed by going to university or college rather than doing something else. Let us assume that the alternative is to take a job that has been offered. The correct list of opportunity costs of higher education would include:

- tuition fees;
- books, stationery, etc.;
- additional accommodation and transport expenses over what would have been incurred by taking the job;
- wages that would have been earned in the job less any student grant or loan interest subsidy received.

Note that tuition fees would not be included if they had been paid by someone else: for example, as part of a scholarship or a government grant.

3. *Why is the cost of food not included?*
4. *Make a list of the benefits of higher education.*
5. *Is the opportunity cost to the individual of attending higher education different from the opportunity costs to society as a whole?*

Estimate your own cost of studying for a degree (or other qualification). For what reasons might you find it difficult to make such a calculation?

2.3 BUSINESS ECONOMICS: THE MACROECONOMIC ENVIRONMENT

KI 2
p 17

Because things are scarce, societies are concerned that their resources are being used as *fully as possible,* and that over time the national output should *grow.*

The achievement of growth and the full use of resources is not easy, however, as demonstrated by the periods of high unemployment and stagnation that have occurred from time to time throughout the world (e.g. in the 1930s, the early 1980s, the early 1990s and the late 2000s). Furthermore, attempts by governments to stimulate growth and employment often have resulted in inflation and a large rise in imports. Even when societies do achieve growth, it can be short lived. Economies typically experience cycles, where periods of growth alternate with periods of stagnation, such periods varying from a few months to a few years.

Macroeconomics, then, studies the determination of national output and its growth over time. It also studies the problems of stagnation, unemployment, inflation, the balance of international payments and cyclical instability, and the policies adopted by governments to deal with these problems.

Macroeconomic problems are closely related to the balance between aggregate demand and aggregate supply. If aggregate demand is *too high* relative to aggregate supply, inflation and balance of payments deficits are likely to result.

- **Inflation** refers to a general rise in the level of prices throughout the economy. If aggregate demand rises substantially, firms are likely to respond by raising their prices. After all, if demand is high, they can probably still sell as much as before (if not more) even at the higher prices, and thus make more profit. If firms in general put up their prices, inflation results.
- **Balance of trade deficits** are the excess of imports over exports. If aggregate demand rises, part of the extra demand will be spent on imports, such as US tablets, Japanese MP3 players, German cars and Chilean wine. Also, if inflation is high, home-produced goods will become uncompetitive with foreign goods. We are likely, therefore, to buy more imports, and people abroad are likely to buy fewer of our exports.

If aggregate demand is *too low* relative to aggregate supply, unemployment and recession may well result.

- A **recession** is defined as where output in the economy declines for two consecutive quarters or more: in other words, where growth becomes negative over that time. A recession is associated with a low level of consumer spending. If people spend less, shops are likely to find themselves with unsold stocks. As a result, they will buy less from the manufacturers, which in turn will cut down on production.
- **Unemployment** is likely to result from cutbacks in production. If firms are producing less, they will need a smaller labour force.

Government macroeconomic *policy*, therefore, tends to focus on the balance of aggregate demand and aggregate supply. It can be **demand-side policy**, which seeks to influence the level of spending in the economy. This in turn will affect the level of production, prices and employment. Or it can be **supply-side policy**. This is designed to influence the level of production directly: for example, by creating more incentives for businesses to innovate.

Macroeconomic policy and its effects on business

Both demand-side and supply-side policy will affect the business environment. Take demand-side policy. If there is a recession, the government might try to boost the level of spending (aggregate demand) by cutting taxes, increasing government spending or reducing interest rates. If consumers respond by purchasing more, then this clearly will have an effect on businesses. So firms will want to be stocked up ready for an upsurge in consumer demand. Therefore, they will want to estimate the effect on their own particular market of a boost to aggregate demand. Studying the macroeconomic environment and the effects of government policy, therefore, is vital for firms when forecasting future demand for their product.

It is the same with supply-side policy. The government may introduce tax incentives for firms to invest, or for people to work harder; it may introduce new training schemes; it may build new motorways. These policies will affect firms' costs and hence the profitability of production. So, again, firms will want to predict how government policies are likely to affect them, so that they can plan accordingly.

The circular flow of income

One of the most useful diagrams for illustrating the macroeconomic environment and the relationships between producers and consumers is the *circular flow of income* diagram. This is illustrated in Figure 2.1.

The consumers of goods and services are labelled 'households'. Some members of households, of course, are also workers and, in some cases, are the owners of other factors of production too, such as land. The producers of goods and services are labelled 'firms'.

Firms and households are in a twin 'demand and supply' relationship.

First, on the right-hand side of the diagram, households demand goods and services, and firms supply goods and services. In the process, exchange takes place. In a money economy (as opposed to a **barter economy**), firms exchange goods and services for money. In other words, money flows from households to firms in the form of consumer expenditure, while goods and services flow the other way – from firms to households.

> ### Definitions
>
> **Rate of inflation (annual)** The percentage increase in the level of prices over a 12-month period.
>
> **Balance of trade** Exports of goods and services minus imports of goods and services. If exports exceed imports, there is a 'balance of trade surplus' (a positive figure). If imports exceed exports, there is a 'balance of trade deficit' (a negative figure).
>
> **Recession** A period where national output falls for a few months or more. The official definition is where real GDP declines for two or more consecutive quarters.
>
> **Unemployment** The number of people who are actively looking for work but are currently without a job. (Note that there is much debate as to who should be counted as officially unemployed.)
>
> **Demand-side policy** Government policy designed to alter the level of aggregate demand, and thereby the level of output, employment and prices.
>
> **Supply-side policy** Government policy that attempts to alter the level of aggregate supply directly.
>
> **Barter economy** An economy where people exchange goods and services directly with one another without any payment of money. Workers would be paid with bundles of goods.

KI 1
p11

BOX 2.3 LOOKING AT MACROECONOMIC DATA

Assessing different countries' macroeconomic performance

	Unemployment (% of workforce)				Inflation (%)				Economic growth (%)				Balance on current account[1] (% of national income)			
	USA	Japan	Germany	UK	USA	Japan	Germany	UK	USA	Japan	Germany	UK	USA	Japan	Germany	UK
1961–70	4.8	1.3	0.6	1.6	2.4	5.6	2.7	4.0	4.3	10.1	4.4	3.1	0.3	1.1	−0.1	0.7
1971–80	6.4	1.8	2.2	3.8	7.0	8.8	5.2	13.1	3.2	4.4	2.9	2.1	−0.4	−0.6	−0.3	−0.4
1981–90	7.1	2.5	6.0	9.6	4.4	1.8	2.6	6.1	3.3	4.6	2.3	2.9	−3.0	2.6	2.9	−1.1
1991–2000	5.6	3.3	8.1	7.9	2.1	0.5	1.8	2.8	3.4	1.3	2.0	2.5	−2.7	2.7	−1.4	−1.3
2001–10	6.1	4.7	8.8	5.6	2.0	−0.8	1.3	1.7	1.6	0.6	0.9	1.5	−4.7	3.7	4.7	−3.4
2011–19[2]	5.9	3.5	4.6	5.9	1.6	0.2	1.3	2.0	2.1	1.1	1.8	1.8	−1.7[3]	2.8	8.4	−4.3

Notes: [1] The current account balance is the balance of trade plus other income flows from and to abroad.
[2] 2018 and 2019 figures based on forecasts.
[3] USA data average 2011–17 only.
Source: Based on *Statistical Annex of the European Economy*, EC, 2018.

Rapid economic growth, low unemployment, low inflation and the avoidance of balance of trade deficits are the major macroeconomic policy objectives of most governments around the world. To help them achieve these objectives they employ economic advisers. But when we look at the performance of various economies, the success of government macroeconomic policies seems decidedly 'mixed'.

The table shows data for the USA, Japan, Germany and the UK from 1961 to 2019.

If the government does not have much success in managing the economy, it could be for the following reasons:

■ Economists have incorrectly analysed the problems and hence have given the wrong advice.
■ Economists disagree and hence have given conflicting advice.
■ Economists have based their advice on inaccurate forecasts.

■ Governments have not heeded the advice of economists.
■ There is little else that governments could have done: the problems were insoluble.

1. Has the UK generally fared better or worse than the other three countries?
2. Was there a common pattern in the macroeconomic performance of each of the four countries over this period of just over 50 years?

Choose one other EU country and, using the data source for the table above, compare its economic performance since 1981 with that of the other four countries in the table. You should look at each of the four indicators.

Figure 2.1 Circular flow of goods and incomes

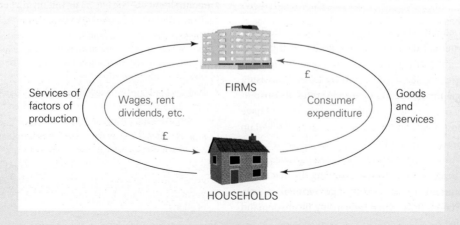

This coming together of buyers and sellers is known as a *market* – whether it be a street market, a shop, an auction, a mail-order system or whatever. Thus we talk about the market for apples, the market for oil, for cars, for houses, for televisions, and so on.

Second, firms and households come together in the market for factors of production. This is illustrated on the left-hand side of the diagram. This time the demand and supply roles are reversed. Firms demand the use of factors of production owned by households – labour, land and capital. Households supply them. Thus the services of labour and other factors flow from households to firms and, in exchange, firms pay households money – namely, wages, rent, dividends and interest. Just as we referred to particular goods markets, so we can also refer to particular factor markets – the market for bricklayers, for secretaries, for hairdressers, for land, etc.

There is, thus, a circular flow of incomes. Households earn incomes from firms and firms earn incomes from households. The money circulates. There is also a circular flow of goods and services, but in the opposite direction. Households supply factor services to firms, which then use them to supply goods and services to households.

Macroeconomics is concerned with the total size of the flow. If consumers choose to spend more, firms will earn more from the increased level of sales. They will probably respond by producing more or raising their prices, or some combination of the two. As a result, they will end up paying more out to workers in the form of wages, and to

shareholders in the form of profits. Households will thus gain additional income. This will then lead to an additional increase in consumer spending and, therefore, a further boost to production.

The effect does not go on indefinitely, however. When households earn additional incomes, not all of it is spent: not all of it recirculates. Some of the additional income will be saved; some will be paid in taxes; and some will be spent on imports (and thus will not stimulate domestic production). The bigger these 'withdrawals', as they are called, the less production will carry on being stimulated.

It is important for firms to estimate the eventual effect of an initial rise in consumer demand (or a rise in government expenditure, for that matter). Will there be a boom in the economy or will the rise in demand merely fizzle out? A study of macroeconomics helps business people to understand the effects of changes in aggregate demand and the effects that such changes will have on their own particular business. It helps with business planning.

We examine the macroeconomic environment and the effects on business of macroeconomic policy in Chapters 26–32.

Definition

Market The interaction between buyers and sellers.

2.4 TECHNIQUES OF ECONOMIC ANALYSIS

When students first come to economics, many are worried about the amount of mathematics they will encounter. Will it all be equations and graphs, with lots of calculations to do and difficult theories to grasp?

Economics can involve a lot of mathematics, but it doesn't have to and, as you will see if you glance through the pages of this text, there are many diagrams and tables, but only a few equations. The mathematical techniques that you will have to master are relatively limited, but they are ones that we use many times in many different contexts. You will

find that, if you are new to the subject, you will very quickly become familiar with these techniques. If you are not new to the subject, perhaps you could reassure your colleagues who are!

In the two Mathematical Appendices (A and B) on the student website, you will find a guide to some of the simple techniques that economists use. We suggest that you look through them at this stage. However, the first one, in particular, should provide a useful reference throughout your study of the book.

SUMMARY

1a The central economic problem is that of scarcity. Given that there is a limited supply of factors of production (labour, land, raw materials and capital), it is impossible to provide everybody with everything they want. Potential demands exceed potential supplies.

1b The subject of economics usually is divided into two main branches: macroeconomics and microeconomics.

2a Microeconomics deals with the activities of individual units within the economy: firms, industries, consumers, workers, etc. Because resources are scarce, people have to make choices. Society has to choose by some means or other *what* goods and services to produce, *how* to produce them and *for whom* to produce them. Microeconomics studies these choices.

2b Rational choices involve weighing up the marginal benefits of each activity against its marginal opportunity costs. If the marginal benefit exceeds the marginal cost, it is rational to choose to do more of that activity.

2c Businesses are constantly faced with choices: how much to produce, what inputs to use, what price to charge, how much to invest, etc. We will study these choices.

3a Macroeconomics deals with aggregates such as the overall levels of unemployment, output, growth and prices in the economy.

3b The macroeconomic environment will be an important determinant of a business's profitability.

REVIEW QUESTIONS

1 Virtually every good is scarce in the sense we have defined it. There are, however, a few exceptions. Under *certain circumstances,* water and air are not scarce. When and where might this be true for (a) water and (b) air? Why is it important to define water and air very carefully before deciding whether they are scarce or abundant? Under circumstances where they are *not* scarce, would it be possible to charge for them?

2 Which of the following are macroeconomic issues, which are microeconomic ones and which could be either, depending on the context?

   a) Inflation.
   b) Low wages in certain service industries.
   c) The rate of exchange between the pound and the euro.
   d) Why the price of cabbages fluctuates more than that of cars.
   e) The rate of economic growth this year compared with last year.
   f) The decline of traditional manufacturing industries.

3 Make a list of three things you did yesterday. What was the opportunity cost of each?

4 A washing machine manufacturer is considering whether to produce an extra batch of 1000 washing machines. How would it set about working out the marginal opportunity cost of so doing?

5 How would a firm use the principle of weighing up marginal costs and marginal benefits when deciding whether (a) to take on an additional worker; (b) to offer overtime to existing workers?

6 We identified three categories of withdrawal from the circular flow of income. What were they? There are also three categories of 'injection' of expenditure into the circular flow of income. What do you think they are?

3
Chapter

Business organisations

Business issues covered in this chapter

- How are businesses organised and structured?
- What are the aims of business?
- Will owners, managers and other employees necessarily have the same aims? How can those working in the firm be persuaded to achieve the objectives of their employers?
- What are the various legal categories of business and how do different legal forms suit different types of business?
- How do businesses differ in their internal organisation? What are the relative merits of alternative forms of organisation?

If you decide to grow strawberries in your garden or allotment, or if you decide to put up a set of shelves in your home, then you have made a production decision. Most production decisions, however, are not made by the individuals who will consume the product. Most production decisions are made by firms: whether by small one-person businesses or by giant multinational corporations, such as General Motors or Sony.

In this chapter we are going to investigate the firm: what is its role in the economy; what are the goals of firms; how do firms differ in respect to their legal status; and in what ways are they organised internally?

3.1 THE NATURE OF FIRMS

As firms have grown and become more complex, so the analysis of them has become more sophisticated. They are seen less and less like a 'black box', where inputs are fed in one end, used in the most efficient way and then output emerges from the other end. Instead, the nature and organisation of firms are seen to be key determinants of how they behave and of the role they play in respect to resource allocation and production.

Complex production

Very few goods or services are produced by one person alone. Most products require a complex production process that will involve many individuals. But how are these individuals to be organised in order to produce such goods and services? Two very different ways are:

- within markets via price signals;
- within firms via a hierarchy of managerial authority.

In the first of these two ways, each stage of production would involve establishing a distinct contract with each separate producer. Assume that you wanted to produce a woollen jumper. You would need to enter a series of separate contracts: to have the jumper designed, to buy the wool, to get the wool spun, to get it dyed, to have the jumper knitted. There are many other stages in the production and distribution process that might also be considered. With each contract a price will have to be determined, and that price will reflect current market conditions. In most cases, such a form of economic organisation would prove to be highly inefficient and totally impractical. Consider the number of contracts that might be necessary if you wished to produce a motor car!

With the second way of organising production, a single **firm** (or just a few firms) replaces the market. The co-ordination of the conversion of inputs into output takes place *within* the firm: not through the market mechanism, but by management issuing orders as to what to produce and the manner in which this is to take place. Hence the distinguishing feature of the firm is that the price mechanism plays little role in allocating resources within it.

The benefits of organising production within firms

The function of the firm is to bring together a series of production and distribution operations, doing away with the need for individuals to enter into narrowly specified contracts. If you want a woollen jumper, you go to a woollen jumper retailer.

According to Ronald Coase,[1] the key advantage of organising production and distribution through firms, as opposed to the market, is that it involves lower **transaction costs**. Transaction costs are the costs of making economic arrangements about production, distribution and sales.

> **KEY IDEA 5**
>
> **Transaction costs.** The costs incurred when firms buy inputs or services from other firms as opposed to producing them themselves. They include the costs of searching for the best firm to do business with, the costs of negotiating, drawing up, monitoring and enforcing contracts, and the costs of transporting and handling products between the firms. These costs should be weighed against the benefits of outsourcing through the market.

The transaction costs associated with individual contracts made through the market are likely to be substantial for the following reasons:

- The *uncertainty* in framing contracts. It is unlikely that decision makers will have perfect knowledge of their production processes, especially given their complexity. Given, then, that such contracts are established on imperfect information, they are consequently subject to error.

- The *complexity* of contracts. Many products require multiple stages of production. The more complex the product, the greater the number of contracts that would have to be made. The specifications within contracts may also become more complex, requiring high levels of understanding and knowledge of the production process, which raises the possibility of error in writing them. As contracts become more complex, they raise a firm's costs of production and make it more difficult to determine the correct price for a transaction.

- *Monitoring* contracts. Entering into a contract with another person may require you to monitor whether the terms of the contract are fulfilled. This may incur a significant time cost for the individual, especially if a large number of contracts require monitoring.

- *Enforcing* contracts. If one party breaks its contract, the legal expense of enforcing the contract or recouping any losses may be significant. Many individuals might find such costs prohibitive and, as a consequence, be unable to pursue broken contracts through the legal system.

What is apparent is that, for most goods, the firm represents a superior way to organise production. The actions of management replace the price signals of the market and overcome many of the associated transaction costs.

Goals of the firm

As we saw in Chapter 1 (page 14), economists traditionally assume that firms aim to maximise profits. But, while critics of the traditional theory tend to accept that this is true of the *owners* of firms, are the owners the people who actually make the decisions about how much to produce and at what price? In many firms, the answer is 'no'.

The divorce of ownership from control

As businesses steadily grew over the nineteenth and twentieth centuries, many owner-managers were forced, however reluctantly, to devolve some responsibility for the running of the business to other individuals. These new managers brought with them technical skills and business expertise, a crucial prerequisite for a modern successful business enterprise.

The managerial revolution that was to follow, in which business owners (shareholders) and managers became

> **Definitions**
>
> **Firm** An economic organisation that co-ordinates the process of production and distribution.
>
> **Transaction costs** The costs incurred when firms buy inputs or services from other firms as opposed to producing them themselves. They include the costs of searching for the best firm to do business with, the costs of drawing up, monitoring and enforcing contracts and the costs of transporting and handling products between the firms.

[1] Ronald H. Coase, 'The Nature of the Firm', *Economica,* Vol. 4, No. 16, Nov. 1937, pp. 386–405. See also: www.econlib.org/library/Enc/bios/Coase.html.

distinct groups, called into question what the precise goals of the business enterprise might now be. This debate was to be further fuelled by the growth of the **joint-stock company** (a structure first recognised in England in the sixteenth century) in which the ownership of the enterprise was progressively dispersed over a large number of shareholders. The growth in the joint-stock company was a direct consequence of business owners looking to raise large amounts of investment capital in order to maintain or expand business activity.

This twin process of managerial expansion and widening share ownership led Berle and Means[2] to argue that the *ownership* of stocks and shares in an enterprise no longer meant *control* over its assets. Subsequently, they drew a distinction between 'nominal ownership', namely getting a return from investing in a business, and 'effective ownership', which is the ability to control and direct the assets of the business. The more dispersed nominal ownership becomes, the less and less likely it is that there will be effective ownership by shareholders. (This issue will be considered in more detail in Chapter 13.)

The modern company is *legally* separate from its owners (as you will discover in section 3.2). Hence the assets are legally owned by the business itself. Consequently, the group *in charge* of the business is that which controls the use of these assets: i.e. the group that determines the business's objectives and implements the necessary procedures to secure them. In most companies this group is the managers.

Berle and Means argued that, as a consequence of this transition from owner to manager control, conflicts are likely to develop between the goals of managers and those of the owners. But what are the objectives of managers? Will they want to maximise profits or will they have some other aim?

Managers may want to maximise their *own* interests, such as pursuing higher salaries, greater power or prestige, greater sales, better working conditions or greater popularity with their subordinates. Different managers in the same firm may well pursue different aims. But these aims may conflict with the owners' aims of profit maximisation.

Managers will still have to ensure that *sufficient* profits are made to keep shareholders happy, but that may be very different from *maximising* profits. Alternative theories of the firm to those of profit maximisation, therefore, tend to assume that large firms are **profit 'satisficers'**. That is, managers strive hard for a minimum target level of profit, but are less interested in profits above this level. (An article from Bloomberg considers some of the background to the theory and more recent evidence relating to Japanese scandals.)[3]

Such theories fall into two categories: first, those theories that assume that firms attempt to maximise some other aim, provided that sufficient profits are achieved; and second, those theories that assume that firms pursue a number of potentially conflicting aims, of which sufficient profit is merely one. (These alternative theories are examined more fully in Chapter 14.)

> ### Pause for thought
>
> *Make a list of six possible aims that a manager of a high street department store might have. Identify some conflicts that might arise between these aims.*

 KEY IDEA 6 *The nature of institutions and organisations is likely to influence behaviour.* There are various forces influencing people's decisions in complex organisations. Assumptions that an organisation will follow one simple objective (e.g. short-run profit maximisation) are thus too simplistic in many cases.

The principal–agent relationship

Can the owners of a firm ever be sure that their managers will pursue the business strategy most appropriate to achieving the owners' goals (traditionally, profit maximisation)? This is an example of what is known as the **principal–agent problem**.

One of the features of a complex modern economy is that people (principals) have to employ others (agents) to carry out their wishes. If you want to go on holiday, it is easier to go to a travel agent to sort out the arrangements than to do it all yourself. Likewise, if you want to buy a house, it is more convenient to go to an estate agent.

The crucial advantage that agents have over their principals is specialist knowledge and information. This is frequently the basis upon which agents are employed. For example, owners employ managers for their specialist knowledge of a market or their understanding of business practice. But this situation of **asymmetric information** – that one party (the agent) knows more than the other (the

> ### Definitions
>
> **Joint-stock company** A company where ownership is distributed between a large number of shareholders.
>
> **Profit satisficing** Where decision makers in a firm aim for a target level of profit rather than the absolute maximum level. By not aiming for the maximum profit, this allows managers to pursue other objectives, such as sales maximisation or their own salary or prestige.
>
> **Principal–agent problem** One where people (principals), as a result of lack of knowledge, cannot ensure that their best interests are served by their agents.
>
> **Asymmetric information** A situation in which one party in an economic relationship knows more than another.

[2] Adolf A. Berle Jr. and Gardiner C. Means, *The Modern Corporation and Private Property* (Macmillan, 1932).

[3] Noah Smith, 'Japan Inc. scandals build a case for corporate reform'; *Bloomberg* (12 October 2017).

principal) – means that it will be very difficult for the principal to judge in whose interest the agent is operating. Are managers pursuing their own goals rather than the goals of the owner?

> **KEY IDEA 7**
>
> **The principal–agent problem.** Where people (principals), as a result of a lack of knowledge, cannot ensure that their best interests are served by their agents. Agents may take advantage of this situation to the disadvantage of the principals.

Principals may attempt to reconcile the fact that they have imperfect information and are, thus, in an inherently weak position, in the following ways:

- *Monitoring* the performance of the agent. Shareholders could monitor the performance of their senior managers through attending annual general meetings. The managers could be questioned by shareholders and, ultimately, replaced if their performance is seen as unsatisfactory.
- Establishing a series of *incentives* to ensure that agents act in the principals' best interest. For example, managerial pay could be closely linked to business performance (e.g. profitability). Schemes such as profit sharing encourage managers (agents) to act in the owners' (principals') interests, thereby aligning their objectives. However, this is likely to be more effective with a larger incentive: e.g. the larger the share in company profits, the more inclined managers will be to act in the owners' interests. However, the larger the incentive the more costly it is likely to be to the owners.

> **Pause for thought**
>
> *Identify a situation where you, as a consumer, are in a principal–agent relationship with a supplier. How can you minimise the problem of asymmetric information in this relationship?*

Within any firm there will exist a complex chain of principal–agent relationships – between workers and managers, between junior managers and senior managers, between senior managers and directors, and between directors and shareholders. All groups will hold some specialist knowledge that might be used to further their own distinct goals. Predictably, the development of effective monitoring and evaluation programmes and the creation of performance-related pay schemes have been two central themes in the development of business practices in recent years – a sign that the principal is looking to fight back.

Staying in business

Aiming for profits, sales, salaries, power, etc. will be useless if the firm does not survive! Trying to *maximise* any of the various objectives may be risky. For example, if a firm tries to maximise its market share by aggressive advertising or price cutting, it might invoke a strong response from its rivals. The resulting war may drive it out of business. Some of the managers may move easily to other jobs and actually may gain from the experience, but the majority are likely to lose. Concern with survival, therefore, may make firms cautious.

Not all firms, however, make survival the top priority. Some are adventurous and are prepared to take risks. Adventurous firms are most likely to be those dominated by a powerful and ambitious individual – an individual prepared to take gambles.

The more dispersed the decision-making power is in the firm, and the more worried managers are about their own survival, the more cautious are their policies likely to be: preferring 'tried and trusted' methods of production, preferring to stick with products that have proved to be popular, and preferring to expand slowly and steadily.

If a firm is too cautious, however, it may not survive. It may find that it loses market share to more innovative or aggressive competitors. Ultimately, a firm must balance caution against keeping up with competitors, ensuring that the customer is sufficiently satisfied and that costs are kept sufficiently low by efficient management and the introduction of new technology.

The efficient operation of the firm may be influenced strongly by its internal organisational structure. We will consider this in more detail (see section 3.3), but first we must consider how the *legal* structure of the firm might influence its conduct within the marketplace. KI 6 p 29

> **Pause for thought**
>
> *Why is a firm facing little competition from rivals likely to have higher profits, but also higher costs, than a firm facing intense competition?*

3.2 THE FIRM AS A LEGAL ENTITY

 KI 6 p 29 The legal structure of the firm is likely to have a significant impact on its conduct, and subsequent performance, within the marketplace. In the UK, there are several types of firm, each with a distinct legal status.

The sole proprietor

Here, the business is owned by just one person. Usually, such businesses are small, with only a few employees. Retailing, construction and farming are typical areas where sole

BOX 3.1 EXPLOITING ASYMMETRIC INFORMATION

Examples of the principal–agent relationship

The issue of asymmetric information and its implications for the principal–agent relationship is not just a problem within firms. It exists in many walks of life where two parties are involved in some sort of transaction, but where one party has more information than the other and it may be in their interests to use that extra information to gain an advantage.

Second-hand cars

Assume you want to buy a second-hand car and go to a second-hand car dealer. When looking at a particular car, you might look at the mileage, the upholstery and whether there are any scratches on the bodywork or any obvious damage. You'll ask about any problems or reliability issues.

But, even if you have expert knowledge about cars, the dealer will have much better information than you as to how good (or bad) it really is. They may 'neglect' to tell you about the rust on the underside of the car, the problems of starting it on a cold morning or its history of unreliability. By omitting certain bad things about the car, they will hope to gain a higher price and thus use the problem of asymmetric information to their advantage.

George Akerlof published a paper in the 1970s, entitled 'The Market for "Lemons"',[1] in which he considered the problem of asymmetric information in the market for used cars. In the paper, he showed how poor information on the part of customers can, in extreme circumstances, lead to the total unravelling of the market – second-hand car dealers consistently try to sell poor quality cars (or 'lemons') as 'reliable' ones and consumers, unable to distinguish poor quality cars, become increasingly mistrustful.

Elections

Whether it is at school, college, university or even in government, you need votes to win an election. Depeding on the context, there will be certain things that are more likely to lead to victory. Perhaps at school, it's campaigning for shorter days or no uniforms. At university, it might be about providing more contact with academic staff and, at a general election, it might be about redistributing income, protecting education or health care, or investing money in regeneration projects.

But here, too, there is a problem of asymmetric information. Whatever the campaign promises, the people seeking election (the agents) generally know better than the electorate (the principals) whether or not their manifesto is viable; whether they will stick to their promises or if they are merely promises to gain votes. There are countless past examples from across the world of broken promises.[2]

Internet dating

The world of online dating has grown significantly over the past few years, with more and more people taking to the web to find their perfect match. But here is another classic example of the problem of asymmetric information. Dating sites (so we're told!) require you to upload a picture and complete some general information about yourself: your likes, dislikes, height, age, education, salary, occupation, location, etc.

However, when you complete that information, only you know how much of it is completely true. There are, inevitably, certain characteristics that make people's profiles more attractive – perhaps you exaggerate your height or salary or take a few years off your age. Whatever 'white lies' you tell, you have much better information as to your own profile than those looking at it. Of course, the same applies to you when you accept a date with someone who has seen your profile – they have more information than you as to whether their picture is recent or taken a decade ago!

Interviews

When you apply for a job, you will probably write lots of wonderful things about yourself. If you are lucky enough to be invited for interview, you will, undoubtedly, repeat those things and elaborate on just how committed you would be if you were offered the job.

■ Would you be willing to stay late, if it was required? Of course you would!
■ What about coming in early or at weekends? No problem!
■ Are you happy working as part of a team? You love working with others!
■ Can you manage and prioritise a heavy workload? Efficiency is your middle name! And so on . . .

You say all of these things to impress the interview panel and thus increase your chances of getting the job. However, you know much better than the interviewers if you really mean these things. When it comes down to it, will you really come in at the weekend if you're not obliged to do so?

Asymmetric information creates an issue, as you, the interviewee, have much better information about your personality, your aims and commitment to the job, than the interviewers. Of course, they can and will ask for references, but hopefully you've been sensible enough to ask only those people who think well of you to supply them!

 Give some other examples of where asymmetric information might cause problems for one party.

 Consider your own interactions with other people over the past week. In which cases were you (a) the principal, (b) the agent, (c) neither as it was not a principal–agent interaction? In the cases of (a) and (b), to what extent did asymmetric information influence the nature and outcome of the interaction?

---

[2]See, for example, Stef W. Kight, '10 big broken promises of past presidents', *Axios* (2 May 2017) and Ryan Koronowski. 'Trump broke 80 promises in 100 days', *Think Progress* (29 April 2017).

---

[1]G. Akerlof, 'The Market for "Lemons": Quality, Uncertainty and the Market Mechanism', *The Quarterly Journal of Economics*, Vol. 84, No. 3. (August 1970)

proprietorships are found. Such businesses are easy to set up and may require only a relatively small initial capital investment. They may well flourish if the owner is highly committed to the business and can respond to changing market conditions. They suffer two main disadvantages, however:

- *Limited scope for expansion.* Finance is limited to what the owner can raise personally, e.g. through savings or a bank loan. Also there is a limit to the size of an organisation that one person can effectively control.
- *Unlimited liability.* The owner is personally liable for any losses that the business might make. This could result in the owner's house, car and other assets being seized to pay off any outstanding debts, should the business fail.

The partnership

This is where two or more people own the business. In most partnerships there is a legal limit of 20 partners. Partnerships are common in the same fields as sole proprietorships. They are also common in the professions: solicitors, accountants, surveyors, etc. With more owners, there is more scope for expansion, as extra finance can be raised. Also, as each partner can specialise in one aspect of the business, larger organisations are often more viable. However, taking on partners does mean a loss of control through shared decision making.

Although, since 2001, it has been possible to form limited liability partnerships, many partnerships still have unlimited liability. This problem could be very serious. The mistakes of one partner could jeopardise the personal assets of all the other partners.

Where large amounts of capital are required and/or when the risks of business failure are relatively high, partnerships without limited liability are not an appropriate form of organisation. In such cases, it is best to form a company (or 'joint-stock company' to give it its full title).

Companies

A company is legally separate from its owners. This means that it can enter into contracts and own property. Any debts are *its* debts, not the owners'. The owners are the shareholders, each of whom receives his or her share of the company's distributed profit: these payments are called 'dividends' and the size will depend on the profit made and the number of shares held.

The owners have only *limited liability*. This means that, if the company goes bankrupt, the owners will lose the amount of money they have invested in the company, but no more. Their personal assets cannot be seized. This has the advantage of encouraging people to become shareholders and, indeed, large companies may have thousands of shareholders – some with very small holdings and others, including institutional shareholders such as pension funds, with very large holdings. Without the protection of limited liability,

many of these investors would never put their money into any company that involved even the slightest risk. It also means that companies can raise significant finance, thus creating greater scope for expansion.

Shareholders often take no part in the running of the firm. They may elect a board of directors which decides broad issues of company policy. The board of directors, in turn, appoints managers who make the day-to-day decisions, which has its own problems, as we have seen. There are two types of company: public and private.

Public limited companies. A public limited company is not a nationalised industry: it is still in the private sector. It is 'public' because it can offer new shares publicly: by issuing a prospectus, it can invite the public to subscribe to a new share issue. In addition, many public limited companies are quoted on a stock exchange, where existing shareholders can sell some or all of their shares. The prices of these shares will be determined by demand and supply. A public limited company must hold an annual shareholders' meeting. Examples of well-known UK public limited companies are Marks & Spencer, BP, Barclays, BSkyB and Tesco.

Private limited companies. Private limited companies cannot offer their shares publicly. Shares have to be sold privately. This makes it more difficult for private limited companies to raise finance and, consequently, they tend to be smaller than public companies. They are, however, easier to set up than public companies. One of the most famous examples of a private limited company was Manchester United Football Club (which used to be a public limited company until it was bought out by the Glazer family in 2005). It then became a public limited company again in August 2012 when 10 per cent of the shares were floated on the New York Stock Exchange.

Consortia of firms

It is common, especially in large civil engineering projects that involve very high risks, for many firms to work together as a consortium. The Channel Tunnel and Thames Barrier are products of this form of business organisation. Within the consortium one firm may act as the managing contractor, while the other members may provide specialist services. Alternatively, management may be shared more equally.

Co-operatives

These are of two types.

Consumer co-operatives. These, like the old high street Co-ops, are officially owned by the consumers. Consumers, in fact, play no part in the running of these co-operatives. They are run by professional managers.

Producer co-operatives. These are firms that are owned by their workers, who share in the firm's profit according to some agreed formula. They are sometimes formed by people in the same trade coming together: for example, producers of handicraft goods. At other times, they are formed by workers buying out their factory from the owners; this is most likely if it is due to close, with a resultant loss of jobs. Producer co-operatives, although still relatively few in number, have grown in recent years. One of the most famous is the department store chain, John Lewis.

Public corporations

These are state-owned enterprises such as the BBC, the Bank of England and nationalised industries.

Public corporations have a legal identity separate from the government. They are run by a board, but the members of the board are appointed by the relevant government minister. The boards have to act within various terms of reference laid down by an Act of Parliament. Profits of public corporations that are not reinvested accrue to the Treasury. Since 1980, most public corporations have been 'privatised': that is, they have been sold directly to other firms in the private sector (such as Austin Rover to British Aerospace) or to the general public through a public issue of shares (such as British Gas). However, in response to turmoil in the financial markets, the UK Government nationalised two banks in 2008, Northern Rock (see Box 15.3) and Bradford & Bingley. It also partly nationalised two others, the Royal Bank of Scotland and the Lloyds Banking Group (HBOS and Lloyds TSB).

The issue of privatisation is considered in Chapter 22 and you can read about current debate regarding the future of Britain's railways on the Sloman News Site.[4]

3.3 THE INTERNAL ORGANISATION OF THE FIRM

The internal operating structures of firms are governed frequently by their size. Small firms tend to be centrally managed, with decision making operating through a clear managerial hierarchy. In large firms, however, the organisational structure tends to be more complex, although technological change is forcing many organisations to reassess the most suitable organisational structure for their business.

Pause for thought

Before you read on, consider in what ways technology might influence the organisational structure of a business.

U-form

In small to medium-sized firms, the managers of the various departments – marketing, finance, production, etc. – are normally directly responsible to a chief executive, whose function is to co-ordinate their activities: relaying the firm's overall strategy to them and being responsible for interdepartmental communication. We call this type of structure *U (unitary) form* (see Figure 3.1).

When firms expand beyond a certain size, however, a U-form structure is likely to become inefficient. This inefficiency arises from difficulties in communication, co-ordination and control. It becomes too difficult to manage the whole organisation from the centre. The problem is that the chief executive suffers from *bounded rationality* – a limit on the rate at which information can be absorbed and processed. When facing complex decisions, typically they make satisfactory rather than optimal decisions, relying on rules-of-thumb and tried and tested methods. As the firm grows, more decisions are required. This leads to less time per decision and, ultimately, poorer decisions. The chief executive effectively loses control of the firm.

KEY IDEA 8

Good decision making requires good information. Where information is poor, or poorly used, decisions and their outcomes may be poor. This may be the result of bounded rationality.

In attempting to regain control, it is likely that a further managerial layer will be inserted. The chain of command thus becomes lengthened as the chief executive must now co-ordinate and communicate via this intermediate managerial level. This leads to the following problems:

- Communication costs increase.
- Messages and decisions may be misinterpreted and distorted.
- The firm experiences a decline in organisational efficiency as various departmental managers, freed from central control, seek to maximise their personal departmental goals.

Definitions

U-form business organisation One in which the central organisation of the firm (the chief executive or a managerial team) is responsible both for the firm's day-to-day administration and for formulating its business strategy.

Bounded rationality When individuals have limited abilities to find and process the relevant information required to make the best decision, i.e. purchase the goods that generate the most consumer surplus.

[4]'Should Britain's railways be nationalised', *The Sloman Economics News site* (6 January 2018).

BOX 3.2   MANAGERS, PAY AND PERFORMANCE

CEO and average worker pay ratios

One key feature of large public limited companies tends to be the very high pay received by the top managers and executives. In the USA, the median pay of top US executives up to the 1980s was around 30 times higher than average wages. According to the AFL-CIO Labour Union in 2016, their median pay was 347 times more than that of employees.

Other data give different figures. For example, a report by the Economic Policy Institute[1] found that the ratio was 20:1 in 1965, 59:1 in 1989 and 271:1 in 2016. It found that CEO compensation had risen by 937 per cent (based on stock options realised) since 1978, which is 70 per cent faster than the rise in the stock market and compares rather favourably with the 11.2 per cent growth in the average worker's compensation.

In the UK, similar trends are observed. The Equality Trust finds that CEOs of the FTSE 100 earned around 190 times the average employee's pay package. In 2014, the High Pay Centre think tank found that by 5 January, the top CEOs in Britain would have earned more than the average UK worker earns in the whole year. Just four years later, on 4 January 2018, known as 'Big Cat Thursday', the High Pay Centre announced that the top CEOs would already have earned more than the average UK worker – it took just 3 working days.[2]

According to Bloomberg,[3] CEOs in companies in India listed on its Sensex Index earn 229 times more than average workers. This is the second biggest gap after the USA (265:1). Other countries, including Norway and Austria, have much smaller gaps. In this dataset, the UK has a 201:1 pay gap, while South Africa, Germany, China and Japan have pay gaps of 180:1, 136:1, 127:1 and 58:1 respectively.

The pay-performance link?

The awards given to executive 'fat cats' have met with considerable protest in recent years. While a large pay differential has always existed, it has grown significantly over the past few decades and, given the negligible pay rises of the average worker since the financial crisis in particular, this widening gap has caused much resentment. But, is the pay gap justified?

There are arguments put forward to justify such generosity, including:

- 'The best cost money.' Failure to offer high rewards may encourage the top executives within an industry to move elsewhere.
- 'High rewards motivate.' High rewards are likely to motivate not only top executives, but also those below them. Managers, especially those in the middle of the business hierarchy, will compete for promotion and seek to do well with such high rewards on offer.

We do live in a world where comparisons are constantly being made. Comparing compensation packages can be used as a means of identifying those CEOs who are above or below average. As Next's CEO said: 'No board wants their CEO to be in the bottom quartile.' However, the culture was somewhat different in Japan, where a number of years ago, a regulatory change required listed securities companies to publish remuneration details of any managers earning above $1 million (approximately). One aim was to increase the pay of underpaid bosses. But such was the embarrassment of being on the list of so-called 'high-earners', some bosses took pay cuts!

But, is there a link between high pay and company performance?

Research suggesting a negative link

Despite the more than doubling of growth in the pay of FTSE 100 CEOs since the 1980s, there has been little change in the share prices of the companies themselves. In a piece of research by Lancaster Management School, commissioned by the UK arm of the CFA Institute, the CEOs of Britain's top 350 companies each earnt an average of £1.9m in 2014 – this represented a rise of 82 per cent compared to the figure 13 years before. Yet the report found that the return on invested capital had risen by less than 1 per cent. The authors concluded:

> Our findings suggest a material disconnect between pay and fundamental value generation.[4]

[1] Lawrence Mishel and Jessica Schieder, *CEO pay remains high relative to the pay of typical workers and high-wage earners*, Economic Policy Institute (20 July 2017).

[2] 'It's Fat Cat Day – Thursday Jan 4 2018'; *High Pay Centre blog* (4 January 2018).

[3] Anders Melin, 'Executive Pay', *Bloomberg* (23 January 2018).

[4] Zlata Rodionova, 'Link between high executive pay and performance 'negligible', study finds'; *Independent* (28 December 2016).

M-form

To overcome these organisational problems, the firm can adopt an *M- (multi-divisional) form* of managerial structure (see Figure 3.2).

This suits medium to large firms. The firm is divided into a number of 'divisions'. Each division could be responsible for a particular product or group of products, or a particular

Definitions

M-form business organisation One in which the business is organised into separate departments, such that responsibility for the day-to-day management enterprise is separated from the formulation of the business's strategic plan.

However, it is important to note that the report also stated that many of the measures used focus on the short term and thus are 'unsophisticated'.

Some go even further and suggest that the high pay of CEOs can be counter-productive and actually can reduce productivity. Andrew Smithers, an economist, says that long-term incentives relating to performance actually encourage short-termism and that such extensive use of these reward mechanisms in the UK relative to Europe (where executive pay is lower) is one reason for Britain's lower productivity.[5]

In July 2016, research from Corporate Governance firm, MSCI, which focused on 10 years of performance and pay data, showed that some of the worst performing companies were run by some of the highest paid executives. The report found:

> . . . little evidence to show a link between the large proportion of pay that such awards represent and long-term company stock performance. In fact, even after adjusting for company size and sector, companies with lower total summary CEO pay levels more consistently displayed higher long-term investment returns'.[6]

The report found that if $100 was invested in the top 20 per cent of companies based on CEO pay, then that money would be worth $265 after 10 years (the length of the study). Conversely, the same investment in the 20 per cent of companies run by the lowest paid CEOs would have generated a $367 return.

A different view

However, others take a different view. Thomas Noe, Professor of Management Studies at Oxford's Saïd Business School, argues that, in the USA, and probably the UK too, most of the increase in executive pay can be accounted for by an increase in company size. For a large company, it can make sense to pay a premium for a chief executive who may deliver a slightly better performance than its rivals. 'You are much more willing to pay for tiny differences in performance, because now they

are getting multiplied by a much bigger base . . . If shareholders were unhappy, they would vote against company pay policies.'[7]

Shareholder pressure

And, in many cases, this has happened. Executive pay has fallen over the past year or more. For example, in the USA, the ratio was 299:1 in 2014, falling to 271:1 in 2016. In the UK, the average pay of CEOs in the FTSE 100 fell by around 17 per cent in 2017, though it still remains at £4.5 million! According to CIPD Chief Executive Peter Cheese:

> The drop in pay in the last year is welcome, although relatively marginal, and will have largely been driven by the growing public and shareholder concerns and the Prime Minister's stronger focus on boardroom excess and plans to reform corporate governance.[8]

Sir Martin Sorrell, the boss of advertising giant WPP, saw his pay fall from £70 million in 2015 to £48 million in 2016, even though his company's advertising revenues and profits increased. By 2021, it should be cut to just over £13 million, following a change in pay policy at WPP and past revolt by key shareholders.

The pay gap remains substantial and, while there are certainly cases of high paid bosses providing excellent returns, there are many examples where high pay is seemingly unrelated to performance.[9]

1. Explain how excessive executive remuneration might illustrate the principal–agent problem.
2. In the UK, many of the highest-paid executives head former public utilities. Why might the giving of very high rewards to such individuals be a source of public concern?

Choose a FTSE 100 company and, from its reports, examine the pay of the CEO or other senior executives. Assess the arguments used for justifying these rewards.

[5] See, for example, Anthony Hilton, 'Bonus culture will hurt UK in the long term', *Evening Standard* (10 May 2016).

[6] Ric Marshall and Linda-Eling Lee, *Are CEOs paid for performance?*, MSCI (July 2016).

[7] Brian Groom, 'Executive pay: The trickle-up effect', *Financial Times* (27 July 2011).

[8] 'Many UK CEOs earn more in three days than a typical worker does in a year', *Reuters*, (3 January 2018).

[9] See, for example: Andrew Hill, 'Bonuses are bad for bankers and even worse for banks' *Financial Times* (25 January 2016).

market (e.g. a specific country). The day-to-day running and even certain long-term decisions of each division would be the responsibility of the divisional manager(s). This leads to the following benefits:

- Reduced length of information flows.
- The chief executive being able to concentrate on overall strategic planning.

- An enhanced level of control, with each division being run as a mini 'firm', competing with other divisions for the limited amount of company resources available.

The flat organisation

The shift towards the M-form organisational structure was motivated primarily by a desire to improve the process of

Figure 3.1 U-form business organisation

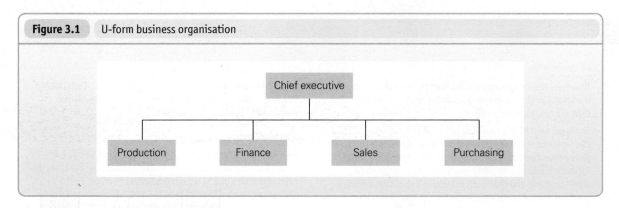

Figure 3.2 M-form business organisation

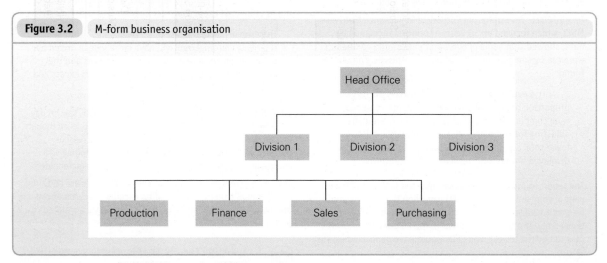

decision making within the business. This involved adding layers of management. Recent technological innovations, especially in respect to computer systems such as email and management information systems, have encouraged many organisations to think again about how to establish an efficient and effective organisational structure. The *flat organisation* is one that fully embraces the latest developments in information technology and, by so doing, is able to reduce the need for a large group of middle managers. Senior managers, through these new information systems, can communicate easily and directly with those lower in the organisational structure. Middle managers are, effectively, bypassed.

The speed of information flows reduces the impact of bounded rationality on the decision-making process. Senior managers are able to re-establish and, in certain cases, widen their span of control over the business organisation.

In many respects, the flat organisation represents a return to the U-form structure. It is yet to be seen whether we also have a return to the problems associated with this type of organisation.

The holding company

Also known as the H-form, this business organisation is closely linked to the expansion and development of multinational enterprises, which have become more prevalent with globalisation. In many respects, it is a variation on the M-form structure. A *holding company* (or parent company) is one that owns a controlling interest in other subsidiary companies, which, in turn, may also have controlling interests in other companies.

H-form organisational structures can be highly complex. While the parent company has ultimate control over its various subsidiaries, it is likely that both tactical and strategic decision making is left to the individual companies within the organisation. Many multinationals are organised along the lines of an international holding company, where overseas subsidiaries pursue their own independent strategy. The Walt Disney Company (Holding Company) represents a good example of an H-form business organisation. Figure 3.3 shows the firm's organisational structure and the range of assets it owns.

Definitions

Flat organisation One in which technology enables senior managers to communicate directly with those lower in the organisational structure. Middle managers are bypassed.

Holding company A business organisation in which the present company holds interests in a number of other companies or subsidiaries.

Figure 3.3 Organisational structure of The Walt Disney Company (Holding Company)

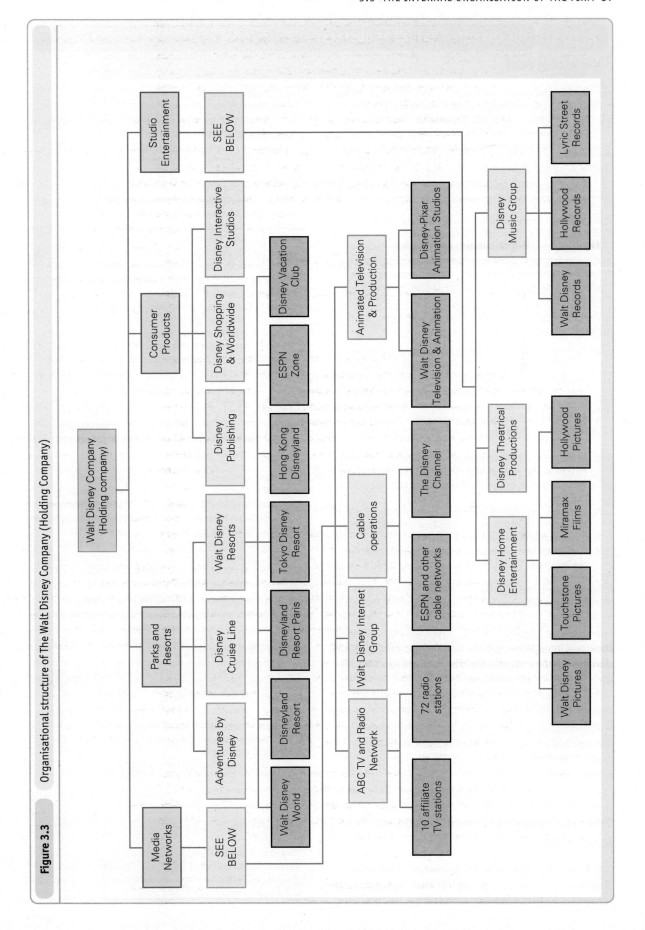

BOX 3.3 THE CHANGING NATURE OF BUSINESS

Knowledge rules

In the knowledge-driven economy, innovation has become central to achievement in the business world. With this growth in importance, organisations large and small have begun to re-evaluate their products, their services, even their corporate culture in the attempt to maintain their competitiveness in the global markets of today. The more forward-thinking companies have recognised that only through such root and branch reform can they hope to survive in the face of increasing competition.[1]

Knowledge is fundamental to economic success in many industries and, for most firms, key knowledge resides in skilled members of the workforce. The result is a market in knowledge, with those having the knowledge being able to command high salaries and often being 'headhunted'. The 'knowledge economy' is affecting people from all walks of life, and fundamentally changing the nature, organisation and practice of business.

The traditional business corporation was based around five fundamental principles:

■ Individual workers needed the business and the income it provided more than the business needed them. After all, employers could always find alternative workers. As such, the corporation was the dominant partner in the employment relationship.

■ Employees who worked for the corporation tended to be full time, and depended upon the work as their sole source of income.

■ The corporation was integrated, with a single management structure overseeing all the various stages of production. This was seen as the most efficient way to organise productive activity.

■ Suppliers, and especially manufacturers, had considerable power over the customer by controlling information about their product or service.

■ Technology relevant to an industry was developed within the industry.

In more recent times, with the advent of the knowledge economy, the principles above have all but been turned on their head.

■ The key factor of production in a knowledge economy is knowledge itself, and the workers that hold such knowledge. Without such workers, the corporation is unlikely to succeed. As such, the balance of power between the business and the worker in today's economy is far more equal.

■ Even though the vast majority of employees still work full time, the diversity in employment contracts, such as

part-time and short-term contracts and consultancy, means that full-time work is not the only option. (We examine this in section 18.4.) The result is an increasing number of workers offering their services to business in non-conventional ways.

■ As companies increasingly supply their products to a global marketplace, many find that they do not have the expertise to do everything themselves – from production though all its stages, research and development, adapting products to specific markets, marketing, sales, etc. With communication costs that are largely insignificant, businesses are likely to be more efficient and flexible if they outsource and de-integrate. Not only are businesses outsourcing various stages of production, but many are also employing specialist companies to provide key areas of management, such as HRM (human resource management): hiring, firing, training, benefits, etc.

■ Whereas, in the past, businesses controlled information, today access to information via sources such as the Internet means that power is shifting towards the consumer.

■ Today, unlike in previous decades, technological developments are less specific to industries. Knowledge developments diffuse and cut across industry boundaries. What this means for business, in a knowledge-driven economy, is that they must look beyond their own industry if they are to develop and grow. We frequently see partnerships and joint ventures between businesses that cut across industry types and technology.

What is clear from the above is that the dynamics of the knowledge economy require a quite fundamental change in the nature of business. Organisationally it needs to be more flexible, helping it to respond to the ever-changing market conditions it faces. Successful companies draw upon their *core* competencies to achieve market advantage and thus, ultimately, specialise in what they do best. Businesses must learn to work with others, either through outsourcing specialist tasks or through more formal strategic partnerships.

Within this new business model, the key assets are the specialist people in the organisation – its knowledge workers. How will businesses attract, retain and motivate the best? Will financial rewards be sufficient or will workers seek more from their work and the organisation they work for?

With such issues facing the corporation we can expect to see a radical reinterpretation of what business looks like and how it is practised over the coming years.

[1] European Commission, Directorate-General for Enterprise, *Innovation Management and the Knowledge-Driven Economy* (ECSC-EC-EAEC Brussels-Luxembourg, 2004).

 How is the development of the knowledge economy likely to affect the distribution of wage income? Will it become more equal or less equal?

Other structures used by multinational companies

Other types of organisational structure for multinational organisations include the **integrated international enterprise**. In this structure, a company's international

Definitions

Integrated international enterprise One in which an international company pursues a single business strategy. It co-ordinates the business activities of its subsidiaries across different countries.

subsidiaries, rather than pursuing independent business strategies, co-ordinate (at a regional or global level) and integrate their activities in pursuit of shared corporate aims and objectives. In such an organisation, the distinction between parent company and subsidiary is of less relevance than the identification of a clear corporate philosophy which dominates business goals and policy.

Another structure is the *transnational association*, which typically is owned and managed by local people, with the business headquarters holding little equity investment in its subsidiaries and providing minimal managerial and technical assistance. The subsidiary produces output (typically components) and sells this by a contractual arrangement to the headquarters, which then assembles, markets or distributes it. The headquarters retains the decisive role within the international business, but the use of

global sourcing means that distinct production sites are used to produce large numbers of single components and this helps to reduce costs.

We shall investigate the organisational structures and issues surrounding multinational corporations more fully (see Chapter 23).

Definitions

Transnational association A form of business organisation in which the subsidiaries of a company in different countries are contractually bound to the parent company to provide output to or receive inputs from other subsidiaries.

Global sourcing Where a company uses production sites in different parts of the world to provide particular components for a final product.

SUMMARY

1a The firm's role in the economy is to eliminate the need for making individual contracts through the market and to provide a more efficient way to organise production.

1b Using the market to establish a contract is not costless. Transaction costs will mean that the market is normally less efficient than the firm as an allocator of resources.

1c The divorce of ownership from control implies that the objectives of owners and managers may diverge and, similarly, the objectives of one manager may differ from another. Hence the goals of firms may be diverse. What is more, as ownership becomes more dispersed, so the degree of control by owners diminishes yet further.

1d Managers might pursue maximisation goals other than profit or look to achieve a wide range of targets in which profit acts as a constraint on other business aims.

1e The problem of managers not pursuing the same goals as the owners is an example of the principal–agent problem. Agents (in this case the managers) may not always carry out the wishes of their principals (in this case the owners). Because of asymmetric information, managers are able to pursue their own aims, just so long as they produce results that will satisfy the owners. The solution for owners is for there to be better means of monitoring the performance of managers and incentives for the managers to behave in the owners' interests.

2a The legal status of the firm will influence both its actions and performance within the marketplace.

2b There are several types of legal organisation of firms: the sole proprietorship, the partnership, the private limited company, the public limited company, consortia of firms, co-operatives and public corporations. In the first two cases, the owners have unlimited liability: the owners are personally liable for any losses the business might make. With companies, however, shareholders' liability is limited to the amount they have invested. This reduced risk encourages people to invest in companies.

3a The relative success of a business organisation will be influenced strongly by its organisational structure. As a firm grows, its organisational structure will need to evolve in order to account for the business's growing complexity. This is particularly so if the business looks to expand overseas.

3b As firms grow, so they tend to move from a U-form to an M-form structure. In recent years, however, with the advance of information technology, many firms have adopted a flat organisation – a return to U-form.

3c Multinational companies often adopt relatively complex forms of organisation, such as the holding company (H-form) structure and more and more firms are de-integrating and outsourcing as a means of improving efficiency.

REVIEW QUESTIONS

1 What is meant by the term 'transaction costs'? Explain why the firm represents a more efficient way of organising economic life than relying on individual contracts.

2 Explain why the business objectives of owners and managers are likely to diverge. How might owners attempt to ensure that managers act in their interests and not in the managers' own interests?

3 Compare and contrast the relative strengths and weaknesses of the partnership and the public limited company.

4 Conduct an investigation into a recent large building project, such as the PyeongChang Winter Olympics or the Football World Cup in Russia or Brazil. Identify what firms were involved and the roles and responsibilities they had.

Outline the advantages and disadvantages that such business consortia might have.

5 If a business is thinking of reorganisation, why and in what ways might new technology be an important factor in such considerations?

6 What problems are multinational corporations, as opposed to domestic firms, likely to have in respect to organising their business activity? What alternative organisational models might multinationals adopt? To what extent do they overcome the problems you have identified?

ADDITIONAL PART A CASE STUDIES ON THE *ECONOMICS FOR BUSINESS* STUDENT WEBSITE (www.pearsoned.co.uk/sloman)

A.1 **The UK defence industry.** A PEST analysis of the changes in the defence industry in recent years.

A.2 **Scarcity and abundance.** If scarcity is the central economic problem, is anything truly abundant?

A.3 **Global economics.** This examines how macroeconomics and microeconomics apply at the global level and identifies some key issues.

A.4 **Buddhist economics.** A different perspective on economic problems and economic activity.

A.5 **Green economics.** This examines some of the environmental costs that society faces today. It also looks at the role of economics in analysing these costs and how the problems can be tackled.

A.6 **Downsizing and business reorganisation.** Many companies in recent years have 'downsized' their operations and focused on their core competencies. This looks particularly at the case of IBM.

A.7 **Positive and normative statements.** A crucial distinction when considering matters of economic policy.

WEBSITES RELEVANT TO PART A

Numbers and sections refer to websites listed in the Web appendix and hotlinked from this text's website at **www.pearsoned.co.uk/sloman**

■ For a tutorial on finding the best economics websites, see site C8 (Internet for Economics).

■ For news articles relevant to Part A, see the Economics News Articles link from the text's website.

■ For general economics news sources, see websites in section A of the Web appendix at the end of the text and particularly A1–9, 35, 36. See also A38, 39, 42, 43, 44 for links to newspapers worldwide.

■ For business news items, again see websites in section A of the Web appendix at the end of the text and particularly A1–4, 8, 20–26, 35, 36.

■ For sources of economic and business data, see sites in section B and particularly B1–5, 27–9, 32, 36, 39, 43.

■ For general sites for students of economics for business, see sites in section C and particularly C1–7.

■ For sites giving links to relevant economics and business websites, organised by topic, see sites I7, 11, 12, 16, 18.

■ For details on companies, see site A3.

Business and markets

The FT Reports . . .

The Financial Times, 26 April 2018

Computerised trading drives up New York cocoa price

By Emiko Terazono

Computers are dominating the trading of cocoa in New York, sparking a dramatic divergence in the longstanding price relationship with the London market.

Speculative funds have driven the price of the commodity in New York up more than 50 per cent since the start of the year to just under $3,000 a tonne. The New York market, traded in dollars, has traditionally been the preferred market for financial players such as hedge funds.

The London market, historically favoured by traders and commercial players buying and selling physical cocoa, has only risen 34 per cent in the same timeframe.

The big shift triggered by the New York buying is that its benchmark, which normally trades at a discount to London, now sits at a record premium.

The pronounced shift in price relationships comes as hedge fund managers with physical trading capabilities and merchant traders have exited the cocoa market.

In the past, such a large price difference would have encouraged a trader to buy physical cocoa in London and send it to New York, hence narrowing the relationship. However, current price movements reflected the absence of such players, said brokers.

Anthony Ward, the commodities trader known in the cocoa market for his large bets, has been among the more well-known fund managers to close his hedge fund, exiting the market at the end of last year. Mr Ward, dubbed 'Chocfinger' due to his influence over the cocoa price, blamed the rising power of algorithmic and systems-based trading for making position-taking based on 'fundamental' supply and demand factors more difficult. . .

The divergence between the two cocoa benchmarks comes as waves of buying and selling by speculative funds, many believed to be driven by algorithms, are rippling across the soft commodities markets. . .

Cocoa is a relatively small market compared with other agricultural commodities such as corn or soyabeans, and it is hard to take large positions without the rest of the market knowing. However, brokers said anonymous computerised strategies now dominate flows in the New York market.

Rather than follow fundamental supply and demand news, many of the funds trade on momentum. Others use algorithms that exploit the shifts in price relationships between different markets or separate contracts of the same commodity.

'[The market] is in the grip of technical, system-led buying,' said Justin Grandison, director of cocoa brokerage at ABN Amro.

Uncertainty is also the defining characteristic of business competition today. Competing in volatile markets can feel a lot like entering the ring against George Foreman in his prime – or, even worse, like stumbling into a barroom brawl. The punches come from all directions, include a steady barrage of body blows and periodic haymakers, and are thrown by a rotating cast of characters who swing bottles and bar stools as well as fists.

Donald Sull, 'How to survive in turbulent markets', *Harvard Business Review*, February 2009, p. 80

Markets dominate economic life, from buying and selling raw materials, to supplying the final product to the customer. It would be difficult to imagine a world without markets. In fact, we talk about economies today as 'market economies', with economic decisions made primarily by business, consumers and employees interacting with each other in a market environment.

The determination of a market price is a complex business and often subject to great fluctuation (as the *Financial Times* article illustrates). This is particularly so when you consider commodities, such as coffee, wheat and orange juice, which are highly dependent upon the weather and subject to considerable speculative buying and selling.

In Part B of this text we shall explore how the market system operates. In Chapter 4 we will consider those factors that influence both demand and supply and how, via their interaction, we are able to derive a market price. We see how markets transmit information from consumers to producers and from producers to consumers. We see how prices act as an incentive – for example, if consumers want more mobile phones, how this increased demand leads to an increase in their price and hence to an incentive for firms to increase their production.

Changes in price affect the quantity demanded and supplied. But how much? How much will the demand for DVDs go up if the price of DVDs comes down? How much will the supply of new houses go up if the price of houses rises? In Chapter 5 we develop the concept of *elasticity* of demand and supply to examine this responsiveness. We also consider some of the issues the market raises for business, such as the effects on a business's revenue of a change in the price of the product, the impact of time on demand and supply and how businesses deal with the risk and uncertainty markets generate. We also look at speculation – people attempting to gain by anticipating price changes.

Key terms

Price mechanism
Demand and demand curves
Income and substitution effects
Supply and supply curves
Equilibrium price and quantity
Shifts in demand and supply curves
Price elasticity of demand
Income elasticity of demand
Cross-price elasticity of demand
Price elasticity of supply
Speculation
Risk and uncertainty
Spot and futures markets

4

The working of competitive markets

- How do markets operate?
- How are market prices determined and when are they likely to rise or fall?
- Under what circumstances do firms have to accept a price given by the market rather than being able to set the price themselves?
- What are the influences on consumer demand?
- What factors determine the amount of supply coming on to the market?
- How do markets respond to changes in demand or supply?

4.1 BUSINESS IN A COMPETITIVE MARKET

If a firm wants to increase its profits, should it raise its prices or should it lower them? Should it increase its output or should it reduce it? Should it modify its product or should it keep the product unchanged? The answer to these, and many other questions, is that it depends on the market in which the firm operates. If the market is buoyant, it may well be a good idea for the firm to increase its output in anticipation of greater sales. It may also be a good idea to raise the price of its product in the belief that consumers will be willing to pay more. If, however, the market is declining, the firm may decide to reduce output, cut prices or diversify into an alternative product.

The firm is, thus, greatly affected by its market environment, an environment that is often outside the firm's control and subject to frequent changes. For many firms, prices are determined not by them, but by the market. Even where they do have some influence over prices, the influence is only slight. They may be able to put prices up a small amount

but, if they raise them too much, they will find that they lose sales to their rivals.

The market dominates a firm's activities. The more competitive the market, the greater this domination becomes. In the extreme case, the firm may have no power at all to change its price: it is what we call a *price taker*. It has to accept the market price as given. If the firm attempts to raise the price above the market price, it will simply be unable to sell its product: it will lose all its sales to its competitors. Take the case of farmers selling wheat. They have to accept the price as dictated by the market. If, individually, they try to sell above the market price, no one will buy.

Definition

Price taker A person or firm with no power to be able to influence the market price.

In competitive markets, consumers too are price takers. When we go into shops we have no control over prices. We have to accept the price as given. For example, when you get to the supermarket checkout, you cannot start haggling with the checkout operator over the price of a can of beans or a tub of margarine.

So how does a competitive market work? For simplicity, we will examine the case of a *perfectly competitive market*. This is where both producers and consumers are too numerous to have any control over prices whatsoever: a situation where everyone is a price taker.

Clearly, in other markets, firms will have some discretion over the prices they charge. For example, a manufacturing company such as Ford will have some discretion over the prices it charges for its Fiestas or Mondeos. In such cases, the firm has some 'market power'. (We will examine different degrees of market power in Chapters 11 and 12.)

The price mechanism

In a *free market* individuals are free to make their own economic decisions. Consumers are free to decide what to buy with their incomes: free to make demand decisions. Firms are free to choose what to sell and what production methods to use: free to make supply decisions. The resulting demand and supply decisions of consumers and firms are transmitted to each other through their effect on *prices*: through the *price mechanism*.

The price mechanism works as follows. Prices respond to *shortages* and *surpluses*. Shortages cause prices to rise. Surpluses cause prices to fall.

If consumers decide they want more of a good (or if producers decide to cut back supply), demand will exceed supply. The resulting *shortage* will cause *the price of the good to rise.* This will act as an incentive to producers to supply more, since production will now be more profitable. At the same time, it will discourage consumers from buying so much. *The price will continue rising until the shortage has thereby been eliminated.* A *Business Insider* article looks at changes in the price of butter in Europe caused by shortages.[1]

If, on the other hand, consumers decide they want less of a good (or if producers decide to produce more), supply will exceed demand. The resulting *surplus* will cause *the price of the good to fall.* This will act as a disincentive to producers, who will supply less, since production will now be less profitable. It will encourage consumers to buy more. *The price will continue falling until the surplus has thereby been eliminated.*

This price, where demand equals supply, is called the *equilibrium price*. By *equilibrium* we mean a point of balance or a point of rest: in other words, a point towards which there is a tendency to move.

The same analysis can be applied to labour markets (and those for other factors of production), except that here the demand and supply roles are reversed. Firms are the demanders of labour. Households are the suppliers. If there is a surplus of a particular type of labour, the wage rate (i.e. the price of labour) will fall until demand equals supply. Many economies fell into recession in 2008 and, in the next few years, the demand for goods and services fell, reducing the demand for labour. The surplus of labour (unemployment) that emerged in many labour markets led to a fall in wage rates in these markets. You can read about the link between wages and surplus labour in a BBC News article.[2]

Likewise, if the demand for a particular type of labour exceeds its supply, the resulting shortage will drive up the wage rate, as employers compete with each other for labour. The higher wages will curb firms' demand for that type of labour and encourage more workers to take up that type of job. As economies have recovered from recession, wages have risen in many labour markets and they should continue to do so until demand equals supply, thus eliminating the shortage in those markets.

As with price, the wage rate where the demand for labour equals the supply is known as the *equilibrium* wage rate.

The response of demand and supply to changes in price illustrates a very important feature of how economies work.

 KEY IDEA 9

People respond to incentives. It is important, therefore, that incentives are appropriate and have the desired effect.

The effect of changes in demand and supply

How will the price mechanism respond to changes in consumer demand or producer supply? After all, the pattern of consumer demand changes over time. For example, people

---

Definitions

Perfectly competitive market (preliminary definition) A market in which all producers and consumers of the product are price takers. There are other features of a perfectly competitive market (these are examined in Chapter 11).

Free market One in which there is an absence of government intervention. Individual producers and consumers are free to make their own economic decisions.

Price mechanism The system in a market economy whereby changes in price in response to changes in demand and supply have the effect of making demand equal to supply.

Equilibrium price The price where the quantity demanded equals the quantity supplied; the price where there is no shortage or surplus.

Equilibrium A position of balance. A position from which there is no inherent tendency to move away.

---

[1]Oscar Williams-Grut, 'The butter market is going crazy', *Business Insider* (30 October 2017).

[2]Matthew West, 'No wage rises until jobless rate falls to 5% says MPC member', *BBC News* (18 June 2014).

may decide they want more downloadable music and fewer CDs. The pattern of supply also changes. For example, changes in technology may allow the mass production of microchips at lower cost, while the production of hand-built furniture becomes relatively expensive.

In all cases of changes in demand and supply, the resulting changes in *price* act as both *signals* and *incentives*.

A change in demand

 A rise in demand for a good creates a shortage, which causes a rise in its price. This then acts as an incentive for firms to supply more of it. They will divert resources from goods with lower prices relative to costs (and hence lower profits) to this good, which is now more profitable.

A fall in demand for a good creates a surplus, which causes a fall in its price. This then acts as an incentive for firms to supply less, as these goods are now less profitable to produce.

A change in supply

A rise in supply creates a surplus and causes a fall in price. This then acts as an incentive for consumers to demand more. A fall in supply creates a shortage, causing a rise in price. This then acts as an incentive for consumers to buy less.

> **KEY IDEA 10**
> *Changes in demand or supply cause markets to adjust.* Whenever such changes occur, the resulting 'disequilibrium' will bring an automatic change in prices, thereby restoring equilibrium (i.e. a balance of demand and supply).

The interdependence of markets

The interdependence of goods and factor markets

 A rise in demand for a good will raise its price and profitability. The higher price will help to curb the rise in demand. It will also encourage firms to supply more. But to do this they will require more inputs. Thus the demand for the inputs will rise, which, in turn, will raise the price of the inputs. The suppliers of these inputs will respond to this incentive by supplying more, which, in turn, will allow the

users of these inputs to produce more goods to meet the higher demand. This can be summarised as follows:

Goods market

- Demand for the good rises.
- This creates a shortage.
- This causes the price of the good to rise.
- This eliminates the shortage by choking off some of the demand and encouraging firms to produce more.

Factor market

- The increased supply of the good causes an increase in the demand for factors of production (i.e. inputs) used in making it.
- This causes a shortage of those inputs.
- This causes their prices to rise.
- This eliminates their shortage by choking off some of the demand and encouraging the suppliers of inputs to supply more.

Goods markets thus affect factor markets. Figure 4.1 summarises this sequence of events. (It is common in economics to summarise an argument like this by using symbols.)

Interdependence exists in the other direction too: factor markets affect goods markets. For example, the discovery of raw materials will lower their price. This will lower the costs of production of firms using these raw materials and increase the supply of the finished goods. The resulting surplus will lower the price of the good, which, in turn, will encourage consumers to buy more.

The interdependence of different goods markets

Many goods markets are also interdependent, such that a rise in the price of one good may encourage consumers to buy alternatives. This will drive up the price of alternatives, which will encourage producers to supply more of the alternatives.

Let us now turn to examine each side of the market – demand and supply – in more detail.

Figure 4.1 The price mechanism: the effect of a rise in demand

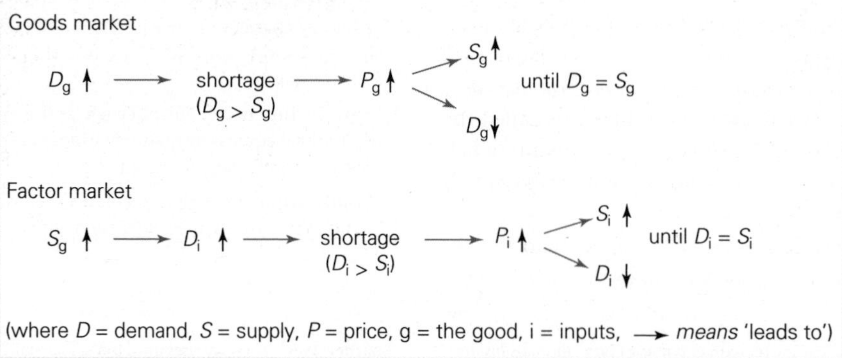

Goods market

$$D_g \uparrow \longrightarrow \text{shortage} \longrightarrow P_g \uparrow \nearrow \; S_g \uparrow \quad \text{until } D_g = S_g$$
$$(D_g > S_g) \qquad\qquad \searrow D_g \downarrow$$

Factor market

$$S_g \uparrow \longrightarrow D_i \uparrow \longrightarrow \text{shortage} \longrightarrow P_i \uparrow \nearrow \; S_i \uparrow \quad \text{until } D_i = S_i$$
$$(D_i > S_i) \qquad\qquad \searrow D_i \downarrow$$

(where D = demand, S = supply, P = price, g = the good, i = inputs, $\longrightarrow$ *means* 'leads to')

4.2 DEMAND

The relationship between demand and price

The headlines announce: 'Major crop failures in Brazil and East Africa: coffee prices soar.' Shortly afterwards, you find that coffee prices have doubled in the shops. What do you do? Presumably, you will cut back on the amount of coffee you drink. Perhaps you will reduce it from, say, six cups per day to two. Perhaps you will give up drinking coffee altogether.

This is simply an illustration of the general relationship between price and consumption: *when the price of a good rises, the quantity demanded will fall*. This relationship is known as the *law of demand*. There are two reasons for this law:

■ People will feel poorer. They will not be able to afford to buy so much of the good with their money. The purchasing power of their income (their *real income*) has fallen. This is called the *income effect* of a price rise.

■ The price has risen *relative to other goods*. People will thus switch to alternative or 'substitute' goods. This is called the *substitution effect* of a price rise.

Similarly, when the price of a good falls, the quantity demanded will rise. People can afford to buy more (the income effect), and they will switch away from consuming alternative goods (the substitution effect).

Therefore, returning to our example of the increase in the price of coffee, we will not be able to afford to buy as much as before, and we will probably drink more tea, cocoa, fruit juices or even water instead.

A word of warning: be careful about the meaning of the words *quantity demanded*. They refer to the amount consumers are willing and able to purchase at a given price over a given time period (for example, a week or a month). They do *not* refer to what people would simply *like* to consume. You might like to own a luxury yacht, but as the price of luxury yachts is in the millions, your demand will almost certainly be zero.

The demand curve

Consider the hypothetical data in Table 4.1. The table shows how many kilos of potatoes per month would be purchased at various prices.

Columns (2) and (3) show the *demand schedules* for two individuals, Tracey and Darren. Column (4), by contrast, shows the total *market demand schedule*. This is the total demand by all consumers. To obtain the market demand schedule for potatoes, we simply add up the quantities

Definitions

Law of demand The quantity of a good demanded per period of time will fall as the price rises and rise as the price falls, other things being equal (*ceteris paribus*).

Income effect The effect of a change in price on quantity demanded arising from the consumer becoming better or worse off as a result of the price change.

Substitution effect The effect of a change in price on quantity demanded arising from the consumer switching to or from alternative (substitute) products.

Quantity demanded The amount of a good that a consumer is willing and able to buy at a given price over a given period of time.

Demand schedule for an individual A table showing the different quantities of a good that a person is willing and able to buy at various prices over a given time period.

Market demand schedule A table showing the different total quantities of a good that consumers are willing and able to buy at various prices over a given time period.

Table 4.1	The demand for potatoes (monthly)		
	Price (pence per kg) (1)	Tracey's demand (kg) (2)	Darren's demand (kg) (3)	Total market demand (tonnes: 000s) (4)
A	20	28	16	700
B	40	15	11	500
C	60	5	9	350
D	80	1	7	200
E	100	0	6	100

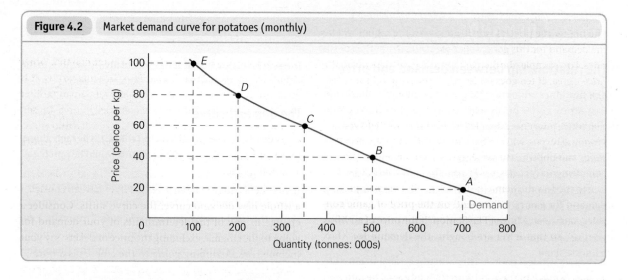

Figure 4.2 Market demand curve for potatoes (monthly)

demanded at each price by *all* consumers: i.e. Tracey, Darren and everyone else who demands potatoes. Notice that we are talking about demand *over a period of time* (not at a *point in* time). Thus we would talk about daily demand or weekly demand or whatever.

The demand schedule can be represented graphically as a ***demand curve***. Figure 4.2 shows the market demand curve for potatoes corresponding to the schedule in Table 4.1. The price of potatoes is plotted on the vertical axis. The quantity demanded is plotted on the horizontal axis.

Point *E* shows that at a price of 100p per kilo, 100 000 tonnes of potatoes are demanded each month. When the price falls to 80p we move down the curve to point *D*. This shows that the quantity demanded has now risen to 200 000 tonnes per month. Similarly, if the price falls to 60p, we move down the curve again to point *C*: 350 000 tonnes are now demanded. The five points on the graph (*A–E*) correspond to the figures in columns (1) and (4) of Table 4.1. The graph also enables us to read off the likely quantities demanded at prices other than those in the table.

A demand curve could also be drawn for an individual consumer. Like market demand curves, individuals' demand curves generally slope downward from left to right (they have negative slopes): the lower the price of a product, the more a person is likely to buy.

Two points should be noted at this stage:

■ In textbooks, demand curves (and other curves too) are, only occasionally, used to plot specific data. More frequently, they are used to illustrate general theoretical arguments. In such cases, the axes will simply be price and quantity, with the units unspecified.
■ The term 'curve' is used even when the graph is a straight line! In fact, when using demand curves to illustrate arguments, we draw them frequently as straight lines – it's easier.

Pause for thought

Referring to Table 4.1, assume that there are 200 consumers in the market. Of these, 100 have schedules like Tracey's and 100 have schedules like Darren's. What would be the total market demand schedule for potatoes now?

Other determinants of demand

Price is not the only factor that determines how much of a good people will buy. Think about your own consumption of any good – which other factors would cause you to buy more or less of it? Here are just some of the factors that might affect demand:

Tastes. The more desirable people find the good, the more they will demand. Your tastes are probably affected by advertising, fashion, observing what your friends and other consumers buy, considerations of health and your experiences from consuming the good on previous occasions. Taste for dairy is rising quickly in China, which is affecting the dairy market, as discussed in an article from *New Food*.[3]

---

[3]George Smith, 'Research reveals global consequences of China's growing taste for dairy', *New Food* (19 February 2018).

Definitions

Demand curve A graph showing the relationship between the price of a good and the quantity of the good demanded over a given time period. Price is measured on the vertical axis; quantity demanded is measured on the horizontal axis. A demand curve can be for an individual consumer or a group of consumers or, more usually, for the whole market.

The number and price of substitute goods (i.e. competitive goods). The higher the price of **substitute goods**, the higher will be the demand for this good as people switch from the substitutes. For example, the demand for coffee will depend on the price of tea. If tea goes up in price, the demand for coffee will rise.

The number and price of complementary goods. **Complementary goods** are those that are consumed together: cars and petrol, shoes and polish, bread and butter. The higher the price of complementary goods, the fewer of them will be bought and hence the less the demand for this good. For example, the demand for games will depend on the price of game consoles, such as an Xbox or PlayStation. If the price of an XBox goes up, so that fewer are bought, the demand for Xbox games will fall.

Income. As people's incomes rise, their demand for most goods will rise. Such goods are called **normal goods**. There are exceptions to this general rule, however. As people get richer, they spend less on **inferior goods**, such as supermarkets' value lines or bus travel, and switch to better-quality goods.

Distribution of income. If, for example, national income were redistributed from the poor to the rich, the demand for luxury goods would rise. At the same time, as the poor got poorer, they might have to turn to buying inferior goods, whose demand would thus rise, too.

**KI 13
p75**

Expectations of future price changes. If people think that prices are going to rise in the future, they are likely to buy more now before the price does go up, so demand will increase.

Although the list above covers the main categories of determinants of demand, there are many other factors that will also affect demand and they will vary depending on the good in question. You can read about some of the key determinants, first for beef in an article[4] based on the findings of a report[5] prepared for the Cattlemen's Beef Board in January 2018 and, second, following a key change in the UK in 2016 that involved a charge on plastic bags.[6]

Pause for thought

1. By referring to each of these six determinants of demand, consider what factors would cause a rise in the demand for butter.
2. Do all these six determinants of demand affect both an individual's demand and the market demand for a product?
3. Identify any other factors that would affect (a) your demand for goods and services and (b) the market demand for goods and services.

Movements along and shifts in the demand curve

A demand curve is constructed on the assumption that 'other things remain equal' (*ceteris paribus*). In other words, it is assumed that none of the determinants of demand, other than price, changes. The effect of a change in price is then simply illustrated by a movement along the demand curve: for example, from point B to point D in Figure 4.2 when price rises from 40p to 80p per kilo.

What happens, then, when one of these other determinants does change? The answer is that we have to construct a whole new demand curve: the curve shifts. Consider a change in one of the determinants of your demand for going to the cinema, excluding the price of tickets: say your income rises. Assuming going to the cinema is a normal good, this increase in income will cause you to go more often at any price: the whole curve will shift to the right. This shows that at each price more cinema tickets will be demanded than before. Thus in Figure 4.3 at a price of P, a

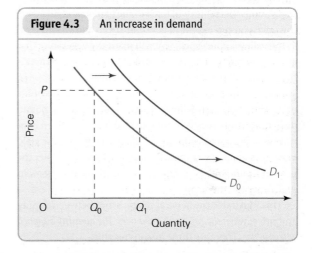

Figure 4.3 An increase in demand

Definitions

Substitute goods A pair of goods that are considered by consumers to be alternatives to each other. As the price of one goes up, the demand for the other rises.

Complementary goods A pair of goods consumed together. As the price of one goes up, the demand for both goods will fall.

Normal goods Goods whose demand rises as people's incomes rise.

Inferior goods Goods whose demand falls as people's incomes rise.

[4]National Cattlemen's Beef Association, 'NCBA Study: Many Factors Impacting Domestic Beef Demand', *Drovers* (1 February 2018).

[5]Glynn T. Tonsor, Jayson L. Lusk and Ted C. Schroeder, *Assessing Beef Demand Determinants*, Cattlemens' Beef Board (18 January 2018).
[6]Rebecca Morelle, 'Plastic bag use plummets in England since 5p charge', *BBC News* (30 July 2016).

quantity of Q_0 was originally demanded. But now, after the increase in demand, Q_1 is demanded. (Note that D_1 is not necessarily parallel to D_0.)

If a change in a determinant other than price causes demand to fall, the whole curve will shift to the left.

To distinguish between shifts in and movements along demand curves, it is usual to distinguish between a change in *demand* and a change in the *quantity demanded*. A shift in demand is referred to as a **change in demand**, whereas a movement along the demand curve as a result of a change in price is referred to as a **change in the quantity demanded**.

> ### Pause for thought
>
> *The price of a can of Coca-Cola rises, but you notice that the demand for Coca-Cola increases. Can you conclude that the demand curve for Coca-Cola is upward sloping?*

4.3 SUPPLY

Supply and price

Imagine you are a farmer deciding what to do with your land. Part of your land is in a fertile valley. Part is on a hillside where the soil is poor. Perhaps, then, you will consider growing vegetables in the valley and keeping sheep on the hillside.

Your decision will depend, to a large extent, on the price that various vegetables will fetch in the market and, likewise, the price you can expect to get from sheep and wool. As far as the valley is concerned, you will plant the vegetables that give the best return. If, for example, the price of potatoes is high, you will probably use a lot of the valley for growing potatoes. If the price gets higher, you may well use the whole of the valley, perhaps being prepared to run the risk of potato disease. If the price is very high indeed, you may even consider growing potatoes on the hillside, even though the yield per acre is much lower there. In other words, the higher the price of a particular crop, the more you are likely to grow in preference to other crops.

This illustrates the general relationship between supply and price: *when the price of a good rises, the quantity supplied will also rise*. There are three reasons for this:

- As firms supply more, they are likely to find that, beyond a certain level of output, costs rise more and more rapidly. Only if price rises will it be worth producing more and incurring these higher costs.
- In the case of the farm we have just considered, once potatoes have to be grown on the hillside, the costs of producing them will increase. Also, if the land has to be farmed more intensively, say by the use of more and more fertilisers, again the cost of producing extra potatoes is likely to rise quite rapidly. It is the same for manufacturers. Beyond a certain level of output, costs are likely to rise rapidly as workers have to be paid overtime and as machines approach their full capacity. If higher output involves higher costs of production, producers will need to get a higher price if they are to be persuaded to produce extra output. We consider how costs rise with rises in output in more detail in Chapter 9.
- The higher the price of the good, the more profitable it becomes to produce. Firms will thus be encouraged to produce more of it by switching from producing less profitable goods.
- Given time, if the price of a good remains high, new producers will be encouraged to set up in production. Total market supply thus rises.

The first three determinants affect supply in the short run. The fourth affects supply in the long run. (We distinguish between short-run and long-run supply later, in section 5.4.)

The supply curve

The amount that producers would like to supply at various prices can be shown in a **supply schedule**. Table 4.2 shows a

> ### Definitions
>
> **Change in demand** The term used for a shift in the demand curve. It occurs when a determinant of demand *other* than price changes.
>
> **Change in the quantity demanded** The term used for a movement along the demand curve to a new point. It occurs when there is a change in price.
>
> **Supply schedule** A table showing the different quantities of a good that producers are willing and able to supply at various prices over a given time period. A supply schedule can be for an individual producer or group of producers, or for all producers (the market supply schedule).

Table 4.2	The supply of potatoes (monthly)		
	Price of potatoes (pence per kg)	**Farmer X's supply (tonnes)**	**Total market supply (tonnes: 000s)**
a	20	50	100
b	40	70	200
c	60	100	350
d	80	120	530
e	100	130	700

monthly supply schedule for potatoes, both for an individual farmer (farmer X) and for all farmers together (the whole market).

The supply schedule can be represented graphically as a *supply curve*. A supply curve may be an individual firm's supply curve or a market supply curve (i.e. that of the whole industry).

Figure 4.4 shows the *market* supply curve of potatoes. As with demand curves, price is plotted on the vertical axis and quantity on the horizontal axis. Each of the points *a–e* corresponds to a figure in Table 4.2. Thus, for example, a price rise from 60p per kilogram to 80p per kilogram will cause a movement along the supply curve from point *c* to point *d*: total market supply will rise from 350 000 tonnes per month to 530 000 tonnes per month.

Not all supply curves will be upward sloping (positively sloped). Sometimes they will be vertical, horizontal, or even downward sloping. This will depend largely on the time period over which firms' response to price changes is considered. This question is examined in Chapter 5.

Pause for thought

1. *How much would be supplied at a price of 70p per kilo?*
2. *Draw a supply curve for farmer X. Are the axes drawn to the same scale as in Figure 4.4?*

Other determinants of supply

Like demand, supply is not determined simply by price. The other determinants of supply are as follows.

The costs of production. The higher the costs of production, the less profit will be made at any price. As costs rise, firms will cut back on production, probably switching to alternative products whose costs have not risen so much.

The main reasons for a change in costs are as follows:

- *Change in input prices:* costs of production will rise if wages, raw material prices, rents, interest rates or any other input prices rise.
- *Change in technology:* technological advances can fundamentally alter the costs of production. Consider, for example, how the microchip revolution has changed production methods and information handling in virtually every industry in the world.
- *Organisational changes:* various cost savings can be made in many firms by reorganising production.
- *Government policy:* costs will be lowered by government subsidies and raised by various taxes.

The profitability of alternative products (substitutes in supply). Many firms produce a range of products and will move resources from the production of one good to another as circumstances change. If some alternative product

Definitions

Supply curve A graph showing the relationship between the price of a good and the quantity of the good supplied over a given time period.

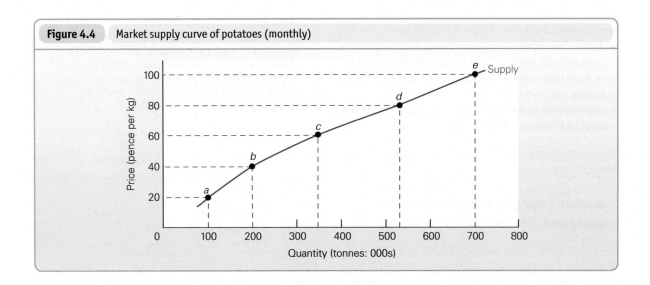

Figure 4.4 Market supply curve of potatoes (monthly)

(a *substitute in supply*) becomes more profitable to supply than before, producers are likely to switch from the first good to this alternative; so supply of the first good falls. Other goods are likely to become more profitable if their prices rise or their costs of production fall. For example, if the price of carrots goes up, or the cost of producing carrots comes down, farmers may decide to produce more carrots. The supply of potatoes is, therefore, likely to fall.

The profitability of goods in joint supply. Sometimes when one good is produced, another good is also produced at the same time. These are said to be *goods in joint supply*. An example is the refining of crude oil to produce petrol. Other grade fuels will be produced as well, such as diesel and paraffin. If more petrol is produced, due to a rise in demand, then the supply of these other fuels will rise, too.

Nature, 'random shocks' and other unpredictable events. In this category we would include the weather and diseases affecting farm output, wars affecting the supply of imported raw materials, the breakdown of machinery, industrial disputes, earthquakes, floods and fire, etc.

The aims of producers. A profit-maximising firm will supply a different quantity from a firm that has a different aim, such as maximising sales.

> ### Pause for thought
>
> *With reference to each of the above determinants of supply, identify what would cause (a) the supply of potatoes to fall and (b) the supply of leather to rise.*

KI 13
p75 *Expectations of future price changes.* If price is expected to rise, producers may temporarily reduce the amount they sell. Instead, they are likely to build up their stocks and release them on to the market only when the price does rise. At the same time, they may plan to produce more, by installing new machines or taking on more labour so that they can be ready to supply more when the price has risen.

The number of suppliers. If new firms enter the market, supply is likely to rise.

Movements along and shifts in the supply curve

The principle here is the same as with demand curves. The effect of a change in price is illustrated by a movement along the supply curve: for example, from point *d* to point *e* in Figure 4.4 when price rises from 80p to 100p. Quantity supplied rises from 530 000 to 700 000 tonnes.

If any other determinant of supply changes, the whole supply curve will shift. A rightward shift illustrates an increase in supply. A leftward shift illustrates a decrease in supply. Thus in Figure 4.5, if the original curve is S_0, the curve S_1 represents an increase in supply (more is supplied at each price), whereas the curve S_2 represents a decrease in supply (less is supplied at each price).

A movement along a supply curve often is referred to as a *change in the quantity supplied*, whereas a shift in the supply curve simply is referred to as a *change in supply*.

> ### Pause for thought
>
> *By referring to the determinants of supply, consider what factors would cause a rightward shift in the supply of family cars.*

> ### Definitions
>
> **Substitutes in supply** These are two goods where an increased production of one means diverting resources away from producing the other.
>
> **Goods in joint supply** These are two goods where the production of more of one leads to the production of more of the other.
>
> **Change in the quantity supplied** The term used for a movement along the supply curve to a new point. It occurs when there is a change in price.
>
> **Change in supply** The term used for a shift in the supply curve. It occurs when a determinant other than price changes.

Figure 4.5   Shifts in the supply curve

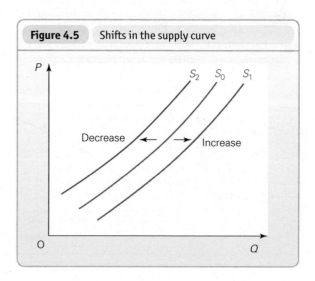

4.4 PRICE AND OUTPUT DETERMINATION

Equilibrium price and output

We can now combine our analysis of demand and supply. This will show how the actual price of a product and the actual quantity bought and sold are determined in a free and competitive market.

Let us return to the example of the market demand and market supply of potatoes, and use the data from Tables 4.1 and 4.2. These figures are given again in Table 4.3.

What will be the price and output that actually prevail? If the price started at 20p per kilogram, demand would exceed supply by 600 000 tonnes ($A - a$). Consumers would be unable to obtain all they wanted and thus would be willing to pay a higher price. Producers, unable or unwilling to supply enough to meet the demand, will be only too happy to accept a higher price. The effect of the shortage, then, will be to drive up the price. The same would happen at a price of 40p per kilogram. There would still be a shortage; the price would still rise. But, as the price rises, the quantity demanded falls and the quantity supplied rises. The shortage is progressively eliminated.

What would happen if the price started at a much higher level: say, at 100p per kilogram? In this case supply would exceed demand by 600 000 tonnes ($e - E$). The effect of this surplus would be to drive the price down as farmers competed against each other to sell their excess supplies. The same would happen at a price of 80p per kilogram. There would still be a surplus; the price would still fall.

In fact, only one price is sustainable. This is the price where demand equals supply: namely 60p per kilogram, where both demand and supply are 350 000 tonnes. When supply matches demand, the market is said to **clear**. There is no shortage and no surplus.

The price, where demand equals supply, is called the *equilibrium price* (see page 45) or market clearing price. In Table 4.3, if the price starts at any level other than 60p per kilogram, there will be a tendency for it to move towards 60p.

The equilibrium price is the only price at which producers' and consumers' wishes are mutually reconciled: where the producers' plans to supply exactly match the consumers' plans to buy.

> **KEY IDEA 11**
>
> *Equilibrium is the point where conflicting interests are balanced.* Only at this point is the amount that demanders are willing to purchase the same as the amount that suppliers are willing to supply. It is a point that will be reached automatically in a free market through the operation of the price mechanism.

Demand and supply curves

The determination of equilibrium price and output can be shown using demand and supply curves. Equilibrium is where the two curves intersect.

Figure 4.6 shows the demand and supply curves of potatoes corresponding to the data in Table 4.3. Equilibrium price is P_e (60p) and equilibrium quantity is Q_e (350 000 tonnes).

At any price above 60p, there would be a surplus. Thus at 80p there is a surplus of 330 000 tonnes ($d - D$). More is supplied than consumers are willing and able to purchase at that price. Thus a price of 80p fails to clear the market. Price will fall to the equilibrium price of 60p. As it does so, there will be a movement along the demand curve from point D to point C, and a movement along the supply curve from point d to point c.

At any price below 60p, there would be a shortage. Thus at 40p there is a shortage of 300 000 tonnes ($B - b$). Price will rise to 60p. This will cause a movement along the supply curve from point b to point c and along the demand curve from point B to point C.

Point Cc is the equilibrium: where demand equals supply.

Movement to a new equilibrium

The equilibrium price will remain unchanged only so long as the demand and supply curves remain unchanged. If either of the curves shifts, a new equilibrium will be formed.

KI 11 p53

Table 4.3	The market demand and supply of potatoes (monthly)		
Price of potatoes (pence per kg)	**Total market demand (tonnes: 000s)**	**Total market supply (tonnes: 000s)**	
20	700 (A)	100 (a)	
40	500 (B)	200 (b)	
60	350 (C)	350 (c)	
80	200 (D)	530 (d)	
100	100 (E)	700 (e)	

> ### Definition
>
> **Market clearing** A market clears when supply matches demand, leaving no shortage or surplus. The market is in equilibrium.

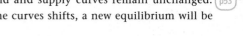

Figure 4.6   The determination of market equilibrium (potatoes: monthly)

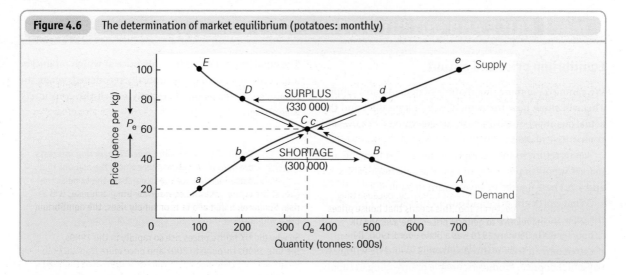

A change in demand

If one of the determinants of demand changes (other than price), the whole demand curve will shift. This will lead to a movement *along* the *supply* curve to the new intersection point.

For example, in Figure 4.7, if a rise in consumer incomes led to the demand curve shifting to D_2, there would be a shortage of $h - g$ at the original price P_{e1}. This would cause price to rise to the new equilibrium P_{e2}. As it did so there would be a movement along the supply curve from point g to point i, and along the new demand curve (D_2) from point h to point i. Equilibrium quantity would rise from Q_{e1} to Q_{e2}.

The effect of the shift in demand, therefore, has been a movement *along* the supply curve from the old equilibrium to the new: from point g to point i.

A change in supply

Likewise, if one of the determinants of supply (other than price) changes, the whole supply curve will shift. This will lead to a movement *along* the *demand* curve to the new intersection point.

For example, in Figure 4.8, if costs of production rose, the supply curve would shift to the left: to S_2. There would be a shortage of $g - j$ at the old price of P_{e1}. Price would rise from P_{e1} to P_{e3}. Quantity would fall from Q_{e1} to Q_{e3}. In other words, there would be a movement along the demand curve from point g to point k, and along the new supply curve (S_2) from point j to point k.

To summarise: a shift in one curve leads to a movement along the other curve to the new intersection point.

Sometimes, a number of determinants might change. This may lead to a shift in *both* curves. When this happens, equilibrium simply moves from the point where the old curves intersected to the point where the new ones intersect.

Pause for thought

What would happen to price and quantity if the demand curve shifted to the left? Draw a diagram to illustrate your answer.

Figure 4.7   The effect of a shift in the demand curve

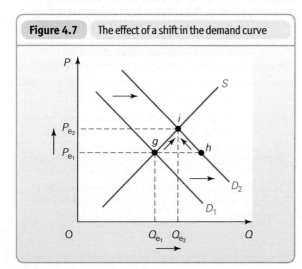

Figure 4.8   The effect of a shift in the supply curve

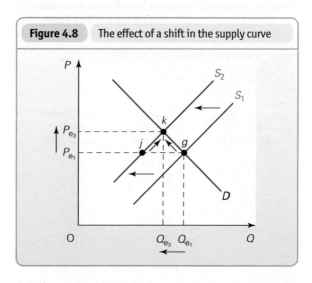

BOX 4.1 UK HOUSE PRICES

The ups and downs of the housing market

If you are thinking of buying a house sometime in the future, then you may well follow the fortunes of the housing market with some trepidation. It is an exceptionally important market to consumers and government, with households spending more on housing as a proportion of their income than on anything else.

Movements in the housing market are rarely out of the news. This is not only because nominal (actual) prices are increasing over the longer term, but, more significantly, because they are increasing in *real* terms too. This means that house prices are increasing *relative* to general prices. The average UK house price in January 1970 was a little over £3900. By January 2017, as shown in the following table, it had risen to around £215 000, an increase of nearly 5400 per cent.

Average UK house price and RPI (January)

	1970	1980	1990	2000	2010	2017
House price (£)	3 920	19 273	58 250	84 620	167 469	215 037
RPI (Jan. 1987 = 100)	10.8	37.4	71.5	100.0	131.1	160.6
House price at constant Jan. 1987 consumer prices (£)	21 736	30 810	48 643	50 539	76 299	79 954

Sources: Consumer Price Inflation time series dataset and UK House Price Index: reports (Office for National Statistics).

Although house prices have increased significantly over the past 50 years, there has also been a great deal of volatility in this market – more so than in general prices across the economy. In the 1970s and 1980s, annual house price inflation rates exceeded 50 and 30 per cent, respectively. Between 1984 and 1989, house prices doubled and this led to a rush to buy houses, with borrowing increasing significantly.

However, this was followed by a protracted period of real and nominal house price falls between 1990 and 1995, where house prices fell by 12.2 per cent, sending many households into *negative equity*. This occurs when the size of a household's mortgage is greater than the value of their house, meaning that, if they sold their house, they would still owe money! Many people, therefore, found themselves in a situation where they were unable to move house.

By the end of the 1990s, house price inflation had returned and we saw a period of protracted house price growth, such that, by the end of 2002, house prices were rising by an annual rate of 26 per cent: good news for sellers, but first-time buyers were struggling to get on the property ladder. The gross house-price-to-earnings ratio for first-time buyers had increased from just over 2 in the mid-1990s to over 5 times the size of a first-time buyer's earnings by 2007.

As the UK economy entered recession in 2008, house prices began to decline again, falling at an annual rate of 17.5 per cent in early 2009. Despite a slight recovery in 2010, followed by a small decline, house prices remained relatively flat until late 2013, when, once more, they began to grow.

This was helped particularly by strong growth in London and the South East of England. Then, in 2016, the UK voted to leave the EU and the growth in house prices once more began to slow.

What causes house price volatility?

House prices are determined by demand and supply. If demand rises (i.e. shifts to the right) or if supply falls (i.e. shifts to the left), the equilibrium price of houses will rise. Similarly, if demand falls or supply rises, the equilibrium price will fall.

So why did UK house prices rise so rapidly in the 1980s, the late 1990s through to 2007 and once more from 2013 to 2016? Why did they also fall in the early 1990s and then fall again from 2008 to 2013 and since the EU referendum? The answer lies primarily in changes in the *demand* for housing. Let us examine the various factors that affected the demand for houses.

Incomes (actual and anticipated)

The second half of the 1980s, 1996 to 2007 and from 2013 to 2016 were periods of rising incomes or recovery. The economy was experiencing an economic 'boom' or a recovery from recession. Many people wanted to spend their extra incomes on housing: either buying a house for the first time or moving to a better one. What is more, many people thought that their incomes would continue to grow, and were thus prepared to stretch themselves financially in the short term by buying an expensive house, confident that their mortgage payments would become more and more affordable over time.

The early 1990s and from 2008 to 2012, by contrast, were periods of low or negative growth, with rising unemployment and falling incomes. People had much less confidence about their ability to afford large mortgages. Similarly, in 2017, rising inflation rates caused real incomes to fall and this, together with uncertainty about the future of the UK outside of the EU, had a negative impact on demand for housing.

The desire for home ownership

The desire for home ownership has increased over the years, fuelled by many television programmes focused on buying and selling property. There has also been an increase in the number of households, due to increased life expectancy and changing demographics, such as more single-parent families and flows of workers from EU countries. In 1981, there were 20 million households in the UK; by 2017, this had increased to 27.3 million.

The cost of mortgages

During the second half of the 1980s, mortgage interest rates generally were falling. This meant that people could afford larger mortgages and thus afford to buy more expensive houses. In 1989, however, this trend was reversed. Mortgage interest rates were now rising. Many people found it difficult to maintain existing payments, let alone to take on a larger mortgage. From 1996 to 2003, mortgage rates generally were reduced again, once more fuelling the demand for houses. From 2003 to 2007, interest rates rose again, but this was not enough to deter the demand for housing.

▶

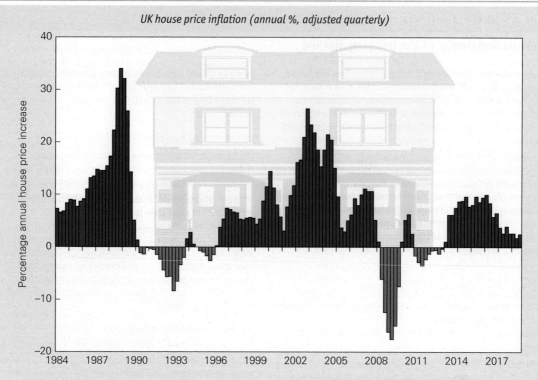

UK house price inflation (annual %, adjusted quarterly)

Source: Based on data in *Halifax House Price Index* (Lloyds Banking Group)

Between 2009 and 2018, interest rates remained low, which reduced the cost of mortgage repayments, but this did not cause an increase in housing demand until 2013, due to the continued economic uncertainty following the financial crisis and cautious mortgage lenders. The recovery in housing demand from around 2013, although driven partly by the recovery of the economy, was helped by continuing low interest rates, but, from the second half of 2016, uncertainty returned to the market due to the result of the EU referendum.

The availability of mortgages

In the late 1980s and from 1997 to 2007, mortgages were readily available. Banks and building societies were prepared to accept smaller deposits on houses and to grant large mortgages as house prices were rising so quickly. In the early 1990s and from the late 2000s, however, banks and building societies were more cautious about granting mortgages. They were aware that, with falling house prices,

rising unemployment and the growing problem of negative equity, there was a growing danger that borrowers would default on payments.

The problem in the late 2000s was compounded by the financial crisis, which meant that banks had less money to lend. Credit criteria remained tight into the early 2010s, so that purchasers had to find historically large deposits. Many mortgage lenders were asking for deposits of at least 25 per cent – over £40 000 for an average house in the UK. This reduced significantly the number of first-time buyers. The deposit requirement eased a little through 2013 and 2014 and government-backed 'Help to Buy'[1] schemes were introduced to help borrowers get a mortgage with a 5 per cent deposit. The easing of credit constraints contributed towards an increase in house prices once again.

Speculation

A belief that house prices will continue to move in a particular direction can exacerbate house price movements. In other

---

[1] www.helptobuy.gov.uk/.

words, speculation tends to increase house price volatility. In the 1980s and from the mid-1990s to 2007, people generally believed that house prices would continue rising. This encouraged people to buy as soon as possible, and to take out the biggest mortgage possible, before prices went up any further. There was also an effect on supply. Those with houses to sell held back until the last possible moment in the hope of getting a higher price. The net effect was for a rightward shift in the demand curve for houses and a leftward shift in the supply curve. The effect of this speculation, therefore, was to help bring about the very effect that people were predicting (see section 5.4).

In the early 1990s, and again from 2008, the opposite occurred. People thinking of buying houses held back, hoping to buy at a lower price. People with houses to sell tried to sell them as quickly as possible before prices fell any further. Again, the effect of this speculation was to aggravate the change in prices – this time a fall in prices.

The impact of speculation has also been compounded by the growth in the 'buy-to-let' industry, with mortgage lenders entering this market in large numbers. There was a huge amount of media attention on the possibilities for individuals to make very high returns.

Supply

While speculation about changing house prices is perhaps the biggest determinant of housing supply in the short term, over the long term, supply depends on house building. Governments' housing policy is often focused on how to encourage the building industry by providing tax and other incentives and streamlining planning regulations. But house building may bring adverse environmental and social problems and people often oppose new housing developments in their area.

Housing supply is a hotly debated topic in the UK, with disagreement over how many, where and who should build new houses. Some of these issues are discussed in articles from the *Financial Times*,[2] *The Guardian*,[3] *Bloomberg*[4] and *The Daily Telegraph*.[5] You can also read more about it from a UK Parliament briefing[6] and from data on new builds from the Ministry of Housing, Communities & Local Government.[7]

A global dimension to falling house prices

The fall in UK house prices in 2008 had global origins. The dramatic growth in mortgage lending in the UK was also a feature of many other industrialised countries at this time, most notably the USA, where there had been similar dramatic rises in house prices.

Banks and other mortgage lenders bundled up these large mortgage debts into 'financial instruments' and sold them on to other global financial institutions so that they could meet their everyday liquidity requirements of paying bills and meeting customers' demands for cash. This worked well while there was economic prosperity and people could pay their mortgages. However, it became apparent in 2007 that many of the mortgages sold, notably in the USA, were to people who could not meet their repayments.

As the number of mortgage defaults increased, the value of the mortgage-laden financial instruments sold on to other financial institutions fell. As banks found it increasingly difficult to meet their liquidity requirements, they reduced the number of mortgages to potential home owners.

Although housing markets in many countries have recovered as more housing finance has become available and as confidence has returned, the world economy has continued to become more interdependent. This means that the state of the global economy and global finance will be felt increasingly in housing markets around the world.

1. Draw supply and demand diagrams to illustrate what was happening to house prices (a) in the second half of the 1980s and from the late 1990s to 2007; (b) in the early 1990s and 2008–12; (c) in London and the South East of England from 2014–16.
2. Are there any factors on the supply side that contribute to changes in house prices? If so, what are they?
3. Find out what has happened to house prices over the past three years. Attempt an explanation of what has happened.

   Undertake an internet search to find out what forecasters are predicting for house prices over the next year and attempt to explain the role played by demand and supply in their forecasts.

[2]John Kay, 'How to solve the UK housing crisis', *Financial Times* (8 November 2017).
[3]Ann Pettifor, 'Why building more homes will not solve Britain's housing crisis', *The Guardian* (27 January 2018).
[4]Ferdinando Giugliano, 'To End U.K. Housing Shortage, Build More Houses. Duh.', *Bloomberg* (30 November 2017).

[5]Isabelle Fraser, 'Number of homes on the market falls to a new low with housing market "stifled" by uncertainty, says Rics', *The Telegraph* (13 July 2017).
[6]Wendy Wilson, 'Housing supply and demand', *Key Issues for the New Parliament 2010,* House of Commons Library Research (2010).
[7]Live tables on housing supply: net additional dwellings, Ministry of Housing, Communities & Local Government.

KI 10
p46

BOX 4.2 STOCK MARKET PRICES

Demand and supply in action

Financial Times Stock Exchange Index (FTSE) and Retail Price Index (RPI): 3/1/1984 = 1000

Note: FTSE figures based on end-of-month values
Sources: Based on data from *Consumer Price Inflation time series dataset* and various, 2018

Firms that are quoted on the stock market can raise money by issuing shares. These are sold on the 'primary stock market'. People who own the shares receive a 'dividend' on them, normally paid six-monthly. This varies with the profitability of the company.

People or institutions that buy these shares, however, may not wish to hold on to them for ever. This is where the 'secondary stock market' comes in. It is where existing shares are bought and sold. There are stock markets, primary and secondary, in all the major countries of the world. There are 2028 companies whose shares are listed on the London Stock Exchange, as of the end of February 2018 and shares are traded each Monday to Friday (excluding bank holidays).

The prices of shares depend on demand and supply. For example, if the demand for Tesco shares at any one time exceeds the supply on offer, the price will rise until demand and supply are equal. Share prices fluctuate throughout the trading day and sometimes price changes can be substantial.

To give an overall impression of share price movements, stock exchanges publish share price indices. The best-known one in the UK is the FTSE 100, which stands for the 'Financial Times Stock Exchange' index of the 100 largest companies' shares. The index represents an average price of these 100 shares. The chart shows movements in the FTSE 100 from 1995 to 2018. The index was first calculated on 3 January 1984 with a base level of 1000 points and it has increased by an average of 7 per cent per year since. Despite this increase, there have been some significant fluctuations in share prices.

The FTSE 100 reached a peak of 6930 points on 30 December 1999 and fell to 3287 on 12 March 2003; it then rose again, reaching a high of 6730 on 12 October 2007. In the midst of the financial crisis, the index fell to a low of 3512 on March 2009, but, by early 2010, it had recovered partially, passing 6000 for a brief period, before levelling out and fluctuating

around an average of 5500 to mid-2012, only to rise above 6000 again at the start of 2013, peaking at 7104 on 27 April 2015, before falling back to around 6000 in early 2016.

Despite the shock of the Brexit vote in June 2016, the FTSE 100 recovered and rose back to 7000 by the end of the year and finished 2017 at 7688. Part of the reason for this was the fall in the sterling exchange rate that occurred because of the uncertainty over the nature of the Brexit deal. With many of the FTSE 100 companies having assets denominated in dollars, a falling sterling exchange rate meant that these dollar assets were now worth more pounds. The rise also reflected a general buoyancy in stock markets around the world, which, in fact, in most major countries rose faster than the FTSE 100.

But what causes share prices to change? Why were they so high in 1999, but only just over half that value just three years later, and why has this trend repeated itself in the late 2000s and what can we expect as the UK prepares to leave the EU? The answer lies in the determinants of the demand and supply of shares.

Demand

There are five main factors that affect the demand for shares.

The dividend yield

This is the dividend on a share as a percentage of its price. The higher the dividend yields on shares, the more attractive they are as a form of saving. One of the main explanations of rising stock market prices from 2003 to 2007 was high profits and resulting high dividends. Similarly, the slowdown in the world economy after 2007 led to falling profits and falling dividends and the global recovery caused them to increase once more.

The price of and/or return on substitutes

The main substitutes for shares in specific companies are other shares. Thus, if, in comparison with other shares, Tesco shares are expected to pay high dividends relative to the share price, people will buy Tesco shares. As far as shares in general are concerned, the main substitutes are other forms of saving. Thus, if the interest rate on savings accounts in banks and building societies fell, people with such accounts would be tempted to take their money out and buy shares instead.

Another major substitute is property. If house prices rise rapidly, as they did from the late 1990s to 2007, this will reduce the demand for shares as many people switch to buying property in anticipation of even higher prices, as we saw in Box 4.1. If house prices level off, this makes shares relatively more attractive as an investment and can boost the demand for them.

Of course, other factors may affect *both* house prices *and* shares in the same way. From late 2007, the 'credit crunch' caused both house prices and share prices to fall dramatically. Investors looked towards other, safer, investments such as gold, government debt (Treasury bills and gilts) or even holding cash.

But then with interest rates, including those on savings accounts, being dramatically cut as a result of Bank of England measures to stimulate the economy in 2009, many people saw shares as an attractive alternative to bank and building society accounts. The stock market began rising again.

Incomes

If the economy is growing rapidly and people's incomes are thus rising rapidly, they are likely to buy more shares. Thus, in the mid-to-late 1990s, when UK incomes were rising at an average annual rate of over 3 per cent, share prices rose rapidly (see chart). As growth rates fell in the early 2000s, so share prices fell.

Similarly, when economic growth improved from 2003 to 2007, share prices increased, but they fell back with the global financial crisis in 2007–8 and the onset of recession and declining real incomes from 2008, only to rise again as the recovery took hold from around 2013 to 2015.

Wealth

'Wealth' is people's accumulated savings and property. Wealth rose in the 1990s and 2000s, and many people used their increased wealth to buy shares. The growth in wealth was halted by the financial crisis and many people looked to 'cash in' their shares, which depressed share prices.

Expectations

In the mid-to-late 1980s and 1990s, and again from 2003 to 2007, people expected share prices to go on rising. They were optimistic about an end to 'boom and bust' and continued growth in the economy. But, as people bought shares, this pushed their prices up even more, thereby fuelling further speculation that they would go on rising and encouraging further share buying.

In the early 2000s, confidence was shaken as growth began to slow and this was further exacerbated by other factors, including the 11 September 2001 attack on the World Trade Center and a range of corporate scandals. Combined, these

factors caused share prices to plummet and, as people anticipated further price falls, so they held back from buying, thereby pushing prices even lower.

A similar thing occurred with the global banking crisis in 2007–8, as fears of impending recession started a dramatic fall in share prices. Uncertainty over how and when the global economy would recover caused share prices to be volatile for a few years. It was only when confidence started to return that share prices begin to rise once more.

However, uncertainty may return with the unknown consequences of the UK's exit from the EU, a still tentative recovery in Japan and in many European countries and the possibility that growth in countries like China and other developing nations may slow. The rise and fall in share prices associated with expectations mirror those seen in the housing market and discussed in Box 4.1.

Supply

The factors affecting supply in the secondary market are largely the same as those affecting demand, but in the opposite direction.

If the return on alternative forms of saving falls, people with shares are likely to hold on to them, as they represent a better form of saving. The supply of shares to the market will fall. If incomes or wealth rise, people again are likely to want to hold on to their shares.

As far as expectations are concerned, if people believe that share prices will rise, they will hold on to the shares they have. Supply to the market will fall, thereby pushing up prices. If, however, they believe that prices will fall (as they did in 2008), they will sell their shares now before prices do fall. Supply will increase, driving down the price.

Share prices and business

Companies are crucially affected by their share price. If a company's share price falls, this is taken as a sign that 'the market' is losing confidence in the company, as we saw with Tesco during the latter part of 2014 and with companies such as easyJet from June 2016 to February 2017. Such falls in share prices make it more difficult for a company to raise finance, not only by issuing additional shares in the primary market, but also from banks.

It can also make the company more vulnerable to a takeover bid. This is where one company seeks to buy out another by offering to buy all its shares. A takeover will succeed if the owners of more than half of the company's shares vote to accept the offered price. Shareholders are more likely to agree to the takeover if the company's share price has not been performing very well.

Further discussion of the stock market and how efficient it is can be found in section 19.5.

If the rate of economic growth in the economy is 3 per cent in a particular year, why are share prices likely to rise by more than 3 per cent that year?

Research what has happened to the FTSE 100 index over the past 12 months (see site B27 on the hotlinks part of the website). Summarise the patterns you find and examine the economic factors helping to drive these patterns.

BOX 4.3 CONTROLLING PRICES

Efforts to curb binge drinking

Throughout this chapter we have been looking at the way in which the price mechanism works in competitive markets. When a determinant of demand and/or supply changes, the price mechanism eliminates any resulting shortage or surplus: price moves to a new equilibrium level which equates demand and supply.

Over the years, there has been a general shift in economies across the world to a more market-based system that allows the price mechanism to work. This means consumers and many producers responding to prices, creating a more efficient market, as we saw in Box 2.2. However, is there an argument against the price mechanism and in favour of government intervention to fix prices? The equilibrium price is not necessarily the 'best' price in a market and we do see governments setting prices either above or below the equilibrium.

When a price is set above the equilibrium, it is known as a *minimum price* (or price floor). Such a price will create a surplus, as the quantity supplied will exceed the quantity demanded, as shown in chart (a). Normally, a surplus would be eliminated by a fall in price but, with a minimum price set above the equilibrium, the surplus persists. One minimum price control that you will be familiar with and may benefit from is the National Minimum Wage, which is covered in more detail in Chapter 18.

When a price is set below the equilibrium, it is known as a *maximum price* (or price ceiling). In this case, a shortage emerges, as the quantity demanded will exceed the quantity supplied, as shown in chart (b). Again, the shortage will persist, as the price mechanism no longer adjusts to eliminate it. Governments in some countries have set maximum prices for various basic foodstuffs. The aim is to help the poor. The problem, however, is that it is likely to create shortages of food. The quantity demanded will be higher and the low price is likely discourage farmers from producing so much.

Minimum price for alcohol

Another market where price controls have been extensively discussed is that of alcohol. In early 2010, the UK House of Commons Health Select Committee proposed a minimum price per unit of alcohol in England and Wales (among other policies) to combat the growing problem of binge drinking.

It was argued that it would reduce the demand for alcohol by heavy drinkers by raising the price of otherwise cheap drinks, such as those found on offer in supermarkets and in bars during 'happy hours'.

The report suggested that a minimum price of alcohol of 50p would save more than 3000 lives per year and would go some

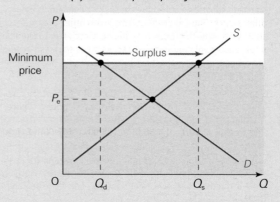

(a) Minimum price: price floor

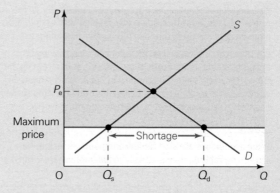

(b) Maximum price: price ceiling

way to tackling the costs to the National Health Service of excessive drinking. Estimates by the Royal College of Physicians suggested that the total cost of excessive drinking is £6 billion, £3 billion of which is directly related to higher costs for the NHS.

However, the minimum price was not introduced. The reason given was a lack of 'concrete evidence'. But, in May 2014, the Coalition Government did introduce a ban that prevented the sale of alcohol below cost price.

In Scotland, however, the approach has been different. In 2012, plans emerged for a 50p minimum unit price on alcohol, but this was challenged in both the European and Scottish Courts by the Scottish Whisky Association – clearly an organisation that would be negatively impacted by such a price. The Scottish Government decided that it was worth the cost of fighting the challenge and, on 15 November 2017, the

UK Supreme Court ruled that the minimum price was legal. The 50p minimum price was introduced on 1 May 2018.[1]

What impact would a 50p MUP have on the price of alcoholic drinks in the UK? The following table provides some examples across a range of products available in supermarkets.

Effect of a 50p MUP on the price of various alcoholic drinks

Product	Volume	Strength (% abv)	Units of alcohol	Current price	Minimum price
Cheap strong spirits	70cl	50.0	35.00	£12.00	£17.50
Cheap spirits	70cl	37.5	26.25	£10.00	£13.13
Cheap wine	750ml	13.0	9.75	£3.99	£4.88
Cheap strong cider	3 litres	7.5	22.50	£3.50	£11.25
Lager (4 pack)	440 ml × 4	5.0	2.20	£4.50	£4.40
Alcopop	70cl	4.0	2.80	£3.00	£1.40

Scotland will become the first country to introduce a minimum price for alcohol, but a few countries do have forms of price regulation in place on alcohol, including Saskatchewan, Canada, and many others are still considering it. Evidence from Canada suggests that a 10 per cent rise in the prices of alcoholic drinks leads to an 8 per cent fall in consumption. While their policy is somewhat different, with the minimum price varying for different drinks, it was one of the studies that furthered the argument in favour of minimum pricing in the UK.[2]

Many other pieces of research also indicate the benefits of a minimum price, including a paper that considered 33 studies, which found that, 'price-based alcohol policy interventions such as MUP are likely to reduce alcohol consumption, alcohol-related morbidity and mortality'.[3]

Critics of the minimum price will continue to argue that it will be ineffective, because those at whom it is primarily aimed (binge drinkers) will be largely unresponsive to the higher price. Instead, it would be the 'sensible' drinkers who suffer from having to pay a higher price for alcohol. The Scottish Whisky Association refer to it as a 'blunt instrument'. Furthermore, there are concerns that it will adversely affect pubs and small supermarkets.

When the minimum price is imposed, it will need to be above the equilibrium for it to have any effect and this will create a surplus, as firms would be willing to supply more at the price floor, but consumers would cut back their demand (or at least that is the idea). Further intervention may then be needed to deal with the resulting surpluses that are always associated with minimum prices. There is the danger that the surpluses may be sold illicitly at cut prices. It will take time to see how effective the minimum price in Scotland will be and what impact, if any, it has on the drinks-industry.

1. What methods could be used by the government to deal with:
   (a) the surpluses from minimum price controls?
   (b) the shortages that result from maximum price controls?
2. How will the policy of a minimum or maximum price control be affected by a change in the relative steepness of the demand and supply curves? (This concept will be considered in more detail in Chapter 5.)
3. Give some examples of items where the government might choose to set a maximum price. What problems might arise from doing so?

Undertake desktop research to examine moves in various countries to introduce minimum unit pricing for alcohol. How do the measures, or proposals, compare? Discuss which are likely to be more effective.

[1] *Alcohol: Minimum Pricing*, House of Commons Library, Research Briefing (9 February 2018).

[2] Nick Triggle, 'The battle over alcohol pricing', *BBC News*, www.bbc.co.uk/news/health-21244194 (30 January 2013).

[3] Sadie Boniface, Jack W. Scannell and Sally Marlow, 'Evidence for the effectiveness of minimum pricing of alcohol: a systematic review and assessment using the Bradford Hill Criteria for causality, *BMJ Journal*, Volume 7 Issue 5, (6 June 2017).

Definitions

Minimum price A price floor set by the government or some other agency. The price is not allowed to fall below this level (although it is allowed to rise above it).

Maximum price A price ceiling set by the government or some other agency. The price is not allowed to rise above this level (although it is allowed to fall below it).

SUMMARY

1a A firm is greatly affected by its market environment. The more competitive the market, the less discretion the firm has in determining its price. In the extreme case of a perfect market, the price is determined by demand and supply and is entirely outside the control of firms and consumers: they are price takers.

1b In a perfect market, price changes act as the mechanism whereby demand and supply are balanced. If there is a shortage, price will rise until the shortage is eliminated. If there is a surplus, price will fall until that is eliminated.

2a When the price of a good rises, the quantity demanded per period of time will fall. This is known as the 'law of demand'. It applies both to individuals' demand and to the whole market demand.

2b The law of demand is explained by the income and substitution effects of a price change.

2c The relationship between price and quantity demanded per period of time can be shown in a table (or 'schedule') or as a graph. On the graph, price is plotted on the vertical axis and quantity demanded per period of time on the horizontal axis. The resulting demand curve is downward sloping (negatively sloped).

2d Other determinants of demand include tastes, the number and price of substitute goods, the number and price of complementary goods, income, the distribution of income and expectations of future price changes.

2e If price changes, the effect is shown by a movement along the demand curve. We call this effect 'a change in the quantity demanded'. If any other determinant of demand changes, the whole curve will shift. We call this effect 'a change in demand'. A rightward shift represents an increase in demand; a leftward shift represents a decrease in demand.

3a When the price of a good rises, the quantity supplied per period of time will usually also rise. This applies both to individual producers' supply and to the whole market supply.

3b There are two reasons in the short run why a higher price encourages producers to supply more: (a) they are now willing to incur higher costs per unit associated with producing more; (b) they will switch to producing this product and away from now less profitable ones. In the long run, there is a third reason: new producers will be attracted into the market.

3c The relationship between price and quantity supplied per period of time can be shown in a table (or schedule) or as a graph. As with a demand curve, price is plotted on the vertical axis and quantity per period of time on the horizontal axis. The resulting supply curve is upward sloping (positively sloped).

3d Other determinants of supply include the costs of production, the profitability of alternative products, the profitability of goods in joint supply, random shocks and expectations of future price changes.

3e If price changes, the effect is shown by a movement along the supply curve. We call this effect 'a change in the quantity supplied'. If any determinant *other* than price changes, the effect is shown by a shift in the whole supply curve. We call this effect 'a change in supply'. A rightward shift represents an increase in supply; a leftward shift represents a decrease in supply.

4a If the demand for a good exceeds the supply, there will be a shortage. This will lead to a rise in the price of the good. If the supply of a good exceeds the demand, there will be a surplus. This will lead to a fall in the price.

4b Price will settle at the equilibrium. The equilibrium price is the one that clears the market, such that demand equals supply. This is shown in a demand and supply diagram by the point where the two curves intersect.

4c If the demand or supply curve shifts, this will lead either to a shortage or to a surplus. Price will, therefore, either rise or fall until a new equilibrium is reached at the position where the supply and demand curves *now* intersect.

REVIEW QUESTIONS

1 Using a diagram like Figure 4.1, summarise the effect of (a) a reduction in the demand for a good; (b) a reduction in the costs of production of a good.

2 Why do the prices of fresh strawberries fall when they are in season? Could an individual producer prevent the price falling?

3 If you were the owner of a clothes shop, how would you set about deciding what prices to charge for each garment at the end-of-season sale?

4 Again referring to Table 4.1, draw Tracey's and Darren's demand curves for potatoes on one diagram. (Note that you will use the same vertical scale as in Figure 4.2, but you will need a quite different horizontal scale.) At what price is their demand the same? What explanations could there be for the quite different shapes of their two demand curves? (This question is explored in Chapter 5.)

5 This question is concerned with the supply of oil for central heating. In each case, consider whether there is a movement along the supply curve (and in which direction) or a shift in it (and whether left or right): (a) new oil fields start up in production; (b) the demand for central heating rises; (c) the price of gas falls; (d) oil companies anticipate an upsurge in the demand for central-heating oil; (e) the demand for petrol rises; (f) new technology decreases the costs of oil refining; (g) all oil products become more expensive.

6 For what reasons might the price of foreign holidays rise? In each case, identify whether these are reasons affecting demand or supply (or both).

7 The price of cod is much higher today than it was 30 years ago. Using demand and supply diagrams, explain why this should be so.

8 What will happen to the equilibrium price and quantity of butter in each of the following cases? You should state whether demand or supply, or both, have shifted and in which direction: (a) a rise in the price of margarine; (b) a rise in the demand for yoghurt; (c) a rise in the price of bread; (d) a rise in the demand for bread; (e) an expected increase in the price of butter in the near future; (f) a tax on butter production; (g) the invention of a new, but expensive, process of removing all cholesterol from butter, plus the passing of a law that states that butter producers must use this process. In each case, assume *ceteris paribus*.

9 The weekly demand and supply schedules for orange dresses (in millions) in a free market are as follows:

Price (£)	8	7	6	5	4	3	2	1
Quantity demanded	6	8	10	12	14	16	18	20
Quantity supplied	18	16	14	12	10	8	6	4

a) What is the equilibrium price and quantity?
b) If there is a change in fashion that causes demand for orange dresses to rise by 4 million at each price, what will be the new equilibrium? Has the equilibrium quantity risen by as much as the increase in demand? Explain why or why not.

10 If both demand and supply change, and if we know in which direction they have shifted but not by how much, why is it that we will be able to predict the direction in which *either* price or quantity will change, but not both? (Clue: consider the four possible combinations and sketch them, if necessary: *D* left, *S* left; *D* right, *S* right; *D* left, *S* right; *D* right, *S* left.)

Chapter 5

Business in a market environment

Business issues covered in this chapter

- How responsive is consumer demand to changes in the market price? How responsive is it to changes in consumer incomes and to the prices of other products?
- How is a firm's sales revenue affected by a change in price?
- How responsive is business output to changes in price?
- How does the responsiveness (or 'elasticity') of demand and supply to changes in price affect the working of markets?
- Why are markets likely to be more responsive in the long run than in the short run to changes in demand or supply?
- What is the difference between stabilising and destabilising speculation and how does this affect the volatility of market prices?
- What is meant by 'risk' and 'uncertainty' and what is their significance to business?
- How do firms deal with uncertainty about future market movements?

In Chapter 4 we examined how prices are determined in perfectly competitive markets: by the interaction of market demand and market supply. In such markets, although the *market* demand curve is downward sloping, the demand curve faced by the individual firm will be horizontal. This is illustrated in Figure 5.1.

The market price is P_m. The individual firm can sell as much as it likes at this market price: it is too small to have any influence on the market – it is a price taker. It will not force the price down by producing more because, in terms of the total market, this extra output would be an infinitesimally small amount. If a farmer doubled the output of wheat sent to the market, it would be too small an increase to affect the world price of wheat!

In practice, however, many firms are not price takers; they have some discretion in choosing their price. Such firms will face a downward-sloping demand curve. If they raise their price, they will sell less; if they lower their price, they will sell more. But firms and economists will want to know more than this. They will want to know just *how much* the quantity demanded will fall. In other words, they will want to know how *responsive* demand is to a rise in price. This responsiveness is measured using a concept called 'elasticity'.

Key Idea 12

Elasticity. The responsiveness of one variable (e.g. demand) to a change in another (e.g. price). This concept is fundamental to understanding how markets work. The more elastic variables are, the more responsive is the market to changing circumstances.

The responsiveness of quantity demanded to a change in price

The demand for an individual firm

For any firm considering changing its price, it is vital to know the likely effect on the quantity demanded. Take the case of two firms facing very different demand curves. Firm A faces little or no competition, whereas Firm B is competing with several other firms. The two demand curves are shown in Figure 5.2.

Firm A can raise its price quite substantially – from £6 to £10 – and yet its level of sales falls only by a relatively small amount – from 100 units to 90 units. With few, or even no, competitors to worry about, the firm probably will be quite keen to raise its price. After all, it could make significantly more profit on each unit sold (assuming no rise in costs per unit), and yet sell only slightly fewer units.

Firm B, however, will think twice about raising its price. Even a relatively modest increase in price – from £6 to £7 – will lead to a substantial fall in sales from 100 units to 40 units as people switch to competitors' products. What is the point of making a bit more profit on those units it manages to sell if, in the process, it ends up selling a lot fewer units? In such circumstances, the firm may contemplate lowering its price.

The responsiveness of market demand

Economists too will want to know how responsive demand is to a change in price: except in this case it is the responsiveness of *market* demand that is being considered. This information is necessary to enable them to predict the effects of a shift in supply on the market price of a product.

Figure 5.3 shows the effect of a shift in supply with two quite different demand curves (D and D'). Assume that, initially, the supply curve is S_1, and that it intersects with both demand curves at point a, at a price of P_1 and a quantity of Q_1.

Now supply shifts to S_2. What will happen to price and quantity? The answer is that it depends on the shape of the demand curve. In the case of demand curve D, there is a relatively large rise in price (to P_2) and a relatively small fall in quantity (to Q_2): equilibrium is at point b. In the case of demand curve D', however, there is only a relatively small rise in price (to P_3), but a relatively large fall in quantity (to Q_3): equilibrium is at point c.

Figure 5.1	Market demand curve for an individual firm under conditions of perfect competition

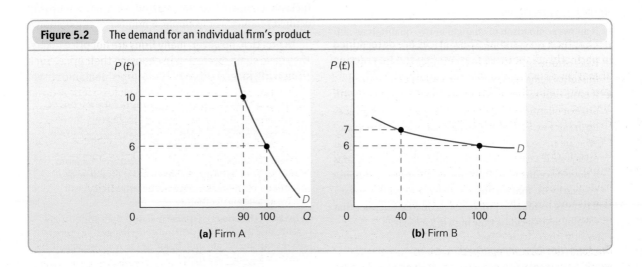

Figure 5.2	The demand for an individual firm's product

(a) Firm A

(b) Firm B

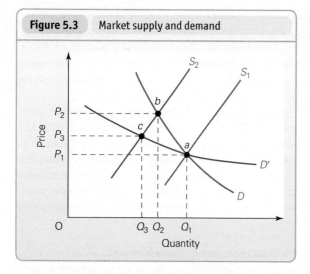

Figure 5.3 Market supply and demand

Defining price elasticity of demand

What we want to compare is the size of the change in quantity demanded of a given product with the size of the change in price. *Price elasticity of demand* does just this. It is defined as follows:

$$P\epsilon_D = \frac{\text{Proportionate (or percentage)}}{\text{Proportionate (or percentage) change in price}}$$

If, for example, a 20 per cent rise in the price of a product causes a 10 per cent fall in the quantity demanded, the price elasticity of demand will be:

$$-10\%/20\% = -0.5$$

Three things should be noted at this stage about the figure that is calculated for elasticity.

The use of proportionate or percentage measures

Elasticity is measured in proportionate or percentage terms for the following reasons:

- It allows comparison of changes in two qualitatively different things, which are thus measured in two different types of unit: i.e. it allows comparison of quantity changes (quantity demanded) with monetary changes (price).
- It is the only sensible way of deciding *how big* a change in price or quantity is. Take a simple example. An item goes up in price by £1. Is this a big increase or a small increase? We can answer this only if we know what the original price was. If a can of beans goes up in price by £1, that is a huge price increase. If, however, the price of a house goes up by £1, that is a tiny price increase. In other words, it is the percentage or proportionate increase in price that we look at in deciding how big a price rise it is.

The sign (positive or negative)

We already know that demand curves are downward sloping. If price increases (a positive figure), the quantity demanded will fall (a negative figure). If price falls (a negative figure), the quantity demanded will rise (a positive figure). Thus price elasticity of demand will be negative: a positive figure is being divided by a negative figure (or vice versa).

The value (greater or less than 1)

If we now ignore the sign and just concentrate on the value of the figure, this tells us how responsive demand is to the change in price; or, in economic terms, whether demand is *elastic* or *inelastic*.

Elastic ($\epsilon > 1$) This is where a change in price causes a proportionately larger change in the quantity demanded. In this case, the price elasticity of demand will be greater than 1, since we are dividing a larger figure by a smaller figure.

Inelastic ($\epsilon < 1$). This is where a change in price causes a proportionately smaller change in the quantity demanded. In this case, the price elasticity of demand will be less than 1, since we are dividing a smaller figure by a larger figure.

Unit elastic ($\epsilon = 1$). **Unit elasticity** is where the quantity demanded changes proportionately the same as price. This will give an elasticity equal to 1, since we are dividing a figure by itself.

The determinants of price elasticity of demand

The price elasticity of demand varies enormously from one product to another. But why do some products have a highly elastic demand, whereas others have a highly *in*elastic demand? What determines price elasticity of demand?

The number and closeness of substitute goods

This is the most important determinant. The more substitutes there are for a good and the closer they are as substitutes, the more people will switch to these alternatives when the price of the good rises and the greater, therefore, will be the price elasticity of demand.

The demand for a product, in general, will be relatively inelastic compared to the demand for a more narrowly defined product. For example, a number of international

---

Definitions

Price elasticity of demand A measure of the responsiveness of quantity demanded to a change in price: the proportionate change in quantity demanded divided by the proportionate change in price.

Elastic If demand is (price) elastic, then any change in price will cause the quantity demanded to change proportionately more. Ignoring the negative sign, it will have a value greater than 1.

Inelastic If demand is (price) inelastic, then any change will cause the quantity demanded to change by a proportionately smaller amount. Ignoring the negative sign, it will have a value less than 1.

Unit elasticity When the price elasticity of demand is unity, this is where quantity demanded changes by the same proportion as the price. Price elasticity is equal to 1.

meta-studies have found that alcohol has a relatively inelastic demand of around − 0.4.[1] This is to be expected, given that there are few substitutes for alcohol and we know that alcohol is an addictive substance – people are still willing to buy, even if price rises.

However, if we look at a more specific product, such as beer, we find that estimates of elasticity tend to be more elastic as here there are other substitutes – not only substitutes for alcohol in general, but also substitutes for beer, such as wine and spirits. Typical estimates for the price elasticity of beer vary between −0.98 and −1.27.[2] This means that when the price of alcohol rises, demand for it will fall, but when the price of a particular type of alcohol, such as beer, rises, demand will fall by more, as there are substitutes for this drink. We would expect the price elasticity of demand for particular types of beer to be even higher and for particular brands to be higher still.

The proportion of income spent on the good

The higher the proportion of our income we spend on a good, the more we will be forced to cut consumption when its price rises: the bigger will be the income effect and the more elastic will be the demand.

Thus salt has a very low price elasticity of demand – estimates suggest it is about − 0.1.[3] This is because we spend such a tiny fraction of our income on salt that we would find little difficulty in paying a relatively large percentage increase in its price: the income effect of a price rise would be very small. By contrast, there will be a much bigger income effect when a major item of expenditure rises in price. For example, if mortgage interest rates rise (the 'price'

of loans for house purchases), people may have to cut down substantially on their demand for housing – being forced to buy somewhere much smaller and cheaper, or to live in rented accommodation.

> ### Pause for thought
>
> *Will the price elasticity of demand for a Peugeot be higher or lower than the price elasticity of demand for all family cars? Explain.*

The time period

When price rises, people may take time to adjust their consumption patterns and find alternatives. The longer the time period after a price change, the more elastic is the demand likely to be.

The Office for Budget Responsibility estimates that the price elasticity of demand for road fuel is −0.07 in the short run and −0.13 in the medium term. Research from America on the price elasticity of electricity demand finds a 1-year figure of −0.14, a 3-year figure of −0.29 and a long-run figure of between −0.29 and −0.39 [4] and research from Korea estimates short-run and long-run price-elasticity figures of −0.36 and −0.55 for diesel demand.[5] In each of these cases, we observe more elastic demand in the long run, when people have time to shop around (for alternative means of transport in the case of road fuel), than we do in the short run.

5.2 THE IMPORTANCE OF PRICE ELASTICITY OF DEMAND TO BUSINESS DECISION MAKING

A firm's sales revenue

One of the most important applications of price elasticity of demand concerns its relationship with a firm's sales revenue. The **total sales revenue (TR)** of a firm is simply price multiplied by quantity: $TR = P \times Q$.

For example, 3000 units (Q) sold at £2 per unit (P) will earn the firm £6000 (TR).

Let us assume that a firm wants to increase its total revenue. What should it do? Should it raise its price or lower it? The answer depends on the price elasticity of demand.

> ### Definition
>
> **Total (sales) revenue (TR)** The amount a firm earns from its sales of a product at a particular price.
> $TR = P \times Q$. Note that we are referring to *gross* revenue: that is, revenue before the deduction of taxes or any other costs.

[1]João Sousa, 'Estimate of price elasticities of demand for alcohol in the United Kingdom', *HMRC Working Paper 16,* HM Revenue & Customs (December 2014).

[2]Y. Meng *et al.*; 'Estimation of own and cross price elasticities of alcohol demand in the UK – A pseudo-panel approach using the Living Costs and Food Survey 2001–2009', *Journal of Health Economics,* 34, White Rose Research Online (2014).

[3]Patrick L. Anderson et al., *Price Elasticity of Demand,* Mackinac Center for Public Policy (13 November 1997).

[4]Tatyana Deryugina, Alexander MacKay and Julian Reif, *The Long-Run Elasticity of Electricity Demand: Evidence from Municipal Electric Aggregation* (16 December 2016).

[5]Kyoung-Min Lim, Myunghwan Kim, Chang Seob Kim and Seung-Hoon Yoo, 'Short-Run and Long-Run Elasticities of Diesel Demand in Korea', *Energies,* 2012, 5 (28 November 2012).

Elastic demand and sales revenue

As price rises, so quantity demanded falls, and vice versa. When demand is elastic, quantity changes proportionately more than price. Thus the change in quantity has a bigger effect on total revenue than does the change in price. This can be summarised as follows:

- *P* rises; *Q* falls proportionately more; therefore *TR* falls.
- *P* falls; *Q* rises proportionately more; therefore *TR* rises.

In other words, total revenue changes in the same direction as *quantity*.

This is illustrated in Figure 5.4. The areas of the rectangles in the diagram represent total revenue. But why? The area of a rectangle is its height multiplied by its length. In this case, this is price multiplied by quantity purchased, which, as we have seen, gives total revenue.

Demand is elastic between points *a* and *b*. A rise in price from £4 to £5 causes a proportionately larger fall in quantity demanded: from 20 to 10. Total revenue *falls* from £80 (the striped area) to £50 (the shaded area).

When demand is elastic, then, a rise in price will cause a fall in total revenue. If a firm wants to increase its revenue, it should *lower* its price.

Pause for thought

If a firm faces an elastic demand curve, why will it not necessarily be in the firm's interests to produce more? (Clue: you will need to distinguish between revenue and profit. We will explore this relationship in Chapter 10.)

Inelastic demand and sales revenue

When demand is inelastic, it is the other way around. Price changes proportionately more than quantity. Thus the change in price has a bigger effect on total revenue than does the change in quantity. To summarise the effects:

- *P* rises; *Q* falls proportionately less; *TR* rises.

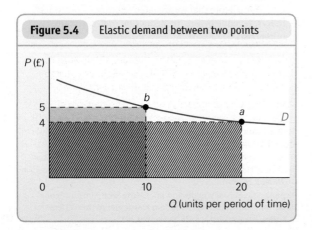

Figure 5.4   Elastic demand between two points

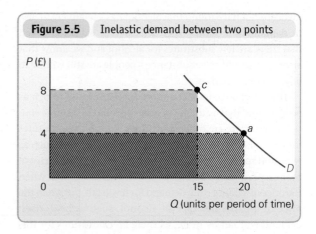

Figure 5.5   Inelastic demand between two points

- *P* falls; *Q* rises proportionately less; *TR* falls.

In other words, total revenue changes in the same direction as price.

This is illustrated in Figure 5.5. Demand is inelastic between points *a* and *c*. A rise in price from £4 to £8 causes a proportionately smaller fall in quantity demanded: from 20 to 15. Total revenue *rises* from £80 (the striped area) to £120 (the shaded area).

If a firm wants to increase its revenue in this case, therefore, it should *raise* its price.

Special cases

Figure 5.6 shows three special cases: (a) a totally inelastic demand ($P\epsilon_D = 0$), (b) an infinitely elastic demand ($P\epsilon_D = 1$) and (c) a unit elastic demand ($P\epsilon_D = -1$).

Totally inelastic demand

This is shown by a vertical straight line. No matter what happens to price, quantity demanded remains the same. It is obvious that the more the price is raised, the bigger will be the revenue. Thus in Figure 5.6(a), P_2 will earn a bigger revenue than P_1.

Infinitely elastic demand

This is shown by a horizontal straight line. At any price above P_1 demand is zero. But at P_1 (or any price below) demand is 'infinitely' large.

This seemingly unlikely demand curve is, in fact, relatively common for individual firms. Many firms that are very small (like the small-scale grain farmer) are price takers. They have to accept the price as given by supply and demand in the *whole market*. If individual farmers were to try to sell above this price, they would sell nothing at all. At this price, however, they can sell to the market all they produce. (Demand is not *literally* infinite, but, as far as the farmer is concerned, it is.) In this case, the more the individual farmer produces, the more revenue will be earned. In Figure 5.6(b), more revenue is earned at Q_2 than at Q_1.

Figure 5.6 **(a)** Totally inelastic demand ($P\epsilon_D = 0$); **(b)** Infinitely elastic demand ($P\epsilon_D = \infty$); **(c)** Unit elastic demand ($P\epsilon_D = -1$)

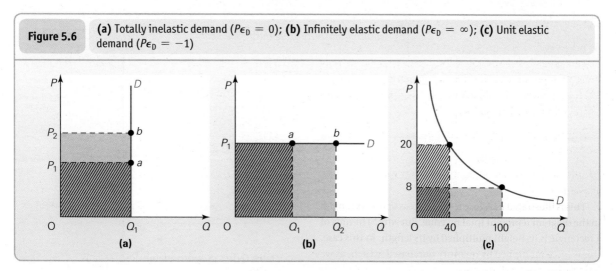

BOX 5.1   THE MEASUREMENT OF ELASTICITY

The average or 'mid-point' formula

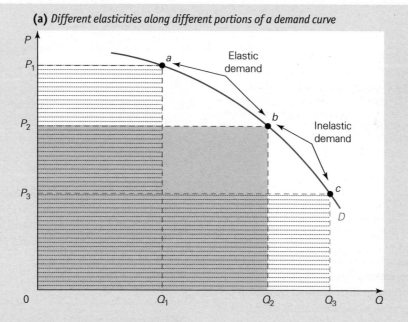

(a) *Different elasticities along different portions of a demand curve*

We have defined price elasticity as the percentage or proportionate change in quantity demanded divided by the percentage or proportionate change in price. But how, in practice, do we measure these changes for a specific demand curve?

A common mistake that students make is to think that you can talk about the elasticity of a whole *curve*. The mistake here is that, in most cases, the elasticity will vary along the length of the curve.

Take the case of the demand curve illustrated in diagram (a). Between points *a* and *b*, total revenue rises ($P_2Q_2 > P_1Q_1$): demand is thus elastic between these two points. Between points *b* and *c*, however, total revenue falls ($P_3Q_3 < P_2Q_2$). Demand here is inelastic.

Normally, then, we can refer to the elasticity of only a *portion* of the demand curve, not of the *whole* curve.

There is, however, an exception to this rule. This is when the elasticity just so happens to be the same all the way along a curve, as in the three special cases illustrated in Figure 5.6.

Although we cannot normally talk about the elasticity of a whole curve, we can, nevertheless, talk about the elasticity between any two points on it. Remember the formula we used was:

$$\frac{\text{\% or Proportionate } \Delta Q}{\text{\% or Proportionate } \Delta P}$$

(where Δ means 'change in').

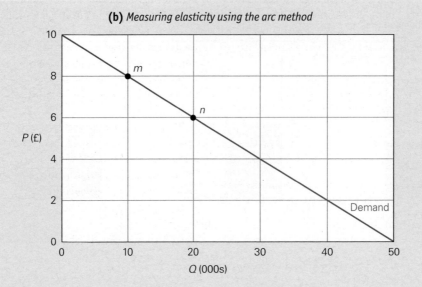

(b) *Measuring elasticity using the arc method*

The way we measure a proportionate change in quantity is to divide that change by the level of Q: i.e. $\Delta Q/Q$. Similarly, we measure a proportionate change in price by dividing that change by the level of P: i.e. $\Delta P/P$. Price elasticity of demand can thus now be rewritten as:

$$\frac{\Delta Q}{Q} \div \frac{\Delta P}{P}$$

But just what value do we give to P and Q? Consider the demand curve in diagram (b). What is the elasticity of demand between points m and n? Price has fallen by £2 (from £8 to £6), but what is the proportionate change? Is it $-2/8$ or $-2/6$? The convention is to express the change as a proportion of the average of the two prices, £8 and £6: in other words, to take the mid-point price, £7. Thus the proportionate change is $-2/7$.

Similarly, the proportionate change in quantity between points m and n is 10/15, since 15 is mid-way between 10 and 20.

Thus, using the *average (or 'mid-point') formula,* elasticity between m and n is given by:

$$\frac{\Delta Q}{\text{average } Q} \div \frac{\Delta P}{\text{average } P} = \frac{10}{10} \div \frac{-2}{7} = -2.33$$

Since 2.33 is greater than 1, demand is elastic between m and n.

1. *Referring again to diagram (b), what is the price elasticity of demand between a price of (a) £6 and £4 and (b) £4 and £2? What do you conclude about the elasticity of a straight-line demand curve as you move down it?*

Unit elastic demand

This is where price and quantity change in exactly the same proportion. Any rise in price will be exactly offset by a fall in quantity, leaving total revenue unchanged. In Figure 5.6(c), the striped area is exactly equal to the shaded area: in both cases total revenue is £800.

You might have thought that a demand curve with unit elasticity would be a straight line at 45° to the axes. Instead, it is a curve called a *rectangular hyperbola.* The reason for its shape is that the proportionate *rise* in quantity must equal the proportionate *fall* in price (and vice versa). As we move down the demand curve, in order for the *proportionate* (or percentage) change in both price and quantity to remain constant, there must be a bigger and bigger *absolute* rise in

quantity and a smaller and smaller absolute fall in price. For example, a rise in quantity from 200 to 400 is the same proportionate change as a rise from 100 to 200, but its absolute size is double. A fall in price from £5 to £2.50 is the same percentage as a fall from £10 to £5, but its absolute size is only half.

Pause for thought

Two customers go to the fish counter at a supermarket to buy some cod. Neither looks at the price. Customer A orders 1 kilo of cod. Customer B orders £3 worth of cod. What is the price elasticity of demand of each of the two customers?

5.3 OTHER ELASTICITIES

As we know, there are many factors that affect our demand for a product besides price. Firms will, thus, be interested to know the responsiveness of demand to a change in these

other variables, such as consumers' incomes and the prices of goods that are substitute or complementary to theirs. They will want to know the **income elasticity of demand** – the responsiveness of demand to a change in consumers' incomes (*Y*); and the ***cross-price elasticity of demand*** – the responsiveness of demand for their good to a change in the price of another (whether a substitute or a complement).

Income elasticity of demand ($Y\epsilon_D$)

We define the income elasticity of demand for a good as follows:

$$Y\epsilon_D = \frac{\text{Proportionate (or percentage) change in demand}}{\text{Proportionate (or percentage) change in income}}$$

For example, if a 2 per cent rise in consumer incomes causes an 8 per cent rise in a product's demand, then its income elasticity of demand will be:

8%/2% = 4

The major determinant of income elasticity of demand is the degree of 'necessity' of the good.

In a developed country, the demand for luxury goods expands rapidly as people's incomes rise, whereas the demand for more basic goods, such as bread, rises only a little. Thus items such as cars and foreign holidays have a high income elasticity of demand, whereas items such as potatoes and bus journeys have a low income elasticity of demand.

The World Health Organisation has investigated the income elasticity of demand for tobacco and has found that 'the positive income elasticity of demand is more likely to be observed in low and middle income countries that are at an earlier stage of the tobacco epidemic. Since many low and middle income countries are growing rapidly, large increases in tobacco consumption is [*sic*] likely to occur over a short period of time.' Estimates vary across countries, including 0.43 in Poland, 0.56 in Turkey, 0.9 in China and 1.6 in Egypt.[6]

As we saw in the last chapter, the demand for inferior goods decreases as income rises. As people earn more, so they switch to better-quality goods. Unlike normal goods, therefore, which have a positive income elasticity of demand, inferior goods have a negative income elasticity of demand (a rise in income leads to a *fall* in demand).

Income elasticity of demand and the firm

Income elasticity of demand is an important concept to firms considering the future size of the market for their product. If the product has a high income elasticity of demand, sales are likely to expand rapidly as national income rises, but may also fall significantly if the economy moves into recession.

Firms may also find that some parts of their market have a higher income elasticity of demand than others, and may thus choose to target their marketing campaigns on this group. For example, middle-income groups may have a higher income elasticity of demand for certain

high-tech products than lower-income groups (which are unlikely to be able to afford such products, even if their incomes rise somewhat) or higher-income groups (which can probably afford them anyway, and thus would not buy much more if their incomes rose). For this reason, changes in the distribution of income can be an important factor for firms to consider when making decisions about which products to sell.

The current state of the economy and expectations of how average incomes could change will also be a key factor for firms to consider in helping them decide where to invest resources, based on their predictions about the types of goods that people will demand.

> ### Pause for thought
>
> *Assume that you decide to spend a quarter of your income on clothes. What is (a) your income elasticity of demand; (b) your price elasticity of demand?*

Cross-price elasticity of demand ($C\epsilon_{Dab}$)

This is often known by its less cumbersome title of 'cross elasticity of demand'. It is a measure of the responsiveness of demand for one product to a change in the price of another (either a substitute or a complement). It enables us to predict how much the demand curve for the first product will shift when the price of the second product changes. For example, knowledge of the cross elasticity of demand for Coca-Cola with respect to the price of Pepsi would allow Coca-Cola to predict the effect on its own sales if the price of Pepsi were to change.

We define cross-price elasticity as follows:

$$C\epsilon_{Dab} = \frac{\begin{array}{c}\text{Proportionate (or percentage)}\\\text{change in demand for good a}\end{array}}{\begin{array}{c}\text{Proportionate (or percentage) change}\\\text{in price of good b}\end{array}}$$

If good b is a *substitute* for good a, a's demand will *rise* as b's price rises. For example, the demand for bicycles will rise as the price of public transport rises. In this case, cross elasticity will be a positive figure. If b is *complementary* to a, however, a's demand will *fall* as b's price rises and thus as the quantity

> ### Definitions
>
> **Income elasticity of demand** The responsiveness of demand to a change in consumer incomes: the proportionate change in demand divided by the proportionate change in income.
>
> **Cross-price elasticity of demand** The responsiveness of demand for one good to a change in the price of another: the proportionate change in demand for one good divided by the proportionate change in price of the other.

---

[6]*Estimating Price and Income Elasticity of Demand,* World Health Organisation (2015).

BOX 5.2 ELASTICITY AND THE INCIDENCE OF TAX

Who bears the tax?

Taxes on goods are known as 'indirect taxes' because they tax people indirectly through higher prices while it is the shops or other firms that actually pay the taxes. Such taxes include value added tax (VAT) and excise duties on cigarettes, petrol and alcoholic drinks. These taxes can be a fixed amount per unit sold (a 'specific tax') or a percentage of the price (an '*ad valorem* tax').

When a tax is imposed, it represents an increase in a firm's costs of production and, in order to protect its profit margins, the firm will want to pass the cost increase on to its customers in the form of a higher price. However, the law of demand tells us that any increase in price will cut the quantity demanded. Therefore, firms must decide just how much of the tax to pass onto consumers in the form of a higher price and how much they should absorb through reduced profit.

This 'incidence' of taxation depends on the demand and supply curves for the product being taxed.

As a tax represents an increase in production costs, the effect will be to shift the firm's supply curve upward to the left, as discussed in section 4.3 and as shown in diagram (a). The supply curve shifts from S_1 to S_2, where the vertical distance between S_1 and S_2 represents the amount of the tax per unit. This is shown by the arrow.

The price that consumers pay is forced up from P_1 to P_2 and the equilibrium quantity sold falls from Q_1 to Q_2. Notice that the rise in price from P_1 to P_2 is smaller than the total size of the tax. This means that the burden of the tax must be shared between consumers and producers. The producer's share of the tax is the difference between the initial price, P_1, and the price $P_{2-\text{tax}}$. Therefore, consumers pay to the extent that price rises, whereas producers pay to the extent that this rise in price is not sufficient to cover the tax.

The consumers' and producers' shares of the tax are shown by the two shaded areas: namely, the shares of the tax per unit multiplied by the number of units sold (Q_2).

Elasticity and the incidence of taxation

A key question for any firm to answer, when faced with a specific tax being imposed on its good, is just how much of the

(a) *The effect of a tax*

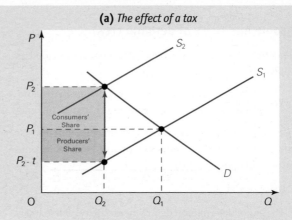

tax the consumer can pay. The more of the tax that is passed on to the consumer, the bigger will be the potential loss in customers. But, if only a small amount is paid by the consumer, the firm will suffer a loss in revenue, as the price it gets to keep will be lower.

The burden faced by each group will depend on the price elasticities of demand and supply.

Take the case of demand. If the demand curve is relatively inelastic, any increase in price will cause a smaller proportionate fall in quantity demanded. As such, the firm will be able to pass a large percentage of the total tax on to its customers in the form of a higher price, knowing that, while demand will fall, it will not fall by much. The incidence of taxation falls mainly on the consumer.

Conversely, if the firm's product has relatively elastic demand, any price increase will cause a proportionately larger fall in quantity demanded and so the firm will be reluctant to increase the price to its customers by too much. In this case, the tax burden will fall primarily on the producer.

In diagram (b), you can see the impact on the consumer's and producer's share of the tax with a relatively inelastic demand curve. The tax shifts the supply from S_1 to S_2 and consumers now

---

of b demanded falls. For example, the demand for petrol falls as the price of cars rises. In this case, cross elasticity will be a negative figure.

Cross-price elasticity of demand and the firm

The major determinant of cross elasticity of demand is the closeness of the substitute or complement. The closer it is, the bigger will be the effect on the first good of a change in the price of the substitute or complement, and hence the greater will be the cross elasticity – either positive or negative.

Firms will wish to know the cross elasticity of demand for their product when considering the effect on the demand for their product of a change in the price of a rival's product (a substitute). If firm b cuts its price, will this make significant inroads into the sales of firm a? If so, firm a may feel forced to cut its prices too; if not, then firm a may keep its price unchanged. The cross-price elasticities of demand between a firm's product and those of each of its rivals are thus vital pieces of information for a firm when making its production, pricing and marketing plans.

(b) *Inelastic demand: the incidence of tax*

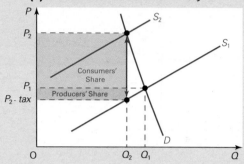

face a significant increase in price from P_1 to P_2. The consumer's share of the tax is, therefore, the difference in these prices multiplied by the new equilibrium quantity, Q_2 (the red area).

The firm still has to pay some of the tax – the difference between P_1 and P_{2-tax} – but this green area is relatively small. It is, therefore, in a firm's interest to make its product relatively price inelastic, by advertising its unique qualities and persuading consumers that there are no substitutes, as this will enable the firm to minimise the amount of tax it has to bear.

1. *Draw a diagram showing an elastic demand curve and explain how this will affect the burden of tax borne by consumers and producers.*

Tax policy

If we combine the red and green areas in diagram (b), we can find the total amount that the firm will pay in tax. This is the same as the amount of revenue earned by the government. So, how can governments use the concept of elasticity to help increase tax revenue? It is easy to see that the less elastic demand is, the smaller will be the fall in quantity sold following the imposition of a tax. This means that the government is able to receive a given per unit tax on a larger quantity when demand is relatively

price inelastic. It therefore has an incentive to impose taxes on products that have a relatively inelastic demand, as a means of generating the highest amount of tax revenue.

This is what we observe in many countries, where products such as cigarettes, petrol and alcohol are the major targets for indirect taxes, as taxes raise a lot of revenue and do not curb demand significantly. Indeed, in the UK, fuel duty (a specific tax) and VAT (an *ad valorem* tax), together account for between 60 and 75 per cent of the cost of petrol, depending on the price of petrol.

The elasticity of supply also has an impact on the burden of tax borne by consumers and producers and crucially on the amount of tax revenue generated. The more elastic supply is, the smaller will be the producer's share of the tax and hence firms have an incentive to make their supply as responsive as possible to a change in price. However, the greatest amount of government revenue will be generated from imposing a tax on a firm that has a relatively inelastic supply curve. Such a tax will cause a relatively small decrease in the quantity sold compared to an elastic supply curve and hence there are many more units to tax.

Combining both demand and supply analysis, government revenue will be at its greatest when both demand and supply are relatively inelastic.

2. *Using the same approach we did for demand in diagram (b), show how the burden of tax borne by consumers and producers will vary as the elasticity of supply is changed.*
3. *Demand tends to be more elastic in the long run than in the short run. Assume that a tax is imposed on a good that was previously untaxed. How will the incidence of this tax change as time passes?*

Investigate the rates of tax on tobacco products in a country of your choice. Whose share of the tax, the producer or the consumer, is likely to be higher at the current rates of tax? If the tax were substantially raised, what would be the revenue implications for the government (a) in the short run and (b) in the long run?

Similarly, a firm will wish to know the cross-price elasticity of demand for its product with any complementary good. Car producers will wish to know the effect of petrol price increases on the sales of their cars.

Price elasticity of supply ($P\epsilon_S$)

Just as we can measure the responsiveness of demand to a change in one of the determinants of demand, so too we can measure the responsiveness of supply to a change in one of the determinants of supply. The *price elasticity of supply*

refers to the responsiveness of supply to a change in price. We define it as follows:

Definition

Price elasticity of supply The responsiveness of quantity supplied to a change in price: the proportionate change in quantity supplied divided by the proportionate change in price.

Figure 5.7	Price elasticity of supply

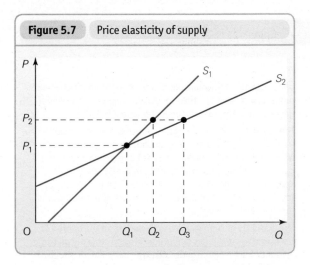

Figure 5.8	Supply in different time periods

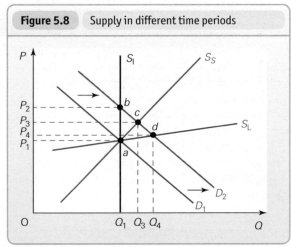

$$P\epsilon_S = \frac{\text{Proportionate(or percentage) change in quantity supplied}}{\text{Proportionate(or percentage)change in price}}$$

Thus if a 15 per cent rise in the price of a product causes a 30 per cent rise in the quantity supplied, the price elasticity of supply will be:

$$30\%/15\% = 2$$

In Figure 5.7, curve S_2 is more elastic between any two prices than curve S_1. Thus, when price rises from P_1 to P_2 there is a larger increase in quantity supplied with S_2 (namely, Q_1 to Q_3) than there is with S_1 (namely, Q_1 to Q_2).

Determinants of price elasticity of supply

The amount that costs rise as output rises. The less the additional costs of producing additional output, the more firms will be encouraged to produce for a given price rise: the more elastic will supply be.

Supply is thus likely to be elastic if firms have plenty of spare capacity, if they can readily get extra supplies of raw

materials, if they can easily switch away from producing alternative products and if they can avoid having to introduce overtime working (at higher rates of pay). If all these conditions hold, costs will be little affected by a rise in output and supply will be relatively elastic. The less these conditions apply, the less elastic supply will be.

Time period (see Figure 5.8)

■ Immediate time period. Firms are unlikely to be able to increase supply by much immediately. Supply is virtually fixed or can vary only according to available stocks. Hence, supply is highly inelastic. In the diagram, S_I is drawn with $P\epsilon_s = 0$. If demand increases to D_2, supply will not be able to respond. Price will rise to P_2. Quantity will remain at Q_1. Equilibrium will move to point *b*.

■ Short run. If a slightly longer time period is allowed to elapse, some inputs can be increased (e.g. raw materials), while others will remain fixed (e.g. heavy machinery). Supply can increase somewhat. This is illustrated by S_S. Equilibrium will move to point *c* with price falling again, to P_3, and quantity rising to Q_3.

■ Long run. In the long run, there will be sufficient time for all inputs to be increased and for new firms to enter the industry. Supply, therefore, is likely to be highly elastic. This is illustrated by curve S_L. Long-run equilibrium will be at point *d* with price falling back even further, to P_4, and quantity rising all the way to Q_4. In some circumstances, the supply curve may even slope downward. (See the section on economies of scale in Chapter 9, pages 156–7.)

Pause for thought

Return to question 2 in Box 4.3, where we considered the impact of minimum and maximum price controls and how the shape of the demand and supply curves could affect the size of the resulting surplus and shortages. How is the price elasticity of demand and supply relevant in the context of a minimum price on alcohol or any other product?

5.4 THE TIME DIMENSION OF MARKET ADJUSTMENT

The full adjustment of price, demand and supply to a situation of disequilibrium will not be instantaneous. It is necessary, therefore, to analyse the time path that

supply takes in responding to changes in demand and that demand takes in responding to changes in supply.

Short-run and long-run adjustment

As we have already seen, elasticity varies with the time period under consideration. The reason is that producers and consumers take time to respond to a change in price. The longer the time period, the bigger the response and thus the greater the elasticity of supply and demand.

This is illustrated in Figures 5.9 and 5.10. In both cases, as equilibrium moves from points *a* to *b* to *c,* there is a large short-run price change (P_1 to P_2) and a small short-run quantity change (Q_1 to Q_2), but a small long-run price change (P_1 to P_3) and a large long-run quantity change (Q_1 to Q_3).

Price expectations and speculation

In a world of shifting demand and supply curves, prices will be moving up and down constantly, as we saw in Boxes 4.1 and 4.2. If prices are likely to change in the foreseeable future, this will affect the behaviour of buyers and sellers *now*. If, for example, it is now December and you are thinking of buying a new winter coat, you might decide to wait until the January sales and, in the meantime, make do with your old coat. If, on the other hand, when January comes you see a new summer jacket in the sales, you might well buy it now and not wait until the summer, for fear that the price will have gone up by then. Thus a belief that prices will go up will cause people to buy now; a belief that prices will come down will cause them to wait.

The reverse applies to sellers. If you are thinking of selling your house and prices are falling, you will want to sell it as quickly as possible. If, on the other hand, prices are rising sharply, you will wait as long as possible so as to get the highest price. Thus a belief that prices will come down will cause people to sell now; a belief that prices will go up will cause them to wait.

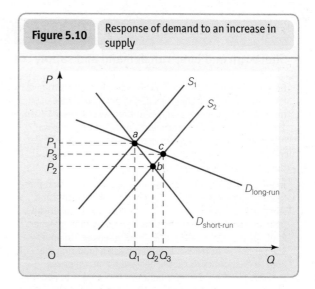

Figure 5.10 Response of demand to an increase in supply

This behaviour of looking into the future and making buying and selling decisions based on your predictions is called ***speculation***. Speculation is often partly based on current trends in price behaviour. If prices are currently rising, people may try to decide whether they are about to peak and go back down again or whether they are likely to go on rising. Having made their prediction, they will then act on it. This speculation will thus affect demand and supply, which, in turn, will affect price. Speculation is commonplace in many markets: the stock exchange (see Box 4.2), the foreign exchange market and the housing market (see Box 4.1) are three examples. Large firms often employ specialist buyers who choose the right time to buy inputs, depending on what they anticipate will happen to their price.

Speculation tends to be ***self-fulfilling***. In other words, the actions of speculators tend to bring about the very effect on prices that speculators had anticipated. For example, if speculators believe that the price of BP shares is about to rise, they will buy more BP shares, shifting demand to the right. But, by doing this, they will ensure that the price *will* rise. The prophecy has become self-fulfilling.

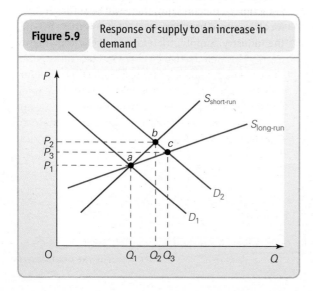

Figure 5.9 Response of supply to an increase in demand

Definitions

Speculation This is where people make buying or selling decisions based on their anticipations of future prices.

Self-fulfilling speculation The actions of speculators tend to cause the very effect that they had anticipated.

BOX 5.3 ADJUSTING TO OIL PRICE SHOCKS

Short-run and long-run demand and supply responses

Between December 1973 and June 1974, the Organisation of Petroleum Exporting Countries (OPEC) put up the price of oil from $3 to $12 per barrel. It was further raised to over $30 in 1979. In the 1980s, the price fluctuated, but the trend was downward. Except for a sharp rise at the time of the Gulf War in 1990, the trend continued through most of the 1990s, at times falling as low as $11.

In the early 2000s, oil prices were generally higher, first fluctuating between $19 and $33 per barrel, before increasing steadily from 2004 to 2006 and then increasing dramatically from January 2007, reaching a peak of nearly $150 in June 2008. By the start of 2009, prices had fallen back to under $50 per barrel, as fears of a world recession following the 2007/8 financial crisis cut the demand for oil. Oil prices recovered as the global economic recovery began, temporarily passing $120 per barrel in early 2011, before falling and then fluctuating around $100 until mid-way through 2014.

There was then another significant fall in prices in the latter half of 2014 and throughout 2015, reaching a low of under $30 per barrel in January 2016. Key causes were the strength of the dollar, an increasing supply of oil from shale, oil sands and other sources, and declining demand. This is discussed in various blogs on the Sloman Economics News site.[1] Up until March 2018 (the time of writing), prices have recovered to stand at just over $60 per barrel. The price movements can be explained using simple demand and supply analysis.

The initial rise in price

In the 1970s, OPEC raised the price from P_1 to P_2 (see diagram (a)). To prevent surplus at that price, OPEC members restricted their output by agreed amounts. This had the effect of shifting the supply curve to S_2, with Q_2 being produced. This reduction in output needed to be only relatively small because the short-run demand for oil was highly price inelastic: for most uses there are no substitutes in the short run.

Long-run effects on demand

The long-run demand for oil was more elastic (see diagram (b)). With high oil prices persisting, people tried to find ways of cutting back on consumption. People bought smaller cars. They converted to gas or solid-fuel central heating. Firms switched to other fuels. Less use was made of oil-fired power stations for electricity generation. Energy-saving schemes became widespread both in firms and in the home.

This had the effect of shifting the short-run demand curve from D_1 to D_2. Price fell back from P_2 to P_3. This gave a long-run demand curve of D_L: the curve that joins points A and C.

The fall in demand was made bigger by a world recession in the early 1980s.

Long-run effects on supply

With oil production so much more profitable, there was an incentive for non-OPEC oil producers to produce oil. Prospecting went on all over the world and large oil fields were discovered and opened up in the North Sea, Alaska, Mexico, China and elsewhere. In addition, OPEC members were tempted to break their 'quotas' (their allotted output) and sell more oil.

The net effect was an increase in world oil supplies. In terms of the diagrams, the supply curve of oil started to shift to the right from the mid-1980s onwards, causing oil prices to fall through most of the period up to 1998. Similar effects occurred between 2014 and 2016, when again we saw significant increases in supply.

Back to square one?

By the late 1990s, with the oil price as low as $10 per barrel, OPEC once more cut back supply. The story had come full circle. This cut-back is once more illustrated in diagram (a).

The trouble this time was that worldwide economic growth was picking up. Demand was shifting to the right. The result was a rise in oil prices to around $33, which then fell back again in 2001 as the world slipped into recession and the demand curve shifted to the left.

There were then some very large price increases, first as a result of OPEC in late 2001 attempting once more to restrict supply (a leftward shift in supply), and, then, before the Iraq War of 2003, because of worries about possible adverse effects on oil supplies (a rightward shift in demand as countries

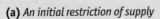

[1]See, in particular, the following posts: 'Oil prices – the ups and the downs'; 'OPEC deal pushes up oil prices'; 'Will there be an oil price rebound?'; 'An oil glut'; and 'A crude indicator of the economy (Part 2)'.

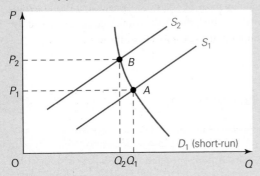

(a) *An initial restriction of supply*

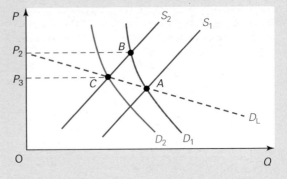

(b) *Long-run demand response*

(c) *Oil market in 2014–16*

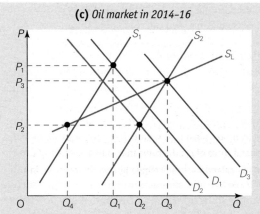

Second, rather than OPEC attempting to push prices up by restricting output, it stated that it would not cut its production, even if the crude oil price were to fall to $30. It hoped, thereby, to make shale oil production unprofitable for many US producers.

These supply-side factors, plus continuing weak demand in the Eurozone and other parts of the world, pushed oil prices below $50.

These effects can be illustrated in diagram (c). The starting point is mid-2014. Global demand and supply are D_1 and S_1; price is above $100 per barrel ($P_1$) and output is Q_1. Demand now shifts to the left (to D_2) as growth in the Eurozone and elsewhere falls; and supply shifts to the right (to S_2). Price falls to around $40 per barrel and, given the bigger shift in supply than demand, output rises to Q_2. At a price of P_2, however, output of Q_2 cannot be sustained: investing in new shale oil wells becomes unprofitable. Thus at P_2, long-run supply (shown by S_L) is only Q_4.

But with growth in the global economy in the latter part of the 2010s, demand shifts to the right: say, to D_3. Price rises to P_3 – possibly around $80 per barrel. This gives a short-run output of Q_3, but at that price it is likely that supply will be sustainable in the long run as it makes investment in shale oil sufficiently profitable. Thus curve D_3 intersects with both S_2 and S_L at this price and quantity.

With both demand and supply being price *inelastic* in the short run, large fluctuations in price are only to be expected. And these are amplified by speculation.

The problem is made worse by an income elastic demand for oil. Demand can rise rapidly in times when the global economy is booming, only to fall back substantially in times of recession.

stocked up on oil). The worries about long-run security of supply continued after the invasion of Iraq and the continuing political uncertainty in the region.

The rises in the price of oil from 2004 through to mid-2008 were fuelled partly by rapidly expanding demand (a rightward shift in short-run demand), especially in countries such as China and India, and by speculation on the future price of oil. On the supply side, producers could not respond rapidly to meet this demand and there was further disruption to supply in some oil-producing countries, including Nigeria and Algeria (a leftward shift in short-run supply). However, the dramatic rise in oil prices fuelled inflation across the world. Consumers and industry faced much higher costs and looked at methods to conserve fuel.

In late 2008, the global financial crisis was followed by recession. The price of oil began to fall back as the demand curve for oil shifted leftwards. It fell from a peak of $147 per barrel in July 2008 to a mere $34 per barrel by the end of the year. But then, as the world economy slowly recovered, and the demand for oil rose, so oil prices rose again. By early 2011, oil was trading at around $128 per barrel.

New sources of supply

The fall in oil prices from the latter part of 2014 until 2016 might seem somewhat surprising. With continuing conflicts in key oil-producing countries, the normal impact would be a rise in prices, as supply falls. But two things were happening on the supply side.

First, new sources of supply were becoming available, in particular large amounts of shale oil from the USA were coming onto the market. This had a large downward effect on prices.

1. *Give some examples of things that could make the demand for oil more elastic. What specific policies could the government introduce to make demand more elastic?*
2. *Demand for oil may be relatively elastic over the longer term and, yet, it could still be observed that, over time, people consume more oil (or only very slightly less) despite rising oil prices. How can we explain this contradiction?*

 Download monthly price data on commodity markets from the World Bank.[2] Create a chart showing the annual rate of oil price inflation from the early 1970s. Write a short commentary summarising the patterns observed in oil price inflation.

[2]www.worldbank.org/en/research/commodity-markets.

Speculation can either help to reduce price fluctuations or aggravate them: it can be stabilising or destabilising.

Stabilising speculation

Speculation will tend to have a ***stabilising*** effect on price fluctuations when suppliers and/or demanders believe that a change in price is only *temporary*.

Assume, for example, that recently there has been a rise in price, caused, say, by an increase in demand. In Figure 5.11 (a), demand has shifted from D_1 to D_2. Equilibrium has moved from point *a* to point *b*, and price has risen from P_1 to P_2. How do people react to this rise in price?

Given that they believe this rise in price to be only temporary, suppliers bring their goods to market now, before price falls again. Supply shifts from S_1 to S_2. Demanders, however, hold back until price does fall. Demand shifts from D_2 to D_3. The equilibrium moves to point *c*, with price falling back towards P_1.

A good example of stabilising speculation is that which occurs in agricultural commodity markets. Take the case of wheat. When it is harvested in the autumn, there will be a plentiful supply. If all this wheat were to be put on the market, the price would fall to a very low level. Later in the year, when most of the wheat would have been sold, the price would then rise to a very high level. This is all easily predictable.

So what do farmers do? The answer is that they speculate. When the wheat is harvested, they know its price will tend to fall and so, instead of bringing it all to market, they put a lot of it into store *anticipating that the price will later rise*. But this holding back of supplies prevents prices from falling. In other words, it stabilises prices.

Later in the year, when the price begins to rise, they will release grain gradually on to the market from the stores. The more the price rises, the more they will release on to the market, *anticipating that the price will fall again by the time of the*

next harvest. But this releasing of supplies will again stabilise prices by preventing them rising so much.

Recently, we have seen the fluctuating market for bitcoin.[7] Created in 2009, it is a digital currency that has exhibited extreme price volatility and has been subject to massive speculation. You can read about this in Box 5.4.

Destabilising speculation

Speculation will tend to have a ***destabilising*** effect on price fluctuations when suppliers and/or buyers believe that a change in price heralds similar changes to come.

Assume again that there has recently been a rise in price, caused by an increase in demand. In Figure 5.11(b), demand has shifted from D_1 to D_2 and price has risen from P_1 to P_2. This time, however, believing that the rise in price heralds further rises to come, suppliers wait until the price rises further. Supply shifts from S_1 to S_2. Demanders buy now before any further rise in price. Demand shifts from D_2 to D_3. As a result, the price continues to rise: to P_3.

Box 4.1 examined the housing market. In this market, speculation is frequently destabilising. Assume that people see house prices beginning to move upward. This might be the result of increased demand brought about by a cut in mortgage interest rates or by growth in the economy. People may well believe that the rise in house prices signals a boom in the housing market: that prices will go on rising.

Definitions

Stabilising speculation This is where the actions of speculators tend to reduce price fluctuations.

Destabilising speculation This is where the actions of speculators tend to make price movements larger.

---

[7] http://pearsonblog.campaignserver.co.uk/?s=bitcoin.

Figure 5.11 Speculation (initial rise in price)

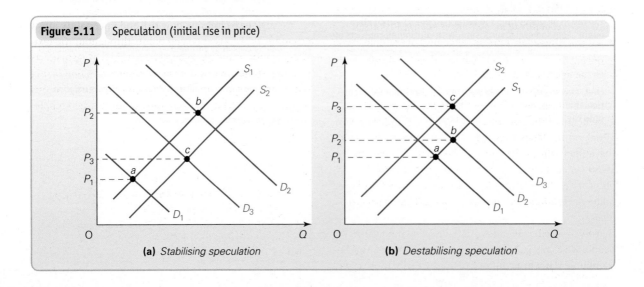

(a) *Stabilising speculation*

(b) *Destabilising speculation*

Potential buyers will thus try to buy as soon as possible before prices rise any further. This increased demand (as in Figure 5.11(b)) will thus lead to even bigger price rises. This is precisely what happened in the UK housing market in 1999–2007.

> ### Pause for thought
>
> *Draw two diagrams like Figures 5.11(a) and (b), only this time assume an initial fall in demand and hence price. The first diagram should show the effects of stabilising specula-tion and the second the effect of destabilising speculation.*

Conclusion

In some circumstances, then, the action of speculators can help keep price fluctuations to a minimum (stabilising speculation). This is most likely when markets are relatively stable in the first place, with only moderate underlying shifts in demand and supply.

> ### Pause for thought
>
> *What are the advantages and disadvantages of speculation from the point of view of (a) the consumer; (b) firms?*

In other circumstances, however, speculation can make price fluctuations much worse. This is most likely in times of uncertainty, when there are significant changes in the deter-minants of demand and supply. Given this uncertainty, peo-ple may see price changes as signifying some trend. They then 'jump on the bandwagon' and do what the rest are doing, further fuelling the rise or fall in price.

5.5 DEALING WITH UNCERTAINTY

Risk and uncertainty

KI 13
p75

When price changes are expected, buyers and sellers will try to anticipate them. Unfortunately, on many occasions, no one can be certain just what these price changes will be. Take the case of stocks and shares. If you anticipate that the price of, say, BP shares is likely to go up substantially in the near future, you may decide to buy some now and then sell them after the price has risen. But you cannot be certain that they will go up in price: they may fall instead. If you buy the shares, therefore, you will be taking a gamble.

Gambles can be of two types. The first is where you know the probability of each possible outcome occurring. Let us take the simplest case of a gamble on the toss of a coin. Heads you win; tails you lose. You know that the probability of win-ning is precisely 50 per cent. If you bet on the toss of a coin, you are said to be operating under conditions of **risk**. *Risk is when the probability of an outcome is known.* Risk itself is a measure of the *variability* of an outcome. For example, if you bet £1 on the toss of a coin, such that heads you win £1 and tails you lose £1, then the variability is −£1 to +£1.

The second form of a gamble is the more usual. This is where the probabilities are not known or are only roughly known. This is the case when investing, or technically 'gam-bling', on the Stock Exchange. You may have a good idea that a share will go up in price, but is it a 90 per cent chance, an 80 per cent chance or what? You are not certain. Gam-bling under these sorts of conditions is known as operating under **uncertainty**. *This is when the probability of an outcome is not known.*

You may well disapprove of gambling and want to dismiss people who engage in it as foolish or morally wrong. But 'gambling' is not just confined to horses, cards, roulette and the like. Risk and uncertainty pervade the whole of economic life and we are always making decisions, despite not knowing an outcome with any certainty. Even the most morally upright person must decide which career to go into, whether and when to buy a house or even something as trivial as whether or not to take an umbrella when going out. Each of these decisions and thousands of others are made under con-ditions of uncertainty (or occasionally risk).

> ### Key Idea 14
>
> ***People's actions are influenced by their attitudes towards risk.*** *Many decisions are taken under condi-tions of risk or uncertainty. Generally, the lower the probability of (or the more uncertain) the desired out-come of an action, the less likely will people be to undertake the action.*

We shall be examining how risk and uncertainty affect economic decisions at several points throughout the text. For example, in the next chapter we will see how it affects people's attitudes and actions as consumers, and how taking out insurance can help to reduce their uncertainty. At this point, however, let us focus on firms' attitudes when supply-ing goods.

> ### Definitions
>
> **Risk** This is when an outcome may or may not occur, but where its probability of occurring is known.
>
> **Uncertainty** This is when an outcome may or may not occur and where its probability of occurring is not known.

BOX 5.4 BUBBLE, BUBBLE, TOIL AND TROUBLE

Housing, stocks and tulips

Speculative bubbles are not uncommon and are not just restricted to the markets you might expect or be familiar with, such as housing, the Internet (the dot-com bubble) or financial commodities.

Housing, land and IT stocks

In the housing market, we have seen bubbles in Japan, the UK, the USA. In Japan, 1989, the housing bubble, triggered by a set of government policy stimulus packages, caused 'the value of the Imperial Palace grounds in Tokyo [to be] greater than that of the real estate in the entire state of California.'[1]

In the USA, house prices increased rapidly between 2002 and 2006, with the average price increasing by some 65 per cent. Then the bubble burst and the average property lost one third of its value.[2] This helped trigger the financial crisis and recession that affected the world.

Many suggest that one of the causes of the US house price bubble was the bursting of the 'dot-com' bubble. With the emergence and growth of the Internet in the 1990s, massive speculation in IT stocks caused the USA's NASDAQ index to rise from around 500 in 1990 to 5000 in March 2000, as money was ploughed into these tech companies. By October 2002, the index had seen 80 per cent of its value wiped out, sending the economy into a recession and this may have been one of the reasons why investors moved their money into housing, believing it was a safer asset.

Tulips and Beanie Babies

Bubbles, however, are not restricted to these areas and nor are they a recent phenomenon. One of the earliest recorded bubbles occurred in the Netherlands and involved tulips. Tulips were a new flower for the Dutch and, following a virus that had the effect of creating new vibrant colours on the petals, demand for them began to increase.

More and more people began to trade in tulips, with different varieties (affected differently by the virus) fetching different prices. The market was seen as having no limits; and so began a wave of speculation that fuelled prices. With more and more people buying tulips, demand increased, as shown in the following figure.

At the same time, suppliers (those growing the tulips) had to replenish their stock for the summer, as they would always do.

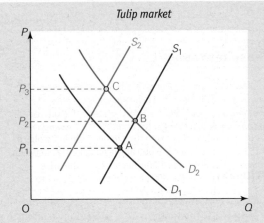

Tulip market

This, however, reduced supply on the market and made tulip bulbs scarcer.

As supply shifted leftwards and demand shifted to the right, prices climbed upward – speculation was destabilising, as everyone thought prices would just keep going up. The higher the prices went, the more people began to trade in tulips, hoping to make their millions by selling tulips to unwitting foreigners.

Between November 1636 and February 1637, there was a 20-fold increase in the price of tulip bulbs, such that a skilled worker's annual salary would not even cover the price of one bulb. Some were even worth more than a luxury home! But, only three months later, their price had fallen by 99 per cent. Some traders refused to pay the high price and others began to sell their tulips. Prices began falling. This dampened demand (as tulips were seen to be a poor investment) and encouraged more people to sell their tulips. Soon the price was in freefall, with everyone selling – another case of destabilising speculation, as everyone thought prices would just go on falling. The bubble had burst.[3]

We even saw a Beanie Baby bubble in the USA in the 1990s, when parents began trading their $5 toys for thousands of dollars and such trade accounted for around 10 per cent of eBay's sales![4]

 Draw a demand and supply diagram that illustrates the changes in the tulip market, showing how prices were affected.

The ups and downs of bitcoin

Created in 2009, bitcoin is an electronic currency that has seen huge price volatility, a bubble that burst and ongoing speculation about its future price.

The supply of national currencies is controlled typically by central banks and the banking sector. In the case of bitcoin,

[1]Elvis Picardo, 'Five of the largest asset bubbles in history'; *Investopedia* (23 June 2015).

[2]Dean Baker, 'The housing bubble pops', *CBS News* (20 September 2007).

[3]Andrew Beattie, 'Market Crashes: The tulip and bulb craze'; *Investopedia* (14 November 2017).

[4]Adam Davidson, '"The Great Beanie Baby Bubble" by Zac Bissonnette'; *The New York Times* (20 March 2015).

however, its supply is determined by 'mining', whereby individuals/groups solve complicated mathematical problems in exchange for new 'blocks' of bitcoins. The maximum number of bitcoins that can be supplied is restricted to B21 million, though this number is not expected to be mined until some time in the next century. However, 99 per cent should have been mined by around 2032, as the number of bitcoins generated per block is halved for every 210 000 blocks created. By March 2018, B16.9 million had been created.

The price of bitcoin had risen from under $300 in October 2015 to a peak of over $19 000 at the end of 2017. Between 14 September 2017 and 17 December 2017, the price increased by just under 600 per cent from $3226.41 to $19 086.64. Despite this upward trend, it has exhibited significant volatility. For example, in the nine weeks to 7 December 2017, the price rose by 399 per cent. By 10 December 2017, the price had fallen at one point by nearly 22 per cent. Within a few hours, it had recovered by 18 per cent. By the start of February 2018, it had plummeted by 56 per cent.

What has caused its price to rise and fall so significantly? In order to answer this question, we need to refer to our old friends – demand and supply.

As we have discussed, the supply of bitcoin is growing (at around 150 per hour), but, as we have seen, it is growing at an increasingly slower rate. Given the relatively stable supply increase, the initial rise in bitcoin must be down to the demand-side.

Although it can be used for transactions in some places, especially on the 'Dark Web', most legitimate vendors do not accept this 'currency' and so the demand for it has come from those viewing it as an investment. They are speculating that the price of bitcoin will rise and, hence, want to put their money into this asset, in the hopes of selling it in the future for a significantly higher price. Bitcoin has, therefore, been subject to destabilising speculation, as the more that people have expected its price to go up, the more people have bought bitcoin, which does indeed push prices further up. This then encourages even more people to buy and, as continued demand pushes up the price, so we begin to see the emergence of a bubble. The price of bitcoin at its peak, therefore, reflected not the actual value of bitcoin, but the enthusiasm of buyers.

A bitcoin bubble?

One thing that we know about bubbles is that they tend to burst, which we saw on 10 December 2017, albeit temporarily, and also at the start of 2018. As a cryptocurrency, bitcoin is very susceptible to media announcements, especially about its future as a currency and any regulations that might emerge.

At the start of 2018, there was much discussion about the future regulation of bitcoin, which deterred investors from

buying and hence reduced demand, thus cutting price. Similar results were observed after India's Minister of Finance announced that the Indian Government did not view electronic currencies, such as bitcoin, as legal tender and would be aiming to eliminate them, especially given their potential role in criminal activities. Facebook announced that it would be banning adverts for cryptocurrencies.

Many officials have issued warnings, including RBS Chairman, Sir Howard Davies, who told Bloomberg: 'All the authorities can do is put up the sign from Dante's Inferno – "abandon hope all ye who enter here"'.[5] These and other similar announcements by high-profile commentators and government officials caused the demand curve for bitcoin to shift to the left and thus depressed the price, as investors became more uncertain about the future of the currency.

Interpreting the bursting of the bitcoin bubble

When a bubble bursts, it is always important to consider how a price fall is interpreted. If people think it is a permanent price fall (or at least a price fall that will be sustained over a long time period) and that further falls will come, then they will rush to sell their bitcoin before it falls any lower. However, this action, an increase in supply, will push prices down further and when these next lot of price falls are observed, more people decide to sell and so it continues. Speculation is destabilising as people believe that prices will continue to fall.

On the other hand, people may view the bubble bursting as a temporary blip – perhaps some are selling to cash in and the expectation is that a new bubble will soon emerge. In this case, when the price does fall, investors do not rush to sell their bitcoin; indeed, some may take the opportunity to invest in it at the slightly lower price. Speculation now is stabilising, as the actions help to stabilise the price.

It is impossible to predict when a bubble will burst and how investors will respond to it. It all depends on people's expectations – what do they think will happen? But this, in turn, depends on what people think others are going to do. My expectations depend on other people's expectations, which depend on other people's expectations, which depend on . . . This is known as a Keynesian Beauty Contest[6] and does suggest that the future of bitcoin is very uncertain.

 Find out what has happened to the price of bitcoin over the past year. Have there been more bubbles and if so, have they burst? In each case, think about whether speculation has played a role and whether it was destabilising or stabilising.

[5]'Bitcoin price tracker: live chart'; *The Telegraph* (6 March 2018).
[6]Richard Thaler, 'Keynes "beauty contest"', *Financial Times* (10 July 2015).

Stock holding. A simple way that suppliers can reduce risks is by holding stocks. Take the case of the wheat farmers we saw in the previous section. At the time when they are planting the wheat in the spring, they are uncertain as to what the price of wheat will be when they bring it to market. If they keep no stores of wheat, they will just have to accept whatever the market price happens to be at harvest time. If, however, they have storage facilities, they can put the wheat into store if the price is low and then wait until it goes up. Alternatively, if the price of wheat is high at harvest time, they can sell it straight away. In other words, they can wait until the price is right.

Pause for thought

The demand for pears is more price elastic than the demand for bread and yet the price of pears fluctuates more than that of bread. Why should this be so? If pears could be stored as long and as cheaply as flour, would this affect the relative price fluctuations? If so, how?

Purchasing information. Consumers and firms can purchase, or simply obtain, information as a means of reducing uncertainty when making decisions about buying products, supplying goods or entering new markets. A firm could commission various forms of market research or purchase the information from specialist organisations. Consumers might access financial advice on the stock market, take advice from an estate agent before buying a house or buy a copy of a consumer magazine, such as *Which?,* before buying a washing machine. Buying and selling information in this way helps substantially to reduce uncertainty.

Better information can also, under certain circumstances, help to make any speculation more stabilising. With poor information, people are much more likely to be guided by rumour or fear, which could well make speculation destabilising as people 'jump on the bandwagon'. If people generally are better informed, however, this is likely to make prices go more directly to a long-run stable equilibrium.

Dealing in futures markets

Another way of reducing or even eliminating uncertainty is by dealing in **futures** or **forward markets**. Let us examine the activities first of sellers and then of buyers.

Sellers

Suppose you are a farmer and want to store grain to sell some time in the future, expecting to get a better price then than now. The trouble is that there is a chance that the price will go down. Given this uncertainty, you may be unwilling to take a gamble.

An answer to your problem is provided by the *commodity futures market.* This is a market where prices are agreed between sellers and buyers *today* for delivery at some specified date in the *future.*

For example, if it is 20 October today, you could be quoted a price *today* for delivery in six months' time (i.e. on 20 April). This is known as the six-month **future price**. Assume that the six-month future price for wheat is £60 per tonne. If you agree to this price and make a six-month forward contract, you are agreeing to sell a specified amount of wheat at £60 on 20 April. No matter what happens to the **spot price** (i.e. the current market price) in the meantime, your selling price has been agreed. The spot price could have fallen to £30 (or risen to £100) by April, but your selling price when 20 April arrives is fixed at £60. There is thus *no risk to you whatsoever of the price going down.* You will, of course, lose out if the spot price is *more* than £60 in April.

Buyers

Now suppose that you are a flour miller. In order to plan your expenditures, you would like to know the price you will have to pay for wheat, not just today, but also at various future dates. In other words, if you want to take delivery of wheat at some time in the future, you would like a price quoted *now*. You would like the risks removed of prices going *up*.

Let us assume that today (20 October) you want to *buy* the same amount of wheat on 20 April that a farmer wishes to sell on that same date. If you agree to the £60 future price, a future contract can be made with the farmer. You are then guaranteed that purchase price, no matter what happens to the spot price in the meantime. There is thus *no risk to you whatsoever of the price going up.* You will, of course, lose out if the spot price is *less* than £60 in April.

The determination of the future price

Prices in the futures market are determined in the same way as in other markets: by demand and supply. For example, the six-month wheat price or the three-month coffee price will be that which equates the demand for those futures with the supply. If the five-month sugar price is currently £200 per tonne and people expect by then, because of an anticipated good beet harvest, that the spot price for sugar will be £150 per tonne, there will be few who will want to buy the futures at £200 (and many who will want to sell). This excess of supply of futures over demand will push the price down.

Definitions

Futures or forward market A market in which contracts are made to buy or sell at some future date at a price agreed today.

Future price A price agreed today at which an item (e.g. commodities) will be exchanged at some set date in the future.

Spot price The current market price.

Speculators

Many people operate in the futures market who will never actually handle the commodities themselves. They are neither producers nor users of the commodities. They merely speculate. Such speculators may be individuals, but they are more likely to be financial institutions.

Let us take a simple example. Suppose that the six-month (April) coffee price is £1000 per tonne and that you, as a speculator, believe that the spot price of coffee is likely to rise above that level between now (October) and six months' time. You thus decide to buy 20 tonnes of April coffee futures now.

But you have no intention of taking delivery. After four months, let us say, true to your prediction, the spot price (February) has risen and, as a result, the April price (and other future prices) have risen too. You thus decide to *sell* 20 tonnes of April (two-month) coffee futures, whose price, let us say, is £1200. You are now 'covered'.

When April comes, what happens? You have agreed to buy 20 tonnes of coffee at £1000 per tonne and to sell 20 tonnes of coffee at £1200 per tonne. All you do is hand the futures contract to buy to the person to whom you agreed to sell. They sort out delivery between them and you make £200 per tonne profit.

If, however, your prediction had been wrong and the price had *fallen,* you would have made a loss. You would have been forced to sell coffee contracts at a lower price than you had bought them for.

Speculators in the futures market thus incur risks, unlike the sellers and buyers of the commodities, for whom the futures market eliminates risk. Financial institutions offering futures contracts will charge for the service: for taking on the risks.

Pause for thought

If speculators believed that the price of cocoa in six months was going to be below the six-month future price quoted today, how would they act?

SUMMARY

1a Price elasticity of demand measures the responsiveness of demand to a change in price. It is defined as the proportionate (or percentage) change in quantity demanded divided by the proportionate (or percentage) change in price.

1b If the quantity demanded changes proportionately more than price, the figure for elasticity will be greater than 1 (ignoring the sign): it is elastic. If the quantity demanded changes proportionately less than price, the figure for elasticity will be less than 1: it is inelastic. If they change by the same proportion, the elasticity has a value of 1: it is unit elastic.

1c Given that demand curves are downward sloping, price elasticity of demand will have a negative value.

1d Demand will be more elastic the greater the number and closeness of substitute goods, the higher the proportion of income spent on the good and the longer the time period that elapses after the change in price.

1e Except for the three special cases of totally inelastic, infinitely elastic and unit elastic demand, demand curves normally have different elasticities along their length. We can thus normally refer only to the specific value for elasticity between two points on the curve or at a single point.

2a Firms need to know the price elasticity of demand for their product whenever they are considering a price change, as the effect on the firm's sales revenue will depend on the product's price elasticity.

2b When the demand for a firm's product is price elastic, a rise in price will lead to a reduction in consumer expenditure on the good and hence to a reduction in the total revenue of the firm.

2c When demand is price inelastic, however, a rise in price will lead to an increase in total revenue for the firm.

3a Income elasticity of demand measures the responsiveness of demand to a change in income. For normal goods it has a positive value. Demand will be more income elastic the more luxurious the good and the less rapidly demand is satisfied as consumption increases.

3b Cross-price elasticity of demand measures the responsiveness of demand for one good to a change in the price of another. For substitute goods the value will be positive; for complements it will be negative. The cross-price elasticity will be greater the closer the two goods are as substitutes or complements.

3c Price elasticity of supply measures the responsiveness of supply to a change in price. It has a positive value. Supply will be more elastic the less costs per unit rise as output rises and the longer the time period.

4a A complete understanding of markets must take into account the time dimension.

4b Given that producers and consumers take a time to respond fully to price changes, we can identify different equilibria after the elapse of different lengths of time. Generally, short-run supply and demand tend to be less price elastic than long-run supply and demand. As a result, any shifts in demand or supply curves tend to have a relatively bigger effect on price in the short run and a relatively bigger effect on quantity in the long run.

4c People often anticipate price changes and this will affect the amount they demand or supply. This speculation will tend to stabilise price fluctuations if people believe that the price changes are only temporary. However, speculation will tend to destabilise these fluctuations (i.e. make them more severe) if people believe that prices are likely to continue to move in the same direction as at present (at least for some time).

▶

5a Much economic decision making is made under conditions of risk or uncertainty.

5b Risk is when the probability of an outcome occurring is known. Uncertainty is when the probability is not known.

5c One way of reducing risks is to hold stocks. If the price of a firm's product falls unexpectedly, it can build up stocks rather than releasing its product on to the market. If the price later rises, it can then release stocks on to the market. Similarly with inputs: if their price falls unexpectedly, firms can build up their stocks, only to draw on them later if input prices rise. Consumers and firms can also access information to help them reduce uncertainty and risk.

5d Another way of eliminating risk and uncertainty is to deal in the futures markets. When firms are planning to buy or sell at some point in the future, there is the danger that price could rise or fall unexpectedly in the meantime. By agreeing to buy or sell at some particular point in the future at a price agreed today (a 'future' price), this danger can be eliminated. The bank or other institution offering the price (the 'speculator') is taking on the risk, and will charge for this service.

REVIEW QUESTIONS

1 Why does price elasticity of demand have a negative value, whereas price elasticity of supply has a positive value?

2 Rank the following in ascending order of elasticity: jeans, black Levi jeans, black jeans, black Levi 501 jeans, trousers, outer garments, clothes.

3 Would a firm want demand for its brand to be more or less elastic? How might a firm set about achieving this?

4 Assume that an iPhone currently sells for £200 and, at this quantity, 10 million units are purchased. The price then falls to £170. If the price elasticity of demand (using the formula *percentage change in quantity demanded/percentage change in price*) is calculated to be −1.5, by how many units will demand increase?

5 Assuming that a firm faces an inelastic demand and wants to increase its total revenue, how much should it raise its price? Is there any limit?

6 Can you think of any examples of goods that have a totally inelastic demand (a) at all prices; (b) over a particular price range?

7 Which of these two pairs are likely to have the highest cross-price elasticity of demand: two brands of coffee, or coffee and tea?

8 Why are both the price elasticity of demand and the price elasticity of supply likely to be greater in the long run?

9 Draw a diagram with two supply curves that have different slopes and cross each other. By adding a demand curve that passes through the supply curves at the point where they cross, show how the shape of the supply curve affects the equilibrium price and quantity following any shift in demand.

10 Redraw Figure 5.11, only this time assume that it was an initial shift in supply that caused the price to change in the first place.

11 Give some examples of decisions you have taken recently that were made under conditions of uncertainty. With hindsight, do you think you made the right decisions? Explain.

12 What methods can a firm use to reduce risk and uncertainty?

13 If speculators believed that the price of cocoa in six months was going to be below the six-month future price quoted today, how would they act?

ADDITIONAL PART B CASE STUDIES ON THE *ECONOMICS FOR BUSINESS* STUDENT WEBSITE (www.pearsoned.co.uk/sloman)

B.1 **The interdependence of markets.** A case study of the operation of markets, examining the effects on a local economy of the discovery of a large shale oil deposit.

B.2 **Adam Smith (1723–90).** Smith, the founder of modern economics, argued that markets act like an 'invisible hand' guiding production and consumption.

B.3 **Shall we put up our price?** Some examples of firms charging high prices in markets where demand is relatively inelastic.

B.4 **Any more fares?** Pricing on the buses: an illustration of the relationship between price and total revenue.

B.5 **Elasticities of demand for various foodstuffs.** An examination of the evidence about price and income elasticities of demand for food in the UK.

B.6 **Income elasticity of demand and the balance of payments.** This examines how a low income elasticity of demand for the exports of many developing countries can help to explain their chronic balance of payments problems.

B.7 **The cobweb.** An outline of the theory that explains price fluctuations in terms of time lags in supply.

B.8 **The role of the speculator.** This assesses whether the activities of speculators are beneficial or harmful to the rest of society.

B.9 **Rationing.** A case study in the use of rationing as an alternative to the price mechanism. In particular, it looks at the use of rationing in the UK during the Second World War.

B.10 Underground or shadow markets. How underground markets can develop when prices are fixed below the equilibrium.

B.11 Rent control. This shows how setting (low) maximum rents is likely to lead to a shortage of rented accommodation.

B.12 Coffee prices. An examination of the coffee market and the implications of fluctuations in the coffee harvest for growers and coffee drinkers.

B.13 Response to changes in petrol and ethanol prices in Brazil. This case examines how drivers with 'flex-fuel' cars responded to changes in the relative prices of two fuels: petrol and ethanol (made from sugar cane).

WEBSITES RELEVANT TO PART B

Numbers and sections refer to websites listed in the Web appendix and hotlinked from this text's website at **www.pearsoned.co.uk/sloman.**

- For news articles relevant to Part B, see the Economics News Articles link from the text's website.

- For general news on markets, see websites in section A, and particularly A2, 3, 4, 5, 8, 9, 20–25, 35, 36. See also site A43 for links to economics news articles from newspapers worldwide.

- For links to sites on markets, see the relevant sections of B1, I7, 14, 17.

- For data on the housing market (Box 4.1), see sites B7–11.

- For student resources relevant to Part B, see sites C1–7, 9, 10, 19.

- For sites favouring the free market, see C17 and E34. See also C18 for the development of ideas on the market and government intervention.

Background to demand

The FT Reports . . .

The Financial Times, 11 October 2015

Online Shopping Boom Leads to Record Increase in Vans

By Michael Pooler

The boom in online shopping and revived construction activity has led to record levels of investment in vans and trucks, as British businesses enlarge their fleets.

Finance for commercial vehicles on lease and hire-purchase agreements rose 10 per cent to £6.5bn in the year ending in August, according to the Finance and Leasing Association, a trade body.

The figures point to the broader economic recovery, as well as a shift in how consumers buy – and receive – goods.

Driving the growth was the buoyant retail sector and an increase in people setting up businesses, said BNP Paribas Leasing Solutions, with some of the strongest demand for vans coming from self-employed workers in the building and associated trades.

'It's very easy to get vehicles financed on very competitive rates these days,' said Brian Templar, of logistics consultancy Davies and Robson.

Following a drop in demand for trucks last year due to changes in legislation, registrations have jumped 36 per cent in 2015. The number of vans on the road has continued to rise thanks to online shopping, with 17 per cent more added this year, according to the Society of Motor Manufacturers and Traders.

This reflects how retailers and logistics companies are making fewer large deliveries to stores but more small deliveries to homes. Online sales account for a fifth of all non-food retail sales in Britain.

'Logistics is the next big battleground in e-commerce. [Retailers] have always delivered larger items like furniture but now they will be able to offer it even for smaller items,' said Anita Balchandani, partner at OC&C. The consultancy put the UK e-commerce market size at £42bn last year and forecasts it will rise to £61bn by 2018.

Argos challenged its online and bricks-and-mortar rivals last week as it became the first high-street brand to launch same-day deliveries seven days a week throughout the country. Amazon Prime Now offers shipments within an hour in Coventry and London, and has been introducing a similar service for frozen and chilled foods in parts of the capital.

Meanwhile Ocado, the upmarket online grocer, spent £12.5m on vehicle leases in 2014, against £9m the previous year.

The need for expanded vehicle fleets was underlined on 'Black Friday' in November last year, when a number of companies were caught out by a record-breaking day of online shopping. Delivery delays resulted.

Evidence of the fierce competition in the parcel delivery market was seen when City Link collapsed into administration last Christmas Eve making about 2400 staff redundant and laying off 1000 self-employed drivers.

Consumers, that is, the 'demand side', are just as important as the supply side: after all, it is they who ultimately pay for the goods and services provided, while the shape and size of their current and future demand choices is critical to the investment decisions that businesses make.

Philip Collins (2009), Chairman of the Office of Fair Trading, *Preserving and Restoring Trust and Confidence in Markets.* Keynote address to the British Institute of International and Comparative Law at the Ninth Annual Trans-Atlantic Antitrust Dialogue, 30 April.

If a business is to be successful, it must be able to predict the strength of demand for its products and be able to respond to any changes in consumer tastes, particularly when the economic environment is uncertain. It will also want to know how its customers are likely to react to changes in its price or its competitors' prices, or to changes in income. In other words, it will want to know the price, cross-price and income elasticities of demand for its product. The better the firm's knowledge of its market, the better will it be able to plan its output to meet demand, and the more able will it be to choose its optimum price, product design, marketing campaigns, etc.

In Chapter 6 we will go behind the demand curve to gain a better understanding of consumer behaviour. We will consider how economists analyse consumer satisfaction and how it varies with the amount consumed. We will then relate this to the shape of the demand curve. The chapter will also consider situations where there is uncertainty over the size of the benefits and costs from consuming a product.

Then, in Chapter 7, we will investigate the behavioural economics of the consumer. In particular we will consider a number of different circumstances where the behaviour of consumers differs from that predicted by standard economic theory. This includes the use of mental short-cuts, loss aversion and present bias.

Chapter 8 explores how data on consumer behaviour can be collected and the problems businesses face in analysing such information. It also investigates how firms can expand and develop their markets by the use of various types of non-price competition. It looks at ways in which firms can differentiate their products from those of their rivals. The chapter also considers how a business sets about deriving a marketing strategy and assesses the role and implications of product advertising. However, as the *Financial Times* article shows, if businesses are successful in expanding their markets, they must have the means of supplying them.

Key terms

Marginal utility
Diminishing marginal utility
Consumer surplus
Rational consumer
Asymmetric information
Adverse selection
Moral hazard
Product characteristics
Indifference curves
Efficiency frontier
Behavioural economics
Bounded rationality
Heuristics
Framing
Reference dependent preferences
Endowment effect
Loss aversion
Present bias
Nudging
Market surveys
Market experiments
Demand function
Forecasting
Non-price competition
Product differentiation
Product marketing
Advertising

Demand and the consumer

Given our limited incomes, we have to make choices about what to buy. You may have to choose between that new economics textbook you feel you ought to buy and going to a rock concert, between a new pair of jeans and a meal out, between saving up for a car and having more money to spend on everyday items, and so on. Business managers are interested in finding out what influences your decisions to consume, and how they might price or package their product to increase their sales.

In this section, it is assumed that as consumers we behave 'rationally': that we consider the relative costs and benefits of our purchases in order to gain the maximum satisfaction possible from our limited incomes. Sometimes, we may act 'irrationally'. We may purchase goods impetuously with little thought to their price or quality. In general, however, it is a reasonably accurate assumption that people behave rationally.

This does not mean that you get a calculator out every time you go shopping! When you go round the supermarket, you are hardly likely to look at every item on the shelf and weigh up the satisfaction you think you would get from it against the price on the label. Nevertheless, you have probably learned over time the sort of things you like and the prices they cost. You can probably make out a 'rational' shopping list quite quickly.

With major items of expenditure, such as a house, a car, a carpet or a foreign holiday, we are likely to take much more care. Take the case of a foreign holiday: you will probably spend quite a long time browsing through brochures comparing the relative merits of various holidays against their relative costs, looking for a holiday that gives good value for money. This is rational behaviour.

6.1   MARGINAL UTILITY THEORY

Total and marginal utility

People buy goods and services because they get satisfaction from them. Economists call this satisfaction 'utility'.

An important distinction must be made between *total utility* and *marginal utility*.

Total utility (*TU*) is the total satisfaction that a person gains from all those units of a commodity consumed within a given time period. Thus, if Tracey drank 10 cups of tea a day, her daily total utility from tea would be the satisfaction derived from those 10 cups.

Marginal utility (*MU*) is the additional satisfaction gained from consuming one *extra* unit within a given period of time. Thus we might refer to the marginal utility that Tracey gains from her third cup of tea of the day or her eleventh cup.

Diminishing marginal utility

Up to a point, the more of a commodity you consume, the greater will be your total utility. However, as you become more satisfied, each extra unit you consume will probably give you less additional utility than previous units. In other words, your marginal utility falls as you consume more. This is known as the *principle of diminishing marginal utility*. For example, the second cup of tea in the morning gives you less additional satisfaction than the first cup. The third cup gives less satisfaction still.

KEY IDEA 15

The principle of diminishing marginal utility. The more of a product a person consumes over a given period of time, the less will be the additional utility gained from one more unit.

Pause for thought

Are there any goods or services where consumers do not experience diminishing marginal utility?

At some level of consumption, your total utility will be at a maximum. No extra satisfaction can be gained by the consumption of further units within that period of time. Thus marginal utility will be zero. Your desire for tea may be fully satisfied at 12 cups per day. A thirteenth cup will yield no extra utility. It may even give you displeasure (i.e. negative marginal utility).

The optimum level of consumption: the simplest case – one commodity

Just how much of a good should people consume if they are to make the best use of their limited income? To answer this question we must tackle the problem of how to measure utility. The problem is that utility is subjective. There is no way of knowing what another person's experiences are really like. Just how satisfying does Brian find his first cup of tea in the morning? How does his utility compare with Tracey's? We do not have utility meters that can answer these questions!

One solution to the problem is to measure utility with money. In this case, total utility becomes the value that people place on their consumption, and marginal utility becomes the maximum amount of money that a person would be prepared to pay to obtain one more unit: in other words, what that extra unit is worth to that person. If Darren is prepared to pay 70p to obtain an extra packet of crisps, then that packet yields him 70p worth of utility: $MU = 70p$.

So how many packets should he consume if he is to act rationally? To answer this we need to introduce the concept of *consumer surplus*.

Marginal consumer surplus

Marginal consumer surplus (MCS) is the difference between the maximum amount that you are willing to pay for one more unit of a good (i.e. your marginal utility) and what you are actually charged (i.e. the price). If Darren was willing to pay 70p for another packet of crisps, which in fact cost him only 55p, he would be getting a marginal consumer surplus of 15p.

$$MCS = MU - P$$

Definitions

Total utility The total satisfaction a consumer gets from the consumption of all the units of a good consumed within a given time period.

Marginal utility The extra satisfaction gained from consuming one extra unit of a good within a given time period. In money terms, it is what you are willing to pay for one more unit of the good.

Principle of diminishing marginal utility As more units of a good are consumed, additional units will provide less additional satisfaction than previous units.

Consumer surplus The excess of what a person would have been prepared to pay for a good (i.e. the utility measured in money terms) over what that person actually pays. Total consumer surplus equals total utility minus total expenditure.

Marginal consumer surplus The excess of utility from the consumption of one more unit of a good (*MU*) over the price paid: $MCS = MU - P$.

Total consumer surplus

Total consumer surplus (TCS) is the sum of all the marginal consumer surpluses you have obtained from all the units of a good you have consumed. It is the difference between the total utility from all the units and your expenditure on them. If Darren consumes four packets of crisps, and if he would have been prepared to spend £2.60 on them and only had to spend £2.20, then his total consumer surplus is 40p.

$$TCS = TU - TE$$

where *TE* is the total expenditure on a good: i.e. $P \times Q$.

(Note that total expenditure (*TE*) is a similar concept to total revenue (*TR*). They are both defined as $P \times Q$. But in the case of total expenditure, *Q* is the quantity *purchased* by the consumer(s) in question, whereas in the case of total revenue, *Q* is the quantity *sold* by the firm(s) in question.)

Rational consumer behaviour

KI 4
p 19

Let us define **rational consumer behaviour** as the attempt to maximise (total) consumer surplus.

The process of maximising consumer surplus can be shown graphically. Let us take the case of Tina's annual purchases of petrol. Tina has her own car, but, as an alternative, she can use public transport or walk. To keep the analysis simple, let us assume that Tina's parents bought her the car and pay the licence duty, and that Tina does not have the option of selling the car. She does, however, have to buy the petrol. The current price is 130p per litre. Figure 6.1 shows her consumer surplus.

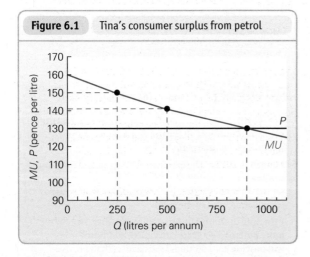

Figure 6.1   Tina's consumer surplus from petrol

If she were to use just a few litres per year, she would use them for very important journeys for which no convenient alternative exists. For such trips she may be prepared to pay up to 160p per litre. For the first few litres, then, she is getting a marginal utility of around 160p per litre, and hence a marginal consumer surplus of around 30p (i.e. 160p − 130p).

By the time her annual purchase is around 250 litres, she would be prepared to pay only around 150p for additional litres. The additional journeys, although still important, would be less vital. Perhaps these are journeys where she could have taken public transport, albeit at some inconvenience. Her marginal consumer surplus at 250 litres is 20p (i.e. 150p − 130p).

Gradually, additional litres give less and less additional utility as fewer and fewer important journeys are undertaken. The 500th litre yields 141p worth of extra utility. Marginal consumer surplus is now 11p (i.e. 141p − 130p).

KI 15
p 89

By the time she gets to the 900th litre, Tina's marginal utility has fallen to 130p. There is no additional consumer surplus to be gained. Her total consumer surplus is at a maximum. She thus buys 900 litres, where $P = MU$.

Her total consumer surplus is the sum of all the marginal consumer surpluses: the sum of all the 900 vertical lines between the price and the *MU* curve. This is represented by the total *area* between the dashed *P* line and the *MU* curve.

This analysis can be expressed in general terms. In Figure 6.2, if the price of a commodity is P_1, the consumer will consume Q_1. The person's total expenditure (*TE*) is P_1Q_1, shown by area 1. Total utility (*TU*) is the area under the marginal utility curve: i.e. areas 1 + 2. Total consumer surplus (*TU* − *TE*) is shown by area 2.

We can now state the general rule for maximising total consumer surplus. If $MU > P$ people should buy more. As they do so, however, *MU* will fall (diminishing marginal utility). People should stop buying more when *MU* has fallen to equal *P*. At that point, total consumer surplus is maximised.

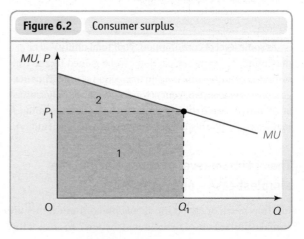

Figure 6.2   Consumer surplus

Definitions

Total consumer surplus The excess of a person's total utility from the consumption of a good (*TU*) over the amount that person spends on it (*TE*): $TCS = TU - TE$.

Rational consumer behaviour The attempt to maximise total consumer surplus.

Marginal utility and the demand curve for a good

An individual's demand curve

Individual people's demand curves for any good will be the same as their marginal utility curve for that good, measured in terms of money.

This is demonstrated in Figure 6.3, which shows the marginal utility curve for a particular person and a particular good. If the price of the good were P_1, the person would consume Q_1: where $MU = P_1$. Thus point a would be one point on that person's demand curve. If the price fell to P_2, consumption would rise to Q_2, since this is where $MU = P_2$. Thus point b is a second point on the demand curve. Likewise, if price fell to P_3, Q_3 would be consumed. Point c is a third point on the demand curve.

Thus as long as individuals seek to maximise consumer surplus and hence consume where $P = MU$, their demand curve will be along the same line as their marginal utility curve.

| Figure 6.3 | An individual person's demand curve |

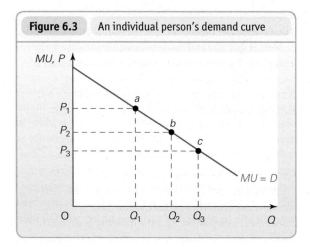

The market demand curve

The market demand curve will simply be the (horizontal) sum of all individuals' demand curves and hence MU curves. Similarly, total consumer surplus is the sum of the consumer

---

| BOX 6.1 | CALCULATING CONSUMER SURPLUS |

What can we learn from eBay?

The idea of a maximum willingness to pay might sound a little strange to most consumers. If you go to a sandwich shop to buy a tuna baguette for £2.50, you are unlikely to consider what you might have been willing to pay if the price had been higher. The only thing we can tell from your decision is that the price must be below the maximum amount you are willing to pay. There is some consumer surplus in the transaction, but it is difficult to tell how much. We have one piece of information, the price; but we do not have the other information – the amount you were willing to pay – required to make the calculation.

Perhaps one of the only situations where most consumers will be asked about their willingness to pay is when they bid for an item on eBay and are asked for their maximum bid price. This information is not revealed to either the other potential buyers or the seller. Instead, it is used by eBay to make the smallest bid required on behalf of the customer in order for them to become the highest bidder.

Take the following simple example. Robert currently has the highest bid for an item of £10. Unknown to the other buyers and the seller, the maximum amount Robert will bid is £15. If Jon sees the item and places a maximum bid of £12, the price will increase to £12.50. Robert would still have the highest bid as his willingness to pay is greater than Jon's willingness to pay. However, with the bid price increasing, Robert's potential consumer surplus will have fallen from £5 to £2.50.

Assume now that Charlotte sees the item with a current highest bid price of £12.50 and bids with a maximum willingness to pay of £20. The price will now adjust to £15.50 and Charlotte will be the highest bidder. The software does not make her bid £20. Instead, it makes it just high enough to

be larger than Robert's maximum willingness to pay of £15. Her consumer surplus if she wins the item at this price would be £4.50.

Unfortunately for economists who want to calculate consumer surplus, eBay does not release data on maximum bid prices. As eBay is a second price auction, all that is observable is a price that is just above the maximum willingness to pay of the consumer who just misses out on winning the auction.

To try to overcome these problems, Bapna *et al.*[1] set up a website that bid on eBay for customers at the last moment – known as sniping. In order to use the site, people had to enter the maximum amount they were willing to pay for items. The authors used the data this software generated on more than 4500 auctions on eBay. They projected that the consumer surplus on eBay auctions was $7 billion in 2003 and $19 billion in 2007.

1. *What are the differences between eBay and other types of auctions?*
2. *Why might some customers not enter their true willingness to pay when placing their maximum bid on eBay?*

Make a diary for a week and, each time you buy something, write down what you paid and how much you would have been willing to pay. Calculate your consumer surplus for the week. Reflect on whether doing this exercise has affected your approach to shopping.

---

[1] R. Bapna, P. Goes, A. Gupta and G. Karuga, 'Predicting bidders' willingness to pay in online multi-unit ascending auctions: Analytical and empirical insights', *INFORMS Journal on Computing*, 20 (2008), pp. 345–55.

surplus of each individual consumer: i.e. the sum of all individuals' area 2 in Figure 6.2.

Market demand and market consumer surplus are shown in Figure 6.4, where it is assumed that market price is P_m.

The shape of the demand curve. The price elasticity of demand, at any given price, will reflect the rate at which *MU* diminishes. If there are close substitutes for a good, it is likely to have an elastic demand, and its *MU* will diminish slowly as consumption increases. The reason is that increased consumption of this product will be accompanied by *decreased* consumption of the alternative product(s). Since total consumption of this product *plus* the alternatives has increased only slightly (if at all), the marginal utility will fall only slowly.

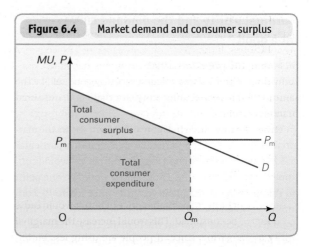

Figure 6.4 Market demand and consumer surplus

BOX 6.2 THE MARGINAL UTILITY REVOLUTION: JEVONS, MENGER, WALRAS

Solving the diamonds–water paradox

What determines the market value of a good? We already know the answer: demand and supply. So if we find out what determines the position of the demand and supply curves, we will, at the same time, be finding out what determines a good's market value.

This might seem obvious. Yet, for years, economists puzzled over just what determines a good's value.

Some economists like Karl Marx and David Ricardo concentrated on the supply side. For them, value depended on the amount of resources used in producing a good. This could be further reduced to the amount of *labour* time embodied in the good. Thus, according to the *labour theory of value,* the more labour that was directly involved in producing the good, or indirectly in producing the capital equipment used to make the good, the more valuable would the good be.

Other economists looked at the demand side. But here they came across a paradox. Adam Smith in the 1760s gave the example of water and diamonds. 'How is it', he asked, 'that water which is so essential to human life, and thus has such a high "value-in-use", has such a low market value (or "value-in-exchange")? And how is it that diamonds which are relatively so trivial have such a high market value?' The answer to this paradox had to wait over 100 years until the marginal utility revolution of the 1870s. William Stanley Jevons (1835–82) in England, Carl Menger (1840–1921) in Austria, and Leon Walras (1834–1910) in Switzerland all independently claimed that the source of the market value of a good was its *marginal* utility, not its *total* utility.

This was the solution to the diamonds–water paradox. Water, being so essential, has a high total utility: a high 'value in use'. But, for most of us, given that we consume so much already, it has a very low marginal utility. Do you leave the cold tap running when you clean your teeth? If you do, it shows just how trivial water is to you *at the margin*. Diamonds, on the other hand, although they have a much lower total utility, have a much higher marginal utility. There are so few diamonds in the world, and thus people have so few of them, that they are very valuable at the margin. If, however, a new technique were to be discovered of producing diamonds

cheaply from coal, their market value would fall rapidly. As people had more of them, so their marginal utility would rapidly diminish.

Marginal utility still only gives the demand side of the story. The reason why the marginal utility of water is so low is that *supply* is so plentiful. Water is very expensive in Saudi Arabia! In other words, the full explanation of value must take into account both demand *and* supply.

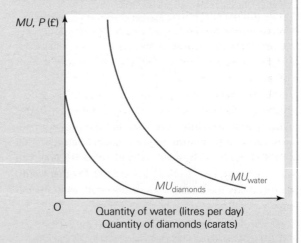

 The diagram illustrates a person's MU curves of water and diamonds. Assume that diamonds are more expensive than water. Show how the MU of diamonds will be greater than the MU of water. Show also how the TU of diamonds will be less than the TU of water. (Remember: TU is the area under the MU curve.)

 Identify two items you buy over the course of the year, one of which is expensive and one of which is cheap. What is the relationship between the marginal and total utility you derive from each?

For example, the demand for a given brand of petrol is likely to have a fairly high price elasticity, since other brands are substitutes. If there is a cut in the price of Texaco petrol (assuming the prices of other brands stay constant), consumption of Texaco will increase a lot. The *MU* of Texaco petrol will fall slowly, since people consume less of other brands. Petrol consumption *in total* may be only slightly greater and hence the *MU* of petrol only slightly lower.

Shifts in the demand curve. How do *shifts* in demand relate to marginal utility? For example, how would the marginal utility of (and hence demand for) margarine be affected by a rise in the price of butter? The higher price of butter would cause less butter to be consumed. This would increase the marginal utility of margarine, since, if people are using less butter, their desire for margarine is higher. The *MU* curve (and hence the demand curve) for margarine thus shifts to the right.

Weaknesses of the one-commodity version of marginal utility theory

A change in the consumption of one good will affect the marginal utility of substitute and complementary goods. It will also affect the amount of income left over to be spent on other goods. Thus a more satisfactory explanation of demand would involve an analysis of choices between goods, rather than looking at one good in isolation. (We examine such choices in section 6.3.)

Nevertheless, the assumptions of diminishing marginal utility and of the consumer making rational choices by considering whether it is 'worth' paying the price being charged are quite realistic assumptions about consumer behaviour. It is important for businesses to realise that the demand for their product tends to reflect consumers' perceptions of the *marginal* utility they expect to gain, rather than the *total* utility.

6.2 DEMAND UNDER CONDITIONS OF RISK AND UNCERTAINTY

The problem of imperfect information

KI 8
p 33

So far we have assumed that, when people buy goods and services, they know exactly what price they will pay and how much utility they will gain. In many cases, this is a reasonable assumption. When you buy a bar of chocolate, you clearly do know how much you are paying for it and have a very good idea how much you will like it. But what about a mobile phone, a tablet, a car, a washing machine or any other *consumer durable*? In each of these cases, you are buying something that will last you a long time and, the further into the future you look, the less certain you will be of its costs and benefits to you.

Take the example of purchasing a laptop computer, which costs £300. If you pay cash, your immediate outlay involves no uncertainty: it is £300. But the computer can break down. In 12 months' time you could face a repair bill of £100. This cannot be predicted and, yet, it is a price you will have to pay, just like the original £300. In other words, when you buy the laptop, you are uncertain as to the full 'price' you will have to pay over its lifetime.

If the costs of the laptop are uncertain, so too are the benefits. You might have been attracted to buy it in the first place by the description in an online advert or at a shop. Once you have used the laptop for a while, however, you might discover things you had not anticipated. Perhaps it takes longer than you anticipated to boot up or to connect to the Internet or to run various types of software/ games.

Buying consumer durables thus involves uncertainty. So, too, does the purchase of assets, whether a physical asset such as a house or financial assets such as shares. In the case of assets, the uncertainty is over their future *price,* which you cannot know for certain.

Attitudes towards risk and uncertainty

KI 14
p 79

So how will uncertainty affect people's behaviour? The answer is that it depends on their attitudes towards taking a gamble. To examine these attitudes, let us assume that people do at least know the *chances* involved when taking a gamble (i.e. the *probabilities involved* in doing so). In other words, the person is operating under conditions of *risk* rather than *uncertainty*. Consider the following example.

Imagine that, as a student, you have only £105 left out of your student loan to spend and have no other income or savings. You are thinking of buying an instant lottery ticket/ scratch card. The lottery ticket costs £5 and there is a 1 in 10, or 10 per cent, chance that it will be a winning ticket. A winning ticket pays a prize of £50. Would you buy the lottery ticket? This will depend on your attitude towards risk.

In order to explain people's attitude towards risk, it is important to understand the concept of expected value. The *expected value* of a gamble is the amount the person would earn on average if the gamble were repeated many times. To calculate the expected value of a gamble you simply multiply each possible outcome by the probability that it will occur. These values are then added together. In this example the

Definitions

Consumer durable A consumer good that lasts a period of time, during which the consumer can continue gaining utility from it.

Expected value The average value of a variable after many repetitions: in other words, the sum of the value of a variable on each occasion divided by the number of occasions.

gamble has only two possible outcomes – you purchase a winning ticket or a losing ticket. There is a 10 per cent chance it is a winning ticket, which will give you a total of £150 to spend (£100 left out of your loan plus a £50 prize). There is a 90 per cent chance it is a losing ticket, in which case you will have only £100 left to spend out of your student loan. Therefore, the expected value of this gamble is:

$$EV = 0.1(150) + 0.9(100) = 105$$

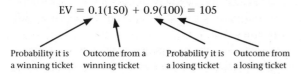

Probability it is a winning ticket   Outcome from a winning ticket   Probability it is a losing ticket   Outcome from a losing ticket

If you do not purchase the ticket, then you will have £105 to spend for sure.

$$EV = 1(105) = 105$$

There are three possible categories of attitude towards risk.

■ *Risk neutral.* If people are risk neutral they will always choose the option with the highest expected value. Therefore, a student who is risk neutral would be indifferent between buying or not buying the instant lottery ticket, as each outcome has the same expected value of £105.
■ *Risk averse.* If people are risk averse they will never choose a gamble if it has the same expected value as the pay-off from not taking a gamble. Therefore, a student who is risk averse would definitely not buy the instant lottery ticket.

It is too simplistic, however, to say that a risk averse person will never take risks. Such a person may choose a gamble if it has a greater expected value than a certain pay-off. If the probability of purchasing a winning instant lottery ticket in the previous example was 20 per cent instead of 10 per cent, then a risk averse student might, nevertheless, buy the ticket, as the expected value of the gamble (£110) would be greater than the certain pay-off (£105).

Whether or not risk averse people do take gambles depends on the *strength* of their aversion to risk, which will vary from one individual to another. The greater people's level of risk aversion, the greater the expected value of a gamble they are willing to give up in order to have a certain pay-off.

The certain amount of money that gives a person the same utility as a gamble is known as the gamble's **certainty equivalent**. The more risk averse people are, the lower the gamble's certainty equivalent for them.

The expected value of a gamble minus a person's certainty equivalent of that gamble is called the **risk premium**. The more risk averse people are, the greater their (positive) risk premium.

■ *Risk loving.* If people are risk loving they would always choose a gamble if it had the same expected value as the

pay-off from not taking the gamble. Therefore, a risk loving student would definitely purchase the instant lottery ticket.

Once again, it is too simplistic to say that risk loving people will always choose a gamble. They may choose a certain pay-off if it has a higher expected value than the gamble. For a risk loving person the certainty equivalent of a gamble is greater than its expected value. For example, if the probability of purchasing a winning instant lottery ticket in the previous example were 1 per cent instead of 10 per cent, then even a risk loving student might choose not to buy the ticket. It would depend on the extent to which that person enjoyed taking risks. The more risk loving people are, the greater the return from a certain pay-off they are willing to sacrifice in order to take a gamble. Because the certainty equivalent of a gamble is *greater* than its expected value, the risk premium is *negative*.

Pause for thought

1. What is the expected value of the above lottery ticket gamble if the chances of purchasing a winning lottery ticket with a prize of £50 are 30 per cent? How much of the expected value of the gamble are risk averse people willing to sacrifice if they decide against purchasing a ticket?
2. What is the expected value of the lottery ticket gamble if the chances of purchasing a winning ticket are 1 per cent? How much of the certain pay-off are risk loving people willing to sacrifice if they decide to purchase the lottery ticket? If they were indifferent between purchasing and not purchasing the ticket, what is their certainty equivalent and risk premium of the gamble?

Diminishing marginal utility of income and attitudes towards risk taking

Avid gamblers may be risk lovers. People who spend lots of money on various online betting websites or at the race track may enjoy the thrill of taking a risk, knowing that there is always the chance that they might win. On average, however, such people will lose. After all, the bookmakers have to take their cut and thus the odds are generally unfavourable.

Definitions

Certainty equivalent The guaranteed amount of money that an individual would view as equally desirable as the expected value of a gamble. If a person is risk averse, the certainty equivalent is less than the expected value.

Risk premium The expected value of a gamble minus a person's certainty equivalent.

KI 15
p89

Most people, however, for most of the time, are risk averse. We prefer to avoid insecurity. But why? Is there a simple reason for this? Economists use marginal utility analysis to explain why.

They argue that the gain in utility to people from an extra £1000 is less than the loss of utility from forgoing £1000. Imagine your own position. You have probably adjusted your standard of living to your income (or are trying to!). If you unexpectedly gained £1000, that would be very nice: you could buy some new clothes or have a weekend away. But, if you lost £1000, it could be very hard indeed. You might have very serious difficulties in making ends meet. Thus, if you were offered the gamble of a 50:50 chance of winning or losing £1000, you would probably decline the gamble.

This risk-averse behaviour accords with the principle of *diminishing marginal utility*. Up to now in this chapter we have been focusing on the utility from the consumption of individual goods: Tracey and her cups of tea; Darren and his packets of crisps. In the case of each individual good, the more we consume, the less satisfaction we gain from each additional unit: the marginal utility falls. But the same principle applies if we look at our *total* consumption. The higher our level of total consumption, the less additional satisfaction will be gained from each additional £1 spent.

What we are saying here is that there is a **diminishing marginal utility of income**. The more you earn, the lower will be the utility from each *extra* £1. If people on £15 000 per year earned an extra £1000, they would feel much better off: the marginal utility they will get from that income will be relatively high. If people already earning £500 000 per year earned an extra £1000, however, their gain in utility will be less.

Why, then, does a diminishing marginal utility of income make us risk averse? The answer is illustrated in Figure 6.5, which shows the *total* utility you get from your income.

The slope of this curve gives the *marginal* utility of your income. As the marginal utility of income diminishes, the curve gets flatter. Assume that you experience 70 units or utils of pleasure from spending £5000 on the goods you like. This is shown as point *a* on Figure 6.5.

If your income now rises from £5000 to £10 000, your total utility increases by 30 utils, from 70 to 100 utils. This is shown as the movement along the total utility curve from point *a* to point *b*. A similar rise in income from £10 000 to £15 000 leads to a move from point *b* to point *c*. This time, however, your total utility has increased by only 16 utils, from 100 to 116 utils. Marginal utility has diminished.

Now assume that your income is £10 000 and you are offered the following gamble: a 50:50 chance of gaining an extra £5000 or losing £5000. Effectively, then, you have an equal chance of your income rising to £15 000 or falling to £5000. The expected value of the gamble is £10 000 – the same as the pay-off from not taking the gamble.

At an income of £10 000, your total utility is 100. If the gamble pays off and increases your income to £15 000, your total utility will rise to 116: i.e. an increase of 16. If it does not pay off, you will be left with only £5000 and a utility of 70 utils i.e. a decrease of 30. Therefore you have a 50:50 chance of experiencing either 116 or 70 utils of pleasure. Your *average* or expected utility will be (116 + 70)/2 = 93 utils.

This point can be illustrated on Figure 6.5 by drawing a straight-line or chord between points *a* and *c*. Points along this chord represent all the possible weighted averages of the

---

Pause for thought

Do you think that this provides a moral argument for redistributing income from the rich to the poor? Does it prove that income should be so redistributed?

Definition

Diminishing marginal utility of income Where each additional pound earned yields less additional utility than the previous pound.

Figure 6.5 Total utility of income

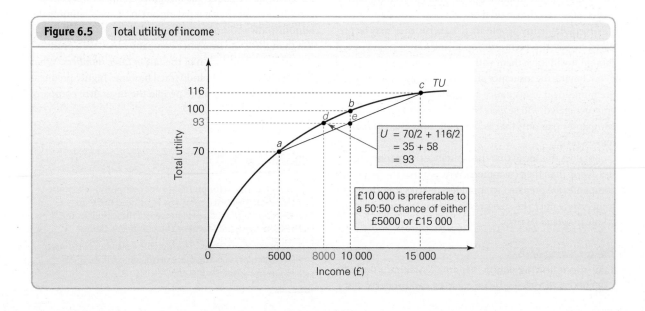

U = 70/2 + 116/2
= 35 + 58
= 93

£10 000 is preferable to a 50:50 chance of either £5000 or £15 000

utility at point *a* and point *c*. In this example, because the probability is 50:50, expected utility is represented half way along the chord at point *e*. As you can see from the *TU* curve, the expected utility from the gamble is the same as the utility experienced from receiving £8000 for certain (point *d*). This is the certainty equivalent of the gamble.

The risk premium is £2000: i.e. the expected value of £10 000 minus the certainty equivalent of £8000. In other words, £10 000 for certain provides greater utility than the gamble. In the case illustrated in Figure 6.5, you would always prefer a certain pay-off as long as it was greater than £8000. Hence risk aversion is part of rational utility-maximising behaviour.

Pause for thought

If people are generally risk averse, why do so many around the world take part in national lotteries?

Most of the time we do not know the exact chances involved in taking a gamble. In other words, we operate under conditions of *uncertainty*. We often have to make judgements about what we think are the different likelihoods of various outcomes occurring. There is evidence that, in some circumstances, people are not very good at making probabilistic judgements and are prone to making systematic errors. (This is discussed in more detail in section 7.1, see pages 113–16.)

Insurance: a way of removing risks

Insurance is the opposite of gambling. It removes the risk. For example, every day you take the risk that you will lose your mobile phone or drop and break it. In either case, you will have to incur the cost of purchasing a new handset to replace it. Alternatively, you can remove the risk by taking out an appropriate insurance policy that pays out the cost of a new handset if the original one gets lost or broken.

Given that many people are risk averse, they may be prepared to pay the premium for an insurance policy, even though it will leave them with less than the expected value of not buying the insurance and taking the gamble. The total premiums paid to insurance companies, and hence the revenue generated, will be *more* than the amount the insurance companies pay out: that is, after all, how the companies make a profit.

But does this mean that the insurance companies are less risk averse than their customers? Why is it that the insurance companies are prepared to shoulder the risks that their customers were not? The answer is that the insurance company is able to *spread its risks*.

The spreading of risks

Take the following simple example. Assume you have £100 000 worth of assets (i.e. savings, car, property, etc.).

You drive your car to university/work every day and there is a 1 in 20 (or 5 per cent) chance that, at some point during the year, you will be responsible for an accident that results in your car being a write-off. Assume the market value of the car is currently £20 000 and remains unchanged for the following 12 months. The expected value of taking the gamble for the year (i.e. not purchasing comprehensive car insurance) is 0.95(100 000) + 0.05(80 000) = £99 000.

If you are risk averse you would be willing to pay more than an additional £1000 to purchase a fully comprehensive car insurance policy that covers you for a year. For example, you may be willing to pay £1100 a year (over and above a simple third-party insurance) for an annual policy that pays out the full £20 000 if you have the accident for which you are responsible. Having paid the extra £1100 out of your total assets of £100 000, you would be left with £98 900 for sure. If you are risk averse, this may give you a higher level of utility than not purchasing the insurance and taking the gamble that you are not responsible for an accident where your car is a write-off.

The insurance company, however, is not just insuring you. It is insuring many others like you at the same time. Assume that it has many customers with exactly the same assets as you and facing the same 5 per cent risk every year of causing an accident that results in their car being a write-off. As the number of its customers increases, the outcome each year will become closer to its expected or average value. Therefore, the insurance company can predict with increasing confidence that, on average, 5 out of every 100 customers will cause an accident every year and make a claim on their own insurance for £20 000, while 95 out of every 100 will not have an accident and not make a claim on their insurance for their own car.

This means that the insurance company will pay out £100 000 in claims for every 100 customers: i.e. five will each make a claim of £20 000. This works out as an average pay-out of £1000 per customer. If each customer is willing to pay £1100 for such a policy, the insurance company will generate more in revenue than it is paying out in claims. Assuming the administrative cost of providing each policy per customer is less than £100, the insurance company can make a profit.

This is an application of the *law of large numbers*. What is unpredictable for an individual becomes highly predictable in the mass. The more people the insurance company

---

Definitions

Spreading risks (for an insurance company) The more policies an insurance company issues and the more independent the risks of claims from these policies are, the more predictable will be the number of claims.

Law of large numbers The larger the number of events of a particular type, the more predictable will be their average or expected outcome.

insures, the more predictable the final outcome becomes. In other words, an insurance company will be able to convert your *uncertainty* into their *risk*.

In reality, people taking out insurance will not all have the same level of wealth and the same chances of having an accident. However, using statistical data, the insurance company will be able to work out the average chances of an event occurring for people in similar situations. Basing premiums on average chances can, however, create some problems for the insurance supplier, which will be discussed later in the chapter.

The independence of risks

The spreading of risks does not just require that there should be a large number of policies. It also requires that the risks should be **independent**. This means that, if one person makes a claim, it does not increase the chances of another person making a claim too. If the risks are independent in the previous example then, if one person has a car accident, the risk of another person having a car accident remains unchanged at 5 per cent.

Now imagine a different example. If any insurance company insured 1000 houses *all in the same neighbourhood,* and there was a major fire in the area, the claims would be enormous. The risks of fire would *not* be independent, as if one house catches fire it increases the chances of the surrounding houses catching fire. If, however, a company provided fire insurance for houses scattered all over the country, the risks *are* independent.

Pause for thought

1. *Why are insurance companies unwilling to provide insurance against losses arising from war or 'civil insurrection'?*
2. *Name some other events where it would be impossible to obtain insurance.*
3. *Explain why an insurance company could not pool the risk of flooding in a particular part of a country. Does your answer imply that insurance against flooding is unobtainable?*

Another way in which insurance companies can spread their risks is by **diversification**. The more types of insurance a company offers (car, house, life, health, etc.), the greater the likelihood the risks would be independent.

Problems for unwary insurance companies

A major issue for insurance companies is that they operate in a market where there is significant asymmetric information (see page 29). Asymmetric information exists in a market if one party has some information that is relevant to the value of that transaction that the other party does not have. In the insurance market, the buyer often has private information about themselves to which the insurance company does not have access.

Asymmetric information often is split into two different types – unobservable characteristics and unobservable actions. Each separate type of asymmetric information generates a different problem. Unobservable characteristics could generate the problem of *adverse selection*; unobservable actions could generate the problem of *moral hazard*. We consider each in turn.

Potential problems caused by unobservable characteristics – adverse selection

Different potential consumers of insurance will have different characteristics. Take the case of car insurance: some drivers may be very skilful and careful, while others may be less able and enjoy the thrill of speeding. Or take the case of life assurance: some people may lead a very healthy lifestyle by eating a well-balanced diet and exercising regularly. Others may eat large quantities of fast food and do little or no exercise.

In each of these cases, the customer is likely to know more about their own characteristics than the insurance company. These characteristics will also influence the cost to the firm of providing insurance. For example, less able drivers are more likely to be involved in an accident and make a claim on their insurance than more able drivers. The problems this might cause can be explained best with a simple numerical example.

In the previous car insurance example (see page 96), we assumed that all the customers had the same characteristics: i.e. they all had a 5 per cent chance per year of being responsible for a car accident, where the damage to their own car costs, on average, £20 000. In reality, because of their different characteristics, the chances of having a car accident will vary from one customer to another. To keep the example simple, we will assume that an insurance company has only two types of potential customer. One half of them are very skilful drivers and have a 1 per cent chance per year of causing an accident, while the other half are less able drivers who each have a 9 per cent chance per year of causing an accident. The problem for the insurance company is that, when a customer purchases the insurance, it does not know if they are a skilful or a less able driver.

When faced with this situation, the insurance company could set a profit-making risk premium on the assumption that half of its customers will be highly competent drivers, while the other half have relatively poor driving skills. Using the law of large numbers, the firm can predict that 1 in 20 (5 per cent) of its customers will make a claim and so the

---

Definitions

Independent risks Where two risky events are unconnected. The occurrence of one will not affect the likelihood of the occurrence of the other.

Diversification A business growth strategy in which a business expands into new markets outside of its current interests.

average pay-out would be £1000 per customer (i.e. £20 000/20). Once again, assuming less than £100 of administrative costs, a premium of £1100 per customer would, in theory, enable the firm to make a profit.

The problem is that the skilful drivers might find this premium very unattractive. For them the expected value of the gamble (i.e. not taking out the insurance) is $0.99(100 000) + 0.01(80 000) = £99 800$. Taking out the insurance would leave them with £98 900: i.e. their initial wealth of £100 000 minus the premium of £1100. Unless they were very risk averse, the maximum amount they would be willing to pay is likely to be far lower than £1100.

On the other hand, the less skilful drivers might find the offer from the insurance company very attractive. Their expected value from taking the gamble is $0.91(100 000) + 0.09(80 000) = £98 200$. Their maximum willingness to pay is likely to be greater than £1100. In fact, if they were all risk averse they would all purchase the policy if it was £1800, as this would leave them with £98 200 – the same as the expected value of the gamble.

The insurance company could end up with only the less able drivers purchasing the insurance. If this happens, then nine out of every 100 customers would make a claim of £20 000 each. The average pay-out per customer would be £1800. Therefore, the firm would be paying out far more in claims than they would be generating from the premiums.

If, however, the insurer *knew* a potential customer was a skilful driver, then it could offer the insurance policy at a much lower price: one that the risk averse careful driver would be willing to pay. If all the customers purchasing the policy were skilful drivers, then only 1 in 100 would make a claim for £20 000. The average claim per customer would be only £200. All the skilful and risk averse customers would be willing to pay more than £200 for the insurance policy.

But, if the insurance company does not know who is careful and who is not, this asymmetric information prevents the mutually beneficial sale of insurance for skilful drivers.

This example has illustrated the problem of *adverse-selection* in insurance markets. This is where customers with the least desirable characteristics from the sellers' point of view (i.e. those with the greatest chance of making a claim) are more likely to take out the insurance policy at a price

based on the average risk of all the potential customers. This can result in the insurance market for low risk individuals collapsing, even though mutually beneficial trade would be possible if symmetric information was present.

We can define adverse selection more generally as follows.

> **Adverse selection.** Where information is imperfect, high-risk groups will be attracted to profitable market opportunities to the disadvantage of the average buyer (or seller). In the context of insurance, it refers to those who are most likely to take out insurance posing the greatest risks to the insurer.

KEY IDEA 16

The potential problem of adverse selection is not unique to the insurance market. Unobservable characteristics are present in many other markets and may relate to the buyer, the seller or the product that is being traded. Table 6.1 provides some examples.

Tackling the problem of adverse selection. Are there any ways that the potential problems caused by adverse selection can be overcome? One way is for the person or party who is uninformed to ask the person or party who is informed for the relevant information. For example, an insurance company may require people to fill out a questionnaire giving details about their lifestyle and family history so that the company can assess the particular risk and set an appropriate premium. There may need to be legal penalties for people caught lying! This process of the uninformed trying to get the information from the informed is called *screening*.

Definition

Adverse selection in the insurance market Where customers with the least desirable characteristics from the seller's point of view are more likely to purchase an insurance policy at a price based on the average risk of all the potential customers.

Table 6.1	Adverse selection in various markets		
Market	**Hidden characteristic**	**Informed party**	**Uninformed party**
The labour market	Innate ability of the worker/ preference for working hard	The potential employee: i.e. the seller of labour services	The employer: i.e. the buyer of labour services
The credit market	Ability of people to manage their money effectively	The customer applying for credit	The firm lending the money
A street market with haggling	How much the person is willing to pay	The customer	The seller of the product
The electronic market: e.g. eBay	The quality/condition of the product	The seller of the product	The buyer of the product

An alternative would be for the person or party who is informed about the relevant characteristics to take action to reveal it to the uninformed person or party. This is called *signalling*. For example, a potentially hardworking and intelligent employee could signal this fact to potential employers by obtaining a good grade in an economics degree or work for a period of time as an unpaid intern.

Pause for thought

What actions can either the buyers or sellers take in each of the examples in Table 6.1 to help overcome some of the potential problems caused by the unobservable characteristics?

Potential problems caused by unobservable actions – moral hazard

Imagine in the previous example if the different characteristics of the drivers were perfectly observable to the insurance company: i.e. the insurance company could identify which drivers were more able or careful and could charge them a lower premium than those who were less able or more careless. The company might still face problems caused by *unobservable actions*.

Once drivers have purchased the insurance, their driving behaviour may change. All types of driver now have an incentive to take less care when they are driving. If they are now responsible for an accident, all the costs will be covered by the insurance policy and so the marginal benefit from taking greater care will have fallen. This will result in the chances of both very careful and careless drivers of having an accident to rise above 1 per cent and 9 per cent respectively.

The problem for the insurer is that these changes in driving behaviour are difficult to observe. The companies may end up in a position where the amount of money claimed by both the skilful and less skilful drivers increases above the revenue they are collecting in premiums based on the risk before the insurance was taken out.

This is called **moral hazard** and can, more generally, be defined as where the actions/behaviour of one party to a transaction change in a way that reduces the pay-off to the other party. It is caused by a change in incentives once a deal has been reached. It can only exist if there are unobservable actions.

Moral hazard. Following a deal, the actions/behaviour of one party to a transaction may change in a way that reduces the pay-off to the other party. In the context of insurance, it refers to people taking more risks when they have insurance than they would have if they did not have insurance.

The problem of moral hazard may occur in many different markets and different situations. For example:

- Once a person has a permanent contract of employment they might not work as hard as the employer anticipated.
- If someone else is willing to pay your debts (e.g. your parents), you are likely to take less care with your spending. A similar type of argument has been used for not cancelling the debts of poor countries.
- If a bank knows that it will be bailed out by the government, i.e. it is too big to fail, it may undertake more risky lending strategies.
- If you hire a car, you may be rough with the clutch or gears, knowing that you will not bear the cost of the extra wear and tear of the car.
- When working in teams, some people may slack, knowing that more diligent members of the team will cover for them (giving them a 'free ride').

Tackling moral hazard. What are the most effective ways of reducing moral hazard? One approach would be for the uninformed party to devote more resources to *monitoring* the actions and behaviour of the informed party – in other words, to reduce the asymmetry of information. Examples include insurance companies employing loss adjusters to assess the legitimacy of claims and lecturers using plagiarism detection software to discourage students from attempting to pass off other people's work as their own. However, monitoring may often be difficult and expensive.

An alternative is to change the terms of the deal so that the party with the unobservable actions has an incentive to behave in ways that are in the interests of the uninformed party. Examples include employees who take sick leave being required to produce a medical certificate to prevent people taking 'sickies' and students doing group project work being assessed on their own contribution to the project rather than being given the same mark as everyone else in the group, thereby discouraging free riding.

Pause for thought

How will the following reduce the moral hazard problem?
1. *A no-claims bonus in an insurance policy.*
2. *Having to pay the first so many pounds of any insurance claim.*
3. *The use of performance-related pay.*

Definition

Moral hazard Where one party to a transaction has an incentive to behave in a way that reduces the pay-off to the other party. The temptation to take more risks when you know that someone else will cover the risks if you get into difficulties. In the case of banks taking risks, the 'someone else' may be another bank, the central bank or the government.

BOX 6.3   ADVERSE SELECTION IN THE INSURANCE MARKET

Can consumer incompetence save the market?

If the buyers in the insurance market have characteristics that are impossible or very costly for the insurance supplier to observe, then the market may suffer from adverse selection. For example, it may be very difficult for an insurer to observe the driving ability of their potential customers. Some will be more able and less likely to have an accident, while others will be less able and more likely to have an accident.

If an insurer cannot tell its customers apart, it will have to base its premiums on the average ability level of all of its potential customers. However, premiums based on this information tend to be above the maximum amount that the more able drivers are willing to pay and below the maximum amount the less able drivers are willing to pay. This results in only the less able drivers purchasing the policy and the insurance company paying out more in claims than the revenue they are generating from the premiums (as we saw on pages 97–8). According to standard economic theory, the market suffers from adverse selection.

However, this argument is based on the assumption that people can accurately assess their own driving skills. Do less able drivers realise that they are less able drivers and therefore more likely to have an accident?

A number of psychologists have argued that people often find it very difficult to judge accurately their own ability and competence in a range of activities. In particular, many people tend to be overconfident and think that they are better than average. This is called *illusory superiority*. For example, in a study by McCormick, Walkey and Green,[1] 178 participants were asked to judge their driving skill compared to other people: 80 per cent believed that their driving ability was above that of the average driver.

The Dunning–Kruegar effect

Although there is a large amount of evidence that many people are overconfident in their own ability, studies have also found that the level of this overconfidence varies considerably between individuals.

In a well-known piece of research, the psychologists Dunning and Kruegar carried out a number of experiments to try to identify the factors that influence the extent of this overconfidence. Participants in their study had to complete a number of exercises that were designed to test their skills in a number of different areas. These included logical reasoning, grammar and judging how funny a series of jokes were!

After completing the test, the participants were asked to judge how well they thought they had done. The study found that the least able participants (i.e. those who achieved the lowest scores on the test) were the most overconfident. The most able (i.e. those who achieved the highest scores on the test) tended to be slightly under-confident but much more accurate. The authors concluded that the skills that make a person good at a particular activity tend to be the same skills that enable them to evaluate if they are good at that same activity. This has become known as the *Dunning–Kruegar effect*.

Similar research has been undertaken to assess how accurately students can judge the quality of their own academic work on the course they are studying. For example, Guest and Riegler[2] examined how accurately undergraduate students of economics could judge the quality of their own assessed essays, with a marks bonus given for accurate estimates. The results were very similar to those of Dunning and Kruegar, with the students who achieved the lowest marks being the most overconfident about the quality of the essay they had written.

These research findings have interesting implications for the predictions of standard economic theory when analysing the impact of unobservable characteristics on a market.

1. If the least able drivers overestimate their driving skills and the most able drivers underestimate their driving skills, what impact will this have on their willingness to pay for an insurance policy?
2. To what extent could the experience of the driver over time have an impact on either their under- or overconfidence?
3. What implications do your answers to question 1 have on the likelihood of adverse selection occurring in a market with unobservable characteristics?

Conduct a survey of 15 to 20 students after they have submitted a piece of work. Ask them to estimate their mark. Later, when the marks are published, ask them what they actually got and to explain any divergence between the actual mark and the estimated one. What general observations can you make about the exercise? If other students are also doing this activity with different groups of students, discuss the differences in findings. Note that it is important to conduct this exercise anonymously, with no students' names being attached to the results.

[1] Iain A. McCormick, Frank H. Walkey and Dianne E. Green, 'Comparative perceptions of driver ability – a confirmation and expansion', *Accident Analysis & Prevention* 18 (3) (1986), pp. 205–8.

[2] Jon Guest and Robert Riegler, 'Learning by doing: Do economics students' self-evaluation skills improve?', *International Review of Economics Education*, 24 (2017), pp. 50–64.

BOX 6.4 DEALING WITH MORAL HAZARD AND ADVERSE SELECTION

Overcoming the problems of supplying high-quality versions of a good

The existence of asymmetric information sometimes can prevent the sale of products/services that would make both buyers and sellers better off. The impact of unobservable characteristics and actions makes it difficult for consumers to separate high-quality from low-quality versions of a good and service. The uncertainty caused by the resulting problems of moral hazard and adverse selection reduce consumers' willingness to pay for the higher-quality versions of the product, which can lead to this segment of the market collapsing.

The potential for an information 'gap' between buyers and sellers is far greater in the market for some types of goods than others. It may be a particular issue for experience goods. These are products or services where it is difficult for consumers to judge how much utility or pleasure they will derive until the good has actually been consumed. For example, it is far easier to anticipate the pleasure from a loaf of bread or packet of pasta before purchase than eating out in a restaurant. Other examples of experience goods include going on holiday, studying a course at university, employing the services of a plumber, garage mechanic, etc.

It is in the interests of both consumers and suppliers of higher-quality versions of these goods to establish institutional or within-market arrangements to address the issue. Some potential solutions include:

Guarantees and warranties

Firms can provide guarantees/warranties that ensure the product is improved, repaired, replaced or refunded if the customer is dissatisfied with the purchase. In many circumstances, this is an effective way for the seller of a high-quality good to signal the information to prospective buyers. If a seller knows they are supplying a low-quality good, it would deter them from offering a warranty because of the potential cost involved.

Establishing a reputation

A single firm can establish a reputation for selling high-quality goods by word of mouth or, perhaps, by creating a valued brand name through advertising. The incentives to create a reputation will be strong when a company plans to stay in business for a long period of time.

One increasingly important way for firms to develop a positive reputation is via online consumer ratings and reviews. Whereas traditional word-of-mouth comments might reach half a dozen potential customers, online ratings can reach thousands. A number of very successful website companies, such as *TripAdvisor, Yelp* and *Angie's List,* provide customer reviews for the public, while the success of online market platforms such as eBay and Amazon is partly attributed to the feedback facilities.

A survey commissioned by the Competition and Markets Authority[1] found that 54 per cent of adults read online reviews. It estimated that £23 billion of consumer spending in the UK was influenced by these reviews. A 2017 study in the USA[2] found that 97 per cent of customers read online reviews when choosing a local business.

Economists have tried to quantify the impact of online ratings using actual sales data. For example Anderson and Magruder[3] found that an extra half-star rating on the Yelp website caused restaurants to sell out 49 per cent more frequently. Cabral and Hortacsu[4] studied the collectables market and found that the first negative online review for a seller resulted in a 7 per cent fall in its sales the following week.

Are comments posted online always a reliable source of information? One drawback is the potential for businesses to post both fake positive reviews about themselves and fake negative reviews about their rivals. Mayzlin, Dover and Chevalier[5] researched this issue in the hotel industry using data from TripAdvisor, where anyone can post a review, and Expedia, where only people who have stayed in the hotel can post a review. Given this important difference, fake reviews are less likely to be posted on Expedia than on TripAdvisor.

The authors found that, on average, a small independently-run hotel had seven more fake positive reviews (out of 120) posted on TripAdvisor than one that was part of a national chain. If a hotel was situated near a small independent rival, it received six more fake negative reviews than one located a long distance away from other hotels.

Why are small independently run hotels more likely to post fake reviews than those that belong to a national chain?

---

[1] *On-line reviews and endorsements* CMA (June 2015).

[2] *Local Consumer Review Survey,* BrightLocal (2017).

[3] Michael Anderson and Jeremy Magruder, 'Learning from the Crowd: Regression Discontinuity Estimates of the Effects of an Online Review Database', *Economic Journal,* Vol.122, No.563, (2012) pp. 957–89.

[4] Luís Cabral and Ali Hortaçsu, 'The Dynamics of Seller Reputation: Evidence from eBay' *The Journal of Industrial Economics,* Vol. 58, (1), (2010) pp. 54–78.

[5] Dina Mayzlin, Yaniv Dover and Judith Chevalier, 'Promotional Reviews: An Empirical Investigation of Online Review Manipulation' *American Economic Review,* Vol. 104, No. 8 (2014) pp. 2421–55.

▶

Trade associations and voluntary ombudsman

Firms can also band together collectively and establish a trade association, which is an organisation founded and funded by businesses that operate in a specific industry. For example, the Association of Plumbing and Heating Contractors (APHC) claims that APHC membership allows professional plumbers and heating contractors to distinguish themselves from rogue traders. The association also states that it is committed to ensuring better standards of workmanship for consumers.

Some associations provide consumers with compensation if one member firm provides a poor-quality product or goes out of business. For example the Association of British Travel Agents (ABTA) guarantees customers will either complete their holiday or obtain a refund, if they have purchased it from a member that has gone bankrupt. By preventing membership of low-quality suppliers, trade associations may be an effective way for businesses to signal the quality of their goods and services to potential customers.

What happens if a customer complains about the quality of a good or service and is unhappy with the response of the firm or lack of one? To deal with these situations, some sectors have established an *Ombudsman*. This is an organisation that helps to resolve complaints by offering independent resolution services for consumers. The services are offered free of charge and aim to remedy the imbalance between the expertise/resources of a business and those of an individual consumer. They should also have complete independence from the firms they have the power to investigate.

Some Ombudsman services are voluntary organisations established by a particular trade organisation, e.g. the Removals Industry Ombudsman. Given that consumers do not pay a fee for the services, how are they funded? Each business covered by an Ombudsman has to pay a fee or levy, which varies depending on the size of the firm. They also have to pay a case fee for each complaint made against them. Financing and establishing an Ombudsman is another way the members of a trade association can signal to customers the quality of the goods and services they provide.

 What are the potential disadvantages of trade associations?

Government intervention

Governments sometimes intervene by requiring the establishment of an ombudsman by law. Examples include the Financial Ombudsman and the Legal Ombudsman. Others are approved by government departments or regulators to meet minimum criteria for that particular sector. Examples include the Property Ombudsman and Ombudsman Services. Ombudsman Services provide independent dispute resolution in three main sectors: communications, energy and property. In 2016, it resolved 72 652 complaints out of 243 272 initial contacts. The following table summarises the information, broken down by each of the three main sectors.

Complaints resolved by Ombudsman Services in the communications sector 2016

Sector	Initial queries	Complaints resolved	Main reasons for complaint (and percentage for that sector)
Communications (telephone, mobile phone and internet services)	99 103	29 503	Billing (30%), contract issues (15%), service (11%)
Energy	88 255	41 622	Billing (74%), transfers (7%), customer service (4%)
Property	5 601	1 166	Valuations/surveys (9%), other complaint (5%), property management (4%)
Other	53 315	361	
Total	246 274	72 652	

On the whole, recent UK governments have avoided the creation of a sector or industry regulator, preferring trade associations and self-regulation. One exception has been the case of the financial services industry. Following a number of scandals, including the mis-selling of pensions and mortgages, the government replaced ineffective self-regulation in 2000 with the Financial Services Authority (FSA) – an independent industry regulator with statutory powers. However, the FSA was widely criticised for failing to prevent the lending boom which led to the financial crisis in 2007. It was abolished in April 2013 and replaced by the Financial Conduct Authority (FCA), which has greater powers. (See section 21.1 for a more general discussion of competition policy and regulation.)

1. *Consider the customer complaints in the communications sector (telephones, Internet, etc.) received by Ombudsman Services (see table). Use the concepts of adverse selection and moral hazard to explain why this sector may be predisposed to a high number of complaints.*
2. *Explain why online market places such as eBay, Amazon and Airbnb have to deal with the possibility of double moral hazard, i.e. moral hazard by both buyers and sellers.*

This section is optional. You may skip straight to the next chapter if you prefer.

To get a better understanding of consumer demand, we need to analyse how consumers choose *between* products (as we concluded in section 6.1). In other words, we must look at products not in isolation, but in relation to other products. Any firm wanting to understand the basis on which consumers demand its products will want to know why they might choose *its* product rather than those of its rivals. A car manufacturer will want to know why consumers might choose one of its models rather than those of its competitors.

 Such choices depend not only on price but also on the characteristics of the products. If you were buying a car, in addition to its price, you would consider features such as style, performance, comfort, reliability, durability, fuel economy, safety and various added features (such as air conditioning, stereo system, air bags, electric windows, etc.). Car manufacturers will thus design their cars to make them as attractive as possible to consumers, relative to the cost of manufacture. In fact, most firms constantly will try to find ways of improving their products to make them more appealing to consumers.

 What we are saying here is that consumers derive utility from the various characteristics that a product possesses. To understand choices, then, we need to look at the attributes of different products and how these influence consumer choices between them. *Characteristics theory* (sometimes called 'attributes theory') was developed by the economist Kelvin Lancaster[2] in the mid-1960s to analyse such choices and to relate them to the demand for a product.

Characteristics theory is based on four key assumptions:

■ All products possess various characteristics.
■ Different brands possess them in different proportions.
■ The characteristics are measurable: they are 'objective'.
■ The characteristics, along with price and consumers' incomes, determine consumer choice.

Identifying and plotting products' characteristics

Let us take a simple case of a product where consumers base their choice between brands on price and just two characteristics. For example, assume that consumers choose between different brands of breakfast cereal on the basis of taste and health-giving properties. To keep the analysis simple, let us assume that taste is related to the amount of sugar in the cereal and that health-giving properties are related to the amount of fibre.

Plotting the characteristics of different brands

The combinations of these two characteristics, sugar and fibre, can be measured on a diagram. In Figure 6.6, the quantity of sugar is measured on the horizontal axis and the quantity of fibre on the vertical axis. One brand, Healthbran, contains a lot of fibre, but only a little sugar. Another, Tastyflakes, contains a lot of sugar, but only a little fibre.

The ratio of the two attributes, fibre and sugar, in each of the two brands is given by the slope of the two rays out from the origin. Thus, by consuming a certain amount of Healthbran, given by point h_1 on the Healthbran ray, the consumer is getting f_1 of fibre and s_1 of sugar. The consumption of more Healthbran is shown by a movement up the ray, say to h_2. At this point, the consumer gets f_2 of fibre and s_2 of sugar. Notice that the ratio of fibre to sugar is the same in both cases. The ratio is given by $f_1/s_1 (= f_2/s_2)$, which is simply the slope of the Healthbran ray.

The consumer of Tastyflakes can get relatively more sugar, but less fibre. Thus consumption at point t_1 gives s_3 of sugar, but only f_3 of fibre. The ratio of fibre to sugar for Tastyflakes is given by the slope of its ray, which is f_3/s_3.

Any number of rays can be put on the diagram, each one representing a particular brand. In each case, the ratio of fibre to sugar is given by the slope of the ray.

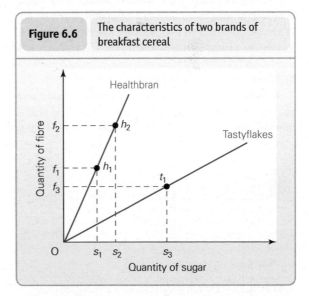

| Figure 6.6 | The characteristics of two brands of breakfast cereal |

Definition

Characteristics (or attributes) theory The theory that demonstrates how consumer choice between different varieties of a product depends on the characteristics of these varieties, along with prices of the different varieties, the consumer's budget and the consumer's tastes.

[2]K. Lancaster, 'A new approach to consumer theory', *Journal of Political Economy*, 74 (April 1966), pp. 132–57.

Changes in a product's characteristics. If a firm decides to change the mix of characteristics of a product, the slope of the ray will change. Thus, if Healthbran were made sweeter, its ray would become shallower.

The budget constraint

The amount that a consumer buys of a brand will depend in part on the consumer's budget and on the price of the product. Assume that, given the current price of Healthbran, Jane's budget for breakfast cereals allows her to buy at h_1 per month: in other words, the amount of Healthbran that gives f_1 of fibre and s_1 of sugar. (This assumes that she buys only Healthbran and not some other brand too.)

A change in the budget. If she allocates more of her income to buying breakfast cereal, and sticks with Healthbran, she would move up the ray: say, to h_2. In other words, by buying more Healthbran, she would be buying more fibre and more sugar. Similarly, a reduction in expenditure on a product would be represented by a movement down its ray.

A change in price. If a product rises in price and the budget allocated to it remains the same, less will be purchased. There will be a movement down its ray.

The efficiency frontier

In practice, many consumers will buy a mixture of brands. Some days you may prefer one type of breakfast cereal, some days you may prefer another type. People get fed up with consuming too much of one brand or variety: they experience diminishing marginal utility from that particular mix of characteristics. You may allocate a certain amount of money for a summer holiday each year, but you may well want to go to a different place each year, since each place has a different mix of characteristics.

Assume that, given her current budget for breakfast cereals, the prices of Healthbran and Tastyflakes allow Jane to buy at either point *a* or point *b* in Figure 6.7. By switching completely from Healthbran to Tastyflakes, her consumption of fibre would go down from f_1 to f_2, and her consumption of sugar would go up from s_1 to s_2. She could, however, spend part of her budget on Healthbran and part on Tastyflakes. In fact, she could consume anywhere along the straight line joining points *a* and *b*. This line is known as the *efficiency frontier*. For example, by buying some of each brand, she could consume at point *c*, giving her f_3 of fibre and s_3 of sugar.

If she did consume at point *c*, how much of the two characteristics would she get from each of the two brands? This is shown in Figure 6.8 by drawing two lines from point *c*, each one parallel to one of the two rays. Consumption of the two brands takes place at points *d* and *e* respectively, giving her f_h units of fibre and s_h units of sugar from Healthbran, and f_t units of fibre and s_t units of sugar from Tastyflakes. The total amount of fibre and sugar from the two brands will be $f_3(= f_h + f_t)$ and $s_3(= s_h + s_t)$.[3]

It is easily possible to show an efficiency frontier between several brands, each with their own particular blend of characteristics. This is illustrated in Figure 6.9, which shows the case of four breakfast cereals, each with different combinations of fibre and sugar.

Figure 6.8	Consuming a mixture of two products

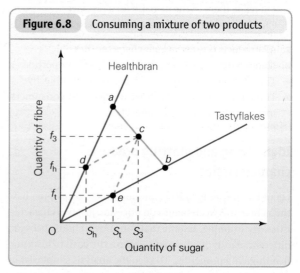

Figure 6.7	The efficiency frontier

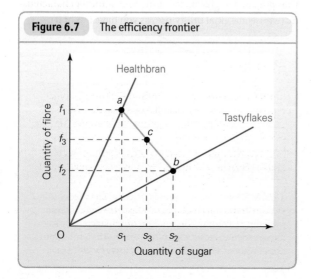

---

[3]This follows because of the shape of the parallelogram O*dce*. Being a parallelogram makes the distance $f_3 - f_h$ equal to $f_t - O$. Thus adding f_h and f_t gives f_3, which must correspond to point *c*. Similarly, the distance $s_3 - s_t$ must equal $s_h - O$. Thus adding sh and s_t gives s_3, which also must correspond to point *c*.

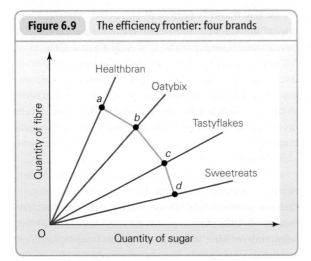

Figure 6.9 The efficiency frontier: four brands

Any of the four points through which the efficiency frontier passes can change if the price of that brand changes. So, if Oatybix went up in price, point *b* would move down the Oatybix ray, thereby altering the shape of the efficiency frontier.

If any of the brands changed their mix of characteristics, then the respective ray would pivot. If the consumer's budget changed, then the whole efficiency frontier would move parallel up or down all the rays.

The optimum level of consumption

Indifference curves

We have seen that, by switching between brands, consumers can obtain different mixtures of characteristics. But what, for any given consumer, is the optimum mixture? This can be shown by examining a consumer's preferences, and the way we do this is to construct *indifference curves*. This is illustrated in Figure 6.11, which shows five indifference curves, labelled I_1 to I_5.

An indifference curve shows all the different combinations of the two characteristics that yield an equal amount of satisfaction or utility. Thus any combination of characteristics along curve I_1 represents the same given level of utility. The consumer is, therefore, 'indifferent' between all points along curve I_1. Although the actual level of utility is not measured in the diagram, the further out the curve, the higher the level of utility. Thus all points on curve I_5 are preferred to all points along curve I_4, and all points along curve I_4 are preferred to all points along curve I_3, and so on. In fact, indifference curves are rather like contours on a map. Each contour represents all points on the ground that are a particular height above sea level. You can have as many contours as you like on the map, depending at what interval you draw them: 100 metres, 25 metres, 10 metres, or whatever. Similarly you could have as many indifference curves as you like on an *indifference map*. In Figure 6.10, we have drawn just five such curves, as that is all that is necessary to illustrate consumer choice, in this example.

The shape of indifference curves. Indifference curves are drawn as downward sloping. The reason is that, if consumers get less of one characteristic, they would need more of the other to compensate, if their total level of utility was to stay the same. Take the case of washing powder. For any given expenditure, you would be prepared to give up only a certain amount of one characteristic, say whiteness, if you got more of another characteristic, such as softness.

Notice that the indifference curves are not drawn as straight lines. They are bowed in towards the origin. The reason is that people generally are willing to give up less and less of one characteristic for each additional unit of another. For example, if you were buying a new PC, you might be prepared to give up some RAM to get extra hard disk space, but for each extra GB of disk space you would probably be prepared to give up less and less RAM. We call this a *diminishing marginal rate of substitution* between the two characteristics. The reason is that you get diminishing marginal utility from any characteristic the more of it you consume, and are thus prepared to give up less and less of another characteristic (whose marginal utility rises as you have less of it).

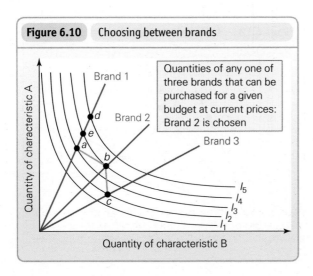

Figure 6.10 Choosing between brands

> Quantities of any one of three brands that can be purchased for a given budget at current prices: Brand 2 is chosen

Definitions

Indifference curve A line showing all those combinations of two characteristics of a good between which a consumer is indifferent, i.e. those combinations that give a particular level of utility.

Indifference map A diagram showing a whole set of indifference curves. The further away a particular curve is from the origin, the higher the level of utility it represents.

Diminishing marginal rate of substitution of characteristics The more a consumer gets of characteristic A and the less of characteristic B, the less and less of B the consumer will be willing to give up to get an extra unit of A.

Indifference curves for different consumers. Different consumers will have different indifference maps. The indifference map in Figure 6.10 is drawn for a particular consumer, say James. If another consumer, Henry, gets relatively more satisfaction from characteristic B than does James, Henry's indifference curves would be steeper. In other words, he would be prepared to give up more units of A to get a certain amount of B than would James.

Pause for thought

Can you think of any instances where the indifference curve will not be bowed in towards the origin?

The optimum combination of characteristics

We are now in a position to see how a 'rational' consumer would choose between brands. Figure 6.10 shows the rays for three brands of a product, with, at given prices, the efficiency frontier passing through points *a, b* and *c*. The consumer would choose to consume Brand 2, since point *b* is on a higher indifference curve than point *a* (Brand 1), which, in turn, is on a higher indifference curve than point *c* (Brand 3).

Sometimes, the consumer will choose to purchase a mixture of brands. This is shown in Figure 6.11, which takes the simple case of just two brands in the market. By consuming at point *a* (i.e. a combination of point *b* on the Brand 1 ray and point *c* on the Brand 2 ray), the consumer is on a higher indifference curve than by consuming only Brand 1 (point *d*) or Brand 2 (point *e*).

Response to changes

We can now show how consumers would respond to changes in price, income, product characteristics and tastes.

Changes in price

Referring back to Figure 6.10, if the price of a brand changes, there is a shift in the efficiency frontier, so that it crosses the ray for that brand at a different point. For example, if the price of Brand 1 fell, there would be a movement of the efficiency frontier up the Brand 1 ray from point *a*. If the price fell far enough that the efficiency frontier now passed through point *d*, the consumer would switch from consuming just Brand 2 to just Brand 1. If the price fell less than this, so that the efficiency frontier passed through point *e*, then the consumer would buy a mixture of both brands. The optimum consumption point would lie on an indifference curve a little above I_4.

We can relate this analysis to the concept of cross-price elasticity of demand (see page 71). If two products are very close substitutes, they will have a high cross-price elasticity of demand. But what makes them close substitutes? The answer is that they are likely to have similar characteristics; their rays will have a similar slope. Even a slight rise in the price of one of them (i.e. a small movement along its ray) can lead the consumer to switch to the other. This will occur when the rays are close together: when they have a similar slope.

Changes in income

If there is a change in consumer incomes, so that people allocate a bigger budget to the product in question, then there will be a parallel movement outwards of the efficiency frontier. Whether this will involve consumers switching between brands depends on the shape of the indifference map.

Changes in the characteristics of a product (real or perceived)

If consumers believe that a brand now yields relatively more of characteristic B than A, the ray will become less steep. How far out will the efficiency point be on this new ray? This depends on the total perceived amount of the two characteristics that is obtained from the given budget spent on this brand.

To illustrate this, consider Figure 6.12. The firm producing Brand 1 changes its specifications so that, for a given budget, a lot more characteristic B can be obtained and a

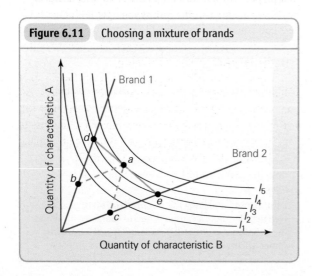

Figure 6.11 Choosing a mixture of brands

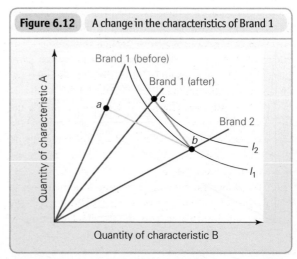

Figure 6.12 A change in the characteristics of Brand 1

little more characteristic A. The result is that the brand's ray shifts inwards and the efficiency frontier that originally connected points *a* and *b* now connects points *c* and *b*. In this case, the consumer represented by the indifference curves shown switches consumption from Brand 2 at point *b* to Brand 1 at point *c*.

If there is a proportionate increase in both characteristics (i.e. the brand has generally improved), the slope of the ray will not change. Instead, there will be a movement of the efficiency frontier outward along the ray. Graphically, the effect is the same as a fall in the price of the product: more of both characteristics can be obtained for a given budget.

Changes in tastes

If consumers' tastes change, their whole indifference map will change. If characteristic B now gives more utility relative to A than before, the curves will become steeper, and the consumer is likely to choose a product that yields relatively more of characteristic B (i.e. one with a relatively shallow ray).

Clearly, firms will attempt to predict such changes in tastes and will try, through product design, advertising and marketing, to shift the ray for their brand in the desired direction (downward in the above case). They will also try to persuade consumers that the product is generally better (i.e. has more of all characteristics) and thereby move outward the point where the efficiency frontier crosses the brand's ray.

Business and the characteristics approach

Characteristics analysis can help us understand the nature of consumer choice. When we go shopping and compare one product with another, it is the differences in the features of the various brands, along with price, that determine which products we end up buying. If firms, therefore, want to compete effectively with their rivals, it is not enough to compete solely in terms of price; it is important to focus on the specifications of their product and how these compare with those of their rivals' products.

Characteristics analysis can help firms study the implications of changing their product's specifications (and of their rivals changing theirs). It also allows firms to analyse the effects of changes in their price or their rivals' prices; the effects of changes in the budgets of various types of consumer; the effects of changes in consumer tastes; and the effects of repositioning themselves in the market.

Take the producer of Brand 1 in Figure 6.13. Clearly the firm would like to persuade consumers like the one illustrated to switch away from Brand 2 to Brand 1. It could do this by lowering its price. But a small reduction in price will have no effect on this consumer. Only when the price has fallen far enough for the efficiency frontier to rise nearly to point *d* will the consumer start switching; and only when the price has fallen further still, so that the efficiency frontier passes through a point a little above point *d,* will the consumer switch completely.

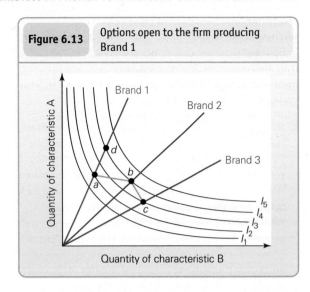

| Figure 6.13 | Options open to the firm producing Brand 1 |

An alternative would be for the firm to reposition its product. It could introduce more of characteristic B into its product, thereby swinging the Brand 1 ray clockwise towards the Brand 2 ray. Clearly, it would have to be careful about its price too. The closer its brand became in quality to Brand 2, the more elastic would demand become, since Brand 1 would now be a closer substitute for Brand 2. In the extreme case of its ray becoming the same as that for Brand 2, its price would have to be low enough for the consumer to buy at or above point *b*. Depending on consumer tastes (and hence the shape of the indifference curves), it may choose to reposition its brand between the Brand 2 and Brand 3 rays. Again, a careful mix of product characteristics and price may enable it to capture a larger share of the market.

Another alternative would be for the firm to attempt to influence consumer tastes. In Figure 6.13, if it could persuade consumers to attach more value to characteristic A, the indifference curves would become shallower (i.e. less characteristic A would now be needed to give consumers a given level of utility). If the curves swung downward enough, point *a* could be now on a higher indifference curve than point *b*. The consumer concerned would switch from Brand 2 to Brand 1. Clearly, the more consumers are influenced in this way, the more sales of Brand 1 will rise.

If a firm is thinking of launching a new product, again it will need to see how the characteristics of its product compare with those of the existing firms in the market. It will need to see where its ray would be compared with those of other firms, and whether the price it is thinking of charging would enable it to take sales away from its rivals.

Pause for thought

Before you read on, what do you think are the limitations of characteristics analysis?

Limitations of characteristics analysis

Characteristics analysis, as we have seen, can help firms to understand their position in the market and the effects of changing their strategy. Nevertheless, it cannot provide firms with a complete analysis of demand. There are four key limitations of the approach:

- It is sometimes difficult to identify and measure characteristics in a clear and unambiguous way. Take the look or design of a product, whether it be furniture, clothing, a painting or a car. What makes it visually appealing depends on the personal tastes of the consumer, and such tastes are virtually impossible to quantify.
- Most products have several characteristics. The analysis we have been examining, however, is limited to just two characteristics: one on each axis. By using mathematical analysis, it is possible to extend the number of characteristics, but the more characteristics that are included in the analysis, the more complex it becomes.
- Indifference curves, while being a good means of understanding consumer choice in theory, have practical limitations. To draw an indifference map for just one consumer would be very difficult, given that consumers often would find it hard to imagine a series of combinations of characteristics between which they were indifferent. To draw indifference curves for millions of consumers would be virtually impossible. At best, therefore, they can provide a rough guide to consumer choice.
- Consumer tastes change. In what ways consumer tastes will change and how these changes will influence the shape of the indifference curves are very difficult to predict.

Despite these problems, there are many useful insights that firms can gain from the analysis. Firms, through their market research, could gain considerable information about consumer attitudes towards their products' characteristics and thus the general shape, if not precise position, of indifference curves.

What is more, many markets divide into different **market segments** with consumers in each segment having similar tastes (and hence similar sets of indifference curves). For example, different models of car fall into different groups (such as medium-sized saloons, high-performance small cars, people carriers and small 'tall' cars), as do different types of restaurant and different types of holiday. Thus a tour operator will first identify the particular segment of the market it is aiming for (e.g. a young person's package holiday with the characteristics of guaranteed sunshine and plenty of nightlife) and then position itself in that particular market relative to its rival tour operators.

What is clear is that firms need good information about the demand for their products and to develop a careful marketing strategy. In Chapter 7, we look at how firms attempt to get information about demand and, in Chapter 8, we examine how firms set about developing, marketing and advertising their products.

Definition

Market segment A part of a market for a product where the demand is for a particular variety of that product.

SUMMARY

1a Economists call consumer satisfaction 'utility'. Marginal utility diminishes as consumption increases. This means that total utility will rise less and less rapidly as people consume more. At a certain point, total utility will reach a maximum, at which point marginal utility will be zero. Beyond this point, total utility will fall; marginal utility will be negative.

1b Consumers will attempt to maximise their total utility. They will do this by consuming more of a good as long as its marginal utility to them (measured in terms of the price they are prepared to pay for it) exceeds its price. They will stop buying additional amounts once *MU* has fallen to equal the price. At this point, the consumer's surplus will be maximised.

1c An individual's demand curve lies along the same line as the individual's marginal utility curve. The market demand curve is the sum of all individuals' marginal utility curves.

2a When people buy consumer durables, they may be uncertain of their benefits and any additional repair and maintenance costs. When they buy financial assets, they may be uncertain of what will happen to their price in the future. Buying under these conditions of imperfect

knowledge is, therefore, a form of gambling. When we take such gambles, if we know the probabilities, we are said to be operating under conditions of *risk*. If we do not know the probabilities, we are said to be operating under conditions of *uncertainty*.

2b People can be divided into risk lovers, risk averters and those who are risk neutral. Because of the diminishing marginal utility of income, it is rational for people to be risk averters (unless gambling is itself pleasurable).

2c Insurance is a way of eliminating risks for policy-holders. Being risk averters, people are prepared to pay premiums in order to obtain insurance. Insurance companies, on the other hand, are prepared to take on these risks because they can spread them over a large number of policies. According to the law of large numbers, what is unpredictable for a single policy-holder becomes highly predictable for a large number of them, provided that their risks are independent of each other.

2d When there is asymmetric information, buyers and/or sellers can experience the problems of adverse selection and moral hazard. For example, insurance companies that offer health insurance without taking into account the health of their potential policy-holders will attract those individuals who are most likely to benefit from a health policy, i.e. those prone to illness and injury. This is the problem of adverse selection. Further, once individuals have taken out an insurance policy, they may engage in more risky behaviour. This is the problem of moral hazard.

3a Consumers buy products for their characteristics. Characteristics can be plotted on a diagram and a ray drawn out from the origin for each product. The slope of the ray gives the amount of the characteristic measured on the vertical axis relative to the amount measured on the horizontal axis.

3b The amount purchased will depend on the consumer's budget. An efficiency frontier can be drawn showing the maximum quantity of various alternative brands (or combinations of them) that can be purchased for that budget.

3c An indifference map can be drawn on the same diagram. The map shows a series of indifference curves, each one measuring all the alternative combinations of two characteristics that give the consumer a given level of utility. The consumer is thus indifferent between all combinations along an indifference curve. Indifference curves further out to the right represent higher levels of utility

and thus preferred combinations. Indifference curves are bowed in to the origin. This reflects a diminishing marginal rate of substitution between characteristics.

3d The optimum combination of characteristics is where the efficiency frontier is tangential to (i.e. just touches) the highest indifference curve. The 'rational' consumer will thus purchase at this point.

3e A change in a product's price, or a change in the consumer's budget, is represented by a movement along the product's ray. A change in the mix of characteristics of a product is represented by a swing in the ray (i.e. a change in its slope). A change in consumer tastes is represented by a shift in the indifference curves. They will become steeper if tastes shift towards the characteristic measured on the horizontal axis.

3f Although (a) some characteristics are difficult or impossible to measure, (b) only two characteristics can be measured on a simple two-dimensional diagram and (c) the position of indifference curves is difficult to identify in practice, characteristics theory gives useful insights into the process of consumer choice. It can help firms analyse the implications of changing their or their rivals' product specifications, changes in consumer tastes and changes in their or their rivals' prices.

REVIEW QUESTIONS

1 How would marginal utility and market demand be affected by a rise in the price of a complementary good?

2 Why do we get less consumer surplus from goods where our demand is relatively price elastic?

3 Explain why the price of a good is no reflection of the *total* value that consumers put on it.

4 Give some numerical examples of risk taking where the expected value of the gamble (a) is greater than the pay-off from the certain outcome; (b) equal to the pay-off from the certain outcome; (c) lower than the pay-off from the certain outcome.

5 If people are generally risk averse, why do so many people around the world take part in national lotteries?

6 Why are insurance companies unwilling to provide insurance against losses arising from war or 'civil insurrection'? Name some other events where it would be impossible to obtain insurance.

7 Assume that the insurance company is able to observe whether or not a potential customer is a skilful driver. If drivers do not take out the insurance, there is a 1 per cent chance they will be involved in an accident that results in the car being written off. Based on this risk, the insurance company charges a premium of £250 per customer. Assume also that, having taken out the insurance, drivers take less care when driving. Using a numerical example, explain how this might cause problems for the insurance company.

8 In March 2011, the European Court of Justice banned insurance companies from charging different premiums to men and women solely because of their gender. This change in the law came into effect in December 2012. What impact might this ruling be having on the market for

car insurance? What actions might an insurance company or a driver take in response to the change in the law?

9 Based on Euro NCAP[1] test results in 2017, the Subaru XV was judged to be one of the safest family cars on the market. If you observed that these cars were *more* likely to be involved in traffic accidents, could this be an example of adverse selection or moral hazard? Explain.

10 In many countries, consumers are not obliged to disclose the results of predictive genetic tests (i.e. those that predict the likelihood of future illnesses as a result of a genetic condition) to an insurer. What impact might this have on the market for health and long-term care insurance?

11 Make a list of characteristics of shoes. Which of these could be measured easily and which are more 'subjective'?

12 If two houses had identical characteristics, except that one was near a noisy airport and the other was in a quiet location and, if the market price of the first house was £300 000 and the second was £400 000, how would that help us to put a value on the characteristic of peace and quiet?

13 Assume that Rachel is attending university and likes to eat a meal at lunchtime. Assume that she has three options of where to eat: the university refectory, a nearby pub or a nearby restaurant. Apart from price, she takes into account the quality of the food and the pleasantness of the surroundings when choosing where to eat.

---

[1] www.euroncap.com/en/press-media/press-releases/euro-ncap-s-best-in-class-cars-of-2017/.

Sketch her indifference map for the two characteristics: food quality and pleasantness of surroundings. Now, making your own assumptions about which locations provide which characteristics, the prices they charge and Rachel's weekly budget for lunches, sketch the rays for the three locations and draw a weekly efficiency frontier. Mark Rachel's optimum consumption point.

Now illustrate the following (you might need to draw separate diagrams):

a) A rise in the price of meals at the local pub, but no change in the price of meals at the other two locations.

b) A shift in Rachel's tastes in favour of food quality relative to pleasantness of surroundings.

c) The refectory is refurbished and is now a much more attractive place to eat.

14 Why would consumption at a point inside the efficiency frontier not be 'rational'?

3 for 2
on longer lasting

Behavioural economics of the consumer

Business issues covered in this chapter

- How can consumers use mental shortcuts to simplify decision making?
- How does the use of such shortcuts lead to predictable behaviour?
- How can businesses present information to boost sales?
- What are the implications for pricing of consumer behaviour?

In this chapter, we examine the possibility that consumers do not always behave in ways that are consistent with the predictions of the rational choice model examined in Chapter 6. For example, they may lack both the time and processing ability to deal effectively with all the information relevant to the choices facing them.

In these situations, consumers may revert to using mental shortcuts often referred to as 'heuristics'. These sometimes prove to be an effective method of dealing with complex problems. However, in other situations, their use results in people making systematic errors.

Consumers may also code potential benefits and costs as either separate gains or losses, rather than considering their effect on their overall income, wealth or satisfaction. The outcomes coded as losses appear to cause far greater levels of discomfort than the pleasure associated with an equivalent-sized gain.

The decisions consumers make are also influenced by the way information is presented. Businesses might be able to take advantage of this to boost their sales. Consumers also seem to have difficulty sticking to their plans. For example, they may plan to eat more healthily and exercise more but suffer from self-control problems. They also care about the pay-offs to others as well as to themselves.

7.1 HOW DOES BEHAVIOURAL ECONOMICS DIFFER FROM STANDARD THEORY?

The field of behavioural economics has developed rapidly over the past 25 years and, in October 2017, Richard Thaler was awarded the Nobel Prize in Economics for his work in the area.[1] In this chapter, the focus is on how behavioural economics can improve our understanding of consumer behaviour. In Chapter 13, we look at the contribution behavioural economics can make in helping to explain the behaviour of firms.

[1] www.nobelprize.org/nobel_prizes/economic-sciences/laureates/2017/press.html.

What is behavioural economics?

Behavioural economics integrates some simple insights from psychology into standard economic theory in an attempt to improve its ability to explain and predict behaviour. It is important to understand that the development of modern behavioural economics is not an attempt to replace mainstream economic theory. It aims, instead, to complement and enhance models that have already been developed.

Standard economic theory

To understand what behavioural economics is, it is useful to think back to an important assumption underpinning many standard economic theories. This is that people successfully attempt to maximise their own self-interest. In other words, they make rational choices. They do this by accurately assessing all the cost and benefits involved when making both simple and complicated decisions. They then successfully make choices that maximise their own happiness. In most standard theories, it is assumed that people's happiness depends only on the pay-offs to themselves. They are not interested in the welfare of others.

However, this does not mean that economists actually believe that everyone in the real world behaves like this. They accept that real human beings make mistakes and often care about the pay-offs to others. What economists assume is that the people in their theoretical models behave in a rational and selfish manner.

But why assume that people in theories, such as consumer choice, behave differently from people in the real world? This is an example of abstraction. If theories built upon this simplified view of human behaviour can effectively explain and predict real-world behaviour, then it is a useful assumption to make.

The alternative would be to assume that people in theories are as complicated as their real-world counterparts. This would introduce much greater complexity into the analysis and make it much more difficult to understand and apply. If the simpler model is doing a good job at explaining and predicting real-world behaviour, why make it any more complicated than it needs to be?

However, in practice, traditional assumptions of rationality and perfect information sometimes lead to errors in prediction. Behavioural economics seeks to allow better understanding and predictions by observing and understanding actual consumer behaviour, while still making relatively simple assumptions.

Evidence of human behaviour and the challenge to standard theory

Laboratory experiments. Results from a number of laboratory experiments inspired a growing interest in behavioural economics. Modern laboratory experiments in economics typically take place in a specially designed computer room in a university.[2] The participants are usually students who make decisions in a simple online environment that attempts to simulate a particular economic model or scenario. They are paid for taking part and receive additional payments depending on the decisions they make during the experiment. This provides incentives for the decisions to be taken seriously. The researcher observes and records the behaviour of the participants for later analysis.

While some laboratory experiments have produced results that are consistent with traditional economic theory, others have not. For example, some studies have found that people really dislike losses and are sometimes willing to reduce their own earnings to avoid outcomes they perceived as unfair. An example is discussed in more detail in Box 7.4.

An advantage of laboratory experiments is that they allow economists to control the decision-making environment. One factor can be changed at a time and the response of the participants observed while holding all other things equal. The biggest disadvantage is that the decisions are made in a very artificial environment and people may behave differently when faced with the same incentives in a real-world setting.

Field experiments. To try to address this issue, an increasing number of economists have used field experiments. A field experiment differs from a laboratory experiment in two main ways. It takes place in the real-world environment where decisions are usually taken (i.e. not a computer room in a university) and the participants are unaware that their behaviour is being observed and recorded by the researcher.

Field experiments have been conducted to study a wide range of behaviours including sports card traders, soft fruit producers and donations to charity. Often, they produce results that are inconsistent with mainstream theory.

Naturally occurring data. Some studies use existing data. These, too, have found evidence that is inconsistent with the rational choice model in a number of areas, including (a) gym membership; (b) the housing market; (c) trading in financial markets; (d) the labour supply decisions of taxi drivers.

Behavioural economists have developed theories, therefore, that are more consistent with the results of this research literature. Some of the most influential are discussed in the remainder of this section.

A lack of processing ability

Consumers might, in principle, want to maximise utility, but may face limits on their ability to find and process the relevant information to make the best decision. This is

---

[2]For example, the Birmingham Experimental Economics Laboratory (BEEL) at Birmingham University and the Lancaster Experimental Economics Laboratory (LExEL) at Lancaster University.

sometimes referred to as **bounded rationality**. Finding and processing information takes time and mental effort and busy consumers may decide it is simply not worth it.

For example, in some circumstances, it may be difficult to compare the price and quality of all the different versions of a good or service offered by different suppliers. This may become more of a problem as the range of alternatives increases.

With many consumption decisions, there is also an element of uncertainty about the exact size and nature of the cost and benefits. This will be particularly true for consumer durables such as laptop computers, mobile phones and TVs. For example, when purchasing a laptop, a customer may be unsure about (a) how well it will perform, (b) how useful it will be and (c) the chances it will break down. Considerable uncertainty may also exist when booking a hotel or holiday. In these circumstances, the consumer will have to make a judgement about the likelihood of different events occurring. For example, what are the chances that a holiday resort/hotel is not as nice as it appears in the brochure or that the weather may be bad? There is evidence that people often find it very difficult to make these types of probability assessments.

Heuristics

To simplify choice problems, consumers often revert to using mental shortcuts that save on their time and effort. These are called **heuristics**. For example, a study by Hoyer found that consumers spent on average 13 seconds deciding what to purchase from a supermarket aisle. The same study also found that only 11 per cent of consumers examined two or more products when purchasing detergent. To make these decisions so quickly, people typically use very simple rules of thumb.

For example, when deciding what make or brand of product to buy, consumers may revert to using the so-called 'halo heuristic'. This simple rule is the assumption that, because a person or business is good at doing one thing, they will also be good at doing something else that may be completely unrelated. Therefore, if a consumer is happy with their experience of consuming a particular brand of a product, they may choose the same brand when deciding to purchase a different product they have never tried before. For example, if you are really happy with your Samsung TV, then you may choose another Samsung product when buying a laptop computer or smartphone for the first time. The halo heuristic generates brand loyalty and is something that companies recognise and strive to develop in their customers.

Consumers can be heavily influenced by the experience of a limited number of friends or relatives when choosing to buy a product. This is called the 'availability heuristic' and is explained in more detail in the next section.

Using heuristics often helps consumers make the best choices while also reducing the time and effort costs of carefully comparing each option. However, their use can sometimes lead to decisions that differ from rational choices in systematic and predictable ways.

Behavioural economics attempts to identify these heuristics and the systematic errors they sometimes cause. Understanding these mental shortcuts is important to those working in the advertising and marketing industry who want to know the most effective ways of influencing people's spending decisions.

Types of heuristic

There are several different types of heuristic that people use. These include the following:

Choice overload or the paradox of choice. When faced with numerous different choices, consumers may respond by using a very simple rule of thumb – avoid making a decision altogether. This results in two possible outcomes:

- Those consumers who have no prior experience of consuming the good fail to make any purchases, even though it would increase their utility.
- Those consumers who have consumed the good previously continue buying the same brand without attempting to search for other options that are better value for money. This leads to purchases with a lower consumer surplus than the alternatives.

A well-known experiment to test this idea of choice overload was conducted by Sheena Iyengar and Mark Lepper who set up a jam tasting stall in a grocery store. People were more likely to buy a jam when there were only six varieties available than when there were 24. This and other evidence on choice overload is discussed in more detail in Box 7.1.

The herding heuristic. Some consumers may use a quick decision rule of copying and imitating the actions of others. In other words, they are strongly influenced by what other people purchase. A fashion might catch on; people might grab an item in a sale because other people seem to be grabbing it as well; people might buy a particular share on the stock market because other people are buying it.

In some circumstances, the herding heuristic may be a good decision rule as other people have better information about the quality of the good or service. However, in some situations, other consumers may not have superior information. They start buying the good because many other people have. Sales soar and prices may be driven well above a level that reflects the utility people end up gaining.

Definitions

Bounded rationality When consumers have limited abilities to find and process the relevant information required to make the best decision, i.e. purchase the goods that generate the most consumer surplus.

Heuristic A mental shortcut or rule of thumb that people use when trying to make complicated choices. They reduce the computational and/or research effort required but sometimes lead to systematic errors.

The anchoring heuristic. This is a tendency for consumers to be overly influenced by the first piece of information they see, even if it is unrelated to the decision. In one famous piece of research by Tversky and Kahneman[3] the participants in an experiment first spun a wheel that randomly generated a number between 0 and 100. They were then asked how many African countries were in the UN. The participants

[3]A. Tversky and D. Kahneman, 'Judgment under uncertainty: Heuristics and Biases', *Science*, Vol 185 (1974), pp. 1124–31.

BOX 7.1   CHOICE OVERLOAD

Is more choice always a good thing for consumers?

According to standard economic theory, more choice is a good thing for the consumer. It helps people find products and services that increase and maximise their utility. However, results from a well-known field experiment conducted by Sheena Iyengar and Mark Lepper[1] suggest that, in some circumstances, too much choice might hamper effective decision making.

To test this idea, the researchers set up a jam tasting stall in a supermarket in California: i.e. in an environment where consumers typically make choices. Every few hours, they switched the number of different varieties on the stall from 6 to 24 and back again. No popular flavours such as strawberry were ever included. As shoppers walked by, they were invited to sample the different jams. After a visit, shoppers were given a $1 discount voucher towards the purchase of any of the jams they had tasted. The experiment was designed so that the usage of these vouchers could be tracked to see if the shoppers who visited the stall when there were 24 varieties of jam were more likely to use their coupons than when there were 6 and *vice versa*. The study produced the following results:

- Shoppers were more likely to visit the stall and taste the jams when 24 varieties were displayed. This suggests that consumers initially find the thought of more choice appealing.
- The average number of different jams tasted remained the same, no matter how many varieties were displayed. Interestingly, no consumers tried more than two different flavours.
- Approximately 30 per cent of the shoppers who visited the stall when there were 6 different varieties of jam used the vouchers as opposed to just 3 per cent who visited when there were 24.

The same authors also carried out a laboratory experiment (i.e. in an artificial classroom environment rather than a grocery store). The participants were split into different groups. Those in one group had to sample chocolate from a choice of 6 different varieties, while those in another group had to sample chocolate from a choice of 30 different varieties. At the end of the experiment, the participants could either accept $5 in cash or $5 worth of chocolates from the brands they had tasted. Only the choices of those who stated they both enjoyed the chocolate and had never tried the brand before were analysed. The researchers found that 48 per cent of those in the 6-variety group opted for the $5 box of chocolates instead

of the cash, while the figure for the 30-variety group was only 12 per cent.

The results from both the field and laboratory experiments suggest that people find effective decision making more difficult when confronted with more choices. In these situations, they often appear to use a simple rule of thumb – do not make a choice at all. Survey evidence also suggests that consumers are less satisfied with their choices when faced with numerous options as opposed to just a few.

Although the study by Iyengar and Lepper is very famous, results from other research on choice overload are mixed. For example, when Scheibehenne, *et al.*.[2] repeated the same jam and chocolate experiments, they did not generate the same results. More choice did not hinder the ability of consumers to make effective choices. They also reviewed the data from 50 different experiments and found large differences between the results. On average, the negative impact of choice overload was very small.

Other research[3] has found that the chances of choice overload is far greater in particular circumstances. It is more likely when:

- consumers do not know very much about the product or service: i.e. they have limited expertise or have not purchased it before;
- the choice has to be made quickly;
- consumers face a choice of 5 items with 20 different characteristics than a choice of 20 items that each has just a couple of attributes.

If choice overload does exist, it will be interesting to see if researchers can find more evidence on what makes it more likely to occur and what the implications are for businesses.

1. Can you think of any limitations with the jam tasting field experiment?
2. Discuss three different ways of trying to measure the extent of choice overload.
3. On what basis would you choose between different providers of internet, phone and TV services?

Devise a survey to establish the basis on which consumers make choices and whether more choice encourages people to purchase more.

[1] Sheena S. Iyengar and Mark R. Lepper, 'When choice is demotivating: can one desire too much of a good thing?', *Journal of Personality and Social Psychology*, 79, No. 6 (2000), pp.995–1006.

[2] Benjamin Scheibehenne, Rainer Greifeneder and Peter M. Todd, 'Can there ever be too many options? A meta-analytic review of choice overload', *Journal of Consumer Research*, 37 (October 2010), pp. 409–25.

[3] Alexander Chernev, Ulf Böckenholt and Joseph Goodman, 'Choice overload: A conceptual review and meta-analysis' *Journal of Consumer Psychology*, 25, No. 2 (2015), pp. 333–58.

seemed to be influenced by this irrelevant random number. Those whose spin resulted in a bigger number answered with a larger number of countries than those whose spin produced a lower number.

The availability heuristic. When assessing the likely size of any uncertain benefits or costs, consumers disproportionately weight single events that are easy to imagine or retrieve from memory. One example of the availability heuristic is the tendency for people to overweight the single experience of a friend or relative and underweight the experience of a large number of customers they have never met. For example, assume that you are thinking of buying a particular laptop and are trying to determine its reliability. A friend has recently purchased the same model and has had to send it back to the manufacturer for costly repairs. This may lead you to underestimate the reliability of this particular model and overestimate the chances of it breaking down. When making the probability assessment, you underweight the information from a survey based on the experience of 10 000 users of the same laptop.

Gamblers, or Monte Carlo, fallacy. This is the false belief that past outcomes have an impact on the likelihood of the next outcome occurring when, in reality, they are independent of one another. For example, assume a coin is tossed on four consecutive occasions and comes up heads each time. You may mistakenly believe that a tail is more likely on the next toss.

Customers in a casino may suffer from this bias. If a ball on a roulette table came up black five times in a row, a number of gamblers may bet on red the next time around believing that it is more likely. This famously happened in Monte Carlo in 1913 when the ball landed on a black space 26 times in a row. Investors may also feel that the stock market must fall if it has reached record high levels for several consecutive days.

> **Pause for thought**
>
> *How good are you at making probabilistic judgements? Here is an interesting example. Suppose that one out of a hundred people in the population has a genetic medical condition. There is a test for this medical condition that is 99 per cent accurate. This means that, if a person has the condition, the test returns a positive test with a 99 per cent probability; and, if a person does not have the condition, it returns a negative result with a 99 per cent probability. If a person's test comes back positive (and you know nothing else about this person), what is the probability that s/he has the medical condition?*

7.2 FRAMING AND THE REFERENCE POINT FOR DECISIONS

Reference dependent preferences – coding outcomes as losses and gains

In standard economic theory, it is assumed that people judge decisions by incorporating benefits and costs into their total income or wealth.[4] For example, imagine that your assets and income give you total current wealth of £100 000. You are now offered a 50:50 gamble of gaining £11 or losing £10. Standard economic theory predicts that you will assess the situation as a 50:50 gamble of having £100 011 or £99 990 of total wealth. When judged in this way, we would expect many people to accept moderate stake gambles such as these.

Reference dependent preferences suggest that people judge decisions differently from this. Instead of incorporating any benefits and costs of a decision into their total wealth, they assess them according to some reference point.

The simplest example of a reference point is a person's current income and wealth. If this were applied to the previous example, then the gamble would be coded as a 50:50 chance of gaining £11 or losing £10. The pay-offs would not be incorporated into total wealth. This is known as *decision isolation.*

The reference point used by people to judge an outcome as a gain or a loss could also be influenced by a range of factors other than the direct effect on their current wealth/income. For example, it might be influenced by the following:

■ *Their expectations.* Imagine that Dean and Jon are both students on an economics course. They have both exerted the same level of effort writing an assessed essay and each receives a mark of 60 per cent. Will they both be equally happy? If Dean expected to get 70 per cent, then this might influence his reference point. He might code the result as a 10 percentage point loss and feel very unhappy. If Jon expected to get a mark of 50 per cent, he might code the result as a gain of 10 percentage points and feel much happier. A similar argument could be made if a worker was expecting to receive a real wage increase of 3 per cent but only received one of 2 per cent.

■ *By making comparisons with others.* If customers obtain a 10 per cent discount on a product, initially they may feel happy and code the outcome as a gain. However, if, subsequently, they find out other customers obtained a 20 per cent discount on the same product, this might

> **Definition**
>
> **Reference dependent preferences** Where people value (or 'code') outcomes as either gains or losses in relation to a reference point.

---

[4]Rational consumers should incorporate any costs and benefits into their total expected lifetime wealth. If, for example, a consumer expected to inherit a large amount of money in the future, we would expect it to influence that person's decisions today.

change their reference point and they might begin to code the outcome as a loss.

■ *Adjusting slowly to a changed income/asset position.* Contestants on the game show, *Who Wants to be a Millionaire?*, who have already won £16 000, may still take a 50:50 gamble of winning another £16 000 (i.e. having a total prize of £32 000) or losing £15 000 (i.e. having a total prize of £1000). When asked why they took the gamble, some participants explain that, even if they lose, they will still have £1000 more than before they played the game. Comments such as these suggest that the contestant's reference point while playing the game remains at their income level *before* playing the game: i.e. every pay-off is coded as a gain. However, as they play the game, their income/asset position is changing. When they take the gamble, they have already won £16 000. If their perception of their income position had fully adjusted, the reference income level would include the £16 000 and the chances of losing would be coded as a £15 000 loss not a £1000 gain.

Loss aversion

The theory of reference dependent preferences leads to another important result: that of *loss aversion*. Outcomes coded as losses are disliked far more than the pleasure received from an equivalent sized gain.

We saw in Chapter 6 how the standard economic theory of diminishing marginal utility of income predicts that people dislike losses more than gains. However, if an outcome is coded as a loss in relation to a reference point, the dislike of this loss seems to be even greater than that predicted by conventional theory. Some estimates suggest that the dislike of a financial loss is at least twice as big as the pleasure associated with an equivalent gain. This would produce a discrete kink or change in the slope of the utility function at the reference point.

The theory of loss aversion is a potential explanation for the *endowment effect*, sometimes known as *divestiture aversion*. This is where people ascribe more value to things when they own them than when they are merely considering purchasing or acquiring them. One explanation for this difference is that ownership of a good influences a person's reference point. If a good is not already owned, its purchase by the consumer is coded as a gain. Once purchased, its

---

Definitions

Loss aversion Where a loss is disliked far more than the pleasure associated from an equivalent sized gain. This dislike of losses is far greater than that predicted by standard economic theory.

Endowment effect (or **divestiture aversion**) The hypothesis that people ascribe more value to things when they own them than when they are merely considering purchasing or acquiring them – in other words, when the reference point is one of ownership rather than non-ownership.

BOX 7.2 THE ENDOWMENT EFFECT

An example of loss aversion and its implications for framing

Consider the following two slightly different situations for the same person, Helen: (a) she is thinking of buying a good such as a coffee mug; (b) she has already purchased it and now owns it. In each case, we can think of a way of measuring her valuation of that good.

In the first case, it could be measured as the maximum amount she is willing to pay for the mug. This is known as her willingness to pay (WTP). In the second case, it could be measured as the minimum amount she needs to be offered for her to be willing to sell it to someone else. This is known as her willingness to accept (WTA).

Apart from a few exceptions, traditional economic theory predicts that ownership of a product should have no impact on peoples' valuation of that product. Therefore, their WTP for the product should be equal to their WTA for the same product.

The endowment effect: when the WTA is greater than WTP

In a famous study, Kahneman, Knetsch and Thaler[1] carried out a series of experiments with students on a Law and Economics degree at Cornell University. They were randomly divided into two equal-sized groups. Students in one group were each given a coffee mug and told that they could sell it if they wished. They were asked for their WTA. Students in the other group could each examine the mugs and make an offer to buy one. They were asked their WTP. The authors found that the median WTA of the students who were given the mugs was $5.25 whereas the median WTP in the other group was only $2.25.

As the students had been allocated randomly into the two groups, standard theory predicts that WTP should be equal to WTA. However, the evidence suggests that those who were given ownership of the mugs at the start of the experiment valued them far more than those who were not.

A similar exercise was carried out with pens. In this experiment, the median WTP remained constant at $1.25, while the median WTA varied between $1.75 and $2.50. Once again, ownership seemed to have an impact on valuation.

One explanation for these results is that ownership of a good influences a person's reference point. Those who do not already own the good perceive (or 'code') its purchase as a *gain* in utility. However, once they have purchased a good, its ownership is included in their reference point. Selling the good would be coded as a *loss*.

---

[1] Daniel Kahneman, Jack L. Knetsch and Richard H. Thaler, 'Experimental Tests of the Endowment Effect and the Coase Theorem', *Journal of Political Economy*, 98(6) (1990), pp. 1325–48.

ownership is included in the consumer's reference point. Selling the good would now be coded as a loss. Box 7.2 examines the endowment effect in more detail.

The theory of loss aversion may also help to explain why consumers seem to be so risk averse for small-stake gambles. In particular, they appear to be willing to buy very highly priced insurance policies for products they have purchased, such as mobile handsets.

Framing

Traditional economic theory predicts that different ways of presenting or framing the same choice to consumers should have no impact on the decisions they make. However, because of processing biases and loss aversion there is lots of evidence that it does.

Businesses might be able to take advantage of this by presenting products in ways that have a positive impact on their sales. Some potential examples of how this might be done are discussed in this section.

Firms might be able to take advantage of the anchoring heuristic by placing irrelevant limits on the quantity of a

good consumers can purchase. For example, in a field experiment conducted by Wansink, Kent and Hoch[5] people purchased 3.3 cans of soup on average from a grocery store. However, when the researchers placed a sign stating 'There is a limit of 12 per person', the average number of cans purchased increased to 7. The first piece of information appears to have influenced their decisions, even though it was irrelevant.

Another example is *partitioned* or *drip pricing*. This is a strategy where, instead of presenting one total combined price for a product, the seller splits the price into one or more components. For example, an airline might highlight the fare, but charge you separately for luggage or even to sit together. There is evidence that consumers anchor their decision to the headline price and fail to adjust to other elements of the price such as delivery costs. This is discussed in more detail in Box 13.1 in Chapter 13.

The availability heuristic suggests that a vivid and memorable story about one very happy customer may have a greater impact on subsequent sales than using simple statistics about the positive experiences of thousands of customers.

The framing of an advert or promotion may also influence consumers' reference points and hence how they code

---

[5]Brian Wansink, Robert J. Kent and Stephen J. Hoch, 'An anchoring and adjustment model of purchase quantity decisions', *Journal of Marketing Research*, Vol. 35 (February 1998), pp. 71–81.

> ### Definition
>
> **Framing** Consumption decisions are influenced by the way that costs and benefits are presented.

Some implications of the endowment effect for marketing

What implications does the endowment effect have for the way a firm presents and markets its products? Can it take advantage of consumers' loss aversion to boost its sales? The following are some possible tactics:

- *Offering a free trial period for the good or service.* Using a product increasingly makes consumers feel that they already own it. This changes their reference point so that not buying the good, when the trial period ends, feels like a loss. This makes it more likely that they will purchase the good.

- *Offering consumers a 30-day return period.* This may seem like a potentially costly policy for the firm but can have a similar impact to the free trial. The returns policy encourages some consumers, who are uncertain about a particular purchase, to buy the product. Once they have purchased the product, the endowment effect suggests they will come to value it more highly. This makes it less likely that they will return the product before the 30-day period ends.

- *Encouraging consumers to imagine themselves already owning and using the product.* This could be done with the

careful use of language in promotions: i.e. stressing what the customer 'will miss out on' rather than what they will gain. Another method is for the firm to create an advertisement that clearly shows someone using the product. Evidence suggests that watching another person use a product encourages a feeling of ownership among consumers.

1. *What explanations other than the endowment effect could help to explain any differences between a buyer's WTP and a seller's WTA?*

2. *Cafés at the University of Winchester offered customers a 25p discount off the advertised price of hot drinks if they used a reusable cup. In 2017, they changed this policy by reducing the price of all hot drinks by 25p. There was an additional charge of 25p for those customers who used a non-reusable cup. Using the concept of loss aversion, do think this new policy will have a stronger impact than the previous one?*

Investigate adverts for a variety of products in different media. To what extent to they provide evidence that the concept of loss aversion is being used in their design?

a purchase. Take the following two ways that the sale of the same good can be framed:

- 'If you purchase this more energy efficient product you will gain £200 per year in lower energy costs.'
- 'If you don't purchase this more energy efficient product you are wasting £200 per year in higher energy costs.'

The first presentation may lead to people perceiving the £200 as a potential gain; the reference point is the current situation before the choice of whether to purchase the good is made. The second presentation is designed to move the reference point to having purchased the good. The word 'wasting' makes it more likely that the consumer will perceive not buying the good as loss.

Other advertisements that have a similar impact are those that stress what consumers 'will miss out on' if they do not purchase the good as opposed to what they gain if they do. If consumers are much more sensitive to a potential loss than

a forgone gain, then presenting the sale of a good in this manner is likely to lead to more sales.

Some other ways of presenting information to take advantage of consumers' loss aversion and boost sales are discussed in Box 7.2.

Present bias and self-control issues

The costs and benefits of purchasing some goods occur in different time periods. If consumers choose to:

> **Pause for thought**
>
> *According to rational choice theory, the money you've already spent – known as 'sunk costs' (see page 147) should be excluded from decision making. However, there is considerable evidence that it does affect consumer behaviour. Using loss aversion, can you explain why this might be the case?*

BOX 7.3   **THE BEST MADE PLANS**

Present bias

Standard economic theory predicts that consumers will behave in a time consistent manner. However, in the real world, often we observe people behaving in a time *inconsistent* way. They plan to do things such as changing their energy supplier, bank account, mobile phone contract and car insurance. They also plan to drink less alcohol, eat more healthily and quit smoking. Unfortunately, they never seem to get around to doing most of these things. When the moment arrives, often they procrastinate and decide to put it off until later.

Take the example of exercise. On Sunday night, Dean is considering whether to go down the gym after work on Monday evening. Although the costs (the exertion of exercising on Monday) occur sooner than the benefits (long-term improvements to his health), he still plans to go. The key point is that, from his point on Sunday, all of these costs and benefits are in the future.

The problem occurs for Dean when Monday evening finally arrives. The costs of going to the gym are now immediate. If he suffers from present bias, he will now weight these immediate costs far more heavily than the future benefits. He changes his mind and watches football on the TV while planning to go to the gym on Tuesday evening instead. From his point of view, on Monday evening, all the costs and benefits of going on Tuesday are once again in the future.

Unfortunately, when Tuesday arrives, the same thing happens again. As soon as the costs become immediate, he weights them much more heavily and decides once more to stay in and watch TV while planning to go on Wednesday evening instead. This process continues with Dean continually planning to go to the gym but never quite making it.

This inability to make accurate predictions of their future behaviour means that present-biased consumers may choose

gym membership contracts that do not maximise their utility. To investigate this possibility, DellaVigna and Malmendier (2006)[1] analysed data from three health clubs in the USA where consumers could choose between a $70 monthly fee with no payment per visit or $10 per visit with no monthly fee. Those consumers who opted for the monthly fee went on average 4.3 times per month. This works out to a price of around $17 per visit. They could have saved around $30 per month by opting for the pay-as-you-go option. The authors found that 80 per cent of those who chose the monthly membership option ended up paying more per visit.

Why did so many consumers make such a poor choice? When asked how often they would visit the gym, on average, consumers forecast they would go 9.5 times per month. If they stuck to their plans, the monthly membership would have been the best option. Unfortunately, because of present bias, consumers have problems anticipating their future behaviour.

The impact of automatic renewal

The tendency to procrastinate because of present bias means that automatic renewal of a deal can have a significant impact on consumer choice. Many insurance policies, mobile phone contracts, TV/Internet contracts and energy supply policies are automatically renewed when an existing deal expires. What happens if the new terms are significantly worse than the initial deal? Do consumers plan to search around for an alternative supplier but never get around to it? In this case,

---

[1] Stefano DellaVigna and Ulrike Malmendier, 'Paying Not to Go to the Gym', *American Economic Review*, Vol. 96, No. 3 (June 2006).

[2] www.fca.org.uk/firms/transparency-insurance-renewals.

- use a credit card to buy a good, the benefits are immediate, whereas the bill does not have to be paid until the future;
- buy a chocolate muffin instead of a same-priced piece of fruit, the nicer flavour from eating the muffin is immediate, whereas the negative health impacts occur in the future;
- exercise at the gym rather than play a computer game, the effort costs of exercising are immediate, whereas the health benefits occur in the future

Evidence suggests that the majority of people tend to be impatient most of the time. Traditional models of economic behaviour capture this idea but also predict something else: if someone plans to do something at some point in the future, they will do so when the time arrives. For example, if a consumer plans to shop around for a new energy supplier or a new mobile phone contract when their current deal expires, they indeed do so. If they plan to start a diet tomorrow, they do so when tomorrow arrives. This is called *time consistency*.

The only reason time-consistent people would change their mind is if new information became known about the relative size of the costs and benefits of their decisions. For example, you plan to shop around for a new energy supplier when your current deal expires but, when it actually does expire, the current supplier offers a much better deal than you anticipated. This is still time consistent behaviour, as the only reason you changed your mind is that information has changed. The opportunity cost of not switching supplier is much smaller than you thought it was going to be before the current deal expired.

> ### Definitions
>
> **Time consistency** Where a person's preferences remain the same over time. If they plan to do something in the future, such as change energy supplier, they do so when the time arrives.

automatic renewal could be an effective way for firms to increase their profits.

In April 2017, the Financial Conduct Authority in the UK issued new regulations[2] on how the details in insurance renewal notices had to be presented to customers to increase the likelihood of them shopping around. Specifically, it required insurers to:

- disclose last year's premium at each renewal, so that it can be compared easily to the new premium offered;
- encourage consumers to check their cover and shop around for the best deal at each renewal;
- identify consumers who have renewed four, or more, consecutive times, and give these consumers an additional prescribed message encouraging them to shop around. This includes consumers who renew after 1 April 2017, who may have renewed four or more times already before these rules come into force.

In the study conducted by DellaVigna and Malmendier, the monthly gym contract was renewed automatically unless customers informed the management of their intention to cancel the membership. The researchers found that, on average, the gap between the last date a person attended the gym and cancelled the contract was 2.31 full months! This meant that people wasted over $180 paying for a service they did not use. Twenty per cent delayed by at least four months!

Alternative contracts

Is it possible for firms to make profits only by designing contracts that take advantage of our self-control problems? What

happens if some consumers are aware that their present bias is costing them money? Could some businesses make profits by[3] helping us to deal with our irrational manner?

In 2010, two Harvard graduates set up a business, Gym-Pact, which bought group gym memberships from a number of existing gyms. Gym-Pact then sold on these memberships; but, rather than a regular deal, they offered 'motivational' contracts to individuals, who pay more if they miss their regular workouts. The pair came up with this idea after studying behavioural economics as part of their degree; they learnt that people react more strongly to immediate certainties than to future possibilities.

This business model turned out to be short-lived. However, the founders did not give up on the principle. By 2014, Gym-Pact had become Pact, a business that brought together members who committed to working out, to logging their food intake and to eating vegetables. Those who succeeded were rewarded with small cash sums, of up to £5 per day. Those who failed were charged for their lack of willpower. Pact made money as the intermediary. However, in 2017, it was forced to close, with money owed to those who had stuck to their commitments.

1. To what extent will the new FCA regulations about how insurance renewal notices are presented to customers encourage people to shop around?
2. Assume you have present bias but are fully aware of the inconsistent nature of your preferences. What actions could you take to make sure you carry out your planned decisions?

Search for motivational apps and consider the extent that they are likely to tackle the problem of present bias.

---

[3] Stefano DellaVigna and Ulrike Malmendier, 'Paying Not to Go to the Gym', *American Economic Review*, Vol. 96, No. 3 (June 2006), pp. 694–719.

Time consistency seems to predict and explain behaviour reasonably well when all the costs and benefits of a decision occur in the future. A consumer's plan of action often remains the same with the passage of time as long as none of the cost and benefits occurs immediately. For example, at 9.00 a.m. today you may plan to eat a healthy lunch tomorrow: i.e. you plan to eat a piece of fruit instead of a chocolate muffin. The plan remains the same throughout today and tomorrow morning. However, when lunchtime finally arrives, you eat the chocolate muffin instead. What has changed? When lunchtime finally arrives, the costs of not eating the chocolate muffin are now immediate – missing out on the greater enjoyment – but the health benefits are still in the future. Once the time arrives to experience the costs or benefits of a decision, many people have a tendency to change their minds. They act in a time inconsistent manner and suffer from self-control problems.

Behavioural economists refer to this as *present bias* (see Box 7.3). If people are impatient, they weight costs and benefits that occur sooner more heavily than those that occur later.

However, present bias is different from simple impatience. The theory predicts that, once any of the costs and benefits are immediate, the relative weighting of these pay-offs becomes much greater. In the previous example, the costs of not eating the chocolate muffin appear to be much greater when it is in front of a consumer! This theory predicts that a consumer can appear both patient when making a decision (i.e. planning to eat healthily when all the costs and benefits occur in the future) and very impatient when making the same decision (i.e. eating unhealthily now).

Read and van Leeuwen[6] (1998) tested this idea by conducting a field experiment. They approached over 200 employees in their normal place of work and informed them they would return a week later to give away a selection of free snacks. The employees simply had to choose in advance whether they wanted a healthy snack (e.g. a piece of fruit) or an unhealthy snack (e.g. a chocolate bar or a packet of crisps). Seventy-four per cent chose the healthy option.

When the researchers returned a week later with the snacks, the employees were asked for their decision again. However, this was now for immediate consumption and they did not have to stick with the same decision they had made the week before. Seventy per cent of the employees now opted for the unhealthy snack.

Present bias helps to explain why many people have difficulty in sticking to commitments. Think of how many people make and then very quickly break New Year's resolutions. Indeed, some behavioural economists have actually created a website called StickK[7] that enables people to make their own commitment contracts to help them to stick to their plans.

> **Pause for thought**
>
> *Can you think of any studying decisions where students often change their mind with the passage of time once the costs or benefits become immediate?*

> **Definition**
>
> **Present bias** Where the relative weight people place on immediate costs and benefits versus those that occur in the future is far greater than predicted by standard economic theory. This leads to time inconsistent behaviour.

---

[6]Daniel Read and Barbara van Leeuwen, 'Predicting Hunger: The Effects of Appetite and Delay on Choice', *Organizational Behavior and Human Decision Processes,* Vol. 76, No. 2 (November 1998).

[7]www.stickk.com/.

7.3 CARING ABOUT THE PAY-OFFS TO OTHERS

In many standard economic theories it is assumed that people are motivated only by pay-offs to themselves. They do not value any pay-offs to others. However, casual observation and evidence from experiments suggests that this is not true. People tip waiters, give to charity and undertake voluntary work. Participants in laboratory experiments reward those that are perceived to have acted fairly while punishing those who have not – see Box 7.4 for more detail. Many consumers have what behavioural economists call *other regarding preferences* and this has significant economic consequences in market transactions.

Altruism, envy and reciprocity

Behavioural economists have tried to develop utility functions that capture the idea that consumers care about the pay-offs to other people as well as themselves.

Having *altruistic* preferences in economics means that you value the pay-offs to others as well as to yourself

---

> **Definitions**
>
> **Altruism (in economics)** Positively valuing the pay-offs to others.

positively. If this relative weighting of the welfare of others is strong enough, then you may be willing to increase their income at personal cost to yourself as it makes you feel happier. Altruism is a type of unconditional kindness as people do not have to be nice to you for you to value their welfare.

Having *spiteful* or *envious* preferences is the opposite of having altruistic preferences. You now value the pay-offs to others negatively and be might be willing to take costly actions to *reduce* their income.

Evidence from experiments suggests that individuals can display both altruistic and spiteful behaviour. Often, they are willing to increase the pay-offs to others at a personal cost to themselves in some situations while reducing the pay-offs to others at a personal cost to themselves in other situations.

To capture these ideas, behavioural economists have developed a number of models of **reciprocity**. Some of these suggest that people may experience an increase in own utility by taking costly actions to (a) increase the income of those who have acted fairly and (b) reduce the incomes of those who have acted unfairly. This is different from tit-for-tat strategies in standard economic theory (see page 219) where people or firms are willing to reward or punish people in a repeated setting in an attempt to increase their own personal pay-off in the long run.

Reciprocity can have implications for firms' pricing strategies. For example, research by Kahneman, Knetch and Thaler[8] found that many consumers thought it was unfair for firms to increase their prices in response to an increase in

> ## Definitions
>
> **Envy (in economics)** Negatively valuing the pay-offs to others.
>
> **Reciprocity (in economics)** Where people's preferences depend on the kind or unkind behaviour of others.

---

[8]Daniel Kahneman, Jack L. Knetch and Richard H. Thaler, 'Fairness as a constraint on profit seeking: Entitlements in the market' *American Economic Review*, Vol. 76(4) (September 1986).

| BOX 7.4 | A SIMPLE EXPERIMENT TO TEST FOR SOCIAL PREFERENCES |

Responding to fair and unfair offers

Imagine taking part in the following laboratory experiment.

You have been randomly assigned to be a *proposer*. This is the initial decision maker in the game. You will be matched with a *responder* – a participant who must respond to the decision you make. Your identity and that of the responder will remain anonymous; you will never know who each other is.

The person in charge of the experiment (the 'experimenter') gives you £20 and asks you to suggest a way of dividing this sum of money between yourself and the responder. Your proposal is communicated by the experimenter (usually online) to the responder.

The responder then has one simple decision to make – either accept or reject the offer. If the responder accepts the offer, the money is divided in the way you propose. If the responder rejects the offer, then you both earn zero and the £20 is returned to the experimenter. A proposer only plays with the same responder on one occasion. There is no opportunity for reputation building by the responder, such as rejecting offers in the hope of influencing future behaviour.

What share of the £20 would you offer to the responder? Would you suggest a 50:50 split or an offer where you keep a larger or smaller share of the money? You could make an offer of 1p and if accepted you would make £19.99.

Now imagine that you have been randomly assigned to be the responder in the game. Would you accept or reject an offer of 1p, £1, £5, or £10? What is the minimum-sized offer you would accept?

The predictions of standard theory

What does standard economic theory predict should happen in the game? If the proposer (a) only cares about their own monetary pay-off and (b) knows the responder feels the same, then they should offer 1p. The responder will accept the offer as 1p is better than nothing and the proposer gets to keep £19.99.

The results of experiments: demonstrating altruism and spite

This game has been played on numerous occasions in many different countries and for different amounts of money. The results are consistent and are completely at odds with the predictions of standard theory. The majority of proposers offer between 40 and 50 per cent of the money, demonstrating a degree of altruism.

Those that do make lower offers find they are rejected frequently. For example, around half of any offers below 20 per cent are declined.

How can these results be explained? It seems that offers of less than 40 per cent are considered unfair by many responders. They decline these offers in order to punish the proposers. The key point about this punishment is that it is costly to the responder. If they decline an offer of 20 per cent in the above game, they are, effectively, sacrificing £4 of potential earnings. As the game is played only once, the punishment cannot be used to create a reputation and enhance the responders' future earnings. Therefore, they appear to be demonstrating social preferences.

1. *In what circumstances would a proposer who only cares about their own monetary pay-offs make an offer of £10 in the above game?*
2. *What are the limitations of using the results from these games to help explain real world behaviour?*

Find out about some other laboratory experiments conducted by economists to test for social preferences. Summarise some of the key findings.

demand for the good. Many consumers indicated that they would take costly action to punish the firm in these circumstances by searching and switching to an alternative supplier. Interestingly, consumers thought it was fair for firms to pass on any increase in costs in the form of higher prices.

Consumers may have particular fairness concerns about the supply conditions of the goods and services that they purchase. They may be willing to pay more for a good that is produced in an environmentally friendly manner and/or where the workers are well treated. An increasing number of firms now engage in corporate social responsibility (CSR) activities. CSR is discussed in more detail in Chapter 20 (see pages 382–7).

> ## Pause for thought
>
> *Can you think of any examples of where people with selfish preferences would engage in costly reward or punishment activities?*

7.4 GOVERNMENT POLICY TO INFLUENCE BEHAVIOUR

Governments, in designing policy, normally will attempt to change people's behaviour. They might want to encourage people to work harder, to save more, to recycle rubbish, to use their cars less, to eat more healthily, and so on. If the policy is to be successful, it is vital for the policy measures to contain appropriate incentives: whether it be a tax rise, a grant or subsidy, a new law or regulation, an advertising campaign or direct help.

But, whether the incentives are appropriate, depends on how people will respond to them and, to know that, the policymakers will need to understand people's behaviour. This is where behavioural economics comes in. People might respond as rational maximisers; but they might not. It is thus important to understand how context affects behaviour and adjust policy incentives appropriately.

Nudging people

One observation of behavioural economists is that people make many decisions out of habit. They use simple heuristics, such as: 'I'll buy the more expensive item because it's bound to be better'; or 'I'll buy this item because it's on offer'; or 'I always take the car to work, so I don't need to consider alternatives'; or 'Other people are buying this, so it must be worth having'.

Given people behave like this, how might they be persuaded to change their behaviour? Governments might want to know this. Are there 'nudges' that will encourage people to act in their own self-interest: e.g. stop smoking, take more exercise or eat more healthy food? Will these 'nudges' impose a cost on those people who are acting in a rational manner?

Opting in versus opting out

An interesting example concerns 'opting in' versus 'opting out'. In some countries, with organ donor cards, or many company pension schemes or charitable giving, people have to opt in. In other words, they have to make the decision to take part. Many, as a result, do not, partly because they never seem to find the time to do so, even though they might quite like to. With the busy lives people lead, it is too easy to think,

'Yes, I'll do that some time', but never actually get round to doing it: i.e. they have present bias.

With an 'opt out' system, people are signed up automatically to the scheme, but can freely choose to opt out. Thus it would be assumed that organs from people killed in an accident who had not opted out could be used for transplants. If you did not want your organs to be used, you would have to join a register. It could be the same with charitable giving. Some firms add a small charitable contribution to the price of their products (e.g. airline tickets or utility bills), unless people opt out.

Similarly, under UK pension arrangements introduced from 2012, firms automatically deduct pension contributions from employees' wages unless they opt out of the scheme.

> Opt-in [pension] schemes have participation rates of around 60 per cent, while otherwise identical opt-out funds retain between 90 and 95 per cent of employees. It is no wonder that Adair Turner, in his report on pensions, urged legislation to push pension schemes to an opt-in default position and that policy is moving in this direction.[9]

This type of policy can improve the welfare of those who make systematic mistakes (i.e. suffer from present bias) while imposing very limited harm on those who act in a time consistent manner. If it is in the interests of someone to opt out of the scheme, they can easily do so. Policies such as these are an example of what behavioural economists call 'soft paternalism'.

The UK Behavioural Insights Team

The UK Coalition Government (2010–15) established the Behavioural Insights Team (BIT)[10] (also unofficially known as the Nudge Unit) in the Cabinet Office in 2010. BIT was

---

[9]Richard Reeves, 'Why a nudge from the state beats a slap' *Observer* (20 July 2008).

[10]www.behaviouralinsights.co.uk/.

partially privatised in 2014 and is now equally owned by the UK Government, the innovation charity Nesta and the Teams' employees.

A major objective of this team is to use ideas from behavioural economics to design policies that enable people to make better choices for themselves. However, it is not simply a behavioural economics unit. BIT uses research findings from a number of different subject areas such as psychology and marketing science to inform its policy recommendations. Indeed, Richard Thaler has argued that some of its initiatives do not always include that much economics.

BIT uses a process to encourage changes in behaviour, which has the acronym EAST. The principles of EAST are:

- Make it *Easy* for people to change their behaviour by requiring them to make minimum effort and by making the changes simple to understand and execute. This was the reasoning behind the adoption of automatic enrolment in pension schemes for employees of large companies, where people had to opt out of they did not want to participate. Participation rates rose from 61 to 83 per cent.
- Make it *Attractive* for people to change their behaviour, or unattractive for them not to, by giving incentives or improving the design of a product or activity. 'When letters to non-payers of car tax included a picture of the offending vehicle, payment rates rose from 40 to 49 per cent.'
- Make it *Social,* by showing other people behaving in the desirable way or encouraging people to make commitments to others. When people were informed by HMRC that most people pay their taxes on time, payment rates increased by as much as 5 percentage points.
- Make it *Timely* by prompting people at a time when they are likely to be the most receptive and by considering the direct costs and benefits of acting at the relevant moment in time. For example, sending text messages just before a payment is due or just before a person has to submit a form increases the response rate.

For government, nudging people to behave in ways that accord with government objectives can be both low-cost and effective.

Pause for thought

1. *How might you nudge members of a student household to be more economical in the use of electricity?*
2. *How could the government nudge people to stop dropping litter?*

SUMMARY

1a Traditional economics is based on the premise that consumers act rationally, weighing up the costs and benefits of the choices open to them. Behavioural economics acknowledges that real-world decisions do not always appear rational; it seeks to understand and explain what economic agents actually do.

1b Behavioural insights can be based on laboratory experiments, field experiments or using existing data on behaviour.

1c People's ability to make rational decisions is bounded by limited information and time. Thus people resort to using heuristics – rules of thumb. Types of heuristics include: avoiding making decisions altogether when faced with too much choice, copying and imitating the actions of others, basing decisions on easily available information, believing that past outcomes have an impact on the current situation.

1d Sometimes people have too much choice – they suffer from choice overload. This may discourage them from buying.

2a Seemingly irrational behaviour may arise from the choice of reference point for decision taking. The reference point used by people to judge an outcome as a gain or a loss can be influenced by a range of factors, including their expectations, comparisons with others and adjusting slowly to new information.

2b People who are loss averse may value things more highly when they own them than when they are considering buying them (the endowment effect) or when the costs or benefits are immediate. This reference dependent loss aversion may result in people giving additional weight to loss than would occur simply from the diminishing marginal utility of income.

2c The choices people make may also depend on how these choices are framed – the way in which they are presented or are perceived. The careful framing of an advert or promotion may influence consumers' reference points and hence how they code a purchase.

2d People may give additional weight to immediate benefits or costs. This is called 'present bias' and can lead to time-inconsistent behaviour, with people changing their mind and not acting in accordance with previous plans.

3 Apparently irrational behaviour may also be the result of taking other people into account. Altruism and spite are two emotions affecting choice here.

4a Governments, in devising policy, increasingly are looking at ways to influence people's behaviour by devising appropriate incentives. Behavioural economics provides useful insights here.

4b People may be able to be 'nudged' into behaving in certain ways. For example, moving from an opting in to an opting out system for schemes such as pensions, organ donation or charitable giving may encourage much greater participation rates.

4c The UK Behavioural Insights Team uses ideas from behavioural economics to design policies to nudge people into making better choices for themselves.

REVIEW QUESTIONS

1 How does behavioural economics differ from standard economic theory?

2 Give some examples of mental shortcuts/heuristics that you use when choosing a product or service. Why do you use them?

3 What is the representativeness heuristic? How might it influence decision making?

4 Outline the so-called 'disposition effect'. Provide an explanation for why it might occur.

5 Sometimes consumers have to pay an extra charge when buying products using a credit card. This makes it cheaper to buy the product using cash. Explain why credit-card companies want retailers to present this to customers as 'a cash bonus' rather than 'a credit-card surcharge'.

6 Using diagrams, explain the difference between loss aversion and diminishing marginal utility of income/wealth.

7 Dean supports Leicester City Football Club and has paid £80 for a ticket to watch them play in a cup final. The maximum amount he is willing to pay for the ticket is £200. He is approached by another Leicester supporter who offers him £400 for the ticket. Even though there are no restrictions on the resale of the tickets, Dean decides not to sell. Is his decision consistent with the predictions of rational decision making in economics? Explain your answer.

8 For many years, the long-term return from investing in stocks and shares has been much greater than from investing in bonds. The size of this return is far greater than can be explained by standard theories of risk aversion so it is called the *equity premium puzzle*. What ideas from behavioural economics might help to explain this puzzle?

9 Using present bias, provide an economic rationale for the government regulating the payday loan market.

10 In the 2011 Budget, the then Chancellor, George Osborne, announced that charitable giving in wills would be exempt from inheritance tax. Do you think this will be an effective way of encouraging more charitable donations?

Chapter 8

Firms and the consumer

Business issues covered in this chapter

- How can businesses set about estimating the strength of demand for their products?
- How do businesses set about gathering information on consumer attitudes and behaviour?
- How do businesses calculate the importance of various factors (such as tastes, consumer incomes and rivals' prices) in determining the level of demand?
- What methods can they use to forecast the demand for their products?
- In what ways can firms differentiate their products from those of their rivals?
- What strategies can firms adopt for gaining market share, developing their products and marketing them?
- What elements are likely to be contained in a marketing strategy?
- How extensive is advertising in the UK?
- What are the effects of advertising and what makes a successful advertising campaign?

Given our analysis in Chapter 6, how might a business set about discovering the wants of consumers and hence the intensity of demand? The more effectively a business can identify such wants, the more likely it is to increase its sales and be successful. The clearer idea it can gain of the rate at which the typical consumer's utility will decline as consumption increases, the better estimate it can make of the product's price elasticity. In the first part of this chapter, we consider the alternative strategies open to business for collecting data on consumer behaviour, and how it can help business managers to estimate patterns of demand.

For most firms, selling their product is not simply a question of estimating demand and then choosing an appropriate price and level of production. In other words, they do not simply take their market as given. Instead, they will seek to *influence* demand. They will do this by developing their product and differentiating it from those of their rivals, and then marketing it by advertising and other forms of product promotion. This is *non-price competition* and many of the issues involved are discussed in the second part of this chapter.

Product differentiation is a key strategic decision for many businesses. Take the case of washing machines. Although all washing machines wash clothes and, as such, are close substitutes for each other, there are many differences between brands. They differ not only in price, but also in their capacity, their styling, their range of programmes, their economy in the use of electricity, hot water and detergent, their reliability, their noise, their after-sales service, etc. Firms will attempt to design their product so that they can stress its advantages (real or imaginary) over the competitor brands.

Just think of the specific features of particular models of car, smart phones or brands of cosmetics, and then consider the ways in which these features are stressed by advertisements. In fact, think of virtually any advertisement and consider how it stresses the features of that particular brand.

8.1 ESTIMATING DEMAND FUNCTIONS

If a business is to make sound strategic decisions, it must have a good understanding of its market. It must be able to predict things such as the impact of an advertising campaign, or the consequences of changing a brand's price or specifications. It must also be able to predict the likely growth (or decline) in consumer demand, both in the near future and over the longer term.

The problem is that information on consumer behaviour can be costly and time-consuming to acquire, and there is no guarantee as to its accuracy. As a result, business managers are frequently making strategic decisions with imperfect knowledge, never fully knowing whether the decision they have made is the 'best' one, i.e. the one that yields the most profit or sales, or best meets some other more specific strategic objective (such as driving a competitor from a segment of a market).

But, despite the fact that the information that a firm acquires is bound to be imperfect, it is, still, usually better than relying on hunches or 'instinct'. Once the firm has obtained information on consumer behaviour, there are two main uses to which it can be put:

■ *Estimating demand functions.* Here the information is used to show the relationship between the quantity demanded and the various determinants of demand, such as price, consumers' incomes, advertising, the price of substitute and complementary goods, etc. Once this relationship (known as a *demand function*) has been established, it can be used to predict what would happen to demand if one of its determinants changed.
■ *Forecasting future demand.* Here the information is used to project future sales potential. This can then be used as the basis for output and investment plans.

In this section we concentrate on the first of these two uses. We examine methods for gathering data on consumer behaviour and then see how these data can be used to estimate a demand function. (Forecasting is considered in section 8.2.)

Methods of collecting data on consumer behaviour

There are three general approaches to gathering information about consumers. These are: *observations of market behaviour*, *market surveys* and *market experiments*.

Market observations

The firm can gather data on how demand for its product has changed over time. Virtually all firms will have detailed information of their sales broken down by week and/or month and/or year. They will probably also have information on how sales have varied from one part of the market to another.

In addition, the firm will need to obtain data on how the various determinants of demand (such as price, advertising and the price of competitors' products) themselves have changed over time. Firms are likely to have much of this information already: for example, the amount spent on advertising and the prices of competitors' products. Other information might be relatively easy to obtain by paying an agency to do the research.

Having obtained this information, the firm can then use it to estimate how changes in the various determinants have affected demand in the past and, hence, what effect they will be likely to have in the future (we examine this estimation process later in this section).

Even the most sophisticated analysis based on market observations, however, will suffer from one major drawback. Relationships that held in the past will not, necessarily, hold in the future. Competitors' products change, technology develops and consumer tastes change.

Market surveys

A vast quantity of information can be collected by carrying out surveys in a city centre or by knocking on people's doors. Questions concerning all aspects of consumer behaviour might be asked, such as those relating to present and future patterns of expenditure, or how a buyer might respond to changing product specifications or price, both of the firm in question and of its rivals.

Market surveys can be targeted at distinct consumer groups, thereby reflecting the specific information requirements of a business. For example, firms selling luxury goods will be interested only in consumers falling within higher income brackets. Other samples might be drawn from a particular age group or gender or from those with a particular lifestyle, such as eating habits.

The major drawback with this technique concerns the accuracy of the information acquired. Accurate information requires various conditions to be met. These include a randomly selected sample of consumers, unambiguous questions, the avoidance of leading questions and truthful

---

Definitions

Non-price competition Competition in terms of product promotion or product development.

Observations of market behaviour Information gathered about consumers from the day-to-day activities of the business within the market.

Market surveys Information gathered about consumers, usually via a questionnaire, that attempts to enhance the business's understanding of consumer behaviour.

Market experiments Information gathered about consumers under artificial or simulated conditions. A method used widely in assessing the effects of advertising on consumers.

responses from those taking part. Also, by the time the product is launched, consumer demand may have changed.

As well as surveying consumers, businesses might survey other businesses or panels of experts within a particular market. Both could yield potentially valuable information to the business.

Market experiments

Rather than asking consumers questions and getting them to *imagine* how they *would* behave, the market experiment involves observing consumer *behaviour* under simulated conditions. It can be used to observe consumer reactions to a new product or to changes in an existing product.

For example, a *laboratory shop* might be set up to simulate a real shopping experience. People could be given a certain amount of money to spend in the 'shop' and their reactions to changes in prices, packaging, display, etc. could be monitored.

The major drawback with such 'laboratories' is that consumers might behave differently because they are being observed. For example, they might spend more time comparing prices than they otherwise would, simply because they think that this is what a *good,* rational consumer should do.

Another type of market experiment involves confining a marketing campaign to a particular town or region. The campaign could involve advertising, giving out free samples, discounting the price or introducing an improved version of the product, but each confined to that particular locality. Sales in that area are then compared with sales in other areas in order to assess the effectiveness of the various campaigns.

> ### Pause for thought
>
> *Before you read on, try to identify some other drawbacks in using market experiments to gather data on consumer behaviour.*

Using the data to estimate demand functions

Once the business has undertaken its market analysis, what will it do with the information? How can it use its new knowledge to aid its decision making?

One way the information might be used is for the business to attempt to estimate the relationship between the quantity demanded and the various factors that influence demand. This would then enable the firm to predict how the demand for the product would be likely to change if one or more of the determinants of demand changed.

We can represent the relationship between the demand for a product and the determinants of demand in the form of an equation. This is called a **demand function**. It can be expressed in general terms or with specific values attached to the determinants.

General form of a demand function

In its general form, the demand function is effectively a list of the various determinants of demand.

$$Q_d = f(P_g; T; P_{s_1}, P_{s_2} \ldots P_{s_n}; P_{C_1}, P_{C_2}, \ldots P_{C_m}; Y; P_{g_{t+1}}^e; U)$$

This is merely saying in symbols that the quantity demanded (Q_d) is a 'function of' (f) – i.e. depends on – the price of the good itself (P_g), tastes (T), the price of a number of substitute goods ($P_{s_1}, P_{s_2}, \ldots P_{s_n}$), the price of a number of complementary goods ($P_{C_1}, P_{C_2}, \ldots P_{C_m}$) total consumer incomes (Y), the expected price of the good (P_g^e) at some future time ($t + 1$) and other factors (U) such as the distribution of income, the demographic profile of the population, etc. The equation is thus just a form of shorthand.

Note that this function could be extended by dividing determinants into sub-categories. For example, income could be broken down by household type, age, gender or any other characteristic. Similarly, instead of having one term labelled 'tastes', we could identify various characteristics of the product or its marketing that determine tastes.

In this general form, there are no numerical values attached to each of the determinants. As such, the function has no predictive value for the firm.

Estimating demand equations

To make predictions, the firm must use its survey or experimental data to assign *values* to each of the determinants. These values show just how much demand will change if any one of the determinants changes (while the rest are held constant). For example, suppose that an electricity distributor believes that there are three main determinants of demand (Q_d) for the electricity it supplies: its price (P), total consumer incomes (Y) and the price of gas (P_g). It will wish to assign values to the terms *a, b, c* and *d* (known as *coefficients*) in the following equation:

$$Q_d = a + bP + cY + dP_g$$

But how are the values of the coefficients to be estimated? This is done using a statistical technique called **regression analysis**. To conduct regression analysis, a number of observations must be used. For example, the electricity company could use its market observations (or the results from various surveys or experiments).

> ### Definition
>
> **Demand function** An equation showing the relationship between the demand for a product and its principal determinants.
>
> **Regression analysis** A statistical technique that shows how one variable is related to one or more other variables.

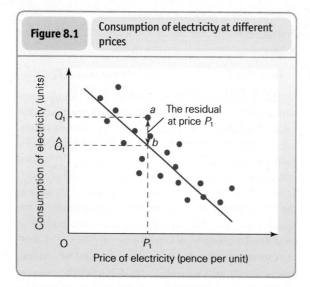

Figure 8.1 Consumption of electricity at different prices

Consumption of electricity (units)

Q_1

$\hat{Q}_1$

a — The residual at price P_1

b

O

P_1

Price of electricity (pence per unit)

Using simple regression analysis. To show how these observations are used, let us consider the very simplest case: that of the effects of changes in just one determinant – for example, price. In this case, the demand equation for the regression analysis would simply be of the form:

$$Q_d = a + dP + \epsilon$$

where '*a*' is a constant which provides an estimate of the quantity demanded if the price is zero; the coefficient '*b*' indicates the strength of the impact of a price change and should be negative because of the law of demand; and ϵ is an error term, which captures the combined impact of *other* factors that influence the demand for electricity but have not been included in the regression.[1]

The observations might be like those illustrated in Figure 8.1. The red points show the amounts of electricity per time period actually consumed at different prices. (Note that the axes are labelled the other way around from the demand curve diagrams in Chapter 4 as it is conventional to put the dependent variable, in this case quantity consumed, on the horizontal axis.)

We could visually try to construct an approximate line of best fit through these points. Alternatively, we could do this much more accurately by using regression analysis. The goal is to find the values of *a* and *b* in the equation:

$$Q_d = a + bP$$

If we did, then we could use the equation to draw the line of best fit. This is shown as the blue line in Figure 8.1. It illustrates the estimated values of the demand for electricity at each price. For example, at a price of P_1 the estimated

consumption is $\hat{Q}_1$, given on the line of best fit at point *b*. Actual demand for electricity, however, is Q_1, at point *a*. The difference between the estimated and the actual value of demand at each price is known as the 'residual', which is also illustrated in Figure 8.1 for P_1.

Simple linear regression analysis produces an equation (i.e. the values of the *a* and *b* terms) that minimises the sum of the squares of the residuals. (We do not explain regression analysis in detail in this text, but most business statistics textbooks cover the topic.)

Multiple regression analysis. Of course, in reality, there are many determinants of the demand for electricity. If we can obtain data on these variables, it is better to include them in the regression equation, otherwise our model might suffer from a problem called 'omitted variable bias'. This can cause the estimated coefficients to be unreliable.

Regression analysis can also be used to determine these more complex relationships: to derive the equation that best fits the data on changes in a number of variables. Unlike a curve on a diagram, which simply shows the relationship between two variables, an equation can show the relationship between *several* variables. Multiple regression analysis can be used to find the 'best fit' equation from data on changes in a number of variables.

For example, regression analysis could be applied to data showing the quantity of electricity consumed at various levels of price (P), consumer incomes (Y) and the price of gas (P_g). An equation similar to the following might be estimated:

$$Q_d = 2000 - 500P + 0.4Y + 200P_g + \epsilon$$

where Q_d is measured in millions of gigawatts per annum, P in pence per kilowatt hour, Y in £ millions, P_g in pence per kilowatt hour and ϵ is the error term. Once again, an error term must be included because, although data have been included on Y and P_g, there may still be other factors that we are unable to observe or measure that influence the demand for electricity.

The equation shows that if, say, the price of electricity were 5p per kilowatt hour, consumer incomes were £20 billion and the price of gas were 2p per kilowatt hour, then the demand for electricity would be 7900 million gigawatts per annum. This is calculated by substituting these values into the equation as follows:

$$Q_d = 2000 - (500 \times 5) + (0.4 \times 20000) + (200 \times 2)$$
$$= 2000 - 2500 + 8000 + 400 = 7900$$

Testing the equation. It is important to test to see if each of the coefficients that have been estimated is significant. This is done typically by completing a 't' test.[2]

---

[1] To be precise, the error term only captures the combined impact of other factors if a number of assumptions are met. These can be found in most introductory statistics textbooks.

[2] A 't' statistic is calculated by dividing the estimated coefficient by its standard error. More detail can be found in most business statistics textbooks.

What happens if the 't' test indicates that the coefficient is not significant? This means that we cannot be sure that the true value of the coefficient is not, in fact, zero instead of the value that has been estimated. In other words, the variable may have no impact on the demand for electricity.

Interpreting the equation. If the estimated coefficients on each of the variables in the regression equation *are* statistically significant, the equation tells us the impact on the demand for electricity of a marginal or one unit change in each determinant, while holding each of the other determinants constant. In the equation above, this would give the effects on the demand for electricity shown in Table 8.1.

The branch of economics that applies statistical techniques to economic data is known as *econometrics*. The problem with using such techniques, however, is that they cannot produce equations and graphs that allow totally reliable predictions to be made. The data on which the equations are based are often incomplete or unreliable, and the underlying relationships on which they are based (often ones of human behaviour) may well change over time. Therefore, these techniques do not provide an exact quantification of the strength of any relationships between variables. They simply provide an estimate. Thus econometrics cannot provide a business manager with 'the answer', but, when properly applied, it is more reliable than relying on 'hunches' and instinct.

Table 8.1	Effect on the demand for electricity of a 1 unit rise in each determinant	
Determinant	**Change**	**Effect on demand for electricity**
Price of electricity (P)	1p per kilowatt rise	Fall by 500 gigawatts
Consumer incomes (Y)	£1 million rise	Rise by 0.4 gigawatts
Price of gas (P_g)	1p per kilowatt rise	Rise by 200 gigawatts

Definition

Econometrics The branch of economics that applies statistical techniques to economic data.

8.2 FORECASTING DEMAND

Demand functions are useful in that they show what will happen to demand *if* one of the determinants changes. But businesses will want to know more than the answer to an 'If . . . then' question. They will want to know what will actually happen to the determinants and, more importantly, what will happen to demand itself as the determinants change. In other words, they will want *forecasts* of future demand. After all, if demand is going to increase, they may well want to invest *now* so that they have the extra capacity to meet the extra demand. But it will be a costly mistake to invest in extra capacity if demand is not going to increase.

We now, therefore, turn to examine some of the forecasting techniques used by business.

Simple time-series analysis

Simple time-series analysis involves directly projecting from past sales data into the future. Thus, if it is observed that sales of a firm's product have been growing steadily by 3 per cent per annum for the past few years, the firm can use this to predict that sales will continue to grow at approximately the same rate in the future. Similarly, if it is observed that there are clear seasonal fluctuations in demand, as in the case of the demand for holidays, ice cream or winter coats, then again it can be assumed that fluctuations of a similar magnitude will continue into the future. In other words, using simple time-series analysis assumes that demand in the future will continue to behave in the same way as in the past.

Using simple time-series analysis in this way can be described as 'black box' forecasting. No *explanation* is offered as to *why* demand is behaving in this way: any underlying model of demand is 'hidden in a black box'. In a highly stable market environment, where the various factors affecting demand change very little or, if they do, change very steadily or regularly, such time-series analysis can supply reasonably accurate forecasts. The problem is that, without closer examination of the market, the firm cannot know whether changes in demand of the same magnitude as in the past will continue into the future.

Successful forecasting, therefore, usually will involve a more sophisticated analysis of trends.

The decomposition of time paths

One way in which the analysis of past data can be made more sophisticated is to identify different elements in the time path of sales. Figure 8.2 illustrates one such time path: the (imaginary) sales of woollen jumpers by firm X. It is shown by the continuous red line, labelled 'Actual sales'.

Four different sets of factors normally determine the shape of a time path like this.

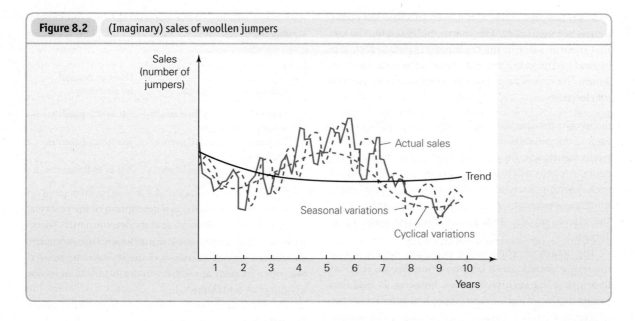

Figure 8.2 (Imaginary) sales of woollen jumpers

Trends. These are increases or decreases in demand over a number of years. In our example, there is a long-term decrease in demand for this firm's woollen jumpers up to year 7 and then a slight recovery in demand thereafter.

Trends may reflect longer-term factors such as changes in population structure, or technological innovation or longer-term changes in fashion. Thus, if wool were to become more expensive over time compared with other fibres, or if there were a gradual shift in tastes away from woollen jumpers and towards acrylic or cotton jumpers, or towards sweatshirts, this could explain the long-term decline in demand up to year 7. A gradual shift in tastes back towards natural fibres, and to wool in particular, or a gradual reduction in the price of wool, could then explain the subsequent recovery in demand.

Alternatively, trends may reflect changes over time in the structure of an industry. For example, an industry might become more and more competitive with new firms joining. This would tend to reduce sales for existing firms (unless the market were expanding very rapidly).

Cyclical fluctuations. In practice, the level of actual sales will not follow the trend line precisely. One reason for this is the cyclical upswings and downswings in business activity in the economy as a whole. In some years, incomes are rising rapidly and thus demand is buoyant. In other years, the economy will be in recession, with incomes falling. The cyclical variations line thus rises above the trend line in boom years and falls below the trend line during a recession.

Seasonal fluctuations. The demand for many products also depends on the time of year. In the case of woollen jumpers, the peak demand is likely to be as winter approaches or just before Christmas. Thus the seasonal variations line is above the cyclical variations line in winter and below it in summer.

Short-term shifts in demand or supply. Finally, the actual sales line will also reflect various short-term shifts in demand or supply, causing it to diverge from the smooth seasonal variations line.

There are many reasons why the demand curve might shift. A competitor might increase its price or there may be a sudden change in fashion, caused, say, by a pop group deciding to wear woollen jumpers for their new video: what was once seen as unfashionable by many people now suddenly becomes fashionable! Alternatively, there may be an unusually cold, hot, wet or dry spell of weather.

Likewise, there are various reasons for sudden shifts in supply conditions. For example, there may be a sheep disease that ruins the wool of infected sheep. As a result, the price of wool goes up and sales of woollen jumpers fall.

These sudden shifts in demand or supply conditions often are referred to as 'random shocks' because they are usually unpredictable and temporarily move sales away from the trend. (Note that *long-term* shifts in demand and supply will be shown by a change in the trend line itself.)

Even with sophisticated time-series analysis, which breaks time paths into their constituent elements, there is still one major weakness: time-series analysis is merely a projection of the *past*. Most businesses will want to anticipate *changes* to sales trends – to forecast any deviations from the current time path. One method for doing this is *barometric forecasting*.

Barometric forecasting

Assume that you are a manager of a furniture business and are wondering whether to invest in new capital equipment. A good barometer of future demand for furniture would be the number of new houses being built. People will tend to buy new furniture some months after the building of their new house has commenced.

It is common for businesses to use *leading indicators* such as 'housing starts' (the number of houses built measured at the time when building starts rather than when it is completed) when attempting to predict the future. In fact, some leading indicators, such as increased activity in the construction industry, rises in Stock Exchange prices, a depreciation of the rate of exchange and a rise in industrial confidence, are good indicators of a general upturn in the economy.

Barometric forecasting is a technique whereby forecasts of demand in industry A are based on an analysis of time-series data for industry (or sector or indicator) B, where changes in B normally precede changes in the demand for A. If B rises by x per cent, it can be assumed (other things being equal) that the demand for A will change by y per cent.

Barometric forecasting is used widely to predict *cyclical* changes: the effects of the upswings and downswings in the economy. It is thus useful not only for individual firms, but also for governments, which need to plan their policies to counteract the effects of the business cycle: the unemployment associated with recessions or the inflation associated with booms in the economy.

Barometric forecasting suffers from two major weaknesses. The first is that it allows forecasting only a few months ahead — as far ahead as is the time lag between the change in the leading indicator and the variable being forecast. The second is that it can give only a general indication of changes in demand. It is simply another form of time-series analysis. Just because a relationship existed in the past between a leading indicator and the variable being forecast, it cannot be assumed that exactly the same relationship will exist in the future.

Normally, then, firms use barometric forecasting merely to give them a rough guide as to likely changes in demand for their product: i.e. whether it is likely to expand or contract and by 'a lot' or by 'a little'. Nevertheless, information on leading indicators is readily available in government or trade statistics.

To get a more precise forecast, firms must turn to their demand function and estimate the effects of predicted changes in the determinants of the demand for their product.

Using demand functions in forecasts

We have seen (section 8.1) how demand functions can be used to show the effects of changes in the determinants of demand. For example, in the following model:

$$Q_d = a - bP + cP_s + dY + eA$$

where the demand for the product (Q_d) is determined by its price (P), the price of a substitute product (P_s), consumer incomes (Y) and advertising (A), the parameters (b, c, d and e) show the effects on Q_d of changes in the determinants.

In order to forecast the demand for its product (the *dependent variable*), the firm will need to obtain values for P, P_s, Y and A (the *independent variables*). The firm itself chooses what price to charge and how much to advertise and, thus, will decide the values of P and A. Forecasts of consumer incomes are readily available from a number of sources, such as the Office for Budget Responsibility and various private forecasting agencies, such as EY's Item Club. As far as P_s is concerned, here the firm will have to make an informed guess about the most likely policies of their competitors.

Obviously, the accuracy of the forecasts will depend on the accuracy of the model as a description of the past relationship between demand and its determinants. Fortunately, this can be tested using various econometric techniques and the reliability of the model can be determined. What is more, once the forecast is made, it can be compared with the actual outcome and the new data can be used to refine the model and improve its predictive power for next time.

The major strength of these econometric models is that they attempt to show how the many determinants affect demand. They also allow firms to feed in different assumptions to see how they will affect the outcome. Thus, one forecast might be based on the assumption that the major competitor raises its price by x per cent, another that it raises its price by y per cent and another that it leaves its price unchanged. The firm can then see how sensitive its sales will be to these possible changes. This is called *sensitivity analysis* and its use allows the firm to assess just how critical its assumptions are: would a rise in its rival's price by x per cent rather than y per cent make all the difference between a profit and a loss or would it make little difference?

Econometric models can be highly complex, involving several equations and many variables. For example, there might be a separate variable for each of the prices and specifications of all the various products in competition with this one.

Definitions

Leading indicators Indicators that help predict future trends in the economy.

Barometric forecasting A technique used to predict future economic trends based upon analysing patterns of time-series data.

Dependent variable That variable whose outcome is determined by other variables within an equation.

Independent variables Those variables that determine the dependent variable, but are themselves determined independently of the equation they are in.

Sensitivity analysis Assesses how sensitive an outcome is to different variables within an equation.

Problems with econometric forecasting

Despite the apparent sophistication of some of the econometric models used by firms or by forecasting agencies, the forecasts are often wrong.

One reason for this is that the variables specified in the model cannot explain all the variation in the demand for the product. As we explained earlier in the chapter, it is normal to include an *error term* (ϵ) in order to take some account of these missing independent variables. But this error term probably will cover a number of unspecified determinants that are unlikely to move together over time. It does not, therefore, represent a stable or predictable 'determinant'. The larger the error term, the less confident we can be about using the equation to predict future demand.

Another reason for the inaccuracy of forecasts is that certain key determinants are difficult, if not impossible, to measure with any accuracy. This is a particular problem with subjective variables like taste and fashion. How can taste be modelled?

Perhaps the biggest weakness of using demand functions for forecasting is that the forecasts are themselves based on forecasts of what will happen to the various determinants. Take the cases of just two determinants: the specifications of competitors' products and consumer tastes. Just what changes will competitors make to their products? Just how will tastes change in the future? Consider the problems a clothing manufacturer might have in forecasting demand for a range of clothing! Income, advertising and the prices of the clothing will all be significant factors determining demand, but so too will be the range offered by other manufacturers and also people's perception of what is and what is not fashionable. But predicting changes in competitors' products and changes in fashion is notoriously difficult.

This is not to say that firms should give up in their attempt to forecast demand. Rather, it suggests that they might need to conduct more sophisticated market research and even then to accept that forecasts can only give an approximate indication of likely changes to demand.

8.3 PRODUCT DIFFERENTIATION

Selling a product is not just about forecasting demand so that the right amount of output can be produced and investment can be planned. It is also about driving demand: developing products and encouraging consumers to buy more. We start by seeing how a firm can differentiate its product from those of its rivals.

Features of a product

A product has many dimensions and a strategy to differentiate a product may focus on one or more of these dimensions.

■ *Technical standards.* These relate to the product's level of technical sophistication: how advanced it is in relation to the current state of technology. This would be a very important product dimension if, for example, you were purchasing a PC.

■ *Quality standards.* These relate to aspects such as the quality of the materials used in the product's construction and the care taken in assembly. These will affect the product's durability and reliability. The purchase of consumer durables, such as televisions, tablets and toys, will be influenced strongly by quality standards.

■ *Design characteristics.* These relate to the product's direct appeal to the consumer in terms of appearance or operating features. Examples of design characteristics are colour, style and even packaging. A major reason for the success of Apple's iPhone has been its design and appearance – something that Samsung has tried to match in recent years with various models of its Galaxy series of smartphones. The demand for fashion products such as clothing is also strongly influenced by design characteristics.

■ *Service characteristics.* This aspect is not directly concerned with the product itself, but with the support and back-up given to the customer after the product has been sold. Servicing, product maintenance and guarantees would be included under this heading. When purchasing a new car, the quality of after-sales service might strongly influence the choice you make.

Any given product will possess a 'bundle' of the above attributes. Within any product category, each brand is likely to have a different mix of technical and quality standards and design and service characteristics. Consumers will select the bundle of attributes or characteristics they most prefer (see section 6.3). The fact that these different dimensions exist means that producers can focus the marketing of their product on factors other than price – they can engage in non-price competition.

Vertical and horizontal product differentiation

When firms are seeking to differentiate their product from those of their rivals (product differentiation), one important distinction they must consider is that between *vertical* and *horizontal* differentiation.

Vertical product differentiation. This is where products differ in quality, with some being perceived as superior and

---

Definition

Vertical product differentiation Where a firm's product differs from its rivals' products with respect to quality.

others as inferior. In general, the better the quality, the more expensive the product will be. Take the case of a mobile phone handset. The cheaper (inferior) models will have just basic functions. More expensive models will have more and better functions, such as higher screen resolution, cameras with more megapixels and faster charging times.

Vertical product differentiation usually will be in terms of the quantity and quality of functions and/or the durability of the product (often a reflection of the quality of the materials used and the care spent in making the product). Thus a garment normally will be regarded as superior if it is better made and uses high-quality cloth. In general, the vertical quality differences between products will tend to reflect differences in production costs.

Horizontal product differentiation. This refers to differences between products that generally are not regarded as superior or inferior, but merely reflections of the different tastes of different consumers. For example, some consumers prefer silver smartphones to black ones while others prefer a red car to a black one.

Horizontal differences within a product range (i.e. style, flavour, colour) do not alter the costs of production significantly and it is common for the different varieties to have the same price: a pot of red paint is likely to be the same price as a pot of black (of the same brand). The point is that the products, although horizontally different, are of comparable quality.

> ### Pause for thought
>
> *Identify two other products that are vertically differentiated, two that are horizontally differentiated and two that are both.*

In practice, most product ranges will have a mixture of horizontal and vertical differentiation. For example, some of the differences between different makes and models of motor car will be vertical (e.g. luxury or basic internal fittings, acceleration and fuel consumption); some will be horizontal (e.g. hatchback or saloon, colour and style).

Market segmentation

Different features of a product will appeal to different consumers. This applies both to vertically differentiated features and to horizontally differentiated ones. Where features are quite distinct, and where particular features or groups of features can be seen to appeal to a particular category of consumers, it might be useful for producers to divide the market into segments. Taking the example of cars again, the market could be divided into luxury cars, large, medium and small family cars, sports cars, multi-terrain vehicles, six-seater people carriers, etc. Each type of car occupies a distinct market segment and, within each segment, the individual models are likely to be both horizontally and vertically differentiated from competitor models.

When consumer tastes change over time, or where existing models do not cater for every taste, a firm may be able to identify a new segment of the market – a *market niche*. Having identified the appropriate market niche for its product, the marketing division within the firm will then set about targeting the relevant consumer group(s) and developing an appropriate strategy for promoting the product. (In the next section we will explore more closely those factors that are likely to influence a business's marketing strategy.)

> ### Definitions
>
> **Horizontal product differentiation** Where a firm's product differs from its rivals' products, although the products are seen to be of a similar quality.
>
> **Market niche** A part of a market (or new market) that has not been filled by an existing brand or business.

8.4 MARKETING THE PRODUCT

What is marketing?

There is no single accepted definition of marketing. Generally, it is agreed, however, that marketing covers the following activities: establishing the strength of consumer demand in existing parts of the market and potential demand in new niches; developing an attractive and distinct image for the product; informing potential consumers of various features of the product; fostering a desire by consumers for the product; and, in the light of all these, persuading consumers to buy the product.

Clearly, marketing must be seen within the overall goals of the firm. There would be little point in spending vast sums of money in promoting a product if it led to only a modest increase in sales and sales revenue.

Product/market strategy

Once the nature and strength of consumer demand (both current and potential) have been identified, the business will set about meeting and influencing this demand. In most cases, it will be hoping to achieve a growth in sales. To do this, one of the first things the firm must decide is its *product/ market strategy*. This will involve addressing two major questions:

- Should it focus on promoting its existing product or should it develop new products?
- Should it focus on gaining a bigger share of its existing market or should it seek to break into new markets?

BOX 8.1	THE BATTLE OF THE BRANDS

The rise, fall and rise of own-label brands

From fairly humble beginnings, supermarket own-label brands (also known as private-label brands) really took off in the late 1980s and early 1990s. By 1995, they accounted for over half of supermarket sales in the UK.

However, by the mid-2000s, own-label brands' share of super-market sales had fallen to around one-third. They became popular again during the 2008–9 recession and sales have continued to increase even when the economy and peoples' real incomes have grown. Research by Nielsen[1] found that private label brands had a market share of 41 per cent in the UK in 2016. The report stated that:

> There is a new retail revolution underway, and it's going to affect the food industry across the globe over the next five years in ways we have never seen before. We're talking about the development of private-label products and the new challenges that this will present for brands and manufacturers across the globe, as retailers develop and market their own products rather than multinational name brands to meet changing consumer needs.

The market penetration of private-label goods has been much greater in some sectors than in others.

For example, market shares vary from close to 100 per cent for fresh fruit to below 10 per cent for products such as baby food and chocolate.

So, how do own-label brands compete? Why have they been far more successful in some categories than others? Why have their fortunes fluctuated over time? Why have their sales increased so rapidly in the last few years?

They don't have significant differences in costs of production . . .

It was thought that branded manufacturers had the advantage of being able to take advantage of large economies of scale in sourcing and production. However, new technologies and close working relationships between retailers and suppliers have allowed supermarkets to provide own-label products in smaller batches but at lower costs, thus offsetting any advantage that brand manufacturers may have once had. Technology has also helped to improve the quality of products, making it possible for own-label producers to imitate the ideas of brand manufacturers and engage in their own innovations.

. . . but they do offer different product characteristics

Own-label products are not a homogenous group all with the same characteristics. Instead, they can be placed into three broad categories – value/economy, standard and premium.

As the name suggests, the value/economy own-label products are the cheapest. Examples of economy own-label products include Tesco's 'Everyday Value', Morrisons' 'M Savers', Sainsbury's 'Basics' and Aldi's 'Everyday Essentials'.

According to research by Mintel in 2014[2], only 1 per cent of people thought that such products were overpriced, compared to 30 per cent for branded products; and 68 per cent thought that they offered value for money, compared with just 10 per cent for branded products. However, only 8 per cent of people associated them with high quality, whereas for branded goods the figure was 52 per cent.

A further survey by Mintel in 2018[3] showed a continued movement by consumers to own-brand products as more people sought to cut their spending and get value for money.

The widest variety of own-label products is the standard range. Their prices fall somewhere between those of the premium and economy products. Slightly more consumers perceive them as being of higher quality than the value range, whereas slightly fewer consumers think they are value for money. Standard own-label products usually just display the name of the supermarket such as Tesco or Sainsbury's, although Asda uses the label 'Chosen by you'.

Premium own-label products are positioned in the higher end of the market and are much more associated with quality than the other own-label products. Compared with branded goods, they are still less likely to be associated with high quality and other positive characteristics, such as being trustworthy and authentic. However, this gap is narrowing in the minds of many customers and they do score better on value for money. In the 2014 Mintel survey, 36 per cent of people felt that they were of high quality and 24 per cent felt they were value for money.

Examples of premium own-label products include Sainsbury's 'Taste the Difference', Tesco's 'Finest' and Morrison's 'The Best'. Interestingly, there appears to be very little difference between any of the own-label and branded products on consumer perceptions such as ethically responsible or caring about my health.

The balance between quality and price remains a difficult combination for supermarkets to get right. A low price on its own is not enough as the sales of standard own-label products are still significantly greater than value own-label products.

An approach adopted by the discounters, Aldi and Lidl, has been to use a large number of own-label brands, each for a different category of products. This gives an impression of a greater range of brands. Also their approach has been to focus on products of an equivalent quality to branded products, albeit cheaper.

Following the success of this strategy by the discounters, in 2016, Tesco started to replace some of its 'Everyday Value' products with a series of its own 'farm' brands including 'Redmere Farms' and Woodside, Willow and Boswell Farms'. However, it came in for heavy criticism for using these

---

[1] The Nielsen Company (US) (2018).
[2] *The Private Label Food Consumer – UK*, Mintel Reports (November 2014).
[3] *The Private Label Food Consumer – UK*, Mintel Reports (September 2018).

'fake farms', with five of them offering a mix of British and imported produce and one exclusively imported.

They take advantage of changing consumer preferences

Many consumers who typically purchased famous brand names started to try cheaper own-label products during the 2009–10 recession. Often, they found the quality of these goods to be very similar and so, when incomes started to rise again, they continued to purchase these cheaper products. Also, many more premium own-label products have been introduced into different sectors in recent years such as wine, coffee and high-quality chilled meals.

More consumers have also demonstrated a preference for organic and natural goods made with healthier ingredients. For example, there has been rapid growth in recent years of 'free-from' products. Own-label product sales have increased significantly in this segment of the market.

Also, so-called millennial consumers (people born between 1980 and 2000) are more likely to try new products and are less attached to brands. They are also more likely to investigate products before making a purchase. Typically, this involves accessing information online. If this group of consumers finds evidence that an own-label product is of similar quality to a famous brand but cheaper, they are more likely to make the purchase.

Brands dominate many market segments ...

While the trend in recent times has been for customers to switch back to own-label brands, it is important to recognise that there is still substantial variability in own-label penetration across products. In some product segments, the penetration of supermarkets' own-brands is considerable (e.g. fresh fruit and vegetables, ready meals, milk and pasta). In others, however, branded products dominate (e.g. baby food, chocolate and carbonated soft drinks). Less than 1 per cent of the sales of baby food and drink products and only around 5 per cent of chocolate and confectionery products are own-label.

Where products are viewed by the customer as fairly homogeneous or require limited technological input, product differentiation or unique selling points (USPs) are difficult for brands to achieve. Fruit, vegetables, milk and pasta are clear examples of this. For example, 4 in 10 consumers believe that own-label dry pasta is as tasty as (or even tastier than) branded varieties, whereas only 28 per cent believe that the branded products are tastier. For these types of products, supermarket own-labels can compete effectively on price. The example of ready meals is, perhaps, more interesting as differentiation is more likely. However, when ready meals were first introduced, they were predominately own-label products and branded versions may have found it difficult to enter the market because of the limited chilled cabinet space in supermarkets.

For other goods that can be more easily differentiated, consumers may identify the quality of a product with a particular brand. Carbonated soft drinks (CSDs) are a good example, with famous names such as Coca-Cola and Pepsi. When surveyed, two-thirds of consumers agreed that they preferred the taste of a branded CSD to an own-label product. This has made it difficult for own-label products to compete and they have managed to obtain a market share of only just over 8 per cent. Another example of perceived quality differences is in the market for washing-up liquid. The Fairy brand is believed to last twice as long as its own-label competitors.

Branded products may also target a particular group (defined by gender, age or socioeconomic status) or reflect a certain style of living (e.g. healthy eating). People are also more likely to choose a branded item when it is being purchased as a treat or a present. In these types of market, brands do not have to compete strictly on price as successful differentiation enables them to charge premium prices. Research by Mintel[4] indicated that 54 per cent of people were willing to pay a higher price for branded chocolate, while 40 per cent were willing to pay a higher price for branded breakfast cereals.

One disadvantage for own-label products is that the advertising expenditure by supermarkets is concerned largely with branding the store rather than a particular product. This makes their promotional expenditures rather diluted. Brand manufacturers, on the other hand, are specialists in targeting their advertising and promotional expenditures towards particular markets. They achieve economies from marketing the brand, with the result that their sales per pound of promotional expenditure are higher. Economies of scale in marketing provide a powerful competitive advantage for brand manufacturers.

Will the suppliers of branded goods be able to fight back against their recent loss of sales to own-label products? It will be interesting to watch how this battle plays out.

1. How has the improvement in the quality of own-brands affected the price elasticity of demand for branded products? What implications does this have for the pricing strategy of brand manufacturers?
2. Why don't brand manufacturers readily engage in the production of supermarket own-label products?
3. Think of some different ways that the suppliers of branded goods could respond to the increase in competition from own-label products.

Do your own research in two supermarkets serving different clientele to establish the balance between own-label and branded products and the ways in which they are displayed and promoted in store. Write a brief report assessing the approach of the two supermarkets.

[4] *The Private Label Food Consumer – UK*, Mintel Reports (November 2014).

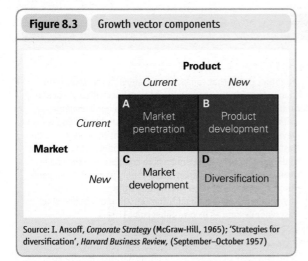

| Figure 8.3 | Growth vector components |

Source: I. Ansoff, *Corporate Strategy* (McGraw-Hill, 1965); 'Strategies for diversification', *Harvard Business Review*, (September–October 1957)

In 1957, Igor Ansoff illustrated these choices in what he called a ***growth vector matrix***. This is illustrated in Figure 8.3.

The four boxes show the possible combinations of answers to the above questions: Box A – *market penetration* (current product, current market); Box B – *product development* (new product, current market); Box C – *market development* (current product, new market); Box D – *diversification* (new product, new market).

- *Market penetration.* In the market penetration strategy, the business will seek not only to retain existing customers, but also to expand its customer base with current products in current markets. Of the four strategies, this is generally the least risky: the business will be able to play to its product strengths and draw on its knowledge of the market. The business's marketing strategy will tend to focus upon aggressive product promotion and distribution. Such a strategy, however, is likely to lead to fierce competition from current business rivals, especially if the overall market is not expanding and if the firm can, therefore, gain an increase in sales only by taking market share from its rivals.
- *Product development.* Product development strategies will involve introducing new models and designs in current markets. This may involve either vertical differentiation (e.g. the introduction of an upgraded model) or horizontal differentiation (e.g. the introduction of a new style).
- *Market development.* With a market development strategy, the business will seek increased sales of current products by expanding into new markets. These may be in a different geographical location (e.g. overseas), or new market segments. Alternatively, the strategy may involve finding new uses and applications for the product.
- *Diversification.* A diversification strategy will involve the business expanding into new markets with new products. Of all the strategies, this is the most risky given the unknown factors that the business is likely to face.

Once the product/market strategy has been decided upon, the business will then attempt to devise a suitable *marketing strategy.* This will involve looking at the marketing mix.

The marketing mix

In order to differentiate the firm's product from those of its rivals, there are four variables that can be adjusted. These are as follows:

- product;
- price;
- place (distribution);
- promotion.

The particular combination of these variables, known as 'the four Ps', represents the business's **marketing mix**, and it is around a manipulation of them that the business will devise its marketing strategy.

Figure 8.4 illustrates the various considerations that might be taken into account when looking at product, price, place and promotion.

- *Product considerations.* These involve issues such as quality and reliability, as well as branding, packaging and after-sales service.
- *Pricing considerations.* These involve not only the product's basic price in relation to those of competitors' products, but also opportunities for practising price discrimination (the practice of charging different prices in different parts of the market: see Chapter 17), offering discounts to particular customers and adjusting the terms of payment for the product.
- *Place considerations.* These focus on the product's distribution network and involve issues such as where the business's retail outlets should be located, what warehouse facilities the business might require and how the product should be transported to the market.
- *Promotion considerations.* These focus primarily upon the amount and type of advertising the business should use. In addition, promotion issues might also include selling techniques, special offers, trial discounts and various other public relations 'gimmicks'.

Figure 8.4 Model of the customer market offering dimensions of the marketing mix

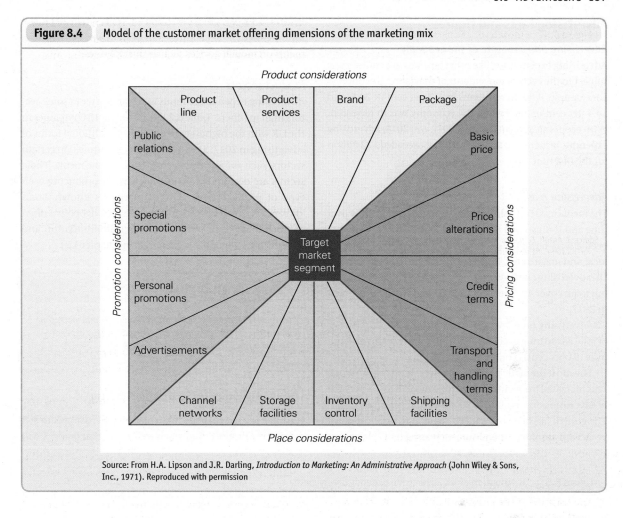

Source: From H.A. Lipson and J.R. Darling, *Introduction to Marketing: An Administrative Approach* (John Wiley & Sons, Inc., 1971). Reproduced with permission

Every product is likely to have a distinct marketing *mix* of these four variables. Thus we cannot talk about an ideal value for one (e.g. the best price) without considering the other three. What is more, the most appropriate mix will vary from product to product and from market to market. If you wanted to sell a Rolls-Royce, you would be unlikely to sell any more by offering free promotional gifts or expanding the number of retail outlets. You might sell more Rolls-Royces, however, if you were to improve their specifications or offer more favourable methods of payment.

What the firm must seek to do is to estimate how sensitive demand is to the various aspects of marketing. The greater the sensitivity (elasticity) in each case, the more the firms

should focus on that particular aspect. It must be careful, however, that changing one aspect of marketing does not conflict with another. For example, there would be little point in improving the product's quality if, at the same time, the product was promoted by the use of marketing gimmicks that led consumers to believe they were buying an inferior, 'mass consumption' product.

Another consideration that must be taken into account is the stage in the product's life cycle (see section 17.6). The most appropriate marketing mix for a new, and hence unfamiliar, product, and one that may be facing little in the way of competition, may well be totally inappropriate for a product that is long established and may be struggling against competitors to maintain its market share.

8.5 ADVERTISING

One of the most important aspects of marketing is advertising. The major aim of advertising is to sell more products, and businesses spend a vast quantity of money on advertising to achieve this goal. By advertising, the business will not only be informing the consumer of the product's existence

and availability, but also deliberately attempting to persuade and entice the consumer to purchase the good. In doing so, it will tend to stress the specific and unique qualities of this firm's product over those of its rivals. This will be discussed in more detail below.

Advertising facts and figures

Advertising and the state of the economy

Advertising expenditure, like other business expenditures, is subject to the cyclical movements of the national economy. For example, it fell in real terms by 6.3 per cent in 2008 and 14.4 per cent in 2009 when the economy was in recession. With economic growth between 2012 and 2018, advertising expenditure increased again. In 2017, it exceeded £22 billion for the first time.

Advertising media

The media used by businesses has changed dramatically over time and is illustrated in Figure 8.5. For example, there has been a long-term decline in the use of the press (national, local and magazines). It peaked at nearly 90 per cent of all UK advertising expenditure in 1953 before gradually declining to just over 40.5 per cent in 2005 and just 12.1 per cent in 2017.

Advertising on television accounts for some 25 per cent of total advertising expenditure. The majority of this expenditure (91 per cent) is on sports advertising.

The most dramatic growth, however, is on the Internet. This increased from virtually nothing in 1998 to 9.5 per cent of advertising expenditure in 2005 and 52.1 per cent in 2017. The growth has been particularly rapid in the last couple of years with absolute expenditure increasing by 17.3 per cent in 2015, 13.3 per cent in 2016 and 14.3 per cent in 2017. The recent growth in expenditure has been driven by advertisements on mobile devices such as smartphones.

Product sectors

Advertising expenditure tends to be far greater in some sectors than in others. Table 8.2 illustrates the 10 companies in the UK with the highest expenditure on traditional forms of advertising in 2017. They tend to be concentrated in certain sectors, such as food, drink, cosmetics and the media. These sectors are dominated by just a few firms producing each type of product. This type of market is known as an 'oligopoly', which is Greek for 'few sellers'. Oligopolists often compete heavily in terms of product differentiation and advertising. (Oligopoly is examined in Chapter 12.)

> **Pause for thought**
>
> *Try to use the ideas of the growth vector matrix and marketing mix to explain the reasons for the high advertising expenditures of a few of the companies in Table 8.2.*

The intended effects of advertising

We have argued that the main aim of advertising is to sell more of the product. But, when we are told that brand X will

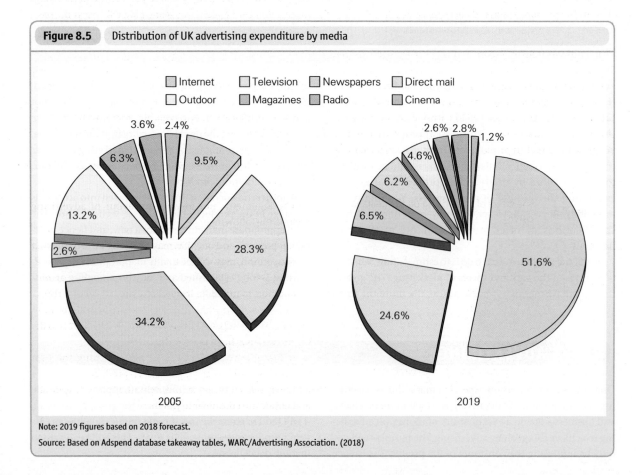

Figure 8.5 Distribution of UK advertising expenditure by media

Legend: Internet · Television · Newspapers · Direct mail · Outdoor · Magazines · Radio · Cinema

2005: 9.5%, 28.3%, 34.2%, 2.6%, 13.2%, 6.3%, 3.6%, 2.4%

2019: 51.6%, 24.6%, 6.5%, 6.2%, 4.6%, 2.6%, 2.8%, 1.2%

Note: 2019 figures based on 2018 forecast.

Source: Based on Adspend database takeaway tables, WARC/Advertising Association. (2018)

Table 8.2	The top 10 advertisers by expenditure in the UK (2017)

Advertiser	Total spending on advertising (£m)
1. BSkyB	197.1
2. Procter & Gamble	196.8
3. BT	144.1
4. Unilever UK	116.8
5. McDonald's	96.2
6. Tesco	89.5
7. Reckitt Benckiser	88.2
8. Virgin Media	72.1
9. Lidl	71.1
10. Samsung	66.6

Source: 'Sky leads traditional media spend', *WARC News and Opinion* (April 2018)

make us more beautiful, enrich our lives, wash our clothes whiter, give us get-up-and-go, give us a new taste sensation or make us the envy of our friends, just what are the advertisers up to? Are they merely trying to persuade consumers to buy more?

In fact, there is a bit more to it than this. Advertisers are trying to do two things:

- shift the product's demand curve to the right;
- make it less price elastic.

This is illustrated in Figure 8.6. D_1 shows the original demand curve with price at P_1 and sales at Q_1. D_2 shows the curve after an advertising campaign. The rightward shift allows an increased quantity (Q_2) to be sold at the original price. If, at the same time, the demand is made less elastic, the firm can also raise its price and still experience an increase in sales. Thus, in the diagram, price can be

Figure 8.6	The effect of advertising on the demand curve

raised to P_2 and sales will be Q_3 – still substantially above Q_1. The total gain in revenue is shown by the shaded area.

How can advertising bring about this new demand curve?

Shifting the demand curve to the right. This will occur if the advertising brings the product to more people's attention and if it increases people's desire for the product.

Making the demand curve less elastic. This will occur if the advertising creates greater brand loyalty (i.e. lowering the product's cross-elasticity of demand). People must be led to believe (rightly or wrongly) that competitors' brands are inferior. This will allow the firm to raise its price above that of its rivals with no significant fall in sales. There will be only a small substitution effect of this price rise because consumers have been led to believe that there are no close substitutes.

The more successful an advertising campaign is, the more it will shift the demand curve to the right and the more it will reduce the price elasticity of demand.

Assessing the effects of advertising

The supporters of advertising claim that not only is it an important freedom for firms, but it also provides specific benefits for the consumer. By contrast, critics of advertising suggest that it can impose serious costs on the consumer and on society in general. In this section we will assess the basis of this difference.

Pause for thought

Before considering the points listed below, see if you can identify the main arguments both for and against the use of advertising.

The arguments put forward in favour of advertising include the following:

- Advertising provides information to consumers on what products are available.
- Advertising may be necessary in order to introduce new products. Without it, firms would find it difficult to break into markets in which there were established brands. In other words, it is a means of breaking down barriers to the entry of new firms and products.
- It can aid product development by helping the firm emphasise the special features of its product.
- It may encourage price competition, if prices feature significantly in the advertisement.
- By increasing sales, it may allow the firm to gain economies of scale (see section 9.4), which in turn will help to keep prices down.

On the other side, the following arguments are put forward against advertising:

- Advertising is designed to persuade people to buy the product. Consumers do not have perfect information and may thus be misled into purchasing goods whose qualities may be inferior to those goods that are not advertised.

- Scarcity is defined as the excess of human wants over the means of fulfilling them. Advertising is used to *create* wants; it could thus be argued to increase scarcity.

- It increases materialism.

- Advertising costs money: it uses resources. These resources could be put to alternative uses in producing more goods.

- If there are no reductions in costs to be gained from producing on a larger scale, the costs of advertising will tend to raise the price paid by the consumer. Even if the firm has potential economies of scale, it may be prevented from expanding its sales by retaliatory advertising from its rivals.

- Advertising can create a barrier to the entry of new firms by promoting brand loyalty to *existing* firms' products. New firms may not be able to afford the large amount of advertising necessary to create a new brand image, whereas existing firms can spread the cost of their advertising over their already large number of sales. In other words, there are economies of scale in advertising that act as a barrier to entry (see page 191–2).

This barrier is strengthened if existing firms sell many brands each (for example, in the washing powder industry many brands are produced by just two firms). This makes it even harder for new firms to introduce a new brand successfully, since the consumer already has so many to choose from.

The fewer the competitors, the less elastic will be the demand for each individual firm, and the higher will be the profit-maximising price (see Chapter 12).

- People are constantly subjected to advertisements, whether on television, in magazines, on bill-boards, etc., and often find them annoying, tasteless or unsightly. Thus advertising imposes costs on society in general. These costs are external to the firm: that is, they do not cost the firm money and, hence, are normally ignored by the firm.

The effects of advertising on competition, costs and prices are largely an empirical issue (an issue of *fact*) and, clearly, these effects will differ from one product to another. However, many of the arguments presented here involve judgements as to whether the effects are socially desirable or undesirable. Such judgements involve questions of taste and morality: things that are questions of opinion and cannot be resolved by a simple appeal to the facts.

BOX 8.2 — THE USE OF SOCIAL MEDIA

A case study

Companies have increasingly made use of social media to support their advertising activity on the television and support long-running campaigns.

One of the clearest examples of this approach was implemented by the price comparison website *Compare the Market*. In January 2009, the company launched its 'Compare the Meerkat' advert on the television. This centred on a CGI-animated Russian Meerkat, Alexandr Orlov, complaining about the confusion between the 'Compare the Meerkat' and the *Compare the Market* websites. The company launched a real 'Compare the Meerkat' website in order to promote its brand further.

The impact of the campaign was immediate. In the week following its first broadcast, the number of Internet searches containing the word 'meerkat' increased by 817 per cent. Within 9 weeks, the requested number of insurance quotes via the *Compare the Market* website increased by 80 per cent.

The company quickly created a Facebook page for the Alexandr Orlov character, which has over half a million fans.

A Twitter account was also established, which has over 60 000 followers!

A series of television adverts continues to follow the story of Alexandr and has introduced new characters including friends and family members. The 'Meerkat Movies' promotion was introduced, which gives customers two-for-one tickets to cinemas.

The online promotion has also continued to expand. Wallpapers, ringtones, text alerts and voicemail messages can be downloaded from the 'Compare the Meerkat' website. A novel – *A Simples Life: The Life and Times of Aleksandr Orlov* – became a best seller. Meerkat cuddly toys were the second best-selling cuddly toys in the UK in both 2015 and 2016.

What are the limitations of advertising in increasing a firm's profits over the long term?

Research some other examples of businesses that have successfully used social media to advertise their products. Discuss why they were successful.

SUMMARY

1a Businesses seek information on consumer behaviour so as to predict market trends and improve strategic decision making.

1b One source of data is the firm's own information on how its sales have varied in the past with changes in the various determinants of demand, such as consumer incomes and the prices of competitors' products.

1c Another source of data is market surveys. These can generate a large quantity of cheap information. Care should be taken, however, to ensure that the sample of consumers investigated reflects the target consumer group.

1d Market experiments involve investigating consumer behaviour within a controlled environment. This method is particularly useful when considering new products where information is scarce.

1e Armed with data drawn from one or more of these sources, the business manager can attempt to estimate consumer demand using various statistical techniques, such as regression analysis.

1f The estimation of the effects on demand of a change in a particular variable, such as price, depends upon the assumption that all other factors that influence demand remain constant. However, factors that influence the demand for a product are constantly changing, hence there will always be the possibility of error when estimating the impact of change.

2a It is not enough to know what will happen to demand if a determinant changes. Businesses will want to forecast what will actually happen to demand. To do this they can use a variety of methods: time-series analysis, barometric forecasting and econometric modelling.

2b Time-series analysis bases future trends on past events. Time-series data can be decomposed into different elements: trends, seasonal fluctuations, cyclical fluctuations and random shocks.

2c Barometric forecasting involves making predictions based upon changes in key leading indicators.

2d If a firm has estimated its demand function (using econometric techniques), it can then feed into this model forecasts of changes in the various determinants of demand and use the model to predict the effect on demand. The two main problems with this approach are: the reliability of the demand function (although this can be tested using econometric techniques) and the reliability of forecasts of changes in the various determinants of demand.

3a When firms seek to differentiate their product from those of their competitors, they can adjust one or more of four dimensions of the product: its technical standards, its quality, its design characteristics and the level of customer service.

3b Products can be vertically and horizontally differentiated from one another. Vertical differentiation is where products are superior or inferior to others. Horizontal differentiation is where products differ, but are of a similar quality.

4a Marketing involves developing a product image and then persuading consumers to purchase it.

4b A business must choose an appropriate product/market strategy. Four such strategies can be identified: market penetration (focusing on current product and market); product development (new product in current market); market development (current product in new markets); diversification (new products in new markets).

4c The marketing strategy of a product involves the manipulation of four key variables: product, price, place and promotion. Every product has a distinct marketing mix. The marketing mix is likely to change over the product's life cycle.

5a Advertising expenditure is cyclical, expanding and contracting with the upswings and downswings of the economy.

5b Most advertising expenditure goes on consumables and durable goods.

5c The aims of advertising are to increase demand and make the product less price elastic.

5d Supporters of advertising claim that it: provides consumers with information; brings new products to consumers' attention; aids product development; encourages price competition; and generates economies of scale through increasing sales.

5e Critics of advertising claim that it: distorts consumption decisions; creates wants; pushes up prices; creates barriers to entry; and produces unwanted side effects, such as being unsightly.

REVIEW QUESTIONS

1 What are the relative strengths and weaknesses of using (a) market observations, (b) market surveys and (c) market experiments as means of gathering evidence on consumer demand?

2 You are working for a record company that is thinking of signing up some new bands. What market observations, market surveys and market experiments could you conduct to help you decide which bands to sign?

3 You are about to launch a new range of cosmetics, but you are still to decide upon the content and structure of your advertising campaign. Consider how market surveys and market experiments might be used to help you assess consumer perceptions of the product. What limitations might each of the research methods have in helping you gather data?

4 Outline the alternative methods a business might use to forecast demand. How reliable do you think such methods are?

5 Imagine that you are an airline attempting to forecast demand for seats over the next two or three years. What, do you think, could be used as leading indicators?

6 How might we account for the growth in non-price competition within the modern developed economy?

7 Distinguish between vertical and horizontal product differentiation. Give examples of goods that fall into each category.

8 Consider how the selection of the product/market strategy (market penetration, market development, product development and diversification) will influence the business's marketing mix. Identify which elements in the marketing mix would be most significant in developing a successful marketing strategy.

9 Imagine that 'Sunshine' sunflower margarine, a well-known brand, is advertised with the slogan, 'It helps you live longer' (the implication being that butter and margarines high in saturates shorten your life). What do you think would happen to the demand curve for a supermarket's own brand of sunflower margarine? Consider both the direction of shift and the effect on elasticity. Will the elasticity differ markedly at different prices? How will this affect the pricing policy and sales of the supermarket's own brand? Could the supermarket respond other than by adjusting the price of its margarine?

10 On balance, does advertising benefit (a) the consumer; (b) society in general?

ADDITIONAL PART C CASE STUDIES ON THE *ECONOMICS FOR BUSINESS* STUDENT WEBSITE (www.pearsoned.co.uk/sloman)

C.1 Bentham and the philosophy of utilitarianism. This looks at the historical and philosophical underpinning of the ideas of utility maximisation.

C.2 Choices within the household. Is what is best for the individual best for the family?

C.3 Taking account of time. The importance of the time dimension in consumption decisions.

C.4 The demand for lamb. An examination of a real-world demand function.

C.5 What we pay to watch sport. Consideration of the demand function for season tickets to watch spectator sports such as football.

WEBSITES RELEVANT TO PART C

Numbers and sections refer to websites listed in the Web appendix and hotlinked from this book's website at **www.pearsoned.co.uk/sloman**

■ For news articles relevant to Part C, see the *Economics News Articles* link from the book's website.

■ For general news on demand, consumers and marketing, see websites in section A, and particularly A2, 3, 4, 8, 9, 11, 12, 23, 24, 25, 36. See also links to newspapers worldwide in A38, 39, 42–44. See also site A41 for links to economics news articles and to search particular topics (e.g. advertising).

■ For data, information and sites on products and marketing, see sites B1, 3, 14, 27.

■ For student resources relevant to Part C, see sites C1–7, 19.

■ For data on advertising, see site E37.

Background to supply

The FT Reports . . .

The Financial Times, 20 April 2018

US airline stocks tumble after warnings of higher fuel costs

By Patti Waldmeir and Pan Kwan Yuk

US airline stocks tumbled on Thursday after two carriers warned of higher fuel costs that could feed through to fare increases.

Shares of American Airlines fell 6.3 per cent after the company lowered its 2018 profit forecast due to an expected $2.3bn rise in fuel costs this year.

Chief executive Doug Parker warned that sharply higher fuel prices were "feeling somewhat more like the 'new normal'" and were likely to impact on the profits of other US carriers too.

Mr Parker said the carrier had decided to cut its full-year guidance after fuel prices rose 12 per cent in the past two weeks. "This is the kind of increase that is going to have an impact on airline financials," he said on an earnings call, predicting that low cost carriers would suffer even more than legacy carriers like American.

Southwest Airlines also warned on fuel costs, predicting a fuel bill in the second quarter of $2.20 per gallon, up 10.5 per cent from the year earlier figure. Its shares closed down 1.0 per cent, additionally hit by news that second quarter bookings had dropped following an inflight engine accident last week in which a Southwest passenger died.

Shares of Delta Air Lines and United Continental were also down on Thursday, each by 2.8 per cent.

US airline stocks had already been under pressure for months as investors worry about an increase in capacity that they fear could lead to a fare war. The NYSE Arca Airline Index was already in technical correction territory, having dropped more than 10 per cent since its March peak.

Mr Parker of American Airlines said that the industry could constrain capacity if costs remain at current levels, and predicted higher fuel would be passed on to consumers in the form of higher fares.

American Airlines said it now expects full-year earnings per share (excluding special items) of $5–$6, compared with an earlier forecast of $5.50–$6.50 despite what it expects to be strong global travel demand for both business and leisure travel.

Southwest said revenue per available seat mile will fall by 1–3 per cent for the current quarter compared to the second quarter last year, largely as a result of the booking downturn that followed the death of Jennifer Riordan on Flight 1380 on April 17.

[Steelworks across Europe] have been hit by falling prices, weak demand and a flood of cheap imports as the slowdown in China stifles the appetite of the world's biggest steel consumer. These have combined with high operating costs to weigh heavily on their finances, raising questions about the sustainability of the UK's domestic industry. While such factors have squeezed the steelmakers across Europe, their British counterparts say they face additional burdens of higher business rates and energy costs, as well as the impact of a strong pound.

'UK steel hit by perfect storm of falling prices and high costs', *Financial Times,* 29 September 2015

In Part D we turn to supply. In other words, we will focus on the amount that firms produce.

In Parts E and F we shall see how the supply decision is affected by the environment in which a firm operates and, in particular, by the amount of competition it faces. We will also consider some of the alternative objectives and aims that firms might pursue.

In this part of the text, however, we take a more general look at supply and its relationship to profit. We assume that maximising profits is the main aim of a firm.

Profit is made by firms earning more from the sale of goods than the goods cost to produce. A firm's total profit ($T\Pi$) is thus the difference between its total sales revenue (TR) and its total costs of production (TC):

$$T\Pi = TR - TC$$

(Note that we use the Greek Π (pi) for 'profit'.)

Businesses can increase their profitability either by increasing their revenue (by selling more of their product or adjusting their price) or by reducing their costs of production. But, as the *Financial Times* article opposite shows, sometimes costs can be outside a company's control, as can demand. In cases where there is a combination of falling demand, low prices and rising costs, losses may become inevitable.

In order, then, to discover how a firm can maximise its profit, or even get a sufficient level of profit, we must first consider what determines costs and revenue. Chapter 9 examines production, productivity and costs. Chapter 10 considers revenue, and then puts costs and revenue together to examine profit. We will discover the output at which profits are maximised and how much profit is made at that output.

Costs of production

Business issues covered in this chapter

- What do profits consist of?
- How are costs of production measured?
- How do we distinguish between fixed and variable factors of production and between fixed and variable costs?
- What is the relationship between inputs and outputs in both the short and long run?
- What is meant by diminishing returns?
- How do costs vary with output in both the short and long run?
- What are meant by 'economies of scale' and what are the reasons for such economies?
- How can a business combine its inputs in the most efficient way?

9.1 THE MEANING OF COSTS

Opportunity cost

KI 3
p 19
When measuring costs, economists use the concept of *opportunity cost*. Opportunity cost is the cost of any activity measured in terms of the sacrifice made in doing it: in other words, the cost measured in terms of the opportunities forgone (see Chapter 2). If a car manufacturer can produce 10 small saloon cars with the same amount of inputs as it takes to produce 6 large saloon cars, then the opportunity cost of producing one small car is 0.6 of a large car. If a taxi and car hire firm uses its cars as taxis, then the opportunity cost includes not only the cost of employing taxi drivers and buying fuel, but also the sacrifice of rental income from hiring its vehicles out.

Measuring a firm's opportunity costs

To measure a firm's opportunity cost, we must first discover what factors of production it has used. Then we must measure the sacrifice involved in using them. To do this it is necessary to put factors into two categories.

Definition

Opportunity cost The cost of any activity measured in terms of the best alternative forgone.

Factors not owned by the firm: explicit costs

The opportunity cost of those factors not already owned by the firm is simply the price that the firm has to pay for them. Thus if the firm uses £100 worth of electricity, the opportunity cost is £100. The firm has sacrificed £100, which could have been spent on something else.

These costs are called *explicit costs* because they involve direct payment of money by firms.

Factors already owned by the firm: implicit costs

When the firm already owns factors (e.g. machinery), it does not, as a rule, have to pay out money to use them. The opportunity costs are thus *implicit costs*. They are equal to what the factors *could* earn for the firm in some alternative use, either within the firm or hired out to some other firm.

Here are some examples of implicit costs:

- A firm owns some buildings. The opportunity cost of using them is the rent it could have received by letting them out to another firm.
- A firm withdraws £100 000 from its savings in order to invest in new plant and equipment. The opportunity cost of this investment is not just the £100 000 (an explicit cost), but also the interest it thereby forgoes (an implicit cost).
- The owner of the firm could have earned £35 000 per annum by working for someone else. This £35 000 is the opportunity cost of the owner's time.

If there is no alternative use for a factor of production, as in the case of a machine designed to produce a specific product, and if it has no scrap value, the opportunity cost of using it is *zero*. In such a case, if the output from the machine is worth more than the cost of all the *other* inputs involved, the firm might as well use the machine rather than let it stand idle.

What the firm paid for the machine – its *historic cost* – is irrelevant. Not using the machine will not bring that money

back. It has been spent. These are sometimes referred to as *sunk costs* (see Box 9.1).

> ### Pause for thought
>
> *Assume that a farmer decides to grow wheat on land that could be used for growing barley. Barley sells for £100 per tonne. Wheat sells for £150 per tonne. Seed, fertiliser, labour and other costs of growing crops are £80 per tonne for both wheat and barley. What are the farmer's costs and profit per tonne of growing wheat?*

Likewise, the *replacement cost* is irrelevant. That should be taken into account only when the firm is considering replacing the machine.

 KEY IDEA 18

> *The 'bygones' principle.* This states that sunk (fixed) costs should be ignored when deciding whether to produce or sell more or less of a product. Only variable costs should be taken into account.

> ### Definitions
>
> **Explicit costs** The payments to outside suppliers of inputs.
>
> **Implicit costs** Costs that do not involve a direct payment of money to a third party, but that, nevertheless, involve a sacrifice of some alternative.
>
> **Historic costs** The original amount the firm paid for factors it now owns.
>
> **Sunk costs** Costs that cannot be recouped (e.g. by transferring assets to other uses).
>
> **Replacement costs** What the firm would have to pay to replace factors it currently owns.

9.2 PRODUCTION IN THE SHORT RUN

The cost of producing any level of output depends on the amount of inputs used and the price that the firm must pay for them. Let us first focus on the quantity of inputs used.

 KEY IDEA 19

> *Output depends on the amount of resources and how they are used.* Different amounts and combinations of inputs will lead to different amounts of output. If output is to be produced efficiently, then inputs should be combined in the optimum proportions.

Short-run and long-run changes in production

If a firm wants to increase production, it will take time to acquire a greater quantity of certain inputs. For example, a

manufacturer can use more electricity by turning on switches, but it might take a long time to obtain and install more machines and longer still to build a second or third factory.

If, then, the firm wants to increase output in a hurry, it will be able to increase the quantity of only certain inputs. It can use more raw materials, more fuel, more tools and possibly more labour (by hiring extra workers or offering overtime to its existing workforce). But it will have to make do with its existing buildings and most of its machinery.

The distinction we are making here is between *fixed factors* and *variable factors*. A *fixed* factor is an input that cannot be increased within a given time period (e.g. buildings). A *variable* factor is one that can.

BOX 9.1   SHOULD WE IGNORE SUNK COSTS?

There's no point crying over spilt milk

'What's done is done.'

'Write it off to experience.'

'You might as well make the best of a bad job.'

These familiar sayings are all everyday examples of a simple fact of life: once something has happened, you cannot change the past. You have to take things as they are *now*. Whether you have made a decision or spent some money, in many cases, you cannot change what has happened and therefore economists argue that rational decision making should ignore the past and consider only current and future costs and benefits.

Sunk costs

Past or 'sunk' costs exist in many walks of life: for consumers, firms, government and society. A classic example is spending £10 on a ticket for the cinema and deciding, after 30 minutes, that you are not enjoying the film. The £10 you have spent is a sunk cost, as, whether you stay through the film or leave, you cannot recoup the cost of the ticket.

When making the decision about whether to stay or go, you might consider: what else you could do if you leave; will the film get better or worse? Will it be embarrassing to walk out; are you with a friend who seems to be enjoying it? All of these factors should form part of your decision, but the money you spent on the ticket should not– it is an historic cost.

What about when you are waiting for a bus? Perhaps you have been waiting for 45 minutes already and are deciding whether to keep waiting or start walking. When making the decision, you shouldn't consider the 45 minutes you have wasted, as you can't get that back!

Consider a government that has decided to invest £500 million in a new IT project over three years. After one year, £150 million has been invested, but the project is not going well. Should the government continue with the project or stop it? When making this decision, the government should consider what else the remaining £350 million could be spent on; would other projects generate better returns; will the IT project turn around and be successful? Rational economic decision making implies that the government should ignore the £150 million that it has spent – it is a sunk cost that cannot be recouped. It is the same for a firm when making a decision or when purchasing inputs. It is no good wishing it had acted differently – the firm must simply make the best decisions moving forwards.

Consider a local convenience store that buys 100 Christmas trees for £10 each on 1 December. At the time of purchase, this represents an opportunity cost of £10 each, since the £10 could have been spent on something else. The shopkeeper estimates that there is enough local demand to sell all 100 trees at £20 each, thereby making a reasonable profit (even after allowing for handling costs).

But the estimate turns out to be wrong. On 23 December, there are still 50 trees unsold. What should be done? At this stage, the £10 paid for the trees is irrelevant. It is an historic or sunk cost, which cannot be recouped: the trees cannot be sold back to the wholesaler!

In fact, the opportunity cost is now zero. It might even be negative if the shopkeeper has to pay to dispose of any unsold trees. It might, therefore, be worth selling the trees at £10, £5 or even £1. Last thing on Christmas Eve, it might even be worth giving away any unsold trees.

KI 3
p 19

Do we behave rationally?

Although rationality requires that we ignore sunk costs, is that really how we behave?

If you have spent £10 on a cinema ticket, almost everyone would think about this when deciding whether to leave. You may say to yourself, 'I've spent £10, I will enjoy it'. Although it may be irrational to consider the money you have spent, in reality, most people will take it into account. Similarly, most people at the bus stop would think 'I've been waiting for 45 minutes, I'm not going to give up now!'

In reality, will a government really ignore the £150 million that it has spent on a pointless IT project? Imagine the media response: 'Government throws away £150 million that could have been spent on healthcare, social care, education, etc.' This is taxpayer's money and, hence, the use of it concerns the public and government will, undoubtedly, take it into account when deciding what to do about the project. Again, this is irrational behaviour.

Will the convenience store really give away the trees? If you had spent £10 on each tree, would you be happy giving them away free? It may be the rational response, but that doesn't mean you behave in that way.

If you fall over and break your leg, there may be little point in saying: 'If only I hadn't done that I could have gone on that skiing holiday', but it doesn't mean you still don't say it! Everyone considers sunk costs, even if doing so makes us irrational.

1. *Why is the correct price to charge (for the unsold trees) the one at which the price elasticity of demand equals* -1*? (Assume no disposal costs.)*

2. *Can you think of other examples when sunk costs are ignored?*

The distinction between fixed and variable factors allows us to distinguish between the **short run** and the **long run**.

The short run is a time period during which at least one factor of production is fixed. This means that, in the short run, output can be increased only by using more variable factors. For example, if a shipping line wanted to carry more passengers in response to a rise in demand, it could accommodate more passengers on existing sailings if there was space. It could increase the number of sailings with its existing fleet by hiring more crew and using more fuel. But, in the short run, it could not buy more ships: there would not be time for them to be built.

The long run is a time period long enough for *all* of a firm's inputs to be varied. Thus, in the long run, the shipping company could have a new ship built to cater for the increase in demand.

The actual length of the short run will differ from firm to firm. It is not a fixed period of time. Thus, if it takes a farmer a year to obtain new land, buildings and equipment, the short run is any time period up to a year and the long run is any time period longer than a year. But, if it takes a shipping company three years to obtain an extra ship, the short run is any period up to three years and the long run is any period longer than three years.

For this and the next section we will concentrate on *short-run* production and costs. We will look at the long run in sections 9.4 and 9.5.

Pause for thought

How will the length of the short run for the shipping company depend on the state of the shipbuilding industry?

Production in the short run: the law of diminishing returns

Production in the short run is subject to *diminishing returns,* which we alluded to first in section 4.3. You may well have heard of 'the law of diminishing returns': it is one of the most famous of all 'laws' of economics. To illustrate how this law underlies short-run production, let us take the simplest possible case where there are just two factors: one fixed and one variable.

Take the case of a farm. Assume the fixed factor is land and the variable factor is labour. Since the land is fixed in supply, output per period of time can be increased only by increasing the number of workers employed. But imagine what would happen as more and more workers crowded on to a fixed area of land. The land cannot go on yielding more and more output indefinitely. After a point, the additions to output from each extra worker will begin to diminish.

We can now state the *law of diminishing (marginal) returns*.

The law of diminishing marginal returns. When increasing amounts of a variable factor are used with a given amount of a fixed factor, there will come a point when each extra unit of the variable factor will produce less additional output than the previous unit.

There is an article on the Sloman News Site, 'Tackling diminishing returns in food production', which provides a good application of this core concept.

The short-run production function: total product

Let us now see how the law of diminishing returns affects total output or *total physical product* (TPP).

The relationship between inputs and output is shown in a *production function*. In the simple case of the farm with only two factors – namely, a fixed supply of land $\overline{Ln}$ and a variable supply of farm workers (Lb) – the production function would be:

$$TPP = f(\overline{Ln}, Lb)$$

This states that total physical product (i.e. the output of the farm) over a given period of time is a function of (i.e. depends on) the quantity of land and labour employed.

The production function can also be expressed in the form of a table or a graph. Table 9.1 and Figure 9.1 show a hypothetical production function for a farm producing wheat. The first two columns of Table 9.1 and the top diagram in Figure 9.1 show how wheat output per year varies as extra workers are employed on a fixed amount of land.

With nobody working on the land, output will be zero (point *a*). As the first farm workers are taken on, wheat output initially rises more and more rapidly. The assumption behind this is that, with only one or two workers, efficiency is low, since the workers are spread thinly across multiple tasks. With more workers, however, they can work as a team – each, perhaps, doing some specialist job and becoming more productive at it – and thus they can use the land more efficiently. In the top diagram of Figure 9.1, output rises more and more rapidly up to the employment of the second worker.

After point *b*, however, diminishing marginal returns set in: output rises less and less rapidly, and the TPP curve correspondingly becomes less steeply sloped.

Definitions

Fixed factor An input that *cannot* be increased in supply within a given time period.

Variable factor An input that *can* be increased in supply within a given time period.

Short run The period of time over which at least one factor is fixed.

Long run The period of time long enough for *all* factors to be varied.

Law of diminishing (marginal) returns When one or more factors are held fixed, there will come a point beyond which the extra output from additional units of the variable factor will diminish.

Total physical product The total output of a product per period of time that is obtained from a given amount of inputs.

Production function The mathematical relationship between the output of a good and the inputs used to produce it. It shows how output will be affected by changes in the quantity of one or more of the inputs.

Table 9.1	Wheat production per year from a particular farm (tonnes)			
	Number of workers (*Lb*)	*TPP*	*APP* (= TPP/Lb)	*MPP* (= ΔTPP/ ΔLb)
a	0	0	–	
				3
	1	3	3	
				7
	2	10	5	
b				14
	3	24	8	
				12
c	4	36	9	
				4
	5	40	8	
				2
	6	42	7	
d				0
	7	42	6	
				–2
	8	40	5	

When point *d* is reached, wheat output is at a maximum: the land is yielding as much as it can. Any more workers employed after that are likely to get in each other's way. Thus, beyond point *d*, output is likely to fall again: eight workers produce less than seven workers.

The short-run production function: average and marginal product

In addition to total physical product, two other important concepts are illustrated by a production function: namely, *average physical product (APP)* and *marginal physical product (MPP)*.

Definitions

Average physical product (*APP*) Total output (*TPP*) per unit of the variable factor (*Qv*) in question: $APP = TPP/Qv$.

Marginal physical product (*MPP*) The extra output gained by the employment of one more unit of the variable factor: $MPP = \Delta TPP/\Delta Qv$.

Figure 9.1 Wheat production per year (tonnes) from a particular farm

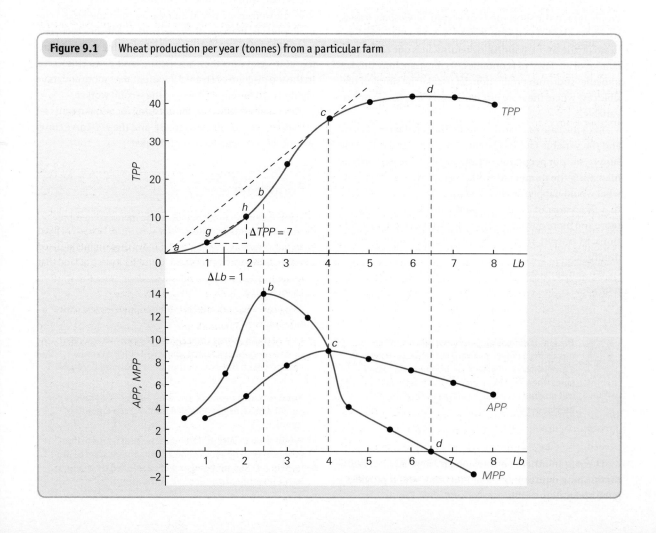

Average physical product

This is output (*TPP*) per unit of the variable factor (*Qv*). In the case of the farm, it is the output of wheat per worker.

$$APP = TPP/Qv$$

Thus in Table 9.1 the average physical product of labour when four workers are employed is $36/4 = 9$ tonnes per year.

Marginal physical product

This is the *extra* output (ΔTPP) produced by employing *one more* unit of the variable factor, (where the symbol Δ denotes 'a change in').

Thus in Table 9.1 the marginal physical product of the fourth worker is 12 tonnes. The reason is that, by employing the fourth worker, wheat output has risen from 24 tonnes to 36 tonnes: a rise of 12 tonnes.

In symbols, marginal physical product is given by:

$$MPP = \Delta TPP/\Delta Qv$$

Thus in our example:

$$MPP = 12/1 = 12$$

The reason why we divide the increase in output (ΔTPP) by the increase in the quantity of the variable factor (ΔQv) is that some variable factors can be increased only in multiple units. For example, if we wanted to know the *MPP* of fertiliser and we found out how much extra wheat was produced by using an extra 20 kg bag, we would have to divide this output by 20 (ΔQv) to find the *MPP* of *one* more kilogram.

Note that in Table 9.1 the figures for *MPP* are entered in the spaces between the other figures. The reason is that *MPP* is the *difference* in output *between* one level of input and another. Thus in the table the differences in output between five and six workers is two tonnes.

The figures for *APP* and *MPP* are plotted in the lower diagram of Figure 9.1. We can draw a number of conclusions from these two diagrams.

- The *MPP* between two points is equal to the slope of the *TPP* curve between those two points. For example, when the number of workers increases from 1 to 2 ($\Delta Lb = 1$), *TPP* rises from 3 to 10 tonnes ($\Delta TPP = 7$). *MPP* is thus 7: the slope of the line between points *g* and *h*.
- *MPP* rises at first: the slope of the *TPP* curve gets steeper.
- *MPP* reaches a maximum at point *b*. At that point the slope of the *TPP* curve is at its steepest.
- After point *b*, diminishing returns set in. *MPP* falls. *TPP* becomes less steep.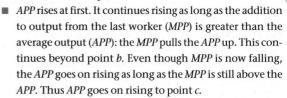
- *APP* rises at first. It continues rising as long as the addition to output from the last worker (*MPP*) is greater than the average output (*APP*): the *MPP* pulls the *APP* up. This continues beyond point *b*. Even though *MPP* is now falling, the *APP* goes on rising as long as the *MPP* is still above the *APP*. Thus *APP* goes on rising to point *c*.
- Beyond point *c*, *MPP* is below *APP*. New workers add less to output than the average. This pulls the average down: *APP* falls.
- As long as *MPP* is greater than zero, *TPP* will go on rising: new workers add to total output.
- At point *d*, *TPP* is at a maximum (its slope is zero). An additional worker will add nothing to output: *MPP* is zero.
- Beyond point *d*, *TPP* falls. *MPP* is negative.

Pause for thought

What is the significance of the slope of the line ac in the top part of Figure 9.1?

9.3 COSTS IN THE SHORT RUN

Having looked at the background to costs in the short run, we now turn to examine short-run costs themselves. We will be examining how costs change as a firm changes the amount it produces and hence responds to short-run market conditions. Obviously, if it is to decide how much to produce, it will need to know just what the level of costs will be at each level of output.

Costs and inputs

A firm's costs of production will depend on the factors of production it uses. The more factors it uses, the greater its costs will be. More precisely, this relationship depends on two elements.

The productivity of the factors. The greater their physical productivity, the smaller will be the quantity of them that is needed to produce a given level of output and, hence, the lower will be the cost of that output. In other words, there is a direct link between *TPP, APP* and *MPP* and the costs of production.

The price of the factors. The higher their price, the higher will be the costs of production. In the short run, some factors are fixed in supply. Therefore, the total costs (*TC*) of these inputs are fixed and thus do not vary with output. Consider a piece of land that a firm rents: the rent it pays will be a *fixed cost*. Whether the firm produces a lot or a little, its rent will not change.

The cost of variable factors, however, does vary with output. The cost of raw materials is a *variable cost*. The more that is produced, the more raw materials are needed and therefore the higher is their total cost.

Definitions

Fixed costs Total costs that do not vary with the amount of output produced.

Variable costs Total costs that do vary with the amount of output produced.

Table 9.2	Total costs for firm X		
Output (Q)	**TFC (£)**	**TVC (£)**	**TC (£)**
0	12	0	12
1	12	10	22
2	12	16	28
3	12	21	33
4	12	28	40
5	12	40	52
6	12	60	72
7	12	91	103

Total cost

The **total cost (TC)** of production is the sum of the *total variable costs* (TVC) and the *total fixed costs* (TFC) of production.

$$TC = TVC + TFC$$

Consider Table 9.2 and Figure 9.2. They show the total costs for an imaginary firm for producing different levels of output (Q). Let us examine each of the three cost curves in turn.

Total fixed cost (TFC)

In our example, total fixed cost is assumed to be £12. Since this does not vary with output, it is shown by a horizontal straight line.

Total variable cost (TVC)

With a zero output, no variable factors will be used. Thus $TVC = 0$. The TVC curve, therefore, starts from the origin.

The shape of the TVC curve follows from the law of diminishing returns. Initially, *before* diminishing returns set in, TVC rises less and less rapidly as more variable factors are added. For example, in the case of a factory with a fixed supply of machinery, initially as more workers are taken on the workers can do increasingly specialist tasks

and make a fuller use of the capital equipment. This corresponds to the portion of the TPP curve that rises more rapidly (up to point *b* in the top diagram of Figure 9.1).

Then, as output is increased beyond point *m* in Figure 9.2, diminishing returns set in. Extra workers (the extra variable factors) produce less and less additional output, so the additional output they do produce costs more and more in terms of wage costs. Thus TVC rises more and more rapidly. The TVC curve gets steeper. This corresponds to the portion of the TPP curve that rises less rapidly (between points *b* and *d* in Figure 9.1).

Total cost (TC)

Since $TC = TVC + TFC$, the TC curve is simply the TVC curve shifted vertically upwards by £12.

Average and marginal cost

Average cost (AC) is the cost per unit of production.

$$AC = TC/Q$$

Thus, if it costs a firm £2000 to produce 100 units of a product, the average cost would be £20 for each unit (£2000/100).

Like total cost, average cost can be divided into the two components, fixed and variable. In other words, average cost equals **average fixed cost** (AFC = TFC/Q) plus **average variable cost** (AVC = TVC/Q).

> ### Definitions
>
> **Total cost (TC)** The sum of total fixed costs (TFC) and total variable costs (TVC): $TC = TFC + TVC$.
>
> **Average (total) cost (AC)** Total cost (fixed plus variable) per unit of output: $AC = TC/Q = AFC + AVC$.
>
> **Average fixed cost (AFC)** Total fixed cost per unit of output: $AFC = TFC/Q$.
>
> **Average variable cost (AVC)** Total variable cost per unit of output: $AVC = TVC/Q$.

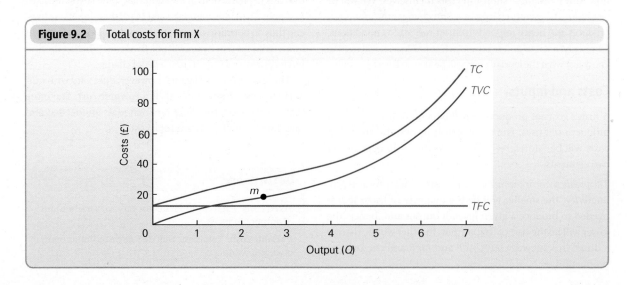

Figure 9.2 Total costs for firm X

$$AC = AFC + AVC$$

Marginal cost (MC) is the *extra* cost of producing *one more unit*: that is, the rise in total cost per one-unit rise in output. Note that all marginal costs are variable, since, by definition there can be no extra fixed costs as output rises.

$$MC = \frac{\Delta TC}{\Delta Q}$$

where Δ means 'a change in'.

For example, assume that a firm is currently producing 1 000 000 boxes of matches a month. It now increases output by 1000 boxes (another batch): $\Delta Q = 1000$. As a result, its total costs rise by £30: $\Delta TC = £30$. What is the cost of producing *one* more box of matches? It is:

$$MC = \frac{\Delta TC}{\Delta Q} = \frac{£30}{1000} = 3p$$

Given the *TFC, TVC* and *TC* for each output, it is possible to derive the *AFC, AVC, AC* and *MC* for each output using the above definitions. For example, using the data in Table 9.2, Table 9.3 can be constructed.

The shapes of the marginal and average cost curves

What will be the shapes of the *MC, AFC, AVC* and *AC* curves? These follow from the nature of the *MPP* and *APP* curves (which we looked at in section 9.2).

KI 20
p 149 *Marginal cost (MC)*. The shape of the *MC* curve follows directly from the law of diminishing returns. Initially, in Figure 9.3, as more of the variable factor is used, extra units of output cost less than previous units. This means that *MC* falls. This corresponds to the portion of the *TVC* curve in Figure 9.2 to the left of point m.

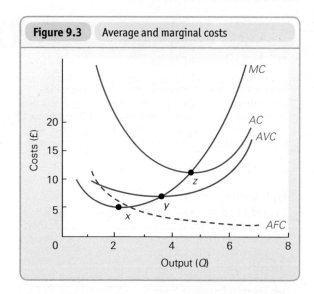

Figure 9.3 Average and marginal costs

Beyond a certain level of output, diminishing returns set in. This is shown as point *x* in Figure 9.3 and corresponds to point *m* in Figure 9.2. Thereafter *MC* rises. Additional units of output cost more and more to produce, since they require ever-increasing amounts of the variable factor.

Average fixed cost (AFC). This falls continuously as output rises, since total fixed costs are being spread over a greater and greater output.

Definition

Marginal cost (MC) The cost of producing one more unit of output: $MC = \Delta TC/\Delta Q$.

Table 9.3	Costs						

Output (Q) (units)	TFC (£)	AFC (TFC/Q) (£)	TVC (£)	AVC (TVC/Q) (£)	TC (TFC + TVC) (£)	AC (TC/Q) (£)	MC (ΔTC/ΔQ) (£)
0	12	–	0	–	12	–	
							10
1	12	12	10	10	22	22	
							6
2	12	6	16	8	28	14	
							5
3	12	4	21	7	33	11	
							7
4	12	3	28	7	40	10	
							12
5	12	2.4	40	8	52	10.4	
							20
6	12	2	60	10	72	12	
							31
7	12	1.7	91	13	103	14.7	

BOX 9.2	HOW VULNERABLE ARE YOU?

The importance of costs

Firms operate in an uncertain business environment and, while some firms grow and succeed, others fail. What is it that makes some firms more vulnerable to the economic environment, while other firms are more insulated? In this box, we look at one aspect of the answer to this question by focusing on the shape of a firm's cost curves and the impact this has on its economic vulnerability.

Type 1 vulnerability

A typical firm will have a U-shaped average cost curve. It falls at first, reflecting rapidly falling average fixed costs, as they are spread over a greater output, plus a more efficient deployment of variable factors of production. Then, as diminishing marginal returns become relatively more important than falling average fixed costs, average costs rise. The speed at which average costs first fall and then rise as output changes is an important determinant of how vulnerable a firm is.

Consider two firms, A and B. Each firm's average cost curve is shown in Figure (a). Assume, for simplicity, that each firm achieves minimum average cost at point x, namely at the same output Q_0 and at the same average cost, AC_0. Now consider what would happen if there was a recession, such that both firms experience a fall in demand and cut output to Q_1.

With a U-shaped AC curve, per unit costs begin to rise, but firm A's costs rise significantly faster than firm B's, because firm A has a steeper AC curve. The same fall in quantity pushes firm A's average costs up from AC_0 to AC_1 (point a) but only causes firm B's costs to increase to AC_2 (point b) as firm B's AC curve is very flat.

Returning to point x, now assume that there is an expansion in demand. Both firms consequently increase output. Again, firm A's costs rise more rapidly than firm B's, because of the shape of the AC curves.

Firm A is thus much more susceptible to any change in demand, as any change in output has a greater effect on its costs and hence on its profit margin and profits, making it a much more vulnerable firm. The steeper its AC curve, the more vulnerable a firm will be.

What are the factors that affect the steepness of the AC curve and hence make one firm more vulnerable than another?

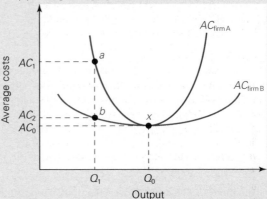

(a) Average cost for firms A and B: change in output

- If a firm has a high ratio of fixed factors to variable factors, then it is likely to face a steeper AC curve at low levels of output. Total fixed costs do not change with output and, hence, if output falls, it implies that its high fixed costs are spread over fewer and fewer units of output and this causes average costs to rise rapidly.
- If a firm is relatively inflexible in its use of inputs, it may find that a cut in production means that efficiency goes down and average cost rises rapidly. Similarly, if it wishes to expand output beyond Q_0, it may find it difficult to do so without incurring considerable extra costs, for example by employing expensive agency staff or hiring expensive machinery.

 Conduct some research on a firm of your choice, looking into its data on costs, and decide whether or not you think this firm would suffer from type 1 vulnerability.

Type 2 vulnerability

Most firms purchase inputs from other companies, but their reliance on other firms and, in some cases, on materials where there is a volatile global market, can vary significantly. The second type of economic vulnerability concerns a firm's reliance on external or bought-in factors of production (inputs).

Average variable cost (AVC). The shape of the AVC curve depends on the shape of the APP curve. As the average product of workers rises, the average labour cost per unit of output (the AVC) falls: up to point y in Figure 9.3. Thereafter, as APP falls, AVC must rise.

Average (total) cost (AC). This is simply the vertical sum of the AFC and AVC curves. Note that, as AFC falls, the gap between AVC and AC narrows. Although AVC and MC curves are usually drawn as a U-shape, they are not always shaped like this.

Case study D.6 on the student website considers alternative shapes for these curves.

Pause for thought

Before you read on, can you explain why the marginal cost curve will always cut the average cost curve at its lowest point?

The relationship between average cost and marginal cost

This is simply another illustration of the relationship that applies between *all* averages and marginals.

Some firms may be heavily dependent on oil or other raw materials and, if the prices of these change, it can have a very big effect on the firm's costs of production, its profit margins and total profit. During an economic boom or period of high growth, production tends to increase and so demand for oil and other raw materials often rises, thereby pushing up these prices. The more dependent a firm is on such inputs, the greater the effect on its costs and the bigger the upward vertical shift in its AC curve. If a firm is less reliant on these raw materials or has alternative inputs, such a change in global prices will cause only a small shift in the firm's AC curve.

In Figure (b), assume both firms X and Y have the same AC curve, given by AC_1. But let us also assume that firm X is very dependent on oil, whereas firm Y is not.

Assume that oil prices now rise. This will lead to a large upward shift in firm X's AC curve from AC_1 to AC_2, but a smaller upward shift in firm Y's AC curve from AC_1 to AC_3. There is a much larger cost penalty imposed on firm X than on firm Y, due to its greater reliance on oil as a factor of production.

In 2010, oil prices rose significantly, so firms that were big users of oil, either directly into the production process or for transporting their inputs and produce, saw their costs rise and their profits eroded. However, from late 2014 into early 2016, oil prices fell considerably and so those firms that were heavily dependent on oil saw their AC curves shift downward significantly, thereby helping to increase their profits. Other firms that were less reliant on oil, however, did not benefit so much from low global prices for oil.

Now look at some data on a firm of your choice and decide whether or not you think this firm would suffer from type 2 vulnerability. Is it the same firm as you discussed in question 1? If your data suggest the firms would be vulnerable in both ways, what might this mean for the firm?

The case of Nippon Steel & Sumitomo Metal Corporation (NSSMC)

Some firms are vulnerable in both ways. They may be heavily dependent on external or bought-in costs and, at the same time, have a high proportion of fixed costs or lack flexibility.

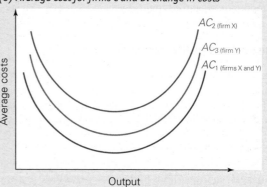

(b) Average cost for firms C and D: change in costs

This might mean that, as economies move from economic boom to economic recession, these firms are always vulnerable to changes in costs of production.

A good example is the Japanese steel producer, NSSMC. Its fixed costs as a percentage of internal costs are very high, suggesting a steep AC curve at low levels of output and hence a vulnerability to a fall in output. However, this firm's external costs also account for a high percentage of its total costs, suggesting heavy reliance on costs that are beyond its control.

During the economic downturn of 2009, NSSMC reduced its output to just above 50 per cent of its maximum capacity. This fall in output made the firm very vulnerable to rising short-run average costs. And, just the previous year, the company had also been in trouble, but this time because costs of production had been rising due to increases in the prices of oil and various raw materials on which the company is very dependent.

These types of vulnerability create uncertainty in the business environment. They can help to explain why some firms are successful and can survive periods of falling output, while others have little chance of survival.

As long as the cost of additional units of output is less than the average, their production must pull the average cost down. That is, if MC is less than AC, AC must be falling. Likewise, if additional units cost more than the average, their production must drive the average up. That is, if MC is greater than AC, AC must be rising. Therefore, the MC crosses the AC, and also the AVC, at their minimum points (point z and y respectively in Figure 9.3).

9.4 PRODUCTION IN THE LONG RUN

In the long run, *all* factors of production are variable. There is time for the firm to build a new factory (maybe in a different part of the country), to install new machines, to use different techniques of production and, in general, to combine its inputs in whatever proportion and in whatever quantities it chooses.

Therefore, when planning for the long run, a firm will have to make a number of decisions: about the scale of its operations, the location of its operations and the techniques of production it will use. These decisions will affect the firm's costs of production and can be completely irreversible, so it is important to get them right.

The scale of production

If a firm were to double all of its inputs – something it could do only in the long run – would this cause its output to double? Or would output more than double or less than double? We can distinguish three possible situations.

- *Constant returns to scale.* This is where a given percentage increase in inputs leads to the same percentage increase in output.
- *Increasing returns to scale.* This is where a given percentage increase in inputs leads to a larger percentage increase in output.
- *Decreasing returns to scale.* This is where a given percentage increase in inputs leads to a smaller percentage increase in output.

Notice the terminology here. The words 'to scale' mean that *all* inputs increase by the same proportion. Decreasing returns to *scale* are, therefore, quite different from *diminishing* marginal returns (where only the *variable* factor increases). The differences between marginal returns to a variable factor and returns to scale are illustrated in Table 9.4.

In the short run, input 1 is assumed to be fixed in supply (at 3 units). Output can be increased only by using more of the variable factor (input 2). In the long run, however, both inputs are variable.

In the short-run situation, diminishing returns can be seen from the fact that output increases at a decreasing rate (25 to 45 to 60 to 70 to 75) as input 2 is increased. In the long-run situation, the table illustrates increasing returns to scale. Output increases at an *increasing* rate (15 to 35 to 60 to 90 to 125) as both inputs are increased.

Economies of scale

The concept of increasing returns to scale is closely linked to that of *economies of scale*. A firm experiences economies of scale if costs per unit of output fall as the scale of production increases. Clearly, if a firm is getting increasing returns to scale from its factors of production, then, as it produces more, it will be using smaller and smaller amounts of factors per unit of output.

Other things being equal, this means that it will be producing at a lower unit cost.

KI 19
p 147

There are a number of reasons why firms are likely to experience economies of scale. Some are due to increasing returns to scale; some are not.

Specialisation and division of labour. In large-scale plants, workers can do more simple, repetitive jobs. With this *specialisation and division of labour*, less training is needed; workers can become highly efficient in their particular job, especially with long production runs; there is less time lost in workers switching from one operation to another; supervision is easier. Workers and managers who have specific skills in specific areas can be employed.

Indivisibilities. Some inputs are of a minimum size. They are indivisible. The most obvious example is machinery. Take the case of a combine harvester. A small-scale farmer could not make full use of one. They become economical to use, therefore, only on farms above a certain size. The problem of *indivisibilities* is made worse when different machines, each of which is part of the production process, are of a different size. Consider a firm that uses two different machines at different stages of the production process: one produces a maximum of 6 units a day; the other can package a maximum of 4 units a day. Therefore, if all machines are to be fully utilised, a minimum of 12 units per day will have to be produced, involving 2 production machines and 3 packaging machines.

The 'container principle'. Any capital equipment that contains things (blast furnaces, oil tankers, pipes, vats, etc.) will tend to cost less per unit of output, the larger its size. This is due to the relationship between a container's volume and its surface area. A container's cost will depend largely on the materials used to build it and hence roughly on its

Table 9.4	Short-run and long-run increases in output				
	Short run			**Long run**	
Input 1	**Input 2**	**Output**	**Input 1**	**Input 2**	**Output**
3	1	25	1	1	15
3	2	45	2	2	35
3	3	60	3	3	60
3	4	70	4	4	90
3	5	75	5	5	125

Definitions

Economies of scale When increasing the scale of production leads to a lower cost per unit of output.

Specialisation and division of labour Where production is broken down into a number of simpler, more specialised tasks, thus allowing workers to acquire a high degree of efficiency.

Indivisibilities The impossibility of dividing a factor of production into smaller units.

surface area. Its output will depend largely on its *volume.* Large containers have a bigger volume relative to surface area than do small containers. For example, a container with a bottom, top and four sides, with each side measuring 1 metre, has a volume of 1 cubic metre and a surface area of 6 square metres (6 surfaces of 1 square metre each). If each side were now to be doubled in length to 2 metres, the volume would be 8 cubic metres and the surface area 24 square metres (6 surfaces of 4 square metres each). Therefore, a fourfold increase in the container's surface area, and thus an approximate fourfold increase in costs, has led to an eightfold increase in capacity.

Greater efficiency of large machines. Large machines may be more efficient, in the sense that more output can be gained for a given amount of inputs. For example, whether a machine is large or small, only one worker may be required to operate it. Also, a large machine may make more efficient use of raw materials.

By-products. With production on a large scale, there may be sufficient waste products to enable them to make some by-product. For example, a wood mill may produce sufficient sawdust to make products such as charcoal briquettes or paper.

Multistage production. A large factory may be able to take a product through several stages in its manufacture. This saves time and cost moving the semi-finished product from one firm or factory to another. For example, a large cardboard-manufacturing firm may be able to convert trees or waste paper into cardboard and then into cardboard boxes in a continuous sequence.

All the above are examples of *plant economies of scale*. They are due to an individual factory or workplace or machine being large. There are other economies of scale that are associated with the firm being large – perhaps with many factories.

Organisational. With a large firm, individual plants can specialise in particular functions. There can also be centralised administration of the firms. Often, after a merger between two firms, savings can be made by *rationalising* their activities in this way.

Spreading overheads. Some expenditures are economic only when the *firm* is large, such as research and development: only a large firm can afford to set up a research laboratory. This is another example of indivisibilities, only this time at the level of the firm rather than the plant. The greater the firm's output, the more these *overhead costs* are spread.

Financial economies. Large firms may be able to obtain finance at lower interest rates than small firms, as they are perceived as having lower default risks or have more power to negotiate a better deal. Additionally, larger firms may be able to obtain

certain inputs more cheaply by purchasing in bulk. This follows from the concept of opportunity cost, as the larger a firm's order, the more likely it is that the supplier will offer a discount, as the opportunity cost of losing the business is getting higher. This helps to reduce the cost per unit.

Economies of scope. Often a firm is large because it produces a range of products. This can result in each individual product being produced more cheaply than if it was produced in a single-product firm. The reason for these *economies of scope* is that various overhead costs and financial and organisational economies can be shared between the products. For example, a firm that produces a whole range of CD players, DVD players and recorders, games consoles, TVs, and so on can benefit from shared marketing and distribution costs and the bulk purchase of electronic components.

Pause for thought

What economies of scale would you expect a large department store to experience? What about Google?

Many companies will experience a variety of economies of scale and you can find examples in practice from a variety of sources. On the Sloman News Site, you will find blogs that discuss economies of scale, such as those experienced by companies using cloud computing (Operating in a cloud), the possibility of achieving economies of scale through take-overs (Taking over?) and whether big supermarkets can use economies of scale to their advantage (Supermarket wars: a pricing race to the bottom). The economies of scale for large cloud providers is also discussed in numerous articles, including an article by Randy Bias[1] and another that considers the case of Microsoft.[2]

Definitions

Plant economies of scale Economies of scale that arise because of the large size of the factory.

Rationalisation The reorganising of production (often after a merger) so as to cut out waste and duplication and generally to reduce costs.

Overheads Costs arising from the general running of an organisation and only indirectly related to the level of output.

Economies of scope When increasing the range of products produced by a firm reduces the cost of producing each one.

---

[1]Randy Bias, 'Understanding cloud datacenter economies of scale', cloudscaling (4 October 2010).

[2]Charles Babcock, 'Microsoft: "incredible economies of scale" await cloud users', *Information Week* (5 November 2011).

BOX 9.3	LIGHTS, CAMERA, ACTION

Location, location, location

Globalisation means that it is easy to source inputs and products from anywhere in the world and this would suggest that location is becoming less important. It is no longer vital for a firm to be located near raw materials or places where they have a competitive cost advantage. After all, why would a firm need to locate itself somewhere particular when it can buy from firms and sell to markets anywhere? Yet, location is still one of the most important factors in determining both firm and industry competitiveness and much of this is driven by the formation of **clusters**.

> Clusters are geographically proximate groups of interconnected companies, suppliers, service providers, and associated institutions in a particular field, linked by commonalities and complementarities.[1]

Professor Michael Porter suggests that clusters are vital for competitiveness in three crucial respects:

- Clusters improve productivity. The close proximity of suppliers and other service providers enhances flexibility.
- Clusters aid innovation. Interaction among businesses within a cluster stimulates new ideas and aids their dissemination.
- Clusters contribute to new business formation. Clusters are self-reinforcing, in so far as specialist factors such as dedicated venture capital, and labour skills, help reduce costs and lower the risks of new business start-up.

Clusters are also one of the key things that create competition between rivals, as they compete for both customers and inputs and this competitiveness is a crucial ingredient for a successful cluster.

Porter's view is that economic development is achieved through a series of stages.

- The factor-driven stage identifies factors of production as the basis of competitive advantage: you have an advantage in those industries where you have a plentiful supply of the relevant factors of production.
- The investment-driven stage of development focuses upon efficiency and productivity as the key to competitive success.
- The third stage is achieved through the production of innovative products and services.

One highly successful cluster will be familiar to everyone: Hollywood.

The success of Hollywood

In the early 1900s, movie companies began to move to what we now know as Hollywood, attracted by the good weather and the cheaper labour costs. The industry initially was dominated by major studios, such as Paramount Pictures, who not only controlled all aspects of movie production, but also owned the theatres where the movies were shown. This meant that they also controlled consumption.[2]

A legal case helped to break up the major studios and created smaller specialist firms which, by all clustering around Hollywood, were still able to receive the benefits of a large studio, without many of the issues experienced by a large firm. It also

[1] M.E. Porter and C.H.M. Ketels, *UK competitiveness: moving to the next stage*, DTI and ESRC (May 2003), p. 5.

[2] M. Gupta, R. Jacobi, J.F. Jamet and L. Malik, 'The LA Motion Picture Industry Cluster', *The Microeconomics of Competitiveness: Firms, clusters and economic development*, Harvard Business School (May 2006).

Diseconomies of scale

When firms get beyond a certain size, costs per unit of output may start to increase. There are several reasons for such *diseconomies of scale*:

- Management problems of co-ordination may increase as the firm becomes larger and more complex and as lines of communication get longer. There may be a lack of personal involvement and oversight by management.
- Workers may feel 'alienated' if their jobs are boring and repetitive and if they feel an insignificant and undervalued small part of a large organisation. Poor motivation may lead to shoddy work.
- Industrial relations may deteriorate as a result of these factors and also as a result of the more complex interrelationships between different categories of worker.
- Production-line processes and the complex interdependencies of mass production can lead to great disruption if there are hold-ups in any one part of the firm.

Whether firms experience economies or diseconomies of scale will depend on the conditions applying in each individual firm.

Location

In the long run, a firm can move to a different location. The location will affect the cost of production, since locations differ in terms of the availability and cost of raw materials, suitable land and power supply, the qualifications, skills and experience of the labour force, wage rates, transport and communications networks, the cost of local services and banking and financial facilities. In short, locations differ in

Definition

Diseconomies of scale Where costs per unit of output increase as the scale of production increases.

meant that consumption and production were separated, creating a more competitive environment.

Another factor that required the companies to adapt was the growing demand and the emergence of new technologies. First, television ownership began to expand and then technology that allowed households to have entire films to watch at their leisure emerged (VHS tapes – the precursor to DVDs!). Such innovations required the industry to adapt, seeing these new forms of entertainment not as a potential threat to the industry, but as a new opportunity to generate revenue.[3]

Making the most of the competitive advantage that Hollywood had already established, the industry quickly grew. Data from 2013 show that the creative industries contributed $504 billion to US GDP, with Hollywood and the video industry together employing 310 000 workers – more than any other industry in California.

This Hollywood cluster has been a great success, but why?

Its location is certainly crucial, having all the geographical features that could be required in a film, together with a climate suitable for filming all year. The growth of Hollywood led many related industries to relocate there and this brought many significant benefits to the whole cluster, including cost advantages.

It attracted huge amounts of human capital, which is a key input for any successful cluster. Aspiring actors and actresses moved to Hollywood, as did those working in production, marketing and distribution, etc. It became the place to be for success in this industry.

As technology developed and movie production became more complex, so Hollywood attracted more and more industries:

electronics, IT, special effects and animation, to name but a few. This, together with the location playing home to thousands of movie stars, created a huge tourism industry, generating millions of dollars each year and providing another key contributing factor to the cluster's success: capital investment.

The film industry in Hollywood has always sought to move with the times, creating the most technologically advanced films that are always in high demand. The local rivalry between studios has been a key factor in driving competitiveness and fostering innovation, for example through special effects and animations: explosions, battle scenes and chases have to be bigger and better! The cluster's success has also been driven by government support, as both state and federal government provide incentives to aid in the growth of the cluster, such as tax credits to support film production and to help cut costs.

One big downside of Hollywood's success, however, is the growing cost of film production. Despite the government incentives that do help to keep costs lower, the popularity of Hollywood as a place to live and work has inflated property prices and wages. Movie making in this successful cluster generates huge revenues, but is also experiencing some of the adverse effects of its own success.

 What other examples of clusters can you find and how have they evolved to be a success?

Definition

Cluster (business or industrial) A geographical concentration of related businesses and institutions.

---

[3] R. Kumar, J. Zwirbulis, A. Narko, M Goszczycki and E. Ersöz, *Hollywood Movie Cluster Analysis*, Warsaw School of Economics, Microeconomics of Competitiveness (January 2014).

terms of the availability, suitability and cost of the factors of production. As you will see in Box 9.3, this is one reason why we see industrial clusters emerging in certain locations, such as Hollywood.

Transport costs are an important influence on a firm's location. Ideally, a firm wants to be as near as possible to both its raw materials and the market for its finished product. When market and raw materials are in different locations, the firm will minimise its transport costs by locating somewhere between the two. In general, if the raw materials are more expensive to transport than the finished product, the firm should locate as near as possible to the raw materials. Normally, this will apply to firms whose raw materials are heavier or more bulky than the finished product. Thus heavy industry, which uses large quantities of coal and various ores, tends to be concentrated near the coal fields or near the ports. If, on the other hand, the finished product is more expensive to transport (e.g. bread or beer), the firm will probably be located as near as possible to its market.

When raw materials or markets are in many different locations, transport costs will be minimised at the 'centre of gravity'. This location will be nearer to those raw materials and markets whose transport costs are greater per mile.

The size of the whole industry

As an *industry* grows in size, this can lead to *external economies of scale* for its member firms. This is where a firm, whatever its own individual size, benefits from the *whole industry* being large. For example, the firm may benefit from having access to specialist raw material or component suppliers, labour with specific skills, firms that specialise in marketing the finished product and banks and other financial institutions with experience of the industry's requirements. What we are referring to here is the *industry's infrastructure*: the facilities, support services, skills and experience that can be shared by its members.

The member firms of a particular industry might experience *external diseconomies of scale*. For example, as an industry grows larger, this may create a growing shortage of specific raw materials or skilled labour. This will push up their prices and hence the firms' costs.

Pause for thought

Would you expect external economies of scale to be associated with the concentration of an industry in a particular region? Explain.

The optimum combination of factors

In the long run, all factors can be varied. The firm can thus choose what techniques of production to use: what design of factory to build, what types of machine to buy, how to organise the factory and whether to use highly automated processes or more labour-intensive techniques. It must be very careful in making these decisions. Once it has built its factory and installed the machinery, these then become fixed factors of production, maybe for many years: the subsequent 'short-run' time period may, in practice, last a very long time!

For any given scale, how should the firm decide what technique to use? How should it decide the optimum 'mix' of factors of production?

The profit-maximising firm will, obviously, want to use the least costly combination of factors to produce any given output. It will, therefore, substitute factors, one for another, if by so doing it can reduce the cost of a given output. What, then, is the optimum combination of factors?

The simple two-factor case

Take first the simplest case where a firm uses just two factors: labour (*L*) and capital (*K*). The least-cost combination of the two will be where:

$$\frac{MPP_L}{P_L} = \frac{MPP_K}{P_K}$$

In other words, it is where the extra product (*MPP*) from the last pound spent on each factor is equal. But why should this be so? The easiest way to answer this is to consider what would happen if they were not equal.

If they were not equal, it would be possible to reduce cost per unit of output, by using a different combination of labour and capital. For example, if:

$$\frac{MPP_L}{P_L} > \frac{MPP_K}{P_K}$$

KI 4
p 19

more labour should be used relative to capital, since the firm is getting a greater physical return for its money from extra workers than from extra capital. As more labour is used per unit of capital, however, diminishing returns to labour set in.

KI 20
p 149

Thus MPP_L will fall. Likewise, as less capital is used per unit of labour, the MPP_K will rise. This will continue until:

$$\frac{MPP_L}{P_L} = \frac{MPP_K}{P_K}$$

At this point, the firm will stop substituting labour for capital.

Since no further gain can be made by substituting one factor for another, this combination of factors or 'choice of techniques' can be said to be the most efficient. It is the least-cost way of combining factors for any given output. Efficiency in this sense of using the optimum factor proportions is known as *technical or productive efficiency*.

The multifactor case

Where a firm uses many different factors, the least-cost combination of factors will be where:

$$\frac{MPP_a}{P_a} = \frac{MPP_b}{P_b} = \frac{MPP_c}{P_c} \cdots = \frac{MPP_n}{P_n}$$

where a . . . n are different factors of production.

The reasons are the same as in the two-factor case. If any inequality exists between the *MPP/P* ratios, a firm will be able to reduce its costs by using more of those factors with a high *MPP/P* ratio and less of those with a low *MPP/P* ratio until the ratios all become equal. A major problem for a firm in choosing the least-cost technique is in predicting future factor price changes.

If the price of a factor were to change, the *MPP/P* ratios would cease to be equal. The firm, to minimise costs, would then like to alter its factor combinations until the *MPP/P* ratios once more become equal. The trouble is that, once it has committed itself to a particular technique, it may be several years before it can switch to an alternative one. Thus, if a firm invests in labour-intensive methods of production and is then faced with an unexpected wage rise, it may regret not having chosen a more capital-intensive technique.

Postscript: decision making in different time periods

We have distinguished between the short run and the long run. Let us introduce two more time periods to complete the picture. The complete list then reads as follows.

Definitions

External economies of scale Where a firm's costs per unit of output decrease as the size of the whole *industry* grows.

Industry's infrastructure The network of supply agents, communications, skills, training facilities, distribution channels, specialised financial services, etc. that support a particular industry.

External diseconomies of scale Where a firm's costs per unit of output increase as the size of the whole industry increases.

Technical or productive efficiency The least-cost combination of factors for a given output.

Very short run (immediate run). All factors are fixed. Output is fixed. The supply curve is vertical. On a day-to-day basis, a firm may not be able to vary output at all. For example, a flower seller, once the day's flowers have been purchased from the wholesaler, cannot alter the amount of flowers available for sale on that day. In the very short run, all that may remain for a producer to do is to sell an already-produced good.

KI 20
p 149

Short run. At least one factor is fixed in supply. More can be produced by increasing the quantity of the variable factor, but the firm will come up against the law of diminishing returns as it tries to do so.

Long run. All factors are variable. The firm may experience constant, increasing or decreasing returns to scale. But, although all factors can be increased or decreased, they are of a fixed *quality*.

Very long run. All factors are variable *and* their quality, and hence productivity, can change. Labour productivity can increase as a result of education, training, experience and social factors. The productivity of capital can increase as a result of new inventions (new discoveries) and innovation (putting inventions into practice).

Improvements in factor quality will increase the output they produce: *TPP*, *APP* and *MPP* will rise. These curves will shift vertically upward.

Just how long the 'very long run' is will vary from firm to firm. It will depend on how long it takes to develop new techniques, new skills or new work practices.

It is important to realise that decisions *for* all four time periods can be made *at* the same time. Firms do not make short-run decisions *in* the short run and long-run decisions *in* the long run. They can make both short-run and long-run decisions today. For example, assume that a firm experiences an increase in consumer demand and anticipates that it will continue into the foreseeable future. It thus wants to increase

output. Consequently, it makes the following four decisions *today*:

- *(Very short run)* It accepts that, for a few days, it will not be able to increase output. It informs its customers that they will have to wait. It may temporarily raise prices to choke off some of the demand.
- *(Short run)* It negotiates with labour to introduce overtime working as soon as possible, to tide it over the next few weeks. It orders extra raw materials from its suppliers. It launches a recruitment drive for new labour so as to avoid paying overtime longer than is necessary.
- *(Long run)* It starts proceedings to build a new factory. The first step may be to discuss requirements with a firm of consultants.
- *(Very long run)* It institutes a programme of research and development and/or training in an attempt to increase productivity.

> **Pause for thought**
>
> 1. *What will the long-run market supply curve for a product look like? How will the shape of the long-run curve depend on returns to scale?*
> 2. *Why would it be difficult to construct a very long-run supply curve?*

Although we distinguish these four time periods, it is the middle two we are concerned with primarily. The reason for this is that there is very little that the firm can do in the very short run. And, in the very long run, although the firm obviously will want to increase the productivity of its inputs, it will not be in a position to make precise calculations of how to do it. It will not know precisely what inventions will be made or just what will be the results of its own research and development.

9.5 COSTS IN THE LONG RUN

When it comes to making long-run production decisions, the firm has much more flexibility. It does not have to operate with plant and equipment of a fixed size. It can expand the whole scale of its operations. All its inputs are variable and thus the law of diminishing returns does not apply. The firm may experience economies of scale or diseconomies of scale or its average costs may stay constant as it expands the scale of its operations.

Since there are no fixed factors in the long run, there are no long-run fixed costs. For example, the firm may rent more land in order to expand its operations. Its rent bill, therefore, goes up as it expands its output. All costs, then, in the long run, are variable costs.

Long-run average costs

Although it is possible to draw long-run total, marginal and average cost curves, we will concentrate on **long-run average cost (LRAC) curves**. These curves can take various shapes, but a typical one is shown in Figure 9.4.

> **Definition**
>
> **Long-run average cost (LRAC) curve** A curve that shows how average cost varies with output on the assumption that *all* factors are variable. (It is assumed that the least-cost method of production will be chosen for each output.)

BOX 9.4 MINIMUM EFFICIENT SCALE

The extent of economies of scale in practice

Two of the most important studies of economies of scale have been those made by C.F. Pratten and Michael Emerson[1] in the late 1980s and by a group advising the European Commission[2] in 1997. Both studies found strong evidence that many firms, especially in manufacturing, experienced substantial economies of scale.

In a few cases, long-run average costs fell continuously as output increased. For most firms, however, they fell up to a certain level of output and then remained constant.

The extent of economies of scale can be measured by looking at a firm's *minimum efficient scale* (*MES*). The *MES* is the size beyond which no significant additional economies of scale can be achieved: in other words, the point where the *LRAC* curve flattens off. In Pratten's studies, he defined this level as the minimum scale above which any possible doubling in scale would reduce average costs by less than 5 per cent (i.e. virtually the bottom of the *LRAC* curve). In the diagram, *MES* is shown at point *a*.

The *MES* can be expressed in terms either of an individual factory or of the whole firm. Where it refers to the minimum efficient scale of an individual factory, the *MES* is known as *the minimum efficient plant size* (*MEPS*).

The *MES* can then be expressed as a percentage of the total size of the market or of total domestic production. Table (a), based on the Pratten study, shows *MES* for plants and firms in

Table (a)

Product	MES as % of production		% additional cost at $1/2$ MES
	UK	EU	
Individual plants			
Cellulose fibres	125	16	3
Rolled aluminium semi-manufactures	114	15	15
Refrigerators	85	11	4
Steel	72	10	6
Electric motors	60	6	15
TV sets	40	9	9
Cigarettes	24	6	1.4
Ball-bearings	20	2	6
Beer	12	3	7
Nylon	4	1	12
Bricks	1	0.2	25
Tufted carpets	0.3	0.04	10
Shoes	0.3	0.03	1
Firms			
Cars	200	20	9
Lorries	104	21	7.5
Mainframe computers	>100	n.a.	5
Aircraft	100	n.a.	5
Tractors	98	19	6

Sources: Based on Michael Emerson, assisted by Michel Aujean, Michel Catinat, Philippe Goybet and Alexis Jacquemin, 'The Economics of 1992', *European Economy* 35, Commission of the European Communities (March 1988), Section 6.1 'Size phenomena: economies of scale'.

[1] C.F. Pratten, 'A survey of the economies of scale', in *Research on the 'Costs of Non-Europe'*, Vol. 2 (Office for Official Publications of the European Communities, 1988) and Michael Emerson, assisted by Michel Aujean, Michel Catinat, Philippe Goybet and Alexis Jacquemin, 'The Economics of 1992', *European Economy* 35, Commission of the European Communities (March 1988), Section 6.1 'Size phenomena: economies of scale'.

[2] European Commission/Economists Advisory Group Ltd, 'Economies of scale', *The Single Market Review*, subseries V, Vol. 4 (Office for Official Publications of the European Communities, 1997).

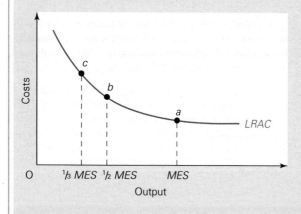

It is often assumed that, as a firm expands, initially it will experience economies of scale and thus face a downward-sloping *LRAC* curve. While it is possible for a firm to experience a continuously decreasing *LRAC* curve, in most cases, after a certain point (Q_1 in Figure 9.4), all such economies will have been achieved and thus the curve will flatten out.

Then, possibly after a period of constant *LRAC* (between Q_1 and Q_2), the firm will get so large that it will start experiencing diseconomies of scale and thus a rising *LRAC*. At this stage, production and financial economies begin to be offset by the managerial problems of running a giant organisation. Evidence does indeed show diseconomies of scale in many businesses arising from managerial problems and industrial relations, especially in growing businesses, but there is little evidence to suggest technical diseconomies.

Table (b)

Plants	MES as % of total EU production
Aerospace	12.19
Tractors and agricultural machinery	6.57
Electric lighting	3.76
Steel tubes	2.42
Shipbuilding	1.63
Rubber	1.06
Radio and TV	0.69
Footwear	0.08
Carpets	0.03

Source: European Commission/Economists Advisory Group Ltd, 'Economies of scale', *The Single Market Review*, subseries V, Vol. 4 (Office for Official Publications of the European Communities, 1997), data from Table 3.3.

various industries. The first column shows *MES* as a percentage of total UK production. The second column shows *MES* as a percentage of total EU production. Table (b), based on the 1997 study, shows *MES* for various plants as a percentage of total EU production.

Expressing *MES* as a percentage of total output gives an indication of how competitive the industry could be. In some industries (such as footwear and carpets), economies of scale were exhausted (i.e. *MES* was reached) with plants or firms that were still small relative to total UK production and even smaller relative to total EU production. In such industries there would be room for many firms and thus scope for considerable competition.

In other industries, however, even if a single plant or firm were large enough to produce the whole output of the industry in the UK, it would still not be large enough to experience the full potential economies of scale: the *MES* is greater than 100 per cent. Examples from Table (a) include factories producing cellulose fibres and car manufacturers.

In such industries there is no possibility of competition. In fact, as long as the *MES* exceeds 50 per cent, there will not be room for more than one firm large enough to gain full economies of scale. In this case, the industry is said to be *a natural monopoly*. As we shall see in the next few chapters, when competition is lacking, consumers may suffer by firms charging prices considerably above costs.

A second way of measuring the extent of economies of scale is to see how much costs would increase if production were reduced to a certain fraction of *MES*. The normal fractions used are $\frac{1}{2}$ or $\frac{1}{3}$ *MES*. This is illustrated in the diagram. Point *b* corresponds to $\frac{1}{2}$ *MES*; point *c* to $\frac{1}{3}$ *MES*. The greater the percentage by which *LRAC* at point *b* or *c* is higher than at point *a*, the greater will be the economies of scale to be gained by producing at *MES* rather than at $\frac{1}{2}$ *MES* or $\frac{1}{3}$ *MES*. For example, in the table there are greater economies of scale to be gained from moving from $\frac{1}{2}$ *MES* to *MES* in the production of electric motors than in cigarettes.

The main purpose of the studies was to determine whether the single EU market is big enough to allow both economies of scale and competition. The tables suggest that, in all cases, other things being equal, the EU market is large enough for firms to gain the full economies of scale *and* for there to be enough firms for the market to be competitive.

The second study also found that 47 of the 53 manufacturing sectors analysed had scope for further exploitation of economies of scale.

In the 2007–13 Research Framework, the European Commission agreed to fund a number of research projects. These will conduct further investigations of *MES* across different industries and consider the impact of the expansion of the EU.

1. *Why might a firm operating with one plant achieve MEPS and yet not be large enough to achieve MES? (Clue: are all economies of scale achieved at plant level?)*
2. *Why might a firm producing bricks have an MES that is only 0.2 per cent of total EU production and yet face little effective competition from other EU countries?*

The effect of these factors is to give an L-shaped or saucer-shaped curve.

Assumptions behind the long-run average cost curve

We make three key assumptions when constructing long-run average cost curves.

Factor prices are given. At each level of output, a firm will be faced with a given set of factor prices. If factor prices *change*,

therefore, both short- and long-run cost curves will shift. For example, an increase in wages would shift the curves vertically upwards.

However, factor prices might be different at *different* levels of output. For example, one of the economies of scale that many firms enjoy is the ability to obtain bulk discount on raw materials and other supplies. In such cases the curve does *not* shift. The different factor prices are merely experienced

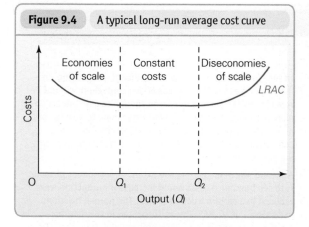

Figure 9.4 A typical long-run average cost curve

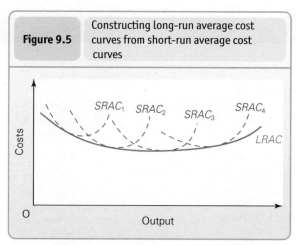

Figure 9.5 Constructing long-run average cost curves from short-run average cost curves

at different points along the curve, and are reflected in the shape of the curve. Factor prices are still given for any particular level of output.

The state of technology and factor quality are given. These are assumed to change only in the very long run. If a firm gains economies of scale, it is because it is able to exploit existing technologies and make better use of the existing factors of production. As technology improves, the curves will shift downwards.

Firms choose the least-cost combination of factors for each output. The assumption here is that firms operate efficiently: that they choose the cheapest possible way of producing any level of output. In other words, at every point along the *LRAC* curve the firm will adhere to the cost-minimising formula:

$$\frac{MPP_a}{P_a} = \frac{MPP_b}{P_b} = \frac{MPP_c}{P_c} \cdots = \frac{MPP_n}{P_n}$$

where a . . . n are the various factors that the firm uses.

If the firm did not choose the optimum factor combination, it would be producing at a point above the *LRAC* curve.

The relationship between long-run and short-run average cost curves

Take the case of a firm that has just one factory and faces a short-run average cost curve illustrated by $SRAC_1$ in Figure 9.5.

In the long run, it can build more factories or expand its existing facilities. If it thereby experiences economies of scale (due, say, to savings on administration), each successive factory will allow it to produce with a new lower *SRAC* curve. Thus, with two factories, it will face curve $SRAC_2$; with three factories curve $SRAC_3$, and so on. Each *SRAC* curve corresponds to a particular amount of the factor that is fixed in the short run: in this case, the factory. (There are many more *SRAC* curves that could be drawn between the ones shown, since factories of different sizes could be built or existing ones could be expanded.)

From this succession of short-run average cost curves, we can construct a long-run average cost curve. This is shown in Figure 9.5 and is known as the ***envelope curve***, since it envelops the short-run curves.

Definition

Envelope curve A long-run average cost curve drawn as the tangency points of a series of short-run average cost curves.

Pause for thought

Will the envelope curve be tangential to the bottom of each of the short-run average cost curves? Explain why it should or should not be.

BOX 9.5 | **FASHION CYCLES**

Costs and prices in the clothing industry

For many products, style is a key component of success. A good example is clothing. If manufacturers can successfully predict or even drive a new fashion, then sales growth can be substantial.

With any new fashion, growth is likely to be slow at first. Then, as the fashion 'catches on' and people want to be seen wearing this fashionable item, sales grow until a peak is

reached. In the case of clothing, if it is 'this year's fashion', then the peak will be reached within a couple of months. Then, as the market becomes saturated and people await the next season's fashions, so sales will fall.

This rise and fall is known as the 'fashion cycle' and is illustrated in the following diagram, which shows five stages:

introduction of a style; growth in popularity; peak in popularity; decline in popularity; obsolescence.

The variation of costs and prices over the fashion cycle

Costs and prices tend to vary with the stages of the fashion cycle. At the introductory stage of a new fashion item, average costs are likely to be high. Within that stage, the fixed costs of design, setting up production lines, etc. are spread over a relatively small output; average fixed costs are high. Also, there is a risk to producers that the fashion will not catch on and thus they are likely to factor in this risk when estimating costs. Finally, those consumers who want to be ahead in fashion and wearing the very latest thing will be willing to pay a high price to obtain such items – they will have relatively inelastic demand. The result of all these factors is that price is likely to be high in the introductory stage.

Assuming the fashion catches on and more units are produced to cater for this higher demand, average costs will begin to fall. This will allow prices to fall and, as a result, cheaper high street retailers will stock the clothes, thus further driving demand.

Beyond the peak, costs are unlikely to fall much further, but intense competition between retailers is likely to continue driving prices down. Demand for the garment in one store will be relatively elastic, as the same garment can be bought in any number of stores. The garments may end up on sales rails. (Note that, with fashions that do not catch on, the price may fall rapidly quite early on as producers seek to cut their losses.)

Then, with the new season's fashions, the cycle begins again.

1. *If consumers are aware that fashion clothing will fall in price as the season progresses, why do they buy when prices are set high at the start of the season? What does this tell us about the shape of the demand curve for a given fashion product (a) at the start, and (b) at the end of the season?*

The greater the importance of fashion for a particular type of garment, the greater the seasonable price variability is likely to be. The taller the 'bell' in the diagram, i.e. the greater the

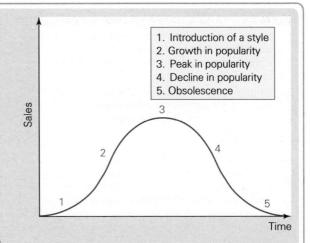

rise and fall in sales, the greater the difference in price between the different stages is likely to be.

Technology and the fashion cycle

We have seen that costs are an important element in the fashion cycle and in prices and sales through the different phases of the cycle. Fixed costs are highly dependent on technology. Advances in the textile industry have included more easily adaptable machines that are relatively easily programmed and design software that allows designers to change fashion parameters on the screen rather than with physical materials. These advances have meant that the fixed costs of introducing new fashions have come down. With lower fixed costs, average costs will tend to decline less steeply as output rises.

2. *How might we account for the changing magnitudes of the fashion price cycles of clothing? What role do fixed costs play in the explanation?*

3. *Despite new technology in the car industry, changing the design and shape of cars has increased as a share of the total production costs. How is this likely to have affected the fashion cycle in the car industry?*

SUMMARY

1a When measuring costs of production, we should be careful to use the concept of opportunity cost.

1b In the case of factors not owned by the firm, the opportunity cost is simply the explicit cost of purchasing or hiring them. It is the price paid for them.

1c In the case of factors already owned by the firm, it is the implicit cost of what the factor could have earned for the firm in its next best alternative use.

2a A production function shows the relationship between the amount of inputs used and the amount of output produced from them (per period of time).

2b In the short run, it is assumed that one or more factors (inputs) are fixed in supply. The actual length of the short run will vary from industry to industry.

2c Production in the short run is subject to diminishing returns. As greater quantities of the variable factor(s) are used, so each additional unit of the variable factor will add less to output than previous units: total physical product will rise less and less rapidly.

2d As long as marginal physical product is above average physical product, average physical product will rise. Once *MPP* has fallen below *APP*, however, *APP* will fall.

3a With some factors fixed in supply in the short run, their total costs will be fixed with respect to output. In the case of variable factors, their total cost will increase as more output is produced and hence as more of them are used.

3b Total cost can be divided into total fixed and total variable cost. Total variable cost will tend to increase less rapidly at first as more is produced, but then, when diminishing returns set in, it will increase more and more rapidly.

3c Marginal cost is the cost of producing one more unit of output. It will probably fall at first (corresponding to the part of the *TVC* curve where the slope is getting shallower), but will start to rise as soon as diminishing returns set in.

3d Average cost, like total cost, can be divided into fixed and variable costs. Average fixed cost will decline as more output is produced, as the total fixed cost is spread over a greater and greater number of units of output. Average variable cost will tend to decline at first, but once the marginal cost has risen above it, it must then rise.

4a In the long run, there are no fixed factors of production and so a firm is able to vary the quantity of all its inputs.

4b If a firm increases all factors by the same proportion, it may experience constant, increasing or decreasing returns to scale.

4c Economies of scale occur when costs per unit of output fall as the scale of production increases. This can be due to a number of factors, some of which are directly caused by increasing (physical) returns to scale, such as specialisation and division of labour. Other economies of scale arise from the financial and administrative benefits of large-scale organisations having a range of products (economies of scope).

4d Long-run costs are also influenced by a firm's location. The firm will have to balance the need to be as near as possible both to the supply of its raw materials and to its market. The optimum balance will depend on the relative costs of transporting the inputs and the finished product.

4e To minimise costs per unit of output, a firm should choose that combination of factors that gives an equal marginal product for each factor relative to its price: i.e. $MPP_a/P_a = MPP_b/P_b = MPP_c/P_c$, etc. (where a, b and c are different factors). If the MPP/P ratio for any factor is greater than that for another, more of the first should be used relative to the second.

5a There are thus no long-run fixed costs, as all factors are variable in the long run.

5b When constructing long-run cost curves, it is assumed that factor prices are given, that the state of technology is given and that firms will choose the least-cost combination of factors for each given output.

5c The *LRAC* curve can be downward sloping, upward sloping or horizontal, depending in turn on whether there are economies of scale, diseconomies of scale or neither. Typically, *LRAC* curves are drawn as saucer-shaped or L-shaped. As output expands, initially there are economies of scale. When these are exhausted, the curve will become flat. When the firm becomes very large, it may begin to experience diseconomies of scale. If this happens, the *LRAC* curve will begin to slope upward again.

5d An envelope curve can be drawn which shows the relationship between short-run and long-run average cost curves. The *LRAC* curve envelops the short-run *AC* curves: it is tangential to them.

REVIEW QUESTIONS

1 Are all explicit costs variable costs? Are all variable costs explicit costs?

2 Roughly how long would you expect the short run to be in the following cases?

   a) A mobile wedding DJ.
   b) Electricity power generation.
   c) A small grocery retailing business.
   d) 'Superstore Hypermarkets plc'.
   In each case, specify your assumptions.

3 Given that there is a fixed supply of land in the world, what implications can you draw from Figure 9.1 about the effects of an increase in world population for food output per head?

4 The following are some costs incurred by a shoe manufacturer. Decide whether each one is a fixed cost or a variable cost or has some element of both.

   a) The cost of leather.
   b) The fee paid to an advertising agency.
   c) Wear and tear on machinery.
   d) Business rates on the factory.
   e) Electricity for heating and lighting.
   f) Electricity for running the machines.
   g) Basic minimum or living wages agreed with the union.
   h) Overtime pay.
   i) Depreciation of machines as a result purely of their age (irrespective of their condition).

5 Assume that you are required to draw a *TVC* curve corresponding to Figure 9.1. What will happen to this *TVC* curve beyond point *d*?

6 Why is the minimum point of the *AVC* curve at a lower level of output than the minimum point of the *AC* curve?

7 Which economies of scale are due to increasing returns to scale and which are due to other factors?

8 Why are many firms likely to experience economies of scale up to a certain size and then diseconomies of scale after some point beyond that?

9 Why are bread and beer more expensive to transport per mile than the raw materials used in their manufacture?

10 Name some industries where external economies of scale are gained. What are the specific external economies in each case?

11 If factor X costs twice as much as factor Y ($P_X/P_Y = 2$), what can be said about the relationship between the *MPPs* of the two factors if the optimum combination of factors is used?

12 Could the long run and the very long run ever be the same length of time?

13 Examine Figure 9.4. What would (a) the firm's long-run total cost curve and (b) its long-run marginal cost curve look like?

14 Under what circumstances is a firm likely to experience a flat-bottomed *LRAC* curve?

Revenue and profit

Business issues covered in this chapter

- How does a business's sales revenue vary with output?
- How does the relationship between output and sales revenue depend on the type of market in which a business is operating?
- How do we measure profits?
- At what output will a firm maximise its profits? How much profit will it make at this output?
- At what point should a business shut down?

In this chapter, we will identify one of the most important points in business economics: the output and price at which a firm will maximise its profits and how much profit will be made at that level. Remember that we defined a firm's total profit ($T\Pi$) as its total revenue minus its total costs of production.

$$T\Pi = TR - TC$$

In the previous chapter, we looked at costs in some detail. We must now turn to the revenue side of the equation. As with costs, we distinguish between three revenue concepts: total revenue (TR), average revenue (AR) and marginal revenue (MR).

10.1 REVENUE

Total, average and marginal revenue

Total revenue (TR)

Total revenue is the firm's total earnings per period of time from the sale of a particular amount of output (Q).

For example, if a firm sells 1000 units (Q) per month at a price of £5 each (P), then its monthly total revenue will be £5000: in other words, £5 × 1000($P \times Q$). Thus:

$$TR = P \times Q$$

Average revenue (AR)

Average revenue is the average amount the firm earns per unit sold. Thus:

$$AR = TR/Q$$

So if the firm earns £5000 (TR) from selling 1000 units (Q), it will earn £5 per unit. But this is simply the price! Thus:

$$AR = P$$

The only exception to this is when the firm is selling its products at different prices to different consumers. In this case *AR* is simply the (weighted) average price.

Marginal revenue (MR)

Marginal revenue is the extra total revenue gained by selling one more unit per time period. So if a firm sells an extra 20 units this month compared with what it expected to sell and, in the process, earns an extra £100, then it is getting an extra £5 for each extra unit sold: *MR* = £5. Thus:

$$MR = \Delta TR/\Delta Q$$

We now need to see how each of these three revenue concepts (*TR*, *AR* and *MR*) varies with output. We can show this relationship graphically in the same way as we did with costs.

The relationship will depend on the market conditions under which a firm operates. A firm that is too small to be able to affect market price will have differently shaped revenue curves from a firm that has some choice in setting its price. Let us examine each of these two situations in turn.

Revenue curves when price is not affected by the firm's output

Average revenue

If a firm is very small relative to the whole market, it is likely to be a **price taker**. That is, it has to accept the price given by the intersection of demand and supply in the whole market. At this price, the firm can sell as much as it is capable of producing, but, if it increases the price, it would lose all its sales to competitors. Charging a lower price would not be rational as the firm can sell as much as it is capable of producing at the prevailing price. This is illustrated in Figure 10.1.

Diagram (a) shows market demand and supply. Equilibrium price is £5. Diagram (b) looks at the demand for an individual firm, which is tiny relative to the whole market. (Look at the difference in the scale of the horizontal axes in the two diagrams.)

Being so small, any change in the firm's output will be too insignificant to affect the market price. The firm thus faces a horizontal demand 'curve' at this price. It can sell any output up to its maximum capacity, without affecting this £5 price.

Average revenue is thus constant at £5. The firm's average revenue curve must, therefore, lie along exactly the same line as its demand curve.

Marginal revenue

In the case of a horizontal demand curve, the marginal revenue curve will be the same as the average revenue curve, since selling one more unit at a constant price (*AR*) merely adds that amount to total revenue. If an extra unit is sold at a constant price of £5, an extra £5 is earned.

Total revenue

Table 10.1 shows the effect on total revenue of different levels of sales with a constant price of £5 per unit.

As price is constant, total revenue will rise at a constant rate as more is sold. The *TR* 'curve' will therefore, be a straight line through the origin, as in Figure 10.2.

> ### Definitions
>
> **Total revenue** A firm's total earnings from a specified level of sales within a specified period: $TR = P \times Q$.
>
> **Average revenue** Total revenue per unit of output. When all output is sold at the same price, average revenue will be the same as price: $AR = TR/Q = P$.
>
> **Marginal revenue** The extra revenue gained by selling one or more unit per time period: $MR = \Delta TR/\Delta Q$.
>
> **Price taker** A firm that is too small to be able to influence the market price.

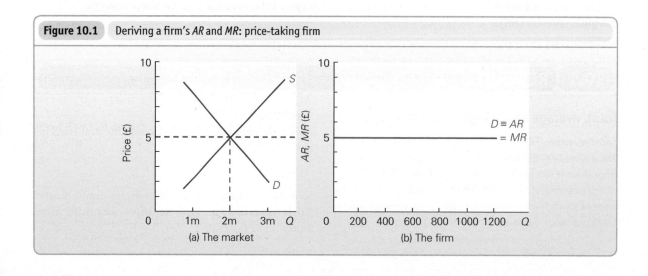

Figure 10.1 Deriving a firm's *AR* and *MR*: price-taking firm

Table 10.1	Deriving total revenue		
Quantity (units)	Price = AR = MR (£)		TR (£)
0	5		0
200	5		1000
400	5		2000
600	5		3000
800	5		4000
1000	5		5000
1200	5		6000
.	.		.

Table 10.2	Revenues for a firm facing a downward-sloping demand curve		
Q (units)	P = AR (£)	TR (£)	MR (£)
1	8	8	
			6
2	7	14	
			4
3	6	18	
			2
4	5	20	
			0
5	4	20	
			−2
6	3	18	
			−4
7	2	14	

Figure 10.2	Total revenue curve for a price-taking firm

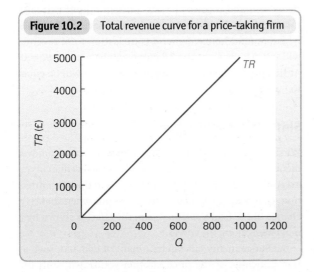

Pause for thought

What would happen to the TR curve if the market price rose to £10? Try drawing it.

Revenue curves when price varies with output

Rather than accepting (or taking) the market price, firms generally would prefer to be a ***price maker***. This means that, if a firm wants to sell more, it must lower its price. Alternatively, it could raise its price, if it was willing to accept a fall in demand. As such, a firm that is a price maker will face a downward-sloping demand curve. Firms will tend to be benefit from being price makers, as discussed in an article from Harvard Business School.[1]

The three curves (*TR, AR* and *MR*) will look quite different when price does vary with the firm's output.

Average revenue

Remember that average revenue equals price. If, therefore, the price has to be reduced to sell more output, average revenue will fall as output increases.

Table 10.2 gives an example of a firm facing a downward-sloping demand curve. The demand curve (which shows how much is sold at each price) is given by the first two columns.

Note that, as in the case of a price-taking firm, the demand curve and the *AR* curve lie along exactly the same line. The reason for this is simple: *AR* = *P*, and thus the curve relating price to quantity (the demand curve) must be the same as that relating average revenue to quantity (the *AR* curve).

Pause for thought

Consider the items you have recently purchased. Classify them into products purchased from markets where sellers were price takers and those where the sellers were price makers.

Marginal revenue

When a firm faces a downward-sloping demand curve, marginal revenue will be less than average revenue and may even be negative. But why?

If a firm is to sell more per time period, it must lower its price (assuming it does not advertise). This will mean

Definition

Price maker (price chooser) A firm that has the ability to influence the price charged for its good or service.

[1]Benson P. Shapiro, 'Commodity busters: be a price maker not a price taker', *Working Knowledge,* Harvard University (10 February 2003).

lowering the price not just for the extra units it hopes to sell, but also for those units it would have sold had it not lowered the price.

Thus the marginal revenue is the price at which it sells the last unit, *minus* the loss in revenue it has incurred by reducing the price on those units it could otherwise have sold at the higher price. This can be illustrated with Table 10.2.

Assume that price is currently £7. Two units are thus sold. If the firm wishes to sell an extra unit, it must lower the price, say to £6. It thus gains £6 from the sale of the third unit, but loses £2 by having to reduce the price by £1 on the two units previously sold at £7. Its net gain is therefore £6 − £2 = £4. This is the marginal revenue: it is the extra revenue gained by the firm from selling one more unit. Try using this method to check out the remaining figures for *MR* in Table 10.2. (Note that in the table the figures for *MR* are entered in the spaces between the figures for the other three columns.)

There is a simple relationship between marginal revenue and *price elasticity of demand*. Remember from Chapter 5 (see page 68) that, if demand is price elastic, a *decrease* in price will lead to a proportionately larger increase in the quantity demanded and hence an *increase* in revenue. Marginal revenue will thus be positive. If, however, demand is inelastic, a decrease in price will lead to a proportionately smaller increase in sales. In this case, the price reduction will more than offset the increase in sales and, as a result, revenue will fall. Marginal revenue will be negative.

If, then, marginal revenue is a positive figure (i.e. if sales per time period are four units or fewer in Figure 10.3), the demand curve will be elastic at that point, since a rise in quantity sold (as a result of a reduction in price) would lead to a rise in total revenue. If, on the other hand, marginal revenue is negative (i.e. at a level of sales of five or more units in

Figure 10.3), the demand curve will be inelastic at that point, since a rise in quantity sold would lead to a *fall* in total revenue.

Thus, even though we have a straight-line demand (*AR*) curve in Figure 10.3, the price elasticity of demand is not constant along it. The curve is elastic to the left of point *r* and inelastic to the right.

Total revenue

Total revenue equals price times quantity. This is illustrated in Table 10.2. The *TR* column from Table 10.2 is plotted in Figure 10.4.

Unlike in the case of a price-taking firm, the *TR* curve is not a straight line. It is a curve that rises at first and then falls. But why? As long as marginal revenue is positive (and hence demand is price elastic), a rise in output will raise total revenue. However, once marginal revenue becomes negative (and hence demand is inelastic), total revenue will fall. The peak of the *TR* curve will be where *MR* = 0. At this point, the price elasticity of demand will be equal to −1.

Shifts in revenue curves

We saw (Chapter 4) that a change in *price* will cause a movement along a demand curve. It is similar with revenue curves, except that here the causal connection is in the other direction. Here we ask what happens to revenue when there is a change in the firm's *output*. Again, the effect is shown by a movement along the curves.

A change in any *other* determinant of demand, such as tastes, income or the price of other goods, will shift the demand curve. By affecting the price at which each level of output can be sold, it will cause a shift in all three revenue curves. An increase in revenue is shown by a vertical shift upward; a decrease by a shift downward.

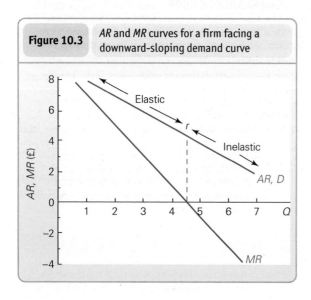

| **Figure 10.3** | *AR* and *MR* curves for a firm facing a downward-sloping demand curve |

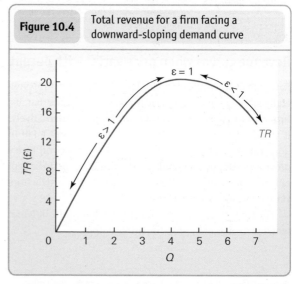

| **Figure 10.4** | Total revenue for a firm facing a downward-sloping demand curve |

BOX 10.1   COSTS, REVENUE AND PROFITS

Strategies to increase total revenue

A firm's profit depends on two key factors: costs and revenue. In this box, we consider some strategies to increase revenue, while also considering the potential effect of such strategies on costs and, in turn, profits.

Total revenue is determined by price and quantity, so a change in either will affect total revenue. How might a firm go about boosting sales at the current price? Firms may look to find new markets for their products. For example, many US, European, Australian and Japanese companies have expanded into Asian markets (as discussed in a PwC blog[1] in the context of Japanese companies).

Another strategy used by firms is product differentiation. This aims to distinguish their product from others and encourage consumers to switch to it. Alternatively, a firm may engage in advertising to try to persuade consumers to buy the product (we explored this in Chapter 8).

With successful implementation of these strategies, at any given price, quantity should now rise and hence so will total revenue. But, does this mean that profits increase?

Advertising, product innovation and market research require time, resources and money and so can be very expensive. While the outcome of such investment might be an increase in total revenue, the means of achieving it will be an increase in total costs. This means that, unless we know the relative increase in total revenue and total costs, the impact on profits is uncertain.

Furthermore, the increase in costs will occur as soon as work starts on the process of product differentiation or market research or at the beginning of an advertising campaign. The increase in revenue may not be felt for some time, as advertising campaigns, entrance into a new market and a differentiated product can take many months before having their anticipated effect. Any firm engaging in such a strategy may, therefore, experience a period of time in which its costs are rising while revenue is remaining fairly constant. In other words, profits decline, until the sales figures respond to the firm's strategy. In 2013, Starbucks implemented a strategy to boost profits, as is discussed in an article by Tucker Dawson[2]; and a travel agency in the north east of the UK also changed its strategy in a bid to increase profits, as discussed in an article by Jonathan Manning.[3]

Pricing, elasticity and profits

Another option for the firm could be to look at its pricing strategy. The Law of Demand tells us that, if the price of a good falls, the quantity demanded will rise. The key question is by how much?

When demand is price inelastic, any decrease in price leads to a proportionately smaller increase in demand and so total revenue would fall (as we saw in Chapter 5). But, if the firm were to *increase* the price of such a product, total revenue would rise.

1. *How will total revenue be affected by (a) a price rise and (b) a price fall if demand for the product was elastic?*

Therefore, if a firm knows its product's price elasticity of demand, it can use this to help it increase total revenue.

But what about the impact on profits? Let us consider a product with an *elastic* demand and think about the impact of a price cut on both revenue and costs. The cut in price will boost revenue, as the quantity demanded rises proportionately more than price falls. But, with an increased demand, the firm may have to increase production, which means its total variable costs will rise and, possibly, its average variable costs too (although average fixed costs will fall). If, however, the firm has sufficient stocks to satisfy the higher demand, then the impact on costs may be less severe. With an elastic demand, the impact on profit depends on whether total revenue increases by more or less than total costs.

But what about the situation where a product has an inelastic demand? This time it is an *increase* in price that will boost total revenue, as the resulting fall in quantity will be proportionately smaller than the rise in price. If production is reduced, it will reduce the firm's demand for raw materials and, in doing so, cut its total variable costs. In this case, the impact on profit is somewhat more predictable, as total revenue is increasing, while total costs are falling.

Whether demand is elastic or inelastic will depend in part on what rivals do. If a firm has an apparently elastic demand because consumers are very responsive to price changes in that industry, it might seem sensible for the firm to cut its price if the anticipated rise in revenue is greater than the rise in costs. But this may trigger a response from rivals; they too may cut prices to avoid losing market share. If this happens, the firm may find that its sales rise by only a little and that its revenue falls, not rises. So pricing strategy must take into account the likely response of competitors. We consider this issue in Chapters 12 and 17.

There are many factors that can influence profitability and, whenever a firm considers a change in strategy, it is important to consider the impact on both costs and revenue and the timing of such changes. This may make the difference between a company's success and failure.

2. *Consider a firm that introduced a new policy of using only environmentally friendly inputs and locally sourced products in its production process. Analyse the impact of this strategy on the firm's costs and revenue. How do you think profits will be affected?*

[1]Arie Nakamura, 'The continuous expansion of Japanese companies in Southeast Asia', *Navigating Growth Markets blog,* PwC Growth Markets Centre (25 August 2017).

[2]Tucker Dawson, 'How Starbucks uses pricing strategy for profit maximization', *Price Intelligently* (30 June 2013).

[3]Jonathon Manning, 'Hays Travel sees profits soar as expansion strategy begins to take off', *ChronicleLive* (19 March 2018).

10.2 PROFIT MAXIMISATION

We are now in a position to put costs and revenue together to find the output at which profit is maximised, and also to find out how much that profit will be. At this point, you may find an article by Renee O'Farrell[2] interesting: it considers the advantages and disadvantages of pursuing a strategy of profit maximisation.

There are two ways of determining the level of output at which a firm will maximise profits. The first and simpler method is to use total cost and total revenue curves. The second method is to use marginal and average cost and marginal and average revenue curves. Although this method is a little more complicated, it makes things easier when we come to compare profit maximising under different market conditions (see Chapters 11 and 12).

We will look at each method in turn. In both cases, we will concentrate on the short run: namely that period in which one or more factors are fixed in supply. In both cases, we take the case of a firm facing a downward-sloping demand curve: i.e. a price maker.

Short-run profit maximisation: using total curves

Table 10.3 shows the total revenue figures from Table 10.2. It also shows figures for total cost. These figures have been chosen so as to produce a TC curve of a typical shape.

Total profit (TΠ) is found by subtracting TC from TR. This can be seen in Table 10.3. Where (TΠ) is negative, the firm is making a loss. Total profit is maximised at an output of three units: where there is the greatest gap between total revenue and total costs. At this output, total profit is £4 (£18 − £14).

The TR, TC and TΠ curves are plotted in Figure 10.5. The size of the maximum profit is shown by the arrows.

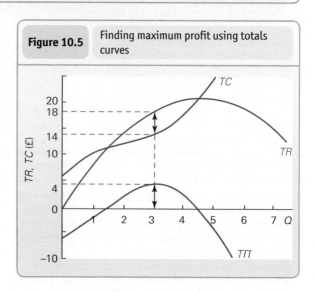

Figure 10.5 Finding maximum profit using totals curves

Short-run profit maximisation: using average and marginal curves

Finding the maximum profit that a firm can make is a two-stage process. The first stage is to find the profit-maximising output. To do this we use the MC and MR curves. The second stage is to find out just how much profit is at this output. To do this we use the AR and AC curves.

Stage 1: Using marginal curves to arrive at the profit-maximising output

There is a very simple **profit-maximising rule**: if profits are to be maximised, MR *must equal MC*. From Table 10.4 it can be seen

> **Definition**
>
> **Profit-maximising rule** Profit is maximised where marginal revenue equals marginal cost.

Table 10.3 Total revenue, costs and profit

Q (units)	TR (£)	TC (£)	TΠ (£)
0	0	6	−6
1	8	10	−2
2	14	12	2
3	18	14	4
4	20	18	2
5	20	25	−5
6	18	36	−18
7	14	56	−42
.	.	.	.

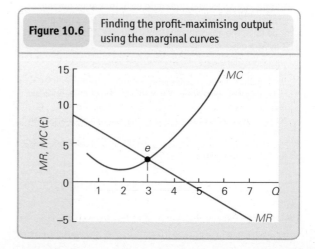

Figure 10.6 Finding the profit-maximising output using the marginal curves

[2]Renee O'Farrell, 'Advantages and disadvantages of profit maximization', *Small Business*Chron.com, Houston Chronicle* (24 June 2011).

Table 10.4 Revenue, costs and profit

Q (units)	P = AR (£)	TR (£)	MR (£)	TC (£)	AC (£)	MC (£)	TΠ (£)	AΠ (£)
0	9	0		6	—		−6	—
			8			4		
1	8	8		10	10		−2	−2
			6			2		
2	7	14		12	6		2	1
			4			2		
3	6	18		14	4.67		4	−1.33
			2			4		
4	5	20		18	4.5		2	−0.5
			0			7		
5	4	20		25	5		−5	−1
			−2			11		
6	3	18		36	6		−18	−3
			−4			20		
7	2	14		56	8		−42	−6

Pause for thought

Why are the figures for MR and MC entered in the spaces between the lines in Table 10.4?

that $MR = MC$ at an output of 3 (Table 10.4 is based on the figures in Table 10.3). This is shown as point *e* in Figure 10.6.

KI 4
p 19

But why are profits maximised when $MR = MC$? The simplest way of answering this is to see what the position would be if MR did not equal MC.

Referring to Figure 10.6, at a level of output below 3, MR exceeds MC. This means that by producing more units there will be a bigger addition to revenue (MR) than to cost (MC). Total profit will *increase. As long as MR exceeds MC, profit can be increased by increasing production.*

At a level of output above 3, MC exceeds MR. All levels of output above 3 thus add more to cost than to revenue and hence *reduce* profit. *As long as MC exceeds MR, profit can be increased by cutting back on production.*

Profits are thus maximised where $MC = MR$: at an output of 3. This can be confirmed by examining the $TΠ$ column in Table 10.4.

Students worry sometimes about the argument that profits are maximised when $MR = MC$. Surely, they say, if the last unit is making no profit, how can profit be at a *maximum*? The answer is very simple. If you cannot *add* anything more to a total, the total must be at the maximum. Take the simple analogy of going up a hill. When you cannot go any higher, you must be at the top.

Stage 2: Using average curves to measure the size of the profit

Once the profit-maximising output has been discovered, we now use the average curves to measure the *amount* of profit at

the maximum. Both marginal and average curves corresponding to the data in Table 10.4 are plotted in Figure 10.7.

First, average profit ($AΠ$) is found. This is simply $AR − AC$. At the profit-maximising output of 3, this gives a figure for $AΠ$ of £6 − £4⅔ = £1⅓ Then total profit is obtained by multiplying average profit by output:

$$TΠ = AΠ \times Q$$

This is shown as the shaded area. It equals £1⅓ × 3 = £4. This can again be confirmed by reference to the $TΠ$ column in Table 10.4.

Some qualifications

Long-run profit maximisation

Assuming that the AR and MR curves are the same in the long run as in the short run, long-run profits will be maximised at the output where MR equals the *long-run MC*. The reasoning is the same as with the short-run case.

Pause for thought

What will be the effect on a firm's profit-maximising output of a rise in fixed costs?

The meaning of 'profit'

One element of cost is the opportunity cost to the owners of the firm incurred by being in business. This is the minimum return that the owners must make on their capital in order to prevent them from eventually deciding to close down and perhaps move into some alternative business. It is a *cost* since, just as with wages, rent, etc., it has to be covered if the firm is to continue producing. This opportunity cost to the owners is sometimes known as **normal profit**, and *is included in the cost curves.*

KI 3
p 19

What determines this normal rate of profit? It has two components. First, someone setting up in business invests capital in it. There is thus an opportunity cost of capital. This is the interest that could have been earned by lending it in some riskless form (e.g. by putting it in a savings account in a bank). Nobody would set up a business unless they expected to earn at least this rate of profit. Running a business is far from riskless, however, and hence a second element is a return to compensate for risk. Thus:

normal profit (%) = rate of interest on a riskless loan + *a risk premium*

The risk premium varies according to the line of business. In those with fairly predictable patterns, such as food retailing, it is relatively low. Where outcomes are very uncertain, such as mineral exploration or the manufacture of fashion garments, it is relatively high.

Thus if owners of a business earn normal profit, they will (just) be content to remain in that industry. If they earn more than normal profit, they will (obviously) prefer to stay in this business. If they earn less than normal profit, then, after a time, they will consider leaving and using their capital for some other purpose.

Given that normal profits are included in costs, any profit that is shown diagrammatically (e.g. the shaded area in Figure 10.7) must therefore be over and above normal profit. It is known by several alternative names: *supernormal profit, pure profit, economic profit, abnormal profit* or sometimes simply *profit*. They all mean the same thing: the excess of profit over normal profit, or where *AR* is greater than *AC*. The article 'Milk prices: who gets the cream?', from the Sloman News Site, considers profitability in the milk industry.

Loss minimising

It may be that there is no output at which the firm can make a profit. Such a situation is illustrated in Figure 10.8: the *AC* curve is above the *AR* curve at all levels of output.

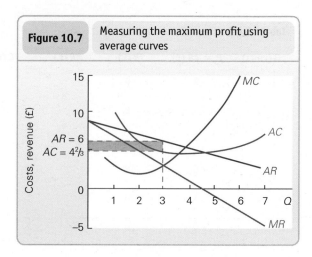

Figure 10.7	Measuring the maximum profit using average curves

In this case, the output where $MR = MC$ will be the loss-minimising output. The amount of loss at the point where $MR = MC$ is shown by the shaded area in Figure 10.8.

Whether or not to produce at all

The short run. Fixed costs have to be paid, even if the firm is producing nothing at all. Rent has to be paid, business rates have to be paid, etc. Providing, therefore, that the firm is more than covering its *variable* costs, it can go some way

---

Definitions

Normal profit The opportunity cost of being in business. It consists of the interest that could be earned on a riskless asset, plus a return for risk-taking in this particular industry. It is counted as a cost of production.

Supernormal profit (also known as **pure profit, economic profit, abnormal profit** or simply **profit**) The excess of total profit above normal profit.

BOX 10.2 — SELLING ICE CREAM WHEN I WAS A STUDENT

John's experience of competition

When I was a student, my parents lived in Exeter in Devon and, at that time, the city's bypass became completely jammed on a summer Saturday as holidaymakers made their way to the coast. Traffic queues were several miles long.

For a summer job, I drove a small ice-cream van. Early on, I had the idea of selling ice cream from a tray to the people queuing in their cars. I made more money on a Saturday than the rest of the week put together. I thought I was on to a good thing.

But news of this lucrative market soon spread and, each week, new ice-cream sellers appeared – each one reducing my earnings! By the middle of August, there were over 30 ice-cream sellers from five different ice-cream companies. Most tried to get to the beginning of the queue, to get ahead of their rivals.

Imagine the scene. A family driving to the coast rounds a bend and is suddenly met with a traffic jam and several

ice-cream sellers all jostling to sell them an ice cream. It was quite surreal. Not surprisingly, many of the potential customers refused to buy, feeling somewhat intimidated by the spectacle. It was not long before most of us realised that it was best to disperse and find a section of the road where there were no other sellers.

But, with so many ice-cream sellers, no one made much money. My supernormal earnings had been reduced to a normal level. I made about the same on Saturday selling to people stuck in queues as I would have done if I had driven my van around the streets.

Imagine that you live in a popular and sunny seaside town and that the local council awarded you the only licence to sell ice cream in the town. Would you be earning normal or supernormal profit? Explain your answer.

Figure 10.8 Loss-minimising output

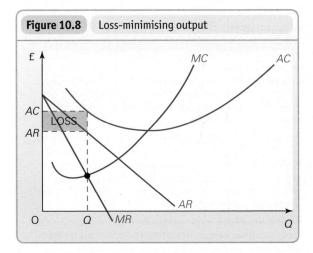

to paying off these fixed costs and therefore will continue to produce.

Therefore, the firm will shut down if the loss it would make from doing so (i.e. the fixed costs that must still be paid) is less than the loss it makes from continuing to produce. That is, a firm will shut down if it cannot cover its variable costs. In Figure 10.9, this will be where the price (*AR*) is below the *AVC* curve: i.e. if it is below the **short-run shut-down point**, where *AR* = *AVC*.

The long run. All costs are variable in the long run. If, therefore, the firm cannot cover its long-run average costs (which include normal profit), it will close down. The **long-run shut-down point** will be where the *AR* curve is tangential to the *LRAC* curve.

Figure 10.9 The short-run shut-down point

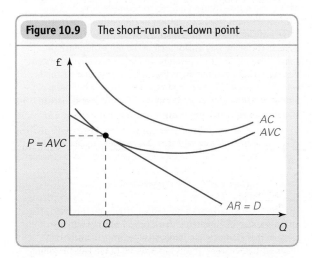

Pause for thought

Why might it make sense for a firm that cannot sell its output at a profit to continue in production for the time being?

Definitions

Short-run shut-down point This is where the *AR* curve is tangential to the *AVC* curve. The firm can only just cover its variable costs. Any fall in revenue below this level will cause a profit-maximising firm to shut down immediately.

Long-run shut-down point This is where the *AR* curve is tangential to the *LRAC* curve. The firm can just make normal profits. Any fall in revenue below this level will cause a profit-maximising firm to shut down once all costs have become variable.

BOX 10.3	MONARCH'S TURBULENCE

What disrupted Monarch's flight path?

In October 2017, Monarch Airlines collapsed, ending its 50-year run as a leading airline for short-haul flights for package holidays in and around Europe. Monarch operated in a competitive market place (more on this in Part E), competing for customers with airlines such as easyJet, Ryanair, Thomas Cook and TUI.

There were several contributing factors to Monarch's demise that affected its costs and revenues and eventually meant that its profits disappeared, replaced with unsustainable losses. The airline had been in difficulty, with its pre-tax profits down from £39.3 million in the year ending October 2015 to £12.9 million in October 2016, but, throughout the latter half

of 2016 and 2017, its profit position changed significantly, despite a cash injection of £165 million from its majority shareholder, Greybull Capital. A series of unfortunate external events added to problems within the business itself and the combination pushed costs up, pulled revenues down and led to a reported pre-tax loss of £291 million in August 2017.

We now consider how Monarch's costs and revenues were affected and you can read about Monarch's troubles in many articles, including in Business Insider,[1] The Guardian,[2] BBC News,[3] the Independent[4] and Management Today.[5]

[1]Will Martin, 'What brought down Monarch, the UK's biggest ever airline collapse?', *Business Insider* (3 October 2017).

[2]Gwyn Topham and Rachel Obordo, 'The collapse of Monarch: inside the doomed airline in its last days', *The Guardian* (2 October 2017).

[3]Karen Hoggan, 'Monarch: Four reasons behind its failure', *BBC News* (2 October 2017).

[4]Simon Calder, 'Monarch airlines goes into administration: what went wrong?', *Independent* (1 October 2017).

[5]Adam Gale, 'What did Monarch do wrong?', *Management Today* (2 October 2017).

▶

Monarch's costs

Airlines are notorious for having high fixed costs through salaries, certain aviation taxes, insurance, etc. and, as we saw in Box 9.2, this makes a firm particularly vulnerable to any fall in output, as it raises costs significantly and thus cuts profits. However, not only did Monarch have the typical fixed costs of an airline, but it tended to have more fixed costs than some of its competitors, because it operated many more aircraft within its fleet. This meant that it incurred much higher costs in a number of areas, including training driven by the need to access more skilled labour. However, given the market in which Monarch was competing, it was really incurring these costs unnecessarily.

A key cost for any airline is fuel, which is priced in dollars. This means that for a UK-based airline such as Monarch, it has to purchase dollars on the foreign exchange market in order to buy a given quantity of fuel. As the exchange rate between pounds and dollars changes, so does the cost of buying the fuel. One of the major causes of Monarch's trouble was Brexit. When the UK voted to leave the EU in June 2016, the pound began to depreciate (we cover this in more detail in Chapter 27). This meant that Monarch needed to buy more and more dollars in order to purchase the same quantity of fuel. The higher cost of fuel, together with the higher cost of aircraft leases, also priced in dollars, pushed up Monarch's annual costs by £50 million and adversely affected profits. Andrew Swaffield, Monarch's Chief Executive commented:

> We take nearly all or our revenue in pounds and a lot of our costs go out in dollars and euros. We pay for aircraft leases and fuel in dollars and things like navigation and ground handling in euros. So we get no revenue benefit from a decline in the pound but we get a big cost increase.

Other British-based airlines were similarly affected, with easyJet noting the fall in the pound cost it £90 million.

 1. *Draw a diagram of Monarch's average cost curves and explain the shape. With the fall in the value of the pound increasing Monarch's costs, illustrate the impact on the cost curves.*

Monarch's revenues

At the same time as Monarch's costs were rising, changes were also occurring on the demand side. While some short-haul airlines had specialised in flights to the Mediterranean, Monarch had focused on travel to slightly different destinations, including Tunisia and Sharm el Sheikh. Due to terrorist activities in such locations and subsequent travel bans and travel advice from the UK Government, Monarch saw demand for its flights begin to decline. As Tim Symes noted:

> A higher terrorism threat has proved to be difficult for trading conditions; Egypt and Turkey provided a key chunk of revenue for [Monarch] and subsequent terror attacks left the airline deprived from the resulting weaker demand.

Consumers were facing a continuing squeeze on their incomes. This was exacerbated by the fall in the pound, which put upward pressure on the sterling price of foreign holidays. Despite offering extremely low fares, Monarch was operating flights that were barely half-full. This impacted dramatically on its revenues. As we shall see in Chapter 18 (see pages 299–300), the general pricing model for budget airlines is to raise ticket prices as flights fill up. A half-full plane, therefore, earns considerably less than half the revenue from a full plane.

Not only did this mean that its revenues were lower, but it was also facing rising per unit costs, as its fixed costs were now having to be spread across fewer people. While you can certainly cut some costs with a half-full flight (e.g. less fuel required), you still need to pay the flight staff, the pilot, the aviation insurance, etc.

While Monarch was experiencing a decline in demand because its destinations were either less popular or banned for travel, competitors, such as easyJet, saw passenger numbers increase. Between 2015 and 2017, numbers flying to Portugal with easyJet rose from 41 million to 53 million and to Spain, the increase was from 215 million to 258 million. Therefore, while easyJet was certainly affected by Brexit and faced rising costs in the same way as Monarch, it did not experience the same adverse effects on revenue. In fact, it actually benefited from the trials of Monarch, as the data suggest that customers who may have been planning to travel to Tunisia or Sharm el Sheikh with Monarch now looked for substitutes and instead travelled to the Mediterranean.

 2. *Draw a diagram that shows the changes that Monarch experienced on both the demand and supply side and hence on costs and revenues. Show how this led to the airline's decline in profits and eventual collapse.*

The short-haul market is highly competitive and this was another issue for Monarch – there simply was not enough room in this market when it moved away from its focus on the long-haul market. It was not offering passengers anything new and, because of its over-capacity, this again meant per-unit costs were higher and it was not able to compete effectively with the other low-cost carriers.

Conclusions

Monarch's market share was insufficient to deal with the rising costs and contracting demand in the market. Furthermore, while some of its competitors did adapt to the changing market conditions, Monarch did not. For example, Ryanair partnered with Air Europa and hence was able to benefit from the long-haul market as well, as customers could now buy such flights via Ryanair.

It was, therefore, a combination of both internal and external factors that led to the demise of Monarch. Its cost strucwture, failure to adapt to changes, the crowded market, Brexit and terrorism all played a part and led to rising costs, falling revenues and, inevitably, unsustainable losses. Monarch was not the only short-haul casualty, as its collapse followed the decisions to file for bankruptcy by Alitalia and Air Berlin in May and August 2017 respectively. As the founder of Greybull Capital said, 'the European short-haul market is certainly a "bloodbath"'.

SUMMARY

1a Just as we could identify total, average and marginal costs, so too we can identify total, average and marginal revenue.

1b Total revenue (*TR*) is the total amount a firm earns from its sales in a given time period. It is simply price times quantity: $TR = P \times Q$.

1c Average revenue (*AR*) is total revenue per unit: $AR = TR/Q$. In other words, $AR = P$.

1d Marginal revenue is the extra revenue earned from the sale of one more unit per time period.

1e The *AR* curve will be the same as the demand curve for the firm's product. In the case of a price taker, the demand curve, and hence the *AR* curve, will be a horizontal straight line and will be the same as the *MR* curve. The *TR* curve is an upward-sloping straight line from the origin.

1f A firm that faces a downward-sloping demand curve must also face the same downward-sloping *AR* curve. The *MR* curve will also slope downward, but will be below the *AR* curve and steeper than it. The *TR* curve will be an arch shape starting from the origin.

1g When demand is price elastic, marginal revenue will be positive and the *TR* curve will be upward sloping. When demand is price inelastic, marginal revenue will be negative and the *TR* curve will be downward sloping.

1h A change in output is represented by a movement along the revenue curves. A change in any other determinant of revenue will shift the curves up or down.

2a Total profit equals total revenue minus total cost. By definition, then, a firm's profits will be maximised at the point where there is the greatest gap between total revenue and total cost.

2b Another way of finding the maximum-profit point is to find the output where marginal revenue equals marginal cost. Having found this output, the level of maximum profit is found by finding the average profit *(AR − AC)* and then multiplying it by the level of output.

2c Normal profit is the minimum profit that must be made to persuade a firm to stay in business in the long run. It is counted as part of the firm's cost. Supernormal profit is any profit over and above normal profit.

2d For a firm that cannot make a profit at any level of output, the point where $MR = MC$ represents the loss-minimising output.

2e In the short run, a firm will close down if it cannot cover its variable costs. In the long run, it will close down if it cannot make normal profits.

REVIEW QUESTIONS

1. Draw a downward-sloping demand curve. Now put in scales of your own choosing for both axes. Read off various points on the demand curve and use them to construct a table showing price and quantity. Use this table to work out the figures for a marginal revenue column. Now use these figures to draw an *MR* curve. Explain the position of your *MR* curve in relation to demand.

2. Copy Figures 10.3 and 10.4 (which are based on Table 10.2). Now assume that incomes have risen and that, as a result, two more units per time period can be sold at each price. Draw a new table and plot the resulting new *AR, MR* and *TR* curves on your diagrams. Are the new curves parallel to the old ones? Explain.

3. What can we say about the slope of the *TR* and *TC* curves at the maximum-profit point? What does this tell us about marginal revenue and marginal cost?

4. Using the following information, construct a table like Table 10.3.

Q	0	1	2	3	4	5	6	7
P	12	11	10	9	8	7	6	5
TC	2	6	9	12	16	21	28	38

Use your table to draw diagrams like Figures 10.5 and 10.7. Use these two diagrams to show the profit-maximising output and the level of maximum profit. Confirm your findings by reference to the table you have constructed.

5. The following table shows the average cost and average revenue (price) for a firm at each level of output.

a) Construct a table to show *TC, MC, TR* and *MR* at each level of output (put the figures for *MC* and *MR* midway between the output figures).

b) Using *MC* and *MR* figures, find the profit-maximising output.

c) Using *TC* and *TR* figures, check your answer to (b).

d) Plot the *AC, MC, AR* and *MR* figures on a graph.

e) Mark the profit-maximising output and the *AR* and *AC* at this output.

f) Shade in an area to represent the level of profits at this output.

Output	1	2	3	4	5	6	7	8	9	10
AC (£)	7.00	5.00	4.00	3.30	3.00	3.10	3.50	4.20	5.00	6.00
AR (£)	10.00	9.50	9.00	8.50	8.00	7.50	7.00	6.50	6.00	5.50

6. Normal profits are regarded as a cost (and are included in the cost curves). Explain why.

7. What determines the size of normal profit? Will it vary with the general state of the economy?

8. A firm will continue producing in the short run, even if it is making a loss, providing it can cover its variable costs. Explain why. Just how long will it be willing to continue making such a loss?

9. Would there ever be a point in a firm attempting to continue in production if it could not cover its *long-run* average (total) costs?

10 The price of pocket calculators and digital watches fell significantly in the years after they were first introduced and, at the same time, demand for them increased substantially. Use cost and revenue diagrams to illustrate these events. Explain the reasoning behind the diagram(s) you have drawn.

11 In 2017 and 2018, M&S, a food and clothing retailer in the UK, decided to close a number of its stores, reassess and reduce its planned expansions, overhaul its clothing and home outlets and focus more of its shop space on food-only outlet, where demand remains relatively high. The hope is to boost sales and increase profits. If it meets these targets, what is likely to have happened to its total costs, total revenue, average costs and average revenue? Give reasons for your answer.

ADDITIONAL PART D CASE STUDIES ON THE *ECONOMICS FOR BUSINESS* STUDENT WEBSITE (www.pearsoned.co.uk/sloman)

D.1 Malthus and the dismal science of economics.

A gloomy warning, made over 200 years ago by Robert Malthus, that diminishing returns to labour would lead to famine for much of the world's population.

D.2 Division of labour in a pin factory.

This is the famous example of division of labour given by Adam Smith in his *Wealth of Nations* (1776).

D.3 Diminishing returns to nitrogen fertiliser.

This case study provides a good illustration of diminishing returns in practice by showing the effects on grass yields of the application of increasing amounts of nitrogen fertiliser.

D.4 Diminishing returns in the bread shop.

An illustration of the law of diminishing returns.

D.5 The relationship between averages and marginals.

An examination of the rules showing how an average curve relates to a marginal curve.

D.6 Deriving cost curves from total physical product information.

This shows how total, average and marginal costs can be derived from a total product information and the price of inputs.

WEBSITES RELEVANT TO PART D

Numbers and sections refer to websites listed in the Web appendix and hotlinked from this text's website at **www.pearsoned.co.uk/sloman**

■ For news articles relevant to Part D, see the *Economics News Articles* link from the text's website.

■ For student resources relevant to Part D, see sites C1–7, 9, 10, 14, 19–21, 25; D3, 19.

■ For a case study examining costs, see site D2.

■ For sites that look at companies, their scale of operation and market share, see D2; E4, 10; G7, 8.

Supply: short-run decision making by firms

The FT Reports . . .

The Financial Times, 30 April 2018

Eliminating competition in order to protect it

FT View

When executives from the US mobile telecoms groups T-Mobile and Sprint presented their merger plans on Sunday, it was clear what was foremost in their minds: competition regulators.

True, they talked about the financial terms of the deal and their plans for taking on larger rivals Verizon and AT&T. But they were most concerned to say that the deal would lead to lower prices and more investment. The tie-up, which would leave the US with three major players in mobile, would not lead to an even cosier oligopoly, but "create a new competitor that has the tenacity and customer focus to unleash real change" – that is, put pressure on the top two huge players.

There is a slightly Alice In Wonderland quality to this idea: that by taking a competitor out of the market, the market will become more competitive. The paradox has not reduced the argument's popularity. It comes up for most big mergers these days: if big company A does not – or is not allowed – to buy big company B, even bigger companies C or D will crush both.

In the case of the proposed merger of J Sainsbury and Asda, there is no question who company C is:

Amazon. Leaders of the number two and three grocers in the UK by market share mentioned the American ecommerce leader only in passing in pitching their tie-up, but the threat is clear. Amazon, though small in UK food now, is expanding and its mere presence creates acute price pressure on the grocery market, as it already has in the US.

Should competition regulators take this sort of argument seriously? T-Mobile and Sprint face an uphill battle: US regulators have balked before at letting the market move from four players to three, on the grounds that consumers will face higher prices. The two companies will argue that what matters now is less price than innovation and therefore having the scale to invest.

Regulators should not buy it. The US market has high tariffs by global standards. Removing one of the companies that has offered cheaper plans will make this worse eventually, whatever is promised now. T-Mobile's recent success shows what a small, under-funded competitor can do to improve a market. Sprint is struggling financially. But whether that is because of the market structure, or because it took on too much debt and has a history of mediocre management is an open question.

Some analysts believe that more upmarket food and drink retailers – from Waitrose to Majestic Wines – are coming under pressure as Aldi and Lidl push into more upmarket products – from fine wines to pulled pork – and their move into more affluent areas . . . Not only is the vicious supermarket price war hurting the big four supermarkets – Tesco, Asda, J Sainsbury and Wm Morrison – but the collateral damage is spreading upmarket . . . "There is not a retail market that I know of anywhere that is insulated, including the people right at the top," says Richard Hyman, the independent retail analyst. "I have seen shoppers in Harvey Nichols with Lidl bags . . . People are much more value-conscious right across the piece."

As we saw in Chapter 10, a firm's profits are maximised where its marginal cost equals its marginal revenue and, from this, using average revenue and cost curves, we can determine the size of the profits. But we will want to know more than this.

What determines the *amount* of profit that a firm will make? Will profits be large, just enough for the firm to survive or so low that it will be forced out of business?

- Will the firm produce a high level of output or a low level?

- Will it be producing efficiently?

- Will the price charged to the consumer be high or low?

- And, more generally, will the consumer benefit from the decisions that a firm makes?

The answers to all these questions depend, at least in part, on the amount of *competition* that a firm faces. A firm in a highly competitive environment will behave quite differently from a firm facing little or no competition.

In Part E we will look at *different types of market structure*: from highly competitive markets ('perfect competition'), to ones with no competition at all ('monopoly'). We will also look at the intermediate cases of 'imperfect competition': monopolistic competition (where there are quite a lot of firms competing against each other) and oligopoly (where there are just a few).

In some markets, having just a few firms may result in highly competitive behaviour, technological advance and lower prices for the consumer. However, it is also the case that firms may collude to restrict competition and the development of new technology, as we will see in this Part and Chapter 21. Consumers may then end up with less choice and paying higher prices.

Competition and choice can also be restricted through mergers and takeovers as the article opposite from the *Financial Times* illustrates.

Key terms

Market structures
Perfect competition
Monopoly
Natural monopoly
Competition for corporate control
Barriers to entry
Contestable markets
Sunk costs
Monopolistic competition
Product differentiation
Oligopoly
Interdependence
Collusive and non-collusive oligopoly
Open and tacit collusion
Price leadership
Benchmark pricing
Game theory
Dominant and non-dominant strategy games
Prisoners' dilemma
Nash equilibrium
Credible threat
First-mover advantage
Decision tree
Countervailing power
Behavioural thories of the firm
Profit satisficing
Organisational slack

Chapter 11

Profit maximisation under perfect competition and monopoly

Business issues covered in this chapter

- How does the structure of an industry affect firms' behaviour and performance?
- What determines the degree of market power of a firm?
- Why does operating under conditions of perfect competition make being in business a constant battle for survival?
- What is the short-run equilibrium for firms under perfect competition and by what process do they move to a long-run equilibrium?
- How do firms get to become monopolies and remain so?
- At what price and output will a monopolist maximise profits and how much profit will it make?
- How well or badly do monopolies serve the consumer compared with competitive firms?
- Why will the size of entry barriers to an industry (the degree of 'contestability' of a market) affect the amount of profit a monopolist can make?

11.1 ALTERNATIVE MARKET STRUCTURES

In this section, we are beginning to think about firms' behaviour and the factors that determine this. Why do we see constant advertising and innovation in some products, while others are rarely promoted and see little development? Why do prices fall in some industries and rise in others? Why is government more concerned with the behaviour of firms in just some industries? We see markets with many competitors and others with few. Why does this happen?

All of these questions can be answered by looking at the structure of the industry and, in particular, at the degree of competition. Before we look at the economic theory behind the different market structures, let us look at some specific industries and consider the different ways that firms behave.

The degree of competition in different markets

The importance of competition. Most markets have a number of firms competing against each other. Go into your local town or city and look around. If you want to buy shoes, there are probably many shops, all selling shoes of different types, quality and price. Alternatively, you could go online and there will be a very high number of suppliers. If you want lunch or a cup of coffee, there are lots of cafés providing choice. The same thing applies for birthday cards, wrapping paper, food, electronic devices and many other products, including services.

If you need a haircut, there are many salons. When writing this section, I (Elizabeth) used Google to search for hairdressers in St Ives (a small town in Cornwall with a population of around 10 000, though a popular tourist destination and covering an area of less than 11 km^2). I found over 15 salons advertised online and there are many others without websites. Expanding the search area only slightly, gave me a huge list of hairdressers – some practically next door to others. If you need a cleaner, gardener or builder, I imagine you could find a number of people advertising their services in the relevant area.

Markets where there are few competitors. In practice, most markets have a number of competitors, each trying to gain customers, though how they do it and the market outcomes, can vary significantly. However, in some markets, there are very few competitors, sometimes just two or three – or occasionally just one firm with no competitors. Or there might be lots of small firms, but with a few big ones dominating.

Let us consider a market that everyone needs: food. There are many places selling food, whether it is your local corner shop, a farm shop, households selling eggs and freshly grown vegetables or Amazon. But, for many people, it is in supermarkets that they do the bulk of their food shopping

Together, the four largest British supermarkets (Tesco, Sainsbury's, Asda and Morrisons) account for over 70 per cent of sales in the food industry. Therefore, while the market has many competitors, it is actually dominated by four big firms, all of whom are in a constant battle to gain and retain customers. If you turn on the TV or radio, often you will see adverts from these supermarkets, advertising price cuts, savings, promotions and deals, all of which aim to gain you as a customer.

The supermarkets each have a sufficiently large share of the market that, if one of them cuts prices, it would cause many customers to switch and buy from the cheaper supplier – after all, the cabbage you buy from Tesco is pretty similar to the one sold in Asda. This means that we do not just see one supermarket advertising its latest price cuts, but we see all of them doing this – they are constantly responding to each other, for example see adverts from a range of supermarkets, such as Tesco, Asda, Aldi and Morrisons. This characteristic is called *interdependence,* which we will discuss further in Chapter 12.

Another related industry where this occurs is fast food restaurants. In the USA, there has been a high degree of advertising and price cutting from chains such as McDonalds, Burger King and Wendy's. Although it is a market with many competitors, there are a number of bigger chains, all of which respond to the tactics employed by their rivals. You can read more about the latest rivalry in Box 11.1.

We see similar things happening with mobile phones, energy companies, petrol stations, razors, cars and other consumer durables, such as sofas: a few big firms constantly advertising price cuts or offers and responding to the actions of each other. This is a form of *imperfect competition* that economists call *oligopoly*. We examine oligopoly in detail in Chapter 12.

Markets with many competitors. There are countless places you can go to buy clothes: Next, Tesco, Top Shop, Selfridges, John Lewis, Bloomingdales, Burton and many, many more. As with shoes, we can then divide the market into different types or quality of clothing, but, even then, there are many places you could buy a pair of jeans, a shirt or a dress.

Although clothing retailers do compete on price, it is not a market where we see as much television advertising, with one retailer telling us that it has cut the price of scarves and another saying that it has slashed the price of jumpers. Retailers here compete in other areas, such as the quality of the product and are less responsive to the strategies employed by their rivals as, although we still see some big firms, there are many more of them, each with a smaller share of the market. For example M&S is the UK's biggest clothing retailer, but it has only an 8.1 per cent share of the market – significantly lower than Tesco who has almost 30 per cent of the food market in the UK.

There are other markets with a similar degree of competition to that of clothing: hairdressers, restaurants, builders, plumbers and many more. Economists call this market structure *monopolistic competition* and, again, it is the structure of the industry that helps to explain the outcomes we see, as we shall discuss throughout part E.

> ## Pause for thought
>
> *Think of ten different products or services and estimate roughly how many firms there are in the market. You will need to decide whether 'the market' is a local one, a national one or an international one. In what ways do the firms compete in each of the cases you have identified?*

By analysing the particular characteristics of each industry's structure and its competitiveness, we can gain a better understanding of how firms behave and why they do so and then use this to explain their overall performance and the outcomes for them and customers, such as the prices consumers pay and the prices suppliers receive. It helps to explain the amount of profits that firms make and whether they can be sustained and also whether firms need to innovate, advertise or respond in any other ways to their rivals.

Factors affecting the degree of competition

So what influences the degree of competition in an industry? There are four key determinants:

- The number of firms.
- The freedom of entry and exit of firms into the industry.
- The nature of the product.
- The shape of the demand curve.

We will consider each factor to determine exactly what impact it has on the degree of competition within a market and then look at how these features vary between different market structures. We should then be able to place different industries into one of four key market structures.

The number of firms. The more firms there are competing against each other, the more competitive any market is likely to be, with each firm trying to steal customers from its rivals. Though there are many ways by which this can be done, one strategy will be to keep prices low. Generally, this will be in the consumer's interest.

If, however, there are only a few firms in the market, there may be less intense price competition, though, as we saw in our earlier discussion and will see throughout the next two chapters, this is not always the case.

The freedom of entry and exit of firms into the industry. A key factor that will affect the number of firms in an industry is how easy it is for a new firm to set up in competition. In some markets, there may be barriers to entry that prevent new firms from entering and this then acts to restrict the number of competing firms in the market. A key question here is, just how great are the barriers to the entry of new firms?

Pause for thought

1. *Consider a situation where you have set up a business selling a brand new product that is not available anywhere else. As the only seller of this product, what could you do in terms of price?*
2. *Why could the ease with which a firm can leave an industry be a factor that determines the degree of competition within that industry?*

The nature of the product. If firms produce an identical product – in other words, if there is no product differentiation within the industry – there is little a firm can do to gain an advantage over its rivals. If, however, firms produce their own particular brand or model or variety, this may enable them to charge a higher price and/or gain a larger market share from their rivals.

The shape of the demand curve. Finally, the degree of competition is affected by the degree of control the firm has over its price. Is the firm a price taker with no control over price? Or can it choose its price? And, if it can, how will changing its price affect its profits? The degree of control clearly is affected by the three factors above, but it has important implications for the shape of the firm's demand curve. How elastic is it? If it puts up its price, will it lose (a) all its sales (a horizontal demand curve), (b) a large proportion of its sales (a relatively elastic demand curve) or (c) just a small proportion of its sales (a relatively inelastic demand curve)?

 Market power benefits the powerful at the expense of others. When firms have market power over prices, they can use this to raise prices and profits above the perfectly competitive level. Other things being equal, the firm will gain at the expense of the consumer. Similarly, if consumers or workers have market power, they can use this to their own benefit.

Market structures

Traditionally, we divide industries into categories based on the factors above, which determine the degree of competition that exists between the firms. There are four such categories.

At the most competitive extreme is a market structure referred to as **perfect competition**. This is a situation where there are a large number of firms competing. Each firm is so small relative to the whole industry that it has no power to influence market price. It is a price taker.

At the least competitive extreme is **monopoly**, where there is just one firm in the industry and hence no competition from *within* the industry, often due to very high barriers to entry.

In the middle there are two forms of **imperfect competition**. **Monopolistic competition** is the more competitive, which involves quite a lot of firms competing and freedom for new firms to enter the industry. Examples of monopolistic competition can be found by flicking through the *Yellow Pages* or typing a good or service into a search engine! The other type of imperfect competition is **oligopoly**, where there are only a few firms and where the entry of new firms is difficult. Some or all of the existing firms will be dominant – that is, they will tend to have

---

Definitions

Perfect competition A market structure in which there are many firms; where there is freedom of entry to the industry; where all firms produce an identical product; and where all firms are price takers.

Monopoly A market structure where there is only one firm in the industry.

Imperfect competition The collective name for monopolistic competition and oligopoly.

Monopolistic competition A market structure where, like perfect competition, there are many firms and freedom of entry into the industry, but where each firm produces a differentiated product and thus has some control over its price.

Oligopoly A market structure where there are few enough firms to enable barriers to be erected against the entry of new firms.

Table 11.1	Features of the four market structures				

Type of market	Number of firms	Freedom of entry	Nature of product	Examples	Implication for demand curve for firm
Perfect competition	Very many	Unrestricted	Homogeneous (undifferentiated)	Cabbages, foreign exchange (these approximate to perfect competition)	Horizontal. The firm is a price taker
Monopolistic competition	Many/several	Unrestricted	Differentiated	Builders, restaurants, hairdressers	Downward sloping, but relatively elastic. The firm has some control over price
Oligopoly	Few	Restricted	1. Undifferentiated or 2. Differentiated	1. Cement 2. Cars, electrical appliances, supermarkets	Downward sloping, relatively inelastic but depends on reactions of rivals to a price change
Monopoly	One	Restricted or completely blocked	Unique	Local water company, many prescription drugs protected by patents	Downward sloping, more inelastic than oligopoly. Firm has considerable control over price

Pause for thought

Based on the characteristics outlined above for each market structure, can you think of a few more examples that fit into each of the four market structures?

a relatively high market share and can influence prices, advertising, product design, etc.

Table 11.1 shows the differences between the four categories.

The structure of the market affects firms' behaviour and the outcomes for price, output, etc. You might be thinking that this sounds familiar to something we considered in Chapter 1, where we looked at the Structure–Conduct–Performance paradigm and you would be right. So let us revisit this idea.

Structure, conduct and performance

KI 1
p 11

The market structure under which a firm operates will determine its behaviour. Firms under perfect competition behave quite differently from firms that have market dominance, such as a monopolist. As we have already seen, the behaviour of firms is different again when there are lots of small firms competing (monopolistic competition) and when there are only a few big firms (oligopoly).

This behaviour, or 'conduct', will, in turn, affect the firm's performance: its prices, profits, efficiency, etc. In many cases, it will also affect other firms' performance: *their* prices, profits, efficiency, etc. The collective conduct of all the firms in the industry will affect the whole industry's performance.

Some economists thus see a causal chain running from market structure, through conduct, to the performance of that industry.

Structure → Conduct → Performance

This does not mean, however, that all firms operating in a particular market structure will behave in exactly the same way. For example, some firms under oligopoly may be highly competitive and engage in fierce price cutting behaviour, such as the supermarkets we discussed, whereas others may collude with each other to keep prices high.

It is for this reason that government policy towards firms – known as 'competition policy' – prefers to focus on the *conduct* of individual firms, rather than simply on the market structure within which they operate. Regulators focus on aspects of conduct such as price fixing and other forms of collusion. Indeed, competition policy in most countries accepts that market structures evolve naturally (e.g. because of economies of scale or changing consumer preferences) and do not necessarily give rise to competition problems.

Nevertheless, market structure still influences firms' behaviour and this, in turn, influences the development of the market structure and industry, even if it does not rigidly determine it. For example, the interaction between firms may influence the development of new products or new production methods and may encourage or discourage the entrance of new firms into the industry.

It is also important to remember that some firms with different divisions and products may operate in more than one market structure. As an example, consider the case of Microsoft. Its Edge browser (which is replacing Internet Explorer) competes with more successful rivals, such as Chrome, Safari and Firefox and, as a result, has little market power in the browser market. Its Office products, by contrast,

BOX 11.1	A FAST FOOD RACE TO THE BOTTOM

Measuring the degree of competition

In the USA, in 2015, industry analysis found that there were over 200 000 fast food restaurants, employing over 4 million people. Despite having thousands of firms, the market is dominated by a few big chains, including McDonalds, Burger King and Wendy's and hence has some of the characteristics of an oligopoly. A similar structure exists in many other countries.

When analysing an industry, it is important to look not just at the number of firms as an indicator of the degree of competition, as in doing that, we could come to misleading conclusions. Another key indicator that should be considered is the level of 'concentration' of firms. This is the market share of the largest so many firms, e.g. the largest 3, 5 or 15, etc. This gives the '3-firm', '5-firm' or '15-firm' concentration ratio. The resulting figures can be used to assess whether or not the largest firms in an industry dominate the market.

For example, in the case of British supermarkets, we saw that the 4-firm concentration ratio was approximately 70 per cent. The concentration ratio in the US fast food industry is not as high, but estimates put the 3-firm concentration ratio at approximately 40 per cent –still quite a high figure. This means that, despite the market having over 200 000 firms, a significant portion is dominated by three chains, creating a nice example of an oligopoly. While in some oligopolies firms can collude with each other and fix prices, in other cases, we observe a highly competitive market. It is the latter that applies to the fast food industry.

1. *What are the advantages and disadvantages of using a 5-firm concentration ratio rather than a 10-firm, 3-firm or even a 1-firm ratio?*

Price competition

Fast food outlets have always been focused on cheaper meals, but, over the past few years, the level of price competition has intensified and it has moved beyond the typical hamburger outlets, hitting places like Pizza Hut. In 2016, McDonalds launched its promotion, 'McPick 2' (choose 2 items from a selection including McChicken and McDouble for $2).

In response, Wendy's launched its '4 for $4' (where customers can choose 4 items from a selection for $4) and, soon after, Burger King announced its promotion of a 5-item meal for $4. Pizza Hut joined the party, offering a 7-item menu for just $5.

Within just a few days, the biggest fast food chains in the USA had responded to each other and were creating new deals at budget prices. The chains freely admitted that they were 'aggressively pursuing value-conscious customers looking for the cheapest meal deals'.[1] The outlets were aiming to be the best value chain, while still making profits and this price war has continued.

In 2018, McDonald's launched a new deal, called the '$1 $2 $3 Menu', allowing customers to choose items from three price points. As demand for fast food is relatively elastic, demand for McDonald's products would have increased significantly, if its competitors had not responded. Customers are price sensitive and hence respond to small price changes and thus we saw McDonald's rivals responding immediately to its new promotion. Wendy's added 20 things onto its menu, all priced at just $1; JACK announced plans for promotions focused on products within the $1 to $5 bracket and Taco Bell then began to sell $1 nacho fries, together with announcing plans for a range of other $1 offers. Analysis from Credit Suisse suggested that McDonald's closest competitors could see sales affected by around 1 per cent following unmatched price changes.[2]

This competitive market has, therefore, seen falling prices and more products offered at a given price. There is, of course, a danger from this race to the bottom for prices, as firms will need to ensure that the price they sell each burger at is sufficient to cover the costs of producing it. With prices on a downward spiral, this difference is getting smaller and,

---

[1]K.J. Mariño, 'Fast Food competition intensifies as Burger King, McDonald's, Wendy's fight for cheapest meal deal', *Latin Post* (5 January 2016).

[2]'McDonald's Corp: Assessing Impact of MCD's New Value Menu + Updated Franchisee Checks', *Americas/United States, Equity Research, Restaurants,* Credit Suisse (19 December 2017).

---

have a much bigger market share and dominate the word processor, presentation and spreadsheet markets.

For the rest of this chapter and the next we explore how the different market structures affect firms' conduct and performance and the implications of this for the consumer.

First, we look at the two extreme market structures: perfect competition and monopoly (this chapter). Then we turn to look at the two intermediate cases of monopolistic competition and oligopoly (Chapter 12).

As we have seen, these two intermediate cases are sometimes referred to collectively as imperfect competition. The vast majority of firms in the real world operate under imperfect competition. It is still worth studying the two extreme cases, however, because they provide a framework within which to understand the real world. They provide important benchmarks for comparison. For example, regulators would find it difficult to identify anti-competitive behaviour if they could not show how outcomes would differ in a more competitive environment.

Some industries tend more to the competitive extreme and thus their performance corresponds, to some extent, to perfect competition. Other industries tend more to the other extreme: for example, when there is one dominant firm and a few much smaller firms. In such cases, their performance corresponds more to monopoly.

in some cases, has turned negative. Why are firms continuing to cut prices if it means their profit margins are falling?

Competitors choose their promotions carefully, focusing on those with more elastic demand, as this is what attracts customers and increases sales. They then hope that customers will spend money on other products, such as drinks, sides or desserts, that will tend to be more profitable. Professor Patricia Smith from the University of Michigan said:

> McDonald's will make money selling burgers for a buck if it can make the burger for less than $1 and sell *lots* and *lots* of burgers . . . Part of the strategy is to attract consumers in to the store and then entice them to buy more than just the burger – fries, drinks, desserts.[3]

Product differentiation

There have been price wars in the UK, too, with many outlets offering highly competitive deals, though certainly not at the same level as those in the USA. In mainland Europe, price competition is less intense again, but we see another characteristic of an oligopoly here, as well as in the UK and USA: namely, product differentiation.

The big chains are constantly innovating with new products, deals and variations to make their burger or pizza just a bit different, including extra cheese, bacon, fries and toys in meal deals. In doing this, firms are attempting to make demand for their products more inelastic. The fast food outlets know how competitive the market is and that, without product differentiation, they would lose customers, sales and hence profits. In the UK and Europe, similar things occur, but we have also seen a different type of product differentiation, focusing on customer demands.

Customers are increasingly conscious of sustainability, locally sourced produce and ethical consumerism, as we will discuss in Chapter 22. Food outlets have responded to this by differentiating their products, not with extra food or toys, but with advertising the local source of their food and its use of sustainable sources, including in the European branches of McDonald's. Martin Caraher, from City University, London, has noted that any significant cuts in prices in Europe would negatively affect McDonald's reputation among its customers who are more focused on ethical consumerism, saying: 'In order to lower their prices, they would have to break a lot of their marketing initiatives that they've implemented here in Europe. They've positioned themselves in a different level of the market'.[4] In the UK, McDonald's aims to make all of its coffee 'ethically sourced' by 2020.

Therefore, although we observe that the fast food industry does always seem to be dominated by a few big firms, indicating an oligopoly, the actions of the competitors are different across the world. They all focus on strategies to gain customers, reflecting the competitiveness of the market, but the way in which they attract and keep customers does vary. In each case, they focus on the key things that customers respond to and, in doing this, they aim to maintain market share.

2. Explain how fast food outlets are changing the shape of their demand curve by engaging in product differentiation.
3. How can fast food outlets sell a burger at $1, when the person making it is earning say $10 and still make profits?

Choose another industry under oligopoly and select two companies. Find out what competitive strategies they use and why.

---

[3]Bryan Lufkin, 'How can a fast food chain ever make money from a $1 burger?', BBC Capital (23 February 2018).

[4]*Ibid.*

11.2   PERFECT COMPETITION

The theory of perfect competition illustrates an extreme form of capitalism. Firms have no power whatsoever to affect the price of the product. The price they face is that determined by the interaction of demand and supply in the whole *market*.

Assumptions

The model of perfect competition is built on four assumptions:

1. Firms are *price takers*. There are so many firms in the industry that each one produces an insignificantly small

proportion of total industry supply and, therefore, has *no power whatsoever* to affect the price of the product. Hence it faces a horizontal (perfectly elastic) demand 'curve' at the market price: the price determined by the interaction of demand and supply in the whole market.

2. There is complete *freedom of entry* into the industry for new firms. Existing firms are unable to stop new firms setting up in business. Setting up a business takes time, however. Freedom of entry, therefore, applies in the long run.

3. All firms produce an *identical product.* The product is 'homogeneous', meaning they are all perfect substitutes for each other and hence firms do not engage in any branding or advertising.

4. Producers and consumers have *perfect knowledge* of the market. That is, producers are fully aware of prices, costs, technology and market opportunities. Consumers are fully aware of price, quality and availability of the product.

These assumptions are very strict. Few, if any, industries in the real world meet these conditions. Certain agricultural markets, perhaps, are closest to perfect competition. The market for fresh vegetables is an example.

Pause for thought

1. *It is sometimes claimed that the market for various stocks and shares is perfectly competitive or nearly so. Take the case of the market for shares in a large company, such as Apple or Google. Go through each of the four assumptions above and see if they apply in this case. (Don't be misled by the first assumption. The 'firm' in this case is not Apple or Google itself, but, rather, the owners of the shares.)*
2. *Is the market for gold or silver perfectly competitive?*

The short-run equilibrium of the firm

In the *short run*, we assume that the number of firms in the industry cannot be increased; there is simply no time for new firms to enter the market.

Figure 11.1 shows a short-run equilibrium for both industry and a firm under perfect competition. Both parts of the diagram have the same scale for the vertical axis. The horizontal axes have totally different scales, however. For example, if the horizontal axis for the firm were measured in, say, thousands of units, the horizontal axis for the whole industry might be measured in millions or tens of millions of units, depending on the number of firms in the industry.

Let us examine the determination of price, output and profit in turn.

Price

The price is determined in the industry by the intersection of market demand and supply. The firm faces a horizontal demand (or average revenue) 'curve' at this price. It can sell all it can produce at the market price (P_e). It would sell nothing at a price above P_e, however, since competitors would be selling identical products at a lower price.

Output

The firm will maximise profit where marginal cost equals marginal revenue ($MR = MC$), at an output of Q_e. Note that, since the price is not affected by the firm's output, marginal revenue will equal price (see page 168 and Figure 10.1).

Pause for thought

If the industry under perfect competition faces a downward-sloping demand curve, why does an individual firm face a horizontal demand curve?

Definition

Short run under perfect competition The period during which there is too little time for new firms to enter the industry.

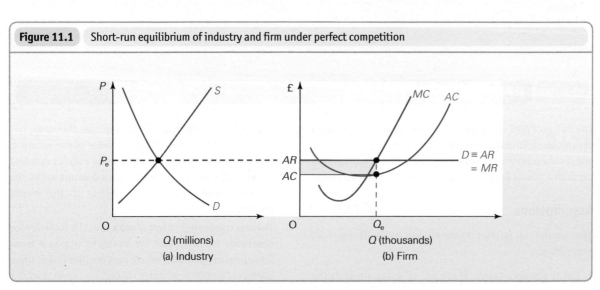

| Figure 11.1 | Short-run equilibrium of industry and firm under perfect competition |

Thus the firm's *MR* 'curve' and *AR* 'curve' (= demand 'curve') are the same horizontal straight line.

Profit

If the average cost (*AC*) curve (which includes normal profit) dips below the average revenue (*AR*) 'curve', the firm will earn supernormal profit. Supernormal profit per unit at Q_e is the vertical difference between *AR* and *AC* at Q_e. Total supernormal profit is the shaded rectangle in Figure 11.1 (i.e. profit per unit times quantity sold).

What happens if the firm cannot make a profit at *any* level of output? This situation would occur if the *AC* curve were above the *AR* curve at all points. This is illustrated in Figure 11.2 where the market price is P_1. In this case, the point where *MC* = *MR* represents the *loss-minimising* point (where loss is defined as anything less than normal profit). This amount of the loss is represented by the shaded rectangle.

KI 18
p 147

Whether the firm is prepared to continue making a loss in the short run or whether it will close down immediately depends on whether it can cover its *variable* costs (as we saw in Chapter 10). Provided price is above average variable cost (*AVC*), the firm will continue producing in the short run: it can pay its variable costs and go some way to paying its fixed costs. It will shut down in the short run only if the market price falls below P_2 in Figure 11.2: i.e. when variable costs of production cannot be covered.

The long-run equilibrium of the firm

In the *long run*, if typical firms are making supernormal profits, new firms will be attracted into the industry. Likewise, if existing firms can make supernormal profits by increasing the scale of their operations, they will do so, since all factors of production are variable in the long run.

The effect of the entry of new firms and/or the expansion of existing firms is to increase industry supply, meaning that at every price level the quantity produced would be higher. This is illustrated in Figure 11.3.

> ### Pause for thought
>
> *Before you read on, can you explain why perfect competition and substantial economies of scale are likely to be incompatible?*

The industry supply curve shifts to the right. This, in turn, leads to a fall in price. Supply will go on increasing, and price falling, until firms are making only normal profits. This will be when price has fallen to the point where the demand 'curve' for the firm just touches the bottom of its long-run average cost curve. Q_L is thus the long-run equilibrium output of the firm, with P_L the long-run equilibrium price.

KI 10
p 46

Since the *LRAC* curve is tangential to all possible short-run *AC* curves (see section 9.5), the full long-run equilibrium will be as shown in Figure 11.4 where:

KI 11
p 53

$$LRAC = AC = MC = MR = AR$$

> ### Definition
>
> **Long run under perfect competition** The period of time that is long enough for new firms to enter the industry.

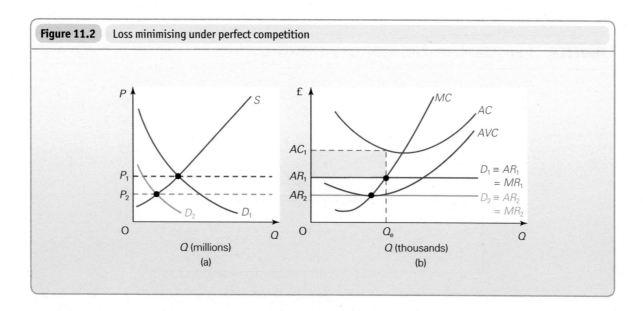

Figure 11.2 Loss minimising under perfect competition

Figure 11.3 Long-run equilibrium under perfect competition

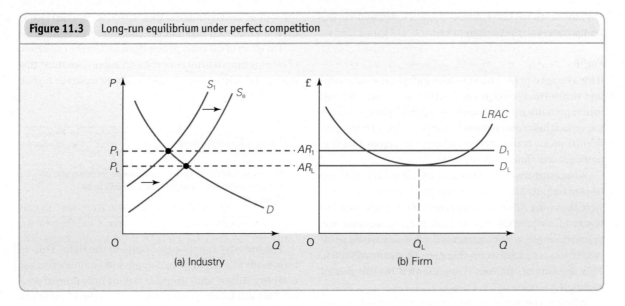

(a) Industry (b) Firm

The incompatibility of perfect competition and substantial economies of scale

Why is perfect competition so rare in the real world – if it even exists at all? One important reason for this has to do with economies of scale.

In many industries, firms may have to be quite large if they are to experience the full potential economies of scale. But perfect competition requires there to be *many* firms. Firms must, therefore, be small under perfect competition: too small in most cases for them to achieve economies of scale.

Once a firm expands sufficiently to achieve economies of scale, it will usually gain market power. It will be able to undercut the prices of smaller firms, which will thus be

driven out of business. Perfect competition is destroyed. Therefore, perfect competition could exist in any industry only if there were no (or virtually no) economies of scale.

Who benefits from perfect competition?

How does perfect competition affect the firm?

Under perfect competition the firm faces a constant battle for survival. If it becomes less efficient than other firms, it will make less than normal profits and be driven out of business. If it becomes more efficient, it will earn supernormal profits, but they will not last for long. Soon other firms, in order to survive themselves, will be forced to copy the more efficient methods of the new firm, which they can do because of the assumption of perfect knowledge.

Figure 11.4 Long-run equilibrium of the firm under perfect competition

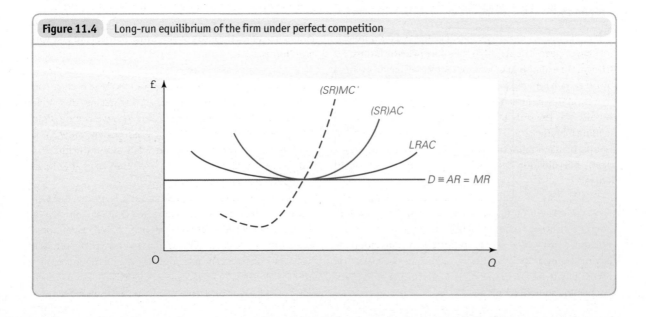

A similar thing happens with product development. If a firm produces a new popular product, it will gain a temporary advantage over its rivals. It may make supernormal profits in the short run, but, once the other firms respond (which they will have to do, in order to avoid making a loss and being driven from the market) and develop this new product, supply of it will rise. This will drive down the price and eliminate the supernormal profits.

How does perfect competition affect the consumer?

What does this constant battle for survival mean for consumers?

Firms are encouraged to invest in new improved technology to ensure survival and, in the long run, they must also produce at the least-cost output to ensure that at least normal profits are made. This idea is known as *productive efficiency*. Producing at the minimum cost and making only normal profits mean that prices are kept at a minimum, which is beneficial to consumers.

Under perfect competition, we also see firms producing the level of output where *price equals marginal cost*. It could be argued that this is the *optimum* level of output.

To show why, consider what would happen if price and marginal cost were not equal. If price were greater than marginal cost, this would mean that consumers were putting a higher value (P) on the production of extra units than they cost to produce (MC). Therefore, more ought to be produced. If price were less than marginal cost,

consumers would be putting a lower value on extra units than they cost to produce. Therefore, less ought to be produced.

When they are equal ($MC = P$), production levels are just right and this is referred to as *allocative efficiency*.

> **KEY IDEA 22**
>
> *Economic efficiency.* This is achieved when each good is produced at the minimum cost and where consumers get maximum benefit from their income.

Perfectly competitive markets thus result in economic efficiency though, as we shall see, it is not always best for the consumer any more than it is for the firm. We develop the arguments in the next section and in Chapter 12.

Definitions

Productive efficiency A situation where firms are producing the maximum output for a given amount of inputs, or producing a given output at the least cost.

Allocative efficiency A situation where the current combination of goods produced and sold gives the maximum satisfaction for each consumer at their current levels of income.

11.3   MONOPOLY

What is a monopoly?

This may seem a strange question because the answer seems obvious. A monopoly exists when there is only one firm in the industry.

But whether an industry can be classed as a monopoly is not always clear. It depends on how narrowly the industry is defined. For example, a textile company may have a monopoly on certain types of fabric, but it does not have a monopoly on fabrics in general. In Box 10.2, we saw how John initially was the only person selling ice creams to people queuing in traffic jams. He had a monopoly on ice creams on that particular stretch of road (until the others copied his idea!), but did not have a monopoly on ice cream in general.

To some extent, the boundaries of an industry are arbitrary. What is more important for a firm is the amount of monopoly *power* it has and that depends on the closeness of substitutes produced by rival industries. A train company may have a monopoly over railway journeys between two towns, but it faces competition in transport from cars, coaches and sometimes planes.

Barriers to entry

For a firm to maintain its monopoly position, there must be barriers to the entry of new firms. Barriers also exist under oligopoly, but, in the case of monopoly, they must be high enough to block the entry of new firms. Barriers can take various forms.

Economies of scale. If the monopolist's average costs go on falling significantly up to the output that satisfies the whole market, the industry may not be able to support more than one producer. This case is known as *natural monopoly*. It is particularly likely if the market is small and/or the industry has relatively high capital/infrastructure costs (i.e. fixed costs) and relatively low marginal costs.

One real-world example is the network of pipelines that supply gas to homes and businesses. If two competing firms each built a national network of pipes, it might be difficult for them both to make a profit as they would share the customers but each have their own separate infrastructure costs. A monopoly that supplies all customers could make a profit as it would have much lower average total costs from supplying the whole market.

BOX 11.2 E-COMMERCE

A modern form of perfect competition?

The relentless drive towards big business in recent decades has seen many markets become more concentrated and increasingly dominated by large producers. However, forces are at work that are undermining this dominance and bringing more competition to markets. One of these forces is *e-commerce*.

In this case study, we will consider just how far e-commerce is returning 'power to the people'.

Moving markets back towards perfect competition?

Let us reconsider three of the assumptions of perfect competition and the impact of e-commerce on them: a large number of firms; freedom of entry; and perfect knowledge.

A large number of buyers and sellers.

E-commerce has allowed many new firms to set up small businesses, often selling via their own websites or using online markets, such as eBay or Amazon. In Quarter 3 of 2018, eBay had 177 million buyers and over 25 million sellers, while Amazon had 2 million third-party sellers (accounting for approximately 50 per cent of sales volume), reaching 310 million customers. The global reach of the Internet increases the number of buyers and sellers that can trade with each other. Firms must now compete with others across the world, as consumers have access to the global marketplace. They must keep an eye on the prices and products of competitors worldwide and be aware of the continual emergence of new smaller businesses.

Freedom of entry.

The costs of starting a business often have been a key obstacle for firms, but e-commerce has created a low-cost market place. Internet companies tend to have lower start-up costs, as often they are run from much smaller premises, including owners' homes, requiring little more than a computer and access to the Internet. With advanced search algorithms, new businesses can also minimise marketing costs, by ensuring their website is easily located by consumers on search engines, such as Google and Bing.

Many of the new online companies focus on specialist products and rely on Internet 'outsourcing' (buying parts, equipment and other supplies through the Internet), rather than making everything themselves. Small businesses also tend to use other companies for transport and distribution, all of which help to keep costs down, thus making more businesses viable.

All of these factors, together with the speed with which a new firm can set up a website and hence a business, mean that the market has never been more open to new competitors. The benefit of e-commerce has, therefore, been to open up the market place and this has had spillover effects on existing firms, who have been forced to become more efficient and, consequently, markets have become more price competitive. Demand curves have tended to become more elastic and we now see a growing range of innovative products. We have also seen a blurring of the line between firms and consumers, given the ease with which people can start a business.

Perfect knowledge.

The Internet has also added to consumer knowledge. There are some obvious ways, such as obtaining facts and figures, through sites such as TripAdvisor and Wikipedia, on where to eat, where to stay, what to read, etc.

However, it has also improved consumer knowledge through greater transparency. Consumers can easily compare the prices and other features of the products they are interested in purchasing by using search engines, such as Google Shopping, NexTag and PriceGrabber.

You can also use comparison websites to find alternative suppliers and their prices. It is now fairly common to see people in shops on the high street browsing competitors' prices on their mobile phones. This has placed high street retailers under intense competitive pressure and we have seen evidence of this through the collapse of some well-known high street retailers, such as Comet, BHS, Maplin and Toys R Us.

Although the competitive pressures seem to have increased in 'B2C' (business-to-consumers) e-commerce, the impact may be even greater in 'B2B' (business-to-business) e-commerce. Many firms are searching constantly for cheaper sources of supply and the Internet provides a cheap and easy means of conducting such searches.

Even if a market could support more than one firm, a new entrant is unlikely to be able to start up on a very large scale. Thus the monopolist that is already experiencing economies of scale can charge a price below the cost of the new entrant and drive it out of business. If, however, the new entrant is a firm already established in another industry, it may be able to survive this competition. For example, Amazon entered the UK online grocery market in 2016.

Economies of scope.   These are the benefits in terms of lower average costs of production, because a firm produces a range of products. For example, a large pharmaceutical company producing a range of drugs and toiletries can use shared research, marketing, storage and transport facilities across its range of products. These lower costs make it difficult for a new single-product entrant to the market, since the large firm will be able to undercut its price and drive it out of the market.

Product differentiation and brand loyalty.   If a firm produces a clearly differentiated product, where the consumer associates the product with the brand, it will be very difficult for a new firm to break into that market. Rank Xerox invented, and patented, the plain paper photocopier. After this legal

1. *Give three examples of products that are particularly suitable for selling over the Internet and three that are not. Explain your answer.*

Before reading ahead, consider your own shopping and buying habits – how much shopping do you do online? What do you think are the limits to e-commerce? Compare your answers with a friend and try to determine the key factors that explain any differences between you and what might be the limits to e-commerce.

What does the future hold?

Statista recorded global online retail sales at $1.3 trillion in 2014; by 2017, this had grown to $2.3 trillion, with predictions that it will reach $4.9 trillion by 2021.[1] The Centre of Retail Research estimates that online retailers have 15–16 per cent of the UK retail market and believe that this growth will continue, with a potential to reach 25 per cent by 2025.[2]

If e-commerce is developing so quickly and costs are much lower for firms by trading online, why do so many big firms retain a physical presence on our high streets and have even increased their number of stores? Why are high street retailers still prepared to pay an extremely high price for a prime location in cities, despite sales in UK stores falling by an estimated 2.5 per cent in 2017?

'Shop shopping' still plays a key role in society; people are able to see, touch and try the good. Behavioural economics tells us that being able to see something and take possession of it immediately is something we are prepared to pay a price for, even with next-day or even same-day delivery available to us. Many people (though not all) also like the experience of shopping and the other activities that complement it and hence are prepared to pay a 'premium'. Therefore, a physical presence is still important, especially in some markets where location really does matter.

However, an online presence has never been more important, with firms investing huge sums of money on their websites and expansion of online ordering to compete more effectively. With technology improving every day and reducing the problems of slow internet connections, busy sites and failures in logistics, online shopping is likely to go in just one direction. But are there any downsides?

Some downsides of e-commerce.

Although greater price transparency should increase competition, there are some concerns that it may actually reduce the incentive for firms to lower prices. Firms can now observe and instantly respond to their rivals cutting prices. Thus the previous advantage that firms might have gained from cutting price are now removed very quickly such that it may remove the incentive and even encourage firms to collude and charge higher prices.

Comparison sites earn revenue by charging a fee every time a customer is referred to a listed firm's website via the price comparison website. These are additional costs and thus firms may push up prices to maintain profitability.

While it is certainly easier and cheaper than ever before to set up a business, it is likely that established firms are also benefiting from the lower costs that technology and online market places bring. Amazon has invested heavily in automating its distribution centres using Kiva robots. However, this type of capital investment will reduce a firm's average costs only if it sells a large volume of products, which is unlikely for new businesses. Furthermore, while search engines can make new businesses more visible to customers, it will still tend to be the more established firms who appear at the top of searches. These factors can lead to the growth of already large firms and make it harder for smaller firms to compete.

Generally, however, the market place is becoming more competitive with e-commerce and more opportunities do now exist for firms and customers to interact in a global market.

2. *Why may the Internet work better for replacement buys than for new purchases?*
3. *As eBay and Amazon have grown in size, they have acquired substantial monopoly power, while simultaneously increasing competition. How can both be true?*

[1]*Retail e-commerce sales worldwide from 2014 to 2021 (in billion US dollars),* Statista (2018).

[2]*'Peak e-commerce', Retail Briefings,* Centre for Retail Research.

monopoly ran out, people still associated photocopiers with Rank Xerox. It is still not unusual to hear someone say that they are going to 'Xerox the article', 'Hoover their carpet' or 'Google it'. The monopolist may also have access to superior technology, helping to distinguish its product from the competition. For example, Google's search ranking algorithm set it apart from its rivals, as many people found Google's search engine more useful than any others.

Lower costs for an established firm. An established monopoly is likely to have developed the most efficient way of producing and marketing its product and this will be very difficult for other competitors to replicate. It may also be aware of the cheapest suppliers and have access to cheaper finance. Together, this means it is likely to be operating on a lower average total cost curve, making it difficult for new entrants to compete on price.

Pause for thought

Illustrate the situation described above using AC curves for both a new entrant and an established firm.

Access to, control over or ownership of key inputs or outlets. In some markets the monopolist might be able to obtain access to key inputs on more favourable terms for a certain period of time. For example, if there was a supplier that provided a much higher quality input than its rivals, the monopolist could either sign a long-term exclusive contract with this firm or take ownership via a merger. For example, in 2012 Amazon purchased Kiva Systems. This company was the leading supplier of robotics for a number of warehouse operators and retailers. After the takeover, Kiva supplied only Amazon and was renamed Amazon Robotics in 2015.

In more extreme cases, the monopolist may gain complete control of a market if there is only one supplier of that input. For many years, the De Beers Group owned both the majority of the world's diamond mines and the major distribution system.

Similarly, if a firm controls the outlets through which the product must be sold, it can prevent potential rivals from gaining access to consumers. For example, approximately 50 per cent of public pubs in the UK operate on tenancy contracts known as the 'tied lease model'. This is effectively an exclusive supply contract, which means that landlords of such pubs have to purchase almost all of their beverages from the pub company (e.g. Enterprise Inns, Punch Taverns and JD Wetherspoon) that owns the pub.

Legal protection. The firm's monopoly position may be protected by patents on essential processes, by copyright, by various forms of licensing (allowing, say, only one firm to operate in a particular area) and by tariffs (i.e. customs duties) and other trade restrictions to keep out foreign competitors. Examples of monopolies, or near monopolies, protected by patents include most new medicines developed by pharmaceutical companies (e.g. anti-AIDS drugs), Microsoft's Windows operating systems and agro-chemical companies, such as Monsanto, with various genetically modified plant varieties and pesticides.

While patents do help monopolists to maintain their market power, they are also essential in encouraging new product innovation, as R&D is very expensive. Patents allow firms that engage in R&D to reap the rewards of that investment.

Mergers and takeovers. The monopolist can put in a takeover bid for any new entrant. The sheer threat of takeovers may discourage new entrants.

Retained profits and aggressive tactics. An established monopolist is likely to have some retained profits behind it. It can use these profits to help it sustain losses over a period of time, while it engages in a price war, mounts an advertising campaign or offers consumers various deals to compete with a new entrant until that firm is forced out of the market. The established firm then regains its monopoly status.

Switching costs. New entrants may struggle to access customers, if customers incur costs when moving to another supplier. These might be monetary or non-monetary costs, such as the time taken to shop around or learn how to use another product. For example, a consumer might have spent a lot of time learning how to use applications with the iOS operating system on an iPhone, which may deter them from switching to a smartphone that uses Google's Android operating system. Another thing that may prevent consumers from switching mobile phones is if they are tied in to a contract or have difficulties in comparing the best deals, which is often the case in the energy sector and banking. For example, a report into the retail banking market by the Competition and Markets Authority in 2016[1] found low switching rates among current account holders, because they found it almost impossible to compare products.

Consumers may also decide not to switch due to *network economies*. For example, people sell on eBay, because it is used by so many people. Similar sites will find it difficult to enter the market, as encouraging consumers to switch sites depends on the number of customers it already has.

Equilibrium price and output

Since there is, by definition, only one firm in the industry, the firm's demand curve is also the industry demand curve.

Compared with other market structures, demand under monopoly will be relatively inelastic at each price. The monopolist can raise its price and consumers have no alternative firm to turn to within the industry. They either pay the higher price or go without the good altogether.

Unlike the firm under perfect competition, the monopolist is thus a 'price maker'. It can choose what price to charge. Nevertheless, it is still constrained by its demand curve. A rise in price will reduce the quantity demanded.

As with firms in other market structures, a monopolist will maximise profit where $MR = MC$. In Figure 11.5, profit is maximised by producing a quantity of Q_m. The supernormal profit obtained is shown by the shaded area.

These profits will tend to be larger the less elastic is the demand curve (and hence the steeper is the MR curve) and thus the bigger is the gap between MR and price (AR).

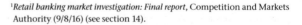

[1]*Retail banking market investigation: Final report*, Competition and Markets Authority (9/8/16) (see section 14).

Definitions

Natural monopoly A situation where long-run average costs would be lower if an industry were under monopoly than if it were shared between two or more competitors.

Switching costs The costs to a consumer of switching to an alternative supplier.

Network economies The benefits to consumers of having a network of other people using the same product or service.

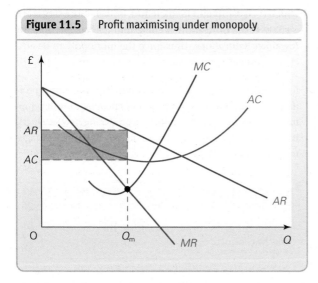

Figure 11.5 Profit maximising under monopoly

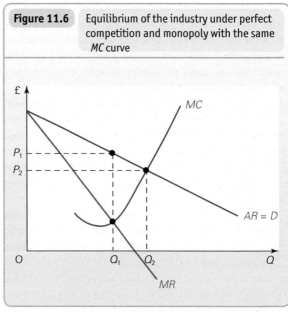

Figure 11.6 Equilibrium of the industry under perfect competition and monopoly with the same *MC* curve

The actual elasticity will depend on whether reasonably close substitutes are available in *other* industries.

The demand for a rail service will be much less elastic (and the potential for profit greater) if there is no bus service between the same destinations.

Since there are barriers to the entry of new firms, a monopolist's supernormal profits will not be competed away in the long run. The only difference, therefore, between short-run and long-run equilibrium is that, in the long run, the firm will produce where $MR = long$-run MC.

KI 21
p 184

Comparing monopoly with perfect competition

Because it faces a different type of market environment, the monopolist will produce a quite different output and at a quite different price from a perfectly competitive industry. Let us compare the two.

KI 21
p 184
The monopolist will produce a lower output at a higher price in the short run. Figure 11.6 compares the profit-maximising position for an industry under monopoly with that under perfect competition. Note that we are comparing the monopoly with the whole *industry* under perfect competition. That way, we can assume, for the sake of comparison, that they both face the same demand curve. We also assume, for the moment, that they both face the same cost curves.

The monopolist will produce Q_1 at a price of P_1. This is where $MC = MR$.

If the same industry were under perfect competition, however, it would produce at Q_2 and P_2 – a higher output and a lower price. But why? The reason for this is that for each of the firms in the industry – and it is at this level that the decisions are made – marginal revenue is the same as price. Remember that the firm under perfect competition faces a perfectly elastic demand (*AR*) curve, which also equals *MR* (see Figure 11.1). Thus producing where $MC = MR$ also

means producing where $MC = P$. When all firms under perfect competition do this, price and quantity in the industry will be given by P_2 and Q_2 in Figure 11.6.

The monopolist may also produce a lower output at a higher price in the long run. Under perfect competition, freedom of entry eliminates supernormal profit and forces firms to produce at the bottom of their *LRAC* curve, keeping long-run prices down. A monopolist, however, because of barriers to entry, can continue to earn supernormal profits in the long run and is not forced to operate at the bottom of the *AC* curve. Thus, other things being equal, long-run prices will tend to be higher, and hence output lower, under monopoly. (In section 20.2, pages 365–6, we examine this in more detail by considering the impact of monopoly on consumer and producer surplus.

Pause for thought

If the shares in a monopoly (such as a water company) were very widely distributed among the population, would the shareholders necessarily want the firm to use its monopoly power to make larger profits?

Costs under monopoly. The sheer survival of a firm in the long run under perfect competition requires that it uses the most efficient known technique and develops new techniques wherever possible. The monopolist, however, sheltered by barriers to entry, can still make large profits even if it is not using the most efficient technique. It has less incentive, therefore, to be efficient.

On the other hand, the monopoly may be able to achieve substantial economies of scale due to larger plant, centralised administration and the avoidance of unnecessary duplication (e.g. a monopoly water company would eliminate the need for several sets of rival water mains under each street). If this results in an *MC* curve substantially below that of the same industry under perfect competition, the monopoly may even produce a *higher* output at a *lower* price.

Another reason why a monopolist may operate with lower costs is that it can use part of its supernormal profits for research and development and investment. It may not have the same *incentive* to become efficient as the perfectly competitive firm that is fighting for survival, but it may have a much greater *ability* to become efficient than a small firm with limited funds.

Although a monopoly faces no competition in the goods market, it may face an alternative form of competition in financial markets. A monopoly, with potentially low costs, which is currently run inefficiently, is likely to be subject to a takeover bid from another company. This *competition for corporate control* may thus force the monopoly to be efficient in order to prevent being taken over.

Innovation and new products. The promise of supernormal profits, protected perhaps by patents, may encourage the development of new (monopoly) industries producing new products. It is this chance of making monopoly profits that encourages many people to take the risk of going into business.

> ### Definition
>
> **Competition for corporate control** The competition for the control of companies through takeovers.

<table>
<tr><td>**11.4**</td><td># POTENTIAL COMPETITION OR POTENTIAL MONOPOLY? THE THEORY OF CONTESTABLE MARKETS</td></tr>
</table>

Potential competition

The theory of contestable markets argues that what is crucial in determining price and output is not whether an industry is *actually* a monopoly or competitive, but whether there is the real *threat* of competition.

If a monopoly is protected by high barriers to entry (e.g. it controls the supply of key raw materials), then it will be able to make supernormal profits with no fear of competition.

If, however, another firm *could* take over from it with little difficulty, it will behave much more like a competitive firm. The threat of competition has a similar effect to actual competition.

As an example, consider a catering company that is given permission by a university to run its cafés and coffee shops. The catering company has a monopoly over the supply of food and drinks to students and staff, assuming there are no other eating places nearby. However, if it starts charging high prices or providing a poor service, the university could offer the running of the coffee shops to an alternative catering company. This threat may force the original catering company to charge 'reasonable' prices and offer a good service.

Perfectly contestable markets

A market is *perfectly contestable* when the costs of entry and exit by potential rivals are zero and when such entry can be made very rapidly. In such cases, the moment the possibility of earning supernormal profits occurs, new firms will enter, thus driving profits down to a normal level. The sheer threat of this happening, so the theory goes, will ensure that the firm already in the market will (a) keep its prices down, so that it just makes normal profits, and (b) produce as efficiently as possible, taking advantage of any economies of scale and any new technology. If the existing firm did not do this, entry would take place and potential competition would become actual competition.

Contestable markets and natural monopolies

So why in such cases are the markets not *actually* perfectly competitive? Why do they remain monopolies?

The most likely reason has to do with economies of scale and the size of the market. To operate at the minimum efficient scale, the firm may have to be so large relative to the market that there is only room for one such firm in the industry. If a new firm does come into the market, then one firm will not survive the competition. The market is simply not big enough for both of them.

If, however, there are no entry or exit costs, new firms will be perfectly willing to enter even though there is only room for one firm, provided they believe that they are more efficient than the existing firm. The existing firm, knowing this, will be forced to produce as efficiently as possible and with only normal profit.

The importance of costless exit

Setting up in a new business usually involves large expenditures on plant and machinery, though as we saw in Box 11.2,

> ### Definitions
>
> **Perfectly contestable market** A market where there is free and costless entry and exit.

BOX 11.3   PREMIER LEAGUE FOOTBALL: THE SKY IS THE LIMIT

The early days of Sky

The structure of English football was changed with the formation of the FA Premier League (EPL) for the 1992/3 football season. One justification for this was the promise of higher payments by TV companies. Live league football had been shown on free-to-air television throughout the 1980s and the clubs were very aware that this was potentially a very lucrative source of revenue.

The first contract to acquire the live and exclusive FA Premier League football broadcasting rights for the United Kingdom and Republic of Ireland was worth £191 million over five seasons. A consequence of Sky being awarded the contract was that live top-flight English league football was no longer available on terrestrial and free-to-air television. Those who wanted to watch live football matches on television had to sign up with Sky, buying both a basic package and the additional Sky sports channels; Sky thus had a monopoly on football broadcasts.

Attempts to reduce monopoly power

Both the Premier League and Sky's coverage proved to be hugely successful with viewers and advertisers and this was reflected in the price paid for subsequent packages. The one starting in 1997 cost Sky £670 million for four seasons, while in 2003 BSkyB, as the company was now formally known, paid over £1 billion for exclusive rights for three seasons.

However, over this period, the European Commission expressed increasing concern about the extent of Sky's monopoly. The Commission started legal proceedings in 2002, filing a statement of objections, but was thwarted when the League agreed a new contract with Sky before ironing out an EC-approved deal.

At this time, Sky did agree to sub-license up to eight 'top quality Premier League matches' each season to another broadcaster in order to win European approval. The Commission trumpeted this pledge as meaning 'that for the first time in the history of the Premier League free-to-air television will have a realistic opportunity to show live Premier League matches'. These hopes were dashed, however, when no rival broadcaster met the asking price set by Sky.

Auctioning the TV rights to the EPL

In 2005, the European Commission announced that Sky's monopoly would be broken. From 2007, the next set of rights, for a three-season period, would be sold in six 'balanced' packages of 23 games per season, with no broadcaster allowed more than five packages. The Commission claimed the deal would give fans 'greater choice and better value'.

However, concern was expressed about the impact on incomes of the Premiership clubs. While some commentators expected a more competitive process to result in roughly the same total income as was paid by Sky in 2003 (just over £1 billion), others suggested that Sky had originally paid a premium for the guarantee that it would be the sole broadcaster and that the introduction of competitive bidding would result in a fall in the revenues paid to clubs.

In May 2006, the bidding process for the rights for 2007–10 was completed. Sky won four of the six available packages and showed 92 live Premiership matches per season, while Setanta, an Irish-based satellite broadcaster, won the remaining two packages and showed 46 games per season. Between them, they paid £1.7 billion. The same process was undertaken in 2009 for the 2010/11 to 2013/14 seasons. This time the rights fetched just short of £1.8 billion.

Despite the opening up of 'competition', the total amount paid for domestic EPL TV rights was to rocket. Auctions took place in 2012 (2013/14 to 2015/16) and in 2015 (2016/17 to 2018/19) with BT now entering the market, after Setanta folded.

In 2012, the total amount paid by BT and Sky rose to over £3 billion and then in 2015 to over £5.1 billion. The 2015 auction was acutely competitive. Both BT and Sky saw the securing of the rights to screen live EPL matches as a means by which it could sell highly profitable broadband and phone services bundled with its respective TV offering. The result was that Sky paid £4.17 billion for five of the auctioned packages of matches (£11.047 million per game) while BT paid £960 million for two packages (£7.619 million per game).

Prior to the 2018 auction (in February), Sky and BT struck a deal to carry each other's content on their TV platforms. For some, this marked the end to what had been an aggressive battle for domination of the UK pay-TV market. BT had struggled to make inroads against Sky's strong position in the market. This was then reflected in the 2018 auction for rights to screen live EPL matches from 2019/20 to 2022/23. The initial announcement revealed that Sky and BT had paid £4.464 billion for five of the seven auctioned packages, with Sky paying £3.579 billion (£9.3 million per game) and BT £885 million (£9.22 million per game).

The final two packages, largely a mix of midweek and bank holiday fixtures, were not allocated initially, having failed to meet the reservation price. There has been some suggestion that the remaining 40 fixtures could be packaged together with other rights, but this would prevent Sky from bidding, given the auction rules. It looked likely, therefore, that these matches would remain unsold until the summer, as the Premier League aimed to secure the best deal.

1. *What other examples of monopoly power exist in football? Could this power be reduced?*
2. *Assess the impact of the pay broadcasters' emergence since the establishment of the English Premier League on (a) football fans, (b) other viewers.*
3. *What are the challenges that would face another telecommunications company wishing to enter the market?*

Undertake desktop research on the allocation of rights to broadcast live top-flight football in another European league. Compare the approach with that used to allocate rights to screen live English Premier League matches and assess its impact on the revenues raised, TV viewers and football fans.

BOX 11.4 'IT COULD BE YOU'

Bidding for the UK National Lottery

Since its launch in November 1994, the UK National Lottery has struck at the heart of the British psyche because it offers the opportunity to win a fortune and support worthwhile ventures. By 2018, the lottery had created over 4750 millionaires and had funded 525 000 projects nationwide, totalling £37 billion. It is one of the most efficient lotteries in Europe, with only 4 per cent of total revenue going on operating costs, 1 per cent retained as profit and the remaining 95 per cent going to good causes and winners.[1]

Sales of lottery tickets initially grew very rapidly and, over the years, various new initiatives have been introduced to stem the subsequent downturn in sales. Camelot, which operates the National Lottery, announced a new Chief Executive, Nigel Railton, after it reported sales falling by 3.2 per cent to £3.2 billion in the six months to September 2017, when compared with the same period the previous year. In the year ending 31 March 2017, total ticket sales were £6925.3 million. Mr Railton said:

> Coming off the back of last year's disappointing sales performance . . . I don't underestimate the challenge ahead of us . . . It is going to take some time to turn things around.[2]

There are plans to enable customers to buy tickets at self-checkouts and also to sell tickets for the first time in Aldi and Lidl. Camelot is also looking at ways to ensure more frequent jackpot winners, which may, in part, target some of the changes that had been made previously, which had made it harder for people to win. One of the big pressures facing Camelot with falling sales is the decline in revenues going to 'good causes'. Hence the company is under pressure to turn things around, especially with the next bidding process expected in 2019, as Camelot's licence expires in 2023.

Bidding for the national lottery requires a detailed business plan. This outlines all aspects of running the lottery, but its main emphasis is on providing likely revenue scenarios from games that would maximise money for good causes and safeguard players.

Camelot has been the only company to run the National Lottery to date, having won the rights in every bidding process. Competitors have been encouraged to bid, but incumbent firms, like Camelot, have considerable advantages over potential rivals when contracts have to be renewed and hence the number of new bidders is likely to be low. Two problems in particular stand out for rivals.

The 'Winner's Curse'.

If a potential entrant outbids the incumbent in an auction to run (say) a local bus service, then it could be that winner has paid too much. After all, the incumbent has more knowledge about running the bus service and the likely revenues that may prevail. This was the case when the consortium between Virgin and Stagecoach won the franchise to run the East Coast main railway line from 2015 to 2023. It later transpired that profits were insufficient to pay the agreed amount of money to the government each year and hence the franchise was terminated three years early (see Box 22.4).

This situation is known as the 'Winner's Curse' and a similar scenario may occur in respect of the lottery. Potential bidders may be put off bidding because they don't have the same knowledge about the UK lottery market and, if they won the franchise, might make less profit than they had anticipated. Arguably, the lottery market might be considered a mature market and more is now known about lottery sales and the gaming market in general. However, there are strong incentives for risk-averse regulators to continue with accepting bids from incumbent firms because they are known to provide a certain level of sales and service.

[1] *The National Lottery, Life Changing,* available at www.national-lottery.co.uk/life-changing.

[2] Murad Ahmed, 'Camelot overhauls Lottery as ticket sales fall', *Financial Times,* 21 November 2017.

---

these costs are falling with the growth of e-commerce. However, once money has been spent on the start-up, it becomes part of the fixed costs. If these fixed costs are no higher than those of the existing firm, then the new firm could win the battle. But, of course, there is always the risk that it might lose.

But does losing the battle really matter? Can the firm not simply move to another market?

It does matter if there are substantial costs of exit. This will be the case if the capital equipment cannot be transferred to other uses. In this case, these fixed costs are known as **sunk costs**. The losing firm will exit the industry, but is left with capital equipment that it cannot use and this may deter the firm from entering in the first place. The market is not perfectly contestable and the established firm can make supernormal profit.

If, however, the capital equipment can be transferred, the exit costs are zero (or at least very low), and new firms will be more willing to risk entering the market. For example, a rival coach company may open up a service on a route previously operated by only one company and where there is still only room for one operator. If the new firm loses the resulting battle, it can still use the coaches it has purchased. It simply uses them for a different route or sells them for a fair price on the second-hand market. The cost of the coaches is not a sunk cost.

Definitions

Sunk costs Costs that cannot be recouped (e.g. by transferring assets to other uses).

The handover problem.

If Camelot were to lose the lottery licence, there would be some large risks in transferring to the new bidder. Arguably, Camelot could sell its infrastructure to the new lottery provider, but there is a valuation dilemma. In terms of opportunity cost, Camelot would value the infrastructure at scrap value (if it has no alternative use for it), whereas a winner with no alternative source for such infrastructure would value Camelot's assets at close to their replacement value. This could lead to some difficult negotiations.

Because of this difficulty, the National Lottery Commission did require bidders for the third lottery licence to provide a new infrastructure, but recognised that this would take time to have in place (imagine trying to replace 30 000 retail terminals as well as to make online, television and mobile games work well). Given this difficulty, it is not surprising that there have been so few rivals bidding for the lottery licences.

Camelot managed to achieve a first-mover advantage (see page 221) by winning the initial lottery licence in 1994. It is now to continue providing the UK National Lottery until 2023 and so will have been sole monopoly provider for 29 years. Removing Camelot after that date could prove to be difficult.

The rationale for a monopoly supplier

Camelot is a monopoly supplier of the UK National Lottery, although it need not be so. The legislation currently allows for two licences, one to operate the infrastructure and another to run the games. It is possible for other companies to run games on the computer network owned by Camelot, much in the same way that Network Rail owns the railway tracks, tunnels, etc. and allows competition between firms on particular routes on the network. Indeed, this option was briefly undertaken by Camelot in 1998, when Vernons Pools sold its 'Easy Play' game using the National Lottery retailer network. Its sales, though, were poor and it was scrapped in May 1999.

However, the government has a strong preference for a single owner of the infrastructure and a single supplier of National Lottery games. The rationale for having a single owner of the infrastructure is fairly standard; this is a natural monopoly and it would be pointless having two lottery computer networks, just as it would be having two separately owned rail lines from Edinburgh to London. With one firm controlling the infrastructure, economies of scale can be reaped.

One of the arguments for having a single supplier of games is known, rather bizarrely, as 'peculiar economies of scale'.[3] This is a situation in which a company that offered a portfolio of innovative lottery games would be more likely to induce additional players to participate in games because they can raise the size of the prize to be won. In other words, good game design can lead to more and bigger jackpots and thus more people buying lottery tickets. This reduces the average costs of supplying tickets and increases the money for good causes.

Arguably, more than one firm may be able to supply an innovative portfolio of games if the market is large enough. However, the government is concerned about the risks involved in regulating relationships between network owners and network users. For example, there might be a lengthy legal dispute if a supplier of games is accused of unacceptable performance but it, in turn, accuses the network owner of poor service. This would then have a detrimental effect on the money raised for good causes. Thus the government has always preferred a single-firm framework for running the National Lottery.

1. *If Camelot is maximising revenue, what is the price elasticity of demand for lottery tickets?*
2. *To what extent is the National Lottery market a contestable market?*

---

[3]See, for example, P. Daffern, 'Assessment of the effects of competition on the National Lottery', *Technical Paper No. 6*, Department of Culture, Media and Sport, 2006.

Costless exit, therefore, encourages firms to enter an industry, knowing that, if unsuccessful, they can always transfer their capital elsewhere.

The lower the exit costs, the more contestable the market. This implies that firms already established in other similar markets may provide more effective competition against monopolists, since they can simply transfer capital from one market to another. For example, studies of airlines in the USA show that entry to a particular route may be much easier for an established airline, which can simply transfer planes from one route to another.

Assessment of the theory

In considering potential competition, and the size of entry barriers and exit costs, the theory of contestable markets does provide some useful insights. The more contestable the market, the greater the pressure on the monopolist to behave competitively. This might bring the 'best of both worlds' for consumers, if the monopolist benefits from economies of scale and, through the threat of potential competition, is forced to pass these costs onto consumers in the form of lower prices.

This potential outcome seems to provide a justification for a *laissez-faire* (non-interventionist) economy, where things are left to the free market and regulated when required (e.g. coach and air routes). Indeed, politicians on the political right seized on the theory, arguing in favour of the free market!

However, in response, others argue that few markets are *perfectly* contestable and hence monopolists can still make supernormal profits in the long run. Furthermore, even though there may be the threat of competition, the established firm may use its own threats to let it be known that, if any firm dares to enter the market, it will face all-out war. This certainly will deter new entrants and allow the established firm to keep prices and profits high. Thus, despite the threat of competition, government intervention may still be needed to regulate markets.

Pause for thought

Think of two examples of highly contestable monopolies (or oligopolies). Are the market outcomes in the public interest?

SUMMARY

1a Most markets fall into the category of imperfect competition, with many firms competing, albeit in often very different ways.

1b The market structure under which a firm operates will affect its conduct and its performance. This is the 'structure-conduct-performance' paradigm.

1c There are four alternative market structures under which firms operate. In ascending order of firms' market power, they are: perfect competition, monopolistic competition, oligopoly and monopoly.

2a The assumptions of perfect competition are: a very large number of firms, complete freedom of entry, a homogeneous product and perfect knowledge of the good and its market by both producers and consumers.

2b In the short run of perfect competition, there is not time for new firms to enter the market, and thus supernormal profits can persist. In the long run, however, any supernormal profits will be competed away by the entry of new firms.

2c The short-run equilibrium for the firm under perfect competition will be where the price, as determined by demand and supply in the market, is equal to marginal cost. At this output, the firm will be maximising profit.

2d The long-run equilibrium in a perfectly competitive market will be where the market price is just equal to firms' long-run average cost.

2e There are no substantial economies of scale to be gained in a perfectly competitive industry. If there were, the industry would cease to be perfectly competitive as the large, low-cost firms drove the small, high-cost ones out of business.

3a A monopoly is where there is only one firm in an industry. In practice, it is difficult to determine where a monopoly

exists because it depends on how narrowly an industry is defined.

3b Barriers to the entry of new firms normally will be necessary to protect a monopoly from competition. Such barriers include economies of scale (making the firm a natural monopoly or at least giving it a cost advantage over new (small) competitors), control over supplies of inputs or over outlets, patents or copyright, exploiting network economies and tactics to eliminate competition (such as takeovers or aggressive advertising).

3c Profits for the monopolist (as for other firms) will be maximised where $MC = MR$.

3d If demand and cost curves are the same in a monopoly and a perfectly competitive industry, the monopoly will produce a lower output and at a higher price than the perfectly competitive industry.

3e On the other hand, any economies of scale may, in part, be passed on to consumers in lower prices, and the monopolist's high profits may be used for research and development and investment, which in turn may lead to better products at possibly lower prices.

4a Potential competition may be as important as actual competition in determining a firm's price and output strategy. This is the theory of contestable markets.

4b The greater the threat of this competition, the lower are the entry and exit costs to and from the industry. If the entry and exit costs are zero, the market is said to be *perfectly* contestable. Under such circumstances, an existing monopolist may be forced to keep its profits down to the normal level if it is to resist entry of new firms. The lower the exit costs, the lower are the sunk costs of the firm.

4c The theory of contestable markets provides a more realistic analysis of firms' behaviour than theories based simply on the *existing* number of firms in the industry.

REVIEW QUESTIONS

1 Why do economists treat normal profit as a cost of production? What determines (a) the level and (b) the rate of normal profit for a particular firm?

2 Why is perfect competition so rare?

3 Why does the market for fresh vegetables approximate to perfect competition, whereas that for frozen or tinned ones does not?

4 Illustrate on a diagram similar to Figure 11.3 what would happen in the long run if price were initially below P_L.

5 We discussed e-commerce in Box 11.2, but are there any other examples of the impact of technological development on the competitiveness of markets or on meeting specific assumptions of perfect competition?

6 As an illustration of the difficulty in identifying monopolies, try to decide which of the following are monopolies: a train-operating company; your local evening newspaper; British Gas; the village post office; Interflora; the London Underground; ice creams in the cinema; Guinness; food sold on trains; the board game 'Monopoly'.

7 Try this brain teaser. A monopoly would be expected to face an inelastic demand. After all, there are no direct substitutes. And, yet, if it produces where $MR = MC$, MR must be positive, demand must therefore be elastic. Therefore the monopolist must face an elastic demand! Can you solve this conundrum?

8 For what reasons would you expect a monopoly to charge (a) a higher price and (b) a lower price than if the industry were operating under perfect competition?

9 'The outcomes of perfect competition are always good, whereas monopolies are always bad.' Discuss this statement.

10 In which of the following industries are exit costs likely to be low: (a) steel production; (b) market gardening; (c) nuclear power generation; (d) specialist financial advisory services; (e) production of fashion dolls; (f) production of a new drug; (g) contract catering; (h) mobile discos; (i) car ferry operators? Are these exit costs dependent on how narrowly the industry is defined?

11 Think of three examples of monopolies (local or national) and consider how contestable their markets are.

Profit maximisation under imperfect competition

Business issues covered in this chapter

- How will firms behave under monopolistic competition (i.e. where there are many firms competing, but where they produce differentiated products)?
- What is the short-run equilibrium under monopolistic competition and what is the process whereby long-run equilibrium is reached?
- Why will firms under monopolistic competition make only normal profits in the long run?
- How do the outcomes of monopolistic competition compare with that of perfect competition?
- How are firms likely to behave when there are just a few of them competing ('oligopolies')?
- What determines whether oligopolies will engage in all-out competition or instead collude with each other?
- What strategic 'games' are oligopolists likely to play in their attempt to out-do their rivals?
- Why might such games lead to an outcome where all the players are worse off than if they had colluded?
- Does oligopoly serve the consumer's interests?

Very few markets in practice can be classified as perfectly competitive or as a pure monopoly. The vast majority of firms do compete with other firms, often quite aggressively, and yet they are not price takers: they do have some degree of market power. Most markets, therefore, lie between the two extremes of monopoly and perfect competition, in the realm of 'imperfect competition'. There are two types of imperfect competition: namely, monopolistic competition and oligopoly (see section 11.1).

12.1 MONOPOLISTIC COMPETITION

Monopolistic competition is towards the competitive end of the spectrum (as we saw in section 11.1). It can best be understood as a situation where there are a lot of firms competing, but where each firm does, nevertheless, have some degree of market power (hence the term 'monopolistic' competition): each firm has some discretion as to what price to charge for its products because they are differentiated from those of other firms.

Assumptions of monopolistic competition

There are three key assumptions about monopolistic competition:

- *Quite a large number of firms.* As a result, each firm has only a small share of the market and, therefore, its actions are unlikely to affect its rivals to any great extent. This means that when a firm makes its decisions, it will not have to worry about how its rivals will react. It assumes that what its rivals choose to do will not be influenced by what it does.

This is known as the assumption of **independence**. As we saw in chapter 11 and we discuss later, this is not the case under oligopoly.

■ *Freedom of entry of new firms.* If any firm wants to set up in business in this market, it is free to do so.

In these two respects, therefore, monopolistic competition is like perfect competition. The third assumption, however, is different from perfect competition.

■ *Differentiated products.* Each firm now produces a product or provides a service that is in some way different from its rivals. This is known as the assumption of **product differentiation**. This gives the firm some degree of market power, meaning it can raise its price without losing all its customers. Thus its demand curve is downward sloping, albeit relatively elastic given the large number of competitors to which customers can turn.

Petrol stations, restaurants, hairdressers and builders are all examples of monopolistic competition – as is the case of busking, which is discussed on the Freakonomics blog,[1] as too was John's experience of selling ice cream (see Box 10.2 on page 174).

When considering monopolistic competition, it is important to take account of the distance consumers are willing to travel to buy a product. In other words, the geographical size of the market matters. For example, Costa is a major coffee retailer, but, in any one location, it experiences intense competition from other coffee shops, cafés, restaurants and bars, as well as other places where other drinks can be purchased. So, in any one local area, there is competition between firms, each offering differentiated products.

---

[1]http://freakonomics.com/2012/05/21/the-economics-of-busking/.

Equilibrium of the firm

Short run

As with other market structures, profits are maximised at the output where $MC = MR$. The diagram will be the same as for the monopolist, except that the AR and MR curves will be more elastic, due to more competition. This is illustrated in Figure 12.1(a). As with perfect competition, it is possible for the monopolistically competitive firm to make supernormal profit in the short run. This is shown as the shaded area.

Just how much profit the firm will make in the short run depends on the strength of demand: the position and elasticity of the demand curve. The further to the right the demand curve is relative to the average cost curve, and the less elastic the demand curve is, the greater will be the firm's short-run profit. Thus a firm facing little competition and whose product is considerably differentiated from its rivals may be able to earn significant short-run profits.

KI 4 p 19

KI 12 p 64

> ## Pause for thought
>
> *Which of these two items is a petrol station more likely to sell at a discount: (a) engine oil; (b) sweets? Why?*

> ## Definitions
>
> **Independence (of firms in a market)** When the decisions of one firm in a market will not have any significant effect on the demand curves of its rivals.
>
> **Product differentiation** When one firm's product is sufficiently different from its rivals', it can raise the price of the product without customers all switching to the rivals' products. This gives a firm a downward-sloping demand curve.

Figure 12.1 Equilibrium of the firm under monopolistic competition: (a) short run; (b) long run

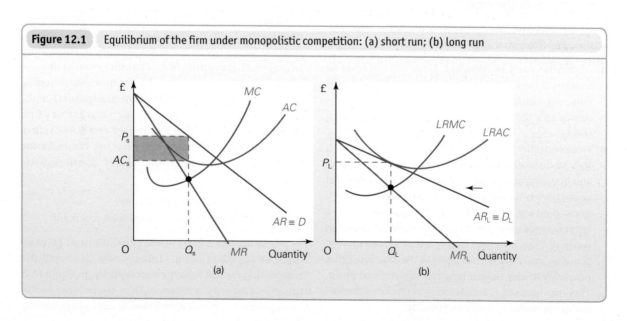

Long run

If typical firms are earning supernormal profit, new firms will enter the industry in the long run. As new firms enter, they will take some of the customers away from established firms. The demand for the established firms' products will, therefore, fall. Their demand (*AR*) curve will shift to the left and will continue doing so as long as supernormal profits remain and thus new firms continue entering.

Long-run equilibrium will be reached when only normal profits remain: when there is no further incentive for new firms to enter. This is illustrated in Figure 12.1(b). The firm's demand curve settles at D_L, where it is tangential to (i.e. just touches) the firm's *LRAC* curve. Output will be Q_L: where $AR_L = LRAC$. (At any other output, *LRAC* is greater than *AR* and thus less than normal profit would be made.)

It is important to note that there is a difference between the transition from the short run to the long run under perfect competition and monopolistic competition, even though the long run equilibrium of normal profits for the firm is the same in both market structures.

- Under perfect competition, when new firms enter (or leave) the market, it is the industry supply curve that shifts, which changes the market price and leaves just normal profits.
- Under monopolistic competition, however, the entry of new firms is reflected by shifting an established firm's demand curve inwards and this eliminates the supernormal profits.

As all firms under monopolistic competition are producing a slightly differentiated product, each firm is different and hence we cannot create an industry demand or supply curve. Instead, we have to focus on the effect on a given firm when new firms enter the market. This can be seen as a limitation of the model, as we discuss next.

Limitations of the model

There are various problems in applying the model of monopolistic competition to the real world:

- Information may be imperfect. Firms will not enter an industry if they are unaware of the supernormal profits currently being made or if they underestimate the demand for the particular product they are considering selling.
- Firms will differ from each other, not only in the product they produce or the service they offer, but also in their size and in their cost structure. What is more, entry may not be completely unrestricted. For example, two petrol stations could not set up in exactly the same place – on a busy crossroads, say – because of local authority planning controls. Thus, although the typical or 'representative' firm may earn only normal profit in the long run, other firms may be able to earn long-run supernormal profit. They may have some cost advantage or produce a product that is impossible to duplicate perfectly.

- Existing firms may make supernormal profits, but, if a new firm entered, this might reduce everyone's profits below the normal level. Thus a new firm will not enter and supernormal profits will persist into the long run. An example would be a small town with two chemist shops. They may both make more than enough profit to persuade them to stay in business. But if a third set up (say midway between the other two), there would not be enough total sales to allow them all to earn even normal profit. This is a problem of indivisibilities. Given the overheads of a chemist shop, it is not possible to set up one small enough to take away just enough customers to leave the other two with normal profits.
- One of the biggest problems with the simple model outlined above is that it concentrates on price and output decisions. In practice, the profit-maximising firm under monopolistic competition will also need to decide the exact variety of product to produce, and how much to spend on advertising it. This will lead the firm to take part in non-price competition (which we examined in Chapter 8).

Pause for thought

Why will additional advertising lead to smaller and smaller increases in sales under monopolistic competition?

Comparing monopolistic competition with perfect competition and monopoly

Comparison with perfect competition

Often, it is argued that monopolistic competition leads to a less efficient allocation of resources than perfect competition.

Figure 12.2 compares the long-run equilibrium positions for two firms. One firm is under perfect competition and thus faces a horizontal demand curve. It will produce an output of Q_1 at a price of P_1. The other is under monopolistic competition and thus faces a downward-sloping demand curve. It will produce the lower output of Q_2 at the higher price of P_2. A crucial assumption here is that a firm would have the *same* long-run average cost (*LRAC*) curve in both cases. Given this assumption, we can make the following two predictions about monopolistic competition:

- Less will be sold and at a higher price.
- Firms will not be producing at the least-cost point.

By producing more, firms would move to a lower point on their *LRAC* curve. Thus firms under monopolistic competition are said to have **excess capacity**. In Figure 12.2, this excess capacity is shown as $Q_1 - Q_2$. In other words, monopolistic competition is typified by quite a large number

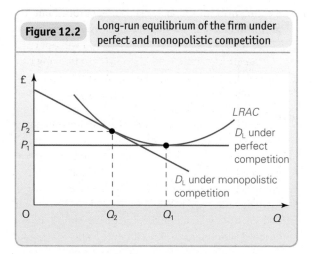

Figure 12.2 Long-run equilibrium of the firm under perfect and monopolistic competition

of firms (e.g. petrol stations), all operating at less than optimum output, and thus being forced to charge a price above that which they could charge if they had a bigger turnover.

Pause for thought

Which would you rather have: five restaurants to choose from, each with very different menus and each having spare tables so that you could always guarantee getting one; or just two restaurants to choose from, charging a bit less but with less choice and making it necessary to book well in advance?

So how does this affect the consumer? Although the firm under monopolistic competition may charge a higher price than under perfect competition, the difference may be very small. Although the firm's demand curve is downward sloping, it is still likely to be highly elastic due to the large number of substitutes. Furthermore, the consumer may benefit from monopolistic competition by having a greater variety of products to choose from. Each firm may satisfy some particular requirement of particular consumers.

Comparison with monopoly

When comparing monopolistic competition with monopoly, we find very similar arguments as we had when comparing perfect competition and monopoly.

On the one hand, freedom of entry for new firms and hence the lack of long-run supernormal profits under monopolistic competition are likely to help keep prices down for the consumer and encourage cost saving. On the other hand, monopolies are likely to achieve greater economies of scale and have more funds for investment and research and development.

Definition

Excess capacity (under monopolistic competition) In the long run, firms under monopolistic competition will produce at an output below that which minimises average cost per unit.

12.2 OLIGOPOLY

Oligopoly occurs when just a few firms between them share a large proportion of the industry. Some of the best-known companies are oligopolists, including Ford, Coca-Cola, Apple, EDF and Tesco. On the Sloman News Site, you will find many blogs written about different oligopolies and it is both useful and interesting to compare the outcomes as, despite all being oligopolies, there can be significant differences in the behaviour of firms.

One of the key differences between oligopolies is in the degree of product differentiation. The firms may produce a virtually identical product (e.g. metals, chemicals, sugar, petrol). In most cases, however, oligopolists produce highly differentiated products (e.g. cars, soap powder, soft drinks, electrical appliances). Much of the competition between such oligopolists is in terms of the marketing of their particular brand. Marketing practices may differ considerably from one industry to another.

The two key features of oligopoly

Despite the differences between oligopolies, there are two crucial features that distinguish an oligopoly from other market structures.

Barriers to entry

Unlike firms under monopolistic competition, there are various barriers to the entry of new firms. These are similar to those under monopoly (see pages 191–4). The size of the barriers, however, will vary from industry to industry. In some cases, entry is relatively easy, whereas in others it is virtually impossible, perhaps due to patent protection or prohibitive research and development costs.

Interdependence of the firms

With only a few firms under oligopoly, each firm will need to take account of the behaviour of the others when making its own decisions. This means that they are mutually dependent: they are *interdependent*. Each firm is affected by its

Definition

Interdependence (under oligopoly) This is one of the two key features of oligopoly. Each firm is affected by its rivals' decisions and its decisions will affect its rivals. Firms recognise this interdependence and take it into account when making decisions.

rivals' actions. If a firm changes the price or specification of its product, for example, or the amount of its advertising, the sales of its rivals will be affected.

The rivals may then respond by changing their price, specification or advertising. No firm can therefore afford to ignore the actions and reactions of other firms in the industry and it is this feature that differentiates oligopolies from the other market structures.

> **KEY IDEA 23** *People often think and behave strategically.* How you think others will respond to your actions is likely to influence your own behaviour. Firms, for example, when considering a price or product change, often will take into account the likely reactions of their rivals.

It is impossible, therefore, to predict the effect on a firm's sales of, say, a change in its price without first making some assumption about the reactions of other firms. Different assumptions yield different predictions about how firms will respond to a given market situation and thus there is no one single theory of oligopoly.

Competition and collusion

The interdependence of oligopolists means firms are pulled in two different directions: to compete and to collude.

Firms will want to maximise their *share* of industry profits. Having analysed its rivals' strategies, a firm may decide to *compete* with its rivals, perhaps by cutting prices or undertaking advertising with the aim of increasing sales. However, if all firms cut prices, each unit sold now earns less revenue; if all firms increase advertising, average costs will rise. Either way, profits are likely to fall.

Thus, the firm may conclude that, rather than competing with its rivals, *collusion* will be more a profitable strategy. If it can come to agreements with the other firms on price, output, product design, etc., the firms may jointly be able to maximise industry profits. They can then split these maximum profits between them. Of course, this may be bad for the consumer and most countries have competition laws that try to prevent open collusion (as we shall see in section 21.1).

Sometimes, if they can get away with it, firms will collude; sometimes they will not. The following sections examine first *collusive oligopoly*, where we consider both formal agreements and tacit collusion, and then *non-collusive oligopoly*.

Collusive oligopoly

KI 21 p 184 When firms under oligopoly engage in collusion, they may agree on prices, market share, advertising expenditure, etc. Such collusion reduces the uncertainty they face. It reduces the fear of engaging in competitive price cutting or retaliatory advertising, both of which could reduce total industry profits and probably each individual firm's profit.

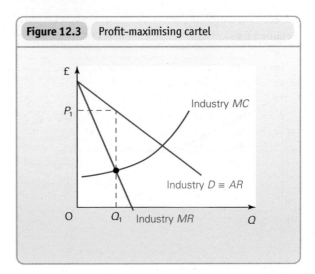

Figure 12.3 Profit-maximising cartel

Cartels

A formal collusive agreement is called a *cartel*. The cartel will maximise profits by acting like a monopolist, with the members behaving as if they were a single firm. This is illustrated in Figure 12.3.

The total market demand curve is shown with the corresponding market *MR* curve. The cartel's *MC* curve is the **KI 4 p 19** *horizontal* sum of the *MC* curves of its members (since we are adding the *output* of each of the cartel members at each level of marginal cost). Profits are maximised at Q_1 where $MC = MR$. The cartel must therefore set a price of P_1 (at which Q_1 will be demanded).

Having agreed on the cartel price, the members may then compete against each other using *non-price competition*, to gain as big a share of resulting sales (Q_1) as they can.

Alternatively, the cartel members may somehow agree to divide the market between them. Each member would be given a **quota**. These quotas could be the same for every firm or they might be allocated according to the current market share of the firm. Whatever the method of allocation, the sum of all the quotas must add up to Q_1. If the quotas

Definitions

Collusive oligopoly When oligopolists agree (formally or informally) to limit competition between themselves. They may set output quotas, fix prices, limit product promotion or development, or agree not to 'poach' each other's markets.

Non-collusive oligopoly When oligopolists have no agreement between themselves – formal, informal or tacit.

Cartel A formal collusive agreement.

Quota (set by a cartel) The output that a given member of a cartel is allowed to produce (production quota) or sell (sales quota).

exceeded Q_1, either there would be output unsold if price remained fixed at P_1 or the price would fall to clear the market.

The most famous example of a cartel is OPEC, which was set up in 1960 by the five major oil-exporting countries and is discussed in more detail in Box 12.1.

Where open collusion is illegal, firms may simply break the law or find ways to get round it. Alternatively, firms may stay within the law, but still *tacitly* collude by watching each other's prices and keeping theirs similar. Firms may tacitly 'agree' to avoid price wars or aggressive advertising campaigns.

Pause for thought

If this 'fair' solution were adopted, what effect would it have on the industry MC curve in Figure 12.3?

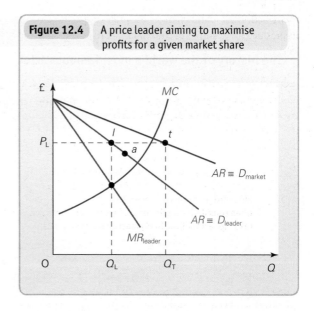

Figure 12.4 A price leader aiming to maximise profits for a given market share

Tacit collusion

One form of **tacit collusion** is where firms keep to the price that is set by an established leader. The leader may be the largest firm: the firm that dominates the industry. This is known as **dominant firm price leadership**. Alternatively, the price leader may simply be the one that has proved to be the most reliable to follow: the one that is the best barometer of market conditions. This is known as **barometric firm price leadership**. Let us examine each of these two types of price leadership in turn.

Dominant firm price leadership. This is a 'sequential game', where one firm (the leader) moves first and then the followers, having observed the leader's choice of price, move second. We will discuss sequential games in more detail in section 12.3. Here we are interested in determining how the leader sets the price. This depends on the assumptions it makes about its rivals' reactions to its price changes. If it assumes that rivals will simply follow it by making exactly the same percentage price changes up or down, then a simple model can be constructed. This is illustrated in Figure 12.4. The leader assumes that it will maintain a constant market share (say 50 per cent).

The leader will maximise profits where its marginal revenue is equal to its marginal cost. It knows its current position on its demand curve (say, point *a*). It then estimates how responsive its demand will be to industry-wide price changes and thus constructs its demand and *MR* curves on that basis. It then chooses to produce Q_L at a price of P_L: at point *l* on its demand curve (where $MC = MR$). Other firms then follow that price. Total market demand will be Q_T, with followers supplying that portion of the market not supplied by the leader: namely, $Q_T - Q_L$.

There is one problem with this model. That is the assumption that the followers will want to maintain a constant market share. It is possible that, if the leader raises its price,

the followers may want to supply more, given that the new price ($= MR$ for a price-taking follower) may well be above their marginal cost. On the other hand, the followers may decide merely to maintain their market share for fear of invoking retaliation from the leader, in the form of price cuts or an aggressive advertising campaign.

Barometric firm price leadership. A similar exercise can be conducted by a barometric firm. Although the firm is not dominating the industry, its price will be followed by the others. It merely tries to estimate its demand and *MR* curves – assuming, again, a constant market share – and then produces where $MR = MC$ and sets price accordingly.

In practice, which firm is taken as the barometer may change frequently. Whether we are talking about oil companies, car producers or banks, any firm may take the initiative in raising prices. If the other firms are merely waiting for someone to take the lead – say, because costs have risen – they will all quickly follow suit. For example, if one of the bigger building societies or banks raises its mortgage rates by 1 per cent, this is likely to stimulate the others to follow suit.

Definitions

Tacit collusion When oligopolists follow unwritten 'rules' of collusive behaviour, such as price leadership. They will take care not to engage in price cutting, excessive advertising or other forms of competition.

Dominant firm price leadership When firms (the followers) choose the same price as that set by a dominant firm in the industry (the leader).

Barometric firm price leadership Where the price leader is the one whose prices are believed to reflect market conditions in the most satisfactory way.

BOX 12.1 **OPEC**

The history of the world's most famous cartel

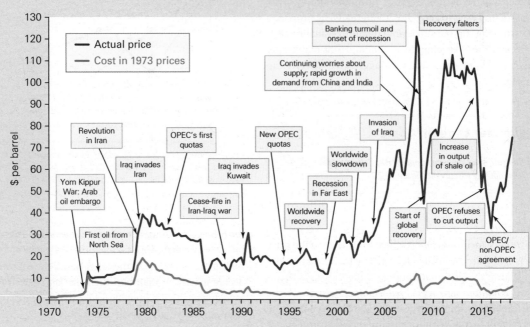

Oil prices (crude oil, monthly average)

Sources: Nominal oil price data from *World Commodity Price Data (The Pink Sheet)*, *Commodity Markets* (World Bank); Price Index from *Data Extracts* (OECD).

OPEC is probably the best known of all cartels. Set up in 1960 by the five major oil-exporting countries (Saudi Arabia, Iran, Iraq, Kuwait and Venezuela), it now has 14 members, including Nigeria, Angola, Libya and Ecuador.

OPEC's main objective is to co-ordinate the supply of oil by its members so as to support an oil price that gives a steady income to producers and a good return on capital. It also aims to ensure a regular supply to consumers.

The years leading up to 1960 had seen the oil-producing countries increasingly in conflict with the international oil companies, which extracted oil under 'concessionary agreement'. Under this scheme, oil companies were given the right to extract oil in return for royalties. This meant that the oil-producing countries had little say over output and price levels.

In Box 5.3, we considered some of the factors behind changes in global oil prices and now we take a closer look at the role of OPEC in influencing the prices.

The early years

Despite the formation of OPEC in 1960, it was not until 1973 that control of oil production was effectively transferred from the oil companies to the oil countries, with OPEC making the decisions on how much oil to produce and thereby determining its oil revenue. By this time OPEC consisted of 13 members.

OPEC's pricing policy over the 1970s consisted of setting a market price for Saudi Arabian crude (the market leader) and leaving other OPEC members to set their prices in line with this: a form of dominant 'firm' price leadership (as discussed on page 207).

As long as demand remained buoyant and was price inelastic, this policy allowed large price increases with consequent large revenue increases. In 1973/4, after the Arab–Israeli war, OPEC raised the price of oil from around $3 per barrel to over $12 (see chart). The price was kept at roughly this level until 1979 and sales of oil remained stable.

After 1979, however, following a further increase in the price of oil from around $15 to $40 per barrel, demand did fall. This was due largely to the recession of the early 1980s which, in turn, was caused largely by governments' responses to the oil price increases.

Quotas

Faced by declining demand, OPEC after 1982 agreed to limit output and allocate production quotas in an attempt to keep the price up. A production ceiling of 16 million barrels per day was agreed in 1984.

However, the cartel was beginning to break down as the world recession led to a fall in the demand for oil, growing output from non-OPEC members and cheating by some OPEC members who exceeded their quota limits. With a glut of oil, OPEC could no longer maintain the price.

The trend of lower oil prices was reversed in the late 1980s as the world economy boomed and the demand for oil rose. Then, in 1990, Iraq invaded Kuwait and the first Gulf War ensued. With the cutting-off of supplies from Kuwait and Iraq, the supply of oil fell and there was a sharp rise in its price.

But with the ending of the war and the recession of the early 1990s, the price rapidly fell again and only recovered slowly as the world economy started expanding once more.

On the demand side, the development of energy-saving technology plus increases in fuel taxes led to a relatively slow growth in consumption. On the supply side, the growing proportion of output supplied by non-OPEC members, plus the adoption in 1994 of a relatively high OPEC production ceiling of 24.5 million barrels per day, meant that supply more than kept pace with demand.

The situation for OPEC deteriorated further in the late 1990s, following the recession in the Far East. Oil demand fell by some 2 million barrels per day and prices declined significantly. OPEC once again intervened and its members agreed to cut production by 4.3 million barrels per day in an attempt to push the price back up to around $18–20 per barrel.

In late 2001, the relationship between OPEC and non-OPEC oil producers changed. The 10 members of the OPEC cartel decided to cut production by 1.5 million barrels a day. This followed an agreement with five of the major oil producers outside of the cartel to reduce their output too, the aim being to cut supply and push oil prices upward and then stabilise them at around $25 per barrel.

The alliance between OPEC and non-OPEC oil producers is the first such instance of its kind in the oil industry. As a result, it seemed that OPEC might now, once again, be able to control the market for oil. However, political conflict in key oil producing countries in the early 2000s led to supply problems and, although OPEC tried to relax its quotas, it found it difficult to adjust supply sufficiently quickly to make any real difference to the price.

Prior to 2008, oil prices had been rising, creating inflationary pressures, but leading to a doubling of the income of OPEC nations in the first half of that year. Then came the financial crisis, which pushed oil prices down dramatically: falling from a high of $144 per barrel in July 2008 to a low of $34 per barrel in December of that year. The lower prices, while good for consumers, were potentially damaging for investment in oil exploration and development and also for investment in alternative energy supplies.

OPEC responded to the falling price by announcing cuts in production, totalling some 14 per cent between August 2008 and January 2009. But with OPEC producing less than a third of global oil output, this represented less than 5 per cent of global production and, consequently, had little effect on the price.

A new competitor

Prices did recover and, between mid-2011 and mid-2014, remained fairly stable at around $100 to $120 per barrel. But then OPEC faced a new competitor in the form of US shale oil production. With a new source of supply, oil prices fell – from $112 per barrel in June 2014 to just $30 per barrel in February 2016.

OPEC responded to this fall in price, not by cutting output, but by announcing that it would retain output. What it was relying on was the fact that production from shale oil wells, although often involving low marginal costs, often lasts only two or three years. Investment in new shale oil wells, by contrast, tends to be relatively expensive. By OPEC maintaining production, it was hoping to use its remaining market power to reduce the supply of competitors over the medium to long term.

However, with revenues from oil falling so dramatically, the strategy was not sustainable. OPEC and non-OPEC producers (such as Russia) reached an agreement in December 2016 to cut production. This was the first time such an agreement had occurred since 2001. The oil price immediately started to increase again.

The agreement that had been due to expire in March 2018, was then extended to the end of 2018. The problem for OPEC is that the increase in oil prices made US shale production profitable once again. A number of rigs that had temporarily shut down became operational again and production therefore increased. It will be interesting to see what influence OPEC can have on the price of oil in the future, given the increase of non-conventional extraction, such as in shale formations and oil sands.

1. What conditions facilitate the formation of a cartel? Which of these conditions were to be found in the oil market in (a) the early 1970s; (b) the mid-1980s; (c) the mid-2000s; (d) the mid-2010s?
2. Could OPEC have done anything to prevent the long-term decline in real oil prices seen from 1982 to 2002?

Download monthly price data on commodity markets[7] from the World Bank. Create a chart showing the annual rate of oil price inflation from the early 1970s. Write a short commentary summarising the patterns observed in oil price inflation.

Other forms of tacit collusion. An alternative to having an established leader is for there to be an established set of simple 'rules of thumb' that everyone follows.

One such example is *average cost pricing*. Here producers, instead of equating *MC* and *MR*, simply add a certain percentage for profit on top of average costs. Thus, if average costs rise by 10 per cent, prices will be raised automatically by 10 per cent. This is a particularly useful rule of thumb in times of inflation, when all firms will be experiencing similar cost increases.

Another rule of thumb is to have certain *price benchmarks*. Thus clothes may sell for £9.99, £24.99 or £39.99 (but not, say, £12.31 or £36.42). If costs rise, then firms simply raise their price to the next benchmark, knowing that other firms will do the same. (Average cost pricing and other pricing strategies are considered in more detail in Chapter 17.)

Rules of thumb can also be applied to advertising (e.g. you do not criticise other firms' products, only praise your own); or to the design of the product (e.g. lighting manufacturers tacitly agreeing not to bring out an everlasting light bulb).

> ### Pause for thought
>
> *If a firm has a typical-shaped average cost curve and sets prices 10 per cent above average cost, what will its supply curve look like?*

Factors favouring collusion

Collusion between firms, whether formal or tacit, is more likely when firms can clearly identify with each other or some leader and when they trust each other not to break agreements. It will be easier for firms to collude if the following conditions apply:

- There are only very few firms, all well known to each other.
- They are open with each other about costs and production methods.
- They have similar production methods and average costs and are thus likely to want to change prices at the same time and by the same percentage.
- They produce similar products and can thus more easily reach agreements on price.
- There is a dominant firm.
- There are significant barriers to entry and thus there is little fear of disruption by new firms.
- The market is stable. If industry demand or production costs fluctuate wildly, it will be difficult to make agreements, partly due to difficulties in predicting market conditions and partly because agreements may frequently have to be amended. There is a particular problem in a declining market where firms may be tempted to undercut each other's price in order to maintain their sales.
- There are no government measures to curb collusion.

In some oligopolies, there may be only a few (if any) factors favouring collusion. In such cases, the likelihood of price competition is greater.

Non-collusive oligopoly: assumptions about rivals' behaviour

Even though oligopolists might not collude formally or tacitly, they will still need to take account of rivals' likely behaviour when deciding their own strategy. Firms will make assumptions about how they believe their rivals will behave and are likely to base these assumptions on past behaviour. There are three well-known models, each based on a different set of assumptions.

Assumption that rivals produce a given quantity: the Cournot model

One assumption is that rivals will produce a particular *quantity*. This is most likely when the market is stable and the rivals have been producing a relatively constant quantity for some time. The task, then, for the individual oligopolist is to decide its own price and quantity given the presumed output of its competitors.

The earliest model based on this assumption was developed by the French economist Augustin Cournot in 1838. The *Cournot model* (which is developed in Web Appendix 4.2) takes the simple case of just two firms (a *duopoly*) producing an identical product: for example, two electricity generating companies supplying the whole country.

This is illustrated in Figure 12.5, which shows the profit-maximising price and output for firm A. The total market demand curve is shown as D_M. Assume that firm A believes that its rival, firm B, will produce Q_{B1} units. Thus firm A perceives its own demand curve (D_{A1}) to be Q_{B1} units less than total market demand. In other words, the horizontal gap between D_M and D_{A1} is Q_{B1} units. Given its perceived demand curve of D_{A1}, its marginal revenue curve will be MR_{A1} and the profit-maximising output will be Q_{A1}, where $MR_{A1} = MC_A$. The profit-maximising price will be P_{A1}.

> ### Definitions
>
> **Average cost pricing** Where a firm sets its price by adding a certain percentage for (average) profit on top of average cost.
>
> **Price benchmark** This is a price that typically is used. Firms, when raising prices, usually will raise them from one benchmark to another.
>
> **Cournot model** A model of duopoly where each firm makes its price and output decisions on the assumption that its rival will produce a particular quantity.
>
> **Duopoly** An oligopoly where there are just two firms in the market.

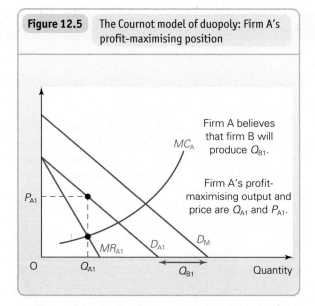

Figure 12.5 The Cournot model of duopoly: Firm A's profit-maximising position

Firm A believes that firm B will produce Q_{B1}.

Firm A's profit-maximising output and price are Q_{A1} and P_{A1}.

If firm A believed that firm B would produce *more* than Q_{B1}, its perceived demand and *MR* curves would be further to the left and the profit-maximising quantity and price would both be lower.

At the same time as firm A makes an assumption about firm B's output, firm B will also be making an assumption about how much it thinks firm A will produce. This is, therefore, a 'simultaneous game', as both firms are making their decisions at the same time, as we will discuss in section 12.3.

Profits in the Cournot model. Industry profits will be *less* than under a monopoly or a cartel. The reason is that price will be lower than the monopoly price. This can be seen from Figure 12.5. If this were a monopoly, then to find the profit-maximising output, we would need to construct an *MR* curve corresponding to the market demand curve (D_M). This would intersect with the *MC* curve at a higher output than Q_{A1} and a *higher* price (given by D_M). Nevertheless, profits in the Cournot model will be higher than under perfect competition, since price is still above marginal cost.

Assumption that rivals set a particular price: the Bertrand model

An alternative assumption is that rival firms set a particular price and stick to it. This scenario is more realistic when firms do not want to upset customers by frequent price changes or want to produce catalogues that specify prices. The task, then, for a given oligopolist is to choose its own price and quantity in the light of the prices set by rivals.

The most famous model based on this assumption was developed by another French economist, Joseph Bertrand, in 1883. Bertrand again took the simple case of a duopoly, but its conclusions apply equally to oligopolies with three or more firms.

The outcome is one of price cutting until all supernormal profits are competed away. The reason is simple. If firm A assumes that its rival, firm B, will hold price constant, then firm A should undercut this price by a small amount and, as a result, gain a large share of the market. At this point, firm B will be forced to respond by cutting its price. We end up with a price war, with prices forced down to the level of average cost, with only normal profits remaining.

As with the Cournot model above, this is also a simultaneous move game, except here the variable of interest is price. The supermarket industry is a good example of a market where price wars are a constant feature: see, for example, the blog on the Sloman News Site titled *Supermarket price wars and the effect on suppliers* and another titled *Pizza Price War*.

Nash equilibrium. The equilibrium outcome in both the Cournot and Bertrand models is not in the *joint* interests of the firms. In each case, total profits are less than under a monopoly or cartel. But, in the absence of collusion, the outcome is the result of each firm doing the best it can given its assumptions about what its rivals are doing. The resulting equilibrium is known as a **Nash equilibrium**, after John Nash, a US mathematician (and subject of the film *A Beautiful Mind*)[2] who introduced the concept in 1951. This concept is particularly important when analysing strategic behaviour by firms, as we do when we consider game theory in section 12.3.

In practice, when competition is intense, as in the Bertrand model, the firms may seek to collude long before profits have been reduced to a normal level. Alternatively, firms may put in a **takeover bid** for their rival(s).

The kinked demand-curve assumption

In 1939, a theory of non-collusive oligopoly was developed simultaneously on both sides of the Atlantic: in the USA by Paul Sweezy and in Britain by R.L. Hall and C.J. Hitch. This **kinked demand theory** has since become, perhaps, the most

[2]www.youtube.com/watch?v=2d_dtTZQyUM.

Definitions

Nash equilibrium The position resulting from everyone making their optimal decision based on their assumptions about their rivals' decisions. Without collusion, there is no incentive for any firm to move from this position.

Takeover bid Where one firm attempts to purchase another by offering to buy the shares of that company from its shareholders.

Kinked demand theory The theory that oligopolists face a demand curve that is kinked at the current price: demand being significantly more elastic above the current price than below. The effect of this is to create a situation of price stability.

BOX 12.2	OLIGOPOLY AND OLIGOPSONY

Market power in oligopolistic industries

Oligopolies are often complex markets and, as we have seen, the behaviour of firms within them can be very different. One thing they often have in common is being of interest to the relevant country's competition authorities. We examine competition policy in section 21.1. In this box, we consider the energy market and then return to consider supermarkets, and focus not on their selling power, but on their buying power. You will also find many other examples of oligopolies discussed on the Sloman News Site.

Who has the energy to switch?

The UK energy sector is dominated by six big firms (the 'Big Six'), which sell to over 90 per cent of UK households. You can find many articles about the energy sector on the Sloman News Site, which consider, among other things, the barriers to entry to the industry (*Energising the energy market*), the referral to the Competition and Markets Authority (CMA) (*An energy price cap*) and the savings that are possible from switching suppliers (*Do people have the energy to switch*).

Barriers to entry

As with most oligopolies, a key problem in the energy sector is the existence of barriers to entry. In this industry, there is both vertical and horizontal integration within firms (see Chapter 15): the Big Six are involved in both the generation of power and the local distribution of it (vertical integration); they also offer 'dual-fuel' deals, where customers can receive a discount from buying electricity and gas from the same supplier (horizontal integration).

The vertical integration, in particular, has made it difficult for smaller suppliers to enter the market, as they have had to buy wholesale from one of the Big Six. They may, as a result, have less favourable terms of access to wholesale supplies, thereby pushing up their costs and necessitating higher prices for customers. This barrier to entry restricts growth in the industry and results in less effective competition. Thus a key focus of the industry regulator, Ofgem (the Office of Gas and Electricity markets: see section 21.1), has been how to reduce the barriers to entry to make the market more competitive. Through an increased number of suppliers, competition should increase and this should keep prices down, thereby benefiting households.

 1. *Does vertical integration matter if consumers still have a choice of supplier and if generators are still competing with each other?*

In June 2014, following months of political pressure, Ofgem referred the industry to the Competition and Markets Authority (CMA) to see if there was a possible breach of a dominant market position. Ofgem asked the CMA to investigate accusations of profiteering by the big six and discuss

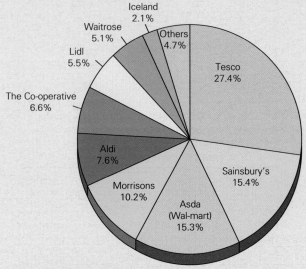

UK supermarket food market share (12 weeks to 9 September 2018)

Source: Based on data from *Kantar Worldpanel*

mechanisms to reduce structural barriers to entry that undermine competition, including the potential breaking up of these dominant firms. The Chief Executive of Ofgem, Dermot Nolan, said:

> A CMA investigation should ensure there are no barriers to stop effective competition bearing down on prices and delivering the benefits of these changes to consumers.[1]

After investigating the issues surrounding vertical integration in particular, the costs to non-vertically integrated suppliers and the benefits to vertically integrated suppliers were identified. However, it was determined that any benefits were likely to be fairly modest in size, especially as many of the vertically integrated firms were moving away from this structure. The CMA concluded:

> Overall, we have not identified any areas in which vertical integration is likely to have a detrimental impact on competition for independent suppliers and generators. In addition, we consider that there may be some efficiencies resulting from vertical integration, which may be passed through to customers. As a result, our conclusion is that firms' vertically integrated structure does not give rise to an AEC [adverse effect on competition].[2]

Consumer inertia

As well as the traditional barriers to entry discussed above, it was felt that new competitors faced another obstacle that

---

[1] 'Ofgem refers the energy market for a full competition investigation', *Press Release*, Ofgem (26 June 2014).
[2] *Energy Market Investigation: Summary of Final Report*, Competition and Markets Authority (24 June 2016, updated 27 February 2018)

restricted competition. In some sense it is a form of brand loyalty, where customers are reluctant to switch to an alternative supplier, making it difficult for new entrants to attract customers.

However, in the case of energy firms, a big criticism levelled at the Big Six was that it was virtually 'impossible' to switch. With so many tariffs available to domestic consumers, this was a case of too much choice, leading to confused customers and inertia in the market, whereby households simply stayed with their existing supplier, even if it was not the cheapest. The suppliers were thus accused of exploiting these 'loyalty' customers and limiting competition, as new firms entering the market would find it very difficult to gain a sufficient number of customers and make a profitable business. The CMA found that, between Quarter 1 2012 and Quarter 2 2014, over 95 per cent of the Big Six's dual-fuel customers could have saved by switching tariff and/or supplier.[3]

Various steps have been taken by Ofgem and, more recently, the CMA to break down the barriers to entry in the industry that arise from inertia. In 2013, Ofgem required energy companies to publish simple 'per-unit' prices to allow customers to compare tariffs more easily and encourage switching and thus competition. From March 2014, the Big Six were required to publish prices up to two years in advance to ensure more effective competition and avoid facing penalties if they did not trade fairly with independent suppliers.

Data still suggest that a significant share of customers lack engagement in the energy market, due to a lack of understanding of the options. In a CMA-commissioned survey of 7000 customers, it was found that:

■ 36 per cent of respondents did not think/know that the tariff, payment method and supplier could be changed;
■ 34 per cent of respondents had never considered switching supplier;
■ 56 per cent of respondents had either never switched supplier, did not know it was possible, or if they had done so;
■ 72 per cent had either never switched tariff with an existing supplier, did not know it was possible, or if they had done so.

More recently, the CMA has noted that those customers on higher incomes and with more education are more likely to be engaged in the market and switch suppliers. They found that:

> 35 per cent of those whose household incomes were above £36 000 had switched supplier in the last three years, compared with 20% of those whose household incomes were below £18 000, and 32 per cent of those with degree level qualifications had switched in the last three years

compared with 18 per cent of those with no qualifications.[4]

Work is continuing to improve the engagement of customers, including Ofgem's programme of providing customers with more information about switching. This includes an Ofgem-controlled database that lists 'disengaged customers' and allows rival suppliers contact them about switching.

The completion of the roll-out of smart meters to domestic customers is due by 2020 and it is hoped that this will improve incentives for energy companies to compete with each other and will 'improve customer engagement by making the relationship between prices and consumption more visible and improve[d] the accuracy of bills.' Ofgem will be monitoring suppliers to ensure that the timetable for the roll-out is met and will have the power to impose penalties on suppliers who fail to comply.

Despite the steps that have been taken, concern still remains that the Big Six retain a more than 90 per cent share of the market. Hence, continued monitoring of the behaviour of firms will be vital.

 2. *The Big Six have been required to open up their finances to greater scrutiny and publish prices up to two years in advance. How will this help to boost competition?*

Super Market' power

In the supermarket industry, some of the most recent focus has been on their power not as sellers, but as buyers. If a wholesale manufacturer of ready-meals, a supplier of sausages or a farmer wants to reach a wide customer base, it will need to deal with the eight largest supermarket chains, which control some 93 per cent of the market (see chart). A market such as this, where there are a few large *purchasers* of goods and services, is known as an *oligopsony*. (A single large buyer of goods, services or factors of production is known as a monopsony and we look at this in Chapter 18, pages 319–20).

Market power

Over the years, a number of unfair practices by the supermarkets towards their suppliers have been identified. These include retrospectively changing contracts and forcing suppliers to fund special offers such as 'buy one, get one free'. Furthermore, there was evidence that firms were regularly

---

Definition

Oligopsony A market with just a few buyers (or employers, in the case of labour markets, as discussed in Chapter 18).

---

[3]*Energy Market Investigation: Updated Issues Statement,* Competition and Markets Authority (18 February 2015)

[4]*Energy Market Investigation: Summary of Final Report,* op. cit.

asking for very substantial payments, in order to be included on 'preferred supplier' lists.

After a lengthy investigation, the Competition Commission (one of the predecessors to the Competition and Markets Authority) concluded that the supermarkets were passing on excessive risks and unexpected costs to their suppliers. As a consequence, a stronger Grocery Supplies Code of Practice (GSCP) was introduced in 2009. This recognised the power that large grocery retailers wield over their smaller suppliers and outlawed the practices detailed above.

In January 2013, the government appointed a 'Groceries Code Adjudicator' (GCA) to make sure the supermarkets were complying with the GSCP. In January 2016, the GCA concluded that Tesco had not been complying with the code. In particular, she concluded that the company had 'knowingly delayed paying money to suppliers in order to improve its own financial position'. In June 2016, Morrisons was also judged to have broken the code by requiring suppliers to make lump-sum payments even though they were not required according to the supply contracts.

Who benefits?

It would be easy to conclude that the power of supermarkets, both as purchasers and as retailers, is so great that they are

a 'bad thing'. However, that would be overly simplistic. There is evidence that they compete on price and that, as a consequence, have held down the cost of food bills in the UK. They have also introduced a variety of products and offer very convenient shopping for many people, particularly those who work full-time.

The grocery market is, therefore, a good example of a sector where growth and market power can be identified as both beneficial and harmful to other economic agents.

3.   *Explain why manufacturers of food products continue to supply supermarkets, despite concerns that they are not always treated fairly.*
4.   *Is the supermarket sector an oligopoly or monopolistically competitive, in your opinion? Justify your answer.*

Visit the Competition and Markets Authority website. Under 'CMA cases', search for cases/investigations involving the grocery sector. Choose a particular case and summarise the economic ideas and principles relevant to the case.

---

famous of all theories of oligopoly. Economists noted that, even when oligopolists did not collude over price, the price charged across the industry often remained relatively stable. The kinked demand curve model was developed to explain this observation and it rests on two asymmetrical assumptions:

■ If a firm cuts its price, its rivals will feel forced to follow suit and cut theirs, to prevent losing customers to the first firm.

■ If a firm raises its price, its rivals will *not* follow suit since, by keeping their prices the same, they will thereby gain customers from the first firm.

On these assumptions, each oligopolist will face a demand curve that is *kinked* at the current price and output (see Figure 12.6(a)). A rise in price will lead to a large fall in sales as customers switch to the now relatively lower-priced rivals. The firm will thus be reluctant to raise its price. Demand is relatively elastic above the kink. On the other hand, a fall in price will bring only a modest increase in sales, since rivals lower their prices too and therefore customers do not switch. The firm will thus also be reluctant to lower its price. Demand is relatively inelastic below the kink. Thus oligopolists will be reluctant to change prices at all.

This price stability can be shown formally by drawing in the firm's marginal revenue curve, as in Figure 12.6(b).

To see how this is done, imagine dividing the diagram into two parts either side of Q_1. At quantities less than Q_1 (the left-hand part of the diagram), the *MR* curve will correspond to the shallow part of the *AR* curve. At quantities greater than Q_1 (the right-hand part), the *MR* curve will correspond to the steep part of the *AR* curve. To see how this part of the *MR* curve is constructed, imagine extending the steep part of the *AR* curve back to the vertical axis. This and the corresponding *MR* curve are shown by the dotted lines in Figure 12.6(b).

As you can see, there will be a gap between points *a* and *b*. In other words, there is a vertical section of the *MR* curve between these two points.

Profits are maximised where $MC = MR$. Thus, if the *MC* curve lies anywhere between MC_1 and MC_2 (i.e. between points *a* and *b*), the profit-maximising price and output will be P_1 and Q_1. Thus prices will remain stable *even with a considerable change in costs*.

Oligopoly and the consumer

If oligopolists act collusively and jointly maximise industry profits, they will, in effect, be acting as a monopoly. In such cases, prices may be very high. This is clearly not in the best interests of consumers.

Figure 12.6 (a) Kinked demand for a firm under oligopoly; (b) stable price under conditions of a kinked demand curve

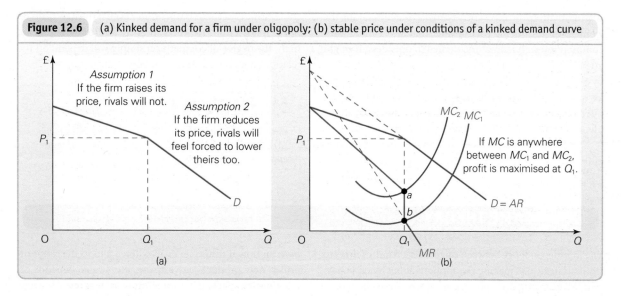

(a)

(b)

Furthermore, in two respects, oligopoly may be more disadvantageous than monopoly:

■ Depending on the size of the individual oligopolists, there may be less scope for economies of scale to lower costs and mitigate the effects of market power.

■ Oligopolists are likely to engage in much more extensive advertising than a monopolist. This will raise costs. Consumers could, thus, end up paying higher prices, though it may lead to product development and better information about the product's characteristics.

These problems will be less severe, however, if oligopolists do not collude, if there is some degree of price competition and if barriers to entry are weak. For example, in the Bertrand model, prices end up being set at the perfectly competitive level.

Moreover, the power of oligopolists in certain markets may, to some extent, be offset if they sell their product to other powerful firms. Thus oligopolistic producers of baked beans or soap powder sell a large proportion of their output to giant supermarket chains, which can use their market power to keep down the price at which they purchase these products. This phenomenon is known as *countervailing power*.

In some respects, oligopoly may be more beneficial to the consumer than other market structures:

Pause for thought

Assume that two brewers announce that they are about to merge. What information would you need to help you decide whether the merger would be in the consumer's interests?

■ Oligopolists, like monopolists, can use part of their supernormal profit for research and development. Unlike monopolists, however, oligopolists will have a considerable *incentive* to do so. If the product design is improved, this may allow the firm to capture a larger share of the market and it may be some time before rivals can respond with a similarly improved product. If, in addition, costs are reduced by technological improvement, the resulting higher profits will improve the firm's capacity to withstand a price war.

■ Non-price competition through product differentiation may result in greater choice for the consumer. Take the case of tablets or mobile phones. Non-price competition has led to a huge range of different products of many different specifications, each meeting the specific requirements of different consumers.

It is difficult to draw any general conclusions about the outcomes in this market structure, since oligopolies differ so much in their behaviour and performance. Although an oligopoly is closer to the non-competitive end of the spectrum, it can still be a highly competitive market structure.

Oligopoly and contestable markets

The theory of contestable markets has been applied to oligopoly as well as to monopoly, and similar conclusions are drawn.

The lower the entry and exit costs for new firms, the more difficult it will be for oligopolists to collude and make supernormal profits. If oligopolists do form a cartel (whether legal or illegal), it will be difficult to maintain it if there is a threat of competition from new entrants. What a cartel has to do in

Definition

Countervailing power When the power of a monopolistic/oligopolistic seller is offset by powerful buyers who can prevent the price from being pushed up.

such a situation is to erect entry barriers, thereby making the 'contest' more difficult. For example, the cartel could form a common research laboratory, denied to outsiders. It might attempt to control the distribution of the finished product by buying up wholesale or retail outlets. Or it might simply let it be known to potential entrants that they will face all-out price, advertising and product competition from all the members if they should dare to set up in competition.

The industry is thus likely to behave competitively if entry and exit costs are low, with all the benefits and costs to the consumer of such competition – even if the new firms do not actually enter. However, if entry and/or exit costs are high, the degree of competition simply will depend on the relations between existing members of the industry.

> ### Pause for thought
>
> *Which of the following markets do you think are contestable: (a) credit cards; (b) brewing; (c) petrol retailing; (d) insurance services; (e) compact discs?*

12.3 GAME THEORY

The interdependence between oligopolists requires firms to think strategically, making assumptions about rivals' behaviour before taking decisions. *Game theory* is used by economists to examine the best strategy that a firm can adopt and how this may affect market outcomes.

This section will focus on how game theory can be used to provide some useful insights into firms' behaviour. It allows us to assess the various strategies that firms might use for dealing with their rivals.

However, it is worth bearing in mind that game theory can be applied to a huge range of other areas. For example, the BBC News article, 'What exactly is "game theory"?',[2] examines the application of game theory by Greek Finance Minister Yanis Varoufakis in 2015 in his approach to negotiations over Greek debt. Game theory can also be applied to negotiations over the UK's exit from the European Union.

Simultaneous one-shot games

When a firm is competing against others, its profit-maximising strategy (under non-collusive oligopoly) depends, in part, on how it thinks its rivals will react to its decisions on prices, new products, advertising, etc. It also depends on whether it expects the competition to be a one-off event (such as firms competing for a specific contract) or repeated.

We focus first on competition that is a one-off event. In the case of firms bidding for a specific contract, each firm will make its decision independently (i.e. submit its bid price); then all the bids will be considered and the contract will be awarded – probably to the lowest bidder; then the game ends. In this case, each firm 'moves' just once and therefore it is modelled as a *single-move or one-shot game*. As both firms are making their decisions at the same time, or without observing the decision of each other, it is also a *simultaneous game*.

Dominant strategy games

Consider a market where there are just two firms with identical costs, products and demand. They are both considering which of two alternative prices to charge. Table 12.1 shows typical profits they could each make.

Let us assume that at present both firms (X and Y) are charging a price of £2 and they are each making a profit of £10 million, giving a total industry profit of £20 million. This is shown in the top left-hand cell (A).

Now assume they are both (independently) considering reducing their price to £1.80. Given the interdependence between them, firm X will need to consider what firm Y

Table 12.1	Profits for firms X and Y at different prices	

		X's price	
		£2	£1.80
Y's price	£2	**A** £10 m each	**B** £5 m for Y £12 m for X
	£1.80	**C** £12 m for Y £5 m for X	**D** £8 m each

> ### Definitions
>
> **Game theory (or the theory of games)** The study of alternative strategies that oligopolists may choose to adopt, depending on their assumptions about their rivals' behaviour.
>
> **Single-move or one-shot games** Where each player (e.g. each firm) makes just one decision (or move) and then the 'game' is over.
>
> **Simultaneous game** Where each player (e.g. each firm) makes its decision at the same time and is therefore unable to respond to other players' moves.

---

[2]Chris Stokel-Walker, 'What exactly is "game theory"?', *BBC News Magazine*.

might do and the impact this will have. Firm Y must do the same. Let us consider X's position. In our simple example, there are just two things that its rival, firm Y, might do. Either Y could cut its price to £1.80, or it could leave its price at £2. What should X do?

To answer this question, we need to take each of firm Y's two possible actions and look at firm X's best response to each. If we assume that firm Y chooses a price of £2, firm X could decide to keep its price at £2, giving it £10m in profit. This is shown by cell A. Alternatively, firm X could cut its price to £1.80 and earn £12m in profit, in cell B. Firm X's best response is, therefore, to cut its price to £1.80, preferring a profit of £12m to one of £10m.

What happens if we now assume that firm Y charges £1.80 – how should firm X best respond? If firm X charged £2, we would end up in cell C and firm X would earn only £5m in profit. On the other hand, firm X could also cut its price to £1.80, moving us to cell D and it would earn £8m profit. By comparing these two profit outcomes, we can see that firm X's best response to firm Y lowering its price to £1.80 is to cut its own price to £1.80 as well, preferring a profit of £8m to a profit of £5m.

Note that firm Y will argue along similar lines, cutting its price to £1.80 as well, no matter what it assumes that firm X will do.

This game is called a ***dominant strategy game***, since the firm's best response is always to play the same (dominant) strategy (namely, cutting the price to £1.80). The result is that we end up in cell D, with each firm earning a profit of £8 million.

As we saw in the Cournot and Bertrand models, this equilibrium outcome, when there is no collusion between players, is known as a *Nash equilibrium*. Both firms do what is best for themselves, given the assumptions made about their rivals' behaviour and neither firm has any incentive to change its behaviour.

Nash equilibrium. The position resulting from everyone making their optimal decision based on their assumptions about their rivals' decisions. Without collusion, there is no incentive for any firm to move from this position.

However, it is important to note that the profits earned by each firm in the Nash equilibrium (cell D) are lower than they would have been had the firms colluded and charged the higher price (cell A). Each firm would have earned £10 million.

But, even with collusion, both firms would be tempted to cheat and cut prices. This is known as the ***prisoners' dilemma*** (see Box 12.3).

More complex simultaneous one-shot games

More complex 'games' can be devised with more than two firms, many alternative prices, differentiated products and

| Table 12.2 | Profits for firms X and Y at different prices |

		X's price	
		£25	£19
Y's price	£20	**A** £6m for Y £6m for X	**B** £2m for Y £5m for X
	£15	**C** £4m for Y £3m for X	**D** £4m for Y £4m for X

various forms of non-price competition (e.g. advertising). We may also see 'games' where the best response for each firm depends on the assumptions made, meaning there is no dominant strategy. Consider the payoff matrix in Table 12.2.

If firm X assumes that firm Y will charge £20, then firm X will earn either £6m in profit if it charges £25 or £5m in profit if it charges £19. Firm X's best response would be to charge £25 (cell A). However, if it assumes that firm Y will charge £15, then firm X's best response now will be to charge £19, preferring £4m in profit (cell D) to £3m in profit (cell C). We no longer have a dominant strategy. Firm X's best response depends on its assumption about Y's price. However, firms X and Y are still choosing their best response, given the assumptions they make about their rival's behaviour and hence we can still arrive at a Nash equilibrium.

Pause for thought

What is firm Y's best response to each of firm X's possible choices in the game shown in Table 12.2? Does it have a dominant strategy in this game?

In many situations, firms will have a number of different options open to them and a number of possible reactions by rivals. Such games can become highly complex and predicting your rivals' behaviour can be crucial in ensuring the best

Definitions

Dominant strategy game Where the same policy is suggested by different strategies.

Prisoners' dilemma Where two or more firms (or people), by attempting independently to choose the best strategy, based upon what other(s) are likely to do, end up in a worse position than if they had co-operated from the start.

BOX 12.3 THE PRISONERS' DILEMMA

Game theory is relevant not just to economics. A famous non-economic example is the prisoners' dilemma.

Nigel and Amanda have been arrested for a joint crime of serious fraud. They are both guilty. Each is interviewed separately and given the following alternatives:

- First, if they say nothing, the court has enough evidence to sentence both to a year's imprisonment.
- Second, if either Nigel or Amanda alone confesses, he or she is likely to get only a three-month sentence but the partner could get up to ten years.
- Third, if both confess, they are likely to get three years each.

These outcomes are illustrated in the diagram. What should Nigel and Amanda do?

Let us consider Nigel's dilemma. Should he confess in order to get the short sentence? This is better than the year he would get for not confessing. There is, however, an even better reason for confessing. Suppose Nigel doesn't confess but, unknown to him, Amanda does confess. Then Nigel ends up with the long sentence (cell B). Better than this is to confess and to get no more than three years (cell D). Nigel's best response is always to confess.

Amanda is in the same dilemma and so the result is simple. When both prisoners act in their own self-interest by confessing, they both end up with relatively long prison terms (cell D). Only when they collude will they end up with relatively short ones, the best combined solution (cell A). However, for each of these prisoners, the more certain they are

that their compatriot will maintain their innocence, the greater the incentive for them to confess and reduce their sentence!

Of course, the police know this and will do their best to prevent any collusion. They will keep Nigel and Amanda in separate cells and try to persuade each of them that the other is bound to confess.

Thus the choice of strategy depends on:

- Nigel's and Amanda's risk attitudes: i.e. are they 'risk lovers' or 'risk averse'?
- Nigel's and Amanda's estimates of how likely the other is to own up.

1. *Why is this a dominant strategy game?*
2. *How would Nigel's choice of strategy be affected if he had, instead, been involved in a joint crime with Adam, Ashok, Diana and Rikki, and they had all been caught?*

Let us now look at two real-world examples of the prisoners' dilemma.

Standing at concerts

When people go to some public event, such as a concert or a match, often they stand in order to get a better view. But, once people start standing, everyone is likely to do so: after all, if they stayed sitting, they would not see at all. In this Nash equilibrium, most people are worse off, since, except for tall people, their view is likely to be worse and they lose the comfort of sitting down.

Too much advertising

Why do firms spend so much on advertising? If they are aggressive, they do so to get ahead of their rivals. If they are cautious, they do so in case their rivals increase their advertising. Although, in both cases, it may be in the individual firm's best interests to increase advertising, the resulting Nash equilibrium is likely to be one of excessive advertising: the total spent on advertising (by all firms) is not recouped in additional sales.

3. *Give one or two other examples (economic or non-economic) of the prisoners' dilemma.*

	Amanda's alternatives	
	Not confess	Confess
Nigel's alternatives — Not confess	**A** Each gets 1 year	**B** Nigel gets 10 years Amanda gets 3 months
Nigel's alternatives — Confess	**C** Nigel gets 3 months Amanda gets 10 years	**D** Each gets 3 years

possible outcome. It now becomes possible to have multiple Nash equilibria.

The better the firm's information about (a) its rivals' costs and demand, (b) the likely reactions of rivals to its actions and (c) the effects of these reactions on its own profit, the better the firm's 'move in the game' is likely to be. It is similar to a card game: the more you know about your opponents' cards and how your opponents are likely to react to your moves, and the better you can calculate the effects of their moves on you, the better your moves in the game are likely to be.

Repeated simultaneous games

Although one-shot games do occur, and not just in business scenarios, many firms actually will compete with each other on a continuous basis. In our earlier example of firms bidding for a contract, once each firm had set its price, the game ended. But, what happens if the game does not end there? Supermarkets and fast food restaurants are frequently amending their prices; Apple and Samsung launch new versions of their mobile phones on an annual basis.

In these cases, we do not have a one-shot game, as the 'players' have to make decisions, over and over again. Such games are now *repeated games*. The big difference is that now each firm or 'player' can see its rivals' actions in previous periods/rounds of the game, even though firms are playing simultaneously in each period. Players can use this information to inform their own strategy and hence it creates a scenario whereby a player's actions in period one may have an impact on its rivals' actions and its own profits in subsequent periods. Firms may face a trade-off between the short run and the long run.

Consider the prisoner's dilemma game from Box 12.3, which was a one-shot game. Even though both Nigel and Amanda would have been better off colluding, neither had an incentive to do so and thus the Nash equilibrium was for both to confess. If we now think of this as a repeated game, will the predicted outcome change? Is there a way in which Nigel and Amanda can be encouraged to co-operate with each other so that they both deny the charges and end up with the most efficient outcome for each of them: they each get one year.

Infinitely repeated games

Perhaps Nigel and Amanda are a modern version of Bonnie and Clyde and are constantly committing crimes, but getting caught! Therefore, they find themselves having to decide between 'confess' and 'deny' on a weekly basis. This is a repeated game and now our two criminals may have an incentive to collude. Before, neither player could be convinced to collude and choose 'deny' because, if their partner confessed, they would then receive up to 10 years in prison. But now, there is an incentive to collude. Let us consider Amanda's decision.

The grim trigger strategy. Assume that Nigel and Amanda have agreed that they will 'deny' if they are ever caught. However, when they are caught for the first time, Amanda changes her mind under questioning and confesses (persuaded by the shorter sentence). Once the sentences are served and they play the game again (commit the next crime and get caught), Nigel may now decide to punish Amanda for breaking their agreement. That is, he may now play 'confess' in all future rounds of the game. This strategy employed by Nigel is known as the *grim trigger strategy*.

It means that Amanda benefits in round one by confessing, as she gets only three months in jail (Nigel did as promised and denied). However, in all future rounds of the game, Nigel and Amanda now both play 'confess' and hence Amanda suffers in the long run, from repeatedly getting three years in jail. She trades off three months in jail in round one, but then suffers from three years in jail in every other round of the game.

If Amanda had not changed her mind and instead played 'deny' in round one, she would have received one year in jail (worse than the three months she served by confessing in period one), but then, in all future rounds, both of them would have continued to deny. Thus, every future round of the game would lead to just one year in jail for Amanda, rather than three.

In this repeated game, both players have an incentive to co-operate with each other from the start, as they want to avoid their partner punishing them in all future rounds. This means that, as long as both players believe they will 'play' again and they value their future payoffs (as little time in jail as possible), we can see a situation where neither player will choose the Nash equilibrium. Instead, both will choose to collude and 'deny'. Through co-operation the most efficient strategy has now been achieved.

The tit-for-tat strategy. You may think that the grim trigger strategy is rather extreme! Another strategy that might be played is what game theorists have found to be the most successful strategy in a repeated game, called the *tit-for-tat strategy*. Just as with the grim trigger strategy, tit-for-tat can also encourage players to co-operate.

In this strategy, each player observes the action of its rival in one period and then copies that action in the next period. Therefore, if Nigel chose to play the tit-for-tat strategy, then, after Amanda confessed in round one, Nigel would confess in round two. If Amanda confessed in round two, Nigel would confess in round three. But, if Amanda denied in round two, then Nigel would deny in round three.

This strategy, therefore, still incorporates the 'punishment' from the grim trigger strategy, but it also introduces the idea of forgiveness. That is: if you confessed in the last round, I'll punish you this round by confessing, but, if you change your mind and deny, I'll forgive your earlier transgression and will deny next time too! A comment from a microeconomics textbook by Thomas Nechyba[3] nicely summarises the idea behind it. He says 'Play nice with the other kids . . . but if someone hits you, you hit them back until they start being nice again.'

In the context of pricing, a tit-for-tat strategy might be for a firm not to be the first to cut prices, but, if one of its rivals cuts its price, this firm will cut its price too. The hope of this first firm is that the other firm will realise this and, not wanting to trigger a price war, will decide not to cut its price. This could be seen as a form of tacit collusion: the implicit threat

---

[3]Thomas J. Nechyba, *Microeconomics: an Intuitive Approach with Calculus*, Cengage (2010).

> ### Definitions
>
> **Grim trigger strategy** Once a player observes that its rival has broken some agreed behaviour, it will never again co-operate with them again.
>
> **Tit-for-tat strategy** Where a firm will cut prices, or make some other aggressive move, *only* if the rival does so first. If the rival knows this, it will be less likely to make an initial aggressive move.

of retaliation prevents firms from cutting prices (or from launching an advertising campaign, etc).

Finitely repeated games

An important thing to consider with repeated games is just how many rounds there will be. In our previous scenario, we didn't consider the last round of the game. That is, we assumed it was an infinitely repeated game and, hence, there was always a chance that the players would meet again.

If, instead, the game is a finitely repeated game, i.e. there are a certain number of rounds, say ten, the outcome of the game reverts to the one-shot game. The reason is that in the final tenth round, both players know that they will never be in this position again and thus the incentive they had to collude has now disappeared. Both players will revert to playing 'confess' in this final period. If, in the ninth period, both players realise that they cannot influence what their partner will do in the tenth period, then they have no incentive to collude in the ninth period. And hence no incentive to collude in the eighth period or the seventh, etc. The Nash equilibrium of 'confess, confess' returns.

This process of working backwards from the last period to think about outcomes in earlier periods is called **backwards induction**.

Pause for thought

Consider the game from Table 12.1, but this time extend it beyond one time period. Explain whether either firm has an incentive to keep the price at £2.00 and, hence, if co-operation can be sustained. (Hint: consider both an infinitely and finitely repeated game).

Sequential games

Most decisions by firms are made by one firm at a time rather than simultaneously by all firms. In Box 11.1, we saw McDonald's move first by announcing its new prices and deals and then other firms responded. This is an example of a 'sequential game', where the 'order of play' is important and firms can now observe the decisions of their rivals.

Take the case of a new generation of large passenger aircraft that can fly further without refuelling. Assume that there is a market for a 500-seater version of this type of aircraft and a 400-seater version, but that the individual markets for each aircraft are not big enough for the two manufacturers, Boeing and Airbus, to share them profitably. Let us also assume that the 400-seater market would give an annual profit of £50 million to a single manufacturer and the 500-seater would give an annual profit of £30 million, but that, if both manufacturers produced the same version, they would each make an annual loss of £10 million.

Definitions

Backwards induction A process by which firms consider the decision in the last round of the game and then work backwards through the game, thinking through the most likely outcomes in earlier rounds.
Decision tree (or game tree) A diagram showing the sequence of possible decisions by competitor firms and the outcome of each combination of decisions.

Figure 12.7 A decision tree

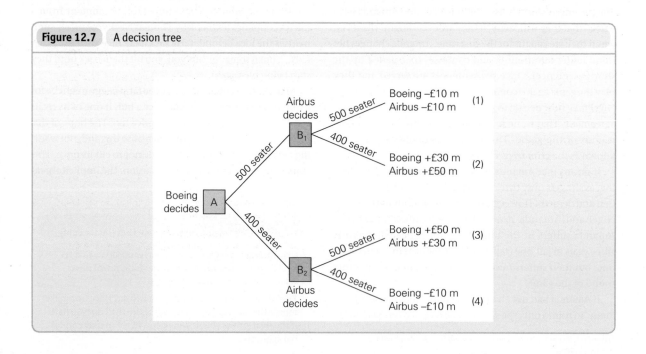

Assume that Boeing announces that it is building the 400-seater plane. What should Airbus do? The choice is illustrated in Figure 12.7. This diagram is called a **decision tree or game tree** and shows the sequence of events.

The small square at the left of the diagram is Boeing's decision point (point A). If it had decided to build the 500-seater plane, we would move up the top branch. Airbus now would have to make a decision (point B_1). If it too built the 500-seater plane, we would move to outcome 1: a loss of £10 million for both manufacturers.

Clearly, with Boeing building a 500-seater plane, Airbus would choose the 400-seater plane: we would move to outcome 2, with Boeing making a profit of £30 million and Airbus a profit of £50 million. Airbus would be very pleased!

Boeing's best strategy at point A, however, would be to build the 400-seater plane. We would then move to Airbus's decision point B_2. In this case, it is in Airbus's interests to build the 500-seater plane. Its profit would be only £30 million (outcome 3), but this is better than a £10 million loss if it too built the 400-seater plane (outcome 4). With Boeing deciding first, the Nash equilibrium thus will be outcome 3.

There is clearly a **first-mover advantage** here. Once Boeing has decided to build the more profitable version of the plane, Airbus is forced to build the less profitable one. Naturally, Airbus would like to build the more profitable one and be the first mover. Which company succeeds in going first depends on how advanced they are in their research and development and in their production capacity.

More complex decision trees. The aircraft example is the simplest version of a decision tree, with just two companies and each one making only one key decision. In many business situations, much more complex trees could be constructed. The 'game' would be more like one of chess, with many moves and several options on each move. If there were more than two companies, the decision tree would be more complex still.

Credible threats and promises

In sequential games, firms may threaten (or promise) that they will act in a certain way as a means of influencing the

outcome of the game. The key question is whether the threat or promise is *credible*.

Often, we see threats being made by the second mover in a game, as it tries to convince the first mover to choose a particular action. The first mover must look down the game tree to the point where the second mover will make its decision and, taking into account the payoffs, it must ask, will the firm really behave in the way it has threatened? If the answer is 'yes', then the threat is credible and the second mover can gain an advantage by influencing the first mover's behaviour. If the answer is 'no', then the threat is non-credible and the firm will ignore it.

Take the simple situation where a large oil company, such as Esso, states that it will match the price charged by any competitor within a given radius. Assume that competitors believe this 'price promise' but also that Esso will not try to *undercut* their price. In the simple situation where there is only one other petrol station in the area, what price should it charge? Clearly, it should charge the price that would maximise its profits, assuming that Esso will charge the *same* price. In the absence of other petrol stations in the area, this is likely to be a relatively high price.

Now assume that there are several petrol stations in the area. What should the company do now? Its best choice is probably to charge the same price as Esso and hope that no other company charges a lower price and forces Esso to cut its price. Assuming that Esso's threat is credible, other companies are likely to reason in a similar way. Prices will, therefore, be kept high, because of the credible threat made by Esso.

> ### Pause for thought
>
> *Assume that there are two major oil companies operating filling stations in an area. The first promises to match the other's prices. The other promises to sell at 1p per litre cheaper than the first. Describe the likely sequence of events in this 'game' and the likely eventual outcome. Could the promise of the second company be seen as credible?*

> ### Pause for thought
>
> *Give an example of decisions that two firms or 'players' could make in sequence, each one affecting the other's next decision.*

> ### Definition
>
> **First-mover advantage** When a firm gains from being the first one to take action.
>
> **Credible threat (or promise)** One that is believable to rivals because it is in the threatener's interests to carry it out.

KI 24
p 217

BOX 12.4 THE HUNGER GAMES

To sleep or not to sleep?

Suzanne Collins published the first book of the trilogy, The Hunger Games in 2008 and, since then, it has been made into four films (with the final book, *Mockingjay* being split into two parts).[1] *The Hunger Games* is the story of Katniss Everdeen, living in an unknown future time where the country has been divided into Districts, ranging from the wealthy Capitol that rules the other 12 Districts. Each year, one girl and one boy from every District are chosen randomly and they must compete to the death against each other in the Hunger Games, which is set in a dangerous and very public arena. Katniss Everdeen volunteers in place of her younger sister and enters the arena with Peeta, the male 'Tribute' and so the use of strategic thinking and game theory begins.[2]

The Hunger Games lasts until all but one 'Tribute' is left alive (although there is a slight deviation in the 74th Hunger Games). However, survival is not just about avoiding being killed by one of the other 'Tributes', as the Games could last for weeks. Survival is also about having enough sleep to sustain yourself. The problem is, when you are asleep, there is the chance of a stealth attack by another competitor, but, if you don't sleep, you become more susceptible to any future attack, due to sleep deprivation.

1. *Try constructing a matrix and determine the Nash equilibrium in this game.*

One thing you might have considered in answering the question above is, even if you don't sleep and everyone else does, will it necessarily mean that you can find and kill another Tribute? One thing that happens in the Games is that a coalition is formed between a group of Tributes – they agree to work together, but still know that they are competing against each other and hence, at some point, each of them will have to try to kill their rivals. They are camping together and so, within that group, they know where everyone is.

2. *Does the Nash equilibrium in the game change if we are now thinking about the decision of one member of the coalition, given the possible responses of the other members of the coalition?*

The value that each member places on sleep and getting closer to the finishing line is obviously a key factor in

determining how any member should behave. Also, with sleep being a natural response to being tired, there are only so many nights when you can go without sleep and the more nights you do this, the more likely it becomes that you will be susceptible to an attack.

Many stabs in the dark

Looking at the matrix that you have constructed and perhaps making some assumptions about the relative value of sleep versus progress, the likely outcome seems to be 'Don't sleep' for everyone. After all, being sleep deprived is better than being dead. This would suggest that all members of the coalition should avoid sleep, knowing that, if they do fall asleep, they are very vulnerable to an attack from another member of the coalition. So, why do the members of the coalition get any sleep?

The Hunger Games goes on for many nights, so it is not just a one-shot game, but a repeated game and, more so, an infinitely repeated game. Perhaps if the Games had to be over in one night, we would see a clear incentive not to sleep. But, in the Hunger Games, no player knows when their last night will be. The members of the coalition will have to make the sleep decision night after night, knowing that every night they don't sleep they may make progress, but will become more vulnerable to other attacks.

Furthermore, as there are multiple members of the coalition, each member will become less trustworthy if others are killed during the night. So, perhaps the best response in this infinitely repeated game is to co-operate from the start and thus trust everyone within the coalition – everyone gets some sleep. However, if one night a member is killed, then the next night we would probably see each player once again best responding by remaining awake. Perhaps here would be a typical 'tit-for-tat' strategy, until a winner emerges.

This is just one more example of the application of game theory to areas beyond traditional economics.

3. *Search for the game show Golden Balls online or go onto YouTube and watch a clip of the very last part of the game '£66,885 Split or Steal?'[3] Try constructing a matrix for this game and working out what the Nash equilibrium is.*

[1] www.thehungergames.co.uk/.

[2] Samuel Arbesman, 'Probability and game theory in The Hunger Games', Wired, 10 April 2012.

[3] www.youtube.com/watch?v=yM38mRHY150.

SUMMARY

1a Monopolistic competition occurs where there is free entry to the industry and quite a large number of firms operating independently of each other. Each firm has some market power as a result of producing differentiated products or services.

1b In the short run, firms can make supernormal profits. In the long run, however, freedom of entry will drive profits down to the normal level. The long-run equilibrium of the firm is where the (downward-sloping) demand curve is tangential to the long-run average cost curve.

1c The long-run equilibrium is one of excess capacity. Given that the demand curve is downward sloping, its tangency point with the *LRAC* curve will not be at the bottom of the *LRAC* curve. Increased production would thus be possible at *lower* average cost.

1d In practice, supernormal profits may persist into the long run: firms have imperfect information; entry may not be completely unrestricted; there may be a problem of indivisibilities; firms may use non-price competition to maintain an advantage over their rivals.

1e Monopolistically competitive firms, because of excess capacity, may have higher costs, and thus higher prices, than perfectly competitive firms, but consumers gain from a greater diversity of products.

1f Monopolistically competitive firms may have less economies of scale than monopolies and conduct less research and development, but the competition may keep prices lower than under monopoly. Whether there will be more or less choice for consumers is debatable.

2a An oligopoly is where there are just a few firms in the industry with barriers to the entry of new firms. Firms recognise their mutual dependence and each firm must consider the reactions of rivals to any changes it makes.

2b Oligopolists may aim to maximise their joint profits. This may create an incentive for collusion, whereby prices are kept high. On the other hand, they will want the biggest share of industry profits for themselves. This may incentivise them to compete.

2c A formal collusive agreement is called a 'cartel'. A cartel aims to act as a monopoly. It can set the price and leave the members to compete for market share or it can assign quotas. There is always a temptation for cartel members to 'cheat' by undercutting the cartel price if they think they can get away with it and not trigger a price war.

2d Firms are more likely to collude: if there are few of them; if they are open with each other; if they have similar products and cost structures; if there is a dominant firm; if there are significant entry barriers; if the market is stable; and if there is no government legislation to prevent collusion.

2e Rather than being part of a formal collusive agreement, firms can collude tacitly. This can take the form of price leadership, whereby firms follow the price set by either a dominant firm in the industry or one seen as a reliable 'barometer' of market conditions. Alternatively, firms can follow various rules of thumb such as average cost pricing and benchmark pricing.

2f As firms under oligopoly are interdependent, there are many theories of oligopoly. In the Cournot model, firms assume that their rivals' output is given. In the Bertrand model, firms assume their rivals' price is given. In these and other theories of oligopoly, firms must take into account their rivals' behaviour and then best respond by choosing the profit-maximising price and output. The assumptions made determine the market price and output.

2g In the kinked-demand curve model, firms are likely to keep their prices stable unless there is a large shift in costs or demand.

2h If all firms make the optimal decision, given the assumptions they make about their rivals' behaviour, then we will arrive at a Nash equilibrium. The outcomes in both the Cournot and Bertrand models are Nash equilibria.

2i Whether consumers benefit from oligopoly depends on: the particular oligopoly and how competitive it is; whether there is any countervailing power; whether the firms engage in extensive advertising and of what type; whether product differentiation results in a wide range of choice for the consumer; how much of the profits are ploughed back into research and development; and how contestable the market is. Since these conditions vary substantially from oligopoly to oligopoly, it is impossible to state just how well or how badly oligopoly in general serves the consumer's interest.

3a Game theory is a way of modelling behaviour in strategic situations where the outcome for an individual or firm depends on the choices made by others. Thus game theory examines various strategies that firms can adopt when the outcome of each is not certain.

3b The simplest type of 'game' is a simultaneous one-shot game. Many games of this kind have predictable outcomes, as a player's best response does not depend on the assumptions made about the other players' behaviour. These are dominant strategy games with a single Nash equilibrium. However, in such games, it is possible that both players could do better by co-operating or colluding.

3c Other simultaneous one-shot games can be more complex, where a firm's best response does depend on the assumptions it makes about its rivals' behaviour. The Nash equilibrium is a useful way to predict the most likely outcome in any of these games.

3d If a simultaneous game is repeated, players can be encouraged to co-operate. The outcome will depend on whether the game is infinite or finite and hence whether players know when the last round will be and on how much they value future payoffs versus short-term gains.

3e In sequential games, play is passed from one 'player' to the other and we can use a decision or game tree to illustrate the decisions and outcomes of the game. In many instances, a firm can gain a strategic advantage over its rival by being the first mover.

3f Firms will respond not only to what firms do, but also to what they say they will do. To this end, a firm's threats or promises must be credible if they are to influence rivals' decisions.

REVIEW QUESTIONS

1 Consider the long-run equilibrium of a monopolistically competitive industry. On a diagram similar to Figure 12.1, show what will happen to output, price and profits in the short run and long run if there is a fall in demand.

2 Imagine there are two types of potential customer for jam sold by a small food shop. One is the person who has just run out and wants some now. The other is the person who looks in the cupboard, sees that the pot of jam is less than half full and thinks, 'I will soon need some more'. How will the price elasticity of demand differ between these two customers?

3 Why may a food shop charge higher prices than supermarkets for 'essential items' and yet very similar prices for delicatessen items?

4 How will the position and shape of a firm's short-run demand curve depend on the prices that rivals charge?

5 Assuming that a firm under monopolistic competition can make supernormal profits in the short run, will there be any difference in the long-run and short-run elasticity of demand? Explain.

6 Firms under monopolistic competition generally have spare capacity. Does this imply that if, say, half of the petrol stations were closed down, the consumer would benefit? Explain.

7 If a market is dominated by a few big firms, does this always imply that consumers will face higher prices?

8 Will competition between oligopolists always reduce total industry profits?

9 In which of the following industries is collusion likely to occur: bricks, beer, margarine, cement, crisps, washing powder, carpets?

10 Draw a diagram like Figure 12.4. Illustrate what would happen if there were a rise in market demand.

11 Devise a box diagram like that in Table 12.1, only this time assume that there are three firms, each considering the two strategies of keeping price the same or reducing it by a set amount. Is the game still a 'dominant strategy game'?

12 Having watched the clip from the film *A Beautiful Mind,* can you work out why the situation that Russell Crowe describes as being a 'Nash equilibrium' is actually not a Nash equilibrium? Specifically, in the example used, would all of the males be best responding if they behave as John Nash suggests they should?

13 Consider the following sequential game: Mr New-Entrant is about to enter a market, where there is an established firm run by Mrs Incumbent. Mr New-Entrant has to decide whether to enter the market aggressively (with deals and lots of advertising) or enter more passively. Once Mr New-Entrant has made his decision and entered the market, Mrs Incumbent has to decide between acquiescing (accepting that there is a new competitor) and fighting (trying to drive Mr New-Entrant out of the market.) If Mr New-Entrant decides to use aggressive tactics, he will make £2m profit if Mrs Incumbent acquiesces and £0.75m profit if she fights, while Mrs Incumbent would make £1m profit if she acquiesces and £0.75m if she fights. On the other hand, if Mr New-Entrant enters the market passively and Mrs Incumbent acquiesces, both will make £0.5m. If Mrs Incumbent chooses to fight despite the passive entrance, she will make £2m profit, while Mr New-Entrant will make £1m.

a) Draw the game tree, clearly identifying who is the first mover, what each player's actions are and what their payoffs are.

b) What is the Nash equilibrium? (Hint: there is more than one.) Which Nash equilibrium do you think is the most likely to occur and why?

c) If Mrs Incumbent threatens that she will fight irrespective of the tactics Mr New-Entrant uses, should Mr New-Entrant believe that this threat is credible? Should this influence his decision?

14 Which of the following are examples of effective counter-vailing power?

a) A power station buying coal from a large local coal mine.

b) A large factory hiring a photocopier from Rank Xerox.

c) Marks & Spencer buying clothes from a garment manufacturer.

d) A small village store (but the only one for miles around) buying food from a wholesaler.

Is it the size of the purchasing firm that is important in determining its power to keep down the prices charged by its suppliers?

Chapter 13

Alternative theories of the firm

Business issues covered in this chapter

- Why is it often difficult for a firm to identify its profit-maximising price and output?
- Why may managers pursue goals other than maximising profit?
- What other goals might they pursue?
- What will be the effect of alternative business objectives on price and output?
- Why might businesses have multiple objectives and, if they do, how do they reconcile conflicts between them?

13.1   PROBLEMS WITH TRADITIONAL THEORY

The traditional profit-maximising theories of the firm have been criticised for being unrealistic. The criticisms are mainly of two sorts: (a) that firms wish to maximise profits, but, for some reason or other, are unable to do so; or (b) that firms have aims other than profit maximisation. Let us examine each in turn.

Difficulties in maximising profit

One criticism of traditional theory sometimes put forward is that firms do not use *MR* and *MC* concepts. This may be true, but firms could still arrive at maximum profit by trial and error adjustments of price or by finding the output where *TR* and *TC* are furthest apart. Provided they end up maximising profits, they will be equating *MC* and *MR*, even if they do not know it!

In mature industries, where all firms have access to similar technology, an evolutionary process may ensure that the firms that survive are the ones closest to profit maximisation.

Firms that are not maximising profits will be forced out of the market by their more profitable rivals. In this case, traditional models will still be useful in predicting price and output.

Lack of information

The main difficulty in trying to maximise profits is a lack of information.

Firms may well use accountants' cost concepts not based on opportunity cost (see section 9.1). If it is thereby impossible to measure true profit, a firm will not be able to maximise profit, except by chance.

Pause for thought

What cost concepts are there other than those based on opportunity cost? Would the use of these concepts be likely to lead to an output greater or less than the profit-maximising one?

More importantly, firms are unlikely to know precisely (or even approximately) their demand curves and hence their *MR* curves. Even though (presumably) they will know how much they are selling at the moment, this gives them only one point on their demand curve and no point at all on their *MR* curve. In order to make even an informed guess about marginal revenue, they must have some idea of how responsive demand will be to a change in price. But how are they to estimate this price elasticity? Market research may help. But even this is frequently very unreliable.

The biggest problem in estimating the firm's demand curve is in estimating the actions and reactions of *other* firms and their effects. Even when firms collude over pricing or output there will still be considerable uncertainty about demand, especially if the firm faces competition from abroad or from other industries.

As we saw in Chapter 12, game theory may help a firm decide its price and output strategy. But, for this to be accurate, it requires that a firm knows the consequences in order for its profits of each possible reaction of its rivals. In reality, no firm will have this information, because it will not know for sure how consumers will respond to each of its rivals' alternative strategies.

Time period

Finally, there is the problem in deciding the *time period* over which the firm should be seeking to maximise profits. Firms operate in a changing environment. Demand curves shift; supply curves shift. Some of these shifts occur as a result of factors outside the firm's control, such as changes in competitors' prices and products or changes in technology. Some, however, change as a direct result of a firm's policies, such as an advertising campaign, the development of a new improved product or the installation of new equipment.

The firm is not, therefore, faced with static cost and revenue curves from which it can read off its profit-maximising price and output. Instead, it is faced with a changing (and often highly unpredictable) set of curves. If it chooses a price and an output that maximise profits this year, it may be entirely the wrong decision months, or even weeks, later.

Take a simple example. The firm may be considering whether to invest in new expensive equipment. If it does, its costs will rise in the short run and thus short-run profits will fall. On the other hand, if the quality of the product thereby increases, demand is likely to increase over the longer run. Also variable costs are likely to decrease if the new equipment is more efficient. In other words, long-run profit is likely to increase, but probably by a highly uncertain amount.

Given these extreme problems in deciding profit-maximising price and output, firms may adopt simple rules of thumb for pricing. (These are examined in Chapter 17.)

Alternative aims

An even more fundamental attack on the traditional theory of the firm is that firms do not even *aim* to maximise profits (even if they could).

The traditional theory of the firm assumes that it is the *owners* of the firm that make price and output decisions. It is reasonable to assume that owners *will* want to maximise profits: this much most of the critics of the traditional theory accept. The question is, however, whether the owners do, in fact, make the decisions.

In public limited companies, there is generally a separation of ownership and control (see Chapter 3). The shareholders are the owners and, presumably, will want the firm to maximise profits so as to increase their dividends and the value of their shares. Shareholders elect directors. Directors, in turn, employ professional managers, who often are given considerable discretion in making decisions. But what are the objectives of managers? Will *they* want to maximise profits or will they have some other aim?

Managers may be assumed to want to *maximise their own utility*. This may well involve pursuits that conflict with profit maximisation. They may, for example, pursue higher salaries, greater power or prestige, better working conditions, greater sales, etc. Different managers in the same firm may well pursue different aims.

Managers will still have to ensure that *sufficient* profits are made to keep shareholders happy, but that may be very different from *maximising* profits.

Alternative theories of the firm to those of profit maximisation, therefore, tend to assume that large firms are **profit satisficers**. That is, managers strive hard for a minimum target level of profit, but are less interested in profits above this level.

Such theories fall into two categories: first, those theories that assume that firms attempt to maximise some other aim, provided that sufficient profits are achieved (these are examined in section 13.3); and second, those theories that assume that firms pursue a number of potentially conflicting aims, of which sufficient profit is merely one (these theories are examined in section 13.4).

Definition

Profit satisficing Where decision makers in a firm aim for a target level of profit rather than the absolute maximum level. By not aiming for the maximum profit, this allows managers to pursue other objectives, such as sales maximisation or their own salary or prestige.

Is firm behaviour consistent with the rational choice model?

Chapter 7 introduced behavioural economics, the field of study that integrates some simple insights from psychology into standard economic theory. We saw how ideas such as heuristics, loss aversion, present bias and reciprocity sometimes predict human behaviour more effectively than the traditional economics approach.

The focus in Chapter 7 was on consumer behaviour. In this chapter, we consider how *behavioural economics* can be applied to the theory *of the firm*. In what ways might managerial decision making deviate from that predicted by the profit-maximising theories of Chapters 11 and 12? For example, how might a firm's actions be affected by managers who have a strong preference for fairness?

Some potential heuristics

As discussed in section 13.1, firms operate in complex environments, dealing with imperfect information and uncertainty about both the present and the future. Trying to work out and implement a profit-maximising strategy in these situations is a cognitively demanding task that places great strain on a manager's computational capacity. Rather like consumers, managers may respond by using heuristics (rules of thumb/mental shortcuts) to simplify things. Some heuristics might include the following:

Copying the strategy of the most profitable businesses in the market. To implement this heuristic, the firm must be able to observe the actions and profits made by its rivals. If some firms follow a strategy of imitation in an oligopolistic market, it might lead to more intense competition, with lower prices and higher output. Some research has also found that firms that simply imitate do at least as well as those that successfully calculate their own profit-maximising strategy.

Focusing on relative rather than absolute profits. It is easier for investors to see if a firm is making more profit than its competitors than if it is making the maximum profit possible. Therefore, a manager's performance may be judged by comparing the firm's profits or other indicators with that of its rivals. For example, growing market share may be seen as a more important indicator of 'success' than simple growth in sales. Comparisons may be made between product design, technology and industrial relations with those of rivals. There may also be financial incentives to behave in this way as bonuses often are based on relative, as opposed to absolute, profits.

This type of behaviour may lead to firms implementing strategies that reduce their own profits (e.g. an aggressive price war) if it reduces the profits of their rivals by a greater amount.

Making a satisfactory/target level of profit. Instead of constantly looking for new opportunities to maximise profits in a dynamic market, managers may, instead, change a firm's strategy only when its profits fall below some target level.

The most influential early exponents of this approach were Richard Cyert and James March[1] (see section 13.4 for more detail). Their research made use of case studies of four multinational firms. They used the observations obtained to develop models of the firm, where decisions resulted from a sequence of behaviours of various managers within the firm.

Their work highlighted the limitations of the traditional assumption of profit maximisation and proved to be highly influential in two ways. First, it led to the study of behaviour, both of firms and the individual decision makers within them. Second, the research methods used have been adopted by experimentalists, not only in economics, but across the social sciences.

Some other potential biases

Over-optimism. Economists have long identified over-optimism as a trait seen in many people. Adam Smith commented that 'the chance of gain is by every man, more or less over-valued, and the chance of loss is by most men under-valued'.[2] A number of factors may make over-optimism even greater among managers than the population as a whole.

Including sunk costs. There is also survey evidence that managers include sunk costs as well as avoidable costs, when making pricing decisions.[3] This can lead to different prices from those set by a profit-maximising firm (we examine cost-based pricing in Chapter 17).

> ### Pause for thought
>
> *Why might managers choose to set prices that cover all costs, including sunk costs?*

> ### Definition
>
> **Behavioural economics of the firm** Attempts to explain why the behaviour of firms deviate from traditional profit maximisation because of (a) the managerial use of mental shortcuts to simplify complex decisions and (b) managerial preferences for fairness.

---

[1] Richard Cyert and James March, *A Behavioural Theory of the Firm* (Blackwell, 1963).

[2] See: Adam Smith, *An Inquiry into the Nature and Causes of the Wealth of Nations*, Book 1, Chapter 10, para. 29.

[3] See, for example: Steve Buchheit and Nick Feltovich, 'Experimental evidence of a sunk—cost paradox: a study of pricing behavior in Bertrand–Edgeworth duopoly', *University of Aberdeen Discussion Paper 2008-4* (April 2008).

Managerial preferences for fairness?

Rather than trying to maximise profits, some managers may have strong preferences for fairness. In particular, they may care about the equitable distribution of returns to all stakeholders in the business including investors, suppliers, customers, employees and the local community where the business is located. Stakeholders are discussed in more detail in Box 13.3, while managerial preferences are considered in more detail in section 20.5, which examines 'corporate social responsibility'.

Can firms make use of behavioural economics?

Firms might be able to make use of behavioural economics if they are profit maximisers but their customers use heuristics that lead to systematic mistakes. Indeed, there is evidence that firms have been making use of some of these principles for many years. For example, they develop marketing strategies that do not concentrate solely on price, but are tailored to consumers' sometimes irrational preferences (see Chapter 8). Examples include offering 'buy one, get one free' and loyalty points. In Box 13.1, we look at some examples of how businesses can bring the lessons of behavioural economics into their pricing and marketing.

Then there is the behaviour of workers. Since, for most firms, labour is a major input, it will be important to account for the motivation of employees – to ensure that they work hard and that their actions are aligned with the interests of the firm. Mechanisms of reward (and possibly punishment) may be most effective, if the behaviour of workers and their preference for fairness is fully understood.

A crucial factor for firms is the behaviour of other firms. Behavioural economics of the firm is thus important not just for economists and policy makers in analysing the motivation and decisions of managers; it is important too for firms in understanding and predicting the behaviour of their competitors and suppliers.

> ### Pause for thought
>
> *Which is easier – for managers to make decisions that maximise profits or for consumers to make decisions that maximise utility? Discuss some of the arguments in favour of each case.*

13.3 ALTERNATIVE MAXIMISING THEORIES

Long-run profit maximisation

The traditional theory of the firm is based on the assumption of *short-run* profit maximisation. Many actions of firms may be seen to conflict with this aim and yet could be consistent with the aim of **long-run profit maximisation**. For example, policies to increase the size of the firm or the firm's share of the market may involve heavy advertising or low prices to the detriment of short-run profits. But, if this results in the firm becoming larger, with a larger share of the market, the resulting economic power may enable the firm to make larger profits in the long run.

At first sight, a theory of long-run profit maximisation would seem to be a realistic alternative to the traditional short-run profit-maximisation theory. In practice, however, the theory is not a very useful predictor of firms' behaviour and is very difficult to test.

A claim by managers that they were attempting to maximise long-run profits could be an excuse for virtually any policy. When challenged as to why the firm had, say, undertaken expensive research, or high-cost investment, or engaged in a damaging price war, the managers could reply: 'Ah, yes, but in the long run it will pay off.' This is very difficult to refute (until it is too late!).

Even if long-run profit maximisation *is* the prime aim, the means of achieving it are extremely complex. The firm will need a plan of action for prices, output, investment, etc., stretching from now into the future (see, for example, Box 13.2). But today's prices and marketing decisions affect tomorrow's demand. Therefore, future demand curves cannot be taken as given. Similarly, today's investment decisions will affect tomorrow's costs. Therefore, future cost curves cannot be taken as given. These shifts in demand and cost curves will be very difficult to estimate with any precision. Quite apart from this, the actions of competitors, suppliers, unions, and so on are difficult to predict. Thus the picture of firms making precise calculations of long-run profit-maximising prices and outputs is a false one.

It may be useful, however, simply to observe that firms, when making current price, output and investment decisions, try to judge the approximate effect on new entrants, consumer demand, future costs, etc., and try to avoid decisions that would appear to conflict with long-run profits. Often, this will simply involve avoiding making decisions (e.g. cutting price) that may stimulate an unfavourable reaction from rivals (e.g. rivals cutting their price).

> ### Definition
>
> **Long-run profit maximisation** An alternative theory which assumes that managers aim to shift cost and revenue curves so as to maximise profits over some longer time period.

BOX 13.1 HOW FIRMS INCREASE PROFITS BY UNDERSTANDING 'IRRATIONAL' CONSUMERS

In Chapter 7, we looked at how behavioural economics can help improve our understanding of consumer behaviour. Some reasons why people's actions may be inconsistent with the prediction of traditional economic theory were examined in detail.

How firms present prices

The analysis suggests that there may be opportunities for businesses to increase profits by taking this 'irrationality' into account. One area that has received a great deal of attention in recent years is the way companies present prices to consumers.

According to the predictions of standard economic theory, different ways of presenting the same price should have no impact on consumer behaviour. However, there is an increasing amount of evidence that it does and that firms can take advantage of these biases to boost their profits.

Partitioned or drip pricing

One example is partitioned or drip pricing. This is a strategy where, instead of presenting one total combined price for a product, the seller splits the price into one or more components. Usually, this includes a base price and then additional fees for factors such as handling, administration, processing, credit/debit card, tax, postage and packaging.

If all the different elements to the total price are displayed simultaneously, it is called partitioned pricing.

Drip pricing is where only part of the price is advertised before the seller gradually includes additional fees as the consumer proceeds through the buying process. It is commonly used in online markets where supplements to the total price appear after customers have worked their way through a series of web pages.

For example, in 2013, the consumer group *Which* carried out a mystery shopping investigation[1] into ticket prices for music, comedy and theatre events. In 76 out of 78 cases, additional booking charges and delivery fees were added towards the end of the transaction. In some instances, these were up to a third of the advertised ticket price.

Evidence on the impact

Is there any evidence that partitioned or drip pricing has an impact on consumer behaviour?

Morwitz, Greenleaf and Johnson (1998)[2] carried out an auction experiment and found that, when a 15 per cent surcharge was separated from the base price, the participants were willing to pay more.

Hossain and Morgan (2006)[3] conducted a field experiment on auctions for CDs and Xbox games on eBay. They found that the sales price in auctions was always greater when a low reserve

price was displayed with high shipping/handling costs as opposed to a high reserve price with low shipping/handling costs.

In a laboratory experiment, Huck and Wallace (2015) found that drip pricing reduced consumer surplus by 22 per cent.[4]

What behavioural biases can help to explain these results?

Anchoring

Consumers anchor to the advertised or headline price as they believe this to be the most important and relevant piece of information. They fail to take full account of and adjust to the other elements of the price (delivery, costs, etc.), which causes them to underestimate the product's total price.

Loss aversion/the endowment effect

Consumers may decide that they want to purchase the product once they see the initial advertised price. This makes them feel like they already own the good and so their reference point changes and they begin to value it more highly: i.e. the endowment effect (see page 116). Loss aversion means they are willing to pay the additional elements to avoid having to give up the purchase.

Some other examples of company pricing strategies that possibly exploit biases in consumers' decision making include:

- *Reference pricing.* The price of the product is displayed alongside another price: i.e. a price the seller claims is more typical. This reference price could be a higher price, either (a) previously charged by the same supplier; (b) charged by other suppliers; (c) suggested by the manufacturer.
- *Time-limited pricing.* The customer is informed that the same offer will not be available at a later date. Therefore, if they delay, they could miss out on the deal.
- *Complex pricing.* The information is displayed in such a way that the consumer has to exert some cognitive effort to work out the price per unit: i.e. buy three for the price of two.
- *Bait pricing.* Consumers are enticed into either a physical or online store by a low price offer, but very few, if any, of these deals actually exist. The seller then tries to sell the same or a similar product for a higher price.

Competition authorities from around the world have started to investigate some of the implications of these pricing strategies for consumer welfare (we examine competition policy in Chapter 21). For example, in 2015, the Australian Competition and Consumer Association ruled that Airbnb, the room letting website, had to include its own charges in the total prices that it advertised on its Australian website.

1. *Is 'Black Friday' an example of any of the pricing strategies discussed in the box?*
2. *What behavioural biases are reference pricing, time-limited pricing, complex pricing and bait pricing trying to exploit?*

Find some real-world examples of these types of pricing strategies. Are they more likely to occur in some sectors than others?

---

[1] Play-fair-on-ticket-fees' *Which?* press release (17 December 2013).

[2] V.G. Morwitz, E.A. Greenleaf and E.J. Johnson, 'Divide and prosper: Consumers' reactions to partitioned prices', *Journal of Marketing Research 35*, pp. 453–63 (1998).

[3] Tanjim Hossain and John Morgan, '. . . Plus Shipping and Handling: Revenue (Non) Equivalence in Field Experiments on eBay', *Advances in Economic Analysis and Policy*, 6, pp. 1–26 (2006).

[4] Steffan Huck and Brian Wallace, 'The impact of price frames on decision making: Experimental evidence', *UCL Working paper* (October 2015).

Managerial utility maximisation

One of the most influential of the alternative theories of the firm, *managerial utility maximisation*, was developed by O.E. Williamson[4] in the 1960s. Williamson argued that, provided satisfactory levels of profit are achieved, managers often have the discretion to choose what policies to pursue. In other words, they are free to pursue their own interests. And what are the managers' interests? To maximise their own utility, argued Williamson.

Williamson identified a number of factors that affect a manager's utility. The four main ones were salary, job security, dominance (including status, power and prestige) and professional excellence.

Of these only salary is *directly* measurable. The rest have to be measured indirectly. One way of doing this is to examine managers' expenditure on various items and, in particular, on *staff*, on *perks* (such as a company car and a plush office) and on *discretionary investment*. The greater the level of expenditure by managers on these items, the greater is likely to be their status, power, prestige, professional excellence and job security and, hence, utility.

Having identified the factors that influence a manager's utility, Williamson developed several models in which managers seek to maximise their utility. He used these models to predict managerial behaviour under various conditions and argued that they performed better than traditional profit-maximising theory.

One important conclusion was that average costs are likely to be higher when managers have the discretion to pursue their own utility. For example, perks and unnecessarily high staffing levels add to costs. On the other hand, the resulting 'slack' allows managers to rein in these costs in times of low demand (see page 235). This enables them to maintain their profit levels. To support these claims, he conducted a number of case studies. These did, indeed, show that staff and perks were cut during recessions and expanded during booms, and that new managers frequently were able to reduce staff levels without influencing the productivity of firms.

Sales revenue maximisation (short run)

Perhaps the most famous of all alternative theories of the firm is that developed by William Baumol in the late 1950s. This is the theory of *sales revenue maximisation*. Unlike the theories of long-run profit maximisation and managerial utility maximisation, it is easy to identify the price and output that meet this aim – at least in the short run.

So why should managers want to maximise their firm's sales revenue? The answer is that the success of managers, and especially sales managers, may be judged according to the level of the firm's sales. Sales figures are an obvious barometer of the firm's health. Managers' salaries, power and prestige may depend directly on sales revenue. The firm's

sales representatives may be paid commission on their sales. Thus sales revenue maximisation may be a more dominant aim in the firm than profit maximisation, particularly if it has a dominant sales department.

Sales revenue will be maximised at the top of the *TR* curve at output Q_1 in Figure 13.1. Profits, by contrast, would be maximised at Q_2. Thus, for given total revenue and total cost curves, sales revenue maximisation will tend to lead to a higher output and a lower price than profit maximisation.

The firm will still have to make sufficient profits, however, to keep the shareholders happy. Thus firms can be seen to be operating with a profit constraint. They are *profit satisficers*.

The effect of this profit constraint is illustrated in Figure 13.2. The diagram shows a total profit curve. (This is found simply by taking the difference between *TR* and *TC* at each output.) Assume that the minimum acceptable profit is

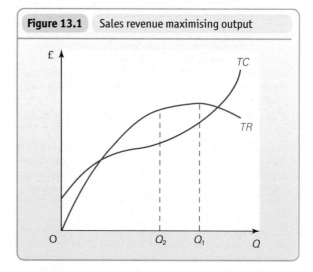

Figure 13.1 Sales revenue maximising output

P (whatever the output). Any output greater than Q_3 will give a profit less than P. Thus the sales revenue maximiser who is also a profit satisficer will produce Q_3 not Q_1. Note, however, that this output is still greater than the profit-maximising output Q_2.

If the firm could maximise sales revenue and still make more than the minimum acceptable profit, it would probably spend this surplus profit on advertising to increase

Definitions

Managerial utility maximisation An alternative theory that assumes that managers are motivated by self-interest. They will adopt whatever policies are perceived to maximise their own utility.

Sales revenue maximisation An alternative theory of the firm that assumes that managers aim to maximise the firm's short-run total revenue.

---

[4] *The Economics of Discretionary Behaviour* (Prentice Hall, 1964), p. 3.

BOX 13.2   IN SEARCH OF LONG-RUN PROFITS

The video games war

Traditional economic theory argues that firms will seek to maximise their short-run profits and, therefore, adopt a range of strategies to achieve this goal. There are, however, plenty of examples from the world of business to suggest that firms often take a longer-term perspective. One example is the long-running video games war between the big three companies in the industry – Sony, Nintendo and Microsoft.

The static games console market

Market share in the static console games market fluctuates between the different models produced by the big three businesses. New console developments, which occur every few years, have a dramatic impact on the shape of the industry. For example, Nintendo was the industry leader with its GameCube until the mid-1990s when Sony launched its PlayStation 1. Sony retained its position as market leader when it released the PlayStation 2 in 2000. This became the most successful static game console of all time and has sold over 155 million units worldwide.

However, Sony faced new competition when Microsoft entered the market for the first time in November 2001 with the Xbox, and became the market leader in 2006 with the introduction of the Xbox360. This seventh generation console was released 12 months ahead of those of its rivals, at a price of £209 for the basic model and £280 for the premium model. Sony suffered technical difficulties with the launch of the PlayStation 3 and failed to deliver it on schedule. It also priced the console significantly above its rival at £425.

Nintendo released the Wii in November 2006 at a price of £179. The company targeted a much wider audience of casual and non-gamers as well as hard-core gamers. Its innovative movement sensor play system helped to catapult it into first place in the market. By 2007, its sales had already surpassed those of the Xbox360, even though it was released a year

later. It sold over 22 million units worldwide in both 2008 and 2009 and has sold over 100 million units in total.

Between 2012 and 2013, the 'big three' released the eighth generation of games consoles onto the market. Nintendo released the Wii U in November 2012. The basic edition of the console was priced at £250 in the UK. Sony released the PlayStation 4 (PS4) in November 2013 for a price of £349 in the UK and $399 in the USA. Microsoft released the Xbox One in the same month for a price of £429 in the UK and $499 in the USA.

As illustrated in chart (a), the sales of the Wii U console have proved rather disappointing for Nintendo and the company reported a loss of £57 million for the second quarter of 2013. The company had forecast sales for 2013/14 of 9 million consoles but sold only 2.7 million, despite cutting the price by $50.

The PS4 has been much more successful. It has outsold its key rivals by quite some margin. In the financial year 2013/14, Sony sold more games consoles than Nintendo for the first time in eight years.

The sales performance of the Xbox One has been in between its two leading rivals. One initial problem was its price – it was $100 more expensive than the PS4 in the USA and £80 more expensive in the UK. Only three months after its launch, Microsoft reduced the price of the console in the UK to £399. It also offered a cheaper version of the product without the Kinect camera for motion tracking.

As of January 2018, the cumulative sales of the PS4, Xbox One and Wii U have been 72.2 million, 34.8 million and 13.6 million respectively.

The market for mobile gaming hardware

Mobile gaming is another sector of the market that has seen some of the most significant changes in the past few years. Traditionally, it was dominated by handheld consoles and, in

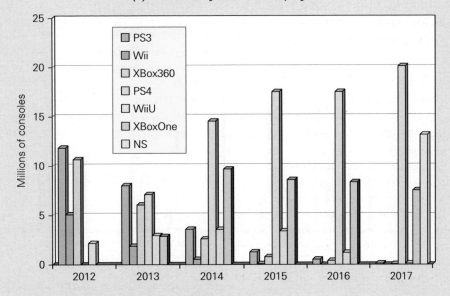

(a) Global sales of static consoles per year

Source: Based on data in 'Global Hardware by Platform', VGChartz, various years

particular, those produced by Nintendo. The original Gameboy was launched in 1989 and sold nearly 120 million units. Nintendo then introduced the DS in 2004, which became the best-selling handheld console of all time with total sales of over 150 million. The 3DS was released in 2011.

Sony also successfully entered this market in 2004 with its own handheld console, the PlayStation Portable PSP, which was described as the first real competitor to challenge Nintendo's domination. It has sold over 82 million units. Sony launched the PS Vita in 2011. Microsoft has never entered this market.

Chart (b) clearly shows how the demand for handheld consoles has fallen dramatically in the past few years. In 2010, approximately 30 million units were sold. This fell to just over 7.5 million in 2017. The major reason for this decline in sales is the increased competition in the mobile gaming sector from smartphones and tablets.

Gaming with smartphones and tablets.

The launch of the iPhone in 2007, which enabled consumers to play games on the device, changed the mobile gaming market dramatically. The growth in the market has been astonishing. In the third quarter of 2017, there were over 9 billion mobile game downloads from the Apple App and Google Play Store.

In 2017, gaming on smartphones and tablets generated global revenues of $39.1bn and 11.4bn.[1]

A hybrid of static and handheld consoles

In March 2017, Nintendo launched its new Switch console. Rather than being either a static or handheld console, it is a hybrid of the two. The Switch console is a tablet that plugs into a docking station that is connected to a TV. When plugged into the docking station, the Switch is, effectively, a static games console. However, the entire tablet can be removed

from the docking station without any interruption to a game being played. It then becomes a handheld console for mobile gaming. Data from Nintendo show that about 30 per cent of customers use it as a handheld console for the majority of the time.

The initial sales of the Switch console have been very impressive. As illustrated in chart (a), over 13 million units were sold in 2017. This is roughly equal to the total sales of Wii U consoles over a five-year period. Nintendo posted an operating profit of $1.1bn for the final quarter of 2017 – a 261 per cent increase on the same period for the previous year.

The secret of success – the quality of the games

Static and mobile console sales are successful only if they have games and other features that are attractive to consumers – they are complementary in consumption. Therefore, the relationship between the companies that produce the games and those that make the consoles is an important one.

The games are actually written and produced by game developers. Writing games is a time-consuming and expensive process. Sometimes, developers receive funding from a games publisher, which then releases and markets the games.

Game developers may be employed by an independent company, a games publisher or one of the console producers. For example, an independent development company called Infinity Ward created the famous game *Call of Duty*. It received significant funding from the publisher Activision to help finance the costs of writing the game. The day after *Call of Duty* was released in 2003, Infinity Ward was purchased by Activision and so became a division of this publisher.

---

[1] 'Quarterly global games market update', *Newzoo*. November 2017.

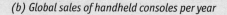

(b) Global sales of handheld consoles per year

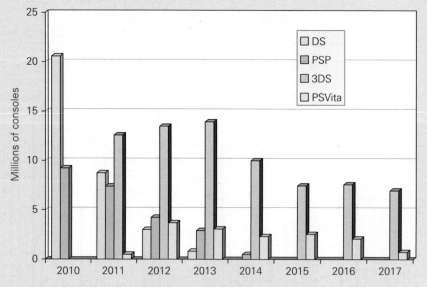

Source: Based on data in 'Global Hardware by Platform', VGChartz, various years

Some games are exclusive to a particular console because the game developers work directly for that company. For example, Nintendo invested heavily in producing the third, fourth and fifth best-selling games in the world in 2017. *Super Mario Odyssey* sold 6.4 million copies, *The Legend of Zelda: Breath of the Wild* sold 5.5 million copies, while *Mario Kart 8 Deluxe* sold 5.4 million copies. The popularity of these releases was a key reason for the initial success of the Switch console.

Games that are released by a publisher often are available on different consoles and so tend to be the most popular. For example, one of best-selling releases in 2017 was *Call of Duty: WWII,* produced by Activision. Over 9.5 million copies were sold for the PS4, while another 4.5 million were sold for the Xbox One. Another very popular game, *FIFA18,* published by Electronic Arts, had global sales of 9.2 million for the PS4 and just under 2.4 million for the Xbox One.

Part of the reason for the poor sales of the Wii U was its failure to attract independent publishers to develop games for the console. Poor initial sales lead to a lack of interest from games developers, which, in turn, lead to poor sales. The

success of the Switch has generated far more interest from independent games developers.

With the increased competition from gaming on smartphones/iPads and PCs, some people predicted the end of the console market in 2013. However, in 2017, games for static/handheld consoles still accounted for 29 per cent of the revenues generated by the global games market. Games for tablets/smartphones accounted for 43 per cent, while those for PCs accounted for 28 per cent.[2]

It will be interesting to see how Microsoft and Sony respond in the future with the release of the next generation of games consoles.

1. *What factors have affected the price elasticity of demand for static and handheld games consoles?*
2. *How does the maximisation of long-run profits conflict with the maximisation of short-run profits?*
3. *What factors might favour collusion in the video games market? What factors might make collusion unlikely?*

_____
[2]*Ibid.*

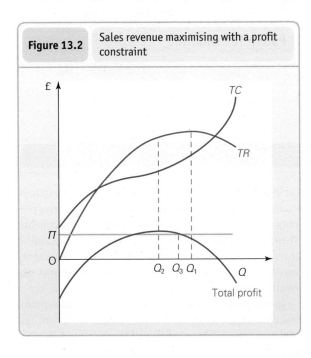

Figure 13.2 Sales revenue maximising with a profit constraint

revenue further. This would have the effect of shifting the *TR* curve upward and also the *TC* curve (since advertising costs money).

Sales revenue maximisation will tend to involve more advertising than profit maximisation. Ideally, the profit-maximising firm will advertise up to the point where the marginal revenue of advertising equals the marginal cost of advertising (assuming diminishing returns to advertising). The firm aiming to maximise sales revenue will go beyond this, since further advertising, although costing more than it earns the firm, will still add to total revenue. The firm will

continue advertising until surplus profits above the minimum have been used up.

Growth maximisation

Rather than aiming to maximise *short-run* revenue, managers may take a longer-term perspective and aim for *growth maximisation* in the size of the firm. They may gain utility directly from being part of a rapidly growing 'dynamic' organisation; promotion prospects are greater in an expanding organisation, since new posts tend to be created; large firms may pay higher salaries; managers may obtain greater power in a large firm.

Growth is probably best measured in terms of a growth in sales revenue, since sales revenue (or 'turnover') is the simplest way of measuring the size of a business. An alternative would be to measure the capital value of a firm, but this will depend on the ups and downs of the stock market and is thus a rather unreliable method.

If a firm is to maximise growth, it needs to be clear about the time period over which it is setting itself this objective. For example, maximum growth over the next two or three years might be obtained by running factories to absolute maximum capacity, cramming in as many machines and workers as possible, and backing this up with massive

Definition

Growth maximisation An alternative theory that assumes that managers seek to maximise the growth in sales revenue (or the capital value of the firm) over time.

advertising campaigns and price cuts. Such policies, however, may not be sustainable in the longer run. The firm simply may not be able to finance them. A longer-term perspective (say, 5–10 years) may, therefore, require the firm to 'pace' itself and, perhaps, to direct resources away from current production and sales into the development of new products that have a potentially high and growing long-term demand.

Equilibrium for a growth-maximising firm

What will a growth-maximising firm's price and output be? Unfortunately, there is no simple formula for predicting this.

In the short run, the firm may choose the profit-maximising price and output – so as to provide the greatest funds for investment. On the other hand, it may be prepared to sacrifice some short-term profits in order to mount an advertising campaign. It all depends on the strategy it considers most suitable to achieve growth.

In the long run, prediction is more difficult still. The policies that a firm adopts will depend crucially on the assessments of market opportunities made by managers. But this involves judgement, not fine calculation. Different managers will judge a situation differently.

One prediction can be made, though. Growth-maximising firms are likely to diversify into different products, especially as they approach the limits to expansion in existing markets. (Alternative growth strategies are considered in Chapter 15.)

Alternative maximising theories and the consumer

It is difficult to draw firm conclusions about how the behaviour of firms in these alternative maximising theories will affect the consumer's interest.

In the case of sales revenue maximisation, a higher output will be produced than under profit maximisation, but the consumer will not, necessarily, benefit from lower prices, since more will be spent on advertising – costs that will be passed on to the consumer.

In the case of growth and long-run profit maximisation, there are many possible policies that a firm could pursue. To the extent that a concern for the long run encourages firms to look to improved products, new products and new techniques, the consumer may benefit from such a concern. To the extent, however, that growth encourages a greater level of industrial concentration through merger, the consumer may lose from the resulting greater level of monopoly power.

As with the traditional theory of the firm, the degree of competition that a firm faces is a crucial factor in determining just how responsive it will be to the wishes of the consumer.

> ### Pause for thought
>
> *How will competition between growth-maximising firms benefit the consumer?*

13.4 MULTIPLE AIMS

Satisficing and the setting of targets

Firms may have more than one aim. For example, they may try to achieve increased sales revenue *and* increased profit. The problem with this is that, if two aims conflict, it will not be possible to maximise both of them. For example, sales revenue probably will be maximised at a different price and output from that at which profits are maximised. Where firms have two or more aims, a compromise may be for targets to be set for individual aims, which are low enough to achieve simultaneously and, yet, which are sufficient to satisfy the interested parties. This is known as 'satisficing' (as opposed to maximising) behaviour.

Such target setting is also likely when the maximum value of a particular aim is unknown. If, for example, the maximum achievable profit is unknown, the firm may well set a target for profit that it feels is both satisfactory and achievable.

Behavioural theories of the firm: the setting of targets

Large firms are often complex institutions with several departments (sales, production, design, purchasing, personnel, finance, etc.). Each department is likely to have its own specific set of aims and objectives, which may possibly come into conflict with those of other departments. These aims, in turn, will be constrained by the interests of shareholders, workers, customers and creditors (collectively known as **stakeholders**), who will need to be kept sufficiently happy.

In many firms, targets are set for production, sales, profit, stockholding, etc. If, in practice, target levels are not achieved, a 'search' procedure will be started to find what went wrong and how to rectify it. If the problem cannot be rectified, managers probably will adjust the target downward. If, on the other hand, targets are easily achieved, managers may adjust them upward. Thus the targets to which

> ### Definition
>
> **Stakeholders (in a company)** People who are affected by a company's activities and/or performance (customers, employees, owners, creditors, people living in the neighbourhood, etc.). They may or may not be in a position to take decisions, or influence decision taking, in the firm.

BOX 13.3   STAKEHOLDER POWER

Who governs the firm?

The concept of the 'stakeholder economy' became fashionable in the late 1990s. Rather than the economy being governed by big business, and rather than businesses being governed in the interests of shareholders (many of whom are big institutions, such as insurance companies and pension funds), the economy should serve the interests of everyone. But what does this mean for the governance of firms?

The stakeholders of a firm include customers, employees (from senior managers to the lowest-paid workers), shareholders, suppliers, lenders and the local and national communities.

The supporters of a stakeholding economy argue that *all* these interest groups ought to have a say in the decisions of the firm. Trade unions or workers' councils ought to be included in decisions affecting the workforce or, indeed, all company decisions. They could be represented on decision-making bodies and perhaps have seats on the board of directors. Alternatively, the workforce might be given the power to elect managers.

Banks or other institutions lending to firms ought to be included in investment decisions. In Germany, where banks finance a large proportion of investment, banks are represented on the boards of most large companies.

Local communities ought to have a say in any projects (such as new buildings or the discharge of effluent) that affect the local environment. Customers ought to have more say in the quality of products being produced, for example by being given legal protection against the production of shoddy or unsafe goods. Where interest groups cannot be directly represented in decision making, then companies ought to be regulated by the government in order to protect the interests of

the various groups. For example, if farmers and other suppliers to supermarkets are paid very low prices, then the purchasing behaviour of the supermarkets could be regulated by some government agency.

But is this vision of a stakeholder economy likely to become reality? Trends in the international economy suggest that the opposite might be occurring. The growth of multinational corporations, with their ability to move finance and production to wherever it is most profitable, has weakened the power of employees, local interest groups and even national governments.

Employees in one part of the multinational may have little in the way of common interests with employees in another. In fact, they may vie with each other, for example over which plant should be expanded or closed down. What is more, many firms are employing a larger and larger proportion of casual, part-time, temporary or agency workers. With these new 'flexible labour markets' such employees have far less say in the company than permanent members of staff: they are 'outsiders' to decision making within the firm (see section 18.4).

Also, the widespread introduction of share incentive schemes for managers (whereby managers are rewarded with shares) increasingly has made profits their driving goal. Finally, the policies of opening up markets and deregulation, policies that were adopted by many governments round the world up to the mid-1990s, have again weakened the power of many stakeholders.

 1.   *Are customers' interests best served by profit-maximising firms, answerable primarily to shareholders, or by firms where various stakeholder groups are represented in decision taking?*

---

managers aspire depend to a large extent on the success in achieving *previous* targets. Targets are also influenced by expectations of demand and costs, by the achievements of competitors and by expectations of competitors' future behaviour. For example, if it is expected that the economy is likely to move into recession, sales and profit targets may be adjusted downward.

If targets conflict, the conflict will be settled by a bargaining process between managers. The outcome of the bargaining, however, will depend on the power and ability of the individual managers concerned. Thus a similar set of conflicting targets may be resolved differently in different firms.

Organisational slack

Since changing targets often involves search procedures and bargaining processes and is, therefore, time-consuming, and since many managers prefer to avoid conflict, targets tend to be changed fairly infrequently. Business conditions, however, often change rapidly. To avoid the need to change

targets, therefore, managers will tend to be fairly conservative in their aspirations. This leads to the phenomenon known as *organisational slack*.

When the firm does better than planned, it will allow slack to develop. This slack can then be taken up if the firm does worse than planned. For example, if the firm produces more than it planned, it will build up stocks of finished goods and draw on them if production subsequently falls. It would not, in the meantime, increase its sales target or reduce its production target. If it did, and production then fell below target, the production department might not be able to supply the sales department with its full requirement.

Thus keeping targets fairly low and allowing slack to develop allows all targets to be met with minimum conflict.

Definition

Organisational slack When managers allow spare capacity to exist, thereby enabling them to respond more easily to changed circumstances.

Organisational slack, however, adds to a firm's costs. If firms are operating in a competitive environment, they may be forced to cut slack in order to survive. In the 1970s, many Japanese firms succeeded in cutting slack by using *just-in-time* methods of production. These involve keeping stocks to a minimum and ensuring that inputs are delivered as required. Clearly, this requires that production is tightly controlled and that suppliers are reliable. Many firms today have successfully cut their warehouse costs by using such methods. (These methods are examined in section 18.4.)

> ### Pause for thought
>
> *Will this type of behaviour tend to lead to profit maximisation?*

Satisficing and the consumer's interest

Firms with multiple goals will be satisficers. The greater the number of goals of the different managers, the greater is the chance of conflict and the more likely it is that organisational slack will develop. Satisficing firms are, therefore,

likely to be less responsive to changes in consumer demand and changes in costs than profit-maximising firms. They may thus be less efficient.

On the other hand, such firms may be less eager to exploit their economic power by charging high prices, to use aggressive advertising or to pay low wages.

The extent to which satisficing firms do act in the public interest will, as in the case of other types of firm, depend to a large extent on the amount and type of competition they face and their attitudes towards this competition. Firms that compare their performance with that of their rivals are more likely to be responsive to consumer wishes than firms that prefer to stick to well-established practices. On the other hand, they may be more concerned to 'manipulate' consumer tastes than the more traditional firm.

> ### Definition
>
> **Just-in-time methods** Where a firm purchases supplies and produces both components and finished products as they are required. This minimises stockholding and its associated costs.

SUMMARY

1a There are two major types of criticism of the traditional profit-maximising theory: (a) firms may not have the information to maximise profits; (b) they may not even want to maximise profits.

1b Lack of information on demand and costs and on the actions and reactions of rivals, and a lack of use of opportunity cost concepts, may mean that firms adopt simple 'rules of thumb' for pricing.

1c In large companies, there is likely to be a divorce between ownership and control. The shareholders (the owners) may want maximum profits, but it is the managers who make the decisions, and managers are likely to aim to maximise their own utility rather than that of the shareholders. This leads to profit 'satisficing'. This is where managers aim to achieve sufficient profits to keep shareholders happy, but this is a secondary aim to one or more alternative aims.

1d Some alternative theories assume that there is a single alternative aim that firms seek to maximise. Others assume that managers have a series of (possibly conflicting) aims.

2a Behavioural economics is relevant for understanding why and how the aims and strategies of firms deviate from traditional profit maximisation. This deviation is, in part, explained by managers using various mental shortcuts or heuristics to simplify complex decisions made in conditions of uncertainty. Some examples include imitation and focusing on relative performance.

2b Many managers are motivated by questions of fairness and the interests of various stakeholders. This can affect their behaviour.

2c Decision makers in firms can make use of behavioural insights about consumers, employees and other stakeholders and about other firms – whether competitors or suppliers.

3a Rather than seeking to maximise short-run profits, a firm may take a longer-term perspective. It is very difficult, however, to predict the behaviour of a long-run profit-maximising firm, since (a) different managers are likely to make different judgements about how to achieve maximum profits, and (b) demand and cost curves may shift unpredictably both in response to the firm's own policies and as a result of external factors.

3b Managers may seek to maximise their own utility, which, in turn, will depend on factors such as salary, job security, power within the organisation and the achievement of professional excellence. Given, however, that managerial utility depends on a range of variables, it is difficult to use the theory to make general predictions of firms' behaviour.

3c Managers may gain utility from maximising sales revenue. However, they will still have to ensure that a satisfactory level of profit is achieved. The output of a firm that seeks to maximise sales revenue will be higher than that for a profit-maximising firm. Its level of advertising will also tend to be higher. Whether price will be higher or lower depends on the relative effects on demand and the cost of the additional advertising.

3d Many managers aim for maximum growth of their organisation, believing that this will help their salaries, power, prestige, etc.

3e As with long-run profit-maximising theories, it is difficult to predict the price and output strategies of a growth-maximising firm. Much depends on the judgements of particular managers about growth opportunities.

4a In large firms, decisions are taken by, or influenced by, a number of different people, including various managers, shareholders, workers, customers, suppliers and creditors. If these different people have different aims, then a conflict between them is likely to arise. A firm cannot maximise more than one of these conflicting aims. The alternative is to seek to achieve a satisfactory target level of a number of aims.

4b Behavioural theories of the firm examine how managers and other interest groups actually behave, rather than merely identifying various equilibrium positions for output, price, investment, etc.

4c If targets were easily achieved last year, they are likely to be made more ambitious next year. If they were not achieved, a search procedure will be conducted to identify how to rectify the problem. This may mean adjusting targets downward, in which case there will be some form of bargaining process between managers.

4d Life is made easier for managers if conflict can be avoided. This will be possible if slack is allowed to develop in various parts of the firm. If targets are not being met, the slack can then be taken up without requiring adjustments in other targets.

4e Satisficing firms may be less innovative, less aggressive and less willing to initiate change. If they do change, it is more likely to be in response to changes made by their competitors. Managers may judge their performance by comparing it with that of rivals.

4f Satisficing firms may be less aggressive in exploiting a position of market power. On the other hand, they may suffer from greater inefficiency.

REVIEW QUESTIONS

1 In the traditional theory of the firm, decision makers often are assumed to have perfect knowledge and to be able to act, therefore, with complete certainty. It is now widely accepted that, in practice, firms will be certain about very few things. Of the following: (a) production costs; (b) demand; (c) elasticity; (d) supply; (e) consumer tastes; (f) technology; (g) government policy, which might they be certain of? Which might they be uncertain of?

2 Why might it present problems for a firm if managers are over-confident? Can you think of any reasons why CEOs might be more inclined to optimism than the population as a whole?

3 Make a list of six aims that a manager of a high street department store might have. Identify some conflicts that might arise between these aims.

4 When are increased profits in a manager's personal interest?

5 Draw a diagram with *MC* and *MR* curves. Mark the output (a) at which profits are maximised; (b) at which sales revenue is maximised.

6 If managers have strong preferences for fairness, will it increase or decrease the chances of collusion?

7 Since advertising increases a firm's costs, will prices necessarily be lower with sales revenue maximisation than with profit maximisation?

8 We have seen that a firm aiming to maximise sales revenue will tend to produce more than a profit-maximising firm. This conclusion certainly applies under monopoly and oligopoly. Will it also apply under (a) perfect competition and (b) monopolistic competition, where, in both cases, there is freedom of entry?

9 A frequent complaint of junior, and some senior, managers is that frequently they are faced with new targets from above, and that this makes their life difficult. If their complaint is true, does this conflict with the hypothesis that managers will try to build in slack?

ADDITIONAL PART E CASE STUDIES ON THE *ECONOMICS FOR BUSINESS* STUDENT WEBSITE (www.pearsoned.co.uk/Sloman)

E.1 A supply chain revolution: B2B electronic marketplaces. This case study examines the growth of firms trading with each other over the Internet (business to business or 'B2B') and considers the effects on competition.

E.2 Measuring monopoly power. An examination of how the degree of monopoly power possessed by a firm can be measured.

E.3 X-inefficiency. A type of inefficiency suffered by many large firms, resulting in a wasteful use of resources.

E.4 Competition in the pipeline. An examination of attempts to introduce competition into the gas industry in the UK.

E.5 Airline deregulation. This case examines whether the deregulation of various routes has led to more competition and lower prices.

E.6 The motor vehicle repair and servicing industry. A case study of monopolistic competition.

E.7 Edward Chamberlin and Joan Robinson. A portrait of the two economists who developed the model of monopolistic competition.

E.8 Bakeries: oligopoly or monopolistic competition. A case study on the bread industry, showing that small-scale local bakeries can exist alongside giant national bakeries.

E.9 Curry wars. An examination of the market for Indian and other ethnic foods.

E.10 Oligopoly in the brewing industry. A case study showing how the UK brewing industry is becoming more concentrated.

E.11 Cut throat competition. An examination of the barriers to entry to the UK razor market.

E.12 What do you maximise? This examines the motivation of managers and compares it with our motivation as individuals.

WEBSITES RELEVANT TO PART E

Numbers and sections refer to websites listed in the Web appendix and hotlinked from this text's website at
www.pearsoned.co.uk/sloman

■ For news articles relevant to Part E, see the Economics News Articles link from the Sloman Economics News site.

■ For general news on companies and markets, see websites in section A, and particularly A1, 2, 3, 4, 5, 8, 9, 18, 23, 24, 25, 26, 35, 36. See also A38–44 for links to newspapers worldwide.

■ For student resources relevant to Part E, see sites C1–7, 9, 10, 14, 19, 25.

■ For models and simulations relevant to Part E, see sites D3, 5, 7, 8, 10, 13, 14, 16–20.

■ For sites that look at companies, their scale of operation and market share, see D2; E4, 10; G7, 8.

■ For sites that look at competition and market power, see B2; E4, 10, 20; G7, 8. See also links in B1; I7, 11, 14 and 17.

Supply: alternative strategies

The FT Reports . . .

The Financial Times, 2 August 2015

Industrial giants caught in LED headlights

Philips, Osram and GE face decline of traditional light bulb units as new technology takes off

By Chris Bryant

Lighting is starting to become part of the "internet of things" – where different devices are all connected on telecoms networks – but for incumbent manufacturers this rapid technological shift is causing huge upheaval.

Industrial giants Philips, Siemens and General Electric for decades enjoyed an oligopoly in the hitherto slow-moving lighting market, which James Stettler, an analyst at Barclays, compares with a "licence to print money", partly because people have to regularly replace their bulbs.

Now LEDs are fast displacing traditional light sources such as incandescent, halogen and fluorescent bulbs, catalysed partly by double-digit annual price declines in components.

Government regulations also have supported the growth of LEDs because of their energy efficiency. They produce light using semiconductors — whereas traditional light bulbs rely on filaments — and therefore consume less electricity.

LEDs also last much longer than old-style bulbs and are far more sophisticated. For example, the new 68-storey International Youth Culture Centre in Nanjing, China, has 700,000 LED lights capable of illuminating the building façade in different colours at night.

Frost & Sullivan estimates the global LED lighting market grew 35 per cent to $32.3bn last year, and it is forecast to more than double to $70bn by 2019. LED as a proportion of the total lighting market is set to near 50 per cent by the end of 2015 and reach 84 per cent by 2020.

The incumbents saw the tech revolution coming and are now among the biggest players, but the rapid growth in LEDs has attracted new low-cost competitors, particularly from Asia.

The incumbents are responding to these challenges in different ways, but broadly speaking they are restructuring legacy, high-volume lighting units and regearing their business models towards "smart" and "connected lighting".

"In 10 years there might not be a single light bulb left. If your core competence isn't needed any more, then you need to adapt — the challenge is to move from being a general lighting company to a solution provider," says Ms Nocchi. . . .

Although sales of traditional light bulbs are in structural decline, the market remains profitable because there is so little competition. The incumbents therefore talk about a "long" or "golden tail".

"From an investor perspective, this is a cash cow and a solid one, despite the top line decline," says Frans van Houten, Philips chief executive.

The competitive forces reveal the drivers of industry competition. A company strategist who understands that competition extends well beyond existing rivals will detect wider competitive threats and be better equipped to address them. At the same time, thinking comprehensively about an industry's structure can uncover opportunities: differences in customers, suppliers, substitutes, potential entrants, and rivals that can become the basis for distinct strategies yielding superior performance. In a world of more open competition and relentless change, it is more important than ever to think structurally about competition.

Michael E. Porter, 'The five competitive forces that shape competition', *Harvard Business Review,* January 2008, p. 93

Many small companies, especially those facing fierce competition, may be forced to pursue profit as their overriding goal, merely to survive. With large companies, however, where mere survival is not the overriding concern, the pursuit of short-run profit is likely to be only one of many business objectives.

The modern business enterprise is often a complex organisation, with many different departments and divisions. What is more, the ownership and control of the firm are often in totally different hands: i.e. shareholders and managers. With many competing interests, there are often several objectives being pursued simultaneously.

In Part F we will consider what these alternative objectives might be and the strategies that businesses might adopt in their pursuit. Having the correct strategy is crucial for business survival. For example, a strategy for lighting manufacturers that worked well for many years may no longer be appropriate as new types of lighting, such as LEDs, replace older types (see the *Financial Times* article on the left).

We start, in Chapter 14, by introducing you to the world of business strategy. We show how crucial the degree of competition is in shaping not only business success but also the strategic approaches open to business.

In Chapter 15, we will focus on one particular strategy: that of growth. Should a firm seek to grow by simply expanding the scale of its operations or should it merge with other firms or enter into alliances with them? Chapter 16 looks at the small-firm sector and compares the objectives and behaviour of small firms with those of their bigger rivals.

Finally, in Chapter 17, we will look at alternative pricing strategies and how they vary with market structure and the different aims that firms might pursue.

Key terms

Porter's five forces
Strategic management
Value chain
Core competence
Internal expansion
External expansion
Transaction costs
Takeover constraint
Horizontal and vertical integration
Vertical restraints
Diversification
Merger
Enterprise
Strategic alliance
Networks
Logistics
SME
Cost-based pricing
Price discrimination
Transfer pricing
Peak-load pricing
Inter-temporal pricing
Product life cycle

An introduction to business strategy

Business issues covered in this chapter

- What are the objectives of strategic management?
- What are the key competitive forces affecting a business?
- What choices of strategy towards competitors are open to a business?
- What internal strategic choices are open to a business and how can it make best use of its core competencies when deciding on its internal organisation?
- How does a business's strategy relate to its vision and mission? What is the role of various stakeholders in shaping strategy?
- Should a business 'go global'?

Most public limited companies have a mission statement in which they identify their main goals. As we saw in the last chapter, these goals will normally be more than simple short-term profit maximisation. Profit is still likely to be important and so companies' stated goals will normally include increasing profit to achieve a good return for their shareholders. Over the longer term this is likely to require an increase in sales and/or more efficient production. This may require developing and improving their products and production methods.

But companies are likely to have other aims too. These may include taking account of environmental concerns, by reducing waste, economising on energy and using sustainable ingredients; developing good relationships with suppliers and customers and treating them fairly; providing a good working environment for employees that respects their rights and provides fair wages and opportunities for career development; recognising the company's role in society and seeking to meet various social obligations.

Take the case of Ben and Jerry's ice cream. According to its mission statement, being successful means producing a high-quality product, returning a profit, presiding over business growth and enhancing shareholder value. The company also claims that a successful business rests upon a 'deep respect for individuals' and that it wants to initiate ways of improving the quality of life, such as by using fair-trade and non-GMO ingredients and by supporting local communities. What strategy or strategies will Ben & Jerry's need to adopt in order to achieve these goals?

Ben & Jerry's was formed in 1978 by Ben Cohen and Jerry Greenfield. In 2000, it was taken over by Unilever, the Anglo-Dutch multinational, but it still maintains its identity and its mission. Since its early years as a two-person operation, Ben & Jerry's has expanded to have operations in 35 countries. However, as its mission statement suggests, the founders of Ben & Jerry's were in search of more than profits from their business activities. With a clear philosophy of social responsibility, the business strategy has been one in which the search for profit has been regulated by a wider set of social and environmental goals.

14.1 WHAT IS STRATEGY?

Defining strategy

Business strategy describes the way in which an organisation addresses its fundamental challenges over the medium to long term. Usually, the term 'strategy' is applied to the decision-making processes of the senior management team, but it can be applied at all levels of the organisation.

The term can also be applied to a number of everyday situations. Thus, an individual may have a strategy to keep fit that involves a healthy diet and going to the gym. A student may have a career strategy that involves passing examinations.

Businesses use strategy in an attempt to be more competitive than their rivals. Sometimes, these strategies are successful: businesses outperform their competitors. Similarly, individuals' strategy may be successful: people keep their weight under control; students pass exams.

Sometimes, however, strategies fail. Businesses underperform; individuals put on weight; students fail their exams. If this is the case, then a re-evaluation of existing goals and strategies has to take place with new strategies being developed to meet long-term objectives. For a business that has failed to perform, this is an opportunity to regain its competitive position.

Clearly the type of business 'strategy' that is appropriate depends upon the context in which the strategy is being developed. In an attempt to capture the diversity of the term, Henry Mintzberg[1] suggests that we need to look at the 'five Ps' of business strategy. A strategy can be:

- a plan;
- a ploy;
- a pattern of behaviour;
- a position with respect to others;
- a perspective.

A plan. This represents the most common use of the term strategy. It involves, as Mintzberg states, a 'consciously intended course of action to deal with a situation'. Plans most commonly operate over a given period of time, in which the business outlines where it would like to be at a given point in the future. This might be in terms of its market share or its level of profitability, or some other combination of criteria upon which business progress or success might be evaluated. As such, plans tend to focus on long-term issues facing the business rather than operational details.

A ploy. In contrast to the long-term nature of the plan, strategy as a ploy is generally short term in its application. It often focuses on a specific manoeuvre by business in order to outwit or counteract the behaviour of rivals. Aggressive pricing policy and the use of special offers by supermarkets is a frequently adopted ploy to gain, or more commonly protect, market share. Such a strategy may have limited objectives and be liable to frequent changes.

A pattern of behaviour. Rather than a consciously planned framework of action, business strategy may, in fact, emerge naturally from a consistent response to events: e.g. introducing a new product variety each year. Such consistent action involves a pattern of behaviour, which takes on a strategic form. Such strategies tend to evolve as circumstances change. There is no clear long-term objective; unlike plan and ploy, here strategy just happens.

A position with respect to others. Here strategy is determined by the position of the business in its market. For example, a firm may attempt to gain or defend market share. Thus a car company such as BMW may set out to defend its position as a manufacturer of high-quality motorcars by focusing on design and performance in its product development and advertising campaigns. Conversely, Aldi and Lidl might focus on defending and developing their claim to have some of the lowest prices in grocery retailing.

A perspective. In this respect, strategy is based upon establishing a common way of perceiving the world, primarily within the organisation itself. It may be that this perspective of the world is based on the views of a forceful leader or a strong senior management team, though it can also involve a consensus between stakeholders in the organisation. Businesses with strong ethical and environmental objectives, such as Ben & Jerry's, would see a shared perspective as an important part of their business strategy. Employees are encouraged to take on board the company's philosophy. This, it is hoped, will not only contribute to the business's success through motivation and commitment, but also encourage employees to feel good about what they do.

Mintzberg notes in his analysis of the term 'strategy' that businesses might adopt any number of approaches to

BOX 14.1 BUSINESS STRATEGY THE SAMSUNG WAY

Staying ahead of the game

Samsung is a major South Korean conglomerate involved in a number of industries, including the machinery and heavy engineering, chemical, financial services and consumer electronic sectors. Across its various divisions, it has over 480 000 employees globally and is a major international investor and exporter.

This case study outlines some of the strategic initiatives that have been taken in recent times by one of its most successful divisions, Samsung Electronics, which has become the world's largest mobile phone producer.

By 2017, it had a 21.9 per cent share of the global mobile phone market, in contrast to its leading rival Apple, which had 15.2 per cent. It shipped 317 million phone handsets, whereas Apple shipped 215 million. Samsung Electronics is also the world's largest producer of TVs and had a global market share of 26.5 per cent in 2017. Its leading rival, LG Electronics, had a market share of 14.6 per cent. It is the second biggest producer of tablet computers with a global market share of 15.2 per cent in 2017 compared with Apple's 26.8 per cent. The company is also one of the leading suppliers of components, such as memory chips for computers and mobile phones. In 2017, it had 308 745 employees.

The division's success over the past few years is quite an achievement as it has managed to reposition itself in the upmarket segment of the consumer electronics industry.

The key features of Samsung's strategy

How has Samsung achieved this? What have been the keys to its success?

First, it had a strong management team led by Lee Kun-hee, the chairman until 2014 and son of Lee Byung-chul who started the original business in 1938. Samsung is an example of a *Chaebol* – a family-owned and managed conglomerate in South Korea. Lee Kun-hee introduced a new management initiative in 1993 that stressed the importance of responding rapidly to competitive threats. He famously instructed Samsung managers to 'change everything but your wife and children'.

Second, there was a dramatic streamlining of the business and the decision-making structure following its poor financial performance in the mid-1990s and an association with low-end brands in televisions and air-conditioning units. The management team took aggressive measures to improve the division's finances by cutting jobs, closing unprofitable factories, reducing inventory levels and selling corporate assets.

Third, Samsung Electronics has invested heavily in research and development (R&D) to increase its product portfolio and reduce the lead time from product conception to product launch. In 2017, the division invested $12.2 billion in R&D.[1] This made it the fourth biggest R&D spending company in the world behind Volkswagen, Alphabet (Google) and Microsoft. In December 2017, it launched Samsung Research. This new division is the result of a reorganisation of the company's Software R&D Centre and Digital Media & Communications. It has 22 R&D units and around 20 000 employees. Some of its key priorities include developments in artificial intelligence and the *Internet of Things*.

The business has also engaged in a number of strategic alliances with major players such Qualcomm, Red Hat and Good Technology to share R&D costs.

One way of measuring the output of successful R&D activity is by looking at the number of patents a business has been awarded. In the USA, Samsung was ranked second behind International Business Machines (IBM) in 2017, ahead of businesses such as Intel, LG Electronics, Microsoft and Google. It successfully registered 6509 patents with the United States Patent Office.[2] It has been in second place behind IBM in every year from 2006 to 2017. In the EU, Samsung was ranked in fourth place in 2017, having filed 2016 cases with the European Patent Office.[3]

Fourth, Samsung is concerned about volumes from which it can achieve economies of scale. To this end, it invests heavily in modern factories that can cope with large production runs. To help achieve these economies, Samsung also supplies components to its competitors as well as making them for its own product range. For example, it sells OLED display panels for Apple's iPhone X. Further, production systems are flexible enough to allow customisation for individual buyers, ensuring that selling prices are above the industry average.

Alongside longer production runs, Samsung uses both internal and external suppliers for components such as memory chips, screens, batteries, etc. The internal divisions do not receive any special treatment. If they cannot compete on price, quality and delivery with external suppliers, then they lose the business. Employees in successful divisions receive large bonuses, while those that make losses for three years or more are sold off or closed down. However, to prevent this

---

[1] *2017 EU Industrial R&D Investment Scoreboard* (European Commission).

[2] *2017 Top 25 USPTO Recipients* (Aztec IP Solutions).

[3] *2017 European Patent Office Annual Report* (European Patent Office).

strategic behaviour. Pursuing strategy as a plan, for example, does not preclude using strategy as a ploy or as a position in respect to others. Businesses may interpret strategy in a number of ways simultaneously. What these different understandings of strategy do is to enable us to analyse different aspects of business behaviour and organisation.

Strategic management

The majority of the time, most managers' primary function is managing the routine day-to-day activities of the business, such as dealing with personnel issues, checking budgets and looking for ways to enhance efficiency. In other

competition between divisions from becoming destructive, a Corporate Strategy Office oversees the whole process.

Finally, Samsung has been developing its global brand name in consumer electronics and marketing, particularly sports marketing. For example, it sponsored the Rugby World Cup in 2015, the 2016 Summer Olympics in Rio de Janeiro and the 2018 Winter Olympics in Pyeongchang.

As a result of these strategies, Samsung rose from 42nd in BusinessWeek/Interbrand's list of the top 100 global brands in 2001 to 6th in 2017.[4]

Recent developments and challenges

The introduction of the large-screen Galaxy brand of smart phones was a key factor underpinning the division's growth between 2010 and 2013. However, this competitive advantage in the high end premium segment of the market was removed in 2014, when Apple successfully launched its larger screen iPhone 6 and iPhone 6 Plus.

It also started to face more intense competition from producers of lower-price Android devices in emerging markets. For example, in 2017, the three leading producers in China were Huawei, Oppo and Vivo, with market shares of 19, 18 and 17 per cent respectively. In contrast, Samsung sold around 12 million handsets, just 2.2 per cent of the market. Samsung has a much stronger presence in the Indian market but lost its top spot in the final quarter of 2017 to Xiaomi. The share of Chinese handset producers in this market increased dramatically from 34 per cent in 2016 to 53 per cent in 2017.

Samsung's annual net profit in 2014 was $21.3 billion – 27 per cent lower than in 2017. Hence it became vitally important for Samsung to differentiate its smartphones from other producers using the Android operating system. It did this successfully with the launch, in March 2015, of the new Galaxy 6 Edge handset with its curved screen. Further design and appearance improvements followed with the introduction of the Galaxy S7 in March 2016. The company also streamlined the number of products it offered, which enabled it to benefit from greater economies of scale.

The business made an operating profit of $13.2 billion in the first six months of 2016, with the mobile division accounting for approximately half of this amount.

However, the launch of the Galaxy Note 7 in August proved a disaster. Although initially it received positive reviews, a problem soon became apparent with its design. Unfortunately, while recharging, batteries could sometimes

---

[4] *Best Global Brands 2017 Rankings* (Interbrand).

overheat, causing the handsets to catch fire. Samsung initially recalled the handsets before finally having to withdraw them from the market. The company announced that the failure of the product cost $5.3 billion of forgone operating profits.

The business also became involved in a huge corruption scandal in 2016. Lee Kun-hee was incapacitated by a heart attack in 2014 and it was widely expected that he would be replaced by his only son Lee Jae-yong, who had become vice-chairman of Samsung Electronics in 2013. However, in August 2017, a court found him guilty of bribing the then South Korean President, Park Geun-hye, in return for political support for a controversial takeover. Initially, he was given a prison sentence of five years but this was later reduced to two-and-a-half years. He was freed in February 2018 as the sentence was suspended, but the case has damaged the company's international reputation.

Many people have begun to question the future role of the Lee family in the management of Samsung Electronics and its governance structures. In an attempt to address this issue, the company announced in March 2018 that it was increasing the number of board members from 9 to 11 and splitting the role of chairman from that of the CEO. It is hoped this will increase the independence of the board and its ability to monitor objectively the company's performance.

Despite all of these problems, the business made record operating profits of $14.1 billion in the fourth quarter of 2017. Its full-year profits were $50 billion – an 83 per cent increase on the previous year.

Approximately two-thirds of this profit came from its sales of memory chips. The demand for Dram and Nand memory chips for mobile devices and computer servers began to increase rapidly in the second half of 2016. This trend continued into 2017, with global demand increasing by 74 per cent and 46 per cent respectively, while average prices increased by 45 per cent and 20 per cent. It is also, as we saw above, the key supplier of OLED screens for Apple's iPhone X. Revenues from its mobile division have also increased.

With concerns over future growth levels for smartphones and memory chips, Samsung Electronics is trying to diversify into different markets. In particular, it has developed components for driverless cars, connected car technologies and the *Internet of Things*.

1. What dangers do you see with Samsung's recent business strategy?
2. Given Mintzberg's five Ps, which would you say fit(s) Samsung's approach to strategy most closely and why?

---

words, they are involved in the detailed operational activities of the business.

Some managers, however, especially those high up in the business organisation, such as the managing director, will be busy in a different way, thinking about big, potentially complex, issues, which affect the whole company. For example,

they might be analysing the behaviour of competitors, evaluating the company's share price or considering ways to expand the business. In other words, these managers are involved in the strategic long-term activities of the business.

Both types of management are equally important in the management process, as each contributes in its own way to the business's overall success. However, what is clear is that strategic and operational management are quite distinct managerial functions.

Strategic management comprises three main components.

- *Strategic analysis* is concerned with examining those factors that underpin an organisation's mission (or purpose) and its long-term vision. These factors are key in determining a business's performance and include internal factors, such as the development of business skills and knowledge, and external factors, such as the competitive environment, resource availability and changes in technology.
- *Strategic choice,* by contrast, is concerned primarily with the formulation and evaluation of alternative courses of action that might be adopted in order to achieve the business's strategic objectives. What strategic choices are available? How suitable are such strategies, given their risks and constraints such as time, cost and the business's values?
- *Strategic implementation* is concerned with how strategic choices might be put into effect. In other words, it considers how a strategy might be translated into action. Who is responsible for its implementation? How will it be managed? How is its success or otherwise to be monitored?

In the following sections of this chapter we are going to consider these three dimensions of strategic management and the issues they raise for the conduct of business. Before we do so, it is worth considering what strategic management means for different business types. How might businesses differ in respect to their analysis, choice and implementation of strategy?

Big business/small business. The strategic requirements of a small local computer assembler and Microsoft are clearly going to be massively different. A small business, operating in a niche market, providing a limited range of products or services, certainly would not require the complex strategic assessment of a large business operating in many markets and providing a whole range of products. Not only would the strategy for a small business usually be simpler, it would probably be easier to formulate, given that the managers of small businesses are often the owners and generally the principal creators of the businesses strategy.

Manufacturing business/service provider business. Although in many respects the strategic commitments of both

a manufacturer and a service-sector business might be similar, in some crucial respects the focus of strategy will differ. Manufacturers will tend to focus a large part of their strategic effort on product issues (technology, design, inputs, etc.), whereas service providers will tend to focus on strategic issues related to the customer, especially in the area of retailing.

Domestic business/multinational business. The crucial difference in strategic thinking between a domestic business and a multinational business concerns the geographic spread of the multinational corporation. The multinational will need to focus its strategy not only in global terms but possibly also within the context of each international market within which it operates. Depending upon the diversity of these markets, this may require a quite distinct strategic approach within each. Similarly, a business serving a national market will have more complex strategic issues to consider than one serving a local market.

Private-sector business/public-sector business. Quite clearly the strategic considerations of the National Health Service will, in many respects, be quite different from, say, Ford, but how different will they be from those of BUPA, the private-sector medical care provider? Increasingly, public-sector organisations, like their private-sector counterparts, are having to adopt a more business-orientated approach to service provision. Stakeholders may be different and profit may not be the principal motivation of business activity, but efficiency, targets and accountability are increasingly becoming public-sector as well as private-sector organisational goals.

For-profit organisations/not-for-profit organisations. Not-for-profit businesses such as charities are, essentially, based upon a mission underpinned by principles of value. In shaping their strategic goals, such values will be paramount in determining the direction and focus of strategic behaviour.

Definition

Strategic management The management of the strategic long-term activities of the business, which includes strategic analysis, strategic choice and strategic implementation.

14.2 STRATEGIC ANALYSIS

In order for an organisation to make strategic decisions, first it must analyse what the organisation is about (its mission) and how it envisages where it wants to be (its vision). In other words, the mission and vision will affect the strategic choices made. Take the case of Ben & Jerry's. Its proclaimed ethical stance limits potential strategic avenues.

Strategic choices also depend on an analysis of (a) the external business environment and (b) the organisation's internal capabilities.

- How much competition does the firm face and what forms does it take?

- What other external factors, such as laws and regulations, technological changes and changes in consumer tastes, are likely to affect the firm's decisions?
- Similarly, what internal factors drive an organisation's performance?

In the case of Ben & Jerry's, the nature of its supply chain is likely to affect not only the quality of the product but also the ability of the company to develop and grow.

Vision and mission

At the beginning of this chapter, we referred to the mission statement of Ben & Jerry's, in which the company clearly expresses a purpose for its business: a purpose that goes far beyond simply making a profit. Such wider social, environmental and ethical considerations are increasingly shaping business thinking, as expectations regarding corporate responsibility grow.

It is now widely expected that a business must look beyond 'the bottom line' (i.e. profitability) and take account of the interests of a wide group of stakeholders, such as employees, customers, creditors and the local community, and not just the owners of the business. It would be a risky business strategy indeed that pursued profit without taking into account the social, environmental and ethical implications that this might entail (see section 20.5). As such, the formulation of strategy must take into account the purpose of the organisation and the values and objectives that such a purpose involves. Organisational purpose is most often found in a business's mission statement, which is, in turn, shaped by a number of distinct influences (see Figure 14.1).

Corporate governance. Corporate governance refers to the way in which a business is run and the structure of decision making. It also includes the monitoring and supervision and, in some cases, regulation of executive decisions. The way a business is run depends on the purposes of the business and in *whose interests* it is run.

Stakeholders. Stakeholders differ in power and influence, but, ultimately, they might all shape the purpose of the organisation in certain respects. Given the wide number of stakeholders, many conflicts of interest can arise.

Business ethics. A business's ethical position might, as in the case of Ben & Jerry's, be driven by the values of its founders. Alternatively, ethics might be determined and shaped by wider cultural values and standards that determine what is and what is not acceptable behaviour. As previously remarked, business today would find it very difficult to pursue a strategy that failed to exhibit a degree of social responsibility.

High-profile cases can have a significant impact on a firm's reputation and standing in both the business community and society in general. For example, Oxfam produces a 'Behind the Brands Scorecard' which ranks the ten biggest food companies based on seven ethical standards. They call on people to use social media to put pressure on these companies to introduce more ethical policies. Since the campaign started in 2013, Oxfam claims that a number of these businesses have improved their practices.

Corporate social responsibility has become an increasingly important issue for many businesses and is discussed in more detail in Chapter 20.

Cultural context. How does the cultural context of the organisation influence its objectives? Not only will national culture be significant here, but also the subculture of managers. Wider questions are also raised, given the growth in multinational business activity and the cross-cultural nature of such organisations. Recognising differing cultural contexts might be crucial in shaping business success within such increasingly global markets.

The business environment

We considered the various dimensions of the business environment and how they shape and influence business activity (Chapter 1). We divided the business environment into four distinct sets of factors: political, economic, social and technological. Such factors comprise what we call a PEST analysis. In this section we will take our analysis of the business environment forward and consider more closely those factors that are likely to influence the competitive advantage of the organisation.

Figure 14.1 Factors influencing organisational purpose

Corporate governance → Organisational purpose ← Stakeholder views

Business ethics → Organisational purpose ← Cultural context

Pause for thought

Give some examples of cultural differences between countries or regions that might influence business strategy.

The Five Forces Model of competition

Developed by Professor Michael Porter of Harvard Business School in 1980, the Five Forces Model sets out to identify those factors that are likely to affect an organisation's competitiveness (see Figure 14.2). This then helps a firm to choose an appropriate strategy to enhance its competitive opportunities and to protect itself from competitive threats. The five forces that Porter identifies are:

- the bargaining power of suppliers;
- the bargaining power of buyers;
- the threat of potential new entrants;
- the threat of substitutes;
- the extent of competitive rivalry.

The bargaining power of suppliers. Most business organisations depend upon suppliers to some extent, whether to provide raw materials or simply stationery. Indeed, many businesses have extensive supply or 'value chain' networks (as we shall discuss later in this section). Such suppliers can have a significant and powerful effect on a business when:

- there are relatively few suppliers in the market, reducing the ability of the firm to switch from one supply source to another;
- there are no alternatives to the supplies they offer;
- the prices of suppliers form a large part of the firm's total costs;
- a supplier's customers are small and fragmented and, as such, have little power over the supplying business.

Car dealers often find that car manufacturers can exert considerable pressure over them in terms of pricing, display and after-sales service.

The bargaining power of buyers. The bargaining power of companies that purchase a firm's products will be greater when:

- these purchasing companies are large and there are relatively few of them;
- there are many other firms competing for their custom and, hence, a firm that produces an undifferentiated product is likely to be more prone to 'buyer power' than one that produces a unique or differentiated product;
- the costs for the purchasing companies of switching to other suppliers are low;
- purchasing companies are able to backward integrate and effectively displace the supplying firm.

The UK grocery-retailing sector, up until recently, was dominated by a small number of large supermarket chains such as Tesco, Sainsbury and Asda Wal-Mart. These exert massive levels of buyer power over farmers and food processing companies. Not only do such supermarkets dominate the market, but also, normally, they can find many alternative supply sources, both domestic and international, at relatively low switching costs. Also, all the supermarkets sell own-brand labels, either produced themselves or through agreement with existing manufacturers, and these are sold at prices often considerably below those of equivalent branded products (see Box 8.1 on page 134).

Figure 14.2 Porter's Five Forces Model

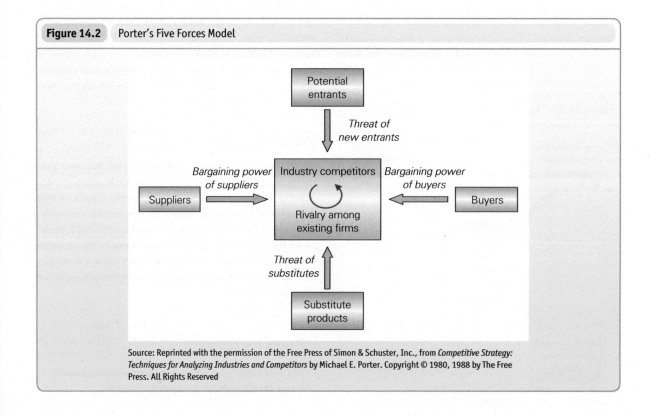

Source: Reprinted with the permission of the Free Press of Simon & Schuster, Inc., from *Competitive Strategy: Techniques for Analyzing Industries and Competitors* by Michael E. Porter. Copyright © 1980, 1988 by The Free Press. All Rights Reserved

The threat of potential new entrants. The ability of new entrants to enter the marketplace depends largely upon the existence and effectiveness of various barriers to entry. These barriers to entry were described fully in section 11.3 (pages 191–4), but are listed here as a reminder:

■ economies of scale and scope;
■ product differentiation;
■ capital requirements;
■ lower costs of established firm;
■ ownership of/control over key factors of production;
■ ownership of/control over wholesale or retail outlets;
■ legal protection;
■ aggressive tactics and retaliation.

Barriers to entry tend to be very industry, product and market specific. Nevertheless, two useful generalisations can be made. First, companies with products that have a strong brand identity often will attempt to use this form of product differentiation to restrict competition; second, manufacturers will tend to rely on economies of scale and low costs as a basis for restricting competitive pressure.

KI 1
p11 *The threat of substitutes.* The availability of substitutes can be a major threat to a business and its profitability. Issues that businesses need to consider in relation to the availability of substitute products are:

■ the ability of and cost to customers of switching to the substitute;
■ the threat of competitors bringing out a more advanced or up-to-date product;
■ the impact that substitute products are likely to have on pricing policy.

Some examples include the impact of tablet computers on the sales of laptop computers and the impact of smartphones on the sales of mobile games consoles.

The extent of competitive rivalry. The previous two chapters focused on market structure and were concerned primarily with how businesses respond to differing levels of competition. Clearly the degree of competition a firm faces is a crucial element in shaping its strategic analysis. Competitive rivalry will be enhanced when there is the potential for new firms to enter the market, when there is a real threat from substitute products and when buyers and suppliers have some element of influence over the firm's performance. In addition to this, competitive rivalry is likely to be enhanced in the following circumstances:

■ Competitors are of equal size.
■ Markets are growing slowly. This makes it difficult to acquire additional sales without taking market share from rivals.
■ There are high fixed costs, which require the firm to gain a large market share in order to break even.

■ Productive capacity in an industry increases in large increments, often resulting in over-production in the short term. This adds to competitive pressure by putting downward pressure on prices.
■ Product differentiation is difficult to achieve; hence product switching by consumers is a real threat.
■ There are high exit costs. When a business invests in non-transferable fixed assets, such as highly specialist capital equipment, it may be reluctant to leave a market. It may thus compete fiercely to maintain its market position. On the other hand, as we have seen in the section on contestable markets (pages 196–200), high exit costs may deter firms from entering a market in the first place and thus make the market less contestable.
■ There exists the possibility for merger and acquisition. This competition for corporate control may have considerable influence on the firm's strategy.

Pause for thought

Given that the stronger the competitive forces, the lower the profit potential for firms, describe what five force characteristics an attractive and unattractive industry might have.

Limitations of the Five Forces Model

One of the great values of the Five Forces Model is that it creates a structured framework for a business to analyse the strategic issues that it faces. However, it does have a number of weaknesses.

First, the Five Forces Model presents a largely static view of the business environment, whereas in reality it is likely to be constantly changing.

Second, the model starts from the premise that the business environment is a competitive threat to the business organisation, which, if the business is to be successful, needs to be manipulated in particular ways. Often, however, success might be achievable not via competition but rather through co-operation and collaboration. For example, a business might set up close links with one of its major buyers; or businesses in an industry might establish links either to build barriers or to share costs via some form of collaborative research and development. In such instances, the business environment of the Five Forces Model might be viewed as a collaborative opportunity rather than a competitive threat. (The section on strategic alliances in Chapter 15 (section 15.6) will offer a fuller evaluation of collaborative business agreements.)

Finally, critics of the model argue that it fails to take sufficient account of the microenvironment of the organisation and its human resources. For example, factors such as country culture and management skills might have a decisive impact on a firm's choice of strategy and its successful implementation.

Value chain analysis and sustainable competitive advantage

As with the Five Forces Model, value chain analysis was developed by Michael Porter and, as such, the two concepts are closely related. A *value chain* shows how value is added to a product as it moves through each stage of production: from the raw material stage to its purchase by the final consumer. Value chain analysis is concerned with evaluating how each of the various operations within and around an organisation, such as handling inputs, manufacturing the product and marketing it, contributes to the competitive position of the business. Ultimately, it is these value-creating activities that shape a firm's strategic capabilities. A firm's value chain can be split into two separate sets of activities: primary and support (see Figure 14.3).

Primary activities

KI 19
p 147

Primary activities are those directly concerned with the production, distribution and sales of the firm's product. Such primary activities can be grouped into five categories:

- *Inbound logistics.* Here we are concerned with the handling of inputs, storage and distribution of such inputs throughout the business.
- *Operations.* These activities involve the conversion of inputs into the final product or service. Operations might include manufacturing, packaging and assembly.
- *Outbound logistics.* These are concerned with transferring the final product to the consumer. Such activities would include warehousing and transport.
- *Marketing and sales.* This section of the value chain is concerned with bringing the product to the consumer's attention and would involve product advertising and promotion.
- *Service.* This can include activities such as installation and repair, as well as customer requirements such as training.

A business might attempt to add value to its activities by improving its performance in one or more of the above categories. For example, it might attempt to lower production costs or be more efficient in outbound logistics.

Support activities

Such primary activities are underpinned by support activities. These are activities that do not add value directly to any particular stage within the value chain. They do, however, provide support to such a chain and ensure that its various stages are undertaken effectively. Support activities include:

- *Procurement.* This involves the acquisition of inputs by the firm.
- *Technological development.* This includes activities within the business that support new product and process developments, such as the use of research departments.

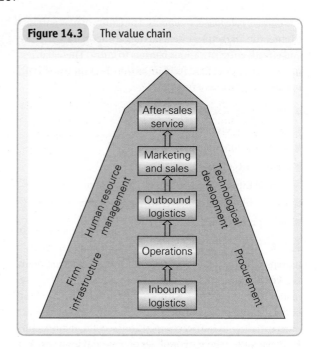

Figure 14.3 The value chain

- *Human resource management.* Activities in this category include things such as recruitment, training and the negotiation and determination of wage rates.
- *Firm infrastructure.* This category includes activities such as financial planning and control systems, quality control and information management.

As well as creating value directly themselves, most firms buy in certain value chain activities, such as employing another firm to do its advertising or using an external delivery firm to distribute its products. The outsourcing of these activities might prove to be far more beneficial to a business than providing the activities itself. You can employ the best advertisers or the most efficient and reliable distributors.

Thus the value system extends beyond the individual organisation and encompasses the value chains of all those individual businesses that the organisation might deal with. The implication is that the value chain and the value system may be highly complex and the competitive position of a business may extend well beyond the immediate value chain of the organisation. This will have significant implications for the formulation and choice of business strategy.

Having now discussed the background to strategic analysis, we can shift our focus to consider strategic choice and implementation. What strategies are potentially open to businesses and how do they choose the right ones and set about implementing them?

Definitions

Value chain The stages or activities that help to create product value.

Logistics The process of managing the supply of inputs to a firm and the outputs from a firm to its customers.

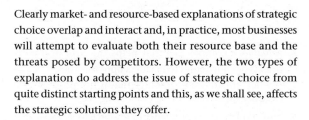

STRATEGIC CHOICE

Theories of strategic choice fall into two main categories: market-based and resources-based.

Market-based theories argue that strategic choices are, ultimately, determined by the competitive environment that the business faces. As such, understanding this competitive environment and identifying appropriate ways to deal with it will determine whether you are successful or not.

Resource-based theory also looks at the firm's competitive position, but focuses on its internal situation. It considers how strategic decision making is affected by the ownership, control and use of an organisation's resources. It is seen that such resources ultimately deliver profits and it is through a manipulation of such resources that a business can maintain and enhance its competitive position.

Clearly market- and resource-based explanations of strategic choice overlap and interact and, in practice, most businesses will attempt to evaluate both their resource base and the threats posed by competitors. However, the two types of explanation do address the issue of strategic choice from quite distinct starting points and this, as we shall see, affects the strategic solutions they offer.

Environment or market-based strategy

As with many other areas in this field, our analysis of market-based theory starts with the observations of Michael Porter. As an extension of his Five Forces Model of competition, Porter argued that there are three fundamental (or 'generic') strategies that a business might adopt:

- cost leadership;
- differentiation;
- focus.

In order to identify which of these was the most appropriate strategy, a business would need to establish two things: (a) the basis of its competitive advantage – whether it lies in lower costs or differentiation; (b) the nature of the target market – is it broad or a distinct market niche?

Cost leadership

As the title implies, a business that is a low-cost leader is able to manufacture and deliver its product more cheaply than its rivals, thereby gaining competitive advantage. The strategic emphasis here is on driving out inefficiency at every stage of the value chain. 'No-frills' budget airlines, such as easyJet and Ryanair, are classic examples of companies that pursue a cost-leadership strategy.

A strategy based upon cost leadership may require a fundamentally different use of resources or organisational structure if the firm is to stay ahead of its rivals. Wal-Mart's hub and spoke distribution system would be an example in point. Here the company distributes its products to shops from regional depots in order to minimise transport costs.

In addition, firms which base their operations on low costs in order to achieve low prices (although that may not necessarily be the aim of low costs) are unlikely to have a high level of brand loyalty. In other words, if customer choice is going to be driven largely by price, demand is likely to be relatively price elastic. Other virtues of the product that might tie in buyers, such as quality or after-sales service, are largely absent from such firms' strategic goals.

Differentiation

A differentiation strategy aims to emphasise and promote the uniqueness of the firm's product. As such, high rather than low prices often are attached to such products. Product characteristics such as quality, design and reliability are the basis of the firm's competitive advantage. Hence a strategy that adds to such differences and creates value for the customer needs to be identified.

Such a strategy might result in higher costs, especially in the short term, as the firm pursues constant product development through innovation, design and research. However, with the ability to charge premium prices, revenues may increase more than costs: in other words, the firm may achieve higher profits. Mobile phone handset producers such as Apple and Samsung provide a good example. Even though they are in fierce competition with each other, both firms focus their strategy on trying to differentiate their products from their rival's. This differentiation is in terms of features and performance, not price. Screen size, camera quality (megapixels), speakers, screen resolution, availability of apps, operating systems, battery life and overall design are all characteristics used in the competitive battle.

Differentiation strategies are not, however, risk free. Pricing differentiated products can be problematic. At what point does the price premium for the product deter potential buyers, such that the differentiated nature of the product is insufficient to outweigh such price considerations? The fact that tastes and fashion change could also have a significant impact upon the sales of a differentiated product.

Laura Ashley clothing was a case in point. In an attempt to differentiate itself from other high street clothing rivals, Laura Ashley promoted a strategy producing rather exclusive clothing for women, rooted in a country lifestyle. During the early 1980s, Laura Ashley's profits grew as its differentiated product attracted a large following. But the fickle nature of fashion had turned by the early 1990s and Laura Ashley's fashion products were seen as dated and stuffy.

But, while its differentiated product and brand image had become somewhat of a liability *in the clothing market,* the company successfully diversified into the home decorations and furniture market. Here the existing brand image was used to create an affluent customer base. By 2018, clothing sales constituted only 17 per cent of the company's revenue.

It further diversified into hotels and tea rooms. However, with an increase in competition from online furnishing retailers, profits fell in the home furnishings division. This problem was exacerbated by a rise in online furnishings retailers and by the fall in the pound following the Brexit vote, as much of the company's products are made in East Asia and were made more expensive by the weaker pound. The strategic question was whether expansion into the hotels and catering market would be sufficient to offset the company's difficulties elsewhere.

Focus strategy

Rather than considering a whole market as a potential for sales, a focus strategy involves identifying market niches and designing and promoting products for such niches. Such a strategy may or may not be applicable to other niches. As such, a business might pursue any number of different strategies simultaneously for different market niches. In such cases, a business that does not hold a competitive advantage in a market in general may be able to identify distinct market segments in which it might exploit some advantage that it might have over its rivals, whether in terms of costs or product difference. Ben & Jerry's ice cream would be a case in point. The mass low-cost ice-cream market is served by a number of large multinational food manufacturers and processors, but the existence of niche high-quality ice-cream markets offers opportunities for companies like Ben & Jerry's and Häagen-Dazs. By focusing on such consumers, they are able to sell and market their product at premium prices.

Niche markets, however profitable, are, by their nature, small and, as such, are limited in their growth potential. Hence firms that focus upon niche market opportunities are likely to have limited growth prospects. There is also the possibility that niches shift or disappear over time. This would require businesses to be flexible in setting out their strategic position.

Sometimes, a focus strategy may be combined with a cost-leadership strategy to develop a niche market into a mass market. Amazon.com, the online bookseller, was, until relatively recently, a business that had a clear cost focus strategy. With low overheads, it was able to sell books at knockdown prices to online customers (its niche market segment) and, over time, thanks to lower costs, lower prices and the spread of the Internet, this has become a mass market.

Resource-based strategy

Resource-based strategy, as already mentioned, focuses on exploiting a firm's internal organisation and production processes in order to develop its competitive advantage. It is the firm's *distinctiveness* that sets it apart from its competitors. If a business does not have a distinctive feature, then it needs to set about creating one.

Core competencies

Core competencies are those skills, knowledge and technologies that underpin the organisation's competitive advantage. These competencies are likely to differ from one business to another, reflecting the uniqueness of each individual organisation and, ultimately, determining its potential for success. Given these differences, how does a firm select an appropriate strategy?

When a firm has unique competencies, its strategy should seek to sustain and exploit these, whether in the design of the product or in its methods of production. In many cases, however, firms do not have any competencies that give them a distinctive competitive advantage, even though they may still be profitable. In such instances, strategy often focuses upon either developing such resources or more effectively using the resources the firm already has.

What defines a core competence?

A core competence must satisfy the following four capabilities to serve as a source of competitive advantage for the business. It must be:

- *valuable*: a competence that helps the firm deal with threats or contributes to business opportunities;
- *rare*: a competence or resource that is not possessed by competitors;
- *costly to imitate*: a competence or resource that other firms find difficult to develop and copy;
- *non-substitutable*: a competence or resource for which there is no alternative.

> **Pause for thought**
>
> *Referring back to Box 14.1, what core competencies does Samsung have? Remember, you must justify a core competence in terms of all four listed criteria.*

Core competencies. The key skills of a business that underpin its competitive advantage. A core competence is valuable, rare, costly to imitate and non-substitutable. Firms normally will gain from exploiting their core competencies.

Clearly, then, whether we adopt a market-based view of strategic choice or a resource-based view, will have significant implications for how a firm can develop and exploit competitive advantage.

> **Definition**
>
> **Core competence** The key skills of a business that underpin its competitive advantage.

Before we consider issues of how to implement strategy, there is one dimension of the business environment that we need to consider and that is the impact of globalisation on the world economy in general and business activity in particular. Few businesses have been left untouched by the phenomenon. So how has globalisation affected strategic analysis and strategic choice?

14.4 BUSINESS STRATEGY IN A GLOBAL ECONOMY

In many respects, a firm's global strategy is simply an extension of its strategy within its own domestic market. However, opening up to global markets can present many new business opportunities: access to new markets, new customers, new supply sources, new ideas and skills. In addition to such opportunities, the global marketplace can also present competitive threats, as new market entrants from abroad arrive with lower costs, innovative products and marketing or some other core competency that the domestic firm finds difficult to match. In this section, we explore the strategic implications for business in facing up to the global economic system.

BOX 14.2 HYBRID STRATEGY

Are the big four UK supermarkets stuck in the middle?

Michael Porter, in his analysis of alternative business strategies, suggested that it could be disastrous for a business to be 'stuck in the middle', having no clear strategic direction.[1] Attempting both to differentiate its product and to offer lower prices would be a serious strategic error. According to Porter, consumers would be confused, as the business would have no clear market identity to which they could relate. His advice was to pick one strategy and stick with it exclusively.

But is a single generic strategy always the best choice? Is a mixed strategy always inappropriate? Consumers often demand a range of product characteristics that cover not only issues such as quality and reliability, but also price and convenience. As such, businesses are often forced to adopt a strategic position that attempts to capture both difference and low prices simultaneously.

Hybrid theories that focus on a combination of strategies are greatly influenced by the market in which the business is operating. Grocery retailing in the UK offers a clear example of hybrid strategy. The various supermarket chains not only look to differentiate themselves from their rivals in terms of the look and feel of their stores, customer service and loyalty schemes such as Sainsbury's Nectar card and Tesco's Clubcard, but also compete fiercely over price.

Then there is the range of their products. At the 'bottom' end of the range, with their own-branded 'basic' products, the supermarkets compete primarily in terms of price (e.g. the Tesco 'Value' and Morrisons 'M Savers' ranges). But, with more upmarket products, they compete in terms of the variety of lines stocked and their quality (e.g. Asda's 'Extra Special' and Sainsbury's 'Taste the Difference' ranges).

A mixed strategy that appears to work well in a market at one point in time might not be so effective if conditions change. This appears to be the case in the grocery market. The impact of the recession and the continued squeeze on consumer incomes during the economic recovery appears to have made many customers more price sensitive.

One downside with following a hybrid strategy is that it means the business has to offer a large number of different products. For example, a large supermarket typically will stock between 30 000 and 40 000 different product lines. This generates

relatively high administration costs and hence higher prices. In contrast, companies such as Lidl and Aldi that focus on a strategy of cost leadership stock far fewer product lines – normally between 2000 and 3000. This generates much lower administration costs and so enables the companies to charge lower prices.

The recent success of the cost leadership strategy of Lidl and Aldi has seen their combined market share increase from 5.2 per cent in 2009 to 12.1 per cent in 2018. The hybrid strategies followed by the 'big four' supermarkets (Tesco, Asda, Morrisons, Sainsbury) that were once so successful have resulted in their combined market share falling from 75.6 per cent in 2009 to 70.3 per cent in 2018. A number of observers have commented that the big four are struggling because they are 'stuck in the middle' between the discounters at the bottom end of the market and companies like Waitrose and Marks & Spencer in the higher-quality segment of the market.

Another problem for the 'big four' is that an increasing number of people are changing the way they buy their groceries. For a number of years, the norm for many customers was to travel to a large out-of-town supermarket and do a weekly shop. Instead, many shoppers are now buying online many of the basic goods they consume regularly, using their mobile phones or tablets. They then make more regular visits to local convenience stores to 'top up' on purchases of fresh goods.

In April 2015, Tesco announced a record annual pre-tax loss of £6.4 billion for the year to the end of February. Around £4.7 billion of these losses were caused by a big fall in the property value of its UK stores – a direct consequence of far fewer people shopping at out-of-town supermarkets. It responded by trying to cut its costs by £1.5 billion and, in October 2017, announced half-yearly profits of £562 million. Lidl and Aldi seem to be having a longer-term impact on the performance of Asda. In 2016, its like-for-like sales fell by 5.7 per cent, while its profits were down by 19 per cent.

1. Choose three supermarket chains and identify the strategy or strategies they adopt. To what extent have they changed over the past few years?

2. Do you feel the classification of business strategy options into cost leadership, differentiation and focus is adequate to describe the strategic approaches that businesses might adopt?

[1] M. E. Porter, *Competitive Advantage: Creating and Sustaining Superior Performance* (Free Press, 1985).

Why go global?

The following are reasons why a business may wish to expand beyond its domestic market.

Market size

International markets can, potentially, offer a business massive new opportunities for growth and expansion. Such markets would be particularly attractive to a business where domestic growth opportunities are limited as a result of either the maturity of the market or shifting consumer taste. Businesses that conduct extensive research and development (R&D) would also be attracted to larger markets as potential returns can be used to offset the firm's R&D investment costs and risk.

Increased profitability

Expanding beyond the domestic economy offers a number of opportunities for increasing profits.

Location economies. The internationalisation of a firm's value chain would enable it to place each value-creating activity in the most appropriate or effective geographic location. So, if production costs are lower in one country, it could locate production there. If another country has the specialist skills to offer superior product design and research facilities, then these functions could be located there. Nike, the US training shoe and sportswear manufacturer, undertakes most of its manufacturing at production sites in South East Asia. However, product innovation and research, along with marketing and promotion, are undertaken largely in the USA.

As businesses relocate many dimensions of their value chain, the structure and organisation of the business takes on a web-like appearance, with its various operations being spread throughout the world.

Pause for thought

Identify some of the potential strengths and weaknesses of businesses having their value chains located in a variety of different countries.

Scope for significant cost reductions. It is widely observed that, over the life cycle of a product, a firm's average costs fall. This is partly the result of economies of scale as the firm gets bigger and plants can specialise in particular functions. Clearly, these cost reductions can be greater by expanding globally.

Cost reductions over time are also the result of what is known as 'learning by doing'. This is where skills and productivity improve with experience. Such learning effects apply not only to workers in production, sales, distribution, etc., but also to managers, who learn to develop more efficient forms of organisation. When a firm expands globally, there may be more scope for learning by doing. For example, if a firm employs low-cost labour in developing countries, initially the

lower cost per worker will, to some extent, be offset by lower productivity. As learning by doing takes place, and productivity increases, so initial small cost advantages may become much more substantial.

Using core competencies. A firm may be able to exploit its core competencies in competing effectively in global markets. The firm might look to expanding first in those countries where it has a clear competitive advantage over already established companies. Wal-Mart's logistic expertise is one example of a business that might exploit such an advantage, in particular overseas markets.

Learning from experience in diverse markets. Successful businesses will learn from their global operations, copying or amending production techniques, organisation, marketing, etc. from one country to another as appropriate. In other words, they can draw lessons from experiences in one country for use in another.

Spreading risk (diversification)

Clearly, one of the main reasons a business might have for going global is to spread risk, avoiding being overly reliant on any specific market or geographic region. As such, falling profitability in one region of the global economy might be effectively offset by improved or more favourable economic conditions elsewhere.

Brewery companies have diversified globally in order to reduce their reliance on domestic markets, which, in recent years, have been growing either very slowly or contracting. For example, AB-InBev, the biggest brewer in the world, acquired SABMiller in 2016 to gain access to the fast-growing beer market in Africa.

Keeping up with rivals

Increasingly, it seems that the globalisation of business is like a game of competitive leapfrog, with businesses having to look overseas in order to maintain their competitive position in respect of their rivals. A fiercely competitive global environment, in which small cost differences or design improvements can mean the difference between business success and failure, ensures that strategic thinking within a global context is high on the business agenda.

It would seem that, at this point, we need to raise a few notes of caution regarding the adoption of a global strategy. It is clearly not without its potential pitfalls. Within any global strategy there exists a high degree of both economic and political risk. Investing in developing economies or emerging markets, such as China, is likely to be much riskier than investing in developed market economies. However, it is often within emerging markets that the greatest returns are achieved. It is essentially this trade-off between potential returns and risk that a firm needs to consider in its strategic decisions.

A global business will need a strategy for effectively embracing foreign cultures and traditions into its working practices, and for devising an efficient system for global logistics. Some businesses may be more suited to deal with such global issues than others.

The global strategy trade-off

A firm's drive to reduce costs and enhance profitability by embracing a global strategy is tempered by one critical consideration – the need to meet the demands of customers in foreign markets. To minimise costs, a firm may seek to standardise its product and its operations throughout the world. However, to meet foreign buyers' needs and respond to local market conditions, a firm may be required to differentiate both its product and its operations, such as marketing. In such cases, customisation will *add* to costs and generate a

degree of duplication within the business. If a business is required to respond to local market conditions in many different markets, it might be faced with significantly higher costs. But if it fails to take into account the uniqueness of the market in which it wishes to sell, it may lose market share.

The trade-off between cost reduction and local responsiveness can be a key strategic consideration for a firm when selling or producing overseas. As a general rule, we tend to find that cost pressures are greatest in those markets where price is the principal competitive weapon. Where product differentiation is high, and attributes such as quality or some other non-price factor predominates within the competitive process, local responsiveness will tend to shape business thinking. In other words, cost considerations will tend to be secondary.

14.5 STRATEGY: EVALUATION AND IMPLEMENTATION

Evaluation

In deciding what strategy to pursue, global or otherwise, the business will need to evaluate the alternatives open to it. How feasible are they? Are they acceptable strategic goals given the business's mission and vision and other stakeholder demands? How will the strategy contribute to the business's competitive position?

If the choice of strategy is deliberate or prescriptive, i.e. planned in advance, then evaluation tools such as investment appraisal and cost–benefit analysis (CBA) might be used to help identify the best strategy (see section 19.3). Most strategies, however, tend to be emergent: in other words, they evolve over time as conditions change and as the success or otherwise of the firm's decisions becomes apparent. The result is that techniques such as investment appraisal have limited value, given the incomplete information available at the time an appraisal is conducted.

Implementation

When a business considers implementing a strategy, often this involves an assessment of three areas:

- resourcing;
- business culture and structure;
- managing change.

Resourcing

All businesses need to evaluate the resource implications of their strategic choices. What resources will be required? Where might they be drawn from within the organisation? What new resources will need to be brought into the organisation? From where will the finance for such resources come? Predictably, the more adventurous the strategy, the greater the impact on resources it is likely to have.

Business culture and structure

Similarly, the more radical the strategic shift, the greater the impact this is likely to have on a business's culture and structure. Is the organisation of the business flexible enough to adapt to the new strategic demands placed upon it? This might be particularly relevant if the strategic shift in the business is towards a greater focus on the global marketplace.

Managing change

Managing change can be both difficult and time-consuming. With change often comes uncertainty for employees, especially if the changes are not understood or managers are not trusted. The greater the uncertainty, the more difficult managing change becomes. In addition to barriers to change from employees, there may be organisational barriers. Entrenched power structures and control systems may be quite unsuitable for the new strategy. There may need to be fundamental organisational restructuring before the new strategy can be implemented.

In this chapter we have introduced you to the basic principles underpinning the determination, choice and evaluation of business strategy. This is a massive subject area and we can only hope to cover a small fraction of the material here. However, from what we have covered you can see how the market environment in which a business operates has a significant impact on its strategic behaviour – and it is such behaviour that ultimately determines its success.

As we have seen, one key factor in determining a business's choice of strategy is its vision and mission – in other words, its aims. In traditional microeconomic theory the firm is assumed to aim for maximum profit. In the next chapter we turn to 'alternative theories of the firm'. These examine the effects of pursuing aims other than simple profit maximisation, especially on prices and output.

SUMMARY

1a Business strategy describes the way in which an organisation addresses its fundamental challenges over the medium to long term.

1b Strategy can be understood in many ways. It can be a plan, a ploy, a pattern of behaviour, a position in respect to others, a perspective or any combination of them.

1c Strategic management differs from operational management (the day-to-day running of the business) as it focuses on issues that affect the whole business, usually over the long term.

1d Strategic management is composed of three components: strategic analysis (factors affecting business performance), strategic choice (the formulation and evaluation of alternative sources of action) and strategic implementation (how strategic choices are put into effect).

1e Different strategic issues will face different types of business, depending on whether they are large or small, manufacturing or service providers, domestic or multinational, private sector or public sector and whether they are for-profit or not-for-profit organisations.

2a The Five Forces Model of competition identifies those factors that are most likely to influence the competitive environment of a business. The five forces are: the bargaining power of suppliers, the bargaining power of buyers, the threat of potential new entrants, the threat of substitutes and the extent of competitive rivalry.

2b The weakness of the Five Forces Model is that not only is it a static view of the business environment, but also it does not see the business environment as a collaborative opportunity but merely as a competitive threat. Critics also argue that it underplays the impact of country culture and management skills on strategic choice and implementation.

2c A business value chain shapes its strategic capabilities. The value chain can be split into primary and support activities. Primary activities are those that directly create value, such as operations and marketing and sales. Support activities are those that underpin value creation in other areas, such as procurement and human resource management.

2d A business's vision and mission are shaped by a number of considerations: in whose interest the business is run, the influence of different stakeholder groups, the prevailing ethical expectations of society or the business owners and the cultural context of the environment in which the organisation operates.

3a Strategic choices are determined either by the competitive nature of the environment within which the organisation operates or by the internal resources controlled by the business. Strategic choice often involves a consideration of both internal and external factors.

3b Environment- or market-based strategies are of three types: cost-leadership strategy, where competitiveness is achieved by lower costs; differentiation strategy, where the business promotes the uniqueness of its product; focus strategy, where competitiveness is achieved by identifying market niches and tailoring products for different groups of consumers.

3c The resource-based view of strategy involves identifying core competencies as the key to a business's competitive advantage. A core competence will be valuable, rare, costly to imitate and non-substitutable.

4a A firm might go global in order to increase market size, increase profitability, spread risk and keep up with rivals.

4b When a firm does go global, it must weigh up the potential benefits against ensuring it meets the local markets' needs. There is a trade-off between cost reduction and local responsiveness.

5a The impact of a chosen strategy is difficult to evaluate, as the strategy often evolves over time as conditions change.

5b When implementing a strategy, a business must consider the following: the resource implications of the strategic choice, how the strategic choice might fit (or not fit) into existing business culture and structure and the difficulties in managing the change resulting from the new strategic direction of the business.

REVIEW QUESTIONS

1 What do you understand by the term 'business strategy'?

2 Explain why different types of business will see strategic management in different ways. Give examples.

3 Outline the Five Forces Model of competition. Identify both the strengths and weaknesses of analysing industry in this manner.

4 Distinguish between a business's primary and support activities in its value chain. Why might a business be inclined to outsource its support activities? Can you see any weaknesses in doing this?

5 Explain what is meant by a business's vision and mission. What implications might different missions have for its strategic decision making?

6 Distinguish between a market-based and a resource-based view of strategic choice.

7 What do you understand by the term 'core competence' when applied to a business?

8 How might going global affect a business's strategic decision making?

9 'Going global, thinking local.' Explain this phrase and identify the potential conflicts for a business in behaving in this way.

10 Why is the choice of business strategy and its potential for success difficult to evaluate?

11 When implementing a business strategy, what issues does it raise for a firm?

Growth strategy

Business issues covered in this chapter

- Why do many businesses want to grow larger?
- What is the relationship between business growth and profitability?
- What constraints on its growth is a business likely to face?
- What alternative growth strategies can a business pursue?
- Why will some firms pursue a growth strategy of internal expansion whereas others will pursue a strategy of merging with or taking over other firms?
- As far as internal expansion is concerned, why will some firms expand through a process of vertical integration whereas others will prefer to diversify?
- Under what circumstances might a business want to form a strategic alliance with other firms?

Whether businesses wish to grow or not, many are forced to. The dynamic competitive process of the market drives producers on to expand in order to remain in the marketplace. If a business fails to grow, this may benefit its more aggressive rivals. They may secure a greater share of the market, leaving the first firm with reduced profits. Thus business growth is often vital if a firm is to survive.

The goal of business growth is closely linked to the key objectives of managers. Managerial status, prestige, promotion and salary might be more directly related to such a goal rather than to that of profit maximisation (as discussed in Chapter 13). Business growth might also be essential if the business is to manage change successfully and deal with many of the inherent uncertainties of the business environment.

In this chapter we shall consider the various growth strategies open to firms and assess their respective advantages and disadvantages. First, however, we need to look at the relationship between a firm's growth and its profitability and also at those factors that are likely to constrain the growth of the business.

15.1 GROWTH AND PROFITABILITY

In using traditional theories of the firm, economists often assume that there is a limit to the expansion of the firm: that there is a level of output beyond which profits will start to fall. The justification for this view can be found on both the supply side and the demand side.

On the supply side, it is assumed that, if a firm grows beyond a certain size, it will experience rising long-run average costs. In other words, the long-run average cost curve is assumed to be U-shaped, possibly with a horizontal section at the bottom (see pages 163–4). This argument often is based on the assumption that it is *managerial* diseconomies of scale that start driving costs up once a firm has expanded beyond a certain point: there are no more plant economies to be achieved (the firm has passed its **minimum efficient scale (MES)** – see Box 9.4; instead, the firm is faced with a more complex form of organisation, with longer lines of management, more difficult labour relations and a greater possibility of lack of effort going unnoticed.

On the demand side, it is assumed that the firm faces a downward-sloping demand curve (and hence marginal revenue curve) for its product. Although this demand curve can be shifted by advertising and other forms of product promotion, finite demand naturally places a constraint on the expansion of the firm.

These two assumptions can be challenged, however. On the supply side, with a multidivisional form of organisation and systems in place for monitoring performance, it is quite possible to avoid diseconomies of scale.

As far as demand is concerned, although the demand (or at least its rate of growth) for any one product may be limited, the firm could diversify into new markets.

It is thus incorrect to say that there is a limit to the size of a business. An individual business may be able to go on expanding its capacity or diversifying its interests indefinitely. There does, however, exist an upper limit on the firm's *rate* of growth – the *speed* at which it can expand its capacity or diversify. The reason behind this constraint is that growth is determined by the profitability of the business. The growth rate/profitability relationship can operate in two ways:

- *Growth depends upon profitability*. The more profitable the firm, the more likely it is to be able to raise finance for investment.

- *Growth affects profitability*. In the short run, growth above a certain rate may reduce profitability. Some of the finance for the investment necessary to achieve growth may have to come from the firm's sales revenue. A firm wishing to expand its operations in an existing market will require greater advertising and marketing; and a firm seeking to diversify may have to spend considerable sums on market research and employing managers with specialist knowledge and skills. In both cases, investment is likely to be needed in new plant and machinery. In other words, the firm may have to sacrifice some of its short-run profits for the long-run gains that greater growth might yield.

But what about long-run profits? Will growth increase or decrease these? The answer depends on the nature of the growth. If growth leads to expansion into new markets in which demand is growing, to increased market power or to increased economies of scale, then growth may well increase long-run profits – not only total profits, but the rate of profit on capital or the ratio of profits to revenue. If, however, growth leads to diseconomies of scale or to investment in risky projects, then growth may well be at the expense of long-run profitability.

To summarise: greater profitability may lead to higher growth, but higher growth, at least in the short run, may be at the expense of profits.

15.2 CONSTRAINTS ON GROWTH

However much a firm may want to grow, it simply might not be possible. There are several factors that can restrict the ability of a business to expand.

Pause for thought

Before you read on, what constraints on its growth do you feel a business might experience?

Financial conditions. Financial conditions determine the ability of a firm to fund its growth. Growth can be financed in three distinct ways: from internal funds, from borrowing or from the issue of new shares.

The largest source of finance for investment in the UK is **internal funds** (i.e. ploughed-back profit). The principal limitation in achieving growth via this means is that such funds are linked to business profitability and this, in turn, is subject to the cyclical nature of economic activity – to the booms and

slumps that the economy experiences. Profitability tends to fall in a recession along with the level of sales. In such times, it is often difficult for a firm to afford new investment.

The *borrowing* of finance to fund expansion may be constrained by a wide range of factors, from the availability of finance in the banking sector to the creditworthiness of the business.

The *issuing of new shares* to fund growth depends not only on confidence within the stock market in general, but

Definitions

Minimum efficient scale (MES) The size of the individual factory or of the whole firm, beyond which no significant additional economies of scale can be gained. For an individual factory, the MES is known as the *minimum efficient plant size (MEPS)*.

Internal funds Funds used for business expansion that come from ploughed-back profit.

on the stock market's assessment of the potential performance of the individual firm in particular. It should be noted that finance from this source is not open to all firms. For most small and medium-sized enterprises (i.e. those not listed on the Stock Exchange), raising finance through issuing new shares must be done privately and, normally, this source of finance is very limited and hence difficult to access.

(We will examine the financing of investment in more detail in sections 19.4 and 19.5.)

Shareholder confidence. Whichever way growth is financed – internal funds, borrowing or new share issues – the likely outcome in the short run is a reduction in the firm's share dividend. If the firm *retains* too much *profit,* there will be less to pay out in dividends. Similarly, if the firm *borrows* too much, the interest payments that it incurs are likely to make it difficult to maintain the level of dividends to shareholders. Finally, if it attempts to raise capital by a *new issue of shares,* the distributed profits will have to be divided between a larger number of shares.

Whichever way it finances investment, therefore, the more it invests, the more the dividends on shares in the short run will probably fall. Unless shareholders are confident that *long*-run profits and hence dividends will rise again, thus causing the share price to remain high in the long run, they may well sell their shares. This will cause share prices to fall. If they fall too far, the firm runs the risk of being taken over and some managers risk losing their jobs.

This risk of takeover gives rise to a concept referred to as the **takeover constraint**. The takeover constraint requires that the growth-maximising firm needs to distribute sufficient profits to avoid being taken over. Hence the rate of business growth is influenced not only by market opportunities but also by shareholder demands and expectations and the fear of takeover.

The converse of this situation is also true. If a business fails to grow fast enough, it may be that a potential buyer sees the firm as a valuable acquisition, whose resources might be put to more profitable use over the longer term. Hence businesses must avoid being overcautious and paying high share dividends, but, as a result, failing to invest and failing to exploit their true potential.

The likelihood of takeover depends in large part on the stock market's assessment of the firm's potential: how is the firm's investment strategy perceived to affect its future performance and profitability? The views of the stock market are reflected in the **valuation ratio** of the firm. This is the ratio of the stock market value of the firm's shares (the number of issued shares times the current share price) to the book value of the firm's assets. This is sometimes referred to as the **price to book ratio**. A low ratio means that the real assets of the business are effectively undervalued: that they can be purchased at a low market price. The

business is thus likely to be more attractive to potential bidders. Conversely, firms with a high valuation ratio are seen as overvalued and are unlikely to be the target of takeover bids.

In the long run, a rapidly growing firm may find its profits increasing, especially if it can achieve economies of scale and a bigger share of the market. These profits can then be used to finance further growth. The firm will still not have unlimited finance, however, and therefore will still be faced by the takeover constraint if it attempts to grow too rapidly.

Demand conditions. Our analysis of business growth has shown that finance for growth is largely dependent upon the business's profitability. The more profit it makes, the more it can draw on internal funds; the more likely financial institutions will be to lend; and the more readily will new share issues be purchased by the market. The profitability of a business is, in turn, dependent upon market demand and demand growth. If the firm is operating in an expanding market, profits are likely to grow and finance will be relatively easy to obtain.

If, on the other hand, the firm's existing market is not expanding, it will find that profits and sales are unlikely to rise unless it diversifies into related or non-related markets. One means of overcoming this demand constraint is to expand overseas, either by attempting to increase export sales or by locating new production facilities in foreign markets.

Managerial conditions. The growth of a firm is usually a planned process and, as such, must be managed. But the management team might lack entrepreneurial vision or various organisational skills.

Equally, as with other resources within the business, the management team might grow or, alternatively, its composition might change in order to reflect the new needs of the growing business. However, new managers take time to be incorporated into, and become part of, an effective management team. They must undergo a period of training and become integrated into their new firm and its culture. It takes time to integrate into a team of managers already

---

Definitions

Takeover constraint The effect that the fear of being taken over has on a firm's willingness to undertake projects that reduce distributed profits.

Valuation ratio or **price to book ratio** The ratio of stock market value to book value. The stock market value is an assessment of the firm's past and anticipated future performance. The book value is a calculation of the current value of the firm's assets.

accustomed to working together. The rate of growth of business is thus constrained by this process of managerial expansion.

In the sections below we will explore the alternative growth strategies open to businesses and the various advantages and limitations that such strategies present.

15.3 ALTERNATIVE GROWTH STRATEGIES

In pursuit of growth, a firm will seek to increase its markets: whether at home or internationally. In either case, the firm will need to increase its capacity. This may be achieved by internal or external expansion.

Internal expansion. This is where a business looks to expand its productive capacity by adding to existing plant or by building new plant. There are three main ways of doing this:

■ The firm can expand or *differentiate its product* within existing markets, by, for example, updating or restyling its product or improving its technical characteristics.

■ Alternatively, the business might seek to expand via *vertical integration*. This involves the firm expanding within the same product market, but at a different stage of production. For example, a car manufacturer might wish to produce its own components. This is known as 'backward' vertical integration (sometimes called 'upstream' integration). Alternatively, it might decide to distribute and sell its own car models. This is described as 'forward' (or 'downstream') vertical integration.

■ As a third option, the business might seek to expand outside of its current product range and move into new markets. This is known as a process of *diversification*.

External expansion. This is where the firm engages with another in order to expand its activities. It may do this in one of two ways:

■ It can join with another firm to form a single legal identity either by merger or by acquisition (takeover).

■ Alternatively, it may form a *strategic alliance* with one or more firms. Here firms retain their separate identities.

The term 'strategic alliance' is used to cover a wide range of alternative collaborative arrangements. A strategic alliance might involve a joint venture between one or more firms to complete a particular project or to produce a particular product. It might also involve firms making an informal or a contractual agreement to supply or distribute goods. A key characteristic of a strategic alliance is that the parties involved retain their own legal identity outside of the alliance.

As with internal expansion, external expansion, whether by merger or alliance, can be vertical or horizontal, or involve diversification. In the case of mergers, we

use the terms 'horizontal merger', 'vertical merger' and 'conglomerate merger'.

Figure 15.1 outlines the main routes to a firm's growth and the various stages at which it can take place. These will be considered in the following sections.

A further dimension of business growth that we should note at this point is that all of the above-mentioned growth paths can be achieved by the business looking beyond its national markets. In other words, the business might decide to become multinational and invest in expansion overseas. This raises a further set of advantages, issues and problems that a business might face. (These will be discussed in Chapter 23 when we consider multinational business.)

We have already considered business expansion through product differentiation (see Chapter 8). In this chapter, therefore, we will focus on the other possibilities facing the firm: internal expansion via vertical integration or diversification, and external expansion via merger or takeover (whether horizontal, vertical or conglomerate). We will also investigate the increasing tendency for business to enter into strategic alliances with other businesses as an alternative to all of the above.

Definitions

Internal expansion Where a business increases its productive capacity by adding to existing plant or by building new plant.

Product differentiation Where a firm's product is in some way distinct from its rivals' products.

Vertical integration A business growth strategy that involves expanding within an existing market, but at a different stage of production. Vertical integration can be 'forward', such as moving into distribution or retail, or 'backward', such as expanding into extracting raw materials or producing components.

Diversification A business growth strategy in which a business expands into new markets outside of its current interests.

External expansion Where business growth is achieved by merger, takeover, joint venture or an agreement with one or more other firms.

Strategic alliance Where two or more firms work together, formally or informally, to achieve a mutually desirable goal.

Figure 15.1 Alternative growth strategy

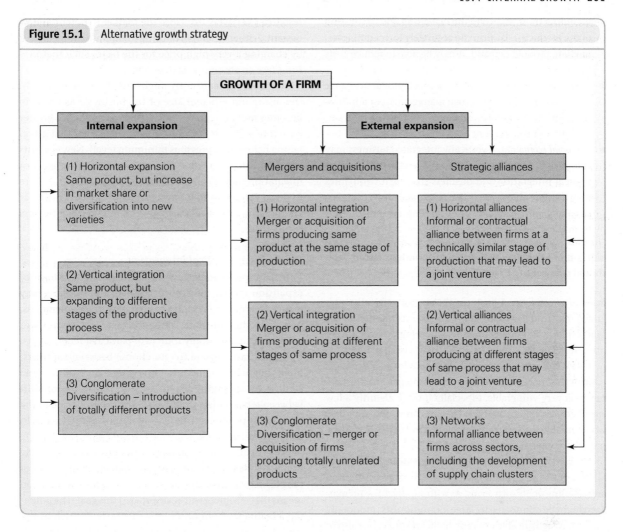

Firms can extend their product range in a number of ways and for a number of reasons. One method is that of horizontal expansion. This involves the firm producing multiple products within a similar and related activity for which there may be economies of scope (see page 192). Likewise, there may be gains for the firm in providing different varieties of the product (as discussed in Chapter 8). Given our extensive discussions on this method of internal growth, therefore, we concentrate in the next two sections on vertical integration and conglomerate diversification.

Growth through vertical integration

We can identify a number of specific reasons why a business might wish to expand via vertical integration. (These reasons also apply to external expansion by merger or acquisition.)

KI 22 *Greater efficiency*. When vertical integration results in a fall in
p191 a business's long-run average costs, it is effectively

experiencing various economies of scale. We can identify four categories under which vertical integration might lead to cost savings:

■ *Production economies*. These occur when a business, through integration, lowers its costs by performing *complementary* stages of production within a single business unit. The classic example of this is the steel manufacturer combining the furnacing and milling stages of production, saving the costs that would have been required to reheat the iron had such operations been undertaken by independent businesses. Clearly, for most firms, performing more than one stage on a single site is likely to reduce transport costs, as semi-finished products no longer have to be moved from one plant to another.

■ *Co-ordination economies*. Such economies arise from the internal structure of the business and its ability to transfer intermediate products between its various divisions. The business is able to avoid purchasing and selling expenses, including those related to the marketing and advertising of the product(s). If a firm can accurately forecast its intermediate product demand, it may be able to reduce costs by holding lower stocks of intermediate products.

- *Managerial economies.* Even though each production stage or division might have its own management or administrative team, economies can be gained from having a single source of supervision.
- *Financial economies.* A vertically integrated business may gain various financial economies. Given the link between vertical integration and business size, such companies may be more able to negotiate favourable deals from key suppliers and secure lower borrowing rates of interest from the financial markets.

(For a more detailed analysis of economies of scale, you should refer back to Chapter 9.)

Reduced uncertainty. A business that is not vertically integrated may find itself subject to various uncertainties in the marketplace. Examples include: uncertainty over future price movements, supply reliability or access to markets.

Backward vertical integration will enable the business to control its supply chain. Without such integration, the firm may feel very vulnerable, especially if there are only a few suppliers within the market. In such cases, the suppliers would be able to exert considerable control over price. Alternatively, suppliers may be unreliable.

Forward vertical integration creates greater certainty in so far as it gives the business guaranteed access to distribution and retailing on its own terms. As with supply, forward markets might be dominated by large monopsonists (monopoly buyers), which are able not only to dictate price, but also to threaten market foreclosure (being shut out from a market). Forward vertical integration can remove the possibility of such events occurring.

Innovation. Having a more integrated supply chain may lead to more innovation and higher rates of technical change. Enclosing multiple stages of production within the same business should improve communication between component producers and consumers. Dialogue between component designers, manufacturers and users leads to increased possibilities for the development of productivity-improving innovations.

Monopoly power. Forward or backward vertical integration may allow the business to acquire a greater monopoly/monopsony position in the market. Depending upon the type of vertical integration, the business might be able to set prices both for final products and for factor inputs.

Barriers to entry. Vertical integration may give the firm greater power in the market by enabling it to erect entry barriers to potential competitors. For example, a firm that undertakes backward vertical integration and acquires a key input

resource effectively can close the market to potential new entrants, either by simply refusing to supply a competitor or by charging a very high price for the factor such that new firms face an absolute cost disadvantage.

A further barrier to entry might arise from an increase in the minimum efficient size of the business. As the firm becomes more integrated, it is likely to experience greater economies of scale (i.e. long-run average costs that go on falling below their previous minimum level). New entrants are then forced to come into the market at the level of integration that existing firms are operating under. Failure to do so will mean that new entrants will be operating at an instant cost disadvantage and hence will be less competitive.

Problems with vertical integration

The major problem with vertical integration as a form of expansion is that the security it gives the business may reduce its ability to respond to changing market demands. A business that integrates, either backward or forward, ties itself to particular supply sources or particular retail outlets. If, by contrast, it were free to choose between suppliers, inputs might be obtained at a lower price than the firm could achieve by supplying itself. Equally, the ability to shift between retail outlets would allow the firm to locate in the best market positions. This may not be possible if it is tied to its own retail network.

As with all business strategy, one course of action may well preclude the pursuit of an alternative. The decision of the business to expand its operations via vertical integration means that resources will be diverted to this goal. The potential advantages from other growth strategies, such as the spreading of risk through diversification, are lost. This is not a problem of vertical integration as such, but it represents the opportunity costs of selecting this strategy to the *exclusion* of others.

KI 3
p19

Tapered vertical integration

How can a firm gain the benefits of vertical integration but avoid the costs? One alternative means of expansion is **tapered vertical integration**. This is where a business begins producing some of an input itself, while still buying some from another firm (often through subcontracting). This growth strategy is different from a situation where you are relying totally on subcontractors to provide supply (which we will explore in section 15.7). For example, Coca-Cola

---

Definition

Tapered vertical integration Where a firm is partially integrated with an earlier stage of production: where it produces *some* of an input itself and buys some from another firm.

and Pepsi are large vertically integrated enterprises. They have, as part of their operations, wholly owned bottling subsidiaries. However, in certain markets, they subcontract to independent bottlers both to produce and to market their product.

The advantages of both making and buying an input are:

- The firm, by making an input or providing a service in-house, will have information concerning the costs and profitability of such an operation. Such information helps in the negotiation of contracts with independent producers. In addition, the firm will be able to use the threat of producing more itself to ensure that independent suppliers do not exploit their supply position, which they might be able to do if they held a monopolistic position within the supply chain. The firm is not totally at the mercy of an independent third party over which it has no control.
- The firm does not require the same level of capital outlay that would be required if it were to rely solely on an input or service produced by itself. As such, it is able to externalise some of the costs and risks of its business operations.

The major drawback with this growth strategy is that shared production might fail to generate economies of scale and is hence less efficient than might otherwise be the case. In other words, if Coca-Cola bottled all its own cola, then it might achieve significantly greater economies of scale than by sharing bottling with other firms. None might be large enough to achieve the efficiency gains that a single production site might generate.

Other significant costs with subcontracting are largely borne by the firm doing the subcontracted work, not by the contractor. Many small and medium-sized enterprises (SMEs), which might see doing subcontracted work for a large firm as a means of expanding their business and hence of growing themselves, find that the relationship between them and the large firm is often a highly unequal one. SMEs find that they not only bear some of the large firm's risk, but are also easily expendable. Such vulnerability intensifies, the greater the proportion of the SME's production that is done for a particular customer. When a high level of reliance occurs, the SME finds that its business is, in essence, vertically integrated with its customer, but without the benefits that such a position should confer.

Growth through diversification

Diversification is the process whereby a firm shifts from being a single-product to a multi-product producer. Such products need not cover similar activities. We can, in fact, identify four directions in which diversification might be undertaken:

- using the existing technological base and market area;
- using the existing technological base and new market area;
- using a new technological base and existing market area;
- using a new technological base and new market area.

Categorising the strategies in this way would suggest that the direction of diversification is dependent largely upon both the nature of technology and the market opportunities open to the firm. But the ability to capitalise on these features depends on the experience, skills and market knowledge of the managers of the business. In general, diversification is likely to occur in areas where the business can use and adapt existing technology and knowledge to its advantage.

A good example of a highly diversified company is Virgin. The brand began as the name of a small record shop in London. It now embraces an airline, trains, banking and finance, gift 'experiences', holidays, hotels, soft drinks, mobile phones, a digital television service, Internet service provision, radio, online books, an online wine store, cosmetics, health clubs, balloon rides and, even, with its Virgin Galactic brand, space travel! Another example is the 'easyGroup': i.e. easyJet, easyGym, easyHotel and easyBus.

Why diversification?

There are three principal factors that might encourage a business to diversify:

- *Stability.* So long as a business produces a single product in a single market, it is vulnerable to changes in that market's conditions. If a farmer produces nothing but potatoes, and the potato harvest fails, the farmer is ruined. If, however, the farmer produces a whole range of vegetable products, or even diversifies into livestock, then he or she is less subject to the forces of nature and the unpredictability of the market. Diversification therefore enables the business to *spread risk.*
- *Maintaining profitability.* Businesses might also be encouraged to diversify if they wish to protect existing profit levels. It may be that the market in which a business is currently located is saturated and that current profitability is perceived to be at a maximum. Alternatively, the business might be in a market where demand is stagnant or declining. In such cases, the business is likely to see a greater return on its investment by diversifying into new product ranges located in dynamic expanding markets.
- *Growth.* If the current market is saturated, stagnant or in decline, diversification might be the only avenue open to the business if it wishes to maintain a high growth performance. In other words, it is not only the level of profits that may be limited in the current market, but also the growth of sales.

15.5 EXTERNAL GROWTH THROUGH MERGER

A *merger* is a situation in which, as a result of mutual agreement, two firms decide to bring together their business operations. A merger is distinct from a **takeover** in so far as a takeover involves one firm bidding for another's shares (often against the will of the directors of the target firm). One firm thereby acquires another.

The distinction between merger and takeover is an important one. For example, an important difference is that, in order to acquire a firm, a business will require finance, whereas a merger simply might involve two firms swapping their existing shares for shares in the newly created merged company. A further difference might concern managerial relations between the two businesses. A merger implies that managers, through negotiation, have reached an agreement acceptable to both sides, whereas a takeover involves one group of managers, working in opposition to another group, looking to fend off the aggressor. The acquired firm usually finds its management team dismissed following such action!

In order to avoid confusion at this stage, we will use the term 'merger' to refer to *both* mergers ('mutual agreements') and takeovers ('acquisitions'), although, where necessary, we will draw a distinction between the two. Before proceeding, we need to give some consideration to the types of merger and acquisition. We distinguished three types in Figure 15.1.

A *horizontal merger*. This where two firms at the same stage of production within an industry merge.

- In February 2015, Facebook completed the acquisition of WhatsApp Messenger, another social media business, for $19 billion.
- A more recent example is the £93 million acquisition of Treetops Nurseries by Busy Bees Childcare in March 2017. Busy Bees is one of the five largest nursery groups in the UK and the takeover increases its number of nurseries to 329.
- Recently, there have been several horizontal mergers in the gambling industry. For example, in March 2018, the Competition and Markets Authority cleared the £4 billion takeover of Ladbrokes Coral by GVC Holdings. Both businesses supply online betting and gaming services.

A *vertical merger*. This is where businesses at different stages of production within the same industry merge. As such, we might identify backward and forward vertical mergers for any given firm involved.

- One very high-profile case is the proposed takeover of Time Warner by AT&T in an $85.4 billion deal. AT&T is the biggest telecommunication business in the world and is the largest provider of fixed-line telephone services and the second largest provider of mobile telephone services in the USA. Time Warner is the third biggest entertainment company in the world and offers a broad range of TV content. It owns HBO (producer of Game of Thrones), Warner Brothers and CNN. In November 2017, the US competition authorities announced that they were going to try to block the deal – the first time this had happened in the case of a vertical merger for 40 years.
- Another example occurred in December 2017, when CVS a US-based pharmacy retailer with a large number of shops, purchased Aetna, one of the USA's largest health insurers for $69 billion.
- In March 2018, the European Commission approved the merger between the Italian business Luxottica and the French firm Essilor. The €48 billion transaction is one of the biggest ever cross-border deals in Europe. Luxottica is the world's largest producer of eyewear frames and owner of brands such as Ray-Ban, Oakley and Sunglass. Essilor is the world's largest manufacturer of lenses.

A *conglomerate merger*. This is where firms in totally unrelated industries merge. These were once common in the 1960s and 1970s as firms tried to diversify, but are far less popular today.

- Two businesses that have recently acquired a large number of companies in a range of different sectors are Amazon and Google. For example, in 2014, Amazon purchased Twitch (a video games business) while Google purchased Nest (a thermostats producer). In 2017, Amazon acquired Whole Foods in a $13.7 billion deal. Whole Foods is an organic food chain that has around 460 stores.

Why merge?

Why do firms want to merge with or take over others? Is it purely that they want to grow: are mergers simply evidence of the hypothesis that firms are growth maximisers? Or are there other motives that influence the predatory drive?

Definitions

Merger The outcome of a mutual agreement made by two firms to combine their business activities.

Takeover Where one business acquires another. A takeover may not necessarily involve mutual agreement between the two parties. In such cases, the takeover might be viewed as 'hostile'.

Horizontal merger Where two firms in the same industry at the same stage of the production process merge.

Vertical merger Where two firms in the same industry at different stages of the production process merge.

Conglomerate merger Where two firms in different industries merge.

Merger for growth. Mergers provide a much quicker means to growth than internal expansion. Not only does the firm acquire new capacity, but it also acquires additional consumer demand. Building up this level of consumer demand by *internal* expansion might have taken a considerable length of time.

For example, Google has used mergers as a key part of its growth strategy. It has purchased over 200 companies as part of its expansion plans in sectors such as robotics, mapping, video broadcasting, telecommunications and advertising. Some of the bigger deals included the acquisitions of YouTube for $1.65bn, DoubleClick for $3.1bn and Motorola for $12.5bn.

Facebook has also used mergers and acquisitions (M&As) as a key part of its growth strategy. Acquisitions include WhatsApp for $19 billion, Instagram for $1 billion, Atlas Advertiser suite for less than $1billion and Oculus VR for $2 billion.[1]

Merger for economies of scale. Once the merger has taken place, the constituent parts can be reorganised through a process of 'rationalisation'. The result can be a reduction in costs. For example, only one head office will now be needed. On the marketing side, the two parts of the newly merged company may now share distribution and retail channels, benefiting from each other's knowledge and operation in distinct market segments or geographical locations.

A company that has built a reputation for doing this successfully is Anheuser-Busch InBev – the largest brewing business in the world. In October 2017, it announced cost savings of $3.2 billion following its acquisition of SABMiller. In its previous takeovers of Anheuser-Busch in 2008 and Grupo Modelo in 2013, the company exceeded its initial cost saving targets by 50 per cent and 65 per cent respectively.

> ### Pause for thought
>
> *Which of the three types of merger (horizontal, vertical and conglomerate) are most likely to lead to (a) reductions in average costs; (b) increased market power?*

KI 21
p 184 *Merger for monopoly power.* Here the motive is to reduce competition and thereby gain greater market power and larger profits. With less competition, the firm will face a less elastic demand and be able to charge a higher percentage above marginal cost. What is more, the new more powerful company will be in a stronger position to regulate entry into the market by erecting effective entry barriers, thereby enhancing its monopoly position yet further.

Merger for increased market valuation. A merger can benefit shareholders of *both* firms if it leads to an increase in the

[1]https://wikivividly.com/wiki/
List_of_mergers_and_acquisitions_by_Facebook.

stock market valuation of the merged firm. If both sets of shareholders believe that they will make a capital gain on their shares, then they are more likely to give the go-ahead for the merger.

Merger to reduce uncertainty. Firms face uncertainty at two levels. The first is in their own markets. The behaviour of rivals may be highly unpredictable. Mergers, by reducing the number of rivals, can correspondingly reduce uncertainty. At the same time, they can reduce the *costs* of competition (e.g. reducing the need to advertise).

The second source of uncertainty is the economic environment. In a period of rapid change, such as often accompanies a boom, firms may seek to protect themselves by merging with others.

Merger due to opportunity. A widely held theory concerning merger activity is that it occurs simply as a consequence of opportunities that may arise: opportunities that often are unforeseen. Therefore, business mergers are largely unplanned and, as such, virtually impossible to predict. Dynamic business organisations will be constantly on the lookout for new business opportunities as they arise.

Other motives. Other motives for mergers include:

- getting bigger so as to become less likely to be taken over oneself;
- merging with another firm so as to defend it from an unwanted predator (the 'White Knight' strategy);
- asset stripping, where a firm takes over another and then breaks it up, selling off the profitable bits and probably closing down the remainder;
- empire building, where owners or managers favour takeovers because of the power or prestige of owning or controlling several (preferably well-known) companies;
- geographical expansion, whose motive is to broaden the geographical base of the company by merging with a firm in a different part of the country or the world;
- reducing levels of taxation: it has been argued that a number of takeovers in the pharmaceutical industry have been motivated by the desire to reduce the company's tax bill. Under certain conditions, if a US firm purchases a business outside of the USA, it can switch its residence for tax purposes to the country of the firm it has acquired. This was one reason why the US pharmaceutical company Pfizer made a $100 billion bid to purchase the UK company AstraZeneca in April 2014. The move could have cut its rate of corporation tax from 27 per cent to 20 per cent. The bid was rejected. Pfizer attempted a similar move to purchase the Irish-based business, Allergan, but, in 2016, once again the deal collapsed.

Mergers generally will have the effect of increasing the market power of those firms involved. This could lead to less choice and higher prices for the consumer. For this reason, mergers have become the target for government competition policy. (Such policy is the subject of Chapter 21.)

BOX 15.1	GLOBAL MERGER ACTIVITY

An international perspective

What have been the trends, patterns and driving factors in mergers and acquisitions[1] (M&As) around the world in recent years? An overview of cross-border M&A is given in diagram (a).

The 1990s

The early 1990s saw relatively low M&A activity as the world was in recession, but, as world economic growth picked up, so worldwide M&A activity increased. Economic growth was particularly rapid in the USA, which became the major target for acquisitions.

There was also an acceleration in the process of 'globalisation'. With the dismantling of trade barriers around the world and increasing financial deregulation, international competition increased. Companies felt the need to become bigger in order to compete more effectively.

In Europe, M&A activity was boosted by the development of the single European market, which came into being in January 1993. Companies took advantage of the abolition of trade barriers in the EU, which made it easier for them to operate on an EU-wide basis. Strong economic growth experienced throughout the EU, combined with the arrival of the euro, led to a booming M&A market in the late 1990s.

By 2000, the number of annual worldwide M&As was some three times the level of 1990. Very large deals included a €29.4 billion merger of pharmaceutical companies Zeneca of the UK and Astra of Sweden in 1998, a €205 billion takeover of telecoms giant Mannesmann of Germany by Vodafone of the UK in 1999 and a €50.8 billion takeover of Orange™ of the UK by France Telecom in 2000.

Other sectors in which merger activity was widespread included financial services and the privatised utilities sector. In the UK, most of the privatised water and electricity companies were taken over by French and US buyers, attracted by the sector's monopoly profits.

The 2000s

The number of cross-border deals peaked at 6497 in 2000 and had a combined total value of over $960 billion. However, a worldwide economic slowdown after 2000 led to a fall in both the number and value of mergers throughout most of the world. The value of cross-border M&As in 2003 was just over $165 billion – a fall of 82.8 per cent from the peak of three years earlier. Activity began to increase again after 2003 as economic growth in the world economy began to accelerate. Two major target regions were (a) the 10 countries that joined the EU in 2004 plus Russia and (b) Asian countries, especially India and China.

In 2007, the number of cross-border mergers reached a new peak of 7582 with a combined total value of $1033 billion. However, the Great Recession of 2008–9 led to both the number and value of cross-border deals falling dramatically. Recession is a difficult time for deal making and the number of withdrawn mergers – that is, where two firms agree in principle to merge but later pull out of a deal – increased. As diagram (a) shows, the value of cross-border M&As in 2009 was just $288 billion – a fall of over 72 per cent from the record high in 2007.

---

[1] By 'acquisitions' we mean takeovers or the acquiring of at least 5 per cent of a company's shares.

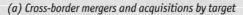

(a) Cross-border mergers and acquisitions by target

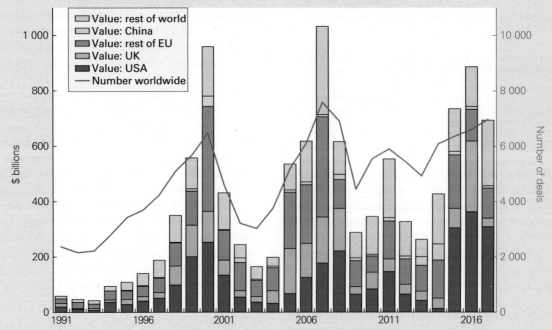

Note: The data cover only those deals that involve an acquisition of an equity of more than 10%

Source: 'Cross Border Mergers & Acquisitions', *World Investment Report Annex Tables* (UNCTAD, June 2018), Tables 5 and 7

The 2010s

With the faltering recovery of 2010 there was a small increase in global M&A. However, the Eurozone crisis and fears about the state of the public finances of the USA had a negative impact on M&A activity in 2012 and 2013.

Economic growth and growing business confidence saw M&A activity grow quickly again in 2015 and 2016. The combined market value of cross-border deals in these two years was $735 billion and $869 billion respectively – the highest values since the financial crisis. The total value of all M&As reached $3.5 trillion in 2017 – the fourth year in a row the figure has surpassed $3 trillion. The ability of firms to borrow money cheaply, because of historically low interest rates, slow rates of internal growth and large cash reserves were seen as important drivers behind this increase. A large number of mergers also appear to be defensive moves by firms facing the threat of new competition from Amazon, Facebook and Netflix.

Given the uncertainty generated by the Brexit vote in the UK and the election of President Trump in the USA, many observers were surprised to see the continued strong growth in merger activity in both 2016 and 2017.

Furthermore, the worldwide pattern of cross-border M&A activity had changed between the mid-1990s and the mid-2010s. Diagram (b) illustrates three interesting trends when comparing the period from 1993 to 1997 with that from 2013 to 2017:

■ First, North America saw a rise in its average global share of cross-border M&As from 20.4 per cent in the mid-1990s to 24.9 per cent in the mid-2010s. Its share measured by value also increased from 31.1 per cent to 33.2 per cent. However, this was caused by it having an unusually high share of cross-border M&A activity by value of 43.4 per cent in 2015 and 42.3 per cent in 2016 and 43.1

per cent in 2017. In 2013 and 2014 its average share by value was just 18.6 per cent.

■ Second, Asian countries (excluding Japan) saw a dramatic growth in their share of the number of cross-border M&As from 8.3 per cent in the mid-1990s to 13.6 per cent in the mid-2010s. The growth in their share by value increased from 4.5 per cent to 12.9 per cent. Two nations in the region, China and India, have been particularly attractive because their economies are growing rapidly; they have low costs, notably cheap skilled labour and low tax rates; and they are becoming more receptive to all forms of foreign direct investment, including M&As. However, M&A investment in both countries fell significantly in 2015 and 2017 – down from $56.8 billion to $12.4 billion in China and $7.9 billion to $1.3 billion in India. The downward trend continued in China in 2017 – down to $11.1 billion and $8.3 billion respectively – whereas in India it rebounded back up to $8.0 billion and $22.8 billion respectively.

■ Third, EU countries saw a reduction in their share of the number of cross-border M&As from 51.4 per cent in the mid-1990s to 41.2 per cent in the mid-2010s; and a fall in their share of the value from 44.1 per cent to 37.4 per cent over the same periods.

Different types and consequences of cross-border M&A activity

The long-run trend is for an increasing number of cross-border M&As as globalisation gathers pace. In the mid-1990s, they accounted for about 16 per cent of all deals, whereas they accounted for approximately 40 per cent in 2016.

The Office for National Statistics reported that, between 2013 and 2017, the average number of acquisitions by UK companies abroad or by foreign companies in the UK was 311 per annum. The figure for internal deals was roughly the same over the same period at 292 per annum. However, the value of

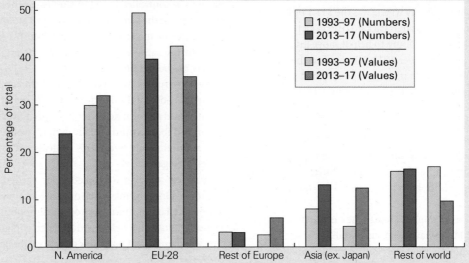

(b) Cross-border mergers and acquisitions by target region (% of total number and value)

Source: 'Cross Border Mergers & Acquisitions', *World Investment Report Annex Tables* (UNCTAD, June 2018), Tables 5 and 7

cross-border deals tends to be much greater and averaged £91.9 billion per annum between 2013 and 2017. The figure for domestic deals was £13.2 billion.[2]

Cross-border M&As can be an effective strategy for firms that want to gain large-scale entry into an overseas market. One motivating factor for AB-InBev's takeover of SABMiller is to gain access to the fast-growing beer market in Africa. However, these types of takeover can raise concerns about national sovereignty: i.e. the extent to which governments have control over their industrial base when foreign firms own businesses in the domestic economy. For example, following concerns expressed by the South African Government, AB-InBev made a commitment to maintain employment in that country at the same level for at least five years.

Horizontal cross-border mergers. These are the most common type of merger. A horizontal merger or acquisition of a domestic firm by an overseas firm may not alter the number of firms competing in the sector if the foreign firm merely replaces an existing firm. Its presence may generate greater competition and innovation in the industry if the new owners bring fresh ideas.

If the foreign firm is already present in the domestic economy and it then takes over a rival, the number of firms in the industry is reduced. This could lead to less competition and higher prices. Alternatively, the newly merged firm may benefit from lower costs that it can pass on, at least in part, to its customers in the form of lower prices.

Vertical cross-border mergers. Vertical cross-border M&As are less common than their horizontal counterparts but also come with potential costs as well as benefits. For example, a backward vertical M&A can help a firm compete globally by reducing its supply costs. Unfortunately, this may be achieved by imposing harsh terms on suppliers in the domestic economy where it operates. Forward vertical M&A into the retail sector can help a foreign firm secure a domestic market and offer customers a better service. However, they may also move away from supplying rival retailers on comparable terms so that customer choice is reduced.

Conglomerate cross-border mergers. There was a wave of these mergers in the 1960s as firms tried to diversify. The results in terms of lower costs and/or growth tended to be very disappointing and they are now far less popular. The tendency instead has been for many companies to try to become more focused, by selling off parts of the business that are not seen as 'core activities'. For example, in October 2012, the conglomerate Kraft Foods split its business into a global snack brand, named Mondelez International, and a food business, named Kraft Foods Group. In 2015, Kraft Foods Group merged with Heinz to become Kraft Heinz. In 2017, Kraft Heinz failed in its attempt to acquire Unilever.

There is no doubt that many M&As have been good for society and are a sign of a healthy capital market. However, evidence suggests that approximately two-thirds of deals fail to achieve the anticipated gains.

 Are the motives for merger likely to be different in a recession from in a period of rapid economic growth?

 Use newspaper and other resources to identify the costs and benefits of a recent cross-border merger or acquisition.

[2]*Mergers and Acquisitions involving UK Companies, Q4 2017*, ONS (March 2018).

Do mergers result in the anticipated gains?

The record of many mergers and acquisitions appears to be rather disappointing. An extreme example of where things appear to have gone badly wrong was the $11.1 billion takeover of Autonomy by Hewlett Packard (HP) in October 2011. HP had purchased Autonomy to help it move into the software market. In November 2012, HP shocked the business world by announcing that the company it had purchased just a year earlier had fallen in value by $8.8 billion. HP accused the management at Autonomy of using illegal accounting activities before the takeover in order deliberately to inflate the true value of the business. Executives at Autonomy accused HP of completely mismanaging the integration of Autonomy into its business after the merger. At the time of writing, both parties were involved in a bitter legal case.

The previous example is an extreme case, so how can you judge if most M&As have been successful?

One common method is to look at what happens to the share price of the acquiring company both before and after the takeover. If the merged company manages to attain all of the perceived benefits from the deal (economies of scale, greater revenue, etc.), then it should become more profitable and this should be reflected in the share price.

However, other factors will affect share prices and this needs to be controlled for. Most studies use the share price of other firms in the same sector as a control group. Thus, if the share price of the merged firm outperforms that of other firms in the same sector, then it can be argued that the merger has been a success.

Recent studies that have adopted this approach have found that about a third of deals increase shareholder value; about a third perform no better than other firms in the same sector; and about a third actually perform worse. This implies that approximately two-thirds of deals fail to achieve the anticipated gains.

A survey of over 350 executives carried out by the Economics Intelligence Unit in 2012 identified the 5 most important factors that resulted in disappointing M&As. These are illustrated below with the percentage of respondents who considered it a major or very major factor:

- Due diligence failed to highlight critical issues (59 per cent).
- Overestimated synergies: i.e. cost reductions, growth in revenue (55 per cent).

- Failed to recognise insufficient strategic fit (49 per cent).
- Failed to assess cultural fit during (46 per cent).

- Problems integrating management teams and retaining staff (46 per cent).

15.6 EXTERNAL GROWTH THROUGH STRATEGIC ALLIANCE

We noted (section 15.3) that a major form of growth for firms was that of strategic alliances – a broad term that covers a number of collaborative arrangements across one or more sectors. These alliances may involve some joint ownership and sharing of resources; they may be contractual arrangements or agreements based on trust between parties to supply and distribute goods. Strategic alliances may be horizontal or vertical, or involve networks of firms across industries (see Figure 15.1 on page 261).

Types of strategic alliance

Horizontal strategic alliances

Horizontal strategic alliances are formal or informal arrangements between firms to co-operate on a particular activity at the same stage of production. This may involve the

establishment of a *joint venture*. For example, in 2018, Amazon, JPMorgan Chase and Berkshire Hathaway announced that they were creating a not-for-profit health care company. Qualcomm and Samsung formed a strategic alliance in January 2018 to develop processors for the transition to 5G.

Figure 15.2 shows the current status of the major strategic alliances in the airline industry. In addition to the global alliances illustrated in Figure 15.2, there are many bilateral

> **Definitions**
>
> **Horizontal strategic alliances** A formal or informal arrangement between firms jointly to provide a particular activity at a similar stage of the same technical process.
>
> **Joint venture** Where two or more firms set up and jointly own a new independent firm.

Figure 15.2 Airline strategic alliances

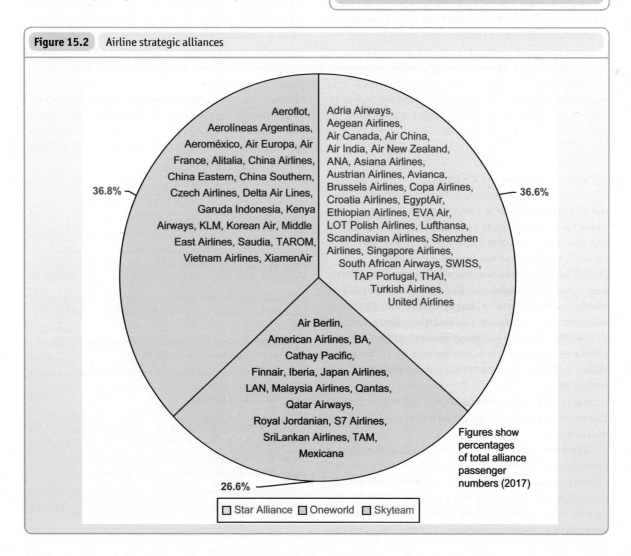

arrangements between the airlines on specific routes. Indeed, many airlines see these as more significant than belonging to one of the three global airline alliances. For example, Emirates, while refusing to join one of the three global alliances, formed a 10-year strategic alliance with Qantas in September 2012 to align ticket prices and flight schedules between Europe and Australia. This agreement led to Qantas switching its stopover destination for many of its European flights from Singapore to Dubai. Previously, it had been in a similar arrangement with BA. This agreement had lasted for 17 years. Qantas also remains in the One World Alliance and continues to cross-sell seats with BA.

Contractual agreements between firms at the same stage of production include the establishment of a *franchise* (though there are also vertical franchise agreements). A franchise usually involves another party agreeing to take on the product format of the franchisor in return for a fee. Two of the most famous examples of companies that have grown by using franchise arrangements are Subway and McDonalds.

Another form of contractual agreement is that of *licensing*. Some lagers, beers and soft drinks are sold in the UK under licence. For example Britvic has had licensing agreements with PepsiCo for the bottling of a number of products including Pepsi, Gatorade and Lipton Ice Tea.

Some informal horizontal agreements might focus upon very specific stages in the supply chain. An example here is the decision by three of the world's largest steel manufacturers, NKK, Kawasaki and ThyssenKrupp, to share information on the technology for producing car panels.

Vertical strategic alliances

Vertical strategic alliances are formal or informal arrangements between firms operating at different stages of an activity to provide jointly a particular product or service. Examples of vertical joint ventures include the company FilmFlex, a video-on-demand service, provided for customers in the UK. This service was provided jointly by Walt Disney Television International and Sony Pictures Television. In the UK, it operates services with Film4, TalkTalk and mobile operator EE. The venture brings film and TV makers into a specialist retail sector. Customers can order and watch a particular film or TV programme from their own home or mobile device when it is convenient for them. Sony and Disney sold FilmFlex to the USA-based company Vubiquity in May 2014.

Where a number of companies join together to provide a good or service, the term *consortium* is used. In recent years, many consortia have been created. A consortium usually is created for very specific projects, such as a large civil engineering work. As such, they have a very focused objective and, once the project is completed, the consortium usually is dissolved. TransManche Link, the Anglo-French company that built the Channel Tunnel, is an example of a defunct consortium. Camelot, the company that runs the UK National Lottery, was previously owned in equal shares by Cadbury Schweppes, De La Rue, Fujitsu Services, Royal Mail Enterprises and Thales Electronics, each of which had particular expertise to bring to the consortium.

It is also possible for firms at different stages of production to form contractual agreements. For example, there are licensing deals between suppliers of mobile phones and software companies such as Adobe. Similarly, Edios and Square Enix create and manufacture games for the PlayStation 3, having been given licences by Sony. Square Enix purchased Eidos for just over £85 million in April 2009 and now produces games for the PlayStation 4. There are also licensing agreements between manufacturers of cosmetics and retailers as well as car manufacturers and car dealers. These are sometimes known in competition policy language as *vertical restraints* because the dealer is restrained by the manufacturer as to how and where it can sell the product.

One of the best-known forms of vertical contractual alliance is that of *outsourcing* or *subcontracting*. When a business outsources, it employs an independent business to manufacture or supply some service rather than conduct the activity itself. Car manufacturers are major subcontractors. Given the multitude and complexity of components that are required to manufacture a car, the use of subcontractors to supply specialist items, such as brakes and lights, seems a logical way to organise the business. Nissan in the UK, for example, has set up a supplier business park so that it can get its inputs at the right price and quality and available 'just-in-time', thereby keeping inventory costs to a minimum. Box 15.2 explores some of the issues associated with outsourcing the Apple iPhone.

Definitions

Franchise A formal agreement whereby a company uses another company to produce or sell some or all of its product.

Licensing Where the owner of a patented product allows another firm to produce it for a fee.

Vertical strategic alliance A formal or informal arrangement between firms operating at different stages of an activity jointly to provide a product or service.

Consortium Where two or more firms work together on a specific project and create a separate company to run the project.

Vertical restraints Conditions imposed by one firm or another, which is either its supplier or its customer.

Outsourcing or **subcontracting** Where a firm employs another firm to produce part of its output or some of its input(s).

Networks

Networks consist of multi-firm alliances across sectors between organisations, some of which may be formal and others informal. Sony is a good example of a company that has expanded abroad over the years through the formation of joint ventures, licensing and informal arrangements with other firms across a number of sectors. Firms in the motor vehicle, electronics, pharmaceutical and other high-tech sectors have similar arrangements.

Some networks of firms are very large and reflect expansion through internal growth as well as via mergers, acquisitions and strategic alliances. Being part of a network may give firms access to technology and resources at lower costs. It may also give greater access to global markets. However, network development is also important at the local level.

Many firms have developed supply-chain clusters to support their operations and they rely increasingly on other organisations from outside the sector, such as banks, insurance companies and government. Thus, the establishment of networks allows firms to develop competitive advantage through their core business activities and other less formal means, including conversations with influential individuals and groups.

Why form strategic alliances?

There are many reasons why firms may decide to set up a strategic alliance. Often, these reasons are specific to a particular time or set of circumstances.

New markets. As a business expands, possibly internationally, it may well be advantageous to join with an existing player in the market. Such a business would have local knowledge and an established network of suppliers and distributors. Similar arguments apply if a business is seeking to diversify. Rather than developing the skills, knowledge and networks necessary to succeed, the process might be curtailed by

establishing an alliance with a firm already operating in the market.

Risk sharing. Many business ventures might just be too risky for a solitary firm. Creating some form of strategic alliance spreads risk and creates opportunity. The Channel Tunnel and the consortium of firms that built it is one such example. The construction of the Channel Tunnel was a massive undertaking and far too risky for any single firm to embark upon. With the creation of a consortium, risk was spread, and the various consortium members were able to specialise in their areas of expertise.

Capital pooling. Projects that might have prohibitively high start-up costs or running costs may become feasible if firms co-operate and pool their capital. In addition, an alliance of firms, with their combined assets and credibility, may find it easier to generate finance, whether from investors in the stock market or from the banking sector.

The past 20 years have seen a flourishing of strategic alliances. They have become a key growth strategy for business both domestically and internationally. They are seen as a way of expanding business operations quickly without the difficulties associated with the more aggressive approach of acquisition or the more lengthy process of merger.

> ### Pause for thought
>
> *What are the difficulties associated with acquisitions and mergers?*

> ### Definitions
>
> **Network** The establishment of formal and informal multi-firm alliances across sectors.

15.7 EXPLAINING EXTERNAL FIRM GROWTH: A TRANSACTION COSTS APPROACH

By way of concluding this chapter, it is worth considering a theoretical approach to understanding how external growth may occur. We examined the transaction cost approach (see Chapter 3) when explaining why firms exist. This approach, developed by the economist Oliver Williamson, can also be useful in illustrating the growth of firms, particularly by strategic alliance or vertical integration.

Consider two firms, one a motor vehicle manufacturer, the other a supplier of car exhausts. These two parties will have invested heavily in a highly specific set of assets, which have little or no alternative use outside of making cars or exhausts, respectively. In other words, they both have sunk costs. Both the car and the exhaust manufacturer will also be involved in frequent transactions with each

other. The car manufacturer sells a lot of cars and so will need a lot of exhausts on a regular basis. In addition, if the economic environment is uncertain and there is information asymmetry in the exchange, then the potential for moral hazard exists (see pages 99–102).

Consider the following. The car manufacturer is looking for a supplier of exhausts. It puts out an invitation to tender for the contract. A number of potential suppliers put in bids and one supplier is chosen because it offers the best price and can deliver the best quality, and does so 'just-in-time' to keep inventory costs low. Once the contract has been signed, the two parties to the exchange become 'locked in' to the contract. It is at this stage that one or both of the parties could act opportunistically and exploit the situation because they

| BOX 15.2 | HOW MANY FIRMS DOES IT TAKE TO MAKE AN IPHONE? |

Quite a lot actually

Outsourcing is a growing and strategically important activity for modern businesses. Making decisions about what products to make in-house and what to outsource has important implications for a firm's profitability and growth.

Take the case of the iPhone. The original iPhone was introduced in 2007, and the iPhone 8 and iPhone X were launched in September 2017. Apple does not manufacture these products but instead outsources the production and assembly of the numerous different parts to various companies spread across countries in three continents. In February 2018, it published a Supplier List.[1] This is a directory of the 200 suppliers that accounted for at least 98 per cent of its procurement expenditure in 2017. Many of the suppliers are based in China, Japan, Taiwan, Thailand, Indonesia, South Korea and the USA. A key issue for Apple is how best to manage this very complex production process.

Apple's main contribution is the design of the device. A specialist team designs the look and feel of the phone and its various features. Apple's engineers design the internal workings of the phone – the hardware and the necessary software – to meet the specifications of the design team. Not surprisingly, there is a lot of negotiation between these two groups before an initial specification is agreed.

At this point, the supply chain team comes into operation. The engineering team will itemise the range of components and other materials that are needed and the assembly requirements. The supply chain team will then have to estimate the costs of sourcing the components and their assembly from a range of potential suppliers.

'Apple's consistently reliable and profitable operations have made their supply chain team . . . one of the most envied in the industry – they develop and source from hundreds of suppliers from around the world; manage assembly contractors; set challenging production schedules and deliver better than most in their industry.'[2]

The suppliers chosen by Apple are those that offer the best deal, where 'best' includes not just cost, but also quality, reliability and capacity.

Take the iPhone X:[3] Qualcomm (USA) and Intel (USA) supply the modems; Skyworks Solutions (USA) supplies other wireless components; NXP Semiconductors (Netherlands) supplies near-field communication chips; Broadcom (Singapore) supplies other wireless components; Toshiba (Japan) supplies flash storage; Sony (Japan) and Foxconn (Taiwan) supply the camera; Samsung (South Korea) supplies the OLED screens; Cirrus Logic (USA) supplies audio components; Dialog Semiconductor (UK) supplies power management chips. Several other manufacturers supply the other parts. It is assembled in China and Brazil by two Taiwanese companies, Foxconn (a subsidiary of Hon Hai Precision Industry) and Pegatron. In 2017, Apple began selling iPhones assembled in India by its partner, Wistron.

With the launch of the iPhone X, some suppliers remained the same, some had bigger roles to play than previously, while

---

[1] https://images.apple.com/supplier-responsibility/pdf/Apple-Supplier-List.pdf.

[2] Ram Ganeshan, 'The iPhone 4 Supply Chain' *Operations Buzz* (28 November 2010).

[3] Andrew Rassweiler, Wayne Lam, Jérémie Bouchaud and David Hsieh, 'iPhone X Costs Apple $370 in Materials IHS Markit Teardown Reveals' *IHS Markit press release* (8 November 2017).

---

have different sets of information about the markets in which they operate.

For example, the motor vehicle manufacturer could say to the supplier of exhausts that car sales are poorer than expected because of a fall in demand. As a result, it might ask the exhaust manufacturer to lower the price at which it sells exhausts. Alternatively, the exhaust manufacturer may claim that it needs a higher price for its exhausts because the cost of steel has risen. The possibility of this renegotiation of the contract arises because each party to the exchange has a different set of information. But what should either party do if they were faced with this problem?

Both firms have invested in highly specific equipment that may have been specially tailored to meet this contract. The value of this equipment would be much lower in a

transaction with a different business partner. It would, therefore, cost both firms money if they were to exit the deal and try to find an alternative supplier or purchaser. Williamson suggested that one party might take over or merge with the other – a vertically integrated merger would occur.

However, it is also possible that the parties engage in some other action short of a merger, largely because they want to carry out business transactions in a more civilised manner. Contracts can be useful devices for managing the exchange process, but they can also be very difficult instruments to apply because they do not allow flexibility.

Williamson suggested, therefore, that many firms would form some intermediate arrangement – a strategic alliance – that might rely partly on contract and also on

some had smaller ones. For example, Apple's decision to switch from using an LCD display to an OLED display benefited Samsung as it is the only company that can produce OLED displays that meet Apple's specification. Apple has also started to design more of its components in-house: e.g. graphics chips.

Power and value added

With such a large share of the market, Apple has considerable market power when negotiating with suppliers. IHS Markit[4] estimates that the cost of materials to produce an iPhone X is approximately $370. The biggest expense is the OLED screen with touch sensor and cover glass, which costs $110. The stainless steel enclosure costs $61, while the rear dual lens camera costs $11. The *TrueDepth* sensing system for facial recognition is estimated to cost $16.70.

When the cost of these materials is subtracted from the price of around $999, this leaves Apple with around $630 of value added to cover assembly, R&D, administration, marketing and distribution. This gross profit margin of around 64 per cent is very similar to that for previous models. Once the total costs are taken into account, Apple makes a margin of approximately 40 per cent on the sale of each handset.

The iPhone has proved to be one of the most profitable products in the world. In February 2018, Apple reported record quarterly profits of $20.1 billion (£14 billion) for October to December 2017. A key factor in explaining these profits was the higher price of the iPhone X. However, its sales have been lower than expected as global sales of smart phones fell in the fourth quarter of 2017 compared with the same period a year earlier. This was the first ever year-on-year decline and suggests that consumers have been slower to upgrade their devices.

Apple's market power works in two ways.

First, with suppliers eager to supply parts to such a large purchaser, Apple can use this competition to drive down component and assembly prices. Most of the parts are fairly generic and Apple thus has a choice of suppliers. However, it did experience supply problems, which led to the launch of the iPhone X being delayed from September until November 2017.

Second, with a buoyant demand for iPhones (and other Apple products), Apple can charge a premium price. It has a monopoly on its specific designs and thus demand for the finished product is relatively inelastic.

The story of iPhones applies also to iPods, iPads and Macs. Each uses parts sourced from around the world and each features unique design properties that give the product a loyal following.

1. *What factors determine the size of the value-added for iPhones? Why do you think the figure is larger for later versions of the iPhone?*
2. *Is value-added the same as normal or supernormal profit?*

[4]*Ibid.*

trust. Parties will have to signal to the other that they want a long-term business relationship as a means of building that trust.

A number of companies, particularly Japanese firms, have these sorts of arrangements. For example, there may be an opportunity for senior executives from each firm to sit on the boards of the other or there may be meetings between business partners to discuss key issues. Indeed, in our example above, buyers from the car manufacturer might go out on visits with their exhaust manufacturer counterparts so that they can explain to raw materials suppliers the consequences of higher prices further up the supply chain.

Further, firms that signal that they are trustworthy business partners and that they have successfully developed resources over the long term are also more likely to engage in joint ventures.

Thus, where there are large and uncertain costs associated with market transactions, it can be beneficial to have some form of merger or an alliance. The conditions in which these might occur are often specific to the parties involved and depend on the nature of the industry as well as the prevailing and anticipated economic conditions.

In this chapter we have considered the growth of firms and the forms it may take. Although we identified various constraints on growth (section 15.2), a word of caution is still required. There can be real dangers associated with a strategy of rapid external business growth in turbulent or largely unknown environments, as the case of Northern Rock in Box 15.3 demonstrates.

BOX 15.3 | THE DAY THE WORLD STOPPED

Northern Rock: a cautionary tale of business growth

In 1997, Northern Rock converted from a building society – a residential mortgage lender owned by its savers and borrowers – into a bank quoted on the stock market. During the next 10 years, it reduced the number of branches from 128 to 76, but expanded its online banking capabilities and mortgage business dramatically.

In January 2007, the bank announced pre-tax profits of £627 million for 2006. Its share of the UK mortgage market had grown steadily, reaching 18.9 per cent by June 2007. Northern Rock had grown from being a small local lender in the north-east of England to being the fifth largest supplier of mortgages in the UK.

However, all was not well. On 13 September 2007, it had to be granted emergency financial support by the Bank of England in its role as 'lender of last resort'. The share price plummeted (see diagram).

The following day saw the beginning of a 'run on the bank', something that had not occurred since Overend, Gurney & Co. collapsed in 1866. Not only were there queues outside the branch offices of Northern Rock, but the online banking website crashed as depositors withdrew their savings.

Over the next few months, the government issued some £25 billion in loans so that the bank could continue operating. In spite of several attempts to find a private-sector 'white knight' to take it over, the government decided to take it into full public ownership on 22 February 2008 and shares were finally suspended.

What went wrong?

Commercial retail banks have two major objectives. They should make profit for their shareholders by engaging in activities that include lending, but have sufficient liquidity (e.g. cash) in order to meet the requirements of their customers (see Chapter 28).

Northern Rock relied far more heavily on mortgage lending for its profits than other commercial banks that had a more diversified range of services. It had an excellent IT system that not only lowered the costs of mortgage services, but also showed mortgage brokers and independent financial advisers the cheap mortgages it had for sale.

While house prices were rising (see Box 4.1) the demand for mortgages kept rising, but this also meant that individuals needed bigger mortgages. If an individual wanted a 100 per cent (or even 125 per cent) mortgage at competitive rates, Northern Rock would provide it, if it thought there was a good chance it would be paid back.

A bank makes profit on the interest that it earns from mortgage customers. However, it has to pay house sellers, and this money can come either from the deposits of savers or by borrowing from elsewhere. Northern Rock largely adopted the latter strategy, because attracting new deposits is a more costly exercise. The bank bundled its mortgages together and packaged them as financial instruments (bonds), which it then sold to investors on money markets around the world at

a favourable interest rate, at least initially. These loans were accepted largely as secure investments in money markets because investors believed that Northern Rock customers were unlikely to default on their mortgages.

This practice of 'securitisation' is legitimate and allowed under international banking regulations, but Northern Rock engaged in extremely high levels of money market lending. According to the BBC, 61 per cent of its lending was from the money market. This was far in excess of its rivals such as HBOS (33 per cent), RBS (23 per cent), Barclays (20 per cent) and Lloyds (16 per cent).[1] By using the money markets to borrow money at low interest rates, it gained a competitive edge over its rivals. The more money it borrowed, the more mortgages it could afford to provide and the more profit it would make.

Mortgage lending, backed by securitised assets, was the 'goose that laid the golden egg', and so Northern Rock continued to focus its business efforts in this direction. Even though there had been some disquiet among financial commentators about this strategy, the risks were viewed at the time as acceptable by the UK financial regulators – the Financial Services Authority (FSA) and the Bank of England.

In 2007, as monetary policy in the UK tightened faster than expected, Northern Rock issued a tranche of mortgages at interest rates that were lower than those it had to pay in the market to finance them. The bank issued a profits warning in June and its share price fell.

Then the market for obtaining finance from securitised assets crumbled as it became clear that similar mortgage-backed assets in the USA had high levels of repayment arrears and property prices were falling rapidly. Anyone who now held a mortgage-backed asset (bond) would be highly unsure whether they could recoup its value in the presence of mortgage defaults. Thus, credit, once freely available, dried up and the term 'credit crunch' has become part of the lexicon of everyday life. Northern Rock now had mortgages that were not covered by money market loans. The goose had been mortally wounded.

The chief executive of Northern Rock had a vivid recollection of the day in 2007 when he realised the business strategy had failed:

> The world stopped on August 9. It's been astonishing, gobsmacking. Look across the full range of financial products, across the full geography of the world, the entire system has frozen.[2]

---

[1] See 'The downturn in facts and figures' BBC News (18 February 2008).

[2] 'Why Northern Rock was doomed to fail', The Telegraph (17 September 2007).

Northern Rock share prices, January 2007 until suspension

September 12th. Northern Rock applies to Bank of England for emergency funding
September 14th. Savers withdraw money.
September 17th. Emergency funds granted.

February 7th. First signs that the US sub-prime market could collapse.

February 22nd 2008. Northern Rock taken into public ownership.

Source: Based on data available from http://news.bbc.co.uk/1/hi/business/7250498.stm

The world is different now

The world of Northern Rock is very different ten and a half years after nationalisation. Questions were asked in the press and parliament about the risks involved in the Northern Rock business strategy and about the role of the FSA, the Bank of England and the Treasury as regulators. Questions were also raised about the Basel II arrangements, which provide guidance, rules and standards in respect of risk management and supervision at an international level (see Chapter 28, pages 565–6).

In 2010, the bank was split into two parts. The first, Northern Rock Asset Management, now called NRAM, holds the bank's historic mortgage portfolio and toxic loans. The second, Northern Rock PLC, holds the retail and wholesale deposit business. These two banks are informally referred to by staff as the 'bad bank' and the 'good bank'. The 'good bank', with its 75 high street branches, was sold to Virgin Money in November 2011, for just under £1 billion. This was substantially below the amount pumped into the bank by the government to secure its solvency. In January 2012, Virgin Money began the process of fully integrating Northern Rock into its business and, in the process, ended the Northern Rock name. By October 2012, all the previous Northern Rock branches had been rebranded as Virgin Money Stores and the two websites were combined into Virginmoney.com.

As of April 2015, the 'bad bank', NRAM, remains under government ownership. This business has no customer branches and is closed to new business. It services only what remains of the residential mortgage book. The remaining assets of NRAM were combined with those of Bradford & Bingley into a single holding company called UK Asset Resolution (UKAR). This is a state-owned limited company which has the objective of managing the remaining mortgages and repaying the government loans that were made as part of the bailout. In July 2012, it sold £465 million of high-quality NRAM mortgages to Virgin Money. In October 2014, UKAR announced that it had sold £1.7 billion of mortgages formerly owned by NRAM (and a further £1 billion formerly owned by Bradford & Bingley) to a consortium led by JPMorgan. In November 2015, the Chancellor of the Exchequer announced that a further £13 billion of mortgages originally owned by Northern Rock had been sold to the US business, Cerberus.[3] Some observers have commented that perhaps the assets of the so-called 'bad bank' have not proved to be as bad as people first thought.

In an attempt to reduce the risk of a similar situation in the future, the government passed the Financial Services Act in 2012. The FSA was abolished and a new regulatory framework for the financial system was established. This created two new regulatory bodies that both became operational on 1 April 2013. These were the Prudential Regulation Authority (PRA) which is a subsidiary of the Bank of England and the Financial Conduct Authority (FCA). Both of these new regulators are under the supervision of the Financial Policy Committee of the Bank of England. It is hoped that this regulatory framework will prevent a 'Northern Rock' from happening again.

 What are the strengths and weaknesses of diversification as a business growth strategy?

 Follow the story of the successors to Northern Rock using materials from the media and consider how they have developed since Northern Rock was split.

---

[3] See 'Northern Rock mortgages sold for £13bn' *BBC News* (13 November 2015)

SUMMARY

1a Business growth and business profitability are likely to be inversely related in the short run. A growing firm will bear certain additional costs, such as higher advertising and marketing bills.

1b In the long run, the relationship could be positive. A growing firm may take advantage of new market opportunities and may achieve greater economies of scale and increased market power. On the other hand, a rapidly growing firm may embark on various risky projects or projects with a low rate of return.

2a Constraints on business growth include: (i) financial conditions, (ii) shareholder confidence, (iii) the level and growth of market demand and (iv) managerial conditions.

2b (i) Financial conditions determine the business's ability to raise finance. (ii) Shareholder confidence is likely to be jeopardised if a firm ploughs back too much profit into investment and distributes too little to shareholders. (iii) A firm is unlikely to be able to grow unless it faces a growing demand: either in its existing market, or by diversifying into new markets. (iv) The knowledge, skills and dynamism of the management team will be an important determinant of the firm's growth.

3a A business can expand either internally or externally.

3b Internal expansion involves one or more of the following: expanding the market through product promotion and differentiation; vertical integration; diversification.

3c External expansion entails the firm expanding by merger/acquisition or by strategic alliance.

4a Vertical integration can reduce a firm's costs through various economies of scale. It can also help to reduce uncertainty, as the vertically integrated business hopefully can secure supply routes and/or retail outlets. This strategy can also enhance the business's market power by enabling it to erect various barriers to entry.

4b A vertically integrated business will trade off the security of such a strategy with the reduced ability to respond to change and to exploit the advantages that the market might present.

4c Through a process of tapered vertical integration, many firms make part of a given input themselves and subcontract the production of the remainder to one or more other firms. By making a certain amount of an input itself, the firm is less reliant on suppliers, but does not require as much capital equipment as if it produced all the input itself.

4d The nature and direction of diversification depend upon the skills and abilities of managers and the type of technology employed.

4e Diversification offers the business a growth strategy that not only frees it from the limitations of a particular market, but also enables it to spread its risks and seek profit in potentially fast-growing markets.

5a There are three types of merger: horizontal, vertical and conglomerate. The type of merger adopted will be determined by the aims of business: that is, whether to increase market power, improve business security or spread risks.

5b There is a wide range of motives for merger. Some have more statistical backing than others.

6a One means of achieving growth is through the formation of strategic alliances with other firms. They are a means whereby business operations can be expanded relatively quickly and at relatively low cost.

6b Types of strategic alliance include: horizontal and vertical strategic alliances and networks. They may take a number of forms: joint ventures, consortia, franchising, licensing, subcontracting and informal agreements based on trust between the parties.

6c Advantages of strategic alliances include easier access to new markets, risk sharing and capital pooling.

7 An important explanation of business growth relates to the transaction costs in markets where there are large sunk costs, frequent transactions and information differences on both sides of the exchange. This is particularly relevant in explaining the development of strategic alliances and vertical integration.

REVIEW QUESTIONS

1 Explain the relationship between a business's rate of growth and its profitability.

2 'Business managers must constantly tread a fine line between investing in business growth and paying shareholders an "adequate" dividend on their holdings.' Explain why this is such a crucial consideration.

3 Distinguish between internal and external growth strategy. Identify a range of factors that might determine whether an internal or external strategy is pursued.

4 What is meant by the term 'vertical integration'? Why might a business wish to pursue such a growth strategy?

5 A firm can grow by merging with or taking over another firm. Such mergers or takeovers can be of three types: horizontal, vertical or conglomerate. Which of the following is an example of which type of merger (takeover)?

a) A soft drinks manufacturer merges with a pharmaceutical company.

b) A car manufacturer merges with a car distribution company.

c) A large supermarket chain takes over a number of independent grocers.

6 To what extent will consumers gain or lose from the three different types of merger identified above?

7 Assume that an independent film company, which has, up to now, specialised in producing documentaries for a particular television broadcasting company, wishes to expand. Identify some possible horizontal, vertical and other closely related fields. What types of strategic alliance might it seek to form and with what types of company? What possible drawbacks might there be for it in such alliances?

The small-firm sector

- How are small- and medium-sized businesses defined?
- How large is the small-firm sector in the UK?
- What competitive advantages do small businesses have?
- What problems are they likely to face?
- What determines how rapidly small businesses are likely to grow?
- What policies towards small businesses do governments pursue?

KI 6
p 29

How often do you hear of small businesses making it big? Not very often and, yet, many of the world's major corporations began life as small businesses. From acorns have grown oak trees! But small and large businesses usually are organised and run quite differently and face very different problems.

In this chapter we consider the place of small firms in the economy: their strengths and weaknesses, their ability to grow and the factors that limit expansion. We also consider the small-business policies of governments, both in the UK and in the European Union.

16.1 DEFINING THE SMALL-FIRM SECTOR

Unfortunately, there is no single agreed definition of a 'small' firm. In fact, a firm considered to be small in one sector of business, such as manufacturing, may be considerably different in size from one in, say, the road haulage business. Nevertheless, the most widely used definition is that adopted by the EU for its statistical data. Three categories of SME (small and medium enterprise) are distinguished. These are shown in Table 16.1.

This subdivision of small firms into three categories allows us to distinguish features of enterprises that vary with the degree of smallness (e.g. practices of hiring and firing, pricing and investment strategies, competition and

collusion, innovation). It also enables us to show changes over time in the size and composition of the small-firm sector. However, we might still question the adequacy of such a definition, given the diversity that can be found in business activity, organisational structure and patterns of ownership within the small-firm sector.

The small-firm sector in the UK

In the UK, firms are divided into four categories by number of employees: micro (0–9 employees), small (0–49 employees) (includes micro), medium (50–249 employees),

Table 16.1 EU SME definitions

Criterion	Micro	Small	Medium
Maximum number of employees	9	49	249
Maximum annual turnover	€2 million	€10 million	€50 million
Maximum annual balance sheet total	€2 million	€10 million	€43 million
Maximum % owned by one, or jointly by several, enterprise(s) not satisfying the same criteria	25%	25%	25%

Note: To qualify as an SME, both the employee and the independence criteria must be satisfied and either the turnover or the balance sheet total criteria

large (250 or more employees). The Department for Business, Energy and Industrial Strategy publishes annual business population estimates, which are available from the web page *Business population estimates 2017*.[1] Table 16.2 is taken from the 2017 dataset.

The most significant feature of the data is that micro businesses (between 0 and 9 employees) accounted for 95.3 per cent of all businesses in 2017 and provided 26.6 per cent of all employment. The table also shows that there were 5 745 585 micro and small businesses out of a total of 5 795 570 businesses: i.e. 99.1 per cent. Micro and small businesses also accounted for 39.5 per cent of employment and 34.7 per cent of turnover. From such information, we can see that the small-firm sector clearly represents a very important part of the UK's industrial structure.

There are significant variations between sectors in the percentage of SMEs, whether by number of firms, employment or turnover. This is illustrated in Table 16.3. The total number of businesses is smaller than in Table 16.2, as it does not include central/local government and non-profit organisations. It includes only businesses in the private sector.

[1]www.gov.uk/government/statistics/business-population-estimates-2017.

Service providers (categories G to S in Table 16.3) contribute the overwhelming number of micro and small firms within the economy, accounting for 4 227 320 businesses, or 74.2 per cent of all small firms.

Changes over time

How has the small-firm sector changed over time? The problems associated with definition and data collection make time-series analysis of the small-firm sector very difficult and prone to various inconsistencies. However, it is possible to identify certain trends.

The Bolton Report on small firms in 1971 estimated that there were approximately 820 000 businesses employing fewer than 200 people. This figure had declined fairly consistently throughout the first part of the twentieth century, before beginning to rise again in the mid-1960s. By the turn of the century, it was estimated that there were just under 3.5 million small firms (i.e. employing fewer than 250 people) in the private sector. This figure had increased to nearly 5.7 million by 2017. The period between 2010 and 2017 was one of particularly rapid growth, with the number of SMEs increasing by 1.2 million.

Pause for thought

What inconsistencies might there be in time-series data on the small-firm sector?

What is the explanation for this rise in small businesses in recent years? A wide range of factors have been advanced to explain this phenomenon, and include the following:

- *The growth in the service sector of the economy*. Many services are, by their nature, small in scale and/or specialist. For example, many small businesses have developed in the area of computer support and back-up.
- *The growth in niche markets*. Rising consumer affluence creates a growing demand for specialist products and services. Some examples are craft-based markets such as

Table 16.2 Number of UK businesses, employment and turnover for the whole economy by number of employees (2017)

Size (number of employees)	Businesses (number)	Employment (000s)	Turnover[a] (£m ex VAT)	Businesses (%)	Employment (%)	Turnover (%)
0–9 (micro)	5 521 760	8 981	837 571	95.3	26.6	20.8
10–49 (small)	223 825	4 382	555 955	3.9	13.0	13.9
50–249 (medium)	40 180	4 008	574 854	0.6	11.8	14.3
250 + (large)	9 805	16 465	2 043 176	0.2	48.6	50.9
All	5 795 570	33 836	4 011 556	100.0	100.0	100.0

[a]Excluding finance sector (Sector K) as data are not available on a comparable basis.

Source: *Business Population Estimates for the UK and Regions* Table 2, www.gov.uk/government/statistics/business-population-estimates-2017 (BEIS, 2017).

Table 16.3 SME share of UK private-sector businesses, employment and turnover by industrial sector (2017)

Industrial sector SIC 2007	Businesses		Employment		Turnover	
	Total number	SME (% share)	Total employment (000s)	SME (% share)	Total turnover (£m)	SME (% share)
All industries	5 694 515	99.9	26 724	60.4	3 740 171	50.9
A Agriculture, forestry and fishing	155 795	99.9	469	94.2	41 275	90.2
B, D, E Mining, electricity, gas, water	38 125	99.6	392	33.2	191 327	18.6
C Manufacturing	265 775	99.5	2 606	57.8	553 902	33.3
F Construction	1 007 500	100.0	2 112	86.5	296 888	74.7
G Wholesale, retail and repairs	542 150	99.8	5 041	45.9	1 249 354	52.6
H Transportation and storage	345 285	99.9	1 502	49.7	199 236	40.0
I Accommodation and food service	202 060	99.7	2 314	59.4	98 154	55.6
J Information and communication	351 485	99.9	1 354	62.0	236 100	44.7
K Financial and insurance activities	86 410	99.6	1 067	28.1	n.a.	n.a.
L Real estate activities	111 870	99.9	490	75.5	57 827	74.9
M Professional, scientific and technical activities	855 625	99.9	2 639	75.4	313 842	63.4
N Administrative and support service activities	478 810	99.8	2 974	48.0	253 024	61.0
P Education	296 305	100.0	563	86.5	22 938	80.7
Q Health and social work	362 115	99.9	1 774	70.8	82 086	74.1
R Arts, entertainment and recreation	276 300	99.9	737	69.1	110 381	25.3
S Other service activities	318 905	100.0	690	91.2	33 837	83.9

Note: n.a. = not available.
Source: *Business Population Estimates for the UK and Regions Table 4*, www.gov.uk/government/statistics/business-population-estimates-2017 (BEIS, 2017).

beer, jewellery and baking. Such goods and services are likely to be supplied by small firms, in which economies of scale and hence price considerations are of less relevance.

- *New working practices which require greater labour force flexibility.* Forms of employment such as **subcontracting** have become more pronounced, as businesses attempt to achieve certain cost and flexibility advantages over their rivals. This often forces individuals either to set up their own companies to provide such services or to become self-employed.

- *Rises in the level of unemployment.* The higher the level of unemployment, the more people turn to self-employment as an alternative to trying to find work with an employer. The rise in unemployment in the 1980s, early 1990s and from 2008 to 2011 were all associated with increases in self-employment. For example, although employee jobs fell after 2007, the numbers of self-employed continued to grow. This increase was the main factor driving the growth of employment between 2008 and 2014. Since 2014, however, the contribution of employee jobs to employment growth has become more of an important factor.

According to the Office for National Statistics, 4.8 million people in the UK were self-employed in their main job in 2017. This represents 15.1 per cent of the total number of people in work and is the highest figure since the data were first collected over 40 years ago. The figure was 13 per cent in 2008 and just 8.7 per cent in 1975.

Definition

Subcontracting The business practice where various forms of labour (frequently specialist) are hired for a given period of time. Such workers are not employed directly by the hiring business, but employed either by a third party or self-employed.

BOX 16.1 CAPTURING GLOBAL ENTREPRENEURIAL SPIRIT

Stimulating the growth of SMEs

There has been considerable interest in the notion of entrepreneurship in recent times and governments around the world increasingly have made it a focus of their economic strategy. But what exactly is an entrepreneur? Entrepreneurs are people who set up businesses. In doing so, they are often sources of new ideas and new ways of doing things. That is, they are at the forefront of invention and innovation, providing new products and developing markets.

The GEM

The Global Entrepreneurship Monitor (GEM) provides a framework for analysing entrepreneurship. It suggests that entrepreneurship is a complex phenomenon that can exist at various stages of the development of a business. So, someone who is just starting a venture and trying to make it in a highly competitive environment is entrepreneurial. And so, too, but in a different way, are established business owners if they are innovative, competitive and growth-minded. Focusing on different stages of the 'entrepreneurial cycle' allows many of the dynamic elements of SMEs to be identified and analysed.

GEM measures the stage of the life cycle of entrepreneurship by dividing entrepreneurs into nascent, new and established business owners. Nascent owners are those who have established a business within the last three months. New owners are those who have been in business between 3 and 42 months. Together, nascent and new business owners make up 'early stage entrepreneurs', while 'established owners'

– those in business for more than 42 months – will have come through the traumas of the initial birth and the early development stages of the firm.

GEM's Global Report[1] measures entrepreneurial activity in a country by the percentage of those aged 18 to 64 who are business owners, whether early stage or established. The 2017/18 report was based on a survey of individuals across 54 different countries. The prevalence of all entrepreneurial activity was highest in Lebanon, where 57.3 per cent of those surveyed indicated that they had entrepreneurial tendencies (see chart (a)). Madagascar also had a very high incidence of 51.2 per cent. This can be contrasted with Qatar, which had one of the lowest occurrences, with only 8.7 per cent of those surveyed indicating an enterprising disposition. The unweighted average for all the countries surveyed was 25.5 per cent.

Among the 20 European Union countries cited in the GEM survey of 2017/18, the UK appears just above midway, with 15.1 per cent noted as early stage or established entrepreneurs. Of the EU countries, 11 had a lower incidence than the UK, while 8 had a higher incidence. The countries with a lower incidence included France (7.6%), Germany (11.5%) and Spain (13.4%), while those with higher incidence included Estonia (30.8%), The Netherlands (18.7%) and Greece (17.3%). The UK was also behind the USA (21.4%) and Canada (25.4%) in all measures of entrepreneurship.

Unfortunately, consistent time-series data are unavailable. Not all countries report every year and the concept of

(a) Entrepreneurial activity

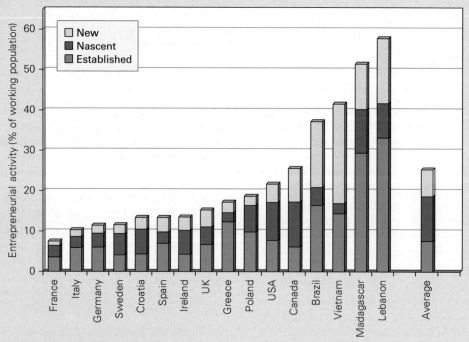

Note: Unweighted average is of 54 countries
Source: Based on data in *Global Entrepreneurship Monitor, 2017/18 Executive Report* (Global Enterprise Research Association, 2015)

[1]'2017/18 Global Report ', *Global Entrepreneurship Monitor*, GERA, www.gemconsortium.org/report (2017).

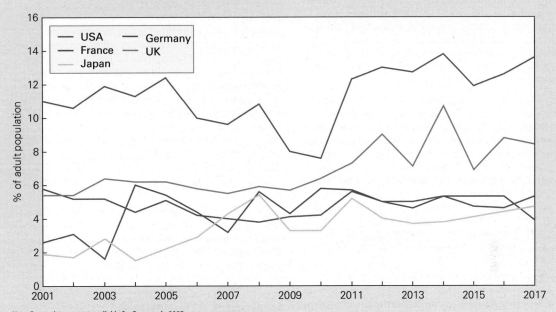

(b) Early stage entrepreneurial activity in selected countries (% adult population)

Note: Survey data was not available for Germany in 2007
Source: Data accessed 2018 from *Key Indicators* database, *Global Entrepreneurship Monitor* (Global Entrepreneurship Research Association)

'established entrepreneurs' was introduced only in 2005. However, there are data relevant for comparison purposes on nascent and new business owners (early stage entrepreneurial activity) for industrialised countries over the period 2001 to 2017. Chart (b) illustrates that the UK is above France, Germany and Japan, but below the USA, in being involved in new venture creation.

The GEM report also includes data on the motivation for starting a business. A necessity-driven entrepreneur is someone who reports that they started a business because there were no better options available to obtain work. An opportunity-driven entrepreneur is someone who reports that they started a business because of a recognised opportunity in the market rather than having no other options for work.

Information from the 2017/18 GEM report indicates that the proportion of early stage entrepreneurs in the UK who established a business because of necessity-driven motives was 13.6 per cent. This compares favourably with a figure of 28.3 per cent in Spain, 20.2 per cent in Greece and 34.7 per cent in Croatia. Also 82.2 per cent of early stage entrepreneurs in the UK reported an opportunity-driven motive for starting their business compared with 68.5 per cent in Spain, 61.4 per cent in Slovakia and 63.2 per cent in Croatia. The figures for the UK were similar to the USA, which had 10.6 per cent and 86.2 per cent respectively.[2]

Challenges for UK entrepreneurs

Thus, the UK seems to be performing fairly well compared to similar nations. However, challenges remain.

Survival rates. First, longer-term survival has to be improved. The Office for National Statistics reported in November 2016 that the three-year survival rate of UK VAT-registered businesses that were established in 2013 (i.e. which were still active in 2016) was 60.8 per cent.[3] This figure has remained relatively stable over the past few years but was 5 per cent lower than the three-year survival rate for those firms that started in 2004.

The five-year survival rate was also low, with only 41.3 per cent of businesses established in 2011 still active in 2016. The five-year survival rate varies substantially by sector, ranging from a high of 54.1 per cent for health-related businesses to a low of 34.6 per cent for businesses in the accommodation and food services industry. It also varied by region, with the South West having the highest survival rate of 47 per cent, while London had the lowest of 41.7 per cent.

Improving survival rates is important because fear of failure is commonly cited as part of the explanation for differences in enterprise and business formation rates between the UK and USA: 36.8 per cent of people seeking entrepreneurial opportunities in the UK, compared with 29.7 per cent in the USA, said that fear of failure would prevent them from starting a business.

Female entrepreneurs. Second, the UK needs to address the issue of low rates of female entrepreneurship. Figures from the GEM report for 2017/18 show that the incidence of female early stage entrepreneurial activity in the UK was 5.2 per cent whereas the figure for the USA was 10.7 per cent and for Canada it was 15 per cent. The Small Business Survey for 2016[4] reports that 20 per

---

[2]*Ibid.*

[3]Business demography, UK: 2016, *ONS Statistical Bulletin,* Office for National Statistics (21 November 2017).

cent of SMEs were women-led – either controlled by a woman or with a management team that is over 50 per cent female. Although low, this figure has increased from 3.2 per cent in 2001.

High-growth firms. Third is how to encourage initially high-growth firms into maintaining that growth. The OECD defines high-growth firms as those with annual growth rates of at least 20 per cent (of either turnover or employment) over a 3-year period, and having more than 10 employees at the beginning of the observation period. A subset of these high-growth firms – those that were less than five years old – are referred to as 'gazelles'.

High-growth SMEs contribute dramatically to an economy's employment, innovation and growth and their presence in large numbers demonstrates a higher order of entrepreneurial dynamism within an economy. They create around a quarter of all new jobs among existing businesses. A 2017 survey of 100 fast-growing firms in the UK revealed that 37 had founders who were 30 or younger when they set up the business and 20

had founders who were female. Over a quarter (29) were e-commerce businesses while 33 were manufacturers. Their average sales growth in the previous three years was 65 per cent and they employed 19 300 staff. Examples in the top 10 included a burger restaurant chain, a TV show producer, an online beauty retailer, a management consultancy and a healthcare recruitment consultancy.[5]

However, it seems very difficult to turn fast-growing small firms in the UK from 'gazelles' into 'gorillas' – firms less than 10 (perhaps 15) years old with a presence in at least 3 countries and employing over 500 people. In the USA, companies such as Google, Facebook, eBay and Amazon stand out as recent examples of firms that have developed from gazelles into gorillas. In the UK, however, these beasts are much more elusive.

1. *Under what economic conditions is 'necessity' entrepreneurship likely to increase?*
2. *Is business failure necessarily a 'bad thing' for a country?*

[4]*Small Business Survey, 2016: businesses with employees*, Department for Business, Energy & Industrial Strategy (July 2017).

[5]'Britain's fastest-growing private companies revealed' , *Fast Track 100 national press release* (3 December 2017).

■ *The role of government.* Government attitudes and policy initiatives shifted in favour of small-business creation during the 1980s. The development of an ***enterprise culture***, in which individuals were to be given the opportunity, and various financial incentives, to start their own businesses, has been one of the principal aims of all governments in recent times. (In section 16.3 we shall consider government policy initiatives in more detail.)

The growth in small businesses in the UK has been pronounced since the early 1970s. But has a similar trend been apparent in other developed economies?

International comparisons

Poor-quality data made international comparisons on small-firm activity and entrepreneurship very difficult in the past. However, this challenge is starting to be met because of their importance in job creation (look at Tables 16.2 and 16.3 again), in productivity, in innovation and, ultimately, economic growth. For example, a consortium of academics in universities across the world has compiled a Global Entrepreneurial Monitor (GEM). This is reported on in Box 16.1.

16.2 THE SURVIVAL, GROWTH AND FAILURE OF SMALL BUSINESSES

Evidence suggests that a small business stands a significantly higher chance of failure than a large business and, yet, many small businesses survive and some grow. What characteristics distinguish a successful small business from one that is likely to fail? The following section looks at this issue.

Competitive advantage and the small-firm sector

The following have been found to be the key competitive advantages that small firms might hold.

■ *Flexibility.* Small firms are better able to respond to changes in market conditions and to meet customer requirements effectively. For example, they may be able to develop or adapt products for specific needs. Small

firms may also be able to make decisions quickly, avoiding the bureaucratic and formal decision-making processes that typify many larger companies.

Pause for thought

Before you read on, try to identify what competitive advantages a small business might have over larger rivals.

Definition

Enterprise culture One in which individuals are encouraged to become wealth creators through their own initiative and effort.

- *Quality of service.* Small firms are better able to deal with customers in a personal manner and offer a more effective after-sales service.
- *Production efficiency and low overhead costs.* Small firms can avoid some of the diseconomies of scale that beset large companies. A small firm can benefit from: management that avoids waste; good labour relations; the employment of a skilled and motivated workforce; lower premises costs. In a survey of SME managers,[2] 80 per cent ranked themselves as having strong people management skills.
- *Product development.* As we have seen, many small businesses operate in niche markets, offering specialist goods or services. The distinctiveness of such products gives the small firm a crucial advantage over its larger rivals. A successful small business strategy, therefore, would be to produce products that are clearly differentiated from those of large firms in the market, thereby avoiding head-on competition – competition that the small firm probably would not be able to survive.
- *Innovation.* Small businesses, especially those located in high-technology markets, are frequently product or process innovators. Such businesses, usually through entrepreneurial vision, manage successfully to match such innovations to changing market needs. Many small businesses are, in this respect, path breakers or market leaders.

Small businesses do, however, suffer from a number of significant limitations.

Problems facing small businesses

The following points have been found to hinder the success of small firms. They are often collectively referred to as the 'liabilities of smallness'.

- *Selling and marketing.* Small firms face many problems in selling and marketing their products, especially overseas. Small firms are perceived by their customers to be less stable and reliable than their larger rivals. This lack of credibility is likely to hinder their ability to trade. This is a particular problem for 'new' small firms that have not had long enough to establish a sound reputation. Only 54 per cent of SME managers ranked themselves as 'strong' at developing and introducing new products or services.[3]
- *Funding R&D.* Given the specialist nature of many small firms, their long-run survival may depend upon developing new products and processes in order to keep pace with changing market needs. Such developments may require significant R&D investment. However, the ability of small firms to attract finance is limited, as many of them have virtually no collateral and frequently they are perceived by banks as a highly risky investment. Only 29 per cent of SME managers ranked themselves as 'strong' at accessing external finance.[4]
- *Management skills.* A crucial element in ensuring that small businesses not only survive but also grow is the quality of management. If key management skills, such as being able to market a product effectively, are limited, then this will limit the success of the business.
- *Economies of scale.* Small firms will have fewer opportunities and scope to gain economies of scale and, hence, their costs are likely to be somewhat higher than those of their larger rivals. This obviously will limit their ability to compete on price.

The question often arises whether it is possible to distinguish between those small businesses that are likely to grow and prosper and those that are likely to fail. In the section below we will consider not only how businesses grow, but also whether there is a key to success.

How do small businesses grow?

It is commonly assumed that all businesses wish to grow. But is it true? Do small businesses want to become big businesses? It may well be that the owners of a small firm have no aspirations to expand the operations of their enterprise. They might earn sufficient profits and experience a level of job satisfaction that would in no way be enhanced with a bigger business operation. In fact, the negative aspects of big business – formalised management structure, less customer contact and a fear of failure – might reduce the owner's level of satisfaction.

If growth is a small business objective, what are the chances of success? Evidence from the UK and the USA suggests that, for every 100 firms established, after a 5-year period only 41 and 51, respectively, will survive; but they are more likely to survive if they have grown.

The process of growth

Small businesses are frequently perceived to grow in five stages: 1) inception; 2) survival; 3) growth; 4) expansion; 5) maturity.[5] Each stage tends to have a particular management structure and style.

In the initial stage, *inception,* the entrepreneur plays the key role in managing the enterprise with little, if any, formalised management structure.

[2]*Longitudinal Small Business Survey Year 2 (2016): Panel report*, Department for Business, Energy & Industrial Strategy (July 2017).
[3]*Ibid.*

[4]*Ibid.*
[5]See, for example: D. J. Storey, *Understanding the Small-Business Sector* (Routledge, 1994).

In the next two stages we see the firm establish itself (the *survival* stage) and then *begin to grow.* The entrepreneur devolves management responsibility to non-owner managers. Such non-owner managers are able to add certain skills to the business which might enhance its chances of growth and success. The entrepreneur is still likely to retain an administrative or co-ordinating function.

The fourth and fifth phases, *expansion* and *maturity,* see the firm become more bureaucratic and rationalised; power within the organisation becomes more dispersed. The business may be divided into sections (either by function or product), with professional managers being in charge of each section. In this decentralised model, the original entrepreneur's role is likely to be reduced to that of oversight – of being largely just a watchdog.

This picture of the growth of small businesses is *descriptive* rather than explanatory. To *explain* why a small firm grows we need to examine a number of factors. It is useful to group them under three headings – the entrepreneur, the firm and strategy.

The entrepreneur

Factors in this section relate predominantly to the attributes and experience of the individual entrepreneur. They include the following:

■ *Entrepreneurial motivation and a desire to succeed.* Motivation, drive and determination are clearly important attributes for a successful entrepreneur. On their own, however, they are unlikely to be sufficient. If motivation is not complemented with things such as good business knowledge and decision making, then a business is likely to fail, irrespective of its owner's motives.

■ *Educational attainment.* Although educational attainment does not necessarily generate business success (indeed, it is often claimed that running a business is not an 'intellectual' activity), the level of education of an entrepreneur is positively related to the rate of growth of the firm.

■ *Prior management experience and business knowledge.* Previous experience by the owner in the same or a related industry is likely to offer a small firm a far greater chance of survival and growth. 'Learning by doing' will enable the new business owner to avoid past mistakes or to take advantage of missed previous opportunities.

The firm

The following are the key characteristics of a small business that determine its rate of growth:

■ *The age of the business.* New businesses grow faster than mature businesses.

■ *The sector of the economy in which the business is operating.* A firm is more likely to experience growth if it is operating in a growing market. Examples include the financial services sector during the 1980s and specialist high-technology sectors today.

■ *Legal forms.* Limited companies have been found to grow faster than sole proprietorships or partnerships. Evidence suggests that limited companies tend to have greater market credibility with both banks and customers.

■ *Location.* Small firms tend to be highly dependent for their performance on a localised market. Being in the right place is thus a key determinant of a small business's growth.

Strategy

Various strategies adopted by the small firm will affect its rate of growth. Strategies that are likely to lead to fast growth include the following:

■ *Workforce and management training.* Training is a form of investment. It adds to the firm's stock of human capital and thereby increases the quantity, and possibly also the quality, of output per head. This, in turn, is likely to increase the long-term growth of the firm.

■ *The use of external finance.* Taking on additional partners or, more significantly, taking on shareholders, will increase the finance available to firms and therefore allow a more rapid expansion.

■ *Product innovation.* Firms that introduce new products have been found, on the whole, to grow faster than those that do not.

■ *Export markets.* Even though small firms tend to export relatively little, export markets can frequently offer additional opportunities for growth. This is especially important when the firm faces stiff competition in the domestic market.

■ *The use of professional managers.* The devolving of power to non-owning managers is identified as a major characteristic of fast-growth small firms. Such managers, as previously mentioned, widen the skills and knowledge base of the organisation and shift the reliance of the business away from the entrepreneur, whose skills might be limited to specific areas.

What the above factors suggest is that, if a small business is to be successful and subsequently grow, it must consider its business strategy – the organisation of the business and the utilisation of individuals' abilities and experience (Box 16.2 looks at an example). It is a combination of these factors that is likely to generate success and only those businesses that co-ordinate such characteristics are likely to grow. Conversely, those businesses that fail to embrace these key characteristics are likely to fall by the wayside.

A potentially crucial factor in aiding success is the contribution and role of public policy. In the next section we shall consider the attitude of the UK Government to small business and the policy initiatives it has introduced. We will also assess how such initiatives differ from, complement or duplicate those provided by the EU.

BOX 16.2 HOTEL CHOCOLAT

A small, fast-growing, ethical business

Hotel Chocolat is a UK-based luxury chocolate manufacturer founded in 1993 by Angus Thirwell and Peter Harris. They had previous experience of the confectionery sector, having established the Mint Marketing Company in 1988, which sold packaged mints to the corporate market. A number of their customers asked them if they sold confectionery other than mints, which led them to move into the chocolate business with the creation of Choc Express in 2003.

Their initial sales were primarily from mail-order catalogues. The company then developed an online store, which helped it to collect much better marketing data than most of its rivals that sold their products through supermarkets.

In 2003, Choc Express was rebranded as Hotel Chocolat and, in 2004, opened its first retail store in Watford. The business now has 100 shops and cafés located across the UK and its *Rabot 1745* restaurant in London. Three chocolate boutiques have been opened in Denmark while a franchise agreement has also been made with a department store in Hong Kong. The business still remains heavily reliant on the domestic market, with 96 per cent of its sales in 2017 taking place in the UK.

As well as through its own website, the chocolates can also be purchased online through Amazon and Ocado. They are also available in John Lewis and Fenwick department stores.

A tasting club was created in 1998, where, for a fee, customers receive a monthly box of new chocolates, which they have to rate on a 'taste scorecard'. This tasting club has over 55 000 members and provides valuable market research data on the public's tastes.

The rapid growth in the business has been helped by its use of 'chocolate bond' crowdfunding. These bonds pay investors' interest, not in money, but in chocolate and have helped to raise over £5 million. In May 2016, the company raised £55.5m through its public sale of shares and listing on the Alternative Investment Market (AIM) of the London Stock Exchange. The two founding partners each made £20 million, while £12 million was used to finance the opening of new stores and improve the company's website.

The company's growth has been based on premium chocolates with authentic, wholesome ingredients: i.e. without artificial flavourings or hydrogenated fats. The product range covers chocolate slabs, boxed chocolates, gift boxes and chocolate fancies, such as chocolate-covered 'Amaretto and Almond Sultanas' and 'Dark with Chilli and Cocoa Nibs'. They also offer products for the corporate sector, vegetarians, vegans and diabetics. A range of beauty products was launched in November 2012 as well as a cookbook entitled *A new way of cooking with chocolate*. The business introduced a cocoa-infused gin advent calendar for Christmas 2017. One of its latest innovations is no added sugar milk chocolate.

The company has also engaged in forward vertical integration. It originally outsourced the production of its chocolates, but now they are all produced at its own factory in Cambridgeshire.

Fair trading

In 2004, Hotel Chocolat engaged in backward vertical integration and purchased a 140-acre cocoa plantation on the Caribbean island of St Lucia. The company refurbished the estate, began to plant new seedlings and worked towards gaining full organic accreditation. In 2011, it opened the Boucan luxury hotel and restaurant on the plantation.

The company realised early on in St Lucia that developing a sustainable industry for the long term, offering a high-quality and consistent supply of cocoa, required that it support local cocoa growers. For over 20 years prior to the purchase of the plantation, cocoa in St Lucia had been in decline. Local growers had no guarantee that harvested crops would be bought and, when crops were sold, payment could take up to six months to arrive. Under these circumstances, cocoa production was loss making.

The company has developed a programme of 'engaged ethics' to develop sustainable production and fair standards. Hotel Chocolat now guarantees that farmers who embrace the programme will be able to sell all the cocoa they produce at 30 to 40 per cent above the market price and will be paid within one week. The company buys all of the cocoa 'wet' (unfermented) to ensure consistent quality, allowing farmers to concentrate on growing and replanting. All of this is supported by advice and technical expertise. By 2011, the company had 120 cocoa growing partners including both new and established farmers.

As it develops the chocolate factory, Hotel Chocolat plans to bring other St Lucians into the supply chain, including chocolate workers, drivers, tour guides, engineers and support staff, all of whom will be trained and developed.

Performing well in a difficult market

Hotel Chocolat chose a good country in which to establish its business, as people in the UK are some of the largest consumers of chocolate in the world. In 2016, they consumed 8.61kg of chocolate per capita.[1]

However, the market environment was very difficult for chocolate producers during 2014–17. Increasingly, health-conscious consumers started to switch away from chocolate to healthier snacks containing less sugar. Mintel reported that the quantity of chocolate purchased in the UK fell by 1 per cent in 2015.[2] The downward trend continued with Euromonitor reporting a 1 per cent fall in the value of sales in 2017.[3] IRI research also found that, in 2017, the sales of famous chocolate brands in the UK such as Cadburys Dairy Milk, Galaxy and Aero fell by 4.2, 5.2 and 12.5 per cent respectively.

The costs of cocoa also increased sharply in commodity markets. The average price of cocoa increased from around $2 per kilogram in February 2013 to over $3 per kilogram for much of

---

[1]*Sweet success for seasonal chocolate*, Mintel Press Office (12 April 2017).

[2]'Mintel in the media', *Mintel blog* (13 July, 2015).

[3]'Chocolate confectionery in the UK', *Country Report*, Euromonitor International (July 2017).

▶

the 2014–16 period. Since then, however, the price has fallen and, from mid-2017 to mid-2018, was around $2 again.

Despite these tough trading conditions, Hotel Chocolat continued to perform strongly. In March 2015, it made greater profits than Thorntons, its main high-street rival. In 2017, the company's revenue increased by 12 per cent and its pre-tax profits doubled to £11.2m.

Hotel Chocolat's approach to excellence in chocolate products clearly has helped it to succeed in difficult market conditions. Many consumers appear to have been more focused on quality rather than the quantity of chocolate they purchased. The business's strong sense of corporate and social responsibility

has also helped it to appeal to an increasing number of ethical consumers.

Unsurprisingly, the firm has received a number of awards. In 2007, *Retail Week* judged Hotel Chocolat the 'Emerging Retailer of the Year' while, in 2016, it won Lloyds Bank 'Mid-Market Business of the Year'.

1. What conditions existed to enable Hotel Chocolat's small business to do so well in such a short period of time?
2. What dangers do you see in the growth strategy adopted by Hotel Chocolat?

16.3 GOVERNMENT ASSISTANCE AND THE SMALL FIRM

SME policy in the UK

Various UK governments have increasingly recognised the strategic importance of small firms to the economy. For example the UK Conservative–Liberal Coalition Government, elected in 2010, stated that its principal economic objective was to develop a strategy that would enable the country to achieve its full economic potential. A key element of the strategy was the encouragement and promotion of entrepreneurial talent; and one way of achieving this was by supporting small- and medium-sized enterprises (SMEs).

Over a number of years, various grants, tax concessions and advisory services have been established to encourage the establishment of new SMEs.

Pause for thought

Why might the government wish to distinguish SME start-up policies from SME growth and performance policies?

A new Department for Business, Energy & Industrial Strategy (BEIS) was created in July 2016. One of its key objectives is to support businesses to start and grow. This includes the aim of making the UK the best place to start and grow a business. The department is also reviewing the most effective methods for improving productivity of SMEs.

The UK Government and the EU also offer grants and other forms of assistance through regional, urban, social and industrial policy that small firms may be able to tap into (see sections 21.2, 21.3, 31.3 and 31.4). In this section we concentrate on the strategic framework and specific policies aimed at SMEs.

Strategic framework

In October 2010, the UK Government launched a new vision for growth and enterprise, entitled 'Local growth: realising every place's potential'. This set out how it intended to support enterprise, innovation, global trade and inward investment. It developed a framework centred around the idea of 'Local Enterprise Partnerships'. These are joint bodies bringing together the private and public sector to promote the economic interests of each part of the country.

In October 2011, Lord Young was appointed as an advisor to the Prime Minister on Enterprise. He undertook a three-part review on enterprise and small firms:

- The first review, Make business your business, was published in May 2012. This report stressed the record number of new start-up businesses and the growing culture of entrepreneurship.
- The second review, Growing your business, was published in 2013 and focused on ways of helping small firms to grow.
- The final review, Enterprise for all, was published in June 2014 and focused on the best ways of developing enterprise in the education system.

Forms of government support to small business in the UK

Raising finance. The Government created the British Business Bank on 1 November 2014. It is a state-owned but independently run body, which manages all government schemes that try to help smaller firms obtain access to finance. It does not lend or invest with businesses directly but instead works with over 80 delivery partners. The current schemes operated by the British Business Bank fall into two broad categories – equity and debt.

Debt finance is where SMEs borrow money from a lender. This money has to be repaid with interest.

Equity finance is where SMEs seek investment from groups or individuals and offer a share of their business in return. Individuals who invest their own money into a new business in return for a share of that business (i.e. ownership equity) are referred to as 'angel investors' (or as 'Dragons' in the popular TV programme, *Dragons' Den*). As well as providing finance, these angel investors may also offer managerial guidance and enable the firm to make use of their business contacts. 'Venture capitalists' invest other people's money that has been pooled into a managed fund. Once again, venture capitalists expect a share of the business in return for the investment.

Examples of debt finance schemes.

■ *Start Up Loans*. These are government-backed unsecured loans of up to £25 000. To be eligible, a person must either have just set up a business or have been trading for less than two years. They must also be unable to obtain finance from other sources. The loan has to be paid off within five years and has a fixed interest rate of 6.2 per cent. Successful applicants also receive 12 months of free mentoring services.

The scheme is run by the Start Up Loans Company, which is a subsidiary of the British Business Bank. The loans are provided by a delivery partner of the company. By the end of September 2017, £358.3 million had been lent through the scheme to more than 50 000 entrepreneurs.

■ *Enterprise Finance Guarantee (EFG)*. Rather than providing support for start-ups, EFG facilitates lending to SMEs that have more of a proven business track record but lack adequate security to obtain a loan. The scheme provides lenders with a government-backed guarantee that covers 75 per cent of the value of an individual loan.

The decision of whether or not to lend the money is still left entirely to the discretion of the private provider. However, given the extra protection afforded by the scheme, loan applications by SMEs have a much greater chance of being successful.

To be eligible for a loan with the EFG, a firm must be UK based, have a turnover no greater than £41 million and be seeking finance of between £1000 and £1.2 million. It must also agree to a repayment period of between 3 months and 10 years.

Since its launch in 2009, over 33 000 EFG loans have been made with a total value of just over £3.5 billion.

Examples of equity finance schemes.

■ *Angel CoFund*. This scheme aims to promote and develop the angel investment market. It offers support for angel investors who have organised themselves into groups or syndicates and are looking to make an equity investment of between £100 000 and £1 million in an eligible SME. The scheme provides government money for up to a maximum of 49 per cent of the investment. Since its launch in November 2011, the fund has invested £37 million in 79 SMEs with supporting investments of £180 million from business angel syndicates.

■ *Enterprise Capital Funds*. This scheme aims to encourage venture capital funds to invest in fast-growing SMEs. The scheme combines both private and public money in Enterprise Capital Funds (ECFs) that are available to SMEs.

Each ECF is run by managers in the private sector and often they are organised on a matched-fund basis – the government invests £1 in a fund for every £1 raised by the fund manager from the private sector. The maximum amount the government will invest in any individual ECF is capped at £50 million or two-thirds of the total fund size.

As of December 2017, 26 ECF funds had been created, which have raised £1 billion to help finance over 400 SMEs. In the November 2017 Budget, the Government committed up to £1 billion to support the ECF programme for 10 years.

Grants. Governments from all political parties have introduced a large range of different grants to support SMEs. These are usually focused on supporting a particular business activity, such as R&D, training and energy usage, or business purpose, such as business growth and exporting. For example, SMEs can apply for innovation funding from the government agency, Innovate UK. This is normally conditional on match funding by business or other partners and is designed to help SMEs find innovative ways of overcoming any barriers that were preventing them from growing.

Tax concessions. Every year, the Chancellor of the Exchequer sets out the tax rates and exemptions for the economy and some of these are designed to encourage enterprise and SME development. Three of the most important allowances for SMEs relate to employer National Insurance Contributions (NICs), business rates and VAT.

The UK Government introduced Employment Allowance in April 2014, which gave all firms the opportunity to claim up to £2000 per year towards the cost of their employer Class 1 NICs. Estimates suggest that 90 per cent of the benefits from this tax cut go to SMEs. In April 2016, the Government announced that it was increasing Employment Allowance to £3000 per year.

Business rates are based on the open-market rental value of premises. Reductions are available if the business uses only one property with a rateable value of less than £15 000. If its value is £12 000 or less, the business does not have to pay any rates. The rate of relief gradually declines from 100 per cent down to zero as the rateable value increases from £12 001 to £15 000. A revaluation occurs every five years where the Valuation Office Agency adjusts rates to reflect any changes in the local property market. The last revaluation came into effect on 1 April 2017. For some SMEs the changes mean they are no longer entitled to rate relief and face big increases in their bills. To help deal with this issue the Government announced that businesses no longer entitled to rate relief because of the revaluation would have any increases in their bills limited to £50 per month from April 2017 until 31 March 2018.

Firms with a turnover of less than £85 000 do not have to pay VAT (i.e. a tax of 20 per cent on the value of sales less the cost of supplies). This might deter some small firms from expanding as once their turnover hits £85 000 they could be faced with a VAT tax bill of up to £17 000 plus the additional administrative burden incurred. The Government announced in March 2018 that it was going to review the system.

Regulations. The Coalition Government introduced the 'red tape challenge' in 2011. Businesses were invited to identify regulations which they believed could be simplified or removed. In January 2014, the Government announced that more than 3000 regulations had been discovered that could be either scrapped or amended. The Better Regulation Executive (BRE) is a unit in the department for Business, Energy & Industrial Strategy that tries to make sure that regulations are less costly to business.

Mentoring. Some evidence suggests that survival rates are higher for small businesses that receive mentoring from more experienced business people. For this reason, UK governments have been willing to fund various mentoring schemes to help SMEs. These include the Get Mentoring project and the GrowthAccelerator initiative.

However, funding for many of these national schemes was withdrawn in 2016 as part of a 17 per cent cut in the budget for the then Department for Business, Innovation & Skills. The Government expects large businesses increasingly to provide the finance for these types of national scheme. For example, Mentorsme is operated by the British Bankers' Association. The Government has also established 39 regional Growth Hubs across the country to provide business support at the local level.

> ### Pause for thought
>
> *Do any sources of market failure exist in the finance market for SMEs?*

Small-firm policy in the EU

The EU adopted the Small Business Act in June 2008, which was its first comprehensive policy framework to support SMEs. The act focused on issues such as access to finance, the time taken to set up a company and how the public sector interacts with SMEs.

In 2011, the original act was revisited and new actions were implemented. These new actions included strengthening loan guarantee schemes, improving access to venture capital markets and streamlining legislation. In September 2014, the European Commission carried out a public consultation exercise to gather feedback on how the Small Business Act could be improved.

One of the more recent and important schemes run by the EU to support SMEs was the Competition and Innovation Framework Programme (CIP) which had a budget of €3.62 billion and operated from 2007 to 2013. It had a number of objectives that were focused on SMEs, including: providing better access to finance, supporting their innovation activities and delivering business support services.

COSME and the Horizon 2020 programme

CIP was replaced by the programme for the Competitiveness of Enterprises and Small and Medium-sized Enterprises (COSME) which has a planned budget of €2.3 billion and runs from 2014–20. A new Executive Agency for Small and Medium-sized Enterprises (EASME) was created in January 2014 to manage most parts of COSME on behalf of the EU. The programme has four key objectives:

- To improve access to finance for SMEs.
- To improve access to markets inside the EU and globally.
- To promote entrepreneurship.
- To improve conditions for the competitiveness and sustainability of EU businesses.

The objectives of COSME are very similar to those of the CIP. However, all the innovation actions and policies that were carried out previously under CIP have now been transferred to the Horizon 2020 (H2020) programme. H2020 will also run from 2014 to 2020 and has a budget of €80 billion to help implement the Innovation Union Initiative.

Some of the policies that have been implemented under the COSME programme include:

- *The Loan Guarantee Facility (LGF)*. This is similar to the EFG scheme in the UK. It provides guarantees for loans to SMEs of up to €150 000, which otherwise might not have taken place because of the lack of collateral. It is estimated that the LGF will enable 330 000 SMEs to obtain loans with a total value of €21 billion. It is also expected that 90 per cent of the firms that benefit from the scheme will have 10 or fewer employees.
- *Equity Facility for Growth (EFG)*. This is similar to Enterprise Capital Funds in the UK and provides financial support for venture capital funds that invest in SMEs. The EU predicts that the scheme will help over 500 firms obtain equity financing.
- *Enterprise Europe Network (EEN)*. The aim of this scheme is to help SMEs get access to different markets. Staff from the SME can get into contact with a local partner from the EEN, who can provide support on issues such as how to obtain market information and overcome any legal obstacles. They can also identify potential business partners across Europe.

An important part of the H2020 programme is the *SME Instrument.* This scheme has a €2.8 billion budget and aims to support the growth of SMEs, which have innovative ideas and EU or global potential. Applicants can receive up to €2.5 million of funding.

The EU's commitment to SMEs clearly has grown in recent years and it has recognised the valuable role that they play within the economy, not only as employers and contributors to output, but in respect of their ability to innovate and initiate technological change – vital components in a successful and thriving regional economy. However, it also recognises that there is more to be done.

SUMMARY

1a The small-firm sector is difficult to define. Different criteria might be used. However, the level of employment tends to be the most widely used.

1b The difficulties in defining what a small firm is mean that measuring the size of the small-firm sector is also difficult and subject to a degree of error. However, it appears that, in the UK, the small-firm sector has been growing since the mid-1960s. This is the result of a variety of influences including: industrial structure, working practices, the level of unemployment, the role of government and consumer affluence.

1c The growth in the small-firm sector in the UK is not mirrored elsewhere in the major European nations other than in Italy.

2a Small firms survive because they provide or hold distinct advantages over their larger rivals. Such advantages include: greater flexibility, greater quality of service, production efficiency, low overhead costs and product innovation.

2b Small businesses are prone to high rates of failure, however. This is due to problems of credibility, finance and limited management skills.

2c Of those small businesses that manage to survive, a small fraction will grow. The growth of business tends to proceed through a series of stages, in which the organisation and management of the firm evolve, becoming less and less dependent upon the owner-manager.

2d Those small businesses that do grow are likely to have distinct characteristics relating to individual abilities, business organisation and business strategy. Combinations of variables from these three categories will tend to favour growth of the SME.

3a Government policy aimed at the small firm within the UK is particularly concerned with business start-ups, although we can also identify initiatives that look to stimulate growth and improve performance.

3b Small business policy within the EU seeks to complement national programmes. It provides a wide range of grants, projects and information for SMEs. A large emphasis is placed upon the development and transmission of technological innovations within the SME sector.

REVIEW QUESTIONS

1 Why is it so difficult to define the small-firm sector? What problems does this create?

2 'Small businesses are crucial to the vitality of the economy.' Explain.

3 Compare and contrast the competitive advantages held by both small and big business.

4 Often, it is argued that the success of a small business depends upon a number of conditions. Such conditions can be placed under the general headings of: the entrepreneur, the firm and the strategy. How are conditions under each of these headings likely to contribute to small business success?

5 Compare and contrast UK and EU approaches to SME policy.

17 Chapter

Prices down and staying down

Pricing strategy

Business issues covered in this chapter

- How are prices determined in practice?
- What determines the power that a firm has to determine its prices?
- Why do some firms base prices on average costs of production?
- Why do firms sometimes charge different prices to different customers for the same product (e.g. seats on a plane)? What forms can such 'price discrimination' take?
- What types of pricing strategy is a firm likely to pursue if it is producing multiple products?
- How does pricing vary with the stage in the life of a product? Will newly launched products be priced differently from products that have been on the market a long time?

How are prices determined in practice? Is there such a thing as an 'equilibrium price' for a product, which will be charged to all customers and by all firms in the industry? In most cases the answer is no.

Take the case of the price of a rail ticket. On asking, 'What's the train fare to London?', you are likely to receive any of the following replies: 'Do you want an "Advance" ticket?' 'Do you want a single or return?' 'How old are you?' 'Do you have a railcard (family & friends, young person's, student, senior)?' 'Do you want an off-peak or Anytime return?' 'Will you be travelling out before 10 am?' 'Will you be leaving London between 4 pm and 6 pm?' 'Do you want to reserve a seat?' 'Do you want to take advantage of our special low-priced winter Saturday fare?'

How you respond to the above questions will determine the price you pay, a price that can vary several hundred per cent from the lowest to the highest. And it is not just train fares that vary in this way: air fares and holidays are other examples. In some situations, selling the same product to different groups of consumers at different prices is an example of *price discrimination*. The key question is whether the different prices can be explained by any differences in the costs of supplying the good. (We shall examine price discrimination in detail later in this chapter.) But prices for a product do not just vary according to the customer. They vary according to a number of other factors as well.

- *The competition that the firm faces.* Firms operating under monopoly or collusive oligopoly are likely to charge very different prices from firms operating in highly competitive markets

KI 1
p11

Definition

Price discrimination Where a firm sells the same or similar product at different prices and the difference in price cannot be fully accounted for by any differences in the costs of supply.

- *Information on costs and demand.* Firms in the real world may have very scant information about the elasticity of demand for their product and for the products of their competitors, and how demand is likely to change. It is the same with information on costs: firms may have only a rough idea of how costs are likely to change over time and over different levels of output. The picture of a firm choosing its price by a careful calculation of marginal cost and marginal revenue may be far from reality.

- *The aims of the firm.* Is the firm aiming to maximise profits, is it seeking to maximise sales or growth or does it have a series of aims? Which aim or aims that it pursues will determine the price it charges?

- *The life cycle of the product.* When a firm launches a product, it may charge a very different price from when the product has become established in the market or, later, when it is beginning to be replaced by more up-to-date products.

In this chapter, we will explore the pricing strategies of business. We will identify different pricing models, show how a firm's pricing policy is likely to change over a product's life cycle, and how and under what circumstances businesses might practise price discrimination. We will also consider a number of other pricing issues, such as those linked to a multi-product business and the use of a practice known as 'transfer pricing'.

17.1 PRICING AND MARKET STRUCTURE

The firm's power over prices

In a free and competitive market, we know that the quantity bought and sold, and the actual price of the product, are determined by the forces of supply and demand. If the quantity demanded is in excess of the quantity supplied, the consequent market shortage will cause the price level to rise. Equally, if the quantity supplied is in excess of the quantity demanded, the resulting market surplus will cause the market price to fall. At some point, we have an equilibrium or market-clearing price, to which the market will naturally move. In such an environment, the firm cannot have a 'pricing strategy': the price is set for it by the market. It is a price taker and has no influence over the setting of prices.

But, even if a firm were able to identify the market demand and supply schedules, which is not at all certain given the problem of acquiring accurate market information, the market equilibrium price is likely to be short lived as market conditions change and demand and supply shift. This would be the case particularly for those goods or services that are fashionable and subject to changing consumer preferences, or where production technology is undergoing a period of innovation, influencing both the cost structure of the product and the potential output decisions open to the business. The best business could hope for, given the uncertainty of demand and supply, is to be flexible enough to continue making a profit when market conditions shift.

When a firm has a degree of market power, however, it will have some discretion over the price it can charge for its product. The smaller the number of competitors, and the more distinct its product is from those of its rivals, the more inelastic the firm's demand will become at any given price. This will provide it with greater control over price.

We saw (Chapter 12) that, in oligopolistic markets, firms are dependent on each other: what one firm does, in terms

of pricing, product design, product promotion, etc., will affect its rivals. The degree of interdependence and the extent to which firms acknowledge it will affect the degree to which they either compete or collude. This, in turn, will affect their pricing strategy. The result is that prices may be very difficult to predict in advance and bear little resemblance to those that would have been determined through the operation of free-market forces.

At one time, there may be an all-out price war, with firms desperately trying to undercut each other in order to grab market share or even drive their rivals out of business. At other times, prices may be very high, with the oligopolists colluding with each other to achieve maximum industry profits. In such cases, the price may be even higher than if the industry were an unregulated monopoly because there might still be considerable *non*-price competition, which would add to costs and hence to the profit-maximising price.

Pause for thought

Would prices generally be lower or higher if a business was aiming to maximise long-run growth rather than short-run profits?

It is clear from this that, under oligopoly, pricing is likely to be highly strategic. One of the key strategic issues is the effect of prices on potential new entrants, and here it is not only the oligopolist, but also the monopolist that must think strategically. If the firm sets its prices at a level that maximises its short-run profits, will this encourage new firms to take the risk of entering the market? If so, should the firm keep its price down and thereby deliberately limit the size of its profits so as not to attract new entrants?

Limit pricing

This policy of *limit pricing* is illustrated in Figure 17.1. To simplify the explanation, it is assumed that both the existing firm and potential new entrant have constant marginal costs. It is also assumed that neither firm has any fixed costs so that $AC = MC$.

Two AC curves are drawn: one for the existing firm and one for a new entrant. The existing firm, being experienced and with a capital base and established supply channels, is shown having a lower AC curve. Any potential new entrant, if it is to compete successfully with the existing firm, must charge the same price or a lower one: i.e. we are assuming there is no product differentiation.

The short-run profit maximising position for the existing firm is to produce where $MC = MR$. This is illustrated at point *a* in Figure 17.1. The firm will produce an output of Q_1 and charge a price of P_1. However, given that the potential new entrant's average costs are below this price, it could enter the industry and earn supernormal profits.

If, instead, the existing firm produced an output of Q_2 at a price of P_L, then it would be more difficult for the potential new entrant to enter the market. If it did enter and the existing firm continued to produce Q_2, then the market price would fall below P_L and the new entrant would make a loss.

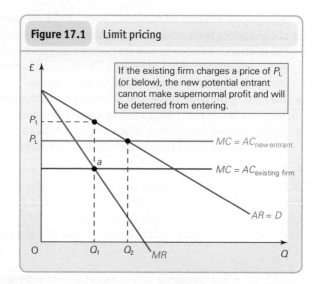

Figure 17.1 Limit pricing

If the existing firm charges a price of P_L (or below), the new potential entrant cannot make supernormal profit and will be deterred from entering.

Thus, provided the existing firm does not raise price above P_L, the other firm, unable to make supernormal profit, will not be attracted into the industry.

P_L may well be below the existing firm's short-run profit-maximising price, but it may prefer to limit its price to P_L to protect its long-run profits from damage by competition.

17.2 ALTERNATIVE PRICING STRATEGIES

What is the typical procedure by which firms set prices? Do they construct marginal cost and marginal revenue curves (or equations) and find the output where they are equal? Do they then use an average revenue curve (or equation) to work out the price at that output?

To do this requires a detailed knowledge of costs and revenues that few firms possess. To work out *marginal* cost, the firm must know how costs will *change* as output changes. In reality, this is highly unlikely. The business environment is in a constant state of change and uncertainty. The costs of production and the potential revenues from sales will be difficult to predict, shaped as they are by many complex and interrelated variables (changes in tastes, advertising, technological innovation, etc.).

Similarly, to work out *marginal* revenue, the firm requires information not just on current price and sales. It must know what will happen to demand if price *changes*. In other words, it must know the price elasticity of demand for its product. Under oligopoly in particular, it is virtually impossible to identify a demand curve for the firm's product. Demand for one firm's product will depend on what its rivals do: and that can never be predicted with any certainty. As a consequence, managers' 'knowledge' of future demand and costs will take the form of estimates (or even 'guesstimates').

Trying to equate marginal costs and marginal revenue, therefore, is likely to be a highly unreliable means of achieving maximum profits (if, indeed, that were the aim).

If, then, the marginalist principle of traditional theory is not followed by most businesses, what alternative pricing strategy can be adopted? In practice, firms look for rules of pricing that are relatively simple to apply.

Cost-based pricing

One alternative to marginalist pricing is average-cost or *mark-up pricing*. In this case, producers derive a price by simply adding a certain percentage (mark-up) for profit on top of average costs (average fixed costs plus average variable costs).

$$P = AFC + AVC + \text{profit mark-up}$$

The size of the profit mark-up will depend on the firm's aims: whether it is aiming for high or even maximum profits or merely a target based on previous profit.

KI 4
p 19

Definitions

Limit pricing Where a business strategically sets its price below the level that would maximise its profits in the short run in an attempt to deter new rivals entering the market. This enables the firm to make greater profits in the long run.

Mark-up pricing A pricing strategy adopted by business in which a profit mark-up is added to average costs.

Choosing the level of output

KI 19
p 147

Although calculating price in this manner does away with the firm's need to know its marginal cost and revenue curves, it still requires the firm to estimate how much output it intends to produce. The reason is that average cost varies with output. If the firm estimates that it will be working to full capacity, its average cost is likely to be quite different from that if it only works at 80 or 60 per cent of capacity.

Businesses tend to base their mark-up on *short-run* average costs. This is because estimates of short-run costs are more reliable than those of long-run costs. Long-run costs are based on *all* factors being variable, including capital. But by the time new capital investment has taken place, factors such as technological change and changes in factor prices will have shifted the long-run average cost curve, thereby making initial estimations inaccurate.

Figure 17.2 shows a firm's typical short-run average cost curves. The *AVC* curve is assumed to be saucer shaped. It falls at first as a result of increasing marginal returns; then is probably flat, or virtually so, over a range of output; then rises as a result of diminishing marginal returns and possibly the need to pay overtime. The flat range of the average variable cost curve reflects the **reserve capacity** held by the business. This is spare capacity that the business can draw upon, if needed, to respond to changes in the market. For example, demand for the product may be subject to seasonal variation. The point is that many businesses can accommodate such changes with very little change in their average variable costs.

Most firms that use average-cost pricing will base their price on this horizontal section of the *AVC* curve (between points *a* and *b* in Figure 17.2). This section represents the firm's *normal* range of output. This normal range of output is that within which the plant has been designed to operate and the business expects to be producing.

Average fixed costs will carry on falling as more is produced: overheads are spread over a greater output. This is illustrated in Figure 17.2. The result is that average (total) cost (*AC*) will continue falling over the range of output where *AVC* is constant, with minimum *AC* being reached at point *c* – beyond the flat section of the *AVC* curve. In practice, many firms do not regard average fixed costs in this way. Instead, they focus on average variable costs and then just add an element for overheads (*AFC*).

Choosing the mark-up

The level of profit mark-up on top of average cost will be influenced by a range of possible considerations, such as fairness and the response of rivals. However, the most significant consideration is likely to be the implications of price for the level of market demand.

If a firm could estimate its demand curve, it could then set its output and profit mark-up at levels to avoid a shortage or surplus. Thus, in Figure 17.3, it could choose a lower output (Q_1) with a higher mark-up (*fg*) or a higher output (Q_2) with a lower mark-up (*hj*). If a firm could not estimate its demand curve, then it could adjust its mark-up and output over time by a process of trial and error, according to its success in meeting profit and sales aims.

KI 12
p 64

One problem here is that prices have to be set in advance of the firm knowing just how much it will sell and therefore how much it will need to produce. In practice, firms usually will base their assumptions about next year's sales on this year's figures, add a certain percentage to allow for growth in demand and then finally adjust this up or down if they decide to change the mark-up.

Definition

Reserve capacity A range of output over which business costs will tend to remain relatively constant.

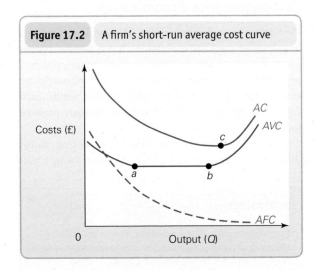

Figure 17.2 A firm's short-run average cost curve

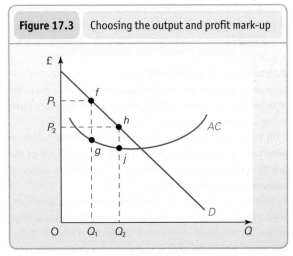

Figure 17.3 Choosing the output and profit mark-up

Variations in the mark-up

In most firms, the mark-up is not rigid. In expanding markets, or markets where firms have monopoly/oligopoly power, the size of the mark-up is likely to be greater. In contracting markets, or under conditions of rising costs and constant demand, a firm may well be forced to accept lower profits and thus reduce the mark-up.

Multi-product firms often have different mark-ups for their different products depending on their various market conditions. Such firms often will distribute their overhead costs unequally among their products. The potentially most profitable products, often those with the least elastic demands, will probably be required to make the greatest contribution to overheads.

The firm is likely to take account of the actions and possible reactions of its competitors. It may well be unwilling to change prices when costs or demand change, for fear of the reactions of competitors (see the kinked demand curve theory on pages 211 and 214). If prices are kept constant and yet costs change, either due to a movement along the *AC* curve in response to a change in demand, or due to a shift in the *AC* curve, the firm must necessarily change the size of the mark-up.

> **Pause for thought**
>
> *If the firm adjusts the size of its mark-up according to changes in demand and the actions of competitors, could its actions approximate to setting price and output where MC = MR?*

17.3 PRICE DISCRIMINATION

Up until this point in the chapter, it has been assumed that a firm sells each unit of its output for the same price. This is called *uniform pricing* and may result in the firm missing out on opportunities to make greater profits. Why? Because some customers value a product more highly than others and thus have a greater willingness to pay. They would still purchase the good if the price were higher.

To exploit this situation, the firm might be tempted to increase prices to try to capture some of this consumer surplus and convert it into profit. However it faces a trade-off. A higher price will increase the profit *per transaction,* but some customers will stop buying its product: i.e. the ones who do not value it so highly. Indeed, if the firm is already producing at an output where *MC = MR*, it loses more from the lost trade than it gains from charging remaining customers the higher price.

This trade-off could be avoided, however, if the firm could charge a higher price to those customers with a high valuation for the product (i.e. gaining a high utility) and a lower price to those consumers with a lower valuation for the product. Firms can do this by implementing a strategy of *price discrimination.*

Defining price discrimination

Care needs to be taken when explaining the precise meaning of this concept, as vague definitions can sometimes lead to it being incorrectly applied.

If the cost to the firm of supplying different customers does not vary then price discrimination is defined as the practice of selling the same or similar products to different customers for different prices.

If the costs of supplying different customers *does* vary, then the definition is slightly more complicated. It is defined as the practice of selling the same or similar product at different prices and the difference in price cannot be fully accounted for by any difference in the costs of supply. If any

differences in the cost of supplying each customer can fully explain the variation in prices, then it is *not* an example of price discrimination.

> **Pause for thought**
>
> *If customers were all charged the same price for a product could this ever be classed as an example of price discrimination? Explain your answer.*

Economists often divide price discrimination into three broad categories: first, second and third degree. In some cases, this division is not always clear and people debate whether to classify a particular example as either second or third degree.

First-degree price discrimination

First-degree price discrimination is also sometimes referred to as 'perfect price discrimination'. It is a pricing strategy where the seller is able to charge each consumer a different price for the same product which is equal to the maximum amount they are prepared to pay. In other words, each consumer pays a different price based on their own personal valuation of the product.

Unfortunately for the firm, only the buyer truly knows the maximum amount they are willing to pay for each unit

> **Definition**
>
> **First-degree price discrimination** Where the seller of the product charges each consumer the maximum price they are prepared to pay for each unit of the good.

of a product: i.e. there is asymmetric information (see pages 29–30). The firm could simply ask the customer 'What is the maximum amount you are willing to pay for the product?'. However, the customer is highly unlikely to provide a truthful response, especially if they believe their answer will influence the price.

The difficulties involved for the firm in overcoming this asymmetric information means that first-degree price discrimination remains more of a theoretical possibility than a viable business strategy. Firms may not be able to charge each person the maximum amount they are willing to pay, but in some circumstances they may be able to charge different customers different prices for the same product. This is called *personalised* or *person-specific pricing* and is a strategy that can approach one of first-degree price discrimination.

It is more likely in any sector where there is scope for some bargaining over price. Through observation and negotiation a seller may be able to 'size up' different customers and obtain some information about their willingness to pay. Examples include stallholders in a street market and second-hand car dealers haggling with their customers.

An experienced and skilful salesperson will be able to extract some consumer surplus but it is highly unlikely they will ever succeed in negotiating a price equal to the maximum amount each customer is willing to pay. The process is also very time-consuming and a supplier will have to judge whether the extra revenue it generates outweighs the extra costs. The potential for personalised pricing in online markets is discussed in Box 17.1.

A model of first-degree price discrimination

Although it is highly unlikely to occur in the real world, perfect price discrimination still provides a useful benchmark against which to judge the impact of other pricing strategies. For this reason it is illustrated in Figure 17.4. To simplify the explanation, we assume that marginal cost (MC) is constant and that there are no fixed costs, so that average cost (AC) = MC.

If the profit-maximising firm charged the same price to all of its customers, it would be P_1 and output would correspondingly be Q_1 (i.e. where $MC = MR$). Area 1 would represent the supernormal profit made by the firm. However, if the firm knew the demand curve for its product and could sell every unit at the maximum price that each consumer was prepared to pay, it could make additional gains.

First, it could make more profit from the same number of sales, Q_1. All of the consumer surplus that existed when it charged one price (area 2) would be converted into profits by a policy of first-degree price discrimination.

Second, its profit-maximising level of output would be greater than Q_1. If the firm could charge each customer a separate price then the MR changes – it is no longer below the AR curve. Instead $MR = AR$, as the firm no longer has to pass any price reductions on to other customers. This means that the new profit-maximising level of output is Q_2. This further increases its total profit by area 3.

The impact on consumers is mixed. Those who previously purchased the product under a single pricing strategy are now paying higher prices than they were before. However, new customers are able to purchase the product under first-degree price discrimination who would not have purchased it if a single price had been charged.

Third-degree price discrimination

Third-degree price discrimination is where a firm charges a different price to different groups of consumers: for example, lower prices for children or senior citizens, or higher prices for products sold in more affluent areas. There is no bargaining, haggling or discussion between buyers and sellers. Instead, the firm needs to find some consumer characteristic, trait or attribute as a basis to split them into different groups.

To be successful, the characteristic must be:

- relatively easy for the firm to observe;
- informative about consumers' willingness to pay, i.e. consumers allocated to one group should generally be less price sensitive at any given price than those allocated to another group; **KI 12 p 64**
- legal to use. In many countries, charging different prices based on a person's ethnicity or gender is unlawful. For

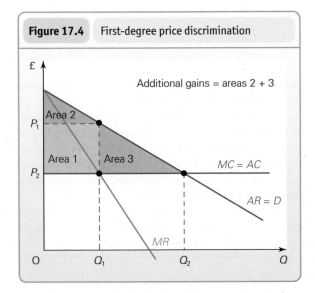

Figure 17.4 First-degree price discrimination

£

Additional gains = areas 2 + 3

Area 2

P_1

Area 1 | Area 3

P_2

$MC = AC$

$AR = D$

MR

O | Q_1 | Q_2 | Q

Definition

Third-degree price discrimination Where a firm divides consumers into different groups based on some characteristic that is relatively easy to observe, legal, informative about their willingness to pay and acceptable. The firm then charges a different price to consumers in different groups, but the same price to all the consumers within a group.

BOX 17.1 ONLINE PERSONALISED PRICING

To what extent is it used and do customers think it is fair?

It is impossible for firms to gather enough information to implement a policy of perfect price discrimination, i.e. charging each customer the maximum amount they are willing to pay. However, some businesses may still be able to charge each person a different price based on certain characteristics and behaviours that are relatively easy to observe. This is called personalised pricing.

It can occur in markets where salespeople observe their customers and haggle over the price. The clothes people wear, the cars they drive, the address where they live and their ethnicity/nationality might enable an experienced salesperson to make an informed guess about their likely income and willingness to pay. The information can be used to set the starting point in any negotiation over the price.

Personalised pricing has never been widespread in traditional *brick and mortar* retailing because of the time-consuming nature of the negotiation process. In many instances, the incremental costs are simply too great and outweigh the extra revenues generated. This will be especially true for firms selling large volumes of goods. Just imagine how long it would take to shop at a supermarket if each customer had to haggle with a member of staff over the price of each item in their trolley! There is also the problem of designing compensation contracts that provide sales staff with appropriate incentives. In many cases, the firm's best strategy is to post the same price for all consumers, who either accept or reject the purchase.

The dramatic growth in the use of e-commerce, however, has opened up new possibilities for firms to observe customers and monitor their individual behaviour. In the UK alone, internet sales as a proportion of total sales have increased from 3.4 per cent in 2007 to 16.3 per cent in 2017.

Every single click a user makes when browsing online generates potentially useful information for the firm. Known as 'digital Big Data', it offers new possibilities but also presents new problems. One issue is that the quantity, speed and variety of this new online information cannot be managed by using traditional methods of analysis.

For example, some of the data is in the form of millions of social media comments that cannot be examined with traditional databases. Many business schools in UK and US universities have responded by offering new courses in business analytics, which are often nicknamed 'Big Data finishing school'.

Digital *Big Data* comes from three main sources:

First-party data. This is generated from the interaction between a supplier and buyer via the supplier's on-line store or website. For example, a firm can use an Internet Protocol (IP) address and/or cookies to identify the following information about a consumer:

- their geographical location, i.e. country and region;
- their internet service provider;
- the type and speed of their internet connection;
- the browser and make of computer/tablet/mobile phone they are using;
- their purchase history.

All of this information can help the firm to build a profile of their different customers without the need for any time-consuming interaction by a salesperson. A big retailer with a large range of goods can also monitor its customers' click history, i.e. the different types of products they browse on the website.

Second-party data. This is first-party data that the business sells and/or exchanges with another firm. For example, a hotel chain might find an airline's first-party data useful.

Third-party data. Some businesses such as Acxiom, Oracle Bluekai, Lotame, Experian and Neustar specialise in collecting data by tracking the browsing behaviour of people across a number of different websites. They do not directly interact with consumers but, instead, pay major retailers for access to their websites so they can build detailed profiles of users as they move around the web. This information is then processed and presented in a usable form that some businesses are willing to pay for.

---

example, 'Ladies nights' have been prohibited in the USA in California, New Jersey, Maryland and Pennsylvania;

- acceptable to the customer. If consumers think the characteristic is an unfair basis on which to group consumers, they may boycott the product.

It should also be impossible, or very costly, for a consumer to change characteristic so they are in the low-price group. For example, a customer is unable to reclassify themselves as a

child or a pensioner in order to qualify for the lower price associated with this characteristic.

Having allocated its customers into these groups, the seller then sets a different price for each group according to its price elasticity of demand at any given price: the group with the lowest price elasticity of demand will be charged the highest price. However, each consumer in the same group pays the same price for the product.

Because the firm is setting the price that a particular consumer has to pay, third-degree is closer to first-degree

Is pricing influenced by different consumer characteristics? Is there any evidence that retailers are systematically using online data on the characteristics of their customers to personalise prices? Mikians, *et al.*[1] analysed data collected over a 20-day period on products for sale at 200 different online retailers including Amazon and Best Buy. This generated over 20 000 observations. The research found:

■ no evidence of retailers personalising prices based on the operating system and/or browser used by their customers;
■ the majority of the retailers did not personalise prices based on the geographic location of the customers;
■ some evidence of price variation by country for computer games and e-books on the Amazon and Steam websites;
■ the office supplies business, Staples, varied prices based on the location of the consumer within the USA.

An investigation carried out by the *Wall Street Journal* also found evidence of price discrimination based on location. For example, Staples offered lower online prices to customers located within 20 miles of rival stores such as *OfficeMax* and *Office Depot*.

Is pricing influenced by browsing behaviour?

Mikians, *et al.* did not find any evidence of price discrimination based on the browsing behaviour of the user. They did, however, find some evidence of price steering. This is where a website alters its search results based on the characteristics and behaviour of the consumer. For example, users who had previously browsed luxury good websites had more expensive products listed at the top of their search results page.

Hannak, *et al.*[2] conducted controlled experiments with fake accounts to see if factors such as the users click history, purchase history and cookies had an influence on prices. In the majority of cases, they found no evidence of any impact.

The evidence suggests that the majority of firms are not using the greater availability of digital Big Data to personalise prices. This is surprising, given how many businesses regularly personalise online advertising.

One potential constraint on the use of personalised pricing is the attitude and response of the public. Turow, Feldman and Meltzer[3] reported that 87 per cent of respondents to a survey of US consumers disagreed with the following statement: 'It is OK if an online store I use charges different people different prices for the same products during the same hour.'

Given its unpopularity, firms who use personalised prices are likely to receive negative comments on social media. Concerns about the potential damage to a business's reputation and fears that consumers will boycott their products may deter managers from implementing the policy in the first place.

1. *Distinguish between first-, second- and third-degree price discrimination.*
2. *Draw a diagram to illustrate the impact of first-degree price discrimination when the costs to the firm are greater than those of using a policy of uniform pricing.*
3. *Explain how the revenue from personalised pricing will differ from first-degree price discrimination.*

[1] J. Mikians, L. Gyarmati, V. Erramilli and N. Laoutaris, 'Detecting price and search discrimination on the internet', *Proceedings of the 11th ACM Workshop on Hot Topics in Networks*, pp. 79–84 (October 2012).

[2] A. Hannak, G. Soeller, D. Lazer, A. Mislove and C. Wilson, 'Measuring price discrimination and steering on E-commerce web sites *Proceedings of the 2014 Conference on Internet Measurement Conference*, pp. 305–18 (November 2014).

[3] J. Turow, L. Feldman and K Meltzer, 'Open to exploitation: America's shoppers on-line and off-line', *Departmental Papers*, Annenberg Public Policy Center of the University of Pennsylvania (June 2005).

than second-degree price discrimination (as we shall see below). First- and third-degree price discrimination are sometimes referred to as examples of 'direct price discrimination'.

Third-degree price discrimination is more feasible than first-degree price discrimination as the informational demands it places on the firm are much lower: i.e. it only needs to have information about how the willingness to pay varies between different groups of customers rather than between each individual consumer. However, the firm still

needs to be able to find an informative, acceptable and easily observable characteristic.

One possibility would be to split consumers into different groups based on their incomes. In many instances, it is highly probable that most consumers with higher incomes would be willing to pay more for a given product than those on lower incomes. They would tend to be less price sensitive at any given price. Therefore, the firm could set a relatively high price for those consumers on higher incomes and a relatively low price for those on lower incomes. For example,

> **Figure 17.5** Third-degree price discrimination

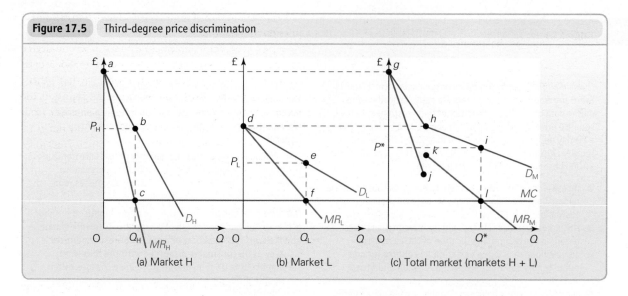

(a) Market H   (b) Market L   (c) Total market (markets H + L)

supermarkets could charge higher prices in stores located in wealthy areas than in those located in poorer areas.

Modelling third-degree price discrimination

Figure 17.5 illustrates a simple example.

Assume a firm decides to split its customers into two different groups – those earning at or above £40 000 per year and those earning less than £40 000. Panel (a) in Figure 17.5 illustrates the demand curve for the firm's product of those earning at or above £40 000, while panel (b) illustrates the demand curve for those earning less than £40 000.

Equilibrium for a single-price firm. If the firm were unable to split its customers into these two different groups, then a market demand curve could be derived. This is illustrated in panel (c) and is obtained by horizontally aggregating the demand curves in panel (a) and (b). The market demand curve is the same as the demand curve in market H from point *g* to *h*. This is because no consumers in market L are willing to pay a price above *d*.

As the price falls below point *d*, consumers in both markets, H and L, are willing to buy the good; so horizontal aggregation of both demand curves must take place from this point onwards. This creates a kink in the market demand curve at point *h*. This kink also creates a discontinuity in the *MR* curve between points *j* and *k*. To simplify the explanation, it is also assumed that the firm's marginal cost is constant and that it has no fixed costs. Thus $AC = MC$.

To understand how a firm would behave if it could only set one price for all of its customers, we need to focus on the market demand curve in panel (c). If it was a profit-maximising firm, then it would produce where the market *MR*: i.e. $MR_M = MC$. This occurs at point *l* in panel (c) of Figure 17.5. It would therefore produce an output of Q^* and sell all of this output at the same price of P^*.

Equilibrium under third-degree price discrimination. What happens if the firm could now charge a different price to the

customers in market H from those in market L? At the single price of P^* the price elasticity of demand in market H is lower than it is in market L. (Note that demand is, nevertheless, elastic in both markets at this price as *MR* is positive.) Therefore, the firm could increase its profits by charging a price above P^* in market H and below P^* in market L. Once again, this can be illustrated in Figure 17.5.

In market H, the profit-maximising firm should produce where $MR_H = MC$. Therefore, it should sell an output of Q_H for a price of P_H.

In market L, it should produce where $MR_L = MC$ at point *f*. Therefore, it should sell an output of Q_L for a price of P_L.

Note that P_L is below P^*, while P_H is above P^*. Also, because the demand curves are linear, the total output sold is the same under third-degree price discrimination as it is under uniform pricing: i.e. $Q^* = Q_H + Q_L$. We will see later in the chapter that this is a key point when considering whether or not price discrimination is in the public interest.

Splitting customers into different groups based on their incomes might be informative about their willingness to pay. However, it might be a difficult characteristic for the firm to directly observe. It might, perhaps, ask to see a copy of the customer's salary slip in order to qualify for the lower price. In reality, however, most people are unlikely to keep this type of proof on their person. They might also object on the grounds that it was an unacceptable invasion of their privacy.

To implement this pricing strategy successfully, the seller might have to find another consumer characteristic that successfully met all four criteria (see the bullet list above). Some possible alternatives are shown in Table 17.1.

> ### Pause for thought
>
> *How would the profit-maximising output and price be determined under third-degree price discrimination if the marginal cost curve was upward sloping? Draw a diagram to illustrate your answer.*

Table 17.1	Examples of third-degree price discrimination

Characteristic	Example
Age	16–25 or senior railcard; half-price children's tickets in the cinema.
Gender	'Ladies' night' in a bar or club where men pay the full price for drinks while women can get the same drinks at a discounted price.
Ethnicity	A study by Levitt and Venkatech found that prostitutes charged black customers less than either white or Hispanic customers.
Location	Pharmaceutical companies often charge different prices for the same medicine/drug in different countries. Consumers in the USA often are charged more than those from other countries.
Occupation	Apple and Microsoft provide price discounts to employees of educational institutions.
Business or individual	Publishers of academic journals charge much lower subscription rates to individuals than university libraries.
Past buying behaviour	Firms often charge new customers a lower price than existing customers for the same product or service as an 'introductory offer'.

Third-degree price discrimination by the non-profit-maximising firm

If a firm does not set a profit-maximising price, either because it has some alternative aim or because it uses cost-based methods of pricing, which, owing to a lack of information, do not lead to the profit-maximising price, then we cannot predict precisely what the discriminatory prices will be. All we can say is that price discrimination will allow the firm to achieve higher revenue and probably higher profits, which most firms will prefer to lower profits.

Pause for thought

To what extent does each of the characteristics in Table 17.1 indicate to the firm differences in consumers' incomes?

Second-degree price discrimination

Second-degree price discrimination is where a firm offers consumers a range of different pricing options for the same or similar products. However, unlike first- and third-degree price discrimination, customers are free to choose the pricing option they want from those on offer. They are not stuck with a price assigned to them by the seller. Whereas first and third degree are sometimes described as examples of direct

price discrimination, second degree is referred to as indirect price discrimination.

Why would a firm implement a policy of second-degree as opposed to third-degree price discrimination? Some of its customers are likely to be more price sensitive than others, but it may be impossible for the firm to identify one from the other. Informative and easy-to-observe characteristics that signal consumers' willingness to pay may simply not exist. An alternative strategy for the firm is to offer a range of prices in such a way that relatively price-insensitive customers voluntarily choose to buy the product for a higher price.

But, why would rational consumers ever choose to pay a higher price than they have to? The key for the strategy to work is for the firm to make the lower prices for the product conditional on other aspects of the sale. Some more commonly used examples include:

The quantity of the product purchased. In order to obtain the good at a lower price, the customer has to purchase a certain quantity of the good or service, Q^*. An example of how such 'quantity discounts' can work is explained in more detail in Box 17.2.

It is important to distinguish between quantity discounts and block pricing. With a quantity discount, the lower price applies to *all* the units purchased, including those below Q^*. With a 'block declining tariff', the lower

Definition

Second-degree price discrimination Where a firm offers consumers a range of different pricing options for the same or similar product. Consumers are then free to choose whichever option they wish, but the lower prices are conditional on some other aspect of the sale such as the quantity or the exact version of the product purchased.

Figure 17.6	Second-degree price discrimination: block declining tariff

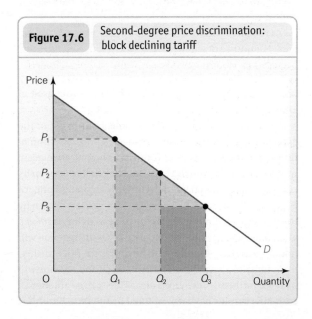

BOX 17.2 A QUANTITY DISCOUNT PRICING STRATEGY

A strategy to get consumers to identify themselves!

Assume that a firm knows that it has two types of customers for its product. Type 'I' customers have a lower price elasticity of demand than type 'E' customers at any given price for the product. Unfortunately for the firm, it has no way of knowing into which category any individual customer falls. There are no easy-to-observe consumer characteristics that would provide some indication of their willingness to pay.

Ideally, the firm would like the customers to sort themselves voluntarily into the two different groups. It could then charge type I consumers a higher price than type E consumers and transfer some consumer surplus into profit. However, if it simply offered the good for sale at two different prices all the consumers, whether they were type I or type E, would simply choose the lower price.

In order to try to get the consumers to self-select voluntarily into the two different groups, the firm could introduce a *quantity discount*. This pricing strategy is illustrated in the figure. To simplify the example, it is assumed that the firm's marginal cost is constant and it has no fixed costs of production, so that $AC = MC$. Consumers can obtain the product for the lower discounted price of P_L if they purchase a minimum quantity of the product (Q^*). The new lower price applies to all the units of the good they purchase and not just those in excess of Q^*. (This is different from a block declining tariff where the lower price would only apply to the incremental units purchased in excess of Q^*.) If the consumers purchase less than Q^*, then they have to pay the higher price of P_H.

Which pricing option will a type I consumer choose?

All consumers, if they are rational, will choose the pricing option that provides them with the most satisfaction: i.e.

A quantity discount

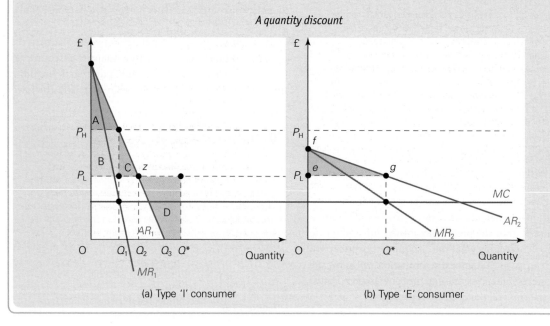

(a) Type 'I' consumer   (b) Type 'E' consumer

price applies only to the incremental units purchased in excess of Q^*.

A block declining tariff allows some, but not all, of the extra consumer surplus from first-degree price discrimination to be obtained. Figure 17.6 illustrates how it can increase revenue. The total demand curve for the product is given by curve D. Assume that the firm is currently charging a price of P_1 and hence selling an output of Q_1. Its revenue is shown by the blue area. If it now reduces the price to P_2 for *additional* sales above Q_1, its sales will increase to Q_2. Its revenue will now increase by the pink area. If it reduces the price further, to P_3, for sales above Q_2, sales will rise to Q_3 and revenue will increase further, by the green area. Thus a large amount of consumer surplus has been captured by the firm. But this is

not as much as under first-degree price discrimination (see Figure 17.4). Consumer surplus of the grey areas still remains.

The use of coupons/vouchers. To be eligible to purchase the good at the lower price, customers have to provide vouchers or coupons they have collected. For this pricing strategy to work, consumers must have to exert some time and effort in collecting the voucher/coupons. In this way, only the price-sensitive customers should find it worth their while.

For example, the vouchers may be on a flyer inside a local newspaper, included in junk mail or on a website. The customer will then have to search through the flyers, web pages or junk mail to see if there are any coupons or vouchers for products they are interested in buying.

the option that gives them the greatest level of consumer surplus.

If type I consumers pay the higher price for the product, P_H, then they will buy Q_1 units of the good – see diagram (a) in the figure. Their consumer surplus would be area A (the green area). If, instead, consumers purchased the quantity required (Q^*) to get the discounted price (P_L) then there are potentially three effects on their welfare. Two are positive and one is negative.

- The first positive effect on consumers' welfare comes from the quantity of the product that they would still have purchased at a price of P_H: i.e. Q_1. The consumer is now able to purchase Q_1 for the lower price of P_L. The extra consumer surplus obtained from buying Q_1 at the lower price is shown by area B (the blue area).
- The second positive effect comes from some of the additional units of the product that the consumer purchases at the discounted price of P_L. From diagram (a) it can be seen that at a price of P_L a type I consumer would purchase Q_2 units of the product: i.e. the quantity where P_L meets the consumer's demand curve. This will generate an increase in consumer surplus as the maximum willingness to pay for these additional units from Q_1 to Q_2 is greater than the price. This gain in consumer surplus is represented in by area C (the orange area).
- The negative effect on consumer welfare comes from the extra units of the product from Q_2 to Q^* that the consumer has to buy to obtain the lower price of P_L. Type I consumers would maximise their consumer surplus by purchasing Q_2 at a price of P_L. However, this lower price is not available to them if they only purchase Q_2. They have to buy Q^* in order to obtain the quantity discount. This means that between Q_2 and Q^* the consumers' maximum willingness to pay for the product is less than the price they have to pay: i.e. the section of the demand curve from point z to Q_3 is below the price of P_L. The quantity from Q_3 to Q^* does not provide the consumer with any utility at all. Their maximum willingness to pay for these additional units is zero. This negative impact on consumer surplus can be represented by area D (the lilac area).

The net gain for a type I customer of purchasing the product at the lower price is area B + area C − area D. Therefore, if area D is greater than areas B + C, this consumer would be worse off from buying the good at the lower price. Such consumers would voluntarily pay the higher price for the product where the total consumer surplus they receive is at its greatest.

Which pricing option will a type E consumer choose?

Type E consumers, with the relatively more price sensitive demand at any given price, as shown in diagram (b) in the figure, would choose to purchase the product at the lower price. They would not buy any of the product at a price of P_H as it is above the maximum amount they are willing to pay for the first unit: i.e. the intercept of the demand curve (AR_2) on the price axis at point f is below P_H. By purchasing Q^* at a price of P_L they can obtain consumer surplus equal to the pink area in diagram (b).

The discount quantity pricing strategy has managed to get the type I customers to identify themselves and self-select to pay a higher price for the same product than a type E customer. In this case, the firm has not had to use an easily identifiable consumer characteristic in order to separate its consumers into different groups.

1. The quantity discount is an example of what type of price discrimination?
2. Explain any conditions that must be met for this type of price discrimination to be a viable strategy for the firm.
3. Both type I and type E consumers are still able to obtain some consumer surplus. Under what type of price discrimination is the firm able to extract all the consumers' surplus and convert it into profit?
4. Redraw the diagram to illustrate a situation where both types of consumer would purchase the product for a lower price.
5. It is assumed in this example that MC is constant. If MC and AC fell as the firm produced more would a quantity discount still be an example of price discrimination? Explain your answer.

Only those consumers who are relatively more price sensitive at the non-discounted price of the product will take the time and effort involved in order to get the voucher. Those who are relatively less price sensitive will not find the search costs involved worthwhile and will end up paying the full price.

When the product is purchased. This is sometimes referred to as **inter-temporal pricing** and is a strategy than can be used where different customers have a different willingness to pay at different points in time. When a product is launched, some consumers are desperate to get hold of it. For example, some consumers want to have the most up-to-date technology and are willing to pay more for a new mobile phone or tablet when it is first released. Over time, the price of such

products is reduced, which enables firms to sell to people who do not value the latest version so highly.

Another example is the pricing of seats on certain airlines. As the plane fills up, so the price of the seat rises. If you book a seat on a budget airline a long time in advance, for example, you may be able to get it at a very low price. If, on the

Definition

Inter-temporal pricing Where the price a firm charges for a product varies over time. It occurs where the price elasticity of demand for a product varies at different points in time.

other hand, you want a seat at the last minute, you may well have to pay a very high price. Although this is the other way around from the case of high-tech products, it again reflects price elasticity of demand. The business traveller who needs to travel the next day for a meeting will have a very low price sensitivity and may well be prepared to pay a very high price indeed.

In both the above cases, customers are not being assigned to a time period by the firm, so it is not classed as an example of third-degree price discrimination. In the high-tech case, the least price-sensitive customers reveal themselves by paying the higher price when the good is first launched, whereas customers who are more price sensitive simply wait for the price to come down. In the case of airlines, the more price sensitive consumers reveal themselves early on, while the less price sensitive ones reveal themselves later.

The version of the product purchased (versioning). Firms can produce different versions of the same core product that have different levels of actual or perceived quality. Examples include first class versus economy seats on aeroplanes or trains; 'value' versus 'finest' ranges of products sold in supermarkets; different specifications of computers or software packages. This is called 'versioning'. One interesting example of versioning is called the 'damaged goods strategy', where firms create a lower-quality version of its good by deliberately damaging the product. It does this by removing some features or reducing its performance characteristics.

For the strategy of versioning to work, the consumer surplus for the relatively less price-sensitive customers from purchasing the more expensive version of the product must be greater than the consumer surplus they would receive if they purchased the cheaper version of the product.

Versioning is only an example of price discrimination if the price differentials between the different versions of the core good are greater than any differences in the marginal cost of producing them. More specifically, the mark-up of price over marginal cost must be greater for the version of the product purchased by the relatively less price-sensitive consumers than for that purchased by the relatively more price-sensitive consumers. This is very likely to be the case with the damaged goods strategy, as the cost of producing the lower-quality version of the good is actually greater than the costs of the higher-quality version, i.e. there is a cost to a firm of damaging its own good.

In some circumstances, firms may be able to combine some of these different factors, such as the version of the product and inter-temporal pricing. For example, some new products are released in a higher quality, more expensive version first. For example, a book written by a celebrity author is often released in the higher-priced hardback form to capture the desire of more avid fans, before being released in the lower-priced paperback version sometime later. Again, the hardback version costs a little bit more to produce than the paperback one (but only a little), but the price difference can be huge.

Other examples of price discrimination

There are various other pricing strategies used by firms that involve an element of price discrimination. They include the following:

Peak-load pricing. This is where people are charged more at times of peak demand and less at off-peak times (see Case study F.6 on the student website). For example, bus and train fares are often highest during the 'rush hours' when consumers want to get to work. Similarly, the price of landline telephone calls is highest during the working day. During 'off-peak' times, prices are lower.

Part of the reason for this practice is the lower price elasticity of demand at peak times. For example, many commuters have little option but to pay higher rail fares at peak times. This is genuine price discrimination. But part of the reason has to do with higher marginal costs incurred at peak times, as capacity limits are reached.

Two-part tariff. This is a pricing system that requires customers to pay an access and a usage price for a product. This practice is used in a variety of settings but particularly in the telecommunications and energy sectors. For example, most customers who use gas have to pay a fixed standing charge per period of time and then pay so much per therm of gas used.

The aim of these schemes is to increase the firm's revenue, by giving it a lump-sum payment per customer (particularly relevant where the firm has high fixed costs) on top of the price per unit. The problem is setting the appropriate two-part tariff. This is particularly difficult when there is a lot of competition between firms and when customers are quite prepared to switch supplier. It is for this reason that there are several mobile phone two-part tariff plans for customers

---

Pause for thought
In 2016, Tesla sold two different versions of its Model S and X electric cars. They both included the same 75KwH battery. However, in the version that was £9000 cheaper, computer software was added that reduced the battery power to 60KwH. This limited the number of miles the car could travel before it needed recharging. Explain why Tesla did this.

Definitions
Peak-load pricing The practice of charging higher prices at times when demand is highest because the constraints on capacity lead to higher marginal cost.
Two-part tariff A pricing system that requires customers to pay both an access and a usage price for a product.

with an average to high usage, as well as a 'Pay-As-You-Go' option aimed at lighter users.

> **Pause for thought**
>
> *What type or types of price discrimination is/are being prac-tised in the cases of (a) peak-load pricing and (b) two-part tariffs?*

Conditions necessary for price discrimination to operate

Given that firms can generate greater revenue and profits by implementing a strategy of price discrimination, why don't all firms implement the policy? Unfortunately, for some firms, it might not be possible for a number of reasons. The following are the conditions necessary for price discrimina-tion to operate.

Conditions necessary for all types of price discrimination

The firm must have some market power. In other words, it must face a downward-sloping demand curve and hence can set its price. Thus price discrimination would be impos-sible under perfect competition, where firms are price takers.

Resale of the product must not be possible between consumers. A potentially profitable strategy of price discrimination may fail if consumers in the low-price market are able to resell the good to those consumers who are in the high-price market.

For example, with second-degree price discrimination, can the customer who obtains the quantity discount sell some of the units they have purchased to another customer who does not purchase enough to receive the discount? Can consumers allocated to one group under a pricing strategy of third-degree price discrimination resell the product to a customer allocated to another group? If resale *is* possible, then entrepreneurial consumers who can obtain the product in the low-price market may purchase large amounts of the good and make a profit selling it to customers in the high-price market. With the advent of online retailing, such as eBay, this might be easy for consumers to do. If this happens, the firm may quickly discover that it does not make any sales at the higher price.

In some cases, the nature of the product means that resale is impossible: e.g. you can't resell a haircut! It is similar with many services or with goods that are consumed at the time of purchase, such as a restaurant meal. In other circum-stances, even though resale may be possible, the transactions costs might outweigh the benefits: for example, the good might be relatively inexpensive so the potential gains from

resale are small or it may be difficult to transport and distrib-ute the goods to the customers in the high-price market.

In other cases, it might be both possible and potentially profitable to resell the good. This is most likely when the good is non-perishable, relatively expensive and easy to transport to consumers in the high-price market: i.e. the transaction costs are low. In these situations, the firm may have to inter-vene more directly to prevent resale between its customers.

Demand elasticity must vary between consumers at any given price. The firm will charge the higher price in the market where demand is less elastic and thus less sensitive to a price rise.

Price discrimination and the public interest

The word 'discrimination' carries with it negative connota-tions, so people often assume that this pricing strategy can never be in the public interest. It is also tempting to think that anything that increases a firm's profits must be at the expense of consumers' welfare. It is true that some consumers will benefit from price discrimination while others will be worse off. However, in certain circumstances, economists may judge that it is in the public interest. The following factors need to be taken into account when assessing the impact of price discrimination on a market.

Distribution effects on those customers who previously purchased the good at a uniform price

Those paying the higher price probably will feel that price discrimination is unfair to them as it lowers their consumer surplus. On the other hand, those who previously purchased the good but are now paying a lower price will feel better off. Their consumer surplus will be higher. Judgements could be made about whether the gains were more socially desirable than the losses.

The impact of any extra sales

In Figure 17.5, the quantity of sales under price discrimina-tion remained the same as under uniform pricing. However, in some circumstances, the quantity of sales may increase. There may be some consumers, such as old-age pensioners, who previously could not afford to buy the good when the firm used uniform pricing. The lower price, made possible by a policy of price discrimination, enables them to purchase the good. These extra sales will have a positive impact on the welfare of society. They will increase both consumer and producer surplus.

Misallocation effects

Price discrimination may cause a negative allocation effect. Under uniform pricing, the product is allocated through the pricing mechanism to those consumers who value it the most, given their incomes. The implementation of third-degree price discrimination could result in some units of the product being reallocated away from those consumers with a higher willingness to pay to those with a lower willingness to pay.

Without any restrictions, mutually beneficial trade could take place between the buyers. Those consumers with a higher valuation of the good could purchase it from those with a lower valuation at a price that would improve the welfare of both parties. However, the seller blocks this resale from taking place and, in the process, reduces society's welfare.

If the number of sales does not increase, then price discrimination is usually judged to be against the public interest because of the misallocation effect. If the pricing strategy does have a positive impact on the number of sales, then economists judge that it might be in the public interest. It all depends on the relative sizes of the positive impact of the extra sales and the negative impact of the misallocation effect.

Competition effects

The analysis of the impact of price discrimination often focuses on a pure monopoly. However, price discrimination could take place in an oligopolistic market. In this case, it is possible that a firm may use price discrimination to drive competitors out of business. This is known as *predatory pricing*. Under this practice, a company charges a price below average cost in one market by cross-subsidising that part of the business with profits from another part of the business. It does this until its rival stops competing in that market.

Predatory pricing, however, is illegal under UK and European competition law. Even though consumers gain from lower prices in the short run, the long-run strategy of predatory firms is to raise their prices once their competitor has been driven from the market.

On the other hand, a firm that engages in price discrimination might use its profits from its high-priced market to break into another market and withstand a possible price war. This would increase competition and hence consumer welfare. Alternatively, it might use the higher profits to invest in new and improved products that enhance consumer choice.

17.4 MULTIPLE PRODUCT PRICING

Thus far in our analysis of pricing strategy, we have been concerned only with a single product produced by a single firm. However, many businesses produce a range of products. Such products might be totally distinct and sold in different markets or the firm might offer a range of models in the same market that differ in design and performance. For example, a vacuum cleaner manufacturer might also produce other household appliances such as irons, as well as offering a range of vacuums with different suction abilities and design features.

Each of these products and product ranges will require its own distinct price, and probably a longer-term pricing strategy. However, multi-product pricing raises a wider set of issues owing to the interrelated nature of demand and production.

Interrelated demand

Many of the large supermarkets or DIY stores are in fierce competition for business. It is quite normal to see them offering 'bargain buys', whose prices are cut dramatically in order to attract customers to the store. Often their price is even below average cost. Such cases are known as *loss leaders*. The hope is that customers will purchase not just the loss leader, but additional amounts of other products with full profit mark-ups, thereby bringing a net gain in profits.

This strategy is known as *full-range pricing* and involves the business assessing the prices of all its products together

and deciding from this how it might improve its profit performance.

One of the most important considerations is the price elasticity of demand for the loss leader. The more elastic it is, the more customers will tend to be attracted into the store by the bargain. The business will also consider additional factors such as advertising the loss leaders and their positioning in the store, so as to attract customers to see other items at full price that they had not intended to buy.

Other demand interrelations that might influence the pricing policy of a business are where a business produces either complementary or substitute products.

If a business produces complementary products, then increased sales of one product, such as Apple's iPod, will raise the revenue gained from the other, such as the use of the iTunes store.

> ### Definitions
>
> **Predatory pricing** Where a firm sets its average price below average cost in order to drive competitors out of business.
>
> **Loss leader** A product whose price is cut by the business in order to attract custom.
>
> **Full-range pricing** A pricing strategy in which a business, seeking to improve its profit performance, assesses the pricing of its goods as a whole rather than individually.

KI 12
p 64

Alternatively, if the products produced by a business are substitutes, such as those of a breakfast cereal manufacturer like Kellogg's, then the increased sales of one product within its range may well detract from the revenue gained from the others.

Businesses like Apple and Kellogg's should therefore determine the prices of all their substitute and complementary products jointly so as to assess the total revenue implications. Here it is vital for the firm to have estimates of the cross-price elasticities of demand for their products (see section 5.3).

Interrelated production

The production of **by-products** is the most common form of interrelated production. A by-product is a good or service that is produced as a consequence of producing another good or service. For example, whey is a by-product of cheese. By-products have their own distinct market demand. However, the by-product is produced only following demand for the main production good: it may well not be profitable to produce as a separate product.

To consider whether the by-product is profitable to sell, it is important to allocate the correct costs to its production. The raw materials and much of the other inputs to produce

it can be considered to have a zero cost, since they have already been paid in producing the main product. But packaging, marketing and distributing the by-product clearly involve costs that have to be allocated directly to it, and the price it sells for must more than cover these costs.

It is not as simple as this, however, since the pricing of the by-product and the subsequent revenue gained from its sale might significantly influence the pricing of the main production good. Given that the two products share joint costs, a business must carefully consider how to allocate costs between them and what pricing policy it is going to pursue.

If it is aiming to maximise profits, it should add the marginal costs from both products to get an *MC* curve for the 'combined' product. Similarly, it should add the marginal revenues from both products at each output to get an *MR* curve for the combined product. It should then choose the combined output where the combined *MC* equals the combined *MR*. It should read off the price at this output for each of the two products from their separate demand curves.

In practice, many firms simply decide on the viability of selling by-products *after* a decision has been made on producing the main product. If the specific costs associated with the by-product can be more than covered, then the firm will go ahead and sell it.

KI 4
p 19

17.5 TRANSFER PRICING

The growth of modern business, both national and international, has meant that its organisation has become ever more complex. In an attempt to reduce the diseconomies that stem from co-ordinating such large business enterprises, the setting of price and output levels is frequently decentralised to individual divisions or profit centres. Such divisions or profit centres are assumed to operate in a semi-independent way, aiming to maximise their individual performance and, in so doing, benefit the business as a whole.

However, the decentralisation of pricing and output decision making can become problematic. This is particularly the case when the various divisions within the firm represent distinct stages in the production process. In these instances, certain divisions may well produce intermediate products that they will sell to other divisions within the business. There then arises the difficulty of how such intermediate products should be priced. This is known as the problem of *transfer pricing*.

One implication of this is that a division that is seeking to maximise its own profits when selling to another division will attempt to exploit its 'monopoly' position and increase the transfer price. As it does so, the purchasing division, unless it, in turn, can pass on the higher cost, will see its profits fall. Indeed, if it could, the purchasing division would seek to drive down the purchase price as low as possible.

This conflict between divisions may not necessarily be in the interests of the business as a whole. The solution to this problem is for divisions to base their pricing of intermediate products on marginal costs. The marginal cost of the final product produced by the business will then be a 'true' marginal cost. If the business is seeking to maximise overall profits, it can then compare this final marginal cost with marginal revenue in order to decide on the level of total output. The lesson is that, for maximum company profits, individual divisions should seek to be efficient and produce with the lowest possible marginal costs, but not seek to maximise their own division's profits.

Transfer pricing and tax liability

Transfer pricing within multinational companies is an area of concern for tax authorities. The price used to

---

Definitions

By-product A good or service that is produced as a consequence of producing another good or service.

Transfer pricing The pricing system used within a business organisation to transfer intermediate products between the business's various divisions.

BOX 17.3	SELLING GOODS SEPARATELY OR TOGETHER? THE IMPACT OF BUNDLING

Bundling is where a firm combines two or more goods and services together and sells the whole package for one price. One sector of the economy where businesses increasingly use this type pricing strategy is in telecommunications.

The figure below shows the proportion of consumers purchasing bundled services from a single provider. It increased from 39 per cent in 2009 to 81 per cent in 2017.[1] The two most popular, and fastest growing combinations of services, are (a) landline phone and fixed broadband – up from 17 per cent to 34 per cent and (b) landline phone, fixed broadband and pay-TV – up from 12 per cent to 33 per cent.

What are the potential advantages to a firm from bundling its products together? The following simple example will illustrate how the price strategy can be used, in effect, to charge different customers different prices for the same goods.

Assume a firm with market power supplies both pay-TV and fixed broadband services. It has only two customers (Dean and Robert) and knows their willingness to pay for both goods. Also, to keep the analysis simple, assume that the firm's marginal costs of supplying both the services is zero.

Dean enjoys pay TV but values his fixed broadband connection more highly. He really likes to spend most of his free time watching YouTube clips and chatting with his friends on social media. Robert, on the other hand, likes his broadband connection but values his pay-TV more highly. He enjoys spending most of his free time watching movies and

---

[1]Note that methodology changes in 2016 and 2017 mean that data are not directly comparable with earlier years.

The take up of bundled telecommunication services, England

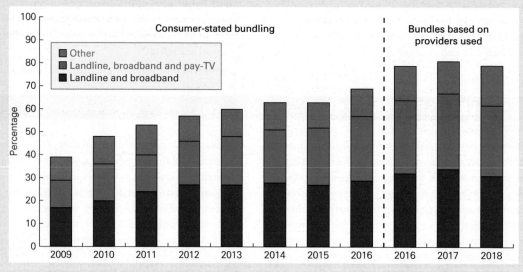

Source: Based on data from *Communications Market Report*, Ofcom (2018)

transfer goods or services between plants and divisions located in different countries is not determined by a market. Instead, the price is often set to avoid tax, ensuring that profits appear in countries where taxes on profits are lowest.

In recent years, there have been many high-profile cases of companies setting transfer prices so as to avoid tax. Companies such as Starbucks, Apple, Amazon and Coca-Cola have charged themselves high prices for the use of things such as logos, brands or business services owned or 'provided by' a subsidiary located in a low-tax country or region, such as Luxembourg, Jersey or the Cayman Islands and have thereby diverted a large proportion of their profits to these 'tax havens'. Often, the 'subsidiary' is little more than a small office with one employee, a telephone and a bank account.

OECD countries have agreed that tax liabilities on profits should be calculated using prices that would have arisen if he transfers had taken place between independent firms, rather than within one firm. In practice, this is difficult to achieve and extremely hard to police. We examine this issue further in section 23.6 (see pages 459–60).

his favourite football team, Austria Vienna, on the television.

Dean's and Robert's willingness to pay for fixed broadband and pay-TV services per are illustrated in the table below.

	Dean	Robert
Pay-TV	£20/month	£30/month
Fixed broadband	£25/month	£15/month

Selling the services separately

Assume, initially, that the firm sells each service separately. Will it make more money by selling its Pay-TV services to just Robert or both Dean and Robert? If it only sells the service to Robert, the firm can charge a price equal to his willingness to pay, i.e. £30/month. Given that marginal costs are zero, the producer surplus from this one sale is also £30. To sell pay-TV to both consumers, the firm needs to set the price equal to Dean's lower willingness to pay −£20/month. Assuming the firm cannot charge different prices to each consumer, its total producer surplus is £40. Therefore, the firm can make a greater surplus by selling TV services to both customers.

What about fixed broadband? If the firm sold the service only to Dean, it could charge £25/month. To sell fixed broadband to both consumers, the firm needs to set the price equal to Robert's lower willingness to pay −£15/month. Once again, the firm can generate a greater producer surplus of £30 by selling to both customers rather than just £25 by only selling to Robert.

The firm's total producer surplus from selling both services to both consumers is £70 (£40 + £30), while total consumer surplus is £20. Dean gains £10 of consumer surplus from his purchase of broadband while Robert gains £10 of consumer surplus from his purchase of pay-TV.

Selling the services as a bundle

What difference does it make if the firm is able to sell pay-TV and fixed broadband together for one price? Dean and Robert are both willing to pay £45/month for both

services if they are bundled together. Therefore, the firm is able to increase its surplus to £90 by combining the services.

The strategy works because the firm is now able, in effect, to charge Robert his willingness to pay of £30/month for the pay-TV component of the bundle and Dean his willingness to pay of £25 for the fixed broadband element. It effectively charges Robert £15/month for the fixed broadband element of the bundle and Dean £20 for the pay-TV element (the prices it would have charged both of them if the products were sold separately). In others words, bundling is a type of price discrimination.

For the strategy to be effective, the consumers' willingness to pay must differ. This is true in this example as Dean's willingness to pay for broadband is greater than Robert's while Robert's willingness to pay for pay-TV is greater than Dean's.

If the goods and services are only available as a bundle and cannot be purchased separately, it is called *pure bundling*.

In many real-world examples, such as those in the telecommunications sector, the consumer can choose to purchase the services either separately or together. This is called *mixed bundling*. This strategy can enable a firm to increase its surplus when the marginal cost of supplying some of the goods in the bundle exceeds the willingness to pay of a number of potential consumers.

1. *What are some of the potential economic advantages of bundling?*
2. *Assume in this example that Robert's willingness to pay for fixed broadband is now £25/month while Dean's is £15/month. What impact does bundling have on the firm's total surplus?*
3. *How could the use of bundling enable a firm to increase its market power?*

Find at least three different real world examples of bundling. In each case, explain if they are examples of pure or mixed bundling.

17.6 PRICING AND THE PRODUCT LIFE CYCLE

New products are launched and then become established. Later, they may be replaced by more up-to-date products. Many products go through such a 'life cycle'. Four stages can be identified in a typical life cycle (see Figure 17.7):

1. Being launched.
2. A rapid growth in sales.
3. Maturity: a levelling off in sales.
4. Decline: sales begin to fall as the market becomes saturated or as the product becomes out of date.

Analogue televisions, audio cassettes and traditional mobile phones have all reached stage 4. Writable DVDs, DIY products and automatic washing machines have reached stage 3. Large LED TVs, speed-dating events, fairtrade herbal teas, induction hobs, music downloads and smartphones are probably still in stage 2. Electric cars, HD multimedia entertainment devices and biodiesel are probably still in stage 1 (at least they were when we wrote this – but things move quickly!).

At each stage, the firm is likely to be faced with quite different market conditions: not only in terms of consumer demand, but also in terms of competition from rivals. What does this mean for pricing strategy?

The launch stage

In this stage, the firm will probably have a monopoly (unless there is a simultaneous launch by rivals).

Given the lack of substitutes, the firm may be able to charge very high prices and make large profits. This will be especially true if it is a radically new product – like the ball-point pen, the home computer and the mobile phone were. Such products are likely to have a rapidly expanding and price-inelastic demand.

> ### Pause for thought
>
> *If entry barriers are high, should a firm always charge a high price during this phase?*

The danger of a high-price policy is that the resulting high profits may tempt competitors to break into the industry, even if barriers are quite high. As an alternative, then, the firm may go for maximum 'market penetration': keeping the price low to get as many sales and as much brand loyalty as possible, before rivals can become established.

Which policy the firm adopts will depend on its assessment of its current price elasticity of demand and the likelihood of an early entry by rivals.

The growth stage

Unless entry barriers are very high, the rapid growth in sales will attract new firms. The industry becomes oligopolistic.

Despite the growth in the number of firms, sales are expanding so rapidly that all firms can increase their sales. Some price competition may emerge, but it is unlikely to be intense at this stage. New entrants may choose to compete in terms of minor product differences, while following the price lead set by the original firm.

The maturity stage

Now that the market has grown large, there are many firms competing. New firms – or, more likely, firms diversifying into this market – will be entering to get 'a piece of the action'. At the same time, the growth in sales is slowing down.

Competition is now likely to be more intense and collusion may well begin to break down. Pricing policy may become more aggressive as businesses attempt to hold on to their market share. Price wars may break out, only to be followed later by a 'truce' and a degree of price collusion.

It is in this stage particularly that firms may invest considerably in product innovation in order to 'breathe new life' into old products, especially if there is competition from new types of product. Thus the upgrading of hi-fi cassette recorders, with additional features such as Dolby S, was one way in which it was hoped to beat off competition from digital cassette recorders.

> ### Pause for thought
>
> *Why have audio cassettes and cassette recorders virtually disappeared while vinyl records and turntables have seen a resurgence in sales?*

The decline stage

Eventually, as the market becomes saturated, or as new superior alternative products are launched, sales will start to fall.

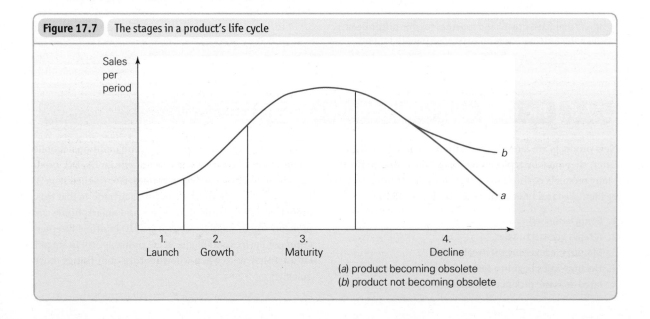

Figure 17.7   The stages in a product's life cycle

(a) product becoming obsolete
(b) product not becoming obsolete

For example, once most households had a fridge, the demand for fridges fell back as people simply bought them to replace worn-out ones or to obtain a more up-to-date one. Initially, in this stage, competition is likely to be intense. All sorts of price offers, extended guarantees, better after-sales service, added features, etc., will be introduced as firms seek to maintain their sales. Some firms may be driven out of the market, unable to survive the competition.

After a time, however, the level of sales may stop falling. Provided the product has not become obsolete, people still need replacements. This is illustrated in Figure 17.7 by line *b*. The market may thus return to a stable oligopoly with a high degree of tacit price collusion.

Alternatively, the product becomes obsolete (line *a*) and sales dry up. Firms will leave the market. It is pointless trying to compete.

SUMMARY

1a Prices are determined by a wide range of factors, principal among which are demand and supply, market structure and the aims of managers.

1b Firms with market power will not always attempt to maximise short-run profits, even if maximum profit is the aim. They may well limit prices so as to forestall the entry of new firms.

2a Traditional economic theory assumes that businesses will set prices corresponding to the output where the marginal costs of production are equal to marginal revenue. They will do so in pursuit of maximum profits.

2b The difficulties that a business faces in deriving its marginal cost and revenue curves suggest that this is unlikely to be a widely practised pricing strategy.

2c Cost-based pricing involves the business adding a profit mark-up to its average costs of production. The profit mark-up set by the business is likely to alter depending upon market conditions, such as the level of consumer demand and the degree of market competition.

3a Many businesses practise price discrimination in an attempt to maximise profits from the sale of a product. There are different types of price discrimination that a business might practise.

3b First-degree price discrimination is where the consumer is charged the maximum he or she is prepared to pay. Second-degree price discrimination is where the same consumer is charged different prices according to the amount, timing or other features of the purchase.

Third-degree price discrimination is where consumers are divided into groups and the groups with the lower price elasticity of demand are charged the higher prices.

3c For a business to practise price discrimination, it must be able to set prices and separate markets so as to prevent resale from the cheap to the expensive market. Also, consumers must have different price elasticities of demand that the firm can exploit in its pricing.

3d Whether price discrimination is in the consumer's interest or not is uncertain. Some individuals will gain and some will lose.

4 Businesses that produce many products need to consider the demand and production interrelations between them when setting prices.

5a The organisation of a business as a series of divisions, each pursuing an independent strategy, has implications for pricing policy, especially when products are sold within a business enterprise.

5b The optimum transfer price between divisions from the point of view of the whole organisation is likely to be equal to marginal cost.

6a Products will be priced differently depending upon where they are in the product's life cycle.

6b New products can be priced cheaply so as to gain market share or priced expensively to recoup cost. Later on in the product's life cycle, prices will have to reflect the degree of competition, which may become intense as the market stabilises or even declines.

REVIEW QUESTIONS

1 Explain why a business will find it difficult to set prices following the $MC = MR$ rule of traditional economic theory.

2 Could an existing firm implement a policy of limit pricing if it had the same cost schedule as potential new entrants? (In the example used in the text it is assumed that the existing firm has lower costs than the potential new entrant.)

3 'Basing prices on average cost is no less problematical than using marginal cost and marginal revenue.' Assess this statement.

4 Outline the main factors that might influence the size of the profit mark-up set by a business.

5 A salesperson often asks a customer the following question 'how much are you thinking of spending?' Why

might the salesperson ask this question? Is it in the interests of the customer to tell him/her the truth?

6 There are websites that collect together information on the various discounts that are available at any given point in time. Some of them make statements like 'Our staff spend several hours every day scouring the Internet for great deals so that you don't have to.' Discuss the implications of these websites for retailers who want to use coupons as a means of implementing a policy of second-degree price discrimination.

7 If a cinema could sell all its seats to adults in the evenings at the end of the week, but only a few on Mondays and Tuesdays, what price discrimination policy would you recommend to the cinema in order for it to maximise its weekly revenue?

8 What factors would make it more difficult for a consumer to resell a good?

9 US publishers often include statements such as the following on the international versions of their textbooks 'This book is authorised for sale in Europe, Asia and Africa only and may not be exported. Exportation from or importation of this book to another region without the publisher's authorisation is illegal'. Explain why they do this.

10 What is the role of a loss leader and what lessons might a business learn when pricing a range of products? Are there any supermarket products that would *not* be suitable to sell as loss leaders?

11 How will a business's pricing strategy differ at each stage of its product's life cycle? First assume that the business has a monopoly position at the launch stage; then assume that it faces a high degree of competition right from the outset.

ADDITIONAL PART F CASE STUDIES ON THE *ECONOMICS FOR BUSINESS* STUDENT WEBSITE (www.pearsoned.co.uk/sloman)

F.1 **Getting smaller.** An historical case study of the downsizing of IBM and the demergers of ICI and Hanson.

F.2 **Enron.** A cautionary tale of business growth.

F.3 **Hypergrowth companies.** Why do some companies grow quickly and are they likely to be a long-term success?

F.4 **Peak-load pricing.** An example of price discrimination: charging more when it costs more to produce.

F.5 **Price discrimination in the cinema.** An illustration of why it might be in a cinema's interests to offer concessionary prices at off-peak times, but not at peak times.

F.6 **How do companies set prices?** The findings of various surveys.

F.7 **Easy pricing.** How low-cost airlines, such as easyJet and Ryanair use price discrimination to increase their revenue.

F.8 **Vouchers and discounts.** This case examines the rise of Groupon and looks at its business practices.

WEBSITES RELEVANT TO PART F

Numbers and sections refer to websites listed in the Web appendix and hotlinked from this text's website at **www.pearsoned.co.uk/sloman**

■ For news articles relevant to Part F, see the *Economics News Articles* link from the student website or go directly to the Sloman Economics News site.

■ For general news relevant to alternative strategies, see websites in section A, and particularly A2, 3, 8, 9, 23, 24, 25, 26, 35, 36. See also A38–44 for links to newspapers worldwide.

■ For student resources relevant to Part F, see sites C1–7, 9, 10, 19.

■ For models and simulations on business strategy see sites D3–9, 13, 14, 16–20.

■ For information on mergers, see sites E4, 10, 18, 20; G7, 8; H2 (see World Investment Report).

■ For data on SME, see the SME database in B3. Also see sites E10 and G7.

■ For information on pricing, see site E10 and the sites of the regulators of the privatised industries: E15, 16, 19, 22.

■ For sites that look at companies, their scale of operation and market share, see D2; E4, 10; G7, 8.

The firm in the factor market

The FT Reports . . .

The Financial Times, 6 January 2018

German employers forced to reveal gender pay gap

By Tobias Buck

German employers will be forced to reveal their gender pay gap to individual workers under a law that comes into force on Saturday.

The measure grants women the right to learn how their salary compares with males in corresponding jobs. It can also be used by men who feel they are disadvantaged compared with female workers, although in practice officials believe that scenario is unlikely. The law applies to the private and public sectors provided the workplace has more than 200 employees.

The new right to information comes into force at a time when gender pay gaps are under scrutiny – and under attack – as never before, across all sectors of the economy.

The issue is particularly acute in Germany, which has one of the worst records in Europe when it comes to equal pay. According to EU data, German women are paid on average 22 per cent less than men, the biggest difference after Estonia and the Czech Republic. The average pay gap across the 28 member states is 16 per cent.

Business leaders have voiced sharp criticism of the new law, which they say imposes an undue burden on companies without an evident pay-off. "Despite an economic boom and record employment the law paints a horror vision of social dislocation and injustice," said Steffen Kampeter, director-general of the BDA employers' federation. "Fact is: In Germany women and men are paid the same for the same work at the same employer." He described the new law as a "massive intervention" and its rules "highly complicated".

The Family Ministry says the gender pay gap is the result of several factors: women tend to be over-represented in low-paying sectors and under-represented in senior positions, for example. Their careers are also often interrupted by long stints devoted to childcare. But the ministry insists that discrimination and a lack of transparency surrounding pay also play a critical role, which the new law is trying to fix.

Germany already prohibits companies from paying different wages to men and women who do the same or similar work. In many cases, however, the workers are unaware of the pay gap or unable to prove that any exists. Under the new law, individuals have the right to ask their employer to explain how their salary measures up to that of a group of comparable employees.

The Entgelttransparenzgesetz law mirrors legislation that exists in 11 other EU member states.

Zero-hours contracts remain a controversial feature of the British workplace, suggesting they may have become embedded in the labour market rather than fading as a temporary recessionary phenomenon. The contracts, which do not guarantee a minimum amount of work, have become a flashpoint in the political debate over the pros and cons of the British labour market. Business groups say they provide useful flexibility for workers and employers, while critics say they are exploitative because they do not guarantee any income security.

'Zero-hours contracts hold their place in UK labour market', *Financial Times*, 2 September 2015

So far, we have considered the role of the firm as a supplier of goods and services. In other words, we have looked at the operation of firms in the goods market. But producing goods and services requires factors of production: labour, capital and raw materials. In Part G, therefore, we turn to examine the behaviour of firms in factor markets and, in particular, the market for labour and the market for capital.

In factor markets, the supply and demand roles are reversed. The firm *demands* factors of production in order to *produce* goods and services. This demand for factors is thus a *derived* demand: one that is derived from consumers' demand for the firm's products. Households, on the other hand, in order to earn the money to buy goods and services, are *supplying* labour. Chapter 18 focuses upon labour and the determination of wage rates. It also shows how the existence of power, whether of employers or trade unions, affects the wage rate and the level of employment in a given labour market. In addition, we consider the problem of low pay and the effects of the minimum wage, tax credits, gender and discrimination and how this affects wages. We finish by considering the implications for the labour market of growing levels of flexibility in employment practices.

In Chapter 19, we will consider the employment of capital by firms and look at the relationship between the business and investment. We will consider how businesses appraise the profitability of investment. We will also examine the various sources of finance for investment. The chapter finishes by examining the stock market. We ask whether it is an efficient means of allocating capital.

Key terms

Derived demand
Wage taker
Wage setter
Marginal revenue product
Monopsony
Bilateral monopoly
Trade union
Collective bargaining
Efficiency wages
Minimum wage rates
Discrimination
The flexible firm
Core and peripheral
  workers
Insiders and outsiders
Capital
Capital services
Investment
Discounting
Net present value
Financial intermediaries
Maturity transformation
Risk transformation
Retail and wholesale
  banking
Efficient capital markets
Weak, semi-strong and
  strong efficiency
Random walk

Labour markets, wages and industrial relations

Business issues covered in this chapter

- How has the UK labour market changed over the years?
- How are wage rates determined in a perfect labour market?
- What are the determinants of the demand and supply of labour and their respective elasticities?
- What forms of market power exist in the labour market and what determines the power of employers and labour?
- What effects do powerful employers and trade unions have on wages and employment?
- What are the causes of low pay and how has the difference in average earnings between men and women changed?
- How has the minimum wage affected business and employment?
- What is meant by a 'flexible' labour market and how has increased flexibility affected working practices, employment and wages?

18.1 MARKET-DETERMINED WAGE RATES AND EMPLOYMENT

The labour market has undergone many changes in recent years. Advances in technology leading to greater automation, changes in the pattern of output, a growing need to be competitive in international markets and various social changes have all contributed to changes in work practices and in the structure and composition of the workforce. (Major changes in the UK are discussed in Case study G.1 on the student website.)

In this chapter, we shall be focusing on wage rates. An obvious question is why do some people earn very high wages, whereas others, who perhaps work just as hard, if not harder, earn much less.

Why, for example, do top sportsmen and sportswomen get paid so much, but, perhaps more interestingly, why do only *some* of them get paid so much? Luis Suárez, Eden Hazard and Sergio Agüero are great footballers and earn very high wages. But have you ever wondered why they earn so much more than Lin Dan and Domagoj Duvnjak? Probably not. They are Chinese and Croatian and are seen as world greats in badminton and handball, respectively.

Economics allows us to develop a theory that explains why the greatest ever sportsman in one discipline can be paid so little relative to merely great sportsmen in other disciplines. You can read about the salaries of footballers and the revenues and costs of their clubs on the Sloman Economics News site in the blog, *Why is it so difficult to make a profit? The problem of players' pay in the English Premier League* and also in this article that looks at the clubs who pay the most: Football salaries: Premier League clubs dominate wages list as Barcelona lead the way.[1]

---

[1] Stephen Crawford, 'Football salaries: Premier League clubs dominate wages list as Barcelona lead the way', available at Goal.com (29 November 2017)

| Figure 18.1 | A perfectly competitive labour market (a) Individual employer (b) Whole market (c) Individual worker – marginal disutility of work |

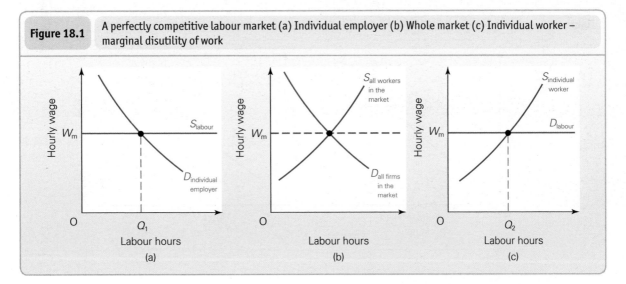

Perfect labour markets

Before we can answer such questions, we first need to consider how wages are determined and, to do this, we must make a similar distinction to that made in the theory of the firm: the distinction between perfect and imperfect markets. Although, in practice, few labour markets are totally perfect, many do at least approximate to it.

The key assumption of a perfect labour market is that everyone is a *wage taker*. In other words, neither employers nor employees have any economic power to affect wage rates. This situation is not uncommon. Small employers are likely to have to pay the 'going wage rate' to their employees, especially where the employee is of a clear category, such as an electrician, a bar worker, a secretary or a porter. As far as employees are concerned, being a wage taker means not being a member of a union and therefore not being able to use collective bargaining to push up the wage rate.

The other assumptions of a perfect labour market are as follows:

- *Freedom of entry.* There are no restrictions on the movement of labour. For example, workers are free to move to alternative jobs or to areas of the country where wage rates are higher. There are no barriers erected by, say, unions, professional associations or the government. of course, it takes time for workers to change jobs and maybe to retrain. This assumption therefore applies only in the long run.
- *Perfect knowledge.* Workers are fully aware of what jobs are available at what wage rates and with what conditions of employment. Likewise, employers know what labour is available and how productive that labour is.
- *Homogeneous labour.* It is usually assumed that, in perfect markets, workers of a given category are identical in terms of productivity. For example, it would be assumed that all bricklayers are equally skilled and motivated.

Wage rates and employment under perfect competition are determined by the interaction of the market demand and supply of labour. This is illustrated in Figure 18.1(b).

Generally, it would be expected that the supply and demand curves slope the same way as in goods markets. The higher the wage paid for a certain type of job, the more workers will want to do that job. This gives an upward-sloping supply curve of labour. On the other hand, the higher the wage that employers have to pay, the less labour they will want to employ. Either they will simply produce less output or they will substitute other factors of production, like machinery, for labour. Thus the demand curve for labour slopes downwards.

Figure 18.1(a) shows how an individual employer has to accept this wage. The supply of labour to that employer is infinitely elastic. In other words, at the market wage W_m, there is no limit to the number of workers available to that employer (but no workers at all will be available below it: they will all be working elsewhere). At the market wage W_m, the employer will employ Q_1 hours of labour.

Figure 18.1(c) shows how an individual worker also has to accept this wage. In this case, it is the demand curve for that worker that is infinitely elastic. In other words, there is as

Definition

Wage taker The wage rate is determined by market forces.

Figure 18.2   (a) The marginal disutility of hours worked; (b) the supply of hours worked

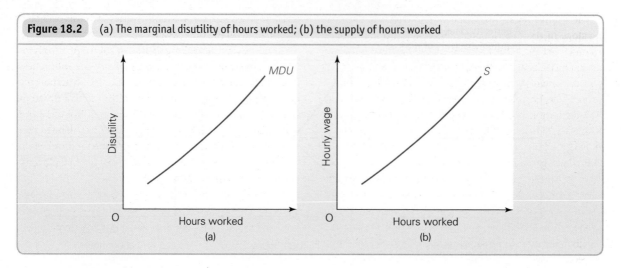

much work as the worker cares to do at this wage (but none at all above it).

We now turn to look at the supply and demand for labour in more detail.

The supply of labour

We can look at the supply of labour at three levels: the supply of hours by an individual worker (Figure 18.1(c)), the supply of workers to an individual employer (Figure 18.1(a)) and the total market supply of a given category of labour (Figure 18.1(b)). Let us examine each in turn.

The supply of hours by an individual worker

Work involves two major costs (or 'disutilities') to the worker:

■ When people work they sacrifice leisure.

■ The work itself may be unpleasant.

Each extra hour worked will involve additional disutility. This ***marginal disutility of work*** (*MDU*) will tend to *increase* as people work more hours. There are two reasons for this. First, the less the leisure they have left, the greater the disutility they experience in sacrificing a further hour of leisure. Second, the unpleasantness they experience in doing the job will tend to increase due to boredom or tiredness.

This increasing marginal disutility (see Figure 18.2(a)) will tend to give an upward-sloping supply curve of hours by an individual worker (see Figure 18.2(b)). The reason is that, in order to persuade people to work more hours, a higher hourly wage must be paid to compensate for the higher marginal disutility incurred. This helps explain why overtime rates are higher than standard rates, as explained in an article about US overtime.[2]

Under certain circumstances, however, the supply of hours curve might bend backward (see Figure 18.3). The

Figure 18.3   Backward-bending supply curve of labour

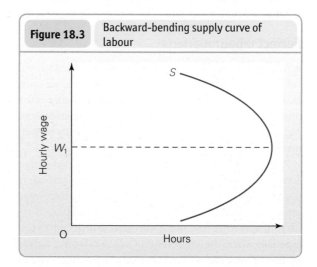

reason is that, when wage rates go up, there will be two opposing forces operating on the individual's labour supply.

On the one hand, with higher wage rates, people will tend to work more hours, since leisure would now involve a greater sacrifice of income and hence consumption. They substitute income for leisure. This is called the ***substitution effect*** of the increase in wage rates.

On the other hand, people may feel that with higher wage rates they can afford to work less and have more leisure. This is called the ***income effect***.

Definitions

Marginal disutility of work The extra sacrifice/ hardship to a worker of working an extra unit of time in any given time period (e.g. an extra hour per day).

Substitution effect of a rise in wages Workers will tend to substitute income for leisure as leisure now has a higher opportunity cost. This effect leads to *more* hours being worked as wages rise.

The relative magnitude of these two effects determines the slope of the individual's supply curve. It is normally assumed that the substitution effect outweighs the income effect, especially at lower wage rates. A rise in wage rates acts as an incentive: it encourages a person to work more hours. It is possible, however, that the income effect will outweigh the substitution effect. Particularly at very high wage rates, people say: 'There's not so much point now in doing overtime. I can afford to spend more time at home.'

If the wage rate becomes high enough for the income effect to dominate, the supply curve will begin to slope backward. This occurs above a wage rate of W_1 in Figure 18.3.

These considerations are particularly important for a government considering tax cuts. Cuts in income tax rates are like giving people a pay rise and thus provide an incentive for people to work harder. This analysis is only correct, however, if the substitution effect dominates. If the income effect dominates, people will work less after the tax cut.

The supply of labour to an individual employer

Under perfect competition, the supply of labour to a particular firm will be perfectly elastic, as in Figure 18.1(a). The firm is a 'wage taker' and thus has no power to influence wages.

The market supply of a given type of labour

Typically, this will be upward sloping. The higher the wage rate offered in a particular type of job, the more people will want to do that job.

The *position* of the market supply curve of labour will depend on the number of people willing and able to do the job at each given wage rate. This depends on three things:

- the number of qualified people;
- the non-wage benefits or costs of the job, such as the pleasantness or otherwise of the working environment, job satisfaction or dissatisfaction, status, power, the degree of job security, holidays, perks and other fringe benefits;
- the wages and non-wage benefits in alternative jobs.

A change in the wage rate will cause a movement along the supply curve. A change in any of these other three determinants will shift the whole curve.

The elasticity of the market supply of labour

How *responsive* will the supply of labour be to a change in the wage rate? If the market wage rate goes up, will a lot more labour become available or only a little? This responsiveness

(elasticity) depends on (a) the difficulties and costs of changing jobs and (b) the time period.

Another way of looking at the elasticity of supply of labour is in terms of the *mobility of labour*: the willingness and ability of labour to move to another job, whether in a different location (geographical mobility) or in a different industry (occupational mobility). The mobility of labour (and hence the elasticity of supply of labour) will be higher when there are alternative jobs in the same location, when alternative jobs require similar skills and when people have good information about these jobs.

It is also much higher in the long run, when people have the time to acquire new skills and when the education system has had time to adapt to the changing demands of industry.

> ### Pause for thought
>
> *During the 2000s, the central and eastern European countries (CEECs) began to join the EU. What effect do you think this expansion of the EU had on the position and elasticity of the supply curve of various types of labour?*

The demand for labour: the marginal productivity theory

The traditional 'neoclassical' theory of the firm assumes that firms aim to maximise profits. The same assumption is made in the neoclassical theory of labour demand. This theory is generally known as the *marginal productivity theory*.

The profit-maximising approach

How many workers will a profit-maximising firm want to employ? The firm will answer this question by weighing up the costs of employing extra labour against the benefits. It will use exactly the same principles as in deciding how much output to produce.

In the goods market, the firm will maximise profits where the marginal cost of an extra unit of *goods* produced equals the marginal revenue from selling it: $MC = MR$.

> ### Definitions
>
> **Income effect of a rise in wages** Workers get a higher income for a given number of hours worked and may thus feel they need to work fewer hours as wages rise.
>
> **Mobility of labour** The ease with which labour can either shift between jobs (occupational mobility) or move to other parts of the country in search of work (geographical mobility).
>
> **Marginal productivity theory** The theory that the demand for a factor depends on its marginal revenue product.

> ### Pause for thought
>
> 1. *Which way will the supply curve shift if the wage rates in alternative jobs rise?*
> 2. *Why, do you think, are some of the lowest-paid jobs the most unpleasant?*

KI 4
p 19

In the labour market, the firm will maximise profits where the marginal cost of employing an extra *worker* equals the marginal revenue that the worker's output earns for the firm: *MC* of labour = *MR* of labour. The reasoning is simple. If an extra worker adds more to a firm's revenue than to its costs,

KI 20
p 149

the firm's profits will increase. It will be worth employing that worker. But, as more workers are employed, diminishing returns to labour will set in (see page 149). Each extra worker will produce less than the previous one and thus earn less revenue for the firm. Eventually, the marginal revenue from extra workers will fall to the level of their marginal cost. At that point, the firm will stop employing extra workers. There are no additional profits to be gained. Profits are at a maximum.

Measuring the marginal cost and revenue of labour

Marginal cost of labour (MCL). This is the extra cost of employing one more worker. Under perfect competition, the firm is too small to affect the market wage. It faces a horizontal supply curve (see Figure 18.1(a) on page 315). In other words, it can employ as many workers as it chooses at the market wage rate. Thus the additional cost of employing one more person will simply be the wage rate: $MC_L = W$.

Marginal revenue of labour (MRPL). The marginal revenue that the firm gains from employing one more worker is called the **marginal revenue product of labour** (MRP_L). The MRP_L is found by multiplying two elements – the marginal physical product of labour (MPP_L) and the marginal revenue gained by selling one more unit of output (MR).

$$MRP_L = MPP_L \times MR$$

The MPP_L is the extra output produced by the last worker. Thus, if the last worker produces 100 tonnes of output per week (MPP_L) and, if the firm earns an extra £2 for each additional tonne sold (MR), then the worker's MRP is £200. This extra worker is adding £200 to the firm's revenue.

KI 20
p 149

The profit-maximising level of employment for a firm

The MRP_L curve is illustrated in Figure 18.4. As more workers are employed, there will come a point when diminishing

returns set in (point *b*). Thereafter, the MRP_L curve slopes downward. The figure also shows the MC_L 'curve' at the current market wage W_m.

> ### Pause for thought
>
> *Why is the MC_L curve horizontal?*

Profits are maximised at an employment level of Q_e, where MC_L (i.e. W) = MRP_L. Why? At levels of employment below Q_e, MRP_L exceeds MC_L. The firm will increase profits by employing more labour. At levels of employment above Q_e, MC_L exceeds MRP_L. In this case, the firm will increase profits by reducing employment.

KI 4
p 19

Derivation of the firm's demand curve for labour

No matter what the wage rate, the quantity of labour demanded will be found from the intersection of W and MRP_L (see Figure 18.5). At a wage rate of W_1, Q_1 labour is demanded (point *a*); at W_2, Q_2 is demanded (point *b*); at W_3, Q_3 is demanded (point *c*).

The MRP_L curve, therefore, shows the quantity of labour employed at each wage rate. But this is just what the demand curve for labour shows. Thus the MRP_L curve is the demand curve for labour.

There are three determinants of the demand for labour:

■ *The wage rate.* This determines the position *on* the demand curve. (Strictly speaking, we would refer here to the wage

> ### Definition
>
> **Marginal revenue product of labour** The extra revenue a firm earns from employing one more unit of labour.
>
> **Derived demand** The demand for a factor of production depends on the demand for the good that uses it.

Figure 18.4	The profit-maximising level of employment

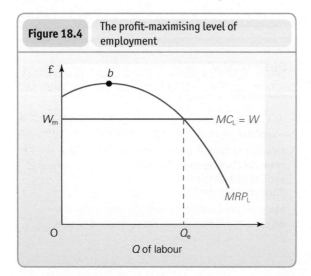

Figure 18.5	Deriving the firm's demand curve for labour

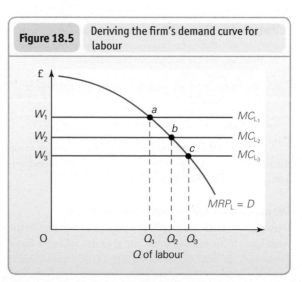

determining the 'quantity demanded' rather than the 'demand'.)

- *The productivity of labour (MPP_L).* This determines the position *of* the demand curve.
- *The demand for the good.* The higher the market demand for the good, the higher will be its market price, and hence the higher will be the *MR,* and thus the MRP_L. This, too, determines the position of the demand curve. It shows how the demand for labour (and other factors) is a **derived demand**: i.e. one derived from the demand for the good. For example, the higher the demand for houses, and hence the higher their price, the higher will be the demand for bricklayers.

Pause for thought

If the productivity of a group of workers rises by 10 per cent, will the wage rate they are paid also rise by 10 per cent? Explain why or why not.

A change in the wage rate is represented by a movement *along* the demand curve for labour. A change in the productivity of labour or in the demand for the good *shifts* the curve.

The elasticity of demand for labour

The elasticity of demand for labour (with respect to changes in the wage rate) will be greater:

The greater the price elasticity of demand for the good. A rise in the wage rate, being a cost of production, will drive up the price of the good. If the market demand for the good is elastic, this rise in price will lead to a significant fall in sales and hence a bigger drop in the number of people employed.

The easier it is to substitute labour for other factors and vice versa. If labour can be readily replaced by other inputs (e.g. machinery), then a rise in the wage rate will lead to a large reduction in labour as workers are replaced by these other inputs.

The greater the wage cost as a proportion of total costs. If wages are a large proportion of total costs and the wage rate rises, total costs will rise significantly; therefore production will fall significantly and so, too, will the demand for labour.

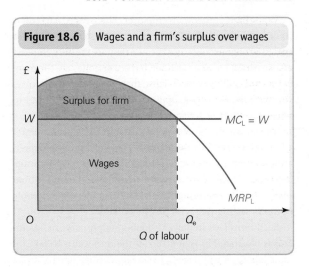

Figure 18.6 Wages and a firm's surplus over wages

The longer the time period. Given sufficient time, firms can respond to a rise in wage rates by reorganising their production processes. For example, they could move towards greater automation on production lines or introduce new technologies.

Wages and profits under perfect competition

The wage rate (*W*) is determined by the interaction of demand and supply in the labour market. This will be equal to the value of the output that the last person produces (MRP_L).

Profits to the individual firm will arise from the fact that the MRP_L curve slopes downward (diminishing returns). Thus the last worker adds less to the revenue of firms than previous workers already employed.

If *all* workers in the firm receive a wage equal to the *MRP* of the *last* worker, everyone but the last worker will receive a wage less than their *MRP*. This excess of MRP_L over *W* of previous workers provides a surplus to the firm over its wages bill (see Figure 18.6). Part of this will be required for paying non-wage costs; part will be the profits for the firm.

Perfect competition between firms will ensure that profits are kept down to *normal* profits. If the surplus over wages is such that *supernormal* profits are made, new firms will enter the industry. The price of the good (and hence MRP_L) will fall, and the wage and hence costs will be bid up, until only normal profits remain.

18.2 POWER IN THE LABOUR MARKET

Power may exist on either side of the labour market. Firms may have market power as employers; workers may have market power is they are members of powerful trade unions. In this section, we consider both types of labour market 'imperfection'.

Firms with market power

In the real world, many firms have the power to influence wage rates – they are not wage takers. When a firm is the only employer of a particular type of labour, this situation is called a **monopsony**. Royal Mail used to be a *monopsony employer of postal workers.*[3] Another example is when a factory is the only employer of certain types of labour in that district. It therefore has local monopsony power.

Definition

Monopsony A market with a single buyer or employer.

---

[3]Until 2005, Royal Mail had a statutory monopoly in the delivery of letters.

When there are just a few employers, this is called *oligopsony* (as we saw in Box 12.2). The big supermarkets are often considered to be oligopsonists, not because they are the only employers of a particular type of labour, but because they are the main buyers of certain products. Thus, they have significant power over farmers and other suppliers and can use that power to force down the prices they pay, thus cutting their costs.

Monopsonists (and oligopsonists) in the labour market are 'wage setters', not 'wage takers'. Thus a large employer in a small town may have considerable power to resist wage increases or even to force wage rates down. On a national scale, the UK's National Health Service has considerable power in setting wages for health workers.

Such firms face an upward-sloping supply curve of labour. This is illustrated in Figure 18.7. If the firm wants to take on more labour, it will have to pay a higher wage rate to attract workers away from other industries. But, conversely, by employing less labour, it can get away with paying a lower wage rate.

The supply curve shows the wage that must be paid to attract a given quantity of labour. The wage it pays is the *average cost* to the firm of employing labour (AC_L): i.e. the cost per worker. The supply curve is also therefore the AC_L curve.

The *marginal* cost of employing one more worker (MC_L) will be above the wage (AC_L): see Figure 18.7. The reason is that the wage rate has to be raised to attract extra workers. The MC_L will thus be the new higher wage paid to the new employee *plus* the small rise in the total wages bill for existing employees; after all, they will be paid the higher wage too.

The profit-maximising employment of labour would be at Q_1, where $MC_L = MRP_L$. The wage (found from the AC_L curve) would thus be W_1.

If this had been a perfectly competitive labour market, employment would have been at the higher level Q_2, with the wage rate at the higher level W_2, where $W = MRP_L$. What, in effect, the monopsonist is doing, therefore, is forcing the wage rate down by restricting the number of workers employed.

Workers with market power: the role of trade unions

How can unions influence the determination of wages and what might be the consequences of their actions?

The extent to which unions will succeed in pushing up wage rates depends on their power and militancy. It also depends on the power of firms to resist and on their ability to pay higher wages. In particular, the scope for unions to gain a better deal for their members depends on the sort of market in which the employers are producing.

Unions facing competitive employers

If the employers are producing under perfect or monopolistic competition, unions can raise wages only at the expense of employment. Firms are earning only normal profit. Thus, if unions force up wages, the marginal firms may make losses, leading to their eventual exit from the industry. Fewer workers

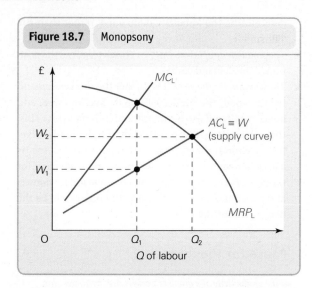

Figure 18.7 Monopsony

will be employed. The fall in output will lead to higher prices. This will enable the remaining firms to pay a higher wage rate.

Figure 18.8 illustrates these effects. If unions force the wage rate up from W_1 to W_2, employment will fall from Q_1 to Q_2. There will be a surplus of people ($Q_3 - Q_2$) wishing to work in this industry, for whom no jobs are available.

Pause for thought

Which of the following unions find themselves in a weak bargaining position for the reasons given?
a) The maritime workers union (Nautilus International).
b) The shopworkers' union (USDAW).
c) The National Union of Mineworkers (NUM).
d The farmworkers' union (part of the Unite Union).

The union is in a doubly weak position. Not only will jobs be lost as a result of forcing up the wage rate, but also there is a danger that these unemployed people could undercut the union wage, unless the union can prevent firms employing non-unionised labour.

In a competitive market, then, the union is faced with the choice between wages and jobs. Its actions will depend on its objectives.

Wages can be increased without a reduction in the level of employment only if, as part of the bargain, the productivity of labour is increased. This is called a *productivity deal*. The *MRP* curve, and hence the demand curve in Figure 18.8, shifts to the right.

Definition

Oligopsony A market with just a few buyers (or employers in the case of labour markets).

Productivity deal Where, in return for a wage increase, a union agrees to changes in working practices that will increase output per worker.

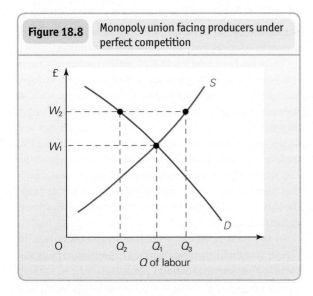

Figure 18.8 Monopoly union facing producers under perfect competition

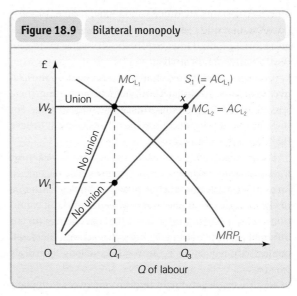

Figure 18.9 Bilateral monopoly

Power on both sides of the labour market: bilateral monopoly

One interesting observation is that the largest and most powerful trade unions are often in industries where there are monopsonist or oligopsonist employers. In such cases, trade unions act as a countervailing power to the large employer.

What will the wage rate and level of employment be under these circumstances? Unfortunately, economic theory cannot give a precise answer to this question. There is no 'equilibrium' level as such. Ultimately, the wage rate and level of employment will depend on the relative bargaining strengths and skills of unions and management.

Strange as it may seem, unions may be in a better position to make substantial gains for their members when they are facing a powerful employer. There is often considerable scope for them to increase wage rates *without* this leading to a reduction in employment, or even for them to increase both the wage rate *and* employment. Figure 18.9 shows how this can be so.

Assume, first, that there is no union. The monopsonist will maximise profits by employing Q_1 workers at a wage rate of W_1 (Q_1 is where $MRP_L = MC_L$).

What happens when a union is introduced into this situation? Wages will now be set by negotiation between unions and management. Once the wage rate has been agreed, the employer can no longer drive the wage rate down by employing fewer workers. If it tried to pay less than the agreed wage, it could well be faced by a strike, and thus have a zero supply of labour!

Similarly, if the employer decided to take on *more* workers, it would not have to *increase* the wage rate as long as the negotiated wage was above the free-market wage: as long as the wage rate was above that given by the supply curve S_1.

The effect of this is to give a new supply curve that is horizontal up to the point where it meets the original supply curve. For example, let us assume that the union succeeds in negotiating a wage rate of W_2 in Figure 18.9. The supply curve will be horizontal at this level to the left of point *x*. To the right of this point, it will follow the original supply curve S_1, since to acquire more than Q_3 workers the employer would have to raise the wage rate above W_2.

If the supply curve is horizontal to the left of point *x* at a level of W_2, so too will be the MC_L curve. The reason is simply that the extra cost to the employer of taking on an extra worker (up to Q_3) is merely the negotiated wage rate: no rise has to be given to existing employees. If MC_L is equal to the wage, the profit-maximising employment ($MC_L = MRP_L$) will now be where $W = MRP_L$. At a negotiated wage rate of W_2, the firm will therefore choose to employ Q_1 workers.

What this means is that the union can push the wage right up from W_1 to W_2 and the firm will still *want* to employ Q_1. In other words, a wage rise can be obtained *without* a reduction in employment.

The union could go further still. By threatening industrial action, it may be able to push the wage rate above W_2 and still insist that Q_1 workers are employed (i.e. no redundancies). The firm may be prepared to see profits drop right down to a normal level rather than face a strike and risk losses. The absolute upper limit to the wage rate will be that at which the firm is forced to close down.

The actual wage rate under bilateral monopoly is usually determined through a process of negotiation or 'collective bargaining'. The outcome of this bargaining will depend on a wide range of factors, which vary substantially from one industry or firm to another.

Collective bargaining

Sometimes, when unions and management negotiate, *both* sides can gain from the resulting agreement. For example, the introduction of new technology may allow higher wages, improved working conditions and higher profits. Usually, however, one side's gain is the other's loss. Higher wages mean lower profits. Either way, both sides will want to gain the maximum for themselves.

The outcome of the negotiations will depend on the relative bargaining strengths of both sides. In bargaining, there are various threats or promises that either side can make. For these to be effective, of course, the other side must believe that they will be carried out.

Union threats might include strike action, *picketing*, *working to rule* or refusing to co-operate with management, for example in the introduction of new technology. Alternatively, in return for higher wages or better working conditions, unions might offer no-strike agreements (or an informal promise not to take industrial action), increased productivity, reductions in the workforce or long-term deals over pay.

In turn, employers might *threaten* employees with plant closure, *lock-outs*, redundancies or the employment of non-union labour. Or they might offer, in return for lower wage increases, various 'perks' such as productivity bonuses, profit-sharing schemes, better working conditions, more overtime, longer holidays or security of employment.

Industrial action imposes costs on both unions and firms. Unions lose pay; firms lose revenue. It is usually in both sides' interests, therefore, to settle by negotiation. Nevertheless, to gain the maximum advantage, each side must persuade the other that it will carry out its threats if pushed. It can be useful to employ game theory here to consider how the actions of each side in the negotiation may be affected by how they think the other side will behave. In addition, the credibility of the threats and promises issued by both the employer and the trade union can affect the behaviour of both sides and hence the outcome of the negotiation.

In 1978/79, the UK experienced a period known as the Winter of Discontent, where strikes took place at the same time across a huge number of sectors. A blog on the Sloman News Site, *The Winter of Discontent: the sequel?*,[4] considers a similar period of industrial unrest that could have occurred in 2009. This is also discussed in Box 18.1, together with the recent strikes in the UK Higher Education System.

The approach described so far has, essentially, been one of confrontation. The alternative is for both sides to concentrate on increasing the total net income of the firm by co-operating on ways to increase efficiency or the quality of the product. This approach is more likely when unions and management have built up an atmosphere of trust over time.

Union membership. Trade union membership varies significantly across the world. Scandinavian countries, such as Finland and Sweden, have membership of around 70 per cent, while other countries, such as France, have less than

10 per cent of its population registered as a trade union member. In the UK, in 2016, 6.6 million people (21 per cent of people in employment) were trade union members.

There has been a decline in trade union membership over the past few decades in many countries across Europe, including those in Central and Eastern Europe, such as Bulgaria, Latvia, Poland and Slovakia. German trade union membership peaked in 1991, but, since then, it has lost 48 per cent of its membership. In the late 1970s, in the UK, trade union membership was at its highest. Throughout the 1980s and 1990s, membership declined significantly, such that membership is now around half that seen at its peak, though over the past 15 years, membership has been more stable.

In the USA, however, according to the US Bureau of Labour Statistics, union membership has remained fairly stable in recent years at around 11 per cent.

The fall in membership in the UK can be explained by a number of factors: the shift to a service-based economy; continued privatisation and the introduction of private-sector management practices, such as local pay bargaining, and contracted-out services into many of the remaining parts of the public sector. More women working and more part-time and casual work, with many people having no guaranteed hours, so-called 'zero-hour contracts', are also contributory factors, as are the negative attitudes of many firms to union recognition.

In Germany, many of the losses in membership were due to reunification; and in Central and Eastern European countries, there was significant restructuring of their economies and a big change in the role of trade unions. You can read an interesting article in *The Economist*, which considers why trade union membership has declined.

Union membership in many countries remains highest in areas of the public sector with high levels of monopsony power, such as education and health care. For example, in the USA, union membership in the public sector is recorded at 34.4 per cent, relative to 6.5 per cent in the private sector. In most countries, it is higher in large firms than in small ones and higher in manufacturing than in services. Despite the higher membership in these sectors, even here union power has declined in most countries.

(Case G.4 on the student website charts the rise and decline of the labour movement in the UK.)

Definitions

Picketing Where people on strike gather at the entrance to the firm and attempt to dissuade workers or delivery vehicles from entering.

Working to rule Workers do no more than they are supposed to, as set out in their job descriptions.

Lock-outs Union members are temporarily laid off until they are prepared to agree to the firm's conditions.

---

[4] E.H. 'Why trade unions are declining', *The Economist* (29 September 2015)

The role of government

The government can influence the outcome of collective bargaining in a number of ways. One is to try to set an example. It may take a tough line in resisting wage demands by public-sector workers, hoping thereby to persuade employers in the private sector to do likewise.

Alternatively, it could set up arbitration or conciliation machinery. For example, in the UK, the Advisory Conciliation and Arbitration Service (ACAS) conciliates in around 1000 disputes each year, roughly half of these involving pay-related issues. It also provides, on request by both sides, an arbitration service, where its findings will be binding.

Another approach is to use legislation. The government could pass laws that restrict the behaviour of employers or unions. It could pass laws that set a minimum wage rate (see pages 327–9) or prevent discrimination against workers on various grounds. Similarly, it could pass laws that curtail the power of unions.

The Conservative Governments between 1979 and 1997 put considerable emphasis on reducing the power of trade unions and making labour markets more 'flexible'. Several Acts of Parliament were passed during these years, which significantly reduced the power of trade unions in the UK. However, in recent years, we have seen many incidents of trade union action in the UK and in many other countries (see Box 18.1).

On the Sloman News Site, you will find blogs written about strikes and industrial action in posts entitled *The Royal Mail, Quiet Underground: Busy Overground, PCS vote to strike, A News blackout* and *Turbulence in the air.*

The efficiency wage hypothesis

We have seen that a union may be able to force an employer to pay a wage above the market-clearing rate. But it may well be in an employer's interests to do so, even in non-unionised sectors.

One explanation for this phenomenon is the *efficiency wage hypothesis*. This states that the productivity of workers rises as the wage rate rises. As a result, employers are frequently prepared to offer wage rates above the market-clearing level, attempting to balance increased wage costs against gains in productivity. But why may higher wage rates lead to higher productivity? There are three main explanations.

Less 'shirking'. In many jobs, it is difficult to monitor the effort that individuals put into their work. Workers may thus get away with shirking or careless behaviour, especially in a large company – a good example of the principal–agent problem (see pages 29–30). The business could attempt to reduce shirking by imposing a series of sanctions, the most serious of which would be dismissal. The greater the wage rate currently received, the greater will be the cost to the individual of dismissal and the less likely it is that workers will shirk. The business will benefit not only from the additional output, but also from a reduction in the costs of having to monitor workers' performance. As a consequence, the *efficiency wage rate* for the business will lie above the market-determined wage rate.

Reduced labour turnover. If workers receive on-the-job training or retraining, then losing a worker once the training has been completed is a significant cost to the business. Labour turnover, and hence its associated costs, can be reduced by paying a wage above the market-clearing rate. By paying such a wage, the business is seeking a degree of loyalty from its employees.

Improved morale. A simple reason for offering wage rates above the market-clearing level is to motivate the workforce – to create the feeling that the firm is a 'good' employer that cares about its employees. As a consequence, workers might be more industrious, show more initiative and be more willing to accept the introduction of new technology (with the reorganisation that it involves).

Pause for thought

Give some examples of things an employer could do to increase the morale of the workforce other than raising wages. How would you assess whether they were in the interests of the employer?

The paying of efficiency wages above the market-clearing wage will depend upon the type of work involved.

Workers who occupy skilled positions are likely to receive efficiency wages considerably above the market wage. This is especially true where the business has invested time in their training, which makes them costly to replace.

By contrast, workers in unskilled positions, where shirking can be easily monitored, little training takes place and workers can be easily replaced, are unlikely to command an 'efficiency wage premium'. In such situations, rather than keeping wage rates high, the business will probably try to pay as little as possible and so minimum wage legislation is likely to be important for such workers, as we shall see in the next section.

Definition

Efficiency wage hypothesis A hypothesis that states that a worker's productivity is linked to the wage he or she receives.

Efficiency wage rate The profit-maximising wage rate for the firm after taking into account the effects of wage rates on worker motivation, turnover and recruitment.

BOX 18.1 | WHAT DO POST, AIRLINES, BINS, BUSES AND UNIVERSITIES HAVE IN COMMON?

The Winter of Discontent

In the winter of 1978/79 (dubbed the 'Winter of Discontent'), the UK economy almost ground to a halt when workers across the country went on strike. Miners, postal workers, refuse workers, grave diggers, healthcare ancillaries, train and bus drivers, gas and electricity workers, lorry drivers for companies such as BP and Esso and workers at Ford all went on strike; there were even unofficial strikes by ambulance drivers.

Industrial action continued into 1980 and 1981 as the UK economy plunged into recession and unemployment rose to 3 million. Then, again, in 1984–5, there was large-scale disruption as the National Union of Miners went on strike over pit closures.

The sequel

It looked as though history was about to repeat itself in 2009 as the world economy plunged into a deep recession in the aftermath of the credit crunch. There were fears that Britain was entering months of industrial unrest, as bus drivers, refuse workers, airline and underground staff and firefighters followed the postal workers' lead and protested at changes to their pay, shift patterns and working conditions.

In the latter half of 2009 and early 2010, industrial action spread rapidly in the UK (and in other countries across the world). From bins to buses and trains to planes, there was massive disruption, affecting everyone and reducing output at a time when the economy was reeling from the financial crisis of 2007–8.

Over 800 drivers in Bolton, Bury and Wigan held numerous 24-hour strikes during 2009 because of disputes with First Bus over pay. At the same time, 1.5 million customers were affected when thousands of Underground workers went on strike and this occurred again in February 2015. These strikes cost businesses, as staff struggled to get to work, meaning lost hours and, as shoppers had problems getting to London, meaning lost sales.

Members of the National Union of Teachers and the National Association of Headteachers boycotted Sats tests in 2010, in part to 'protect their terms and conditions of employment'[1] and in Leeds, 92 per cent of refuse workers went on strike for several weeks after refusing the Council's offer relating to their working week and pay. Piles of rubbish built up, which, although not imposing direct costs on business, did adversely affect them. It was an 'external cost' imposed on consumers as it reduced the incentive to shop. We consider external costs in Chapter 20.

Research by the London Chamber of Commerce suggested that the postal strikes alone cost London more than £500 million in lost business.[2] The airline strikes that occurred in March 2010 were estimated to have cost BA between £40 and £45 million[3] and, during the same period, Germany's Lufthansa had to cancel thousands of flights, when 4000 pilots went on strike, with fears of foreign pilots being used to maintain the airline's profitability. Estimates suggest this cost the company some £21.9 million per day.

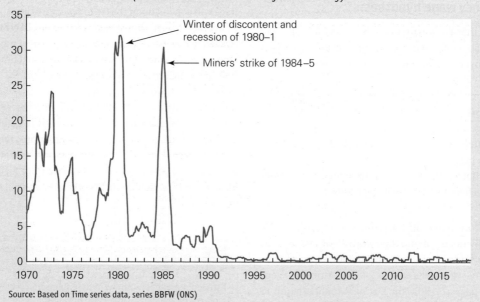

Annual working days lost through industrial disputes in the UK (millions)
(cumulative 12-month totals adjusted monthly)

Source: Based on Time series data, series BBFW (ONS)

---

[1]'Headteachers vote to boycott Sats tests', *The Guardian*, 16 April 2010.

[2]Tom Sands, 'Postal strike costs London £500m', *Parcl2Go.com News*, 26 October 2009.

[3]'BA strike: talks between airline and union resume', *BBC News*, 7 April 2010.

The trilogy

With the election of the Coalition Government and the start of its 'austerity policies', many trade unions quickly began to mobilise. Public-sector unions were particularly vocal in response to curbs on their pay and pensions and further industrial action ensued. In mid-2010, the Public and Commercial Services Union threatened to relaunch strikes, which had begun in March involving 200 000 civil servants, but which had been suspended for the election. In March 2013, the Public and Commercial Services Union (PCS) voted to strike in response to job losses, changes in pensions and public-sector pay being frozen for two years for those earning above £21 000.

Further postal strikes took place over the 2013 Easter weekend and again in the run-up to Christmas in 2014. Baggage handlers at Stansted airport threatened to walk out following shift changes which could adversely affect their pay. This followed a four-day strike over the Jubilee weekend in June 2012.

Civil servants were called in to cover UK border control posts, which was the first time that the government recruited other members of the civil service to break a strike by immigration officials. Further strikes by a variety of airlines and air traffic controllers have also occurred, with several in France.[4]

UK higher education

In February and March 2018, academics from 61 UK universities begun a prolonged period of strike action. There was significant disruption in many universities and in many departments, with lectures cancelled, changes to assessments due to content not being taught and a negative impact on the experience for many students.

While many strikes occur because of pay or working conditions, the strikes in the Higher Education sector relate to changes to the pensions received by academics, who will see a significant fall in their pension pot that can be claimed upon retirement. The University and College Union indicated that the planned changes would cost academics £10 000 per year. Academics argued that they had chosen to work in a relatively low-paid sector, expecting a more generous pension on retirement and that these changes would markedly affect their standard of living, the recruitment of top researchers, the quality of teaching and the overall student experience.

The strike certainly gained media attention, not least because of the negative impact on students. Picket lines were set up and despite the freezing temperatures and snow on the ground, striking academics were not deterred.

Although support was wide-reaching and did gain significant momentum, receiving support from non-striking academics, the public and many students, there were many others who were critical, including some students, who understandably argued that their education, and even their future, was being affected. With tuition fees capped at £9000 and most universities charging this fee, there were calls from students to receive refunds or compensation, as they felt like they were now 'customers'. One student from the University of York noted:

We pay a large amount for our tuition fees and we expect the university in return to provide us with the appropriate education and to pay the staff effectively enough to give us an education. They want students to pay but don't want to give us consumer rights . . . If I were to pay for a water bill, and the water didn't come through, I would expect compensation and it's exactly the same with universities.[5]

The impact of the strikes was felt not just in the UK, but concern was also expressed in other countries, particularly China which has 170 000 nationals studying at UK universities.

The strike did have an impact and, by the middle of week two, employers had agreed to meet the union through ACAS, leading to initial talks. However, no agreement was reached and further strikes were planned, with suggestions that they would take place across the examination period, thus adding to the disruption of students, with potentially big implications in terms of graduation.

Universities responded in a variety of ways, using old lecture recordings, requiring cancelled lectures to be rescheduled to avoid pay losses by striking staff, as well as substitute lecturers. Some universities threatened to punish striking academics, even threatening that they would be the ones to compensate the students. While compensation was unlikely, these strikes did have serious implications for future litigation and provided a stark insight into the state of Higher Education in the UK and the growing weariness over austerity, which many argue is to blame for the strikes.

Despite the range of industrial action we have observed over the past nine years, it has been small in terms of the number of days lost compared with the strikes of the early and mid-1980s (see chart). Indeed, there has been growing recognition that employers and employees can learn from each other and, with co-operation, everyone can be made better off.

However, negotiations across the UK have failed to resolve many issues and estimates across all affected industries show substantial economic costs incurred by recent industrial action and possible action to come.

And the nature of industrial action has been changing. Rather than involving prolonged periods of strike action, with many working days lost, industrial action has become 'smarter'. Action short of strikes is used more frequently and strikes are often called just for selected days.

1. Are strikes the best course of action for workers? In the cases outlined above, would you have advised any other responses by either side?
2. Which strike do you think was the most costly to (a) consumers, (b) businesses and (c) the economy? Explain.
3. Why do strains on public finances lead to industrial unrest?

Choose a recent industrial dispute and examine: (a) the arguments used by both sides to justify their position; (b) the courses of action taken by both sides; (c) the sequence of events; and (d) how it was resolved (if it has been).

---

[4]'French air-traffic strike: a formidable power to disrupt', *The Independent,* 5 May 2015.

[5]Sally Weale, 'Students demand compensation from universities over lecturer strikes', *Guardian,* 7 February 2018.

18.3 LOW PAY AND DISCRIMINATION

Low pay

Identifying workers as being low paid clearly involves making certain value judgements about what constitutes 'low'.

One way is to consider pay relative to living standards. The problem here, though, is that pay is only one of the determinants of living standards. Pay of a certain level may give a reasonable living standard for a single person, especially if he or she has property, such as a house and furniture. The same pay may result in dire poverty for a large household with several dependants living on that one income and considerable outgoings.

It is more usual, therefore, to define low pay relative to average rates of pay. Low pay will be anything below a certain percentage of the average wage rate. The larger the percentage selected, the bigger the low-paid sector will become.

A decency threshold. The Council of Europe defines low pay as anything below 60 per cent of a country's mean net (i.e. post-tax) earnings. It refers to this as the 'decency threshold'. Previously, the decency threshold was defined as anything below 68 per cent of a country's mean gross wage rate, which gave a higher figure. If a minimum hourly wage were to be based on even the new lower decency threshold, then in the UK it would be set at around £8.60 and would raise wages for about 35 per cent of workers. Other studies have identified the low-pay threshold at two-thirds of *median* hourly earnings of *male* workers.[5] A minimum hourly wage set at this level would also be around £8.60 for full-time workers.

Changes in relative wages over time. Another approach to the analysis of low pay is to see how the wage rates of the lowest-paid workers have changed over time compared to the average worker. Evidence from various editions of the Annual Survey of Hours and Earnings (National Statistics) indicates that inequality in pay in the UK has widened.

In 1979, the lowest 10 per cent of wage earners received a wage that was 70 per cent of the median wage. Data for 2017 give the median weekly wage for full-time workers at £550.40. However, the lowest 10 per cent of workers earn less than £319.70, or just 58 per cent of the median wage. On the other hand, the top 10 per cent of earners received a weekly wage of more than £1092.40, which is 198 per cent of the median weekly wage.

Between 2016 and 2017, workers in the bottom 5 per cent of the income distribution saw the largest increase in pay at 3.6 per cent, while the top 5 per cent of earners saw their pay rise by 2.5 per cent.[6]

Low pay in particular sectors/industries. Low pay tends to be concentrated in certain sectors and occupations. Sales, customer service workers, accommodation and food service workers are classic examples, as seen in Table 18.1. Weekly wages of workers in the latter two occupations are only 52.3 per cent of the UK average. Low pay also occurs disproportionately between women and men. In 2017, the median weekly wage for women was £493.60, while the figure for men was 19.8 per cent higher at £591.50.

The growth in low pay

A number of factors have contributed to the progressive rise in the size of the low-paid sector and the widening disparity between high- and low-income earners over the past 30 years.

With technological development, it is the demand for skilled labour that has increased, thus pushing up their wages, while demand for unskilled labour has fallen, pushing down wages.

Developing nations, such as China, Brazil and India, have also contributed to the growth in low pay by exporting goods that compete with domestic products. Over time, this has led to the decline of those industries struggling to compete with cheap imports from these countries. The impact of the decline in such industries is that skilled workers in countries like the UK have lost their jobs, becoming unskilled workers in different sectors. This increase in supply of unskilled labour pushed wages down.

There has also been a general shift in power from workers to employers, which really began with the high unemployment that existed in the early 1980s and 1990s. With such high jobless rates, wages of unskilled and semi-skilled workers in particular were forced downwards and have never fully recovered, despite falling unemployment in the late 1990s and early 2000s.

A rise in part-time employment, from 20.5 per cent of employees in 1984 to 26.5 per cent in 2018, has been a key change in the UK. There had also been a growing number of workers moving to 'zero-hour' contracts, where there is no guaranteed work in any week. This number had been rising for some time, but it has since fallen back slightly from an estimated 1.7 million people on these contracts in May 2016 to 1.4 million in May 2017. The percentage of people working on such contracts grew from 0.6 per cent in 2011 to around 5 per cent today. As part-time workers have not

---

[5] The *mean* hourly wage is the arithmetical average: i.e. the total level of gross wage payments divided by the total number of hours worked by the population (over a specified time period). The *median* hourly wage is found by ranking the working population from lowest to highest paid, and then finding the hourly pay of the middle person in the ranking.

[6] *All Employees* – ASHE: Table 1, Office for National Statistics (26 October 2017)

traditionally received the same rights, privileges and hourly pay as their full-time equivalents, this has contributed towards the growth in the low-pay sector.

Another relatively recent phenomenon has been the growth in the 'gig' economy (see Box 18.3 on page 336). This is where people are treated as self-employed, being paid by the job (just as a musician might be paid for a gig), even though they may work for only one company. Delivery workers are a good example of people in the gig economy. Such people tend not to have the same employment rights as other workers, such as holidays, sick pay and payment for downtime. Their overall annual wages, therefore, can be very low

One policy that has gone some way to arresting the growth in low pay in many countries is the use of a national minimum wage. But, is it enough and is it an effective method of protecting the low paid?

Minimum wages

Minimum wages are used widely in developed countries and can be another way of defining low pay. As of January 2018, 22 of the 28 EU member countries had a national minimum wage. These rates varied considerably. But, three broad groupings can be identified: one where minimum wages were lower than €500 a month, which is comprised only of new EU member states (Bulgaria, Romania, Lithuania, the Czech Republic, Hungary, Latvia, Slovakia, Estonia, Croatia and Poland); an intermediate set, largely made up of Southern European countries, where minimum wages range from €650 to less than €900 a month (Portugal, Greece, Malta, Spain and Slovenia) and a final set of the most affluent nations, where the national minimum wage was €1450 or above per month (United Kingdom, France, Ireland, Germany, The Netherlands, Belgium and Luxembourg).

The UK minimum wage in April 2018 was £7.83 per hour for those aged 25 and over (inspired by the Living Wage Campaign), £7.38 for those between 21 and 24, £5.90 per hour for those aged 18–20 and £4.20 for under-18s. Luxembourg has the highest minimum wage at €1998.6, which is almost 8 times as high as Bulgaria's, which lies at €260.80. However, if minimum wages are then adjusted to take into account price levels in each country, this does help to even out some of the differences, though they still remain significant. Adjusting the minimum wages into 'purchasing power parity standards' (i.e. in terms of what the wages can buy at prevailing prices) means Luxembourg's minimum wage is now just 3 times higher than in Bulgaria.

In the year January 2017 to January 2018, there was a real rise in the statutory minimum wage in 18 of the 22 EU countries, with the highest growth in the low-range countries, topped by Romania, whose minimum wage grew by 50.4 per cent in real terms.

Other countries also have minimum wages, including Japan, where the rate was ¥848/hour (£5.60/hour) in 2018, having increased from ¥771.33/hour in 2010.

Figure 18.10 shows the minimum wage rates in a number of countries in 2016. The red bars show real minimum hourly wage rates. They are adjusted for inflation and given in 2015

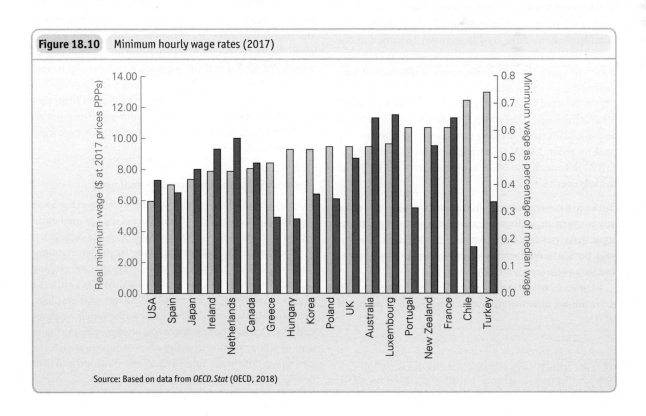

Figure 18.10   Minimum hourly wage rates (2017)

Source: Based on data from *OECD.Stat* (OECD, 2018)

prices and converted to US dollars at 'purchasing-power parity (PPP)' exchange rates, which adjust the market exchange rate to reflect purchasing power, i.e. the exchange rates at which one dollar would be worth the same in purchasing power in each country. This allows more meaningful comparisons between countries. The blue bars show minimum hourly wage rates as a percentage of each country's median hourly wage rate.

Regional Minimum Wages. In the USA, there is a federal minimum wage of $7.25, which has remained unchanged since 2009, but there are additional minimum wages by state, with 18 US states increasing their wage in 2018 and 6 states having no specific minimum wage.

One of the reasons why wage costs have increased in China is the implementation of minimum wages. As with the USA, minimum wages vary across the country, with some regions having wages that are now higher than those in the lowest countries in the EU, including Bulgaria, while others remain similar to wage levels in countries such as Vietnam and India. Throughout 2017, many Chinese regional authorities did raise their minimum wages, in part because they have had greater authority to make adjustments. Indeed, most regions do set different wage levels for different areas, depending on factors such as the stage of development, a rural or urban location, prices and the cost of living. You can read more about China's minimum wage in a China Briefing article.[7]

A living wage. Although the UK minimum wage has increased since its introduction in 1999, many critics still argue that it is insufficient and is not a 'living wage' (despite the government using the name 'National Living Wage' for the minimum wage rate for those aged 25 and over). In particular, due to variations in the cost of living in different parts of the UK, there are suggestions that minimum wages should vary depending on where you live, as we saw in the USA and China. In recent years, there has been a campaign in the UK for a 'living wage' – one which is based on the cost of living and would lift those working full time out of poverty. It is paid by around 4000 UK employers and is estimated at £10.20 in London and £8.75 in other parts of the UK for all workers over 18.

Critics of a national minimum wage argue that it can cause unemployment and with it a *rise* in poverty. Supporters argue that it not only helps to reduce poverty among the low paid, but also has little or no adverse effects on employment and may even *increase* employment.

In order to assess the background to this debate, we need to revisit our earlier analysis of the demand and supply of labour.

[7]Alexander Chipman Koty and Zhou Qian, *A Complete Guide to 2017 Minimum Wage Levels Across China,* China Briefing (15 November 2017)

Minimum wages in a competitive labour market

In a competitive labour market, workers will be hired up to the point where the marginal revenue product of labour (MRP_L), i.e. the demand for labour, is equal to the marginal cost of labour (MC_L), which gives the supply curve. Referring back to Figure 18.8, the free-market equilibrium wage is W_1 and the level of employment is Q_1. A national minimum wage, set at W_2, will reduce the level of employment to Q_2 and increase the supply of labour to Q_3, thereby creating unemployment of the amount $Q_3 - Q_2$.

The level of unemployment created as a result of the national minimum wage will be determined not only by the level of the minimum wage, but also by the elasticity of labour demand and supply. The more elastic the demand and supply of labour, the bigger the unemployment effect will be. Evidence suggests that the demand for low-skilled workers is likely to be relatively wage sensitive. The most likely reason for this is that many of the goods or services produced by low-paid workers are very price sensitive, the firms frequently operating in very competitive markets. It would seem at first sight, therefore, that any increase in wage rates is likely to force up prices and thereby reduce output and employment.

It is important to be careful in using this argument, however. What is relevant is not so much the price elasticity of demand for *individual* firms' products, but rather for the products of the low-paid sector as a whole. If one firm alone raised its prices, it might well lose a considerable number of sales. But with minimum wage legislation applying to *all* firms, if all the firms in an industry or sector put up their prices, demand for any one firm would fall much less. Here the problem of consumers switching away from a firm's products, and hence of that firm being forced to reduce its workforce, would mainly occur (a) if there were cheaper competitor products from abroad, where the new minimum wage legislation would not apply, or (b) if other firms produced the products with more capital-intensive techniques, involving fewer workers to whom the minimum wage legislation applied.

Minimum wages and monopsony employers

In an imperfect labour market where the employer has some influence over rates of pay, the impact of the national minimum wage on levels of employment is even less clear-cut.

The situation is illustrated in Figure 18.10 (which is similar to Figure 18.9). A monopsonistic employer will employ Q_1 workers: where MC_L is equal to MRP_L. At this point, the firm is maximising its return from the labour it employs. Remember that the MC_L curve lies above the supply of labour curve (AC_L), since the additional cost of employing one more unit of labour involves paying all existing employees the new wage. The wage rate paid by the monopsonist will be W_1.

| Figure 18.11 | Effect of a minimum wage under monopsony |

If the minimum wage is set above W_1 (but below W_2), the level of employment within the firm is likely to grow! Why should this be so? The reason is that the minimum wage cannot be bid down by the monopsonist cutting back on its workforce. Assume, for example, that the minimum wage was set at a rate of W_3. The minimum wage rate is thus both the new AC_{L2} and also the new MC_{L2}: the additional cost of employing one more worker (up to Q_2) is simply the minimum wage rate. The $MC_{L2} = AC_{L2}$ line is thus a horizontal straight line up to the original supply curve ($S_1 = AC_1$). The level of employment that maximises the monopsonist's profits will be found from the intersection of this new $MC_L = AC_L$ line with the MRP_L curve: namely, an employment level of Q_2. In fact, with a wage rate anywhere between W_1 and W_2 this intersection will be to the right of Q_1: i.e. the imposition of a minimum wage rate will *increase* the level of employment.

Clearly, if the minimum wage rate were very high, then, other things being equal, the level of employment would fall. This would occur in Figure 18.10 if the minimum wage rate were above W_3. But, even this argument is not clear-cut, given that (a) a higher wage rate may increase labour productivity by improving worker motivation and (b) other firms, with which the firm might compete in the product market, will also be faced with paying the higher minimum wage rate. The resulting rise in prices is likely to shift the MRP_L curve to the right.

On the other hand, to the extent that the imposition of a minimum wage rate reduces a firm's profits, this may lead it to cut down on investment, which may threaten long-term employment prospects.

Evidence on the effect of minimum wages

Which of the views concerning the effects of a national minimum wage are we to believe? Evidence from various countries suggests that modest increases in the minimum wage have had a neutral effect upon employment. It has been found that there exists a 'range of indeterminacy' over which wage rates can fluctuate with little impact upon levels of employment. Even above this 'range', research findings have suggested that, whereas some employers might reduce the quantity of labour they employ, others might respond to their higher wage bill, and hence higher costs, by improving productive efficiency.

Since the introduction of minimum wages in many countries, there is little evidence to suggest that employers have responded by employing fewer workers. Costs have certainly risen, most recently in China, but despite minimum wages rising in many countries and regions relative to both median and mean hourly wage rates, unemployment rates have remained fairly stable.

Part of this will be due to fairly buoyant economies, but also to the difficulties in substituting labour in many industries. Fairly small increases in minimum wages have therefore had little effect on unemployment, though in the UK firms did express their concern about costs and prices if they were forced to pay the much higher living wage. The issue, then, seems to be how *high* can the minimum wage be set before unemployment begins to rise?

Another approach to poverty is through the use of tax credits. Poor people, depending on their incomes, are given 'tax credits'. These are effectively a form of benefit to boost people's incomes. Tax credits are examined in Box 18.2.

Gender and the labour market

Women earn less than men. How much less depends on how earnings are measured and on whether we include full-time and part-time employees. The most widely used measure of the gender pay gap is based on the percentage difference in the *average* gross hourly earnings of employees. Figures in the Annual Survey of Hours and earnings (ASHE) show that,

BOX 18.2 UK TAX CREDITS

An escape from the poverty trap?

Although the minimum (and 'living') wage has gone some way to tackling the problem of low pay in the UK, it is not the only policy that aims to help those on low incomes. In 1999, at the same time as the Labour Government introduced the National Minimum Wage in the UK, tax credits were also created. They were first introduced in the form of Working Families Tax Credit (WFTC), but this was replaced in 2003 by Working Tax Credit[1] (WTC) and Child Tax Credit[2] (CTC). WTC provides support for working people on low incomes, while CTC provides support to families with children.

WTC requires people to work at least 30 hours per week in order to be eligible for the basic benefit of £1960 in 2018/19 (people with children, the over 50s returning to work, the over 60s and disabled people must work at least 16 hours per week). WTC is a cash benefit that not only provides support to people on low incomes, but also encourages work. The payment provides an incentive for people to move from part-time to full-time work (or at least to work enough hours to meet the threshold). Recipients of WTC also get paid 70 per cent of eligible childcare costs and so this benefit also provides help to parents who might otherwise find it difficult to be part of the labour force.

CTC provides support to families with children. Unlike WTC, eligibility is not dependent on someone working in the family and it is paid in addition to WTC. In 2018/19, for families with children born before 6 April 2017, £3325 per year was paid for their first child and £2780 for each subsequent child. For families with the first child born after 5 April 2017, payment for that child was reduced to £2780. Some campaign groups argued[3] that the restriction and reduction of CTC could push

200 000 more children into poverty. However, austerity in the UK has affected almost all areas of spending and the Office for Budget Responsibility estimates[4] that the cuts will save the Treasury some £70 million per year by 2020/21.

In 2017/18, it is estimated that just short of 4 million families received one of these tax credits. The cost to the government was £27 billion.

Tax credits and incentives

Tax credits were designed to improve incentives to work, by reducing the **poverty trap**. The poverty trap is where people are discouraged from working or getting a better job because they would lose any extra income, or most of it, through taxes and lost benefits.

As earnings rise above a certain amount, the tax credit received falls by 41 per cent for each extra pound earned. This is known as the *taper*. This taper rate is lower than with previous types of means-tested benefits. As such, tax credits aimed to reduce the financial penalties for parents taking up work or working more hours.

But, despite this aim, the disincentive to work remains high. With a benefit taper rate of 41 per cent, the combined marginal tax-plus-lost-benefit rate (the 'marginal deduction rate') is typically around 73 per cent (20 per cent income tax + 12 per cent national insurance + 41 per cent lost benefit), depending also on other means-tested benefits received.

What is more, a lower taper rate brings *more* families into the tax credit system. While this is good, in terms of providing support for them, the result is more of a disincentive for

---

[1] https://www.gov.uk/working-tax-credit.
[2] https://www.gov.uk/child-tax-credit.
[3] https://www.bbc.co.uk/news/education-39455078.
[4] https://assets.publishing.service.gov.uk/government/uploads/system/uploads/attachment_data/file/597335/PU2055_Spring_Budget_2017_web_2.pdf.

Definition

Poverty trap Where poor people are discouraged from working or getting a better job because any extra income they earn will be largely or entirely taken away in taxes and lost benefits.

---

in the UK in 2017, the gender pay gap across all employees was between 17.4 per cent (mean average) and 18.4 per cent (median average), though as Figure 18.12 shows, it has narrowed.

A similar picture can be seen throughout the EU. In 2016, women's *mean* average hourly pay was 83.7 per cent of men's for the EU economy (excluding the UK), though with significant variation between countries. In Romania and Italy, it was only 5.2 and 5.3 per cent respectively, whereas in Estonia and Germany, it was 25.3 and 21.5 per cent, respectively, with Denmark's at 15 per cent. You can read more about the gender pay gap in a 2014 report, produced by the European Commission.[8] In the USA, Pew Research

Centre Analysis[9] of median hourly earnings found that, in 2015, a woman needed to work an extra 44 days to earn what a man earned, though for the younger workers, there was a significant narrowing of the gap and both gaps had declined over time.

The latest data from the USA indicate that women earn about 79 per cent of their male counterparts and, in Japan, the figure is 73 per cent.

The inequality between male and female earnings can be explained by many factors and, as you can see in Table 18.1, which looks at data from the UK, there are significant variations within particular occupations.

So why has this inequality persisted? There are a number of possible reasons:

■ The marginal productivity of labour in typically female occupations may be lower than in typically male

---

[8] *Tackling the Gender Pay Gap in the European Union*, Publications Office of the European Union (2014).
[9] Rakesh Kochhar, 'How Pew Research measured the gender pay gap', *Fact Tank*, Pew Research Center (11 December 2013)

parents in such families to work extra hours or to take a better job, since the marginal deduction rate is now higher. In other words, although they are better off, they will take home less for each extra hour worked.

WTC and CTC illustrate the general problem of providing support to poor people that is affordable for taxpayers without creating disincentives to work. The more gently the support tapers off (and hence the less the disincentive to earn extra money), the costlier it is to finance and hence the higher the tax rates that are needed elsewhere.

A major criticism of the way in which tax credits were employed was the complexity of the system. This complexity had two consequences: first, it reduced take up and second, it made the system administratively costly and prone to errors.

A universal approach

In 2011, Iain Duncan Smith, the then Secretary of State for Work and Pensions, announced plans to make fundamental reforms to the benefit system with the introduction of a new Universal Credit (UC). His intention was radically to 'simplify the system to make work pay and combat worklessness and poverty'.[1]

The new credit was described as an integrated working-age credit providing a basic allowance with additional elements for children, disability, housing and caring. It was launched in 2013 with a series of local pilots.

It differs from the system it is gradually replacing in that it supports people both in and out of work, replacing Working Tax Credit, Child Tax Credit, Housing Benefit, Income Support, income-based Jobseeker's Allowance and income-related Employment and Support Allowance. (Note that, although it is called Universal Credit, it is not a universal benefit and is means-tested.)

It is hoped that the design of the Universal Credit will address **some of** the concerns around tax credits:

- Lessening the impact of the poverty trap through smoother taper rates and ensuring work pays.
- Removing the distortions that over-reward individuals working a certain number of hours, notably 16 or 30 hours with Working Tax Credits.
- Bringing together in-work and out-of-work benefits, reducing the risks and transactions costs for those moving into work.
- Reducing administrative costs, with benefits being overseen by a single body, the Department for Work and Pensions, rather than by the multiple agencies involved previously.

UC is gradually being introduced into different areas of the country. The scheme is not expected to be fully implemented until 2022 – five years later than originally planned. Its implementation has suffered numerous setbacks and has been dogged by design errors, problems with IT systems and cost over-runs.

Furthermore, a number of people receiving UC have suffered considerable hardship. Claimants have to wait six weeks for their first payment and some families have found it difficult to cope. In February 2018, 770 000 people were receiving UC.[2] When the scheme finally becomes fully operational, this number will increase to approximately 7 million and will cost around £63 billion of government spending. You can read more about the Universal Credit in a Guardian article.[3]

1. Economists sometimes refer to an 'unemployment trap'. People are discouraged from taking work in the first place. Explain how such a 'trap' arises.
2. Will the Universal Credit create an unemployment trap? What are the best ways of eliminating, or at least reducing, the unemployment trap?

Do a Web search to find out how the roll-out of universal credit is progressing and discuss whether issues that have arisen have to do with the design of the system and incentive mechanisms involved.

[1]Universal Credit: Welfare that works, DWP,
[2]Universal Credit Statistics, DWP (8 February 2018),
[3]Patrick Butler, 'Universal Credit: what is it and what exactly is wrong with it?', *The Guardian* (25 January 2018),

occupations. This may, in small part, be due to simple questions of physical strength. More often, however, it is due to the fact that women tend to work in more labour-intensive occupations. If there is less capital equipment per female worker than there is per male worker, then the marginal product of a woman is likely to be less than that of a man. The existence of this *occupational segregation* means women are far more likely to be employed in relatively poorly paid occupations and thus the gender pay gap is to be expected. Evidence from the EU as a whole suggests that occupational segregation is a significant factor in explaining pay differences.

- Many women take career breaks to have children. For this reason, employers are sometimes more willing to invest money in training men (thereby increasing their marginal productivity), and more willing to promote men. A study

by the Institute for Fiscal Studies (IFS)[10] estimated that, for every year a woman takes away from work, her earnings fall by 2 per cent below those who remain in work.

- Women tend to be less geographically mobile than men. If social norms are such that the man's job is seen as somehow more 'important' than the woman's, then a couple will often move if that is necessary for the man to get promotion. The woman, however, will have to settle for whatever job she can get in the same locality as her partner. Additionally, this may reduce a woman's bargaining power when negotiating for wage increases in her current job, if her employer knows that her outside options are more limited than a man's would be.

[10]William Elming, Robert Joyce and Monica Costa Dias, 'The gender wage gap', *Briefing Note (BN186)*, Institute for Fiscal Studies (23 August 2016)

Figure 18.12 Mean gross hourly earnings of full-time employees

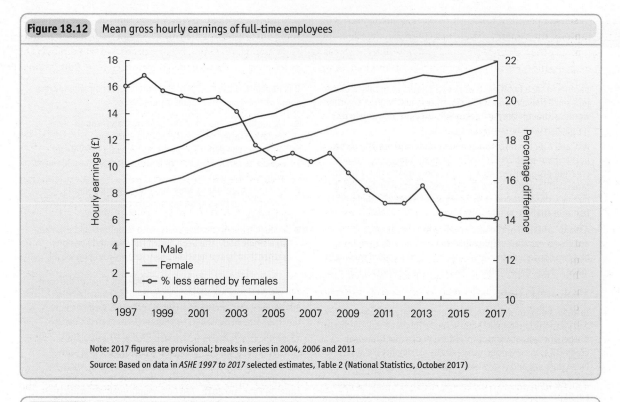

Note: 2017 figures are provisional; breaks in series in 2004, 2006 and 2011

Source: Based on data in *ASHE 1997 to 2017* selected estimates, Table 2 (National Statistics, October 2017)

Table 18.1 Average gross hourly pay, excluding overtime, for selected occupations, full-time UK employees on adult rates, 2017

	Men	Women	
Occupation	£ per hour		Women's pay as % of men's
Legal professionals	39.35	27.14	69.0
Chief executives and senior officials	56.11	41.78	74.5
Architects	23.88	18.75	78.5
Medical practitioners	37.04	30.48	82.3
HE lecturers	30.33	25.24	83.2
Laboratory technicians	12.63	11.31	89.5
Management consultants and business analysts	24.34	21.98	90.3
Accountants	22.52	20.47	90.9
Sales assistants and retail cashiers	9.98	9.09	91.1
Senior police officers	31.38	28.76	91.7
Chefs	10.10	9.37	92.8
Librarians	16.52	15.34	92.9
Secondary school teachers	23.74	22.10	93.1
Bar staff	8.15	7.74	95.0
Bus drivers	11.69	11.13	95.2
Nurses	17.72	17.16	96.8
Social workers	18.69	18.23	97.5
Hairdressers and barbers	8.34	8.18	98.1
All occupations	**17.95**	**15.42**	**85.9**
Average gross weekly pay (incl. overtime)	717.90	578.00	80.5
Average weekly hours worked (incl. overtime)	40.10	37.50	
Average weekly overtime	1.40	0.50	

Source: *Annual Survey of Hours and Earnings: 2017 provisional and 2016 revised results* (National Statistics, October 2017)

- A smaller proportion of women workers are members of unions than men. Even when they are members of unions, they are often in jobs where unions are weak (e.g. clothing industry workers, shop assistants and secretaries). For example, in the USA in 2017, male union membership was just under 12 per cent and had risen over the past year, while female union membership stood at just 10 per cent and had declined.

- Women are more likely to be in part-time work and thus have less bargaining power, less influence and less chance of obtaining promotion relative to men. While the gender pay gap across part-time workers tends to be smaller and is sometimes reversed (men paid less than women), the IFS study noted the longer-term detrimental effect on women's earning when switching from full-time to part-time employment. When this happens, while their wage does not fall immediately, over time, their growth in earnings falls behind those of people working full time.

- Custom and practice. Despite equal pay legislation, many jobs done wholly or mainly by women continue to be low paid, irrespective of questions of productivity.

- Prejudice and discrimination. Although unequal pay (where men and women receive different rates of pay for doing exactly the same job) is illegal, it probably does still exist and is likely to be a contributing factor to the gender pay gap. Furthermore, in many jobs, women are discriminated against when it comes to promotion, especially to senior positions.

> ## Pause for thought
>
> *If we were to look at weekly rather than hourly pay and included the effects of overtime, what do you think would happen to the pay differentials in Table 18.1?*

Which of the above reasons could be counted as economically 'irrational' (i.e. paying different wage rates to women and men for other than purely economic reasons)? Certainly the last two would qualify. Paying different wage rates on these grounds would *not* be in the profit interests of the employer.

Some of the others, however, are more difficult to classify. The causes of inequality in wage rates may be traced back beyond the workplace: perhaps to the educational system or to a culture that discourages women from being so aggressive in seeking promotion or to more generous maternity than paternity leave. Even if it is a manifestation of

profit-maximising behaviour by employers that women in some circumstances are paid less than their male counterparts, the reason why it is more profitable for employers to pay men more than women may indeed reflect discrimination elsewhere or at some other point in time.

Has the gender pay gap narrowed?

There has been a general decline in the gender pay gap over the past few decades in many countries. There are many reasons for this, including: a growth in the number of women working full time; increased awareness across the population leading to greater pressure on companies and governments to take action; a rise in women's education; and changes in government policy.

Research by the IFS in 2016 highlighted the increasing proportion of women who are now educated to A Level and degree standard as a key explanatory variable in the closing of the gender pay gap. However, the IFS also found that there had been little change in the gender pay gap for the highly educated. One reason identified for this is that, despite equal pay legislation, women are still discriminated against when it comes to promotion, especially to senior positions.

For example, an update to the 2010 Davies review was published in 2015.[11] The Davies review examined the under-representation of women on the boards of FTSE 100 and 350 companies. Of the FTSE 100 companies, only 12.5 per cent of board members were female. The report suggested various measures to increase the number of female board members, including discussions with board chairs on the issue, Women on Boards conferences, pressure from investors and requiring companies to report on their diversity policies.

The update showed that figure did improve dramatically and the target Lord Davies set for 2015 (25 per cent female board membership) was met, with a figure of 26.1 per cent. Subsequently, a new target of 33 per cent was set for 2020 and an update, in March 2018, showed that almost 29 per cent of FTSE 100 board positions are now held by women.

There is debate about whether female board members has a positive impact on business performance and, while the evidence is somewhat mixed, you can read about it via BBC News' article: '100 women: do women on boards increase profits?'[12]

> ## Pause for thought
>
> *If employers were forced to give genuinely equal pay for equal work, how would this affect the employment of women and men? What would determine the magnitude of these effects?*

---

[11]'Improving the Gender Balance on British Boards', *Women on Boards Davies Review, Five Year Summary,* KPMG and Cranfield University (October 2015)

[12]'100 women: Do women on boards increase profits?', *BBC News* (2 October 2017)

18.4 THE FLEXIBLE FIRM AND THE MARKET FOR LABOUR

The past 35 years have seen sweeping changes in the ways that firms organise their workforce. Three world recessions combined with rapid changes in technology have led many firms to question the wisdom of appointing workers on a permanent basis to specific jobs. Instead, they want to have the greatest flexibility possible to respond to new situations. If demand falls, they want to be able to 'shed' labour without facing large redundancy costs. If demand rises, they want rapid access to additional labour supplies. If technology changes, say with the introduction of new computerised processes, they want to have the flexibility to move workers around or to take on new workers in some areas and lose workers in others.

What many firms seek, therefore, is flexibility in employing and allocating labour. What countries are experiencing is an increasingly flexible labour market, as workers and employment agencies respond to the new 'flexible firm'.

There are three main types of flexibility in the use of labour:

- *Functional flexibility*. This is where an employer is able to transfer labour between different tasks within the production process. It contrasts with traditional forms of organisation where people were employed to do a specific job and then stuck to it. A functionally flexible labour force will tend to be multi-skilled and relatively highly trained.
- *Numerical flexibility*. This is where the firm is able to adjust the size and composition of its workforce according to changing market conditions. To achieve this, the firm is likely to employ a large proportion of its labour on a part-time or casual basis or even subcontract out specialist requirements, rather than employing such labour skills itself.
- *Financial flexibility*. This is where the firm has flexibility in its wage costs. In large part, it is a result of functional and numerical flexibility. Financial flexibility can be achieved by rewarding individual effort and productivity rather than paying a given rate for a particular job. Such rates of pay are increasingly negotiated at the local level rather than being nationally set. The result is not only a widening of pay differentials between skilled and unskilled workers, but also growing differentials in pay between workers within the same industry but in different parts of the country.

Figure 18.13 shows how these three forms of flexibility are reflected in the organisation of a *flexible firm*, an organisation quite different from that of the traditional firm.

The most significant difference is that the labour force is segmented. The core group, drawn from the *primary labour market*, will be composed of *functionally* flexible workers, who have relatively secure employment and are generally on full-time permanent contracts. Such workers will be relatively well paid and receive wages reflecting their scarce skills.

The periphery, drawn from the *secondary labour market*, is more fragmented than the core and can be subdivided into a first and a second peripheral group. The first peripheral group is composed of workers with a lower level of skill than those in the core, skills that tend to be general rather than firm-specific. Thus workers in the first peripheral group can usually be drawn from the external labour market. Such workers may be employed on full-time contracts, but they will generally face less secure employment than those workers in the core. An example is workers in the hotel industry, many of whom have little job security and who are on short-term or zero-hour contracts.[13]

The business gains a greater level of numerical flexibility by drawing labour from the second peripheral group. Here workers are employed on a variety of short-term, part-time contracts, often through a recruitment agency. Some of these workers may be working from home or online from another country, such as India, where wage rates are much lower. Workers in the second peripheral group have little job security.

As well as supplementing the level of labour in the first peripheral group, the second periphery can also provide high-level specialist skills that supplement the core. In this instance, the business can subcontract or hire self-employed labour, minimising its commitment to such workers. The business thereby gains both functional and numerical flexibility simultaneously.

Definitions

Functional flexibility Where employers can switch workers from job to job as requirements change.

Numerical flexibility Where employers can change the size of their workforce as their labour requirements change.

Financial flexibility Where employers can vary their wage costs by changing the composition of their workforce or the terms on which workers are employed.

Flexible firm A firm that has the flexibility to respond to changing market conditions.

Primary labour market The market for permanent full-time core workers.

Secondary labour market The market for peripheral workers, usually employed on a temporary or part-time basis, or a less secure 'permanent' basis.

KI 6
p 29

KEY IDEA 26

Flexible firm. A firm that has the flexibility to respond to changing market conditions by changing the composition of its workforce and its working practices.

---

[13] Margaret Deery and Leo K. Jago, *The Core and the Periphery: An Examination of the Flexible Workforce Model in the Hotel Industry*, Centre for Hospitality and Tourism Research, Victoria University, Melbourne (2002).

Figure 18.13 The flexible firm

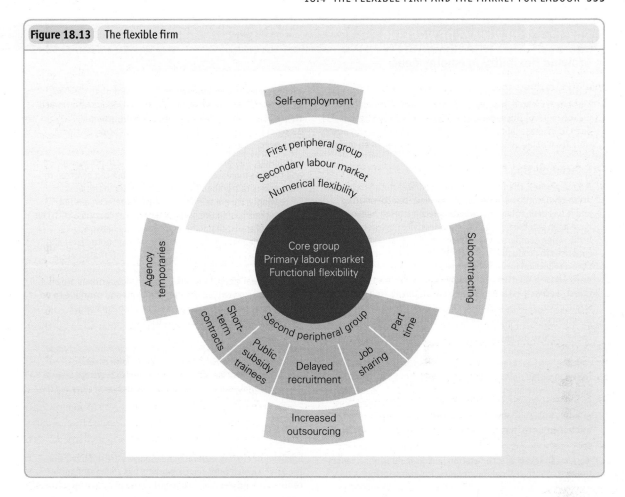

Pause for thought

How is the advent of flexible firms likely to alter the gender balance of employment and unemployment?

The Japanese model

The application of new flexible working patterns has become more prevalent in businesses in the UK and elsewhere in Europe and North America. In Japan, flexibility has been part of the business way of life for many years and was crucial in shaping the country's economic success in the 1970s and 1980s. In fact, we now talk of a Japanese model of business organisation, which many of its competitors seek to emulate.

The model is based around four principles:

■ *Total quality management (TQM).* This involves all employees working towards continuously improving all aspects of quality, both of the finished product and of methods of production.

■ *Elimination of waste.* According to the 'just-in-time' (JIT) principle, businesses should take delivery of just sufficient quantities of raw materials and parts, at the right time and place. Stocks are kept to a minimum and hence the whole system of production runs with little, if any, slack. For example, supermarkets today have smaller storerooms relative to the total shopping area than they did in the past and take more frequent deliveries.

■ *A belief in the superiority of team work in the core group.* Collective effort is a vital element in Japanese working practices. Team work is seen not only to enhance individual performance, but also to involve the individual in the running of the business and thus to create a sense of commitment.

■ *Functional and numerical flexibility.* Both are seen as vital components in maintaining high levels of productivity.

The principles of this model are now widely accepted as being important in creating and maintaining a competitive business in a competitive marketplace.

BOX 18.3 NEW WAYS OF WORKING

Growing flexibility in employment

The labour market has changed beyond recognition, with new jobs being created, new ways of working and growing flexibility and much of this is due to technology. One key effect has been to increase labour market flexibility, as people can now work from home almost as effectively as they can in an office.

Telecommuting

Mobile phones, the Internet, Skype, conference calls, etc. all mean that more and more people are now '**telecommuting**' and it has been found that where 'telecommuting networks' have been established, gains in productivity have been significant, when compared with office workers. Most studies indicate rises in productivity of over 35 per cent and at the same time a reduction in staff absenteeism. With fewer interruptions and less chatting with fellow workers, less working time is lost. Add to this the stress-free environment, free from the strain of commuting and the individual worker's performance is enhanced and workers are found to be more attentive.

There are also broader gains, including reduced time in commuting, savings via lower maintenance, heating and lighting costs, as well as some broader gains to society. For example, telecommuting opens up the labour market to a wider group of workers who might find it relatively difficult to leave the home – groups such as single parents and the disabled. This not only improves efficiency, as a better use is made of the full labour force, but enhances equity as well.

Also, there are environmental gains, as fewer journeys to work mean less traffic congestion and less pollution. A report found that if the 50 million potential teleworkers in the USA worked from home 50 per cent of the time, the reduction in greenhouse gases would be comparable to all workers in New York State no longer using the roads.[1]

In the 2017 State of Telecommuting in the U.S. Employee Workforce report,[2] it was found that in the previous 10 years, the number of people telecommuting in the USA had increased by 115 per cent. Gallup's report on the State of the American Workplace found that, in 2016, 43 per cent of US workers reported working remotely.[3] According to the ONS, in the UK in 2017, there were 4.3 million workers who worked from home or with home as a base. This represented 13.6 per cent of the 31.9 million people in work, up from 11.1 per cent in 1998.[4]

Technology has, therefore, permitted a rise in home working and this has increased labour mobility. Work can be taken to the workers rather than the workers coming to the work. Increasingly, we are seeing international telecommuting, with workers basing themselves in different counties. With the creation of transoceanic fibre optical cable networks, international data transmission has become both faster and cheaper. Some familiar examples include international teleworkers in call centres, especially those employed by multinational companies. Also, increasingly workers are able to purchase property in cheaper countries and continue to do their jobs remotely, taking advantage of cheap budget airlines if they need to go into the office.

1. *What effect is telecommuting likely to have on (a) trade union membership and (b) trade union power?*
2. *How are the developments referred to in this box likely to affect relative house prices between capital cities and the regions?*

Online recruitment

The days of pounding the streets, looking in employment agencies or circling adverts in newspapers are not over, but the way in which firms recruit workers has changed significantly over the years, with increasing use of online recruitment technologies as a means of enhancing labour market flexibility. Firms have their own online vacancy boards and use social networking sites to target different audiences. Those searching for jobs use a range of online sites, such as Monster and Fish4jobs to register for job alerts by email or mobile phone and to register their CV.

KI 26
p 334

---

[1] Kate Lister and Tom Harnish, *The State of Telework in the U.S.* Telework Research Network (June 2011).

[2] *2017 State of Telecommuting in the U.S. Employee Workforce*, Global Workplace Analytics and FlexJobs (June 2017).

[3] Greg Kratz, 'Report Summary: "State of the American Workplace," Gallup', *1 Million for Work Flexibility* (13 April 2017).

[4] Data showing employment and home workers, for the period Labour Force Survey January to March 2015 to 2017 and Annual Population Survey October 2016 to September 2017, ONS (18 January 2018).

This new recruitment process has improved the efficiency with which information is relayed to the employers and suppliers of labour and increases their search horizons. As well as reaching a wider and more targeted audience, recruitment costs are lowered and the recruitment cycle is shortened and made more efficient by the use of Internet technologies. On the downside, it does appear that e-recruitment is leading to more unsuitable candidates applying for vacancies, which does cost money.

According to the Chartered Institute of Personnel and Development:

> Technology plays an increasingly important role in recruitment, ranging from attracting candidates through to the selection process. Electronic techniques are also being used to slim down the number of potential candidates. In particular, using online recruitment can mean employers receive large numbers of applications from unsuitable candidates, so it can be helpful also to use technology to help manage the application forms.[5]

3. *Explain how a flexible firm's flexibility would be enhanced by online recruitment.*
4. *If a firm is trying to achieve flexibility in its use of labour, do you think this would be harder or easier in a period of recession? Explain why.*

The gig economy

Workers in the gig economy are self-employed, but are often contracted to an employer. They are paid by the job (or 'gig': like musicians), rather than being paid a wage. Much of the work is temporary, although many in the gig economy, such as taxi drivers and delivery people stick with the same job. The gig economy is just one further manifestation of the growing flexibility of labour markets, which have also seen a rise in temporary employment, part-time employment and zero-hour contracts. A report by the Resolution Foundation[6] found that the numbers of self-employed workers has risen to 5 million since the financial crisis. This is a growth of 22 per cent.

The gig economy provides a number of benefits for workers, as they have greater flexibility in their choice of hours and many

work wholly or partly from home. Many do several 'gigs' simultaneously, which gives variety and interest. This flexible working also provides a greater opportunity for people to work the optimum number of hours, such that they work up to the point where the marginal benefit from work, in terms of pay and enjoyment, equals the marginal cost, in terms of effort and sacrificed leisure. However, there is less job security and fewer benefits and pay tends to be much lower, as they have much less bargaining power than the traditional worker.

From the firm's point of view, many of these disadvantages to the workers are advantages for them. Gig workers typically have been cheaper to employ, as they do not need to be paid sick pay, holiday pay or redundancy.

However, various court cases are currently under way with challenges to this. In 2017, two tribunal hearings in the UK went against employers, ruling that those working for them should be classed as 'workers' and not 'independent contractors' and consequently, as workers, they were entitled to the national minimum wage, rest breaks and holiday pay. These rulings may therefore change some of the benefits firms observe from using gig workers, as one of the key benefits is now reduced. However, other benefits remain for firms, as they do have greater flexibility in determining how much work individuals should do: the firm chooses the amount of service it buys in a similar way that consumers decide how much to buy.

5. *Give some examples of work that is generally or frequently done in the gig economy.*

Labour markets have, therefore, become increasingly flexible and more efficient over the past few decades and, with technology continuing to improve, it is likely that we will move towards newer and faster ways of working.

Choose a particular company that employs people on a flexible basis. What benefits does it gain from so doing? What are the advantages and disadvantages for people working for the company on flexible terms?

---

[5]'Selection methods', *CIPD Factsheet,* Chartered Institute of Personnel and Development (July 2018).

[6]Dan Tomlinson and Adam Corlett, *A tough gig? The nature of self-employment in 21st Century Britain and policy implications,* Resolution Foundation (February 2017).

Definition

Telecommuting Working from home or locally and being linked to work via the Internet.

SUMMARY

1a The UK labour market has undergone many changes with the growth of technology, changes in the social structure and the movement towards service-sector employment, leading to a more flexible labour market.

1b Wages in a competitive labour market are determined by the interaction of demand and supply. The individual's supply of labour will be determined by the substitution and income effects from a given increase in the wage rate. At low wage levels, it is likely that individuals will substitute work for leisure. At high wage levels, it is possible that individuals will work less and consume more leisure time, giving a backward-bending supply curve of labour by the individual.

1c The elasticity of labour supply will depend largely upon the geographical and occupational mobility of labour. The more readily labour can transfer between jobs and regions, the more elastic the supply.

1d The demand for labour is traditionally assumed to be based upon labour's productivity. Marginal productivity theory assumes that the employer will demand labour up to the point where the cost of employing one additional worker (MC_L) is equal to the revenue earned from the output of that worker (MRP_L). The firm's demand curve for labour is its MRP_L curve.

1e The elasticity of demand for labour is determined by: the price elasticity of demand for the good that labour produces; the substitutability of labour for other factors; the proportion of wages to total costs; and time.

2a In an imperfect labour market, where a business has monopoly power in employing labour, it is known as a monopsonist. Such a firm will employ workers to the point where the $MRP_L = MC_L$. Since the wage is below the MC_L, the monopsonist, other things being equal, will employ fewer workers at a lower wage than would be employed in a perfectly competitive labour market.

2b If a union has monopoly power, its power to raise wages will be limited if the employer operates under perfect or monopolistic competition in the goods market. A rise in wage rates will force the employer to cut back on employment, unless there is a corresponding rise in productivity.

2c In a situation of bilateral monopoly (where a monopoly union faces a monopsony employer), the union may have considerable scope to raise wages above the monopsony level, without the employer wishing to reduce the level of employment. There is no unique equilibrium wage. The wage will depend on the outcome of a process of collective bargaining between union and management.

2d The efficiency wage hypothesis states that a business might hold wages above the market-clearing wage rate so as to: reduce shirking; reduce labour turnover; improve the quality of labour recruited; and stimulate worker morale. The level of efficiency wage will be determined largely by the type of job the worker does and the level and scarcity of skill they possess.

3a Low pay is difficult to define. There is no accepted definition. The widening disparity in wages between high- and low-income earners is due to: unemployment resulting from recession; unemployment resulting from a shift in technology; the growth in part-time employment; and changes in labour market legislation.

3b A statutory minimum wage is one way of tackling the problem of low pay and many countries do have a national minimum wage in place.

3c It is argued, however, that, in a perfect labour market, where employers are forced to accept the wage as determined by the marketplace, any attempt to impose a minimum wage above this level will create unemployment. In an imperfect labour market, where an employer has some monopsonistic power, the impact of a minimum wage is uncertain. The impact will depend largely upon how much workers are currently paid below their MRP and whether a higher wage encourages them to work more productively.

3d Differences between male and female earnings between occupations can, in part, be explained by differences in the types of work that men and women do; they are occupationally segregated. Differences within occupations are less easily accounted for. It would seem that some measure of discrimination is being practised, though the wage gap is narrowing.

4a Changes in technology have had a massive impact upon the process of production and the experience of work. Labour markets and business organisations have become more flexible: functionally, numerically and financially. The flexible firm will incorporate these different forms of flexibility into its business operations, with a core workforce, supplemented by workers and skills drawn from a periphery, who are likely to be on part-time and temporary contracts.

4b The application of the flexible firm model is closely mirrored in the practices of Japanese business. Commitments to improve quality, reduce waste, build teamwork and introduce flexible labour markets are seen as key components in the success of Japanese business organisation.

REVIEW QUESTIONS

1 If a firm faces a shortage of workers with very specific skills, it may decide to undertake the necessary training itself. If, on the other hand, it faces a shortage of unskilled workers, it may well offer a small wage increase in order to obtain the extra labour. In the first case, it is responding to an increase in demand for labour by attempting to shift the supply curve. In the second case, it is merely allowing a movement along the supply curve. Use a demand and supply diagram to illustrate each case. Given that elasticity of supply is different in each case, do you think that these are the best policies for the firm to follow?

2 The wage rate a firm has to pay and the output it can produce varies with the number of workers as follows (all figures are hourly):

Number of workers	1	2	3	4	5	6	7	8
Wage rate (AC_L) (£)	3	4	5	6	7	8	9	10
Total output (TPP_L)	10	22	32	40	46	50	52	52

Assume that output sells at £2 per unit.

a) Copy the table and add additional rows for TC_L, MC_L, TRP_L and MRP_L. Put the figures for MC_L and MRP_L in the spaces between the columns.

b) How many workers will the firm employ in order to maximise profits?

c) What will be its hourly wage bill at this level of employment?

d) How much hourly revenue will it earn at this level of employment?

e) Assuming that the firm faces other (fixed) costs of £30 per hour, how much hourly profit will it make?

f) Assume that the workers now form a union and that the firm agrees to pay the negotiated wage rate to all employees. What is the maximum to which the hourly wage rate could rise without causing the firm to try to reduce employment below that in (b) above? (See Figure 18.9.)

g) What would be the firm's hourly profit now?

3 How do you think the supply of labour curve will be affected by the UK's vote to leave the EU?

4 If, unlike a perfectly competitive employer, a monopsonist has to pay a higher wage to attract more workers, why, other things being equal, will a monopsonist pay a lower wage than a perfectly competitive employer?

5 The table at the top of the next column shows figures for a monopsonist employer. Fill in the missing figures for columns (3) and (4). How many workers should the firm employ if it wishes to maximise profits?

6 What are some of the reasons why the marginal revenue product can differ between workers in different jobs?

Number of workers (1)	Wage rate (£) (2)	Total cost of labour (£) (3)	Marginal cost of labour (£) (4)	Marginal revenue product (£) (5)
1	100	100		
			110	230
2	105	210		
			120	240
3	110	230		
				240
4	115			
				230
5	120			
				210
6	125			
				190
7	130			
				170
8	135			
				150
9	140			
				130
10	145			

7 To what extent could a trade union succeed in gaining a pay increase from an employer with no loss in employment?

8 Do any of the following contradict marginal productivity theory: wage scales related to length of service (incremental scales), nationally negotiated wage rates, discrimination, firms taking the lead from other firms in determining this year's pay increase?

9 Using the analysis of sections 18.1 and 18.2, explain why a Premier League footballer will be paid such a high wage.

10 Apply the same analysis to top handball, lacrosse or badminton players. Why are they paid a relatively low wage compared to Premier League footballers, despite their exceptional talent and skill?

11 What is the efficiency wage hypothesis? Explain what employers might gain from paying wages above the market-clearing level.

12 'Minimum wages will cause unemployment.' Is this so?

13 How might we explain why men continue to earn more than women?

14 Identify the potential costs and benefits of the flexible firm to (a) employers and (b) employees.

Investment and the employment of capital

Business issues covered in this chapter

- What determines the amount of capital a firm will employ?
- How can a firm judge whether a proposed investment should go ahead? What techniques are there for investment appraisal?
- How can investment be financed? What types of financial institution are involved in financing investment?
- What are the relative merits of alternative sources of finance?
- What are the functions of the stock market?
- Is the stock market efficient as a means of allocating capital?

19.1 THE PRICING OF CAPITAL AND CAPITAL SERVICES

Capital includes all manufactured products that are used to produce goods and services. Thus capital includes such diverse items as a blast furnace, a bus, a cinema projector, a laptop, a factory and a screwdriver.

The capital goods described above are physical assets and are known as *physical* capital. The word 'capital' is also used to refer to various *paper* assets, such as shares and bonds. These are the means by which firms raise finance to purchase physical capital and are known as *financial* capital. Being merely paper assets, however, they do not count as factors of production. Nevertheless, financial markets have an important role in determining the level of investment in physical capital and we shall be examining these markets in the final two sections of this chapter.

The price of capital versus the price of capital services

A feature of most manufactured factors of production is that they last a period of time. A machine may last 10 years;

a factory may last 20 years or more. This leads to an important distinction: the income for the owner from *selling* capital and the income from *using* it or *hiring* it out.

- Income can be earned from selling capital and this is known as its *price*. It is a once-and-for-all payment. Thus a factory might sell for £1 million, a machine for £20 000 or a screwdriver for £1.
- Income can be gained from using capital, for example as part of the production process and this is known as its *return*. Alternatively, income can be gained from hiring out capital and this is known as its *rental*. This income therefore represents the value or price of the *services* of capital, expressed per period of time. Thus a firm might have to pay a rental of £1000 per year for a photocopier.

Obviously, the price of capital will be linked to the value of its services: to its return. A highly productive machine will sell for a higher price than one producing a lower output and hence yielding a lower return.

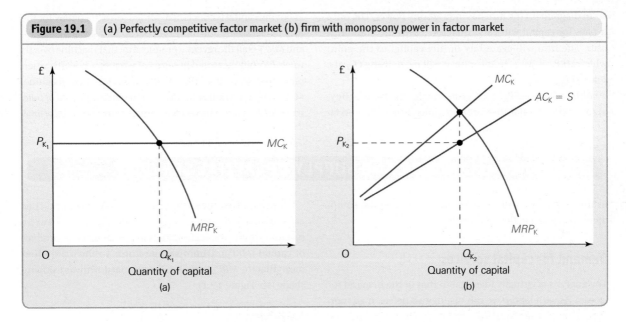

Figure 19.1 (a) Perfectly competitive factor market (b) firm with monopsony power in factor market

The discussion of the rewards to capital leads to a very important distinction: that between stocks and flows.

A *stock* is a quantity of something held. You may have £1000 in a savings account. A factory may contain 100 machines. These are both stocks: they are quantities held at a given point in time. A *flow* is an increase or decrease in quantity over a specified time period. You may save £10 per month. The factory may invest in another 20 machines next year.

> **KEY IDEA 27**
>
> *Stocks and flows.* A stock is a quantity of something at a given point in time. A flow is an increase or decrease in something over a specified period of time. This is an important distinction and a common cause of confusion.

Wages, rental and interest are all rewards to *flows*. Wages are the amount paid not to purchase a person (as a slave!), but for the services of that person's labour for a period of time. Rental is the amount paid per period of time to use the services of machinery or equipment, not to buy it outright. Likewise, interest is the reward paid to people per year for the use of their money.

Pause for thought

Which of the following are stocks and which are flows?
a. *Unemployment.*
b. *Redundancies.*
c. *Profits.*
d. *A firm's stock market valuation.*
e. *The value of property after a period of inflation.*

An important example of stocks and flows arises with capital and investment. If a firm has 100 machines, that is a stock of capital. It may choose to build up its stock by investing. Investment is a flow concept. The firm may choose to

invest in 10 new machines each year. This may not add 10 to the stock of machines, however, as some may be wearing out (a negative flow).

The profit-maximising employment of capital

On the demand side, the same rules apply for capital as for labour, if a firm wishes to maximise profits. Namely, it should demand additional capital (K) up to the point where the **marginal cost of capital** equals its **marginal revenue product**: $MC_K = MRP_K$. This same rule applies whether the firm is buying the capital outright or merely hiring it.

Figure 19.1 illustrates the two cases of perfect competition and monopsony. In both diagrams the MRP curve slopes downward. This is just another illustration of the law of diminishing returns, but this time applied to capital. If a firm increases the amount of capital while *holding other factors constant,* diminishing returns to capital will occur. Diminishing returns will apply equally, whether the firm is buying the extra capital or hiring it.

In diagram (a) the firm is a price taker. The capital price is given at P_{K1}, with profits maximised at Q_{K1} where $MRP_K = P_K$ (since $P_K = MC_K$).

Definitions

Stock The quantity of something held.

Flow An increase or decrease in quantity over a specified period.

Marginal cost of capital The cost of one additional unit of capital.

Marginal revenue product of capital The additional revenue earned from employing one additional unit of capital.

In diagram (b) the firm has monopsony power. The price it pays for capital will vary, therefore, with the amount it uses. The firm will again buy or hire capital to the point where $MRP_K = MC_K$. In this case, it will mean using Q_{K1} at a price of P_{K1}

Although the $MRP_K = MC_K$ rule remains the same for buying and hiring capital, there are some differences to note. As far as buying capital is concerned, MC_K is the extra outlay for the firm in *purchasing* one more unit of capital – say, a machine – and MRP_K is all the revenue produced by that machine over its *whole life* (but measured in terms of what this is worth when purchased: see section 19.3). In the case of hiring the machine, MC_K is the extra outlay for the firm in rental *per period of time*, while MRP_K is the extra revenue earned from it *per period of time*.

19.2 THE DEMAND FOR AND SUPPLY OF CAPITAL SERVICES

In this section we will consider the *hiring* of capital equipment for a given period of time.

Demand for capital services

The analysis is virtually identical to that of the demand for labour. As with labour we can distinguish between an individual firm's demand for capital services (K) and the whole-market demand for capital services.

Individual firm's demand

Take the case of a small painting and decorating firm that requires some scaffolding in order to complete a job. It could use ladders, but the job would take longer to complete. It goes along to a company that hires out scaffolding and is quoted a daily rate.

If it hires the scaffolding for one day, it can perhaps shorten the job by two or three days. If it hires it for a second day, it can perhaps save another one or two days. Hiring it for additional days may save extra still. But diminishing returns are occurring: the longer the scaffolding is up, the less intensively it will be used and the less additional time it will save. Perhaps, for some of the time, it will be used when ladders could have been used equally easily.

The time saved allows the firm to take on extra work. Thus each extra day the scaffolding is hired gives the firm extra revenue. This is the scaffolding's marginal revenue product of capital (MRP_K). Diminishing returns to the scaffolding mean that the MRP_K curve has the normal downward-sloping shape (see Figure 19.1).

Market demand

The market demand for capital services depends on the demand by individual firms (determined by the productivity of the capital and the price of the product it produces). The higher the MRP_K for individual firms, the greater will be the market demand.

Supply of capital services

It is necessary to distinguish (a) the supply *to* a single firm, (b) the supply *by* a single firm and (c) the market supply.

Supply to a single firm

This is illustrated in Figure 19.2(a). The small firm renting capital equipment is probably a price taker. If so, it faces a horizontal supply curve at the going rental rate (R_e). This is the firm's AC_K and MC_K curve. If, however, it has monopsony

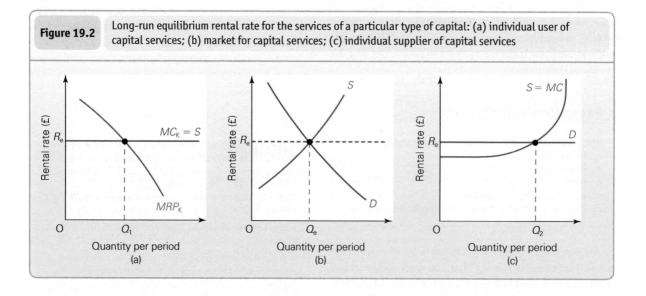

Figure 19.2 Long-run equilibrium rental rate for the services of a particular type of capital: (a) individual user of capital services; (b) market for capital services; (c) individual supplier of capital services

power, it will face an upward-sloping supply curve as in Figure 19.1(b).

Supply by a single firm

This is illustrated in Figure 19.2(c). Here the firm supplying the capital equipment is likely to be a price taker, facing a horizontal demand curve. It has to accept the going rental rate (R_e) established in the market. If it tries to charge more, then customers are likely to turn to rival suppliers.

It will maximise profit by supplying an amount Q_2, where the market rental rate is equal to the marginal cost of supplying the equipment. This is the profit-maximising rule for perfect competition that we established on pages 188–9.

There is a problem, however, in working out the marginal cost of renting out capital equipment: the piece of equipment probably cost a lot to buy in the first place, but lasts a long time. How are these large costs to be apportioned to each new rental? The answer is that it depends on the time period under consideration.

The short run. In the short run, the hire company is not buying any new equipment: it is simply hiring out its existing equipment. In the case of our scaffolding firm, the marginal costs of doing this will include the following:

- *Depreciation.* Scaffolding has second-hand value. Each time the scaffolding is hired out it deteriorates and thus its second-hand value falls. This loss in value is called 'depreciation'.
- *Maintenance and handling.* When equipment is hired out, it can get damaged and thus incur repair costs. The equipment might need servicing. Also, hiring out equipment involves labour time (e.g. in the office) and possibly transport costs.

Pause for thought

Assume now that the firm has monopoly power in hiring out equipment and thus faces a downward-sloping demand curve. Draw in two such demand curves on a diagram like Figure 19.2(c), one crossing the MC curve in the horizontal section and one in the vertical section. How much will the firm supply in each case and at what price? (You will need to draw in MR curves too.) Is the MC curve still the supply curve?

These marginal costs are likely to rise relatively slowly. In other words, for each extra day, a piece of equipment is hired out, the company will incur the same or only slightly higher additional costs. This gives a relatively flat supply curve of capital services in Figure 19.2(c) up to the hire company's maximum capacity. Once the scaffolding firm is hiring out all its scaffolding, the supply curve becomes vertical.

The long run. In the long run, the hire company will consider purchasing additional equipment. It can, therefore, supply as much as it likes in the long run. The supply curve will be relatively elastic or, if it is a price taker itself (i.e. if the scaffolding firm simply buys scaffolding at the market price), the supply curve will be horizontal (i.e. perfectly elastic). This long-run supply curve will be vertically higher than the short-run curve, since the long-run *MC* includes the cost of purchasing each additional piece of equipment.

Market supply

This is illustrated in Figure 19.2(b). The market supply curve of capital services is the sum of the quantities supplied by all the individual firms.

In the short run, the market supply will be relatively inelastic, given that it takes time to manufacture new equipment and that stocks of equipment currently held by manufacturers are likely to be relatively small. Moreover, hire companies may be unwilling to purchase (expensive) new equipment immediately following a rise in demand: after all, the upsurge in demand may turn out to be short lived.

In the long run, the supply curve will be more elastic because extra capital equipment can be produced.

Determination of the price of capital services

As Figure 19.2(b) shows, in a perfect market the market rental rate for capital services will be determined by the interaction of market demand and supply.

If there is monopsony power on the part of the users of hired capital, this will have the effect of depressing the rental rate below the MRP_K (see Figure 19.1(b)), as we saw in the case of a monopsony buyer of labour. If, on the other hand, there is monopoly power on the part of hire companies, the analysis is similar to that of monopoly in the goods market (see Figure 11.5 on page 195). The firm, by reducing the supply of capital for hire, can drive up the rental rate. It will maximise profit where the marginal revenue from hiring out the equipment is equal to the marginal cost of so doing: at a rental rate (price) *above* the marginal cost.

Pause for thought

What will happen to the demand for capital services and the equilibrium rental if the price of some other factor, say labour, changes? Assume that wage rates fall. Trace through the effects on a three-section diagram like that of Figure 19.2. (Clue: a fall in wages will have two significant effects: it will reduce costs and hence the price of the product, so that more will be sold; and it will make labour cheaper relative to capital. How will these two things affect the demand for capital?)

19.3 INVESTMENT APPRAISAL

The alternative to hiring capital is to buy it outright. This section examines the demand and supply of capital for purchase.

The demand for capital: investment

How many planes will an airline want to buy? Should a steelworks install another blast furnace? Should a university purchase technology to facilitate recorded lectures? Should McDonald's build an out-of-town restaurant? Should it install an extra oven? These are all **investment** decisions. Investment is the purchasing of additional capital.

The demand for capital, or 'investment demand', by a profit-maximising firm is based on exactly the same principles as the demand for labour or the demand for capital services. The firm must weigh up the marginal revenue product of that investment (i.e. the money it will earn for the firm) against its marginal cost.

However, capital is durable. It goes on producing goods and, hence, yielding revenue for the firm for a considerable period of time. Calculating these benefits, therefore, involves taking account of their *timing*.

There are two ways of approaching this question of timing: the **present value approach** and the **rate of return approach**. In both cases, the firm is comparing the marginal benefits with the marginal costs of the investment.

Present value approach

To work out the benefit of an investment (its *MRP*), the firm must estimate all the future earnings it will bring and then convert them to a *present value*, as money earned in the future will not be worth the same as money earned today. Let us take a simple example to illustrate this.

Assume that a firm is considering buying a machine. It will produce profits of £1000 per year for four years and then wear out and sell for £1000 as scrap. What is the benefit of this machine to the firm? At first sight, the answer would seem to be £5000. This, after all, is the total income earned from the machine. Unfortunately, it is not as simple as this. The reason is that money earned in the future is less beneficial to the firm than having the same amount of money today: after all, if the firm has the money today, it can earn interest on it by putting it in the bank or reinvesting it in some other project. (Note that this has nothing to do with inflation. In the case we are considering, we are assuming constant prices.)

To illustrate this, assume that you have £100 today and can earn 10 per cent interest by putting it in a bank. In one year's time, that £100 will have grown to £110, in two years' time to £121, in three years' time to £133.10, and so on. This process is known as **compounding**.

It follows that, if someone offered to give you £121 in two years' time, it would be no better than giving you £100 today, since, with interest, £100 invested today would grow to £121 in two years. What we say, then, is that, with a

10 per cent interest rate, £121 in two years' time has a *present value* of £100.

The procedure of reducing future values back to a present value is known as **discounting**.

> **KEY IDEA 28**
>
> ***The principle of discounting.*** People generally prefer to have benefits today than in the future. Thus future benefits have to be reduced (discounted) to give them a present value.

When we do discounting, the rate that we use is called the **rate of discount**: in this case 10 per cent. The formula for discounting is given by:

$$PV = \sum \frac{X_t}{(1 + r)^t}$$

Where
PV	is the present value	
X_t	is the earnings from the investment in year t	
r	is the rate of discount (expressed as a decimal: i.e. 10 per cent = 0.1)	
$\sum$	is the sum of each of the years' discounted earnings.	

So what is the present value of the investment in the machine that produced £1000 for four years and then is sold as scrap for £1000, with a discount rate of 0.1? According to the formula it is:

$$\frac{£1000}{1.1} + \frac{£1000}{(1.1)^2} + \frac{£1000}{(1.1)^3} + \frac{£2000}{(1.1)^4}$$

$$= £909 + £826 + £751 + £1366$$

$$= £3852$$

Definitions

Investment The purchase by the firm of equipment or materials that will add to its stock of capital.

Present value approach to appraising investment This involves estimating the value *now* of a flow of future benefits (or costs).

Rate of return approach The benefits from investment are calculated as a percentage of the costs of investment. This rate is then compared to the rate at which money has to be borrowed in order to see whether the investment should be undertaken.

Compounding The process of adding interest each year to an initial capital sum.

Discounting The process of reducing the value of future flows to give them a present valuation.

Rate of discount The rate that is used to reduce future values to present values.

Thus the present value of the investment (i.e. its *MRP*) is £3852, *not* £5000 as it might seem at first sight. In other words, if the firm had £3852 today and deposited it in a bank at a 10 per cent interest rate, the firm would earn exactly the same as it would by investing in the machine.

So is the investment in the machine worthwhile? It is now simply a question of comparing the £3852 benefit with the cost of buying the machine. If the machine costs less than £3852, it will be worth buying. If it costs more, the firm would be better off keeping its money in the bank and earning the 10 per cent rate of interest.

The difference between the present value of the benefits (*PV*$_b$) of the investment and its cost (*C*) is known as the *net present value (NPV)*.

$$NPV = PV_b - C$$

If the *NPV* is positive, the investment is worthwhile. However, it is worth noting that, even if an investment has a positive *NPV*, a firm may still choose not to invest. A firm may be considering multiple investments and hence may have to allocate its resources to one particular investment and forego another, even if both have a positive *NPV*.

Pause for thought

What is the present value of a machine that lasts three years, earns £100 in year 1, £200 in year 2 and £200 in year 3, and then has a scrap value of £100? Assume that the rate of discount is 5 per cent. If the machine costs £500, is the investment worthwhile? Would it be worthwhile if the rate of discount were 10 per cent?

Rate of return approach

The alternative approach when estimating whether an investment is worthwhile is to calculate the investment's *rate of return*. This rate of return is known as the firm's *marginal efficiency of capital (MEC)* or *internal rate of return (IRR)*.

We use the same formula as for calculating present value:

$$PV = \sum \frac{X_t}{(1 + r)^t}$$

and then calculate what value of *r* would make the *PV* equal to the cost of investment: in other words, the rate of discount that would make the investment just break even. Say this worked out at 5 per cent. What we would be saying is that the investment will just cover its costs if the current rate of interest (rate of discount) is 5 per cent. In other words, this investment is equivalent to receiving 20 per cent interest: it has a 5 per cent rate of return (*IRR*).

So should the investment go ahead? Yes, if the actual rate of interest (*i*) is less than 5 per cent. In such a case, the firm is better off investing its money in this project than keeping its money in the bank: i.e. if *IRR* > *i*, the investment should go ahead.

This is just one more application of the general rule that if *MRP*$_K$ > *MC*$_K$ then more capital should be used: only in this case *MRP*$_K$ is expressed as a rate of return (*IRR*) and the *MC*$_K$ is expressed as a rate of interest (*i*).

The risks of investment

One of the problems with investment is that the future is uncertain. The return on an investment will depend on the value of the goods it produces, which will depend on the goods market. For example, the return on investment in the car industry will depend on the demand and price of cars. But future markets cannot be predicted with accuracy: they depend on consumer tastes, the actions of rivals and the whole state of the economy. Investment is thus risky.

Risk may also be incurred in terms of the output from an investment. Take the case of prospecting for oil. An oil company may be lucky and have a major strike, but it may simply drill dry well after dry well. If it does get a major strike and hence earn a large return on its investment, these profits will not be competed away by competitors prospecting in other fields because they too still run the risk of drilling dry holes.

How is this risk accounted for when calculating the benefits of an investment? The answer is to use a higher rate of discount. The higher the risk, the bigger the premium that must be added to the rate.

Government investment decisions

Just as firms have decisions to make about which investments to pursue, so do governments. A government may be considering investing in a new hospital, a new transport network or communications infrastructure (see Box 19.1).

Private firms nearly always will be focused on those investments that have a positive *NPV*, while governments may have other objectives and concerns. Also, many of the future benefits of a government investment may be very difficult to determine, not just in terms of the monetary value, but also in terms of who will benefit. The investment may also be very long term and so benefits that might arise in 50 years are incredibly difficult to estimate – after all, the future is very uncertain.

Finally, governments are concerned about re-election and thus will be focused on the public – what do the voters want? This might imply that a government investment project with a negative net present value still goes ahead because of the non-monetary benefits, the necessity to maintain

Definitions

Net present value (NPV) of an investment The discounted benefits of an investment minus the cost of the investment.

Marginal efficiency of capital (MEC) or internal rate of return (IRR) The rate of return of an investment: the discount rate that makes the net present value of an investment equal to zero.

BOX 19.1 INVESTING IN ROADS

A permit scheme for roadworks

Road networks are in constant need of maintenance and repair and, whatever country you are in, we are all familiar with the delays, congestion and general costs of roadworks. Typically we complain about them while they are taking place, even if there may be significant positive benefits for us once they are completed. Many different agencies can be involved in roadworks and one of the big issues is often a lack of co-ordination between them, such that disruption seems to occur for a much longer period than is absolutely necessary.

In the UK, Leicestershire County Council (LCC) proposed a 'Permit Scheme for Road Works and Street Works' to start from January 2018, with the aim of decreasing the number of roadworks taking place, thus reducing disruption and promoting better collaboration between the agencies involved.[1] The County Council produced an economic appraisal covering a 25-year period of such a Permit Scheme being in place. It included an evaluation of the operating and capital costs that would be incurred, the reduction in the costs due to fewer roadworks and the future benefits from reductions in delays and congestion, fewer accidents, lower emissions and other effects. The whole proposal was part of the Council's aim to improve transport planning and network management and 'maximise the safe and efficient use of road space'.

Department for Transport (DfT) guidance, based on previous cost–benefit reports, assumes that providing this type of permit scheme increases the efficiency of street work management by 5 per cent. This means that the cost saving assumed from this permit scheme is 5 per cent of the total cost of street works for the year.

Evaluating the costs and benefits or the permit scheme

The council used Highways England's software package QUADRO[2] to appraise the permit scheme and consider potential cost savings and benefits from using the road network more efficiently. The idea of the appraisal is to compare the costs and benefits of the Road Works and Street Works Permit Scheme with a 'do-nothing' scenario to see if the permit scheme is worth pursuing.

The DfT's 'Transport Analysis Guidance'[3] requires the yearly costs and benefits of all transport schemes to be converted to 2010 market prices and for all future costs and benefits to be discounted to the same present value year. It uses a discount rate of 3.5 per cent for the first 30 years of the project and 3 per cent thereafter, as advised by the Treasury's Green Book.[4] It also requires that all future values are in 'real cost' terms, such that it allows for wage inflation over and above general inflation. Finally, these discounted factor costs are converted to market prices by multiplying them by the indirect tax correction factor to allow for the average rate of taxation within the economy.

The costs considered were in two categories: the set up and implementation costs and the ongoing yearly costs of the permit scheme. A figure of £150 000 was allocated for the set up/implementation costs and the ongoing yearly costs were calculated as follows:

The running costs in Table (a) are incurred every year for the 25-year appraisal period and are provided at 2017 prices. These figures are then summed for the 25-year period and each is discounted using the 3.5 per cent per year compound discount rate and multiplied by the average rate of taxation within the economy (1.19) to convert them to 2010 market prices. In doing this, LCC was able to calculate the costs of running the scheme for the 25-year period. For example, the annual permit income in Table (a) is £941 814. When this is summed for 25 years, discounted and converted to 2010 prices, the total income is £12.163 million, as shown in Table (b).

Additional costs and benefits

In addition to the costs and income outlined in Table (a), QUADRO was used to calculate other costs and benefits of the permit scheme relative to the 'do-nothing' scenario. Each cost and benefit was given a monetary estimate in the same way that was outlined above. These are five of the key factors that were assessed:

- Fewer roadworks will reduce delays and mean fewer diversions, saving road users time and reducing their

---

[1] 'Permit Scheme for Road Works and Street Works: Cost Benefit Analysis', Leicestershire County Council (April 2017).

[2] https://tamesoftware.co.uk/quadro/quadro.html.

[3] *Transport Analysis Guidance: The Transport Appraisal Process,* Department for Transport (January 2014).

[4] *The Green Book: Central Government Guidance on Appraisal and Evaluation,* HM Treasury (2018).

Table (a)   LCC permit scheme: ongoing yearly costs (2017 prices)

Item	Statutory utility companies	LCC handling SU permits	LCC Highways: highway works maintenance
Permit handling cost	£182,982*	£914,911**	£453,033
Permit income		−£941,814	
Permit fees	£941,814**		
Total	£1,124,796	−£26,903	£453,033

*Assumed to be a fifth of LCC handling costs, based on previous studies for Nottinghamshire and Derbyshire County Councils.
**Taken directly from the LCC cost matrix as yearly costs.

costs. Guidance indicates that a proportion (i.e. 10 per cent) of the travel-time savings calculated by QUADRO can be used to gain a measure of the time savings.

- Using the lower guidance figure of 10 per cent will also generate reliability benefits. They are calculated to be £2.99 million.
- The improvement in the efficiency and reliability of the road network would, through fewer and shorter traffic controls, as well as fewer diversions, reduce greenhouse gas emissions.
- The greater efficiency and reliability of the road network would reduce the revenue earned by HM Treasury from taxes on fuel, which is thus a disbenefit to society.
- Fewer accidents would occur due to a reduction in roadworks, thus benefiting society.

Calculating the net present value

Having included the relevant costs and benefits, the yearly cost of the roadworks calculated by QUADRO, including carbon and indirect tax benefits, was £38.346 million compared to the 'no roadworks' scenario. Based on DfT guidance of a 5 per cent saving from such a scheme (though this is thought to be conservative), the saving was calculated at £1.917 million/year.

The 25-year economic appraisal was then used to find the *net present value of benefits (PVB)* of the scheme, which was a summation of all the associated benefits or disbenefits to society. This included the effects on carbon emissions, accidents, travel time, road-user operating costs (e.g. less fuel, wear and tear), reliability benefits, permit fees and administration costs. This amounted to £20.6 million.

The appraisal also found the *net present value costs (PVC)* of the scheme, which are a sum of all of the costs (negative or positive) to public accounts. This included the set up and implementation costs, the ongoing costs and the permit income. The total was £5.6 million.

Finally, these figures were used to calculate the *net present value (NPV)* of £15 million.

Table (b) summarises costs and benefits from the permit scheme, based on the preferred scenario by LCC.

The conclusion, therefore, was that the scheme represented very high value for money. The DfT benchmark for the economic viability of a road scheme is that a benefit to cost ratio (BCR) in excess of 2 provides high value for money. This Road and Street Works Permit Scheme was found to have a benefit to cost ratio (BCR) of 3.66 (dividing the PVB by the PVC) and hence the economic appraisal provided support for the scheme to go ahead.

 Although Leicestershire County Council included a variety of costs and benefits that were then monetised (as noted above), other costs and benefits were not included. What other costs and benefits do you think could be included and what explanation might there be for why they were not part of the economic appraisal?

Table (b)	Leicestershire County Council economic appraisal summary

Item	Value
Noise	Not Assessed
Local air quality	Not Assessed
Carbon benefits	0.083
Journey quality	Not Assessed
Physical activity	Not Assessed
Accident benefits	0.903
Economic efficiency – consumer users (time + VOCs)	18.945
Economic efficiency – business users (time + VOCs)	12.398
Reliability benefits @ 10% of time savings	2.990
Provider benefits (SU's)	−14.527
Wider public finances (indirect tax revenues)	−0.220
(1) Net present value of benefits (PVB)	**20.572**
Broad transport budget (local transport authority)	17.780
Permit income	−12.163
(2) Net present value costs (PVC)	**5.610**
Overall impact	
(3) Net present value (NPV) = (1) − (2)	**14.962**
(4) Benefit/cost ratio (BCR) = (1)/(2)	**3.667**

Note: All entries are at 2010 market prices and discounted to a 2010 present value year, in £ million; except for the BCR figure as noted. Monetary benefits are appraised over a 25-year period.

international competitiveness, the long-run benefits it might generate, the demand from voters for the government to be seen to be enhancing or improving some public service, and so on.

The supply of capital

It is important to distinguish between the supply of *physical* capital and the supply of *finance* to be used by firms for the purchase of capital.

Supply of physical capital. The principles here are just the same as those in the goods market. It does not matter whether a firm is supplying lorries (capital) or cars (a consumer good): it will still produce up to the point where $MC = MR$ if it wishes to maximise profits.

Supply of finance. When firms borrow to invest, this creates a demand for finance (or 'loanable funds'). The supply of loanable funds comes from the deposits that individuals and firms make in financial institutions. These deposits are savings, the level of which depends on the rate of interest that depositors receive. The higher the rate of interest, the more people will be encouraged to save. This is illustrated by an upward-sloping supply curve of loanable funds, as shown in Figure 19.3.

Saving also depends on the level of people's incomes, their expectations of future price changes and their general level of 'thriftiness' (their willingness to forgo present consumption in order to be able to have more in the future). A change in any of these other determinants will shift the supply curve.

Determination of the rate of interest

KI 11
p53 The rate of interest is determined by the interaction of supply and demand in the market for loanable funds. This is illustrated in Figure 19.3.

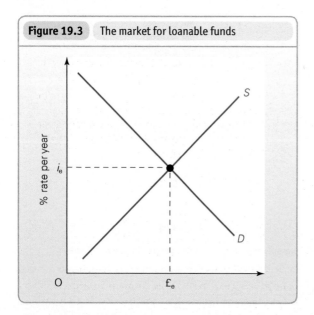

Figure 19.3 The market for loanable funds

As we have seen, supply represents accumulated savings. The demand curve includes the demand by households for credit and the demand by firms for funds to finance their investment. This demand curve slopes downward for two reasons. First, households will borrow more at lower rates of interest. It effectively makes goods cheaper for them to buy. Second, it reflects the falling rate of return on investment as investment increases. This is simply due to diminishing returns to investment. As rates of interest fall, it becomes profitable for firms to invest in projects that have a lower rate of return: the quantity of loanable funds demanded thus rises.

Equilibrium will be achieved where demand equals supply at an interest rate of i_e and a quantity of loanable funds $£_e$.

How will this market adjust to a change in demand or supply? Assume that there is a rise in demand for capital equipment, due, say, to an improvement in technology which increases the productivity of capital. There is thus an increase in demand for loanable funds. The demand curve shifts to the right in Figure 19.3. The equilibrium rate of interest will rise and this will encourage more savings. The end result is that more money will be spent on capital equipment.

Calculating the costs of capital

When calculating the net present value or internal rate of return of an investment, it is clearly important for the firm to estimate the cost of the investment. The cost includes both the cost of the equipment that the firm buys and the costs of raising the finance to pay for the investment.

As we shall see in the next section, a firm can finance investment from three major sources:

- retaining profits;
- borrowing from the banking sector – either domestic or overseas;
- issuing new shares (equities) or debentures (fixed-interest loan stock).

It is quite common for a firm to raise finance for a particular project from a mixture of all three sources. The problem is that each source of finance has a different cost. What is needed, then, for each project is a weighted average of the interest rate (or equivalent) charged or implied by each component of finance.

For investment financed by retained profits, the opportunity cost depends on what would have been done with the profits as the next best alternative. It might be the interest forgone by not putting the money into a bank or other financial institution or by not purchasing assets. If the next best alternative was to distribute the profits to shareholders, then the opportunity cost would be the cost associated with the increased risks of the firm's share price falling and the consequent risks of a takeover by another company. (Share prices would fall if shareholders, disillusioned with the reduced dividends, sold their shares: see page 259) For a bank loan or for debentures, the cost is simply the rate of interest paid on the loan. The only estimation problem here is that of

KI 3
p19

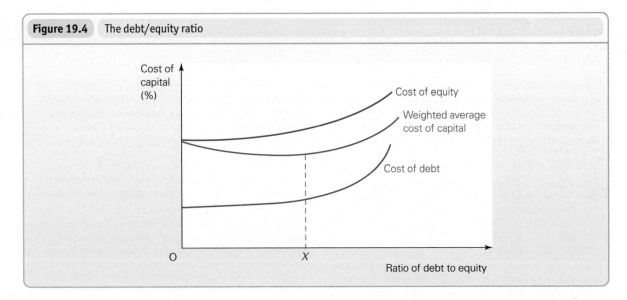

Figure 19.4 The debt/equity ratio

forecasting future rates of interest on loans where the rate of interest is variable.

For equity finance, the cost is the rate of return that must be paid to shareholders to persuade them not to sell their shares. This will depend on the rate of return on shares elsewhere. The greater the return on shares generally, the higher must be the dividends paid by any given firm in order to persuade its shareholders not to switch into other companies' shares.

Leverage and the cost of capital

The cost of capital will increase as the risks for those supplying finance to the company increase: they will need a higher rate of return to warrant incurring the higher risks. One of the most important determinants of the risk to suppliers of finance is the company's leverage. *Leverage* is a measure of the extent to which the company relies on debt finance (i.e. loans) as opposed to equity finance.

There are two common measures of leverage. The first is the *gearing ratio*. This is the ratio of debt finance (debentures and borrowing from banks) to total finance. The other is the *debt/equity ratio*. This is the ratio of debt finance to equity finance (Box 19.2 looks at some other key ratios).

The greater the company's leverage, the higher will be the risks to creditors and hence the higher will be the interest charged (see Figure 19.4). But why should this be so? The reason is that interest on loans (bank loans and debentures) has to be paid, irrespective of the company's profits. If there is a downturn in the company's profits then, if it has 'low

gearing' (i.e. a low debt/equity ratio), it can simply cut its dividends and, as a result, will find it relatively easy to make its interest payments. If, however, it is 'highly geared', it may find it impossible to pay all the interest due, even by cutting dividends, in which case it will be forced into receivership.

Given that a highly geared company poses greater risks to creditors, they will demand a higher interest rate to compensate. Similarly, with shareholders: given that dividends are likely to fluctuate more with a highly geared company, shareholders will require a higher average dividend over the years. In other words, investors in a highly geared company – whether banks, debenture holders or shareholders – will demand a higher *risk premium*. As gearing increases, so the risk premium, and hence the average cost of capital, will rise at an accelerating rate (see Figure 19.4).

KI 14
p 79

Definitions

Leverage The extent to which a company relies upon debt finance as opposed to equity finance.

Gearing ratio The ratio of debt finance to total finance.

Debt/equity ratio The ratio of debt finance to equity finance.

Risk premium As a business's gearing rises, investors require a higher average dividend from their investment. It is measured as the expected value of a gamble minus a person's certainty equivalent.

19.4 FINANCING INVESTMENT

It is often claimed that the UK has 'fair weather' bankers: that is, bankers who are prepared to lend when things are going well, but less inclined to lend when times are hard. This

criticism has intensified in recent years, with banks accused of holding back recovery in the economy by being reluctant to lend to many businesses, especially SMEs. They are also

BOX 19.2 THE RATIOS TO MEASURE SUCCESS

Using numbers to decide

Whenever a firm makes a decision, numerous factors will be considered. Market opportunities will be analysed, the actions of competitors predicted and the economic environment studied. However, crucial to any decision will be the health of the business itself. Owners and managers will need to look at all the firm's numbers before taking any action and there are some ratios that will give a business some key information.

Typically, we classify ratios into groups based on the information that they show. In this box, we split the ratios into three categories: profitability, financial efficiency and liquidity, and outline the main ratios within each category.

Profitability ratios

These ratios do exactly what they suggest: they provide information about a business's profitability. By measuring a firm's ability to generate earnings and profits, they indicate the success of a firm over time and provide a means of comparison with its competitors. The three main profitability ratios are:

■ *Gross profit margin*: this measures the ratio of gross profit to sales revenue. Gross profit is calculated by subtracting the variable costs of goods sold from gross revenue and so measures the profitability of a company before fixed costs (overheads) are taken into account. It is expressed as a percentage and is calculated as:

$$\text{Gross profit margin} = \frac{\text{Gross profit}}{\text{Sales turnover}} \times 100$$

■ *Net profit margin*: this measures the ratio of net profit to sales revenue. Net profit is revenue minus all costs: that is, not only the variable costs of production (to give gross profit), but also fixed costs, such as rent, insurance, heating and lighting, salaries (unrelated to output) and also taxes. It gives us information about how effective a firm is at turning sales into profits and thus whether or not a business adds value during the production process. Net profit margin is also expressed as a percentage and is calculated as:

$$\text{Net profit margin} = \frac{\text{Net profit}}{\text{Sales turnover}} \times 100$$

■ *Return on capital employed (ROCE)*: this measures the efficiency with which a business uses its funds to generate returns. Capital employed refers to the company's total assets minus its current liabilities and the ROCE is calculated as:

$$\text{ROCE} = \frac{\text{Earnings (before interest and taxes)}}{\text{Capital employed}} \times 100$$

While all three ratios are important and having high gross and net profit margins are good indicators that a firm is performing effectively, it is particularly important for a firm to compare these two profitability ratios, as looking at them separately often can lead to misleading conclusions. For example, if a firm's gross profit margin is rising, but its net profit margin is falling, then it means that the firm is generating more profit from its sales, but that its costs are increasing at an even faster rate. That is, the company may be becoming less efficient.

Just as it is important to examine the trends in profit margins, analysing a firm's ROCE over time is also essential and an upward trend suggests that the firm is earning more in revenue for every £1 of capital employed in the business. Profit margins and ROCE should always be compared between firms within an industry and it is always worth remembering that what is seen as a high profit margin or ROCE in one industry may be a low one in another industry.

1. *What steps might a firm take to improve (a) gross profit margin, (b) net profit margin and (c) ROCE?*

Financial efficiency ratios

These are ratios that analyse the efficiency with which a business manages its resources and assets. Once again, there are three key ratios:

■ *Asset turnover*: this ratio looks at the assets (or resources) that a firm has and analyses the amount of sales that are generated from this asset base. Consider a pizza kitchen that has a given level of assets (e.g. work-space, ovens). This ratio will measure the level of sales generated relative to this asset base. The higher the sales, the more efficiently this firm is using its assets; so a higher asset turnover figure is a good indicator of financial efficiency. It is calculated as:

$$\text{Asset turnover} = \frac{\text{Sales}}{\text{Net assets}} \times 100$$

■ *Stock turnover*: this measures the frequency with which a firm orders in new stock. Holding stock can be extremely costly, as it means that money has already been spent on purchasing or producing the items, but no income has been received from their sale. Thus, a higher figure for stock turnover implies that less money is tied up in stock. This particular ratio will vary significantly from one industry to another and you would expect some industries to have a very high level of stock turnover, due to the nature of the products they are selling. For example, firms whose

accused of taking a short-term perspective in their lending practices and of being over-eager to charge high rates of interest on loans, thereby discouraging investment.

But the problem for business does not end there. Dealers on the stock market are also accused of focusing their speculative behaviour on short-run returns (see Box 4.2), thereby

generating volatility in share prices and creating business caution, as firms seek ways of maintaining shareholder confidence in their stock (usually through paying high dividends).

In this section, we will consider the sources from which business might draw finance, and the roles played by the various UK

sales are subject to fluctuation (due, say, to the weather) may need to hold higher stocks. Therefore, although it is suggested that a higher figure for stock turnover is better, it is not always the case. Stock turnover is calculated as:

$$\text{Stock turnover} = \frac{\text{Cost of sales}}{\text{Average stock held}}$$

■ *Debtor and creditor days*: these two ratios measure the effectiveness of a firm in collecting payments from and making payments to other traders. Many businesses offer trade credit, where you can buy something today, but pay for it later. Such incentives can be crucial, but it can cause problems when you are the firm offering the trade credit. Debtor days show how long a firm's customers, on average, take to pay their bill and creditor days show how long a firm takes to pay the bills that it owes. As you will probably realise, comparing these two figures is essential. Ideally, debtor days should be lower than creditor days, as this implies that firm A receives the money it is owed before it has to make payments to those to whom it owes money. They are calculated as follows:

$$\text{Debtor days} = \frac{\text{Trade debtors}}{\text{Revenue}} \times 365$$

and

$$\text{Creditor days} = \frac{\text{Trade payables}}{\text{Cost of sales}} \times 365$$

With the business environment under continuous financial pressure, using resources efficiently is vital. Businesses in all sectors will want to analyse trends in these financial efficiency ratios, as a means of identifying areas where improvements can be made.

2. *What type of figure would you expect a greengrocer to have for its stock turnover? How might this compare with a furniture store?*

3. *What are the advantages and disadvantages of offering trade credit?*

Liquidity ratios

Many businesses have debts, but the key question is whether they have the ability to repay them. We have already considered two key ratios – gearing and the debt/equity ratio (see page 349) – which are very important, especially for those considering investing in a firm. Two additional liquidity ratios provide further information:

■ *Current ratio*: this ratio is a basic measure of how a firm's current assets compare with its current liabilities. If a firm's assets are higher than its liabilities, this suggests that the firm has sufficient funds for the day-to-day running of the business. It is calculated as:

$$\text{Current ratio} = \frac{\text{Current assets}}{\text{Current liabilities}}$$

■ *Acid test ratio* (or *quick ratio*): this is very similar to the current ratio. However, instead of comparing all current assets with liabilities, the acid test ratio excludes stocks, sometimes called 'inventories' (e.g. raw materials), as these cannot readily be turned into cash and hence are termed 'illiquid'. First, they would have to be made into the finished product before any cash could be earned. The calculation is therefore very similar to the current ratio:

$$\text{Acid test ratio} = \frac{\text{Current assets} - \text{Stock}}{\text{Current liabilities}}$$

Some businesses will need to carry much higher levels of stocks (or 'inventories') than others and therefore will have a low acid test ratio relative to their current ratio. For example, most manufacturers will need to have a much higher proportion of stocks than most service-sector firms, such as solicitors or accountants. This does not make their businesses necessarily more risky. Ratios need to be judged, therefore, according to what would be expected in a particular industry.

Since the financial crisis of 2007/8, firms have become more focused on having sufficient liquidity, as all firms need cash to survive. A current ratio of between 1.5 and 2 suggests that a firm has sufficient cash, without having excessive working capital. Again, comparing this ratio over time and with other firms in the same sector is important to give an indication of relative performance.

4. *Would you expect the current ratio or the acid test to have a higher figure for any given firm?*

The ratios discussed in this box, together with gearing and debt/equity, should never be analysed independently, but should always be compared with firms in the same industry. Failing to do so and interpreting them incorrectly can give misleading results, but they still remain a good numerical measure to assess business performance. Before undertaking any changes relating to market penetration, scale of operation, diversification, etc., a firm will consider the above ratios (and many more) to ensure that it is making the best use of its existing resources and that it has sufficient funds to carry out its plans.

financial institutions. We will assess the extent to which 'short-termism' is an endemic problem in the capital market.

Sources of business finance

The firm can finance growth by borrowing, by retaining profits or by a new issue of shares (see section 19.3).

Internal funds

As we noted (see Chapter 15), the largest source of finance for investment in the UK is firms' own internal funds (i.e. retained profits). Given that business profitability depends in large part on the general state of the economy, internal funds as a source of business finance are likely to show considerable cyclical variation. When profits are squeezed in a recession, this source of investment will decline – but so also will the *demand* for investment: after all, what is the point in investing if your market is declining?

Furthermore, if retained profits are used, the firm will have less profit available to pay out in dividends. This could cause shareholders to consider selling their shares, which could cause a fall in share prices.

External funds

Other sources of finance, which include borrowing and the issue of shares and debentures, are known as 'external funds'. These are then categorised as short-term, medium-term or long-term sources of finance.

Short-term finance. This is usually in the form of a short-term bank loan or overdraft facility and is used by firms as a form of working capital to aid them in their day-to-day business operations. Another way of borrowing for a short period of time is for a firm to issue *commercial bills of exchange* (see page 561).

Medium-term finance. Again, this is provided largely by banks and is usually in the form of a loan with set repayment targets. It is common for such loans to be made at a fixed rate of interest, with repayments being designed to fit in with the business's expected cash flow. Bank lending tends to be the most volatile source of business finance and has been particularly sensitive to the state of the economy, especially over the past 10 years. While part of the reason is the lower demand for loans during a recession, part of the reason is the caution of banks in granting loans if prospects for the economy are poor. This caution was also exacerbated by the banking crisis.

The more money that is borrowed, the greater the repayments required and, hence, the more difficult it becomes for a firm to maintain the level of dividends to shareholders. Once again, shareholders may decide to sell their shares, pushing the share price down.

Long-term finance. Especially in the UK, this tends to be acquired through the stock and bond markets. The proportion of business financing from this source clearly depends on the state of the stock market and, in turn, on the economy.

In the late 1990s, with a buoyant stock market, the proportion of funds obtained through share issue increased. Then with a decline in stock market prices from 2000 to 2003, this proportion fell, only to rise again as the stock market surged ahead after 2004. From late 2007 through to early 2009, however, with growing worries about difficulties of raising finance following the 'credit crunch' (see Chapter 28) and fears of an impending recession, the stock market plummeted once more. The stock market did recover, though it took quite a few years to return to the pre-crisis level, as we saw in Box 4.3, and this gave rise to hope that firms would be able to fund the investment needed to increase growth back to pre-recession levels.

Despite the traditional reliance on the stock market for external long-term sources of finance in the UK, there has been a growing involvement of banks in recent years, though criticisms of their caution and short-termism still remain.

This change brings the UK closer to other European countries, notably Germany and France. In these countries, banks provide a significant amount of *long-term,* fixed interest rate finance. While this tends to increase companies' gearing ratios and thus increases the risk of bankruptcy, it does provide a much more stable source of finance and creates an environment where banks are much more committed to the long-run health of companies. For this reason, the net effect may be to *reduce* the risks associated with financing investment.

Other sources of long-term finance include various forms of grants from government, local authorities and the EU, often for specific purposes, such as R&D or training, or just for SMEs.

Another source is 'venture capital', where an established business or a 'business angel' invests in a new or small business seeking to expand in exchange for a share of the business. A Financial Times article[1] considers a new programme in the EU called VentureEU,[2] whereby the European Commission and European Investment Fund are providing €410 million to help new innovative companies in the EU compete with fast growing tech companies in China and the USA.

Another source of finance is that from outside the country. This might be direct investment by externally based companies in the domestic economy or from foreign financial institutions. In either case, a major determinant of the amount of finance from this source is the current state of the economy and predictions of its future state relative to other countries. One of the major considerations here is anticipated changes in the exchange rate (see Chapter 27). If the exchange rate is expected to rise, this will increase the value of any given profit in terms of foreign currency. As would be expected, this source of finance is particularly volatile.

Conflict between financing growth and shareholders' interests

Whether a firm chooses to raise finance for growth through retained profits, the issue of new shares or borrowing, there could be an adverse effect on dividends and thus on the firm's share price.

Shareholders are concerned with their dividends and, if they see their dividends fall as a result of the firm's decision to grow, they may choose to sell their shares, unless they are confident that *long-run* profits and hence dividends will rise again. If shareholders do sell their shares, the supply curve of shares will shift to the right, pushing the share price down.

Firms must, therefore, weigh up the benefits of growth with the potential costs of a falling share price. The problem

---

[1]Chris Flood, 'Europe announces €410m boost for venture capital investing', *Financial Times* (10 April 2018).

[2]http://europa.eu/rapid/press-release_IP-18-2763_en.htm.

is that, if share prices fall too far, firms may become susceptible to being taken over and of certain managers losing their jobs. This is known as the *takeover constraint* (section 15.2, page 259) and, to avoid it, growth-maximising firms need to ensure that they have sufficient profits to distribute in the short run. This is the idea of profit 'satisficing': making sufficient profits to keep shareholders happy, as we discussed in Chapter 14.

The role of the financial sector

Before we look at the financial institutions operating within the UK and assess their differing financial roles, it should be noted that they all have the common function of providing a link between those who wish to lend and those who wish to borrow. In other words, they act as the mechanism whereby the supply of funds is matched to the demand for funds.

As *financial intermediaries*, these institutions provide four important services.

Expert advice

Financial intermediaries can advise their customers on financial matters: on the best way of investing their funds and on alternative ways of obtaining finance. This should help to encourage the flow of savings and the efficient use of them. As far as businesses are concerned, banks often play a central role in advising on investment and on possible mergers and acquisitions. They also support small firms, for example in assisting with the development of business plans. There is considerable competition between banks in terms of the advisory services that they offer to businesses.

Expertise in channelling funds

Financial intermediaries have the specialist knowledge to be able to channel funds to those areas that yield the highest return. This, too, encourages the flow of saving as it gives savers the confidence that their savings will earn a good rate of interest. Financial intermediaries help to ensure that projects that are potentially profitable, at least in the short run, are able to obtain finance. They thereby help to increase allocative efficiency. Box 19.3 looks at the finance of innovation and some of the issues involved.

Maturity transformation

Many people and firms want to borrow money for long periods of time and yet many depositors want to be able to withdraw their deposits on demand or at short notice. If people had to rely on borrowing directly from other people, there would be a problem: the lenders would not be prepared to lend for a long enough period. If you had £100 000 of savings, would you be prepared to lend it to a friend to buy a house if the friend was going to take 25 years to pay it back? Even if there was no risk whatsoever of your friend defaulting, most people would be totally unwilling to tie up their savings for so long.

This is where a bank or building society comes in. It borrows money from a vast number of small savers, who are able to withdraw their money on demand or at short notice. It then lends the money to house purchasers for a long period of time by granting mortgages (typically these are paid back over 20 to 30 years).

This process whereby financial intermediaries lend for longer periods of time than they borrow is known as *maturity transformation*. They are able to do this because with a large number of depositors it is highly unlikely that they would all want to withdraw their deposits at the same time. On any one day, although some people will be withdrawing money, others will be making new deposits.

There is still the problem, however, that long-term loans by banks, especially to industry, often carry greater risks. With banking tradition, especially in the UK, being to err on the side of caution, this can limit the extent to which maturity transformation takes place and can result in a less than optimum amount of investment finance, when viewed from a long-term perspective.

> ### Pause for thought
>
> *What dangers are there in maturity transformation for (a) financial institutions; (b) society generally?*

Risk transformation

You may be unwilling to risk lending money directly to another person in case they do not pay up. Financial intermediaries, however, by lending to large numbers of people, are willing to risk the odd case of default. They can absorb the loss because of the interest they earn on all the other loans. This spreading of risk is known as *risk transformation*. What is more, financial intermediaries may have the expertise to be able to assess just how risky a loan is.

> ### Pause for thought
>
> *Which of the above are examples of economies of scale?*

> ### Definition
>
> **Takeover constraint** The effect that the fear of being taken over has on a firm's willingness to undertake projects that reduce distributed profits.
>
> **Financial intermediaries** The general name for financial institutions (banks, building societies, etc.) which act as a means of channelling funds from depositors to borrowers.
>
> **Maturity transformation** The transformation of deposits into loans of a longer maturity.
>
> **Risk transformation** The process whereby banks can spread the risks of lending by having a large number of borrowers.

BOX 19.3   FINANCING INNOVATION

A flourishing domestic economy is, in no small part, the result of firms successfully innovating and responding to the changing conditions and technologies within the marketplace. Through such adaptation and innovation the economy prospers, stimulating growth, income and employment. Conversely, an economy that fails to innovate and respond to change is likely to be set upon the rocky road to stagnation and decline.

Given the stark contrast in these alternative realities, not only is the development of new ideas and their diffusion throughout the economy crucial to its vitality, but also it is essential that the financial system supports such innovation and does so in the most efficient way. It must ensure not only that finance is available, but also that it goes to those projects with the greatest potential.

Unfortunately, the projects with the greatest potential may involve considerable risk and uncertainty. Because of this, the private sector may be unwilling to fund their development. It may also be unwilling to finance various forms of research, where the outcomes are uncertain: something that is inevitable in much basic research.

As a result of this reluctance by the private sector, innovation funding traditionally has operated at three levels:

- **Level one**: government financing of 'upstream' or basic research, where outcomes are likely to yield few, if any, financial returns.
- **Level two**: self-financed business R&D (i.e. financed out of ploughed-back profit), where the profitability of such R&D activity is difficult to assess, especially by those outside of the business, and thus where banks and other financial institutions would be reluctant to provide finance.
- **Level three**: external financing using accepted financial assessment criteria for risk and uncertainty.

In this traditional model, the state's role in financing innovation and investment does not end at the level of basic research. It will also compensate for market failures at later stages of the innovation-financing process. For example, it may adopt measures to improve the self-financing capacity of firms (e.g. tax relief) or measures to facilitate easier access to external finance (e.g. interest rate subsidies) or measures to extend and protect the ownership of intellectual property rights (e.g. tightening up and/or extending patent or copyright legislation).

The offshore wind generation sector

The offshore wind generation sector is an excellent example of a sector that has been moving through the levels. When compared to onshore facilities, offshore wind farms offer considerable potential. There is more energy to capture and planning regulations are less restrictive. However, this potential needs to be offset against the high costs of offshore production. Nevertheless, since 2012, the costs of offshore wind have fallen 32 per cent and they are continuing to decline, as the technology is improving rapidly.

A significant amount of investment has gone into the UK's offshore wind capacity, particularly as it has been seen as 'the most scalable of the UK's bulk renewable technologies'. Importantly, offshore wind was seen as one of the UK's key investments to help meet the UK's 2020 green energy targets. According to the Crown Estate, 10 per cent of the UK's electricity supply will be met by the offshore wind industry by 2020, as targeted. The Offshore Wind Operational Report[1] (June 2017) found that, thanks to this industry, the UK's CO_2 emissions have fallen by 8.6 million tonnes and the sector generated the electricity for 5.3 million homes (approximately 20 per cent of total homes in the UK). The report found that 'by the end of

---

[1]'Offshore wind operational report', January–December 2017, The Crown Estate, (2017).

In addition to channelling funds from depositors to borrowers, certain financial institutions have another important function. This is to provide a means of transmitting payments. Thus, by the use of debit cards, credit cards, cheques, standing orders, etc., money can be transferred from one person or institution to another without having to rely on cash.

The banking system

Banking can be divided into two main types: *retail banking* and *wholesale banking*. Most banks today conduct both types of business and are thus known as 'universal banks'.

Retail banking. This is the business conducted by the familiar high street banks, such as Barclays, Lloyds, HSBC, Royal Bank of Scotland and Santander. They operate bank accounts for individuals and businesses, attracting deposits and granting loans at published rates of interest. Some of these accounts are accessed through the banks' branches and some via telephone or Internet banking.

Definitions

Retail banking Branch, telephone, postal and Internet banking for individuals and businesses at published rates of interest and charges. Retail banking involves the operation of extensive branch networks.

Wholesale banking Where banks deal in large-scale deposits and loans, mainly with companies and other banks and financial institutions. Interest rates and charges may be negotiable.

2017, there were 33 fully operational offshore windfarms (1762 turbines) in UK waters, with a further eight windfarms under construction.'[2]

The private sector has been unwilling to invest in this sector, due to the high degree of risk and uncertainty, given the emerging nature of this technology. As such, public subsidy has been essential to meet the required degree of investment and this has occurred over the past 15 years. This public investment has led to the UK becoming the world leader in offshore wind in terms of its capacity and the UK is now consistently ranked as the best place in the world to invest in this new means of generating energy.

While this success does not mean the removal of public subsidy and investment, a growing number of international equity investors have already invested in UK operational or construction projects in the sector. As the technology continues to develop and becomes more commercially viable, the sector will move into level three and the government subsidy may well be fully removed. Further details of the UK's investment in offshore wind can be found in a UK Trade and Investment report.[3]

Effects of financial liberalisation

The traditional model of financing innovation appears to be changing and, along with it, the role of governments in the process is diminishing.

The most significant of these changes can be found in the liberalisation of global finance. Three of the major effects of this on innovation financing are as follows:

- Channels of finance have diversified, widening the range of potential investment sources.
- Financial innovations have increased the ability of potential innovators to locate and negotiate favourable financial deals.
- Government regulations over capital market activities have diminished.

The implications of these changes have been to increase the efficiency and flexibility of the financial system. This has resulted in a reduction in international differences in the costs of capital for any businesses having access to global financing. Projects with high earning potential, but high risk, have been able to raise finance from a wider range of sources, national and international.

Although such financial globalisation has not removed the need for state support, it appears that financial changes are certainly diminishing its significance as a supporter of innovation finance.

1. *What market failures could account for a less than optimal amount of innovation in the absence of government support?*
2. *If financial markets were perfectly competitive and could price risk accurately, would there be any case at all for government support of innovation?*

---

[2]David Foxwell , 'UK offshore wind on track to 2020 target', *Offshore Wind Journal* (17 April 2018).

[3]UK Offshore Wind: Opportunities for trade and investment', Department for International Trade, November 2014 (2014).

Wholesale banking. Wholesale banking involves receiving large deposits from and making large loans to companies or other banks and financial institutions; these are known as *wholesale deposits and loans*.

As far as companies are concerned, these may be for short periods of time to account for the non-matching of a firm's payments and receipts from its business. They may be for longer periods of time, for various investment purposes. As wholesale deposits and loans involve very large sums of money, banks compete against each other for them and negotiate individual terms with the firm to suit the firm's particular requirements.

In the past, there were many independent wholesale banks, known as *investment banks*. These included famous names such as Morgan Stanley, Rothschild, S.G. Hambros and Goldman Sachs. Since the deregulation of the mid-1980s,

banks have diversified their business and now provide a range of financial services, such as insurance, share dealing, pensions, mortgages and estate agency. We have also seen many of the independent investment banks merging with universal banks so that they now conduct both retail and wholesale activities.

Concerns about universal banks. One of the major causes of the banking crisis of 2008 was the growth in dealing in highly complex financial products by the investment arms of these

Definition

Wholesale deposits and loans Large-scale deposits and loans made by and to firms at negotiated interest rates.

universal banks. Many of these products bundled up sound assets with highly risky ones, such as mortgage loans to borrowers in the USA who had little chance of repaying, especially with the fall in US house prices. These 'toxic' assets caused serious problems for many banks and forced governments around the world to intervene to rescue ailing banks (we look at this in more detail in Chapter 28).

The UK's Coalition Government set up the Independent Commission on Banking (ICB) in 2010. It was charged with investigating the structure of the banking system and proposed *functional separation,* whereby retail banking was ring-fenced from wholesale banking. It was argued that, for the stability of the financial system, it was necessary to isolate the core activities of retail banks from the potential contagion from risky wholesale banking activities.

The principal recommendations of the ICB were accepted and the Financial Services (Banking Reform) Act became law in December 2013. The Act defines core activities as facilities for accepting deposits, facilities for withdrawing money or making payments from deposit accounts and the provision of overdraft facilities. It gives regulators the power to exercise ring-fencing rules to ensure the effective provision of core activities. These include restricting the power of a ring-fenced body to enter into contracts and payments with other members of the banking group. The Act also gives the regulator restructuring powers so as to split banks up to safeguard their future.

Inter-bank lending. Banks also lend and borrow wholesale funds to and from each other. Banks that are short of funds

borrow large sums from others with surplus funds, thus ensuring that the banking sector as a whole does not have funds surplus to its requirements. The rate at which they lend to each other is known as the IBOR (inter-bank offer rate). The IBOR has a major influence on the other rates that banks charge. As inter-bank loans can be anything from overnight to 12 months, the IBOR will vary from one length of loan to another and, as rates vary, the cost of borrowing for firms also changes. At the time of writing, we have seen the start of interest rate rises in the USA and UK and this has led to firms switching to shorter loans as a means of cutting their loan costs, as discussed in an article from Reuters.[3]

In the Eurozone, the IBOR is known as Euribor, with the weighted average of all overnight rates known as Eonia. In the UK, it is known as LIBOR (where 'L' stands for 'London') and its importance is highlighted in an article from Bloomberg, together with a look at SOFR, the Secured Overnight Financing Rate published by the Federal Reserve Bank of New York.[4] In 2012, allegations emerged that there had been false reporting of LIBOR rates. As the LIBOR rate is a reference rate for financial products, this had potentially serious implications for the interest rates being charged and therefore for the financial well-being of customers.

From April 2018, the Bank of England took over the administration of an alternative interbank benchmark rate. Known as SONIA, the Sterling Overnight Index Average measures the rate at which interest is paid on sterling unsecured loans of one business day. SONIA is, therefore, expected to become the new benchmark determining commercial interest rates.

19.5 THE STOCK MARKET

In this section, we will look at the role of the stock market and consider the advantages and limitations of raising finance through it. We will also consider whether the stock market is efficient.

The role of the Stock Exchange

The London Stock Exchange operates as both a primary and secondary market in capital.

The primary market. As a **primary market**, the Stock Exchange provides a means for public limited companies (see page 32) to raise finance by issuing new shares, whether to new shareholders or to existing ones. To raise finance on the Stock Exchange, a business must be 'listed'. The Listing Agreement involves directors agreeing to abide by a strict set of rules governing behaviour and levels of reporting to shareholders. Companies must have at least three years' trading experience

and make at least 25 per cent of their shares available to the public.

> ### Definition
>
> **Primary market in capital** Where shares are sold by the issuer of the shares (i.e. the firm) and where, therefore, finance is channelled directly from the purchasers (i.e. the shareholders) to the firm.

---

[3]Kristen Haunss, 'Companies switch to one-month Libor to cut loan costs', *Reuters* (13 April 2018).

[4]Matt Levine, 'Banks will miss LIBOR when it's gone', *Bloomberg* (11 April 2018)

KI 14
p 79

KI 29
p 357

At the end of October 2018, there were 943 UK and 223 international companies on the Main Market List, with a market value of £3.89 trillion. During 2017, companies on this list raised £20.8 billion of equity capital on the London Stock Exchange, £3.4 billion of which was raised by international companies.

As well as those on the Main Market List, there are some 928 companies on what is known as the Alternative Investment Market (AIM). Companies listed here tend to be young, but with growth potential and do not have to meet the strict criteria or pay such high costs as companies on the Main Market List.

In 2017, companies on the AIM list raised £6.4 billion of new capital, which is higher than in 2016 when £4.8 billion was raised, but, despite year-on-year growth since 2010 (except in 2016), it is still considerably down on pre-crisis 2007 when £16.2 billion was raised. The reason for this fall had been the persistence of economic uncertainty created by the recession that began in 2008.

The secondary market. As a **secondary market**, the Stock Exchange operates as a market where investors can sell existing shares to one another. In 2018, on an average day's trading, around £5.5 billion worth of trades in listed equities took place.

The advantages and disadvantages of using the stock market to raise capital

As a market for raising capital, the stock market has a number of advantages:

- It brings together those who wish to invest and those who seek investment. It thus represents a way that savings can be mobilised to create output and does so in a relatively low-cost way.
- Firms that are listed on the stock exchange are subject to strict regulations. This is likely to stimulate investor confidence, making it easier for business to raise finance.
- The process of merger and acquisition is facilitated by having a share system. It enables business to pursue this more effectively as a growth strategy.

The main weaknesses of the stock market for raising capital are:

- The cost to a business of getting listed can be immense, not only in a financial sense, but also in being open to public scrutiny. Directors' and senior managers' decisions often will be driven by how the market is likely to react, rather than by what they perceive to be in the business's best interests. They always have to think about the reactions of those large shareholders in the City that control a large proportion of their shares.
- It is often claimed that the stock market suffers from *short-termism*. Investors on the Stock Exchange are more concerned with a company's short-term performance and its share value. In responding to this, the business might neglect its long-term performance and potential.

Is the stock market efficient?

One of the arguments made in favour of the stock market is that it acts as an arena within which share values can be accurately or efficiently priced. If new information comes on to the market concerning a business and its performance, this will be transferred quickly and rationally into the business's share value. This is known as the *efficient market hypothesis*. So, for example, if an investment analyst found that, in terms of its actual and expected dividends, a particular share was under-priced and thus represented a 'bargain', the analyst would advise investors to buy. As people then bought the shares, their price would rise, pushing their value up to their full worth. So, by attempting to gain from inefficiently priced securities, investors will encourage the market to become more efficient.

> **KEY IDEA 29**
>
> *Efficient capital markets.* Capital markets are efficient when the prices of shares accurately reflect information about companies' current and expected future performance.

So how efficient is the stock market in pricing securities? Is information rationally and quickly conveyed into the share's price? Or are investors able to prosper from the stock market's inefficiencies?

We can identify three levels of efficiency.

Weak form of efficiency. Share prices often move in cycles that do not reflect the underlying performance of the firm. If information is imperfect, those with a better understanding of such cycles gain from buying shares at the

---

Definitions

Secondary market in capital Where shareholders sell shares to others. This is thus a market in 'second-hand' shares.

Short-termism Where firms and investors take decisions based on the likely short-term performance of a company, rather than on its long-term prospects. Thus, firms may sacrifice long-term profits and growth for the sake of quick return.

Efficient (capital) market hypothesis The hypothesis that new information about a company's current or future performance will be quickly and accurately reflected in its share price.

trough and selling them at the peak of the cycles. They are taking advantage of the market's inefficiency.

The technical analysis used by investment analysts to track share cycles is a complex science, but more and more analysts are using the techniques. As they do so and knowledge becomes more perfect, so the market will become more efficient and the cycles will tend to disappear. But why?

As more people buy a company's shares as the price falls towards its trough, so this extra demand will prevent the price falling so far. Similarly, as people sell as the price rises towards its peak, so this extra supply will prevent the price rising so far. This is an example of stabilising speculation (see pages 78 and Box 5.4). As more and more people react in this way, so the cycle all but disappears. When this happens, *weak efficiency* has been achieved.

The semi-strong form of efficiency. **Semi-strong efficiency** is when share prices adjust fully to publicly available information. In practice, not all investors will interpret such information correctly: their knowledge is imperfect. But, as investors become more and more sophisticated, and as more and more advice is available to shareholders (through stockbrokers, newspapers, published accounts, etc.), and as many shares are purchased by professional fund managers, so the interpretation of public information becomes more and more perfect and the market becomes more and more efficient in the semi-strong sense.

If the market were efficient in the semi-strong sense, then no gain could be made from studying a company's performance and prospects, as any such information *already* would be included in the current share price. In selecting shares, you would do just as well by pinning the financial pages of a newspaper on the wall, throwing darts at them and buying the shares the darts hit!

The strong form of efficiency. If the stock market showed the *strong form of efficiency*, then share prices would reflect fully *all* available information – whether public or not. For this to be so, all 'inside' information would have to be reflected in the share price the moment the information is available.

If the market is *not* efficient at this level, then people who have access to privileged information will be able to make large returns from their investments by acting on such information. For example, directors of a company would know if the company was soon to announce better than expected profits. In the meantime, they could gain by buying shares in the company, knowing that the share price would rise when the information about the profits became public. Gains made from such 'insider dealing' are illegal, but proving whether individuals are engaging in it is very difficult. Nevertheless, there are people in prison for insider dealing: so it does happen! An article from Reuters[5] about a MIT

research scientist and another from Bloomberg[6] about an Argentinian investigation into insider trading give examples.

Given the penalties for insider dealing and the amount of private information that firms possess, it is unlikely that all such information will be reflected in share prices. Thus the strong form of stock market efficiency is unlikely to hold.

If stock markets were fully efficient, the expected returns from every share would be the same. The return is referred to as the *yield*: this is measured as the dividends paid on the share as a percentage of the share's market price. For example, if you hold shares whose market price is £1 per share and you receive an annual dividend of 3p per share, then the yield on the shares is 3 per cent. But why should the expected returns on shares be the same? If any share was expected to yield a higher-than-average return, people would buy it; its price would rise and its yield would correspondingly fall.

It is only unanticipated information, therefore, that would cause share prices to deviate from that which reflected expected average yields. Such information must, by its nature, be random and, as such, would cause share prices to deviate randomly from their expected price or follow what we call a *random walk*. Evidence suggests that share prices do tend to follow random patterns.

Pause for thought

Would the stock market be more efficient if insider dealing were made legal?

Definitions

Weak efficiency (of share markets) Where share dealing prevents cyclical movements in shares.

Semi-strong efficiency (of share markets) Where share prices adjust quickly, fully and accurately to publicly available information.

Strong efficiency (of share markets) Where share prices adjust quickly, fully and accurately to all available information, both public and that available only to insiders.

Yield on a share The dividend received per share expressed as a percentage of the current market price of the share.

Random walk Where fluctuations in the value of a share away from its 'correct' value are random, i.e. have no systematic pattern. When charted over time, these share price movements would appear like a 'random walk' – like the path of someone staggering along drunk!

---

[5]Jonathan Stempel and Brendan Pierson, 'MIT scientist gets 15 months prison for insider trading', *Reuters* (30 March 2018).

[6]Carolina Millan and Ignacio Olivera Doll, 'Argentina Probes Trades of Andes Shares for Insider Trading', *Bloomberg* (12 April 2018).

SUMMARY

1a We need to distinguish between factor prices and factor services. A factor's price is income from its sale, whereas a factor's service is the income from its use.

1b The profit-maximising employment of capital will be at the point where the marginal cost of capital equals the marginal revenue product.

2a The demand for capital services will be equal to MRP_K. As a result of diminishing returns, this will decline as more capital is used.

2b The supply of capital services to a firm will be horizontal or upward sloping, depending on whether the firm is perfectly competitive or has monopsony power.

2c The supply curve of capital services by a firm in the short run will be relatively elastic up to capacity supply. In the long run, the supply curve will be very elastic, but at a higher rental rate than in the short run, given that the cost of purchasing the equipment must be taken into account in the rental rate.

2d The market supply of capital services is likely to be highly inelastic in the short run, given that capital equipment tends to have very specific uses and cannot normally be transferred from one use to another. In the long run it will be more elastic.

2e The price of capital services is determined by the interaction of demand and supply.

3a The demand for capital for purchase will depend on the return it earns for the firm. To calculate the return, all future earnings from the investment have to be reduced to present value by discounting at a market rate of interest. If the present value exceeds the cost of the investment, the investment is worthwhile. Alternatively, a rate of return from the investment (IRR) can be calculated and then this can be compared with the return that the firm could have earned by investing elsewhere.

3b The supply of finance for investment depends on the supply of loanable funds, which in turn depends, in large part, on the rate of interest.

3c The rate of interest is determined by the demand and supply of loanable funds.

3d The costs of capital supplied to the firm will rise the more it is in debt and hence the more risky the investment becomes.

4a Business finance can come from internal and external sources. Sources external to the firm include borrowing, the issue of shares, venture capital and government grants.

4b The role of the financial sector is to act as a financial intermediary between those who wish to borrow and those who wish to lend.

4c UK financial institutions specialise in different types of deposit taking and lending. It is useful to distinguish between retail and wholesale banking.

5a The stock market operates as both a primary and secondary market in capital. As a primary market it channels finance to companies as people purchase new shares. It is also a market for existing shares.

5b It helps to stimulate growth and investment by bringing together companies and people who want to invest in them. By regulating firms and by keeping transaction costs of investment low, it helps to ensure that investment is efficient.

5c It does impose costs on firms, as it is expensive for firms to be listed and the public exposure may make them too keen to 'please' the market. It can also foster short-termism.

5d The stock market is relatively efficient. It achieves weak efficiency by reducing cyclical movements in share prices. It achieves semi-strong efficiency by allowing share prices to respond quickly and fully to publicly available information. Whether it achieves strong efficiency by adjusting quickly and fully to *all* information (both public and insider), however, is more doubtful.

REVIEW QUESTIONS

1 Draw the MRP_K, AC_K and MC_K curves for a firm that has monopsony power when hiring capital equipment. Mark the amount of capital equipment it will choose to hire and show what hire charge it will pay.

2 Using a diagram like Figure 19.2, demonstrate what will happen under perfect competition (in the short run) when there is an increase in the productivity of a particular type of capital. Consider the effects on the demand, price (rental rate) and quantity supplied of the services of this type of capital. In what way will the long-run effect differ from the short-run one that you have illustrated?

3 If capital supply is totally inelastic, what determines the rental value of capital equipment in the short run?

4 Assume that an engineering company already has a stock of machinery and tools. Which of the following are opportunity costs of hiring out its machinery and tools? (a) the cost of replacing the equipment; (b) the depreciation of the equipment; (c) maintenance costs of the equipment; (d) handling costs from hiring out the equipment.

5 Suppose an investment costs £12 000 and yields £5000 per year for three years. At the end of the three years, the equipment has no value. Work out whether the investment will be profitable if the rate of discount is: (a) 5%; (b) 10%; (c) 20%.

6 If a project's costs occur throughout the life of the project, how will this affect the appraisal of whether the project is profitable?

7 What factors would cause a rise in the market rate of interest?

8 What is meant by the two terms 'gearing ratio' and 'debt/equity ratio'? What is their significance?

9 Explain the various roles that financial intermediaries play within the finance sector.

10 In what circumstances is the stock market likely to be 'efficient' in the various senses of the term?

ADDITIONAL PART G CASE STUDIES ON THE *ECONOMICS FOR BUSINESS* STUDENT WEBSITE (www.pearsoned.co.uk/sloman)

G.1 **Labour market trends.** This case study describes the changing patterns of employment in the UK, from the rise in service-sector employment and fall in manufacturing employment, to the rise in part-time working and a rise in female participation rates.

G.2 **Stocks and flows.** This examines one of the most important distinctions in economics and one that we shall come across on several occasions.

G.3 **Poverty in the past.** Extreme poverty in Victorian England.

G.4 **The rise and decline of the labour movement.** A brief history of trade unions in the UK.

G.5 **How useful is marginal productivity theory?** How accurately does the theory describe employment decisions by firms?

G.6 **Profit sharing.** An examination of the case for and against profit sharing as a means of rewarding workers.

G.7 **Holidays: good for workers; bad for employers?** An examination of holiday entitlements in the USA and Europe and their effects on workers and business.

G.8 **How can we define poverty?** This examines different definitions of poverty and, in particular, distinguishes between absolute and relative measures of poverty.

G.9 **Net present value in cost–benefit analysis.** A numerical example using discounting techniques to show how net present value is calculated.

G.10 **Catastrophic risk.** This examines the difficulties in assigning a monetary value to the remote chance of a catastrophe happening (such as an explosion at a nuclear power station).

WEBSITES RELEVANT TO PART G

Numbers and sections refer to websites listed in the Web appendix and hotlinked from this text's website at **www.pearsoned.co.uk/sloman**

■ For news articles relevant to Part G, see the *Economics News Articles* link from the text's website.

■ For general news on labour and capital markets, see websites in section A, and particularly A1–5, 7, 8, 21–26, 35, 36. See also A38–44 for links to economics news articles from newspapers worldwide.

■ For data on labour markets, see links in B1 or 3, especially to *UK Labour Market* on the National Statistics site. Also see links in B19. Also see the resources > statistics links in H3.

■ For information on international labour standards and employment rights, see site H3.

■ You can search for data on *Labour Economics* in site J5.

■ Links to the TUC and Confederation of British Industry sites can be found at E32 and 33.

■ For information on poverty and inequality, see sites B18; E9, 13, 32; G5.

■ For information on taxes, benefits and the redistribution of income, see E9, 25, 30, 36; G5, 13. See also *The Virtual Chancellor* at D1.

■ For information on stock markets, see sites F18 and A3, 36, 40.

■ For student resources relevant to Part G, see sites C1–7, 9, 10, 19; D3, 7, 8, 12–14, 16–18, 20.

The relationship between government and business

The FT Reports . . .

The Financial Times, 6 January 2015

Global fines for price-fixing hit $5.3bn record high

By Caroline Binham, Legal Correspondent

Fines meted out to companies for price-fixing reached a record high in 2014, as antitrust authorities cracked down on cartels that rigged the markets for products ranging from auto parts to sausages.

Competition agencies across the world levied fines totalling $5.3bn last year, a 31 per cent increase on 2013's own record-breaking total. Several authorities in emerging markets and Europe took their most rigorous action to date against individual and corporate cartel members, according to data compiled by Allen & Overy, the law firm.

France and Germany both imposed their highest fines, with French authorities levying a $1.2bn penalty on a single cartel, and Germany fining three cartels nearly $1bn in total.

Hotels and bistros were revealed as the preferred venue for price-fixing deals. Investigators found that the price of wurst was being rigged by a cartel that included leading makers Herta, Böklunder, and Wiesenhof, which met at the Atlantic hotel in Hamburg. Similarly, French authorities raided a Parisian restaurant as part of a probe into the price fixing of household and personal-care products, involving such companies as L'Oréal and Unilever.

Brazil emerged as one of the toughest enforcers of competition law, imposing fines of $1.6bn over the year, including its highest ever single fine of $1.4bn, levied on a cement cartel. A Brazilian court also imposed the longest jail sentence for price-fixing last year, ordering a Brazilian executive found guilty of bid rigging between two airlines to spend more than 10 years in prison and pay a $156m fine.

'Individual accountability is slowly becoming a mantra of more and more authorities globally, with antitrust offenders now facing prison time on multiple continents,' said John Terzaken, an antitrust partner at A&O. 'This is a particularly sobering reality for senior executives responsible for global business lines, who risk severe sanctions for their own conduct as well as for wilfully ignoring violations of their subordinates.' . . .

Auto-parts makers across the globe have also come under scrutiny from competition authorities, in what Mr Terzaken called 'unquestionably the broadest and deepest international cartel case on record.' Agencies from the EU, South Korea, China and Canada fined companies ranging from SKF of Sweden to Hitachi and Mitsubishi of Japan, as part of parallel probes into the industry in 2014.

While I have been a lifelong capitalist, I could never accept that laissez-faire is a good solution for a society. It was John Ralston Saul who said that 'unregulated competition is just a naïve metaphor for anarchy' – we don't need that. What we need are regulated markets. And the challenge is to maximise our prosperity by finding the most efficient ways to regulate them.

Neelie Kroes, European Commission Competition Commissioner, 'Competition, the crisis and the road to recovery', Address at the Economic Club of Toronto, 30 March 2009

Despite the fact that most countries today can be classified as 'market economies', governments, nevertheless, intervene substantially in the activities of business in order to protect the interests of consumers, workers or the environment.

Firms might collude to fix prices, use misleading advertising, create pollution, produce unsafe products or use unacceptable employment practices. In such cases, government is expected to intervene to correct for the failings of the market system: for example, by outlawing collusion, by establishing advertising standards, by taxing or otherwise penalising polluting firms, by imposing safety standards on firms' behaviour and products or by protecting employment rights.

In Part H, we explore the relationship between business and government. In Chapter 20, we will consider how markets might fail to achieve ideal outcomes and what government can do to correct such problems. We will also consider how far firms should go in adopting a more socially responsible position.

In Chapter 21, we will focus upon the relationship between the government and the individual firm and consider three policy areas: monopolies and oligopolies, research and technology, and training. In their attempt to control price fixing by monopolies and oligopolies, competition authorities in many countries may impose fines on firms, as the *Financial Times* article shows.

In Chapter 22, we will broaden our analysis and look at government policy aimed at the level of the market and its impact upon all firms. Here we will consider environmental policy, transport policy and the issue of privatisation and regulation.

Perhaps, like Neelie Kroes (see the quote above), you believe that markets need government intervention in order to make them more efficient. There is, however, a problem. Unless government intervention is carefully designed, it can have unintended consequences. The 'cure' might even be worse than the 'disease'.

Key terms

Social efficiency
Equity
Market failure
Externalities
Private and social costs and benefits
Deadweight welfare loss
Public goods
Free-rider problem
Merit goods
Government intervention
Coase theorem
Laissez-faire
Social responsibility
Competition policy
Restrictive practices
Technology policy
Training policy
Environmental policy
Green taxes
Tradable permits
Cost–benefit analysis
Road pricing
Transport policy
Privatisation
Regulation
Price-cap regulation
Deregulation
Franchising

20 Chapter

Reasons for government intervention in the market

Business issues covered in this chapter

- To what extent does business meet the interests of consumers and society in general?
- In what sense are perfect markets 'socially efficient' and why do most markets fail to achieve social efficiency?
- In what ways do governments intervene in markets and attempt to influence business behaviour?
- Can taxation be used to correct the shortcomings of markets or is it better to use the law?
- What are the drawbacks of government intervention?
- What is meant by 'corporate social responsibility' and what determines firms' attitudes towards society and the environment?
- What is the relationship between business ethics and business performance?

20.1 MARKETS AND THE ROLE OF GOVERNMENT

Government intervention and social objectives

In order to decide the optimum levels of government intervention, it is first necessary to identify the various social goals that intervention is designed to meet. Two of the major objectives of government policy identified by economists are *social efficiency* and *equity*.

Social efficiency. If the marginal benefits to society – or 'marginal social benefits' (*MSB*) – of producing any given good or service exceed the marginal costs to society or 'marginal

social costs' (*MSC*), it is said to be socially efficient to produce more. For example, if people's gains from having a high speed railway, such as HS2 in the UK, exceed *all* the additional costs to society (both financial and non-financial) then it is socially efficient to construct the railway.

If, however, the marginal social costs of producing any good or service exceed the marginal social benefits, then it is socially efficient to produce less.

It follows that, if the marginal social benefits of any activity are equal to the marginal social costs, then the current level is the optimum. To summarise: for social efficiency in the production of any good or service:

$MSB > MSC \rightarrow$ produce more
$MSC > MSB \rightarrow$ produce less
$MSB = MSC \rightarrow$ keep production at its current level

Similar rules apply to consumption. For example, if the marginal social benefits of consuming more of any good or

Definitions

Social efficiency Production and consumption at the point where $MSB = MSC$.

Equity The fair distribution of a society's resources.

service exceed the marginal social costs, then society would benefit from more of the good being consumed.

Social efficiency is an example of 'allocative efficiency': in other words, the best allocation of resources between alternative uses.

> **KEY IDEA 30**
>
> *Allocative efficiency in any activity is achieved where any reallocation would lead to a decline in net benefit.* It is achieved where marginal benefit equals marginal cost. Private efficiency is achieved where marginal private benefit equals marginal private cost *(MB = MC)*. Social efficiency is achieved where marginal social benefit equals marginal social cost *(MSB = MSC)*.

In the real world, the market rarely leads to social efficiency: the marginal social benefits of most goods and services do not equal the marginal social costs. In this chapter, we examine why the free market fails to lead to social efficiency and what the government can do to rectify the situation. We also examine why the government itself may fail to achieve social efficiency.

> **KEY IDEA 31**
>
> *Markets generally fail to achieve social efficiency.* There are various types of market failure. Market failures provide one of the major justifications for government intervention in the economy.

Equity. Most people would argue that the free market fails to lead to a *fair* distribution of resources, if it results in some people living in great affluence while others live in extreme poverty. Clearly what constitutes 'fairness' is a highly contentious issue. Nevertheless, most people would argue that the government does have some duty to redistribute incomes from the rich to the poor through the tax and benefit system, and perhaps to provide various forms of legal protection for the poor (such as a minimum wage rate).

> **KEY IDEA 32**
>
> *Equity is where income is distributed in a way that is considered to be fair or just.* Note that an equitable distribution is not the same as a totally equal distribution and that different people have different views on what is equitable.

Although our prime concern in this chapter is the question of social efficiency, we will be touching on questions of distribution too.

20.2 # TYPES OF MARKET FAILURE

Market power

Whenever markets are imperfect, whether as pure monopoly or monopsony or whether as some form of imperfect competition, the market will fail to equate *MSB* and *MSC*.

Let us assume that all the costs and benefits to society accrue solely to the firm and its customers (we drop this assumption in the section on externalities below). This means that the firm's marginal cost is the marginal social cost (*MC = MSC*) and the price (*AR*), i.e. what consumers are willing to pay for one more unit is the marginal social benefit (*AR = MSB*).

Take the case of monopoly. A monopoly will produce less than the socially efficient output. This is illustrated in Figure 20.1. A monopoly faces a downward-sloping demand curve and therefore marginal revenue (*MR*) is below average revenue (= *MSB*).

Profits are maximised at an output of Q_1, where marginal revenue equals marginal cost (see Figure 11.6 on page 195). If there are no other sources of market failure, the socially efficient output will be at the higher level of Q_2, where *MSB = MSC*.

Deadweight loss under monopoly

One way of analysing the welfare loss that occurs in any market is to use the concepts of *consumer* and *producer surplus*.

The two concepts are illustrated in Figure 20.2. The diagram shows an industry that is initially under perfect competition and then becomes a monopoly (but faces the same revenue and cost curves).

Consumer surplus. **Consumer surplus** from a good is the difference between the total utility (satisfaction) received by consumers and their total expenditure on the good (see pages 89–92).

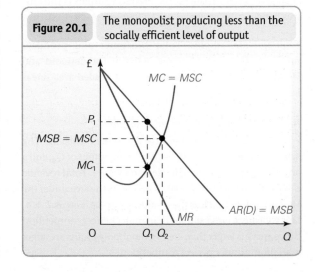

Figure 20.1 The monopolist producing less than the socially efficient level of output

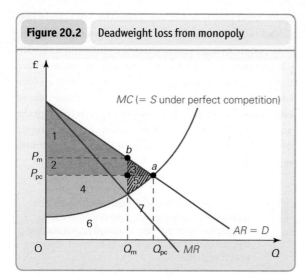

Figure 20.2 Deadweight loss from monopoly

It can be thought of as the difference between the maximum amount people are willing to pay for a good and the price they actually do pay. Under *perfect competition,* the industry will produce an output of Q_{pc} at a price of P_{pc}, where $MC(= S) = P(= AR)$: i.e. at point *a.* Consumers' total utility is given by the area under the demand (MU) curve (the sum of all the areas 1–7). Consumers' total expenditure is $P_{pc} \times Q_{pc}$ (areas 4 + 5 + 6 + 7). Consumers' surplus is thus the area between the price and the demand curve (areas 1 + 2 + 3).

Producer surplus. **Producer surplus** is similar to profit. It is the difference between total revenue and total variable cost. (It will be greater than profit if there are fixed costs.) It can be thought of as the difference between the minimum price required in order for a firm to supply a good and the price that is actually paid. Total revenue is $P_{pc} \times Q_{pc}$ (areas 4 + 5 + 6 + 7). Total variable cost is the area under the MC curve (areas 6 + 7). The reason for this is that each point on the marginal cost curve shows what the last unit costs to produce. The area under the MC curve thus gives all the marginal costs starting from an output of zero to the current output: i.e. it gives total variable costs. Producer surplus is thus the area between the price and the MC curve (areas 4 + 5).

Total (private) surplus. Total consumer plus producer surplus is therefore the area between the demand and MC curves. This is shown by the total shaded area (areas 1 + 2 + 3 + 4 + 5).

The effect of monopoly on total surplus

What happens when the industry is under *monopoly*? The firm will produce where $MC = MR$, at an output of Q_m and a price of P_m (at point *b* on the demand curve). Total revenue is $P_m \times Q_m$ (areas 2 + 4 + 6). Total cost is the area under the MC curve (area 6). Thus the producer surplus is areas 2 + 4. This is clearly a *larger* surplus than under perfect competition (since area 2 is larger than area 5): monopoly profits are larger than profits under perfect competition.

Consumer surplus, however, will be much smaller. With consumption at Q_m, total utility is given by areas 1 + 2 + 4 + 6, whereas consumer expenditure is given by areas 2 + 4 + 6. Consumer surplus, then, is simply area 1. (Note that area 2 has been transformed from consumer surplus to producer surplus.)

Total surplus under monopoly is therefore areas 1 + 2 + 4: a smaller surplus than under perfect competition. 'Monopolisation' of the industry has resulted in a loss of total surplus of areas 3 + 5. The producer's gain has been more than offset by the consumers' loss. This loss of surplus is known as *deadweight welfare loss* of monopoly.

KI 31
p 365

Externalities

Markets tend to work more effectively when the benefits and costs to the consumers and producers directly involved in the transaction are the same as the benefits and costs to society. But this may not always be the case. There may be benefits or costs to people *other* than the consumer or producer. We call these benefits and costs *external benefits* and *external costs*. Together, we refer to them as *externalities*.

So far in this text it has been assumed that there are no externalities. As far as consumption is concerned, we have assumed that the only people who benefit are the customers who purchase the good and derive pleasure from it. We used consumer surplus as a way of measuring consumers' satisfaction or benefit from consuming the product.

Likewise, we have assumed that all the opportunity costs to society in the production of a good are incurred by the firm producing it. These include the payments for the time/

Definitions

Consumer surplus The difference between the maximum a person would have been prepared to pay for a good (i.e. the utility measured in money terms) over what that person actually pays. Total consumer surplus equals total utility minus total expenditure.

Producer surplus The difference between the minimum price required for a firm to supply a good and the price that is actually paid. Total producer surplus is the excess of firms' total revenue over total (variable) costs.

Deadweight welfare loss The loss of consumer plus producer surplus in imperfect markets (when compared with perfect competition).

External benefits Benefits from production (or consumption) experienced by people *other* than the producer (or consumer) directly involved in the transaction.

External costs Costs of production (or consumption) borne by people *other* than the producer (or consumer) directly involved in the transaction.

Externalities Costs or benefits of production or consumption experienced by people *other* than the producers and consumers directly involved in the transaction. They are sometimes referred to as 'spillover' or 'third-party' costs or benefits.

effort of the workers in the form of wages, the cost of raw materials and the opportunity cost of using capital goods. Society misses out on the best alternative things that these factor inputs could have produced. We used producer surplus as a way of measuring the benefit to firms from production.

External effects of consumption and production. But sometimes consumption and production *do* affect other people. In this case, the marginal social benefit (*MSB*) will be different from the marginal private benefit (*MPB*) and/or the marginal social cost (*MSC*) will be different from the marginal private cost (*MPC*).

Take the case of consumption. Imagine a situation where your consumption of a good (e.g. using a mobile phone while driving) has either a positive or negative impact on people around you (other than the firm that sold you the good). This could be on other consumers or other firms. In the mobile phone example, it is the increased risk of an accident for other drivers. In other words, there are either *external* benefits or costs of your actions. In this situation, the full benefit to society from your consumption of the good are different from the private benefits that you receive.

These external or 'third-party' effects from consumption are called *consumption externalities*. When we add consumption externalities to private benefits we get *social benefits*.

Now imagine a situation where you are the owner of a firm. Each unit you produce generates costs or benefits that are experienced by your firm. However, production may also generate benefits or costs for other people. These could be the general public, other than your direct consumers, or other firms that are not your suppliers or customers. Once again, there are external benefits or costs, but this time from the firm's actions. The full costs or benefits to society from the production of the good in this case are different from the private costs borne by the firm.

These external effects of production are called *production externalities*. When we add production externalities to private costs we get *social costs*.

In a market environment without any government intervention, where everyone is acting purely in their own interests, these external costs and benefits will not be taken into account.

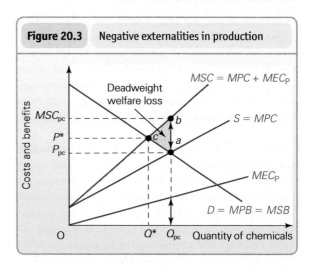

Figure 20.3 Negative externalities in production

KEY IDEA 33
Externalities are spillover costs or benefits. They are experienced by people not directly involved in the market transaction that created them. Where these exist, even an otherwise perfect market will fail to achieve social efficiency.

In the following section, we will consider four different types of externality. Each one will be considered in isolation, although it would be possible to have more than one in any

particular market. It will be assumed in each case that, apart from the existence of an externality, the market is otherwise perfect.

External costs of production (MSC > MPC) with no external costs/benefits of consumption (MSB = MPB)

When firms in the chemical industry dump waste into a river or pollute the air, the community bears additional costs to those borne by the firms. There are marginal external costs (*MEC*$_P$) of chemical production. This is illustrated in Figure 20.3. In this example, we assume that they begin with the first unit of production and increase at a constant rate.

The marginal *social* costs (*MSC*) of chemical production will equal the marginal private costs (*MPC*) plus the *MEC*$_P$. This means that the *MSC* curve is above the *MPC* curve. The vertical distance between them is equal to the *MEC*$_P$. It is also assumed that there are no externalities in consumption, which means that the marginal social benefit (*MSB*) curve is the same as the marginal private benefit (*MPB*) curve.

Competitive market forces, with producers and consumers responding only to private costs and benefits, will result in a market equilibrium at point *a* in Figure 20.3, i.e. where demand (*MPB*) equals supply (*MPC*). The market equilibrium price is P_{pc}, while the market equilibrium quantity is Q_{pc}.

At P_{pc}, *MPB* is thus equal to *MSB*. The market price reflects both the private and social benefits from the last unit consumed. However, the presence of external costs in

---

Definitions

Consumption externalities Spillover effects on other people of consumers' consumption.

Social benefit Private benefit plus consumption externalities.

Production externalities Spillover effects on other people of firms' production.

Social cost Private cost plus production externalities.

production means that $MSC > MPC$. The market price is equal to MPC but less than MSC.

The socially optimal output would be Q^*, where $P = MSB = MSC$. This is illustrated at point c and clearly shows how external costs of production in a perfectly competitive market result in overproduction, i.e. $Q_{pc} > Q^*$. From society's point of view, too much waste is being dumped in rivers.

At the market equilibrium (Q_{pc}), there is a deadweight welfare loss when compared with the socially optimal output (Q^*). In this context, deadweight welfare loss represents the excess of social costs over social benefits at all outputs above Q^* but below or equal to Q_{pc}. It is illustrated by the area abc. Put another way, reducing output from Q_{pc} to Q^* would represent a gain in social surplus equal to the area abc

One of the reasons why external costs cause problems in a free-market economy is because no one has legal ownership of factors such as the air or rivers. Therefore, nobody has the ability either to prevent or to charge for their use as a dumping ground for waste. Such a 'market' is *missing*. Control must, therefore, be left to the government, local authorities or regulators.

Other examples of external costs of production include extensive use of pesticides in agriculture that damage water quality, global warming caused by CO_2 emissions from power stations/factories, the transportation of goods by HGVs adding to congestion and the noise caused by aircraft.

External benefits of production (MSC < MPC) with no external costs/benefits of consumption (MSB = MPB)

If companies in the forestry industry plant new woodlands, there is a benefit not only to the companies themselves, but also to the world through a reduction of CO_2 in the atmosphere (forests are a carbon sink). In this case, there are marginal external benefits (MEB_P) of production. These are shown in Figure 20.4. We assume that they begin with the first tree planted but that the marginal benefit declines with

each additional tree. In other words, the MEB_P is a downward-sloping line.

> ### Pause for thought
>
> *In Figure 20.3, the impact of a negative externality in production is illustrated on the market as a whole. Illustrate the impact of a negative externality in production on one profit maximising firm in a perfectly competitive market. Explain any assumptions you have made about the nature of the external costs.*

Given these positive externalities, the marginal *social* cost (MSC) of providing timber is less than the marginal private cost: $MSC = MPC - MEB_P$. This means that the MSC curve is *below* the MPC curve. The vertical distance between the curves is equal to the MEB_P. Once again, it is assumed that there are no externalities in consumption so that $MSB = MPB$.

Competitive market forces will result in an equilibrium output of Q_{pc}, where market demand ($= MPB$) equals market supply ($= MPC$) (point a). The socially efficient level of output, however, is Q^*: i.e. where $MSB = MSC$ (point c). The external benefits of production thus result in a level of output *below* the socially efficient level. From society's point of view, not enough trees are being planted. The deadweight welfare loss caused by this underproduction is illustrated by the area abc. Output is not being produced between Q_{pc} and Q^* even though $MSB > MSC$.

Another example of external benefits in production is that of research and development. An interesting recent example has been the development of touch-screen technology for tablets and mobile phones. If other firms have access to the results of the research, then clearly the benefits extend beyond the firm that finances it. Since the firm receives only the private benefits, it may conduct a less than optimal amount of research. In turn, this may reduce the pace of

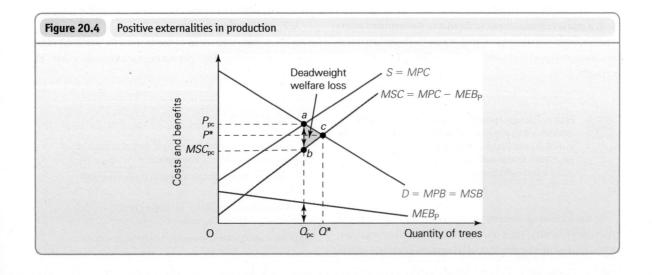

Figure 20.4 Positive externalities in production

innovation and so negatively affect economic growth over the longer term. Other examples included the transportation of goods by train and the firms investing in training.

External costs of consumption (MSB < MB) with no external costs/benefits of production (MSC = MPC)

Drinking alcohol can sometimes lead to marginal external costs of consumption. For example, there are the extra nightly policing costs to deal with the increased chance of social disorder. Public health costs may also be greater as a direct consequence of people's drinking behaviour: e.g. through an increase in hospitalisations. It may also lead to a number of alcohol-related road accidents. These marginal external costs of consumption (MEC_c) result in the marginal social benefit of alcohol consumption being lower than the marginal private benefit: i.e. $MSB = MPB - MEC_c$.

This is illustrated in Figure 20.5, where the MSB curve is below the MPB curve. In this example it is assumed that there are no externalities in production so that $MSC = MPC$.

Competitive market forces will result in an equilibrium output of Q_{pc} (point a) whereas the socially efficient level of output is Q^*, i.e. where $MSB = MSC$ (point c). The external costs of consumption result in level of output *above* the

socially efficient level: i.e. $Q_{pc} > Q^*$. From society's point of view, too much alcohol is being produced and consumed. The deadweight welfare loss caused by this overconsumption is illustrated by the area *abc*.

Other possible examples of negative externalities of consumption include mobile phone usage while driving, speeding and drink driving, smoking indoors, the use of cars for leisure purposes such as shopping, playing loud music and dropping litter – especially chewing gum.

External benefits of consumption (MSB > MPB) with no external costs/benefits of production (MSC = MPC)

How do people travel to a city centre to go shopping on a Saturday? How do people travel to a football match? If they use the train, then other people benefit, as there is less congestion and exhaust fumes and fewer accidents on the roads. These marginal external benefits of consumption (MEB_c) result in the marginal social benefit of rail travel being *greater* than the marginal private benefit (i.e. $MSB = MPB + MEB_c$).

This is illustrated in Figure 20.6, where the MSB curve is above the MPB curve. The vertical distance between the

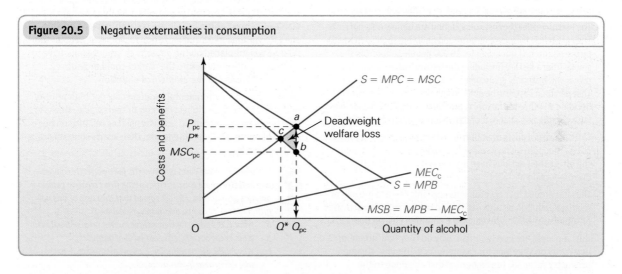

Figure 20.5   Negative externalities in consumption

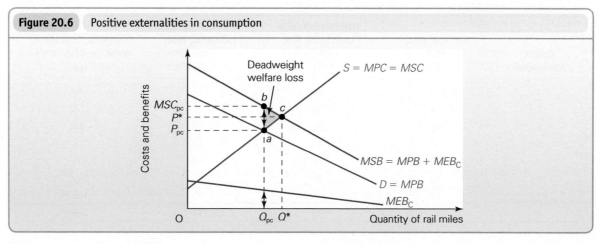

Figure 20.6   Positive externalities in consumption

curves is equal to the MEB_c. Once again, it is assumed that there are no externalities in production so that $MSC = MPC$.

External benefits of consumption result in a level of output below the socially efficient level, i.e. $Q_{pc} < Q^*$. From society's point of view, not enough journeys are being made on the train. The deadweight welfare loss caused by this underconsumption is illustrated by the area *abc*.

Other examples of external benefits of consumption include the beneficial effects for other people from someone using a deodorant, parents getting their children vaccinated, somebody wearing attractive clothing and people planting flowers in their front garden.

To summarise: whenever there are external benefits, there will be too little produced or consumed. Whenever there are external costs, there will be too much produced or consumed. The market will not equate MSB and MSC.

The above arguments have been developed in the context of perfect competition with prices determined by demand and supply. Externalities can also occur in all other types of market.

> ### Pause for thought
>
> *Give other examples of each of the four types of externality.*

BOX 20.1   CAN THE MARKET PROVIDE ADEQUATE PROTECTION FOR THE ENVIRONMENT?

In recent years, people have become acutely aware of the damage being done to the environment by pollution. But if the tipping of chemicals and sewage into the rivers and seas and the spewing of toxic gases into the atmosphere cause so much damage, why does it continue? If we all suffer from these activities, both consumers and producers alike, then why will a pure market system not deal with the problem? After all, a market should respond to people's interests.

The reason is that the costs of pollution are largely *external* costs. They are borne by society at large and only very slightly (if at all) by the polluter. If, for example, 10 000 people suffer from the smoke from a factory (including the factory owner), then that owner will bear only approximately 1/10 000 of the suffering. That personal cost may be quite insignificant when the owner is deciding whether the factory is profitable. And if the owner lives far away, the personal cost of the pollution will be zero.

Thus the *social* costs of polluting activities exceed the *private* costs. If people behave selfishly and only take into account the effect their actions have on themselves, there will be an *overproduction* of polluting activities.

Thus it is argued that governments must intervene to prevent or regulate pollution or, alternatively, to tax the polluting activities or subsidise measures to reduce the pollution (see section 22.1).

But, if people are purely selfish, why do they buy 'green' products? Why do they buy, for example, 'eco-friendly' cleaning products? After all, the amount of damage done to the

environment from their own personal use of 'non-friendly' products would be absolutely minute. The answer is that many people have social preferences. They care about the impact of their actions on other people as well as on themselves. They are not totally selfish – see Chapter 7 for more detail.

Nevertheless, to rely on people's concern for others may be a very unsatisfactory method of controlling pollution. The relative weight placed on selfish pay-offs is likely to be high in a market economy where people are constantly being encouraged to consume more and more goods. For most people, the relative weight placed on the pay-offs to others would have to increase significantly before the market could provide a sufficient answer to the problem of pollution.

Certain types of environmental problem may get high priority in the media, such as global warming or toxic waste. However, the sheer range of polluting activities makes reliance on people's awareness of the problems and their social consciences far too arbitrary.

 The table gives the costs and benefits for a perfectly competitive industry where the activities of the firms create a certain amount of pollution. (It is assumed that the costs of this pollution to society can be accurately measured.)

a.   *What is the perfectly competitive market price and output?*

b.   *What is the socially efficient level of output?*

c.   *Why might the marginal pollution costs increase in the way illustrated in this example?*

Output (000s units)	Price per unit (MSB) (£)	Marginal (private) costs to the firm (MC) (£)	Marginal external (pollution) costs (MEC) (£)	Marginal social costs (MSC = MC + MEC) (£)
1	180	30	20	50
2	160	30	22	52
3	140	35	25	60
4	120	45	30	75
5	100	60	40	100
6	80	80	55	135
7	60	105	77	182
8	40	135	110	245

Public goods

There is a category of goods where the positive externalities are so great that the free market, whether perfect or imperfect, may not produce at all. They are called **public goods**. In order to understand exactly what a public good is, it is important to discuss two of their key characteristics – **non-rivalry** and **non-excludability**. Before looking specifically at public goods, let us explore the concepts of rivalry and excludability.

The degree of rivalry

Rivalry occurs when one person's consumption of a good reduces the amount available for other consumers. Goods vary in their degree of rivalry.

Perfectly rivalrous goods. At one extreme, some goods are perfectly rivalrous. A good has this characteristic if as one or more people increase their consumption of the product, it prevents all other or 'rival' consumers from enjoying it. This is typical with non-durable goods such as food, alcohol and fuel. For example, imagine that you have purchased a bar of chocolate for your own consumption. Each chunk of the chocolate bar that you eat means that there is less available for other or 'rival' consumers to enjoy. They cannot eat the same piece that you have eaten! The good gets 'used up' when it is consumed.

Many durable goods, such as mobile phones, also have this property. For example, if you use your mobile phone, it usually prevents other people from using it. Although the mobile phone does not get 'used up', only one person can usually consume the benefits it provides at a time: i.e. sending a text or calling someone.

Perfectly non-rivalrous goods. At the other extreme, some goods are perfectly non-rivalrous. A good has this characteristic if as one or more people increase their consumption of the product it has no impact on the ability of other or 'rival' consumers to enjoy the good. For example, imagine that you turn on your tablet or television to watch a live football match or an episode of your favourite TV programme. Your decision to watch the programme has no impact on the ability of other people to enjoy watching the same programme on a different device. The television set or tablet may be rivalrous but the broadcast is not.

Goods with a degree of rivalry and non-rivalry. In reality, many goods and services will be neither perfectly rival nor non-rival. For example, it may be possible for more than one person to enjoy watching a video clip on a mobile phone. However a 'crowding effect' will soon occur. As additional people try watching the video, it will prevent others from seeing it on the same phone.

There are a number of goods and services that may have the characteristic of being relatively non-rival with low numbers of consumers before becoming more rivalrous at high levels of consumption. For example, some goods cover a comparatively small geographic range. Here overcrowding and, hence, rivalry will set in with relatively few consumers. Viewing a carnival procession, for example, may be non-rivalrous with just a few people watching, but quickly any given location along the route will become crowded and getting a good view becomes rivalrous. In other cases, such as access to the Internet, rivalry might only set in beyond very high levels of usage, when global demand is exceptionally high.

Rather than trying to categorise many goods as either rival or non-rival it makes more sense to think of them as having different *degrees* of rivalry. They could be placed on a scale of rivalry as illustrated along the horizontal axis in Figure 20.7.

The ease of excludability

Excludability occurs when the supplier of a good can restrict who consumes it. This is the case for goods sold in the market. Suppliers only allow those consumers who are prepared to pay for the good to have it. For those goods already in the hands of consumers, excludability occurs when they can prevent other people benefiting too. Just as with rivalry, goods vary in their ease of excludability.

Definitions

Public good A good or service that has the features of non-rivalry and non-excludability and, as a result, would not be provided by the free market.

Non-rivalry Where the consumption of a good or service by one person will not prevent others from enjoying it.

Non-excludability Where it is unfeasible or simply too costly to implement a system that would effectively prevent people who have not paid from enjoying the benefits from consuming a good.

Figure 20.7	Different degrees of rivalry and ease of excludability

Easily excludable goods. At one extreme, some goods have the property of being very easily excludable. In this case, a relatively low-cost and effective system can be implemented which guarantees that only those people who have paid for the good are able to enjoy the benefits it provides. The system must also prevent anyone who does not pay from obtaining any of the benefits that consuming the good provides. For example, although television broadcasts have a high degree of non-rivalry, a relatively straightforward and reasonably effective system of encryption could be implemented to exclude non-payers from watching the programmes. If this was not possible, then pay-television channels and pay-per-view broadcasting could not exist. YouTube has also introduced a number of subscription channels.

> ### Pause for thought
>
> *How rivalrous in consumption are each of the following: (a) a can of drink; (b) public transport; (c) the reduced probability of crime in a neighbourhood from a given level of policing; (d) the sight of flowers in a public park?*

Advances in technology may also change the ease of excludability for any given good or service over time.

Perfectly non-excludable goods. At the other extreme, there may be some goods for which excludability is impossible: i.e. they have the property of being non-excludable. A good has this characteristic if it is too costly or simply not feasible to implement a system that would, effectively, prevent those people who have not paid from enjoying the benefits it provides.

In some circumstances, it may be theoretically possible to exclude non-payers but, in reality, the transaction costs involved are too great. For example, it may be very difficult to prevent anyone from fishing in the open ocean or enjoying the benefits of walking in a country park. Once again, many goods will be neither perfectly excludable nor non-excludable. In these cases, it makes more sense to think about the differing levels of ease with which non-payers can be excluded from consuming the good. This is also illustrated in Figure 20.7, this time along the vertical axis.

Pure private goods

Good X in Figure 20.7 is a pure private good. It is very easy to exclude any non-payers from consuming the product, while it is also perfectly rivalrous. A pure private good is one where the benefits can be enjoyed only by the consumer who owns (or rents) them.

In reality, many goods will be close to point X and have significant degrees of rivalry and ease of excludability. Products that fall into this category can normally be provided by the market mechanism.

Pure public goods

Good Z in Figure 20.7, by contrast, has the characteristics of being perfectly non-rival and completely non-excludable.

This is a known as a *pure public good*. Once a given quantity of a pure public good is produced, everyone can obtain the same level of benefits it provides. Therefore, the marginal cost of supplying another customer with a given quantity of a public good is zero. However, this should not be confused with the marginal cost of producing another unit of the good. This would involve using additional resources; so the marginal cost of producing another unit would be positive.

Another way to think about the characteristics of pure public goods is that they cannot be sold in separate units to different customers. For example, it is impossible for you to consume five units of a pure public good while somebody else consumes an additional two units of the good. Once five units are produced for one person's consumption, those same five units are freely available for everyone else to consume.

There is some debate whether pure public goods actually exist or whether they are purely a theoretical idea. Perhaps one of the closest real-world examples is that of national defence. Once a given investment in national defence has been made, additional people can often benefit from the protection it provides at no additional cost. It would also be very difficult to exclude anyone within a country from obtaining the benefits from the increase in security.

> ### Pause for thought
>
> *To what extent is national defence a pure public good? Can it ever be rivalrous or excludable in consumption?*

Impure public goods

Good W in Figure 20.7 is an example of an *impure public good*. It has a low level of rivalry, without being perfectly rivalrous, and it is difficult, but not impossible, to exclude non-payers. In reality, many public goods will fall into this category, with some being more impure than others. We will see later that, as the degree of rivalry and ease of excludability fall, it becomes increasingly difficult for the good to be provided by the market mechanism.

Club goods. Good Y has a low degree of rivalry but exclusion is relatively easy. This is called a *club good*. Wireless Internet connection in a café could be an example of a club good if a password is required. Other examples include subscription TV services, such as Netflix or Amazon Prime.

> ### Definitions
>
> **Pure public good** A good or service that has the features of being perfectly non-rivalrous and completely non-excludable and, as a result, would not be provided by the free market.
>
> **Impure public good** A good that is partially non-rivalrous and non-excludable.
>
> **Club good** A good that has a low degree of rivalry but is easily excludable.

Common good or resources. Good V has a high degree of rivalry but the exclusion of non-payers is very difficult. This is called a ***common good or resource***. The high degree of rivalry means that the quantity or quality of the common resource available to one person is negatively affected by the number of other people who consume or make use of the same resource. Because it is difficult to exclude non-payers, a common resource is also potentially available to everyone, free of charge.

Fishing in the open ocean is an example. In the absence of intervention, fishing boats can catch as many fish as is possible. There is no 'owner' of either the fish or the sea to stop them. As one fishing boat catches more fish, it means there is less available for other fishing boats: fish are *rivalrous*. Other examples include the felling of trees in the rainforests and the use of the atmosphere as a common 'dump' for emissions.

If producers/consumers only consider the costs and benefits to themselves, then it is inevitable that common resources will be overused. As the good is free, a rational self-interested individual will keep consuming or using it until the marginal private benefit is zero, even though they are reducing the quantity or quality available for others; they are consuming past the point where $MSC = MSB$. This is the extreme case of a negative externality where the cost of the resource to the user is zero.

The inevitability of the outcome is known as the ***tragedy of the commons***. Depleted fish stocks, disappearing rainforests and a heavily polluted atmosphere all provide evidence to support the tragedy of the commons.

However, is it inevitable that all common resources will be overused? The Nobel Prize winning economist Elinor Ostrom discovered many real-world common resources that were consumed in a sustainable manner. Her work is discussed in more detail in Box 20.2.

The efficient level of output for a pure public good

The socially efficient level of output is the quantity at which the marginal social benefit is equal to the marginal social cost. In a competitive market without externalities the marginal social benefit curve is the same as the market demand curve.

The market demand curve for a private good illustrates the sum of all the quantities demanded by all consumers at each possible price. Different consumers will each want to purchase varying amounts at each price. These different individual demands at each price are simply added together in order to derive the market demand curve for a private good. This is known as horizontal aggregation or summation of individual demand curves.

The market demand curve for a pure public good cannot be derived in the same way, because consumers are unable to purchase and consume different quantities of the good. Once a given amount of a pure public good is produced for one customer, every other customer can consume that same amount at no additional cost.

Therefore, instead of thinking about how much people are willing to buy at each different price, we have to work out how much people are willing to pay *in total* for each possible level of output. In other words, we have to add together the maximum amount each consumer is willing to pay for each possible level of output. This is illustrated in Figure 20.8

To keep the example simple, it is assumed that there are just two consumers of the public good – Dean and Jon. In most real-world examples, there would be many more. The maximum amount Dean would be willing to pay to consume the tenth unit of the good is illustrated at point *a* on his demand curve (D_D) and is £30. The maximum amount Jon would be willing to pay for the tenth unit of the good is illustrated at point *b* on his demand curve (D_J) and is £50.

Therefore, if we simply add these willingness-to-pay figures together, we obtain the marginal benefit to society from producing the tenth unit of the public good. This is illustrated at point *c* and is £80. This provides us with one point on the marginal social benefit curve. If we continue this exercise for each different level of output, the marginal social benefit (*MSB*) can be derived as illustrated in Figure 20.8. The curve has been derived in this example by vertically aggregating Dean and Jon's individual demand curves: $MSB = D_D + D_J$.

Producing a public good normally would have the same characteristics as producing a private good. Costs would vary with output in a very similar manner. Therefore, the marginal cost (*MC*) for the market as a whole would be derived in the same way as it would be for a private good, i.e. by adding together the quantities that each firm would want to supply at each price – the horizontal summation of all the individual firms' marginal cost curves. Hence it is drawn as an upward-sloping line.

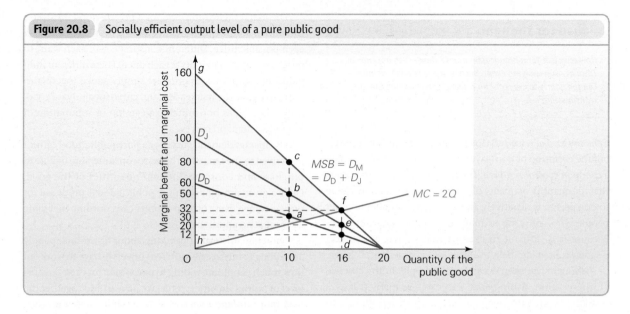

Figure 20.8 Socially efficient output level of a pure public good

Assuming there are no externalities in production, the private marginal cost curve is the same as the social marginal cost curve ($MC = MSC$). The socially efficient quantity can be found where $MC = MSB$ which is at point f at an output of 16.

Provision of pure public goods and the free-rider problem

Assume a private firm produced 16 units of the good and charged Jon a price of £20 per unit (point e) and Dean £12 per unit (point d). These prices would equal their maximum willingness to pay for 16 units. If Jon acts in a perfectly rational and selfish manner, we can predict that he will not pay for the good. Why? Because once the 16 units are produced, he can consume them whether he has paid for them or not. He can act as a *free-rider* by enjoying the benefits of a good that have been paid for by Dean.

Unfortunately, for Jon, if Dean thinks the same way, then he will not pay for the good either. If neither of them pays for the good, then the firm will not generate any revenue and quickly go out of business. As a result, both Dean and Jon will be worse off. Because of the free-riding problem, firms cannot produce the good and make a profit in a private market; so the output will be zero. The social inefficiency this creates can be illustrated by the area of deadweight welfare loss in Figure 20.8 – i.e. the shaded area fgh.

With just two people, it may be possible for the consumers to agree on contribution levels. However, as the number of people who benefit from the public good gets larger, free-riding becomes more likely. This will make it increasingly difficult for private firms to produce public goods in an unregulated market without any government support. If they charge a price they are, in effect, asking for a voluntary contribution from each customer who can consume the good whether they have paid or not. If no voluntary contributions are forthcoming, then the good will not be provided.

The more closely an impure public good resembles a pure public good, the more likely the free-riding problem becomes. It is then increasingly unlikely that the market mechanism will produce the socially efficient level of the good. In these circumstances, the good may have to be provided by the government or by the government subsidising private firms. (Note that not all goods and services produced by the public sector come into the category of public goods and services: thus education and health are publicly provided, but they *can* be, and indeed are, privately provided as well.)

Pause for thought

When studying at school, college or university, often students are asked to produce assessed group work. To what extent is group work an example of an impure public good? How could any potential free-riding problems be overcome?

KEY IDEA 34

The free-rider problem. This occurs when people are able to enjoy the benefits from consuming a good that someone else has bought without having to pay anything towards the cost of providing it themselves. This problem can lead to a situation where a good or service is not produced even though the benefits to society outweigh the costs of producing it.

Definition

Free-rider problem When people enjoy the benefits from consuming a good without paying anything towards the cost of providing it.

BOX 20.2	A COMMONS SOLUTION

Making the best use of common resources

To avoid the tragedy of the commons (see page 373), one solution is to change the status of such resources. There are two obvious ways of doing this.

The first is for the government or an inter-governmental agency either to take over the resources or to regulate their use. Thus a national or local government could pass laws preventing people from tipping waste onto common land or into rivers. Alternatively, groups of governments could act collectively to regulate activities. An example here is the EU's common fisheries policy or international agreements to ban whaling.

The second is to privatise such resources. Common land could be sold or given to private landowners. Such land would then have the property of excludability. This solution clearly raises questions of fairness. How should the land be divided up? If it is sold, how should the previous users of the resource be compensated – if at all? In the 'enclosure movement' in Britain in the eighteenth and nineteenth centuries, common lands were often acquired by wealthy aristocracy and hedges put around them. Poor peasants, who had previously used the land, either had to rent it from the landlords or left the land and were forced to take low-paid work in the cities.

But is there any way for resources to stay as common resources without them being overexploited? After all, economic theory would seem to suggest that the overexploitation of such resources is inevitable: that common ownership will end in tragedy.

Social attitudes towards common resources

In practice, many common resources are used sustainably without government regulation.

> When economists began to look at how systems of commonly managed resources actually worked, they found to their surprise that they often worked quite well. Swiss Alpine pastures; Japanese forests; irrigation systems in Spain and the Philippines. All these were examples of commons that lasted for decades. Some irrigation networks held in common were more efficiently run than the public and private systems that worked alongside them. Though there were failures, too, it seemed as if good management could stave off the tragedy.[1]

The crucial factor here is whether a sense of individual responsibility can be fostered and whether mechanisms can be found for the users to act collectively to manage the resources – a form of quasi-government. Also, there has to be some agreement about what is a fair use of such resources and, in many cases, rules will have to be developed.

> In *Governing the Commons*, which was published in 1990, Elinor Ostrom of Indiana University described the rules needed to keep a commons going. She showed that there are almost always elaborate conventions over who can use resources and when. What you take out of a commons has to be proportional to what you put in. Usage has to be compatible with the commons' underlying health (i.e., you cannot just keep grazing your animals regardless). Everyone has to have some say in the rules. And people usually pay more attention to monitoring abuses and to conflict resolution than to sanctions and punishment.[2]

Sometimes, the rules of behaviour can be deeply embedded in culture. Thus indigenous peoples operating on marginal lands, such as the Aborigines in Australia or the San in the Kalahari, have a culture that respects common resources and puts sustainability at the heart of its philosophy.

> Land is fundamental to the wellbeing of Aboriginal people. The land is not just soil or rocks or minerals, but a whole environment that sustains and is sustained by people and culture. For Indigenous Australians, the land is the core of all spirituality and this relationship and the spirit of 'country' is central to the issues that are important to Indigenous people today.[3]

But, if rules are not embedded in culture, how can they be made to stick? One way is through the development of pressure groups, such as Friends of the Earth or local community action groups.

> Mrs Ostrom suggests the so-called 'miracle of the Rhine' – the clean-up of Europe's busiest waterway – should be seen as an example of successful commons management because it was not until local pressure groups, city and regional governments and non-governmental organisations got involved that polluters were willing to recognise the costs they were imposing on others, and cut emissions. An inter-governmental body (the International Commission for the Protection of the Rhine) did not have the same effect.[4]

The importance of Elinor Ostrom's work was recognised when she was awarded the Nobel Prize in Economics Sciences in 2009.

1. Is there any way in which people's behaviour towards the global commons can be changed so as to reduce the problem of climate change?
2. List some factors that would make successful management of common resources achievable. You might want to think about the number of people, the stability of the population and the role of traditions. What others can you identify?

---

[1] 'Commons Sense', *The Economist*, 31 July 2008.
[2] *Ibid*.
[3] Aboriginal and Torres Strait Islanders Fact Sheet (http://wordpress.as.edu.au/year8l2013/files/2013/09/Aboriginal-Culture.pdf).
[4] 'Commons Sense', *The Economist*, 31 July 2008.

Ignorance and uncertainty

Perfect competition assumes that consumers, firms and factor suppliers have perfect knowledge of costs and benefits.

In the real world, there is often a great deal of ignorance and uncertainty. Thus people are unable to equate marginal benefit with marginal cost.

Consumers purchase many goods only once or a few times in a lifetime. Cars, washing machines, televisions and other consumer durables fall into this category. Consumers may not be aware of the quality of such goods until they have purchased them, by which time it is too late. Advertising may contribute to people's ignorance by misleading them as to the benefits of a good.

Firms are often ignorant of market opportunities, prices, costs, the productivity of workers (especially white-collar workers), the activity of rivals, etc. Many economic decisions are based on expected future conditions. Since the future can never be known for certain, many decisions may turn out to be wrong.

Asymmetric information

One form of imperfect information is when different sides in an economic relationship have different amounts of information. This is known as 'asymmetric information' (see pages 29–31) and is at the heart of the principal–agent problem.

Take the case of a firm (the principal) using the services of a bank (the agent) to finance its investments. The bank is likely to have a much better knowledge of its range of products and of the current state of financial markets and may mis-sell products to the firm in order to earn a larger profit for the bank. For example, it could provide loans at fixed rates of interest, knowing that rates were likely to fall. The firm would end up being locked into paying a higher rate of interest than if it had taken out a variable rate loan and the bank would consequently make more profit. This practice came to light in 2012, with banks accused of mis-selling such products to some 28 000 SMEs.

Immobility of factors and time lags in response

Even under conditions of perfect competition, factors may be very slow to respond to changes in demand or supply. Labour, for example, may be highly immobile both occupationally and geographically. This can lead to large price changes and hence to large supernormal profits and high wages for those in the sectors of rising demand or falling costs. The long run may be a very long time coming!

In the meantime, there will be further changes in the conditions of demand and supply. Thus the economy is in a constant state of disequilibrium and the long run never comes. As firms and consumers respond to market signals and move towards equilibrium, so the equilibrium position moves and the social optimum is never achieved.

The problem of time lags. Many economic actions can take a long time to take effect. This can cause problems of instability and an inability of the economy to achieve social efficiency.

Whenever monopoly/monopsony power exists, the problem is made worse as firms or unions put up barriers to the entry of new firms or factors of production.

Protecting people's interests

Dependants. People do not always make their own economic decisions. They are often dependent on choices made by others. Parents make decisions on behalf of their children; partners on each other's behalf; younger adults on behalf of old people. A free market will respond to these, however good or bad they may be and whether or not they are in the interests of the dependants. Thus the government may feel it necessary to intervene in order to protect the interests of those whose welfare depends on choices made by others.

Poor economic decision making by individuals on their own behalf. The government may feel that people need protecting from poor economic decisions that they make on their *own* behalf. These are sometimes referred to as internalities – impacts of poor decision making that are incurred by the consumer, rather than others, at some point in the future. As we discussed in Chapter 7, this may be a particular problem when the benefits from consuming a good are immediate while the costs happen at some point in the future. People place too much weight on the immediate benefits and too little weight on the long-run costs of their decisions. Products where this might be an issue include tobacco, alcohol and fast/unhealthy food.

On the other hand, the government may feel that people consume too little of things that are good for them: things such as education, health care and sports facilities. Such goods are known as *merit goods*.

> ### Definition
>
> **Merit goods** Goods that the government feels that people will under-consume and that therefore ought to be subsidised or provided free.

20.3 GOVERNMENT INTERVENTION IN THE MARKET

Faced with all the problems of the free market, what is a government to do?

There are several policy instruments that the government can use. At one extreme, it can totally replace the market by providing goods and services itself. At the other extreme, it can merely seek to persuade producers, consumers or workers to act differently. Between the two extremes, the

Government intervention may be able to rectify various failings of the market. Government intervention in the market can be used to achieve various economic objectives which may not be best achieved by the market. Governments, however, are not perfect and their actions may bring adverse, as well as beneficial, consequences.

government has a number of instruments it can use to change the way markets operate. These include taxes, subsidies, laws and regulatory bodies. In this section, we examine these different forms of government intervention.

Taxes and subsidies

KI 31
p 365 When there are imperfections in the market, social efficiency will not be achieved. Marginal social benefit (*MSB*) will not equal marginal social cost (*MSC*). A different level of output would be more desirable.

Taxes and subsidies can be used to correct these imperfections. Essentially, the approach is to tax those goods or activities where the market produces too much and subsidise those where the market produces too little.

Taxes and subsidies to correct for monopoly. If the problem of monopoly that the government wishes to tackle is that of *excessive profits,* it can impose a lump-sum tax on the monopolist: that is, a tax of a fixed absolute amount irrespective of how much the monopolist produces or the price it charges. Since a lump-sum tax is an additional *fixed* cost to the firm, and hence will not affect the firm's marginal cost, it will not reduce the amount that the monopolist produces (which *would* be the case with a per-unit tax). An example of such a tax was the 'windfall tax' imposed by the UK Labour Government in 1997. This was on the profits of various privatised utilities. Then, in 2005, there was another tax on the 'excess' profits of oil companies operating in the North Sea. These had been the result of large increases in world oil prices. In 2017, a labour MP called for a windfall tax on the profits of companies involved in the private finance initiative (PFI) (see pages 661–2).

If the government is concerned that the monopolist produces *less* than the socially efficient output, it could give the monopolist a per-unit *subsidy* (which would encourage the monopolist to produce more). But would this not *increase* the monopolist's profit? The answer to this is to impose a harsh lump-sum tax in addition to the subsidy. The tax would not undo the subsidy's benefit of encouraging the monopolist to produce more, but it could be used to reduce the monopolist's profits below the original (i.e. pre-subsidy) level.

KI 33
p 367 *Taxes and subsidies to correct externalities.* The rule here is simple: the government should impose a tax equal to the marginal external cost (or grant a subsidy equal to the marginal external benefit). This is known as a Pigouvian tax (or Pigouvian subsidy) named after the economist Arthur Pigou. A real-world example of taxes that are partly justified by the existence of external costs in consumption are excise duties on various products, such as tobacco, alcohol and gambling. For example, in 2018/19, the rate of excise tax on cigarettes consists of a fixed element of £4.57 per packet of 20 plus a variable element of 16.5 per cent of the retail price. This is in addition to the standard rate of VAT.

Previously, we examined the impact of external costs of pollution created by the chemical industry as a whole.

We will now focus on one firm in that industry, which otherwise is perfectly competitive. Our firm is thus a price taker. Assume that this particular chemical company emits smoke from a chimney and thus pollutes the atmosphere. This creates external costs for the people who breathe in the smoke. The marginal social cost of producing the chemicals thus exceeds the marginal private cost to the firm: $MSC > MC$.

This is illustrated in Figure 20.9. In this example, it is assumed the marginal external pollution cost begins with the first unit of production but remains constant. Hence the MEC_P is drawn as a horizontal line. The vertical distance between the MC and MSC curves is equal to the MEC_P. The firm produces Q_1 where $P = MC$ (its profit-maximising output), but in doing so takes no account of the external pollution costs it imposes on society.

If the government now imposes a tax on production equal to the marginal pollution cost, it will effectively 'internalise' the externality. The firm will have to pay an amount equal to the external cost it creates. It will therefore now maximise profits at Q_2, which is the socially optimum output where $MSB = MSC$.

Advantages of taxes and subsidies

Many economists favour the tax/subsidy solution to market imperfections (especially the problem of externalities) because it still allows the market to operate. It forces firms to take on board the full social costs and benefits of their actions. It is also adjustable according to the magnitude of the problem.

What is more, by taxing firms for polluting, say, they are encouraged to find cleaner ways of producing. The tax thus acts as an incentive over the longer run to reduce pollution: the more a firm can reduce its pollution, the more taxes it can save. **KI 9** **p 45**

Likewise, when *good* practices are subsidised, firms are given the incentive to adopt more good practices.

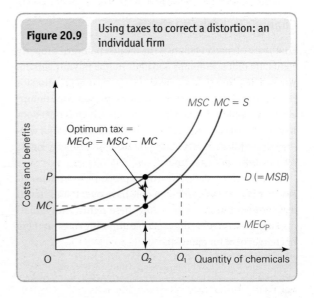

| Figure 20.9 | Using taxes to correct a distortion: an individual firm |

Disadvantages of taxes and subsidies

Infeasible to use different tax and subsidy rates. Each firm produces different levels and types of externality and operates under different degrees of imperfect competition. It would be expensive and administratively very difficult, if not impossible, to charge every offending firm its own particular tax rate (or grant every relevant firm its own particular rate of subsidy).

> **Pause for thought**
>
> *Why is it easier to use taxes and subsidies to tackle the problem of car exhaust pollution than to tackle the problem of peak-time traffic congestion in cities?*

Lack of knowledge. Even if a government did decide to charge a tax equal to each offending firm's marginal external costs, it would still have the problem of measuring that cost and apportioning blame. The damage to lakes and forests from acid rain has been a major concern since the beginning of the 1980s. But just how serious is that damage? What is its current monetary cost? How long lasting is the damage?

Just what and who are to blame? These are questions that cannot be answered precisely. It is thus impossible to fix the 'correct' pollution tax on, say, a particular coal-fired power station.

KI 8
p 33 Despite these problems, it is, nevertheless, possible to charge firms by the amount of a particular emission. For example, firms could be charged for chimney smoke by so many parts per million of a given pollutant. Although it is difficult to 'fine-tune' such a system so that the charge reflects the precise number of people affected by the pollutant and by how much, it does go some way to internalising the externality.

Changes in property rights

KI 33
p 367 One cause of market failure is the limited nature of property rights. If someone dumps a load of rubble in your garden, you can insist that it is removed and claim compensation for the disutility it has caused you. If, however, someone dumps a load of rubble in his or her *own* garden, which is next door to yours, what can you do? You can still see it from your window. It is still an eyesore. But you have no property rights over the next-door garden.

Property rights define who owns property, to what uses it can be put, the rights other people have over it and how it may be transferred. By *extending* these rights, individuals may be able to prevent other people imposing costs on them or charge them for doing so.

> **Pause for thought**
>
> *If the sufferers had no property rights, show how it would still be in their interests to 'bribe' the firm to produce the socially efficient level of output.*

The socially efficient compensation rate would be one that was equal to the marginal external cost (and would have the same effect as the government charging a tax on the firm of that amount, see Figure 20.9). The ***Coase theorem***[1] states that, when there are well-defined property rights and there are no bargaining or negotiation costs, then the socially efficient charge *will* be levied. But why?

Let us take the case of river pollution by a chemical works that imposes a cost on people fishing in the river. If property rights to the river were now given to the fishing community, they could impose a charge on the chemical works per unit of output. If they charged *less* than the marginal external cost, they would suffer more from the last unit (in terms of lost fish) than they were being compensated. If they charged *more,* and thereby caused the firm to cut back its output below the socially efficient level, they would be sacrificing a level of compensation that would be greater than the marginal suffering. It will be in the sufferers' best interests, therefore, to charge an amount *equal* to the marginal externality.

Alternatively, the property rights to the river could be awarded to the chemical works. In this situation, the fishing community could offer payments to the firm on condition that it did not pollute the river.

One interesting result is that the efficient solution to the problem caused by the externality does not depend on which party is assigned the property rights, i.e. the fishing community or the chemical works. All that matters is that the property rights are fully assigned to either one or the other and that there are no bargaining costs.

In most instances, however, this type of solution is totally impractical. It is impractical when *many* people are *slightly* inconvenienced, especially if there are many culprits imposing the costs. For example, if I were disturbed by noisy lorries outside my home, it would not be practical to negotiate with every haulage company involved. What if I wanted to ban the lorries from the street, but my next-door neighbour wanted to charge them 10p per journey? Who gets their way?

The extension of private property rights becomes a more practical solution where the culprits are few in

> **Definition**
>
> **Coase theorem** When there are well-defined property rights and zero bargaining costs, then negotiations between the party creating the externality and the party affected by the externality can bring about the socially efficient market quantity.

---

[1] Named after Ronald Coase, who developed the theory. See his article, 'The problem of social cost', *Journal of Law and Economics,* Vol. 3 (1960), pp. 1–44.

number, are easily identifiable and impose clearly defined costs. Thus a noise abatement act could be passed which allowed me to prevent my neighbours playing noisy radios, having noisy parties or otherwise disturbing the peace in my home. The onus would be on me to report them. Or I could agree not to report them if they paid me adequate compensation.

But, even in cases where only a few people are involved, there may still be the problem of litigation. I may have to incur the time and expense of taking people to court. Justice may not be free and there is thus a conflict with equity. The rich can afford 'better' justice. They can employ top lawyers. Thus, even if I have a right to sue a large company for dumping toxic waste near me, I may not have the legal muscle to win.

KI 32
p 365 Finally, there is the broader question of *equity*. Although the socially efficient outcome does not depend

on who the property rights are assigned to, the equity of the outcome will. The extension of private property rights may favour the rich (who tend to have more property) at the expense of the poor. Ramblers may get great pleasure from strolling across a great country estate, along public rights of way. This may annoy the owner. If the owner's property rights were now extended to exclude the ramblers, is this a social gain?

Of course, equity considerations can also be dealt with by altering property rights, but in a different way. *Public* property like parks, open spaces, libraries and historic buildings could be extended. Also the property of the rich could be redistributed to the poor. Here it is less a question of the rights that ownership confers and more a question of altering the ownership itself.

BOX 20.3   DEADWEIGHT LOSS FROM TAXES ON GOODS AND SERVICES

The excess burden of taxes

Subsidies can be used to correct for social inefficiencies caused by positive externalities, monopoly power and public goods. However, the government might have to impose or raise taxes on other goods in order to finance any subsidies. These taxes might have adverse effects themselves. One such effect is the deadweight loss that results when taxes are imposed on goods and services in a perfectly competitive market.

The diagram below shows the demand and supply of a particular good. Equilibrium is initially at a price of P_1 and a level of sales of Q_1 (i.e. where $D = S$). Now an excise tax is imposed on this market in order to raise revenue to fund a subsidy in another market. The supply curve shifts upwards by the amount of the tax, to S + tax. Equilibrium price rises to P_2 and equilibrium quantity falls to Q_2. Producers receive an after-tax price of P_2 − tax.

Consumer surplus falls from areas 1 + 2 + 3, to area 1 (the upper grey area). Producer surplus falls from areas 4 + 5 + 6 to area 6 (the lower grey area). Does this mean, therefore, that total surplus falls by areas 2 + 3 + 4 + 5? The answer is no, because there is a gain to the government from the tax revenue (and hence a gain to the population from the resulting government expenditure). The revenue

from the tax is known as the **government surplus**. It is given by areas 2 + 4 (the blue area).

But, even after including government surplus, there is still a fall in total surplus of areas 3 + 5 (the pink area). This is the deadweight loss of the tax. It is sometimes known as the **excess burden** of the tax.

Does this loss of total surplus from taxation imply that taxes on goods to fund subsidies are always a 'bad thing'? The answer is no. A comparison would have to be made between the negative impact of the tax in one market with the positive impact of the subsidy it funded in the other market. We have also assumed that there were no market failures in the market where the tax was imposed. This might not be true. For example, if there is a negative externality, then the tax could have a positive impact on social efficiency in the market in which it was implemented.

In the real world of imperfect markets and inequality, taxes can do more good than harm. As we have shown in this section, they can help to correct for externalities. They can also be used as a means of redistributing incomes. Nevertheless, the excess burden of taxes is something that ideally ought to be considered when weighing up the desirability of imposing taxes on goods and services or of increasing their rate.

1. *How would the burden of taxation change if (a) demand was more inelastic and (b) supply was more inelastic?*
2. *How far can an economist contribute to this highly political debate over the desirability of an excise tax?*

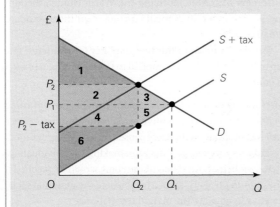

Definitions

Government surplus (from a tax on a good) The total tax revenue earned by the government from sales of a good.

Excess burden (of a tax on a good) The amount by which the loss in consumer plus producer surplus exceeds the government surplus.

Laws prohibiting or regulating undesirable structures or behaviour

Laws are frequently used to correct market imperfections. Laws can be of three main types: those that prohibit or regulate behaviour that imposes external costs; those that prevent firms providing false or misleading information; and those that prevent monopolies and oligopolies from abusing their market power and regulate their behaviour (see Chapter 21).

Advantages of legal restrictions

■ They are usually simple and clear to understand and often are relatively easy to administer. For example, various polluting activities could be banned or restricted by placing quotas on the amounts firms can produce.

■ When the danger is very great, it might be much safer to ban various practices altogether (e.g. the use of various toxic chemicals) rather than to rely on taxes or on individuals attempting to assert their property rights through the civil courts.

■ When a decision needs to be taken quickly, it might be possible to invoke emergency action. For example, in a city like Athens it has been found to be simpler to ban or restrict the use of private cars during a chemical smog emergency than to tax their use.

■ Because consumers suffer from imperfect information, consumer protection laws can make it illegal for firms to sell shoddy or unsafe goods, or to make false or misleading claims about their products.

Disadvantages of legal restrictions

The main problem is that legal restrictions tend to be a rather blunt weapon. If, for example, a firm were required to reduce the effluent of a toxic chemical to 20 tonnes per week, there would be no incentive for the firm to reduce it further. With a tax on the effluent, however, the more the firm reduced the effluent, the less tax it would pay. Thus with a system of taxes there is a *continuing* incentive to cut pollution, to improve safety, or whatever.

Regulatory bodies

Rather than using the blunt weapon of general legislation to ban or restrict various activities, a more 'subtle' approach can be adopted. This involves the use of various regulatory bodies. Having identified possible cases where action might be required (e.g. potential cases of pollution, misleading information or the abuse of monopoly power), the regulatory body would probably conduct an investigation and then prepare a report containing its findings and recommendations. It might also have the power to enforce its decisions or this might be up to some higher authority.

An example of such a body is the Competition and Markets Authority, the work of which will be examined in section 21.1. Other examples are the bodies set up to regulate the privatised utilities: e.g. Ofwat (the Office of Water Services) and Ofgem (the Office of Gas and Electricity Markets). These are examined in section 22.3.

The advantage of this approach is that a case-by-case method can be used and, as a result, the most appropriate solution adopted. However, investigations may be expensive and time-consuming; only a few cases may be examined; and offending firms may make various promises of good behaviour which, if not followed up by the regulatory body, may not in fact be carried out.

Price controls

Price controls can be used either to raise prices above, or to reduce them below, the free-market level.

Prices set below the market equilibrium. The government, or another body, could set prices below the market level to prevent a monopoly or oligopoly from charging prices above the socially efficient level. This is one of the major roles of the regulatory bodies for the privatised utilities.

For example, in April 2017, *Ofgem* introduced a price cap on the energy bills of over four million customers who use pre-payment meters. The rationale for the policy was the relatively high prices in this segment of the market caused by a lack of effective competition. Called the safeguard tariff, this price cap was extended in February 2018 to low-income customers who were receiving the Warm Home Discount and in December 2018 to all customers on the a standard variable tariff.

Another example of this type of policy is the interest rate cap of 0.8 per cent per day applied to the payday loan market in January 2015.

Prices set below the market equilibrium. The government could set prices *above* the competitive market equilibrium to reduce the level of social inefficiency caused by a negative externality and/or poor economic decision making by individuals on their own behalf. An efficient outcome would be reached if a minimum price was set at a level where the marginal social benefit was equal to the marginal social cost.

One example of this type of policy is the decision by the Scottish Government to introduce minimum unit pricing for alcohol on 1 May 2018.

Price controls could be used with the objective of redistributing incomes. Thus (high) farm prices can be used to protect the incomes of farmers and minimum wage legislation can help those on low incomes. On the consumption side, low maximum rents might be put in place with the intention of helping those on low incomes afford housing. However, as was argued in Box 4.3, price controls can cause shortages and surpluses.

Provision of information

When ignorance is a reason for market failure, the direct provision of information by the government or one of its agencies may help to correct that failure. An example is the information on jobs provided by job centres to those looking for work. They thus help the labour market to work better and increase the elasticity of supply of labour. Another example is the provision of consumer information: for example, on the effects of smoking or of eating certain foodstuffs. Another is the provision of government statistics on prices, costs, employment, sales trends, etc. This enables firms to plan with greater certainty.

The direct provision of goods and services

In the case of public goods and services, such as flood defence and national defence, the market mechanism may fail to provide the socially efficient amount because of the free-riding problem. Governments may have to finance the optimal provision of the public good by requiring compulsory payments from members of society. One way of obtaining the compulsory payments is through the central/local tax system. Central government, local government or some other public agency could then manage the production of the goods and services directly. Alternatively, they could pay private firms to do so.

The government could also provide goods and services directly which are *not* public goods. Examples include health and education. There are four reasons why such things are provided free or at well below cost.

Social justice. Society may feel that these things should not be provided according to ability to pay. Rather they should be provided as of right: an equal right based on need.

Large positive externalities. People other than the consumer may benefit substantially. If a person decides to get treatment for an infectious disease, other people benefit by not being infected. A free health service thus helps to combat the spread of disease.

Dependants. If education were not free and if the quality of education depended on the amount spent and if parents could choose how much or little to buy, then the quality of children's education would depend not just on their parents' income, but also on how much they cared. A government may choose to provide such things free in order to protect children from 'bad' parents. A similar argument is used for providing free prescriptions and dental treatment for all children.

Ignorance. Consumers may not realise how much they will benefit. If they have to pay, they may choose (unwisely) to go without. Providing health care free may persuade people to consult their doctors before a complaint becomes serious.

20.4 THE CASE FOR LESS GOVERNMENT INTERVENTION

Government intervention in the market can itself lead to problems. The case for less government intervention is not that the market is the *perfect* means of achieving given social goals, but rather that the problems created by intervention are greater than the problems overcome by that intervention.

Drawbacks of government intervention

Shortages and surpluses. If the government intervenes by fixing prices at levels other than the equilibrium, this will create either shortages or surpluses.

If the price is fixed *below* the equilibrium, there will be a shortage. For example, if the rent of council houses is fixed below the equilibrium in order to provide cheap housing for poor people, demand will exceed supply. In the case of such shortages, the government will have to adopt a system of waiting lists, rationing or giving certain people preferential treatment. Alternatively, it will have to allow allocation to be on a first-come, first-served basis or allow queues to develop. Underground markets are likely to occur.

If the price is fixed *above* the equilibrium price, there will be a surplus. For example, if the price of food is fixed above the equilibrium in order to support farmers' incomes, supply will exceed demand. Either government will have to purchase such surpluses and then perhaps store them, throw them away or sell them cheaply in another market, or it will have to ration suppliers by allowing them to produce only a certain quota or allow them to sell to whomever they can.

Poor information. The government may not know the full costs and benefits of its policies. It may genuinely wish to pursue the interests of consumers or any other group and yet may be unaware of people's wishes or misinterpret their behaviour.

Bureaucracy and inefficiency. Government intervention involves administrative costs. The more wide-reaching and detailed the intervention, the greater the number of people and material resources that will be involved. These resources may be used wastefully.

Lack of market incentives. If government intervention removes market forces or cushions their effect (by the use of subsidies, welfare provisions, guaranteed prices or wages, etc.), it may remove certain useful incentives. Subsidies may allow inefficient firms to survive. Welfare payments may discourage effort. The market may be imperfect, but it does tend to encourage efficiency by allowing the efficient to receive greater rewards.

Shifts in government policy. The economic efficiency of industry may suffer if government intervention changes too frequently. It makes it difficult for firms to plan if they cannot predict tax rates, subsidies, price and wage controls, etc.

Lack of freedom for the individual. Government intervention involves a loss of freedom for individuals to make economic choices. The argument is not just that the pursuit of individual gain is seen to lead to the social good, but that it is desirable in itself that individuals should be as free as possible to pursue their own interests with the minimum of government interference: that minimum being largely confined to the maintenance of laws consistent with the protection of life, liberty and property.

Advantages of the free market

Although markets in the real world are not perfect, even imperfect markets can be argued to have positive advantages over government provision or even government regulation. These might include the following.

Automatic adjustments. Government intervention requires administration. A free-market economy, on the other hand, leads to the automatic, albeit imperfect, adjustment to demand and supply changes.

Dynamic advantages of capitalism. The chances of making high monopoly/oligopoly profits will encourage entrepreneurs to invest in new products and new techniques. Prices may be high initially, but consumers will gain from the extra choice of products. Furthermore, if profits are high, new firms will sooner or later break into the market and competition will ensue.

> ### Pause for thought
>
> *Are there any features of the free market that would discourage innovation?*

A high degree of competition even under monopoly/ oligopoly. Even though an industry at first sight may seem to be highly monopolistic, competitive forces may still work as a result of the following:

- A fear that excessively high profits might encourage firms to attempt to break into the industry (assuming that the market is contestable).
- Competition from closely related industries (e.g. coach services for rail services or electricity for gas).
- The threat of foreign competition.
- Countervailing power (see page 215). Large powerful producers often sell to large powerful buyers. For example, the power of detergent manufacturers to drive up the price of washing powder is countered by the power of supermarket chains to drive down the price at which they purchase it. Thus power is to some extent neutralised.
- The competition for corporate control (see page 196).

20.5 FIRMS AND SOCIAL RESPONSIBILITY

As discussed in previous chapters, traditional economic theory assumes that firms are trying to maximise profits and are not concerned with the impact of their activities on the wider community. However, many of the most famous companies in the world now regularly publish reports that outline their progress towards achieving a set of broader societal goals. For example, Google issues an Environmental Report, BMW produces a Sustainable Value Report, Lego publishes a Responsibility Report and The Walt Disney Company produces a Corporate Citizenship Report – all of them annually.

The approach to decision making described in these reports is widely referred to as *corporate social responsibility (CSR)* and many businesses have increased their investment

in this area. For example, in a 2016 global survey of CEOs carried out by *PriceWaterhouseCoopers*[2] 64 per cent of respondents stated that they planned to increase expenditure on CSR in the future and that it was increasingly becoming a core part of their businesses.

> ### Definition
>
> **Corporate social responsibility** Where a business integrates social, environmental, ethical and human rights concerns into its actions in close collaboration with its stakeholders.

[2] 'Redefining business success in a changing world', *19th Annual Global CEO Survey* PwC (January 2016).

Most of the CSR activities undertaken by firms can be grouped under four broad headings:

Environmental activities. These include polices to use energy more efficiently, reduce wastage, increase recycling, increase the use of energy from renewable sources and reduce CO_2 emissions. For example:

- In 2017, Google announced that all of its energy usage across its entire global operations would come from renewable sources.
- The BMW Group reported that, between 1995 and 2015, it reduced average CO_2 emissions by 39.5 per cent.
- Lego has set itself a target of producing all of its core products and packaging with sustainable materials by 2030.
- Microsoft has implemented a global internal carbon fee model, whereby it charges each business unit a fee based on the carbon emissions of its business operations. 'This provides a powerful incentive to find carbon-saving alternatives and invest in carbon-reducing innovations.'[3]

Donating money/equipment/employees' time to charities, good causes and local community projects. Research by the Charities Aid Foundation found that FTSE 100 companies donated £1.9bn to charities in 2016, with 26 businesses donating at least 1 per cent of their pre-tax profits. However, these figures have been falling in recent years with donations in 2017 over 25 per cent lower than in 2013.

Firm-specific examples include: Microsoft Philanthropies, a division of Microsoft, donating $1.2 billion worth of software and services to non-profit organisations in 2017; and the Walt Disney Company donating $400 million to non-profit organisations in 2016. Another increasingly popular initiative is for organisations to offer a number of days of paid volunteering leave. For example, Apple launched its 'Global Volunteer Program' in 2015.

Fair and ethical treatment of employees. This could include paying 'fair' wages, reducing the gender pay gap, employing more people from ethnic minorities, increasing the percentage of female senior managers, offering more generous maternity and paternity leave and providing greater support for employee physical/mental wellbeing.

Firm-specific examples include: Microsoft's *CARES* employee assistance programme, which offers free access to personal/family counselling and stress management. Microsoft was also one of the first businesses to offer domestic partner benefits for its LGBT employees. Virgin Group, Netflix, Amazon and Google have also extended the period of their paid maternity and paternity leave in the past few years.

Fair/ethical treatment of suppliers. This could include activities such as negotiating 'fair' contracts with suppliers, only dealing with suppliers which meet certain CSR benchmarks and providing support for suppliers to meet CSR benchmarks.

Firm-specific examples include: Toyota implementing a Group Procurement Policy in 2015, which stated that all of its suppliers must comply with laws, regulations and social norms as well as giving proper consideration to environmental issues; Apple publishing an annual Supplier Responsibility Progress Report and launching an Environmental Health

> ### Pause for thought
>
> *Why does there appear to have been such big increases in spending on CSR over the last few years?*

& Safety (EHS) Academy, which runs courses for managers of its suppliers.

Each of these broad types of CSR activity involve businesses making costly investments. Environmental activities involve expenditures to reduce external costs below the level legally required by government regulation. Donating money to good causes is a voluntary contribution to a public good. Treating both employees and suppliers in a 'fair' manner may involve contracts that do not maximise firms' profits. All of this behaviour seems inconsistent with some of the predictions of standard economic theory discussed in this chapter.

How have economists tried to explain this growing expenditure by organisations on CSR activities? Is it necessarily in the interests of society if firms take the broader impact of their actions into account when deciding on which policies or strategies to follow? These issues are discussed below

Some different views of corporate social responsibility

Benabou and Tirole (2010)[4] discuss three different visions or CSR. We look at each in turn.

Insider-initiated philanthropy or the classical view

According to this view, business managers should be responsible only for meeting the objectives of their shareholders, and shareholders are concerned only with maximising the financial returns on their investments. Therefore, managers should be solely concerned with trying to maximise profits.

Under certain conditions, market competition between these profit-maximising firms and self-interested consumers results in social efficiency. If any market failures do occur, such as externalities, the abuse of market power or public goods, intervention should be based upon the preferences of the public. The most effective way these can be expressed is through the democratic process, so the policies should be implemented by the elected government (not firms).

[3]Brad Smith, 'Greener datacenters for a brighter future: Microsoft's commitment to renewable energy', *Microsoft on the Issues blog* (19/5/2016)

[4]Roland Bénabou and Jean Tirole, 'Individual and Corporate Social Responsibility', *Economica*, Vol. 77, 1–19 (2010).

Government intervention may also be justified if the distribution of income and wealth does not align with the preferences of society.

According to this view, a business should not extend its influence over wider social issues, as it lacks the appropriate public accountability to do so.

If businesses do engage in CSR activities, this reflects the preferences of their managers, which are unlikely to be the same as those of either the general public or shareholders. The famous Nobel Prize winning economist, Milton Friedman, argued that managers should not use other people's money (i.e. the returns to shareholders) to invest in good causes that they happen to value themselves.

Socially responsible investments are also costly and will cause the business to make lower profits. This means that managers are failing in their key responsibility to meet the objectives of shareholders, i.e. to maximise profits. This type of behaviour would be possible only when there are imperfect labour and capital markets. If these markets were highly competitive, then the threat of either being fired by the board of directors or redundancy following a takeover should prevent CEOs from making any CSR investments in the first place.

This whole approach to CSR is neatly summarised by the following famous quote from Milton Friedman: 'The social responsibility of business is to increase profits'.

Delegated philanthropy

Many **stakeholders** may have preferences that are not aligned with government policy. For example, they may have voted for political parties with very different policies from those of the government or the government may not have successfully implemented the policies it promised in its manifesto. Therefore, many potential investors, employees and customers may have preferences over issues such as the environment that are not being met. They may be willing to trade off some of their narrower monetary returns in order to interact with firms who help them achieve their wider social objectives. In this view, businesses are effectively outlets through which people can express their values.

If the monetary value of the trade-offs that different stakeholders are willing to make is greater than the costs to the firm, then it may actually become profitable to invest in CSR activities. It improves the welfare of all the parties involved. This view of CSR is far more positive than the insider-initiated approach.

How can different primary stakeholders such as investors, customers and employees effectively pay to interact with firms who invest in CSR activities?

Investors. Are some people willing to accept lower expected returns from investments in businesses that spend large amounts of money on CSR?

Recent reports from the biggest investment company in the world suggest that this might be the case. BlackRock manages funds of approximately $6 trillion. In January 2018,

its CEO (Larry Fink) stated that it would no longer invest in businesses unless they delivered both good financial performance and invested heavily in CSR.

There has also been rapid growth in so called *Impact Investing.* This is defined as investing in businesses with the intention of generating measurable social and/or environmental impacts alongside a financial return. The 2017, Annual Impact Investor Survey[5] reported that 208 respondents had invested $114bn in impact investing assets.

Numerous socially responsible investment funds now exist that attempt to align with investors' personal or ethical values. The FTSE4Good Index was established in 2001 because of the demand from investors for information on the performance of companies heavily involved in socially responsible investments (SRI). The index only includes businesses that meet a variety of environmental, social and governance criteria.

Customers. Are customers willing to pay higher prices for products/brands produced by companies that have a good record of investing in CSR?

In a 2015 Nielsen survey[6] of over 30 000 consumers in 60 countries, 66 per cent of respondents stated that they were willing to pay higher prices for products and services provided by companies that were committed to investing in projects that had a positive social and/or environmental impact. Interestingly, the figure for those earning $20 000 or less was 68 per cent, while for those earning above $50 000 it was 63 per cent.

An international study,[7] published by Unilever in 2017, found that 33 per cent of consumers purchased brands because they believed the producers were engaged in positive social or environmental activities. Also, 21 per cent stated that they would choose a brand if its sustainable credentials were made very clear on the packaging.

Employees. Are employees willing to accept lower wages to work for employers who demonstrate a strong commitment to engage in socially responsible practices? Are they more

---

Definition

Stakeholders (in a company) People who are affected by a company's activities and/or performance (customers, employees, owners, creditors, people living in the neighbourhood, etc.). They may or may not be in a position to take decisions, or influence decision taking, in the firm.

---

[5]*Annual Impact Investor Survey*, Global Impact Investing Network 2017 (May 2017)

[6]'Consumer-Goods' Brands that Demonstrate Commitment to Sustainability Outperform those that Don't', *Nielsen Press Release* (12 October 2015).

[7]'Report shows a third of consumers prefer sustainable brands', *Unilever Press Release* (5/1/2017)

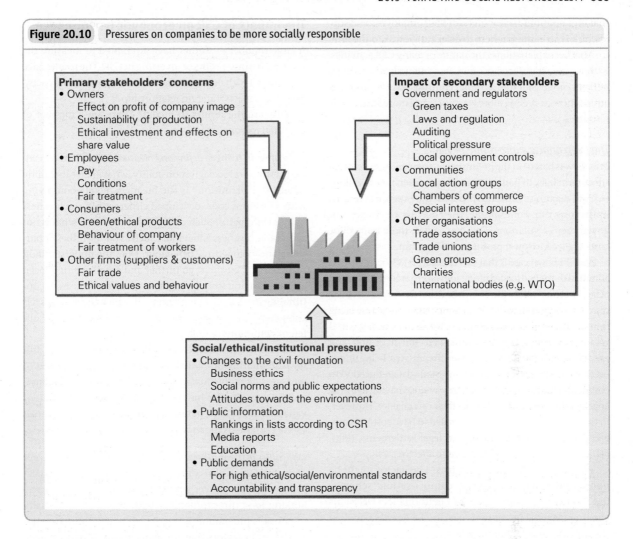

Figure 20.10 Pressures on companies to be more socially responsible

Primary stakeholders' concerns
- Owners
  - Effect on profit of company image
  - Sustainability of production
  - Ethical investment and effects on share value
- Employees
  - Pay
  - Conditions
  - Fair treatment
- Consumers
  - Green/ethical products
  - Behaviour of company
  - Fair treatment of workers
- Other firms (suppliers & customers)
  - Fair trade
  - Ethical values and behaviour

Impact of secondary stakeholders
- Government and regulators
  - Green taxes
  - Laws and regulation
  - Auditing
  - Political pressure
  - Local government controls
- Communities
  - Local action groups
  - Chambers of commerce
  - Special interest groups
- Other organisations
  - Trade associations
  - Trade unions
  - Green groups
  - Charities
  - International bodies (e.g. WTO)

Social/ethical/institutional pressures
- Changes to the civil foundation
  - Business ethics
  - Social norms and public expectations
  - Attitudes towards the environment
- Public information
  - Rankings in lists according to CSR
  - Media reports
  - Education
- Public demands
  - For high ethical/social/environmental standards
  - Accountability and transparency

likely to remain loyal to these businesses even if higher levels of remuneration are available elsewhere?

In the 2016 Cone Communications Millennial Employee Engagement Study, 75 per cent of respondents stated they would be willing to take a pay cut to work for a responsible company, 83 per cent stated they would be more loyal to a company that helps them contribute to social/environmental issues, while 76 per cent would consider a company's social and environmental commitments when deciding where to work.

In a 2016 study[8] of 1700 business students from across 40 countries, 90 per cent of the respondents stated that they were willing to sacrifice some percentage of their future salary to work for an employer that engaged in CSR activities; 14 per cent stated that they were willing to sacrifice more than 40 per cent of their future income.

Other secondary stakeholders and the general public may place further demands on companies as social norms of what

is regarded as 'acceptable' corporate behaviour change over time.

The pressures from all stakeholders are summarised in Figure 20.10. An example of a company that built its reputation on being socially and environmentally responsible – The Body Shop – is discussed in more detail in Box 20.4.

Pause for thought

Discuss some of the limitations of the research results on the willingness of different stakeholder groups to pay to interact with firms which engage in CSR activities.

Why do stakeholders choose to delegate CSR to organisations rather than taking more direct actions? For example, they could make their own donations to good causes or make payments to boost the incomes of low-paid workers. One explanation is that it reduces the informational/transaction costs. To make appropriate donations, stakeholders would need detailed information about a whole range of contracts

KI 9
p45

---

[8] Debbie Haski-Leventhal and Julian Concato, 'The State of CSR and RME in Business Schools and the Attitudes of their Students', *Third bi-annual study, 2016*, Macquarie Graduate School of Management and Prime.

that organisations have with both their employees and suppliers. It is far easier for them to delegate the task to the firm.

Another explanation is the nature of many CSR activities. Rather than a transfer of incomes, they often involve changes in firms' *behaviour*: for example, emitting less CO_2 into the atmosphere, recycling more waste or using more sustainable resources.

The overcoming short-termism view

This view is based on the premise that companies suffer from short-term bias. In particular, managers often take decisions to try to maximise short-run profits at the expense of returns in the long run. For example, they may try to circumvent government regulations. This may reduce more immediate costs but lead to lower profits in the long run.

A well-known case is that of Volkswagen (VW). In 2015, it admitted that it had loaded illegal software to around 11 million of its diesel cars worldwide. This meant that the cars emitted less nitrogen oxide and, within legal limits, when they were being tested in laboratory conditions, i.e. when the steering wheel was not turning. The emissions were much greater and exceeded legal limits, however, when the cars were being driven on the road. This falsification of emissions data reduced VWs costs in the short run, as the company avoided having to install appropriate components to make their cars greener. However, in the long run, the scandal is estimated to have cost Volkswagen between \$25bn and \$30bn in legal settlements, fines, vehicle buybacks and modifications to affected cars.

What causes this short-term bias? One factor might be poorly designed managerial compensation schemes (e.g. bonuses) based on short-run performance. Decisions about managerial promotion may also be heavily based on the firm's most recent information.

Putting value on CSR may help to overcome this short-term bias and maximise the value of profits in the long run. Socially responsible investors are effectively monitoring the managers to make sure they do not become overly focused on short-run profits.

A slightly different standpoint is to view CSR as a *strategic* move, which attempts to improve the firm's competitive position in the long run. A company may believe that the impact on its costs from making socially responsible investments is lower than the impact on its rivals. If rivals feel obliged to match any socially responsible investments to maintain the appeal of their brands, it might put them at a relative cost disadvantage.

The impact of CSR on economic performance

A large number of studies have attempted to measure the impact on firms' profits of investing in CSR. The results have been mixed with different studies finding positive impacts,[9] negative impacts[10] and no relationship.[11]

Why are the results so mixed? There are a number of potential reasons.

Difficulties in trying to define and measure CSR. When considering ethics and social responsibility, what are we including within this definition? Is the business merely complying with a business code, developed either within the business or by a third party? Such codes essentially state 'what is not acceptable business behaviour', such as taking bribes or pursuing anti-competitive behaviour. Does the understanding of an 'ethical business' go further and entail positive social actions, ranging from giving money to good causes to contributing to particular programmes in which the business has competency? A study by Dahlsrud (2008)[12] identified 37 different definitions of CSR!

Even if a definition can be agreed upon, there are still measurement issues. Much of the information needed to measure CSR is non financial and it is not reported in a standardised way. Studies have used a whole range of different variables, including reputation ratings/indices, content analysis of corporate reports and surveys.

Difficulties in trying to measure firms' performance. The concept of profitability is also contentious, most crucially in respect to the time frame over which the assessment takes place. Linking long-run profitability with an ethical or socially responsible programme is fraught with difficulties. How are all the other factors that influence business performance over the longer term accounted for? How do you attribute a given percentage or contribution to profit to the adoption of a more socially responsible business position? Can it ever be this precise or are we merely left with suggesting that a link exists?

The simultaneous impact of a mix of different motives. In reality, socially responsible investments will be driven by all three views considered above. These have conflicting implications for firms' performance. It would be very difficult to identify if one particular motivation was more important than another in any particular case.

[9]Rodgers, W., Choy, H.L. and Guiral, A. 'Do investors value a firm's commitment to social activities?', *Journal of Business Ethics, 114,* 607–23 (2013).

[10]Peng, C.W. and Yang, M.L., 'The effect of corporate social performance on financial performance: The moderating effect of ownership concentration', *Journal of Business Ethics,123,* 171–82 (2014).

[11]Soana, M.G. 'The relationship between corporate social performance and corporate financial performance in the banking sector', *Journal of Business Ethics, 104,* 133–48 (2011).

[12]Dahlsrud, A. 'How corporate social responsibility is defined: An analysis of 37 definitions', *Corporate Social Responsibility and Environmental Management, 15,* 1–13 (2008).

BOX 20.4   THE BODY SHOP

Is it 'worth it'?

The Body Shop shot to fame in the 1980s. It stood for environmental awareness and an ethical approach to business. But its success had as much to do with what it sold as what it stood for. It sold natural cosmetics, Raspberry Ripple Bathing Bubbles and Camomile Shampoo, products that were immensely popular with consumers.

Its profits increased from a little over €1.7 million in 1985 to €65.3 million in 2014. Sales, meanwhile, grew even more dramatically over the same period from €8.4 million to €873.4 million. By the end of 2014, the company had over 2800 stores in over 60 countries.

What makes this success so remarkable is that The Body Shop did virtually no advertising. Its promotion largely stemmed from the activities and environmental campaiging of its founder, Anita Roddick, and the company's uncompromising claims that it sold only 'green' products and conducted its business operations with high ethical standards. It actively supported green causes, such as saving whales and protecting rainforests, and it refused to allow its products to be tested on animals. Perhaps most surprising in the world of big business was its high-profile initiative 'trade not aid', whereby it claimed to pay 'fair' prices for its ingredients, especially those supplied from people in developing countries, who were open to exploitation by large companies.

The growth strategy of The Body Shop focused on developing a distinctive and highly innovative product range and, at the same time, identifying such products with major social issues of the day such as the environment and animal rights.

Its initial expansion was based on a process of franchising.

> ... franchising. We didn't know what it was, but all these women came to us and said, 'if you can do this and you can't even read a balance sheet, then we can do it'. I had a cabal of female friends ... and they started opening little units, all called The Body Shop. I just supplied them with gallons of products – we only had 19 different products, but we made it look like more as we sold them in five different sizes![1]

In 1984, the company went public. In the 1990s, however, sales growth was less rapid and, in 1998, Anita Roddick stepped down as chief executive, but for a while she and her husband remained as co-chairs. Sales began to grow rapidly again from 2004 to 2006 from €553 million to €709 million.

Acquisition of The Body Shop by L'Oréal

To the surprise of many people, the French cosmetics giant, L'Oréal, which was 26 per cent owned by Nestlé, purchased The Body Shop in 2016. The event resulted in the magazine, *Ethical Consumer,* downgrading The Body Shop's ethical rating from 11 out of 20 to a mere 2.5 and called for a boycott of the company. Three weeks after the sale, the daily *BrandIndex* recorded an 11 point drop in The Body Shop's consumer satisfaction rating from 25 to 14.

There were a number of reasons for this. L'Oréal's animal-testing policies were in conflict with those of The Body Shop and L'Oréal had been accused of being involved in price fixing with other French perfume houses. L'Oréal's part-owner, Nestlé, had also been subject to various criticisms for ethical misconduct, including the promotion of formula milk to mothers with babies in developing countries and the use of slave labour in cocoa farms in West Africa.

Anita Roddick argued that, by taking over The Body Shop, L'Oréal would have to develop a more ethical approach to business. The company responded by adopting a new Code of Business Ethics in 2007 and gained some external accreditation for its approach to sustainability and ethics. It was ranked as one of the world's 100 most ethical companies by Ethisphere in 2007 and, in 2016, it was again part of this list for the seventh time.

The business set itself three targets as part of its environmental strategy (2005–15), including a 50 per cent reduction in greenhouse gas emissions, water consumption and waste per finished product. It made a donation of £1.2 million to the US Environment Protection Agency to help bring an end to animal testing and, in March 2013, it announced a 'total ban on the sale in Europe of any cosmetic product that was tested on animals or containing an ingredient that was tested on animals after this date'. It also promised that 'By 2020, we will innovate so that 100 per cent of products have an environmental or social benefit'.

Sadly, Anita Roddick died in 2007 and so was not able to witness these changes.

L'Oréal also looked to inject greater finance into the company, aimed at improving the marketing of products. In autumn 2006, a transactional website was launched and there were greater press marketing campaigns. Profits continued to rise in 2006 and 2007 but fell back from €64 million in 2007 to €36 million in 2008 as recession hit the high streets. They fell by a further 8 per cent in 2009, but then grew significantly in the following three years: by 20.3, 4.3 and 13.8 per cent respectively.

However, from 2013 onwards, the financial performance of The Body Shop deteriorated. Profits fell by 38 per cent in 2016 to just €34 million, with sales falling by 5 per cent. In June 2017, L'Oréal announced that it had agreed to sell The Body Shop for €1 bn (£877m) to Natura Cosmeticos, the largest Brazilian cosmetics business. Natura was awarded 'B corp' status[2] in 2014 as it met certain standards for environmental performance, accountability and transparency. Commenting on the purchase of The Body Shop, the co-chair of Natura's board said:

> The complementarity of our international footprints, the sustainable use of biodiversity in our products, a belief in ethics in management and fair relations with communities and a high degree of innovation constitutes the pillars of the journey on which we are now embarking.

It will be interesting to see if The Body Shop's performance significantly improves under new ownership.

1. *What assumptions has The Body Shop made about the 'rational consumer'?*
2. *How has The Body Shop's economic performance been affected by its attitudes towards ethical issues? (You could do an Internet search to find further evidence about its performance and the effects of its sale to L'Oréal and then Natura Cosmeticos.)*

---

[1] Anita Roddick interview, Startups.co.uk

[2] Companies awarded B Corps status are certified by the non-profit B Lab as meeting rigorous standards of social and environmental performance, accountability, and transparency, see: https://bcorporation.uk/about-b-corps.

SUMMARY

1. Government intervention in the market sets out to attain two goals: social efficiency and equity. Social efficiency is achieved at the point where the marginal benefits to society for either production or consumption are equal to the marginal costs of either production or consumption. Issues of equity are difficult to judge due to the subjective assessment of what is, and what is not, a fair distribution of resources.

2a. Monopoly power will (other things being equal) lead to a level of output below the socially efficient level. It will lead to a deadweight welfare loss: a loss of consumer plus producer surplus.

2b. Externalities are spillover costs or benefits. Whenever there are external costs, the market will (other things being equal) lead to a level of production and consumption above the socially efficient level. Whenever there are external benefits, the market will (other things being equal) lead to a level of production and consumption below the socially efficient level.

2c. Public goods will be underprovided by the market or, in the case of pure public goods, will not be provided at all. The problem is that they have large external benefits relative to private benefits and, without government intervention, it would not be possible to prevent people having a 'free ride' and thereby escaping contributing to their cost of production.

2d. Ignorance and uncertainty may prevent people from consuming or producing at the levels they would otherwise choose. Information may sometimes be provided (at a price) by the market, but it may be imperfect; in some cases, it may not be available at all.

2e. Markets may respond sluggishly to changes in demand and supply. The time lags in adjustment can lead to a permanent state of disequilibrium and to problems of instability.

2f. In a free market, there may be inadequate provision for dependants and an inadequate output of merit goods.

3a. Taxes and subsidies are one means of correcting market distortions. They can be used to affect monopoly price, output and profit. Subsidies can be used to persuade a monopolist to increase output to the competitive level. Lump-sum taxes can be used to reduce monopoly profits without affecting price or output.

3b. Externalities can be corrected by imposing tax rates equal to the size of the marginal external cost and granting rates of subsidy equal to marginal external benefits.

3c. Taxes and subsidies have the advantages of 'internalising' externalities and of providing incentives to reduce external costs. On the other hand, they may be impractical to use when different rates are required for each case or when it is impossible to know the full effects of the activities that the taxes or subsidies are being used to correct.

3d. An extension of property rights may allow individuals to prevent others from imposing costs on them. This is not practical, however, when many people are affected to a small degree or where several people are affected but differ in their attitudes towards what they want doing about the 'problem'.

3e. Laws can be used to regulate activities that impose external costs, to regulate monopolies and oligopolies and to provide consumer protection. Legal controls are often simpler and easier to operate than taxes and are safer when the danger is potentially great. However, they tend to be rather a blunt weapon.

3f. Regulatory bodies can be set up to monitor and control activities that are against the public interest (e.g. anti-competitive behaviour of oligopolists). They can conduct investigations of specific cases, but these may be expensive and time-consuming and may not be acted on by the authorities.

3g. The government may provide information in cases where the private sector fails to provide an adequate level. It may also provide goods and services directly. These could be either public goods or other goods where the government feels that provision by the market is inadequate. The government could also influence production in publicly owned industries.

4a. Government intervention in the market may lead to shortages or surpluses; it may be based on poor information; it may be costly in terms of administration; it may stifle incentives; it may be disruptive if government policies change too frequently; it may not represent the majority of voters' interests if the government is elected by a minority, if voters did not fully understand the issues at election time or if the policies were not in the government's manifesto; it may remove certain liberties.

4b. By contrast, a free market leads to automatic adjustments to changes in economic conditions; the prospect of monopoly/oligopoly profits may stimulate risk taking and hence research and development and innovation, and this advantage may outweigh any problems of resource misallocation; there may still be a high degree of actual or potential competition under monopoly and oligopoly.

5a. More and more companies are adopting broader societal goals beyond simple profit maximisation. Such an approach is known as corporate social responsibility (CSR)

5b. Many of the CSR activities undertaken by firms can be grouped under four broad headings: environmental activities, contributing to good causes, fair and ethical treatment of employees and fair and ethical treatment of suppliers.

5c. There are three broad views on the role of CSR: the insider-initiated philanthropy or the classical view, where CSR is seen as inappropriate, with any market imperfections best tackled by government; the delegated philanthropy view, where managers should respond to the interests and views or a range of stakeholders, rather than simply focusing on profit; and the overcoming short-termism view, where managers should take a longer-term perspective and look to the long-term health of the company and its stakeholders.

5d. It is difficult to measure the precise impact of CSR on firms' performance because: it is difficult to define and measure CSR; it is difficult to measure firms' performance; CSR may be motivated by different views on its role.

1   Assume that a firm discharges waste into a river. As a result, the marginal social costs (*MSC*) are greater than the firm's marginal (private) costs (*MC*). The following table shows how *MC, MSC, AR* and *MR* vary with output.

Output	1	2	3	4	5	6	7	8
MC(£)	23	21	23	25	27	30	35	42
MSC(£)	35	34	38	42	46	52	60	72
TR(£)	60	102	138	168	195	219	238	252
AR(£)	60	51	46	42	39	36.5	34	31.5
MR(£)	60	42	36	30	27	24	19	14

   a)   How much will the firm produce if it seeks to maximise profits?

   b)   What is the socially efficient level of output (assuming no externalities on the demand side)?

   c)   What is the marginal external cost at this level of output?

   d)   What size tax would be necessary for the firm to reduce its output to the socially efficient level?

   e)   Why is the tax less than the marginal externality?

   f)   Why might it be equitable to impose a lump-sum tax on this firm?

   g)   Why will a lump-sum tax not affect the firm's output (assuming that in the long run the firm can still make at least normal profit)?

2   Assume that a market is perfectly competitive and that at low levels of demand the consumption of the good generates no external costs or benefits (e.g. consuming alcohol). However, once a certain level of consumption is reached (Q*), consumption of any additional units results in rising marginal external costs. Draw a diagram to illustrate the impact of these external costs on the economic efficiency of the market. Clearly indicate any deadweight welfare loss.

3   Name some goods or services provided by the government or local authorities that are not public goods.

4   Illustrate the impact of a negative externality in production on a pure monopoly. What implications does this have for government intervention?

5   Draw a diagram to illustrate why the use of the market might lead to the overconsumption of natural resources.

6   Where would you place each of the following in Figure 20.7: (a) hamburgers; (b) a fire service in a rural area; (c) a TV subscription service, such as Netflix or Amazon Prime.

7   Assume that you wanted the information given in (a)–(g) below. In which cases could you: (i) buy perfect information; (ii) buy imperfect information; (iii) be able to obtain information without paying for it; (iv) not be able to obtain information?

   a)   Which tablet/computer is the most reliable?

   b)   Which of two jobs that are vacant is the most satisfying?

   c)   Which builder will repair my roof most cheaply?

   d)   Which builder will make the best job of repairing my roof?

   e)   Which builder is best value for money?

   f)   How big a mortgage would it be wise for me to take out?

   g)   What course of higher education should I follow?

      In which cases are there non-monetary costs to you of finding out the information? How can you know whether the information you acquire is accurate or not?

8   List the different types of information a firm might want to know and consider whether (a) it could buy the information and (b) how reliable that information might be.

9   Why might it be better to ban certain activities that cause environmental damage rather than to tax them?

10   Consider the advantages and disadvantages of extending property rights so that everyone would have the right to prevent people imposing any costs on them whatsoever (or charging them to do so).

11   How suitable are legal restrictions in the following cases?

   a)   Ensuring adequate vehicle safety (e.g. that tyres have sufficient tread or that the vehicle is roadworthy).

   b)   Reducing traffic congestion.

   c)   Preventing the use of monopoly power.

   d)   Ensuring that mergers are in the public interest.

   e)   Ensuring that firms charge a price equal to marginal cost.

12   Evaluate the following statement: 'Despite the weaknesses of a free market, the replacing of the market by the government generally makes the problem worse.'

13   In what ways might business be socially responsible?

14   Is it in the interests of society for firms to invest heavily in CSR activities?

Government and the firm

Business issues covered in this chapter

- How do governments attempt to prevent both the abuse of monopoly power and collusion by oligopolists through competition policy?
- How effective is competition policy?
- Why does a free market fail to achieve the optimal amount of research and development?
- What can the government do to encourage technological development and innovation?
- Why is training so important for a country's economic performance?
- Why do governments pursue a training policy and not just leave it to employers?
- How do training policies differ between countries?

KI 36
p 376 In this chapter, we shall consider the relationship between government and the individual firm. This relationship is not simply one of regulation and control, but can involve the active intervention of government in attempting to improve the economic performance of business. We shall consider government attitudes and policy towards enhancing research and technology, and training, as well as the more punitive area of business regulation through the use of legislation on the abuse of market power, collusion and mergers.

21.1 COMPETITION POLICY

Competition, monopoly and the public interest

KI 21
p 184 Most markets in the real world are imperfect, with firms having varying degrees of market power. Will they use this power in ways that is not in the public interest? This question has been addressed by successive governments in framing legislation to deal with monopolies and oligopolies.

It might be thought that market power is always 'a bad thing', certainly as far as the consumer is concerned. After all, it enables firms to make supernormal profit, thereby 'exploiting' the consumer. The greater the firm's power, the higher prices will be relative to the costs of production. Also, a lack of competition removes the incentive to become more efficient.

But market power is not necessarily a bad thing. Firms may not fully exploit their position of power – perhaps for fear that very high profits eventually would lead to other firms overcoming entry barriers, or perhaps because they are not aggressive profit maximisers. Even if they do make large supernormal profits, they may still charge a lower price than more competitive sectors of the industry because of their economies of scale. Finally, they may use their profits for research and development and for capital investment. The consumer might then benefit from improved products at lower prices.

Competition policy could seek to ban various structures. For example, there could be restrictions on mergers leading to newly combined firms having market shares above a certain level. Most countries, however, prefer to focus on whether the *practices* of particular monopolists or oligopolists are anti-competitive. Some of these practices may be made illegal, such as price fixing by oligopolists; others may be assessed on a case-by-case approach to determine whether or not they should be permitted. Such an approach does not presume that the mere possession of market power is against the public interest, but rather that certain uses of that power may be.

Pause for thought

Try to formulate a definition of 'the public interest'.

The three broad areas of competition policy

There are three broad areas of competition policy

Abuse of the existing power of monopolies and oligopolies: monopoly policy

Monopoly policy seeks to prevent firms from abusing a dominant market position, i.e. misusing their economic power. Although it is referred to as 'monopoly' policy, it also applies to large oligopolists facing very limited competition. Once a position of dominance has been identified, the competition agencies usually weigh up the gains and losses to the public of the firm's behaviour.

As we saw in Figure 11.6 (on page 195), faced with the same cost curves as an industry under perfect competition, a monopoly will charge a higher price, produce a lower output and make a larger profit. This is called an *exploitative abuse* – a business practice that directly harms the customer. Other examples include reductions in product quality, limited product ranges and poor levels of customer service. However, a monopolist may achieve substantial economies of scale, with lower costs and a price below the competitive price. It may also retain profits for investment and research and development (R&D). This may result in better products and/ or lower prices.

However, governments (or regulatory authorities, if separate from the government) have tended to avoid investigating allegations of exploitative abuses because of the challenges involved with accurately identifying and correcting for this type of behaviour. For example, measuring the mark up of price over costs is very difficult in reality and requires the processing of large amounts of complex information supplied by the firm involved. Regulating prices is also a complicated process. Therefore price regulation tends to be left to cases of natural monopoly (i.e. the privatised utilities) which have specific regulators – see chapter 22 for more details. For these reasons, competition agencies tend to focus on investigating allegations of *exclusionary abuses*.

Exclusionary abuses. These are business practices that limit or prevent effective competition from either actual or potential rivals. Exclusionary abuses may be a necessary condition before firms can implement the more direct exploitative abuses. A business that successfully limits or prevents competition today may be able to charge higher prices in the future.

Some of the more frequently cited examples of exclusionary abuses in competition cases include:

- *Exclusivity rebates/discounts.* Customers are offered special deals if they agree to make 'all or most' of their purchases of the product from the dominant firm. See Box 21.1 for some interesting real world examples.
- *Tying.* This is where a firm controlling the supply of a first product (the tying product) insists that its customers buy a second product (the tied product) from it rather than from its rivals. One of the most famous cases of tying was Microsoft's decision to include its media player and Web browser (Internet Explorer) with the sale of its Windows operating system. In 2004, the European competition authorities judged that this was an abuse of a dominant market position.
- *Predatory pricing.* Prices are set by a dominant firm below its average variable costs with the sole intent of driving its competitor(s) out of business. One famous case was that of AKZO Chemie BV, which was found guilty of abusing its dominant position in the organic peroxides market by selectively cutting prices below cost.
- *Refusal to supply and margin squeeze.* This occurs where a vertically integrated firm has a dominant position in an upstream market (e.g. components) but faces competition in later stages of the production process (e.g. assembly). If competitors in the downstream market are completely reliant on the supply of some input from the dominant firm in the upstream market, then the dominant firm could *refuse to supply* them. Its aim would be to drive them out of business, thereby giving it a dominant position in the downstream market. A more subtle approach for the dominant firm would be to charge high prices for the input so that its rivals are unable to cover their costs and go out of business. This is called *margin squeeze*.

Definitions

Exploitative abuse Business practices that directly harm the customer. Examples include high prices and poor quality.

Exclusionary abuses Business practices that limit or prevent effective competition from either actual or potential rivals.

Tying Where a firm is prepared to sell a first product (the tying good) only on the condition that its consumers buy a second product from it (the tied good).

Margin squeeze Where a vertically integrated firm with a dominant position in an upstream market deliberately charges high prices for an input required by firms in a downstream market to drive them out of business.

■ *Vertical restraints.* This is where a supplying firm imposes conditions on a purchasing firm (or *vice versa*). For example, a manufacturer may impose rules on retailers about displaying the product or the provision of after-sales service or it may refuse to supply certain outlets (e.g. perfume manufacturers refusing to supply discount chemist shops).

> **Pause for thought**
>
> *Are all such business practices necessarily against the interests of consumers?*

The growth of market power through mergers and acquisitions: merger policy

Competition authorities typically have powers to control merger and acquisition (M&A) activity. In many cases, M&As are beneficial for consumers and the economy as a whole as the newly combined firms may be able to rationalise and reduce costs. For example, central services such as finance and human resources can be consolidated. Greater financial strength may allow the merged firm to drive down the prices charged by its suppliers and the combined profits may allow larger-scale investment and R&D.

However, in some cases, M&As result in significant reductions in competition. This may lead to the newly combined firm abusing its dominant position in the market. Also, by reducing the number of firms, M&As may increase the chances of collusion.

Most competition authorities carry out a relatively quick initial review of M&As and clear the majority of cases where the impact on competition is judged to be negligible. When the potential impact on competition is more serious, the authorities carry out a more detailed investigation to see whether the potential benefits of the merger outweigh the costs. In only a few cases, the M&A is actually prohibited.

Collusion: restrictive practice policy

In most countries, the approach towards oligopolistic collusion, known as *restrictive practices*, tends to be more prohibitive than for mergers and monopoly power. This is because it is far less likely that agreements to restrict, limit or prevent competition will ever be in the interests of society. Typically, they lead to higher joint profits for the firms and higher prices for the customer.

Examples of restrictive practices that are commonly cited in competition cases include:

■ *Horizontal price fixing.* These are direct or indirect agreements between rival firms to fix prices above competitive levels. There are a number of different ways that firms can make price agreements:
  – Set a minimum level below which prices will not be reduced.
  – Adhere to a published price list.

  – Increase prices by a fixed absolute or percentage amount.
  – Charge customers the same amount for delivery.
  – Pass on all the additional costs of extra regulations in higher prices.
■ *Market sharing.* These are agreements on how to distribute markets or customers between the firms. This could be done by geographical area, type of product or type of customer. For example, two or more supermarket chains could agree to open only one supermarket in each district.
■ *Limit production.* Firms agree quotas on how much each should produce.
■ *Bid rigging.* In response to a call for tenders, firms agree to discuss bids with one another rather than submitting them independently. One or more of them may agree not to submit a bid, withdraw a bid or submit a bid at an artificially high price.
■ *Information sharing.* Firms share sensitive information with one another, such as future plans on pricing, product design and output.

> **Pause for thought**
>
> *Are all such agreements necessarily against the interests of consumers?*

Banning formal cartels is relatively easy. Preventing tacit collusion is another matter. It may be very difficult to prove that firms are making informal agreements behind closed doors.

Competition policy in the European Union

Relevant EU legislation is contained in Articles 101 and 102 of the 2009 Treaty of the Functioning of the European Union (TFEU). Additional regulations covering mergers came into force in 1990 and were amended in 2004. Further minor amendments have since been introduced and many of these focus on specific market regulations.

Article 101 is concerned with restrictive practices and Article 102 with the abuse of market power. The Articles focus on firms trading between EU members and so do not cover monopolies or oligopolies operating solely within a

> **Definitions**
>
> **Vertical restraints** Conditions imposed by one firm on another which is either its supplier or its customer.
>
> **Restrictive practices** Where two or more firms agree to engage in activities that restrict competition.
>
> **Bid rigging** Where two or more firms secretly agree on the prices they will tender for a contract. These prices will be above those that would have been submitted under a genuinely competitive tendering process.

member country. They are implemented by the European Commission (EC), which monitors compliance, investigates behaviour and imposes fines where unlawful conduct is identified.

Firms can appeal against EC judgments to the *General Court* – formerly known as the *Court of First Instance*. The General Court has the power to overturn decisions made by the EC and is able to amend the size of any fines. The EC and/or the firms involved in the case can appeal against decisions made by the *General Court* to the *European Court of Justice*. However, appeals to the *European Court of Justice* can be made only on points of law. See Box 21.1 for an example.

EU restrictive practices policy

Article 101 covers *agreements* between firms, *joint decisions* and concerted *practices* that prevent, restrict or distort competition. In other words, it covers all types of oligopolistic collusion that are judged to be against the interests of consumers.

The legislation is designed to prevent collusive *behaviour* not oligopolistic *structures* (i.e. the simple existence of co-operation between firms). For example, agreements between oligopolists are allowed to continue under Article 101(3). This states that they must meet all of the following conditions: (a) they directly enhance the quality of the good/service for the customer; (b) they are the only way to do so; (c) they do not eliminate competition; (d) consumers receive a fair share of the resulting benefits.

If companies are found guilty of undertaking any anti-competitive practices that are in contravention of Article 101, such as those discussed on page 392, they are ordered to cease the activity with immediate effect and are subject to financial penalties.

Fines. Table 21.1 illustrates the largest fines imposed by the EC on individual businesses involved in cartel activity.

Five of the largest eight fines relate to just one case. The EC ruled in July 2016 and September 2017 that the truck producers MAN, Volvo/Renault, Daimler, Iveco DAF and Scania were guilty of operating a cartel. In particular, they colluded over (a) the factory price of trucks (b) the speed at which new

emission technologies would be introduced and (c) how the compliance costs of stricter EU emissions rules would be passed onto to their customers.

What determines the size of these fines? The size of the initial fine imposed on an organisation depends on a number of factors including:

- the size of its annual sales affected by the anti-competitive activities – referred as the 'relevant sales';
- its market share/the combined market share of all the participating firms and the geographical area of the affected sales;
- the length of time the firm has engaged in the anti-competitive activities: i.e. how many years and months;
- whether it has been found guilty of engaging in anti-competitive practices in the past;
- whether it initiated the formation of the cartel: i.e. been the ring leader.

Fines are also capped and cannot be greater than 10 per cent of a firm's annual total turnover.

> ## Pause for thought
>
> *Why do you think the EC imposed such large fines in the case of the truck producers?*

Reducing fines through co-operation with Commission. The size of the initial or basic fine can be reduced if members of a cartel provide information that helps the Commission with its investigations. Such firms would be granted a 'Leniency Notice'. To qualify, they have to provide information about cartel meetings and details of how the anti-competitive practices operated. The first company to supply this type of information can be granted full immunity (Type 1A leniency) if its co-operation brings the case to the Commission's attention. If the case is already being investigated, the first company to provide detailed information could *possibly* receive full immunity at the discretion of the Commission (Type 1B leniency). In the truck manufacturing case, MAN was awarded full immunity under Type 1A leniency as it had

Table 21.1	Highest EC cartel fines per firm		
Year	**Firm**	**Case**	**Amount in €**
2016	Daimler	Trucks	1 008 766 000
2017	Scania	Trucks	880 523 000
2016	DAF	Trucks	752 679 000
2008	Saint-Gobain	Car glass	715 000 000
2012	Philips	TV/computer monitor tubes	705 296 000
2012	LG Electronics	TV/computer monitor tubes	687 537 000
2016	Volvo/Renault	Trucks	670 448 000
2016	Iveco	Trucks	494 606 000

revealed the existence of the cartel to the Commission in the first place and so did not have to pay a fine.

Other companies supplying information can be given reduced fines (Type 2 leniency). The second company to come forward with this type of information can receive a reduction of up to 50 per cent, the third of up to 30 per cent and any firm after this of up to 20 per cent. In the truck producers case, Volvo/Renault, Daimler and Iveco were granted reductions of 40, 30 and 10 per cent respectively under Leniency Notices.

Firms can receive a further 10 per cent reduction if they accept the Commission's decision and the financial penalties imposed on them. This is referred to as a Settlement. By speeding up the final decision process, it can reduce administrative costs and avoid the legal costs of any possible appeals. Volvo/Renault, Daimler, Iveco and DAF were all granted 10 per cent reductions. However, Scania maintained its innocence and opted not to reach a Settlement agreement. This meant that the investigation into its behaviour took another 14 months to conclude. Finally, in September 2017, the EC announced that it had found the business guilty of colluding with the other five truck producers and imposed a fine of €880 million. Given its lack of co-operation, Scania was not entitled to a 10 per cent reduction in the size of the fine.

EU monopoly policy

Article 102 relates to the abuse of market power and has also been extended to cover mergers. The implementation of the policy follows a two-stage process.

First, the EC has to define the relevant market: i.e. identify which products and suppliers are close substitutes for one another. Then it has to decide if the firm has a dominant position in this market. To do so, it looks at factors such as market shares, the position of competitors, the bargaining strength of customers, measures of profitability and the existence of any significant barriers to entry.

Second, if the evidence confirms that the firm does have a dominant position, the EC then assesses whether the firm is using its market power to restrict competition. As previously discussed, the focus tends to be on exclusionary as opposed to exploitative abuses of power.

If a business is found guilty of engaging in exclusionary abuses that contravene Article 102 (such as those discussed on pages 391–2), they are ordered to cease the activities with immediate effect and are subject to financial penalties.

The fines for any infringements of Article 102 are calculated in a very similar manner to those for infringements of Article 101. There is also some guidance on how a dominant firm can defend its behaviour on efficiency grounds. The business has to prove that its conduct meets all of the following conditions:

- Any efficiencies are the direct result of the exclusionary conduct.

- The same efficiencies could not be achieved by the firm engaging in different behaviour that is less anti-competitive.
- The efficiencies produced by the exclusionary conduct outweigh any of its negative effects.
- The conduct does not result in the removal of all or most of the competition in the market.

EU merger policy

Under current regulations (2004), M&As are prohibited if they significantly impede effective competition in the EU (the 'SIEC' test). This could occur through individual dominance (the M&A leads to a strengthening in the market power of one firm) or through collective dominance (the reduction in the number of firms following the M&A makes collusion likely).

Therefore, the EU investigates 'large' mergers that have an 'EU dimension'. A merger is judged as having an 'EU dimension' when no more than two-thirds of each firm's EU-wide business is conducted in a single member state. If a firm does conduct more than two-thirds of its business in one country, then investigation of the merger would be the responsibility of that member state's competition authority.

Thresholds. M&As are deemed 'large' if they exceed one or other of two turnover thresholds.

The first threshold is exceeded if (a) the firms involved have combined worldwide sales greater than €5 billion and (b) at least two of the firms individually have sales of more than €250 million within the EU.

The second threshold is exceeded if (a) the firms involved have combined worldwide sales of more than €2.5 billion; (b) in each of at least three Member States, combined sales of all firms involved are greater than €100 million; (c) in each of the three Member States, at least two of the firms each have domestic sales greater than €25 million; and (d) EU-wide sales of each of at least two firms is greater than €100 million.

If either of these thresholds is exceeded and the merger or acquisition is judged to have an EU dimension, then formal notification of the intention has to be made by the firms to the European Commission. There were 380 notifications in 2017 and the figure has been around 300 per year since 1998.

Investigations. Once a notification is made, the Commission must carry out a preliminary investigation (Phase 1), which is normally completed within 25 working days. At the end of Phase 1, the majority of cases (over 90 per cent) are usually settled and the merger is either allowed to proceed unconditionally or subject to certain conditions being met. These conditions usually relate to the sale of some of the assets of the newly formed business.

In a small number of cases, competition concerns are raised at the end of Phase 1 and a decision is made to refer the proposed merger to a formal, in-depth investigation

BOX 21.1 EXPENSIVE CHIPS OR ARE THEY?

Some of the biggest fines in EU monopoly policy history

Intel

In May 2004, the European Commission (EC) launched a formal investigation into the business conduct of Intel following a number of objections submitted by Advanced Micro Devices. These complaints focused on the behaviour of Intel in the market for microprocessors. These computer chips, also known as Central Processing Units (CPUs), are the most important hardware component in the manufacture of computers. AMD argued that Intel had used its dominance in this market to act in ways that contravened Article 102 of the Treaty on the Functioning of the European Union (TFEU).

EU monopoly policy follows a two-stage process and is similar to the approach adopted by most national competition agencies such as the Competition and Markets Authority in the UK.

Stage 1

The first element in stage one of the policy is the identification of the relevant market. After its analysis, the EC concluded that the relevant geographical market was global while the relevant product market was x86 CPUs.

Having identified the relevant market, the next phase of stage one is to assess whether the firm has a dominant position. This involves looking at a number of factors such as market shares, the position of competitors, barriers to entry/expansion and measures of profitability.

Data indicated that Intel's share of the x86 CPU market was approximately 70 per cent or more over the whole six-year period investigated from October 2002 to December 2007. The EC typically treats market shares of over 50 per cent as one important indicator of market power. The competition authorities also found evidence of substantial barriers to entry. In particular, the production of CPUs requires considerable sunk investments in R&D, manufacturing facilities and branding. They noted that no new businesses had entered the market in the previous 10 years, while a number had exited. This left Intel with only one significant rival – AMD. All of this evidence led the EC to conclude that Intel did have a dominant position in the market for x86 CPUs.

Having a dominant position is not in itself unlawful under Article 102. However, the legislation does state that firms in a dominant position have a special responsibility not to abuse their market power by restricting competition either in the market in which they are dominant or in adjacent markets.

Stage 2

In stage 2 of the investigation, the authorities focus on the behaviour of the firm. Final judgments are made about business practices that are potential examples of market abuse. Intel was found guilty of engaging in the following two activities that were seen as examples of exclusionary abuses.

- Discounts were given to four major computer manufacturers (Dell, Lenovo, HP and NEC) and to the retailer Media-Saturn on the condition that these businesses purchased all or most of their x86 CPUs from Intel.
- Direct payments were made to HP, Acer and Lenovo on the condition that they postponed or cancelled the launch of products containing x86 CPUs manufactured by AMD.

The fine

In 2009, the EC imposed a record fine of €1.06bn.[1] The size of the penalty reflected the fact that the unlawful behaviour affected the sales of x86 CPUs in the whole of European Economic Area (EEA). It was also less than 10 per cent of Intel's annual turnover.

The size of a fine can be reduced if the firm co-operates with the Commission by more than the minimum that is legally required and also terminates the abusive conduct as soon as the Commission intervenes. Neither of these factors were relevant in the Intel case, so no reductions to the fine were applied.

The appeal process

Intel challenged the decision by appealing to the General Court, which, in June 2014, announced that it was upholding the EC's decision.[2] Intel then lodged an appeal against the judgment of the General Court with the European Court of Justice. The company argued that the General Court had failed to examine properly all of its arguments concerning the case and, in particular, the extent to which discounts could restrict competition. In September 2017, the European Court of Justice upheld one of Intel's arguments and so referred the case back to the General Court.[3] At the time of writing (14 years after the investigation began), a final decision by the General Court had yet to be published.

Qualcomm – a similar case

Qualcomm is the world's largest supplier of LTE baseband chipsets for smart phones and tablets. These chipsets enable the devices to connect to mobile networks. In 2011, Qualcomm agreed to make significant payments to Apple on the condition that only Qualcomm chipsets were used in all iPhones and iPads. If Apple launched a device with a chipset from another supplier, such as Intel, the payments would no longer be made.

In January 2018, the EC ruled that this conduct was an abuse of market dominance by Qualcomm as it prevented rival chipset manufacturers from effectively competing in the market. The firm was ordered to pay a fine of €997 million.[4] It immediately announced plans to appeal against the decision in the General Court.

1. What methods are commonly used by competition authorities to define the relevant market? Discuss some of the problems involved.
2. Why might a firm involved in a monopoly case, such as Intel, try to convince the competition authorities to define the relevant market as broadly as possible?
3. Using some examples, explain the difference between exploitative and exclusionary abuse.

[1] 'Commission imposes fine of €1.06bn on Intel', *press release*, European Commission (13 May 2009).

[2] 'Commission welcomes General Court judgment upholding its decision', *press release*, European Commision (12 June 2014).

[3] 'The Court of Justice sets aside the judgment of the General Court', *press release*, Court of Justice of the European Union (6 September 2017).

[4] 'Commission fines Qualcomm 997 milllion for abuse of a dominant market position', *press release*, European Commission (24 January 2018).

(Phase 2). In 2017, seven of the 380 notifications made to the EC proceeded to Phase 2. These investigations normally must be completed within 90 working days or 110 in more complex cases.

At the end of Phase 2 there are three possibilities: (a) the merger is allowed to proceed with no conditions attached; (b) the merger is allowed to proceed subject to certain conditions being met; (c) the merger is prohibited.

Assessment of the process. It has been argued that the EC is too easily influenced by firms, allowing M&As to go ahead with few, if any, restrictions. Indeed, since the current M&A control measures were put in place in 1990, over 6800 mergers have been notified, but only around 250 have been referred to Phase 2 of the process and, of these, only 27 had been prohibited (as of January 2018).

The only merger or acquisition prohibited in 2016 was the proposed acquisition of mobile network operator O2 by Hutchinson (owner of Three). Two M&As were prohibited in 2017. These were (a) the proposed takeover of the cement business Cemex Croatia by the two German companies, HeidelbergCement and Schwenk; and (b) the proposed merger between the London Stock Exchange Group and Deutsche Börse AG.

The small number of prohibited mergers highlights a problem for EU policy makers: there is a trade-off between encouraging competition within the EU and supporting European companies to become world leaders. The ability to compete in *world* markets normally requires companies to be large, which may result in them having monopoly power within the EU.

The EC appears to be taking a tougher stance towards M&A activity under the Competition Commissioner, Margrethe Vestager. For example, deals increasingly are being scrutinised for their impact on innovation as opposed to just the traditional focus on price and product choice. There are also more stringent rules requiring asset sales that are used as a remedy for competition issues that have been raised.

UK competition policy

There have been substantial changes to UK competition policy since the first legislation was introduced in 1948. The current approach is based on the 1998 Competition Act and the 2002 Enterprise Act, together with Part 3 of the 2013 Enterprise and Regulatory Reform Act.

The Competition Act brought UK policy in line with EU policy, detailed above. The Act has two key sets (or 'chapters') of prohibitions. Chapter I prohibits various restrictive practices and mirrors EU Article 101. Chapter II prohibits various abuses of monopoly power and mirrors Article 102. The Enterprise Act strengthened the Competition Act and introduced new measures for the control of mergers.

The 2013 Enterprise and Regulatory Reform Act set up of a new body, The Competition and Markets Authority (CMA), to carry out investigations into particular firms or markets suspected of not working in the best interests of consumers and being in breach of one or more of the Acts. The CMA carries out much of the work that previously was undertaken by the former Office of Fair Trading and the Competition Commission. Firms affected by a CMA ruling have the right of appeal to the independent Competition Appeal Tribunal (CAT), which can uphold or overturn the ruling.

UK restrictive practices policy

The 1998 Competition Act brought UK restrictive practices policy into line with EU policy. In particular, the calculation of fines for anti-competitive behaviour (such as those discussed on page 392) was made comparable to the approach used by the European Commission. A leniency programme was also developed with Type A and B immunity corresponding to EC Type 1A and 1B leniency (see pages 393–4) and Type C immunity corresponding to EC Type 2 leniency. The following two recent cases help to illustrate how UK restrictive practices policy operates.

In March 2017, the CMA published its final ruling on its investigation into anti-competitive practices in the modelling industry.[1] It ruled that five modelling agencies and their trading association were guilty of regularly exchanging information and fixing minimum prices for modelling fees. Fines totalling £1.5 million were imposed on the businesses involved and none of them qualified for either settlement or leniency reductions.

In the same month, the CMA also published its final ruling on its investigation into anti-competitive practices in the supply of furniture products. It found three businesses guilty of market sharing, price fixing and bid-rigging.[2] Thomas Armstrong (Timber) Ltd and Hoffman Thornwood Ltd, admitted their involvement in these activities and were fined a total of £2.8 million. This figure included a 20 per cent reduction as part of the new settlement procedure. The third business, BHK Ltd, was not fined as it received Type A immunity under the CMA's leniency programme.

The biggest difference between UK and EU policy was created with the passing of the 2002 Enterprise Act. This made it a *criminal* offence for individuals to implement arrangements that enabled price fixing, market sharing, restrictions in production and bid-rigging irrespective of whether there are appreciable effects on competition. Convicted offenders can receive a prison sentence of up to five years and/or an unlimited fine. Prosecutions can be brought by the Serious Fraud Office or the CMA.

---

[1] www.gov.uk/cma-cases/conduct-in-the-clothing-footwear-and-fashion-sector.

[2] www.gov.uk/government/news/cma-continues-crackdown-on-cartels.

Assessing the policy. When the 2002 Act was introduced, it was anticipated that it would result in between six and ten prosecutions per year. In reality, the authorities have found the policy more difficult to implement and only four cases were prosecuted between 2002 and 2017 with only two successful outcomes.

In order to address some of the issues, the 2013 Act included a number of legal amendments to try to make it easier for the CMA to bring successful prosecutions against executives involved in cartel behaviour.

UK monopoly policy

The Chapter II prohibition of the 1998 Competition Act closely mirrors Article 102 of the TFEU. Investigations by the CMA follow the same two-stage process to establish whether the firm (a) has a dominant position and, if so, (b) is using its dominant position to carry out either exploitative or exclusionary abuses. Fines are calculated in a very similar manner to the EC and can be up to 10 per cent of worldwide turnover. One difference between UK and EC policy is that the CMA has the power to ban senior managers from serving as a director of a UK company for up to 15 years.

A recent example of an exploitative abuse case occurred in the pharmaceutical sector. In December 2016, the CMA judged that the pharmaceutical manufacturer Pfizer and distributor Flyn Pharma were guilty of charging excessive and unfair prices for the anti-epilepsy drug, Phenytoin Sodium. In September 2012, the price of a 100mg packet of these tablets was increased from £2.83 to £67.50! The CMA imposed a record high fine on Pfizer of £84.2 million.

A similar provisional judgment was made against Concordia in November 2017. The prices for liothyronine tablets, an essential thyroid drug, increased from around £4.46 per packet in 2007 to £258.19 per packet in July 2017.

In common with other competition authorities, UK agencies have tended to focus on behaviour that is alleged to have excluded competitors from the market. For example, in February 2016, GlaxoSmithKline, the manufacturer of the anti-depressant drug Paroxetine, was fined over £37 million by the CMA for making payments to suppliers of non-branded versions of this same drug in return for these businesses delaying their entry into the market.

UK merger policy

The framework for merger and acquisition (M&A) policy is set out in the 2002 Enterprise Act. A merger or acquisition can be investigated by the CMA if the resulting company meets one of two conditions: (a) it has a UK turnover that exceeds £70 million or (b) it has a market share of 25 per cent or above. The CMA's assessment is made solely on competition issues. More specifically, M&As can be prevented if they are likely to result in a substantial lessening of competition (SLC).

The final judgment is left to the CMA, apart from in a few exceptional circumstances when a minister can intervene. This is where the proposed merger or acquisition would have an impact on national security, media plurality or the stability of the financial system. For example, in September 2017, the Secretary of State for Digital, Culture, Media and Sport referred the proposed acquisition of Sky Plc by 21st Century Fox to the CMA because of concerns over the impact of the deal on media plurality. In January 2018, the CMA[3] published its provisional finding that the takeover should be prohibited. However, the final decision rests with the government.

One unusual aspect of UK policy is that there are no obligations on the participating firms to pre-notify the authorities about a merger that meets either of the two conditions. A voluntary notice can be made or the CMA can initiate an investigation following information received from third parties. Typically, around 30 to 40 per cent of merger investigations are instigated by the CMA as no notification had been made by the firms involved.

A merger can also be completed before it has been officially cleared by the CMA. If the CMA then decides to prevent it, the firms face the costs of having to split the business back into two separate entities. The 2013 Act increased the CMA's power to force companies to reverse integration activities undertaken prior to an investigation.

The investigation. In other respects, UK policy is similar to EU policy. The CMA conducts a preliminary or Phase 1 investigation to see whether competition is likely to be threatened. The 2013 Act introduced a statutory deadline of 40 working days to complete Phase 1 of the process.

At the end of this period, the CMA has to decide whether there is a significant chance that the merger would result in a substantial lessening of competition (SLC). Sometimes, the firms involved will offer to take certain actions to help address any competition concerns. These are known as Undertakings in Lieu (UILs) and usually involve commitments to sell some of the assets of the newly formed business.

If SLC issues still remain, the CMA begins Phase 2 of the process, which is a much more in-depth assessment. At the end of this process, if no SLC issues are raised, or if they are addressed by any UILs, the merger is allowed to go ahead.

In 2017/18, only 9 out of 62 Phase 1 cases were referred for a Phase 2 investigation; 37 cases were cleared unconditionally; 12 were cleared after UILs were accepted and 4 other cases were cleared because the market was deemed to be too small (the 'de minimis' condition).

Consider the case of the acquisition of Punch Taverns Holdco (a) Limited by Heineken UK in June 2017. A Phase 1 investigation raised some competition concerns. The deal meant Heineken UK taking over 1895 pubs to add to the 1047 it already owned in its Star Pubs & Bars estate. The CMA investigation identified 33 local areas where this would lead to a substantial lessening of competition between pubs. Before the acquisition was referred for a Phase 2 investigation, Heineken made a UIL to sell off some pubs in each of the 33 areas. The UIL was accepted and the CMA cleared the deal in August 2017.

---

[3] www.gov.uk/government/news/cma-provisionally-finds-foxsky-deal-not-in-the-public-interest.

There is a 24-week statutory time limit for Phase 2 decisions to be made. This can be extended in special circumstances by up to eight weeks. At the end of Phase 2, the CMA makes one of the following decisions:

■ *Unconditional clearance of the merger.* In 2017/18 this happened in 37 out of the 62 cases. For example, in November 2017, the merger of Just Eat and Hungryhouse was cleared after a Phase 2 investigation.[4] These two businesses are web-based food ordering platforms and the CMA concluded that there would still be plenty of competition in the market after the merger from businesses such as Deliveroo, Uber Eats and Amazon.

■ *Conditional clearance subject to the firms taking certain actions that are legally binding.* These are referred to as 'remedies' and typically involve commitments to sell certain parts of the newly merged business. For example, in March 2017, the CMA published its final conclusions following its phase 2 investigation into the acquisition of Wincor by Diebold Nixdorf.[5] These businesses supply customer-operated ATMs (cash machines) and the CMA concluded that the deal would lead to a substantial lessening of competition in this market – there were only three major suppliers before the merger. To remedy these competition concerns, the CMA ordered Diebold Nixdorf to sell either Diebold's or Wincor's UK customer-operated ATM business to a new approved owner. In June 2017, Diebold Nixdorf sold Diebold's ATM business in the UK to Cennox. The CMA accepted this remedy.

■ *Prohibition of the merger.* In the 14 years between 2004/5 and 2017/18 only 10 mergers were prohibited out of the 143 Phase 2 investigations that took place. In October 2016, the takeover of Trayport,[6] a company that produces software for utilities trading, by Intercontinental Exchange was prohibited by the CMA.

Pause for thought

If anti-monopoly legislation is effective enough, is there ever any need to prevent mergers from going ahead?

Assessment of EU and UK competition policy

Most commentators favour the way monopoly policy in both the EU and UK concentrates on anti-competitive practices and their effects rather than simply on the existence of market dominance. Economic power is only a problem when it is abused. If, by contrast, it enables firms to achieve economies of scale or more finance for investment, the result can be of benefit to consumers.

The stricter and more prohibitive approach taken towards restrictive practices also gains widespread approval. The policing and penalties for infringements of Article 101 have become more severe in recent years. For example, the fines imposed by the EC for the period 1990–4 totalled just under €350 million. For the period 2010–14, the figure was over €7.5 billion. The Leniency Notice is also seen as a good way of trying to deal with the problem of uncovering instances of collusion.

Merger policy remains the most controversial area of competition policy, with criticisms that far too many are allowed to go ahead. Specific areas of contention with UK policy are whether: (a) firms should be forced to notify the authorities of proposed mergers and be prevented from undertaking any integration activities until the merger is cleared; (b) there should be a return to a broad public interest test rather than judging mergers purely by their impact on competition.

A review of the whole UK competition regime published in February 2016 by the National Audit Office was critical of the relatively few number of cases investigated. During the period 2012–14, the UK authorities issued enforcement fines of £65 million (in 2015 prices). Over the same period, the German competition authorities issued fines of £1.4 billion. One explanation for this smaller number of cases may be fear of failure by the CMA. Many firms believe that they have a far greater chance of getting infringement decisions overturned in the UK than in other countries. This fear of successful appeals may deter the CMA from beginning the cases in the first place.

At the time of writing, there is some uncertainty about the impact of the UK's exit from the European Union on competition policy. The current system is referred to as a 'One Stop Shop'. Cases are investigated by either the CMA or the EC but not by both of them. If the UK leaves the Single Market, then both the CMA and EC may have to investigate the same cases. This could result in a big increase in the workload of the CMA. Firms may also face a situation where two different agencies are producing contradictory conclusions: i.e. one prohibits while the other clears the same merger.

Pause for thought

If two or more firms were charging similar prices, what types of evidence would you look for to prove that this was collusion rather than coincidence?

---

[4]www.gov.uk/government/news/
  cma-clears-just-eat-hungryhouse-merger.
[5]www.gov.uk/cma-cases/diebold-wincor-nixdorf-merger-inquiry.

[6]www.gov.uk/cma-cases/intercontinental-exchange-trayport-
  merger-inquiry.

The impact of technology, not only on the practice of business but also on the economy in general, is vividly illustrated by the development and use of the Internet. In 1997, worldwide some 40 million people and 25 000 firms used the Internet. By 2017, there were over 3.5 billion users (around 47 per cent of the world's population).

The commercial possibilities of the Internet range from the selling of information and services to global forms of catalogue shopping. The Internet is just one example of how technology and technological change are shaping the whole structure and organisation of business (see Chapter 3 on the flat organisation), the experience of work for the worker, the productivity of business and, hence, the competitive performance of national economies.

If a business fails to embrace new technology, its productivity and profitability will almost certainly lag behind those businesses that do.

It is the same for countries. Unless they embrace new technology, the productivity gap between them and those that do is likely to widen. Once such a gap has been opened, it will prove very difficult to close. Those countries ahead in the technological race will tend to get further ahead as the dynamic forces of technology enhance their competitiveness, improve their profits and provide yet greater potential for technological advance. In other words, the rate of technological advance can have dramatic effects on a country's living standards. This helps to explain why understanding the nature and drivers of technological advance is an important part of the literature on long-term economic growth. So how can countries compete more effectively in the technological race? *Technology policy* refers to a series of government initiatives to affect the process of technological change and its rate of adoption. The nature of the policy will depend on which stage of the introduction of new technology it is designed to affect. Three stages can be identified:

- *Invention.* In this initial stage, research leads to new ideas and new products. Sometimes the ideas arise from general research; sometimes the research is directed towards a particular goal, such as the development of a new type of car engine or computer chip.

- *Innovation.* In this stage, the new ideas are put into practice. A firm will introduce the new technology and, hopefully, will gain a commercial advantage from so doing.

- *Diffusion.* In the final stage, the new products and processes are copied, and possibly adapted, by competitor firms. The effects of the new technology thus spread throughout the economy, affecting general productivity levels and competitiveness.

Technology policy can be focused on any or all of these stages of technological change.

Technological change and market failure

Why is a technology policy needed in the first place? The main reason is that the market system might fail to provide those factors vital to initiate technological change and there are a number of reasons for this, including the following.

R&D free riders. If an individual business can benefit from the results of *other* businesses conducting R&D, with all its associated costs and risks, then it is less likely to conduct R&D itself. It will simply 'free ride' on such activity. R&D spending by one firm, if the results are published, could provide benefits to its rivals (a positive externality in production). As a consequence, it would be in the interest of the firm conducting R&D to keep its findings secret or under some kind of property right, such as a patent, so as to gain as much competitive advantage as possible from its investment.

Although it is desirable to encourage firms to conduct R&D, and for this purpose it may be necessary to have a strict patent system in force, it is also desirable that there is the maximum *social* benefit from such R&D. This would occur only if such findings were widely disseminated. It is thus important that technology policy finds the optimum balance between the two objectives of (a) encouraging individual firms to conduct research and (b) disseminating the results.

Monopolistic and oligopolistic market structures. The more a market is dominated by a few large producers, the less incentive they will have to conduct R&D and innovate as a means of reducing costs or developing innovative new products or experiences for consumers. The problem is most acute under monopoly. Nevertheless, despite a lower incentive to innovate, the higher profits of firms with monopoly power will at least provide a source of finance that might enable them to conduct more research. The problems of having to borrow money to finance R&D are discussed below.

Duplication. Not only is it likely that there is too little R&D being conducted, there is also the danger that resources may be wasted in duplicating research. The more firms there are conducting R&D, the greater the likelihood of some form of duplication. Given the scarcity of R&D resources, any duplication would be a highly inefficient way to organise production.

> ## Definition
>
> **Technology policy** Involves government initiatives to affect the process and rate of technological change.

Risk and uncertainty. Because the payoffs from R&D activity are so uncertain, there will tend to be a natural caution on the part of both the business conducting R&D and (if different) the financier. Only R&D activity that has a clear market potential, or is of low risk, is likely to be considered. It has been found that financial markets in particular will tend to adopt a risk-averting strategy and fail to provide an adequate pool of long-term funds. (This is another manifestation of the 'short-termism' we considered in section 19.4.)

Forms of intervention

Attempts to correct the above market failures and develop a technology policy might include the use of the following.

The patent system. The strengthening of legal rights over the development of new products will encourage businesses to conduct R&D, as they will be able to reap greater rewards from successful R&D investment.

> ### Pause for thought
>
> *Before you read on, can you identify the main forms of intervention the government might use in order to encourage and support R&D?*

Public provision. In an attempt to overcome the free-rider problem and the inefficiency of R&D duplication, government might provide R&D itself, either through its own research institutions or via funding to universities and other research organisations. This is of particular importance in the case of basic research, where the potential outcomes are far less certain than those of applied research.

R&D subsidies. If the government provided subsidies to businesses conducting R&D activity, it would not only reduce the cost and hence the risk for business, but could also ensure that the outcome from the R&D activity is more rapidly diffused throughout the economy than might otherwise be expected. This would help improve general levels of technological innovation.

Co-operative R&D. Given that the benefits of technological developments are of widespread use, the government could encourage co-operative R&D. The government could take various roles here, from being actively involved in the R&D process to acting as a facilitator, bringing private-sector businesses together. The key advantages of this policy are that it will not only reduce the potential for duplication, but also encourage the pooling of scarce R&D resources.

Diffusion policies. Such policies tend to be of two types: the provision of information concerning new technology and the use of subsidies to encourage businesses to adopt new technology.

Other policies. A wide range of other policies, primarily adopted for other purposes, might also influence R&D. These might include: education and training policy; competition policy; national defence policies and initiatives; and policies on standards and compatibility.

Technology policy in the UK and EU

The UK's poor technological performance since 1945 can be attributed to many factors, from a lack of entrepreneurial vision on the part of business to the excessive short-termism of the UK's financial institutions. There also appears to have been a failure on the part of government to initiate suitable strategies to overcome such problems.

In the UK, the attitude towards technology policy has tended to be market-driven, with the role of government relatively limited. More interventionist strategies typically have been kept to a minimum, focusing largely on military and defence technologies. Recent UK governments have looked to provide financial support for R&D by enabling companies to reduce their profits liable to corporation tax by a proportion of their R&D expenditure (see section 31.2).

Despite a sizeable number of UK-based companies regularly making a list of the world's largest R&D-spending companies, the UK's R&D performance compares less favourably when measured relative to GDP. In part, this reflects the limited R&D expenditure by government. But, it also reflects the low R&D intensity across the private sector. In other words, total R&D expenditure by British firms is low *relative* to the income generated by sales (see Box 21.2). Since 1995, UK gross expenditure on research and development as a percentage of GDP has been lower than that of its main economic rivals (see Figure 21.1). For instance, the UK's share of R&D expenditure in GDP typically has been only 72 per cent of that in Germany and only 57 per cent of that in Japan.

As Figure 21.1 shows, the aggregate level of R&D spending across the member states of the EU is relatively low, averaging only 1.75 per cent of GDP since 1995. Member countries, however, have been encouraged to invest 3 per cent of their GDP in R&D (2 per cent private investment, 1 per cent public finding). The principal EU fund for allocating funds for R&D is the *EU Framework for Research and Technological Development*. The budget for the Seventh Framework Programme from 2007 to 2013 was €50.5 billion, while that for the Eighth Framework Programme from 2014 to 2020, 'Horizon 2020', has been raised to €80 billion.

The framework programmes are designed, among other things, to foster collaboration in research, including between academia and industry, to fund frontier science, help develop knowledge and science clusters, provide

Figure 21.1 Gross expenditure on R&D as a percentage of GDP

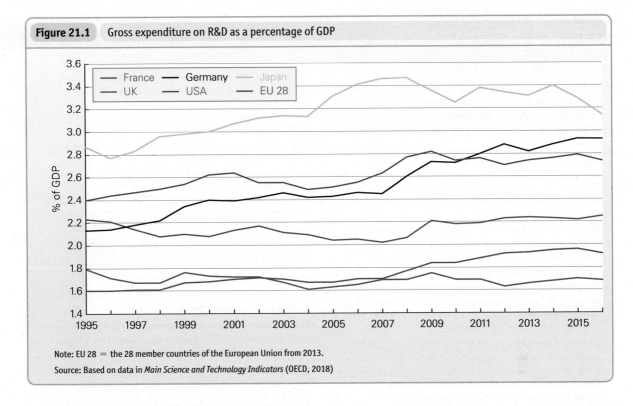

Note: EU 28 = the 28 member countries of the European Union from 2013.

Source: Based on data in *Main Science and Technology Indicators* (OECD, 2018)

scholarships for young researchers and to fund R&D by small businesses. In doing so, the intention is to improve the EU's competitive stance and to promote new growth and jobs.

The hope is that this interventionist approach will raise the productive potential of the wider EU economy not only in the short term, but also in the longer term.

21.3 POLICIES TOWARDS TRAINING

Improvements in training can yield significant gains in productivity. Indeed, the UK's past failure to invest as much in training as many of its major competitors is seen as a key explanation for the country's relatively poor economic performance.

There are various ways in which a government can intervene to influence the amount of training and we discuss various policies later in this section. Public investment in training can be financed through general taxation. Governments in some countries have introduced taxes and levies on firms where the money raised is earmarked for expenditure on training – so-called hypothecated taxes. Examples include France, Denmark and Austria.

But what is the economic rationale for government intervention? Why not leave training to the market? What are the potential sources of market failure?

Economics of the training market

Expenditure on training is an investment in human capital which has short-run costs but generates long-run benefits. These costs and benefits tend to be shared between employers and employees. But these investments will tend to fall below the socially optimal level. To see why the market will provide too little investment in training, it is important to analyse the training decision from the viewpoint of both employees and employers.

Under-investment by employees

Rational employees will pay some of the economic costs of their own training if the discounted value of the long-run economic benefits are greater than the more immediate costs.

How can employees contribute towards the costs? In theory, trainees (or their families) could make direct payments to their employer. Although this was commonplace in the apprenticeship system of the eighteenth and nineteenth centuries, it is rarely observed in modern labour markets. It is far more likely for trainees to pay in a more indirect manner. They do this by accepting wage rates below their productivity while training.

The benefits to the trained employees in the long run are higher wages. These could be earned by either remaining with the businesses that provided the skills or leaving to work for other firms.

BOX 21.2 THE R&D SCOREBOARD

For many years, it has been suggested that the UK's poor international competitive record has been in no small part due to its failure to invest in research and development. The UK's R&D intensity – that is, the ratio of R&D spending to sales – has been considerably lower than most of its main economic rivals.

Each year, the European Union publishes the *EU Industrial R&D Investment Scoreboard*. This report gives details of the R&D expenditures by the top R&D spending companies both in the EU and worldwide. It also investigates emerging trends and patterns in R&D spending.

The data used in the majority of the report are based on the 2500 largest R&D-spending companies in the world. Here we look at some of the patterns that emerge from the 2017 Scoreboard, which is based on data for 2016/17.

The 2500 firms can be grouped into five main categories: in 2016/17, 567 were based in the EU, 822 were based in the USA, 376 were based China, 365 were based in Japan and 370 were from the rest of the world.

A separate part of the report focuses on the top 1000 R&D investing companies based in the EU. Out of these 1000 firms, 290 were based in the UK, 224 in Germany, 108 in France, 82 in Sweden and 46 in the Netherlands.

Geographical concentration

In 2016/17, R&D spending by the world's top 2500 companies was €741.6 billion. This represented an increase of 5.8 per cent over the previous year, which, in turn, was 6.8 per cent more than the year before that. It was the sixth consecutive year the figure had increased significantly.

There were significant geographical differences. The US and EU companies in the sample reported average annual increases of 7.2 and 7 per cent respectively, while those in Japan reported a fall of 3 per cent. The Chinese companies reported a rapid annual growth of 18.8 per cent, while those from the rest of the world reported a more modest growth rate of 2.3 per cent.

The three biggest R&D investing countries in the EU are Germany, the UK and France. Based on 2016 data from the leading 1000 businesses in the EU, German companies spent €76bn, UK companies spent €31bn, while those in France

spent €26bn. The annual growth rates in Germany, the UK and France were 6.7 per cent, 9.2 per cent and 3.4 per cent respectively.

R&D intensity

Across the highest-spending 2500 companies, R&D intensity stood at 4.1 per cent in 2016/17. In other words, the total value of firms' R&D expenditure was equivalent to 4.1 per cent of their sales. The figure for EU companies was 3.5 per cent, which compares unfavourably to the USA, which had a figure of 6.2 per cent. However, it was the same as the figure for Japan and greater than the 2.8 per cent for Chinese firms. The figure for UK companies was 2.9 per cent, which was below the EU average but greater than the 2.6 in France. Germany and The Netherlands both had R&D intensity figures of 4.3 per cent.

R&D by firm and sector

R&D spending is concentrated among a relatively small number of firms. The top 100 companies accounted for 53.1 per cent of the total R&D spending of the 2500 firms in the study.

The table below shows the ranking of the biggest 20 R&D spending companies worldwide. Volkswagen came top of the list, spending over €13.7 billion, with Alphabet (Google) in second place, spending €12.9 billion. The top ranked UK-based companies were AstraZeneca in 22nd place, spending just over €5.3 billion, and GlaxoSmithKline in 38th place, spending €3.9 billion.

The table also illustrates the intensity of R&D, as measured relative to sales. Based on this measure, Intel and Facebook would be first and second with Volkswagen in 15th place.

Investment is also heavily concentrated in the following four sectors, which account for 75 per cent of R&D expenditure by the Scoreboard companies: *ICT producers, Health industries, Automobiles and other transport* and *ICT services*.

Out of the top 20 companies listed in the table, six were in *automobile and parts* (Volkswagen, General Motors, Daimler, Toyota, Ford and Robert Bosch) five were in the *pharmaceutical* and *biotechnology* (Roche, Johnson & Johnson, Novartis, Pfizer and Merck), four were in *software and computer service* (Alphabet, Microsoft, Oracle and

---

What factors might deter or prevent employees from making investments in their own human capital, even when the higher wages are greater than the costs?

- Employees might have imperfect information and underestimate the impact of training on their future earnings.
- Low wages while training may not provide enough income for employees to pay all their living costs (i.e. housing, food and heating), making it necessary to borrow money. However, because of imperfect capital markets, lenders may be unwilling to lend to young people who have limited collateral.

- Imperfect competition in the labour market leads to lower levels of competition among employers for trained employees' labour services. This will increased the likelihood of trained workers earning wages below their productivity.

Pause for thought

Think of some other reasons why employees might be deterred from investing in training even when the discounted value of the higher wages are greater than the costs.

Research and development by firm

Sector	Country	Expenditure (€m)	Intensity (% of net sales)
Volkswagen	Germany	13.7	6.3
Alphabet (Google)	USA	12.9	15.0
Microsoft	USA	12.4	14.5
Samsung Electronics	S. Korea	12.2	7.7
Intel	USA	12.1	21.5
Huawei	China	10.4	19.2
Apple	USA	9.5	4.7
Roche	Switzerland	9.2	19.6
Johnson & Johnson	USA	8.6	12.7
Novartis	Switzerland	8.5	18.2
General Motors	USA	7.7	4.9
Daimler	Germany	7.5	4.9
Toyota Motors	Japan	7.5	3.3
Pfizer	USA	7.4	14.7
Ford Motor	USA	6.9	4.8
Merck US	USA	6.5	17.2
Oracle	USA	5.8	16.3
Cisco Systems	USA	5.7	12.6
Facebook	USA	5.6	21.4
Robert Bosch	Germany	5.6	7.6

Source: Based on data from *2017 EU Industrial R&D Investment Scoreboard*, http://iri.jrc.ec.europa.eu/scoreboard17.
html (European Commission)

Facebook), four were in *technology hardware & equipment* (Intel, Huawei, Apple and Cisco System) and one in *electronics and electrical equipment* (Samsung Electronics). Both of the top-ranked UK companies were in the *pharmaceuticals and biotechnology* sector. The sectors with the fastest growth of R&D investment in 2016/17 were *ICT services* (11.7 per cent) followed by *health* and *ICT producers* (6.9 and 6.8 per cent respectively).

1. What are the economic costs and benefits of R&D spending to the national economy? Distinguish between the short and long run.
2. R&D is only one indicator, albeit an important one, of innovation potential. What other factors are likely to affect innovation?
3. What is the economic case for and against government intervention in the field of R&D?

Under-investment by employers

Similar to employees, rational employers will pay some of the economic costs of training if the discounted value of the long-run economic benefits to them are greater than the more immediate costs. Employers contribute towards the costs of training by paying trainees wages above their net marginal productivity. Net marginal productivity in this context refers to the value of any work activities carried out by the trainee minus the costs of training, such as course fees. The benefits to the firm are the greater profits generated in the long-run.

How do firms earn higher profits from training their employees? Higher profits are earned if the firm is able to retain the trained employees at wages below their productivity. The longer trained employees remain with the firm, and the larger the gap between wages and productivity, the greater this extra profit and the greater the incentive for firms to provide training. However, employers will be reluctant to contribute towards the costs of training if their employees are likely to leave soon after the training is completed.

If trained employees join other firms for higher rates of pay that are still below their productivity, then this is a clear example of a positive externality in production. One firm incurs the costs, while other firms capture some of the benefits: i.e. the extra profit. Often, this is referred to as the 'poaching problem'.

What factors increase the likelihood of trained employees leaving and hence making it difficult for firms to capture any returns on their investments?

- The lower the wage rate paid to trained workers, the more likely they are to find another employer willing to pay them a higher wage.
- The more transferable the skills acquired by employees and the greater the levels of competition in the labour market, the more difficult it is for employers to pay wage rates below productivity and retain trained workers.
- The more transparent the value of the skills acquired by workers are to other firms, the more likely that they will seek to 'poach' such workers. For example, if formal certification of training increases its transparency, trained workers will find it easier to get jobs elsewhere.

Training may also provide wider society-level benefits. It may enable firms to become more innovative by investing in new products and processes. It might also prevent skill shortages and so enable the economy to grow more quickly.

In summary, economic theory suggests a number of reasons why expenditure by employers and employees in the training market may fall below the socially optimal level. It provides a potential rationale for government policies such as (1) providing both employers and employees with more information on the potential benefits of training; (2) introducing government-backed loans for employees who need to borrow to finance their training; (3) paying subsidies to firms that do invest in training, while taxing those who do not; (4) directly providing training in colleges at zero or low cost to students.

Training policy in the UK

Training policy in the UK has gone through numerous initiatives and changes over the last 50 years. The latest in a long line of reviews, the *Report of the Independent Panel on Technical Education,*[7] concluded in 2016:

> Successive UK governments have spent much of the last 50 years tinkering with vocational education. An almost continuous agenda of reform and remodelling has been pursued without a clear vision or sufficient commitment to ensure reforms took root.[8]

Despite all of these initiatives, evidence suggests that the skill levels of workers in the UK remains much lower than those in similar countries. For example:

- The OECD forecasts that, by 2020, the UK will be ranked 28th out of 33 countries for the development of intermediate professional and technical skills among its workforce.[9]

- England and Northern Ireland are ranked in the bottom 4 OECD countries for literacy and numeracy skills of 16 to 24 year olds.
- The incidence of apprenticeships is much lower than in other countries. For example, there are 11 apprentices per thousand employees in England. The figures for France, Austria, Australia and Germany are 17, 33, 39 and 40 respectively.[10]
- The post-secondary technical education sector in England is much smaller than in most comparable countries.

It is often argued that these low skill levels are one of the major reasons why the UK's productivity performance (in terms of output per hour) is so poor. It is approximately 20 per cent below the average in the other G7 countries.

Major initiatives on training policy over the last 50 years can be grouped into three broad areas: vocational/technical qualifications, government-funded training schemes and the institutional bodies tasked with implementing the policies. Some of the more important and recent policy developments in these three areas include the following.

Qualifications

National Vocational Qualifications (NVQs) were launched in 1991. One of the initiative's key objectives was to give employees access to nationally recognised qualifications so they could clearly signal to employers any work-based skills they had acquired. If successful, this would increase the incentives for employees to undertake more training and hence earn higher wages.

The qualifications ranged from level 1 (demonstrating competence in a range of routine activities) through to level 5 (demonstrating competence in complex activities across a wide variety of contexts).

Many employees completed NVQs, but often with very little return. Research by economists found that males with NVQs at level 1 and 2 actually earned 12 to 23 per cent below other males with similar characteristics (apart from not having the qualifications!).[11]

In 2010, the Government commissioned a review of vocational education led by Professor Alison Wolf.[12] Her report concluded that around 350 000 16 to 19 year olds were

[7]David Sainsbury, et al., 'Report of the Independent Panel on Technical Education', GOV.UK (April 2016).

[8] *Ibid.,* p. 23.

[9]Derek L Bosworth and Adam Leech, 'UK Skills Levels and International Competitiveness 2014', UKCES, *Evidence Report 96* (October 2015).

[10]*English Apprenticeships: Our 2020 Vision*, HM Government (December 2015).

[11]L. Dearden, L. McGranahan and B. Sianesi, 'An in-depth analysis of the return to National Vocational Qualifications obtained at Level 2', *CEE Discussion Paper, No.46* (December 2004).

[12]Alison Wolf, *Review of Vocational Education – The Wolf Report,* (GOV.UK, March 2011)

working towards vocational qualifications that were of little value and not recognised by employers. As a result of these findings, the Government started to remove funding for these qualifications.

In July 2016, the Independent Panel on Technical Education[13] published its final report and the Government announced its Post-16 Skills Plan on the same day. A key proposal in this plan is to group together occupations with similar training requirements into 15 different routes. A new T-level qualification will be developed for each of these routes, which should be the equivalent of three A Levels. Employers, professional bodies and education providers will be responsible for developing the content of these new qualifications which should be closely aligned to Apprenticeship Standards.

Interestingly, the review of technical education concluded that competition between different awarding bodies had been harmful, i.e. they had competed against one another by offering easier versions of the same qualification. The Government plans to address this issue by having just one awarding body for each of the new T-level qualifications. Current awarding bodies will be given the opportunity to bid against one another to win an exclusive licence to provide a particular T-level qualification for a given period of time.

Pause for thought

What are the advantages and disadvantages of giving one body an exclusive licence to award a particular T-level or A Level qualification for a given period of time?

Institutional bodies

Learning Skills Councils (LSCs) were established in 2001 and had a budget of over £10 billion. They were responsible for planning and funding training in sixth forms and further education colleges, work-based training for young people aged 16–24, adult and community learning and developing links between education and business.

The LSCs were replaced in April 2010 by two organisations – the Skills Funding Agency (SFA) and the Young People's Funding Agency (YPFA). The SFA took over the role of supporting and allocating government money for training, while the YPFA managed the provision of further education for 16–19 year olds in England. The YPFA lasted only two years before being replaced in 2012 by the Education Funding Agency (EFA).

In April 2017, the EFA and SFA were replaced by the Education and Skills Funding Agency. This new organisation combines the roles of the former SFA and EFA and is responsible for overseeing £63 billion of government funding.

The growing importance of publicly-funded apprenticeships in the UK

Earlier government-funded training schemes

Modern apprenticeships. These were first launched in 1994 with the aim of reversing the decline in apprenticeship numbers which had fallen from 243 700 in 1966 to just 53 000 in 1990. Traditionally, apprenticeships were developed and run by employers. Modern apprenticeships involved far greater levels of government intervention with subsidy payments available to help finance the costs of training that met certain criteria. Publicly-funded apprenticeships will be discussed in far more detail in the next section as they have become the most important part of the UK Government's training policy.

Train to Gain (T2G). T2G was a major programme introduced in 2006, which had the aim of significantly improving the skills of adult workers by subsidising their participation in eligible training programmes. The scheme used public money to pay the course fees and wage costs for employees aged 25 or over who did not have level 2 qualifications (5 GCSEs at grade A–C).

In 2008, it was extended for those workers who did have level 2 qualifications. By 2009, it had financed the training of 1.4 million employees and had a budget of £925 million. Evidence of significant deadweight effects (i.e. financing of training that would otherwise have been funded by employers) led to the programme being abolished in 2010.

Expanding training

Reviews of UK training policy carried out by Lord Leitch (2006),[14] Professor Alison Wolf (2011),[15] Dolphin and Lanning (2011),[16] Doug Richard (2012)[17] and Lord Sainsbury (2016)[18] all agreed on one recommendation – the number of publicly-funded apprenticeships should be increased and the scheme should be significantly reformed.

What is the case for expanding the scheme? Evidence suggests that employees who complete low-level vocational

[14]Lord Leitch, 'Prosperity for all in the global economy - world class skills: final report', *Leitch Review of Skills* (HM Treasury, December 2006).
[15]Op.cit.
[16]Tony Dolphin and Tess Lanning, *Rethinking Apprenticeships*, IPPR (November 2011).
[17]Doug Richard, *Richard Review of Apprenticeships*, GOV.UK (November, 2012).
[18]Op. cit.

[13]Op. cit.

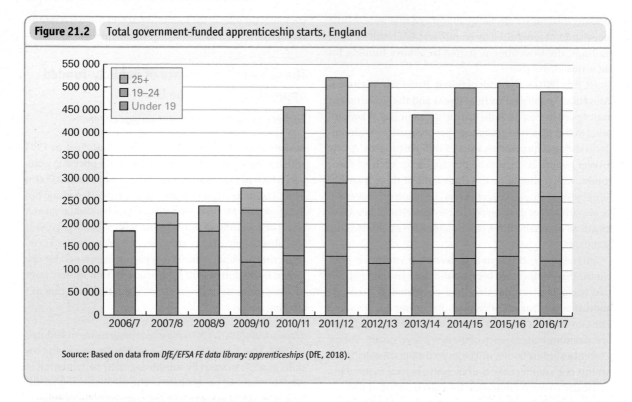

Figure 21.2 Total government-funded apprenticeship starts, England

Source: Based on data from *DfE/EFSA FE data library: apprenticeships* (DfE, 2018).

qualifications as part of an apprenticeship earn higher wages. This contrasts with the experience of those people who complete the same qualifications outside of an apprenticeship. Other arguments are that they (1) improve the transition into work for young people not attending university, (2) encourage employers to engage more fully with the training and (3) help to reduce youth unemployment. Countries with more extensive apprenticeship programmes, such as Germany, Austria and Norway, have much lower rates of youth unemployment than the UK.

Various governments have responded to this recommendation. The number of employees on apprenticeship schemes increased from 175 000 in 2005/6 to 912 200 in 2016/17. Between 2009/10 and 2011/12, the number of apprenticeship starts for those aged 25 and over grew rapidly from 49 000 to 229 000 (see Figure 21.2). Much of this increase was driven by the Government's decision to abolish the Train to Gain programme for adult workers in 2010 and redirect some of the funding into the apprenticeship scheme. In 2015, the Government set itself a target of increasing the number of apprenticeship starts to 3 million by 2020.

What is the case for reforming the scheme? The following are the major criticisms:

■ *The relevance of the training provided.* In traditional apprenticeships, employers play a key role in the design of the schemes, which ensures the training is relevant and highly valued. However, publicly-funded apprenticeships have to meet external requirements, such as an Apprenticeship Framework. These set minimum standards detailing both the training and qualifications the employees should receive. The content, design and assessment of

most Frameworks was determined by Sector Skills Councils, training providers and qualification bodies. Most employers played a very limited role in the whole process. This often led to the development of skills that were not highly valued by employers.

■ *The level of the training provided.* Apprenticeships can be taken at three different levels

— Intermediate – Level 2, equivalent to 5 GCSEs;

— Advanced – Level 3, equivalent to 2 A Levels;

— Higher – Levels 4–7, equivalent to undergraduate and post graduate level.

The level of government funding available to training providers was dependent on a key measure of performance – the proportion of trainees who passed and completed the courses. This type of outcome-based funding gave the training providers an incentive to focus on supplying lower level intermediate apprenticeships: i.e. the qualifications trainees were least likely to fail. As Figure 21.3 clearly illustrates, training providers responded to the funding arrangements in this manner. For most of this period, approximately two-thirds of apprenticeship starts were at Intermediate Level with less than 5 per cent at the Higher Level. The situation improved slightly in 2016/17 with 52 per cent of starts at Intermediate Level, 40 per cent at Advanced Level and 7 per cent at the Higher Level.

■ *The short duration of many of the schemes.* This was a particular issue during the 2010/12 period, when many were completed in less than a year. In some cases, Intermediate Level apprenticeships lasted less than 12 weeks. Typically, they last two years in most European countries.

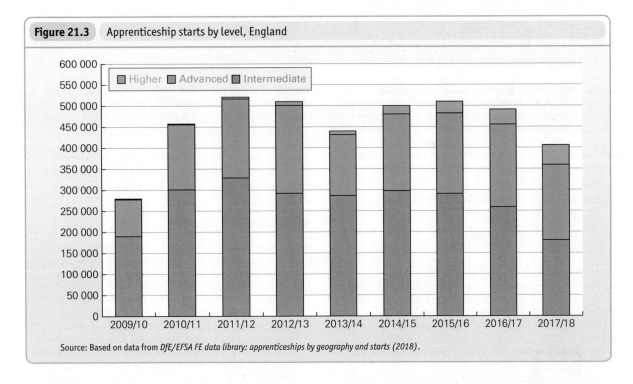

Figure 21.3 Apprenticeship starts by level, England

Source: Based on data from *DfE/EFSA FE data library: apprenticeships by geography and starts (2018)*.

■ *The methods of assessment.* Assessment under an Apprenticeship Framework involved the trainee completing numerous qualifications, of a short duration, on a continual basis throughout the programme. There was no end-point assessment to make sure the trainee could pull together all of the skills they had learned and demonstrate the competences required for a skilled job.

Recent reforms

The UK Government has introduced a number of reforms in response to these criticisms.

In October 2013, the 'Trailblazers' initiative was launched. Trailblazers are a self-selecting group of employers within a sector, who work together to determine the content and assessment of new apprenticeship standards. A Trailblazer group must include representatives from at least 10 different businesses with at least two that employ fewer than 50 people. Sector Skills Councils, training providers and qualification awarding bodies can be involved with the development of the standards but, unlike the Frameworks, they do not take the leading role.

Building on its Trailblazers initiative, the Government launched the Institute for Apprenticeships in April 2017, which replaced the National Apprenticeship Service as the main administrative body for the programme. The Institute for Apprenticeships is an employer-led body responsible for:

■ supporting the development of new Apprenticeship Standards with Trailblazer groups. Apprenticeship Standards will gradually replace the existing system of Apprenticeship Frameworks by 2020;

■ developing and maintaining the criteria for the approval of new Apprenticeship Standards. All Standards must (a)

be in a skilled occupation; (b) require substantial and sustained training, lasting a minimum of 12 months, with at least 20 per cent of the training taking place off-the-job; (c) develop transferable skills, including those in maths and English; (d) lead to full competency in an occupation; and (e) provide training that allows employees to apply for professional recognition where it exists;

■ accepting or rejecting Apprenticeship Standards submitted by Trailblazer groups for approval;

■ advising the government on the maximum level of funding that should be available for each Standard.

The last point refers to changes in the way the system is funded.[19] Large employers in England now have to pay an 'apprenticeship levy' and the money goes into an online apprenticeship service account. The employer can then reclaim this money and use it towards the course fees of their apprentices – this policy is discussed in more detail in Box 21.3. Scotland, Wales and Northern Ireland each have their own devolved system of apprenticeship provision and funding.

Recent changes to the publicly-funded apprenticeship scheme in the UK represent the latest in a long series of policy initiatives that have tried to rectify the long standing skills problem. The introduction of the apprenticeship levy represents one of the biggest interventions in the training market in the last 50 years. It will be interesting to see if this latest set of policy reforms proves to be more successful than any of its predecessors.

[19]www.gov.uk/government/publications/apprenticeship-levy-how-it-will-work/apprenticeship-levy-how-it-will-work.

BOX 21.3 THE APPRENTICESHIP LEVY

The latest attempt to tackle the UK's skills shortage?

The apprenticeship levy was introduced in England in April 2017 and involves much greater levels of government intervention in the financing of training. The Government argues that, without this intervention, employers' expenditure on training will continue to fall below its socially optimal level because of fears over losing trained employees to other firms. In other words, there are positive externalities in production that create a market failure.

It has also proved to be a controversial policy, which is unpopular with many employers.

This box will discuss two key questions: how exactly does it work and what impact will it have?

How exactly does the scheme work?

The apprenticeship levy is a new payment that large employers have to make into an online service account. It is calculated as 0.5 per cent of that part of the employer's annual wage bill that exceeds £3 million. The Government estimated that, in 2017/18, approximately 19 000 employers would have to pay the levy. This is only a small proportion of all employers, as over 98 per cent have an annual wage bill of less than £3 million and so are exempt from the charge. However, the scheme could have a big impact on the labour market as some of the 19 000 organisations are very large employers. Some estimates suggest that 60 per cent of all employees work in an organisation that will have to pay the levy.

In many ways, the levy is an additional tax on employers' wage bills. However, unlike a traditional payroll tax, such as employer national insurance contributions, the firm has up to two years to reclaim the money and use it towards the costs of certain types of training. In particular, it can be used with an additional 10 per cent subsidy from the Government to finance the course fees of employees participating in an approved apprenticeship – known as an Apprenticeship Standard.

All Apprenticeship Standards are allocated to one of 15 new funding bands by the Institute for Apprenticeships. Each one of these funding bands has an upper limit, which ranges from £1500 to £27 000. As long as the agreed course fees for the Apprenticeship Standards are below the upper limits, the levy money and subsidy can be used to contribute towards the costs. Any part of the course fee that exceeds its upper limit has to be paid separately by the employer.

In theory, those large employers who benefit from recruiting trained employees from other firms will now pay the levy but not reclaim any of the money, i.e. they are not paying any training costs. To some extent, this could help to correct for the positive externality in production.

What is the impact on smaller employers who do not pay the levy – those with annual wage bills below £3 million? These businesses are able to claim large government subsidies to pay towards the cost of Apprenticeship Standards. The employer pays 10 per cent of the course fee, while the remaining 90 per cent is financed by the Government. Once again,

any part of the course fee that exceeds the upper limit of the funding band for the Apprenticeship Standard has to be paid separately by the employer without any government support.

The large subsidies should encourage more small- and medium-sized enterprises to invest in training their staff on approved apprenticeships. However, the pay-offs for those that recruit trained workers from other employers remain the same. Therefore, the policy does not address this aspect of the externality.

What will be the other impacts of the scheme?

- *Wages and profits.* If the available Apprenticeship Standards are not suitable for the training requirements of the employer, the levy simply will be an additional cost that reduces its profits. Recently, the skills adviser for the British Retail Consortium stated that some retailers are 'writing the levy off as a tax'. However, as with other taxes, firms may be able to pass some of the costs onto their employees in the form of lower wages. The extent to which they can do this depends on the wage elasticity of demand and supply. In 2015, the Office for Budget Responsibility[1] forecast that, by 2020/21, most of the economic incidence of the levy would be passed onto employees. This would lead to a 0.3 per cent fall in average earnings over the period.
- *Deadweight effect.* Some employers may respond by slightly altering and/or retitling existing training scheme so they meet the criteria of an Apprenticeship Standard and public funding. In this case, taxpayers money is used to finance training that employers otherwise would have funded.
- *Substitution effect.* Some employers may respond by significantly changing the way they train their employees to meet the criteria for public funding. In particular, off-the-job training may be substituted for existing on-the-job training. This distortionary effect might be very damaging if on-the-job training is the most effective way of providing certain skills.

The early response of employers to the scheme has not been promising. Between August 2017 and June 2018 the number of apprenticeship starts was 341 700. This was down from 472 500 (28 per cent) for the equivalent period in 2016–17. At the time of writing, the 3 million target for 2020 seems unlikely to be met.

1. The Government subsidises course fees for qualifications taken by a trainee as part of an apprenticeship. However, course fees represent only one element of the costs of training a worker. What are the other economic costs?
2. Can you think of any other potential effects of the apprenticeship levy in addition to those discussed in the box?
3. Draw a normal form game to illustrate how training financed by employers can be represented as an example of the prisoners' dilemma. Explain how a training levy/tax can change the Nash equilibrium.

Find out how training taxes/levies operate in at least two other countries. Compare and contrast the schemes with the apprenticeship levy in England.

---

[1] 'Economic and Fiscal Outlook - November 2015', Office for Budget Responsibility, p. 47.

SUMMARY

1a Competition policy in most countries recognises that monopolies, mergers and restrictive practices can bring both costs and benefits to the consumer. Generally, though, restrictive practices tend to be more damaging to consumers' interests than simple monopoly power or mergers.

1b European Union legislation applies to firms trading between EU countries. Article 101 applies to restrictive practices. Article 102 applies to dominant firms. There are also separate merger control provisions.

1c UK legislation is covered largely by the 1998 Competition Act, the 2002 Enterprise Act and Part 3 of the 2013 Enterprise and Regulatory Reform Act. The Chapter I prohibition of the 1998 Act applies to restrictive practices and is similar to Article 101. The Chapter II prohibition applies to dominant firms and is similar to Article 102. The 2002 Act made certain cartel agreements a criminal offence and required mergers over a certain size to be investigated. The body, which today conducts investigations under these various Acts, is the Competition and Markets Authority (CMA). It is independent of government.

1d The focus of both EU and UK legislation is on anti-competitive practices rather than on the simple existence of agreements between firms or market dominance. Practices that are found after investigation to be detrimental to competition are prohibited and heavy fines can be imposed, even for a first offence. Since 2008, the EU has operated a streamlined settlement procedure for firms suspected of operating in cartels. Co-operation results in fines being reduced, and firms acting as 'whistle-blowers' can receive immunity from fines.

2a The importance of technology in determining national economic success is growing. There is now a need for government to formulate a technology policy to ensure that the national economy has every chance to remain competitive.

2b Technological change, when left to the market, is unlikely to proceed rapidly enough or to a socially desirable level. Reasons for this include R&D free riders, monopolistic market structures, duplication of R&D activities and risk and uncertainty.

2c Government technology policy might involve intervention at different levels of the technology process (invention, innovation and diffusion). Such intervention might involve extending ownership rights over new products, providing R&D directly or using subsidies to encourage third parties. Government might also act in an advisory/co-ordinating capacity.

2d Technology policy in the UK has tended to emphasise the market as the principal provider of technological change. Where possible, government's role has been kept to a minimum. Within the EU, policy has been more interventionist and a wide range of initiatives have been launched to encourage greater levels of R&D.

3a A well-trained workforce contributes to economic performance by enhancing productivity, encouraging and enabling change and, in respect of supplying scarce skills to the workplace, helps to reduce wage costs.

3b Training policy in the UK has gone through numerous changes in the past 25 years. At times, the level of government intervention has increased and, at other times, training provision has been predominately left to employers. The result of all the changes seems to be a system that delivers less than the optimum amount of training. In other countries, such as Germany, the state plays a far greater role in training provision.

3c The apprenticeship system has become a very important part of the UK Government's policy on vocational training. The number of employees doing an apprenticeship has increased rapidly over the past few years.

REVIEW QUESTIONS

1 What are the possible advantages of a vertical merger?

2 What are the advantages and disadvantages of the current system of controlling restrictive practices?

3 Using competition authority investigations by the EC and CMA, find some real-world examples of the different types of horizontal price fixing discussed in the chapter.

4 Try to find an example of a collective agreement that has been accepted by the European Commission under Article 101(3) TFEU.

5 What turnover thresholds have to be met before a firm has to notify the EC about its intention either to merge with or to acquire a rival?

6 Should governments or regulators always attempt to eliminate the supernormal profits of monopolists/oligopolists?

7 Discuss some of the implications for competition policy if the UK decides to leave the European Economic Area (EEA).

8 We can distinguish three clear stages in the development and application of technology: invention, innovation and diffusion. How might forms of technology policy intervention change at each stage of this process?

9 Governments and educationalists generally regard it as desirable that trainees acquire transferable skills. Why may many employers disagree?

10 If employees leave shortly after they are trained and work for another company for a wage equal to their productivity, is this an example of the poaching problem? Explain your answer.

11 In what circumstances could employers manage to obtain a return on their investment even when their employees leave shortly after a programme of training is completed?

12 Explain the economic rationale for the Advanced Learner Loans (www.gov.uk/advanced-learner-loan) scheme run by the Government.

13 Identify some potential limitations with the latest set of policy initiatives for apprenticeships in the UK.

Government and the market

Business issues covered in this chapter

■ Why is a free market unlikely to lead to environmentally sustainable development?
■ What policies can governments pursue to protect the environment and what are their impacts on business?
■ What determines the allocation of road space?
■ What are the best policies for reducing traffic congestion?
■ What forms has privatisation taken and has it been beneficial?
■ How are privatised industries regulated and how has competition been increased in these industries?

In the previous chapter, we considered examples of the relationship between the government and the individual firm. In this chapter, we turn to examine government policy at the level of the whole market. Although such policies are generally directed at a whole industry or sector, nevertheless, they still affect individual businesses and, indeed, the effects may well vary from one firm to another.

22.1 ENVIRONMENTAL POLICY

Scarcely a day goes by without some environmental issue or other featuring in the news: another warning about global warming; a company fined for illegally dumping waste; a drought or flood blamed on pollution/global warming; smog in some major cities. Also attempts by policy makers to improve the environment are often controversial and hit the headlines: for example, the impact of government climate change policies on the size of people's energy bills.

Why does the environment appear to be so misused and policies that attempt to improve the situation so controversial? To answer these questions, we have to understand the nature of the economic relationship between humans and the natural world.

The environment as a resource

We all benefit from the environment in three ways:

■ as an amenity to be enjoyed;
■ as a source of primary products (food, raw materials and other resources);
■ as a place where we can dump waste.

Unfortunately, these three different uses are often in conflict with each other. For example, we extract and burn fossil fuels, such as coal, oil and gas, for power generation and industrial uses. However, the extraction of these fuels may have a negative impact on the amenity value of the environment. One only has to think of some of the concerns raised by people about the impact of drilling for shale gas on their local communities. The burning of fossil fuels also creates greenhouse gases that are emitted into the atmosphere and cause climate change. Some of the CO_2 gets absorbed into the oceans, which increases their level of acidity and kills marine life.

Policies that try to reduce our current use of the environment as a source of primary products and/or reduce the volume of emissions we generate come at cost. These higher costs are often passed on to consumers in the form of higher prices – an outcome they often dislike and complain about.

The subject of environmental degradation lies clearly within the realm of economics, since it is a direct consequence of production and consumption decisions. So how can economic analysis help us to understand the nature of the problem and design effective policies that will result in the optimal use of the environment? What will be the impact of these policies on business?

Market failures

An unregulated market system may fail to provide adequate protection of the environment for a number of reasons.

Externalities. Pollution could be classified as a 'negative externality' of production or consumption (as we saw in section 20.2). In the case of production, there are marginal external costs (*MEC*), which means that the marginal social costs (*MSC*) are greater than the marginal private costs (*MC*) to the polluter. The failure of the market system to equate *MSC* and marginal social benefit (*MSB*) is due to either consumers or firms lacking the appropriate property rights.

The environment as a common resource. The air, the seas and many other parts of the environment are not privately owned. It is argued that they are global 'commons'. As such, it is extremely difficult to exclude non-payers from consuming the benefits they provide. Because of this property of 'non-excludability' (see page 371–2), the environment often can be consumed at a zero price. If the price of any good or service to the user is zero, there is no incentive to economise on its use.

Many parts of the environment, however, are *scarce*: there is *rivalry* in their use. As people increase their use of the environment, it may prevent other or rival consumers from enjoying it. Overfishing in the open oceans can lead to the depletion of fish stocks (see Case Study H23 on the student website).

Ignorance. There have been many cases of people causing environmental damage without realising it, especially when the effects build up over a long time. Even when the problems are known to scientists, consumers and producers may not appreciate the full environmental costs of their actions. Firms may want to act in a more 'environmentally friendly' manner but lack the appropriate knowledge to do so.

Intergenerational problems. The environmentally harmful effects of many activities are long term, whereas the benefits are immediate. Thus consumers and firms are frequently prepared to continue with various practices and leave future generations to worry about their environmental consequences. The problem, then, is a reflection of the importance that people attach to the present relative to the future.

> ### Pause for thought
>
> *Look through the categories of possible market failings in Sections 8.1 to 8.4. Are there any others, in addition to the four we have just identified, that will result in a socially inefficient use of the environment?*

In order to ensure that the environment is taken sufficiently into account by both firms and consumers, the government must intervene. It must devise an appropriate *environmental policy*.

Such a policy will involve measures to ensure that at least a specified minimum level of environmental quality is achieved. Ideally, the policy would ensure that all externalities are fully 'internalised'. This means that firms and consumers are forced to pay the *full* costs of production or consumption: i.e. their marginal private costs *plus* any external costs. It also needs to make sure that the effects of actions taken by the current generation on the welfare of future generations are fully taken into account when devising policy. For more detail see Box 22.1.

Problems with policy intervention

Valuing the environment

The principal difficulty facing government in constructing its environmental policy is that of *valuing* the environment and, hence, of estimating the costs of its pollution. If policy is based upon the principle that the polluter pays, then an accurate assessment of pollution costs is vital if the policy is to establish a socially efficient level of production.

Three common methods used for valuing environmental damage are: the financial costs to *other* users; revealed preferences; and 'contingent valuation' (or stated preference).

The financial costs to other users. In this method, environmental costs are calculated by considering the financial costs imposed on other businesses or individuals by polluting activities. For example, if firm A feeds chemical waste into

> ### Definition
>
> **Environmental policy** Initiatives by government to ensure a specified minimum level of environmental quality.

BOX 22.1   A STERN REBUKE ABOUT CLIMATE CHANGE INACTION

Economists can offer solutions, but they can't solve the problem

The analysis of global warming is not just for climate scientists. Economists have a major part to play in examining its causes and consequences and the possible solutions. And these solutions are likely to have a major impact on business.

Perhaps the most influential study of climate change in recent times was the Stern Review. This was an independent review led by Sir Nicholas Stern, the then head of the Government Economic Service and former chief economist of the World Bank. Here was an economist using the methods of economics to analyse perhaps the most serious problem facing the world.

> Climate change presents a unique challenge for economics: it is the greatest and widest-ranging market failure ever seen. The economic analysis must therefore be global, deal with long time horizons, have the economics of risk and uncertainty at centre stage, and examine the possibility of major, non-marginal change.[1]

Dealing with long time horizons presents some interesting problems. The benefits to society from acting on climate change today will occur in the future. The problem is that the cost of these policies will be felt today, e.g. higher prices and less consumption. In order to carry out an assessment of environmental policies, the future benefits need to be *discounted* so that they can be compared with the current costs. The problem is in choosing the most appropriate social discount rate. Unfortunately, many economists disagree!

What makes matters worse is that the results obtained from any economic assessment that involve costs and benefits over such a long period of time are very sensitive to the discount rate used. Stern used a relatively low social discount rate, which meant that the future benefits and costs were more highly valued. Other economists criticised the report, claiming that a much higher discount rate should have been chosen.

First the bad news

According to the Stern Report, if no action were taken, global temperatures would rise by some 2–3°C within the next 50 years. As a result, the world economy would shrink by an average of up to 20 per cent. The economies of the countries most seriously affected by floods, drought and crop failure could shrink by considerably more. Rising sea levels could displace some 200 million people; droughts could create tens or even hundreds of millions of 'climate refugees'. Because of the low discount rate used, these future costs were weighted heavily.

Then the good

However, Stern concluded that these consequences could be averted – and at relatively low cost – if action were taken early enough. According to the report, a sacrifice of just 1 per cent of global GDP (global income) could be enough to stabilise greenhouse gases to a sustainable level. To achieve this, action would need to be taken to cut emissions from their various sources (see the chart). This would involve a mixture of four things:

- Reducing consumer demand for emissions-intensive goods and services.
- Increased efficiency, which can save both money and emissions.
- Action on non-energy emissions, such as avoiding deforestation.
- Switching to lower-carbon technologies for power, heat and transport.

As one might expect from a report produced by an economist, the policy proposals focused on altering incentives. This could involve taxing polluting activities; subsidising green alternatives, including the development of green technology; establishing a price for carbon through trading carbon (see section on tradable permits on pages 417–21) and regulating its production; and encouraging behavioural change through education, better labelling of products and encouraging public debate.

Heeding the warnings?

So, nearly 10 years after the Stern Report, how much progress has been made? The OECD is very concerned about the environmental impact on growth and is pressing for a global response. So are national governments therefore acting with urgency?

In 2014, the Intergovernmental Panel on Climate Change (IPCC) issued its *Fifth Assessment Report (AR5)*[2] – the first one had been published in 1990. This major document consists of three working group reports and an overarching synthesis. The first working group looked at the physical science; the second considered impacts, adaptation and vulnerability; while the third focused on mitigation of climate change. Economists contributed substantially to both the second and third groups.

---

[1] 'Stern Review on the Economics of Climate Change, Executive Summary', HM Treasury (2006).

[2] *The Fifth Amendment Report (AR5)*, IPCC (2014).

---

a local stream, then firm B, which is downstream and requires a clean water supply, may have to introduce a water purification process. The expense of this to firm B can be seen as an external cost of firm A.

    The main problem with this method is that not all external costs entail a direct financial cost for the sufferers. Many external costs may therefore be overlooked.

Revealed preferences. If the direct financial costs of pollution are difficult to identify, let alone calculate, then an alternative approach to valuing the environment might be to consider how individuals or businesses change their behaviour in response to environmental changes. Such changes in behaviour frequently carry a financial cost, which makes calculation easier. For example, the building of a new

The report on impact[3] confirmed that the effects of climate change are already occurring on all continents and across the oceans. It concluded that the world is ill-prepared for risks from a changing climate.

As with Stern, it stated that that there are currently opportunities to respond to such risks, though this will be difficult to manage with high levels of warming.

The report details the impacts of climate change to date, the future risks from a changing climate and the opportunities for effective action to reduce risks. It identifies vulnerable people, industries and ecosystems around the world. It finds that risk from a changing climate comes from vulnerability (lack of preparedness) and exposure (people or assets in harm's way) overlapping with hazards (triggering climate events or trends). Each of these three components can be a target for smart actions to decrease risk.

Adaptation to reduce the risks from a changing climate is now starting to occur, but with a stronger focus on reacting to past events than on preparing for a changing future. According to Chris Field, the Co-Chair of Working Group II:

> Climate-change adaptation is not an exotic agenda that has never been tried. Governments, firms, and communities around the world are building experience with adaptation. This experience forms a starting point for bolder, more ambitious adaptations that will be important, as climate and society continue to change.[4]

Less than a month after this report, the working group on mitigation published its own findings.[5] It summarised the diverse options open to policy makers and reaffirmed the conclusion that the worst effects of climate can be prevented, if action is taken.

Part of the Mitigation report takes the form of a summary for policy makers. It acknowledges that substantial reductions in emissions will require major changes in investment patterns. The report finds that some progress in policy development has been achieved, particularly at a national level. These policies are often at sectoral level and involve the regulatory, financial and information measures that economists have recommended for some time.

There is, however, a substantial time lag between the implementation of policies and the impact on the environment. AR5 found that, since 2008, emission growth has not yet deviated from the previous trend.

The IPPC is currently working on its sixth Assessment Report, which will be published in 2022.

Political developments

In the meantime, there have been developments on the political front. In 2015, at the UN climate change conference in Paris (COP21), an agreement was reached amongst the 195 countries present. The Paris Agreement committed countries to limiting global warming to 'well below' 2°C and preferably to no more than 1.5°C. above pre-industrial levels.

However, with the election of Donald Trump, the US administration has become much more sceptical about climate change. The president said the USA would exit the 2015 Paris Agreement and has taken measures to slow the switch from coal. US carbon dioxide emissions increased 3.4 per cent in 2018.

Brazil too, under its new president, Jair Bolsanaro, elected in 2018, is much more sceptical about climate change and is reluctant to take measures to reduce greenhouse gas emissions, such as curbing the destruction of the Amazonian rain forest. The Australian government is similarly sceptical and rejects the IPCC's call to phase out coal power by 2050, saying that Australia will continue to exploit its coal reserves.

But despite these developments, in December 2018, at the UN climate change conference in Poland (COP24), 196 countries agreed to a rulebook for targeting, measuring and verifying emissions. However, the measures already agreed which would be covered by the rulebook will be insufficient to meet the 2°C, let alone the 1.5°C, target agreed in 2015 in Paris (see the blog on the Sloman news site, *Laying down the rules to address climate change: the outcome of COP24*).

1. *Would it be in the interests of a business to reduce its carbon emissions if this involved it in increased costs?*
2. *How is the concept of 'opportunity cost' relevant in analysing the impact of business decisions on the environment?*
3. *The Stern Report was produced in 2006. Why has progress to date been slow? Does this reflect a lack of political will or scepticism about the extent of climate change?*

---

[3] 'Climate Change 2014: Impacts, Adaptation, and Vulnerability, from Working Group II of the IPCC' (2014).

[4] 'IPPC Report: "severe and pervasive" impacts of climate change will be felt everywhere' UN and Climate Change, United Nations (31 March 2014).

[5] 'Climate Change 2014: Mitigation from Climate Change, from Working Group III of the IPCC', IPCC (2014).

---

superstore on a greenfield site overlooked by your house might cause you to move. Moving house entails a financial cost, including the loss in value of your property resulting from the opening of the store. Clearly, in such a case, by choosing to move, you would be regarding the cost of moving to be less than the cost to you of the deterioration in your environment.

Contingency valuation. In this method, people likely to be affected are asked to evaluate the effect on them of any proposed change to their environment. In the case of the superstore, local residents might be asked how much they would be willing to pay in order for the development not to take place or, alternatively, how much they would need to be compensated if it were to take place.

The principal concern with this method is how reliable the answers to the questionnaires would be. There are two major problems:

■ *Ignorance.* People will not know just how much they will suffer *until* the project goes ahead.

■ *Dishonesty.* People will tend to exaggerate the compensation they would need. After all, if compensation is actually going to be paid, people will want to get as much as possible. But, even if it is not, the more people exaggerate the costs to them, the more likely it is that they can get the project stopped.

These problems can be lessened if people who have already experienced a similar project elsewhere are questioned. They are more knowledgeable and have less to gain from being dishonest.

Research on contingency valuation has focused heavily on the questioning process and how monetary values of costs and benefits might be accurately established. Of all the methods, contingency valuation has grown most in popularity over recent years, despite its limitations.

Other problems

As well as the problems of value, other aspects of environmental damage make policy making particularly difficult. These include the following:

■ *Spatial issues.* The place where pollution is produced and the places where it is deposited may be geographically very far apart. Pollution crosses borders (e.g. acid rain) or can be global (e.g. greenhouse gases). In both cases, national policies might be of little value, especially if you are a receiver of others' pollution! In such circumstances, international agreements would be needed and these can be very difficult to reach.

■ *Temporal issues.* Environmental problems such as acid rain and the depletion of the ozone layer have been occurring over many decades. Thus the full effect of pollution on the environment may be identifiable only in the long term. As a consequence, policy initiatives are required to be forward looking and proactive, if the cumulative effects of pollution are to be avoided. Most policy tends to be reactive, however, dealing with problems only as they arise. In such cases, damage to the environment may have been done already.

■ *Irreversibility issues.* Much environmental damage might be irreversible: once a species is extinct, for example, normally it cannot be reintroduced.

Environmental policy options

Environmental policy can take many forms. However, it is useful to put the different types of policy into three broad categories: (a) those that attempt to work through the market by changing property rights or by changing market signals (e.g. through the use of charges, taxes or subsidies); (b) those that involve the use of laws, regulations and controls

(e.g. legal limits on the volume of sulphur dioxide emissions); (c) those that attempt to combine the approaches (e.g. 'cap and trade'). The following sections will examine each of these three categories in more detail.

Market-based policies

Extending private property rights

If those suffering from pollution or causing it are granted property rights, they can charge the polluters for the right to pollute. According to the Coase theorem (see pages 378–9) this could result in the socially efficient level of output being produced. For example, if the sufferers are awarded the property rights, they can impose a charge on the polluter that is greater than the sufferers' marginal pollution cost but less than the polluter's marginal profit. Similarly, if the polluting firm is given the right to pollute, victims could offer a payment to persuade it not to pollute.

Extending property rights in this way is normally impractical whenever there are many polluters and many victims. But the principle of the victims paying polluters to reduce pollution is sometimes followed by governments. Thus, under Article 11 of the 1997 Kyoto Protocol, the developed countries agreed to provide financial assistance to the developing countries to help them reduce greenhouse gas emissions.

Introducing charges for the use of the environment

Previously, we discussed how the environment can be thought of as a common or natural resource where the user pays no price. For example, the emissions created by a coal-burning power station can be spewed into the atmosphere at no cost to the firm, even though it imposes costs on society. A firm could also use resources from the environment in its production process at a zero price. For example, it could extract water, cut down trees for timber or extract minerals out of the ground (assuming it owned or rented the land). With a zero price, these resources will tend to be depleted at a rate that is not optimal for society: i.e. too quickly.

To overcome these problems, the government could introduce charges for the use of the environment which, otherwise, would be free to the user.

Environmental ('green') taxes and subsidies

Rather than charging for the use of the environment, a tax could be imposed on the output (or consumption) of a good whenever external environmental costs are generated. Such taxes are known as *green taxes*. In this case, the good already has a price but it does not fully reflect the full costs to society.

> ### Definition
>
> **Green tax** A tax on output or consumption to charge for the adverse effect on the environment. The socially efficient level of a green tax is equal to the marginal environmental cost of production.

To achieve the socially efficient output level, the rate of tax should be equal to the marginal external cost (see Figure 20.9 on page 377). As such, it should fully internalise the costs of the externality.

An alternative is to subsidise activities that reduce pollution (such as the installation of loft insulation). Here the rate of subsidy should be equal to the marginal external benefit.

Taxes and charges have the advantage of relating the size of the penalty to the amount of pollution. This means that there is continuous pressure to cut down on production or consumption of polluting products or activities in order to save tax.

One approach is to modify *existing* taxes. In most developed countries, there are now higher taxes on high-emission cars.

Increasingly, however, countries are introducing *new* 'green' taxes or charges in order to discourage pollution as goods are produced, consumed or disposed of. Table 22.1 shows the wide range of green taxes and charges used around the world and Figure 22.1 shows green tax revenues as a percentage of GDP in various countries.

As you can see, they are higher than average in The Netherlands and the Scandinavian nations, reflecting the strength of their environmental concerns. They are lowest in the USA. By far the largest green tax revenues come from fuel taxes. Fuel taxes are relatively high in the UK and so, therefore, are green tax revenues.

Problems with taxes and charges

There are various problems with using taxes and charges in the fight against pollution.

Identifying the socially efficient tax rate. It will be difficult to identify the marginal pollution cost of each firm, given that each one is likely to produce different amounts of pollutants for any given level of output. Even if two firms produce identical amounts of pollutants, the environmental damage might be quite different, because the ability of the environment to cope with it will differ between the two locations. Also, the number of people suffering will differ (a factor that is very important when considering the *human* impact of pollution). What is more, the harmful effects are likely to build up over time and predicting these effects is fraught with difficulty.

Problems of demand inelasticity. The less elastic the demand for the product at its current price, the less effective a tax is at reducing production and hence in cutting pollution. Thus taxes on petrol would have to be very high indeed to make significant reductions in the consumption of petrol and hence significant reductions in the exhaust gases that contribute towards global warming and acid rain.

Redistributive effects. The poor spend a higher proportion of their income on domestic fuel than the rich. A 'carbon tax' on such fuel will, therefore, have the effect of redistributing incomes away from the poor. The poor also spend a larger proportion of their income on food than do the rich. Taxes on agriculture, designed to reduce intensive use of fertilisers and pesticides, again will tend to hit the poor proportionately more than the rich.

However, not all green taxes hit the poor more than the rich. The rich spend a higher proportion of their income on motoring than the poor. Thus petrol and other motoring taxes could help to reduce inequality.

Problems with international trade. If a country imposes pollution taxes on its industries, its products will become less competitive in world trade. To compensate for this, the industries may need to be given tax rebates for exports. Also taxes would need to be imposed on imports of competitors' products from countries where there is no equivalent green tax.

Table 22.1	Types of environmental taxes and charges

Motor fuels
  Leaded/unleaded
  Diesel (quality differential)
  Carbon/energy taxation
  Sulphur tax
Other energy products
  Carbon/energy tax
  Sulphur tax or charge
  NO_2 charge
  Methane charge
Agricultural inputs
  Fertilisers
  Pesticides
  Manure
Vehicle-related taxation
  Sales tax depends on car size
  Road tax depends on car size

Other goods
  Batteries
  Plastic carrier bags
  Glass containers
  Drink cans
  Tyres
  CFCs/halons
  Disposable razors/cameras
  Lubricant oil charge
  Oil pollutant charge
  Solvents
Waste disposal
  Municipal waste charges
  Waste-disposal charges
  Hazardous waste charges
  Landfill tax or charges
  Duties on waste water

Air transport
  Noise charges
  Aviation fuels
Water
  Water charges
  Sewage charges
  Water effluent charges
  Manure charges
Direct tax provisions
  Tax relief on green investment
  Taxation on free company cars
  Employer-paid commuting expenses taxable
  Employer-paid parking expenses taxable
  Commuter use of public transport tax deductible

Figure 22.1 Green tax revenues as a percentage of GDP

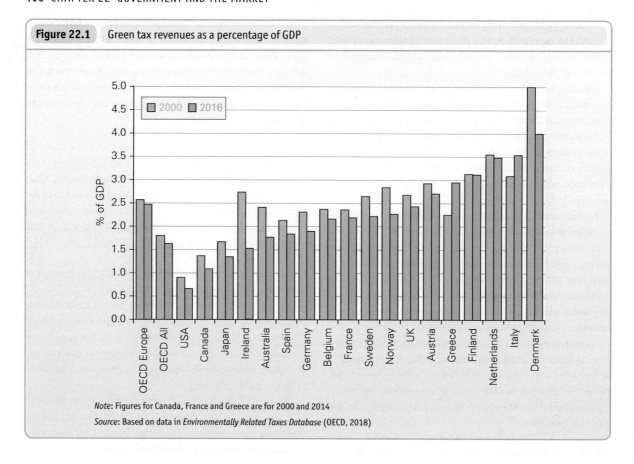

Note: Figures for Canada, France and Greece are for 2000 and 2014

Source: Based on data in *Environmentally Related Taxes Database* (OECD, 2018)

Evidence on the adverse effect of environmental taxes on a country's exports is inconclusive, however. Over the long term, in countries with high environmental taxes (or other tough environmental measures), firms will be stimulated to invest in low-pollution processes and products. Later, this will give such countries a competitive advantage if *other* countries then impose tougher environmental standards.

Effects on employment. Reduced output in the industries affected by green taxes will lead to a reduction in employment. If, however, the effect was to encourage investment in new cleaner technology, employment might not fall. Furthermore, employment opportunities could be generated elsewhere if the extra revenues from the green taxes were spent on alternative products, such as buses and trains rather than cars.

Non-market-based policies

Command-and-control systems (laws and regulations)

The traditional way of tackling pollution has been to set maximum permitted levels of emission or resource use, or minimum acceptable levels of environmental quality, and then to fine firms contravening these limits. Measures of this type are known as ***command-and-control (CAC) systems***. Clearly, there have to be inspectors to monitor the amount of pollution and the fines have to be large enough to deter firms from exceeding the limit.

Virtually all countries have environmental regulations of one sort or another. For example, the EU has over 200 items of legislation covering areas such as air and water pollution, noise, the marketing and use of dangerous chemicals, waste management, the environmental impacts of new projects (such as power stations, roads and quarries), recycling, depletion of the ozone layer and global warming.

Typically, there are three approaches to devising CAC systems.[1]

- ***Technology-based standards.*** The focus could be on the amount of pollution generated, irrespective of its environmental impact. As technology for reducing pollutants improves, so tougher standards could be imposed,

---

Definitions

Command-and-control (CAC) systems The use of laws or regulations backed up by inspections and penalties (such as fines) for non-compliance.

Technology-based standards Pollution control that requires firms' emissions to reflect the levels that could be achieved from using the best available pollution control technology.

---

[1]See R.K. Turner, D. Pearce and I. Bateman, *Environmental Economics* (Harvester Wheatsheaf, 1994), p. 198.

based on the 'best available technology' (as long as the cost was not excessive). Thus car manufacturers could be required to ensure that new car engines meet lower CO_2 emission levels as the technology enabled them to do so.

■ *Ambient-based standards.* Here the focus is on the environmental impact. For example, standards could be set for air or water purity. Depending on the location and the number of polluters in that area, a given standard would be achieved with different levels of discharge. If the object is a cleaner environment, then this approach is more efficient than technology-based standards.

■ *Social-impact standards.* Here the focus is on the effect on people. Thus tougher standards would be imposed in densely populated areas. Whether this approach is more efficient than that of ambient-based standards depends on the approach to sustainability. If the objective is to achieve social efficiency, then human-impact standards are preferable. If the objective is to protect the environment for its own sake (a 'deeper green' approach), then ambient standards would be preferable.

KI 8
p33
Assessing CAC systems. Given the uncertainty over the environmental impacts of pollutants, especially over the longer term, it is often better to play safe and set tough emissions or ambient standards. These could always be relaxed at a later stage if the effects turn out not to be so damaging, but it might be too late to reverse damage if the effects turn out to be more serious. Taxes may be a more sophisticated means of reaching a socially efficient output, but CAC methods are usually more straightforward to devise, easier to understand by firms and easier to implement.

KI 9
p45
Where command-and-control systems are weak is that they fail to offer business any incentive to do better than the legally specified level. By contrast, with a pollution tax, the lower the pollution level, the less tax there will be to pay. There is thus a continuing incentive for businesses progressively to cut pollution levels and introduce cleaner technology.

Voluntary agreements

Rather than imposing laws and regulations, the government can seek to enter into voluntary agreements (VAs) with firms for them to cut pollution. Such agreements may involve a formal contract and hence be legally binding or they may be looser commitments by firms. VAs will be helped if (a) companies believe that this will improve their image with customers and hence improve sales and (b) there is an underlying threat by the government of introducing laws and regulations should VAs fail

Firms often prefer VAs to regulations, because they can negotiate such agreements to suit their own particular circumstances and build them into their planning. The result is that the firms may be able to meet environmental objectives at a lower cost. This clearly helps their competitive position.

The effectiveness of VAs depends on how tightly specified the agreements are and how easy they are for government inspectors to monitor. It also depends on there being genuine goodwill from firms. Without it, they may try to draw up agreements in a way that allows them to cut emissions by less than the level originally intended by the government.

Education

People's attitudes are very important in determining the environmental consequences of their actions. Fortunately, for the environment, people are not always out to simply maximise their own self-interest. If they were, then why would they buy more expensive 'green' products, such as environmentally friendly detergents? The answer is that many people like to do their bit, however small, towards protecting the environment. There is evidence that attitudes have changed markedly over the past few years.

This is where education can come in. If children, and adults for that matter, were made more aware of environmental issues and the consequences of their actions, then people's consumption habits could change and more pressure would be put on firms to improve their 'green credentials'.

Tradable permits (a CAC and market-based system)

A policy measure that has grown in popularity in recent years is that of *tradable permits*, also known as a 'cap-and-trade' system. This is a combination of command-and-control and market-based systems.

Capping pollution

Initially, some criteria have to be set in order to determine which factories, power plants and installations will be covered by the scheme. Policy makers then have to set a limit or 'cap' on the total volume of pollutants these organisations will be collectively allowed to produce before any financial penalties are incurred.

Definitions

Ambient-based standards Pollution control that requires firms to meet minimum standards for the environment (e.g. air or water quality).

Social-impact standards Pollution control that focuses on the effects on people (e.g. on health or happiness).

Tradable permits Firms are issued or sold permits by the authorities that give them the right to produce a given level of pollutants. Firms that do not have permits to match their emission levels can purchase additional permits to cover the difference, while those that reduce their emission levels can sell any surplus permits for a profit.

BOX 22.2 TRADING OUR WAY OUT OF CLIMATE CHANGE

The EU carbon trading system

The EU introduced a carbon Emissions Trading Scheme (EU ETS) in January 2005 as its principal policy to meet environmental targets set by the international treaty, the Kyoto Protocol (which entered into force in February 2005). Article 17 of this treaty supported the use of emissions trading and a similar scheme had already reduced emissions of both sulphur dioxide and nitrous oxide in the USA. The EU ETS created a market in carbon permits or allowances. Its ultimate objective is to give companies greater financial incentives to reduce their emissions of CO_2.

Phases I and II

The first phase of the scheme ran from January 2005 until December 2007. Around 12 000 industrial plants across 27 countries were allocated approximately 2.2 billion CO_2 permits, called Emission Unit Allowances (EUAs). Each EUA issued to a firm gives it the right to emit 1 tonne of carbon dioxide into the atmosphere. The factories covered by the scheme were collectively responsible for around 40 per cent of the EU's CO_2 emissions each year.

Companies that do not have enough EUAs to match their annual emissions can purchase additional EUAs to cover the difference, while those that reduce their emissions are able to sell any surplus EUAs for a profit. Companies are able to trade directly with each other or via brokers operating throughout Europe.

At the end of December 2007, all existing allowances became invalid and the second Trading Period began. This lasted until the end of 2012. Although it was run under the same general principles as Trading Period 1, it also allowed companies to use 'Joint Implementation'[1] and 'Clean Development Mechanism'[2] credits earned under the Kyoto Protocol's project-based mechanisms (see Case study H.22 on the student website). In other words, companies could offset emissions in the EU against emission reductions they achieve in countries outside the EU.

Phase III

Phase III of the EU ETS came into force on 1 January 2013 and operates until 2020. It built on the experience gained from operating Phases I and II of the system and included two significant changes.

Move to an EU-wide cap. The cap on total emissions in both Phases I and II[3] of the system were set in a decentralised manner. Each member state had to develop a National Allocation

Plan (NAP). The NAP set out the total cap on emissions for that country, the total quantity of EUAs that would be issued and how they would be assigned to each industrial plant or factory. Each NAP had to be approved by the European Commission before it could be implemented. The numerous NAPs have been replaced in Phase III of the EU ETS by a single EU-wide cap on the volume of emissions and on the total number of EUAs to be issued. The size of this EU-wide cap is to be reduced by 38 264 246 tonnes per year so that emissions in 2020 are 21 per cent lower than 2005.

Move to auctioning permits. In Phase I and II of the EU ETS, the majority of EUAs were freely allocated to the plants and factories covered by the scheme. The grandfathering method (see page 420) was used to determine the number of EUAs each factory would receive: i.e. it was based on their current emissions. The European Commission allowed member states to auction up to a maximum of 5 per cent of the EUAs in Phase 1 and 10 per cent in Phase II. However, this option was seldom chosen with an average of 96 per cent of EUAs freely allocated during Phase II.

Phase III saw a big increase in the proportion of EUAs auctioned. Since 2013, most of the firms in the power sector have already had to purchase all of their allowances by auction. The average number of EUAs auctioned during the whole of Phase III is just under 50 per cent. Only firms in manufacturing and the power industry in certain member states continue to be allocated the majority of their allowances at no charge.

It has also been recommended by the EU that half of the revenue generated from the auctions should be used to fund measures to reduce greenhouse gas emissions.

Assessing the first three phases of the ETS

The introduction of world's largest market-based policy to address climate change was welcomed by many economists and policy makers. However, others have raised concerns about a number of issues.

The allocation of permits. Some people were very critical about the free allocation of allowances in Phases I and II of the scheme. The people who designed the scheme thought it was important because (a) firms needed time to adjust and (b) the impact on firms' costs might make it difficult for them to compete with companies outside of the EU. However, after the system was introduced, there were accusations that firms in the power sector had simply used the free allocation of permits to make 'windfall profits'. The much greater use of auctioning in Phase III of the scheme helped to address some of these concerns.

The size of the cap. The impact of the scheme depends on the demand for EUAs relative to the total number issued by the authorities: i.e. the size of the overall cap. If the supply of

---

[1] https://unfccc.int/process/the-kyoto-protocol/mechanisms/ joint-implementation.

[2] https://cdm.unfccc.int/about/index.html.

[3] https://ec.europa.eu/clima/policies/ets/pre2013_en.

allowances significantly exceeds demand in the secondary market, then the price will fall to a relatively low level and firms will lack the necessary incentives to invest in new energy-efficient technology.

This was a big problem in Phase I of the scheme as the price of EUAs fell from a peak of €30 to just €0.02. Although the situation improved, the price remained below €10/tonne from late 2011 until 2017. This is thought to be well below the price necessary to incentivise big changes in producer behaviour.

Why has the price been so low? One simple explanation is that the initial number of EUAs issued was based on projected levels of economic activity before the global financial crisis. This number was not adjusted following the fall in economic activity that occurred as a result of the crisis. Thus there was strong downward pressure on prices.

Another reason was the decentralised manner in which the EUAs initially were allocated through the National Allocation Plans. This gave some countries a strong incentive to game the system by setting an aggregate cap in its NAP that was greater than the volume of emissions actually being produced. By doing this, costs could be kept down for firms operating in that country, which would help to maintain its national economic competitiveness. Businesses may also have successfully lobbied governments by exaggerating claims about the potentially negative impact of issuing too few EUAs on costs and future competitiveness. Phase III of the system attempted to address this issue by replacing NAPs with a single EU-wide cap.

The excess supply of allowances has remained an issue, with an estimated 2.1 billion surplus in 2013. To try to deal with this problem, the EU introduced a policy of *backloading* in February 2014. This led to the auction of 900 million allowances being delayed until 2019. *Backloading* was a temporary measure to boost the price of EUAs as it only postponed the auctioning of allowances – it did not actually reduce them.

In October 2015, the EU agreed to introduce a Market Stability Reserve[4] (MSR) to operate from the beginning of 2019. This is a long-term measure to help the EU ETS system deal with imbalances between demand and supply. The MSR controls the volume of allowances auctioned at any point in time based on the total number in circulation. For example, if the total number of allowances in circulation exceeds 833 million, then the quantity of allowances auctioned each year will be reduced by 12 per cent of this total. Any allowances that are not auctioned are placed into the MSR. If the

number in circulation is too low, allowances are released from the MSR. This will happen if the number in circulation falls below 400 million. The 900 million *backloaded* allowances will be moved to the MSR in 2019 instead of being auctioned.

Phase IV

After two-and-a-half years of negotiations, proposals were finally agreed in November 2017 for Phase IV of the EU ETS, which operates from 2021 to 2030. This includes the following changes:

- The annual cap on the total number of EUAs will decrease at the faster rate of 48 million tonnes per year compared to 38 million tonnes per year in Phase III.
- Under a revised MSR, if surplus emissions exceed 833 million, then the number auctioned each year will be reduced by 24 per cent of the total number in circulation compared with 12 per cent in Phase III.
- Also, if the number of allowances in the MSR is greater than the total number auctioned, the previous year they will be *permanently* removed from the market.

Overall, it is still difficult to assess the impact of the ETS, even though it is coming to the end of Phase III of the scheme. Disaggregating the effect of emissions allowances from the effects of other economic factors and policy changes is enormously complicated. However, there is general agreement that the systems and processes set in place do have the potential to be effective. It will be interesting to see if the changes in Phase IV of the programme have the desired impact.

The UK's decision to leave the European Union has raised questions as to whether it would continue to be part of the EU ETS or introduce its own scheme that potentially could be aligned to the EU ETS. Norway, Iceland and Liechtenstein all participate in the EU ETS, while Switzerland has aligned its own scheme so that allowances can be traded between the two. Another policy option would be for the UK to make much greater use of green taxes.

1. *Consider a situation where all firms are of identical size and each is allocated credits that allows it to produce 10 per cent less than its current emissions. How would this compare with a situation where permits are allocated to 90 per cent of firms only? Consider both efficiency and equity in your answer.*
2. *What is carbon leakage? Can it be used to justify the free allocation of EUAs?*

Find out what has happened to the market price of EUAs over the last 12 months. Graph the data and comment on any trends.

---

[4]https://ec.europa.eu/clima/policies/ets/reform_en.

Pollution permits. Once an aggregate cap has been set, pollution permits, sometimes called allowances, are either issued or sold to the firms. Each allowance held by a firm gives it the right to produce a given volume or weight of pollutants. The total volume of all the allowances (permits) issued by the authorities in a given year should be equal to the size of the aggregate cap set on total emissions. The quantity of allowances awarded in subsequent years to each firm is then reduced by a certain percentage – the cap is tightened – to give firms an incentive to invest in more environmentally friendly technology.

All firms covered by the scheme must monitor and report the level of pollutants caused by their production activity. At the end of the year they must then submit enough allowances to the authorities to match the level of pollutants they have emitted. Each allowance can be used only once. If a firm fails to submit enough allowances then it is subject to heavy fines.

How are permits allocated between firms? One method is to base the number of permits allocated to an individual plant, factory or installation on its current level of pollution. The number of allowances awarded in subsequent years of the scheme is then calculated by requiring all firms to reduce their pollution levels by the same percentage. This approach is known as ***grandfathering***. The major criticism of this method is that it seems unfair on those firms that have already invested in cleaner technology. Why should they be required to make the same reductions in the future as firms currently using older polluting technology?

An alternative approach is to auction the allowances. Firms with low rates of emissions will need fewer permits per unit of output and thus will be prepared to pay more per permit. This then acts as an incentive for firms to invest in cleaner technology.

The EU ETS scheme. The biggest cap-and-trade system in the world is the European Union's Emissions Trading Scheme (EU ETS) – for more details see Box 22.2. It covers energy-intensive installations in four broad sectors that have emissions above certain threshold levels. The four sectors are energy (electricity, oil, coal), ferrous metals (iron, steel), minerals (cement, glass, ceramics) and wood pulp (paper and card). The EU set a total cap on the aggregate CO_2 emissions produced by organisations in these sectors of 2 039 152 882 tonnes for 2013. This cap then declines at an annual rate of 1.74 per cent of the average total quantity of allowances issued between 2008 and 2012. This works out to a fall of 38 264 246 allowances per year.

Trading under a cap-and-trade system

The 'trade' part of a 'cap-and-trade' scheme refers to the ability of firms to buy and sell allowances in a secondary market once they have been allocated by the authorities. However, in what circumstances would a firm wish either to buy or to sell an allowance?

Take the example of an organisation that estimates it will not have enough permits at the end of the year to match its forecast level of emissions. It has two options. First, it could invest in new technology that reduces the level of pollutants created by its production process. Alternatively, it could leave its production process unchanged and purchase extra permits. Obviously, its final decision will depend on the relative cost of introducing more energy-efficient technology versus the price of purchasing any additional permits.

In order to buy allowances in the secondary market, there must be other firms that have excess permits and hence are willing to sell. These may be firms that have recently made large investments in a more energy-efficient production process. If an organisation forecasts that it will have more permits than the number required, then it can sell the excess allowances in the secondary market.

The price that firms either pay to buy or receive from selling the allowances in the secondary market will depend on the levels of demand and supply. The levels of demand and supply will be heavily influenced by the initial number of permits allocated by the authorities, the state of the economy and developments in technology.

The principle of tradable permits can be used as the basis of international agreements on pollution reduction. Each country could be required to achieve a certain percentage reduction in a pollutant (e.g. CO_2 or SO_2), but any country exceeding its reduction could sell its right to these emissions to other (presumably richer) countries.

A similar principle can be adopted for using natural resources. Thus fish quotas could be assigned to fishing boats or fleets or countries. Any parts of these quotas not used could then be sold.

Assessing the system of tradable permits

It is argued that one major advantage of the cap-and-trade system over most CAC methods is that it can reduce pollution at a much lower cost to society. This can be illustrated by using the following simple example.

Assume there are just two firms that each own one plant that pollutes the environment. They currently emit a total of 2000 tonnes of CO_2 into the atmosphere each year – 1000 tonnes by each firm. Decreasing emissions of CO_2 would cost firm A £100 per tonne, whereas it would cost firm B £200 per tonne.

Assume that the Government wishes to reduce emissions from 2000 to 1600 tonnes. It could do this by setting an

---

> ### Definition
>
> **Grandfathering** Where the number of emission permits allocated to a firm is based on its *current* levels of emission (e.g. permitted levels for all firms could be 80 per cent of their current emission levels).

emissions cap on both firms of 800 tonnes of CO_2. Each would be given permits for that amount. Without the possibility of trading the permits, firm A would have to spend £20 000 to comply with the cap (200 tonnes × £100), while firm B would have to spend £40 000 (200 tonnes × £200). Thus the cost to society of reducing total emissions from 2000 to 1600 tonnes is £60 000.

With trading, however, the cost can be reduced below £60 000. If the two firms traded permits at a price somewhere between £100 and £200 per tonne, say £150, both could gain. Firm A would have an incentive to reduce its emissions to 600 tonnes, costing £40 000 (400 × £100). It could then sell the unused permits (200 tonnes) to firm B for £30 000 (200 × £150), which could then maintain emissions at 1000 tonnes. The net cost to firm A is now only £10 000 (£40 000 – £30 000), rather than the £20 000 from reducing its production to 800 without trade. The cost to Firm B is £30 000, rather than the £40 000 from reducing its production to 800.

Society will have achieved the same total reduction in pollution (i.e. from 2000 tonnes to 1600 tonnes) but at a much lower cost: i.e. £40 000 instead of £60 000. The smaller increase in costs means that price increases in the sector for consumers will be lower than they would otherwise have been.

One potential drawback of using tradable permits, however, is that it could result in pollution being concentrated in certain geographic areas.

Comparison with CAC systems. In theory, the same outcome could be obtained in a CAC system if the policy makers knew the compliance costs of the different firms. In this case, an emission standard of 600 tonnes could be placed on firm A and a 1000 tonnes on firm B. However, this would require the authorities collecting enormous amounts of detailed information on plant-specific costs in order to calculate the appropriate emissions standard for each business. The cap-and-trade system allows policy makers to achieve the same outcome without the need to collect such large amounts of detailed information.

Comparison with green taxes/charges. An interesting comparison can also be made between green taxes/charges and tradable permits. With the cap-and-trade scheme, the authorities determine the quantity of pollutants, while the market determines the price. With a green tax, the authorities determine the price of pollutants, while the market determines the quantity. In certain circumstances, green taxes and tradable permits will produce the same outcome.

Pause for thought

1. To what extent will the introduction of tradable permits lead to a lower level of total pollution (as opposed to its redistribution)?
2. What determines the size of the administrative costs of a system of tradable permits? For what reasons might green taxes be cheaper to administer than a system of tradable permits?

Environmental policy in the UK and EU

UK policy

In the UK, current policy is embodied in the 1990 Environmental Protection Act, the 1995 Environment Act (which set up the Environment Agency), the 2003 Waste and Emissions Trading Act and the 2005 Neighbourhoods and Environment Act. The Acts are an attempt to establish an integrated pollution control strategy. This has been the approach in other European countries, notably The Netherlands.

Following a number of energy White Papers and Reviews, the UK Government introduced the Climate Change and Sustainable Energy Act and Climate Change Programme in 2006. This obliged the Government to report to Parliament on greenhouse gas emissions and measures taken to reduce these emissions.

Climate Change Act. In 2008, the Climate Change Act established legally binding targets on the UK to achieve reductions in greenhouse gases of at least 80 per cent by 2050 on 1990 levels, and a 26 per cent reduction in CO_2 emissions by 2020. A key policy to help the UK achieve these reductions is its involvement in the EU ETS.

Climate Change levy. Then, in April 2001, a Climate Change Levy (CCL) was introduced. The CCL is a tax on the use of energy by businesses in the industrial, commercial, agricultural and public services sectors. It is added to a company's fuel bill for electricity, gas, liquefied petroleum and solid fuels. For 2018/19, the rate per kilowatt hour was set at 0.583 pence for electricity and 0.203 pence for gas. The rate per kilogram was set at 1.304 pence for liquefied petroleum and 1.591 pence for any other taxable commodity covered by the scheme. It is estimated that the CCL adds around 3 to 6 per cent to the energy bills of the affected companies.

The CCL has been criticised on a number of grounds. Some people argue that it would have been more effective to introduce an upstream tax on energy *production* rather than a downstream tax on energy *consumption* by business. The Government, in 2001, favoured the downstream approach as it argued that the charges could be targeted on business, leaving households exempt from the tax. However, some of the increase in costs are highly likely to have been passed on to consumers in the form of higher prices. The policy has also been criticised because the CCL rates do not reflect the carbon content of the fuels.

Reductions in the main rates of the CCL can be obtained by energy-intensive businesses if they enter into a voluntary Climate Change Agreement (CCA) with the Environment Agency. According to the Environment Agency's first Biennial Progress Report,[2] approximately 7800 sites had

---

[2] 'Climate Change Agreements: biennial progress report 2015 and 2016', Environment Agency, (16 November 2017).

entered into these agreements spread across 53 sectors during 2015/16. The agreements set targets for firms to increase energy efficiency and reduce CO_2 emissions. If the targets are achieved, firms can claim up to a 90 per cent reduction in the CCL for electricity and 65 per cent for their use of other energy sources.

Renewals Obligation. Another important government policy to reduce emissions is the Renewals Obligation (RO). Introduced in 2002, it places an obligation on UK electricity suppliers to source a given percentage of the electricity they supply from renewable sources. The proportion is set by the government each year and has increased annually from 11.1 per cent in 2010/11 to 46.8 per cent in 2018/19.

Energy Company Obligation. The Energy Company Obligation (ECO) was introduced in January 2013 to reduce domestic energy consumption by placing obligations on large energy suppliers to fund energy improvements in people's homes – e.g. installing insulation. As of November 2016, 1.6 million people had benefited from the scheme and over 55 per cent of these were on low incomes. The Government announced that the scheme would run for another five years from April 2017.

Carbon price floor. In the Autumn Statement of 2011, the Government announced plans to introduce a carbon price floor. This was prompted by concerns about the volatility and relatively low prices for EUAs in the EU ETS. It has been argued that a stable price of £30 per tonne of CO_2 emissions is required for strong enough incentives for investment in low-carbon electricity generation.

The aim of the carbon price floor was to ensure that electricity power generators burning fossil fuels paid a minimum price of around £16 per tonne of CO_2 they emitted in 2013/14. The minimum price was set to increase by £2 per year, so that by 2020 it would be £30 per tonne.

The policy works by charging suppliers of coal and gas to the electricity market a 'top-up' tax if the price of EUAs falls below the carbon price floor. This 'top-up' tax is added to the existing Climate Change Levy (CCL) and is called the carbon price support (CPS) rate of the CCL. The rate is based on the carbon content of primary fuels.

The precise size of the tax is actually set two years in advance. It is calculated by comparing the two-year future traded price of EUAs with the carbon price floor (CPF). The tax is set as the difference between these two figures: i.e. the CPF minus the future traded price of EUAs.

Given that the CPS rates are set in advance and the EUA price fluctuates, it is not a strict price cap. For example, if the EUR price falls in the future then the actual carbon price paid will be below the minimum price set by the government.

Because the CPF was introduced only in the UK, there were concerns that it was harming the competitiveness of UK firms. As a result, the Chancellor announced in the 2014 Budget that the floor would remain frozen at £18 from 2016 to 2020. The freeze was extended to 2021 in the 2016 budget. This policy does seem to have had significant impact, as carbon emissions from the generation of electricity have fallen far faster in the UK than in other developed countries. Between 2012 and 2016, coal-fired power generation in Britain fell by 80 per cent.

The challenge for the government continues to be one of finding policies that reduce emissions while being mindful of their impact on energy prices and the competitiveness of UK firms. Ofgem estimates that just over 8 per cent of an average dual energy bill is due to environmental and social obligation costs.

EU policy

A major plank of EU environmental policy is its carbon trading scheme. The broader framework for environmental policy has been detailed in EU Environment Action Programme. There has been a series of such programmes since 1973. The Seventh Programme came into force in January 2014 and will run until 2020. The programme identifies three priority areas to which environmental policy should be directed: protect, conserve and enhance the EU's natural capital; boost resource-efficient, low-carbon growth; reduce threats to human health and well-being linked to pollution, chemical substances and the impacts of climate change.

Natural capital refers to the soil, productive land, seas/fresh water, clean air and biodiversity of the EU. In order to transform the EU into a resource-efficient, low-carbon economy, the programme identifies three key requirements: full delivery of the climate and energy package to achieve the 20-20-20 targets; significant improvements to the environmental performance of products; reductions in the environmental impact of consumption such as cutting food waste. The third priority on human health and well-being is in response to a study by the World Health Organization, which estimated that up to 20 per cent of all deaths in Europe could be caused by environmental factors.

The programme also includes four objectives that will help it to deliver on its three key priory areas. These 'enabling' objectives are: better implementation of existing legislation; improving the knowledge base and making it more available for EU citizens and policy makers; better investments for the environment based on market signals that reflect the true costs to the environment; full integration of environmental requirements into other policies. This will involve systematically assessing the environmental impact of any policy initiatives.

22.2 TRANSPORT POLICY

Traffic congestion is a problem faced by many countries, especially in large cities and at certain peak times. This problem has become more acute as our lives have become increasingly dominated by the motor car. Sitting in a traffic jam is both time-wasting and frustrating. It adds considerably to the costs and stress of modern living.

And it is not only the motorist that suffers. Congested streets make life less pleasant for the pedestrian and increased traffic leads to increased accidents. What is more, the inexorable growth of traffic has led to significant problems of pollution. Traffic is noisy and car fumes are unpleasant and lead to substantial environmental damage.

Between 1960 and 2016, the number of vehicle miles travelled on roads in Great Britain increased from 69.8 billion to 323.7 billion (364 per cent). The length of public roads over the same period increased from 194 180 miles to 246 510 miles (27 per cent), although some roads were widened. In 2016, 89 per cent of passenger kilometres and 76 per cent of domestic freight tonnage kilometres in Great Britain were by road, whereas rail accounted for a mere 10 per cent of passenger traffic and 9 per cent of freight tonnage. Of road passenger kilometres, 94 per cent were by car in 2016 and, as Table 22.2 shows, this proportion had grown significantly up to 1992 before showing a slight fall in recent years.

Average weekly household expenditure on transport in 2015/16 was £72.70, equating to 13.7 per cent of total expenditure. Out of this total figure on transport, households spent £19.40 (26.7 per cent) on fuel, £8.70 (12 per cent) on repairs and services, £24.80 (34.1 per cent) on the purchase of new cars and vans, £6.10 (8.4 per cent) on train/bus fares and £11.00 (15.1 per cent) on air and other travel.

But should the Government do anything about the problem? Is traffic congestion a price worth paying for the benefits we gain from using cars? Or are there things that can be done to ease the problem without greatly inconveniencing the traveller?

The existing system of allocating road space

The allocation of road space depends on both demand and supply. Demand is by individuals who base their decisions on largely private considerations. Supply, by contrast, is usually by the central government or local authorities. Let us examine each in turn.

Demand for road space (by car users)

The demand for road space can be seen largely as a *derived* demand. What people want is not the car journey for its own sake, but to get to their destination. The greater the benefit they gain at their destination, the greater the benefit they gain from using their car to get there.

The demand for road space, like the demand for other goods and services, has a number of determinants. If congestion is to be reduced, it is important to know how responsive demand is to a change in any of these: it is important to consider the various elasticities of demand.

Price. This is the *marginal cost* to the motorist of a journey. It includes petrol, oil, maintenance, depreciation and any toll charges.

The price elasticity of demand for motoring at current prices seems to be relatively low. There can thus be a substantial rise in the price of petrol and there will be only a modest fall in traffic.

Estimates of the short-run price elasticity of demand for road fuel in industrialised countries typically range from −0.1 to −0.5. Long-run elasticities are somewhat higher, but are still generally inelastic.[3] The low price elasticity of demand suggests that any schemes to tackle traffic congestion that merely involve raising the costs of motoring will have only limited success.

KI 12
p 64

---

[3] See: *Road Traffic Demand Elasticities*, Department for Transport (2014).

Table 22.2	Passenger transport in Great Britain: percentage of passenger kilometres by mode of transport					
Year	Cars, vans and taxis	Motor cycles	Buses and coaches	Bicycles	Rail	Air
1952	26.6	3.2	42.2	10.5	17.4	0.1
1962	56.5	3.3	24.5	3.1	13.2	0.4
1972	75.9	0.9	13.9	0.9	7.9	0.5
1982	80.5	2.0	9.5	1.3	6.1	0.6
1992	86.0	0.7	6.3	0.7	5.6	0.7
2002	85.5	0.7	6.0	0.6	6.2	1.1
2016	83.4	0.6	4.2	0.7	10.0	1.1

Source: Based on data from table TSGB0101, *Transport Statistics of Great Britain 2017*, Department for Transport (November 2017).

In addition to the monetary costs, there are also the time costs of travel. Data from the Department for Transport indicated that, in 2016, the average time spent travelling to work by car in Great Britain was 26 minutes. However, if the workplace was in Central London, this figure increased to 55 minutes. The opportunity cost of sitting in a car is the next best alternative activity you could have pursued during this time – relaxing, working, sleeping or even studying economics! Congestion, by increasing the duration of the journey, increases the opportunity cost.

Income. The demand for road space also depends on people's income. As incomes rise, so car ownership and hence car usage increase substantially. Demand is elastic with respect to income. Figure 22.2 shows the increase in car ownership in various countries.

Price of substitutes. If bus and train fares came down, people might switch from travelling by car. However, the cross-price elasticity of demand is likely to be relatively low. For many journeys, people regard bus and trains as a poor substitute for travelling in their own car. Cars often are considered to be more comfortable and convenient.

The price of substitutes also includes the time taken to travel by these alternatives. The quicker a train journey is compared with a car journey, the lower will be its time cost to the traveller and thus more people will switch from car to rail. Data from the Department of Transport[4] showed that, on average in 2016, 68 per cent of people travelled to work by car. However, if the workplace was in Central London,

[4] www.gov.uk/government/statistical-data-sets/
tsgb01-modal-comparisons\#table-tsgb0101.

then this figure fell to 8 per cent. Most journeys, instead, were made by train.

Price of complements. Demand for road space will depend on the price of cars. The higher the price of cars, the fewer people will own cars and so there will not be so many on the road.

> ### Pause for thought
>
> *Go through each of the determinants we have identified so far and show how the respective elasticity of demand makes the problem of traffic congestion difficult to tackle.*

Demand will also depend on the price of complementary services, such as parking. A rise in car parking charges will reduce the demand for car journeys. But here again the cross-elasticity is likely to be relatively low. In most cases, the motorist will either pay the higher charge or park elsewhere, such as in side streets.

Tastes/utility. Another factor explaining the preference of many people for travelling by car is the pleasure they gain from driving compared with alternative modes of transport. Car ownership is regarded by many people as highly desirable and, once accustomed to travelling in their own car, most people are highly reluctant to give it up.

One important feature of the demand for road space is the very large fluctuations. There will be periods of peak demand, such as during the rush hour or at holiday weekends. At such times, roads can get very congested with drivers spending

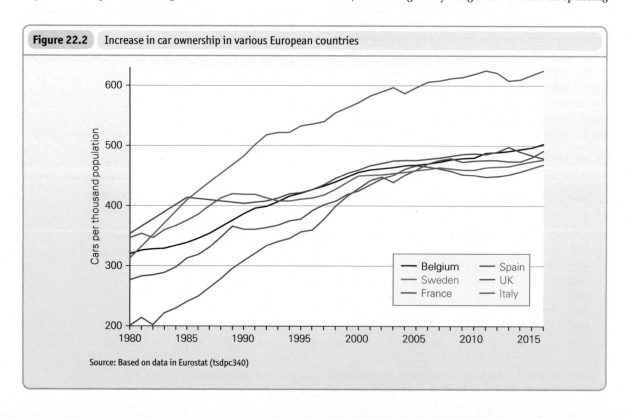

Figure 22.2 Increase in car ownership in various European countries

Source: Based on data in Eurostat (tsdpc340)

hours at a standstill. At other times, however, the same roads may be virtually empty.

Supply of road space

The supply of road space can be examined in two contexts: the short run and the long run.

The short run. In the short run, the supply of road space is constant. When there is no congestion, supply is more than enough to satisfy demand. There is spare road capacity. At times of congestion, however, there is pressure on this fixed supply. Maximum supply for any given road is reached at the point where there is the maximum flow of vehicles per minute along the road.

The long run. In the long run, the authorities can build new roads or improve existing ones. This will require an assessment of the costs and benefits of such schemes.

Identifying a socially efficient level of road usage (short run)

The existing system of *government* provision of roads and *private* ownership of cars is unlikely to lead to an optimum allocation of road space. So how do we set about identifying just what the social optimum is?

In the short run, the supply of road space is fixed. The question of the short-run optimum allocation of road space, therefore, is one of the optimum usage of existing road space. It is a question of *consumption* rather than supply. For this reason, we must focus on the road user, rather than on road provision.

KI 20
p 149 A socially efficient level of consumption occurs where the marginal social benefit of consumption equals its marginal social cost ($MSB = MSC$). So what are the marginal social benefits and costs of using a car?

Marginal social benefit of road usage

Marginal social benefit equals marginal private benefit plus any externalities.

Marginal private benefit is the direct benefit to the car user and is reflected in the demand for car journeys, the determinants of which we examined above. External benefits are few. The one major exception occurs when drivers give lifts to other people.

Marginal social cost of road usage

Marginal social cost equals marginal private cost plus any externalities.

Marginal private costs to the motorist were identified when we looked at demand. They include the costs of petrol, wear and tear and tolls. They also include the time costs of travel.

KI 33
p 367 There may also be substantial external costs. These include the following.

Congestion costs: time. When a person uses a car on a congested road, it will add to the congestion. This will, therefore, slow down the traffic even more and increase the journey time of *other* car users.

Congestion costs: monetary. Congestion increases fuel consumption and the stopping and starting increases the costs of wear and tear. So, when a motorist adds to congestion, there will be additional monetary costs imposed on other motorists.

Environmental costs. When motorists use a road, they reduce the quality of the environment for others. Cars emit fumes and create noise. This is bad enough for pedestrians and other car users, but can be particularly distressing for people living along the road. Driving can cause accidents, a problem that increases as drivers become more impatient as a result of delays. Also, as we saw in section 22.1, exhaust emissions contribute to global warming and acid rain. In 2015, road transport in the UK generated 111.5 million tonnes of CO_2 equivalent emissions. This was 22.5 per cent of total domestic emissions of 495.7 million tonnes.

The socially efficient level of road usage

The optimum level of road use is where the marginal social KI 30
p 365 benefit is equal to the marginal social cost. In Figure 22.3, costs and benefits are shown on the vertical axis and are measured in money terms. Thus any non-monetary costs or benefits (such as time costs) must be given a monetary value. The horizontal axis measures road usage in terms of cars per minute passing a specified point on the road.

For simplicity, it is assumed that there are no external benefits from car use and that therefore marginal private and marginal social benefits are the same. The MSB curve is shown as downward sloping. The reason for this is that different road users put a different value on this particular journey. If the marginal (private) cost of making the journey were high, only those for whom the journey had a high marginal benefit would travel along the road. If the marginal cost of making the journey fell, more people would make the journey: people would choose to make the journey at the

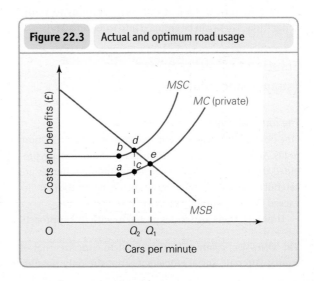

Figure 22.3   Actual and optimum road usage

point at which the marginal cost of using their car had fallen to the level of their marginal benefit. Thus the greater the number of cars in a given time period, the lower the marginal benefit.

The marginal (private) cost curve (*MC*) is likely to be constant up to the level of traffic flow at which congestion begins to occur. This is shown as point *a* in Figure 22.3. Beyond this point, marginal cost is likely to rise as time costs increase and as fuel consumption rises.

The marginal *social* cost curve (*MSC*) is drawn above the marginal private cost curve. The vertical difference between the two represents the external costs. Up to point *b*, external costs are simply the environmental costs. It is assumed that these environmental external costs remain constant. Beyond point *b*, there are also external congestion costs, since additional road users slow down the journey of *other* road users. These external costs get progressively greater as the level of traffic increases.

The actual level of traffic flow will be at Q_1, where marginal private costs and benefits are equal (point *e*). The socially efficient level of traffic flow, however, will be at the lower level of Q_2, where marginal social costs and benefits are equal (point *d*). In other words, the existing system of allocating road space is likely to lead to an excessive level of road usage.

Identifying a socially optimum level of road space (long run)

In the long run, the supply of road space is not fixed. The authorities must, therefore, assess what new road schemes (if any) to adopt. This will involve the use of some form of *cost–benefit analysis*.

The socially efficient level of construction will be where the marginal social benefit from construction is equal to the marginal social cost. This means that schemes should be adopted as long as their marginal social benefit exceeds their marginal social cost. But how are these costs and benefits assessed in practice? Case study H.15 on the student website examines the procedure used in the UK.

We now turn to look at different solutions to traffic congestion. These can be grouped into three broad types.

Solution 1: direct provision (supply-side solutions)

The road solution

One obvious solution to traffic congestion is to build more roads. At first sight, this may seem an optimum strategy, provided the costs and benefits of road-building schemes are carefully assessed and only those schemes where the benefits exceed the costs are adopted.

However, there are serious problems with this approach.

The objective of equity. The first problem concerns that of equity. After all, social efficiency is not the only possible

economic objective. For example, when an urban motorway is built, those living beside it will suffer from noise and fumes. Motorway users gain, but the local residents lose. The question is whether this is fair.

The more the government tries to appeal to the car user by building more and better roads, the less people will use public transport and thus the more public transport will decline. Those without cars lose and these tend to be from the most vulnerable groups – the poor, the elderly, children and the disabled.

Congestion may not be solved. Increasing the amount of road space may encourage more people to use cars. A good example is the London orbital motorway, the M25. In planning the motorway, not only did the Government underestimate the general rate of traffic growth, but it also underestimated the direct effect it would have on encouraging people to use the motorway rather than some alternative route, some alternative means of transport or even not making the journey at all. It also underestimated the effect it would have on encouraging people to live further from their place of work and to commute along the motorway. The result is that there is now serious congestion on the motorway and many sections have been widened from the original dual three-lane model to dual four, five and, in some parts, six lanes.

Thus new roads may simply generate extra traffic, with little overall effect on congestion.

The environmental impact of new roads. New roads lead to loss of agricultural land, the destruction of many natural habitats, noise, the splitting of communities and disruption to local residents. To the extent that they encourage a growth in traffic, they add to atmospheric pollution and a depletion of oil reserves.

Government or local authority provision of public transport

An alternative supply-side solution is to increase the provision of public transport. If, for example, a local authority ran a local bus service and decided to invest in additional buses, open up new routes, including park-and-ride, and operate a low-fare policy, these services might encourage people to switch from using their cars.

To be effective, this would have to be an attractive alternative. Many people would switch only if the buses were frequent, cheap, comfortable and reliable, and if there were enough routes to take people close to where they wanted to go.

> **Definition**
>
> **Cost–benefit analysis** The identification, measurement and weighing up of the costs and benefits of a project in order to decide whether or not it should go ahead.

A policy that has proved popular with many local authorities is to adopt park-and-ride schemes. Here the authority provides free out-of-town parking and cheap bus services from the car park to the town centre. These schemes are likely to be more effective when used in combination with charges for private cars entering the inner city.

Solution 2: regulation and legislation

An alternative strategy is to restrict car use by various forms of regulation and legislation.

Restricting car access

One approach involves reducing car access to areas that are subject to high levels of congestion. For example, in 2015, Oslo announced plans to ban all private vehicles from the city centre by 2019. Paris has also introduced a number of car free days. The following measures are more widely used: bus and cycle lanes, no entry to side streets, 'high-occupancy vehicle lanes' (confined to cars with two or more occupants) and pedestrian-only areas.

However, there is a serious problem with these measures. They tend not to solve the problem of congestion, but merely to divert it. Bus lanes tend to make the car lanes more congested; no entry to side streets tends to make the main roads more congested; and pedestrian-only areas often make the roads round these areas more congested.

Parking restrictions

An alternative to restricting road access is to restrict parking. If cars are not allowed to park along congested streets, this will improve the traffic flow. Also, if parking is difficult, this will discourage people from using their cars to travel into city centres. Apart from being unpopular with people who want to park, there are some serious drawbacks with parking restrictions. The problems with this solution include:

- people may well 'park in orbit', driving round and round looking for a parking space and, in the meantime, adding to congestion;
- people may park illegally – this may add to, rather than reduce, congestion and may create a safety hazard;
- people may feel forced to park down side streets in residential areas, thereby causing a nuisance for local residents.

Solution 3: changing market signals

The solution favoured by many economists is to use the price mechanism. As we have seen, one of the causes of traffic congestion is that road users do not pay the full marginal social costs of using the roads. If they could be forced to do so, a social optimum usage of road space could be achieved.

In Figure 22.3, this would involve imposing a charge on motorists of $d - c$. By 'internalising' the congestion and environmental externalities in this way, traffic flow will be reduced to the social optimum of Q_2.

So how can these external costs be charged to the motorist? There are several possible ways.

Extending existing taxes

Three major types of tax are levied on the motorist: fuel tax, taxes on new cars and car licences. Could increasing these taxes lead to the optimum level of road use being achieved?

Increasing the rates of new car tax and car licences may have some effect on reducing the total level of car ownership, but probably will have little effect on car use. The problem is that these taxes do not increase the marginal cost of car use. They are fixed costs. Once you have paid these taxes, there is no extra to pay for each extra journey you make. They do not discourage you from using your car.

Unlike the other two, fuel taxes are a marginal cost of car use. The more you use your car, the more fuel you consume and, therefore, the more fuel tax you pay. They are also mildly related to the level of congestion, since fuel consumption tends to increase as congestion increases. Nevertheless, they are not ideal. The problem is that all motorists would pay an increase in fuel tax, even those travelling on uncongested roads. To have a significant effect on congestion, there would have to be a very large increase in fuel taxes and this would be unfair on those who are not causing congestion, especially those who have to travel long distances. There is also a political problem. Most motorists already regard fuel taxes as too high and would resent paying even higher rates.

> ## Pause for thought
>
> *Would a tax on car tyres be a good way of restricting car usage?*

Road pricing

Charging people for using roads is a direct means of achieving an efficient use of road space. The higher the congestion, the higher should be the charge.

Variable tolls. Tolls are used in many countries and could be adapted to reflect marginal social costs. One obvious problem, however, is that, even with a system of automatic tolls, there could be considerable tailbacks at peak times. Another problem is that it may simply encourage people to use minor roads into cities, thereby causing congestion on these roads. Cities have networks of streets and thus, in most cases, it is not difficult to avoid the tolls. Finally, if the tolls are charged on people entering a city, they will not affect local commuters. It is often these short-distance commuters within a city who are most likely to be able to find some alternative means of transport and so could make a substantial contribution to reducing congestion.

Area charges. One simple and practical means of charging people to use congested streets is the area charge. People would have to pay (normally by the day) for using their car in a city centre. Earlier versions of this scheme involved people having to purchase and display a ticket on their car, rather like a 'pay-and-display' parking system.

More recently, electronic versions have been developed. The London Congestion Charge is an example. Car drivers must pay £11.50 per day to enter the inner London area (or 'congestion zone') any time between 7.00 and 18.00, Monday to Friday. Payment can be made in advance or on the same day by various means, including post, Internet, telephone, text message, mobile phone SMS and at various shops and petrol stations. Drivers can obtain a £1 discount per day if they use an auto payment system. The charge increases to £14 if payment is delayed to the following charging day.

Cars entering the congestion zone have their number plate recorded by camera and a computer check then leads to a penalty charge of £160 being sent to those who have not paid by midnight the following day (reduced to £80 if payment is made within 14 days).

A report by Transport for London estimated that traffic levels had fallen by 10 per cent in the first 10 years of the London Congestion Charge, although average traffic speeds have fallen. One unanticipated benefit of the scheme is that it appears to have reduced the number of traffic accidents by 40 per cent.

The London Congestion Charge is not a marginal one, however, in the sense that it does not vary with the degree of congestion or the amount of time spent or distance travelled by a motorist within the zone. This is an intrinsic problem of area charges. Nevertheless, their simplicity makes the systems easy to understand and relatively cheap to operate.

The charge does not address pollution directly. However, there is an 'Ultra Low Emission Discount', which means that cars or vans (not exceeding 3.5 tonnes) that emit 75g/km of CO_2 or less and meet the Euro V standard for air quality are eligible for a 100 per cent discount.

A Low Emission Zone (LEZ) was also launched in 2008. This introduced a charge on lorries, buses, coaches minibuses and vans that entered the LEZ and did not meet Euro III and Euro IV emission standards. It operates 24 hours a day, 7 days a week.

Increasing concerns over air pollution led to the introduction of a toxicity charge (T-charge) in October 2017. This is an additional £10 fee for vehicles that enter the congestion zone between 7.00 and 18.00 and fail to meet Euro IV emission standards. There are plans to replace the 'T-charge' with the Ultra Low Emission Zone (ULEZ) in April 2019. This will operate 24 hours a day, 7 days a week. Any vehicle entering the congestion zone that fails to meet the Euro IV emission standards for petrol and Euro VI emission standards for Diesel will have a daily charge of £12.50.

There does appear to be a growing commitment to use charges to deal with the external costs of both congestion and emissions.

Variable electronic road pricing. The scheme most favoured by many economists and traffic planners is that of variable electronic road pricing. It is the scheme that most directly can relate the price that the motorist is charged to the specific level of marginal social cost. The greater the congestion, the greater the charge imposed on the motorist. Ideally, the charge would be equal to the marginal congestion cost plus any marginal environmental costs additional to those created on non-charged roads.

Various systems have been adopted in various parts of the world or are under consideration. One involves devices in the road that record the number plates of cars as they pass; alternatively, cars must be fitted with sensors. A charge is registered to that car on a central computer. The car owner then receives a bill at periodic intervals, in much the same way as a telephone bill. Several cities around the world are already operating such schemes, including Barcelona, Dallas, Orlando, Lisbon, Oklahoma City and Oslo.

Another system involves having a device installed in the car into which a 'smart card' (like a telephone or photocopying card) is inserted. The cards have to be purchased and contain a certain number of units. Beacons or overhead gantries automatically deduct units from the smart cards at times of congestion. If the card is empty, the number of the car is recorded and the driver fined. Such a system was introduced in 1997 on Stockholm's ring road and, in 1998, in Singapore (see Box 22.3).

With both these types, the rate can easily be varied electronically according to the level of congestion (and pollution too). The rates could be in bands and the current bands displayed by the roadside and/or broadcast on local radio so that motorists would know what they were being charged.

The most sophisticated scheme, still under development, involves equipping all vehicles with a receiver. Their position is located by satellites, which then send this information to a dashboard unit that deducts charges according to location, distance travelled, time of day and type of vehicle. The charges can operate through either smart cards or central computerised billing. It is likely that such schemes initially would be confined to lorries.

Despite the enthusiasm for such schemes among economists, there are, nevertheless, various problems associated with them:

■ Estimates of the level of external costs are difficult to make.
■ Motorists will have to be informed in advance what the charges will be, so that they can plan the timing of their journeys.
■ There may be political resistance. Politicians may be reluctant to introduce road pricing for fear of losing popular support.

BOX 22.3   ROAD PRICING IN SINGAPORE

Part of an integrated transport policy

Singapore has some 280 vehicles per kilometre of road (this compares with 271 in Hong Kong, 222 in Japan, 77 in the UK, 75 in Germany and 37 in the USA). The average car in Singapore is driven some 17 500 kilometres per year, but with low car ownership (see below), this translates into a relatively low figure for kilometres travelled by car per person. What is more, cars flow relatively freely: the average car speed during peak hours is estimated to be as high as 29 km/h on main roads and 64 km/h on expressways. Part of the reason is that Singapore has an integrated transport policy. This includes the following:

- A 204-kilometre-long rapid transit (RTS) rail system with five main lines (mass rail transport (MRT)) and three light rail lines (LRT) connecting to the MRT, 165 stations and subsidised fares. Trains are comfortable, clean and frequent. Stations are air-conditioned.
- A programme of building new estates near RTS stations.
- Cheap, frequent buses, serving all parts of the island.
- A modest expansion of expressways.

But it is in respect to road usage that the Singaporean authorities have been most innovative.

Area licences

The first innovation came in 1975 when the Area Licensing Scheme (ALS) was introduced. The city centre was made a restricted zone. Motorists who wished to enter this zone had to buy a ticket (an 'area licence') at any one of 33 entry points. Police were stationed at these entry points to check that cars had paid and displayed. This scheme was extended to the major expressways in 1995 with the introduction of the Road Pricing Scheme (RPS).

The Vehicle Quota System

In 1990, the Government also introduced restrictions on the number of new cars, known as the Vehicle Quota System. In order to register and drive a new vehicle in Singapore, the owner has to purchase a Certificate of Entitlement (COE), which is valid for 10 years. The quantity of COEs issued by the Government is limited and the number available each year is announced in April. The COEs are then sold to the public via monthly auctions, which are operated in a similar manner to those on the eBay system. Buyers specify a maximum price and bids are automatically revised upwards until that maximum price is reached. The price of COEs increases until the quantity demanded is just equal to the number of certificates on offer.

Partly, as a result of the quota system, there are only 114 private cars per 1000 population. As was shown in Figure 22.2, this is only a fraction of the figure for European countries.

A problem with the licences is that they are a once-and-for-all payment, which does not vary with the amount people use their car. In other words, their marginal cost (for additional miles driven) is zero. Many people feel that, having paid such a high price for their licence, they ought to use their car as much as possible in order to get value for money!

Electronic road pricing

With traffic congestion steadily worsening, it was recognised that something more had to be done. In 1998 a new Electronic Road Pricing Scheme (ERP) replaced the Area Licensing Scheme for restricted areas and the Road Pricing Scheme for expressways. This alternative not only saves on police labour costs, but also enables charge rates to be varied according to levels of congestion, times of the day and locality. How does it work?

All vehicles in Singapore are fitted with an in-vehicle unit (IU). Every journey made requires the driver to insert a smart card into the IU. On specified roads, overhead gantries read the IU and deduct the appropriate charge from the card. If a car does not have sufficient funds on its smart card, the car's details are relayed to a control centre and a fine is imposed. The system has the benefit of operating on three-lane highways and does not require traffic to slow down.

The ERP system operates on roads subject to congestion and charges can vary every 5, 20 or 30 minutes according to predicted traffic flows. Rates are published in advance for a three-month period: for example from 5 February 2018 until 6 May 2018. A review of traffic conditions takes place every quarter and the results can lead to rates being adjusted in future periods. The system is thus very flexible to allow traffic to be kept at the desired level.

One potential problem with charging different rates at different times is that some drivers may substantially speed up or slow down as they approach the gantries to avoid paying higher ERP charges. To try to overcome this problem, the ERP rates are adjusted gradually for the first five minutes of a time slot with either new higher or lower charges.

The authorities in Singapore are now testing the use of a Global Navigation Satellite System. This would remove the need for the overhead gantries. It would also make it possible to alter the size of the charge with the length of the congested road the driver has travelled along.

The ERP system was expensive to set up, however. Cheaper schemes have been adopted elsewhere, such as Norway and parts of the USA. These operate by funnelling traffic into a single lane in order to register the car, but they have the disadvantage of slowing the traffic down.

One message is clear from the Singapore solution: road pricing alone is not enough. Unless there are fast, comfortable and affordable public transport alternatives, the demand for cars will be highly price inelastic. People have to get to work!

 Explain how, by varying the charge debited from the smart card according to the time of day or level of congestion, a socially optimal level of road use can be achieved.

- If demand is relatively inelastic, the charges might have to be very high to have a significant effect on congestion.
- The costs of installing road-pricing equipment could be very high.
- If road pricing was introduced only in certain areas, shoppers and businesses would tend to move to areas without the charge.
- A new industry in electronic evasion may spring up!

Subsidising alternative means of transport

An alternative to charging for the use of cars is to subsidise the price of alternatives, such as buses and trains. But cheaper fares alone may not be enough. The Government may also have to invest directly in or subsidise an *improved* public transport service: more frequent services, more routes, more comfortable buses and trains.

Subsidising public transport need not be seen as an alternative to road pricing: it can be seen as complementary. If road pricing is to persuade people not to travel by car, the alternatives must be attractive. Unless public

transport can be made to be seen by the traveller as a close substitute for cars, the elasticity of demand for car use is likely to remain low. This problem is recognised by the UK Government, which encourages local authorities to use various forms of road pricing and charges on businesses for employee car parking spaces on condition that the revenues generated are ploughed back into improved public transport. All local authorities have to produce five-year Local Transport Plans covering all forms of transport. These include targets for traffic reduction and increases in public transport.

Subsidising public transport can also be justified on grounds of equity. It benefits poorer members of society who cannot afford to travel by car.

It is unlikely that any one policy can provide the complete solution. Certain policies or combinations of policies are better suited to some situations than others. It is important for governments to learn from experiences both within their own country and in others, in order to find the optimum solution to each specific problem.

22.3 PRIVATISATION AND REGULATION

One solution to market failure, advocated by some on the political left, is nationalisation. If industries are not being run in the public interest by the private sector, then bring them into public ownership. This way, so the argument goes, the market failures can be corrected. Problems of monopoly power, externalities, inequality, etc. can be dealt with directly if these industries are run with the public interest, rather than private gain, at heart.

In the late 1940s and early 1950s, the Labour Government of the time nationalised many of the key transport, communications and power industries, such as the railways, freight transport, airlines, coal, gas, electricity and steel.

However, by the mid-1970s, the performance of the nationalised industries was being increasingly questioned. A change of policy was introduced in the early 1980s, when successive Conservative Governments engaged in an extensive programme of 'privatisation', returning virtually all of the **nationalised industries** to the private sector. These included telecommunications, gas, water, steel, electricity and the railways. By 1997, the year the Conservatives left office, with the exception of the rail industry in Northern Ireland and the water industry in Northern Ireland and Scotland, the only nationalised industry remaining in the UK was the Post Office (including post offices and mail). The Post Office and Royal Mail was split in 2012 and Royal Mail was privatised in October 2013. Post Office Ltd remains state owned but, under the 2011 Postal Services Act, there is the option for it to become a mutual organisation in the future.

Other countries have followed similar programmes of privatisation in what has become a worldwide phenomenon. Privatisation has been seen as a means of revitalising ailing

industries and as a golden opportunity to raise revenues to ease budgetary problems.

In the 2017, general election, however, the Labour Party stated that, if elected, it would renationalise the train operating companies, the water industry, the energy industries and Royal Mail. A national opinion poll carried out in August 2017 by Populus for the Legatum Institute found that 83 per cent of respondents were in favour of renationalising the water industry, while 77 per cent were in favour of renationalising the energy industry.

The arguments for and against privatisation

The following are the major arguments that have been used for and against privatisation.

Arguments for privatisation

Market forces. The first argument is that privatisation will expose these industries to market forces, from which will flow the benefits of greater efficiency, faster growth and greater responsiveness to the wishes of the consumer.

If privatisation involved splitting an industry into competing companies, this greater competition in the goods

---

Definition

Nationalised industries State-owned industries that produce goods or services that are sold in the market.

market may force the companies to drive down costs and reduce prices in order to stay in business.

Privatised companies do not have direct access to government finance. To finance investment they must now go to the market: they must issue shares or borrow from banks or other financial institutions. In doing so, they will be competing for funds with other companies and thus must be seen as capable of using these funds profitably.

Market discipline will also be enforced by shareholders. Shareholders want a good return on their shares and will thus put pressure on the privatised company to perform well. If the company does not make sufficient profits, shareholders will sell their shares. The share price will fall, and the company will be in danger of being taken over. The market for corporate control (see page 196) thus provides incentives for firms to be efficient. There has been considerable takeover activity in the water and electricity industries with many acquisitions, often by non-UK companies.

Reduced government interference. In nationalised industries, managers frequently may be required to adjust their targets for political reasons. At one time they may have to keep prices low as part of a government drive against inflation. At another they may have to raise their prices substantially in order to raise extra revenue for the government and help finance tax cuts. Privatisation frees the company from these constraints and allows it to make more rational economic decisions and plan future investments with greater certainty.

Financing tax cuts. The privatisation issue of shares directly earns money for the government and thus reduces the amount it needs to borrow. Effectively, then, the government can use the proceeds of privatisation to finance tax cuts. There is a danger here, however, that, in order to raise the maximum revenue, the government will want to make the industries as potentially profitable as possible. This may involve selling them as monopolies. But this, of course, would probably be against the interests of the consumer.

Arguments against privatisation

Natural monopolies. Some industries have the characteristic of being a natural monopoly. Having just one company leads to much lower average costs in the industry than having a number of firms. In these situations, it would not be in the interests of society to introduce competition when privatisation takes place. The market forces argument for privatisation largely breaks down if a public monopoly is simply replaced by a private monopoly, as in the case of the water companies, each of which has a monopoly in its own area. Critics of privatisation argue that at least a public-sector monopoly is not out to maximise profits and thereby exploit the consumer.

The public interest. Will the questions of externalities and social justice not be ignored after privatisation? Critics of privatisation argue that only the most glaring examples of externalities and injustice can be taken into account, given that the whole ethos of a private company is different from that of a nationalised one: private profit rather than public service is the goal. Externalities, they argue, are extremely widespread and need to be taken into account by the industry itself and not just by an occasionally intervening government. A railway or an underground line, for example, may considerably ease congestion on the roads, thus benefiting road as well as rail users. Other industries may cause substantial external costs. Nuclear power stations may produce nuclear waste that is costly to dispose of safely and/or provides hazards for future generations. Coal-fired power stations may pollute the atmosphere and cause acid rain.

In assessing these arguments, a lot depends on the toughness of government legislation and the attitudes and powers of regulatory agencies after privatisation.

> ### Pause for thought
>
> *To what extent can the problems with privatisation be seen as arguments in favour of nationalisation?*

Regulation

Identifying the short-run optimum price and output

Privatised industries, if left free to operate in the market, may have large degrees of monopoly power; may create externalities; and may be unlikely to take into account questions of fairness. An answer to these problems is for the government or some independent agency to regulate their behaviour so that they produce at the socially optimum price and output. This has been the approach adopted for the major privatisations in the UK.

Regulation in practice

To some extent, the behaviour of privatised industries may be governed by general monopoly and restrictive practice legislation. For example, following a two-year investigation into the energy industry, in 2016 the Competition & Markets Authority (CMA) (see section 21.1) published a report with various recommendations.[5]

In addition to the CMA, there is a separate regulatory office to oversee the structure and behaviour of each of the privatised utilities. These regulators are as follows: the Office of Gas and Electricity Markets (Ofgem), the Office of Communications (Ofcom), the Office of Rail and Road (ORR) and the Water Services Regulation Authority (Ofwat).

---

[5] *Modernising the Energy Market,* Competition and Markets Authority (24 June 2006).

BOX 22.4 THE RIGHT TRACK TO REFORM?

Reorganising the railways in the UK

Few train routes across Europe are profitable and thus they have to be subsidised by governments. Such has been the strain placed upon public finances that European governments in recent years have been looking for ways of reforming their railways. The most radical approach has been adopted in the UK.

Privatisation of the rail system in the UK

The 1993 Railways Act detailed the privatisation programme. The management of rail infrastructure, such as track, signalling and stations, was separated from the responsibility for running trains. The plan was to have 25 passenger train operating companies (TOCs), each having a franchise lasting between 7 and 15 years. These companies would have few assets, being forced to rent track and lease stations from the infrastructure owner (Railtrack) and to lease trains and rolling stock from three new rolling-stock companies. Initially, the 25 franchises were operated by just 11 companies with one, National Express, winning nine of the franchises.

Railtrack was responsible for maintaining and improving the rail infrastructure, but rather than providing this in-house, it had to purchase the necessary services from private contractors.

A Rail Regulator was appointed with the responsibility of both promoting competition and protecting consumer interests. This position was abolished in 2004 and replaced by the *Office of Rail Regulation,* which was later renamed the *Office of Rail and Road*.

Developments in the UK since privatisation

Problems with the operation of the rail infrastructure

Following the Hatfield rail disaster in October 2000, when fatalities occurred as a result of a faulty rail, the industry was reduced to a virtual state of crisis. Extensive repair work was required across the whole network and Railtrack had lost most of its in-house expertise in engineering because of the policy of using private contractors.

In response to the situation, part of the industry was 'semi' renationalised, when Railtrack, the privatised track owner, was put into receivership in 2002. It was replaced by

Network Rail, which is a not-for-profit company, wholly dependent upon the UK Treasury for any shortfall in its funds. The shareholders of Railtrack were replaced by an oversight group of 100 members appointed from the TOCs, engineering firms and members of the public. Any profits are reinvested in the rail infrastructure.

Network Rail has taken over control of infrastructure maintenance following concerns about the quality of the work carried out by private firms awarded contracts by Railtrack. It is responsible for 20 000 miles of track, 40 000 bridges/viaducts and thousands of tunnels, signals, level crossings and points. It also manages rail timetabling and 18 of the largest stations. Its performance too has been the subject of much criticism. For example, in March 2018, the *Office of Rail and Road* fined it £733 000 for its failure to repair defective track. This led to a freight train derailment near Gloucester in 2013.

Problems with the TOCs and the franchise system

Some private-sector TOCs performed so poorly that their franchise contracts had to be taken over temporarily by a state-owned operator. For example, in June 2003, the Strategic Rail Authority (SRA) decided to withdraw the operating licence of the French company, Connex South Eastern. The franchise was taken over temporarily by the publicly-owned South Eastern Trains from November 2003 until March 2006 before being returned to a private operator.

Perhaps the most troubled franchise has been the East Coast Main Line between London and Scotland. National Express was awarded a contract to run the service from December 2007 until February 2015. However, the company defaulted in July 2009 and the franchise had to be taken back into public ownership. It was run by East Coast, a subsidiary of Directly Operated Railways, which itself was established by the Department for Transport as an operator of last resort.

In March 2015, the service was re-privatised when a franchise contract was awarded to Virgin Train East Coast. This was a joint venture between Stagecoach (90 per cent) and Virgin (10 per cent), which agreed to run the service from 2015 to 2023 for a fee of £3.3bn. However, in November 2017, the Government agreed to allow the joint venture to exit the contract in 2020 – three years before it was originally supposed

---

As well as supervising the competitive behaviour of the privatised utilities, the specific regulatory offices set the conditions under which the industries have to operate. For example, the ORR sets the terms under which rail companies have access to track and stations. The terms set by the regulator can be reviewed by negotiation between the regulator and the industry. If agreement cannot be reached, the CMA has an appeal court and its decision is binding.

The regulator for each industry also sets limits to the prices that certain parts of the industry can charge. These parts are those where there is little or no competition: for example, the charges made to electricity and gas retailers by National Grid, the owner of the electricity grid and major gas pipelines. This is discussed in more detail below.

For many years after privatisation, the price-setting formulae were largely of the '*RPI* minus *X*' variety (although other factors, including competition and excessive profits,

to end. The business has been losing money as passenger numbers have been lower than expected. Sir Richard Branson, head of the Virgin Group, argues that the problems result from Network Rail's failure to deliver planned upgrades to the line. At present, the future management of the franchise is uncertain.

As new franchises came up for renewal, some contracts were merged, so that by 2018, the 25 franchises had been reduced to 20. It was recognised that the benefits of economies of scale and co-ordinated services within a region exceeded any reduction in competition from having fewer franchises and fewer operators.

Another interesting feature has been the change in the types of business that have been awarded the contracts. Back in 1996, at the start of the franchise era, these were largely private-sector companies such as National Express, Stagecoach, Virgin Rail and Prism Rail. As of April 2018, 14 of the 20 franchises are now operated by a foreign state-owned business or a joint venture with a foreign state-owned firm. For example, Arriva Trains, which operates five franchises, is a subsidiary of Deutsche Bahn – the German state-owned railway company.

Turning the railways around?

The Government took more direct control of the railways by winding up the Strategic Rail Authority in December 2006 and passing most of its functions, including the awarding of franchises, to the Department of Transport. At the same time, government spending in the mid-2000s was also much higher than it had been in the 1980s and 1990s. Total government support peaked at £7.51 billion in 2006/7 (at 2016/17 prices) before falling back to £4.23 billion in 2016/17.

Part of the Government's strategy has been to increase the extent to which customers and the TOCs finance the railway. Fare increases regularly have been in excess of inflation. In 2016/17, £9.7 billion of rail funding came from passenger fares (74 per cent) whereas £3.4 billion (26 per cent) came from public funding. In 2010/11, only 55.6 per cent of funding had come from passenger fares.

With improvements in the infrastructure, investment by the TOCs in new rolling stock and building more slack into timetables, rail punctuality improved and passenger numbers and freight tonnage increased. In the year ending the third quarter of 2017/18, 88.5 per cent of trains were recorded as arriving on time, compared with 79 per cent in 2002/3. Between 1994/95 and 2016/17, passenger kilometres increased from 28.7 billion to 65.4 billion – an increase of 128 per cent. The total volume of rail freight, however, was 17.2 billion net tonne kilometres in 2016/17, down from a peak of 22.7 billion in 2013/14. The main reason for this decline was the fall in the quantity of coal being transported.

Research by the Boston Consulting Group, ranked the UK as the 8th best performing rail system in Europe based on its Rail Performance Index.[1] This index is based on three different dimensions of performance – the intensity of use (i.e. passenger and goods volume), the quality of service (i.e. punctuality) and safety (i.e. accidents per train kilometre travelled). Whereas the UK performed well on safety, third out of 25 nations, it scored poorly on the quality of service. It had the joint sixth worst standard of service in Europe.

The McNulty report[2] published in 2011 concluded that the cost of running the railways in the UK was greater than in other countries because of the more fragmented nature of the industry structure.

Has the model been adopted elsewhere?

Other countries, such as Japan and Germany, have rejected the UK model in favour of maintaining a vertically integrated rail network, where rail infrastructure and train services are managed by the same company.

Nevertheless, some aspects of the UK model have been adopted under EC Directive 91/440, which allows European train operators access to the rail networks of other companies. This means that several companies (say, from different EU countries) can offer competing services on the same international route.

 Why are subsidies more likely to be needed for commuter and regional services than for medium-to-long-distance passenger services?

[1] *The 2017 European Railway Performance Index*, The Boston Consulting Group (April 2017).

[2] *Realising the Potential of GB Rail: Report of the Rail Value for Money Study: Summary Report*, Department for Transport and ORR (May 2011).

are also taken into account). This type of regulation allowed industries to raise their prices by the rate of increase in the retail price index (i.e. a measure of the rate of inflation) *minus* a certain percentage (X) to take account of expected increases in efficiency. Thus, if the rate of inflation were 3 per cent and, if the regulator considered that the industry (or firm) could be expected to reduce its costs by 2 per cent ($X = 2\%$), then price rises would be capped at 1 per cent. The $RPI - X$ system is thus an example of **price-cap**

regulation, which incentivises the industry to pass cost savings on to the consumer.

In March 2008, Ofgem began a two-year review of regulation in the energy industry called *RPI–X@20*. In 2010, it announced plans for a new system of price regulation called *RIIO* (Revenue = Incentives + Innovation + Outputs). It was introduced in 2013, and under the system, firms' prices and hence permitted revenue (R) depend on innovation (I), incentives (I), and the quality of output in addition to costs.

The *RIIO* approach is similar to *RPI–X* but places much greater weight on the quality of the output supplied and allows the climate change agenda to be addressed as part of the price control process. It is discussed in more detail in the following section.

Advantages of the system of regulation in the UK

The system that has evolved in the UK has various advantages over that employed in the USA and elsewhere, where regulation often focuses on the level of *profits* (see Case Study H.17 on the student website).

- It is a discretionary system, with the regulator able to judge individual examples of the behaviour of the industry on their own merits. The regulator has a detailed knowledge of the industry which would not be available to government ministers or other bodies such as the CMA. The regulator could thus be argued to be the best body to decide on whether the industry is acting in the public interest.
- The system is flexible, since it allows for the licence and price formula to be changed as circumstances change.
- Both 'RPI minus *X*' and the *RIIO* formula provide incentives for privatised firms to be as efficient as possible. If they lower their costs, then, in theory, they should make larger profits, which they can retain. If, on the other hand, they do not succeed in reducing costs sufficiently, they will make a loss. There is thus a continuing pressure on them to cut costs. (In the traditional US system, where *profits* rather than *prices* are regulated, there is little incentive to increase efficiency, since any cost reductions must be passed on to the consumer in lower prices and do not, therefore, result in higher profits.)

Problems with and reforms of the system of regulation in the UK

There are, however, some inherent problems with the way in which regulation operates in the UK.

The RPI–X system. The *RPI–X* system of regulation has a number of weaknesses. These were identified in the *RPI–X@20 review.*

- It motivated organisations to reduce their costs but did not provide strong enough incentives for them to deliver a high quality service to their customers.
- Where some aspects of the quality of service were taken into account, they were different from those most highly valued by the network's customers.

Definition

Price-cap regulation Where the regulator puts a ceiling on the amount by which a firm can raise its price.

- There was a tendency to focus on reforming certain parts of the regulatory structure rather than thinking about the impact on the framework as a whole.
- The five-year duration of each price regulation was too short and deterred long-run investment. Indeed, not enough attention was given to longer-run and more dynamic elements of competition such as innovation.
- If price regulation *underestimates* the scope for cost reductions, then firms may be able to make excessive profits. For example, Ofgem reported that, during the final period of *RPI–X* regulation, all the gas distribution and network companies made greater than expected profits. Also, the House of Commons Public Accounts Committee criticised Ofwat for regularly underestimating the water companies' scope for cost reduction, enabling them to make excess profits of £1.2 billion between 2010 and 2015.
- If price regulation *overestimates* the scope for cost reductions, the reduction in firms' profits might lead to reduced investment and innovation.

In response to these limitations, Ofgem decided that the terms of the new *RIIO* system would apply for eight (not five) years. What is more, the new approach tries to incentivise the network companies to deliver more clearly defined outputs. Their ability to raise prices is conditional on their performance in the following areas – levels of customer satisfaction, reliability, the conditions for connection, the environmental impact, social obligations and safety. One challenge for the regulator, however, is to find effective performance measures for each of these different attributes of the network companies' output.

Pause for thought

Think of some different methods that Ofgem could use to measure network companies' performance on customer satisfaction, environmental impacts and social obligations.

The new *RIIO* price controls were supposed to be much tougher. However, in 2017, Citizens Advice claimed that the transmission and network operators made excess profits of £7.5 billion over an eight-year period because the *RIIO* price controls were not demanding enough.[6] In particular, it accused Ofgem of (a) overestimating the risk for investors, (b) assuming interest rates would be much higher than they actually were and (c) giving incentives for firms to inflate

---

[6] 'Energy networks making £7.5bn in unjustified profit over 8 years, Citizens Advice finds', *Citizens Advice press release* (12 July 2017).

their project cost projections by allowing them to keep a share of any underspend. It called for the £7.5 billion of 'unjustified' profit to be paid back to consumers.

Additional problems with regulation. Regulation is becoming increasingly complex. This makes it difficult for the industries to plan and may lead to a growth of 'short-termism'. One of the claimed advantages of privatisation was to give greater independence to the industries from short-term government interference and allow them to plan for the longer term. In practice, one type of 'interference' may have been replaced by another.

As regulation becomes more detailed and complex and, as the regulator becomes more and more involved in the detailed running of the industry, so managers and regulators will become increasingly involved in a game of strategy: each trying to outwit the other. Information will become distorted and time and energy will be wasted in playing this game of cat and mouse.

There may be the opposite danger of *regulatory capture*. As regulators become more and more involved in their industry and get to know the senior managers at a personal level, so they are increasingly likely to see the managers' points of view and become less and less tough. Commentators do not believe that this has happened yet: the regulators are generally independently minded. But it remains a potential danger.

Alternatively, regulators could be captured by government. Instead of being totally independent, there to serve the interests of the consumer, they might bend to pressures from the government to do things that might help the government win the next election.

One way in which the dangers of ineffective or over-intrusive regulation can be avoided is to replace regulation with competition wherever this is possible. Indeed, one of the major concerns of the regulators has been to do just this. (See Case study H.16 on the student website for ways in which competition has been increased in the electricity industry.)

Increasing competition in the privatised industries

Where natural monopoly exists (see pages 191–2), competition is undesirable in a free market. In such a case, regulation is an appropriate way of curbing excess profits. The industry *could* be broken up by the government, with firms prohibited from owning more than a certain percentage of the industry. However, this would lead to higher costs of production with firms operating at a higher point on their long-run average cost curve.

But many parts of the privatised industries are not natural monopolies. For example, competition has been introduced into the retail market for gas and electricity. In 2018, there were approximately 40 different suppliers of energy, including the so-called 'Big Six' (SSE, Npower, E.ON, British Gas, Scottish Power and EDF Energy). These businesses purchase gas and electricity from companies that either produce energy (e.g. power stations that generate electricity) and/or import energy (e.g. natural gas transported through pipelines connecting the UK with mainland Europe). The CMA concluded that wholesale markets are competitive and working well for consumers.

The energy purchased by the suppliers needs to be transported to the final customer through the transmission and distribution network. The transmission network consists of high voltage cables and high-pressure underground pipes, enabling the electricity and gas to travel at high speed and over long distances around the UK. The distribution network transports the gas and electricity at lower pressure and voltage from the transmission network to people's homes. The huge infrastructure costs of building and maintaining this network make it a natural monopoly. The energy suppliers pay the owners of the network a fee to transport gas and electricity through the pipes and cables. As competition is not feasible in this part of the market, the fees charged by the monopolists are subject to the *RIIO* price controls discussed in the previous section.

In some parts of an industry where there is a natural monopoly, attempts have been made to introduce the threat of potential competition by creating contestable monopolies (see section 11.4). One way of doing this is by granting operators a licence for a specific period of time. This is known as *franchising*. This has been the approach used for the railways (see Box 22.4). Once a company has been granted a franchise, it has the monopoly of passenger rail services over specific routes. But the awarding of the franchise can be highly competitive, with rival companies putting in competitive bids, in terms of both price and the quality of service.

As competition was introduced into the retail market of many of the privatised industries, the system of price regulation was gradually eliminated. For example, in 2002 Ofgem removed all price controls on energy suppliers with its chief executive stating that, 'The evidence is overwhelming that competition is effective across all social groups and all methods of payment.'

> ### Definitions
>
> **Regulatory capture** Where the regulator is persuaded to operate in the industry's interests rather than those of the consumer.
>
> **Franchising** Where a firm is granted the licence to operate a given part of an industry for a specified length of time.

Is competition effective?

Despite the introduction of competition, the economic performance of the privatised industries has remained a controversial issue. Many people claim they are examples of failing markets characterised by large firms abusing their dominant position. The CMA report on the energy industry (see above)[7] concluded that customers were paying £1.4 billion a year more than they would have, if the retail market had been fully competitive.

Concerns about this lack of effective competition have led to an increasing number of calls for the reintroduction of price controls.

In April 2017, Ofgem introduced a temporary price cap for energy customers using prepayment meters. It lasts until 2020 and caps prices for around 4 million consumers. Called the safeguard tariff, the level varies depending on the meter type and region. It is reviewed every six months.

In February 2018, the safeguard tariff was extended so that it covered all those consumers who were in receipt of the Warm Home Discount – a payment received by approximately 1 million people on benefits. Also in February 2018, the Government introduced the Domestic Gas and Electricity Bill. This legislation places a requirement on Ofgem to extend the safeguard tariff to roughly 11 million customers on a standard variable tariff – the default pricing scheme for customers who do not shop around. Interestingly, after the two-year enquiry by the CMA, the majority of its panel members concluded that a price cap on the standard variable tariff would undermine competition.

Sixteen years after they were abolished, price caps are back in the retail market of the energy industry. Ofgem will have to monitor carefully the impact of these new price controls.

SUMMARY

1a The market fails to achieve a socially efficient use of the environment because large parts of the environment are a common resource, because production or consumption often generates environmental externalities, because of ignorance of the environmental effects of our actions and because of a lack of concern for future generations. Environmental policy attempts to ensure that the full costs of production or consumption are paid for by those who produce and consume.

1b The environment is difficult to value, so it is difficult to estimate the costs of environmental pollution. This is a major problem in being able to devise an efficient environmental policy.

1c Environmental policy can be either market based or non-market based, or a mixture of the two. Market-based solutions include extending property rights and imposing charges for using the environment or taxes/subsidies per unit of output. The use of taxes, subsidies and charges is to correct market signals. Non-market-based solutions involve the use of regulations and controls over polluting activities.

1d The problem with using charges, taxes and subsidies is in identifying the appropriate rates, since these will vary according to the environmental impact.

1e Command-and-control systems, such as making certain practices illegal or putting limits on discharges, are a less sophisticated alternative to taxes or subsidies. However, they may be preferable when the environmental costs of certain actions are unknown and it is wise to play safe.

1f Tradable permits are a mix of command-and-control and market-based systems. Firms are either given or sold permits to emit a certain level of pollution and then these can be traded. A firm that can relatively cheaply reduce its pollution below its permitted level can sell excess permits to another firm that finds it more costly to do so. The system is an efficient and administratively cheap way of limiting pollution to a designated level. It can, however, lead to pollution being concentrated in certain areas and can reduce the pressure on firms to find cleaner methods of production.

2a The allocation of road space depends on demand and supply. Demand depends on the price to motorists of using their cars, incomes, the cost of alternative means of transport, the price of cars and complementary services (such as parking), and the comfort and convenience of car transport. The price and cross-price elasticities of demand for car usage tend to be low: many people are unwilling to switch to alternative modes of transport. The income elasticity, on the other hand, is high. The demand for cars and car usage grows rapidly as incomes grow.

2b With road space fixed (at least in the short term), allocation depends on the private decisions of motorists. The problem is that motorists create two types of external cost: pollution costs and congestion costs. Thus $MSC > MC$. Because of these externalities, the actual use of road space (where $MB = MC$) is likely to be greater than the optimum (where $MSB = MSC$).

2c There are various types of solution to traffic congestion. These include direct provision by the government or local

---

[7] *Modernising the Energy Market,* Competition and Markets Authority (24 June 2016).

authorities (of additional road space or better public transport); regulation and legislation (such as restricting car access – by the use of bus and cycle lanes, no entry to side streets and pedestrian-only areas – and various forms of parking restrictions); and changing market signals (by the use of taxes, by road pricing, and by subsidising alternative means of transport).

2d Problems associated with building additional roads include the decline of public transport, attracting additional traffic on to the roads and environmental costs.

2e The main problem with restricting car access is that it tends merely to divert congestion elsewhere. The main problem with parking restrictions is that they may actually increase congestion.

2f Increasing taxes is effective in reducing congestion only if it increases the *marginal* cost of motoring. Even when it does, as in the case of additional fuel tax, the additional cost is only indirectly related to congestion costs, since it applies to all motorists and not just those causing congestion.

2g Road pricing is the preferred solution of many economists. By the use of electronic devices, motorists can be charged whenever they add to congestion. This should encourage less essential road users to travel at off-peak times or to use alternative modes of transport, while those who gain a high utility from car transport can still use their cars, but at a price. Variable tolls and area charges are alternative forms of congestion pricing, but are generally less effective than the use of variable electronic road pricing.

2h If road pricing is to be effective, there must be attractive substitutes available. A comprehensive policy, therefore, should include subsidising efficient public transport. The revenues required for this could be obtained from road pricing.

3a From around 1983, the Conservative Government in the UK embarked on a large programme of privatisation. Many other countries followed suit.

3b The economic arguments for privatisation include: greater competition, not only in the goods market but in the market for finance and for corporate control; reduced government interference; and raising revenue to finance tax cuts.

3c The economic arguments against privatisation are largely the market failure arguments that were used to justify nationalisation. In reply, the advocates of privatisation argue that these problems can be overcome through appropriate regulation and increasing the amount of competition.

3d Regulation in the UK has involved setting up regulatory offices for the major privatised utilities. These generally operate informally, using negotiation and bargaining to persuade the industries to behave in the public interest. They also set the terms under which the firms can operate (e.g. access rights to the respective grid).

3e As far as prices are concerned, the industries are required to abide by an '*RPI* minus *X*' formula. This forces them to pass potential cost reductions on to the consumer. At the same time, they are allowed to retain any additional profits gained from cost reductions greater than *X*. This provides them with an incentive to achieve even greater increases in efficiency.

3f Many parts of the privatised industries are not natural monopolies. In these parts, competition may be a more effective means of pursuing the public interest. Various attempts have been made to make the privatised industries more competitive, often at the instigation of the regulator. Nevertheless, considerable market power remains in the hands of many privatised firms, and thus the need for regulation will continue.

REVIEW QUESTIONS

1 Why is it so difficult to value the environment? What are the implications of this for government policy on the environment?

2 Is it a good idea to use the revenues from green taxes to subsidise green alternatives (e.g. using petrol taxes for subsidising rail transport)?

3 Compare the relative merits of increased road fuel taxes, electronic road pricing and tolls as means of reducing urban traffic congestion. Why is the price inelasticity of demand for private car transport a problem here, whichever of the three policies is adopted? What could be done to increase the price elasticity of demand?

4 How would you set about measuring the external costs of road transport?

5 Consider the argument that whether an industry is in the public sector or private sector has far less bearing on its performance than the degree of competition it faces.

6 To what extent do the various goals of privatisation conflict?

7 Is it desirable after an industry has been privatised for profitable parts of the industry to cross-subsidise unprofitable parts if they are of public benefit (e.g. profitable railway lines cross-subsidising unprofitable ones)?

8 Should regulators of utilities that have been privatised into several separate companies permit (a) horizontal mergers (within the industry); (b) vertical mergers; (c) mergers with firms in other related industries (e.g. gas and electricity suppliers)?

9 Assess some of the arguments for and against the imposition of price controls in the retail energy market.

ADDITIONAL PART H CASE STUDIES ON THE *ECONOMICS FOR BUSINESS* STUDENT WEBSITE (www.pearsoned.co.uk/sloman)

H.1 **The police as a public service.** The extent to which policing can be classified as a public good.

H.2 **Should health care provision be left to the market?** An examination of the market failures that would occur if health care provision were left to the free market.

H.3 **Corporate social responsibility.** An examination of social responsibility as a goal of firms and its effect on business performance.

H.4 **Public choice theory.** This examines how economists have attempted to extend their analysis of markets to the field of political decision making.

H.5 **Fixing prices of envelopes at mini-golf meetings.** The European Commission's investigation into the market for both standardised and customised paper envelopes in the EU.

H.6 **Taking your vitamins – at a price.** A case study of a global vitamins cartel.

H.7 **Fixing the price of car parts.** Investigations of global cartels in the car parts industry by competition authorities around the world.

H.8 **Productivity performance and the UK economy.** A detailed examination of how the UK's productivity compares with that in other countries.

H.9 **Technology and economic change.** How to get the benefits from technological advance.

H.10 **The economics of non-renewable resources.** An examination of how the price of non-renewable resources rises as stocks become depleted, and of how the current price reflects this.

H.11 **A deeper shade of green.** This looks at different perspectives on how we should treat the environment.

H.12 **Perverse subsidies.** An examination of the use of subsidies around the world that are harmful to the environment.

H.13 **Can the market provide adequate protection for the environment?** This explains why markets generally fail to take into account environmental externalities.

H.14 **Environmental auditing.** Are businesses becoming greener? A growing number of firms are subjecting themselves to an 'environmental audit' to judge just how 'green' they are.

H.15 **Restricting car access to Athens.** A case study that examines how the Greeks have attempted to reduce local atmospheric pollution from road traffic.

H.16 **Evaluating new road schemes.** The system used in the UK of assessing the costs and benefits of proposed new roads.

H.17 **Selling power to the people.** Attempts to introduce competition into the UK electricity industry.

H.18 **Regulation US-style.** This examines rate-of-return regulation: an alternative to price-cap regulation.

H.19 **Competition on the buses.** An examination of the impact of the deregulation of UK bus services in the mid-1980s.

H.20 **A lift to profits?** The EC imposes a record fine on four companies operating a lift and escalator cartel.

H.21 **Are we all green now?** Changing attitudes to the environment.

H.22 **Selling the environment.** An examination of the Kyoto Protocol and successive attempts to reach international agreement on tackling climate change.

H.23 **HS2: is it really worth it?** The case for and against High Speed Rail in the UK.

WEBSITES RELEVANT TO PART H

Numbers and sections refer to websites listed in the Web appendix and hotlinked from this text's website at *www.pearsoned.co.uk/sloman*

■ For news articles relevant to Part H, see the *Economics News Articles* link from the text's website.

■ For general news on market failures and government intervention, see websites in section A, and particularly A1–5, 9, 21, 23–26, 31. See also links to newspapers worldwide in A38–44.

■ For information on taxes and subsidies, see E18, 25, 30, 36; G13. For use of green taxes, see E2, 14, 30; G11; H5.

■ For information on health and the economics of health care (Case study H.2 on the student website: see above), see E8; H8, 9.

■ For sites favouring the free market, see C17; E34. See also C18 for the development of ideas on the market and government intervention.

■ For information on training, see E5; G14; H3.

■ For policy on the environment and transport, see E2, 7, 11, 14, 29; G10, 11, 19. See also H11.

■ UK and EU departments relevant to competition policy can be found at sites E4, 10; G7, 8.

■ UK regulatory bodies can be found at sites E4, 11, 15, 16, 19, 21, 22, 26, 29.

■ For student resources relevant to Part H see sites C1–7, 9, 10, 19.

■ For simulations, experiments and games relevant to Part H, see sites D12–14, 16–20.

Business in the international environment

The FT Reports . . .

The Financial Times, 3 June 2018

G7 countries condemn US in rebuke over tariffs

By Sam Fleming

America's G7 allies on Saturday condemned Donald Trump's decision to hit his trading partners with tariffs on steel and aluminium in a remarkable public rebuke of the group's most powerful member following days of escalating tensions over trade.

A so-called chair's summary released by G7 host nation Canada after meetings of finance ministers and central bankers on Saturday called for decisive action to address the tariffs in a forthcoming gathering of the group's leaders.

Many ministers attending the G7 meetings in Whistler highlighted the 'negative impact of unilateral trade actions by the United States,' the statement said. 'Concerns were expressed that the tariffs imposed by the United States on its friends and allies, on the grounds of national security, undermine open trade and confidence in the global economy.'

It is rare to see such a bitter rift in the G7, a group of democracies that traces its roots back to the 1970s — much less open criticism by its membership of the US, which normally is a leading force in guiding its agenda. But Mr Trump's decision to pursue protectionist measures against countries that count themselves as America's closest economic and military partners has infuriated and alarmed politicians in other capitals.

'Unfortunately the actions of the United States this week risk undermining the very values that traditionally have bound us together,' said Canada's finance minister Bill Morneau in a statement.

The public criticism of the US in Whistler further raises the stakes ahead of a summit of leaders including Mr Trump next week in Charlevoix. It comes as leading US partners including Canada and the EU prepare retaliatory measures following America's decision to impose tariffs on steel and aluminium imports.

Mr Morneau told reporters following the meetings that there had been consensus outside the US that the Trump administration's actions were 'destructive to our ability to get things done'. US treasury secretary Steven Mnuchin had been asked to convey the 'regret and disappointment' felt by G7 partners to the president, he said.

Mr Mnuchin acknowledged the sentiments expressed by America's partners but insisted after the gathering that the US was not abdicating its position at the helm of the world economy. 'I don't think in any way the US is abandoning its leadership in the global economy — quite the contrary,' he said in a press conference, citing the strength of the recent recovery following Republican-led tax cuts in December.

However, in the meetings finance ministers repeatedly urged the US to reverse its decision to impose levies on metal imports. Taro Aso, Japan's finance minister, called the US action 'deeply deplorable' in comments to reporters. Bruno Le Maire, the French finance minister, referred acerbically to the G6 plus one. The discussions, he said later, had been tense and difficult. 'We cannot understand the American decisions on steel and aluminium. The ball is in the US court,' he said on Twitter.

US allies on both sides of the Atlantic have angrily cited their close ties with the US and shared sacrifices in past wars alongside the country as they condemned America's steps. Brussels has said it will enact retaliatory tariffs on US exports and bring a case to the WTO, while Canada said it would impose tariffs on up to $12.8bn worth of US imports.

Nevertheless, as the G7 finance minister and central bank governors' meetings wrapped up on Saturday, Mr Trump reiterated his demands on trade on social media, saying the US must 'at long last be treated fairly on Trade'.

He added: 'If we charge a country ZERO to sell their goods, and they charge us 25, 50 or even 100 per cent to sell ours, it is UNFAIR and can no longer be tolerated. That is not Free or Fair Trade, it is Stupid Trade!'

The debate in Whistler came as US commerce secretary Wilbur Ross holds talks in China this weekend aimed at reaching an accord with Beijing over the two countries' trade differences. Mr Trump cast those discussions into further doubt earlier in the week by threatening to impose tariffs on $50bn of Chinese goods.

The G7 consists of Canada, France, Germany, Italy, Japan, the United Kingdom, and the United States.

Free trade and open borders have long been considered the golden path towards prosperity. But globalization didn't keep its side of the deal. Worldwide, the enraged losers of borderless trade are calling for protectionist walls, while the establishment is under pressure to backpedal, fast.

Torsten Riecke and Jens Münchrath, 'It's time to rewind', *Handelsblatt Global*, 19 August 2016, https://global.handelsblatt.com/politics/its-time-to-rewind-593767

With falling barriers to international trade, with improved communications and with an increasingly global financial system, so nations have found that their economies have become ever more intimately linked. Economic events in one part of the world, such as changes in interest rates or a downturn in economic growth, will have a myriad of knock-on effects for the international community at large – from the international investor, to the foreign exchange dealer, to the domestic policy maker, to the business that exports or imports or that has subsidiaries abroad.

In Part I, we explore the international environment and its impact on business. Chapter 23 considers the issue of *globalisation* and the rise and spread of multinational enterprises within the world economy. It not only looks at why certain businesses become multinational, but evaluates their impact upon host nations, within both the developed and the developing worlds.

Key terms

Globalisation
Foreign direct investment (FDI)
Multinational corporation
Transnationality index
Comparative advantage
The gains from trade
Terms of trade
Protectionism
Tariffs
Quotas
Infant and senile industries

In Chapter 24, we focus on *international trade*. We consider why trading is advantageous and why, nevertheless, certain countries feel the need to restrict trade and protect domestic industries by raising tariffs or dumping goods on foreign markets at prices below marginal cost (see the *Financial Times* article opposite).

Finally, in Chapter 25, we examine one of the most significant trends in international trade over the past 50 years – namely, the rise of the *trade bloc*. We outline the advantages and disadvantages of regional trading. We also look briefly at trading blocs in North America and South East Asia and the Pacific. Then, as an extended case study, we consider the position of the European Union and the effects of the creation of a single European market on both businesses and consumers.

World Trade Organization (WTO)
Trade bloc
Preferential trading
Free trade areas, customs unions and common markets
Trade creation and diversion
North America Free Trade Association (NAFTA)
Asian-Pacific Economic Co-operation forum (APEC)
European Union (EU)
Single European market

Globalisation and multinational business

Business issues covered in this chapter

- What is meant by globalisation and what is its impact on business?
- What is driving the process of globalisation?
- Does the world benefit from the process of the globalisation of business?
- What forms do multinational corporations take?
- What is the magnitude and pattern of global foreign direct investment and how has it changed?
- For what reasons do companies become multinational ones? Are there any disadvantages for companies of operating internationally?
- How can multinationals use their position to gain the best deal from the host state?
- What is the impact on developing countries of multinational investment?

23.1 GLOBALISATION: SETTING THE SCENE

The nature of global production continually evolves. In the past, many multinational companies (also known as transnational companies) located much of their manufacturing in developing countries. Now, increasingly, they locate service and 'knowledge-based' jobs there too. Such jobs range from telesales to research and development.

Some of these jobs require high levels of skills and training, once seen as the preserve of the rich economies and the source of their competitive advantage in international trade. However, countries such as India and China, as well as many others, produce a massive number of well-trained and well-educated engineers and IT specialists every year. Such workers are predictably cheap to employ compared to their US, European and Japanese counterparts, many of whom have lost their jobs or find their wages being driven down. But it is not all bad news for the developed economies. By outsourcing to developing countries, many companies have

seen their costs fall and their profits rise. At the same time, consumers benefit from lower prices.

For developing economies, such as India and China, the benefits of this new wave of globalisation are substantial. Foreign companies invest in high-value-added, knowledge-rich production, most of which is subsequently exported. Economic growth is stimulated and wages rise. Increased consumption then spreads the benefits more widely throughout the economy. There are, however, costs. Many are left behind by the growth and inequalities deepen. There are also often significant environmental externalities as rapid growth leads to increased pollution and environmental degradation.

The exodus of jobs from developed to developing countries is a good example of the process of globalisation. In this chapter, we are going to explore what *globalisation* is, how it is evolving, the impacts it is likely to have on different groups of people throughout the world and the motivations behind the increasing 'multi-nationalisation' of business.

Defining globalisation

Economically, we are bound through trade, investment, production and finance. Politically, we are bound through organisations such as the United Nations, the World Trade Organization (WTO), the International Monetary Fund (IMF) and the G20. Through such organisations, we attempt to establish frameworks and rules to govern almost every aspect of our lives. Culturally, we are subject to the same advertising and branding; we migrate; we go on holiday; we share ideas, fashions and music; we compete in global sporting events, such as the Olympics; and, increasingly, we communicate globally through the Internet.

Globalisation is, then, the *process* of developing these links. As Phillipe Legrain suggests, globalisation is 'shorthand for how our lives are becoming increasingly intertwined with those of distant people and places around the world – economically, politically and culturally'.[1]

Globalisation is, therefore, a multi-dimensional concept. The OECD defines **economic globalisation** as 'a process of closer economic integration of global markets: financial, product and labour'.[2] Similarly, the IMF refers to economic globalisation as 'the increasing integration of economies around the world, particularly through the movement of goods, services, and capital across borders'. They argue that this definition can be broadened further to include 'the movement of people (labour) and knowledge (technology) across international borders'.[3]

Supporters and critics of globalisation alike tend to agree that globalisation is nothing new. There has always been a degree of economic, financial, political and cultural interdependence. But what has made globalisation an increasingly important issue is the speed at which these interdependences have grown. The acceleration of globalisation has led some to characterise the past couple of decades or so as a period of **hyper-globalisation**. This has been partly the result of unprecedented technological change, particularly in respect to transport and communication and, partly, at least until more recently, the result of a political drive to remove barriers between countries and embrace foreign influences.

Business, caught within this process of globalisation, invariably will seek to take advantage of what it has to offer, which is essentially a borderless world or one that is increasingly so. A global economy enables a business to locate the different dimensions of its value chain wherever it might get the best deal to lower costs or improve quality or both. Globalisation encourages this process of relocation and the framing of business strategy within a global context.

What drives globalisation?

Within any global system, certain industries and markets are likely to be more prone to the forces of globalisation than others. This becomes apparent when you attempt to identify the conditions influencing the globalisation process. These globalisation drivers can be categorised in a number of ways. George Yip suggests that the globalisation potential of an industry – that is, its ability to set global strategy and compete in a global marketplace – can be analysed under four headings:

- market drivers;
- cost drivers;
- government drivers;
- competitive drivers.

These are shown in Table 23.1.

Market drivers. Market drivers focus on the extent to which markets throughout the world are becoming similar. The more similar consumers are in respect to income and taste, the more significant globalisation market drivers will become.

Cost drivers. Cost drivers present the business with the potential to reorganise its operations globally and reduce costs as a consequence. Global economies of scale and transport and distribution issues will be significant.

Government drivers. Governments often play a key role in driving the process of globalisation. The speed of globalisation is likely to be faster when governments openly welcome trade and inward investment.

Global political agreements, such as those made at the WTO covering world trade and related issues (see section 24.4), not only directly affect the operation of markets, but also help establish global rules and protocols.

Competition drivers. As competitiveness builds, whether in the domestic market or overseas, businesses will be forced to consider how to maintain their competitive position. This often involves embracing a global business strategy, which invariably contributes towards globalisation. Global business networks and cross-border strategic alliances are key reflections of this growing competitive global process.

What is clear is that globalisation is both shaped and driven by a wide variety of conditions. These conditions will vary from industry to industry, reflecting why certain industries

---

Definitions

Economic globalisation (OECD definition) The process of closer economic integration of global markets: financial, product and labour.

Hyper-globalisation A term used to describe the rapid pace of globalisation seen in recent years.

---

[1] P. Legrain, *Open World: The Truth about Globalisation* (Abacus, 2003).

[2] A. Gurria, *Managing globalisation and the role of the OECD* (OECD, 2006).

[3] IMF staff, *Globalization: A Brief Overview* (OECD, 2008).

Table 23.1 The drivers of globalisation

Market drivers
- Per capita income converging among industrialised nations
- Convergence of lifestyles and tastes
- Organisations beginning to behave as global customers
- Increasing travel creating global consumers
- Growth of global and regional channels
- Establishment of world brands
- Push to develop global advertising

Cost drivers
- Continuing push for economies of scale
- Accelerating technological innovation
- Advances in transportation
- Emergence of newly industrialised countries with productive capability and low labour costs

- Increasing cost of product development relative to market life

Government drivers
- Reduction of tariff barriers
- Reduction of non-tariff barriers
- Creation of blocs
- Decline in role of governments as producers and customers
- Privatisation in previously state-dominated economies
- Shift to open-market economies from closed communist systems in Eastern Europe
- Increasing participation of China and India in the global economy

Competitive drivers
- Continuing increases in the level of world trade

- Increased ownership of corporations by foreign acquirers
- Rise of new competitors intent upon becoming global competitors
- Growth of global networks making countries interdependent in particular industries
- More companies becoming globally centred rather than nationally centred
- Increased formation of global strategic alliances

Other drivers
- Revolution in information and communication
- Globalisation of financial markets
- Improvements in business travel

Source: G. Yip, *Total Global Strategy* (Prentice Hall, 1995)

---

are more global than others. Furthermore, these conditions will vary over time, so affecting the nature and magnitude of cross-border activities.

Globalisation: the good and the bad

Even though supporters and critics of globalisation are in agreement that globalisation is nothing new, and that it is primarily driven by technological change and shifting political attitudes, they are far from agreeing about the consequences of globalisation and whether these are beneficial or harmful.

The supporters

Supporters of globalisation argue that it has massive potential to benefit the entire global economy. With freer trade and greater competition, countries and businesses within them are encouraged to think, plan and act globally. Technology spreads faster; countries specialise in particular products and processes and thereby exploit their core competitive advantages.

Both rich and poor, it is argued, benefit from such a process. Supporters point to the falling proportion of those in developing countries living in extreme poverty. According to World Bank estimates, 10 per cent of the world's population lived on less than US$1.90 a day in 2015 compared to 36 per cent in 1990 (at 2015 prices).

Pause for thought

The World Bank quantifies 'extreme poverty' based on information on basic needs collected from the 15 poorest countries. What are the arguments for and against monetising poverty in this way?

Politically, globalisation brings us closer together. Political ties help stabilise relationships and offer the opportunity for countries to discuss their differences. However imperfect the current global political system might be, the alternative of independent nations is seen as potentially far worse. The globalisation of culture is also seen as beneficial, as a world of experience is opened, whether in respect of our holiday destinations, the food we eat, the music we listen to or the movies we watch.

Supporters of globalisation recognise that not all countries benefit equally from globalisation: those that have wealth will, as always, possess more opportunity to benefit from the globalisation process, whether from lower prices, global political agreements or cultural experience. However, long term, supporters of globalisation see it ultimately as being for the benefit of all – rich and poor alike.

The critics

Critics of globalisation argue that it contributes to growing inequality and further impoverishes poor nations. As an economic philosophy, globalisation allows multinational corporations (MNCs), based largely in the USA, Europe and Japan, to exploit their dominant position in foreign markets. Without effective competition in these markets, such companies are able to pursue profit with few constraints.

By 'exploiting' low-wage labour, companies are able to compete more effectively on world markets. As competitive pressures intensify and companies seek to cut costs further, this can put downward pressure on such wages.

The effects of globalisation are, of course, not confined to developing countries. The *internationalisation of production* has helped to accelerate the pace of industrial change in many advanced economies. The outsourcing of production overseas and the development of international supply chains has often meant painful adjustment for those affected, particularly in traditional industries trying to compete on a global stage.

The *internationalisation of finance* has meant a significant rise in cross-border financial flows. Critics argue that this has both increased the significance of foreign financial market participants, such as foreign banks, and the systemic importance of the financial system in advanced economies.

The internationalisation of the more developed financial systems of advanced economies has contributed to the growth of the balance sheets of people, businesses and governments. When this growth becomes unsustainable, as witnessed by the financial crisis of the late 2000s, the adverse effects on the well-being of these countries and its citizens can be stark. We discuss the financial crisis of the late 2000s in Chapter 28.

In political terms, critics of globalisation see the world being dominated by big business. Multinationals put pressure on their home governments to promote their interests in their dealings with other countries, thereby heightening the domination of rich countries over the poor.

Critics are no less damning of the cultural aspects of globalisation. They see the world dominated by multinational brands, Western fashion, music and TV. Rather than globalisation fostering a mix of cultural expression, critics suggest that cultural differences are being replaced by the dominant (Western) culture of the day.

The above views represent the extremes and, to a greater or lesser degree, both have elements of truth within them. The impact of globalisation on different groups is not even and never will be. However, to suggest that big business rules is also an exaggeration. Clearly, big business is influential, but it is a question of degree. Influence will, invariably, fluctuate over time, between events and between and within countries.

For many years, the momentum has been for barriers to trade to have come down. This has enabled hyper-globalisation with profound effects on both multinational business and the peoples of the world. More recently, we have seen a rise in protectionist rhetoric and policy actions. These are partly a response to these effects and to their distributional impact. This raises an intriguing question: could the period of hyper-globalisation be coming to an end? If so, this would have important implications for businesses and for their internationalisation strategies.

In the following sections, we consider why it is that businesses decide to go multinational and evaluate what impact they have on their host countries. Before we do this, we shall first offer a definition of multinational business and assess the importance of multinational investment within the global economy.

23.2 WHAT IS A MULTINATIONAL CORPORATION?

Despite their gigantic size and importance within the global economy, *multinational corporations* (MNCs) defy simple definition. At the most basic level, an MNC is a business that owns and controls foreign subsidiaries in more than one country. It is this ownership and control of productive assets in other countries that makes the MNC distinct from an enterprise that does business overseas simply by exporting goods or services.

To achieve control over foreign productive assets, MNCs engage in foreign direct investment (FDI) (rather than merely portfolio investment).[4] This may involve building a new subsidiary overseas, expanding an existing one or acquiring an existing business operation through either merger or acquisition.

According to the 2018 World Investment Report, the 100 largest non-financial MNCs in 2017 (as ranked by the value of their foreign assets) had total assets of $14.50 trillion of which $9 trillion were in foreign affiliates. These MNCs had a combined turnover of $7.96 trillion of which foreign sales contributed $5.2 trillion and they employed 16.65 million people of which 9.8 million were in their foreign affiliates.

An indicator of the global importance and reach of MNCs is provided by the *Transnational Index* (TNI). The UN calculates the TNI as the average of three ratios: foreign assets to total assets, foreign sales to total sales and foreign employment to total employment. The index, therefore, varies between 0 and 100 per cent, where 100 per cent indicates that 100 per cent of assets, sales and employment are attributable to foreign associates. Across the 100 largest non-financial MNCs in 2017, the average TNI was 66.1 per cent. This compares with 52.3 per cent in 1999.

The foreign affiliates of *all* MNCs in 2017 had assets of $103.4, trillion, employing 73.2 million people with sales of $30.8 trillion, equivalent to 39 per cent of global GDP. Back in 1990, foreign affiliates has assets of $5.8 trillion, employing 27 million people with sales of $6.8 trillion, equivalent to 29 per cent of GDP. Again, this points to the long-term increase in the global presence of MNCs.

---

[4]Portfolio investment involves purchasing shares and other financial assets in overseas organisations, but with little or no strategic and operational control over their investment decisions.

> ### Definitions
>
> **Multinational corporations** Businesses that own and control foreign subsidiaries in more than one country.
>
> **Transnational Index** An index of the global presence of multinational corporations (MNCs) based on the ratios of foreign assets to total assets, foreign sales to total sales and foreign employment to total employment.

Table 23.2 shows how some of the largest MNCs have turnovers that exceed the national income of many smaller economies!

In 2017, the global stock of foreign direct investment (FDI) was around $31.5 trillion, the equivalent of 39 per cent of global GDP. Of this, 64 per cent was located in developed economies (with 33 per cent in Europe), 33 per cent in developing economies and 3 per cent in transitional economies. The share of the global stock of FDI located in developed economies has declined in recent times. In 1990, developed economies hosted 77 per cent of the global stock of FDI compared with just 23 per cent in developing and transitional economies.

Diversity among MNCs

There is an immense diversity among MNCs.

Size. Any list of the world's largest firms is dominated by multinationals. As we saw in Table 23.2, their turnovers can be enormous. And, yet, there are also thousands of very small, often specialist multinationals, which are a mere fraction of the size of the giants.

The nature of business. MNCs cover the entire spectrum of business activity, from manufacturing to extraction, agricultural production, chemicals, processing, service provision and finance. There is no 'typical' line of activity of a multinational.

Overseas business relative to total business. MNCs differ in respect of how extensive their overseas operations are relative to their total business. 24 per cent of Walmart's sales in 2017 came from overseas subsidiaries, while 87 per cent of Samsung's sales came from its foreign affiliates. Some smaller MNCs also have a large global presence. The UK pharmaceutical firm AstraZeneca had a transnationality index in 2017 of 81.3 per cent, but had sales of only 4 per cent of those achieved by Walmart who had a transnationality index of 29.3 per cent.

Production locations. Some MNCs are truly 'global', with production located in a wide variety of countries and regions. Other MNCs, by contrast, only locate in one other region or in a very narrow range of countries.

There are, however, a number of potentially constraining factors on the location of multinational businesses. For example, businesses concerned with the extraction of raw materials will locate as nature dictates. Businesses that provide services

Table 23.2	Comparison of the 12 largest companies (by turnover) and selected countries (by GDP): 2017			
MNC rank	**Country or company**	**Company headquarters**	**Industry**	**GDP ($bn) or turnover ($bn)**
	USA			*19 485*
	China			*11 244*
	UK			*2 628*
1	Walmart Stores	USA	Retailing	500
	Belgium			*494*
	Austria			*417*
2	State Grid	China	Power	349
	Ireland			*332*
3	Sinopec	China	Energy	327
4	China National Petroleum	China	Energy	326
5	Royal Dutch Shell	Netherlands/UK	Energy	312
	Chile			*277*
6	Toyota Motors	Japan	Motor vehicles	265
7	Volkswagen	Germany	Motor vehicles	260
	Finland			*253*
8	BP	UK	Energy	245
9	Exxon Mobil	USA	Energy	244
10	Berkshire Hathaway	USA	Financials	242
	Egypt			*237*
11	Apple	USA	Technology	229
	Vietnam			*220*
12	Samsung	S. Korea	Technology	212
	Greece			*201*
	Iceland			*24*

Note: GDP figures are at market exchange rates.

Sources: Companies: *Fortune Global 500* (2018); Countries: *World Economic Outlook* database, IMF (October 2018)

will tend to locate in the rich markets of developed regions of the world economy, where the demand for services is high. Others locate according to the factor intensity of the stage of production. Thus, a labour-intensive stage might be located in a developing country where wage rates are relatively low, while another stage that requires a high level of automation might be located in an industrially advanced country.

Ownership patterns. As businesses expand overseas, they are faced with a number of options. They can decide to go it alone and create wholly owned subsidiaries. Alternatively, they might share ownership, and hence some of the risk, by establishing joint ventures. In such cases, the MNC might have a majority or minority stake in the overseas enterprise. Increasingly, though, MNCs are looking at a third option: non-equity modes of operation. In this scenario, the MNC has no ownership stake in the partner firm overseas, but exerts control over operations through contractual arrangements such as franchising or strategic alliances. This non-equity mode of operation by MNCs begins to challenge our understanding and, hence, our definition of MNCs.

In certain countries, where MNC investment is regulated, many governments insist on owning or controlling a share in the enterprise. Whether this is a majority or minority stake varies from country to country. It also depends on the nature of the business and its perceived national importance.

There have been two significant developments in terms of ownership in recent times. First, there has been a rise in state-owned MNCs. These are MNCs where the government has a significant interest in the parent enterprise and its foreign affiliates. Operationally, this means that government has at least 10 per cent of the voting power or is the single largest shareholder. Second, there has been a growth in sovereign wealth funds (SWFs). These are state-owned organisations investing internationally in a range of assets, such as shares, bonds and property. They have tended to focus their growth in the retail and commercial property sectors.

Organisational structure. We discussed (see Chapter 3) the variety of organisational forms that MNCs might adopt – from the model where the headquarters or parent company is dominant and the overseas subsidiary subservient, to that where international subsidiaries operate as self-standing organisations, bound together only in so far as they strive towards a set of global objectives.

The above characteristics of MNCs reveal that they represent a wide and very diverse group of enterprises. Beyond sharing the common link of having production activities in more than one country, MNCs differ widely in the nature and forms of their overseas business and in the relationship between the parent and its subsidiaries.

> ### Pause for thought
>
> *Given the diverse nature of multinational business, how useful is the definition given (on page 446) for describing a multinational corporation?*

23.3 TRENDS IN MULTINATIONAL INVESTMENT

Successful multinational businesses are constantly adapting to the economic environment. In recent times, they have been shrinking the size of their headquarters, removing layers of bureaucracy and reorganising their global operations into smaller autonomous profit centres. Gone is the philosophy that big companies inevitably will do better than small ones. Many modern multinationals are organisations that combine the advantages of size (i.e. economies of scale) with the responsiveness and market knowledge of smaller firms.

The key for the modern multinational is flexibility and to be at one and the same time both global and local.

The size of multinational investment

We can estimate the size of multinational investment by looking at figures for foreign direct investment (FDI). Figure 23.1 shows FDI inflows in billions of dollars. Global FDI inflows in 2017 were $1.43 trillion, the equivalent to 1.8 per cent of global GDP. This compares with $205 billion in 1990, the equivalent to 0.9 per cent of global GDP.

From the chart, we also observe relatively rapid rates of increase in FDI between 1998 and 2000 and again between 2004 and 2007. In 2000, global FDI flows were the equivalent of 4 per cent of global GDP and, in 2007, they were the equivalent of 3.3 per cent of global GDP. Both periods saw a surge in cross-border merger and acquisition (M&A) activity as can be seen in Figure 23.2.

Between 1990 and 2000, there was a three-fold increase in the number and ten-fold increase in the value of global M&As. This saw the value of M&As reach $960 billion (2.8 per cent of GDP) by 2000. After initially easing on the back of slower global growth, M&A activity then increased as growth rebounded, reaching a new peak in 2007 of over $1.03 trillion (1.8 per cent of global GDP).

Global FDI inflows fell sharply following the financial crisis of the late 2000s, falling by around 20 per cent in both 2008 and 2009. This was mirrored by a 72 per cent fall in the value of cross-border M&As to just $288 billion.

The post-crisis period was marked by significant volatility in FDI flows. The value of global FDI flows increased by 44 per cent in 2015, but fell by 23 per cent in 2017. Consequently, by 2017, global inward FDI flows remained 25 per cent below their 2007 peak. Yet this masks significant differences between FDI flows to developed and developing countries. Inward FDI flows to developed countries were 45 per cent lower, while flows into transition economies were

Figure 23.1 FDI inflows ($ billions)

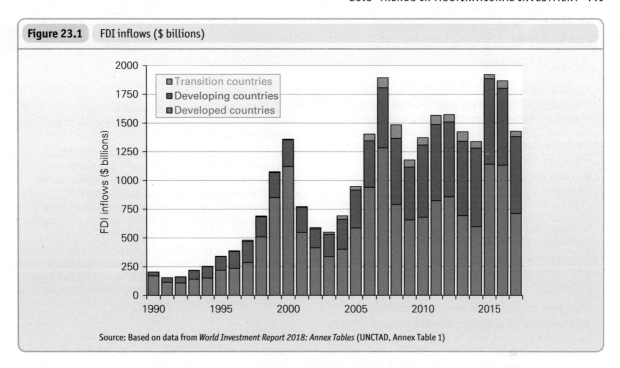

Source: Based on data from *World Investment Report 2018: Annex Tables* (UNCTAD, Annex Table 1)

Figure 23.2 Number and value of net cross-border M&As

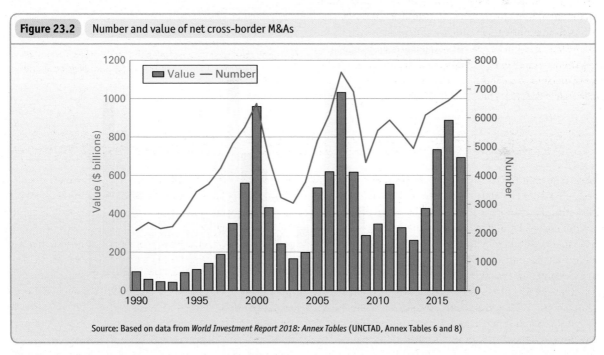

Source: Based on data from *World Investment Report 2018: Annex Tables* (UNCTAD, Annex Tables 6 and 8)

46 per cent lower. However, FDI flows into developing countries were 28 per cent higher.

Box 23.1 looks in more detail at the two principal forms of FDI: M&A activity and greenfield FDI investment (a MNC setting up a new subsidiary or expanding an existing one).

The significance of inward investment relative to total investment (or 'gross fixed capital formation' – GFCF) is shown in Figure 23.3. Increasing globalisation has meant that the trend in inward investment as a proportion of GFCF has been upwards for both developed and developing nations. However, for the majority of the period since the

1990s the proportion of inward FDI to total investment has been lower in developed than in developing and transition economies.

Historically, developed economies have been the main destination for FDI. However, this pattern is changing, especially following the financial crisis of the late 2000s and the subsequent economic downturn. As Table 23.3 shows, in recent times, just under half of FDI has been in the developing world (including transition economies). Given the low levels of income of many developing countries and their powerless position in world trade, this amount is very large

BOX 23.1	M&As AND GREENFIELD FDI

Modes of FDI entry

There are two principal forms of foreign direct investment (FDI), known as 'modes of FDI entry'. The first is *greenfield investment*. This involves multinational companies investing in a new subsidiary overseas or expanding an existing one. The second mode of entry is through *cross-border mergers and acquisitions* (M&As).

In recent years, the values of greenfield FDI and investment through M&As have been broadly similar. In 2017, for example, greenfield FDI was $720.3 billion, while cross-border M&As were worth $694.0 billion. However, if we take a longer-term perspective, from 2003 to 2017, greenfield investment was worth $7.2 trillion compared with $4.5 trillion through M&As. Furthermore, M&A investment tends to be more volatile than greenfield FDI.

The geography of M&As and greenfield FDI

We now analyse the geography of the two modes of FDI entry.

Cross-border M&As

Consider chart (a) which shows the value of cross-border M&As by the *destination* economy, i.e. the economy of the acquired company.

The host economy for the majority of cross-border M&As is a developed economy. However, the size of this majority had been on the decline. In the early 1990s, developed countries were the destination of up to 95 per cent (by value) of cross-border M&As. By 2014, this had fallen to 68 per cent. However, in 2014 and 2015, the share surged again to around the 90 per cent mark. In 2017, the share was 82 per cent.

Consider now the *origin* of M&A activity. Following the financial crisis, investors from developing and transition economies became an increasingly important source of global M&A activity. From 2000 to 2008, 15 per cent of M&As (by value) typically originated from these economies. In the period from 2009 to 2017, this rose to 34 per cent and was as high as 54 per cent in 2013.

(a) *Value of cross-border M&As by destination ($ billions)*

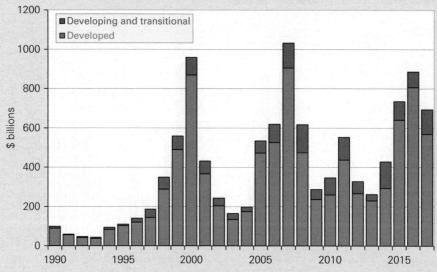

Source: Based on data from *World Investment Report 2018: Annex Tables* (UNCTAD, Annex Table 5)

Percentage of FDI (by value) originating from developed economies

		2003	2005	2007	2009	2011	2013	2015	2017
M&As	Developed	85.9	83.4	84.0	66.5	78.0	46.0	79.9	66.9
	Europe	32.0	58.7	57.5	46.0	31.3	−11.2	42.4	28.4
	USA	36.4	16.9	17.5	8.4	24.9	22.7	17.4	16.6
Greenfield FDI	Developed	81.5	78.6	74.4	73.2	70.6	65.7	64.3	66.4
	Europe	37.1	38.2	48.0	43.7	39.1	36.6	36.3	39.4
	USA	27.5	22.8	15.7	17.1	17.7	16.3	15.5	16.6

Source: Based on data from *World Investment Report 2018: Annex Tables* (UNCTAD, Annex Tables 6 and 13)

(b) *Value of Greenfield FDI projects by destination ($ billions)*

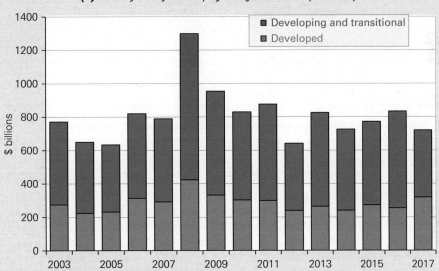

Source: Based on data from *World Investment Report 2018: Annex Tables* (UNCTAD, Annex Table 14)

Greenfield FDI

Chart (b) shows the value of greenfield FDI projects by *destination*. From it, we observe that developing and transition economies have attracted typically around two-thirds of global greenfield FDI investment since 2003.

Despite the growth of cross-border M&A activity in developing and transition economies, the value of greenfield FDI remains substantially higher in these economies. Over the period from 2009 to 2017, the value of greenfield FDI investment in developing and transition economies was six times greater than that from cross-border M&A activity, whereas in developed countries it was around 33 per cent less.

As the table shows, developing and transition economies during the 2010s have been the source of around one-third of global greenfield FDI. When viewed alongside the growing funds these countries now contribute to global M&A activity, it is clear that developing and transition economies are now important participants in cross-border investment.

 What factors might explain the significance of developing and transition economies not only as a destination for FDI but also increasingly as a source of FDI?

 Download data from the Annex Tables of UNCTAD's World Investment Report on merger and acquisition (M&A) activity by seller and greenfield FDI by destination. Construct two time series charts showing the proportions of these two forms of FDI flowing into the UK.

Figure 23.3   FDI inflows (% of gross fixed capital formation)

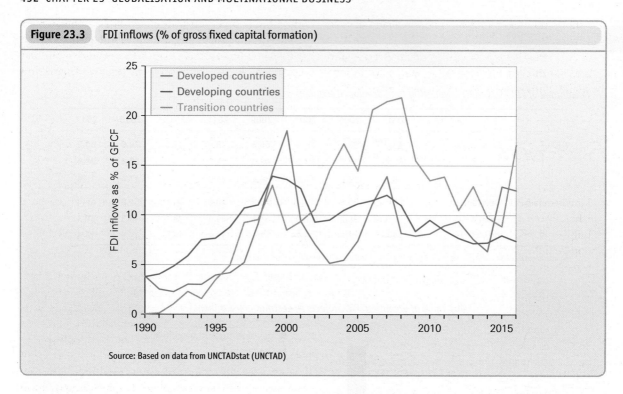

Source: Based on data from UNCTADstat (UNCTAD)

Table 23.3   Distribution of world FDI inflows, 1990–2017 (percentage of world FDI inflows)

Region	1990–2	1993–7	1998–2000	2001–3	2004–7	2008–9	2010–12	2013–17
Developed countries	**74.5**	**61.6**	**78.5**	**67.5**	**63.7**	**54.4**	**52.2**	**52.6**
Europe	49.6	35.3	48.1	47.3	42.6	30.0	31.8	25.9
Australia	3.3	2.0	0.7	1.5	1.7	2.9	3.4	2.8
France	10.0	6.2	3.6	2.4	2.1	2.6	1.4	2.1
Germany	1.1	2.1	7.8	6.1	2.9	1.3	3.6	1.3
Ireland	0.7	0.5	1.6	3.5	−1.0	0.5	2.5	4.0
Japan	1.1	0.2	0.8	1.2	0.5	1.3	0.0	0.5
United Kingdom	11.3	5.9	9.1	3.7	12.0	6.9	3.5	3.7
United States	16.7	20.2	24.9	14.3	14.7	16.4	13.9	19.4
Developing countries	**25.1**	**37.1**	**20.8**	**30.5**	**32.3**	**39.0**	**43.2**	**43.6**
Africa	2.0	2.1	1.1	2.8	2.7	4.4	3.2	3.2
Latin America & Caribbean	7.1	10.2	8.1	9.1	7.3	8.3	12.3	10.4
Developing Asia	15.8	24.8	11.6	18.6	22.2	26.2	27.5	29.8
Least developed	0.7	0.6	0.5	1.3	0.8	1.3	1.5	1.8
Brazil	0.8	1.9	3.1	2.5	1.8	2.6	5.7	4.0
China	3.8	11.4	4.4	8.2	6.5	7.7	8.0	8.4
Hong Kong	1.5	2.6	2.8	2.5	3.5	4.3	5.3	7.3
India	0.1	0.5	0.3	0.8	1.1	3.1	1.9	2.4
Malaysia	2.4	1.9	0.3	0.4	0.5	0.3	0.7	0.7
Singapore	2.4	3.0	1.2	2.0	2.5	1.2	3.5	4.3
South Korea	0.7	0.6	0.9	1.0	1.1	0.8	0.6	0.7
Mexico	2.4	2.8	1.5	3.8	2.4	1.8	1.7	2.2
Transition economies	**0.4**	**1.3**	**0.7**	**2.0**	**4.1**	**6.6**	**4.6**	**3.7**
Russia	0.2	0.6	0.3	0.8	2.3	3.7	2.2	2.1

Note: Shaded areas represent years of weak or declining global FDI; classifications based on UNCTAD country classifications, http://unctadstat.unctad.org/EN/Classifications.html.
Source: Based on data from *World Investment Report 2018: Annex Tables* (UNCTAD)

and shows the dominance of MNCs in many of these economies.

In 2017, the USA was the world's largest recipient of FDI, accounting for 19.3 per cent of global FDI inflows. Mainland China was second (9.5 per cent) and Hong Kong the third (7.3 per cent). Although FDI is generally less concentrated than in the past, Africa still only accounted for 2.9 per cent of global FDI in 2017 and much of this was to the resource-rich countries of Nigeria, Angola and South Africa.

23.4 WHY DO BUSINESSES GO MULTINATIONAL?

The global marketplace can provide massive opportunities for firms to expand. Once markets within the domestic economy have become saturated and opportunities for growth diminish, dynamic firms may seek new markets and hence new opportunities by expanding production overseas.

Expansion overseas may enable companies to reduce costs, perhaps by utilising new supply sources, new ideas and skills. A vertically integrated multinational, for example, may be able to locate each part of the production process in the country where the relevant factor prices are lowest.

Businesses can look to expand in one of two ways: through either internal or external expansion (see Chapter 15). MNCs are no exception to this rule. They can expand overseas, either by creating a new production facility from scratch, such as Nissan in the north-east of England (greenfield FDI), or by merging with or taking over existing foreign producers, such as the acquisition of ASDA by Walmart (M&A FDI). They can also engage in an international strategic alliance (e.g. the joint venture in 2006 between Finland's Nokia and Japan's Sanyo to produce mobile phones for the North American market or the 2014 alliance between Sony and Panasonic).

The decision whether to go multinational will depend on the nature of firms' business and their corporate strategy. MNCs are a diverse group of enterprises and their motives for going overseas will vary. We will examine two theories that have been used to explain the development of the MNC: *the product life cycle* and *the Eclectic Paradigm*.

The product life cycle and the multinational company

The product life cycle hypothesis was discussed at length (Chapter 17). However, it is worth reviewing its elements here in order to identify how an MNC, by altering the geographical production of a good, might extend its profitability.

A product's life cycle can be split into four phases: launch, growth, maturity and decline.

The launch phase. This will tend to see the new product produced in the economy where the product is developed. It will be exported to the rest of the world. At this stage of the product's life cycle, the novelty of the product and the monopoly position of the producer enable the business to charge high prices and make high profits.

The growth phase. As the market begins to grow, other producers will seek to copy or imitate the new product. Prices begin to fall. In order to maintain competitiveness, the business will look to reduce costs and, at this stage, might consider shifting production overseas to lower-cost production centres.

Maturity. At the early stage of maturity, the business is still looking to sell its product in the markets of the developed economies. Thus it may still be happy to locate some of its plants in such economies. As the original market becomes increasingly saturated, however, the MNC will seek to expand into markets overseas which are at an earlier stage of development. Part of this expansion will be by the MNC simply exporting to these economies, but, increasingly, it will involve relocating its production there too.

Maturity and decline. By the time the original markets are fully mature and moving into decline, the only way to extend the product's life is to cut costs and sell the product in the markets of developing countries. The location of production may shift once again, this time to even lower-cost countries. By this stage, the country in which the product was developed will almost certainly be a net importer (if there is a market left for the product), but it may well be importing the product from a subsidiary of the same company that produced it within that country in the first place!

Thus the product life cycle model explains how firms might first export and then engage in FDI. It explains how firms transfer production to different locations to reduce costs and enable profits to be made from a product that could have become unprofitable if its production had continued from its original production base.

The theory was developed in the 1960s when MNC activity was less sophisticated than it is today. It can be useful in explaining horizontally and vertically integrated MNCs, but it cannot explain the more modern forms of MNC growth through strategic alliances. We thus turn to the second theory.

The Eclectic Paradigm

John Dunning[5] developed an organising framework, known as the Eclectic Paradigm. This helps to explain the pattern and growth of international production as well as

[5]J.H. Dunning, *The Globalisation of Business* (Routledge, 1993).

identifying the gains to firms from being multinational. Dunning identifies three categories of gains:

■ MNCs can exploit their core competencies in competing with companies in other countries. These are described by Dunning as 'ownership advantages': in other words, advantages deriving from *ownership-specific assets*.

■ They can exploit *locational advantages* in host countries, such as the availability of key raw materials or high demand for the good.

■ They may also derive *internalisation advantages*. These occur when the MNC gains from investing overseas rather than exporting to an overseas agent or licensing a foreign firm (i.e. using a market solution). In other words, the MNC gains from keeping control of the product within its organisation.

As firms and nations evolve, the distribution of ownership, location and internalisation advantages between firms and nations change so that we observe ever-changing patterns of international production.

Ownership advantages

An MNC may be able to exploit its ownership of assets that reflect its core competencies and which give the business a specific advantage over its foreign rivals in their home markets. Such advantages might include the following:

The ownership of superior technology. Such ownership will not only enhance the productivity levels of the MNC, but probably also contribute to the production of superior-quality products.

Research and development capacity. MNCs are likely to invest heavily in R&D in an attempt to maintain their global competitiveness. The global scale of their operations allows them to spread the costs of this R&D over a large output (i.e. the R&D has a low average fixed cost). MNCs, therefore, are often world leaders in process innovation and product development.

Product differentiation. MNCs often combine innovation with successful product differentiation in international markets. They may invest heavily in advertising and often develop global brand names (e.g. Kellogg's, IKEA, Samsung).

Entrepreneurial and managerial skills. Managers in MNCs are often innovative in the way they do business and organise the value chain. With the arrival of Japanese multinationals in the UK, it became instantly apparent that Japanese managers conducted business in a very different way from their British counterparts. The most fundamental difference concerned working practices. Japanese MNCs quickly established themselves as among the most efficient and productive businesses in the UK (see section 18.4 on the flexible firm).

Pause for thought

Before reading on, can you think of the host country locational advantages that might be attractive to MNCs?

Locational advantages

MNCs will take advantage of the most appropriate locations to make their goods and services. Locational advantages are those features of a host economy that MNCs believe will lower costs, improve quality and/or facilitate greater sales relative to investing in their home country. In addition, by going overseas, a firm must be effective at using its ownership-specific advantages over domestic firms, otherwise the locational advantage is muted. MNCs will consider a range of factors when comparing potential locations.

The availability of raw materials. Nations, like individuals, are not equally endowed with factors of production. Some nations are rich in labour, some in capital, some in raw materials. In other words, individual nations might have specific advantages over others. Because such factors of production are largely immobile, especially between nations, businesses respond by becoming multinational: that is, they locate where the necessary factors of production they require can be found. In the case of a business that wishes to extract raw materials, it has little choice but to do this.

The relative cost of inputs. Although it is possible that firms seek out lower-cost land and capital, perhaps because of host government subsidies, one of the main reasons firms want to move overseas is because labour is relatively cheaper. For example, a firm might locate an assembly plant in a developing country (i.e. a country with relatively low labour costs), if that plant uses large amounts of labour relative to the value added to the product at that stage. Thus foreign countries, with different cost conditions, are able to provide business with a more competitive environment within which to produce its products.

As an example, take the case of Nike, the American sportswear manufacturer. It looks to exploit cost differences

Definitions

Ownership-specific assets Assets owned by the firm, such as technology, product differentiation and managerial skills, which reflect its core competencies.

Locational advantages Those features of a host economy that MNCs believe will lower costs, improve quality and/or facilitate greater sales.

Internalisation advantages Where the net benefits of extending the organisational structure of the MNC by setting up an overseas subsidiary are greater than those of arranging a contract with an external party.

between countries. Nike has organised itself globally so that it can respond rapidly to changing cost conditions in its international subsidiaries. Its product development operations are carried out in the USA, but all of its production operations are subcontracted out to over 40 overseas locations, mostly in South and South East Asia. If wage rates, and hence costs, rise in one host country, then production can be transferred to a more profitable subsidiary.

As businesses, like Nike, relocate many dimensions of their value chain, the structure and organisation of the business takes on a web-like appearance, with its various operations being spread throughout the world. So long as companies have adequate information regarding the cost conditions of its subsidiaries, management decision making concerning the location of production simply will tend to follow the operation of market forces.

In recent times, Nike has tended to consolidate its existing supply base, while attempting to maintain sufficient flexibility in what is a very dynamic sector. The consolidation allows it to develop more focused and sustainable relationships with suppliers. This is one example of a trade-off that MNCs need to consider when assessing the benefits from the internationalisation of production.

The quality of inputs. The location of multinational operations does not simply depend on factor prices: it also depends on factor quality. For example, a country might have a highly skilled or highly industrious workforce and it is this, rather than simple wage rates, that attracts multinational investment. The issue here is still largely one of costs. Highly skilled workers might cost more to employ per hour, but if their productivity is higher, they might well cost less to employ per unit of output. It is also the case, however, that highly skilled workers might produce a better-quality product, and thus increase the firm's sales.

If a country has both lower-priced factors and high-quality factors, it will be very attractive to multinational investors. In recent years, the UK Government has sought to attract multinational investment through having lower labour costs and more flexible employment conditions than its European rivals, while still having a relatively highly trained labour force compared with those in developing countries. However, as the relocation of many call-centre and IT jobs to developing countries shows, such advantages are disappearing fast in many sectors. Though here it is worth noting that, due to many customer complaints, a number of large companies are bringing their call centres back to the UK, including BT, Santander and EE.

Avoiding transport and tariff costs. Locating production in a foreign country can also reduce costs in other ways. For example, a business locating production overseas would be able to reduce transport costs if those overseas plants served local or regional markets or used local raw materials.

One of the biggest cost advantages concerns the avoidance of tariffs (customs duties). If a country imposes tariffs on imports, then by locating *within* that country (i.e. behind the 'tariff wall'), the MNC gains a competitive advantage over its rivals, which are attempting to import their products from outside the country and are thus having to pay the tariff. MNCs may, therefore, be able to pass their cost savings on to consumers in the form of lower prices or maintain prices and increase their profit margins. These, in turn, could be used for R&D.

Following the UK vote to exit the EU, the tariff negotiations for trade with EU countries were of paramount importance for businesses located in the UK. The outcome of these negotiations would be a factor influencing firms' thinking about their location.

Government policy towards FDI. In order to attract FDI, a government might offer an MNC a whole range of financial and cost-reducing incentives, many of which help reduce the fixed (or 'sunk') costs of the investment, thereby reducing the investment's risk. The granting of favourable tax differentials and depreciation allowances, and the provision of premises, are all widely used government strategies to attract foreign business.

The general economic climate in host nations. FDI is more likely to occur if a nation has buoyant economic growth, large market size, high disposable income, an appropriate demographic mix, low inflation, low taxation, few restrictive regulations on business, a good transport network, an excellent education system, a significant research culture, etc. In highly competitive global markets, such factors may make the difference between success and failure.

The financial crisis of the late 2000s, the subsequent economic downturn and fiscal measures to reduce levels of government borrowing (see Chapter 30) affected developed economies, particularly in Europe, especially hard. This only helped to make developing economies even more attractive to foreign investors (see Table 23.3), including investors based in developing economies.

Internalisation advantages

As well as ownership and locational advantages, FDI can bring internalisation advantages. These are where the benefits of setting up an overseas subsidiary (thereby internalising its production in that country) are greater than the costs of arranging a contract with an external party (e.g. an overseas import agent or a firm in a host country that would make the product under licence).

FDI occurs where (in the language of sections 3.1 and 15.7, see page 28) the *transaction costs* of using the market in an overseas country are too high. Thus, the problems of finding the right partner to contract with, agreeing the terms of the contract, determining the price of the transaction and monitoring the contractual agreement are all compounded in foreign locations where different cultures and legal systems create uncertainties for firms considering expansion overseas. In order to minimise opportunistic behaviour in such situations (i.e. to reduce moral hazard), the firm will engage in FDI rather than exporting via an overseas import agent or licensing a domestic firm in the host nation.

Of course, many firms that start to venture into overseas markets will engage in exporting, rather than FDI, and use an import agent. However, it is also the case that many of the first multinational subsidiaries are sales and distribution outlets. The first plant set up by Hoover in the UK during the 1930s, for example, was a sales establishment through which it distributed its vacuum cleaners. Hoover found it more profitable to control sales than to use a third party.

Many firms go through a sequence from exporting to overseas investment. Toyota, for example, exported its cars to the UK using local motor vehicle retailers to distribute them prior to establishing a greenfield manufacturing site in Burnaston in Derbyshire in the early 1990s. Honda also set up a manufacturing plant in Swindon, Wiltshire, in 1992, after years of exporting cars to the UK.

The usefulness of the Eclectic Paradigm
The Eclectic Paradigm is thus a useful tool for explaining why MNCs arise. It explains how firms use combinations of ownership, locational and internalisation advantages to engage in various forms of FDI and strategic alliance.

Horizontally integrated multinationals. It can explain the development of **horizontally integrated multinationals**. Firms initially may manufacture in their home nation and export to a foreign location but then decide to switch out of exporting and establish a subsidiary producing the same product overseas.

Thus, FDI may be part of a sequence of expansion into new markets. The sequence may begin with exporting and then involve investment in one or more countries. Firms see that by combining their ownership-specific assets (e.g. technology and managerial skills) with locational advantages in the host nation (e.g. market size and government grants) their revenue streams will be greatest from internalising those assets and establishing an overseas subsidiary instead of exporting to it.

Alternatively, firms that engage in a cross-border horizontal merger or acquisition may do so to take advantage of the potential synergies in ownership-specific assets.

Vertically integrated multinationals. Likewise, the eclectic paradigm can also explain **vertically integrated multinationals** with various stages of production taking place in different countries. We can follow similar reasoning to that presented in section 15.7. Consider two firms – one a manufacturer and the other a raw material producer – each with its own set of ownership-specific assets, but located in different

countries. Further, these two firms are locked into a contract whereby they trade with each other on a frequent basis and have invested heavily in maintaining the relationship. If there is incomplete information or uncertainty about the other's activities and one firm feels that the other is not fulfilling its side of the bargain, then vertical FDI may take place. Here the driving force in the FDI process is the internalisation advantage achieved by vertical integration because the transaction costs of continuing the market relationship are too high.

Oil companies such as Shell and Exxon Mobil (Esso) are good examples of vertically integrated multinationals, undertaking in a global operation the extraction of crude oil, controlling its transportation, refining it and producing by-products, and controlling the retail sale of petrol and other oil products.

Conglomerate multinationals. Many of the big MNCs have become **conglomerate multinationals** and the Eclectic Paradigm helps to explain this organisational form. Conglomerates exist because firms have specialised managerial talent (i.e. ownership-specific advantages). Such managers can deal with establishing and running large, complex organisations. Further, there are internalisation advantages from establishing a conglomerate MNC because operating across a number of unrelated sectors and locations using market solutions would be prohibitively costly. Conglomerate expansion overseas allows the firm to spread its risks and gain other economies of scope (see page 157).

Unilever is a good example of a conglomerate multinational. It is a British–Dutch MNC employing over 170 000 people in 190 countries, producing various food, home care and personal care products. It has around 400 brands, including: Wall's and Ben & Jerry's ice cream; Knorr soups; Bovril and Marmite; Hellman's mayonnaise; Lipton and PG Tips tea; Flora, Blue Band and Rama margarines and spreads; Signal toothpaste; Domestos, Cif, Omo, Persil and Comfort; TRESemmé and Sunsilk shampoos; VO5, Toni & Guy, and Brylcreem hair products; Vaseline, Dove, Simple and Lux soaps; Pond's skin care products; Impulse, Lynx, Sure and Brut fragrances and antiperspirants.

Joint ventures. Finally, the Eclectic Paradigm offers insights into the establishment of joint ventures (see page 269).

Definitions

Horizontally integrated multinational A multinational that produces the same product in many different countries.

Vertically integrated multinational A multinational that undertakes the various stages of production for a given product in different countries.

Conglomerate multinational A multinational that produces different products in different countries.

Evidence shows that new-product joint ventures, where risks and development costs are high, occur among the larger MNCs that have complementary ownership-specific assets.[6] Because the costs and risks are great, these investments are likely to take place in markets with high perceived growth. This would help to explain, for example, the decision by Sony and Panasonic in 2014 to join forces to produce displays for tablet devices.

Joint ventures also occur among new and smaller MNCs that have limited ownership-specific assets. These firms look for suitable partners that can complement their resources in countries with high market potential. In addition, all joint ventures require that there are limited contractual disadvantages in signing an agreement to share resources and develop products, indicating that the joint venture relationship is built on trust as well as sound strategic reasoning.

Problems facing multinationals

Although multinational corporations are successful in developing overseas subsidiaries, they also face a number of problems resulting from their geographical expansion:

- *Language barriers.* The problem of working in different languages is a necessary barrier for the MNC to overcome. Clearly, this problem varies according to the degree to which a common language is spoken. Further, if a UK MNC tends to employ expatriates, communication will be more difficult and local staff may feel alienated and thus be less productive.
- *Selling and marketing in foreign markets.* Strategies that work at home might fail overseas, given wide social and cultural differences. Many US multinationals, such as McDonald's and Coca-Cola, are frequently accused of imposing US values in the design and promotion of their products, irrespective of the country and its culture. This can lead to resentment and hostility in the host country, which may, ultimately, backfire on the MNC.

To meet foreign buyers' needs and respond to local market conditions, a firm may be required to differentiate both its product and its operations, such as marketing. Therefore, while an MNC may look to minimise costs by standardising its product and its operations throughout the world, a failure to take into account the uniqueness of the market in which it wishes to sell may lose its market share.

The trade-off between the cost reduction and local responsiveness can be a key strategic consideration for a firm to take into account when selling or producing overseas. Where product differentiation is high, and attributes such as quality or some other non-price factor predominates within the competitive process, local responsiveness will tend to shape business thinking.

- *Communication and co-ordination between subsidiaries.* Diseconomies of scale may result from an expanding global business. Lines of communication become longer and more complex. The greater the attempted level of control exerted by the parent company, the greater are these problems likely to be: in other words, the more the parent company attempts to conduct business as though the subsidiaries were regional branches. Multinational organisational structures where international subsidiaries operate largely independently of the parent state will tend to minimise such problems.
- *Attitudes of host governments.* Governments often will try to get the best possible deal for their country from multinationals. This could result in governments insisting on part ownership in the subsidiary (either by themselves or by domestic firms), tight rules and regulations governing the MNC's behaviour or harsh tax regimes. In response, the MNC can always threaten to locate elsewhere.

Within any global strategy, there will be a degree of economic and political risk. However, as MNCs look to invest more in developing economies or emerging markets such as China, this risk will increase, as there are more and more uncertainties. However, it is often within emerging markets that the greatest returns are achieved. It is essentially this trade-off between potential returns and risk that a firm needs to consider in its strategic decisions (see Box 23.2).

A global business will need a strategy for effectively embracing foreign cultures and traditions in its working practices and for devising an efficient global supply chain. Some businesses may be more suited to deal with such global issues than others.

23.5 THE ADVANTAGES OF MNC INVESTMENT FOR THE HOST STATE

As mentioned previously, host governments are always on the lookout to attract foreign direct investment and are prepared to put up considerable finance and make significant concessions to attract overseas business. So what benefits do MNCs bring to the economy?

Employment

If MNC investment is in new plants (as opposed to merely taking over an existing company), this will generate employment. Most countries attempt to entice MNCs to depressed regions where investment is low and

---

[6] See S. Agarwal and S.N. Ramaswami, 'Choice of foreign market entry mode: impact of ownership, location and internalization factors', *Journal of International Business Studies,* Vol. 23, No. 1 (1992), pp. 1–28. See also A. Madhok, 'Revisiting multinational firms' tolerance for joint ventures: a trust-based approach', *JIBS,* Vol. 26, No. 1 (1995), pp. 117–37.

BOX 23.2 ATTRACTING FOREIGN INVESTMENT

The Global Opportunity Index

Since 2013, the Milken Institute has published a Global Opportunity Index, which considers the key factors that make a nation an attractive location for multinational investment. As we continue to see the pattern of FDI flows change, this index provides some interesting insights into just some of the factors making it happen.

The Global Opportunity Index

The Global Opportunity Index (GOI) ranks nations according to their attractiveness to foreign investors. It provides useful information to both companies and countries. For companies, it provides information on which countries have the most potential, with low costs, good protection for business, strong economic performance and good returns. For countries, it provides guidance as to how they can implement government policy in the most effective way to attract more investment.

The methodology for the 2017 GOI tracks the performance across countries based on 51 variables aggregated under 5 categories. Each variable is measured on a scale of 0 to 10, with 10 being the best scenario. Within each category, each variable is given equal weight and then aggregated. The categories are:

Economic fundamentals: this measures the extent to which a country's macroeconomic environment is conducive to FDI. A value of 10 indicates very strong economic fundamentals.

Financial services: this measure the size and access to financial services in a country. A value of 10 indicates a financial system fully supportive of business.

Business perception: this measures the explicit and implicit costs associated with business operations, with 10 indicating very low costs of doing business in a country.

Institutional framework: this measures the extent to which a country's institutions provide support to business. A value of 10 indicates a supportive framework for business.

International standards and policy: this assesses the effectiveness of a country's institutions, policymaking and legal framework in facilitating the free flow of trade and investment. A value of 10 indicates a country that fully facilitates international integration and activity.

The 2017 rankings

The following table shows the *overall* GOI ranking for a selection of countries for 2017, as well as that for each category. Hong Kong is found to be the most attractive destination for investment, the UK second and Singapore third.

GOI ranking	Country	Economic fundamentals	Financial services	Business perception	Institutional framework	International standards and policy
1	Hong Kong	1	2	3	4	14
2	UK	38	5	15	5	8
3	Singapore	7	20	2	2	19
4	Australia	10	3	9	14	33
5	Switzerland	12	10	40	17	1
6	Norway	9	15	1	7	49
7	Japan	45	1	8	20	28
8	United States	11	13	13	10	27
13	Ireland	5	32	16	6	41
16	Germany	27	14	27	19	16
18	New Zealand	41	64	4	1	22
23	France	49	21	18	29	31
41	China	28	7	48	76	102
50	Russia	68	35	54	97	39
75	India	56	78	116	44	86
105	Brazil	123	27	163	104	118
147	Ethiopia	153	170	111	150	140
170	Chad	160	164	170	154	169

Source: based on *Global Opportunity Index*, The Milken Institute

Four of the top ten most attractive countries are Asia-Pacific economies: Hong Kong, Singapore, Australia and Japan. A key element of their attractiveness lies in the perception that they are low-cost locations for doing business and have business-friendly institutions and standards.

The UK is the highest-ranked European country. While it performs consistently well across most of the categories, within Europe it was ranked highest in 2017 in the financial services category. Going forward, it remains to be seen what impact the vote to leave the EU and its new trading

arrangements will have on the UK's attractiveness to multinational investors.

What measures might a country adopt to improve its attractiveness to foreign investors?

Undertake a literature search based around the determinants of Foreign Direct Investment. Write a short literature review summarising your findings.

unemployment is high. Often, these will be regions where a major industry has closed (e.g. the coal mining regions of South Wales). The employment that MNCs create is both direct, in the form of people employed in the new production facility, and indirect, through the impact that the MNC has on the local economy. This might be the consequence of establishing a new supply network or simply the result of the increase in local incomes and expenditure and, hence, the stimulus to local business.

It is possible, however, that jobs created in one region of a country by a new MNC venture, with its superior technology and working practices, might cause a business to fold elsewhere, thus leading to increased unemployment in that region.

> ## Pause for thought
>
> *Why might the size of these regional 'knock-on effects' of inward investment be difficult to estimate?*

The balance of payments

A country's balance of payments (see Chapter 27) is likely to improve on a number of counts as a result of inward MNC investment. First, the investment will represent a direct flow of capital into the country. Second, and perhaps more important (especially in the long term), MNC investment is likely to result in both *import substitution* and export promotion. Import substitution will occur as products, previously purchased as imports, are now produced domestically. Export promotion will be enhanced as many multinationals use their new production facilities as export platforms. For example, many Japanese MNCs invest in the UK in order to gain access to the European Union. Concerns about whether leaving the EU would discourage such inward investment was one of issues raised during the referendum campaign on whether the UK should remain in or leave the EU.

The beneficial effect on the balance of payments, however, will be offset to the extent that profits earned from the investment are repatriated to the parent country, and to the extent that the exports of the MNC displace the exports of domestic producers.

Technology transfer

Technology transfer refers to the benefits gained by domestic producers from the technology imported by the MNC. Such benefits can occur in a number of ways. The most common is where domestic producers implement or replicate the production technology and working practices of the MNC. This is referred to as the 'demonstration effect' and has occurred widely in the UK as British businesses have attempted to emulate many of the practices brought into the country by Japanese multinationals.

In addition to replicating best practice, technology might also be transferred through the training of workers. When workers move jobs from the MNC to other firms in the industry, or to other industrial sectors, they take their newly acquired technical knowledge and skills with them.

Taxation

MNCs, like domestic producers, are required to pay tax and therefore contribute to public finances. Given the highly profitable nature of many MNCs, the level of tax revenue raised from this source could be highly significant (but see section 23.6 on ways in which MNCs can avoid tax).

> ## Definitions
>
> **Import substitution** The replacement of imports by domestically produced goods or services.
>
> **Technology transfer** Where a host state benefits from the new technology that an MNC brings with its investment.

23.6 THE DISADVANTAGES OF MNC INVESTMENT FOR THE HOST STATE

Thus far we have focused on the positive effects resulting from multinational investment. However, multinational investment may not always be beneficial in either the short or the long term.

Uncertainty. MNCs are often 'footloose', meaning that they can simply close down their operations in foreign countries and move. This is especially likely with older plants, which would need updating if the MNC were to remain, or with plants that can be easily sold without too much loss. Also, during the maturity and decline stage of the product life cycle, cost-cutting may be essential and the MNC may move production to even lower cost countries.

The ability to close down its business operations and shift production, while being a distinct economic advantage to the MNC, is a prime concern facing the host nation. If a country has a large foreign multinational sector within the economy, it will become very vulnerable to such footloose activity and face great uncertainty in the long term. It may thus be forced to offer the multinational 'perks' (e.g. grants, special tax relief or specific facilities) in order to persuade it to remain. These perks are clearly costly to the taxpayer.

Control. The fact that an MNC can shift production locations not only gives it economic flexibility, but enables it to exert various controls over its host. This is particularly so in many developing countries, where MNCs are not only major employers but, in many cases, the principal wealth creators. Thus attempts by the host state to improve worker safety or impose pollution controls, for example, may be against what the MNC sees as its own best interests. It might thus oppose such measures or even threaten to withdraw from the country if such measures are not modified or dropped. The host nation is in a very weak position.

Transfer pricing. MNCs, like domestic producers, are always attempting to reduce their tax liabilities. One unique way that an MNC can do this is through a process known as *transfer pricing* (see pages 305–6). The practice of transfer pricing is pervasive and governments are losing vast sums in tax revenue every day because of it. The practice enables the MNC to reduce its profits in countries with high rates of profit tax and increase them in countries with low rates of profit tax. This can be achieved by simply manipulating its internal pricing structure.

For example, take a vertically integrated MNC where subsidiary A in one country supplies components to subsidiary B in another. The price at which the components are transferred between the two subsidiaries (the 'transfer price') will, ultimately, determine the costs and hence the levels of profit made in each country. Assume that in the country where subsidiary A is located, the level of corporation tax is half that of the country where subsidiary B is located. If components are transferred from A to B at very high prices, then B's costs

will rise and its profitability will fall. Conversely, A's profitability will rise. The MNC clearly benefits as more profit is taxed at the lower rather than the higher rate. Had it been the other way around, with subsidiary B facing the lower rate of tax, then the components would be transferred at a low price. This would increase subsidiary B's profits and reduce A's.

The practice of transfer pricing was mostly starkly revealed in *The Guardian* newspaper in February 2009. Citing a paper that examined the flows of goods priced from US subsidiaries in Africa back to the USA, it stated that 'the public may be horrified to learn that companies have priced flash bulbs at $321.90 each, pillow cases at $909.29 each and a ton of sand at $1993.67, when the average world trade price was 66 cents, 62 cents and $11.20 respectively'[7].

The environment. Many MNCs are accused of simply investing in countries to gain access to natural resources, which are subsequently extracted or used in a way that is not sensitive to the environment. Host nations, especially developing countries, that are keen for investment are frequently prepared to allow MNCs to do this. They often put more store on the short-run gains from the MNC's presence than on the long-run depletion of precious natural resources or damage to the environment. Governments, like many businesses, often have a very short-term focus: they are concerned more with their political survival (whether through the ballot box or through military force) than with the long-term interests of their people.

23.7 MULTINATIONAL CORPORATIONS AND DEVELOPING ECONOMIES

Many of the benefits and costs of MNC investment that we have considered so far are most acutely felt in developing countries. The poorest countries of the world are most in need of investment and yet are most vulnerable to exploitation by multinationals and have the least power to resist it. There tends, therefore, to be a love–hate relationship between the peoples of the developing world and the giant corporations that are seen to be increasingly dominating their lives: from the spread of agribusiness into the countryside through the ownership and control of plantations, to international mining corporations despoiling vast tracts of land; from industrial giants dominating manufacturing, to international banks controlling the flow of finance; from international tour operators and hotels bringing the socially disruptive effects of affluent tourists from North America, Japan, Europe and Australasia, to the products of the rich industrialised countries fashioning consumer tastes and eroding traditional culture.

Although MNCs employ only a small proportion of the total labour force in most developing countries, they have a powerful effect on these countries' economies, often dominating the import and export sectors. They also often exert considerable power and influence over political leaders and

their policies and over civil servants and frequently are accused of 'meddling' in politics.

It is easy to see the harmful social, environmental and economic effects of multinationals on developing countries and, yet, governments in these countries are so eager to attract overseas investment that they are frequently prepared to offer considerable perks to MNCs and to turn a blind eye to many of their excesses.

Does MNC investment aid development?

Whether investment by multinationals in developing countries is seen to be a net benefit or a net cost to these countries depends on what are perceived to be their development goals. If maximising the growth in national income is the goal, then MNC investment has probably made a positive contribution. If, however, the objectives of development are seen as more wide-reaching, and include goals such as greater equality, the relief of poverty, a growth in the provision of basic needs (such as food, health care, housing and sanitation) and a general

---

[7]Prem Sikka, 'Shifting profits across borders', *The Guardian* (12 February 2009).

growth in the freedom and sense of well-being of the mass of the population, then the net effect of multinational investment could be argued to be anti-developmental.

Advantages to the host country

In order for countries to achieve economic growth, there must be *investment*. In general, the higher the rate of investment, the higher will be the rate of economic growth. The need for economic growth tends to be more pressing in developing countries than in advanced countries. One obvious reason is their lower level of income. If they are ever to aspire to the living standards of the rich North, then income per head will have to grow at a considerably faster rate than in rich countries and for many years. Another reason is the higher rates of population growth in developing countries – often some 2 percentage points higher than in the rich countries. This means that for income per head to grow at merely the *same* rate as in rich countries, developing countries will have to achieve growth rates 2 percentage points higher.

Investment requires finance. But developing countries are generally acutely short of funds: FDI can help to make up the shortfall. Specifically, there are key 'gaps' that FDI can help to fill.

The savings gap. A country's rate of economic growth (*g*) depends crucially on two factors:

- The amount of extra capital that is required to produce an extra unit of output per year: i.e. the marginal capital/output ratio (*k*). The greater the marginal capital/output ratio, the lower will be the output per year that results from a given amount of investment.
- The proportion of national income that a country saves (*s*). The higher this proportion, the greater the amount of investment that can be financed.

There is a simple formula that relates the rate of economic growth to these two factors. It is known as the **Harrod–Domar model** (after the two economists Sir Roy Harrod and Evsey Domar, who independently developed the model). The formula is:

$$g = s/k$$

Thus, if a developing country saved 10 per cent of its national income (*s* = 10%) and, if £4 of additional capital were required to produce £1 of extra output per annum (*k* = 4), then the rate of economic growth would be 10%/4 = 2.5 per cent.

If that developing country wanted to achieve a rate of economic growth of 5 per cent, then it would require a rate of saving of 20 per cent (5% = 20%/4). There would thus be a shortfall of savings: a *savings gap*. Most, if not all, developing countries perceive themselves as having a savings gap. Not only do they require relatively high rates of economic growth in order to keep ahead of population growth and to break out of poverty, but they also tend to have relatively low rates of saving. Poor people cannot afford to save much out of their income.

This is where FDI comes in. It can help to fill the savings gap by directly financing the investment required to achieve the target rate of growth.

The foreign exchange gap. There are many items, especially various raw materials and machinery, that many developing countries do not produce themselves and yet which are vital if they are to develop. Such items have to be imported. But this requires foreign exchange, and most developing countries suffer from a chronic shortage of foreign exchange. Their demand for imports grows rapidly: they have a high income elasticity of demand for imports – for both capital goods and consumer goods. Yet their exports tend to grow relatively slowly. Reasons include: the development of synthetic substitutes for the raw material exports of developing countries (e.g. plastics for rubber and metal) and the relatively low income elasticity of demand for certain primary products (the demand for things such as tea, coffee, sugar cane and rice tends to grow relatively slowly).

FDI can help to alleviate the shortage of foreign exchange: it can help to close the *foreign exchange gap*. Not only will the MNC bring in capital which might otherwise have had to be purchased with scarce foreign exchange, but also any resulting exports by the MNC will increase the country's future foreign exchange earnings.

Public finance gap. Governments in developing countries find it difficult to raise enough tax revenues to finance all the projects they would like to. MNC profits provide an additional source of tax revenue.

Skills and technology gaps. The capital that flows into the developing countries with MNC investment often embodies the latest technology, access to which the developing country would otherwise be denied. MNCs bring management expertise and often provide training programmes for local labour. Hence, MNCs may not only provide capital but also potentially help to increase the *productivity* of capital and labour, particularly through the spread of knowledge and ideas.

These productivity effects are commonly referred to as positive **productivity externalities** and can help to modernise

KI 33
p 367

Definitions

Harrod–Domar model A model that relates a country's rate of economic growth to the proportion of national income saved and the ratio of capital to output.

Savings gap The shortfall in savings to achieve a given rate of economic growth.

Foreign exchange gap The shortfall in foreign exchange that a country needs to purchase necessary imports such as raw materials and machinery.

Productivity externalities Where the productivity of an individual is affected by the average productivity of other individuals.

and promote economic development in developing countries. Productivity externalities may take the form, for example, of knowledge externalities (also known as knowledge spillovers) or new-good externalities. The significance of these positive externalities is likely to depend on a country's **absorptive capacity**. In simple terms, this refers to the ability of a country to use and therefore benefit from positive productivity spillovers. This could depend on existing levels of human capital, the development of financial markets and a country's infrastructure.

> ### Pause for thought
>
> *How could the access that domestic firms have to credit affect a country's absorptive capacity?*

Disadvantages to the host country

Whereas there is the potential for MNCs to make a significant contribution to closing the above gaps, in practice, they often close them only slightly or even make them bigger! The following are the main problems:

 ■ They may use their power in the markets of host countries to drive domestic producers out of business, thereby lowering domestic profits and domestic investment.

■ They may buy few, if any, of their components from domestic firms, but import them instead: perhaps from one of their subsidiaries.

 ■ The bulk of their profits may simply be repatriated to shareholders in the rich countries, with little, if any, reinvested in the developing country. This, plus the previous point, will tend to make the foreign exchange gap worse.

■ Their practice of transfer pricing may give little scope for the host government to raise tax revenue from them. Governments of developing countries are effectively put in competition with each other, each trying to undercut the others' tax rates in order to persuade the MNC to price its intermediate products in such a way as to make its profits in their country.

■ Similarly, governments of developing countries compete with each other to offer the most favourable terms to MNCs (e.g. government grants, government contracts, tax concessions and rent-free sites). The more favourable the terms, the less the gain for developing countries as a whole.

 ■ The technology and skills brought in by the multinationals may be fiercely guarded by the MNC. Therefore, the adoption of foreign technology and know-how more widely across the economy is frustrated. The economy

> ### Definition
>
> **Absorptive capacity** The ability of a country and its firms to incorporate and benefit from positive productivity spillovers.

does not benefit fully from the knowledge spillovers that could otherwise promote economic development. What is more, the dominance of the domestic market by MNCs may lead to the demise of domestic firms and indigenous technology, thereby worsening the skill and technology base of the country.

In addition to these problems, MNCs can alter the whole course of development in ways that many would argue are undesirable. By locating in cities, they tend to attract large numbers of migrants from the countryside looking for work, but of those only a small fraction will find employment in these industries. The rest swell the ranks of the urban unemployed, often dwelling in squatter settlements on the outskirts of cities and living in appalling conditions.

More fundamentally, they are accused of distorting the whole pattern of development and of worsening the gap between the rich and poor. Their technology is capital intensive (compared with indigenous technology). The result is too few job opportunities. Those who are employed, however, receive relatively high wages and are able to buy their products. These are the products consumed in affluent countries – from cars, to luxury foodstuffs, to household appliances – products that the MNCs often advertise heavily, and where they have considerable monopoly/oligopoly power. The resulting 'coca-colanisation', as it has been called, creates wants for the mass of people, but wants that they have no means of satisfying.

> ### Pause for thought
>
> *What problems is a developing country likely to experience if it adopts a policy of restricting, or even preventing, access to its markets by multinational business?*

What can developing countries do?

Can developing countries gain the benefits of FDI while avoiding the effects of growing inequality and inappropriate products and technologies? If a developing country is large and is seen as an important market for the multinational, if it would be costly for the multinational to relocate, and if the government is well informed about the multinational's costs, then the country's bargaining position will be relatively strong. It may be able to get away with relatively high taxes on the MNC's profits and tight regulation of its behaviour (e.g. its employment practices and its care for the environment). If, however, the country is economically weak and the MNC is footloose, then the deal it can negotiate is unlikely to be very favourable.

The bargaining position of developing countries would be enhanced if they could act jointly in imposing conditions on multinational investment and behaviour. However, given the diverse nature of developing countries' governments and economies and the pro-free market, deregulated world of the early twenty-first century, such agreements seem to be becoming even less likely.

BOX 23.3	GROCERS GO SHOPPING IN THE EASTERN AISLE

Carrefour has a fresh snake counter alongside the fish department in its Chinese stores. Walmart boasts that in its Chinese stores you can find local delicacies such as whole roasted pigs and live frogs. Are fresh snakes and live frogs what's needed to succeed in China? It would seem so. Global companies thinking local, customising themselves to each market, are increasingly seen as the key to success in Asia and elsewhere around the world.

The expansion of European and US grocer retailers into global markets has been under way for a number of years. Driven by stagnant markets at home with limited growth opportunities, the major players in Europe, such as Walmart from the USA, Carrefour and Casino from France, Tesco from the UK, Ahold from Holland and Metro from Germany, have been looking to expand their overseas operations – but with mixed success.

Eastern expansion

In recent times, Asia has been the market's growth sector, with China a particular attraction. In the five years to 2013, the Chinese supermarket sector grew at an average annual rate of 12.3 per cent, although the rate has slowed slightly since.

But, it has not just been China where foreign retailers have invested. Tesco, for example, entered the Thai market in 1998. Tesco Lotus, the company's regional subsidiary, is now the country's number-one retailer. In 2015, it had over 1700 stores across Thailand, employing over 50 000 full-time staff. Meanwhile, Carrefour and Walmart have also opened hundreds of new outlets within the region in recent times.

The advantages that international retailers have over their domestic competitors are expertise in systems, distribution, the range of products and merchandising. However, given the distinctive nature of markets within Asia, business must learn to adapt to local conditions. Joint ventures and local knowledge are seen as the key ingredients to success.

With the rapid expansion of hypermarkets throughout Asia, the retail landscape has undergone revolutionary change. With a wide range of products all under one roof, from groceries to pharmaceuticals to white goods, and at cut-rate prices, local neighbourhood stores have often stood little chance in the competitive battle. 'Mom and pop operations have no economies of scale.' As well as local retailers, local suppliers are also facing a squeeze on profits, as hypermarkets demand lower prices and use their buying power as leverage.

Such has been the dramatic impact these stores have had upon the retail and grocery sector that a number of Asian economies, such as Malaysia and Thailand, have introduced restrictions on the building of new outlets.

China, one of the toughest markets to enter, had restricted foreign companies to joint venture arrangements until 2004. Tesco's answer to these restrictions had been to go into a 50:50 partnership with Taiwanese food supplier Ting Hsing.

Initially, the stores were not the Tesco supermarkets with which customers in the UK are familiar. Instead, they had an orange colour scheme and few brands that the average UK shopper would recognise. In 2006, Tesco increased its stake to 90 per cent and, with this, came the familiar Tesco branding.

This marked a period of expansion by Tesco and other global retailers in China. By 2016, Carrefour, the biggest international retailer in the Chinese market, had over 254 hypermarkets, up from 24 in 2000.

Eastern challenges

The expansion into China and other Asian markets was not to be without difficulties for global retailers. Tesco decided to leave Japan in 2012, after nine years in the market[1] while, in 2014, Carrefour announced that it was leaving India, less than four years after having opened its first store in the country, blaming underperformance, due, in part, to being required to make infrastructure investment and source many of its products locally.[2]

Even in markets like China, the pace of growth of expansion has tended to slow. In 2013, Tesco announced that it was pulling its solo brand out of China and, by May 2014, Tesco had completed the establishment of a joint venture with state-run China Resources Enterprise (CRE).[3] The venture brought together Tesco's 131 stores in China with CRE's nearly 3000 outlets and left Tesco owning 20 per cent of the business and CRE 80 per cent.

With relatively slower economic growth in China and complex local market conditions, Tesco, Carrefour and Walmart began to pull back on their global expansions. Going forward, it is likely that the pace of future expansion abroad will be at a slower rate. Philip Clarke, Tesco's CEO, said about China:

> 'It's more of a marathon than a sprint. Many retailers putting down more space in the market; few seeing that translate into profitable growth.'[4]

A Bloomberg industry analyst added:

> The rate of same-store sales increases is not what they [chains] were expecting it to be. The rate of addition of capacity has probably exceeded the growth of the market.[5]

 What are the ownership, location and internalisation advantages associated with retail FDI in Asia?

 Undertake desktop research on developments in the UK supermarket sector. Prepare a short PowerPoint presentation to summarise these developments.

---

[1] 'Tesco to leave Japanese market after nine years', *BBC News* (18 June 2012).

[2] 'Carrefour to exit India Business', *BBC News* (8 July 2014).

[3] 'Tesco completes the establishment of Joint Venture with CRE', *Tesco News Release* (29 May 2014).

[4] 'Tesco stumbles with Wal-Mart as China shoppers buy local', *Bloomberg* (19 October 2012)

[5] *Ibid.*

SUMMARY

1a Globalisation is a multi-dimensional concept. Economic globalisation can be defined as the process of closer economic integration in financial, goods and labour markets. The process of globalisation can have profound effects on economies.

1b There are various drivers of globalisation, including market, cost, government and competitive drivers.

1c Supporters of globalisation point to its potential to lead to faster growth and greater efficiency through trade, competition and investment. It also has the potential to draw the world closer together politically.

1d Critics of globalisation argue that it contributes to growing inequality and further impoverishes poor nations. It also erodes national cultures and can have adverse environmental consequences.

1e The acceleration of globalisation over recent decades has led some to refer to it as a period of hyper-globalisation. However, with the rise of protectionist rhetoric and policies the rate of further economic globalisation in the near future is less certain.

2 There is great diversity among multinationals in respect of size, nature of business, size of overseas operations, location, ownership and organisational structure.

3a Foreign direct investment (FDI) tends to fluctuate with the ups and downs of the world economy. For example, in 2008/9, with a slowdown in global economic growth, worldwide FDI fell. Over the years, however, FDI has grown substantially and has accounted for a larger and larger proportion of total investment.

3b Developing countries have tended to become an increasingly important destination for FDI and source of FDI.

4a Why businesses go multinational depends largely upon the nature of their business and their corporate strategy.

4b One theoretical explanation of MNC development is the product life cycle hypothesis. In this theory, a business will shift production around the world seeking to reduce costs and extend a given product's life. The phases of a product's life will be conducted in different countries. As the product nears maturity and competition grows, reducing costs to maintain competitiveness will force businesses to locate production in low-cost markets, such as developing economies.

4c A more modern approach to explaining international production and MNC development is provided by the Eclectic Paradigm. According to this approach, firms have certain ownership-specific advantages (core competencies), such as managerial skills, product differentiation and technological advantages, which they can use in the most appropriate locations. They internalise their ownership-specific advantages and engage in FDI because the costs and risks are lower than licensing an overseas firm or using an import agent (i.e. engaging in an external market transaction).

4d Although becoming an MNC is largely advantageous to the business, it can experience problems with language barriers, selling and marketing in foreign markets, attitudes of the host state and the communication and co-ordination of global business activities.

4e An MNC often will find a trade-off between producing a standardised product in order to cut costs and producing a customised product in order to take account of local demand conditions.

5 Host states find multinational investment advantageous in respect to employment creation, contributions to the balance of payments, the transfer of technology and the contribution to taxation.

6 Host states find multinational investment disadvantageous in so far as it creates uncertainty; foreign business can control or manipulate the country or regions within it; tax payments can be avoided by transfer pricing; and MNCs might misuse the environment.

7a The benefits of MNCs to developing countries depend upon the developing countries' development goals.

7b MNCs bring with them investment and are a source of positive productivity externalities, both of which are important determinants of economic growth. They also provide the host state with foreign exchange, which might be crucial in helping purchase vital imports.

7c MNCs might prove to be disadvantageous to developing economies if they drive domestic producers out of business, source production completely from other countries, repatriate profits, practise transfer pricing to avoid tax, force host states to offer favourable tax deals or subsidies for further expansion and guard technology to prevent its transfer to domestic producers.

REVIEW QUESTIONS

1 What do you understand by the term 'economic globalisation'? What measures could be used as indicators of economic globalisation?

2 Using the UNCTAD FDI database in the statistics section of the UNCTAD website at (http://unctadstat.unctad.org/EN/), find out what has happened to FDI flows over the past five years (a) worldwide; (b) to and from developed countries; (c) to and from developing countries; (d) to and from the UK. Explain any patterns that emerge.

3 What are the advantages and disadvantages to an economy, like that of the UK, of having a large multinational sector?

4 How might the structure of a multinational differ depending upon whether its objective of being multinational is to reduce costs or to grow?

5 If reducing costs is so important for many multinationals, why is it that many locate production not in low-cost developing economies, but in economies within the developed world?

6 'Going global, thinking local.' Explain this phrase and identify the potential conflicts for a business in behaving in this way.

7 Explain the link between the life cycle of a product and multinational business.

8 Assess the advantages and disadvantages facing a host state when receiving MNC investment.

9 Debate the following: 'Multinational investment can be nothing but good for developing economies seeking to grow and prosper.'

International trade

Business issues covered in this chapter

- How has international trade grown over the years? Have countries become more or less interdependent?
- What are the benefits to countries and firms of international trade?
- Which goods should a country export and which should it import?
- Why do countries sometimes try to restrict trade and protect their domestic industries?
- What is the role of the World Trade Organization (WTO) in international trade?

Without international trade we would all be much poorer. There would be some items like coffee, cotton clothes, foreign holidays and uranium that we would, simply, have to go without. Then there would be other items like pineapples and spacecraft that we could produce only very inefficiently.

International trade has the potential to benefit *all* participating countries. This chapter explains why.

Totally free trade, however, may bring problems to countries or to groups of people within those countries. Many people argue strongly for restrictions on trade. Textile workers see their jobs threatened by cheap imported cloth. Car manufacturers worry about falling sales as customers switch to Japanese models or other East Asian ones. This chapter, therefore, also examines the arguments for restricting trade. Are people justified in fearing international competition or are they merely trying to protect some vested interest at the expense of everyone else?

24.1 TRADING PATTERNS

Until very recently, international trade had been growing as a proportion of countries' national income for many years. This is illustrated in Figure 24.1, which shows the ratio of the sum of world exports and imports of goods and services to world GDP or 'gross domestic product' (the way we measure national output – see section 26.1 and the Appendix to Chapter 26). Since 1960, the ratio has risen from around 25 per cent to around 60 per cent.

With most nations committed to freer trade and with the World Trade Organization (see section 24.4) overseeing

the dismantling of trade barriers, international trade was able to grow as a proportion of world GDP. One effect of this has been to increase countries' interdependence and their vulnerability to world trade fluctuations. An example of this was the global recession of the late 2000s: world output fell by 2.1 per cent in 2009 (at market exchange rates).

Going forward, there are doubts over world attitudes towards free trade (see section 23.1). With the growth in protectionist measures, led by the Trump administration,

Figure 24.1 World trade in goods and services (imports plus exports), % of GDP

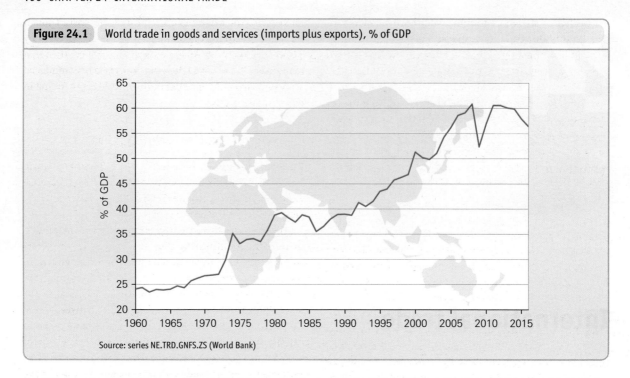

Source: series NE.TRD.GNFS.ZS (World Bank)

it is possible that world trade may have peaked as a proportion of GDP – at least for the time being.

The composition of international trade

Trade in goods

Merchandise exports include exports of manufactures, agricultural products and fuels and mining products. Of these, manufactured products have, in recent years, contributed around 70 per cent of the value of merchandise exports, 20 per cent of fuels and mining products and 10 per cent of agricultural products.

In 1980, the value of world merchandise exports was estimated at $2 trillion. By 2017, this had grown to $17.7 trillion. Part of this growth in money terms merely reflects rises in prices. Figure 24.2 helps to put this into

Figure 24.2 World merchandise exports, $bn and % of world GDP

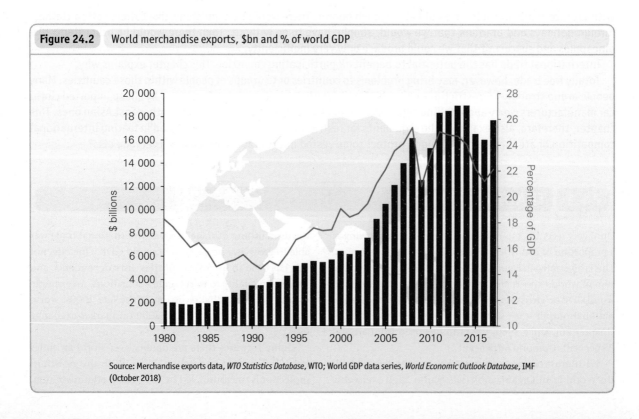

Source: Merchandise exports data, *WTO Statistics Database*, WTO; World GDP data series, *World Economic Outlook Database*, IMF (October 2018)

perspective by showing the dollar value of world merchandise exports alongside this value as a percentage of world GDP. In fact, the ratio of merchandise exports to GDP fell from 18 per cent in 1980 to 14.4 per cent in 1991. There then followed a period of rapid global export growth, which saw the value of exports rise by more than twice that of global output. Consequently, by 2008, the value of world merchandise exports had grown to 25.4 per cent of GDP. However, following the financial crisis of 2007–8, this trend was reversed. By 2017, the value of world merchandise exports stood at 22.1 per cent of GDP.

Trade in services

Commercial services include manufacturing services on physical inputs (e.g. oil refining, assembly of electronics and packing), maintenance and repair, transport, construction, insurance and financial services, telecommunications and private health and education services.

Figure 24.3 shows the value of exports in commercial services since 1980. In 1980, the value of the exports of commercial services was $367 billion and, by 2017, this nominal figure (i.e. not corrected for inflation) had grown to $5.28 trillion. Though the flows are much smaller than those of merchandise goods, there has, nonetheless, been a significant increase in the value of international flows of commercial services. In 2017, the value of exports of commercial services was equivalent to 6.6 per cent of world GDP, almost double the 3.3 per cent figure in 1980.

Reflecting a similar trend in merchandise exports, the growth in the trade of commercial services was particularly rapid during the 1990s and up to the financial crisis. Though the value of exports of commercial service fell in 2009 by 11 per cent, their subsequent growth was stronger than that in merchandise exports. Therefore, the trade in commercial services was to hold up better during the 2010s than that in merchandise goods.

The geography of international trade

Developed countries have, until recently, dominated world trade. In 1980, the percentage of world merchandise exports originating from developed countries was 70 per cent; in 2016, it was 55 per cent.

The reason for this changing global pattern of trade is that many of the countries with the most rapid *growth* in exports can now be found in the developing world. The growth in merchandise exports from the group of developing nations collectively known as the BRICS[1] (Brazil, Russia, India, China and South Africa) has been especially rapid. Between them, they accounted for just 5.5 per cent of the value of world exports in 1992. In 2017, they accounted for 18.2 per cent of world exports. More recently, other countries, such as Mexico, Turkey, Indonesia, Cambodia and Vietnam, have joined the ranks of rapidly growing 'newly industrialised' developing countries.

[1]Sometimes, the term is used to refer just to the first four countries. When South Africa is excluded, the term is written BRIC (or the BRICs) rather than BRICS.

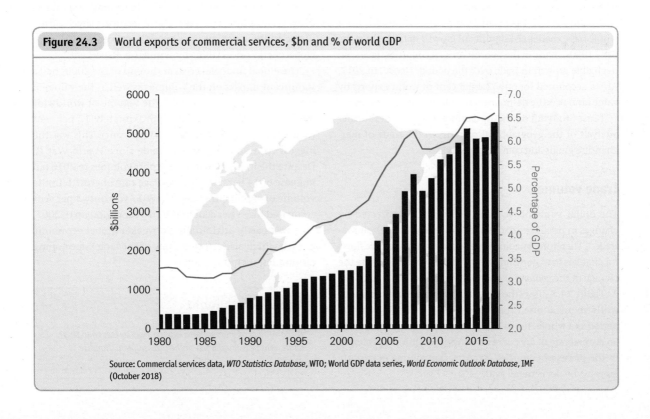

Figure 24.3 World exports of commercial services, $bn and % of world GDP

Source: Commercial services data, *WTO Statistics Database*, WTO; World GDP data series, *World Economic Outlook Database*, IMF (October 2018)

Figure 24.4 Share of world merchandise exports, by value (2017)

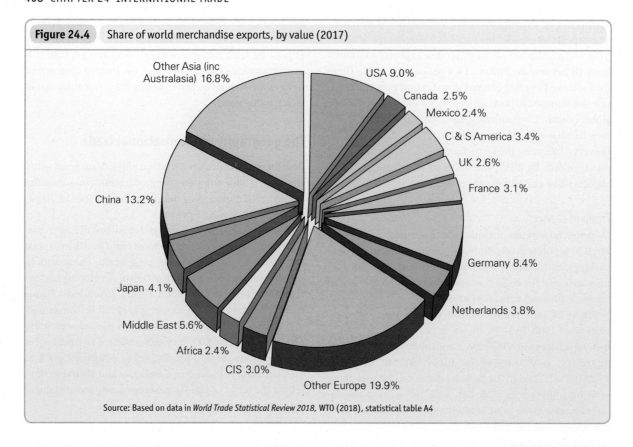

Source: Based on data in *World Trade Statistical Review 2018*, WTO (2018), statistical table A4

Figure 24.4 shows the geographical origin of *exports* in 2017. Despite a more rapid growth in trade values in other regions in recent times, Europe remains an important geographical centre for trade. In 2017, it accounted for 37.8 per cent of world exports by value (and was the destination for 37.1 per cent of imports). While Africa as a whole has experienced significant growth in trade since the early 1990s, many of the poorest African countries have seen negligible growth in trade over the period. Hence, in 2017, Africa accounted for only 2.4 per cent of world exports by value (and was the destination for 3.0 per cent of imports).

(Case Study I.3 on the student website provides further analysis of the geographical patterns in the trade of merchandise goods and commercial services.)

Trade volumes

The dollar value of recorded global trade is affected by changes in prices and exchange rates as well as the volumes traded. Therefore, by adjusting the dollar value of trade flows for changes in export and import prices, we can estimate the change in the *volumes* of goods being traded.

Figure 24.5 shows the growth in the value and volume of world merchandise exports from 1980 to 2017. Over the period as a whole, the value of merchandise exports grew at an annual rate of 5.9 per cent. After accounting for changes in the prices of countries' exports, the volume of exports grew by 4.4 per cent per year.

The chart also shows the year-to-year percentage changes in the values and volumes of merchandise exports. There are some significant differences between the change in values and volumes. Take, for example, 2015, when the value of merchandise exports *fell* by 13.2 per cent. In contrast, the volume of exports *rose* by 2.4 per cent. The difference is largely attributable to the large fall in commodity prices in 2015 with global energy prices falling by as much as 45 per cent.

The global financial crisis at the end of the 2000s had a significant impact on the volume (as well as the value) of merchandise exports. In 2009, the volume of worldwide merchandise exports fell by approximately 12 per cent (while their value declined by 23 per cent). This was the biggest contraction in global trade since World War II. Despite the initial rebound in export volumes in 2010 (an increase of 14 per cent), the average rate of growth in the volume of exports from 2011 to 2017 was only 3 per cent compared to 5.9 per cent in the 10-year period up to 2007. This was partly attributable to weaker global economic growth which also affected some of the larger developing economies, including China.

Pause for thought

If the volume of merchandise exports falls by less than their value, what has happened to the prices of merchandise exports'?

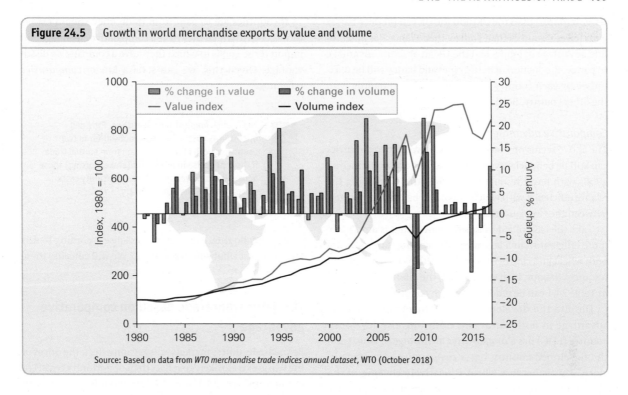

Figure 24.5 Growth in world merchandise exports by value and volume

Source: Based on data from *WTO merchandise trade indices annual dataset*, WTO (October 2018)

24.2 THE ADVANTAGES OF TRADE

Specialisation as the basis for trade

Why do countries trade with each other and what do they gain out of it? The reasons for international trade are really only an extension of the reasons for trade *within* a nation. Rather than people trying to be self-sufficient and do everything for themselves, it makes sense to specialise.

Firms specialise in producing certain types of goods. This allows them to gain economies of scale and to exploit their entrepreneurial and management skills and the skills of their labour force. It also allows them to benefit from their particular location and from the ownership of any particular capital equipment or other assets they might possess. With the revenues that firms earn, they buy in the inputs they need from other firms and the labour they require. Firms thus trade with each other.

Countries also specialise. They produce more than they need of certain goods. What is not consumed domestically is exported. The revenues earned from the exports are used to import goods that are not produced in sufficient amounts at home.

But which goods should a country specialise in? What should it export and what should it import? The answer is that it should specialise in those goods in which it has a *comparative advantage*. Let us examine what this means.

The law of comparative advantage

Countries have different endowments of factors of production. They differ in population density, labour skills, climate, raw materials, capital equipment, etc. These differences tend to persist because factors are relatively immobile between countries. Obviously, land and climate are totally immobile, but even with labour and capital there tend to be more restrictions (physical, social, cultural or legal) on their international movement than on their movement within countries. Thus the ability to supply goods differs between countries.

What this means is that the relative costs of producing goods will vary from country to country. For example, one country may be able to produce one fridge for the same cost as six tonnes of wheat or three MP4 players, whereas another country may be able to produce one fridge for the same cost as only three tonnes of wheat but four MP4 players. It is these differences in relative costs that form the basis of trade.

At this stage, we need to distinguish between *absolute advantage* and *comparative advantage*.

Absolute advantage

When one country can produce a good with fewer resources than another country, it is said to have an **absolute advantage** in that good. If France can produce grapes with fewer resources than the UK, and the UK can produce barley with fewer resources than France, then France has an absolute advantage in grapes and the UK an absolute advantage in barley. Production of both grapes and barley will be maximised by each country specialising and then trading with the other country. Both will gain.

Comparative advantage

The above seems obvious, but trade between two countries can still be beneficial even if one country could produce *all* goods with fewer resources than the other, providing the *relative* efficiency with which goods can be produced differs between the two countries.

Take the case of a developed country that is absolutely more efficient than a less developed country at producing both wheat and cloth. Assume that, with a given amount of resources (labour, land and capital), the alternatives shown in Table 24.1 can be produced in each country.

Despite the developed country having an absolute advantage in both wheat and cloth, the less developed country (LDC) has a *comparative advantage* in wheat and the developed country has a *comparative* advantage in cloth. This is because wheat is relatively cheaper in the LDC: only 1 metre of cloth has to be sacrificed to produce 2 kilos of wheat, whereas 8 metres of cloth would have to be sacrificed in the developed country to produce 4 kilos of wheat. In other words, the opportunity cost of wheat is **KI 3** **p19** 4 times higher in the developed country (8/4 compared with 1/2).

On the other hand, cloth is relatively cheaper in the developed country. Here the opportunity cost of producing 8 metres of cloth is only 4 kilos of wheat, whereas in the LDC 1 metre of cloth costs 2 kilos of wheat. Thus the opportunity cost of cloth is 4 times higher in the LDC (2/1 compared with 4/8).

To summarise: countries have a comparative advantage in those goods that can be produced at a lower opportunity cost than in other countries.

Pause for thought

Draw up a similar table to Table 24.1, only this time assume that the figures are: LDC 6 wheat or 2 cloth; DC 8 wheat or 20 cloth. What are the opportunity cost ratios now?

If countries are to gain from trade, they should export those goods in which they have a comparative advantage and import those goods in which they have a comparative disadvantage. Given this, we can state a *law of comparative advantage*.

 Key Idea 37 *The law of comparative advantage.* Provided opportunity costs of various goods differ in two countries, both of them can gain from mutual trade if they specialise in producing (and exporting) those goods that have relatively low opportunity costs compared with the other country.

But why do they gain if they specialise according to this law? And just what will that gain be? We will consider these questions next.

The gains from trade based on comparative advantage

Before trade, unless markets are very imperfect, the prices of the two goods are likely to reflect their opportunity costs. For example, in Table 24.1, since the less developed country can produce 2 kilos of wheat for 1 metre of cloth, the *price* of 2 kilos of wheat will roughly equal 1 metre of cloth.

Assume, then, that the pre-trade exchange ratios of wheat for cloth are as follows:

LDC : 2 wheat for 1 cloth

Developed country : 1 wheat for 2 cloth (i.e. 4 for 8)

Both countries will now gain from trade, provided the exchange ratio is somewhere between 2:1 and 1:2. Assume, for the sake of argument, that it is 1:1. In other words, 1 wheat trades internationally for 1 cloth. How will each country gain?

The LDC gains by exporting wheat and importing cloth. At an exchange ratio of 1:1, it now has to give up only 1 kilo of wheat to obtain a metre of cloth, whereas before trade it had to give up 2 kilos of wheat.

The developed country gains by exporting cloth and importing wheat. Again, at an exchange ratio of 1:1, it now

---

Definitions

Absolute advantage A country has an absolute advantage over another in the production of a good if it can produce it with fewer resources than the other country.

Comparative advantage A country has a comparative advantage over another in the production of a good if it can produce it at a lower opportunity cost: i.e. if it has to forgo less of other goods in order to produce it.

Law of comparative advantage Trade can benefit all countries if they specialise in the goods in which they have a comparative advantage.

Table 24.1	Production possibilities for two countries				
		Kilos of wheat		**Metres of cloth**	
Less developed country	Either	2	or	1	
Developed country	Either	4	or	8	

has to give up only 1 metre of cloth to obtain a kilo of wheat, whereas before it had to give up 2 metres of cloth.

Thus both countries have gained from trade.

The actual exchange ratios will depend on the relative prices of wheat and cloth after trade takes place. These prices will depend on total demand for and supply of the two goods. It may be that the trade exchange ratio is nearer to the pre-trade exchange ratio of one country than the other. Thus the gains to the two countries need not be equal.

Pause for thought

Show how each country could gain from trade if the LDC could produce (before trade) 3 wheat for 1 cloth and the developed country could produce (before trade) 2 wheat for 5 cloth and, if the exchange ratio (with trade) was 1 wheat for 2 cloth. Would they both still gain if the exchange ratio was (a) 1 wheat for 1 cloth; (b) 1 wheat for 3 cloth?

The limits to specialisation and trade

Does the law of comparative advantage suggest that countries will completely specialise in just a few products? In practice, countries are likely to experience *increasing* opportunity costs. The reason for this is that, as a country increasingly specialises in one good, it will have to use resources that are less and less suited to its production and that were more suited to other goods. Thus ever-increasing amounts of the other goods will have to be sacrificed. For example, as a country specialises more and more in grain production, it will have to use land that is less and less suited to growing grain.

These increasing costs as a country becomes more and more specialised will lead to the disappearance of its comparative cost advantage. When this happens, there will be no point in further specialisation. Thus, whereas a country like Germany has a comparative advantage in capital-intensive manufactures, it does not produce only manufactures. It would make no sense not to use its fertile lands to produce food or its forests to produce timber. The opportunity costs of diverting all agricultural labour to industry would be very high.

Other reasons for gains from trade

Decreasing costs. Even if there are no initial comparative cost differences between two countries, it will still benefit both to specialise in industries where economies of scale can be gained, and then to trade. Once the economies of scale begin to appear, comparative cost differences will also appear, and thus the countries will have gained a comparative advantage in these industries.

This reason for trade is particularly relevant for small countries where the domestic market is not large enough to support large-scale industries. Thus exports form a much

higher percentage of GDP in small countries such as Singapore than in large countries such as the USA.

Differences in demand. Even with no comparative cost differences and no potential economies of scale, trade can benefit both countries if demand conditions differ.

If people in country A like beef more than lamb and people in country B like lamb more than beef, then, rather than A using resources better suited for lamb to produce beef, and B using resources better suited for producing beef to produce lamb, it will benefit both to produce beef *and* lamb and to export the one they like less in return for the one they like more.

Increased competition. If a country trades, the competition from imports may stimulate greater efficiency at home. This extra competition may prevent domestic monopolies/oligopolies from charging high prices. It may stimulate greater research and development and the more rapid adoption of new technology. It may lead to a greater variety of products being made available to consumers.

Trade as an 'engine of growth'. In a growing world economy, the demand for a country's exports is likely to grow over time, especially when these exports have a high income elasticity of demand. This will provide a stimulus to growth in the exporting country.

Non-economic advantages. There may be political, social and cultural advantages to be gained by fostering trading links between countries.

The terms of trade

What price will our exports fetch abroad? What will we have to pay for imports? The answer to these questions is given by the terms of trade. The **terms of trade** are defined as:

$$\frac{\text{Average price of exports}}{\text{Average price of imports}}$$

expressed as an index, where prices are measured against a base year in which the terms of trade are assumed to be 100. Thus, if the average price of exports relative to the average price of imports has risen by 25 per cent since the base year, the terms of trade will now be 125. The terms of trade for selected countries are shown in Figure 24.6 (with 2010 as the base year).

If the terms of trade rise (export prices rising relative to import prices), they are said to have 'improved', since

---

Definition

Terms of trade The price index of exports divided by the price index of imports and then expressed as a percentage. This means that the terms of trade will be 100 in the base year.

Figure 24.6   Terms of trade for selected countries (2010 = 100)

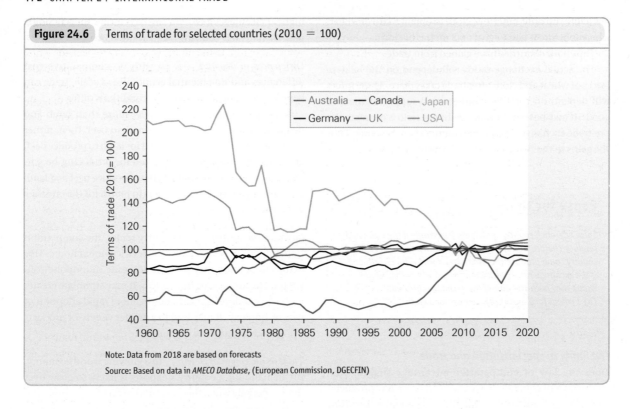

Note: Data from 2018 are based on forecasts

Source: Based on data in *AMECO Database*, (European Commission, DGECFIN)

fewer exports now have to be sold to purchase any given quantity of imports. Changes in the terms of trade are caused by changes in the demand and supply of imports and exports, and by changes in the exchange rate.

> **Pause for thought**
>
> *In Figure 24.6, which countries have experienced an improvement in their terms of trade in recent years?*

24.3 ARGUMENTS FOR RESTRICTING TRADE

We have seen how trade can bring benefits to all countries. But when we look around the world, we often see countries erecting barriers to trade. Their politicians know that trade involves costs as well as benefits.

Possible barriers to imports include the following:

- *tariffs* (i.e. customs duties) on imports;
- *quotas* (i.e. restrictions on the amount of certain goods that can be imported);
- *subsidies on domestic products* to give them a price advantage over imports;
- *administrative regulations* designed to exclude imports, such as customs delays or excessive paperwork;
- *procurement procedures* whereby governments favour domestic producers when purchasing equipment (e.g. defence equipment).

Alternatively, governments may favour domestic producers by subsidising their exports in a process known as **dumping**. The goods are 'dumped' at artificially low prices in the foreign market.

In looking at the costs and benefits of trade, the choice is not the stark one of whether to have free trade or no trade at all. Although countries may sometimes contemplate having completely free trade, typically countries limit their trade. However, they certainly do not ban it altogether.

Arguments in favour of restricting trade

Arguments having some general validity

The infant industry argument.   Some industries in a country may be in their infancy but have a potential comparative advantage. This is particularly likely in developing countries.

> **Definition**
>
> **Dumping** Where exports are sold at prices below marginal cost – often as a result of government subsidy.

Such industries are too small yet to have gained economies of scale; their workers are inexperienced; there is a lack of back-up facilities – communications networks, specialist research and development, specialist suppliers, etc. – and they may have only limited access to finance for expansion. Without protection, these **infant industries** will not survive competition from abroad.

Protection from foreign competition, however, will allow them to expand and become more efficient. Once they have achieved a comparative advantage, the protection can then be removed to enable them to compete internationally. A risk here, however, is that the protectionist measure is not removed once the industry has become established and thus the incentive for efficiency may disappear.

The senile industry argument. This is similar to the infant industry argument. It is where industries with a potential comparative advantage have been allowed to run down and can no longer compete effectively. They may have considerable potential but be simply unable to make enough profit to afford the necessary investment without some temporary protection. This is one of the most powerful arguments used to justify the use of special protection for the automobile and steel industries in the USA. The crucial question is whether, with sufficient investment, these US industries do have a potential comparative advantage or whether the US Government is merely supporting industries with a comparative disadvantage for political reasons.

Pause for thought

How would you set about judging whether an industry had a genuine case for infant/senile industry protection?

To reduce reliance on goods with little dynamic potential. Many developing countries have traditionally exported primaries: foodstuffs and raw materials. The world demand for some of these, however, is fairly income inelastic and thus tends to grow relatively slowly. In such cases, free trade is not an engine of growth. Instead, it may encourage countries' economies to become locked into a pattern of primary production, thereby preventing them from expanding in sectors like manufacturing, which have a higher income elasticity of demand. There may thus be a valid argument for protecting or promoting manufacturing industry.

To prevent 'dumping' and other unfair trade practices. A country may engage in dumping by subsidising its exports. Alternatively, firms may practise price discrimination by selling at a higher price in home markets and a lower price in foreign markets in order to increase their profits. Either way, prices may no longer reflect comparative costs. Thus the world would benefit from tariffs being imposed by importers to counteract the subsidy.

It can also be argued that there is a case for retaliating against countries that impose restrictions on your exports. In the *short* run, both countries are likely to be made worse off by a contraction in trade. But, if the retaliation persuades the other country to remove its restrictions, it may have a longer-term benefit. In some cases, the mere threat of retaliation may be enough to get another country to remove its protection.

To prevent the establishment of a foreign-based monopoly. Competition from abroad could drive domestic producers out of business. The foreign company, now having a monopoly of the market, could charge high prices with a resulting misallocation of resources. The problem could be tackled either by restricting imports or by subsidising the domestic producer(s).

All the above arguments suggest that governments should adopt a 'strategic' approach to trade. **Strategic trade theory** argues that protecting certain industries allows a net gain in the *long* run from increased competition in the market (see Box 24.1). This argument has been used to justify, for example, the huge financial support given to the aircraft manufacturer Airbus, a consortium based in four European countries. The subsidies have allowed it to compete with Boeing, which otherwise would have a monopoly in many types of passenger aircraft. Airlines and their passengers worldwide, it is argued, have benefited from the increased competition.

To spread the risks of fluctuating markets. A highly specialised economy – Zambia with copper, Cuba with sugar – will be highly susceptible to world market fluctuations. Greater diversity and greater self-sufficiency, although maybe leading to less efficiency, can reduce these risks.

To reduce the influence of trade on consumer tastes. The assumption of fixed consumer tastes dictating the pattern of production through trade is false. Multinational companies through their advertising and other forms of sales promotion may influence consumer tastes. Many developing countries object to the insidious influence of Western consumerist values expounded by companies such as Coca-Cola and

Definitions

Infant industry An industry that has a potential comparative advantage, but that is, as yet, too underdeveloped to be able to realise this potential.

Strategic trade theory The theory that protecting/supporting certain industries can enable them to compete more effectively with large monopolistic rivals abroad. The effect of the protection is to increase long-run competition and may enable the protected firms to exploit a comparative advantage that they could not have done otherwise.

McDonald's. Thus some restriction on trade may be justified in order to reduce this 'producer sovereignty'.

To prevent the importation of harmful goods.   A country may want to ban or severely curtail the importation of things such as drugs, pornographic literature and live animals.

To take account of externalities.   Free trade will tend to reflect private costs. Both imports and exports, however, can involve externalities. The mining of many minerals for export may adversely affect the health of miners; the production of chemicals for export may involve pollution; the importation of juggernaut lorries may lead to structural damage to houses; shipping involves large amounts of CO_2 emissions (estimates typically put this at between 3 to 5 per cent of total world emissions).

Arguments having some validity for specific groups or countries

The arguments considered so far are of general validity: restricting trade for such reasons could be of net benefit to the world. There are two other arguments, however, that are used by individual governments for restricting trade, where their country will gain, but at the *expense* of other countries, such that there will be a net loss to the world.

The first argument concerns taking advantage of *market power in world trade.* If a country or a group of countries has

---

BOX 24.1   STRATEGIC TRADE THEORY

An argument for protection?

Lester Thurow is professor of management and economics and former dean in the Sloan School of Management at the Massachusetts Institute of Technology (MIT). He is also an economics journalist and editor and one of the USA's best-known and most articulate advocates of 'managed trade'.

Thurow (and others) have been worried by the growing penetration of US markets by imports from Japan and Europe and also from China and many other developing countries. Their response is to call for a carefully worked-out strategy of protection for US industries.

The strategic trade theory that they support argues that the real world is complex. It is wrong, they claim, to rely on free trade and existing comparative advantage. Particular industries will require particular policies of protection or promotion tailored to their particular needs:

- Some industries will require protection against unfair competition from abroad – not just to protect the industries themselves, but also to protect the consumer from the oligopolistic power that the foreign companies will gain if they succeed in driving the domestic producers out of business.
- Other industries will need special support in the form of subsidies to enable them to modernise and compete effectively with imports.
- New industries may require protection to enable them to get established – to achieve economies of scale and build a comparative advantage.
- If a particular foreign country protects or promotes its own industries, it may be desirable to retaliate in order to persuade the country to change its mind.

The arguments of strategic trade theorists are criticised by economic liberals. If the USA is protected from cheap imports from Asia, they claim, all that will be achieved is a huge increase in consumer prices. The car, steel, telecommunications and electrical goods industries might find their profits bolstered, but this is hardly likely to encourage them to be more efficient.

Another criticism of managed trade is the difficulty of identifying just which industries need protection, and how much and for how long. Governments do not have perfect knowledge. What is more, the political lobbyists from various interested groups are likely to use all sorts of tactics – legal or illegal – to persuade the government to look favourably on them. In the face of such pressure, will the government remain 'objective'? No, say the liberals.

So how do the strategic trade theorists reply? If it works for China and Japan, they say, it can work for the USA. What is needed is a change in attitudes. Rather than industry looking on the government as either an enemy to be outwitted or a potential benefactor to be wooed, and government looking on industry as a source of votes or tax revenues, both sides should try to develop a partnership – a partnership from which the whole country can gain.

But whether sensible, constructive managed trade is possible, given the political context in which decisions would need to be made, is a highly debatable point. 'Sensible' managed trade, say the liberals, is just pie in the sky. However, under the presidency of Donald Trump, who avowed to 'put America first', calls for specific protection of certain industries in the USA were to receive a more sympathetic hearing than from previous administrations. But whether increased protection, such as that of the steel and aluminium sectors, will help to increase efficiency and regain comparative advantage remains to be seen.

 Airbus, a consortium based in four European countries, has received massive support from the four governments in order to enable it to compete with Boeing, which until the rise of Airbus had dominated the world market for aircraft. To what extent are (a) air travellers and (b) citizens of the four countries likely to have gained or lost from this protection? (See Case Study I.6 on the student website.)

 Undertake a literature search on the topic of strategic trade theory. Construct a short PowerPoint presentation summarising for a non-specialist the key ideas from this literature.

monopsony power in the purchase of imports (i.e. they are individually or collectively a very large economy, such as the USA or the EU), then they could gain by restricting imports so as to drive down their price. Similarly, if countries have monopoly power in the sale of some export (e.g. OPEC countries with oil), then they could gain by restricting exports, thereby forcing up the price.

The second argument concerns giving *protection to declining industries*. The human costs of sudden industrial closures can be very high. In such circumstances, temporary protection may be justified to allow the industry to decline more slowly, thus avoiding excessive unemployment in various localities. Such policies will be at the expense of the consumer, who will be denied access to cheaper foreign imports. Nevertheless, such arguments have gained huge support from populist movements in the USA and elsewhere and protection for such industries forms part of President Trump's 'America first' policies.

'Non-economic' arguments for restricting trade. A country may be prepared to forgo the direct economic advantages of free trade in order to achieve objectives that are often described as 'non-economic':

- It may wish to maintain a degree of self-sufficiency in case trade is cut off or disrupted – for instance, in times of war. This may apply particularly to the production of food and armaments.
- It may decide not to trade with certain countries with which it disagrees politically.
- It may wish to preserve traditional ways of life. Rural communities or communities built around old traditional industries may be destroyed by foreign competition.
- It may prefer to retain as diverse a society as possible, rather than one too narrowly based on certain industries.

Pursuing such objectives, however, will involve costs. Preserving a traditional way of life, for example, may mean that consumers are denied access to cheaper goods from abroad. Society must therefore weigh up the benefits against the costs of such policies.

Some arguments for protection, however, simply don't add up. The arguments are fallacious. Some of these are identified in Box 24.2.

Problems with protection

Tariffs and other forms of protection impose a cost on society. Figure 24.7 illustrates the case of a good that is partly home produced and partly imported. Domestic demand and supply are given by D_{dom} and S_{dom}. It is assumed that firms in the country produce under perfect competition and that therefore the supply curve is the sum of the firms' marginal cost curves.

Let us assume that the country is too small to affect world prices: it is a price taker. The world price is given, at P_w. At P_w, Q_2 is demanded, Q_1 is supplied by domestic suppliers and hence $Q_2 - Q_1$ is imported.

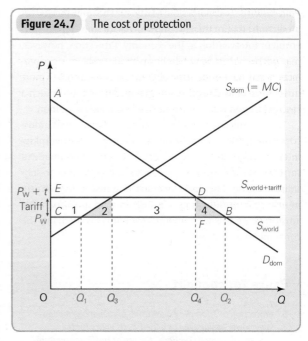

Figure 24.7 The cost of protection

Now a tariff is imposed. This increases the price to consumers by the amount of the tariff. Price rises to $P_w + t$. Domestic production increases to Q_3, consumption falls to Q_4, and hence imports fall to $Q_4 - Q_3$.

What are the costs of this tariff to the country? Consumers are having to pay a higher price and hence consumer surplus falls from area ABC to ADE (see pages 89–92 if you are unsure about consumer surplus). The cost to consumers in lost consumer surplus is thus $EDBC$ (i.e. areas $1 + 2 + 3 + 4$). *Part* of this cost, however, is redistributed as a *benefit* to other sections in society. *Firms* get a higher price, and thus gain extra profits (area 1): where profit is given by the area between the price and the MC curve. The *government* receives extra revenue from the tariff payments (area 3), i.e. $Q_4 - Q_3 \times$ tariff. These revenues can be used, for example, to reduce taxes.

But *part* of this cost is not recouped elsewhere. It is a net cost to society (areas 2 and 4).

Area 2 represents the extra costs of producing $Q_3 - Q_1$ at home, rather than importing it. If $Q_3 - Q_1$ were still imported, the country would only be paying P_w. By producing it at home, however, the costs are given by the domestic supply curve (= MC). The difference between MC and P_w (area 2) is thus the efficiency loss on the production side.

Area 4 represents the loss of consumer surplus by the reduction in consumption from Q_2 to Q_4. Consumers have saved area FBQ_2Q_4 of expenditure, but have sacrificed area DBQ_2Q_4 of utility in so doing – a net loss of area 4.

Ideally, the government should weigh up such costs against any benefits that are gained from protection.

Apart from these direct costs to the consumer, there are several other problems with protection. Some are a direct effect of the protection; others follow from the reactions of other nations.

Protection as 'second-best'. Many of the arguments for protection amount merely to arguments for some type of government intervention in the economy. Protection, however, may not be the best way of dealing with the problem, since protection may have undesirable side effects. There may be a more direct form of intervention that has no side effects. In such a case, protection will be no more than a *second-best* solution.

For example, using tariffs to protect old inefficient industries from foreign competition may help prevent unemployment in those parts of the economy, but the consumer will suffer from higher prices. A better solution would be to subsidise retraining and investment in those areas of the country in *new efficient* industries – industries with a comparative advantage. In this way, unemployment is avoided, but the consumer does not suffer.

Pause for thought

1. *Protection to allow the exploitation of monopoly/monopsony power can be seen as a 'first-best' policy for the country concerned. Similarly, the use of tariffs to counteract externalities directly involved in the trade process (e.g. the environmental costs of an oil tanker disaster) could be seen to be a first-best policy. Explain why.*
2. *Most of the other arguments for tariffs or other forms of protection that we have considered can really be seen as arguments for intervention, with protection being no more than a second-best form of intervention. Go through each of the arguments and consider what would be a 'first-best' form of intervention.*

Impact on global income. If a country, like the USA, imposes tariffs or other restrictions, imports will be reduced. But these imports are other countries' exports. A reduction in their exports will lead to a fall in rest-of-the-world income. This, in turn, will lead to a reduction in demand for US exports. This, therefore, tends to undo the benefits of the tariffs.

Retaliation. If the USA imposes restrictions on, say, imports from the EU, then the EU may impose restrictions on imports from the USA. Any gain to US firms competing with EU imports is offset by a loss to US exporters. What is more, US consumers suffer, since the benefits from comparative advantage have been lost.

The increased use of tariffs and other restrictions can lead to a trade war, with each country cutting back on imports from other countries. In the end, with retaliation (also referred to as beggar-my-neighbour policies), everyone loses.

Protection may allow firms to remain inefficient. By removing or reducing foreign competition, tariffs etc. may reduce firms' incentive to reduce costs. Thus, if protection is being given to an infant industry, the government must ensure that the lack of competition does not prevent it 'growing up'. Protection should not be excessive and should be removed as soon as possible.

Bureaucracy. If a government is to avoid giving excessive protection to firms, it should examine each case carefully. This can lead to large administrative costs. It could also lead to corrupt officials accepting bribes from importers to give them favourable treatment.

BOX 24.2   GIVING TRADE A BAD NAME

Arguments that don't add up

'Why buy goods from abroad and deny jobs to workers in this country?' This is typical of the concerns that many people have about an open trade policy. However, these concerns often are based on arguments that do not stand up to close inspection. Here are four of them.

'Imports should be reduced since they lower the standard of living. The money goes abroad rather than into the domestic economy.' Imports are consumed and thus add directly to consumer welfare. Also, provided they are matched by exports, there is no net outflow of money. Trade, because of the law of comparative advantage, allows countries to increase their standard of living: to consume beyond their production possibility curve.

'Protection is needed from cheap foreign labour.' Importing cheap goods from, say, China, allows more goods to be consumed. The UK uses fewer resources by buying these goods through the production and sale of exports than by producing them at home. However, there will be a cost to certain UK workers whose jobs are lost through foreign competition.

'Protection reduces unemployment.' At a microeconomic level, protecting industries from foreign competition may allow

workers in those industries to retain their jobs. But, if foreigners sell fewer goods to the UK, they will not be able to buy so many UK exports. Thus unemployment will rise in UK export industries. Overall unemployment, therefore, is little affected and, in the meantime, the benefits from trade to consumers are reduced. Temporary protection given to declining industries, however, may help to reduce structural unemployment.

'Dumping is always a bad thing, and thus a country should restrict subsidised imports.' Dumping may well reduce world economic welfare: it goes against the law of comparative advantage. The importing country, however, may well gain from dumping. Provided the dumping is not used to drive domestic producers out of business and establish a foreign monopoly, the consumer gains from lower prices. The losers are the taxpayers in the foreign country and the workers in competing industries in the home country.

 Are distributional arguments valid economic reasons for trade restrictions?

 Go through each of these five arguments and prepare a short presentation replying to the criticisms of them.

24.4 THE WORLD TRADING SYSTEM AND THE WTO

After the Wall Street crash of 1929 (when share prices on the US stock exchange plummeted), the world plunged into the Great Depression. Countries found their exports falling dramatically and many suffered severe balance of payments difficulties. The response of many countries was to restrict imports by the use of tariffs and quotas. Of course, this reduced other countries' exports, which encouraged them to resort to even greater protectionism. The net effect of the Depression and the rise in protectionism was a dramatic fall in world trade. The volume of world trade in manufactures fell by more than a third in the three years following the Wall Street crash. Clearly, there was a net economic loss to the world from this decline in trade.

After the Second World War, there was a general desire to reduce trade restrictions, so that all countries could gain the maximum benefits from trade. There was no desire to return to the beggar-my-neighbour policies of the 1930s.

In 1947, 23 countries got together and signed the General Agreement on Tariffs and Trade (GATT). By 2018, there were 164 members of its successor organisation, the World Trade Organization, which was formed in 1995. Between them, the members of the WTO account for around 98 per cent of world trade.

The aims of GATT, and now the WTO, have been to liberalise trade. But whereas GATT focused on the trade in goods, the WTO and its agreements also relate to the trade in services and in inventions and designs, sometimes referred to as intellectual property.

WTO rules

The WTO requires its members to operate according to various principles. These include the following:

- *Non-discrimination.* Under the 'most-favoured-nations clause', any trade concession that a country makes to one member must be granted to *all* signatories. The only exception is with free-trade areas and customs unions (such as the EU). Here countries are permitted to abolish tariffs between themselves while still maintaining them with the rest of the world.
- *Reciprocity.* Any nation benefiting from a tariff reduction made by another country must reciprocate by making similar tariff reductions itself.
- *The general prohibition of quotas.*
- *Fair competition.* If unfair barriers are erected against a particular country, the WTO can sanction retaliatory action by that country. The country is not allowed, however, to take such action without permission.
- *Binding tariffs.* Countries cannot raise existing tariffs without negotiating with their trading partners.

Unlike the GATT, the WTO has the power to impose sanctions on countries breaking trade agreements. If there are disputes between member nations, these will be settled by the WTO and, if an offending country continues to impose trade restrictions, permission will be granted for other countries to retaliate.

For example, in March 2002, the Bush administration imposed tariffs on steel imports into the USA in order to protect the ailing US steel industry (see Case Study 1.15 on the student website). The EU and other countries referred the case to the WTO, which, in December 2003, ruled that they were illegal. This ruling made it legitimate for the EU and other countries to impose retaliatory tariffs on US products. President Bush consequently announced that the steel tariffs would be abolished.

Following tariffs imposed by the Trump administration in January 2018 targeted on Chinese steel and aluminium imports to the USA, China lodged a request with the WTO for consultations with the USA over the issue. Then, following the widespread imposition of tariffs on steel and aluminium by the Trump administration in June 2018, Canada, Mexico the European Union each launched their own legal challenges at the WTO.

> ### Pause for thought
>
> *Could US action to protect its steel industry from foreign competition be justified in terms of the interests of the USA as a whole (as opposed to the steel industry in particular)?*

The greater power of the WTO has persuaded many countries to bring their disputes to it. From January 1995 to October 2018, 570 disputes were brought to the WTO (compared with 300 to GATT over the whole of its 48 years). With the rise in protectionism since 2016, the number has accelerated.

Trade rounds

Periodically, member countries have met to negotiate reductions in tariffs and other trade restrictions. There have been eight 'rounds' of such negotiations since the signing of GATT in 1947. The last major round to be completed was the Uruguay Round, which began in Uruguay in 1986, continued at meetings around the world and culminated in a deal being signed in April 1994. By that time, the average tariff on manufactured products was 4 per cent and falling. In 1947, the figure was nearly 40 per cent. The Uruguay Round agreement also involved a programme of phasing in substantial reductions in tariffs and other restrictions up to the year 2002 (see Case study I.6 on the student website).

Despite the reduction in tariffs, many countries have still tried to restrict trade by various other means, such as quotas and administrative barriers. Also, barriers have been particularly high on certain non-manufactures. Agricultural protection in particular has come in for sustained criticism by developing countries. High fixed prices and subsidies given to farmers in the EU, the USA and other advanced countries mean that the industrialised world continues to export food to many developing countries which have a comparative advantage in food production! Farmers in developing countries often find it impossible to compete with subsidised food imports from the rich countries.

The most recent round of trade negotiations began in Doha, Qatar, in 2001 (see Box 24.3). The negotiations have focused on both trade liberalisation and measures to encourage development of poorer countries. In particular, the Doha Development Agenda, as it is called, is concerned with measures to make trade fairer so that its benefits are spread more evenly around the world. This would involve improved access for developing countries to markets in the rich world. The Agenda is also concerned with the environmental impacts of trade and development.

The negotiations were due to be completed originally in 2005, but deadlines continued to be missed. However, some progress was made at Ministerial Conferences in 2013 and 2015, as Box 24.3 explains.

BOX 24.3 | THE DOHA DEVELOPMENT AGENDA

A new direction for the WTO?

Globalisation, based on the free play of comparative advantage, economies of scale and innovation, has produced a genuinely radical force, in the true sense of the word. It essentially amplifies and reinforces the strengths, but also the weaknesses, of market capitalism: its efficiency, its instability, and its inequality. If we want globalisation not only to be efficiency-boosting but also fair, we need more international rules and stronger multilateral institutions.[1]

In November 1999, the members of the World Trade Organization met in Seattle in the USA. What ensued became known as the 'battle of Seattle'. Anti-globalisation protesters fought with police; the world's developing economies fell out with the world's developed economies; and the very future of the WTO was called into question. The WTO was accused of being a free trader's charter, in which the objective of free trade was allowed to ride rough-shod over anything that might stand in its way. Whatever the issue – the environment, the plight of developing countries, the dominance of trade by multinationals – free trade was king.

As Pascal Lamy, then EU Trade Commissioner, made clear in the quote above, rules had to be strengthened, and the WTO had to ensure that the gains from trade were fairer and more sustainable.

The rebuilding process of the WTO began in Doha, Qatar, in 2001. The meeting between the then 142 members of the WTO concluded with the decision to launch a new round of WTO trade talks, to be called the 'Doha Development Agenda'. As with previous trade rounds, the talks were designed to increase the liberalisation of trade. However, this time such a goal was to be tempered by a policy of strengthening assistance to developing economies.

Other areas identified for discussion included: greater liberalisation of agriculture; rules to govern foreign direct investment; the co-ordination of countries' competition policies; the use and abuse of patents on medicines and the needs of developing countries.

The talks were originally scheduled for completion by January 2005, but this deadline was extended several times as new talks were arranged and failed to reach agreement. A particular sticking point was the unwillingness of rich countries, and the USA and the EU in particular, to liberalise trade in agricultural products, given the pressure from their domestic farmers. The USA was unwilling to make substantial cuts in agricultural subsidies and the EU in agricultural tariffs.

There was also an unwillingness by large developing countries, such as India and Brazil, to reduce protection of their industrial and service sectors. What is more, there were large divergences in opinion between developing countries on how much they should reduce their own agricultural protection.

Breakdown of the talks

The talks seemed finally to have broken down at a meeting in Geneva in July 2008. Despite the willingness of developing countries to reduce industrial tariffs by more than 50 per cent, and by the USA and the EU to make deep cuts in agricultural subsidies and tariffs, the talks foundered over the question of agricultural protection for developing countries. This was item 18 on a 'to-do' list of 20 items; items 1 to 17 had already been agreed. China and India wanted to protect poor farmers by retaining the ability to impose temporary tariffs on food imports in the event of a drop in food prices or a surge in imports. The USA objected. When neither side would budge, the talks collapsed.

Many commentators, however, argued that failure was no catastrophe. The gain from total liberalisation of trade would

[1] 'Global policy without democracy' (speech by Pascal Lamy, EU Trade Commissioner, given in 2001).

have boosted developing countries' GDP by no more than 1 per cent. And anyway, tariffs were generally falling and were already at an all-time low. But with the global economic downturn of 2008/9, there were worries that protectionism would begin to rise again. This was a classic prisoner's dilemma (see page 217–19). Policies that seemed to be in the interests of countries separately would be to the overall detriment of the world. The Nash equilibrium of such a 'game', therefore, is one where countries are generally worse off. As it turned out, the worries were largely unfounded – at least in the short term

The Bali and Nairobi Packages

In December 2013, an agreement was reached on a range of issues at the WTO's Bali Ministerial Conference and these were adopted in November 2014 by the General Council. The agreement means a streamlining of trade, making it 'easier, faster and cheaper', with a focus on the promotion of development: boosting the trade of the least developed countries and allowing developing countries more options for providing food security, as long as this does not distort international trade.

This was the first significant agreement of the round and went some way to achieving around 25 per cent of the goals set for the Doha Round.

Then, in December 2015, at the Ministerial Conference in Nairobi, another historic agreement was made on various trade initiatives that should provide particular benefits to the WTO's poorest members. This 'Nairobi Package' contains six Ministerial Decisions on agriculture, cotton and issues related to least-developed countries, including a commitment to abolish export subsidies for farm exports. Such subsidies had been widely used by developed countries as a means of protecting their agricultural sector.

The end of the road?

While many issues remain outstanding, some progress has been made. However, many governments, including the USA, have indicated that this could well be the end of the road for the Doha Round. Indeed, the Trump presidency was seen to reflect a new wave of protectionism around the world, with populist movements blaming free trade for the decline of many traditional sectors, with a loss of jobs and increased social deprivation.

 Does the process of globalisation mean that the role of the WTO is becoming less and less important?

 Conduct a literature search around the topic of international trade and inequality. Summarise your findings in a PowerPoint presentation that could be presented to an audience of non-specialists in this area, and that would last for around 10–15 minutes.

SUMMARY

1a World trade had, for many years, grown significantly faster than the growth in world output. This is reflected in a significant long-term increase in the ratio of global trade to GDP. However, following the financial crisis of the late 2000s and the subsequent economic slowdown, the ratio has fallen slightly. With a rise in protectionist rhetoric and actions it could be that the ratio will remain below its 2007-peak, at least in the short-term.

1b Developed nations have tended to dominate world trade. However, the share of world trade accounted for by developing countries has risen rapidly in recent times. The growth in exports from the BRICS (Brazil, Russia, India, China and South Africa), as well as from other 'newly industrialised' developing nations, such as Mexico, Turkey, Indonesia, Cambodia and Vietnam, has been especially rapid in recent years.

1c The composition of world trade is dominated largely by merchandise exports, especially manufacturing products. However, the trade in services has expanded over recent years and was generally less affected by the aftermath of the financial crisis.

2a Countries can gain from trade if they specialise in producing those goods in which they have a comparative advantage, i.e. those goods that can be produced at relatively low opportunity costs. This is merely an extension of the argument that gains can be made from the specialisation and division of labour.

2b If two countries trade, then, provided that the trade price ratio of exports and imports is between the pre-trade price ratios of these goods in the two countries, both countries can gain.

2c With increasing opportunity costs, there will be a limit to specialisation and trade. As a country increasingly specialises, its (marginal) comparative advantage will eventually disappear.

2d Gains from trade also arise from decreasing costs (economies of scale), differences in demand between countries, increased competition from trade and the transmission of growth from one country to another. There may also be non-economic advantages from trade.

2e The terms of trade give the price of exports relative to the price of imports expressed as an index, where the base year is 100.

3a Countries use various methods to restrict trade, including tariffs, quotas, exchange controls, import licensing, export taxes and legal and administrative barriers. Countries may also promote their own industries by subsidies.

3b Reasons for restricting trade that have some validity in a world context include the infant industry argument, the problems of relying on exporting goods whose market is growing slowly or even declining, dumping and other unfair trade practices, the danger of the establishment of a foreign-based monopoly, the need to spread the risks of fluctuating export prices, and the problems that free trade may adversely affect consumer tastes, may allow the importation of harmful goods and may not take account of externalities.

3c Often, however, the arguments for restricting trade are in the context of one country benefiting even though other countries may lose more. Countries may intervene in trade in order to exploit their monopoly/monopsony power or to protect declining industries.

3d Finally, a country may have other objectives in restricting trade, such as remaining self-sufficient in certain strategic products, not trading with certain countries of which it disapproves, protecting traditional ways of life or simply retaining a non-specialised economy.

3e Arguments for restricting trade, however, are often fallacious. In general, trade brings benefits to countries and protection to achieve one objective may be at a very high opportunity cost. Even if government intervention to protect certain parts of the economy is desirable, restricting trade is unlikely to be a first-best solution to the problem, since it involves side-effect costs. What is more, restricting trade may harm global economic growth; it may encourage retaliation; it may allow inefficient firms to remain inefficient; it may involve considerable bureaucracy.

4a Most countries of the world are members of the WTO and, in theory, are in favour of moves towards freer trade.

4b The WTO is more powerful than its predecessor, GATT. It has a disputes procedure and can enforce its rulings. In practice, however, countries have been very unwilling to abandon restrictions if they believe that they can gain from them, even though they might be at the expense of other countries.

4c WTO members periodically meet in rounds of talks, which may last many years. The latest, the Doha Round, has focused on trade liberalisation and aims to spread the benefits of trade across developing countries. It has yet to be concluded, but progress has been made since 2013. There is some doubt, however, as to whether any further progress will be made and whether the round, therefore, is effectively over.

REVIEW QUESTIONS

1 What is likely to be the impact of rising levels of intra-regional trade for the world economy?

2 Imagine that two countries, Richland and Poorland, can produce just two goods, computers and coal. Assume that, for a given amount of land and capital, the output of these two products requires the following constant amounts of labour:

	Richland	Poorland
1 computer	2	4
100 tonnes of coal	4	5

Assume that each country has 20 million workers.

a) Draw the production possibility curves for the two countries (on two separate diagrams).

b) If there is no trade and, in each country, 12 million workers produce computers and 8 million workers produce coal, how many computers and tonnes of coal will each country produce? What will be the total production of each product?

c) What is the opportunity cost of a computer in (i) Richland; (ii) Poorland?

d) What is the opportunity cost of 100 tonnes of coal in (i) Richland: (ii) Poorland?

e) Which country has a comparative advantage in which product?

f) Assuming that price equals marginal cost, which of the following would represent possible exchange ratios?
(i) 1 computer for 40 tonnes of coal;
(ii) 2 computers for 140 tonnes of coal;
(iii) 1 computer for 100 tonnes of coal;
(iv) 1 computer for 60 tonnes of coal;
(v) 4 computers for 360 tonnes of coal.

g) Assume that trade now takes place and that 1 computer exchanges for 65 tonnes of coal. Both countries specialise completely in the product in which they have a comparative advantage. How much does each country produce of its respective product?

h) The country producing computers sells 6 million domestically. How many does it export to the other country?

i) How much coal does the other country consume?

3 Why doesn't the USA specialise as much as General Motors or Texaco? Why doesn't the UK specialise as much as Unilever? Is the answer to these questions similar to the answer to the questions, 'Why doesn't the USA specialise as much as Luxembourg?', and 'Why doesn't Unilever specialise as much as the local florist?'

4 To what extent are the arguments for countries specialising and then trading with each other the same as those for individuals specialising in doing the jobs to which they are relatively well suited?

5 The following are four items that are traded internationally: wheat; computers; textiles; insurance. In which one of the four is each of the following most likely to have a comparative advantage: India; the UK; Canada; Japan? Give reasons for your answer.

6 Go through each of the arguments for restricting trade (both those of general validity and those having some validity for specific countries) and provide a counter-argument for not restricting trade.

7 If countries are so keen to reduce the barriers to trade, why do many countries frequently attempt to erect barriers?

8 Debate the following: 'All arguments for restricting trade boil down to special pleading for particular interest groups. Ultimately, there will be a net social cost from any trade restrictions.'

9 If rich countries stand to gain substantially from freer trade, why have they been so reluctant to reduce the levels of protection of agriculture?

10 Make out a case for restricting trade between the UK and Japan. Are there any arguments here that could not equally apply to a case for restricting trade between Scotland and England or between Liverpool or Manchester?

25 Chapter

Trading blocs

Business issues covered in this chapter

- Why do countries form free trade areas and other types of trading alliance, and what forms can they take?
- Do they result in a creation of trade or a mere diversion of trade from outside to inside the area?
- What trading alliances exist around the world and what are their features?
- How has the EU evolved and to what extent is it a true common market?
- How has the single market in the EU benefited companies and member states?
- What might be the long-term economic impact on the UK economy of the decision to leave the EU?

The world economy seems to have been increasingly forming into a series of trade blocs, based upon regional groupings of countries: a European region centred on the European Union, an Asian region on Japan, a North American region on the USA and a Latin American region. Such trade blocs are examples of *preferential trading arrangements*. These arrangements involve trade restrictions with the rest of the world and lower or zero restrictions between the members.

Although trade blocs clearly encourage trade between their members (intra-regional trade has been growing significantly faster than trade between regions), many countries outside these blocs complain that they benefit the members at the expense of the rest of the world. For many developing economies, in need of access to the most prosperous nations in the world, this represents a significant check on their ability to grow and develop.

In this chapter, we shall first consider why groups of countries might wish to establish trade blocs and what they seek to gain beyond the benefits that result from free and open trade. We will then look at the world's trade blocs as they currently stand, paying particular attention to the European Union, which is by far the most advanced in respect of establishing a high level of regional integration.

We finish by considering some of the possible economic implications for the UK from the vote in 2016 to leave the European Union. The focus here is on the longer-term economic effects of the UK's new trading relationship with the EU and the rest of the world.

Definition

Preferential trading arrangement A trading arrangement whereby trade between the signatories is freer than trade with the rest of the world.

25.1 PREFERENTIAL TRADING

Types of preferential trading arrangement

There are three possible forms that such trading arrangements might take.

Free trade areas

A *free trade area* is where member countries remove tariffs and quotas between themselves, but retain whatever restrictions *each member chooses* with non-member countries. Some provision will have to be made to prevent imports from outside coming into the area via the country with the lowest external tariff.

Customs unions

A *customs union* is like a free trade area, but, in addition, members must adopt *common* external tariffs and quotas with non- member countries.

Common markets

A *common market* is where member countries operate as a *single* market. Like a customs union, there are no tariffs and quotas between member countries and there are common external tariffs and quotas. But a common market goes further than this. A full common market includes the following features:

- *A common system of taxation.* In the case of a *perfect* common market, this will involve identical rates of tax in all member countries.
- *A common system of laws and regulations governing production, employment and trade.* For example, in a perfect common market, there would be a *single* set of laws governing issues such as product specification (e.g. permissible artificial additives to foods or levels of exhaust emissions from cars), the employment and dismissal of labour, mergers and takeovers, and monopolies and restrictive practices.
- *Free movement of labour, capital and materials and of goods and services.* In a perfect common market, this will involve a total absence of border controls between member states, the freedom of workers to work in any member country and the freedom of firms to expand into any member state.
- *The absence of special treatment by member governments of their own domestic industries.* Governments are large purchasers of goods and services. In a perfect common market, they should buy from whichever companies within the market offer the most competitive deal and not show favouritism towards domestic suppliers: they should operate a *common procurement policy.*

The definition of a common market is sometimes extended to include the following two features of *economic and monetary union.*

- *A fixed exchange rate between the member countries' currencies.* In the extreme case, this would involve a single currency for the whole market.
- *Common macroeconomic policies.* To some extent, this must follow from a fixed exchange rate, but in the extreme case it will involve a single macroeconomic management of the whole market, and hence the abolition of separate fiscal or monetary intervention by individual member states. We will examine European economic and monetary union in section 32.3.

The direct effects of a customs union: trade creation and trade diversion

By joining a customs union (or free trade area), a country will find that its trade patterns change. Two such changes can be distinguished: trade creation and trade diversion.

Trade creation

Trade creation is where consumption shifts from a high-cost producer to a low-cost producer. The removal of trade barriers allows greater specialisation according to comparative advantage. Instead of consumers having to pay high prices for domestically produced goods in which the country has a comparative disadvantage, the goods can now be obtained more cheaply from other members of the customs union. In return, the country can export to them goods in which it has a comparative advantage.

Trade diversion

Trade diversion is where consumption shifts from a lower-cost producer outside the customs union to a higher-cost producer within the union.

> ### Definitions
>
> **Free trade area** A group of countries with no trade barriers between themselves.
>
> **Customs union** A free trade area with common external tariffs and quotas.
>
> **Common market** A customs union where the member countries act as a single market with free movement of labour and capital, common taxes and common trade laws.
>
> **Trade creation** Where a customs union leads to greater specialisation according to comparative advantage and thus a shift in production from higher-cost to lower-cost sources.
>
> **Trade diversion** Where a customs union diverts consumption from goods produced at a lower cost outside the union to goods produced at a higher cost (but tariff free) within the union.

Assume that the most efficient producer of good *y* in the world is Russia – outside the EU. Assume that, before membership of the EU, Poland paid a similar tariff on good *y* from any country, and thus imported the product from Russia rather than from the EU.

After Poland joined the EU, however, the removal of the tariff made the EU product cheaper, since the tariff remained on the Russian product. Consumption thus switched to a higher-cost producer. There was, thus, a net loss in world efficiency.

As far as Poland was concerned, consumers still gained, since they were paying a lower price than before. However, there was a loss to domestic producers (from the reduction in protection, and hence reduced prices and profits) and to the government (from reduced tariff revenue). These losses may have been smaller or larger than the gain to consumers: in other words, there may have still been a net gain to Poland, but there could have been a net loss, depending on the circumstances.

> ### Pause for thought
>
> *Is joining a customs union more likely to lead to trade creation or trade diversion in each of the following cases? (a) The union has a very high external tariff. (b) Cost differences are very great between the country and members of the union.*

Longer-term effects of a customs union

Over the longer term, there may be other gains and losses from being a member of a customs union.

Longer-term advantages

- Increased market size may allow a country's firms to exploit *(internal) economies of scale.* This argument is more important for small countries, which therefore have more to gain from an enlargement of their markets.

- *External economies of scale.* Increased trade may lead to improvements in the infrastructure of the members of the customs union (better roads, railways, financial services, etc.). This, in turn, could then bring greater long-term benefits from trade between members and from external trade too, by making the transport and handling of imports and exports cheaper.

- The bargaining power of the whole customs union with the rest of the world may allow member countries to gain *better terms of trade.* This, of course, necessarily will involve a degree of political co-operation between the members.

- *Increased competition* between member countries may stimulate efficiency, encourage investment and reduce monopoly power. Of course, a similar advantage could be gained by the simple removal of tariffs with any competing country.

- Integration may encourage a *more rapid spread of technology.*

Longer-term disadvantages

- *Resources may flow from the country* to more efficient members of the customs union or to the geographical centre of the union (so as to minimise transport costs). This can be a major problem for a common market (where there is free movement of labour and capital). The country could become a depressed 'region' of the community.

- If integration encourages greater co-operation between firms in member countries, it may also encourage *greater oligopolistic collusion,* thus keeping prices higher to the consumer. It may also encourage mergers and takeovers, which would increase monopoly power.

- *Diseconomies of scale.* If the union leads to the development of very large companies, they may become bureaucratic and inefficient.

- *The costs of administering* the customs union may be high. This problem is likely to worsen the more intervention there is in the affairs of individual members.

25.2 PREFERENTIAL TRADING IN PRACTICE

Preferential trading has the greatest potential to benefit countries whose domestic market is too small, taken on its own, to enable them to benefit from economies of scale and where they face substantial barriers to their exports. Most developing countries fall into this category and, as a result, many have attempted to form preferential trading arrangements.

Examples in Latin America and the Caribbean include the Latin American Integration Association (LAIA), the Andean Community, the Central American Integration System (SICA) and the Caribbean Community (CARICOM). A Southern Common Market (MerCoSur) was formed in 1991, consisting of Argentina, Brazil, Paraguay and Uruguay. Venezuela joined in 2012. It has a common external tariff and most of its internal trade is free of tariffs.

The Association of South-East Asian Nations (ASEAN) was formed in 1967 when six nations (Brunei, Indonesia,

Malaysia, the Philippines, Singapore and Thailand) agreed to work towards an ASEAN Free Trade Area (AFTA). Between 1984 and 1999, they were joined by four new members (Vietnam, Laos, Myanmar and Cambodia). ASEAN has a population of over 650 million people and is dedicated to increased economic co-operation within the region.

By 2010, virtually all tariffs between the six original members had been eliminated and both tariff and non-tariff barriers are falling quickly for both original and new members. The ASEAN Economic Community (AEC) was established in 2015, ahead of schedule.

In Africa, the Economic Community of West African States (ECOWAS) has been attempting to create a common market between its 15 members, which has a combined population of around 350 million. The West African franc is used in eight of the countries and another six plan to introduce a common currency, the Eco. However, the launch of this has been delayed several times and it is now not expected until at least 2020. The ultimate goal is to combine the two currency areas and adopt a single currency for all member states.

North America Free Trade Agreement (NAFTA)/ United States-Mexico-Canada Agreement (USMCA)

NAFTA and its successor, the United States-Canada-Mexico Agreement (USCMA) is one of the two most powerful trading blocs in the world (the other being the EU). It came into force in 1994 and consists of the USA, Canada and Mexico. The three countries have agreed to abolish tariffs between themselves in the hope that increased trade and co-operation will follow. Tariffs between the USA and Canada were phased out by 1999 and tariffs between all three countries were eliminated as of 1 January 2008. Many non-tariff restrictions remain, although, under the original agreement, new ones were not to be permitted.

While NAFTA has a market size similar to that of the EU, it is, however, at most only a free trade area and not a common market. Unlike the EU, it does not seek to harmonise laws and regulations, except in very specific areas such as environmental management and labour standards. Member countries are permitted total legal independence, subject to the one proviso that they must treat firms of other member countries equally with their own firms – the principle of 'fair competition'. Nevertheless, NAFTA has encouraged a growth in trade between its members, most of which is trade creation rather than trade diversion.

The election of Donald Trump as President was to be a pivotal moment for NAFTA. During his campaign, he had described NAFTA as the 'worst trade deal in US history'. Shortly after to coming to office, he committed to renegotiating NAFTA. His administration's concerns included the US trade deficit with Mexico, the amount of imported material in goods, such as cars, that qualify under the original NAFTA agreement, and the mechanism to review trade disputes between NAFTA members. The renegotiation talks began in August 2017, with several rounds of talks subsequently taking place.

On 1 June 2018, the Trump administration imposed tariffs on steel and aluminium imports of 25 per cent and 10 per cent respectively from a number of countries, including Canada and Mexico. This led to retaliation, including from Canada and Mexico, with tariffs imposed on a range of US products. These tariffs became central to the NAFTA negotiations.

After difficult negotiations, a deal was eventually reached on 30 September 2018. NAFTA was to be renamed, the United States-Mexico-Canada Agreement (USMCA). But, rather than being radically different from NAFTA, USMCA was a relatively modest reworking of NAFTA.

There were three main changes. The first is that a greater proportion of motor vehicles traded between any of the three countries must have 75 per cent of their components made within USMCA (not the previous 62.5 per cent) and that at least between 40 and 45 per cent of a vehicle's components must be made by workers earning at least US$16 per hour to qualify for zero tariffs. The second change is an agreement by Canada to give US dairy farmers access to 3.6 per cent of Canada's dairy market. The third strengthens various standards inadequately covered in NAFTA. But despite the rhetoric, most of the NAFTA agreement remained unchanged. At the time of the agreement, the steel and aluminium tariffs remained in place.

The Asia-Pacific Economic Cooperation forum (APEC)

The most significant move towards establishing a more widespread regional economic organisation in East Asia appeared with the creation of the Asia-Pacific Economic Co-operation (APEC) in 1989. APEC links 21 economies of the Pacific Rim, including Asian, Australasian and North and South American countries (19 countries, plus Hong Kong and Taiwan). These countries account for over half of the world's total output and almost half of the world's trade. At the 1994 meeting of APEC leaders, it was resolved to create a free trade area across the Pacific by 2010 for the developed industrial countries and by 2020 for the rest.

This preferential trading area is by no means as advanced as NAFTA and is unlikely to move beyond a free trade area. Within the region there exists a wide disparity across a range of economic and social indicators. Such disparities create a wide range of national interests and goals. Countries are unlikely to share common economic problems or concerns. In addition, political differences and conflicts within the region are widespread, reducing the likelihood that any organisational agreement beyond a simple economic one would succeed.

The Trans-Pacific Partnership

The Trans-Pacific Trade Partnership (TPP) agreement was signed in February 2016 by 12 countries – Australia, Brunei, Canada, Chile, Japan, Malaysia, Mexico, New Zealand, Peru, Singapore, the USA and Vietnam, but not China. However, on coming into office in January 2017, Donald Trump withdrew the USA from the agreement.

The agreement is more than a simple free-trade agreement. In terms of trade, it involves the removal of many non-tariff barriers as well as most tariff barriers. It also has elements of a single market. For example, it contains many robust and enforceable environmental protection, human rights and labour standards measures. It also allows for the free transfer of capital by investors in most circumstances.

However, it also established an 'investor–state dispute settlement' (ISDS) mechanism. This allows companies from any of the TPP countries to sue governments of any other countries in the agreement for treaty violations, such as giving favourable treatment to domestic companies, the seizing of companies' assets or controls over the movement of capital. Critics of ISDS claim that it gives too much power to companies and may prevent governments from protecting their national environment or domestic workers and companies.

The other 11 TPP countries signed up to a revised, though largely unchanged, version of the agreement in March 2018. Each of these countries then began the process of officially ratifying the deal. Other countries, including South Korea, Indonesia, the Philippines, Thailand, Taiwan and Colombia, have expressed an interest in joining. However, a key question is whether a growing international antipathy to trade deals will extend beyond the USA to these and other prospective members.

The longest established and most comprehensive preferential trading arrangement is the EU. In the remainder of this chapter we will consider the development of the EU and its implications for business.

25.3 THE EUROPEAN UNION

KI 36
p 376
The European Economic Community (EEC) was formed by the signing of the Treaty of Rome in 1957 and came into operation on 1 January 1958.

The original six member countries of the EEC (Belgium, France, Italy, Luxembourg, The Netherlands and West Germany) had already made a move towards integration with the formation of the European Coal and Steel Community in 1952. This had removed all restrictions on trade in coal, steel and iron ore between the six countries. The aim had been to gain economies of scale and allow more effective competition with the USA and other foreign producers.

The EEC extended this principle and aimed eventually to be a full common market with completely free trade between members in all products and with completely free movement of labour, enterprise and capital.

All internal tariffs between the six members had been abolished and common external tariffs established by 1968. But this still only made the EEC a *customs union*, since a number of restrictions on internal trade remained (legal, administrative, fiscal, etc.). Nevertheless, the aim was eventually to create a full common market.

In 1973, the UK, Denmark and Ireland became members. Greece joined in 1981, Spain and Portugal in 1986 and Sweden, Austria and Finland in 1995. Then, in May 2004, a further 10 countries joined: Cyprus, the Czech Republic, Estonia, Hungary, Latvia, Lithuania, Malta, Poland, Slovakia and Slovenia. Bulgaria and Romania joined in 2007. The last new member is Croatia, which joined in 2013. With the UK scheduled to leave the EU in 2019, there will then be 27 members.

From customs union to common market

The EU is clearly a customs union. It has common external tariffs and no internal tariffs. But is it also a common market? For years, there have been certain common economic policies.

Common Agricultural Policy (CAP). The EU has traditionally set common high prices for farm products. This has involved charging variable import duties to bring foreign food imports up to EU prices and intervention to buy up surpluses of food produced within the EU at these above-equilibrium prices. Although the main method of support has shifted to providing subsidies (or 'income support') unrelated to current output, this still represents a common economic policy of agricultural support.

Regional policy. EU regional policy provides grants to firms and local authorities in relatively deprived regions of the Union.

Competition policy. EU policy here has applied primarily to companies operating in more than one member state (see section 21.1). For example, Article 101 of the Treaty of Lisbon (see pages 392–4) prohibits agreements between firms operating in more than one EU country (e.g. over pricing or sharing out markets) which adversely affect competition in trade between member states.

KI 21
p 184

Harmonisation of taxation. VAT is the standard form of indirect tax throughout the EU. However, there are substantial differences in VAT rates between member states, as there are with other tax rates.

Social policy. In 1989, the European Commission presented a *Social Charter* to the EU heads of state (see Case study I.15 on the student website). This spelt out a series of worker and social rights that should apply in all member states. These rights were grouped under 12 headings covering areas such as the guarantee of decent levels of income for both the employed and the non-employed, freedom of movement of labour between EU countries, freedom to belong to a trade union and equal treatment of women and men in the labour market. The Social Charter was only a recommendation and each element had to be approved separately by the European Council of Ministers.

KI 32
p 365

The Social Chapter of the Maastricht Treaty (1991) attempted to move the Community forward in implementing the details of the Social Charter in areas such as maximum working hours, minimum working conditions, health and safety protection, the provision of information to and consultation with workers and equal opportunities.

Pause for thought

Does the adoption of laws enforcing improved working conditions necessarily lead to higher costs per unit of output?

Despite these various common policies, in other respects, the Community of the 1970s and 1980s was far from a true common market: there were all sorts of non-tariff barriers, such as high taxes on wine by non-wine-producing countries, special regulations designed to favour domestic producers, governments giving contracts to domestic producers (e.g. for defence equipment), and so on.

The Single European Act of 1986, however, sought to remove these barriers and to form a genuine common market by the end of 1992. One of the most crucial aspects of the Act was its acceptance of the principle of **mutual recognition**. This is the principle whereby if a firm or individual is permitted to do something under the rules and regulations of *one* EU country, it must thereby also be permitted to do it in all other EU countries. This means that firms and individuals can choose the country's rules that are least constraining. It also means that individual governments can no longer devise special rules and regulations that keep out competitors from other EU countries.

Box 25.1 considers further the features of the European Single Market.

The benefits and costs of the single market

It is difficult to quantify the benefits and costs of the single market, given that many occur over a long period. Also, it is difficult to know to what extent the changes taking place are the direct result of the single market.

In 2012, the European Commission published *20 Years of the European Single Market*. This stated that: 'EU27 GDP in 2008 was 2.13 per cent or €233 billion higher than it would have been if the Single Market had not been launched in 1992. In 2008 alone, this amounted to an average of €500 extra in income per person in the EU27. The gains come from the Single Market programme, liberalisation in network industries such as energy and telecommunication, and the enlargement of the EU to 27 member countries.'

Even though the precise magnitude of the benefits is difficult to estimate, it is possible to identify the *types* of benefit that have resulted, many of which have been substantial.

Trade creation.   Costs and prices have fallen as a result of a greater exploitation of comparative advantage. Member countries can now specialise further in those goods and services that they can produce at a comparatively low opportunity cost.

Reduction in the direct costs of barriers.   This category includes administrative costs, border delays and technical regulations.

Their abolition or harmonisation has led to substantial cost savings.

Economies of scale. With industries based on a Europe-wide scale, many firms and their plants can be large enough to gain the full potential economies of scale. Yet the whole European market is large enough for there still to be adequate competition. Such gains have varied from industry to industry, depending on the minimum efficient scale of a plant or firm (see Box 9.4 on p. 162). Economies of scale have also been gained from mergers and other forms of industrial restructuring.

Greater competition. Increased competition between firms has led to lower costs, lower prices and a wider range of products available to consumers. This has been particularly so in newly liberalised service sectors such as transport, financial services, telecommunications and broadcasting. In the long run, greater competition can stimulate greater innovation, the greater flow of technical information and the rationalisation of production.

Despite these gains, the single market has not received universal welcome within the EU. Its critics argue that, in a Europe of oligopolies, unequal ownership of resources, rapidly changing technologies and industrial practices, and factor immobility, the removal of internal barriers to trade has merely exaggerated the problems of inequality and economic power. More specifically, the following criticisms are made.

Radical economic change is costly.   Substantial economic change is necessary to achieve the full economies of scale and efficiency gains from a single European market. These changes necessarily involve redundancies – from bankruptcies, takeovers, rationalisation and the introduction of new technology. The severity of this 'structural' and 'technological' unemployment (see section 26.4) depends on (a) the pace of economic change and (b) the mobility of labour – both occupational and geographical. Clearly, the more integrated markets become across the EU, the less the costs of future economic change.

Adverse regional effects.   Firms are likely to locate as near as possible to the 'centre of gravity' of their markets and sources of supply. If, before barriers are removed, a firm's prime market is the UK, it might well locate in the Midlands or the north of England. If, however, with barriers now removed, its market has become Europe as a whole, it may choose to

Definition

Mutual recognition The EU principle that one country's rules and regulations must apply throughout the Union. If they conflict with those of another country, individuals and firms should be able to choose which to obey.

BOX 25.1 — **FEATURES OF THE EUROPEAN SINGLE MARKET**

Removing the frictions to trade

Since 1 January 1993, trade within the EU has operated very much like trade within a country. In theory, there should be no more difficulty for a firm in Marseilles to sell its goods in Berlin than in Paris. At the same time, the single market allows free movement of labour and involves the use of common technical standards.

The features of the single market are summed up in two European Commission publications.[1] They are:

- Elimination of border controls on goods within the EU: no more long waits.
- Free movement of people across borders.
- Common security arrangements.
- No import taxes on goods bought in other member states for personal use.
- The right for everyone to live in another member state.
- Recognition of vocational qualifications in other member states: engineers, accountants, medical practitioners, teachers and other professionals able to practise throughout Europe.
- Technical standards brought into line and product tests and certification agreed across the whole EU.
- Common commercial laws – making it attractive to form Europe-wide companies and to start joint ventures.
- Public contracts to supply equipment and services to state organisations now open to tenders across the EU.

So, what does the single market mean for individuals and for businesses?

Individuals

Before 1993, if you were travelling in Europe, you had a 'duty-free allowance'. This meant that you could only take goods up to the value of €600 across borders within the EU without having to pay VAT in the country into which you were importing them. Now you can take as many goods as you like from one EU country to another, provided they are for your own consumption. But, to prevent fraud, member states may ask for evidence that the goods have been purchased for the traveller's own consumption if they exceed specified amounts.

Individuals have the right to live and work in any other member state. Qualifications obtained in one member state must be recognised by other member states.

Firms

Before 1993, all goods traded in the EU were subject to VAT at every internal border. This involved some 60 million customs clearance documents resulting in a cost of some €70 per consignment.[2]

This has all now disappeared. Goods can cross from one member state to another without any border controls: in fact, the concepts of 'importing' and 'exporting' within the EU no longer officially exist. All goods sent from one EU country to another will be charged VAT only in the country of destination. They are exempt from VAT in the country where they are produced.

One of the important requirements for fair competition in the single market is the convergence of tax rates. Although income tax rates, corporate tax rates and excise duties still differ between member states, there has been some narrowing in the range of VAT rates. Higher rates of VAT on luxury goods were abolished and countries are supposed to have no more than three other rates below the standard rate on 'socially necessary' goods, such as food and water supply. One of these three rates can be zero, while the other two should be at least 5 per cent. There are, however, some countries that do not abide by this, having more than two lower rates above zero and not all of at least 5 per cent.

There is now a lower limit of 15 per cent on the standard rate of VAT. Standard rates in January 2018, nonetheless, varied from 17 per cent in Luxembourg to 27 per cent in Hungary. During the early 2010s, several countries, including the UK, Ireland, Greece, Italy, Hungary and Portugal, increased their standard rate of VAT as a means of reducing their budget deficits (see Section 13.1). One effect of this has been that the vast majority of EU countries now have a standard rate of VAT between 20 and 25 per cent.

 In what ways would competition be 'unfair' if VAT rates differed widely between member states?

 Using the Public Finances Databank from the Office for Budget Responsibility, create a chart showing for the UK the percentage of public-sector current receipts collected from VAT (net of refunds) over time. Briefly summarise the findings of your chart and discuss their significance.

[1] *A Single Market for Goods* (Commission of the European Communities, 1993); *10 Key Points about the Single European Market* (Commission of the European Communities, 1992).

[2] See *A Single Market for Goods* (Commission of the European Communities, 1993).

---

locate in the south of England or in France, Germany or the Benelux countries instead. The creation of a single European market thus tends to attract capital and jobs away from the edges of the Union to its geographical centre.

In an ideal market situation, areas like the south of Italy or Bulgaria should attract resources from other parts of the Union. Being relatively depressed areas, wage rates and land prices are lower. The resulting lower industrial costs should encourage firms to move there. In practice, however, as capital and labour (and especially young and skilled workers) leave the extremities

of the Union, so these regions are likely to become more depressed. If, as a result, their infrastructure is neglected, they then become even less attractive to new investment.

The development of monopoly/oligopoly power. The free movement of capital can encourage the development of giant 'Euro-firms' with substantial economic power. Indeed, recent years have seen some very large European mergers (see Box 15.1). This can lead to higher, not lower prices and less choice for the consumer. It all depends on just how effective

BOX 25.2 | **THE SINGLE MARKET SCOREBOARD**

Keeping a tally on progress to a true single market

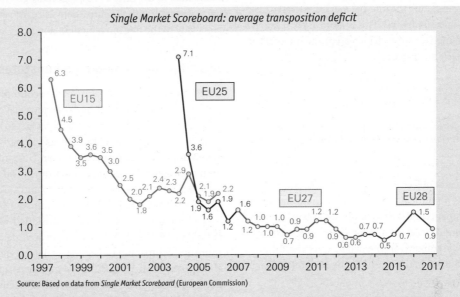

Single Market Scoreboard: average transposition deficit

Source: Based on data from *Single Market Scoreboard* (European Commission)

This success or otherwise of implementing EU internal market directives is measured by Single Market Scoreboard. The Scoreboard tracks the transposition deficit for each country. This is the percentage of directives that have failed to be implemented into national law by their agreed deadline.

The Scoreboard has been published since 1997. In addition to tracking the deficit for each country, it also shows the average deficit across all EU countries. The chart shows that the average deficit was falling until May 2002, but then rose somewhat. Part of the problem is that new directives are being issued as existing ones are being implemented.

After 2004, the transposition deficit tended to fall, even with the accession of ten new members in 2004 and two more in 2007. An average deficit target of 1 per cent was set in 2007 and this was reached by 2008. The average deficit fell further in 2009 to 0.7 per cent but then rose to 0.9 per cent in 2010 and to 1.2 in 2011.

Behind the rise in the average deficit in 2010 and 2011 was a reduction in the speed with which directives were being enacted. To tackle delays, a target of 'zero tolerance' operates for delays of two years or more in transposing directives. Overly long delays are seen as impairing the functioning of Single Market.

In the 2011 Single Market Act, the European Commission proposed a target transposition deficit of close to 0.5 per cent. The transposition deficit began to decline and, by November 2014, the EU average had fallen to 0.5 per cent.

It was then to prove difficult to meet the target consistently. In 2015, the transposition deficit had increased to 0.7 per cent, but there was a more substantial increase in 2016 when the deficit rose to 1.5. As a result, 20 of the 28 EU Member States exceeded the 1 per cent target with only one Member State (Malta) meeting the 0.5 per cent target proposed by the European Commission as part of the 2011 Act.

In its analysis on the trends in the transposition deficit published in 2017, the Commission notes:

> The EU average deficit has been decreasing steadily for the last 19 years (since 1997) and was more or less stable

since November 2012 (between 0.5% and 0.7%). This time, the situation has changed, with a doubled deficit (from 0.7% to 1.5%) that stands at the May 2007 level. This increase is exceptional due to the large number of directives to be transposed in the months preceding the cut-off date for calculating the Member States' performance. We can reasonably expect that the transposition rate will return to normal shortly.[1]

This indeed happened, with the transposition deficit falling back in 2017 to 0.9 per cent.

As well as the transposition deficit, the Scoreboard also measures the *conformity deficit*: the percentage of transposed directives where infringement proceedings for non-conformity have been initiated by the Commission.

The proposed target for the conformity deficit in the 2011 Single Market Act is 0.5 per cent. In recent times, this deficit has been relatively stable. The level of the EU average conformity deficit stood at 0.7 per cent from November 2013 to December 2016. In December 2017, it fell to 0.6 per cent, with nine Member States having a deficit of 0.5 per cent or less.

1. *What value are scoreboards for member states and the European Commission?*
2. *Why do you think that it is so important that legislation, such as that governing the internal market, is in place in all member states at the same time?*

Examine the latest version of the Single Market Scoreboard. How have the transposition and conformity deficits changed since the previous Scoreboard? Explain the differences in transposition and compliance between different Member States.

---

[1]*Single Market Scoreboard (Performance per governance tool): Transposition,* 07/2017 edition (for reporting period 12/2015-12/2016) (European Commission).

competition is and how effective EU competition policy is in preventing monopolistic and collusive practices.

Trade diversion. Just as trade creation has been a potential advantage of completing the internal market, so trade diversion has been a possibility too. This is more likely if *external* barriers remain high (or are even increased) and internal barriers are *completely* abolished.

> ### Pause for thought
>
> *Why may the newer members of the EU have the most to gain from the single market, but also the most to lose?*

Perhaps the biggest objection raised against the single European market is a political one: the loss of national sovereignty. Governments find it much more difficult to intervene at a microeconomic level in their own economies. This was one of the key arguments in the debate over the Britain's future within Europe in the run-up to the EU referendum in 2016 (see section 25.4).

Completing the internal market

Despite the reduction in barriers, the internal market is still not 'complete'. In other words, various barriers to trade between member states still remain.

To monitor progress what is now known as the Single Market Scoreboard was established in 1997. This shows progress towards the total abandonment of any forms of internal trade restrictions (see Box 25.2). It shows the percentage of EU Single Market Directives still to be transposed into national law: the 'transposition deficit'. It also identifies the number of infringements of the internal market that have taken place. The hope is that the 'naming and shaming' of countries will encourage them to make more rapid progress towards totally free trade within the EU.

Despite the general success in reducing the transposition deficits, national governments have continued to introduce *new* technical standards, several of which have had the effect of erecting new barriers to trade. Also, infringements of single market rules by governments have not always been dealt with. The net result is that, although trade is much freer today than in the early 1990s, especially given the transparency of pricing with the euro, there still exist various barriers, especially to the free movement of goods.

The effect of the new member states

Given the very different nature of the economies of many of the new entrants to the EU, and their lower levels of GDP per head, the potential for gain from membership has been substantial. The gains come through trade creation, increased competition, technological transfer and inward investment, both from other EU countries and from outside the EU.

A study in 2004[1] concluded that Poland's GDP would rise by 3.4 per cent and Hungary's by almost 7 per cent. Real wages would rise, with those of unskilled workers rising faster than those of skilled workers, in accordance with these countries' comparative advantage. There would also be benefits for the then 15 existing EU members from increased trade and investment, but these would be relatively minor in comparison to the gains to the new members.

A European Commission Report[2] produced in April 2009, five years after the enlargement, found that the expansion had been a win–win situation for both old and new members. There had been significant improvements in the standard of living in new member states and they had benefited from modernisation of their economies and more stabilised institutions and laws. In addition, enterprises in old member states had enjoyed opportunities for new investment and exports, and there had been an overall increase in trade and competition between the member states.

In future years, now that the euro is used by 19 of the member states, with the possibility of others adopting it at some time, trade within the remaining 27 EU countries is likely to continue to grow as a proportion of GDP. (We examine the benefits and costs of the single currency and the whole process of economic and monetary union in the EU in Section 32.3.)

25.4 THE UK AND BREXIT

On 23 June 2016, the UK held a referendum on whether to remain a member of the EU: 72.1 per cent of the electorate voted and, by a majority of 51.9 per cent to 48.1 per cent, Britain voted to leave the EU.

In the run-up to the vote, there was heated debate on the merits and costs of membership and of leaving ('Brexit'). Although many of the arguments were concerned with sovereignty, security and other political factors, many of the arguments centred on whether there would be a net *economic* gain from either remaining or leaving.

However, as we noted in the previous two sections, assessing the benefits of membership of customs unions and, in this case, of the EU is fraught with difficulties. Hence,

---

[1] M. Maliszewska, *Benefits of the Single Market Expansion for Current and New Member States* (Centrum Analiz Spoleczno-Ekonomicznych, 2004).

[2] 'Five Years of an Enlarged EU – Economic Achievements and Challenges', *European Economy 1 2009* (Commission of the European Communities).

forecasting the economic impact of the decision is difficult. The effects of either remaining or leaving were likely to be very different in the long run from the short run and, of course, long-run forecasts are highly unreliable as the economy is likely to be affected by so many unpredictable events.

Nonetheless, the tools of economics provide a framework in which we can discuss the *potential* economic benefits and costs of the UK's membership of the European Union as compared with the alternatives outside the EU.

Alternative trading arrangements

An analysis of the longer-term economic effects of the UK leaving the European Union was to depend on the nature of its future trading relationship with the EU. Three main possibilities were suggested.

The first was 'the Norwegian model', where Britain leaves the EU, but joins the European Economic Area (EEA), giving access to the single market, but removing regulation in some key areas, such as fisheries and home affairs.

The second possibility was the negotiation of *bilateral agreements*. These fall under three types:

- 'The Swiss model' where the UK negotiates a series of bilateral agreements with the EU, including selective or general access to the single market.
- 'The Canadian model' where the UK forms a comprehensive trade agreement with the EU to lower customs tariffs and other barriers to trade.
- 'The Turkish model' where the UK forms a customs union with the EU. In Turkey's case, the agreement relates principally to manufactured goods.

The third possibility was that the UK would make a complete break from the EU and simply use its membership of the WTO to make trade agreements. Table 25.1 summarises

Table 25.1		Alternative trading relationships with the EU		
		Tariffs	**Customs union and external trade**	**Non-tariff barriers /other policy and regulatory issues**
EU membership		Full tariff-free trade	Common external tariffs No customs costs Access to EU Free Trade Agreements (FTAs)	Alignment of regulations, standards and specifications Non-discriminatory access for markets or services
EEA (Norway)		Some tariffs on agriculture and fisheries	Custom costs apply No access to EU Free Trade Agreements (FTAs)	Limited coverage of agricultural and fisheries Compliance with most EU rules and standards, including free movement of people and social policy
Bilateral agreements	Switzerland	Some tariffs on agriculture	Custom costs apply No access to EU Free Trade Agreements (FTAs)	Minimises non-tariff barriers in areas covered by agreements Limited coverage of services No financial services passport Complies with EU rules in sector covered by agreements, including free movements of people and social policy
	Canada	Some tariffs on agriculture Tariffs for transitional period on manufactured goods	Custom costs apply No access to EU Free Trade Agreements (FTAs)	No financial services passport Compliance with EU standards for firms importing into EU
	Turkey	Tariff exemptions apply only to manufactured goods and processed agricultural goods	No custom costs for manufactured goods Align external trade policy with EU	No financial services passport No special access for services Adopts EU product standards Compliance with environmental standards linked to goods and to rules on competition and state aid
WTO membership		EU external tariffs apply	Custom costs apply No access to EU Free Trade Agreements (FTAs)	No financial services passport Compliance with EU standards for firms importing into EU

Source: Adapted from *EU Referendum: HM Treasury analysis key facts,* HM Treasury (18 April 2016)

these alternative trading relationships between the UK and the EU.

The UK Government, in due course, announced its intention to leave the single market and the EU customs union. In a speech in January 2017, UK Prime Minister, Theresa May, stated that the UK 'cannot possibly' remain in the single market, as that would mean 'not leaving the EU at all. So we do not seek membership of the Single Market. Instead we seek the greatest possible access to it through a new, comprehensive, bold and ambitious Free Trade Agreement'.[3]

Formal Brexit talks began following the triggering of Article 50 in March 2017. The talks would, therefore, shape a new trading relationship between the UK and EU. At their heart would be what happened at the 'UK/EU border'. Would firms face tariffs? Would the UK be able to reach an agreement with the EU that would allow it to make trade deals with other countries? Then there was the need to avoid physical border checks between Northern Ireland and the Republic of Ireland.

Long-term growth, trade and Brexit

The effects of the decision to leave the EU and the new trading relationship between the UK and EU will take many years to become clear. Many of these effects will depend on the impact that the decision has for the UK's long-term rate of economic growth, i.e. the average rate of growth over many years.

When looking at growth over many years, it is important to recognise that we are concerned primarily with the growth in an economy's productive potential. While we will discuss this issue more in subsequent chapters (including an introduction to long-term growth in section 26.6), it is generally recognised that the quantity, quality and effectiveness of inputs that businesses are able to use in production are crucial in determining the rate at which an economy grows over the longer term.

Adverse effects of Brexit

In its 2016 analysis of the possible long-term implications of Brexit, the UK Treasury argued that the country's *openness to trade and investment* had been a key factor behind the growth in the economy's potential output.[4] Hence, maintaining this openness, it argued, would be important for long-term growth and so for raising living standards. Positive effects from openness might include:

- Increasing market opportunities which enable firms to exploit internal economies of scale (see page 156–7).

- Increasing competition encourages firms to improve their productivity to maintain their market share and so encourages the adoption of new technologies and processes.
- Technology transfer (see page 459). Technological know-how can be passed between firms in international supply chains, through internationally-mobile workers or new international entrants.

> ### Pause for thought
>
> *How can the internationalisation of production and finance impact on the pace of technological progress?*

The Treasury's analysis attempted to estimate the average impact on households of the UK leaving the EU by modelling the adverse impacts on the supply-side of the economy from lower levels of openness. To do so, it considered three new relationships with the EU (see Table 25.1).

With a Norwegian-type deal, households would be £2600 worse off each year; a Swiss deal would lead to a £4300 annual loss of GDP per household; and a complete exit would create a household loss per annum of £5200. It found that tax receipts would be lower and that the overall benefit to the UK of being in the EU, relative to another arrangement, would be between 3.4 per cent and 9.5 per cent of GDP, depending on the exact 'new deal'.

The OECD suggested that Brexit would be like a tax, pushing up the costs and weakening the economy. Its analysis indicated that, by 2020, GDP would be at least 3 per cent lower than it otherwise would have been, making households £2200 worse off. By 2030, these figures would be 5 per cent and £3200. It continued that:

> In the longer term, structural impacts would take hold through the channels of capital, immigration and lower technical progress. In particular, labour productivity would be held back by a drop in foreign direct investment and a smaller pool of skills. The extent of forgone GDP would increase over time . . . The effects would be even larger in a more pessimistic scenario and remain negative even in the optimistic scenario.[5]

The OECD analysis points to the *structural change* the UK economy will experience. The growth in openness experienced by the UK economy has occurred within the context of EU membership. Membership has influenced the patterns of trade and investment. It has provided the framework in

---

[3]Speech given by Theresa May at Lancaster House, 17 January 2017.

[4]*EU Referendum: HM Treasury analysis key facts,* HM Treasury (18 April 2016).

[5]*The economic consequences of Brexit: a taxing decision,* OECD (25 April 2016).

which businesses have operated – for example, the development of supply chains across EU member countries. Structural changes accompanying Brexit, the OECD argued, would have negative supply-side effects.

Opportunities from Brexit

Despite the pessimistic forecasts from the vast majority of economists about a British exit, there was a group of eight economists in favour of Brexit.[6] They claimed that leaving the EU would lead to a stronger economy, with higher GDP, a faster growth in real wages, lower unemployment and a smaller gap between imports and exports. The main argument to support the claims was that the UK would be more able to pursue trade creation freed from various EU rules and regulations.

---

[6]www.economistsforbrexit.co.uk (now Economists for Free Trade: www.economistsforfreetrade.com/).

In reply, many economists argue that the EU has much greater bargaining power to achieve more favourable trade deals than the UK could by acting alone.

While disagreement about the impact on the UK's exit from the EU was to be expected, there was agreement that these effects would work primarily through their impact on the supply-side.

However, perhaps less clear was the likely *distributional* effects of the UK's exit. Trade can impact on different sectors differently. For example, people working in agriculture, often on low incomes, will be affected either positively or negatively by a replacement of the Common Agricultural Policy with a system of domestic support. Just what the distributional effect will be depends on what the new arrangements will be.

Consequently, a more complete analysis of trading relationships and hence of Brexit also needs to account for distributional effects.

KI 32
p 365

SUMMARY

1a Countries may make a partial movement towards free trade by the adoption of a preferential trading system. This involves free trade between the members, but restrictions on trade with the rest of the world. Such a system can be either a simple free trade area, a customs union (where there are common restrictions with the rest of the world) or a common market (where in addition there is free movement of capital and labour and common taxes and trade laws).

1b A preferential trading area can lead to trade creation where production shifts to low-cost producers within the area or to trade diversion where trade shifts away from lower-cost producers outside the area to higher-cost producers within the area.

1c Preferential trading may bring dynamic advantages of increased external economies of scale, improved terms of trade from increased bargaining power with the rest of the world, increased efficiency from greater competition between member countries and a more rapid spread of technology. On the other hand, it can lead to increased regional problems for members, greater oligopolistic collusion and various diseconomies of scale. There may also be large costs of administering the system.

2 There have been several attempts around the world to form preferential trading systems. The two most powerful are the European Union and the North America Free Trade Association (NAFTA).

3a The European Union is a customs union in that it has common external tariffs and no internal ones. But virtually from the outset it has also had elements of a common market, particularly in the areas of agricultural policy, regional policy and competition policy and, to some extent, in the areas of tax harmonisation, transport policy and social policy.

3b The Single European Act of 1986 sought to sweep away any remaining restrictions and to establish a genuine free market within the EU: to establish a full common market. Benefits from completing the internal market have included trade creation, cost savings from no longer

having to administer barriers, economies of scale for firms now able to operate on a Europe-wide scale and greater competition leading to reduced costs and prices, greater flows of technical information and more innovation.

3c The actual costs and benefits of EU membership to the various countries vary with their particular economic circumstances – for example, the extent to which they gain from trade creation or lose from adverse regional effects – and with their contributions to and receipts from the EU budget.

3d These costs and benefits in the future will depend on just how completely the barriers to trade are abolished, on the extent of monetary union and on the effects of the enlargement of the Union.

4a Following a referendum in June 2016 the UK voted to leave the European Union. The longer-term economic effects for the UK were expected to depend crucially on the nature of its future trading relationship with the EU.

4b Much of the economic analysis of Brexit has focused on the long-term implications for growth and living standards. Economic theory gives us a framework through which we can analyse the possible supply-side effects of Brexit.

4c Economists have argued largely that the decision to leave would result in negative effects on the supply-side of the economy. Brexit, they argue, would impede cross-border trade with its EU's partners and so reduce the UK's openness to trade and investment. This then adversely affects productivity growth and so living standards.

4d Some economists, however, have argued that outside of the EU the UK would be free of EU rules and regulations and would be able to create trade. The supply-side benefits would help to raise long-term growth and living standards.

4e Trade and the openness of economies has distributional effects. A more complete economic assessment of Brexit therefore requires that we consider such effects.

REVIEW QUESTIONS

1 What factors will determine whether a country's joining a customs union will lead to trade creation or trade diversion?

2 Assume that a group of countries forms a customs union. Is trade diversion in the union more likely or less likely in the following cases?

(a) Producers in the union gain monopoly power in world trade.

(b) Modern developments in technology and communications reduce the differences in production costs associated with different locations.

(c) The development of an internal market within the union produces substantial economies of scale in many industries.

3 Are NAFTA and APEC likely to develop along the same lines as the EU? Explain your answer.

4 Why is it difficult to estimate the magnitude of the benefits of completing the internal market of the EU?

5 Look through the costs and benefits that we identified from the single European market. Do the same costs and benefits arise from a substantially enlarged EU?

6 To what extent do non-EU countries gain or lose from the existence of the EU?

7 If there have been clear benefits from the single market programme, why do individual member governments still try to erect barriers, such as new technical standards?

8 Consider the process of Brexit negotiations since the triggering of Article 50 (to leave the EU) in April 2017. What model of trade relations with the EU27 is likely to be/was the end result of the negotiations?

9 Is a 'hard Brexit' (reverting to WTO rules and negotiating bilateral trade deals) necessarily an inferior alternative to remaining in the European single market or, at least, in the customs union?

ADDITIONAL PART I CASE STUDIES ON THE *ECONOMICS FOR BUSINESS* STUDENT WEBSITE (www.pearsoned.co.uk/sloman)

I.1 **Investing in Wales.** The factors influencing the investment in Wales by the Korean multinational, LG.

I.2 **The Maharaja Mac.** An examination of activities of McDonald's in India.

I.3 **Trading patterns.** An examination of the geographical patterns in the trade of merchandise goods and commercial services.

I.4 **Ethical business.** An examination of the likelihood of success of companies that trade fairly with developing countries.

I.5 **Free trade and the environment.** Do whales, the rainforests and the atmosphere gain from free trade?

I.6 **The Uruguay round.** An examination of the negotiations that led to substantial cuts in trade barriers.

I.7 **The Battle of Seattle.** This looks at the protests against the WTO at Seattle in November 1999 and considers the arguments for and against the free trade policies of the WTO.

I.8 **The World Trade Organization.** This looks at the various opportunities and threats posed by this major international organisation.

I.9 **High oil prices.** What is their effect on the world economy?

I.10 **Crisis in South East Asia.** Causes of the severe recession in many South East Asian countries in 1997/8.

I.11 **A miracle gone wrong.** Lessons from East Asian crisis of the late 1990s.

I.12 **From NAFTA to USMCA.** Who are the winners and losers from NAFTA and its successor, USMCA?

I.13 **The benefits of the Single Market.** Evidence of achievements and the Single Market Action Plan of 1997.

I.14 **The social dimension of the EU** The principles of the Social Charter.

I.15 **Steel barriers.** Looking after the US steel industry.

I.16 **Banana, banana.** An examination of the dispute between the USA and the EU over banana imports.

WEBSITES RELEVANT TO PART I

Numbers and sections refer to websites listed in the Web appendix and hotlinked from this text's website at **www.pearsoned.co.uk/sloman**

■ For news articles relevant to Part I, see the *Economics News Articles* link from the text's website.

■ For general news on business in the international environment, see websites in section A and particularly A1–5, 7–9, 20–25, 31. See also links to newspapers worldwide in A38, 39, 43 and 44, and the news search feature in Google at A41. See also links to economics news in A42.

■ For articles on various aspects of trade and developing countries, see A27, 28; H4, 7, 9, 10, 13, 14, 16–19; I9, 21.

■ For international data on imports and exports, see site H16 > *Documents, Data and Resources* > *Statistics*. See also *World Economic Outlook* in B31 and trade data in B24. See also I17.

■ For UK data, see B1, *1. National Statistics > Business, Industry and Trade > International trade.* See also B4 and 34. For EU data, see B38, 47.

■ For discussion papers on trade, see H4 and 7.

■ For trade disputes, see H16.

■ For various pressure groups critical of the effects of free trade and globalisation, see H11, 13, 14.

■ For information on various preferential trading arrangements, see H20–23.

■ For EU sites, see G1, 7, 20.

■ For information on trade and developing countries, see H4, 7, 9, 10, 13, 14, 16–19; I9, 21.

■ For information and data on trade, development, finance and cross-border investment flows see site H2.

■ For student resources relevant to Part I, see sites C1–7, 9, 10, 19.

The macroeconomic environment

The FT Reports. . .

The Financial Times, 13 May 2018 FT

Consumer spending continues to decline despite UK wage pick-up

By Delphine Strauss in London

UK consumer spending is still declining despite the recent pick-up in wage growth, according to an analysis of credit and debit card payments that suggests the arrival of spring weather has not brought much let-up for Britain's battered retail sector. Household expenditure — adjusted for inflation and seasonal effects — was 2 per cent lower in April compared with the same month one year earlier, according to payment processing company Visa, which published its UK consumer spending index on Monday.

Spending has now fallen on this measure for 11 of the past 12 months, and is on track for its worst annual performance since 2012.

'With inflation beginning to fall and wages growing faster than expected in recent months, it would have been easy to assume we might be over the worst of the consumer squeeze,' said Mark Antipof, chief commercial officer at Visa. 'It is clear that consumers remain in belt-tightening mode.'

High street retailers have fared worst, with Visa's index — which is compiled by data company IHS Markit — showing face to face spending down 5.4 per cent year-on-year in April, while e-commerce dropped just 0.1 per cent. Recommended Gavyn Davies Gavyn Davies: The 'unreliable' Bank of England is right to be cautious

This matches the trend seen in official data for the first quarter, with the Office for National Statistics reporting falling sales volumes in each of the first three months of the year. The data also confirms the structural shift in the retail sector, from in-store sales to online shopping, and from spending on 'stuff' to expenditure on leisure.

Many retailers were hoping that sales would pick up once the unusually bitter weather that kept shoppers off the streets in February and March — a cold front blown in from Siberia, and dubbed the Beast from the East — had passed. The British Retail Consortium's monthly footfall monitor, also published on Monday, suggests that better weather has brought only a modest upturn that will not be enough to revive the sector's fortunes. It showed footfall down 3.3 per cent year-on-year in April, with no growth in any region.

The Bank of England said last week that stronger wage growth and falling inflation should start to support increased household spending, following a two year squeeze on real incomes. But it also suggested that some people might choose to rebuild savings, rather than spending more freely, especially if they felt less confident about the economic outlook or their own circumstances.

Although Visa's index has often painted a gloomier picture of consumer spending in absolute terms than official data, its trend correlates well with ONS figures and with measures of consumer confidence. The figures are based on all expenditure on Visa cards, but adjusted to strip out transactions such as tax payments and refunds, and to take account of changing payment habits.

Banks are dangerous institutions. They borrow short and lend long. They create liabilities which promise to be liquid and hold few liquid assets themselves. That though is hugely valuable for the rest of the economy. Household savings can be channelled to finance illiquid investment projects while providing access to liquidity for those savers who may need it.

Mervyn King, Former Governor of the Bank of England, 'Finance: a return from risk', speech to the Worshipful Company of International Bankers, at the Mansion House, 17 March 2009 (www.bankofengland.co.uk); see www.bankofengland.co.uk/mfsd/iadb/notesiadb/Revisions.htm for the Revisions Policy

The success of an individual business depends not only on its own particular market and its own particular decisions but also on the whole macroeconomic environment in which it operates, as can be seen in the *Financial Times* article opposite.

If the economy is booming, then individual businesses are likely to be more profitable than if the economy is in recession. If the exchange rate rises (or falls), this will have an impact on the competitiveness of businesses trading overseas and on the costs and profitability of business in general. Similarly, business profitability will be affected by interest rates, the general level of prices and wages and the level of unemployment.

It is thus important for managers to understand the forces that affect the performance of the economy. In the remaining chapters of the text, we will examine these macroeconomic forces and their effects on the business sector.

In Chapter 26, we examine the macroeconomic environment in which businesses operate. We identify the main macroeconomic variables that determine this environment. In particular, we look at the crucial issue of economic volatility. It is this volatility that generates what we know as 'the business cycle'. We consider how this volatility affects other macroeconomic variables such as unemployment and inflation and hence how they are interrelated.

Key terms

Nominal and real GDP
Business cycle
Actual and potential economic growth
Output gap
Aggregate demand
Aggregate supply
Unemployment
Inflation
Financialisation
Balance sheet effects
Circular flow of income
Injections and withdrawals
Long-term economic growth
Labour productivity
Human capital

Chapter 27 looks at macroeconomic issues arising from a country's economic relationships with the rest of the world. In particular, it looks at the balance of payments and the role of exchange rates in influencing economic performance.

Chapter 28 looks at the significance of the financial system for both individual businesses and the economy. In particular, it looks at the behaviour of financial institutions and the role of money. The chapter analyses the financial crisis of the late 2000s, the initial responses of policy-makers to limit the adverse impact and the subsequent responses to try to prevent a similar crisis reoccurring. You will be able to judge whether 'Banks are dangerous institutions', as Mervyn King states.

Finally, in Chapter 29, we examine various theories about how the economy operates and the implications for business. We look at the relationship between output, unemployment and inflation and examine the possible causes of the business cycle. We also see the important role played by the expectations of both business and consumers.

Key terms

The balance of payments
The exchange rate
Fixed and floating
  exchange rates
Functions of money
Assets and liabilities (of
  banks)
Central bank
Money market
Money supply
Credit creation
Deposits multiplier
Money multiplier
Demand for money
Keynesian
New classical
Aggregate expenditure
Marginal propensity to
  consume
The multiplier
The accelerator
The quantity theory of
  money
Expectations
The Phillips curve
Real business cycles

The macroeconomic environment of business

Business issues covered in this chapter

- What determines the level of activity in the economy and hence the overall business climate?
- Why do economies experience periods of boom followed by periods of recession? What determines the length and magnitude of these 'phases' of the business cycle?
- If a stimulus is given to the economy, what will be the effect on business output?
- What are the causes of unemployment and how does unemployment relate to the level of business activity?
- What are the causes of inflation and how does inflation relate to the level of business activity?
- What factors are important for longer-term growth and rising living standards?
- What is meant by 'GDP' and how is it measured?

We have seen how the success or failure of a business can be affected by the market conditions in the industry in which it operates and by the strategic choices that it makes. Yet the macroeconomic environment is very important too. Recent history shows this very clearly indeed. Many countries experienced a significant economic slowdown in the late 2000s in the aftermath of the financial crisis. In some countries, such as the USA and the UK, economic output fell very sharply. A greater understanding of the macroeconomic environment and how it is influenced can therefore help firms to plan and make decisions to boost their profitability.

KI 36
p 376   In this chapter, we will identify what the main macroeconomic variables are. This allows us to 'paint a picture' of the macroeconomic environment in which firms operate and which, of course, they help to shape. We look at how the main macroeconomic variables are related by developing a simple model of the macroeconomy – the circular flow of income model. We shall also have a preliminary look at how policy makers, such as the government and the central bank, can influence these variables in order to create a more favourable environment for business. Macroeconomic policy will be discussed in more detail in Part K.

26.1 INTRODUCTION TO THE MACROECONOMIC ENVIRONMENT

The macroeconomic environment can be described by a series of interrelated macroeconomic variables. We can group them under the following headings:

- economic growth
- unemployment
- inflation
- the economic relationships with the rest of the world
- the financial well-being of individuals, businesses and other organisations, governments and nations, and the relationship between the financial system and the economy.

Key macroeconomic issues

Short-term economic growth and the business cycle

Economic growth describes the rate of change in the level of an economy's output from period to period. The rate of economic growth measures the percentage change in output. This is usually measured over short periods, such as 12 or 3 months. If we measure the **rate of economic growth** over a 12-month period, we are measuring the economy's annual rate of growth while, if we measure it over a 3-month period, we are measuring the quarterly rate of growth.

To be able to measure how quickly an economy is growing, we need a means of measuring the value of a nation's output. The measure we use is **gross domestic product (GDP)**. (The Appendix to this chapter explains how it is calculated.) However, to be able to compare changes in output from one period to the next we must eliminate those changes in GDP that result simply from changes in prices. In other words, we use *real* rather than *nominal* GDP figures to analyse changes in the volume of output.

The distinction between nominal and real figures. Nominal figures are those using current prices, interest rates, etc. Real figures are figures corrected for inflation.

Nominal GDP, sometimes called 'money GDP', measures GDP in the prices of the time (also known as 'current prices'). So, for example, nominal GDP in 2018 would be the value of a country's output at 2018 prices. The same principle applies to other years. Hence, no account is made for the effect of inflation, rather the effect of inflation is incorporated within these figures.

In contrast, **real GDP** figures do adjust for inflation. They do this by measuring GDP in the prices that ruled in some particular year – the *base year*. Thus, we could measure each year's GDP in, say, 2015 prices (known as 'GDP at constant 2015 prices'). This then enables us to see how much *real* GDP had changed from one period to another by eliminating increases (or decreases) in money GDP due simply to increases (or decreases) in prices. In other words, we are able to see the **real growth in GDP**.

Figure 26.1 shows annual rates of economic growth (annual percentage changes in real GDP) for a sample of economies. As you can see, there has been considerable volatility in their growth rates. Economies also experience fluctuations in other macroeconomic indicators, such as unemployment, inflation and international trade.

Economies suffer from inherent instability. As a result, economic growth and other macroeconomic indicators tend to fluctuate.

Because of their inherent instability, economies experience a cycle in levels of economic activity. This cycle is known as the **business cycle (or trade cycle)**. In some periods, an economy will be booming; in others, economic growth will be low or even negative. This volatility of growth is true not only of national economies, such as the UK and the USA, but also country groups such as the Eurozone, and also the world economy. Therefore, there is an **international business cycle**. This suggests that countries' business cycles have both a national and a global dimension. What is more, this global dimension has increased in importance, resulting in a growing synchronicity of countries' business cycles.

> **Definitions**
>
> **Rate of economic growth** The percentage increase in output, normally expressed over a 12-month period.
>
> **Gross domestic product (GDP):** The value of output produced within a country, typically over a 12-month period.
>
> **Nominal GDP:** GDP measured in current prices. These figures take no account of the effect of inflation.
>
> **Real GDP:** GDP measured in constant prices that ruled in a chosen base year, such as 2000 or 2015. These figures *do* take account the effect of inflation. When inflation is positive, real GDP figures will grow more slowly than nominal GDP figures.
>
> **Real growth values** Values of the rate of growth of GDP or any other variable after taking inflation into account. The real value of the growth in a variable equals its growth in money (or 'nominal') value minus the rate of inflation.
>
> **Business cycle or trade cycle** The periodic fluctuations of national output round its long-term trend. Periods of rapid growth are followed by periods of low growth or even decline in national output.

Figure 26.1   Annual economic growth rates

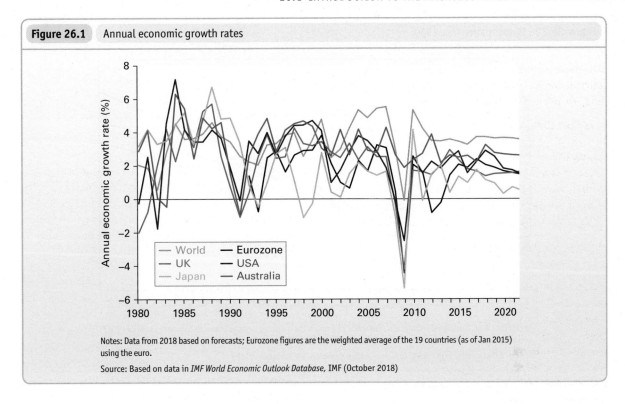

Notes: Data from 2018 based on forecasts; Eurozone figures are the weighted average of the 19 countries (as of Jan 2015) using the euro.

Source: Based on data in *IMF World Economic Outlook Database,* IMF (October 2018)

Longer-term economic growth

Although growth rates fluctuate, most economies experience positive growth over the longer term. In other words, most economies have output paths that trend upwards over time. This can be seen in Figure 26.2 which plots the *levels* of real GDP and hence the output paths over time for the same economies analysed in Figure 26.2.[1]

Figure 26.2 also highlights differences in the longer-term rates of growth of economies. For growth to be sustained over the longer term, an economy's capacity must increase. Hence, differences in long-term economic growth rates reflect differences in the growth of the productive capacity of economies. We discuss this further in section 26.6.

Unemployment

The inherent instability of economies has implications for the number of people in work and so for the number unable to find work. After all, higher levels of economic activity will tend to decrease unemployment numbers, while reduced economic activity will tend to increase them.

Unemployment numbers, however, reflect more than just the position in the business cycle. For example, many countries have seen significant effects on their labour markets from rapid industrial change, technological advance

and globalisation. While some new jobs are created, others are lost. Many people made redundant find they are not qualified for the new jobs being created.

Maximising employment opportunities and reducing unemployment is a key macroeconomic aim of governments, not only for the sake of the unemployed themselves, but also because unemployment represents a waste of human resources and because unemployment benefits are a drain on government revenues.

Measuring unemployment. Unemployment can be expressed either as a number (e.g. $1\frac{1}{2}$ million) or as a percentage (e.g. 5 per cent).

The most usual definition that economists use for the **number unemployed** is: *those of working age who are without work, but who are available for work at current wage rates.*

If the figure is to be expressed as a percentage, then it is a percentage of the total **labour force**. The labour force is defined as *those in employment plus those unemployed.* Thus, if

---

[1]Note that the vertical axis is plotted on a log scale. This allows us to get better picture of growth rates, as they are reflected in the slope of the curves. If a normal arithmetic scale were used instead, a line showing a constant growth rate would get progressively steeper. For example, a doubling of an output index from 100 to 200 over a given number of years would give a line twice as steep as the doubling from 50 to 100 over the same number of years, even though the growth rate would be the same in both cases.

> ### Definitions
>
> **International business cycle** The tendency for groups of economies and the global economy to experience synchronised fluctuations in economic growth rates.
>
> **Number unemployed (economist's definition)** Those of working age who are without work, but who are available for work at current wage rates.
>
> **Labour force** The number employed plus the number unemployed.

Figure 26.2   Output paths since 1980

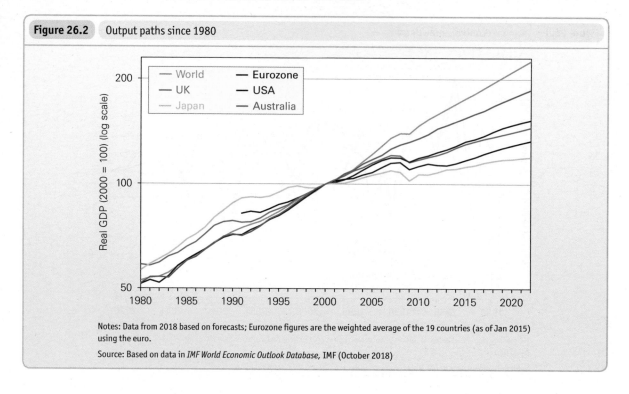

Notes: Data from 2018 based on forecasts; Eurozone figures are the weighted average of the 19 countries (as of Jan 2015) using the euro.

Source: Based on data in *IMF World Economic Outlook Database,* IMF (October 2018)

---

30 million people were employed and 1.5 million people were unemployed, the ***unemployment rate*** would be:

$$\frac{1.5}{30 + 1.5} \times 100 = 4.76\%$$

Historical experience of unemployment. Many advanced economies saw unemployment rates in the 1980s and early 1990s that were significantly higher than in the previous three decades. Then, in the late 1990s and early 2000s, it fell in some countries, such as the UK and USA.

However, with the global economic crisis of the late 2000s, many countries experienced rising rates of unemployment. This was exacerbated in the early 2010s by attempts, particularly across Europe, to reduce levels of government borrowing, which depressed rates of economic growth.

These patterns are captured in Figure 26.3 for a selection of advanced economies.

In the UK, in recent years, there has been a move towards more flexible contracts, with many people's wages not keeping up with inflation and many working fewer hours than they would like. This has helped to reduce the rate of unemployment, but has created a problem of ***underemployment***.

Inflation

By inflation we mean a general rise in prices throughout the economy. Government policy here is to keep inflation both low and stable. One of the most important reasons for this is that it will aid the process of economic decision making. For example, businesses will be able to set prices and wage rates and make investment decisions with far more confidence.

Generally, inflation tends to rise in periods of rapid economic growth: firms respond to the higher demand, partly by raising output, but partly also by raising prices. Conversely, in a recession, inflation is likely to fall: firms, faced with falling demand and rising stocks, are likely to be unwilling to raise prices and may even cut them.

We have become used to low ***inflation rates*** and, in some countries, like Japan, periods of deflation, with a general fall in prices. Even though inflation rates rose in many countries in 2008 and then again in 2010–11, figures remained much lower than in the past; in 1975, UK inflation reached 23 per cent. This can be seen clearly in Figure 26.4, which plots annual rates of

---

Definitions

Unemployment rate The number unemployed expressed as a percentage of the labour force.

Underemployment When people work fewer hours than they would like at their current wage rate. *International Labour Organisation (ILO) definition:* a situation where people currently working less than 'full time' (40 hours in the UK) would like to work more hours (at current wage rates), either by working more hours in their current job, or by switching to an alternative job with more hours or by taking on an additional part-time job or any combination of the three. *Eurostat definition*: where people working less than 40 hours per week would like to work more hours in their current job at current wage rates.

Rate of inflation (annual) The percentage increase in prices over a 12-month period.

Figure 26.3	Standardised unemployment rates

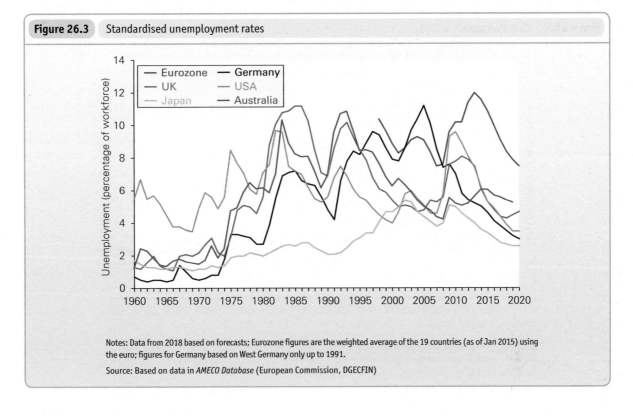

Notes: Data from 2018 based on forecasts; Eurozone figures are the weighted average of the 19 countries (as of Jan 2015) using the euro; figures for Germany based on West Germany only up to 1991.

Source: Based on data in *AMECO Database* (European Commission, DGECFIN)

consumer price inflation (annual percentage change in consumer prices) in the same advanced economies.

In most advanced economies today, *central banks*, such as the Bank of England and the European Central Bank, have a target for the rate of inflation that they are charged with meeting. In the UK, the target for the growth of consumer prices is 2 per cent. The Bank of England then adjusts interest rates to try to keep inflation on target (we see how this works in Chapter 28).

Foreign trade and global economic relationships

A county's macroeconomic environment is influenced both by domestic conditions and by its economic relationships with other countries. These relationships evolve as the global economy develops and the world order changes. As we saw in Chapter 24, the rapid economic growth in economies such as China and India has had a major effect on patterns of world trade and development.

Then, as we saw in Chapter 25, there is the evolution of international economic co-operation as countries or groups of countries come together to shape their economic relationships with each other. Following the UK referendum on EU membership in 2016, the result to leave meant that, over time, a new set of economic relationships between the UK and its foreign partners would emerge.

The balance of payments. One way of viewing the economic relationship between a country and other economies is through its *balance of payments account*. This records all transactions

between the residents of that country and the rest of the world. These transactions enter as either debit items or credit items. The debit items include all payments *to* other countries: these include the country's purchases of imports, the spending on investment it makes abroad and the interest and dividends paid to people abroad who have invested in the country. The credit items include all receipts *from* other countries: from the sales of exports, from inward investment expenditure and from interest and dividends earned from abroad.

The sale of exports and any other receipts from abroad earn foreign currency. The purchase of imports or any other payments abroad use up foreign currency. If we start to spend

KI 27
p 341

Definitions

Central bank A country's central bank is banker to the government and the banks as a whole (see section 28.2). In most countries, the central bank operates monetary policy by setting interest rates and influencing the supply of money. The central bank in the UK is the Bank of England; in the Eurozone it is the European Central Bank (ECB) and in the USA it is the Federal Reserve Bank (the 'Fed').

Balance of payments account A record of the country's transactions with the rest of the world. It shows the country's payments to or deposits in other countries (debits) and its receipts or deposits from other countries (credits). It also shows the balance between these debits and credits under various headings.

Figure 26.4 Inflation rates

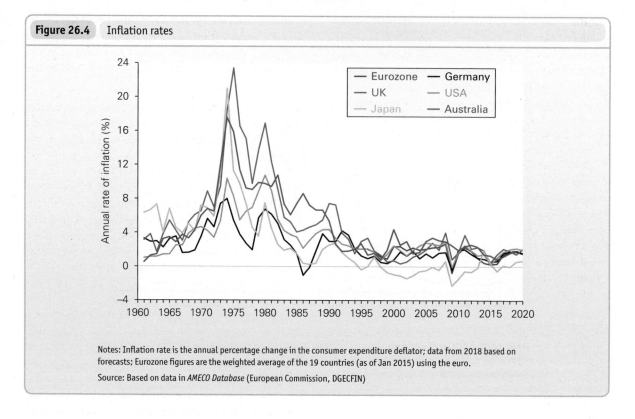

Notes: Inflation rate is the annual percentage change in the consumer expenditure deflator; data from 2018 based on forecasts; Eurozone figures are the weighted average of the 19 countries (as of Jan 2015) using the euro.

Source: Based on data in *AMECO Database* (European Commission, DGECFIN)

more foreign currency than we earn, one of two things must happen. Both are likely to be a problem.

- *The balance of payments will go into deficit.*   In other words, there will be a shortfall of foreign currencies. The government will, therefore, have to borrow money from abroad or draw on its foreign currency reserves to make up the shortfall. This is a problem because, if it goes on too long, overseas debts will mount, along with the interest that must be paid and/or reserves will begin to run low.
- *The exchange rate will fall.*   The **exchange rate** is the rate at which one currency exchanges for another. For example, the exchange rate of the pound into the dollar might be £1 = $1.25.

If the government does nothing to correct the balance of payments deficit, then the exchange rate must fall: for example, to $1.20 or $1.15 or lower. (We will show just why this is so in Chapter 27.) A falling exchange rate is a problem because it pushes up the price of imports and may fuel inflation. This was the experience of the UK in the aftermath of the vote to leave the European Union, when the pound fell sharply. Also, if the exchange rate fluctuates, this can cause great uncertainty for traders and can damage international trade and economic growth.

Financial well-being

The financial system is an integral part of most economies. Financial markets, financial institutions and financial products have become increasingly important in determining the economic well-being of nations, organisations, government

and people. The increasing importance of the financial system in everyday lives and to economies is known as *financialisation*.

One indicator of financialisation is the extent to which many of us now interact with financial institutions and make use of financial products. Financialisation is, perhaps, most frequently associated with the levels of indebtedness of individuals, businesses and organisations to financial institutions.

The importance of financial stability and the problem of financial distress.   It is important for policy-makers to ensure the stability of the financial system and the general financial well-being of *economic agents* (people, firms, government, etc). This importance was most starkly demonstrated by the events surrounding the financial crisis of 2007–9, when many banks

 KI 40 p 505

Definitions

Exchange rate The rate at which one national currency exchanges for another. The rate is expressed as the amount of one currency that is necessary to purchase one unit of another currency (e.g. £1 = €1.30).

Financialisation A term used to describe the process by which financial markets, institutions and instruments become increasingly significant in economies.

Economic agents The general term for individuals, firms, government and organisations when taking part in economic activities, such as buying, selling, saving, investing or in any other way interacting with other economic agents.

looked as if they might become bankrupt. The crisis illustrated how the financial distress of financial institutions can lead to global economic turmoil. Because of the global interconnectedness of financial institutions and markets, problems can spread globally like a contagion.

And it was not just financial institutions that were distressed in the late 2000s, we also witnessed financially distressed households and businesses, many of whom were burdened by unsustainable levels of debt.

Subsequently, financial distress was to affect government too, especially in advanced economies. Governments were burdened by growing levels of debt as they spent more to offset rapidly weakening private-sector spending. At the same time, tax revenues fell because of lower or even negative economic growth. The consequence was a prolonged period during which many governments felt it necessary to tighten their budgets. And this constraint on government spending was to put a further brake on economic growth.

> **KEY IDEA 40**
>
> **Balance sheets affect people's behaviour.** The size and structure of governments', institutions' and individuals' liabilities (and assets too) affect economic well-being and can have significant effects on behaviour and economic activity.

Financial accounts. In analysing financial well-being or distress, there are three key accounts that can be considered. These are compiled for the main sectors of the economy: the household, corporate and government sectors, and the whole economy.

- First, there is the *income account* which records the various *flows* of income (a credit) alongside the amounts either spent or saved (debits). Economic growth refers to the annual real growth in a country's income flows (i.e. after taking inflation into account).
- Next, there is the *financial account.* There are two elements here. First, we can record financial *flows,* which determine the net acquisition of financial wealth by each sector. These comprise new saving, borrowing or repayments. Reductions in the flows of borrowing, in countries like the UK and USA, were very important in explaining the credit crunch and subsequent deep recession of the late 2000s/early 2010s.

  The other element of the financial account is its ***balance sheet***. A balance sheet is a record of *stocks* of ***assets*** and ***liabilities*** of individuals or institutions. An asset is something owned by or owed to you. A liability is a debt: i.e. something you owe to someone else. In the case of the financial account, we have a complete record of the stocks of financial assets (arising from saving) and financial liabilities (arising from borrowing) of a sector, and include things such as currency, bank deposits, loans, bonds and shares. The flows of borrowing during the 2000s meant that many individuals and organisations experienced a significant increase in stocks of financial liabilities.
- Finally, there is the *capital account,* which records flows and stocks of *physical* assets and liabilities. Again, there

are two elements. The first records the capital *flows* of the various sectors, which occur when acquiring or disposing of physical assets, such as property and machinery. The second records the *stock* of physical wealth held by the various sectors.

The national balance sheet. This is a measure of the wealth of a country (i.e. the nation's financial and physical stock of net assets). It shows the *composition* of a country's wealth and the contribution of each of the main *sectors* of the economy.

The balance of a sector's or country's stock of financial and non-financial assets over its financial liabilities is referred to as its ***net worth***. An *increase* in the net worth of the sectors or the whole country implies greater financial well-being. However, during the 2000s, many sectors experienced increases in net worth as asset values rose, despite the rising stock of financial liabilities. Subsequently, the increase in the stock of liabilities was not financially sustainable and asset prices were to fall.

Figure 26.5 is based on the national balance sheet for the UK[2] since 1995. It shows the country's stock of net worth, including its value relative to annual national income (GDP). In 2016, the net worth of the UK was £9.8 trillion, equivalent to 5 times the country's annual GDP. The stock of net worth fell in both 2008 and 2009 at the height of the financial crisis and the economic slowdown. This reduced the country's net worth by nearly 9 per cent. It then fell again shortly afterwards in 2012.

These various accounts are part of an interconnected story detailing the financial well-being of a country's households, companies and government. To illustrate how, consider what would happen if, over a period of time, you were to spend more than the income you receive. This would result in your income account deteriorating.

To finance your excess spending, you could perhaps draw on any financial wealth that you had accumulated through saving. Alternatively, you might fund some of your spending through a loan from a bank. Either way, your financial balance sheet will deteriorate. Or you may dispose of some physical assets, such as property, in which case your capital balance will deteriorate. However excess spending is financed, net worth declines.

The importance of balance-sheet effects in influencing behaviour and, hence, economic activity has been increasingly

---

[2] www.ons.gov.uk/economy/nationalaccounts/uksectoraccounts/datasets/nationalbalancesheet.

> ## Definitions
>
> **Balance sheet** A record of the stock of assets and liabilities of an individual or institution.
>
> **Asset** Possessions of an individual or institution, or claims held on others.
>
> **Liability** Claims by others on an individual or institution; debts of that individual or institution.
>
> **Net worth** The market value of a sector's stock of financial and non-financial wealth.

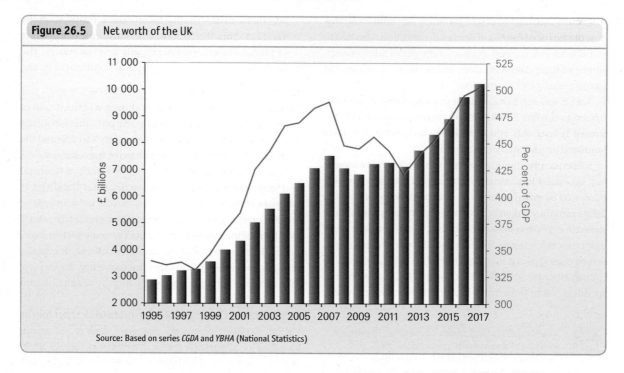

Figure 26.5   Net worth of the UK

Source: Based on series *CGDA* and *YBHA* (National Statistics)

recognised by both economists and policy-makers, especially since the financial crisis of 2007–9. Understanding these effects and their consequences is crucial in devising the most appropriate policies.

KI 40
p 505

Macroeconomic policy objectives

From the above issues we can identify a series of macroeconomic policy objectives that policy makers, including governments, might typically pursue:

- High and stable economic growth.
- Low unemployment.
- Low rates of inflation.
- The avoidance of balance of payments deficits and excessive exchange rate fluctuations.
- A stable financial system.
- The avoidance of excessively financially distressed sectors of the economy, including government.

KI 41
p 506
Unfortunately, these policy objectives may conflict. For example, a policy designed to accelerate the rate of economic growth may result in a higher rate of inflation, a balance of payments deficit and excessive borrowing. Governments are thus often faced with awkward policy choices, illustrating how societies face trade-offs between economic objectives.

In understanding these choices and their implications, it is important to analyse the determinants of the key issues that shape the macroeconomic environment. In this chapter, we will examine economic growth, unemployment and inflation. In Chapter 27, we will focus on the balance of payments and its relation to the exchange rate before then, in Chapter 28, considering the financial system and the financial well-being of economic agents (i.e. households, businesses and governments).

> **KEY IDEA 41**
>
> *Societies face trade-offs between economic objectives.* For example, the goal of faster growth may conflict with that of greater equality; the goal of lower unemployment may conflict with that of lower inflation (at least in the short run). This is an example of opportunity cost: the cost of achieving more of one objective may be achieving less of another. The existence of trade-offs means that policy makers must make choices.

26.2   ECONOMIC VOLATILITY AND THE BUSINESS CYCLE

KI 39
p 500
A fundamental characteristic of economies is their volatility. They experience not only periods of expansion but sometimes also periods when growth is negative – when output levels contract. For many, the defining feature of the business cycle is the absence of growth in times of *recession*. A recession officially is defined as a period of two or more

Definitions

Recession A period where national output falls for a few months or more. The official definition is where real GDP declines for two or more consecutive quarters.

consecutive quarters when the economy experiences declining volumes of output.

Actual and potential growth

The published statistics on growth show ***actual growth: the percentage change in national output over a period of time. This usually is measured*** over a year (12 months) or a quarter (3 months).

We should be careful to distinguish between ***actual*** and potential economic growth. ***Potential growth*** is the speed at which the economy *could* grow. It is the percentage increase in the economy's *capacity* to produce over a period of time: the rate of growth in ***potential output***.

> **KEY IDEA 42**
>
> ***Living standards are limited by a country's ability to produce.*** Potential national output depends on the country's resources, technology and productivity.

Potential output (i.e. potential GDP) is the level of output when the economy is operating at 'normal capacity utilisation'. This allows for firms having a planned degree of spare capacity to meet unexpected demand or for hold-ups in supply. It also allows for some unemployment as people move from job to job. Because potential output is normal-capacity output, it is somewhat below full-capacity output, which is the absolute maximum that could be produced with firms working flat-out.

The difference between actual and potential output is known as the ***output gap***. Thus, if actual output exceeds potential output, the output gap is positive: the economy is operating above normal capacity utilisation. If actual output is below potential output, the output gap is negative: the economy is operating below normal capacity utilisation. Box 26.1 looks at the output gap since 1970 for five major industrial economies.

Assume that the actual growth rate is less than the potential growth rate. This will lead to an increase in spare capacity and probably an increase in unemployment. In turn, the output gap will become less positive or perhaps more negative, depending on the economy's starting point.

In contrast, if the actual growth rate were to exceed the potential growth rate, there would be a reduction in spare capacity and the output gap would become less negative or more positive. However, periods when actual growth exceeds potential growth can only be temporary. In the long run, the actual growth rate will be limited to the potential growth rate.

The business cycle

The hypothetical business cycle

Actual growth tends to fluctuate. In some years, there is a high rate of economic growth: the country experiences a boom. In other years, economic growth is low or even negative: the country experiences a recession. This cycle of expansion and slowdown causes fluctuations in the path of output.

Figure 26.6 illustrates a hypothetical business cycle. While it is a stylised representation of the business cycle, it is useful for illustrating four identifiable 'phases' of the cycle.

1. *The upturn.* In this phase, a stagnant economy begins to recover and growth in actual output resumes.
2. *The rapid expansion.* During this phase, there is rapid economic growth: the economy is booming. A fuller use is made of resources and the gap between actual and full-capacity output narrows.
3. *The peaking out.* During this phase, growth slows down or even ceases.
4. *The slowdown, recession or slump.* During this phase, there is little or no growth or even a decline in output. Increasing slack develops in the economy.

Long-term output trend. A line can be drawn showing the trend of national output over time (i.e. ignoring the cyclical fluctuations around the trend). This is shown as the dashed line in Figure 26.6. If, over time, firms on average operate with a 'normal' degree of capacity utilisation, the trend output line will be the same as the potential output line. If the average level of capacity that is unutilised stays constant from one cycle to another, the trend line will have the same slope as the full-capacity output line. In other words, the trend (or potential) rate of growth will be the same as the rate of growth of capacity.

If, however, the level of unutilised capacity changes from one cycle to another, then the trend line will have a different slope from the full-capacity output line. For example, if unemployment and unused industrial capacity *rise* from one peak to another, or from one trough to another, then the trend line will move further away from the full-capacity output line (i.e. it will be less steep).

> ### Pause for thought
>
> *If the average percentage (as opposed to the average level) of full-capacity output that was unutilised remained constant, would the trend line have the same slope as the potential output line?*

> ### Definitions
>
> **Actual growth** The percentage annual increase in national output actually produced, usually measured over a 3-month or 12-month period.
>
> **Potential growth** The percentage annual increase in the in the output that would be produced if all firms were operating at their normal level of capacity utilisation.
>
> **Potential output** The output that could be produced in the economy if all firms were operating at their normal level of capacity utilisation.
>
> **Output gap** Actual output minus potential output.

| BOX 26.1 | OUTPUT GAPS |

An alternative measure of excess or deficient demand

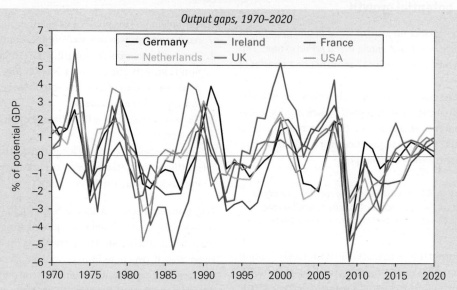

Output gaps, 1970–2020

Note: data from 2018 based on forecasts; figures for Germany based on West Germany only up to 1991.
Source: Based on data from *AMECO database* (European Commission, DGECFIN)

If the economy grows, how fast and for how long can it grow before it runs into inflationary problems? On the other hand, what minimum rate must be achieved to avoid rising unemployment?

To answer these questions, economists have developed the concept of 'output gaps'.[1] The output gap is the difference between actual output and potential output.

If actual output is below potential output (the gap is negative), there will be a higher than normal level of unemployment as firms are operating below their normal level of capacity utilisation. There will, however, be a downward pressure on inflation, resulting from a lower than normal level of demand for labour and other resources. If actual output is above potential output (the gap is positive), there will be excess demand and a rise in inflation.

Generally, the gap will be negative in a recession and positive in a boom. In other words, output gaps follow the course of the business cycle.

But how do we measure output gaps? There are two principal statistical techniques.

De-trending techniques.

This approach is a purely mechanical exercise which involves smoothing the actual GDP figures. In doing this, it attempts to fit a trend growth path along the lines of the dashed line in Figure 26.6. The main disadvantage of this approach is that it is not grounded in economic theory and therefore does not take into consideration those factors that economists consider to be important in determining output levels over time.

Production function approach.

Many forecasting bodies use an approach that borrows ideas from economic theory. Specifically, it uses the idea of a

production function which relates output to a set of inputs. Estimates of potential output are generated by using statistics on the size of a country's capital stock, the potential available labour input and, finally, the productivity or effectiveness of these inputs in producing output.

In addition to these statistical approaches, use could be made of business surveys. In other words, we ask businesses directly. However, survey-based evidence can provide only a broad guide to rates of capacity utilisation and whether there is deficient or excess demand.

International evidence

The chart shows output gaps for five economies from 1970, estimated using a production function approach. What is apparent from the chart is that all the economies have experienced significant output gaps, both positive and negative. This helps to illustrate that economies are inherently volatile. However, while output gaps vary from year to year, over the longer term the average output gap tends towards zero.

The chart shows how the characteristics of countries' business cycles can differ, particularly in terms of depth and duration. But, we also see evidence of an international business cycle (see pages 500–1), where national cycles appear to share characteristics. This global component of countries' business cycles is particularly stark in the late 2000s and early 2010s. Increasing global interconnectedness from financial and trading links meant that the financial crisis of the late 2000s spread like a contagion.

1. How might the behaviour of firms differ during periods of negative and positive output gaps?
2. Are all business cycles the same?

KI 39
p 500

Using the AMECO database, calculate the average output gap for France, Germany, Ireland, UK, USA for the period 2009-11 before then using their values to construct a column chart. Briefly summarise your findings.

[1] See C. Giorno, *et al.*, 'Potential output, output gaps and structural budget balances', *OECD Economic Studies*, No. 24 (1995), p. 1.

Figure 26.6 A hypothetical business cycle

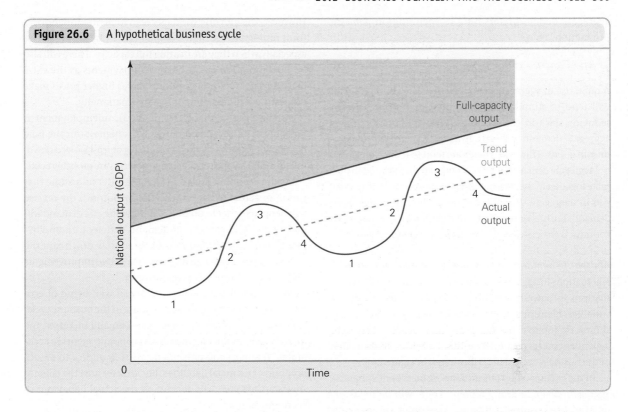

Business cycle in practice

The business cycle illustrated in Figure 26.6 is a 'stylised' cycle. The patterns in output are nice and smooth and regular. Drawing it this way allows us to make a clear distinction between each of the four phases. In practice, business cycles are highly irregular. They are irregular in two ways.

The length of the phases. Some booms are short-lived, lasting only a few months or so. Others are much longer, lasting perhaps three or four years. Likewise, some recessions are short, while others are long. Sometimes, a recession can be closely followed by another recession with the economic upturn only short-lived. Economists refer to this as a double-dip recession. Such a situation occurred when the recession of 1973/4 was followed by another recession in 1975.

The magnitude of the phases. Sometimes, in phase 2, there is a very high rate of economic growth, considerably higher than the economy's longer-term average. On other occasions, in phase 2, growth is much gentler. Sometimes, in phase 4, there is a recession, with an actual decline in output as occurred in 2008/9. On other occasions, phase 4 is merely a 'pause', with growth simply being low.

The business cycle and aggregate demand and aggregate supply

The fluctuations in economic activity that characterise the business cycle reflect, in one way or another, fluctuations in total spending. In analysing the business cycle, it is therefore important to analyse both the *sources* of volatility in

spending and the *processes* or mechanisms by which this volatility works through the economy and affects output and other macroeconomic variables, such as inflation and employment. These processes may help to smooth the business cycle or, alternatively, amplify the peaks and troughs of the cycle.

Aggregate demand and its components

Much of the analysis on the business cycle focuses on understanding fluctuations in *aggregate demand* (AD). This is the total spending on goods and services made within the country ('domestically produced goods and services'). Periods of rapid growth are associated with periods of rapid expansion of aggregate demand. Periods of recession are associated with a decline in aggregate demand.

Aggregate demand consists of spending by four groups of people: consumers on goods and services (C), firms on investment (I), the government on goods, services and investment (such as education, health and new roads) (G) and people abroad on this country's exports (X). From these four, we have to subtract any imports (M), since

Definitions

Aggregate demand (*AD*) Total spending on goods and services made in the economy. It consists of four elements: consumer spending (C), investment (I), government spending (G) and the expenditure on exports (X), less any expenditure on foreign goods and services (M): $AD = C + I + G + X - M$

aggregate demand refers only to spending on *domestic* production. Thus:[3]

$$AD = C + I + G + X - M$$

A rapid rise in aggregate demand will create shortages. This will tend to stimulate firms to increase output, thereby reducing slack in the economy. Likewise, a reduction in aggregate demand will leave firms with increased stocks of unsold goods. They will, therefore, tend to reduce output.

Aggregate demand and actual output therefore tend to fluctuate together in the *short run*. A boom is associated with a rapid rise in aggregate demand: the faster the rise in aggregate demand, the higher the short-run growth rate. A recession, by contrast, is associated with a reduction in aggregate demand.

Aggregate demand and key macroeconomic variables

Fluctuations in aggregate demand will not only result in fluctuations in output, but also in other key macroeconomic variables, identified in section 26.1. This is because in the short term (up to about two years) they are also likely to be dependent on aggregate demand and so vary with the course of the business cycle. This is illustrated in Figure 26.7.

In the expansionary phase of the business cycle (phase 2), aggregate demand grows rapidly. There will be relatively rapid growth in output, with a positive output gap emerging, and unemployment will fall as firms take on more labour.

However, the growing shortages lead to higher inflation, as firms respond to the higher demand partly by raising prices, especially when they are nearing full capacity. There will also be a deterioration in the balance of payments as the extra demand 'sucks in' more imports and as higher prices make domestic goods less competitive internationally.

At the peak of the cycle (phase 3), unemployment is probably at its lowest and output at its highest (for the time being). But growth has already ceased or at least slowed down. Inflation and balance of payments problems are probably acute.

As the economy moves into phase 4 (let us assume that this is an actual recession with falling output), the reverse will happen to that in phase 2. Falling aggregate demand will make growth negative and demand-deficient unemployment higher, but inflation is likely to slow down and the balance of payments will improve. These two improvements may take some time to occur, however.

We might also expect the financial well-being of economic agents to change over the course of the business cycle. For example, in phase 2, as aggregate demand increases, the increase in national income allows economic agents to accumulate financial and non-financial assets and/or to reduce holdings of financial liabilities. But, exactly how the balance sheets are affected will depend on the actual behaviour of economic agents.

---

[3]An alternative way of specifying this is to focus on just the component of each that goes to domestic firms. We use a subscript 'd' to refer to this component (i.e. with the imported component subtracted). Thus $AD = C_d + I_d + G_d + X_d$ (where X_d excludes that part of exports that consists of imported components or raw materials).

> ### Pause for thought
>
> *If the behaviour of financial institutions was to change over the course of the business cycle, how might this affect the business cycle?*

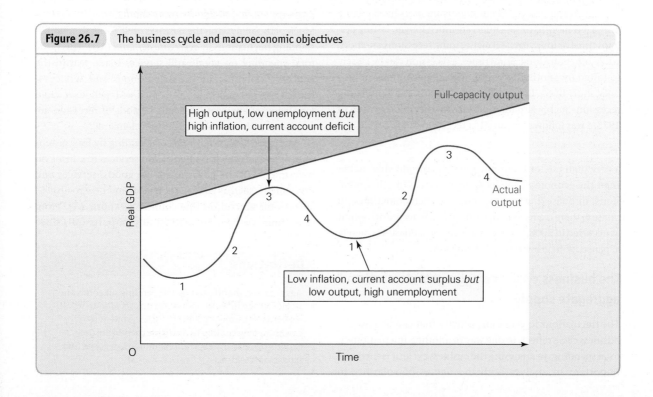

Figure 26.7 The business cycle and macroeconomic objectives

Aggregate supply

While much of the economic analysis of the business cycle stresses the importance of fluctuations in aggregate demand, economists recognise that fluctuations in *aggregate supply* (*AS*) can also cause fluctuations in in output. Aggregate supply is the total amount of goods and services that firms within the country plan to supply at current prices.

Sudden sharp changes to input prices could affect firms' output decisions. For instance, increases in input costs, such as those in employing labour, could result in firms reducing production levels. On the other hand, reductions in input costs could lead firms to increase production levels.

Firms' expectations might be important too. The expectation, for example, of an economic downturn could result not only in firms scaling back current operations but in reducing investment in such things as machinery, buildings or staff training. This raises the possibility that a contraction in the economy arising from declining aggregate demand could be amplified further by changes in aggregate supply, should firms expect lower levels of aggregate demand to persist. Alternatively, expectations of future higher levels of aggregate demand could see firms not only increase current production levels but make investment decisions to increase future production levels.

Aggregate supply takes on increasing importance when we think about long-term economic growth, i.e. growth over many years. We consider the growth in potential output in the final section of this chapter.

26.3 THE CIRCULAR FLOW OF INCOME

The economic choices of people, businesses and organisations can have profound effects for the macroeconomy. One model that allows us to develop an understanding of the impact of these choices for short-term economic growth, and that does so by focusing on aggregate demand, is the *circular flow of income model*. This is shown in Figure 26.8.

In the diagram, the economy is divided into two major groups: *firms* and *households*. Each group has two roles. Firms are producers of goods and services; they are also the employers of labour and other factors of production. Households (which is the word we use for individuals) are the consumers of goods and services; they are also the suppliers of labour and various other factors of production, such as land. In the diagram, there is an inner flow and various outer flows of income between these two groups.

Before we look at the various parts of the diagram, a word of warning. Do not confuse *money* and *income*. Money is a stock concept. At any given time, there is a certain quantity of money in the economy (e.g. £1 trillion). But that does not tell us the level of national *income*. Income is a flow concept (as is expenditure). It is measured as so much *per period of time*.

The relationship between money and income depends on how rapidly the money *circulates*: its 'velocity of circulation'. (We will examine this concept in detail later on.) If there is £1 trillion of money in the economy and each £1 on average is paid out as income twice each year, then annual national income will be £2 trillion.

Pause for thought

Would this argument still hold if prices rose?

The inner flow, withdrawals and injections

The inner flow

Firms pay money to households in the form of wages and salaries, dividends on shares, interest and rent. These payments are in return for the services of the factors of production – labour, capital and land – that are supplied by households. Thus, looking at Figure 26.8, on the left-hand side of the diagram, money flows directly from firms to households as 'factor payments'.

Households, in turn, pay money to domestic firms when they *consume domestically produced goods and services* (C_d). This is shown on the right-hand side of the inner flow. There is thus a circular flow of payments from firms to households to firms and so on.

If households spend *all* their incomes on buying domestic goods and services, and if firms pay out *all* this income they receive as factor payments to domestic households, and if the velocity of circulation does not change, the flow will continue at the same level indefinitely. The money just goes round and round at the same speed and incomes remain unchanged.

In the real world, of course, it is not as simple as this – if it were, economies would not be characterised by the instability we are trying to understand. Not all income gets passed on round the inner flow; some is *withdrawn*. At the same

Definition

Aggregate supply The total amount that firms plan to supply at any given level of prices.

Consumption of domestically produced goods and services (C_d) The direct flow of money payments from households to firms.

Figure 26.8   The circular flow of income

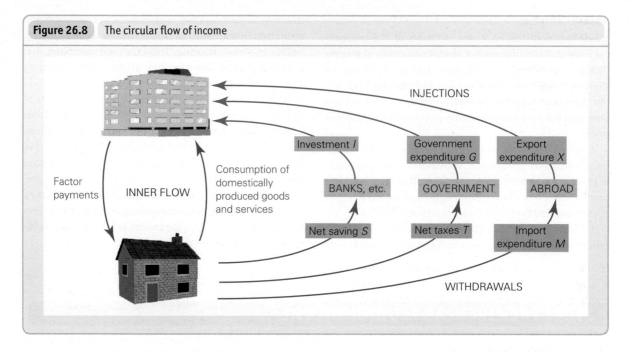

time, incomes are injected into the flow from outside. Let us examine these withdrawals and injections.

Withdrawals

Only part of the incomes received by households will be spent on the goods and services of domestic firms. The remainder will be withdrawn from the inner flow. Likewise, only part of the incomes generated by firms will be paid to domestic households. The remainder of this will also be withdrawn. There are three forms of **withdrawals (W)** (or 'leakages' as they are sometimes called).

Net saving (S).   Saving is income that households choose not to spend but to put aside for the future. Savings are normally deposited in financial institutions such as banks and building societies. This is shown in the bottom right of the diagram. Money flows from households to 'banks, etc.'. What we are seeking to measure here, however, is the net flow from households to the banking sector. We therefore have to subtract from saving any borrowing or drawing on past savings by households in order to get the *net* saving flow. Of course, if household borrowing exceeded saving, the net flow would be in the other direction: it would be negative.

Net taxes (T).   When people pay taxes (to either central or local government), this represents a withdrawal of money from the inner flow in much the same way as saving: only in this case people have no choice. Some taxes, such as income tax, are paid out of household incomes. Others, such as Value Added Tax (VAT) and excise duties, are paid out of consumer expenditure. Others, such as corporation tax, are paid out of firms' incomes before being received by households as dividends on shares. (For simplicity, however, we show taxes being withdrawn at just one point. It does not affect the argument.)

When, however, people receive *benefits* from the government, such as working tax credit, child benefit and pensions, the money flows the other way. Benefits are thus equivalent to a 'negative tax'. These benefits are known as **transfer payments**. They transfer money from one group of people (taxpayers) to others (the recipients).

In the model, 'net taxes' (*T*) represent the *net* flow to the government from households and firms. It consists of total taxes minus benefits.

Pause for thought

How would a rise in government benefit payments, all other things being equal, affect the flow of withdrawals?

Import expenditure (M).   Not all consumption is of totally home-produced goods. Households spend some of their incomes on imported goods and services or on goods and services using imported components. Although the money that consumers spend on such goods initially flows to domestic retailers, eventually it will find its way abroad, either when the retailers or wholesalers themselves import

---

Definitions

Withdrawals *(W)* (or leakages) Incomes of households or firms that are not passed on round the inner flow. Withdrawals equal net saving (*S*) plus net taxes (*T*) plus import expenditure (*M*): $W = S + T + M$.

Transfer payments Moneys transferred from one person or group to another (e.g. from the government to individuals) without production taking place.

them or when domestic manufacturers purchase imported inputs to make their products. This expenditure on imports constitutes the third withdrawal from the inner flow. This money flows abroad.

Total withdrawals are simply the sum of net saving, net taxes and the expenditure on imports:

$$W = S + T + M$$

Injections

Only part of the demand for firms' output arises from consumers' expenditure. The remainder comes from other sources outside the inner flow. These additional components of aggregate demand are known as **injections (J)**. There are three types of injection.

Investment on domestically produced capital (I_d). This consists of investment in plant and equipment. It also includes the building up of stocks of inputs, semi-finished or finished goods. When firms invest, they obtain the money from various financial institutions, either from past savings or from loans, or through new issues of shares.

Government purchases of domestically produced goods and services (G_d). When the government spends money on goods and services produced by domestic firms, this counts as an injection. Examples of such government expenditure are spending on roads, hospitals and schools. (Note that government expenditure in this model does not include state benefits, hence, the use of the term 'government purchases'. Benefits, as we saw above, are transfer payments and are the equivalent of negative taxes and have the effect of reducing the T component of withdrawals.)

As well as providing goods and services by purchasing from firms, governments own and run operations themselves. The government therefore becomes a purchaser on behalf of the public, for example of health and education services. The wages of public-sector staff will be a component of the government's expenditure and are a flow of factor payments to households.

As with investment, not all government purchases (G) are on totally home-produced goods and services. Expenditures on items made overseas contribute towards import expenditure (M).

Export expenditure (X_d). Money flows into the circular flow from abroad when residents abroad buy our exports of goods and services. Note that, as with the other two injections, only those parts of exports made in the country should be counted. Any imported materials or components into the exports should be deducted.

Total injections are thus the sum of investment, government purchases and exports, in each case with any imported component subtracted:

$$J = I_d + G_d + X_d$$

Aggregate demand, as we have seen, is the total spending on domestic firms. In other words, it is the spending by the household sector on domestically produced goods and services (C_d), plus the three injections:[3]

$$AD = C_d + J$$

The relationship between withdrawals and injections

There are indirect links between saving and investment via financial institutions, between taxation and government expenditure via the government (central and local) and between imports and exports via foreign countries. These links, however, do not guarantee that $S = I_d$ or $T = G_d$ or $M = X_d$.

Take investment and saving. The point here is that the decisions to save and invest are made by different people and thus they plan to save and invest different amounts. Likewise, the demand for imports may not equal the demand for exports. As far as the government is concerned, it may choose not to make $T = G_d$. It may choose not to spend all its net tax revenues on domestic goods and services; or it may choose to spend more on domestic goods and services than it receives in net taxes. If necessary, it could borrow money to make up any shortfall.

Thus planned injections (J) may not equal planned withdrawals (W).

Equilibrium in the circular flow

The circular flow of income model helps us to understand how fluctuations in aggregate demand can cause fluctuations in national income. When injections do not equal withdrawals, a state of *disequilibrium* will exist: aggregate demand will rise or fall and so will national income. Disequilibrium results in a chain reaction that brings the economy back to a state of equilibrium where injections are equal to withdrawals.

Take the case where injections exceed withdrawals. Perhaps there has been a rise in business confidence and hence a rise in investment; or perhaps there has been a tax cut so that withdrawals have fallen and consumption rises.

Definitions

Injections (J) Expenditure on the production of domestic firms coming from outside the inner flow of the circular flow of income. Injections equal investment (I_d) plus government expenditure (G_d) plus expenditure on exports (X_d) (less any imported components of these three elements).

---

[3]Note that this definition of aggregate demand $(AD = C_d + J)$ is equivalent to the one we gave (on page 510), i.e. $AD = C + I + G + X - M$, since both the terms C_d and J exclude expenditure on imports.

The level of expenditure will rise: there will be a rise in aggregate demand.

This extra spending will increase firms' sales and thus encourage them to produce more. Total output in the economy will rise. Moving anti-clockwise around the circular flow, this will result in firms paying out more in wages, salaries, profits, rent and interest (i.e. factor payments). In other words, national income will rise.

But, as national income rises, so households will not only spend more on domestic goods (C_d), but also save more (S), pay more taxes (T) and buy more imports (M). In other words, withdrawals will rise too. This will continue until they have risen to equal injections. At that point, national income will stop rising and so will withdrawals. Equilibrium has been reached. Thus equilibrium is where:

$$W = J$$

Similarly, if withdrawals exceed injections, the resulting fall in national income will lead to a fall in withdrawals. Again, this will continue until $W = J$.

The circular flow of income and our key macroeconomic variables

The links between our key macroeconomic variables can be understood further through the circular flow model. Central to these are the relationship that each variable has with aggregate demand. Again, consider the case where injections exceed withdrawals. This will cause the level of expenditure to rise. The extra aggregate demand will generate extra incomes and *actual* national income will rise. If this rise in actual income exceeds any rise there may have been in potential income, there will be the following effects upon the key macroeconomic variables:

■ There will be economic growth. The greater the initial excess of injections over withdrawals, the bigger will be the rise in national income.
■ Unemployment will fall as firms take on more workers in order to meet the extra demand for output.
■ The rate of inflation will tend to rise. The more the gap is closed between actual and potential income, the more difficult will firms find it to meet extra demand, and the more likely they will be to raise prices.
■ The exports and imports part of the balance of payments will tend to deteriorate. The higher demand sucks more imports into the country, and higher domestic inflation makes exports less competitive and imports relatively cheaper compared with home-produced goods. Thus imports will tend to rise and exports will tend to fall (*net exports fall*).
■ An increase in national income allows economic agents to accumulate financial and non-financial assets and/or to reduce holdings of financial liabilities.

Changes in injections and withdrawals thus have a crucial effect on the whole macroeconomic environment in which businesses operate. We will examine some of these effects in more detail in the following chapters.

> **Pause for thought**
>
> *What will be the effect on each of the key macroeconomic variables if planned injections are less than planned withdrawals?*

26.4 UNEMPLOYMENT

Measuring unemployment

As we saw in section 26.1, unemployment can be expressed either as a number (e.g. 2 million) or, more commonly, as a percentage (e.g. 5 per cent). When expressed as a percentage, it is as a percentage of the total labour force, i.e. those in employment plus those unemployed. We are then able to talk about unemployment rates.

To be able to compare unemployment rates both over time and between countries, we use a *standardised unemployment rate*. Sometimes known as ILO unemployment, this is the measure used by the International Labour Organisation (ILO) and the Organisation for Economic Co-operation and Development (OECD), two international organisations that publish unemployment statistics for many countries.

In this measure, the unemployed are defined as people of working age who are without work, available to start work and *actively seeking employment* or waiting to take up an appointment. The figures are compiled from the results of national labour force surveys. In the UK, the labour force survey is conducted quarterly.

Countries also compile unemployment statistics using administrative measures, typically based on unemployment-related benefits. This is known as *claimant unemployment*.

> **Definitions**
>
> **Standardised unemployment rate** The measure of the unemployment rate used by the ILO and OECD. The unemployed are defined as people of working age who are without work, available for work and actively seeking employment.
>
> **Claimant unemployment** Those in receipt of unemployment-related benefits.

Table 26.1	Average unemployment by decade (%)						
	1960s	**1970s**	**1980s**	**1990s**	**2000s**	**2010s**	**1960–2019**
Australia	1.7	3.8	7.6	8.8	5.5	5.5	5.5
Canada	5.0	6.7	9.4	9.5	7.0	6.9	7.4
Denmark	1.3	3.2	6.7	6.9	4.6	6.5	4.9
France	1.7	3.1	7.6	9.7	8.4	9.6	6.7
Germany	0.7	2.0	5.8	7.7	8.9	4.8	5.0
Ireland	5.3	7.5	14.2	12.1	5.7	10.7	9.2
Italy	4.8	5.9	8.4	10.2	7.9	10.9	8.0
Japan	1.3	1.7	2.5	3.1	4.7	3.6	2.8
Netherlands	0.9	3.8	8.4	6.3	4.4	5.6	4.9
Spain	2.4	4.5	16.3	18.0	11.2	20.5	12.1
UK	1.6	3.5	9.5	8.0	5.4	6.1	5.7
USA	4.8	6.2	7.3	5.8	5.5	6.2	6.0

Note: data from 2018 based on forecasts.
Source: *AMECO* (European Commission, Economic and Financial Affairs)

The claimant count is simply a measure of all those in receipt of unemployment-related benefits. In the UK, claimants receive Universal Credit.

Claimant statistics have the advantage of being very easy to collect. However, they exclude all those of working age available for work at current wage rates, but who are *not* eligible for benefits. If the government changes the eligibility conditions so that fewer people are now eligible, this will reduce the number of claimants and hence the official number unemployed, even if there has been no change in the numbers with or without work.

Changing eligibility conditions makes historical comparisons using claimant statistics more difficult. Furthermore, different countries adopt different approaches to unemployment benefit. In turn, this makes country comparisons more difficult. Recognising these difficulties, the standardised unemployment rate has become the generally accepted measure of unemployment.

Unemployment patterns

Cyclical movements

Levels of economic activity vary across the business cycle. Hence, unemployment fluctuates too. In recessions, such as those experienced by most countries in the early 1980s, early 1990s and the late 2000s, unemployment tends to rise. In boom years, such as the late 1980s, late 1990s and mid-2000s, it tends to fall. Figure 26.3 helps to illustrate the cyclical movements in unemployment for selected countries

Longer-term movements

As well as experiencing fluctuations in unemployment, most countries have experienced long-term changes in average unemployment rates. This is illustrated in Table 26.1, which

shows average unemployment rates across a sample of countries since the 1960s.

It shows how, in the 1980s and early 1990s, unemployment rates were significantly higher than in the 1960s and 1970s. Then, in the late 1990s and early 2000s, it fell in some countries, such as the UK and USA. In others, such as Germany and France, it remained stubbornly high. However, the global financial crisis and subsequent economic slowdown meant that unemployment rates were to rise generally in the late 2000s and into the early 2010s.

Pause for thought

How might cyclical movements and longer-term changes in unemployment interact to affect unemployment rates?

Composition of unemployment

In many countries, female unemployment traditionally has been higher than male unemployment. Causes have included differences in education and training, discrimination by employers, more casual or seasonally-related employment among women and other social factors. In many countries, as highlighted in Table 26.2, the position has changed in recent years. An important reason has been the decline in many of the older industries, such as coal and steel, which employed mainly men. Across the whole EU, male and female unemployment rates are virtually the same.

Table 26.2 does, however, show some stark differences across different age groups. Unemployment rates in the under-25 age group are typically higher than the average, and substantially so in many countries. Higher youth

| Table 26.2 | Standardised unemployment rates by age and gender, average 2009–17 |

	All ages			Less than 25 years			25 to 74 years		
	Total	Male	Female	Total	Male	Female	Total	Male	Female
Eurozone (19 countries)	10.6	10.4	10.8	21.9	22.5	21.3	9.4	9.1	9.7
Belgium	7.9	8.1	7.8	21.2	21.9	20.4	6.7	6.8	6.6
France	9.8	9.8	9.7	23.8	24.2	23.3	8.3	8.2	8.3
Germany	5.4	5.7	5.0	8.2	9.0	7.4	5.1	5.3	4.8
Greece	21.0	18.0	24.9	45.6	40.4	51.6	19.3	16.5	22.9
Ireland	12.1	13.6	10.3	24.1	28.6	19.0	10.3	11.4	8.9
Italy	10.5	9.6	11.6	34.8	33.3	37.0	8.7	8.0	9.9
Netherlands	5.9	5.5	6.2	11.1	11.5	10.7	4.9	4.5	5.3
Norway	4.1	3.3	9.3	10.6	8.0	2.8	3.1	2.5	0.0
Poland	8.4	8.0	8.8	22.3	21.2	23.9	7.1	6.6	7.5
Portugal	12.7	12.6	12.9	30.9	29.8	32.2	11.2	11.1	11.3
Spain	21.5	20.8	22.4	46.5	47.4	45.4	19.5	18.6	20.5
Sweden	7.7	7.9	7.5	22.2	23.3	21.0	5.6	5.8	5.5
UK	6.6	7.1	6.1	17.7	19.8	15.3	4.8	5.0	4.6
USA	7.1	7.4	6.7	14.4	15.9	12.8	5.9	6.2	5.7

Source: Based on data from *Employment and Unemployment (LFS)* (Eurostat, European Commission)

unemployment rates can be explained by the suitability (or unsuitability) of the qualifications of school leavers, the attitudes of employers to young people and the greater willingness of young people to spend time unemployed looking for a better job or waiting to start a further or higher education course.

The costs of unemployment

The most obvious cost of unemployment is to the *unemployed themselves*. There is the direct financial cost of the loss in their earnings, measured as the difference between their previous wage and their unemployment benefit. Then there are the personal costs of being unemployed. The longer people are unemployed, the more dispirited they may become. Their self-esteem is likely to fall and they are more likely to succumb to stress-related illness.

Then there are the costs to the *family and friends* of the unemployed. Personal relations can become strained and there may be an increase in domestic violence and the number of families splitting up.

Then there are the *broader costs to the economy*. Unemployment benefits are a cost borne by taxpayers. There may also have to be extra public spending on benefit offices, social services, health care and the police. What is more, unemployment represents a loss of output. Apart from the lack of income to the unemployed themselves, this under-utilisation of resources leads to lower incomes for other people too:

- Firms lose the profits that could have been made, had there been full employment.
- The government loses tax revenues, since the unemployed pay no income tax and national insurance and, given that the unemployed spend less, they pay less VAT and excise duties.
- Other workers lose any additional wages, they could have earned from higher national output.

The costs of unemployment are, to some extent, offset by benefits. If workers voluntarily quit their job to look for a better one, then they must reckon that the benefits of a better job more than compensate for their temporary loss of income. From the nation's point of view, a workforce that is prepared to quit jobs and spend a short time unemployed will be a more adaptable, more mobile workforce – one that is responsive to changing economic circumstances. Such a workforce will lead to greater allocative efficiency in the short run and more rapid economic growth over the longer run.

Long-term involuntary unemployment is quite another matter. The costs clearly outweigh any benefits, both for the individuals concerned and for the economy as a whole. A demotivated, deskilled pool of long-term unemployed is a serious economic and social problem.

Unemployment and the labour market

We now turn to the causes of unemployment. These causes fall into two broad categories: *equilibrium* unemployment

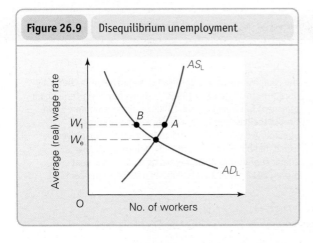

Figure 26.9 Disequilibrium unemployment

Figure 26.10 Equilibrium unemployment

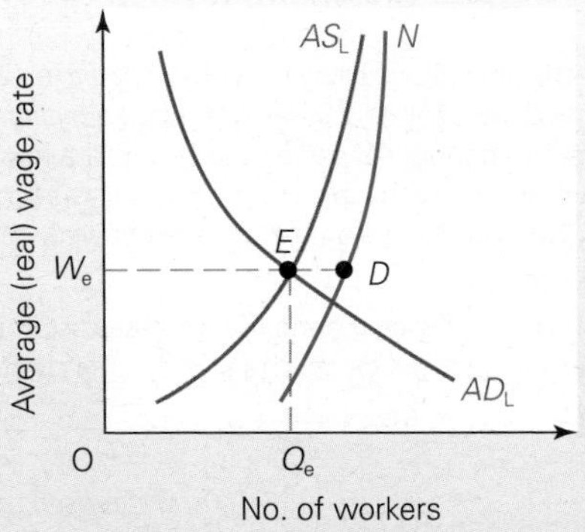

and *disequilibrium* unemployment. To make clear the distinction between the two, it is necessary to look at how the labour market works.

Figure 26.9 shows the aggregate demand for labour and the aggregate supply of labour: that is, the total demand and supply of labour in the whole economy. The *real* average wage rate is plotted on the vertical axis. This is the average wage rate expressed in terms of its purchasing power: in other words, after taking inflation into account.

The *aggregate supply of labour curve* (AS_L) shows the number of workers *willing to accept jobs* at each wage rate. This curve is relatively inelastic, since the size of the workforce at any one time cannot change significantly. Nevertheless, it is not totally inelastic because (a) a higher wage rate will encourage some people to enter the labour market (e.g. parents raising children) and (b) the unemployed will be more willing to accept job offers rather than continuing to search for a better-paid job.

The *aggregate demand for labour curve* (AD_L) slopes downward. The higher the wage rate, the more will firms attempt to economise on labour and to substitute other factors of production for labour.

The labour market is in equilibrium at a wage of W_e in Figure 26.9, where the demand for labour equals the supply. If the wage were above W_e, the labour market would be in a state of disequilibrium. At a wage rate of W_1, there is an excess supply of labour of $A - B$. This is called *disequilibrium unemployment*.

For disequilibrium unemployment to occur, two conditions must hold:

- The aggregate supply of labour must exceed the aggregate demand.
- There must be a 'stickiness' in wages. In other words, the wage rate must not immediately fall to W_e.

Even when the labour market *is* in equilibrium, however, not everyone looking for work will be employed. Some people will hold out, hoping to find a better job. The curve N in Figure 26.10 shows the total number in the labour force. The horizontal difference between it and the aggregate supply of

labour curve (AS_L) represents the excess of people looking for work over those actually willing to accept jobs. Q_e represents the equilibrium level of employment and the distance $D - E$ represents the **equilibrium level of unemployment**. This is sometimes known as the *natural level of unemployment*.

Types of disequilibrium unemployment

There are three possible causes of disequilibrium unemployment.

Real-wage unemployment

This is disequilibrium unemployment caused by real wages being driven up above the market-clearing level. In Figure 26.9, the wage rate is driven up above W_e. Some argue that it is the result of trade unions using their monopoly power to drive up wages or preventing the unemployed from competing wages down. Others argue that the minimum wage has a similar effect.

Even though unions have the power to drive up wages in some industries, their power to do so has waned in recent years. Labour markets have become more flexible (see

Definitions

Aggregate supply of labour curve A curve showing the total number of people willing and able to work at different average real wage rates.

Aggregate demand for labour curve A curve showing the total demand for labour in the economy at different average real wage rates.

Disequilibrium unemployment Unemployment resulting from real wages in the economy being above the equilibrium level.

Equilibrium ('natural') unemployment The difference between those who would like employment at the current wage rate and those willing and able to take a job.

KI 38
p 500

BOX 26.2   THE DURATION OF UNEMPLOYMENT

Taking a dip in the unemployment pool

A few of the unemployed may never have had a job and maybe never will. For most, however, unemployment lasts only a certain period. For some, it may be just a few days while they are between jobs. For others, it may be a few months. For others – the long-term unemployed – it could be several years.

Long-term unemployment normally is defined as those who have been unemployed for over 12 months. The chart shows

the composition of standardised unemployment in the UK by duration since the early 1990s. It shows how long-term unemployment fell from the mid-1990s until the economic downturn in the late 2000s. As a result, the percentage of unemployed people classified as long-term unemployed, which had hit 45 per cent in 1994, fell to just below 20 per cent during 2004, before rising to 37 per cent during 2012. By 2018 it had fallen back to 25 per cent.

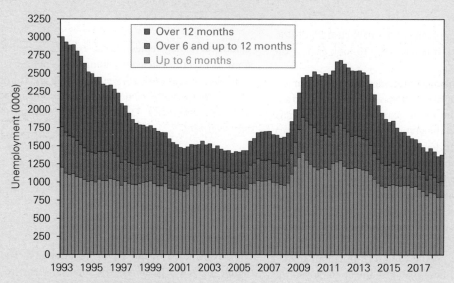

UK standardised unemployment by duration

■ Over 12 months
■ Over 6 and up to 12 months
■ Up to 6 months

Note: Figures relate to people aged 16 and over
Source: Based on series YBWF, YBWG and YBWH (Office for National Statistics)

---

section 18.4). What is more, the process of globalisation has meant that many firms face intense competition from rivals in China, India and many other countries. This makes it impossible for them to concede large pay increases. In many cases, they can simply use labour in other countries if domestic labour is too expensive. For example, many firms employ call-centre workers in India, where wages are much lower.

As far as the national minimum wage is concerned, evidence from the UK suggests that the rate has not been high enough to have significant adverse effects on employment (see page 329).

Demand-deficient or cyclical unemployment

Demand-deficient or *cyclical unemployment* is associated with recessions, such as that of 2008–9. As the economy moves into recession, consumer demand falls. Firms find

that they are unable to sell their current level of output. For a time, they may be prepared to build up stocks of unsold goods, but, sooner or later, they will start to cut back on production and cut back on the amount of labour they employ. In Figure 26.9, the AD_L curve shifts to the left. The deeper the recession becomes and the longer it lasts, the higher will demand-deficient unemployment become.

Definition

Demand-deficient or cyclical unemployment Disequilibrium unemployment caused by a fall in aggregate demand with no corresponding fall in the real wage rate.

But what determines the average duration of unemployment? There are three important factors here.

The number unemployed (the size of the stock of unemployment)

Unemployment is a 'stock' concept: it measures a quantity of people unemployed at a particular point in time. The higher the stock of unemployment, the longer will tend to be the duration of unemployment. There will be more people competing for vacant jobs.

The rate of inflow and outflow from the stock of unemployment

The people making up the unemployment total are constantly changing. Each week, some people are made redundant or quit their jobs. They represent an inflow to the stock of unemployment. Other people find jobs and thus represent an outflow from the stock of unemployment. Unemployment often is referred to as 'the pool of unemployment'.

If the inflow of people into the unemployment pool exceeds the outflow, the pool of unemployed people will rise. The duration of unemployment will depend on the rate of inflow and outflow.

The bigger the flows are relative to the total number unemployed, the less will be the average duration of unemployment. This is because people move into and out of the unemployment pool more quickly and, hence, their average stay will be shorter.

The phase of the business cycle

The duration of unemployment will also depend on the phase of the business cycle. At the onset of a recession, unemployment will rise, but, as yet, the average length of unemployment is likely to have been relatively short. Once a recession has lasted for a period of time, however, people will, on average, have been out of work longer; and this long-term unemployment is likely to persist even when the economy is pulling out of recession.

1. If the number unemployed exceeded the total annual outflow, what could we conclude about the average duration of unemployment?
2. Make a list of the various inflows to and outflows from employment from and to (a) unemployment (b) outside the workforce.

From the Office for National Statistics (www.ons.gov.uk/), download series YBWH (unemployed over 12 months) and MGSC (total unemployed) and calculate the percentage of the total unemployed who have been unemployed for over 12 months. Plot this on a line chart and then write a short summary of your findings.

Only later, as the economy recovers and begins to grow again, so demand-deficient unemployment will start to fall. Therefore, the level of demand-deficient unemployment varies across the business cycle. This explains why it is frequently referred to as 'cyclical unemployment'. Figure 26.3 illustrates this cyclical nature of unemployment.

Growth in the labour supply

If labour supply rises with no corresponding increase in the demand for labour, the equilibrium real wage rate will fall. If the real wage rate is 'sticky' downwards, unemployment will occur. This tends not to be such a serious cause of unemployment as demand deficiency, since the supply of labour changes relatively slowly. Nevertheless, there is a problem of providing jobs for school leavers each year with the sudden influx of new workers on to the labour market.

Equilibrium unemployment

If you look at Table 26.1 (on page 515), you can see how unemployment in many countries was higher in the 1980s and 1990s than in the previous two decades. Part of the reason for this was the growth in equilibrium unemployment. In the 2000s, unemployment fell in many countries – at least until the financial crisis of 2007/8. Again, part of the reason for this was a change in equilibrium unemployment, but this time a fall.

Although there may be overall *macro*economic equilibrium, with the *aggregate* demand for labour equal to the *aggregate* supply, and thus no disequilibrium unemployment, at a *micro*economic level supply and demand may not match. In other words, there may be vacancies in some parts of the economy, but an excess of labour (unemployment) in others. This is equilibrium unemployment. There are various types of equilibrium unemployment.

Frictional (search) unemployment

Frictional unemployment occurs when people leave their jobs, either voluntarily or because they are sacked or made redundant, and are then unemployed for a period of time while they are looking for a new job. They may not get the first job they apply for, despite a vacancy existing. The employer may continue searching, hoping to find a better-qualified person. Likewise, unemployed people may choose not to take the first job they are offered. Instead, they may continue searching, hoping that a better one will turn up.

KI 8
p 33 The problem is that information is imperfect. Employers are not fully informed about what labour is available; workers are not fully informed about what jobs are available and what they entail. Both employers and workers, therefore, have to search: employers search for the right labour and workers search for the right jobs.

Structural unemployment

Structural unemployment occurs where the structure of the economy changes. Employment in some industries may expand while in others it contracts. There are two main reasons for this.

A change in the pattern of demand. Some industries experience declining demand. This may be due to a change in consumer tastes. Certain goods may go out of fashion. Or it may be due to competition from other industries. For example, consumer demand may shift away from coal and to other fuels. This will lead to structural unemployment in mining areas.

A change in the methods of production (technological unemployment). New techniques of production often allow the same level of output to be produced with fewer workers. This is known as 'labour-saving technical progress'. Unless output expands sufficiently to absorb the surplus labour, people will be made redundant. This creates **technological unemployment**. An example is the job losses in the banking industry caused by the increase in the number of cash machines and by the development of telephone and Internet banking.

Structural unemployment often occurs in particular regions of the country. When it does, it is referred to as **regional unemployment**. This is most likely to occur when particular industries are concentrated in particular areas. For example, the decline in the South Wales coal-mining industry led to high unemployment in the Welsh valleys.

> ### Pause for thought
>
> *Why is structural unemployment sometimes referred to as 'mismatch unemployment'?*

Seasonal unemployment

Seasonal unemployment occurs when the demand for certain types of labour fluctuates with the seasons of the year. This problem is particularly severe in holiday areas such as Cornwall, where unemployment can reach very high levels in the winter months.

26.5 INFLATION

Inflation refers to rising price levels; deflation refers to falling price levels. The annual rate of inflation measures the annual percentage *increase* in prices. If the rate of inflation is negative, then prices are falling and we are measuring the rate of deflation.

Typically, inflation relates to *consumer* prices. The government publishes a 'consumer prices index' (CPI) each month and the rate of inflation is the percentage increase in that index over the previous 12 months.

A broader measure of inflation relates to the rate at which the prices of all domestically produced goods and services are changing. The price index used in this case is known as the **GDP deflator**. Figure 26.11 shows the annual rates of change in the GDP deflator for a selection of countries. As you can see, inflation was particularly severe in the mid-1970s, but rates have been relatively low in more recent years and, indeed, Japan experienced a period of prolonged deflation.

You will also find rates of inflation reported for a variety of goods and services. For example, inflation rates are published for wages (wage inflation), commodity prices, food prices, house prices, import prices, prices after taking taxes into account, and so on.

Figure 26.12 shows three inflation rate measures for the UK from 2001. Of the three inflation rates, the annual

> ### Definitions
>
> **Frictional (search) unemployment** Unemployment that occurs as a result of imperfect information in the labour market. It often takes time for workers to find jobs (even though there are vacancies) and, in the meantime, they are unemployed.
>
> **Structural unemployment** Unemployment that arises from changes in the pattern of demand or supply in the economy. People made redundant in one part of the economy cannot immediately take up jobs in other parts (even though there are vacancies).
>
> **Technological unemployment** Structural unemployment that occurs as a result of the introduction of labour-saving technology.
>
> **Regional unemployment** Structural unemployment occurring in specific regions of the country.
>
> **Seasonal unemployment** Unemployment associated with industries or regions where the demand for labour is lower at certain times of the year.
>
> **GDP deflator** The price index of all final domestically produced goods and services: i.e. all items that contribute towards GDP.

| **Figure 26.11** | Economy-wide inflation rates |

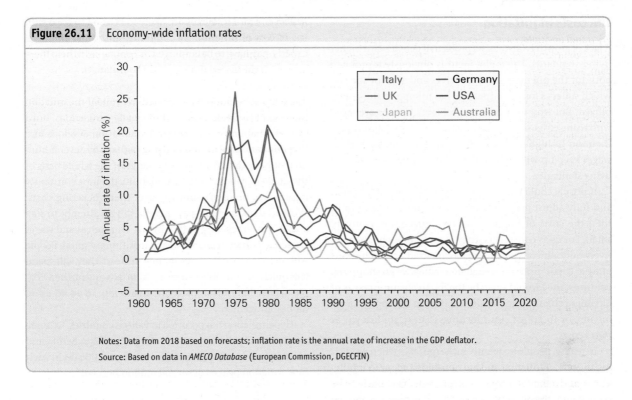

Notes: Data from 2018 based on forecasts; inflation rate is the annual rate of increase in the GDP deflator.

Source: Based on data in *AMECO Database* (European Commission, DGECFIN)

| **Figure 26.12** | Selection of annual UK inflation rates |

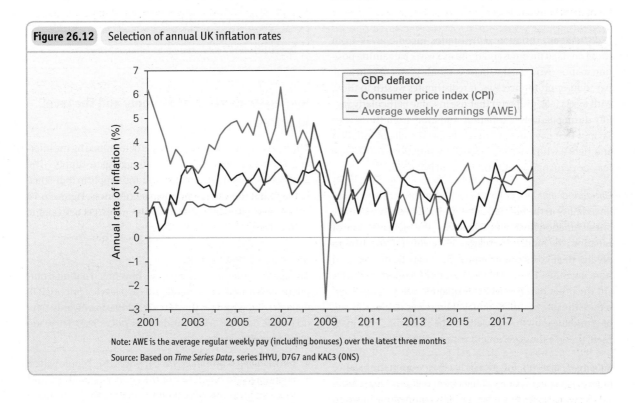

Note: AWE is the average regular weekly pay (including bonuses) over the latest three months

Source: Based on *Time Series Data*, series IHYU, D7G7 and KAC3 (ONS)

growth of average weekly earnings shows the most variability. This has implications for the purchasing power of workers. We can see, for example, a marked erosion of purchasing power in 2009 following the financial crisis and again, to some degree, during 2014.

Before we proceed, a word of caution: be careful not to confuse a rise or fall in *inflation* with a rise or fall in *prices*. A rise in inflation means a *faster* increase in prices. A fall in inflation means a *slower* increase in prices (but still an increase as long as inflation is positive).

The costs of inflation

A lack of growth is obviously a problem if people want higher living standards. Unemployment is obviously a problem both for the unemployed themselves and also for society, which suffers a loss in output and has to support the unemployed. But why is inflation a problem? If firms are faced with rising costs, does it really matter if they can simply pass them on in higher prices? Similarly, for workers, if their wages keep up with prices, there will not be a cut in their living standards.

If people could correctly anticipate the rate of inflation and fully adjust prices and incomes to take account of it, then the costs of inflation would, indeed, be relatively small. For us as consumers, they would simply be the relatively minor inconvenience of having to adjust our notions of what a 'fair' price is for each item when we go shopping. For firms, they would again be the relatively minor costs of having to change price labels, or prices in catalogues or on menus, or to adjust slot machines. These are known as **menu costs**.

In reality, people frequently make mistakes when predicting the rate of inflation and are not able to adapt to it fully. This leads to the following problems, which are likely to be more serious the higher the rate of inflation becomes and the more the rate fluctuates.

Redistribution. Inflation redistributes income away from those on fixed incomes and those in a weak bargaining position to those who can use their economic power to gain large pay, rent or profit increases. It redistributes wealth to those with assets (e.g. property) that rise in value particularly rapidly during periods of inflation, and away from those with savings that pay rates of interest below the rate of inflation and hence whose value is eroded by inflation. Pensioners may be particularly badly hit by rapid inflation.

Uncertainty and lack of investment. Inflation tends to cause uncertainty in the business community, especially when the rate of inflation fluctuates. (Generally, the higher the rate of inflation, the more it fluctuates.) If it is difficult for firms to predict their costs and revenues; they may be discouraged from investing. This will reduce the rate of economic growth. On the other hand, as will be explained below, policies to reduce the rate of inflation may themselves reduce the rate of economic growth, especially in the short run. This may, then, provide the government with a policy dilemma.

Balance of payments. Inflation is likely to worsen the balance of payments. If a country suffers from relatively high inflation rates, its exports will become less competitive in world markets. At the same time, imports will become relatively cheaper than home-produced goods. Thus exports will fall and imports will rise. As a result, the balance of payments will deteriorate and/or the exchange rate will fall or interest rates will have to rise. Each of these effects can cause problems. This is examined in more detail in the next chapter.

Resources. Extra resources are likely to be used to cope with the effects of inflation. Accountants and other financial experts may have to be employed by companies to help them cope with the uncertainties caused by inflation.

The costs of inflation may be relatively mild if the inflation rate is kept to single figures. They can be very serious, however, if inflation gets out of hand. If inflation develops into 'hyperinflation', with prices rising perhaps by several hundred or even thousand per cent per year, the whole basis of the market economy will be undermined. Firms constantly raise prices in an attempt to cover their rocketing costs. Workers demand huge pay increases in an attempt to stay ahead of the rocketing cost of living. Thus prices and wages chase each other in an ever-rising inflationary spiral. People will no longer want to save money. Instead, they will spend it as quickly as possible before its value falls any further. People may even resort to barter in an attempt to avoid using money altogether.

Hyperinflation has occurred in various countries. Extreme examples include Germany in the early 1920s, Serbia and Montenegro in 1993–5 and Zimbabwe in 2006–8. In each case, inflation peaked at several million per cent.

Pause for thought

Do you personally gain or lose from inflation? Why?

Aggregate demand and supply and the level of prices

The level of prices in the economy is determined by the interaction of aggregate demand and aggregate supply. The analysis is similar to that of demand and supply in individual markets, but there are some crucial differences. Figure 26.13 shows aggregate demand and supply curves. Let us examine each in turn.

Aggregate demand curve

The aggregate demand curve shows how much national output (real GDP) will be demanded at each level of prices (GDP deflator). But why does the *AD* curve slope downwards: why do people demand fewer products as prices rise? There are three main reasons:

■ *International substitution effect.* If prices rise, people will be encouraged to buy fewer of the country's products and more imports instead (which are now relatively cheaper);

Definition

Menu costs of inflation The costs associated with having to adjust price lists or labels.

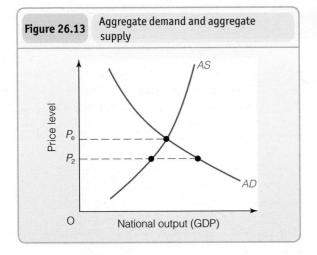

Figure 26.13 Aggregate demand and aggregate supply

Equilibrium

The equilibrium price level will be where aggregate demand equals aggregate supply. To demonstrate this, consider what would happen if aggregate demand exceeded aggregate supply: for example, at P_2 in Figure 26.13. The resulting shortages throughout the economy would drive up prices. This would cause a movement up along both the AD and AS curves from points a and b respectively until $AD = AS$ (at P_e).

KI 11
p 53

Shifts in the AD or AS curves

If there is a change in the price level, there will be a movement *along* the AD and AS curves. If any other determinant of AD or AS changes, the respective curve will shift. The analysis here is very similar to shifts and movements along demand and supply curves in individual markets (see pages 49–50 and 52).

KI 10
p 46

The aggregate demand curve will shift if there is a change in any of its components: consumption, investment, government expenditure or exports minus imports. Thus, if the government decides to spend more, if consumers spend more as a result of lower taxes or if business confidence increases so that firms decide to invest more, the AD curve will shift to the right.

> ### Pause for thought
>
> *Give some examples of events that could shift (a) the AD curve to the left (b) the AS curve to the left.*

---

also the country will sell fewer exports. Thus aggregate demand will be lower.

■ *Inter-temporal substitution effect.* As prices rise, people will need more money to pay for their purchases. With a given supply of money in the economy, this will have the effect of driving up interest rates (we will explore this in Chapter 28). The effect of higher interest rates will be to discourage borrowing and encourage saving. Both will have the effect of reducing spending and hence reducing aggregate demand.

■ *Real balance effect.* If prices rise, the real value of people's savings will be eroded. They may thus save more (and spend less) to compensate.

The above three effects are *substitution effects* of the rise in prices (see page 47). They involve a switch to *alternatives* – either imports or saving.

There may also be an *income effect*. This will occur provided consumers' incomes do not rise as fast as prices, causing a fall in consumers' *real* incomes. Consumers cut down on consumption as they cannot afford to buy so much. Firms, on the other hand, with falling real wage costs, are likely to find their profit per unit rising. However, they are unlikely to spend much more on investment, if at all, as consumer expenditure is falling. The net effect is a fall in aggregate demand.

Aggregate supply curve

The aggregate supply curve slopes upwards – at least in the short run. In other words, the higher the level of prices, the more will be produced. To understand why, it important to recognise that, in drawing the *short-run* aggregate supply curve (sometimes referred to as the *SRAS* curve), various things are assumed to remain constant. These include wage rates and other input prices, technology as well as the total supply of factors of production (land, labour and capital). Therefore, with input prices being constant, as the prices of firms' products rise, their profitability will rise too. This will encourage them to produce more.

The short-run aggregate supply curve will shift if there is a change in any of the variables that are held constant when we plot the curve. Several of these variables, notably technology, the labour force and the stock of capital, change only slowly – normally shifting the curve gradually to the right. This represents an increase in potential output.

By contrast, wage rates and other input prices can change significantly in the short run and are, thus, the major causes of shifts in the short-run supply curve. For example, a general rise in wage rates throughout the economy reduces the amount that firms wish to produce at any level of prices. The aggregate supply curve shifts upwards to the left. A similar effect will occur if other costs, such as oil prices or indirect taxes, increase.

Causes of inflation

Demand-pull inflation

Demand-pull inflation is caused by continuing rises in aggregate demand. In Figure 26.13, the AD curve shifts to the

---

> ### Definition
>
> **Demand-pull inflation** Inflation caused by persistent rises in aggregate demand.

| BOX 26.3 | OUTPUT GAPS AND INFLATION |

Do output gaps explain inflation?

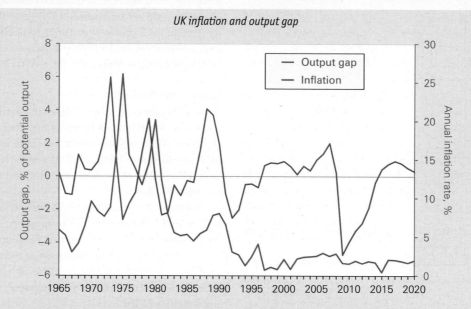

UK inflation and output gap

Notes: Data from 2018 based on forecasts; inflation rate is the annual rate of increase in the GDP deflator.
Source: Based on data in *AMECO Database* (European Commission, DGECFIN)

The output gap measures the difference between an economy's actual level of output and its potential or normal-capacity output (see Box 26.1). A positive output gap shows that the level of actual output is *greater* than the potential level, while a negative output gap shows that the level of output is below the potential level.

The magnitude of the output gap, which usually is expressed as a percentage of potential output, enables us to assess the extent of any demand deficiency (negative output gap) or excess demand (positive output gap).

The 'mainstream view' of the slope of the short-run aggregate supply (see curve *AS* in Figure 26.13 on page 523) is that it is determined by the amount of slack in the economy. As the economy approaches or exceeds its potential output, the aggregate supply curve becomes steeper as firms' marginal costs rise faster. Consequently, increases in demand at output levels close to or in excess of an economy's potential output will exert more upward pressure on prices than if the economy has a more significant amount of slack. This suggests that the rate of price inflation is positively related to the size of the output gap.

The chart plots the output gap (as a percentage of potential output) and the annual rate of economy-wide inflation, i.e. the rate of increase of the GDP deflator, for the UK since 1965.

For the period from 1965 to the end of the 1980s, there is evidence of a positive correlation between output gaps and inflation rates, albeit that turning points in the rates of inflation lag those in the size of output gaps. In other words, it took time for price pressures to work fully through the economy.

This reflects, in part, the fact that some prices, such as wage rates, are adjusted periodically.

Since the 1990s, however, the relationship between output gaps and inflation rates is less clear. Indeed, the period is characterised by relative low rates of inflation regardless of the size of output gaps. This demonstrates that there are several potential influences on inflation rates.

One explanation is a *reduction in global cost-push pressures*. First, labour markets have become more competitive and flexible. Second, firms have faced greater international competition from EU-member states, China and many other countries in an increasingly globalised market.

Another explanation is *inflation rate expectations*. The adoption of clear and credible inflation targets by central banks, such as the Bank of England, has influenced firms when setting prices and in their negotiations with workers over wage rates. It has helped to anchor price and wage setting to the inflation rate target, irrespective of the state of the economy.

1. *What factors may have resulted in the generally lower inflation rates experienced by the UK from the 1990s?*
2. *Do credible inflation rate targets guarantee low inflation?*

Download the latest available version of Forecasts for the UK economy, which is a monthly comparison of independent forecasts complied by HM Treasury. Then, compare the average forecast for the annual CPI inflation rate for the periods available with the Bank of England's target of 2 per cent (plus or minus 1 percentage point).

right, and continues doing so. Firms will respond to the rise in aggregate demand partly by raising prices and partly by increasing output (there is a move up along the *AS* curve). Just how much they raise prices depends on how much their costs rise as a result of increasing output. This, in turn, depends upon how close actual output is to potential output. The less slack there is in the economy, the more will firms respond to a rise in demand by raising their prices (the *steeper* will be the *AS* curve).

Demand-pull inflation typically is associated with a booming economy. Many economists therefore argue that it is the counterpart of demand-deficient (cyclical) unemployment. When the economy is in recession, demand-deficient unemployment will be high, but the rate of demand-pull inflation will be low. When, on the other hand, the economy is near the peak of the business cycle, the rate of demand-pull inflation will be high, but demand-deficient unemployment will be low. Box 26.3 looks at the relationship between inflation and output gaps, which are a measure of excess or deficient demand.

Cost-push inflation

Cost-push inflation is associated with continuing rises in costs and hence continuing leftward (upward) shifts in the *AS* curve. Such shifts occur when costs of production rise *independently* of aggregate demand. If firms face a rise in costs, they will respond partly by raising prices and passing the costs on to the consumer, and partly by cutting back on production (there is a movement back along the *AD* curve).

Just how much firms raise prices and cut back on production depends on the shape of the aggregate demand curve. The less elastic the *AD* curve, the less sales will fall as a result of any price rise and, hence, the more firms will be able to pass on the rise in their costs to consumers as higher prices.

Note that the effect on output and employment is the opposite of demand-pull inflation. With demand-pull inflation, output and hence employment tend to rise. With cost-push inflation, however, output and employment tend to fall.

It is important to distinguish between *single* shifts in the aggregate supply curve (known as 'supply shocks') and *continuing* shifts. If there is a single leftward shift in aggregate supply, there will be a single rise in the price level. For example, if the government raises the excise duty on petrol and diesel, there will be a single rise in road fuel prices and hence in industry's fuel costs. This will cause *temporary* inflation while the price rise is passed on through the economy. Once this has occurred, prices will stabilise at the new level and the rate of inflation will fall back to zero again. If cost-push inflation is to continue over a number of years, therefore, the aggregate supply curve must *continually* shift to the left. If the rate of cost-push inflation is to *rise,* these shifts must get more rapid.

Rises in costs may originate from a number of different sources, such as trade unions pushing up wages, firms with monopoly power raising prices in order to increase their profits or increases in international commodity prices. With the process of globalisation and increased international

competition, cost-push pressures have tended to decrease in recent years. One major exception is the price of various commodities and especially oil. For example, the near tripling of oil prices from $51 per barrel in January 2007 to $147 per barrel in July 2008 and again from $41 a barrel in January 2009 to $126 a barrel in April 2011 put upward pressure on costs and prices around the world.

Demand-pull and cost-push inflation can occur together, since wage and price rises can be caused both by increases in aggregate demand and by independent causes pushing up costs. Even when an inflationary process *starts* as either demand-pull or cost-push, it is often difficult to separate the two. An initial cost-push inflation may encourage the government to expand aggregate demand to offset rises in unemployment. Alternatively, an initial demand-pull inflation may strengthen the power of certain groups, which then use this power to drive up costs. Either way, the result is likely to be continuing rightward shifts in the *AD* curve and leftward shifts in the *AS* curve. Prices will carry on rising.

Expectations and inflation

Workers and firms take account of the *expected* rate of inflation when making decisions.

Imagine that a union and an employer are negotiating a wage increase. Let us assume that both sides expect a rate of inflation of 5 per cent. The union will be happy to receive a wage rise somewhat above 5 per cent. That way the members would be getting a *real* rise in incomes. The employers will be happy to pay a wage rise somewhat below 5 per cent.

After all, they can put their price up by 5 per cent, knowing that their rivals will do approximately the same. The actual wage rise that the two sides agree on will thus be somewhere around 5 per cent.

Now let us assume that the expected rate of inflation is 10 per cent. Both sides will now negotiate around this benchmark, with the outcome being somewhere round about 10 per cent.

Thus, the higher the expected rate of inflation, the higher will be the level of pay settlements and price rises, and hence the higher will be the resulting actual rate of inflation.

In recent years, the importance of expectations in explaining the actual rate of inflation has been increasingly recognised by economists. (We examine this in Chapter 29.)

Pause for thought

How might the announcements of policymakers affect people's expectations of inflation?

Definition

Cost-push inflation Inflation caused by persistent rises in costs of production (independently of demand).

26.6 LONG-TERM ECONOMIC GROWTH

 Much of our focus to this point has been on the economic volatility that affects the macroeconomic environment. Yet, when we step back and look at the longer span of history, this volatility takes on less significance. What we see is that economies tend to experience long-term economic growth.

These twin characteristics of growth are nicely captured in Figure 26.14, which plots for the UK both the *level* of real GDP and annual percentage *changes* in real GDP. It shows that, while the rate of economic growth is volatile, the volume of output grows over time.

 The rate of long-term economic growth in developed nations, such as the UK, has meant that average living standards have improved markedly. When measured in terms of real GDP per head, all developed nations are considerably richer today than they were, say, fifty or sixty years ago.

 The picture, however, is not one of universal improvement. People are not necessarily happier; there are many stresses in modern living; the environment is in many respects more polluted; inequality has increased in most countries, especially over the past twenty years; for many people, work is more demanding and the working day is longer than in the past; there is more crime and more insecurity. Hence, 'more' is not always 'better'.

Nevertheless, most people *want* more consumer goods; they want higher incomes. We briefly examine what causes long-term economic growth and how it can be increased. We leave you to judge whether a materially richer society is a better society.

Comparing the growth performance of different countries

When viewing economic growth over the longer term, aggregate supply takes on increasing importance. This is because a rapid rise in aggregate demand is not enough to ensure a continuing high level of growth over a *number* of years. Without an expansion of potential output too, rises in actual output eventually must come to an end as spare capacity is used up. Therefore, an explanation of long-run growth lies on the supply side. Countries' economic *capacity* must increase.

Table 26.3 shows a series of average economic growth rates: the average annual growth in real GDP (total output), real GDP per worker (a measure of the productivity of labour) and real GDP per capita (real GDP per head of the population). The average growth rates are for several developed countries since the 1960s.

As you can see from Table 26.3, there are considerable differences in the rates of growth experienced by the different countries. The effect of even very small differences can

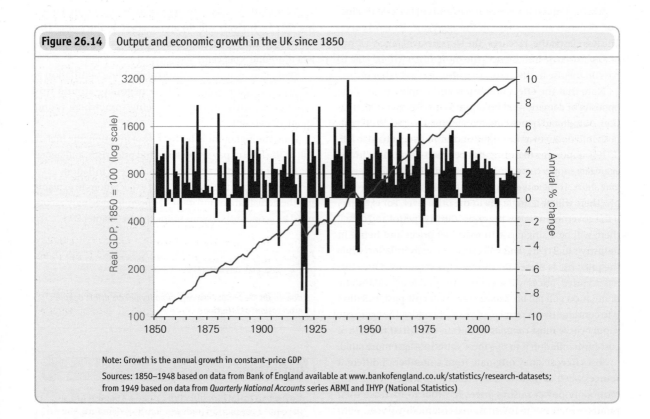

Figure 26.14 Output and economic growth in the UK since 1850

Note: Growth is the annual growth in constant-price GDP

Sources: 1850–1948 based on data from Bank of England available at www.bankofengland.co.uk/statistics/research-datasets; from 1949 based on data from *Quarterly National Accounts* series ABMI and IHYP (National Statistics)

Table 26.3	Average annual growth rates (%) 1961–2019		
	Real GDP	**Real GDP per worker**	**Real GDP per capita**
Ireland	4.90	3.65	3.93
Japan	3.78	3.11	3.23
Spain	3.38	2.64	2.62
Norway	3.11	2.03	2.41
Austria	2.75	2.23	2.34
France	2.79	2.26	2.14
Germany	2.42	1.84	2.10
Italy	2.40	2.14	2.08
Netherlands	2.79	1.84	2.08
USA	3.06	1.59	2.01
UK	2.37	1.82	1.95
Denmark	2.36	1.75	1.93
Australia	3.44	1.46	1.89
Canada	3.14	1.27	1.87
New Zealand	2.68	1.04	1.46

Note: Figures from 2018 based on forecasts; German figures based on West Germany only up to 1991.
Source: Based on data from *AMECO* database (European Commission, DGECFIN)

have a significant effect when looked at over many years. This is particularly important when we are thinking about the impact of growth on a country's *living standards*.

Pause for thought

Is it possible to have economic growth without an increase in output per worker? Explain.

In the context of living standards, it is the growth in real GDP *per capita* that is important (as shown in the last column of the table). An increase in the population will, other things being equal, lower living standards because more people will be sharing a given amount of real national income. Hence, when analysing economic growth over time, it is real GDP per capita that we tend to focus on.

Pause for thought

Why may the rates of growth in average output per worker and in average output per head of the population differ?

Although recent generations have come to expect economic growth, it is a relatively new phenomenon. For most of the last two thousand years, countries have experienced virtually static output per head over the long term. Economic growth has become significant only once countries have undergone an industrial revolution and it is only with the technological advances of the twentieth and now the twenty-first centuries that long-term growth rates of 2 per cent or more have been achieved.

The causes of long-term economic growth

Table 26.3 shows the importance of the growth in real GDP (output) per worker on the growth in real GDP per capita and hence for a country's living standards. Over the long term, the rate of growth of the workforce generally reflects population growth – although, with an ageing population, it tends to lag behind somewhat. Therefore, the growth in output per capita is principally the result of increases in output per worker.

Output per worker is a measure of ***labour productivity***: it is an indicator of how effective workers are in the production process. Since the growth in output per worker is the key to understanding the growth in output per capita, it then follows that the growth of labour productivity is crucial in determining a country's long-run economic growth.

But, what explains the growth in labour productivity? In fact, there are three key sources of growth in labour productivity:

■ An increase in the *quantity of physical capital (K)*. Here we are referring to the accumulation of capital, such as

KI 42 p 507

Definition

Labour productivity Output per unit of labour: for example, output per worker or output per hour worked.

BOX 26.4 THE UK'S STOCK OF HUMAN CAPITAL

Estimating the capabilities of the labour force

The OECD (2001) defines human capital as 'the knowledge, skills, competencies and other attributes embodied in individuals or groups of individuals acquired during their life that facilitate the creation of personal, social and economic well-being'.[1] Hence, trends in human capital have implications for a range of economic-related issues, including economic growth, unemployment, life satisfaction, the inequality of income, wealth and opportunity and also for social cohesiveness. But, how we do we go about measuring human capital?

Measuring human capital

In estimating an individual's human capital, a common approach is to estimate the present value of an individual's

[1] Tom Healy and Sylvain Côté, The Well-being of Nations: the role of human and social capital, Centre for Educational Research and Innovation (OECD, 2001)

remaining lifetime labour income. This can be done for representative individuals in categories defined by gender, age and educational attainment. An assumption is then made about the working life of individuals. In compiling the UK estimates, it is assumed that the remaining lifetime labour income of individuals aged 65 and over is zero. Then an approach known as *backwards recursion* is applied.

Backwards recursion involves first estimating the remaining lifetime labour income of someone aged 64 with a particular gender, age and educational level. The remaining lifetime income in this case is simply their current annual labour income for the year from their 64th birthday. For someone aged 63, it is their current annual labour income for the year from their 63rd birthday plus the present value of the remaining lifetime income of someone aged 64 with the same gender, age and educational level. This continues

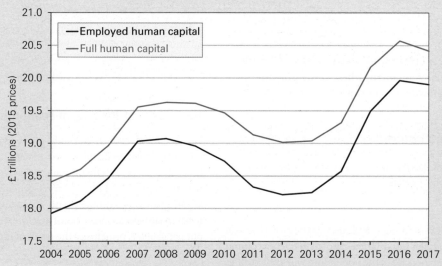

Employed and full human capital (2015 prices)

Source: Based on data in *Human Capital Estimates, UK 2004 to 2017* (Office for National Statistics, 1 October 2018)

machinery/equipment and office/factory space, that arises through investment. The better equipped workers are, the more productive they will be.

- An increase in *human capital*. Here we are referring to the knowledge, skills, competencies and other attributes of individuals that impact on their ability to produce goods and services and to generate ideas.
- *Technological progress.* Developments of computer technology, of new techniques in engineering, of lighter, stronger and cheaper materials, of digital technology in communications and of more efficient motors have all contributed to a massive increase in the productivity of

capital. Machines today can produce much more output than machines in the past that cost the same to manufacture. Therefore, workers are able to produce considerably more today, even allowing for the increases that have taken place in physical and human capital.

Definition

Human capital The knowledge, skills, competencies and other attributes embodied in individuals or groups of individuals that are used to produce goods and services.

back to someone aged 16. In calculating the remaining lifetime labour income of representative individuals, account is also taken of the probability that their level of education attainment may rise and, with it, their expected future earnings.

Further working assumptions are necessary to complete the calculations. Two of the most important are that: the rate of labour productivity growth is 2 per cent per annum and the discount rate is 3.5 per cent per annum, as recommended by HM Treasury's Green Book[2] (2003) when undertaking appraisal and evaluation studies in central government.

Two measures of the stock of human capital are estimated. The first is for *employed* human capital. It is based on estimating the lifetime labour income of those in employment. The second is *full* human capital. It includes the human capital of both the employed and unemployed. This assumes that the human capital of those currently unemployed should be valued at the remaining lifetime labour income of employed individuals with the same characteristics (gender, age and educational attainment). It ignores any so-called scarring effects from being unemployed, such as the depreciation of job-specific or transferable skills. Such effects are likely to increase the longer the duration of unemployment.

Estimates of human capital

The chart shows Office of National Statistics (ONS) estimates of employed and full human capital in the UK from 2004 to 2017 at 2015 prices. Both follow broadly similar patterns. Between 2004 and 2007, prior to the financial crisis, the stock of human capital increased by an average of 2 per cent per annum in real terms, i.e. after adjusting for inflation.

---

[2]www.gov.uk/government/publications/
the-green-book-appraisal-and-evaluation-in-central-government.

Employed and full human capital fell in each year from 2009 to 2013. The fall in full human capital was, however, slightly less pronounced because of the impact of rising unemployment on the employed human capital estimates.

On the back of a resumption of real wage growth and a rise in employment, the value of the stock of human capital, particularly employed human capital, began growing from 2014. It then fell back slightly in 2017 as real wage growth stalled, particularly among younger workers. Nonetheless, by 2017 the value of full human capital stock had reached £20.4 trillion at 2015 prices while that for employed human capital had reached £19.9 trillion. This represented a real increase of 11 per cent on 2004, though the ratio of human capital to GDP (national income) remained unchanged at around 10 per cent.

In decomposing the real increase of 11 per cent in the stock of full human capital between 2004 and 2017, the ONS (2018) estimated that improvements to the level and distribution of qualifications of the working-age population resulted in an 8 per cent increase in human capital. Growth of the working-age population contributed a further 8 per cent increase, though the relative ageing of the working population decreased human capital by 1.7 per cent. The largest negative effect came from a real decline in earnings which reduced growth by 3.4 per cent.

1. *In what ways are human capital and physical capital complementary?*
2. *Other than by educational attainment, in what ways might we wish to analyse the distribution of human capital?*

Using data from Human capital estimates: supplementary tables from the ONS, calculate the percentage shares of human capital originating from the different regions and countries of the UK. Summarise your findings in a short briefing note.

A model of economic growth

Capital accumulation

As countries accumulate capital (*K*) through investment, they have more manufactured equipment to help in production. This is referred to as ***capital accumulation***. If we ignore the problem of machines wearing out or becoming obsolete and needing replacing, then the stock of capital will increase by the amount of investment. The rise in output (ΔY) that results from capital accumulation (ΔK) will depend on the productivity of capital.

The *Harrod–Domar model* assumes that the rate of growth in real national income (*g*) via capital accumulation depends on two things:

- The marginal capital/output ratio (*k*). This is the amount of extra capital (ΔK) divided by the extra annual output

> ### Definition
>
> **Capital accumulation** An increase in the amount of capital that an economy has for production.

that it produces (ΔY). Thus $k = \Delta K / \Delta Y$. The lower the value of k, the higher is the productivity of capital (i.e. the less extra capital you need to produce extra output).

- The proportion of national income that is invested (i), which, assuming that all saving is invested, will equal the proportion of national income that is saved (s).

With a constant labour force, the formula for growth becomes:

$$g = i/k \text{ (or } g = s/k)$$

Thus, if 20 per cent of national income went in new investment ($i = 20\%$) and, if each £1 of new investment yielded 25p of extra income per year ($k = 4$), then the growth rate would be 5 per cent.

A simple example will demonstrate this. If national income is £2 trillion (i.e. £2000 billion), then £400 billion will be invested ($i = 20\%$). This will lead to extra annual output of £100 billion ($k = 4$). Thus national income grows to £2.1 trillion (i.e. £2100 billion): a growth of 5 per cent.

But what determines the rate of investment? There are a number of determinants. These include the confidence of business people about the future demand for their products, the ability of firms to finance investment projects, the profitability of business, the tax regime, the rate of growth in the economy and the rate of interest.

Over the long term, if investment is to increase, then *saving* must increase in order to finance that investment. Put another way, people must be prepared to forgo a certain amount of consumption in order to allow resources to be diverted into producing more capital goods: factories, machines, etc.

Note that, if investment is to increase, there may also need to be a steady increase in *aggregate demand*. In other words, if firms are to be encouraged to increase their capacity by installing new machines or building new factories, they may need first to see the *demand* for their products growing. Here a growth in *potential* output is the result of a growth in aggregate demand and hence *actual* output.

Some qualifications to the model

To gain a better understanding of how increases in physical capital (capital accumulation) affect long-term economic growth, we need to make three qualifications to the Harrod–Domar model. These qualifications provide additional insights into the relationship between the growth in capital *per worker* and output *per worker*. As we saw earlier, the growth in output per worker generally mirrors the growth in output per head of the population. If economic growth is to give an indication of living standards, it has to be measured per head of the population.

Diminishing returns to capital. The first qualification is that as capital per worker increases, so diminishing returns to capital are likely to set in. For example, if, in an office, you start equipping workers with PCs, at first output will increase very rapidly. But, as more and more workers have their own PC

rather than having to share, so the rate of increase in output slows down. When everyone has their own, output is likely to be at a maximum. Any additional PCs (of the same specification) will remain unused. Thus, for a given workforce, as the capital stock increases, so the marginal capital/output ratio (k) will rise and the growth rate will fall.

Required investment for replacement purposes. The second qualification is that the larger the capital stock, the greater the amount of investment that will be required for replacement purposes. This means that a smaller proportion of a given amount of investment is available for increasing the size of the capital stock at higher capital stock levels. Instead, more and more replacement investment is needed simply to maintain existing stock levels.

Growth in the workforce. The final qualification is to allow for changes in the size of the workforce. For growth to be sustained, the capital to labour ratio (K/L), which is also known as the level of **capital intensity**, must rise. A rise in capital intensity is known as **capital deepening**. For this to occur, the rate of capital accumulation must be greater than the growth in the workforce. Thus levels of investment need to be higher the more rapidly the workforce and the population are growing.

Increases in the productivity of resources

Technological improvements can increase the marginal productivity of capital. Much of the investment in new machinery is not just in extra machines, but in superior machines producing a higher rate of return. Consider the microchip revolution of recent years. Modern computers can do the work of many people and have replaced many machines that were cumbersome and expensive to build. Improved methods of transport have reduced the costs of moving goods and materials. Improved communications (such as the Internet) have reduced the costs of transmitting information. The high-tech world of today would seem a wonderland to a person of 100 years ago.

As a result of technical progress, the productivity of capital has tended to increase over time. Similarly, as a result of new skills, improved education and training, and better health, the productivity of labour has also tended to increase over time. If part of saving is used for investment in education and training, then a country's stock of human capital can rise so increasing the productivity of its workers.

Box 26.4 looks at recent estimates of the stock of human capital in the UK.

Definitions

Capital intensity The amount of physical capital that workers have to operate with and which can be measured by the amount of capital per worker (K/L).

Capital deepening An increase in the amount of capital per worker (K/L).

Pause for thought

Will the rate of actual growth have any effect on the rate of potential growth?

Policies to achieve growth

KI 36
p 376 How can governments increase a country's growth rate? Policies differ in two ways.

First, they may focus on the demand side or the supply side of the economy. In other words, they may attempt to create sufficient *aggregate demand* to ensure that firms wish to invest and that potential output is realised. Or, alternatively, they may seek to increase *aggregate supply* by concentrating on measures to increase potential output: measures to encourage research and development, innovation and training. (Chapter 30 looks at demand-side policies, while Chapter 31 looks at supply-side ones.)

Second, they may be market-orientated or interventionist policies. Many economists and politicians, especially those on the political right, believe that the best environment for encouraging economic growth is one where private enterprise is allowed to flourish: where entrepreneurs are able to reap substantial rewards from investment in new techniques and new products. Such economists therefore advocate policies designed to free up the market. Others, however, argue that a free market will be subject to considerable cyclical fluctuations and market distortions. Such economists, therefore, tend to advocate intervention by the government to reduce these fluctuations and compensate for market failures.

SUMMARY

1a The macroeconomic environment is characterised by a series of interrelated macroeconomic variables. These include: economic growth, unemployment, inflation, the balance of payments, exchange rates, the financial well-being of economic agents (i.e. households, businesses, governments and nations) and the stability of the financial system (e.g. flows of credit).

1b A fundamental characteristic of economies is that they are inherently volatile. This is evidenced by fluctuations in short-term economic growth rates. These fluctuations cause an economy's output path to fluctuate, generating what economists call the business cycle.

2a Actual growth must be distinguished from potential growth. The actual growth rate is the percentage annual increase in the output that is actually produced, whereas potential growth is the percentage annual increase in the capacity of the economy to produce (whether or not it is actually produced).

2b Actual growth will fluctuate with the course of the business cycle. The cycle can be broken down into four phases: the upturn, the rapid expansion, the peaking-out and the slowdown or recession. In practice, the length and magnitude of these phases will vary: the cycle is thus irregular.

2c Actual growth is determined by potential growth and by the level of aggregate demand. If actual output is below potential output, actual growth can temporarily exceed potential growth, if aggregate demand is rising sufficiently. In the long term, however, actual output can grow only as fast as potential output will permit.

2d Explanations of the business cycle tend to focus on fluctuations in aggregate demand. This requires an understanding of the behaviour of the components of aggregate demand. When looking at longer-term growth, aggregate supply takes on increasing importance.

3a The circular flow of income model depicts the flows of money around the economy. The inner flow shows the direct flows between firms and households. Money flows from firms to households in the form of factor payments and back again as consumer expenditure on domestically produced goods and services.

3b Not all income gets passed on directly around the inner flow. Some is withdrawn in the form of saving, some is paid in taxes and some goes abroad as expenditure on imports.

3c Likewise, not all expenditure on domestic firms is by domestic consumers. Some is injected from outside the inner flow in the form of investment expenditure, government expenditure and expenditure on the country's exports.

3d Planned injections and withdrawals are unlikely to be the same. If injections exceed withdrawals, national income will rise, unemployment will tend to fall, inflation will tend to rise and the balance of payments will tend to deteriorate. The reverse will happen if withdrawals exceed injections.

4a The two most common measures of unemployment are claimant unemployment (those claiming unemployment-related benefits) and ILO/OECD standardised unemployment (those available for work and actively seeking work or waiting to take up an appointment).

4b The costs of unemployment include the financial and other personal costs to the unemployed person, the costs to relatives and friends and the costs to society at large in terms of lost tax revenues, lost profits and lost wages to other workers, and in terms of social disruption.

4c Unemployment can be divided into disequilibrium and equilibrium unemployment.

4d Disequilibrium unemployment occurs when the average real wage rate is above the level that will equate the aggregate demand and supply of labour. It can be caused by unions or government pushing up wages (real-wage unemployment), by a fall in aggregate demand but a downward 'stickiness' in real wages (demand-deficient unemployment) or by an increase in the supply of labour.

4e Equilibrium unemployment occurs when there are people unable or unwilling to fill job vacancies. This may be due

▶

to poor information in the labour market and hence a time lag before people find suitable jobs (frictional unemployment), to a changing pattern of demand or supply in the economy and hence a mismatching of labour with jobs (structural unemployment – specific types being technological and regional unemployment) or to seasonal fluctuations in the demand for labour.

5a Inflation redistributes incomes from the economically weak to the economically powerful; it causes uncertainty in the business community and, as a result, reduces investment; it tends to lead to balance of payments problems and/or a fall in the exchange rate; it leads to resources being used to offset its effects. The costs of inflation can be very great indeed in the case of hyperinflation.

5b Equilibrium in the economy occurs when aggregate demand equals aggregate supply. Inflation can occur if there is a rightward shift in the aggregate demand curve or an upward (leftward) shift in the aggregate supply curve.

5c Demand-pull inflation occurs as a result of increases in aggregate demand. This can be due to monetary or non-monetary causes.

5d Cost-push inflation occurs when there are increases in the costs of production independent of rises in aggregate demand. Such cost increases could be from higher wages, higher commodity prices, higher profits, etc. not related to demand.

5e Cost-push and demand-pull inflation can interact to form spiralling inflation.

5f Expectations play a crucial role in determining the rate of inflation. The higher people expect inflation to be, the higher it will be.

6a When analysing the long-term rate of economic growth, we focus on the growth in real national income per capita (per head of the population). This is because it provides a better indicator of patterns in living standards than does the growth in total real national income.

6b A key determinant of the growth in real national income per capita is the growth in real national income per worker (labour productivity). There are three principal determinants of labour productivity: the quantity of physical capital, the quantity of human capital and technological progress.

REVIEW QUESTIONS

1 The following table shows index numbers for real GDP (national output) for various countries (2010 = 100). Using the formula $g = (Y_t - Y_{t-1})/Y_{t-1} \times 100$ (where g is the rate of growth, Y is the index number of output, t is any given year and $t - 1$ is the previous year):

	2010	2011	2012	2013	2014	2015	2016	2017	2018
Eurozone	100	101.6	100.7	100.5	101.8	103.9	105.8	108.3	110.8
UK	100	101.5	103.0	105.1	108.3	110.8	113.0	115.0	116.8
USA	100	101.6	103.9	105.6	108.3	111.4	113.1	115.6	119.0
Japan	100	99.9	101.4	103.4	103.8	105.2	106.2	108.0	109.4

Source: *AMECO* database (European Commission, DGECFIN)

a) (i) Work out the growth rate (g) for each country for each year from 2011 to 2018.
   (ii) Plot the figures on a graph.
   (iii) Describe the patterns that emerge.

b) (i) For each country work out the percentage increase in real GDP between 2010 and 2018.
   (ii) Prepare a column chart showing the percentage increase in output over this period with the countries ranked from largest to smallest by the size of increase.
   (iii) Comment on your findings.

2 In 1974, the UK economy shrank by 2.5 per cent before shrinking by a further 1.5 per cent in 1975. However, the figures for GDP showed a rise of 13 per cent in 1974 and 24 per cent in 1975. What explains these apparently contradictory results?

3 How might we assess the financial well-being of households?

4 How regular are the cyclical patterns in real GDP during the course of a business cycle? In what ways could these patterns vary?

5 Figure 26.6 shows a decline in actual output in recessions. Redraw the diagram, only this time show a mere slowing down of growth in phase 4.

6 At what point of the business cycle is the country now? What do you predict will happen to growth over the next two years? On what basis do you make your prediction?

7 In terms of the UK circular flow of income, are the following net injections, net withdrawals or neither? If there is uncertainty, explain your assumptions.

a) Firms are forced to take a cut in profits in order to give a pay rise.
b) Firms spend money on research.
c) The government increases personal tax allowances.
d) The general public invests more money in building societies.
e) UK investors earn higher dividends on overseas investments.
f) The government purchases US military aircraft.
g) People draw on their savings to finance holidays abroad.

h) People draw on their savings to finance holidays in the UK.
i) The government runs a budget deficit (spends more than it receives in tax revenues) and finances it by borrowing from the general public.
j) The government runs a budget deficit and finances it by printing more money.
k) As consumer confidence rises, households decrease their precautionary saving.

8 Would it be desirable to have zero unemployment?

9 What major structural changes have taken place in the UK economy over recent years that have contributed to structural unemployment?

10 What would be the benefits and costs of increasing the rate of unemployment benefit?

11 What is the difference between a rise in the level of prices and a rise in the rate of inflation?

12 Do any groups of people gain from inflation?

13 If everyone's incomes rose in line with inflation, would it matter if inflation were 100 per cent or even 1000 per cent per annum?

14 Imagine that you had to determine whether a particular period of inflation was demand-pull, cost-push or a combination of the two. What information would you require in order to conduct your analysis?

15 For what possible reasons may one country experience a persistently faster rate of economic growth than another?

APPENDIX1: APPENDIX: MEASURING NATIONAL INCOME AND OUTPUT

Three routes: one destination

To assess how fast the economy has grown, we must have a means of *measuring* the value of the nation's output. The measure we use is called *gross domestic product* (GDP).

GDP can be calculated in three different ways, which should all result in the same figure. These three methods are illustrated in the simplified circular flow of income shown in Figure 26.15.

The product method

This first method of measuring GDP is to add up the value of all the goods and services produced in the country, industry by industry. In other words, we focus on firms and add up all their production. This method is known as the *product method*.

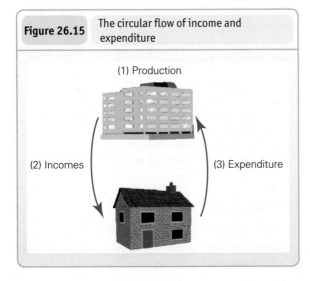

| **Figure 26.15** | The circular flow of income and expenditure |

(1) Production

(2) Incomes (3) Expenditure

In the national accounts, these figures are grouped together into broad categories such as manufacturing, construction and distribution. The figures for the UK economy for 2016 are shown in the top part of Figure 26.16.

When we add up the output of various firms, we must be careful to avoid *double counting*. For example, if a manufacturer sells a television to a retailer for £200 and the retailer sells it to the consumer for £300, how much has this television contributed to GDP? The answer is *not* £500. We do not add the £200 received by the manufacturer to the £300 received by the retailer: that would be double counting. Instead, we count either just the final value (£300) or the value added at each stage (£200 by the manufacturer + £100 by the retailer).

The sum of all the values added by all the various industries in the economy is known as *gross value added (GVA) at basic prices*.

How do we get from GVA to GDP? The answer has to do with taxes and subsidies on products and is shown in the bottom part of Figure 26.16. Taxes paid on goods and services (such as VAT and duties on petrol and alcohol) and any subsidies on products are *excluded* from gross value added (GVA), since they are not part of the value added in

Definitions

Gross value added (GVA) at basic prices The sum of all the values added by all industries in the economy over a year. The figures exclude taxes on products (such as VAT) and include subsidies on products.

Gross domestic product (GDP) (at market prices) The value of output produced within a country over a 12-month period in terms of the prices actually paid. GDP = GVA + taxes on products − subsidies on products.

Figure 26.16	UK GDP: 2016

UK GVA (product-based measure): 2016	£m	% of GVA
Agriculture, forestry and fishing	10 528	0.6
Mining and quarrying;	21 505	1.2
Manufacturing	176 996	10.1
Electricty, gas, steam and air conditioning supply	28 454	1.6
Water supply, sewerage, waste management and remediation	17 458	1.0
Construction	108 124	6.2
Distribution, transport, hotels and restaurants	321 587	18.4
Information and communications	106 740	6.1
Financial and insurance	115 280	6.6
Real estate activities	242 789	13.9
Professional and support services	215 312	12.3
Total government, health and education	309 922	17.7
Other services and miscellaneous	75 131	4.3
GVA (gross value added at basic prices)	**1 749 826**	**100.0**
UK GVA by category of income: 2016		
Compensation of employees (wages and salaries)	968 898	55.4
Operating surplus of corporations (gross profit, rent and interest)	417 223	23.8
Mixed income & gross operating surplus of non-corporate sector	334 991	19.1
Tax less subsidies on production (other than those on products)	28 714	1.6
GVA (gross value added at basic prices)	**1 749 826**	**100.0**
UK GDP: 2016		
GVA (gross value added at basic prices)	1 749 826	
plus VAT and other taxes on products	239 568	
less Subsidies on products	−2 631	
GDP (at market prices)	**1 986 763**	

Source: *Blue Book Tables - Series* (ONS, 2017)

production. Nevertheless, GDP is commonly measured at *market prices*: i.e. at the prices actually paid at each stage of production. Thus **GDP at market prices** (sometimes referred to simply as GDP) is GVA *plus* taxes on products *minus* subsidies on products.

The income method

The second approach is to focus on the incomes generated from the production of goods and services. A moment's reflection will show that this must be the same as the sum of all values added at each stage of production. Value added is simply the difference between a firm's revenue from sales and the costs of its purchases from other firms. This difference is made up of wages and salaries, rent, interest and profit. In other words, it consists of the incomes earned by those involved in the production process.

Since GVA is the sum of all values added, it must also be the sum of all incomes generated: the sum of all wages and salaries, rent, interest and profit.

The second part of Figure 26.16 shows how these incomes are grouped together in the official statistics. As you can see, the total is the same as that in the top part Figure 26.16, even though the components are quite different.

Note that we do not include *transfer payments* such as social security benefits and pensions. Since these are not payments for the production of goods and services, they are excluded from GVA. Conversely, part of people's gross income is paid in income taxes. Since it is this *gross* (pre-tax) income that arises from the production of goods and services, we count wages, profits, interest and rent *before* the deduction of income taxes.

As with the product approach, if we are working out GVA, we measure incomes before the payment of taxes on products or the receipt of subsidies on products, since it is these pre-tax-and-subsidy incomes that arise from the value added by production. When working out GDP, however, we add in these taxes and subtract these subsidies to arrive at a *market price* valuation.

Pause for thought

If a retailer buys a product from a wholesaler for £80 and sells it to a consumer for £100, then the £20 of value that has been added will go partly in wages, partly in rent and partly in profits. Thus £20 of income has been generated at the retail stage. But the good actually contributes a total of £100 to GDP. Where, then, is the remaining £80 worth of income recorded?

The expenditure method

The final approach to calculating GDP is to add up all expenditure on final output (which will be at market prices). This will include the following:

- Consumer expenditure (*C*). This includes all expenditure on goods and services by households and by non-profit institutions serving households (NPISH) (e.g. clubs and societies).
- Government expenditure (*G*). This includes central and local government expenditure on final goods and services. Note that it includes non-marketed services (such as health and education), but excludes transfer payments, such as pensions and social security payments.
- Investment expenditure (*I*). This includes investment in capital, such as buildings and machinery. It also includes the value of any increase (+) or decrease (−) in inventories, whether of raw materials, semi-finished goods or finished goods.
- Exports of goods and services (*X*).
- Imports of goods and services (*M*). These have to be subtracted from the total in order to leave just the expenditure on domestic product. In other words, we subtract the part of consumer expenditure, government expenditure and investment that goes on imports. We also subtract the imported component (e.g. raw materials) from exports.

GDP (at market prices) $= C + G + I + X - M$

Table 26.4 shows the calculation of UK GDP by the expenditure approach.

From GDP to national income

Gross national income

Some of the incomes earned in the country will go abroad. These include wages, interest, profit and rent earned in this country by foreign residents and remitted abroad, and taxes on production paid to foreign governments and institutions (e.g. the EU). On the other hand, some of the incomes earned by domestic residents will come from abroad. Again, these can be in the form of wages, interest, profit or rent, or in the form of subsidies received from governments or institutions abroad.

Gross domestic product, however, is concerned with those incomes generated within the country, irrespective of ownership. If, then, we are to take 'net income from abroad' into account (i.e. these inflows minus outflows), we need a new measure. This is *gross national income (GNY)*.[4] It is defined as follows:

GNY at market prices $=$ GDP at market prices
$+$ net income from abroad

Thus GDP focuses on the value of domestic production, whereas GNY focuses on the value of incomes earned by domestic residents.

Net national income

The measures we have used so far ignore the fact that each year some of the country's capital equipment will wear out or become obsolete: in other words, they ignore capital *depreciation*. If we subtract an allowance for depreciation (or 'capital consumption') we get *net national income (NNY)*:

NNY at market prices $=$ GNY at market prices
$-$ depreciation

Table 26.5 shows GDP, GNY and NNY figures for the UK.

Table 26.4	UK GDP at market prices by category of expenditure, 2016	
	£ million	% of GDP
Consumption expenditure of households and NPISH (*C*)	1 292 379	65.8
Government final consumption (*G*)	369 660	18.8
Gross capital formation (*I*)	333 146	17.0
Exports of goods and services (*X*)	554 378	28.3
Imports of goods and services (*M*)	−595 415	−30.3
Statistical discrepancy	8 803	0.4
GDP at market prices	**1 963 311**	**100.0**

Source: *UK Economic Accounts time series dataset* (ONS)

Table 26.5	UK GDP, GNY and NNY and households' disposable income at market prices: 2016
	£ million
Gross domestic product (GDP)	**1 963 311**
Plus net income from abroad	−50384
Gross national income (GNY)	**1 912 927**
Less capital consumption (depreciation)	240 255
Net national income (NNY)	**1 672 672**
Households' disposable income[1]	**1 338 442**

[1]Includes NPISH sector.
Source: UK Economic Accounts time series dataset *and Blue Book time series dataset* (ONS)

Definitions

Gross national income (GNY) GDP plus net income from abroad.

Depreciation (capital) The decline in value of capital equipment due to age or wear and tear.

Net national income (NNY) GNY minus depreciation.

---

[4]In the official statistics, this is referred to as *GNI*. We use *Y* to stand for income, however, to avoid confusion with investment.

Households' disposable income

Finally, we come to a term called *households' disposable income.* It measures the income people have available for spending (or saving): i.e. after any deductions for income tax, national insurance, etc. have been made. It is the best measure to use if want to see how changes in household income affect consumption.

How do we get from GNY at market prices to households' disposable income? We start with the incomes that firms receive[9] from production (plus income from abroad) and then deduct that part of their income that is *not* distributed to households. This means that we must deduct taxes that firms pay – taxes on goods and services (such as VAT), taxes on profits (such as corporation tax) and any other taxes – and add in any subsidies they receive. We must then subtract allowances for depreciation and any undistributed profits. This gives us the gross income that households receive from firms in the form of wages, salaries, rent, interest and distributed profits.

---

[9]We also include income from any public-sector production of goods or services (e.g. health and education) and production by non-profit institutions serving households.

To get from this what is available for households to spend we must subtract the money households pay in income taxes and national insurance contributions, but add all benefits to households such as pensions and child benefit.

Households' disposable income	=	GNY at market prices
		− taxes paid by firms
		+ subsidies received by firms
		− depreciation
		− undistributed profits
		− personal taxes
		+ benefits

Households' disposable income is shown at the bottom of Table 26.5.

Definition

Households' disposable income The income available for households to spend, i.e. personal incomes after deducting taxes on incomes and adding benefits.

SUMMARY TO APPENDIX

1 National income is usually expressed in terms of gross domestic product. This is simply the value of domestic production over the course of the year. It can be measured by the product, expenditure or income methods.

2 The product method measures the values added in all parts of the economy.

3 The income method measures all the incomes generated from domestic production: wages and salaries, rent and profit.

4 The expenditure method adds up all the categories of expenditure: consumer expenditure, government expenditure, investment and exports. We then have to deduct the element of each that goes on imports in order to arrive at expenditure on domestic products. Thus $GDP = C + G + I + X - M$.

5 GDP at market prices measures what consumers pay for output (including taxes and subsidies on what they buy). Gross value added (GVA) measures what factors of production actually receive. GVA, therefore, is GDP at market prices minus taxes on products plus subsidies on products.

6 Gross national income (GNY) takes account of incomes earned from abroad (+) and incomes earned by people abroad from this country (−). Thus GNY = GDP plus net income from abroad.

7 Net national income (NNY) takes account of the depreciation of capital. Thus NNY = GNY − depreciation.

8 Households' disposable income is a measure of household income after the deduction of income taxes and the addition of benefits.

REVIEW QUESTIONS TO APPENDIX

1 Should we include the sale of used items in the GDP statistics? For example, if you sell your car to a garage for £2000 and it then sells it to someone else for £2500, has this added £2500 to GDP, nothing at all or merely the value that the garage adds to the car, i.e. £500?

2 What items are excluded from national income statistics that would be important to take account of if we were to get a true indication of a country's standard of living?

	BUY	SELL
EURO	1.3977	1.0422
USA	1.5684	
TURKEY	4.4936	3.29 7
AUSTRALIA	2.0389	1.5 16
N ZEALAND	2.1734	1.8113
CANADA	2.0090	1.4894
UAE	5.7142	4.2364
THAILAND	54.3866	39.3834
S AFRICA	22.2880	16.5239
SINGAPORE	2.0916	1.5146

The balance of payments and exchange rates

Business issues covered in this chapter

- What is meant by 'the balance of payments' and how do trade and financial movements affect it?
- How are exchange rates determined?
- What are the implications for business of changes in the exchange rate?
- What is the relationship between the balance of payments and exchange rates?
- How do governments and/or central banks seek to influence the exchange rate and what are the implications for other macroeconomic policies and for business?

In Part I, we examined the role of international trade for a country and for business, and saw how trade has grown rapidly since 1945. The world economy has become progressively more interlinked, with multinational corporations dominating a large proportion of international business. In this chapter, we return to look at international trade and the financial flows associated with it. In particular, we shall examine the relationship between the domestic economy and the international trading environment. This will involve considering both the balance of payments and the exchange rate.

We will first explain what is meant by the balance of payments. In doing so, we will see just how the various monetary transactions between the domestic economy and the rest of the world are recorded.

Then we will examine how rates of exchange are determined and how they are related to the balance of payments. Then we will see what causes exchange rate fluctuations and what will happen if the government intervenes in the foreign exchange market to prevent these fluctuations. Finally, we will consider how exchange rates have been managed in practice.

27.1 THE BALANCE OF PAYMENTS ACCOUNT

KI 27
p 341
A country's balance of payments account records all the flows of money between residents of that country and the rest of the world. *Receipts* of money from abroad are regarded as *credits* and are entered in the accounts with a positive sign. *Outflows* of money from the country are regarded as *debits* and are entered with a negative sign.

There are three main parts of the balance of payments account: the *current account*, the *capital account* and the *financial account*. Each part is then subdivided. We shall look at each part in turn, and take the UK as an example. Table 27.1 gives a summary of the UK balance of payments for 2017, while also providing an historical perspective. KI 27 p 341

Table 27.1	UK balance of payments		

	2017		Average 1987–2017 as % of GDP
	£m	% of GDP	
CURRENT ACCOUNT			
Balance on trade in goods	–137 035	–6.7	–4.1
Balance on trade in services	114 295	5.6	2.6
Balance of trade	**–22 740**	**–1.1**	**–1.5**
Income balance	–32 797	–1.6	–0.3
Net current transfers	–20 962	–1.0	–0.8
Current account balance	**–76 499**	**–3.7**	**–2.6**
CAPITAL ACCOUNT			
Capital account balance	**–1 721**	**–0.1**	**0.0**
FINANCIAL ACCOUNT			
Net direct investment	–63 279	–3.1	–0.7
Portfolio investment balance	62 553	3.1	2.9
Other investment balance	84 219	4.1	0.6
Balance of financial derivatives	–10 342	–0.5	0.0
Reserve assets	–6 799	–0.3	–0.2
Financial account balance	**66 352**	**3.2**	**2.6**
Net errors and omissions	**11 868**	**0.6**	**0.1**
Balance	*0*	*0.0*	*0.0*

Source: Based on data from Balance of Payments time series and series YBHA (Office for National Statistics)

The current account

The *current account* records payments for imports and exports of goods and services, plus incomes flowing into and out of the country, plus net transfers of money into and out of the country. It is normally divided into four subdivisions.

The trade in goods account. This records imports and exports of physical goods (previously known as 'visibles'). Exports result in an inflow of money and are therefore a credit item. Imports result in an outflow of money and are therefore a debit item. The balance of these is called the *balance on trade in goods* or *balance of visible trade* or *merchandise balance*. A *surplus* is when exports exceed imports. A *deficit* is when imports exceed exports.

The trade in services account. This records imports and exports of services (such as transport, tourism and insurance). Thus the purchase of a foreign holiday would be a debit since it represents an outflow of money, whereas the purchase by an overseas resident of a UK insurance policy would be a credit to the UK services account. The balance of these is called the *services balance*.

The balance of both the goods and services accounts together is known as the *balance on trade in goods and services* or simply the *balance of trade.*

The balance of trade directly affects the level of aggregate demand. To see this, we return to the circular flow of income model (introduced in Section 26.3). A balance of trade deficit, which as Table 27.1 shows, has been the norm in the UK for some time, represents a net leakage from the circular flow. This is because imports (a withdrawal) are greater than exports (an injection). Their effect is to reduce aggregate demand. Conversely, a balance of trade surplus is a net injection for an economy. Trade surpluses act to increase aggregate demand.

In equilibrium, injections must equal withdrawals. Thus a net withdrawal on the balance of trade must be offset by a net injection elsewhere: either investment exceeding saving and/or government expenditure exceeding tax revenue. This is why we often see countries with trade deficits also

Definitions

Current account of the balance of payments The record of a country's imports and exports of goods and services, plus incomes and transfers of money to and from abroad.

Balance on trade in goods or **balance of visible trade** or **merchandise balance** Exports of goods minus imports of goods.

Services balance Exports of services minus imports of services.

Balance on trade in goods and services or **balance of trade** Exports of goods and services minus imports of goods and services.

Figure 27.1 Current account balance in selected industrial countries

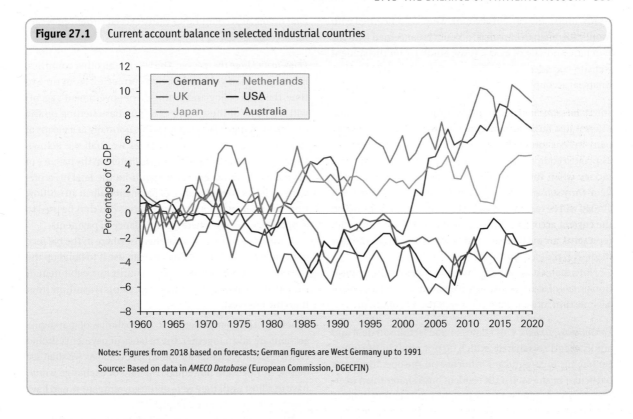

Notes: Figures from 2018 based on forecasts; German figures are West Germany up to 1991

Source: Based on data in *AMECO Database* (European Commission, DGECFIN)

running government budget deficits. The USA and the UK are two notable examples of countries with 'twin deficits'.

Income flows. These consist of wages, interest and profits flowing into and out of the country. For example, dividends earned by a foreign resident from shares in a UK company would be an outflow of money (a debit item).

Current transfers of money. These include government contributions to and receipts from the EU and international organisations, and international transfers of money by private individuals and firms. Transfers out of the country are debits. Transfers into the country (e.g. money sent from Greece to a Greek student studying in the UK) would be a credit item.

The *current account balance* is the overall balance of all the above four subdivisions. A *current account surplus* is where credits exceed debits. A *current account deficit* is where debits exceed credits.

Figure 27.1 shows the current account balance expressed as a percentage of GDP for a sample of countries. In conjunction with Table 27.1, we can also see that the UK has consistently run a current account deficit over the past three decades or so. This has been driven by a large trade deficit in goods.

The capital account

The *capital account* records the flows of funds into the country (credits) and out of the country (debits), associated with the acquisition or disposal of fixed assets (e.g. land or intangibles, such as patents and trademarks), the transfer of funds

by migrants, the payment of grants by the government for overseas projects, debt forgiveness by the government and the receipt of money for capital projects (e.g. from the EU's Agricultural Guidance Fund).

As Table 27.1 shows, the balance on the capital account is small in comparison to that on the current and financial accounts.

The financial account[1]

The *financial account* of the balance of payments records cross-border changes in the holding of shares, property, bank deposits and loans, government securities, etc. In other

---

Definitions

Balance of payments on current account The balance on trade in goods and services plus net incomes and current transfers.

Capital account of the balance of payments The record of transfers of capital to and from abroad.

Financial account of the balance of payments The record of the flows of money into and out of the country for the purpose of investment or as deposits in banks and other financial institutions.

---

[1]Prior to October 1998, this account was called the 'capital account'. The account that is *now* called the capital account used to be included in the transfers section of the current account. This potentially confusing change of names was adopted in order to bring the UK accounts in line with the system used by the International Monetary Fund (IMF), the EU and most individual countries.

words, unlike the current account, which is concerned with money incomes, the financial account is concerned with the purchase and sale of assets. (Case Study J.7 on the student website considers some of the statistics behind the UK's financial account.)

Direct investment. This involves a significant and lasting interest in a business in another country. If a foreign company invests money from abroad in one of its branches or associated companies in the UK, this represents an inflow of money when the investment is made and is thus a credit item. (Any subsequent profit from this investment that flows abroad will be recorded as an investment income outflow on the current account.) Investment abroad by UK companies represents an outflow of money when the investment is made. It is thus a debit item.

Note that what we are talking about here is the acquisition or sale of assets: e.g. a factory or farm, or the takeover of a whole firm, not the imports or exports of equipment.

Portfolio investment. This relates to transactions in debt and equity securities (shares), which do not result in the investor having any significant influence on the operations of a particular business. If a UK resident buys shares in an overseas company, this is an outflow of funds and is hence a debit item.

Other investment and financial flows. While direct and portfolio investments are concerned primarily with long-term investment, these consist primarily of various types of short-term monetary flows between the UK and the rest of the world. Deposits by overseas residents in banks in the UK and loans to the UK from abroad are credit items, since they represent an inflow of money. Deposits by UK residents in overseas banks and loans by UK banks to overseas residents are debit items. They represent an outflow of money.

Short-term monetary flows are common between international financial centres to take advantage of differences in countries' interest rates and changes in exchange rates.

In the financial account, credits and debits are recorded *net*. For example, UK investment abroad consists of the net acquisition of assets abroad (i.e. the purchase less the sale of assets abroad). Similarly, foreign investment in the UK consists of the purchase less the sale of UK assets by foreign residents. By recording financial account items net, the flows seem misleadingly modest. For example, if UK residents deposited an extra £100 billion in banks abroad but drew out £99 billion, this would be recorded as a mere £1 billion net outflow on the other investment and financial flows account. In fact,

total financial account flows vastly exceed current plus capital account flows.

Flows to and from the reserves. The UK, like all other countries, holds reserves of gold and foreign currencies. From time to time, the Bank of England (acting as the government's agent) will sell some of these reserves to purchase sterling on the foreign exchange market. It does this normally as a means of supporting the rate of exchange (as we shall see below). Drawing on reserves represents a *credit* item in the balance of payments accounts: money drawn from the reserves represents an *inflow* to the balance of payments (albeit an outflow from the reserves account). The reserves can thus be used to support a deficit elsewhere in the balance of payments.

Conversely, if there is a surplus elsewhere in the balance of payments, the Bank of England can use it to build up the reserves. Building up the reserves counts as a debit item in the balance of payments, since it represents an outflow from it (to the reserves).

When all the components of the balance of payments account are taken together, the balance of payments should exactly balance: credits should equal debits. As we shall see below, if they were not equal, the rate of exchange would have to adjust until they were or the government would have to intervene to make them equal.

When the statistics are compiled, however, a number of errors are likely to occur. As a result, there will not be a balance. To 'correct' for this, a **net errors and omissions** item is included in the accounts. This ensures that there will be an exact balance. The main reason for the errors is that the statistics are obtained from a number of sources, and there are often delays before items are recorded and sometimes omissions too.

Figure 27.2 graphically summarises the main accounts of the UK's balance of payments: current, capital and financial accounts. It presents each as a percentage of national income (see also right-hand column of Table 27.1). In conjunction with the net errors and omissions item, which

---

Pause for thought

With reference to Table 27.1 and Figure 27.2, compare the 2017 balance of payments figures (as percentages of GDP) with the averages for the period from 1987. In what ways were the 2017 figures more or less favourable than the averages since 1987?

Pause for thought

Where would interest payments on short-term foreign deposits in UK banks be entered on the balance of payments account?

Definition

Net errors and omissions A statistical adjustment to ensure that the two sides of the balance of payments account balance. It is necessary because of errors in compiling the statistics.

Figure 27.2 UK balance of payments as a percentage of GDP

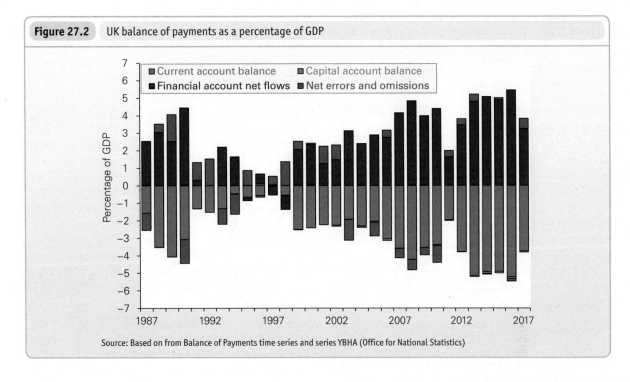

Source: Based on from Balance of Payments time series and series YBHA (Office for National Statistics)

averages close to zero over the long run, we can see how the accounts combine to give a zero overall balance. For much of the period since the late 1980s, current account deficits have been offset by surpluses on the financial account. (The persistence of the UK's current account deficit is discussed further in Case Study J.6 on the student website.)

27.2 THE EXCHANGE RATE

An exchange rate is the rate at which one currency trades for another on the foreign exchange market.

If you want to go abroad, you will need to exchange your pounds into euros, dollars, Swiss francs or whatever. To do this you may go to a bank. The bank will quote you that day's exchange rates: for example, €1.15 to the pound or $1.35 to the pound. It is similar for firms. If an importer wants to buy, say, some machinery from Japan, it will require yen to pay the Japanese supplier. It will thus ask the foreign exchange section of a bank to quote it a rate of exchange of the pound into yen. Similarly, if you want to buy some foreign stocks and shares or if companies based in the UK want to invest abroad, sterling will have to be exchanged into the appropriate foreign currency.

Likewise, if Americans want to come on holiday to the UK or to buy UK assets, or American firms want to import UK goods or to invest in the UK, they will require sterling. They will be quoted an exchange rate for the pound in the USA: say, £1 = $1.35. This means that they will have to pay $1.25 to obtain £1 worth of UK goods or assets.

Exchange rates are quoted between each of the major currencies of the world. These exchange rates are constantly changing. Minute by minute, dealers in the foreign exchange dealing rooms of the banks are adjusting the rates of exchange. They charge commission when they exchange currencies. It is therefore important for them to ensure that they are not left with a large amount of any currency unsold. What they need to do is to balance the supply and demand of each currency: to balance the amount they purchase to the amount they sell. To do this they will need to adjust the price of each currency, namely the exchange rate, in line with changes in supply and demand.

Pause for thought

How did the pound 'fare' compared with the US dollar, Australian dollar and the yen in the period from 1980? What conclusions can be drawn about the relative movements of these three currencies?

Not only are there day-to-day fluctuations in exchange rates, but also there are long-term changes in them. Figure 27.3 shows the average monthly exchange rates between the pound and various currencies since 1980.

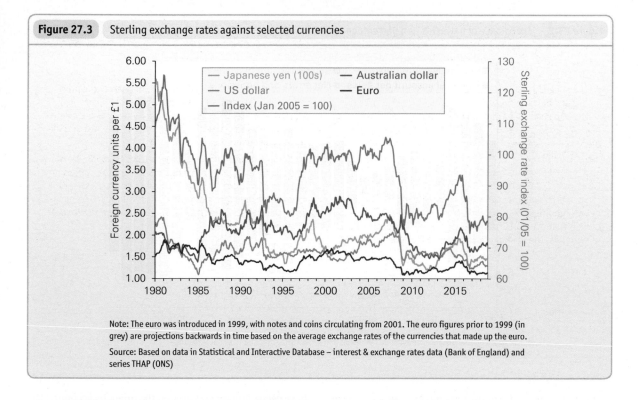

Figure 27.3 Sterling exchange rates against selected currencies

Note: The euro was introduced in 1999, with notes and coins circulating from 2001. The euro figures prior to 1999 (in grey) are projections backwards in time based on the average exchange rates of the currencies that made up the euro.

Source: Based on data in Statistical and Interactive Database – interest & exchange rates data (Bank of England) and series THAP (ONS)

One of the problems in assessing what is happening to a particular currency is that its rate of exchange may rise against some currencies (weak currencies) and fall against others (strong currencies). In order to gain an overall picture of its fluctuations, therefore, it is best to look at a weighted average exchange rate against all other currencies. This is known as the *exchange rate index* or the *effective exchange rate*.[2] The weight given to each currency in the index depends on the proportion of trade done with that country. Figure 27.3 also shows the sterling exchange rate index based on January 2005 = 100.

The determination of the rate of exchange in a free market

In a free foreign exchange market, the rate of exchange is determined by demand and supply. Thus the sterling exchange rate is determined by the demand and supply of pounds. This is illustrated in Figure 27.4.

For simplicity, assume that there are just two countries: the UK and the USA. When UK importers wish to buy goods from the USA or when UK residents wish to invest in the USA, they will *supply* pounds on the foreign exchange market in order to obtain dollars. In other words, they will go to banks or other foreign exchange dealers to buy dollars in exchange for pounds. The higher the exchange rate, the more dollars they will obtain for their pounds. This will, effectively, make US goods cheaper to buy and investment more profitable. Thus the *higher* the exchange rate, the *more*

pounds will be supplied. The supply curve of pounds, therefore, typically slopes upward.

When US residents wish to purchase UK goods or to invest in the UK, they will require pounds. They *demand* pounds by selling dollars on the foreign exchange market. In other words, they will go to banks or other foreign exchange dealers to buy pounds in exchange for dollars. The lower the dollar price of the pound (the exchange rate), the cheaper it will be for them to obtain UK goods and assets, and hence the more pounds they are likely to demand. The demand curve for pounds, therefore, typically slopes downward.

The equilibrium exchange rate will be where the demand for pounds equals the supply. In Figure 27.4, this will be at an exchange rate of £1 = $1.30. But what is the mechanism that equates demand and supply?

If the current exchange rate were above the equilibrium, the supply of pounds being offered to the banks would exceed the demand. For example, in Figure 27.4, if the exchange rate were $1.40, there would be an excess supply of pounds of $a - b$. Banks would not have enough dollars to exchange for all these pounds. But the banks make money by *exchanging* currency, not by holding on to it. They would

[2]www.bis.org/statistics/eer.htm.

> **Definition**
>
> **Exchange rate index** or **effective exchange rate** A weighted average exchange rate expressed as an index, where the value of the index is 100 in a given base year. The weights of the different currencies in the index add up to 1.

BOX 27.1   NOMINAL AND REAL EXCHANGE RATES

Searching for a real advantage

KI 38
p 500

We have seen, on several occasions, just how important the distinction between nominal and real is. But, what does this distinction mean when applied to exchange rates? A *nominal* bilateral exchange rate is simply the rate at which one currency exchanges for another. All exchange rates that you see quoted in the newspapers, on television or the Internet, or at travel agents, banks or airports, are nominal rates. Up to this point, we have considered solely nominal rates.

The *real* exchange rate is the exchange rate index adjusted for changes in the prices of exports (measured in the domestic currency) and imports (measured in foreign currencies). In other words, the nominal rate is adjusted for the *terms of trade*. The terms of trade are defined as the price index of exports divided by the price index of imports (P_X/P_M), expressed as a percentage, where prices are measured against a base year. In the base year, the terms of trade are assumed to be 100.

The terms of trade improve if a country has a higher rate of inflation for its exports than the weighted average inflation rate of the imports it buys from other countries. As they do, its real exchange rate index (RERI) rises relative to its nominal exchange rate index (NERI). The *real exchange rate index* can thus be defined as:

$$RERI = NERI \times P_X/P_M$$

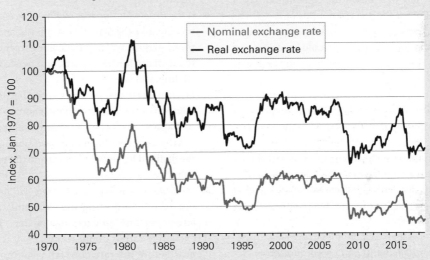

Sterling nominal and real exchange rate indices (January 1970=100)

Note: Exchange rate indices are BIS narrow indices comprising 26 and 27 countries for the nominal and real indices respectively; re-based by the authors, Jan 1970 = 100
Source: Based on data from *effective exchange rate indices* (Bank for International Settlements)

KI 38
p 500

Thus, if (a) a country's inflation is 5 per cent higher than the trade-weighted average of its trading partners (P_X/P_M rises by 5 per cent per year) and (b) its nominal exchange rate depreciates by 5 per cent per year (NERI falls by 5 per cent per year), its real exchange rate index will stay the same.

Take another example: if a country's export prices rise faster than the foreign currency prices of its imports (P_X/P_M rises), its real exchange rate will appreciate relative to its nominal exchange rate.

The real exchange rate thus gives us a better idea of the *quantity* of imports a country can obtain from selling a given quantity of exports. If the real exchange rate rises, the country can get more imports for a given volume of exports.

The chart shows the nominal and real exchange rate indices of sterling. As you can see, the real exchange rate has tended to rise over time relative to the nominal exchange rate. This is because the UK has, typically, had a higher rate of inflation than the weighted average of its trading partners.

The real exchange rate also gives a better idea than the nominal exchange rate of how competitive a country is. The lower the real exchange rate, the more competitive will be the country's exports. From the chart, we can see that the UK became less competitive between 1996 and 2001 and remained at similarly uncompetitive levels until 2008, thanks not only to a rise in the nominal exchange rate index, but also to higher inflation than its trading partners. However, as the financial crisis of the late 2000s unfolded, sterling depreciated sharply. Between July 2007 and October 2009, the nominal and real exchange rate indices fell by 26 per cent and 23 per cent respectively. They both depreciated again following the vote to leave the EU, with each falling by around 12 per cent between June and October of 2016.

If differences in inflation rates were to be reflected in longer-term changes in real exchange rates, what pattern should we observe in real exchange rates? Is this supported by the data in the chart?

 Download the broad-based effective exchange rate indices from the Bank for International Settlements for the euro, US dollar and British pound. Construct a time-series chart from January 1999, showing the nominal indices for the three currencies and then another chart showing the real indices. Prepare a short PowerPoint presentation containing these charts, which explains the concept of exchange rate indices and the economic significance of the patterns within the charts.

Definitions

Terms of trade The price index of exports divided by the price index of imports and then expressed as a percentage. This means that the terms of trade will be 100 in the base year.

Real exchange rate index (RERI) The nominal exchange rate index (NERI) adjusted for changes in the relative prices of exports and imports:
$$\text{RERI} = \text{NERI} \times P_X/P_M.$$

---

thus lower the exchange rate in order to encourage a greater demand for pounds and reduce the excessive supply. They would continue lowering the rate until demand equalled supply.

Similarly, if the rate were below the equilibrium, say at \$1.20, there would be a shortage of pounds of $c - d$. The banks would find themselves with too few pounds to meet all the demand. At the same time, they would have an excess supply of dollars. The banks would thus raise the exchange rate until demand equalled supply.

In practice, the process of reaching equilibrium is extremely rapid. The foreign exchange dealers in the banks are continually adjusting the rate as new customers make new demands for currencies. What is more, each bank has to watch closely what the others are doing. They are constantly in competition with each other and thus have to keep their rates in line. The dealers receive minute-by-minute updates on their computer screens of the rates being offered round the world.

Shifts in the currency demand and supply curves

KI 10 p 46 Any shift in the demand or supply curves will cause the exchange rate to change. This is illustrated in Figure 27.5, which this time shows the euro/sterling exchange rate. If the demand and supply curves shift from D_1 and S_1 to D_2 and S_2 respectively, the exchange rate will fall from €1.40 to €1.20. A fall in the exchange rate is called a *depreciation*. A rise in the exchange rate is called an *appreciation*.

But why should the demand and supply curves shift? The following are the major possible causes of a depreciation:

- *A fall in domestic interest rates.* UK rates would now be less competitive for savers and other depositors. More UK residents would be likely to deposit their money abroad (the supply of sterling would rise) and fewer people abroad would deposit their money in the UK (the demand for sterling would fall).

- *Higher rates of inflation in the domestic economy than abroad.* UK exports will become less competitive. The demand for sterling will fall. At the same time, imports will become relatively cheaper for UK consumers. The supply of sterling will rise.

- *A rise in domestic incomes relative to incomes abroad.* If UK incomes rise, the demand for imports, and hence the supply of sterling, will rise. If incomes in other countries fall, the demand for UK exports, and hence the demand for sterling, will fall.

- *Relative investment prospects improving abroad.* If investment prospects become brighter abroad than in the UK, perhaps because of better incentives abroad or because of worries about an impending recession in the UK, again, the demand for sterling will fall and the supply of sterling will rise.

- *Speculation that the exchange rate will fall.* If businesses involved in importing and exporting, and also banks and other foreign exchange dealers, think that the exchange rate is about to fall, they will sell pounds now before the rate does fall. The supply of sterling will thus rise.

Pause for thought

Go through each of the above reasons for shifts in the demand for and supply of sterling and consider what would cause an appreciation of the pound.

Definitions

Depreciation (currency) A fall in the free-market exchange rate of the domestic currency with foreign currencies.

Appreciation A rise in the free-market exchange rate of the domestic currency with foreign currencies.

Figure 27.4   Determination of the rate of exchange

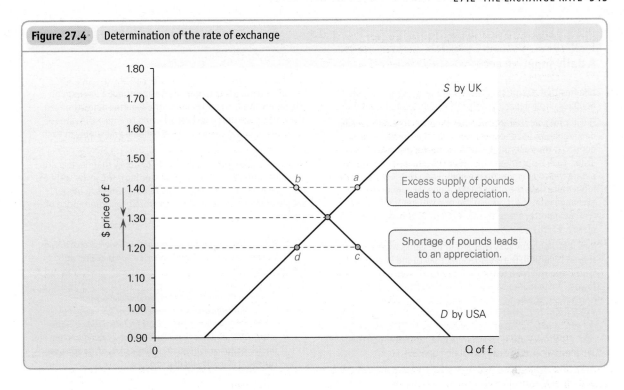

Excess supply of pounds leads to a depreciation.

Shortage of pounds leads to an appreciation.

Figure 27.5   Floating exchange rates: movement to a new equilibrium

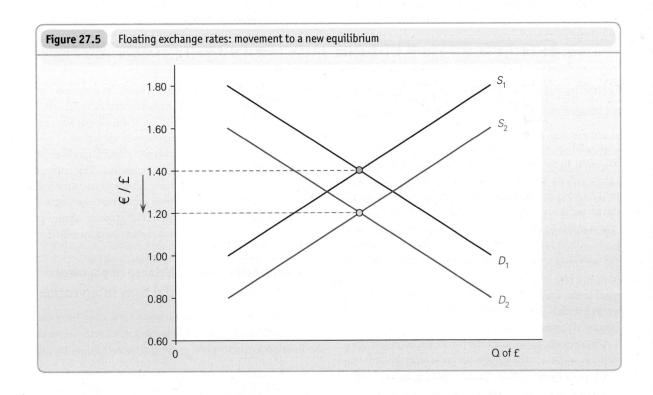

BOX 27.2   DEALING IN FOREIGN EXCHANGE

A daily juggling act

Imagine that a large car importer in the UK wants to import 5000 cars from Japan costing ¥15 billion. What does it do?

It will probably contact a number of banks' foreign exchange dealing rooms in London and ask them for exchange rate quotes. It thus puts all the banks in competition with each other. Each bank will want to get the business and thereby obtain the commission on the deal. To do this it must offer a higher rate than the other banks, since the higher the ¥/£ exchange rate, the more yen the firm will get for its money. (For an importer a rate of, say, ¥160 to £1 is better than a rate of, say, ¥140.)

Now it is highly unlikely that any of the banks will have a spare ¥15 billion. But a bank cannot say to the importer: 'Sorry, you will have to wait before we can agree to sell them to you.' Instead, the bank will offer a deal and then, if the firm agrees, the bank will have to set about obtaining the ¥15 billion. To do this it must offer Japanese who are *supplying* yen to obtain pounds at a sufficiently *low* ¥/£ exchange rate. (The lower the ¥/£ exchange rate, the fewer yen the Japanese will have to pay to obtain pounds.)

The banks' dealers thus find themselves in the delicate position of wanting to offer a *high* enough exchange rate to the

car importer in order to gain its business, but a *low* enough exchange rate in order to obtain the required amount of yen. The dealers are thus constantly having to adjust the rates of exchange in order to balance the demand and supply of each currency.

In general, the more of any foreign currency that dealers are asked to supply (by being offered sterling), the lower will be the exchange rate they will offer. In other words, a higher supply of sterling pushes down the foreign currency price of sterling.

 Assume that an American firm wants to import Scotch whisky from the UK. Describe how foreign exchange dealers will respond.

 Download the latest edition of the Triennial Central Bank Survey of foreign exchange markets (www.bis.org/publ/rpfx16.htm) published by the Bank for International Settlements (BIS). Briefly summarise the levels of activity on the foreign exchange markets, including details of the principal currencies being bought and sold.

27.3   EXCHANGE RATES AND THE BALANCE OF PAYMENTS

Exchange rates and the balance of payments: no government or central bank intervention

In a free foreign exchange market, the balance of payments will *automatically* balance. But why?

The credit side of the balance of payments constitutes the demand for sterling. For example, when people abroad buy UK exports or assets, they will demand sterling in order to pay for them. The debit side constitutes the supply of sterling. For example, when UK residents buy foreign goods or assets, the importers of them will require foreign currency to pay for them. They will thus supply pounds. A *floating exchange rate* will ensure that the demand for pounds is equal to the supply. It will thus also ensure that the credits on the balance of payments are equal to the debits: that the balance of payments balances.

This does not mean that each part of the balance of payments account separately balances, but simply that any current account deficit must be matched by a capital plus financial account surplus and vice versa.

For example, suppose initially that each part of the balance of payments did separately balance. Then let us assume that interest rates rise. This will encourage larger short-term financial inflows as people abroad are attracted to deposit money in the UK: the demand for sterling would shift to the right (e.g. from D_2 to D_1 in Figure 27.5). It will also cause smaller

short-term financial outflows as UK residents keep more of their money in the country: the supply of sterling shifts to the left (e.g. from S_2 to S_1 in Figure 27.5). The financial account will go into surplus. The exchange rate will appreciate.

As the exchange rate rises, this will cause imports to be cheaper and exports to be more expensive. The current account will move into deficit. There is a movement up along the new demand and supply curves until a new equilibrium is reached. At this point, any financial account surplus is matched by an equal current (plus capital) account deficit.

Exchange rates and the balance of payments: with government or central bank intervention

The government or central bank may be unwilling to let the country's currency float freely. Frequent shifts in the demand and supply curves would cause frequent changes in the

---

Definition

Floating exchange rate When the government does not intervene in the foreign exchange markets, but simply allows the exchange rate to be freely determined by demand and supply.

BOX 27.3   **THE IMPORTANCE OF INTERNATIONAL FINANCIAL MOVEMENTS**

How a current account deficit can coincide with an appreciating exchange rate

Since the early 1970s, most of the major economies of the world have operated with floating exchange rates. The opportunities that this gives for speculative gain have led to a huge increase in short-term international financial movements. Vast amounts of money transfer from country to country in search of higher interest rates or a currency that is likely to appreciate. This can have a bizarre effect on exchange rates.

If a country pursues an expansionary fiscal policy (i.e. cutting taxes and/or raising government expenditure), the current account will tend to go into deficit as extra imports are 'sucked in'. What effect will this have on exchange rates? You might think that the answer is obvious: the higher demand for imports will create an extra supply of domestic currency on the foreign exchange market and hence drive down the exchange rate.

In fact, the opposite is likely. The higher interest rates resulting from the higher domestic demand can lead to a massive inflow of short-term finance. The financial account can thus move sharply into surplus. This is likely to outweigh the current account deficit and cause an *appreciation* of the exchange rate.

Exchange rate movements, especially in the short term, are largely brought about by changes on the financial rather than the current account.

 Why do high international financial mobility and an absence of exchange controls severely limit a country's ability to choose its interest rate?

 Undertake a literature search on the topic of interest rates and exchange rate movements. Write a short review of your findings.

---

exchange rate. This, in turn, might cause uncertainty for businesses, which might curtail their trade and investment.

The central bank may thus intervene in the foreign exchange market. But what can it do? The answer to this will depend on its objectives. It may simply want to reduce the day-to-day fluctuations in the exchange rate or it may want to prevent longer-term, more fundamental shifts in the rate.

Reducing short-term fluctuations

Assume that the UK Government believes that an exchange rate of €1.20 to the pound is approximately the long-term equilibrium rate. Short-term leftward shifts in the demand for sterling and rightward shifts in the supply, however, are causing the exchange rate to fall below this level (see Figure 27.5). What can the Government do to keep the rate at €1.20?

Using reserves.   The Bank of England can sell gold and foreign currencies from the reserves to buy pounds. This will shift the demand for sterling back to the right. However, with the growth of short-term international financial flows it is, in practice, very difficult for individual central banks to influence exchange rates significantly by buying and selling currencies. The *combined* actions of central banks might, however, be more successful.

Borrowing from abroad.   The government can negotiate a foreign currency loan from other countries or from an international agency, such as the International Monetary Fund. It can then use these moneys to buy pounds on the foreign exchange market, thus again shifting the demand for sterling back to the right.

Raising interest rates.   If the Bank of England raises interest rates, it will encourage people to deposit money in the UK and encourage UK residents to keep their money in the country. The demand for sterling will increase and the supply of

sterling will decrease. However, the changes in interest rates necessary to manage the exchange rate may come into conflict with other economic objectives, such as keeping the rate of inflation on target.

Maintaining a fixed rate of exchange over the longer term

Governments may choose to maintain a fixed rate over a number of months or even years. The following are possible methods it can use to achieve this (we are assuming that there are downward pressures on the exchange rate: e.g. as a result of higher aggregate demand and higher inflation).

Contractionary policies.   This is where the government deliberately curtails aggregate demand by either *fiscal policy* or *monetary policy* or both.

Contractionary fiscal policy will involve raising taxes and/or reducing government expenditure. Contractionary monetary policy involves raising interest rates. Note that in this case we are not just talking about the temporary raising of interest rates to prevent a short-term outflow of money from the country, but the use of higher interest rates to reduce borrowing and hence dampen aggregate demand.

A reduction in aggregate demand will work in two ways:

- It reduces the level of consumer spending. This will directly cut imports since there will be reduced spending on Japanese electronics, German cars, Spanish holidays, and so on. The supply of sterling coming on to the foreign exchange market thus decreases.
- It reduces the rate of inflation. If inflation falls below that of other countries, this will make UK goods more competitive abroad, thus increasing the demand for sterling. It will also cut back on imports as UK consumers switch to the now more competitive home-produced goods. The supply of sterling falls.

Supply-side policies. This is where the government attempts to increase the long-term competitiveness of UK goods by encouraging reductions in the costs of production and/or improvements in the quality of UK goods. For example, the government may attempt to improve the quantity and quality of training and research and development.

Controls on imports and or foreign exchange dealing. This is where the government restricts the outflow of money, either by restricting people's access to foreign exchange or by the use of tariffs (customs duties) and quotas. For instance, the Icelandic Government put in place controls on foreign currency exchanges in the aftermath of the collapse of its largest banks in 2008 in order to bolster the krona and to build up foreign reserves.

> ### Pause for thought
>
> *What problems might arise if the government were to adopt this third method of maintaining a fixed exchange rate?*

27.4 FIXED VERSUS FLOATING EXCHANGE RATES

Are exchange rates best left free to fluctuate and be determined purely by market forces or should the government or central bank intervene to fix exchange rates, either rigidly or within bands?

Advantages of fixed exchange rates

Surveys reveal that most business people prefer relatively rigid exchange rates: if not totally fixed, then pegged for periods of time or at least where fluctuations are kept to a minimum. The following arguments are used to justify this preference.

Certainty. With fixed exchange rates, international trade and investment become much less risky, since profits are not affected by movements in the exchange rate.

KI 14
p 79

Assume a firm correctly forecasts that its product will sell in the USA for $1.50. It costs 80p to produce. If the rate of exchange is fixed at £1 = $1.50, each unit will earn £1 and hence make a 20p profit. If, however, the rate of exchange were not fixed, exchange rate fluctuations could wipe out this profit. If, say, the rate appreciated to £1 = $2 and, if units continued to sell for $1.50, they would now earn only 75p each, and hence make a 5p loss.

Little or no speculation. Provided the rate is *absolutely* fixed – and people believe that it will remain so – there is no point in speculating. For example, between 1999 and 2001, when the old currencies of the Eurozone countries were still used, but were totally fixed to the euro, there was no speculation that the German mark, say, would change in value against the French franc or the Dutch guilder.

Prevents governments pursuing 'irresponsible' macroeconomic policies. If a government deliberately and excessively expands aggregate demand – perhaps in an attempt to gain short-term popularity with the electorate – the resulting balance of payments deficit will force it to constrain demand again (unless it resorts to import controls).

Governments cannot allow their economies to have a persistently higher inflation rate than competitor countries without running into balance of payments crises, and hence a depletion of reserves. Fixed rates thus force governments (in the absence of trade restrictions) to keep the rate of inflation roughly to world levels.

Disadvantages of fixed exchange rates

Exchange rate policy may conflict with the interests of domestic business and the economy as a whole. A balance of payments deficit can occur even if there is no excess demand. For example, there can be a fall in the demand for the country's exports as a result of an external shock or because of increased foreign competition. If protectionism is to be avoided and if supply-side policies work only over the long run, the government (or central bank) will be forced to raise interest rates. This is likely to have two adverse effects on the domestic economy:

KI 41
p 506

- Higher interest rates may discourage business investment. This, in turn, will lower firms' profits in the long term and reduce the country's long-term rate of economic growth. The country's capacity to produce will be restricted and businesses are likely to fall behind in the competitive race with their international rivals to develop new products and improve existing ones.
- Higher interest rates will have a dampening effect on the economy by making borrowing more expensive and thereby cutting back on both consumer demand and investment. This can result in a recession with rising unemployment.

The problem is that, with fixed exchange rates, domestic policy is entirely constrained by the balance of payments. Any attempt to cure unemployment by cutting interest rates will simply lead to a balance of payments deficit and thus force governments to raise interest rates again.

Competitive contractionary policies leading to world depression. If deficit countries pursued contractionary policies, but surplus countries pursued expansionary policies, there would be no overall world contraction or expansion. Countries may be quite happy, however, to run a balance of payments surplus and build up reserves. Countries may thus competitively deflate – all trying to achieve a balance of payments surplus. But this is beggar-my-neighbour policy. Not all countries can have a surplus. Overall, the world must be in balance. The result of these policies is to lead to general world recession and a restriction in growth.

Problems of international liquidity. If trade is to expand, there must be an expansion in the supply of currencies acceptable for world trade (dollars, euros, pounds, gold, etc.): there must be adequate **international liquidity**. Countries' reserves of these currencies must grow if they are to be sufficient to maintain a fixed rate at times of balance of payments disequilibrium. Conversely, there must not be excessive international liquidity. Otherwise, the extra demand that would result would lead to world inflation. It is important under fixed exchange rates, therefore, to avoid too much or too little international liquidity.

The problem is how to maintain adequate control of international liquidity. The supply of dollars, for example, depends largely on US policy, which may be dominated by its internal economic situation rather than by a concern for the well-being of the international community. Similarly, the supply of euros depends on the policy of the European Central Bank, which is governed by the internal situation in the Eurozone countries.

Inability to adjust to shocks. With sticky prices and wage rates, there is no swift mechanism for dealing with sudden balance of payments crises – like that caused by a sudden increase in oil prices. In the short run, countries will need huge reserves or loan facilities to support their currencies. There may be insufficient international liquidity to permit this. In the longer run, countries may be forced into a depression, by having to deflate. The alternative may be to resort to protectionism or to abandon the fixed rate and *devalue.*

Speculation. If speculators believe that a fixed rate simply cannot be maintained, speculation is likely to be massive. If, for example, there is a large balance of payments deficit, speculative selling will worsen the deficit, and may itself force a devaluation. For example, speculation of this sort had disastrous effects on the Argentinean peso in 2002 (see Case Study J.11) and on the Mexican peso in 1995 and the Thai baht in 1997 (see Case Study J.12).

Advantages of a free-floating exchange rate

The advantages and disadvantages of free-floating rates are, to a large extent, the opposite of fixed rates.

Automatic correction. The government simply lets the exchange rate move freely to the equilibrium. In this way, balance of payments disequilibria are automatically and instantaneously corrected without the need for specific government policies.

No problem of international liquidity and reserves. Since there is no central bank intervention in the foreign exchange market, there is no need to hold reserves. A currency is automatically convertible at the current market exchange rate.

Insulation from external economic events. A country is not tied to a possibly unacceptably high world inflation rate, as it could be under a fixed exchange rate. It is also to some extent protected against world economic fluctuations and shocks.

Governments are free to choose their domestic policy. Under a floating rate, the government can choose whatever level of domestic demand it considers appropriate and simply leave exchange rate movements to take care of any balance of payments effect. Similarly, the central bank can choose whatever rate of interest is necessary to meet domestic objectives, such as achieving a target rate of inflation. The exchange rate will simply adjust to the new rate of interest – a rise in interest rates causing an appreciation, a fall causing a depreciation.

This freedom for the government and central bank is a major advantage, especially when the effectiveness of contractionary policies under fixed exchange rates is reduced by downward wage and price rigidity and when competitive contractionary policies between countries may end up causing a world recession.

Disadvantages of a free-floating exchange rate

Despite these advantages, there are still some potentially serious problems with free-floating exchange rates.

Unstable exchange rates. The less elastic are the demand and supply curves for the currency in Figure 27.4, the greater the change in exchange rate that will be necessary to restore equilibrium following a shift in either demand or supply. In the long run, in a competitive world with domestic substitutes for imports and foreign substitutes for exports, demand and supply curves are relatively elastic. Nevertheless, in the short run, given that many firms have contracts with specific overseas suppliers or distributors, the demands for imports and exports are less elastic.

Speculation. In an uncertain world, where there are few restrictions on currency speculation, where the fortunes and

> **Definitions**
>
> **International liquidity** The supply of currencies in the world acceptable for financing international trade and investment.
>
> **Devaluation** Where the government refixes the exchange rate at a lower level.

BOX 27.4 THE EURO/DOLLAR SEE-SAW

Ups and downs in the currency market

For periods of time, world currency markets can be quite peaceful, with only modest changes in exchange rates. But with the ability to move vast sums of money very rapidly from one part of the world to another and from one currency to another, speculators can suddenly turn this relatively peaceful world into one of extreme turmoil.

In this box we examine the huge swings of the euro against the dollar since the euro's launch in 1999.

First the down . . .

On 1 January 1999, the euro was launched and exchanged for $1.16. By October 2000, the euro had fallen to $0.85. The main cause of this 27 per cent depreciation was the growing fear that inflationary pressures were increasing in the USA and that, therefore, the Federal Reserve Bank would have to raise interest rates. At the same time, the Eurozone economy was growing only slowly and inflation was well below the 2 per cent ceiling set by the ECB. Thus, there was pressure on the ECB to cut interest rates.

The speculators were not wrong. As the following diagram shows, US interest rates rose and ECB interest rates initially fell and, when eventually they did rise (in October 1999), the gap between US and ECB interest rates soon widened again.

In addition to the differences in interest rates, a lack of confidence in the recovery of the Eurozone economy and a

continuing confidence in the US economy encouraged investment to flow to the USA. This inflow of finance (and lack of inflow to the Eurozone) further pushed up the dollar relative to the euro.

The low value of the euro against the dollar meant a high value of other currencies, including the pound, relative to the euro. This made it very difficult for companies outside the Eurozone to export to Eurozone countries and also for those competing with imports from the Eurozone (which had been made cheaper by the fall in the euro).

In October 2000, with the euro trading at around 85¢ the ECB plus the US Federal Reserve Bank, the Bank of England and the Japanese Central Bank all intervened on the foreign exchange market to buy euros. This arrested the fall and helped to restore confidence in the currency.

. . . then the up

The position changed completely in 2001. With the US economy slowing rapidly and fears of an impending recession, the Federal Reserve Bank reduced interest rates 11 times during the year: from 6.5 per cent at the beginning of the year to 1.75 per cent at the end (see the diagram). Although the ECB also cut interest rates, the cuts were relatively modest: from 4.75 at the beginning of the year to 3.25 at the end. With Eurozone interest rates now considerably above US rates, the euro began to rise.

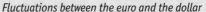

Fluctuations between the euro and the dollar

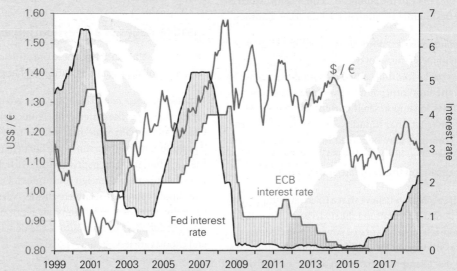

Notes: Federal reserve rate is the federal funds *effective* rate; ECB interest rate is the main refinancing operations rate
Sources: $/€ based on series XUMAERD, *Statistical Interactive Database* (Bank of England); interest rate data from *Federal Reserve Bank* and *European Central Bank*

In addition, a massive deficit on the US current account and a budget deficit nearing 4 per cent of GDP made foreign investors reluctant to invest in the US economy. In fact, investors were pulling out of the USA. One estimate suggests that European investors alone sold $70 billion of US assets during 2002. The result of all this was a massive depreciation of the dollar and appreciation of the euro, so that, by December 2004, the euro had risen to $1.36: a 60 per cent appreciation since July 2001!

In 2004–5, with the US economy growing strongly again, the Fed raised interest rates several times, from 1 per cent in early 2004 to 5.25 by June 2006. With growth in the Eurozone averaging just 1.8 per cent in 2004–5, the ECB kept interest rates constant at 2 per cent until early 2006. The result was that the euro depreciated against the dollar in 2005. But then the rise of the euro began again as the US growth slowed and Eurozone growth rose and people anticipated a narrowing of the gap between US and Eurozone interest rates.

In 2007 and 2008, worries about the credit crunch in the USA led the Fed to make substantial cuts in interest rates to stave off recession. In August 2007, the US federal funds rate was 5.25 per cent. It was then reduced on several occasions to stand at between 0 and 0.25 per cent by December 2008. The ECB, in contrast, kept the Eurozone rate constant at 4 per cent for the first part of this period and even raised it to 4.25 temporarily in the face of rapidly rising commodity prices. As a result, short-term finance flooded into the Eurozone and the euro appreciated again, from $1.37 in mid-2007 to $1.58 in mid-2008.

... then the steps down

Eventually, in September 2008, with the Eurozone on the edge of recession and predictions that the ECB would cut interest rates, the euro at last began to fall. It continued to do so as the ECB cut rates. However, with monetary policy in the Eurozone remaining tighter than in the USA, the euro began to rise again, only falling once more at the end of 2009 and into 2010 as US growth accelerated and speculators anticipated a tightening of US monetary policy.

Growing worries in 2010 about the level of government deficits and debt in various Eurozone countries, such as Greece, Portugal, Spain, Italy and Ireland, contributed to speculation and thus growing volatility of the euro. Throughout the first part of 2010, investors became increasingly reluctant to hold the euro as fears of debt default mounted. As such, the euro fell substantially from $1.44 in January 2010 to $1.19 in June. This was a 17 per cent depreciation.

Then, as support was promised by the ECB and IMF to Greece in return for deficit reduction policies, and similar support could be made available to other Eurozone countries with severe deficits, fears subsided and the euro rose again. By the end of October 2010, the euro was trading at $1.39. In April 2011, the euro rose to a high of $1.44.

Then began a dramatic fall in the euro as concerns grew over the Eurozone's sluggish recovery and continuing high debt levels. Speculators thus believed that Eurozone interest rates would have to continue falling. The ECB cut the main interest rate from 1.5 per cent in October 2011 in a series of steps to 0.05 per cent by September 2014.

With the ECB reducing interest rates and people increasingly predicting the introduction of quantitative easing (QE) (central banks increasing the money supply (see Box 30.4)), the euro depreciated during 2014. Between March and December 2014, it depreciated by 11 per cent against the dollar, while the euro exchange rate index depreciated by 4 per cent. With the announced programme of QE being somewhat larger than markets expected, in the week following the announcement in January 2015, the euro fell a further 2.3 per cent against the dollar, and the euro exchange rate index also fell by 2.3 per cent. The result was that the euro was trading at its lowest level against the US dollar since April 2003.

With the long-awaited rise in US interest rates starting in December 2015, a fall in the main EU rate to zero per cent in March 2016 and the announcement that the ECB's quantitative easing programme would continue to at least the end of 2017, the euro remained weak through 2016. Then, from 2017, the euro began to pick up against the dollar. This was despite a series of increases in the federal funds rate and the end-point for the ECB's quantitative easing programme being moved back to the end of 2018. The expectation now, with economic growth rates in the Eurozone rising close to levels in the USA, was that the ECB would soon begin to tighten monetary policy, albeit quite slowly.

The path of the euro shows that interest-rate volatility and divergence in interest rates between the USA and the Eurozone have been a major factor in the exchange-rate volatility between the euro and the dollar – itself a cause of uncertainty in international trade and finance. However, more recently concerns over the economic and fiscal health of national Eurozone governments have played a particularly important role in explaining fluctuations in the euro.

How important are relative interest rates in the long run in the determination of bilateral exchange rates, such as that between the dollar and the euro?

Find out what has happened to the euro/dollar exchange rate over the past 12 months. You can find the data from the Bank of England's Statistical Interactive Database. Explain why the exchange rate has moved the way it has.

policies of governments can change rapidly and where large amounts of short-term deposits are internationally 'footloose', speculation can be highly destabilising in the short run. At times of international currency turmoil such speculation can be enormous.

There has been a huge growth in international financial markets, with an average of between $3 trillion and $5 trillion worth of foreign exchange traded each day on foreign exchange markets. Such sums are greatly in excess of countries' foreign exchange reserves! If people think that the exchange rate will fall, then they will sell the currency and this will cause the exchange rate to fall even further, perhaps overshooting the eventual equilibrium.

An example of such overshooting occurred between July 2008 and March 2009 when the pound depreciated 14 per cent against the euro, 28 per cent against the US dollar, 34 per cent against the yen and the exchange rate index fell 17 per cent (see Figure 27.3). The nominal sterling exchange rate index fell by 17 per cent (see Figure in Box 27.1). Speculators were predicting that interest rates in the UK would fall further than in other countries and stay lower for longer. This was because recession was likely to be deeper in the UK, with inflation undershooting the Bank of England's 2 per cent target and perhaps even becoming negative. But the fall in the exchange rate represented considerable overshooting and the exchange rate index rose 8 per cent between March and June 2009.

This is just one example of the violent swings in exchange rates that have occurred in recent years. They occur even under managed floating exchange rate systems where governments have attempted to dampen such fluctuations!

The continuance of exchange rate fluctuations over a number of years is likely to encourage the growth of speculative holdings of currency. This can then cause even larger and more rapid swings in exchange rates.

> ## Pause for thought
>
> *If speculators on average gain from their speculation, who loses?*

Uncertainty for traders and investors. The uncertainty caused by currency fluctuations can discourage international trade and investment. To some extent, this problem can be overcome by using the *forward exchange market*. Here traders agree with a bank *today* the rate of exchange for some point in the future (say, six months' time). This allows traders to plan future purchases of imports or sales of exports at a known rate of exchange. Of course, banks charge for this service, since they are taking on the risks themselves of adverse exchange rate fluctuations.

 But dealing in the futures market only takes care of short-run uncertainty. Banks will not be prepared to take on the

risks of offering forward contracts for several years hence. Thus firms simply have to live with the uncertainty over exchange rates in future years. This may discourage long-term investment. For example, the possibility of exchange rate appreciation may well discourage firms from investing abroad, since a higher exchange rate will mean that foreign exchange earnings will be worth less in the domestic currency.

As Figure 27.3 showed, there have been large changes in exchange rates. Such changes make it difficult not only for exporters but importers, too, will be hesitant about making long-term deals. For example, a UK manufacturing firm signing a contract to buy US components in March 2008, when $2.00 worth of components could be purchased for £1, would find it a struggle to make a profit some five years later when less than $1.50 worth of US components could be purchased for £1!

Lack of discipline on the domestic economy. Governments may pursue irresponsibly inflationary policies (e.g. for short-term political gain). This will have adverse effects over the longer term as the government will, at some point, have to deflate the economy again, with a resulting fall in output and rise in unemployment.

Exchange rates in practice

Most countries today have a relatively free exchange rate. Nevertheless, the problems of instability that this can bring are well recognised and thus many countries seek to regulate or manage their exchange rate.

There have been many attempts to regulate exchange rates since 1945. By far the most successful was the Bretton Woods system, which was adopted worldwide from the end of the Second World War until 1971. This was a form of *adjustable peg* exchange rate, where countries pegged (i.e. fixed) their exchange rate to the US dollar, but could repeg it at a lower or higher level ('devalue' or 'revalue' their exchange rate) if there was a persistent and substantial balance of payments deficit or surplus.

With growing world inflation and instability from the mid-1960s, it became increasingly difficult to maintain fixed exchange rates and the growing likelihood of devaluations and revaluations fuelled speculation. The system was abandoned in the early 1970s. What followed was a period of

> ## Definitions
>
> **Forward exchange market** Where contracts are made today for the price at which a currency will be exchanged at some specified future date.
>
> **Adjustable peg** A system whereby exchange rates are fixed for a period of time, but may be devalued (or revalued) if a deficit (or surplus) becomes substantial.

exchange rate management known as *managed flexibility*. Under this system, exchange rates were not pegged but allowed to float. However, central banks intervened from time to time to prevent excessive exchange rate fluctuations. This system largely continues to this day.

However, on a regional basis, especially within Europe, there were attempts to create greater exchange rate stability. The European system, which began in 1979, involved establishing exchange rate bands: upper and lower limits within which exchange rates were allowed to fluctuate. The name given to the EU system was the *exchange rate mechanism*

(ERM). The hope was that, eventually, this would lead to a single European currency. With a single currency there can be no exchange rate fluctuations between the member states, any more than there can be fluctuations between the Californian and New York dollar or between the English, Scottish and Welsh pound.

The single currency, the euro, finally came into being in January 1999 (although notes and coins were not introduced until January 2002). (We examine the euro and its effects on the economies of the member states, and those outside too, in section 32.3.)

Definitions

Managed flexibility (dirty floating) A system of flexible exchange rates, but where the government intervenes to prevent excessive fluctuations or even to achieve an unofficial target exchange rate.

ERM (exchange rate mechanism) A semi-fixed system whereby participating EU countries allowed fluctuations against each other's currencies only within agreed bands. Collectively they floated freely against all other currencies.

SUMMARY

1a The balance of payments account records all payments to and receipts from foreign countries. The current account records payments for imports and exports, plus incomes and transfers of money to and from abroad. The capital account records all transfers of capital to and from abroad. The financial account records inflows and outflows of money for investment and as deposits in banks and other financial institutions. It also includes dealings in the country's foreign exchange reserves.

1b The whole account must balance, but surpluses or deficits can be recorded on any specific part of the account. Thus the current account could be in deficit but it would have to be matched by an equal and opposite capital plus financial account surplus.

2a The rate of exchange is the rate at which one currency exchanges for another. Rates of exchange are determined by demand and supply in the foreign exchange market. Demand for the domestic currency consists of all the credit items in the balance of payments account. Supply consists of all the debit items.

2b The exchange rate will depreciate (fall) if the demand for the domestic currency falls or the supply increases. These shifts can be caused by a fall in domestic interest rates, higher inflation in the domestic economy than abroad, a rise in domestic incomes relative to incomes abroad, relative investment prospects improving abroad or the belief among speculators that the exchange rate will fall. The opposite in each case would cause an appreciation (rise).

3a The government can attempt to prevent the rate of exchange from falling by central bank purchases of the domestic currency in the foreign exchange market, either by selling foreign currency reserves or by using foreign loans. Alternatively, the central bank can raise interest rates. The reverse actions can be taken if the government wants to prevent the rate from rising.

3b In the longer term, it can prevent the rate from falling by pursuing contractionary policies, protectionist policies or supply-side policies to increase the competitiveness of the country's exports.

4a Fixed exchange rates bring the advantage of certainty for the business community, which encourages trade and foreign investment. They also help to prevent governments from pursuing irresponsible macroeconomic policies.

4b Fixed exchange rates bring the disadvantages of conflicting policy goals, the tendency to lead to competitive contractionary policies, the problems of ensuring adequate international liquidity to enable intervention and the restrictions that fixed rates place upon countries when attempting to respond to system shocks.

4c The advantages of free-floating exchange rates are that they automatically correct balance of payments disequilibria; they eliminate the need for reserves; and they give governments a greater independence to pursue their chosen domestic policy.

4d On the other hand, a completely free exchange rate can be highly unstable, especially when the elasticities of demand for imports and exports are low; also speculation may be destabilising. This may discourage firms from trading and investing abroad. What is more, a flexible exchange rate, by removing the balance of payments constraint on domestic policy, may encourage governments to pursue irresponsible domestic policies for short-term political gain.

4e There have been various attempts to manage exchange rates, without them being totally fixed. One example was the Bretton Woods system: a system of pegged exchange rates, but where devaluations or revaluations were allowed from time to time. Another was the ERM, which was the forerunner to the euro. Member countries' currencies were allowed to fluctuate against each other within a band.

REVIEW QUESTIONS

1 The table below shows the items in the UK's 2000 balance of payments.

   a) Fill in the missing totals for (i) the balance of trade, (ii) the current account balance, (iii) the portfolio investment balance and (iv) for net errors and omissions.

   b) UK's GDP in 2000 was estimated at £1 089 131 million. Calculate each item on the balance of payments as a percentage of GDP.

   c) Compare the value of each item in £ millions and as percentages of GDP with those for 2017 in Table 27.1.

	£ millions
Current account:	
Balance on trade in goods	−33 688
Balance on trade in services	13 611
Balance of trade	
Income balance	4 159
Net current transfers	−9 759
Current account balance	
Capital account:	
Capital account balance	393
Financial account:	
Net direct investment	−77 620
Portfolio investment balance	
Other investment balance	3 701
Balance of financial derivatives	1 553
Reserve assets	−3 915
Financial account net flows	25 053
Net errors and omissions	

2 Assume that there is a free-floating exchange rate. Will the following cause the exchange rate to appreciate or depreciate? In each case, you should consider whether there is a shift in the demand or supply curves of sterling (or both) and which way the curve(s) shift(s).

   a) More electronic goods are imported from Japan.
      Demand curve *shifts left/shifts right/does not shift*
      Supply curve *shifts left/shifts right/does not shift*
      Exchange rate *appreciates/depreciates*

   b) Non-UK residents increase their purchases of UK government securities.
      Demand curve *shifts left/shifts right/does not shift*
      Supply curve *shifts left/shifts right/does not shift*
      Exchange rate *appreciates/depreciates*

   c) UK interest rates fall relative to those abroad.
      Demand curve *shifts left/shifts right/does not shift*
      Supply curve *shifts left/shifts right/does not shift*
      Exchange rate *appreciates/depreciates*

   d) The UK experiences a higher rate of inflation than other countries.
      Demand curve *shifts left/shifts right/does not shift*
      Supply curve *shifts left/shifts right/does not shift*
      Exchange rate *appreciates/depreciates*

   e) The result of a further enlargement of the EU is for investment in the UK by the rest of the EU to increase by a greater amount than UK investment in other EU countries.
      Demand curve *shifts left/shifts right/does not shift*
      Supply curve *shifts left/shifts right/does not shift*
      Exchange rate *appreciates/depreciates*

   f) Speculators believe that the rate of exchange will fall.
      Demand curve *shifts left/shifts right/does not shift*
      Supply curve *shifts left/shifts right/does not shift*
      Exchange rate *appreciates/depreciates*

3 What is the relationship between the balance of trade and the circular flow model?

4 Explain how the current account of the balance of payments is likely to vary with the course of the business cycle.

5 Is it a 'bad thing' to have a deficit on the direct investment part of the financial account?

6 Why may credits on a country's short-term financial account create problems for its economy in the future?

7 What is the relationship between the balance of payments and the rate of exchange?

8 What are the major advantages and disadvantages of fixing the exchange rate with a majority currency such as the US dollar?

9 Consider the argument that in the modern world of large-scale short-term international financial movements, the ability of individual countries to affect their exchange rate is very limited.

10 To what extent can dealing in forward exchange markets remove the problems of a free-floating exchange rate?

11 What adverse effects on the domestic economy may follow from (a) a depreciation of the exchange rate and (b) an appreciation of the exchange rate?

12 What will be the effects on the domestic economy under free-floating exchange rates if there is a rapid expansion in world economic activity? What will determine the size of these effects?

28 Chapter

The financial system, money and interest rates

Business issues covered in this chapter

- What are the functions of money?
- Why do banks play such a crucial role in the functioning of economies?
- What determines the amount of money in the economy? What causes it to grow and what is the role of banks in this process?
- What is the relationship between money and interest rates? What is the role of various financial institutions in this relationship?
- How will a change in the money supply affect the level of aggregate demand? How will this, in turn, affect the level of business activity?

In this chapter, we are going to look at the important role that money and financial institutions play in the economy. Changes in the behaviour of financial institutions and in the amount of money can have a powerful effect on all the major macroeconomic indicators, such as inflation, unemployment, economic growth, exchange rates, the balance of payments and the financial well-being of different sectors of the economy. Furthermore, the financial crisis of the late 2000s has helped to demonstrate the systemic importance of financial institutions to the economy.

The chapter begins by defining what is meant by money and examining its functions. Then we look at the operation of the financial sector and its role in determining the supply of money. It is here where we consider the possible causes of the financial crisis, its impact on financial institutions and some of the responses by central banks to the problems faced by financial institutions and, as a result, the economy.

We then turn to look at the demand for money. Here we are not asking how much money people would like. What we are asking is: how much of people's assets do they want to hold in the form of money?

Next, we put supply and demand together to show how free-market interest rates are determined. Finally, we see how changes in money supply and/or interest rates affect aggregate demand and the level of business activity. By using a framework known as the quantity theory of money, we see how monetary changes can have important, but possibly uncertain, effects on spending and national output.

28.1 THE MEANING AND FUNCTIONS OF MONEY

KI 27
p 341
Before going any further, we must define precisely what we mean by 'money' – not as easy a task as it sounds. Money is more than just notes and coins. In fact, the main component of a country's money supply is not cash, but deposits in banks and other financial institutions. The bulk of the deposits appear merely as bookkeeping entries in the banks' accounts.

This may sound very worrying. Will a bank have enough cash to meet its customers' demands? The answer in the vast majority of cases is yes. Only a small fraction of a bank's total deposits will be withdrawn at any one time and banks always seek to ensure that they have the ability to meet their customers' demands.

The chances of banks running out of cash are very low indeed. The only circumstance where this could become possible is if people lost confidence in a bank and started to withdraw money in what is known as a 'run on the bank'. This happened with the Northern Rock Bank in September 2007. But, in these circumstances, the central bank or government would intervene to protect people's deposits by making more cash available to the bank or, as a last resort, by nationalising the bank (as happened with Northern Rock in February 2008).

KI 14
p 79

What is more, the bulk of all but very small transactions are not conducted in cash at all. By the use of debit cards, credit cards, tap-and-pay-enabled mobile phones and cheques, most money is simply transferred from the purchaser's to the seller's bank account without the need for first withdrawing it in cash.

What items should be included in the definition of money? To answer this, we need to identify the *functions* of money.

The functions of money

The main purpose of money is for buying and selling goods, services and assets, i.e. as a **medium of exchange**. It also has two other important functions. Let us examine each in turn.

A medium of exchange

In a subsistence economy where individuals make their own clothes, grow their own food, provide their own entertainments, etc., people do not need money. If people want to exchange any goods, they will do so by barter. In other words, they will do swaps with other people.

The complexities of a modern developed economy, however, make barter totally impractical for most purposes. What is necessary is a medium of exchange that is generally acceptable as a means of payment for goods and services and as a means of payment for labour and other factor services. 'Money' is any such medium.

To be a suitable physical means of exchange, money must be light enough to carry around, come in a number of denominations, large and small, and not be easy to forge. Alternatively, money must be in a form that enables it to be transferred *indirectly* through some acceptable mechanism. For example, money in the form of bookkeeping entries in bank accounts can be transferred from one account to another by the use of mechanisms such as debit cards and direct debits.

A means of storing wealth

Individuals and businesses need a means whereby the fruits of today's labour can be used to purchase goods and services in the future. People need to be able to store their wealth: they want a means of saving. Money is one such medium in which to hold wealth. It can be saved.

A means of evaluation

Money allows the value of goods, services and assets to be compared. The value of goods is expressed in terms of prices and prices are expressed in money terms. Money also allows dissimilar things, such as a person's wealth or a company's assets, to be added up. Similarly, a country's GDP is expressed in money terms. Money thus serves as a 'unit of account'.

A means of establishing the value of future claims and payments

People often want to agree today the price of some future payment. For example, workers and managers will want to agree the wage rate for the coming year. Firms will want to sign contracts with their suppliers specifying the price of raw materials and other supplies. Money prices are the most convenient means of measuring future claims.

Pause for thought

Why may money prices give a poor indication of the value of goods and services?

What should count as money?

What items, then, should be included in the definition of money? Unfortunately, there is no sharp borderline between money and non-money.

Definition

Medium of exchange Something that is acceptable in exchange for goods and services.

Cash (notes and coin) obviously counts as money. It readily meets all the functions of money. Goods (fridges, cars and cabbages) do not count as money. But what about various financial assets such as savings accounts, bonds and shares? Do they count as money? The answer is: it depends on how narrowly money is defined.

Countries thus use several different measures of money supply. All include cash, but they vary according to what additional items are included. To understand their significance and the ways in which money supply can be controlled, it is first necessary to look at the various types of account in which money can be held and at the various financial institutions involved.

> **Pause for thought**
>
> *Why are debit cards not counted as money?*

28.2 THE FINANCIAL SYSTEM

In order to understand the role of the financial sector in determining the supply of money, it is important to distinguish different types of financial institution. Each type has a distinct part to play in determining the size of the money supply.

The banking system

Retail and wholesale banking

By far the largest element of money supply is bank deposits. It is not surprising then that banks play an absolutely crucial role in the monetary system. Banking can be divided into two main types: *retail banking* and *wholesale banking* (see Chapter 19). Most banks today conduct both types of business and are thus known as 'universal banks'.

Retail banking is the business conducted by the familiar high street banks, such as Barclays, Lloyds, HSBC, TSB, Santander, Royal Bank of Scotland and NatWest (part of the RBS group). They operate bank accounts for individuals and businesses, attracting deposits and granting loans at published rates of interest.

The other major type of banking is **wholesale banking**. This involves receiving large deposits from and making large loans to companies or other banks and financial institutions; these are known as *wholesale deposits and loans*. (See section 19.4 for a more detailed account of their activities.)

In the past, there were many independent wholesale banks, known as *investment banks*. These included famous names such as Morgan Stanley, Rothschild, SG Hambros and Goldman Sachs. With the worldwide financial crisis of 2008, however, most of the independent investment banks merged with universal banks, which conduct both retail and wholesale activities.

The rise of large universal banks has caused concern, however. In the UK, in 2010, the Coalition Government set up the Independent Commission on Banking (ICB). It was charged with investigating the structure of the banking system. The ICB proposed the *functional separation of banks*: the ring-fencing of retail from wholesale banking. It argued that, to ensure the stability of the financial system, the core activities of retail banks needed isolating from the potential contagion from risky wholesale banking activities.

The principal recommendations of the ICB were accepted and the Financial Services (Banking Reform) Act became law in December 2013. The Act defines *core activities* as facilities for accepting deposits, facilities for withdrawing money or making payments from deposit accounts and the provision of overdraft facilities. It gives regulators the power to exercise ring-fencing rules to ensure the effective provision of core activities. These include restricting the power of a ring-fenced body to enter into contracts and payments with other members of the banking group. The Act also gives the regulator restructuring powers so as to split banks up to safeguard their future.

It was agreed that the ringfencing of UK banking groups would become effective from the start of January 2019. The UK Government decided that banks with more than £25 billion of core retail deposits would be ring-fenced. Banks that were to be functionally separated from the rest of their groups were to be known as ring-fenced banks or RFBs.

Building societies

Building societies are UK institutions that, historically, have specialised in granting loans (mortgages) for house purchase.

> ## Definitions
>
> **Retail banking** Branch, telephone, postal and Internet banking for individuals and businesses at published rates of interest and charges. Retail banking involves the operation of extensive branch networks.
>
> **Wholesale banking** Where banks deal in large-scale deposits and loans, mainly with companies and other banks and financial institutions. Interest rates and charges may be negotiable.
>
> **Functional separation of banks** The ringfencing by banks of core retail banking services, such as deposit-taking, from riskier investment banking activities.

BOX 28.1 | FINANCIAL INTERMEDIATION

What is it that banks do?

Banks and other financial institutions are known as *financial intermediaries*. They all have the common function of providing a link between those who wish to lend and those who wish to borrow. In other words, they act as the mechanism whereby the supply of funds is matched to the demand for funds. In this process, they provide four important services.

Expert advice

Financial intermediaries can advise their customers on financial matters: on the best way of investing their funds and on alternative ways of obtaining finance. This should help to encourage the flow of savings and the efficient use of them.

Expertise in channelling funds

Financial intermediaries have the specialist knowledge to be able to channel funds to those areas that yield the highest return. This too encourages the flow of savings as it gives savers the confidence that their savings will earn a good rate of interest. Financial intermediaries also help to ensure that projects that are potentially profitable will be able to obtain finance. They help to increase allocative efficiency.

Maturity transformation

Many people and firms want to borrow money for long periods of time, and yet many depositors want to be able to withdraw their deposits on demand or at short notice. If people had to rely on borrowing directly from other people, there would be a problem here: the lenders would not be prepared to lend for a long enough period. If you had £100 000 of savings, would you be prepared to lend it to a friend to buy a house if the friend was going to take 25 years to pay it back? Even if there was no risk whatsoever of your friend defaulting, most people would be totally unwilling to tie up their savings for so long.

This is where a bank or building society comes in. It borrows money from a vast number of small savers, who are able to

withdraw their money on demand or at short notice. It then lends the money to house purchasers for a long period of time by granting mortgages (typically these are paid back over 20 to 30 years). This process whereby financial intermediaries lend for longer periods of time than they borrow is known as *maturity transformation*. They are able to do this because with a large number of depositors it is highly unlikely that they would all want to withdraw their deposits at the same time. On any one day, although some people will be withdrawing money, others will be making new deposits.

Risk transformation

You may be unwilling to lend money directly to another person in case they do not pay up. You are unwilling to take the risk. Financial intermediaries, however, by lending to large numbers of people, are willing to risk the odd case of default. They can absorb the loss because of the interest they earn on all the other loans. This spreading of risks is known as *risk transformation*. What is more, financial intermediaries may have the expertise to be able to assess just how risky a loan is.

Transmitting payments

In addition to channelling funds from depositors to borrowers, certain financial institutions have another important function. This is to provide a means of transmitting payments. Thus by the use of debit cards, credit cards, cheques, direct debits etc., money can be transferred from one person or institution to another without having to rely on cash.

 Which of the above are examples of economies of scale?

 Draw up a list of financial intermediaries and their functions in your local area.

They compete for the savings of the general public through a network of high street branches. Unlike banks, they are not public limited companies, their 'shares' being the deposits made by their investors. In recent years, many of the building societies have converted to banks (including all the really large building societies except the Nationwide).

In the past, there was a clear distinction between banks and building societies. Today, however, they have become much more similar, with building societies now offering current account facilities and cash machines, and retail banks granting mortgages. As with the merging of retail and wholesale banks, this is all part of a trend away from the narrow specialisation of the past and towards the offering of a wider and wider range of services. This was helped by a process of *financial deregulation*.

MFIs

Banks and building societies are both examples of what are called *monetary financial institutions (MFIs)*. This term is

Definitions

Financial deregulation The removal of or reduction in legal rules and regulations governing the activities of financial institutions.

Monetary financial institutions (MFIs) Deposit-taking financial institutions including banks, building societies and central banks.

Financial intermediaries The general name for financial institutions (banks, building societies, etc.) which act as a means of channelling funds from depositors to borrowers.

Maturity transformation The transformation of deposits into loans of a longer maturity.

Risk transformation The process whereby banks can spread the risks of lending by having a large number of borrowers.

used to describe all deposit-taking institutions, which also includes central banks (e.g. the Bank of England).

Deposit taking and lending

Balance sheets

Banks and building societies provide a range of *financial instruments*. These are financial claims, either by customers on the bank (e.g. deposits) or by the bank on its customers (e.g. loans). They are best understood by analysing the balance sheets of financial institutions, which itemise their liabilities and assets.

A financial institution's **liabilities** are those financial instruments involving a financial claim on the financial institution itself. As we shall see, these are largely *deposits* by customers, such as current and savings accounts. Its **assets** are financial instruments involving a financial claim on a third party: these are *loans,* such as personal and business loans and mortgages.

The total liabilities and assets for UK banks and building societies are set out in the balance sheet in Table 28.1. The aggregate size of the balance sheet at the end of Q3 2018 was equivalent to around four times the UK's annual GDP. This is perhaps the simplest indicator of the significance of banks in modern economies, like the UK.

Both the *size* and *composition* of banks' balance sheets have become the focus of the international community's effort to ensure the stability of countries' financial systems. The growth of the aggregate balance sheet in the UK is considered in Box 28.2. We now focus on the composition of the balance

sheet, looking in more detail at the various types of liabilities and assets.

Liabilities

Customers' deposits in banks (and other MFIs) are liabilities to these institutions. This means simply that the customers have the claim on these deposits and thus the institutions are legally liable to meet the claims.

There are four major types of deposit: sight deposits, time deposits, 'repos' and certificates of deposit.

Sight deposits are any deposits that can be withdrawn on demand by the depositor without penalty. In the past, sight accounts did not pay interest. Today, however, there are some sight accounts that do.

The most familiar form of sight deposits are current accounts at banks. Depositors are normally issued with cheque books and/or debit cards (e.g. Visa debit or Mastercard's Maestro) which enable them to spend the money directly without first having to go to the bank and draw the

> ### Definitions
>
> **Financial instruments** Financial products resulting in a financial claim by one party over another.
>
> **Liabilities** Claims by others on an individual or institution; debts of that individual or institution.
>
> **Assets** Possessions of an individual or institution, or claims held on others.
>
> **Sight deposits** Deposits that can be withdrawn on demand without penalty.

Table 28.1 Balance sheet of UK MFIs (end of September 2018)

Sterling liabilities	£bn	%	Sterling assets	£bn	%
Sight deposits		46.2	Notes and coins	9.8	0.3
UK MFIs	46.6		Balances with UK central bank		12.7
UK public sector	17.1		Reserve balances	472.9	
UK private sector	1450.4		Cash ratio deposits	7.6	
Non-residents	199.2		Loans		8.2
Time deposits		29.1	UK MFIs	191.3	
UK MFIs	272.5		UK MFIs' CDs, etc.	2.8	
UK public sector	15.3		Non-residents	114.3	
UK private sector	631.2		Bills and acceptances	10.5	0.3
Non-residents	158.9		Reverse repos	331.4	8.8
Repos	176.2	4.7	Investments	425.9	11.3
CDs and other short-term papers	264.1	7.1	Advances	2131.4	56.3
Capital and other internal funds	445.9	12.0	Other assets	85.1	2.3
Other liabilities	32.6	0.9			
Total sterling liabilities	3710.0	100.0	**Total sterling assets**	3783.0	100.0
Foreign currency liabilities	4325.3		Total foreign currency assets	4252.3	
Total liabilities	8035.3		Total assets	8035.3	

Source: Based on data in *Bankstats* (Bank of England), Table B1.4, Data published October 2018

money out in cash. In the case of debit cards, the person's account is electronically debited when the purchase is made and the card is 'swiped' across the machine. This process is known as EFTPOS (electronic funds transfer at point of sale).

An important feature of current accounts is that banks often allow customers to be overdrawn. That is, they can draw on their account and make payments to other people in excess of the amount of money they have deposited.

Time deposits require notice of withdrawal. However, they normally pay a higher rate of interest than sight accounts. With some types of account, a depositor can withdraw a certain amount of money on demand, but will have to pay a penalty of so many days' interest. They are not cheque-book or debit-card accounts. The most familiar forms of time deposits are the deposit and savings accounts in banks and the various savings accounts in building societies. No overdraft facilities exist with time deposits.

A substantial proportion of time deposits are from the *banking sector*: i.e. other banks and other financial institutions. Inter-bank lending grew over the years as money markets were deregulated and as deposits increasingly moved from one currency to another to take advantage of different rates of interest between different countries. A large proportion of overseas deposits are from foreign banks.

Sale and repurchase agreements ('repos'). If banks have a temporary shortage of funds, they can sell some of their financial assets to other banks or to the central bank – the Bank of England in the UK and the European Central Bank in the Eurozone (see below), and later repurchase them on some agreed date, typically a fortnight later. These *sale and repurchase agreements (repos)* are, in effect, a form of loan, the bank borrowing for a period of time using some of its financial assets as the security for the loan. One of the major assets to use in this way are government bonds, normally called 'gilt-edged securities' or simply 'gilts' (see below). Sale and repurchase agreements involving gilts are known as *gilt repos*. Gilt repos play a vital role in the operation of monetary policy (see section 30.1).

Certificates of deposit. **Certificates of deposit** (CDs) are certificates issued by banks to customers (usually firms) for large deposits of a fixed term (e.g. £100 000 for 18 months). They can be sold by one customer to another, and thus provide a means whereby the holders can get money quickly if they need it without the *banks* that have issued the CD having to supply the money. (This makes them relatively 'liquid' to the depositor but 'illiquid' to the bank: we examine this below.) The use of CDs has grown rapidly in recent years. Their use by firms has meant that, at a wholesale level, sight accounts have become *less* popular.

Capital and other funds. This consists largely of the share capital in banks. Since shareholders cannot take their money out of banks, it provides a source of funding to meet sudden

increases in withdrawals from depositors and to cover bad debts.

It is vital that banks have sufficient capital. As we shall see, an important part of the response to the financial crisis has been to require banks to hold relatively larger amounts of capital. At the end of 2008, the aggregate amount of sterling capital held by banks based in the UK was equivalent to 9.7 per cent of their sterling liabilities. By 2018, this had risen to around 12 per cent.

Assets

Banks' financial assets are its claims on others. There are three main categories of assets.

Cash and reserve balances in the central bank (Bank of England in the UK, ECB in the Eurozone). Banks need to hold a certain amount of their assets as cash. This is used largely to meet the day-to-day demands of customers. This, however, is typically less than 1 per cent of their total sterling assets as the demand for cash at any one time represents only a tiny fraction of total deposits in banks.

They also keep 'reserve balances' in the central bank. In the UK, these earn interest at the Bank of England's repo rate (or 'Bank Rate' as it is called), if kept within an agreed target range. These are like the banks' own current accounts and are used for clearing purposes (i.e. for settling the day-to-day payments between banks). They can be withdrawn in cash on demand. With interbank lending being seen as too risky during the crisis of 2008, many banks resorted to depositing surplus cash in the Bank of England, even though the Bank Rate was lower than interbank interest rates.

In the UK, banks and building societies are also required to deposit a small fraction of their assets as 'cash ratio deposits' with the Bank of England. These cannot be drawn on demand and earn no interest.

As you can see from Table 28.1, cash and balances in the Bank of England account for a fairly small proportion of banks' assets. The vast majority of banks' assets remain in the form of various types of loan – to individuals and firms, to other financial institutions and to the government. These are 'assets' because they represent claims that the banks have on

---

Definitions

Time deposits Deposits that require notice of withdrawal or where a penalty is charged for withdrawals on demand.

Sale and repurchase agreements (repos) An agreement between two financial institutions whereby one, in effect, borrows from another by selling its assets, agreeing to buy them back (repurchase them) at a fixed price and on a fixed date.

Certificates of deposit Certificates issued by banks for fixed-term interest-bearing deposits. They can be resold by the owner to another party.

other people. Loans can be grouped into two types: short and long term.

Short-term loans. These are in the form of market loans, bills of exchange or reverse repos. The market for these various types of loan is known as the ***money market***.

- ***Market loans*** are made primarily to other banks or financial institutions. They consist of (a) money lent 'at call' (i.e. reclaimable on demand or at 24 hours' notice), (b) money lent 'at short notice' (i.e. money lent for a few days) and (c) CDs (i.e. certificates of deposit made in other banks or building societies).

- ***Bills of exchange*** are loans either to companies (commercial bills) or to the government (Treasury bills). These are, as explained in section 19.4, in effect, an IOU, with the company issuing them (in the case of commercial bills) or the Bank of England (in the case of Treasury bills) promising to pay the holder a specified sum on a particular date (typically three months later). Since bills do not pay interest, they are sold below their face value (at a 'discount') but redeemed on maturity at face value. This enables the purchaser, in this case the bank, to earn a return. The market for new or existing bills is therefore known as the ***discount market***.
- ***Reverse repos***. When a sale and repurchase agreement is made, the financial institution *purchasing* the assets (e.g. gilts) is, in effect, giving a short-term loan. The other party agrees to buy back the assets (i.e. pay back the loan) on a set date. The assets temporarily held by the bank making the loan are known as 'reverse repos'.

Longer-term loans. These consist primarily of loans to customers, both personal customers and businesses. These loans, also known as *advances,* are of four main types: fixed-term (repayable in instalments over a set number of years, typically six months to five years), overdrafts (often for an unspecified term), outstanding balances on credit-card accounts and mortgages (typically for 25 years).

Banks also make *investments*. These are partly in government bonds ('gilts'), which are effectively loans to the government. The government sells bonds, which then pay a fixed sum each year in interest. Once issued, bonds can then be bought and sold on the Stock Exchange. Banks are normally only prepared to buy bonds that have less than five years to maturity. Banks also invest in other financial institutions, including subsidiary financial institutions.

Taxing the banks

Bank levy. In January 2011, the UK introduced the bank levy: a tax on the *liabilities* of banks and building societies operating in the UK. The tax was to be applied to the global balance sheet of banks with their HQs in the UK and for subsidiaries of non-UK banks just to their UK activities.

The levy is founded on two key principles. First, the revenues raised should be able to meet the full fiscal costs of any future support for financial institutions. Second, it should provide banks with incentives to reduce risk-taking behaviour and so reduce the likelihood of future financial crises.

The UK bank levy has two rates: a full rate on taxable liabilities with a maturity of less than 1 year and a half rate on taxable liabilities with a maturity of more than 1 year. This differential is intended is to discourage excessive short-term borrowing by the banks in their use of wholesale funding.

Not all liabilities are subject to the levy. First, it is not imposed on the first £20 billion of liabilities. This is to encourage small banks (note that the largest UK banks, such as HSBC, Barclays and RBS, each have liabilities of over £2 trillion). Second, various liabilities are excluded. These are: (a) gilt repos; (b) retail deposits insured by public schemes such as the UK's Financial Services Compensation Scheme, which guarantees customers' deposits of up to £85 000; (c) a large part of a bank's capital known as Tier 1 capital (see below) – the argument here is that it is important for banks to maintain sufficient funds to meet the demands of its depositors.

Banks are also able to offset against their taxable liabilities holdings of highly liquid assets, such as Treasury bills and cash reserves at the Bank of England. These exclusions and deductions are designed to encourage banks to engage in less risky lending.

The levy rates initially were set at 0.075 and 0.0375 per cent, with the intention that the levy raise at least £2.5 billion each year. As the aggregate balance sheets of banks began to shrink, the rates were increased several times. Then, in the 2015 Budget, it was announced that the levy rates, which at time were 0.21 and 0.105 per cent, were to be gradually reduced until, in 2021, they would be 0.1 and 0.05 per cent. Also, with concerns about the effect of the levy on the international competitiveness of UK global banks, it was announced that, from 2021, the levy would apply only to UK balance sheets.

Definitions

Money market The market for short-term loans and deposits.

Market loans Loans made to other financial institutions.

Bill of exchange A certificate promising to repay a stated amount on a certain date, typically three months from the issue of the bill. Bills pay no interest as such, but are sold at a discount and redeemed at face value, thereby earning a rate of discount for the purchaser.

Discount market An example of a money market in which new or existing bills are bought and sold.

Reverse repos When gilts or other assets are *purchased* under a sale and repurchase agreement. They become an asset of the purchaser.

Bank corporation tax surcharge. The 2015 Budget also saw the announcement of a new 8 per cent corporation tax surcharge on banks. This marked a shift in the tax base from banks' balance sheets to their profits. The 8 per cent surcharge was introduced in January 2016 for all banks with annual profits over £25 million. With the main corporation tax rate at 18 per cent when introduced, the surcharge on banks meant that their effective corporation tax rate was 26 per cent. The Office for Budget Responsibility estimated at the time of the announcement that the surcharge would raise £6.5 billion between 2016/17 and 2020/21, while the revenues from the Bank Levy would fall from £3.1 billion to £2.2 billion.

Profitability, liquidity and capital adequacy

As we have seen, banks keep a range of liabilities and assets. The balance of items in this range is influenced by three important considerations: profitability, liquidity and capital adequacy.

Profitability

Profits are made by lending money out at a higher rate of interest than that paid to depositors. The average interest rate received by banks on their assets is greater than that paid by them on their liabilities.

Liquidity

The *liquidity* of an asset is the ease with which it can be converted into cash without loss. Cash itself, by definition, is perfectly liquid.

Some assets, such as money lent at call to other financial institutions, are highly liquid. Although not actually cash, these assets can be converted into cash on demand with no financial penalty. Other short-term interbank lending is also very liquid. The only issue here is one of confidence that the money will actually be repaid. This was a worry in the financial crisis of 2008/9, when many banks stopped lending to each other on the interbank market for fear that the borrowing bank might become insolvent.

Other assets, however, are much less liquid. Personal loans to the general public or mortgages for house purchase can only be redeemed by the bank as each instalment is paid. Other advances for fixed periods are only repaid at the end of that period. This was why securitisation of mortgages became popular with banks as it effectively made their mortgage assets tradable and hence more liquid (see Box 28.3).

Banks must always be able to meet the demands of their customers for withdrawals of money. To do this, they must hold sufficient cash or other assets that can be readily turned into cash. In other words, banks must maintain sufficient liquidity.

The balance between profitability and liquidity

Profitability is the major aim of banks and most other financial institutions. However, the aims of profitability and liquidity tend to conflict. In general, the more liquid an asset, the less profitable it is, and vice versa. Personal and business loans to customers are profitable to banks, but highly illiquid. Cash is totally liquid, but earns no profit. Thus financial institutions like to hold a range of assets with varying degrees of liquidity and profitability.

For reasons of *profitability,* banks will want to 'borrow short' (at low rates of interest, such as people's deposits in current accounts) and 'lend long' (at higher rates of interest, such as on personal loans or mortgages). The difference in the average maturity of loans and deposits is known as the *maturity gap*. In general terms, the larger the maturity gap between loans and deposits, the greater the profitability. For reasons of *liquidity,* however, banks will want a relatively small gap: if there is a sudden withdrawal of deposits, banks will need to be able to call in enough loans.

The ratio of an institution's liquid assets to total assets (or liabilities) is known as its *liquidity ratio*. For example, if a bank had £100 million of assets, of which £10 million were liquid and £90 million were illiquid, the bank would have a 10 per cent liquidity ratio. If a financial institution's liquidity ratio is too high, it will make too little profit. If the ratio is too low, there is a risk that customers' demands may not be able to be met: this would cause a crisis of confidence and possible closure. Institutions thus have to make a judgement as to what liquidity ratio is best – one that is neither too high nor too low.

Balances in the central bank, short-term loans (i.e. those listed above) and government bonds with less than 12 months to maturity (and hence tradable now at near their face value) would normally be regarded as liquid assets.

As Box 28.2 explains, over the years, banks had reduced their liquidity ratios (i.e. the ratio of liquid assets to total assets). This was not a problem as long as banks could always finance lending to customers by borrowing on the interbank market. In 2008, however, banks became increasingly worried about bad debt. They thus felt the need to increase their liquidity ratios and hence cut back on lending and chose to keep a higher proportion of deposits in liquid form. In the UK, for example, banks substantially increased their level of reserves in the Bank of England.

Secondary marketing and securitisation

As we have seen, one way of reconciling the two conflicting aims of liquidity and profitability is to hold a mixture of

---

> ## Definitions
>
> **Liquidity** The ease with which an asset can be converted into cash without loss.
>
> **Maturity gap** The difference in the average maturity of loans and deposits.
>
> **Liquidity ratio** The proportion of a bank's total assets held in liquid form.

BOX 28.2 **GROWTH OF BANKS' BALANCE SHEETS**

The rise of wholesale funding

Banks' traditional funding model relied heavily on deposits as the source of funds for loans. However, new ways for financial institutions to access funds to generate new loans evolved, especially in the years preceding the financial crisis of 2008. These reflected the deregulation of financial markets and the rapid pace of financial innovation.

Seeds of the 2007–8 crisis

Increasingly, financial institutions made greater use of *wholesale funds*. These are funds obtained mainly from other financial institutions. This coincided too with the emergence of a process known as *securitisation*. This involves the conversion of non-marketable banks' assets, such as residential mortgages, which have regular income streams (e.g. from payments of interest and capital), into assets that could be traded, known as 'tradable financial instruments'. These asset-backed securities provide lenders who originate the loans with a source of funds for further loans. Therefore, securitisation became another means by which lenders could raise capital. Securitisation is discussed further in Box 28.3.

With an increasing use of money markets by financial institutions, vast sums of funds became available for lending. One consequence of this is illustrated in the chart: the expansion of the aggregate balance sheet. The balance sheet grew from £2.6 trillion (2.75 times GDP) in 1998 to £8.5 trillion (5.5 times GDP) in 2010.

The growth in banks' balance sheets was accompanied by a change in their composition.

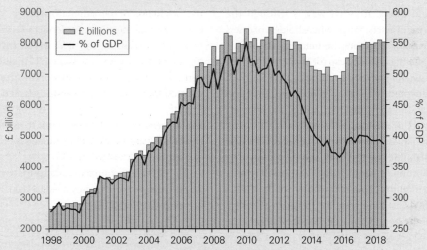

Aggregate balance sheet of UK banks and building societies

Note: Since 2010, all loans securitised by MFIs are recorded on MFI balance sheets.
Sources: (i) Data showing liabilities of banks and building societies based on series LPMALOA and RPMTBJF (up to the end of 2009) and RPMB3UQ (from 2010) from *Statistical Interactive Database,* Bank of England (data published 29 October 2018, not seasonally adjusted).
(ii) GDP based on series YBHA, Office for National Statistics (GDP figures are the sum of the latest four quarters).

First, the profile of banks' assets became less liquid as they extended more long-term credit to households and firms. Assets generally became more risky too, as banks increasingly granted mortgages of 100 per cent or more of the value of houses – a problem for banks if house prices fell and they were forced to repossess.

Second, there was a general increase in the use of fixed-interest bonds as opposed to ordinary shares (equities) for raising capital. The ratio of bonds to equity capital is known as *gearing* (or *leverage*) *ratio.* The increase in leverage meant that banks were operating with lower and lower levels of loss-absorbing capital, such as ordinary shares. If banks run at a loss, dividends on shares can be suspended; the payment of interest on fixed interest bonds cannot. This meant that, as the crisis unfolded, policy makers were facing a liquidity problem, not among one or two financial institutions, but across the financial system.

The market failure we are describing is a form of *co-ordination failure*. When one bank pursues increased earnings by borrowing from and lending to other financial institutions, this is not necessarily a problem. But, if many institutions build their balance sheets by borrowing from and lending to *each other,* then it becomes a problem for the whole financial system. The apparent increase in liquidity for individual banks, on which they base credit, is not an overall increase in liquidity for the financial system as a whole. The effect is to create a credit bubble.

The dangers of the bubble for the financial system and beyond were magnified by the increasingly tangled web of inter-dependencies between financial institutions, both nationally and globally. There was a danger that this complexity was

Definitions

Gearing or **leverage** (US term) The ratio of debt capital to equity capital: in other words, the ratio of borrowed capital (e.g. bonds) to shares.

Co-ordination failure When a group of firms (e.g. banks) acting independently could have achieved a more desirable outcome if they had co-ordinated their decision making.

masking fundamental weaknesses of many financial institutions and too little overall liquidity.

The financial crisis

Things came to a head in 2007 and 2008. Once one or two financial institutions failed, such as Northern Rock in the UK in September 2007 and Lehman Brothers in the USA in September 2008, the worry was that failures would spread like a contagion. Banks could no longer rely on each other as their main source of liquidity.

The problems arising from the balance sheet expansion, increased leverage and a heightened level of maturity mismatch meant that central banks around the world, including the Bank of England, were faced with addressing a liquidity problem of huge proportions. They had to step in to supply central bank money to prevent a collapse of the banking system.

Subsequently, the Basel Committee on Banking Supervision[1] (see pages 566–9) agreed a set of measures, to be applied globally, designed to ensure the greater financial resilience of banks and banking systems.

The chart shows that, during the 2010s, there was a decline in the size of the aggregate balance sheet of banks resident in the UK. By the end of 2015, the balance sheet had fallen to 3.6 times GDP. It stabilised during 2017–18 at around 4 times GDP.

 Why do you think banks became reluctant to deposit moneys with other banks during the financial crisis of the late 2000s?

 Using the Bank of England Statistical Interactive Database download monthly data on MFI total sterling assets (RPMB3XP). Construct a bar chart showing the series across time. Briefly summarise your findings.

[1] www.bis.org/bcbs/.

---

liquid and illiquid assets. Another way is through the *secondary marketing* of assets. This is where holders of assets sell them to someone else before the maturity date. This allows banks to close the maturity gap for *liquidity* purposes, but maintain the gap for *profitability* purposes.

Certificates of deposit (CDs) are a good example of secondary marketing. CDs are issued for fixed-period deposits in a bank (e.g. one year) at an agreed interest rate. The bank does not have to repay the deposit until the year is up. CDs are thus illiquid liabilities for the bank and they allow it to increase the proportion of illiquid assets without having a dangerously high maturity gap. But the holder of the CD, in the meantime, can sell it to someone else (through a broker). It is thus liquid to the holder. Because CDs are liquid to the holder, they can be issued at a relatively *low* rate of interest and thus allow the bank to increase its profitability.

Another example of secondary marketing is when a financial institution sells some of its assets to another financial institution. The advantage to the first institution is that it gains liquidity. The advantage to the second one is that it gains profitable assets. The most common method for the sale of assets has been through a process known as *securitisation*.

Securitisation occurs when a financial institution pools some of its assets, such as residential mortgages, and sells them to an intermediary known as a *special purpose vehicle (SPV)*. SPVs are legal entities created by the financial institution. In turn, the SPV funds its purchase of the assets by issuing bonds to investors (noteholders). These bonds are known as *collateralised debt obligations (CDOs)*. The sellers (e.g. banks) get cash now rather than having to wait and can use it to fund loans to customers. The buyers make a profit if the income yielded by the CDOs is as expected. Such bonds can be very risky, however, as the future cash flows may be *less* than anticipated.

The securitisation chain is illustrated in Figure 28.1. The financial institution looking to sell its assets is referred to as

the 'originator' or the 'originator-lender'. Working from left to right, we see the originator-lender sells its assets to another financial institution, the SPV, which then bundles assets together into CDOs and sells them to investors (e.g. banks or pension funds) as bonds. Now working from right to left, we see that by purchasing the bonds issued by the SPV, the investors provide the funds for the SPV's purchase of the lender's assets. The SPV is then able to use the proceeds from the bond sales (CDO proceeds) to provide the originator-lender with liquidity.

The effect of secondary marketing is to reduce the liquidity ratio that banks feel they need to keep. It has the effect of increasing their maturity gap.

Dangers of secondary marketing. There are dangers to the banking system, however, from secondary marketing. To the extent that banks individually feel that they can operate with a lower liquidity ratio, so this will lead to a lower national liquidity ratio. This may lead to an excessive expansion of credit (illiquid assets) in times of economic boom.

Definitions

Secondary marketing Where assets are sold before maturity to another institution or individual.

Securitisation Where future cash flows (e.g. from interest rate or mortgage payments) are turned into marketable securities, such as bonds.

Special purpose vehicle (SPV) Legal entities created by financial institutions for conducting specific financial functions, such as bundling assets together into fixed-interest bonds and selling them.

Collateralised debt obligations (CDOs) These are a type of security consisting of a bundle of fixed-income assets, such as corporate bonds, mortgage debt and credit-card debt.

Figure 28.1 Securitisation chain

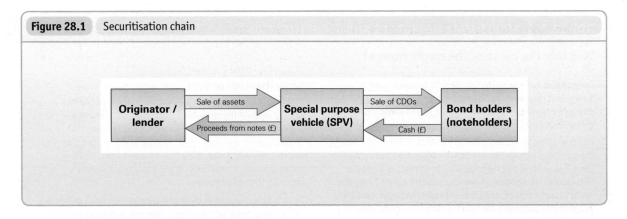

Also, there is an increased danger of banking collapse. If one bank fails, this will have a knock-on effect on those banks that have purchased its assets. In the specific case of securitisation, the strength of the chain is potentially weakened if individual financial institutions move into riskier market segments, such as **sub-prime** residential mortgage markets. Should the income streams of the originator's assets dry up – for instance, if individuals default on their loans – then the impact is felt by the whole of the chain. In other words, institutions and investors are exposed to the risks of the originator's lending strategy.

The issue of securitisation and its impact on the liquidity of the financial system during the 2000s is considered in Box 28.3.

Capital adequacy

In addition to sufficient liquidity, banks must have sufficient capital (i.e. funds) to allow them to meet all demands from depositors and to cover losses if borrowers default on payment. Capital adequacy is a measure of a bank's capital relative to its assets, where the assets are weighted according to the degree of risk. The riskier the assets, the greater the amount of capital that will be required.

A measure of capital adequacy is given by the **capital adequacy ratio (CAR)**. This is given by the following formula:

$$CAR = \frac{\text{Common Equity Tier 1 capital} + \text{Additional Tier 1 capital} + \text{Tier 2 capital}}{\text{Risk-weighted assets}}$$

Common Equity Tier 1 (CET1) capital includes bank reserves (from retained profits) and ordinary share capital ('equities'), where dividends to shareholders vary with the amount of profit the bank makes. Such capital thus places no burden on banks in times of losses as no dividend need be paid. What is more, unlike depositors, shareholders cannot ask for their money back.

Additional Tier 1 (AT1) capital consists largely of preference shares. These pay a fixed dividend (like company bonds), but although preference shareholders have a prior claim over ordinary shareholders on company profits, dividends need not be paid in times of loss.

Tier 2 capital is subordinated debt with a maturity greater than five years. Subordinated debt holders have a claim on a company only after the claims of all other bondholders have been met.

Risk-weighted assets are the total value of assets, where each type of asset is multiplied by a risk factor. Under the internationally agreed Basel II[1] accord, cash and government bonds have a risk factor of zero and are thus not included. Interbank lending between the major banks has a risk factor of 0.2 and is thus included at only 20 per cent of its value; residential mortgages have a risk factor of 0.35; personal loans, credit-card debt and overdrafts have a risk factor of 1; loans to companies carry a risk factor of 0.2, 0.5, 1 or 1.5, depending on the credit rating of the company. Thus the greater the average risk factor of a bank's assets, the greater will be the value of its risk-weighted assets, and the lower will be its CAR.

The greater the CAR, the greater the capital adequacy of a bank. Under Basel II, banks were required to have a CAR of at least 8 per cent (i.e. 0.08). They were also required to meet two supplementary CARs. First, banks needed to hold a ratio of Tier 1 capital to risk-weighted assets of at least 4 per cent and, second, a ratio of ordinary share capital to risk-weighted assets of at least 2 per cent. It was felt that these three ratios would provide banks with sufficient capital to meet the demands from depositors and to cover losses if borrowers defaulted. The financial crisis, however, meant a rethink (as we shall see below on pages 566–9).

Definition

Sub-prime debt Debt where there is a high risk of default by the borrower (e.g. mortgage holders who are on low incomes facing higher interest rates and falling house prices).

Capital adequacy ratio The ratio of a bank's capital (reserves and shares) to its risk-weighted assets.

Macro-prudential regulation Regulation which focuses on the financial system as a whole and which monitors its impact on the wider economy and ensures that it is resilient to shocks.

---

[1] www.bis.org/publ/bcbsca.htm.

BOX 28.3 RESIDENTIAL MORTGAGES AND SECURITISATION

Was this the cause of the credit crunch?

The conflict between profitability and liquidity may have sown the seeds for the credit crunch that affected economies across the globe in the second half of the 2000s.

To understand this, consider the size of the 'advances' item in the banking sector's balance sheet – around 55 per cent of the value of sterling (see Table 28.1). The vast majority of these are to households. Advances secured against property have, in recent times, accounted for around 80 per cent by value of all household advances. *Residential mortgages* involve institutions lending long.

Securitisation of debt

One way in which individual institutions can achieve the necessary liquidity to expand the size of their mortgage lending (illiquid assets) is through securitisation. Securitisation grew especially rapidly in the UK and USA. In the UK, this was particularly true among banks; building societies have, historically, made greater use of retail deposits to fund advances.

Securitisation is a form of financial engineering. It provides banks (originator-lenders) with liquidity and enables them to engage in further lending opportunities. It provides the

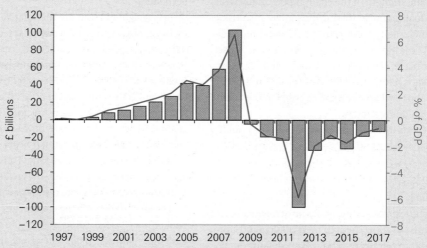

Net securitisations of secured lending to individuals

Note: Data up to 2010 relate to changes in other specialist lenders' sterling net securitisations of secured lending to individuals and housing associations. From 2010, data relate to changes in resident MFI sterling securitised loans secured on dwellings to individuals.
Sources: Based on data from *Statistical Interactive Database*, Bank of England, series LPMVUJD (up to 2010) and LPMB8GO (data published 30 August 2018) and series YBHA, National Statistics.

Strengthening international regulation of capital adequacy and liquidity

Capital adequacy

In light of the financial crisis of 2007–9, international capital adequacy requirements were strengthened by the *Basel Committee on Banking Supervision* with a first draft in 2010/11. The new 'Basel III'[2] capital requirements, as they are called, will be phased in by 2022. They are summarised in Figure 28.2.

Raising minimum levels of capital adequacy

The new framework raises the minimum levels of capital adequacy of all financial institutions. From its introduction in 2013, banks continued to need a CAR of at least 8 per cent

(i.e. 0.08). However, from 2015, they were required to operate with a ratio of CET1 to risk-weighted assets of at least 4.5 per cent. Then, from 2016 began a phased introduction of a *capital conservation buffer* raising the CET1 ratio to no less than 7 per cent by 2022. This will take the overall CAR to at least 10.5 per cent.

Counter-cyclical buffer

The new framework places more emphasis on national regulators assessing the financial resilience across all financial institutions under its jurisdiction, particularly in the context of the macroeconomic environment. This is *macro-prudential regulation*.

If necessary, regulators can apply a *counter-cyclical buffer* to all banks so increasing the CET1 ratio by up to a further 2.5 per cent. This allows financial institutions to build up a

[2]www.bis.org/bcbs/basel3.htm.

special purpose vehicles with the opportunity to issue profitable securities.

In the period up to 2010, most securitisations in the UK saw the original loans moving off the balance sheet of MFIs and onto the balance sheet of the SPV issuing the Collateralised Debt Obligations (CDOs). From 2010, however, all securitisations are detailed on the balance sheets of monetary financial institutions (MFIs), including previous securitisations which, as a result, have been brought back on to the balance sheets of MFIs.

The chart shows the rapid growth in the flows of securitised *secured* loans in the UK from under £3 billion in 1999 to over £100 billion by 2008. This increase reflected the strong demand among investors for CDOs. The attraction of these fixed-income products for the noteholders was the potential for higher returns than on (what were) similarly rated products. However, investors have no recourse should people with mortgages fall into arrears or, worse still, default on their mortgages.

Risks and the sub-prime market

The securitisation of assets is not without risks for all those in the securitisation chain and,consequently, for the financial system as a whole.

The pooling of advances in itself *reduces* the cash-flow risk facing investors. However, there is a **moral hazard** problem here (see page 99). The pooling of the risks may encourage originator-lenders to lower their credit criteria by offering higher income multiples (advances relative to annual household incomes) or higher loan-to-value ratios (advances relative to the price of housing).

Towards the end of 2006, the USA witnessed an increase in the number of defaults by households on residential mortgages. This was a particular problem in the *sub-prime market* – higher-risk households with poor credit ratings. Similarly, the number falling behind with their payments rose. This was on the back of rising interest rates.

These problems in the US sub-prime market were the catalyst for the liquidity problem that beset financial systems in 2007 and 2008. Where these assets were securitised, investors, largely other financial institutions, suffered from the contagion arising from arrears and defaults.

Securitisation also internationalised the contagion. Investors are global so that supporting CDOs for, say, a US family's residential mortgage, are, effectively, travelling across national borders. This resulted in institutions writing off debts, a deterioration of their balance sheets, the collapse in the demand for securitised assets and the drying up of liquidity.

The chart shows the collapse of the market for securitised secured lending in the UK after the financial crisis. Indeed, the 2010s were to be characterised by banks *buying back* CDOs from SPVs, including unsold ones. A similar pattern was observed in many other countries. This process was accelerated by central banks, which began to accept securitised assets in exchange for liquidity, either as part of programmes of quantitative easing to increase the amount of money in the economy (see Box 30.4) or other liquidity insurance mechanisms (see page 571 for a discussion of liquidity insurance in the UK).

 Does securitisation necessarily involve a moral hazard problem?

 Does securitisation necessarily involve a moral hazard problem? Using the Bank of England Statistical Interactive Database download monthly data on the stocks of securitised loans secured on dwellings (LPMB7GT) and of other securitised loans (LPMB7GU). Construct a stacked column chart showing the size and composition of the securitised debt stock of MFIs resident in the UK.

capital buffer during periods of high economic growth to allow it to be drawn on in times of recession or financial difficulty. It should also reduce the likelihood of financial institutions amplifying the business cycle through pro-cyclical behaviour, for example by easing credit conditions during periods of already strong growth and tightening credit in a recession.

Capital buffers for systemically important banks

Global systemically important banks. Large global financial institutions, known as **global systemically important banks (G-SIBs)**, will be required to operate with a CET1 ratio of up to 3.5 per cent higher than other banks, depending on banks' size and global reach. This additional capital buffer is known as the *systemic risk buffer (SRB)* or the *G-SIB capital surcharge.* The buffer recognises the likelihood that the

failure of such larger institution could trigger a global financial crisis.

Definitions

Global systemically important banks (G-SIBs) Banks identified by a series of indicators as being significant players in the global financial system.

Moral hazard Where one party to a transaction has an incentive to behave in a way that reduces the pay-off to the other party. The temptation to take more risks when you know that someone else will cover the risks if you get into difficulties. In the case of banks taking risks, the 'someone else' may be another bank, the central bank or the government.

Figure 28.2 Basel III minimum capital requirements, by 1/1/2022

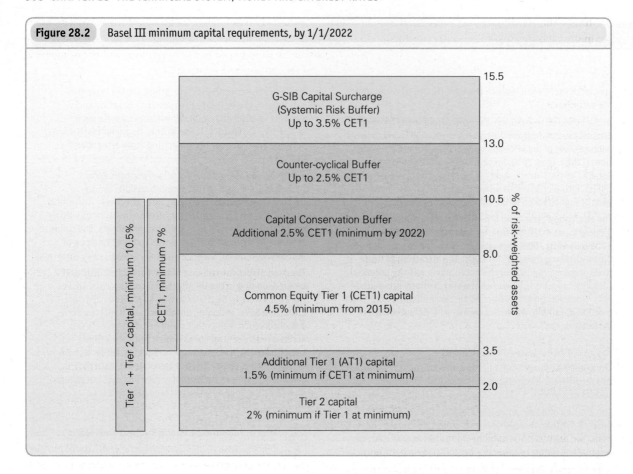

With a G-SIB systemic buffer of potentially up to 3.5 per cent, the overall CAR for G-SIBs from 2022 based on the Basel III requirement would be as high as to 16.5 per cent (see Figure 28.2).

Domestic systemically important banks. Several countries have also adopted a systemic risk buffer on financial institutions identified by their national authorities as **domestic systemically important banks (D-SIBs)**.

In the UK, it was decided that individual ring-fenced banks (RFBs) and large building societies that hold more than £25 billion in deposits would be required to hold a systemic risk buffer. UK bank groups identified as G-SIBs containing a ring-fenced bank are therefore subject to two systemic risk buffers: the systemic risk buffer for G-SIBs at the group level and the domestic systemic risk buffer at the level of the ring-fenced bank.

The UK's domestic systemic risk buffer depends on the size of risk-weighted assets, with the initial plan for additional capital requirement of up to 3 per cent of these assets. However, depending on the judgment of the Financial Policy Committee, whose job is to ensure the financial resilience of the UK financial sector, the asset bands and the systemic risk buffer rates applied can be reviewed and adjusted if necessary.

> ### Pause for thought
>
> *What indicators might help regulators determine whether a bank is systemically important?*

Leverage ratio

To supplement the risk-based capital requirements, the Basel III framework introduced from 2018 a *non-risk-based leverage ratio* (i.e. separate from the ratios listed in Figure 28.2). This was described by regulators as complementary to the risk-based framework; it is intended to prevent a build-up of debt to fund banks' activities.

The leverage ratio buffer requires financial institutions to operate with a Tier 1 capital-to-asset ratio of 3 per cent. In

> ### Definitions
>
> **Domestically systemically important banks (D-SIBs)** Banks identified by national regulators as being significant banks in the domestic financial system.

contrast to the risk-based ratios, the assets in the denominator in this ratio are *not* weighted by risk factors.

Standardising the measure of risk

The impact of the Basel III's capital adequacy requirements was to increase the capital cushions of many banks significantly. Indeed, it seemed that banks generally were making good progress, with some meeting the 2022 requirements well ahead of time.

Despite this, an issue that was to remain outstanding for some time was the *calculation* of risk-weighted assets. Because of the complexity of banks' asset structures, which tend to vary significantly from country to country, it can be difficult to ensure that banks are meeting the Basel III requirements. The problem can then be made worse by the use of internal models by financial institutions, which can apply different approaches to assessing and evaluating risks.

It was therefore proposed that banks would have to compare their own calculations with a 'standardised' model'. Their own calculations of risk-based assets would then not be allowed to fall below a set percentage, known as 'the output floor', of the standardised approach. The argument then centred on how high the output floor should be set.

Those arguing for a higher output floor pointed to the importance of a credible regulatory framework. An over-reliance on inconsistently applied internal risk assessment methods would, they said, undermine the credibility of the regulatory framework. However, others argued that a high output floor could penalise financial institutions by treating assets as equally risky across countries. For example, Germany argued that since mortgage defaults have been rare, German mortgage debt should be given a lower weighting than US mortgage debt, where defaults have been more common. Hence, by setting the output floor too high, banks could be judged to be undercapitalised.

In December 2017, the Basel Committee finally agreed that the output floor for the risk weighting of assets would be set at 72.5 per cent, meaning that individual countries could not set the risk of an asset, such as a mortgage, at less than 72.5 per cent of the level set by international regulators in their standardised models. This will, however, be phased in with an output floor of 50 per cent from 2022, increasing each year until reaching 72.5 per cent in 2027.

Liquidity

The financial crisis drew attention for the need of banks not only to hold adequate levels of capital but also to manage their liquidity better. The Basel III framework includes a *liquidity coverage ratio* (LCR). This requires that financial institutions have high quality liquid assets (HQLAs) to cover the expected net cash flow over the next 30 days. From its implementation in 2015, the minimum LCR ratio (HQLAs relative to the expected 30-day net cash flow) will rise from 60 per cent to 100 per cent by 2022.

> **Pause for thought**
>
> *Why are government bonds that still have 11 months to run regarded as liquid, whereas overdrafts granted for a few weeks are not?*

Net stable funding ratio

As part of Basel III, a minimum *net stable funding ratio* (NSFR) became a regulatory standard from 2018. The NSFR is the ratio of stable liabilities to assets likely to require funding (i.e. assets where there is a likelihood of default or which could not be 'monetised' and thereby converted into money through their sale). The aim of having a minimum NSFR is to limit excessive risk from maturity transformation by taking a longer-term view of the funding profile of banks relative to their assets.

On the liabilities side, these will be weighted by their expected reliability – in other words, by the stability of these funds. This weighting will reflect the maturity of the liabilities and the likelihood of lenders withdrawing their funds. For example, Tier 1 and 2 capital will have a weighting of 100 per cent; term deposits with less than one year to maturity will have a weighting of 50 per cent; and unsecured wholesale funding will have a weighting of 0 per cent. The result of these weightings is a measure of stable funding.

On the assets side, these will be weighted by the likelihood that they will have to be funded over the course of one year. This means that they will be weighted by their liquidity, with more liquid assets requiring less funding. Thus cash will have a zero weighting, while more risky assets will have weightings up to 100 per cent. The result is a measure of required funding.

Banks will need to hold a minimum stable-liabilities-to-required-funding ratio (NSFR) of 100 per cent.

The central bank

The Bank of England is the UK's central bank. The European Central Bank (ECB) is the central bank for the countries using the euro. The Federal Reserve System (the Fed) is the USA's central bank. All countries have a central bank and they fulfil two vital roles in the economy.

The first is to oversee the whole monetary system and ensure that banks and other financial institutions operate as stably and as efficiently as possible.

The second is to act as the government's agent, both as its banker and in carrying out monetary policy.

The Bank of England traditionally worked in very close liaison with the Treasury and there used to be regular meetings between the Governor of the Bank of England and the Chancellor of the Exchequer. Although the Bank may have disagreed with Treasury policy, it always carried it out. With the election of the Labour Government in 1997, however, the Bank of England was given operational independence: independence to decide the course of monetary policy. In particular, this meant that the Bank of England and not the government would now decide interest rates.

Another example of an independent central bank is the European Central Bank (ECB). The ECB operates monetary policy for the countries using the euro and it alone, not the member governments, determines common interest rates for these countries. Similarly, the Fed is independent of both President and Congress and its chairman is generally regarded as having great power in determining the country's economic policy.

Although the degree of independence of central banks from government varies considerably around the world, there has, nevertheless, been a general trend to make central banks more independent.

Within their two broad roles, central banks typically have a number of different functions. Although we will consider the case of the Bank of England, the same principles apply to other central banks, such as the ECB and the Fed.

It issues notes

The Bank of England is the sole issuer of banknotes in England and Wales (in Scotland and Northern Ireland retail banks issue banknotes). The amount of banknotes issued by the Bank of England depends largely on the demand for notes from the general public. If people draw more cash from their bank accounts, the banks will have to draw more cash from their balances in the Bank of England.

It acts as a bank

To the government. It keeps the two major government accounts: 'The Exchequer' and the 'National Loans Fund'. Taxation and government spending pass through the Exchequer. Government borrowing and lending pass through the National Loans Fund. The government tends to keep its deposits in the Bank of England to a minimum. If the deposits begin to build up (from taxation), the government will probably spend them on paying back government debt. If, on the other hand, the government runs short of money, it will simply borrow more.

To the banks. Banks' deposits in the Bank of England consist of reserve balances and cash ratio deposits (see Table 28.1). The reserve balances are used largely for clearing purposes

between the banks, but are also a means by which banks can manage their liquidity risk. Therefore, the reserve balances provide banks with an important buffer stock of liquid assets.

To overseas central banks. The Bank of England holds deposits of sterling (and similarly the European Central Bank holds deposits of euros) made by overseas authorities as part of their official reserves and/or for purposes of intervening in the foreign exchange market in order to influence the exchange rate of their currency (see pages 571–2).

It operates the country's monetary policy

The Bank of England's Monetary Policy Committee[3] (MPC) sets interest rates (the rate on gilt repos) at its regular meetings. This nine-member committee consists of four experts appointed by the Chancellor of the Exchequer and four senior members of the Bank of England, plus the Governor in the chair.

The Bank of England conducts *open-market operations* to keep interest rates in line with the level decided by the MPC. By purchasing securities (gilts and/or Treasury bills), for example through reverse repos (repos to the banks), the Bank of England provides liquidity, thereby putting downward pressure on interest rates. If it is looking to raise interest rates, the Bank of England will sell securities to banks, so reducing banks' reserves in the Bank. In the process of influencing interest rates through open-market operations, the Bank of England affects the size of the money supply. (This is explained in Chapter 30.)

As the financial crisis unfolded, it became increasingly difficult for the Bank to meet its monetary policy objectives while maintaining financial stability. New policies were thus adopted. October 2008 also saw the Bank of England stop short-term open-market operations. The key priority was now ensuring sufficient liquidity and so the focus switched to longer-term OMOs.

March 2009 saw the Bank begin a programme of *quantitative easing (QE)*[4] (see Box 30.4). The aim was to increase the amount of money in the financial system and thereby stimulate bank lending and hence aggregate demand. QE involved the Bank creating electronic money

---

Definitions

Open-market operations The sale (or purchase) by the authorities of government securities in the open market in order to reduce (or increase) money supply and thereby affect interest rates.

Quantitative easing When the central bank increases the monetary base through an open market purchase of government bonds or other securities. It uses electronic money (reserve liabilities) created specifically for this purpose.

---

[3] www.bankofengland.co.uk/monetary-policy.
[4] www.bankofengland.co.uk/monetary-policy/quantitative-easing.

and using it to purchase assets, mainly government bonds, predominantly from non-deposit-taking financial institutions, such as unit trusts, insurance companies and pension funds. These institutions would then deposit the money in banks, which could lend it to businesses and consumers for purposes of spending.

It provides liquidity, as necessary, to banks

Financial institutions engage in maturity transformation (see Box 28.1), which means that they are typically borrowing funds for a shorter time period than that for which they are loaning funds. While most customer deposits can be withdrawn instantly, financial institutions will have a variety of lending commitments, some of which span many years. Hence, the Bank of England acts as a 'liquidity backstop' for the banking system. It attempts to ensure that there is always an adequate supply of liquidity to meet the legitimate demands of depositors in banks.

Banks' reserve balances provide them with some liquidity insurance. However, the Bank of England needs other means by which to provide both individual banks and the banking system with sufficient liquidity. The financial crisis, for instance, saw incredible pressure on the aggregate liquidity of the financial system. The result is that the UK has three principal insurance facilities: index long-term repos, discount window facility and contingent term repo facility.

Index long-term repos (ILTRs). Each month, the Bank of England provides MFIs with reserves for a six-month period secured against collateral and indexed against the Bank Rate. Financial institutions can borrow reserves against different levels of collateral. These levels reflect the quality and liquidity of the collateral. The reserves are distributed through an auction where financial institutions indicate, for their particular level of collateral, the number of basis points over the Bank Rate (the 'spread') they are prepared to pay. The resulting equilibrium interest rate, paid by all those borrowing, is that which balances the demand from MFIs with the supply of reserves made available. The Bank of England may subsequently provide a greater quantity of reserves if, from the bids, it observes a greater demand for it to provide liquidity insurance.

Discount window facility (DWF). This on-demand facility allows financial institutions to borrow government bonds (gilts) for 30 days against different classes of (less liquid) collateral. They pay a fee to do so. The size of the fee is determined by both the type and quantity of collateral being traded. The gilts can then be used in repo operations as a means of securing liquidity. Financial institutions can look to roll over the gilts obtained from the DWF beyond the normal 30 days if they are still short of liquidity.

Contingent term repo facility (CTRP). This is a facility that the Bank of England can activate in exceptional circumstances. As with the ILTRs, financial institutions can obtain liquidity secured against different levels of collateral through an auction. However, the terms, including the maturity of the funds, are intended to be more flexible.

It oversees the activities of banks and other financial institutions

The Bank of England requires all recognised banks to maintain adequate liquidity: this is called *prudential control*.

In May 1997, the Bank of England ceased to be responsible for the detailed supervision of banks' activities. This responsibility passed to the Financial Services Authority (FSA). But the financial crisis of the late 2000s raised concerns about whether the FSA, the Bank of England and HM Treasury were sufficiently watchful of banks' liquidity and the risks of liquidity shortage. Some commentators argued that a much tighter form of prudential control should have been imposed.

In 2013, the FSA was wound up and a new regulatory framework came into force, with an enhanced role for the Bank of England.

First, the Bank's *Financial Policy Committee (FPC)* was made responsible for *macro-prudential regulation*. This is regulation that takes a broader view of the financial system (see pages 565–7). It considers, for instance, the resilience of the financial system to possible shocks and its capacity to create macroeconomic instability through excessive credit creation.

Second, the prudential regulation of individual firms was transferred from the FSA to the *Prudential Regulation Authority (PRA)*, a subsidiary of the Bank of England.

Third, the *Financial Conduct Authority (FCA)* took responsibility for consumer protection and the regulation of markets for financial services. The FCA is an independent body accountable to HM Treasury.

It operates the government's exchange rate policy

The Bank of England manages the country's gold and foreign currency reserves. This is done through the *exchange equalisation account*. By buying and selling foreign

---

Definitions

Prudential control The insistence by the monetary authorities (e.g. the Bank of England) that banks maintain adequate liquidity.

Exchange equalisation account The gold and foreign exchange reserves account in the Bank of England.

currencies on the foreign exchange market, the Bank of England can affect the exchange rate (see Chapter 27).

> **Pause for thought**
>
> *Would it be possible for an economy to function without a central bank?*

The role of the money markets

Money markets enable participants, such as banks, to lend to and borrow from each other. The financial instruments traded are short-term ones. As we have seen, central banks use money markets to exercise control over interest rates. But they are very important too in widening the lending and borrowing opportunities for financial institutions.

We take the case of the London money market, which is normally divided into the 'discount and repo' markets and the 'parallel' or 'complementary' markets.

The discount and repo markets
The discount market. The discount market is the market for commercial or government bills. In the UK, government bills are known as Treasury bills and operations are conducted by the Debt Management Office, usually on a weekly basis. Treasury bills involve short-term lending, say for one or three months, which, in conjunction with their low default risk, make them highly liquid assets.

The discount market is also known as the traditional market because it was the market in which many central banks traditionally used to supply central bank money to financial institutions. For instance, if the Bank of England wanted to increase liquidity in the banking system, it could purchase from the banks' Treasury bills which had yet to reach maturity. This process is known as **rediscounting**. The Bank of England would pay a price below the face value, thus effectively charging interest to the banks. The price could be set so that the 'rediscount rate' reflected the interest rate set by the MPC (see section 30.2).

The repo market. The emergence of the repo market is a more recent development dating in the UK back to the 1990s. Repos have become an important potential source of wholesale funding for financial institutions. They are also an important means by which central banks can affect the liquidity of the financial system both to implement monetary policy and to ensure financial stability.

By entering into a repo agreement, the Bank of England buys gilts from the banks (thereby supplying them with money) on the condition that the banks buy the gilts back at a fixed price and on a fixed date. The repurchase price will be above the sale price. The difference is the equivalent of the interest that the banks are being charged for having what amounts to a loan from the Bank of England. The repurchase price (and hence the 'repo rate') is set by the Bank of England to reflect the rate chosen by the MPC.

The financial crisis caused the Bank to modify its repo operations to manage liquidity for both purposes of monetary policy and increasingly to ensure financial stability. These changes included a widening of the securities eligible as collateral for loans, a suspension of short-term repo operations and an increased focus on longer-term repo operations.

So central banks, like the Bank of England, are prepared to provide central bank money through the creation of reserves. The central bank is thus the ultimate guarantor of sufficient liquidity in the monetary system and is known as **lender of last resort**.

The parallel money markets
Like repo markets, complementary or parallel money markets have grown rapidly in recent years. In part, this reflects the opening up of markets to international dealing, the deregulation of banking and money market dealing, and the desire of banks to keep funds in a form that can be readily switched from one form of deposit to another or from one currency to another.

Examples of parallel markets include the markets for *certificates of deposit* (CDs), *foreign currencies markets* (dealings in foreign currencies deposited short term in the country) and the interbank market. Of these, the *interbank market* is particularly important. It has, traditionally, been a major source of liquidity.

The interbank market. This involves wholesale loans from one bank to another from one day to up to several months. Interbank lending has traditionally been a major source of liquidity. Bank with surplus liquidity lend to other banks, which then use this as the basis for loans to individuals and companies.

The rate at which banks lend to each other has a major influence on the other rates that banks charge. Interbank loans typically can be anything from overnight to 12 months and hence there is a series of rates corresponding to these different maturities.

During the financial crisis of 2008, interbank lending rates in many countries, including the UK, rose significantly above central bank lending rates. At the same time, lending virtually ceased as banks became worried that the bank they were lending to might default.

> **Definitions**
>
> **Rediscounting bills of exchange** Buying bills before they reach maturity.
>
> **Lender of last resort** The role of the Bank of England as the guarantor of sufficient liquidity in the monetary system.

In the UK, the interbank rate has traditionally been measured by the LIBOR (the London interbank offered rate), varying by the length of loan. (In the Eurozone, the interbank rate is known as the Euribor, with the weighted average of all overnight rates known as Eonia). Interbank rates are the cost of borrowing between banks and have to be reported by the banks. However, in 2012, allegations came to light claiming that there had been false reporting of LIBOR rates. Because the LIBOR rate is a reference rate for financial products, this has potentially serious implications for the interest rates being charged and therefore for the financial well-being of customers.

From April 2018, the Bank of England took over the administration of an alternative interbank benchmark rate.

Known as SONIA, the Sterling Overnight Index Average measures the rate at which interest is paid on sterling unsecured loans of one business day. SONIA is therefore expected to become the new benchmark determining commercial interest rates.

> ### Pause for thought
>
> *Why should Bank of England determination of the rate of interest in the discount and repo markets also influence rates of interest in the parallel markets?*

28.3 THE SUPPLY OF MONEY

If money supply is to be monitored and possibly controlled, it is obviously necessary to measure it. But what should be included in the measure? Here we need to distinguish between the *monetary base* and *broad money*.

The **monetary base** (or 'high-powered money' or 'narrow money') consists of cash (notes and coin) in circulation outside the central bank.[5] In 1970, the stock of notes and coin in circulation in the UK was around £4 billion, equivalent to 7 per cent of annual GDP. By 2018, this had grown to over £80 billion, but equivalent to only about 4 per cent of annual GDP.

The monetary base gives us a very poor indication of the effective money supply, however, since it excludes the most important source of liquidity for spending: namely, bank deposits. The problem is which deposits to include. We need to answer three questions:

- Should we include just sight deposits or time deposits as well?
- Should we include just retail deposits or wholesale deposits as well?
- Should we include just bank deposits or building society (savings institution) deposits as well?

In the past, there has been a whole range of measures, each including different combinations of these accounts.

However, financial deregulation, the abolition of foreign exchange controls and the development of computer technology have led to huge changes in the financial sector throughout the world. This has led to a blurring of the distinctions between different types of account. It has also made it very easy to switch deposits from one type of account to another. For these reasons, the most usual measure that countries use for money supply is **broad money**, which, in most cases, includes both time and sight deposits, retail and wholesale deposits and bank and building society deposits.

In the UK, this measure of broad money is known as M4. In most other European countries and the USA, it is known as M3. There are, however, minor differences between countries in what is included.

In 1970, the stock of M4 in the UK was around £25 billion, equivalent to 48 per cent of annual GDP. By 2018, this had grown to £2.4 trillion, equivalent to about 115 per cent of annual GDP.

As we have seen, bank deposits of one form or another constitute by far the largest component of (broad) money supply. To understand how money supply expands and contracts, and how it can be controlled, it is thus necessary to understand what determines the size of bank deposits. Banks can themselves expand the amount of bank deposits, and hence the money supply, by a process known as 'credit creation'.

---

[5]Before 2006, there used to be a measure of narrow money called M0. This included cash in circulation outside the Bank of England and banks' non-interest-bearing 'operational balances' in the Bank of England, with these balances accounting for a tiny proportion of the whole. Since 2006, the Bank of England has allowed banks to hold interest-bearing reserve accounts, which are much larger than the former operational balances. The Bank of England thus decided to discontinue M0 as a measure and focus on cash in circulation as its measure of the monetary base.

> ### Definitions
>
> **Monetary base** Notes and coin in circulation, i.e. outside the central bank.
>
> **Broad money** Cash in circulation plus retail and wholesale bank and building society deposits.

The creation of credit

To illustrate this process in its simplest form, assume that banks have just one type of liability – deposits – and two types of asset – balances with the central bank (to achieve liquidity) and advances to customers (to earn profit).

Banks want to achieve profitability while maintaining sufficient liquidity. Assume that they believe that sufficient liquidity will be achieved if 10 per cent of their assets are held as balances with the central bank. The remaining 90 per cent will then be in advances to customers. In other words, the banks operate a 10 per cent liquidity ratio.

Assume initially that the combined balance sheet of the banks is as shown in Table 28.2. Total deposits are £100 billion, of which £10 billion (10 per cent) are kept in balances with the central bank. The remaining £90 billion (90 per cent) are lent to customers.

Now assume that the government spends more money – £10 billion, say, on roads or education. It pays for this with cheques drawn on its account with the central bank. The people receiving the cheques deposit them in their banks. Banks return these cheques to the central bank and their balances correspondingly increase by £10 billion. The combined banks' balance sheet now is shown in Table 28.3.

But this is not the end of the story. Banks now have surplus liquidity. With their balances in the central bank having increased to £20 billion, they now have a liquidity ratio of 20/110 or 18.2 per cent. If they are to return to a 10 per cent liquidity ratio, they need retain only £11 billion as balances at the central bank (£11 billion/£110 billion = 10 per cent). The remaining £9 billion they can lend to customers.

Assume now that customers spend this £9 billion in shops and the shopkeepers deposit the cheques in their bank accounts. When the cheques are cleared, the balances in the central bank of the customers' banks will duly be debited by £9 billion, but the balances in the central bank of the shopkeepers' banks will be credited by £9 billion: leaving *overall balances in the central bank unaltered*. There is still a surplus of £9 billion over what is required to maintain the 10 per cent liquidity ratio. The new deposits of £9 billion in the shopkeepers' banks, backed by balances in the central bank, can thus be used as the basis for *further* loans. Ten per cent (i.e. £0.9 billion) must be kept back in the central bank, but the remaining 90 per cent (i.e. £8.1 billion) can be lent out again.

When the money is spent and the cheques are cleared, this £8.1 billion will still remain as surplus balances in the central

bank and can therefore be used as the basis for yet more loans. Again, 10 per cent must be retained and the remaining 90 per cent can be lent out. This process goes on and on until, eventually, the position is as shown in Table 28.4.

The initial increase in balances with the central bank of £10 billion has allowed banks to create new advances (and hence deposits) of £90 billion, making a total increase in money supply of £100 billion.

This effect is known as the **bank (or bank deposits) multiplier**. In this simple example with a liquidity ratio of $\frac{1}{10}$ (i.e. 10 per cent), the bank deposits multiplier is 10. An initial increase in deposits of £10 billion allowed total deposits to rise by £100 billion. In this simple world, therefore, the deposits multiplier is the inverse of the liquidity ratio (L).

$$\text{Bank deposits multiplier} = 1/L$$

The bank multiplier is an example of **cumulative causation.** This term refers to the processes by which an initial event results in an ultimate effect that is much larger. In this case, the process of credit creation results in an

Definitions

Bank (or bank deposits) multiplier The number of times greater the expansion of bank deposits is than the additional liquidity in banks that caused it: $1/L$ (the inverse of the liquidity ratio).

Table 28.3	The initial effect of an additional deposit of £10 billion

Liabilities	£bn	Assets	£bn
Deposits (old)	100	Balances with the central bank (old)	10
Deposits (new)	10	Balances with the central bank (new)	10
		Advances	90
Total	110	Total	110

Table 28.2	Banks' original balance sheet

Liabilities	£bn	Assets	£bn
Deposits	100	Balances with the central bank	10
		Advances	90
Total	100	Total	100

Table 28.4	The full effect of an additional deposit of £10 billion

Liabilities	£bn	Assets	£bn
Deposits (old)	100	Balances with the central bank (old)	10
Deposits (new: initial)	10	Balances with the central bank (new)	10
(new: subsequent)	90		
		Advances (old)	90
		Advances (new)	90
Total	200	Total	200

KI 27
p 341

KI 43
p 575

ultimate increase in money supply that is larger than the initial increase in deposits. The bank deposits multiplier therefore measures the number of times greater the final increase in deposits is than the initial increase in deposits.

 Key Idea 43 *The principle of cumulative causation.* An initial event can cause an ultimate effect which is much larger.

Pause for thought

If banks choose to operate with a 5 per cent liquidity ratio and receive an extra £100 million of cash deposits: (a) What is the size of the deposits multiplier? (b) How much will total deposits have expanded after the multiplier has worked through? (c) How much will total credit have expanded?

The creation of credit: the real world

In practice, the creation of credit is not as simple as this. There are three major complications.

Banks' liquidity ratio may vary

Banks may choose a different liquidity ratio. At certain times, banks may decide that it is prudent to hold a bigger proportion of liquid assets. For example, if banks are worried about increased risks of default on loans, they may choose to hold a higher liquidity ratio to ensure that they have enough to meet customers' needs. This was the case in the late 2000s when many banks became less willing to lend to other banks for fear of the other banks' assets containing sub-prime debt. Banks, as a result, hoarded cash and became more cautious about granting loans.

KI 13 p75

On the other hand, there may be an upsurge in consumer demand for credit. Banks may be very keen to grant additional loans and thus make more profits, even though they have acquired no additional assets. They may simply go ahead and expand credit and accept a lower liquidity ratio.

Customers may not want to take up the credit on offer. Banks may wish to make additional loans, but customers may not want to borrow. There may be insufficient demand. But will the banks not then lower their interest rates, thus encouraging people to borrow? Possibly, but if they lower the rate they charge to borrowers, they must also lower the rate they pay to depositors. But then depositors may switch to other institutions such as building societies.

Banks may not operate a simple liquidity ratio

The fact that banks hold a number of fairly liquid assets, such as money at call, bills of exchange and certificates of deposit, makes it difficult to identify a simple liquidity ratio. If the banks use extra cash to buy such liquid assets, can they then use these assets as the basis for creating credit? It is largely up to banks' judgements on their overall

liquidity position. In practice, therefore, the size of the bank deposits multiplier will vary and is thus difficult to predict in advance.

Some of the extra cash may be withdrawn by the public

If extra cash comes into the banking system and, as a result, extra deposits are created, part of them may be held by households and non-bank firms (known in this context as the **non-bank private sector**) as cash *outside* the banks. In other words, some of the extra cash leaks out of the banking system. This will result in an overall multiplier effect that is smaller than the full bank deposits multiplier. The overall multiplier is known as the **money multiplier**. It is defined as the change in total money supply expressed as a proportion of the change in the monetary base that caused it: $\Delta M_s/\Delta M_b$ (where M_s is total broad money supply and M_b is the monetary base).

KI 43 p575

The broad money multiplier in the UK

In the UK, the principal money multiplier measure is the broad money multiplier. This is given by $\Delta M4/\Delta M_b$, where M_b in this case is defined as cash in circulation with the public and in banks' interest-bearing deposits (reserve accounts) at the Bank of England.

 KI 43 p575

Another indicator of the broad money multiplier is simply the ratio of the *level of* (as opposed to the *change in*) M4 relative to the cash in circulation with the public and banks' reserve accounts at the central bank. This 'levels' relationship is shown in Figure 28.4 and helps us to analyse the longer-term relationship between the stocks of broad money and the monetary base.

From Figure 28.3 we can see how the broad money multiplier grew rapidly during the 1980s and into the beginning of the 1990s. From the early 1990s to the mid-2000s, the level of M4 relative to the monetary base fluctuated in a narrow range.

From May 2006, the Bank of England began remunerating banks' reserve accounts at the official Bank Rate. This encouraged banks to increase their reserve accounts at the Bank of England and led to a sharp fall in the broad money multiplier. It then declined further from 2009. The significant decline in 2009, in 2011–12 and again in 2016–17 coincided with the Bank of England's programme of asset purchases (quantitative easing) which led to a large increase in banks' reserves at the Bank of England. The point is that the increase in the monetary base did not lead to the same percentage increase in broad

Definitions

Non-bank private sector Household and non-bank firms. The category thus excludes the government and banks.

Money multiplier The number of times greater the expansion of money supply (M_s) is than the expansion of the monetary base (M_b) that caused it: $\Delta M_s/\Delta M_b$.

Figure 28.3 UK broad money multiplier

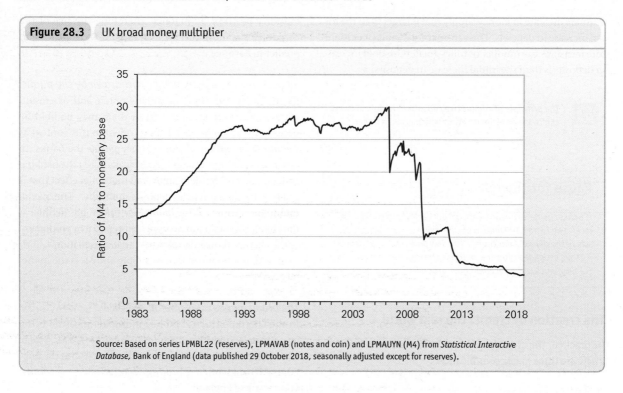

Source: Based on series LPMBL22 (reserves), LPMAVAB (notes and coin) and LPMAUYN (M4) from *Statistical Interactive Database*, Bank of England (data published 29 October 2018, seasonally adjusted except for reserves).

Figure 28.4 Annual rate of growth of M4

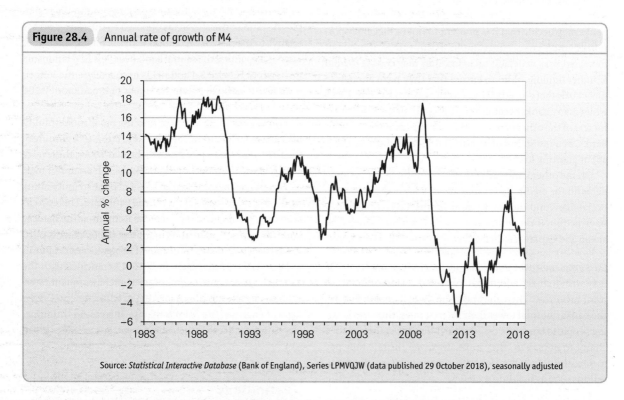

Source: *Statistical Interactive Database* (Bank of England), Series LPMVQJW (data published 29 October 2018), seasonally adjusted

money, as banks were more cautious about lending and chose to keep higher reserves. (The policy of quantitative easing is discussed more in Chapter 30.)

In the next section, we look at factors that help explain movements in the money multiplier and changes in the money supply.

Pause for thought

Which would you expect to fluctuate more, the money multiplier ($\Delta M_s/\Delta M_b$), *or the simple ratio,* M_s/M_b?

What causes money supply to rise?

Money supply can rise for a number of reasons. We consider five sets of circumstances that can cause the money supply to *rise*.

Central bank action

The central bank may decide that the stock of money is too low and that this is keeping up interest rates and holding back spending in the economy. In such circumstances, it may choose to create additional money.

As we saw above (pages 570–1), this was the case following the 2007/8 financial crisis when the Bank of England and the US Federal Reserve Bank embarked on programmes of *quantitative easing*. This involved the central bank creating electronic (narrow) money and using it to purchase assets, mainly government bonds. When the recipients of the money (mainly non-bank financial institutions) deposited it in banks, the banks could lend it to businesses and consumers for purposes of spending and, through the bank deposits multiplier, broad money supply would increase.

As we can see from Figure 28.4, however, this was not enough to prevent UK broad money supply falling for much of the first half of 2010s.

An inflow of funds from abroad

When sterling is used to pay for UK exports and is deposited in UK banks by the exporters, credit can be created on the basis of it. This leads to a *multiplied* increase in money supply.

The money supply will also expand if depositors of sterling in banks overseas then switch these deposits to banks in the UK. This is a direct increase in the money supply. In an open economy like the UK, movements of sterling and other currencies into and out of the country can be very large. This can lead to large fluctuations in the money supply.

A public-sector deficit

A public-sector deficit is the difference between public-sector expenditure and public-sector receipts. To meet this deficit, the government has to borrow money by selling interest-bearing securities (Treasury bills and gilts). The precise amount of money the public sector requires to borrow in any one year is known in the UK as the **public-sector net cash requirement (PSNCR)**. (We will focus on public-sector spending and taxation in Chapter 30.)

In general, the bigger the public sector's deficit, the greater will be the growth in the money supply. Just how the money supply will be affected, however, depends on who buys the securities.

Consider first the case where government securities are purchased by the non-bank private sector (i.e. to the general public and non-bank firms). The money supply will remain unchanged. When people or firms buy the bonds or bills, they will draw money from their banks. When the government spends the money, it will be redeposited in banks.

There is no increase in money supply. It is just a case of existing money changing hands.

This is not the case, however, when the securities are purchased by the banking sector, including the central bank. Consider the purchase of Treasury bills by commercial banks: there will be a multiplied expansion of the money supply. The reason is that, although banks' balances at the central bank will go down when the banks purchase the bills, they will go up again when the government spends the money. In addition, the banks will now have additional liquid assets (bills), which can be used as the basis for credit creation.

The government could attempt to minimise the boost to money supply by financing the deficit through the sale of gilts, since, even if these were partly purchased by the banks, they could not be used as the basis for credit creation.

The above reasons for an expansion of broad money supply (M4) are reasons why the monetary base itself might expand. The final two reasons focus on how the money supply can increase if more *credit* is created for a given monetary base. These reasons therefore would see a rise in the money multiplier, such as the UK saw in the late 1980s/early 1990s and then again in the first half of the 2000s (see Figure 28.4).

Banks choose to hold a lower liquidity ratio

If banks collectively choose to hold a lower liquidity ratio, they will have surplus liquidity. The banks have tended to choose a lower liquidity ratio over time because of the increasing use of direct debits and debit-card and credit-card transactions.

Surplus liquidity can be used to expand advances, which will lead to a multiplied rise in broad money supply (e.g. M4).

An important trend up to the late 2000s was the growth in *interbank lending*. Short-term loans to other banks (including overseas banks) may be used by a bank as the basis for expanding loans and thereby starting a chain of credit creation. But, although these assets are liquid to an *individual bank,* they do not add to the liquidity of the banking system *as a whole*. By using them for credit creation, the banking system is operating with a lower *overall* liquidity ratio.

This was a major element in the banking crisis of 2008. By operating with a collectively low liquidity ratio, banks were vulnerable to people defaulting on debt, such as mortgages. The problem was compounded by the holding of sub-prime debt in the form of securitised assets. Realising the vulnerability of other banks, banks became increasingly unwilling to lend to each other. The resulting decline in interbank

> ### Definitions
>
> **Public-sector net cash requirement (PSNCR)** The (annual) deficit of the public sector (central government, local government and public corporations) and thus the amount that the public sector must borrow.

lending reduced the amount of credit created and so depressed the money supply.

> ### Pause for thought
>
> *What effects do debit cards and cash machines (ATMs) have on (a) banks' prudent liquidity ratios (b) the size of the bank deposits multiplier?*

The non-bank private sector chooses to hold less cash

Households and non-bank firms may choose to hold less cash. Again, the reason may be a greater use of cards, direct debits, etc. This means that a greater proportion of the cash base will be held as deposits in banks rather than in people's wallets, purses or safes outside banks. The extra cash deposits allow banks to create more credit.

> ### Pause for thought
>
> *Identify the various factors that could cause a fall in the money supply.*

The flow of funds equation

KI 27
p 341

A flow-of-funds equation can be used to analyse the contributions to money growth made by the public-sector's budget balance, i.e. the balance between pubic-sector spending and taxation, lending by financial institutions and flows of funds to and from abroad.

The following flow-of-funds equation is the one most commonly used in the UK, that for M4. It consists of four components:

ΔM4	*equals*	PSNCR	(Item 1)
	minus	Sales of public-sector debt to (or plus purchases of public-sector debt from) the non-bank private sector	(Item 2)
	plus	Banks' and building societies' sterling net lending to the UK private sector	(Item 3)
	plus	External effect	(Item 4)

Public-sector borrowing (item 1) will lead to a direct increase in the money supply, but not if it is funded by selling bonds and bills to the non-bank private sector. Such sales (item 2) have therefore to be subtracted from the public-sector net cash requirement (PSNCR). But, conversely, if the government buys back old bonds from the non-bank private sector, this will further increase the money supply.

The initial increase in liquidity from the sale of government securities to the banking sector is given by item 1. This increase in their liquidity will enable banks to create credit. To the extent that this extra lending is to the UK private sector (item 3), money supply will increase, and by a multiple of the initial increase in liquidity (item 1).

Bank lending may also increase (item 3), even if there is no increase in liquidity or even a reduction in liquidity (item 1 is zero or negative). This happens if banks respond to increases in the demand for loans by accepting a lower liquidity ratio or if, through securitisation and other forms of secondary marketing, individual banks gain extra liquidity from each other, even though there is no total increase in liquidity in the banking system. Item 3 will be reduced if banks either choose to, or because of regulatory requirements, hold more capital.

Finally, if there is a net inflow of funds from abroad (item 4), this too will increase the money supply.

Figure 28.5 shows the components of changes in broad money (M4) in the UK since 1995. It illustrates very clearly the contribution from bank lending to the strong growth of the money supply during the 2000s, up to the financial crisis. However, the curbing of lending by banks following the financial crisis, and then the requirement to hold larger capital buffers as part of the new Basel framework (see pages 566–9), dampened monetary growth. This helped to offset the otherwise expansionary impact on the money supply of the large public-sector deficits in the first half of the 2010s. Thereafter, a resurgence in lending along with still large public-sector deficits helped to boost the growth in broad money.

Credit cycles

Monetary growth is, as we have seen, affected by bank lending. An analysis of the flows of credit extended by financial institutions shows that they can vary considerably from period to period. This variation is consistent with the idea of a *credit cycle*. A credit cycle therefore helps to explain some of the patterns we see in the money supply. Some economists go much further and argue that a credit cycle is fundamental to explaining the business cycle.

KI 39
p 500

Credit cycles can be seen readily in Figure 28.6. The chart shows the annual flows of credit from monetary financial institutions (MFIs) to households and private non-financial corporations in the UK from the 1960s. The flows are measured relative to GDP, allowing us to make better comparisons of the magnitude of credit flows over time.

> ### Definition
>
> **Credit cycle** The expansion and contraction of credit flows over time.

Figure 28.5 Components of changes in M4

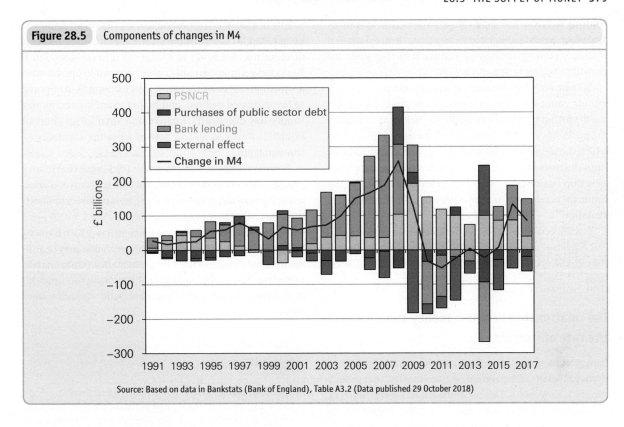

Source: Based on data in Bankstats (Bank of England), Table A3.2 (Data published 29 October 2018)

Figure 28.6 Annual flows of credit from MFIs

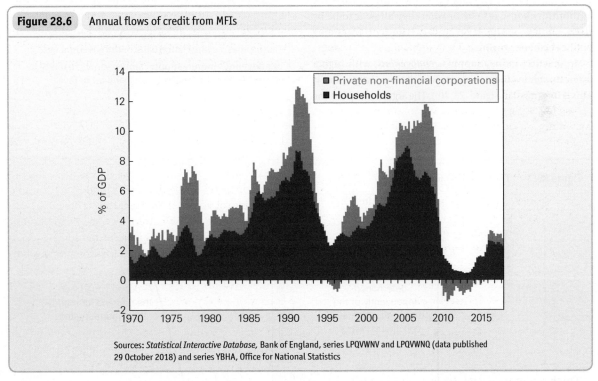

Sources: *Statistical Interactive Database,* Bank of England, series LPQVWNV and LPQVWNQ (data published 29 October 2018) and series YBHA, Office for National Statistics

As you can see, there were especially large flows of credit from MFIs in the late-1980s and the early/mid-2000s. In each case, this was then followed by a period of significantly weaker credit growth and, for non-financial corporations, even net repayments of outstanding lending.

The financial crisis helped to stimulate interest into the causes of credit cycles and their relationship with the macroeconomic environment. One possibility, it is argued, is that banks' lending behaviour is pro-cyclical lending, meaning that they increase lending volumes when economic growth is strong but reduce lending volumes when growth is weak. Therefore, lending either boosts aggregate demand when it is already growing strongly or weakens it further when the growth in aggregate demand is weak.

Because of the importance of aggregate demand in determining national income in the short run, pro-cyclical lending behaviour by financial institutions will tend to amplify the business cycle. The banking sector creates a process by which the sources of volatility in the economy, such as those from fluctuations in aggregate demand, have an amplified effect on national income. This process is known as the *financial accelerator*. It is another example of cumulative causation.

Box 28.4 considers another perspective on credit cycles: *The Financial Instability Hypothesis*. The argument here is that credit cycles are the primary *source* of the business cycle.

The relationship between money supply and the rate of interest

Simple monetary theory often assumes that the supply of money is totally independent of interest rates: that money supply is *exogenous*. This is illustrated in Figure 28.7(a). The supply of money is assumed to be determined by the government or central bank ('the authorities'): what the authorities choose it to be or what they allow it to be by their choice of the level and method of financing public-sector borrowing.

In practice, money supply is *endogenous*, with higher interest rates leading to increases in the supply of money. This is illustrated in Figure 28.7(b). The argument is that the

supply of money is responding to the demand for money. If people start borrowing more money, the resulting shortage of money in the banks will drive up interest rates. But if banks have surplus liquidity or are prepared to operate with a lower liquidity ratio, they will create extra credit in response to the increased demand and higher interest rates: money supply has expanded. If banks find themselves short of liquidity, they can always borrow from the central bank through repos.

Some economists go further still. They argue that money supply is not only endogenous, but also the 'curve' is effectively horizontal; money supply expands passively to match the demand for money.

It is likely, however, that the shape will *vary* with the confidence of banks. In periods of optimism, banks may be willing to expand credit to meet the demand from customers. In periods of pessimism, such as that following the financial crisis, banks may be unwilling to grant credit when customers seek it.

Definitions

Financial accelerator When a change in national income is amplified by changes in the financial sector, such as changes in interest rate differentials or the willingness of banks to lend.

Exogenous money supply Money supply that does not depend on the demand for money but is set by the authorities (i.e. the central bank or the government).

Endogenous money supply Money supply that is determined (at least in part) by the demand for money.

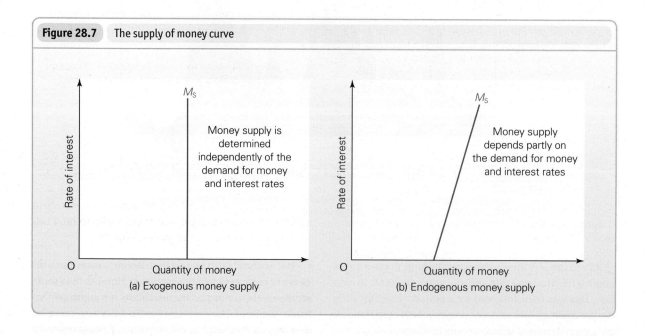

Figure 28.7 The supply of money curve

(a) Exogenous money supply — Money supply is determined independently of the demand for money and interest rates

(b) Endogenous money supply — Money supply depends partly on the demand for money and interest rates

BOX 28.4   MINSKY'S FINANCIAL INSTABILITY HYPOTHESIS

Are credit cycles inevitable?

Destabilising financial cycles

Born of Belarusian parents, Hyman Minsky (1919–96) was a US economist. He is known for his work on understanding the relationship between the financial system and the macroeconomy.

His *financial instability hypothesis* proposes that the volume of credit flows goes through stages which are, ultimately, destabilising for the economy.

In the expansionary stage, flows of credit increase rapidly. This feeds the growth in aggregate demand and, as incomes expend, so people and businesses borrow more, further stimulating the growth in demand.

But, as people and businesses take on more and more debt, so their borrowing becomes unsustainable. This then results in a period of consolidation when they seek (or are required by banks) to reduce their debts. Spending growth is thus subdued and the growth in aggregate demand ends or slows down.

Minsky argued that financial cycles are an inherent part of the economic cycle and are the primary source of fluctuations in real GDP. He argued that the accumulation of debt by people and businesses is not only pro-cyclical, but destabilising.

While Minsky himself focused on the accumulation of debt by businesses, the role of the mortgage market in generating unsustainable stocks of household debt during the 2000s has meant that his ideas are now frequently applied across the whole of the private sector.

From tranquillity to bust

The extension of credit by financial institutions can be seen to go through three different stages: financial tranquillity, financial fragility and financial bust. During each of these stages, both the credit criteria of banks and the ability of borrowers to afford their debts vary.

Minsky argued that credit flows will tend to increase during a period of sustained growth. This causes banks and investors to develop a heightened euphoria and confidence in the economy and in the returns of assets. Economists today refer to this as *irrational exuberance*, which results in people and businesses taking on bigger debts to acquire assets. These debts increasingly stretch their financial well-being. A point

is reached, perhaps triggered by an economic shock or a tightening of economic policy, when the euphoria stops and then confidence is replaced with pessimism. This moment is now commonly referred to as a *Minsky moment*.

The result of a Minsky moment is that lenders reduce their lending and people look to increase their net worth (i.e. reduce debts or increase savings) to ensure their financial well-being. However, the result of these individual actions causes a decline in spending and in national income. The collapse in aggregate demand from financial destress therefore leads to a *balance-sheet recession* or economic downturn (see page 582). Furthermore, with the sale of assets to improve people's financial well-being, the value of assets falls. This paradoxical reduction of net worth is known as the *paradox of debt*.

Minsky believed that credit cycles are inevitable in a free-market economy. Hence, the authorities will need to act to moderate credit cycles. The significance given to macroprudential regulation by policy-makers (see section 28.2) in the response to the financial crisis is recognition of the dangers posed to the economy by credit cycles.

A super cycle

While Minsky argued that the ingredients for economic volatility arising from financial instability are ever-present, some argue that other factors are needed for this instability to develop into a financial crisis. These factors may be part of a longer cycle of events. We could view the processes of financial deregulation and innovation that characterised the two to three decades leading up to the financial crisis as part of this longer cycle.

One interpretation of the financial crisis of the late 2000s is that it was the result of the interaction of the normal Minsky cycle (i.e. short-run variations in the accumulation of credit) with a longer cycle of events or a 'Minsky super-cycle'.

 What demand-side and supply-side factors influence the flows of net lending by financial institutions to the non-bank private sector?

 Undertake an internet news search for reference to the concept of a Minsky Moment. Summarise the findings of your search.

28.4   THE DEMAND FOR MONEY

The demand for money refers to the desire to *hold* money: to keep your wealth in the form of money, rather than spending it on goods and services or using it to purchase financial assets such as bonds or shares. It is usual to distinguish three reasons why people want to hold their assets in the form of money.

The transactions motive. Since money is a medium of exchange, it is required for conducting transactions. But

since people only receive money at intervals (e.g. weekly or monthly) and not continuously, they require to hold balances of money in cash or in current accounts.

The precautionary motive. Unforeseen circumstances can arise, such as a car breakdown. Thus individuals often hold some additional money as a precaution. Firms, too, keep precautionary balances. This may be because of uncertainties about the timing of their receipts and payments. If a large customer is late in making a payment, a firm may be unable to pay its suppliers unless it has spare liquidity. But firms may also hold precautionary balances because of uncertainty surrounding the economic environment in which they operate.

The assets or speculative motive. Money is not just a medium of exchange, it is also a means of storing wealth (see page 556). Keeping some or all of your wealth as money in a bank account has the advantage of carrying no risk. It earns a relatively small, but safe rate of return. Some assets, such as company shares or bonds, may earn you more on average, but there is a chance that their price will fall. In other words, they are risky.

What determines the size of the demand for money?

What would cause the demand for money to rise? We now turn to examine the various determinants of the size of the demand for money (M_D). In particular, we will look at the role of the rate of interest. First, however, let us identify the other determinants of the demand for money.

Money national income. The more money people earn, the greater will be their expenditure and hence the greater the transactions demand for money. A rise in money ('nominal') incomes in a country can be caused either by a rise in real GDP (i.e. real output), by a rise in prices or by some combination of the two.

The frequency with which people are paid. The less frequently people are paid, the greater the level of money balances that will be required to tide them over until the next payment.

Financial innovations. The increased use of credit cards, debit cards and cash machines, plus the advent of interest-paying current accounts, have resulted in changes in the demand for money. The use of credit cards reduces both the transactions and precautionary demands. Paying once a month for goods requires less money on average than paying separately for each item purchased. Moreover, the possession of a credit card reduces or even eliminates the need to hold precautionary balances for many people.

On the other hand, the increased availability of cash machines, the convenience of debit cards and the ability to earn interest on current accounts have all encouraged people to hold more money in bank accounts. The net effect has been an increase in the demand for money.

Speculation about future returns on assets. The assets motive for holding money depends on people's expectations. If they believe that share prices are about to fall on the stock market,

they will sell shares and hold larger balances of money in the meantime. The assets demand, therefore, can be quite high when the price of securities is considered certain to fall. Some clever (or lucky) individuals anticipated the 2007–8 stock market decline. They sold shares and 'went liquid'.

Generally, the more risky such alternatives to money become, the more people will want to hold their assets as money balances in a bank or building society.

People also speculate about changes in the exchange rate. If businesses believe that the exchange rate is about to appreciate (rise), they will hold greater balances of domestic currency in the meantime, hoping to buy foreign currencies with them when the rate has risen (since they will then get more foreign currency for their money).

The rate of interest (or rate of return) on assets. In terms of the operation of money markets, this is the most important determinant. It is related to the opportunity cost of holding money. The opportunity cost is the interest forgone by not holding higher interest-bearing assets, such as shares, bills or bonds. With most bank accounts today paying interest, this opportunity cost is less than in the past and thus the demand for money for assets purposes has increased.

Definitions

Financial instability hypothesis During periods of economic growth, economic agents (firms and individuals) tend to borrow more and MFIs are more willing to lend. This fuels the boom. In a period of recession, economic agents tend to cut spending in order to reduce debts and MFIs are less willing to lend. This deepens the recession. Behaviour in financial markets thus tends to amplify the business cycle.

Irrational exuberance Where banks and other economic agents are over confident about the economy and/or financial markets and expect economic growth to remain stronger and/or asset prices to rise further than warranted by evidence. The term is associated with the economist Robert Shiller and his book *Irrational Exuberance* (2000) and with the former US Federal Reserve Chairman, Alan Greenspan.

Minsky moment A turning point in a credit cycle, where a period of easy credit and rising debt is replaced by one of tight credit and debt consolidation.

Balance sheet recession An economic slowdown or recession caused by private-sector individuals and firms looking to improve their financial well-being by increasing their saving and/or paying down debt.

Paradox of debt (or paradox of deleveraging) The paradox that one individual can increase his or her net worth by selling assets, but, if this is undertaken by a large number of people, aggregate net worth declines because asset prices fall.

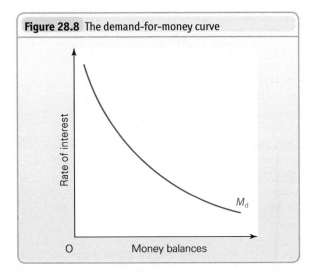

Figure 28.8 The demand-for-money curve

The demand-for-money curve

The demand-for-money curve with respect to interest rates is shown in Figure 28.8. It is downward sloping, showing that lower interest rates will encourage people to hold additional money balances (mainly for speculative purposes).

> **Pause for thought**
>
> *Which way is the demand-for-money curve likely to shift in each of the following cases? (a) Prices rise, but real incomes stay the same. (b) Interest rates abroad rise relative to domestic interest rates. (c) People anticipate that share prices are likely to fall in the near future.*

But what is the relationship between money demand and the rate of interest? Generally, if rates of interest rise, they will rise more on shares, bills and bonds than on bank accounts. The demand for money will thus fall. The demand for money is thus *inversely* related to the rate of interest.

A change in interest rates is shown by a movement along the demand-for-money curve. A change in any other determinant of the demand for money (such as national income or expectations about exchange rate movements) will cause the whole curve to shift: a rightward shift represents an increase in demand; a leftward shift represents a decrease.

28.5 EQUILIBRIUM

Equilibrium in the money market

KI 11
p 53

Equilibrium in the money market occurs when the demand for money (M_d) is equal to the supply of money (M_s). This equilibrium is achieved through changes in the rate of interest.

In Figure 28.9, assume that the demand for and supply of money are given by M_s and M_d. The equilibrium rate of interest is i_e and the equilibrium quantity of money is M_e. But why?

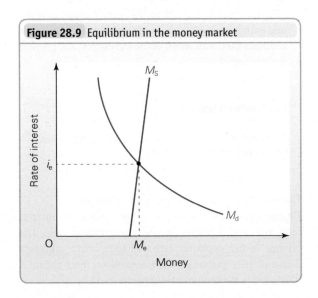

Figure 28.9 Equilibrium in the money market

If the rate of interest were above i_e, people would have money balances surplus to their needs. They would use these to buy shares, bonds and other assets. This would drive up the price of these assets. But the price of assets is inversely related to interest rates. The higher the price of an asset (such as a government bond), the less will any given interest payment be as a percentage of its price (e.g. £10 as a percentage of £100 is 10 per cent, but as a percentage of £200 is only 5 per cent). Thus a higher price of assets will correspond to lower interest rates.

As the rate of interest fell, so there would be a contraction of the money supply (a movement down along the M_s curve) and an increase in the demand for money balances, especially speculative balances (a movement down along the M_d curve). The interest rate would go on falling until it reached i_e. Equilibrium would then be achieved.

Similarly, if the rate of interest were below i_e, people would have insufficient money balances. They would sell securities, thus lowering their prices and raising the rate of interest until it reached i_e.

A shift in either the M_s or the M_d curve will lead to a new equilibrium quantity of money and rate of interest at the new intersection of the curves. For example, a rise in the supply of money will cause the rate of interest to fall, whereas a rise in the demand for money will cause the rate of interest to rise.

KI 10
p 46

In practice, there is no one single interest rate. Rather, equilibrium in the money markets will be where demand

Figure 28.10 Selected interest rates

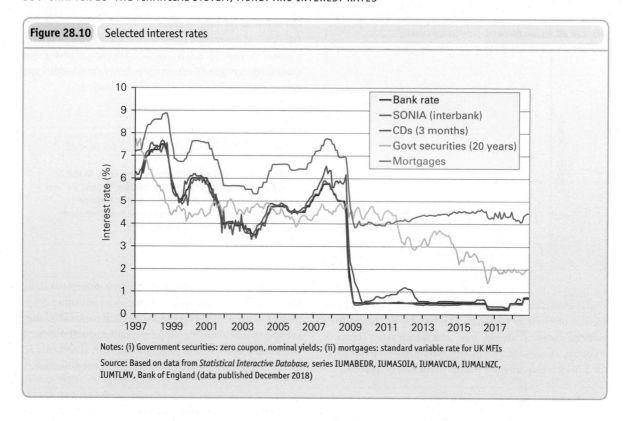

Notes: (i) Government securities: zero coupon, nominal yields; (ii) mortgages: standard variable rate for UK MFIs

Source: Based on data from *Statistical Interactive Database*, series IUMABEDR, IUMASOIA, IUMAVCDA, IUMALNZC, IUMTLMV, Bank of England (data published December 2018)

and supply of the various financial instruments separately balance. Generally, however, different interest rates tend to move roughly together as the overall demand for money and other liquid assets (or their supply) changes.

Figure 28.10 gives some examples of interest rates on various financial instruments. It shows how the various rates of interest generally move together, especially those with shorter maturities. As we saw in section 28.2, the Bank of England conducts open-market operations to affect the general structure of the economy's interest rates and, in turn, the inflation rate. We can see how significant reductions to the policy rate (Bank Rate) following the financial crisis were mirrored by falls in other interest rates.

The link between the money and goods markets

A rise in money supply will cause a rise in aggregate demand. There are two principal ways in which a rise in money supply causes a rise in aggregate demand. The first is via changes in interest rates – known as the interest-rate transmission mechanism. The second is via changes in the exchange rate – known as the exchange-rate transmission mechanism.

The interest-rate transmission mechanism

KI 10
p 46 The interest rate transmission mechanism is illustrated in the top part of Figure 28.11. It is a three-stage process:

- A rise in money supply will lead to a fall in the rate of interest: this is necessary to restore equilibrium in the money market. This would be illustrated by a rightward shift in the M_s line in Figure 28.9, with the rate of interest falling to the point where this new M_s curve crossed the M_d curve.

- This fall in the rate of interest then encourages firms to invest (I), since it is cheaper to borrow money to finance new buildings, machines, etc. It also encourages consumers to spend, since borrowing through credit cards and personal loans is now cheaper. At the same time, it discourages saving (S) since saving now gives a poorer return.

- The net effect of these changes in injections (increase) and withdrawals (fall) is a rise in aggregate demand and a resulting rise in national income and output, and possibly a rise in prices too.

Pause for thought

What elasticities are relevant when analysing the interest-rate transmission mechanism?

The exchange-rate transmission mechanism

Changes in the money supply will not only affect interest rates, they will also have an effect on exchange rates. The change in the exchange rate will then affect aggregate demand. This 'exchange-rate transmission mechanism' is illustrated in the bottom part of Figure 28.11.

Figure 28.11 Monetary transmission mechanism

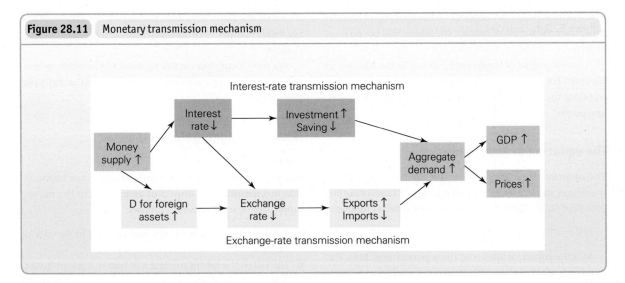

Assume again that the money supply increases. This has the following effects:

- *Part* of the excess money balances is used to purchase foreign assets. This therefore leads to an increase in the supply of domestic currency coming on to the foreign exchange markets.
- As we have already seen, the excess supply of money in the domestic money market pushes down the rate of interest. This reduces the return on domestic assets below that on foreign assets. This, like the first effect, leads to an increased demand for foreign assets and thus an increased supply of domestic currency on the foreign exchange market. It also reduces the demand for domestic assets by those outside the country, and thus reduces the demand for the domestic currency. This causes the exchange rate to fall (*depreciate*).
- The fall in the exchange rate (e.g. from £1 = €1.20 to £1 = €1.10) means that people abroad have to pay less for a pound. This makes UK exports (an injection) cheaper and hence more are sold. People in the UK, by contrast, get less foreign currency for a pound. This makes imports (a withdrawal) more expensive and hence fewer are purchased.
- Again, the net effect of these changes in injections and withdrawals is a rise in aggregate demand.

28.6 MONEY, AGGREGATE DEMAND AND INFLATION

There is considerable debate around the impact of changes in the money supply on output and inflation. The debate can be understood in terms of the transmission mechanisms that we looked at in the previous section, illustrated in Figure 28.11.

There are two key questions.

- First, to what extent will a change in money supply affect interest rates and how much, in turn, will a change in interest rates affect aggregate demand? In other words, what is the strength of the interest rate and exchange rate transmission mechanisms?
- Second, how much will a change in aggregate demand affect real output and how much will it merely result in higher prices?

The 1970s saw the rise of monetarism. The most famous advocate of monetarism was Milton Friedman, who argued that inflation can be attributed entirely to increases in the money supply. The faster money supply expands, the higher will be the rate of inflation. New classical economists of today take a similar view. Excessive expansion of the money supply will lead simply to inflation. According to monetarist and new classical economists, therefore, in answer to the first question, the mechanisms are strong: a rise in money supply directly affects aggregate demand. But any rise in aggregate demand will lead not to an increase in output (at least, according to monetarists, not in the long run) but merely to higher prices.

Keynesians, by contrast, see a much looser association between money and prices. The amount that a rise in money supply leads to higher aggregate demand and higher output depends on circumstances.

The debate can best be understood in terms of the *quantity theory of money*. The theory is simply that the level

Definitions

Quantity theory of money The price level (P) is directly related to the quantity of money in the economy (M).

of prices in the economy depends on the quantity of money: the greater the supply of money, the higher will be the level of prices.

A development of the quantity theory is the *equation of exchange*. Focusing on this equation is the best way of understanding the debate over the relationship between money and prices.

The equation of exchange

 The *equation of exchange* shows the relationship between the money value of spending and the money value of output (nominal GDP). This identity may be expressed as follows:

$$MV = PY$$

M is the supply of money in the economy (e.g. M4). *V* is its *velocity of circulation*. This is the number of times per year that money is spent on buying goods and services that have been produced in the economy that year (real GDP). *P* is the level of prices of domestically produced goods and services, expressed as an index, where the index is 1 in a chosen base year (e.g. 2000). Thus, if prices today are double those in the base year, *P* is 2. *Y* is *real* national income (real GDP): in other words, the quantity of national output produced in that year measured in base-year prices.

 PY is thus nominal GDP, i.e. GDP measured at current prices (see section 26.1, page 500). For example, if GDP at base-year prices (*Y*) is £1 trillion and the price index is 2, then GDP at current prices (*PY*) is £2 trillion.

Pause for thought

If the money supply is cut by 10 per cent, what must happen to the velocity of circulation if there is no change in GDP at current prices?

MV is the total spending on the goods and services that make up GDP – in other words, (nominal) aggregate demand. For example, if money supply is £500 billion, and money, as it passes from one person to another, is spent on average four times a year on national output, then total spending (*MV*) is £2 trillion a year. But this too *must* equal GDP at current prices. The reason is that what is spent on output (by consumers, by firms on investment, by the government or by people abroad on exports) must equal the value of goods produced (*PY*).

The equation of exchange (or 'quantity equation') is true by definition. *MV* is *necessarily* equal to *PY* because of the way the terms are defined. Thus a rise in *MV must* be accompanied by a rise in *PY*.

What a change in *M* does to *P*, however, is a matter of debate. The controversy centres on the impact of changes in the money supply on aggregate demand and then on the impact of changes in aggregate demand on output. We have

seen that the latter depends crucially on the nature of the aggregate supply. We develop this further in the next chapter.

We now focus now on the relationship between money supply and aggregate demand, beginning with the short-run relationship.

Money and aggregate demand

The short run

According to the interest-rate and exchange-rate transmission mechanisms, the impact of an increase in the money supply can be summarised as follows:

- A rise in money supply will lead to a fall in the rate of interest.
- The fall in the rate of interest will lead to a rise in investment and other forms of borrowing. It will also lead to a fall in the exchange rate and hence a rise in exports and a fall in imports.
- The rise in investment, and the rise in exports and fall in imports, will mean a rise in aggregate demand.

However, there is considerable debate over how these transmission mechanisms function.

How interest-rate elastic is money demand? The demand for money as a means of storing wealth (the assets motive) can be large and highly responsive to changes in interest rates on alternative assets. Indeed, large sums of money move around the money market as firms and financial institutions respond to and anticipate changes in interest rates. Therefore, the demand-for-money curve in Figure 28.8 could be relatively flat. This is important because, following an increase in money supply, only a relatively small fall in interest rates on bonds and other assets may be necessary to persuade people to hold all the extra money in bank accounts. This greatly slows down the average speed at which money circulates. The fall in *V* may virtually offset the rise in *M*.

Indeed, this was one of the consequences of the large increases in money supply under the programmes of quantitative easing. These were adopted by central banks around the world in an attempt to stimulate recovery from the recession in 2009–11 that followed the financial crisis. But, although money supply rose, much of it was held in additional reserves rather than being spent.

Definitions

Equation of exchange *MV = PY*. The total level of spending on GDP (*MV*) equals the total value of goods and services produced (*PY*) that go to make up GDP.

Velocity of circulation The number of times annually that money on average is spent on goods and services that make up GDP.

The more sensitive is the demand for money to changes in the rate of interest, the less impact changes in money supply have on aggregate demand.

How stable is the money demand function? Another criticism is that the demand for money is unstable and so the demand-for-money curve (in Figure 28.8) is frequently moving. People hold speculative balances of money when they anticipate that the prices of other assets, such as shares, bonds and bills, will fall (and hence the rate of return or interest on these assets will rise).

There are many factors that could affect such expectations, such as changes in foreign interest rates, changes in exchange rates, statements of government intentions on economic policy, good or bad industrial news or newly published figures on inflation or money supply. With an unstable demand for money, it is difficult to predict the effect of a change in money supply on interest rates and so on aggregate demand.

It has been largely for this reason that most central banks have preferred to control interest rates directly, rather than indirectly by controlling the money supply. (We examine the conduct of monetary policy in Chapter 30.)

KI 12
p 64 *How interest-rate elastic is spending?* The problem here is that investment may be insensitive to changes in interest rates. Businesses are more likely to be influenced in their decision to invest by predictions of the future buoyancy of markets. Interest rates do have *some* effect on businesses' investment decisions, but the effect is unpredictable, depending on the confidence of investors.

Where interest rates are likely to have a stronger effect on spending is via mortgages. If interest rates go up, and mortgage rates follow suit, people will suddenly be faced with higher monthly repayments (debt servicing costs) and will therefore have to cut down their expenditure on goods and services.

KI 12
p 64 *How interest-rate sensitive is the exchange rate?* Also the amount that the exchange rate will depreciate is uncertain, since exchange rate movements, as we saw in Chapter 27, depend crucially on expectations about trade prospects and about future world interest rate movements. Thus the effects on imports and exports are also uncertain.

To summarise: the effects on total spending of a change in the money supply *might* be quite strong, but they could be weak. In other words, the effects are highly unpredictable.

$$M\uparrow \rightarrow V\downarrow(?) \rightarrow MV?$$

Keynesians use these arguments to criticise the use of monetary policy as a means of managing aggregate demand.

The long run

In the long run, there is a stronger link between money supply and aggregate demand. In fact, monetarists claim that in the long run V is determined *totally independently* of the money supply (M). Thus an increase in M will leave V unaffected and hence will directly increase expenditure (MV):

$$M\uparrow \rightarrow M\overline{V}\uparrow$$

where the bar over the V term means that it is **exogenously** determined: i.e. determined *independently* of M. But why do they claim this?

If money supply increases over the longer term, people will have more money than they require to hold. They will spend this surplus. Much of this spending will go on goods and services, thereby directly increasing nominal aggregate demand.

The theoretical underpinning for this is given by the *theory of portfolio balance*. People have a number of ways of holding their wealth. They can hold it as money, as financial assets such as bills, bonds and shares or as physical assets such as houses, cars and televisions. In other words, people hold a whole portfolio of assets of varying degrees of liquidity – from cash to central heating.

If money supply expands, people will find themselves holding more money than they require: their portfolios are 'unnecessarily liquid'. Some of this money will be used to purchase financial assets and some, possibly after a period of time, to purchase *goods and services*. As more assets are purchased, this will drive up their price. This will effectively reduce their 'yield'. For bonds and other *financial* assets, this means a reduction in their rate of interest. For goods and services, it means an increase in their price relative to their usefulness or 'utility'.

The process will stop when a balance has been restored in people's portfolios. In the meantime, there will have been extra consumption and hence an increase in aggregate demand.

Definition

Exogenous variable A variable whose value is determined independently of the model of which it is part.

SUMMARY

1   Money's main function is as a medium of exchange. In addition, it is a means of storing wealth, a means of evaluation and a means of establishing the value of future claims and payments.

2a Central to the financial system are the retail and wholesale arms of banks. Between them they provide the following important functions: giving expert advice, channelling capital to areas of highest return, maturity transformation, risk transformation and the transmission of payments. During the financial crisis, the systemic importance of some of these banks meant they had to be rescued by governments. They were seen as too important or too big to fail (TBF).

2b Banks' liabilities include both sight and time deposits. They also include certificates of deposit and repos. Their assets include: notes and coin, balances with the central bank, market loans, bills of exchange (Treasury bills and commercial bills), reverse repos, advances to customers (the biggest item – including overdrafts, personal loans, credit card debt and mortgages) and investments (government bonds and interbank investments). In the years up to 2008, they had increasingly included securitised assets.

2c Banks aim to make profits, but they must also have a sufficient capital base and maintain sufficient liquidity. Liquid assets, however, tend to be relatively unprofitable and profitable assets tend to be relatively illiquid. Banks therefore need to keep a balance of profitability and liquidity in their range of assets. They also need to have adequate levels of capital to meet the demands of depositors and to cover potential losses from investments or if borrowers default on payments.

2d The regulatory framework provided by the Basel committee on Banking Supervision has been strengthened following the financial crisis. The key features of Basel III include: increasing the level and quality of capital (capital adequacy), constraining leverage and hence the build-up of debt to fund activities, improving bank liquidity and limiting pro-cyclical lending behaviour. Additional capital and leverage buffers are applied to global systemically important banks (GSIBs).

2e The Bank of England is the UK's central bank. It issues notes; it acts as banker to the government, to banks and to various overseas central banks; it ensures sufficient liquidity for the financial sector; it operates the country's monetary and exchange rate policy.

2f The money market is the market in short-term deposits and loans. It consists of the discount and repo markets and the parallel money markets.

2g Through repos the Bank of England provides liquidity to the banks at the rate of interest chosen by the Monetary Policy Committee (Bank Rate). It is always prepared to lend in this way in order to ensure adequate liquidity in the economy. The financial crisis saw the Bank of England supply adapt its operations in the money market and introduce new ways of providing liquidity insurance, including the Discount Window Facility (DWF) and longer-term repos.

2g The parallel money markets consist of various markets in short-term finance between various financial institutions.

3a Money supply can be defined in a number of different ways, depending on what items are included. A useful distinction is between narrow money and broad money. Narrow money includes just cash and possibly banks' balances at the central bank. Broad money also includes deposits in banks and possibly various other short-term deposits in the money market. In the UK, M4 is the preferred measure of broad money. In the Eurozone it is M3.

3b Bank deposits are a major proportion of broad money supply. The expansion of bank deposits is the major element in the expansion of the money supply.

3c Bank deposits expand through a process of credit creation. If banks' liquid assets increase, they can be used as a base for increasing loans. When the loans are redeposited in banks, they form the base for yet more loans and thus a process of multiple credit expansion takes place. The ratio of the increase of deposits to an expansion of banks' liquidity base is called the 'bank multiplier'. It is the inverse of the liquidity ratio.

3d In practice, it is difficult to predict the precise amount by which money supply will expand if there is an increase in cash. The reasons are that banks may choose to hold a different liquidity ratio; customers may not take up all the credit on offer; there may be no simple liquidity ratio given the range of near-money assets; and some of the extra cash may leak away into extra cash holdings by the public.

3e (Broad) money supply will rise if: (a) banks choose to hold a lower liquidity ratio and thus create more credit for an existing amount of liquidity; (b) the non-bank private sector chooses to hold less cash; (c) the government runs a deficit and some of it is financed by borrowing from the banking sector; (d) there is an inflow of funds from abroad.

3f The flow-of-funds equation shows the components of any change in money supply. A rise in money supply equals the public-sector net cash requirement (PSNCR) *minus* sales of public-sector debt to the non-bank private sector, *plus* banks' lending to the private sector (less increases in banks' capital), *plus* inflows of money from abroad.

3g Bank lending exerts an important influence on monetary growth. Credit flows fluctuate in a way that is consistent with a credit cycle. The financial crisis has heightened interest in why credit cycles arise and in their impact on the macroeconomic environment.

3h Simple monetary theory assumes that the supply of money is independent of interest rates. In practice, a rise in interest rates often will lead to an increase in money supply. But, conversely, if the government raises interest rates, the supply of money may fall in response to a lower demand for money.

4a The three motives for holding money are the transactions, precautionary and assets (or speculative) motives.

4b The demand for money will be higher: (a) the higher the level of money national income (i.e. the higher the level of real national income and the higher the price level); (b) the less frequently people are paid; (c) the greater the advantages of holding money in bank accounts, such as access to cash machines and the use of debit cards; (d) the more risky alternative assets become and the more likely they are to fall in value, and the more likely the exchange rate is to rise; and (e) the lower the opportunity cost of holding money in terms of interest forgone on alternative assets.

4c The demand for money curve with respect to interest rates is downward sloping.

5a Equilibrium in the money market is where the supply of money is equal to the demand. Equilibrium is achieved through changes in the interest rate and the exchange rate.

5b The interest rate mechanism works as follows: a rise in money supply causes money supply to exceed money demand; interest rates fall; this causes investment (an injection) and consumer spending to rise and saving (a withdrawal) to fall; this causes a rise in national income.

5c The exchange rate mechanism works as follows: a rise in money supply causes interest rates to fall; the rise in money supply, plus the fall in interest rates, causes an increased supply of domestic currency to come on to the foreign exchange market; this causes the exchange rate to depreciate; this causes increased exports (an injection) and reduced imports (a withdrawal) and hence a rise in national income.

6a The quantity equation $MV = PY$ can be used to analyse the possible relationships between money and prices.

6b In the short run, the velocity of circulation (V) may vary inversely, but unpredictably, with the money supply (M). The reason is that changes in money supply will have unpredictable and possibly rather weak effects on interest rates, and, similarly, changes in interest rates will have unpredictable and probably rather weak effects on aggregate demand. Thus spending (MV) will change by possibly only a small and rather unpredictable amount.

6c In the long run, there is a stronger link between money supply and aggregate demand.

REVIEW QUESTIONS

1 Imagine that the banking system receives additional deposits of £100 million and that all the individual banks wish to retain their current liquidity ratio of 20 per cent.

   a) How much will banks choose to lend out initially?
   b) What will happen to banks' liabilities when the money that is lent out is spent and the recipients of it deposit it in their bank accounts?
   c) How much of these latest deposits will be lent out by the banks?
   d) By how much will total deposits (liabilities) eventually have risen, assuming that none of the additional liquidity is held outside the banking sector?
   e) How much of these are matched by (i) liquid assets; (ii) illiquid assets?
   f) What is the size of the bank multiplier?
   g) If one half of any additional liquidity is held outside the banking sector, by how much less will deposits have risen compared with (d) above?

2 What is meant by the terms *narrow money* and *broad money*? Does broad money fulfil all the functions of money?

3 Why do banks hold a range of assets of varying degrees of liquidity and profitability?

4 What is meant by the securitisation of assets? How might this be (a) beneficial and (b) harmful to banks and the economy?

5 What were the causes of the credit crunch and the banking crisis of the late 2000s?

6 Define the term 'liquidity ratio'. How will changes in the liquidity ratio affect the process of credit creation? Why might a bank's liquidity ratio vary over time?

7 What is measured by the CET1 ratio? What measures would a bank need to take in order to increase its CET1 ratio?

8 Analyse the possible effects on banks' balance sheets of the following:

   a) the Basel III regulatory requirements;
   b) the UK bank levy.

9 What is meant by macro prudential regulation? How has this concept influenced changes to the Basel regulatory framework?

10 Assume that banks choose to operate a 20 per cent liquidity ratio and receive extra cash deposits of £10 million. Assume also that the general public does not wish to hold a larger total amount of cash balances outside the banks.

   a) How much credit will ultimately be created?
   b) By how much will total deposits have expanded?
   c) What is the size of the bank deposits multiplier?

11 What is mean by a credit cycle? What impact do such cycles have on monetary growth?

12 Why might the relationship between the demand for money and the rate of interest be an unstable one?

13 What effects will the following have on the equilibrium rate of interest? (You should consider which way the demand and/or supply curves of money shift.)

   a) Banks find that they have a higher liquidity ratio than they need.
   b) A rise in incomes.
   c) A growing belief that interest rates will rise from their current level.

14 If V is constant, will (a) a £10 million rise in M give a £10 million rise in MV and (b) a 10 per cent rise in M give a 10 per cent rise in MV? (Test your answer by fitting some numbers to the terms.)

15 If both V and Y are constant, will (a) a £10 million rise in M lead to a £10 million rise in P and (b) a 10 per cent rise in M lead to a 10 per cent rise in P? (Again, try fitting some numbers to the terms.)

Business activity, unemployment and inflation

Business issues covered in this chapter

- Why does an increase in aggregate demand of £x lead to a rise in GDP of more than £x?
- How flexibly does aggregate supply respond to changes in aggregate demand?
- What is the relationship between unemployment and inflation? Is the relationship a stable one?
- How do business and consumer expectations affect the relationship between inflation and unemployment? How are such expectations formed?
- How does a policy of targeting the rate of inflation affect the relationship between inflation and unemployment?
- Why have many governments chosen to delegate the operation of monetary policy to central banks?
- Why is private-sector spending volatile?
- What determines the course of a business cycle and its turning points?

In this chapter, we examine what determines the level of business activity and why it fluctuates. We also look at the effects of business activity on employment and inflation.

We start, in section 29.1, by looking at the determinants of GDP and, in particular, the role of aggregate demand. We do this by introducing the simple 'Keynesian' model (named after the great economist, John Maynard Keynes (1883–1946). (See Case study J.18 on the student website.) We consider how business activity might respond to changes in the level of aggregate demand.

Section 29.2 builds on the analysis of section 29.1 by focusing on the flexibility of aggregate supply in response to changes in aggregate demand. Some economists argue that changes in aggregate demand may have little or no effect on output and employment, even in the short run, but may have a significant effect on prices. In contrast, some economists argue that there could be quite significant effects on economic activity and that these effects could persist.

In sections 29.3 and 29.4, we turn to the problems of unemployment and inflation and the relationship between the two. An important influence on both of them is what people *expect* to happen. Generally, if people are optimistic and believe that the economy will grow and unemployment will fall, this will happen. Similarly, if people expect inflation to stay low, it will do. In other words, people's expectations tend to be self-fulfilling. Getting people to expect low rates of inflation is something that can lead central banks to adopt inflation rate targets (the subject of section 29.4).

Finally, we consider the volatility of private-sector spending in more detail. We examine the determinants of consumer spending and firms' investment and their contribution to economic volatility.

29.1 THE SIMPLE KEYNESIAN MODEL OF BUSINESS ACTIVITY

One of our key macroeconomic variables is the economy's output which is measured by GDP (see the appendix to Chapter 26). The income generated from GDP is referred to as 'national income'. Hence, the terms GDP and national income are often used interchangeably.

The circular flow of income model (introduced in Chapter 26) allows us to see the flows of income between the various sectors of the economy and how they affect aggregate demand. This is important because many economists believe that it is fluctuations in aggregate demand that lie behind the business cycle.

In this section, after briefly revisiting the circular flow model, we develop the simple Keynesian model of the determination of national income (GDP). We can then analyse more closely the impact of changes of aggregate demand on national income. We assume initially that prices are constant and so there is no inflation. Later in the section, we see how a change in aggregate demand could affect both output *and* prices.

Revisiting the circular flow of income model

Figure 29.1 shows a simplified version of the circular flow, with injections entering at just one point and, likewise, withdrawals leaving at just one point (this simplification does not affect the argument).

If injections (J) do not equal withdrawals (W), a state of disequilibrium exists. What will bring them back into equilibrium is a change in national income (GDP) and employment.

Start with a state of equilibrium, where injections equal withdrawals. If there is now a rise in injections – say firms decide to invest more – aggregate demand (i.e. the consumption of domestic products (C_d) plus injections (J)) will be higher. Firms will respond to this increased demand by using more labour and other resources and thus paying out more

incomes (Y) to households. Household consumption will rise and so firms will sell more.

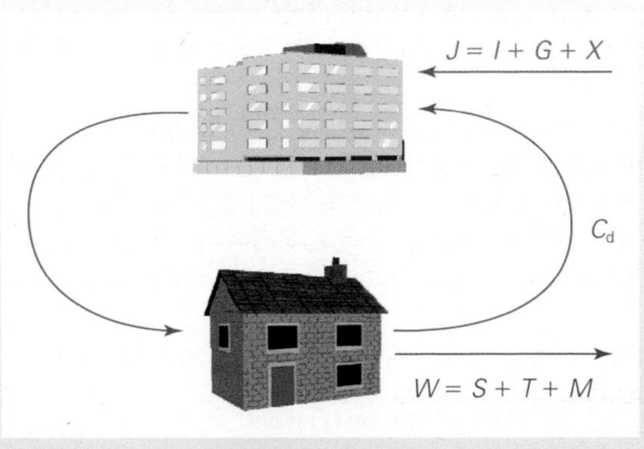

Firms will respond by producing more and thus using more labour and other resources. Household incomes will rise again. Consumption and hence production will rise again, and so on. There will thus be a multiplied rise in incomes and employment. This is known as the ***multiplier effect***.

The process, however, does not go on for ever. Each time household incomes rise, households save more, pay more taxes and buy more imports. In other words, withdrawals rise. When withdrawals have risen to match the increase in injections, equilibrium will be restored and national income (GDP) and employment will stop rising. The process can be summarised as follows:

$$J > W \rightarrow Y\uparrow \rightarrow W\uparrow \text{ until } J = W$$

Similarly, an initial fall in injections (or rise in withdrawals) will lead to a multiplied fall in national income and employment:

$$J < W \rightarrow Y\downarrow \rightarrow W\downarrow \text{ until } J = W$$

Thus equilibrium in the circular flow of income can be at *any* level of national income and employment.

The simple Keynesian model

The circular flow model is a demand-driven model of the economy. Changes in aggregate demand drive changes in national income. But to analyse the determination of national income, we need to model the income flows that affect aggregate demand. Then we can identify the equilibrium level of national income.

Equilibrium can be shown on a 'Keynesian 45° line diagram' also known as the 'Keynesian Cross'. Keynes argued that equilibrium national income is determined by aggregate demand. Equilibrium can be at any level of capacity. If aggregate demand is buoyant, equilibrium can be where businesses are operating at full capacity with full employment. If aggregate demand is low, however, equilibrium can be at well below full capacity with high unemployment (i.e. a recession). Keynes argued that it is important, therefore, for governments to manage the level of aggregate demand to avoid recessions.

The Keynesian Cross diagram plots various elements of the circular flow of income, such as consumption,

KI 11
p 53

Figure 29.1 The circular flow of income

$$J = I + G + X$$

$$C_d$$

$$W = S + T + M$$

Definition

Multiplier effect An initial increase in aggregate demand of £xm leads to an eventual rise in national income that is greater than £xm.

withdrawals, injections and aggregate demand, against national income.

In Figure 29.2, two continuous lines are shown. The 45° line out from the origin plots $C_d + W$ against national income. It is a 45° line because, by definition, $Y = C_d + W$. To understand this, consider what can happen to the income earned from GDP (national income): either it must be spent on domestically produced goods (C_d) or it must be withdrawn from the circular flow – there is nothing else that can happen to it. Thus if national income (Y) were £2 trillion billion, then $C_d + W$ must also be £2 trillion. If you draw a line such that whatever value is plotted on the horizontal axis (Y) is also plotted on the vertical axis ($C_d + W$), the line will be at 45° (assuming that the axes are drawn to the same scale).

The other continuous line plots aggregate demand. In this diagram, it is known as the *aggregate expenditure line* (E). It consists of $C_d + J$: in other words, the total spending on domestic firms.

To show how this line is constructed, consider the dashed line. This shows C_d. It is flatter than the 45° line. The reason is that for any given rise in GDP and hence people's incomes, only *part* will be spent on domestic products, while the remainder will be withdrawn: i.e. C_d rises less quickly than GDP (Y). The E line consists of $C_d + J$. But we have assumed that J is constant with respect to changes in national income. Thus the E line is simply the C_d line shifted upward by the amount of J.

If aggregate expenditure exceeded national income (the value of national output), at say Y_1, there would be excess demand in the economy (of $a - b$). In other words, people would be buying more than was currently being produced. Firms would thus find their stocks dwindling and would therefore increase their level of production. In doing so, they would employ more factors of production. GDP would thus

rise. As it did so, C_d and hence E would rise. There would be a movement up along the E line. But because not all the extra incomes earned from the rise in GDP would be consumed (i.e. some would be withdrawn), expenditure would rise less quickly than income: the E line is flatter than the Y line. As income rises towards Y_e, the gap between the Y and E lines gets smaller. Once point e is reached, $Y = E$. There is then no further tendency for GDP to rise.

If GDP (national income) exceeded aggregate expenditure, at say Y_2, there would be insufficient demand for the goods and services currently being produced ($c - d$). Firms would find their stocks of unsold goods building up. They would thus respond by producing less and employing less factors of production. GDP would thus fall and go on falling until Y_e was reached.

The multiplier

When aggregate expenditure rises, this will cause GDP to rise. But by how much? The answer is that there will be a *multiplied* rise in GDP, i.e. it will rise by more than the rise in aggregate expenditure. The size of the **multiplier** is given by the letter k, where:

$$k = \Delta Y / \Delta E$$

Thus, if aggregate expenditure rose by £10 billion (ΔE) and, as a result, GDP rose by £30 billion (ΔY), the multiplier

KI 43
p 575

> ### Definitions
>
> **Multiplier** The number of times a rise in GDP (ΔY) is bigger than the initial rise in aggregate expenditure (ΔE) that caused it. Using the letter k to stand for the multiplier, the multiplier is defined as $k = \Delta Y / \Delta E$

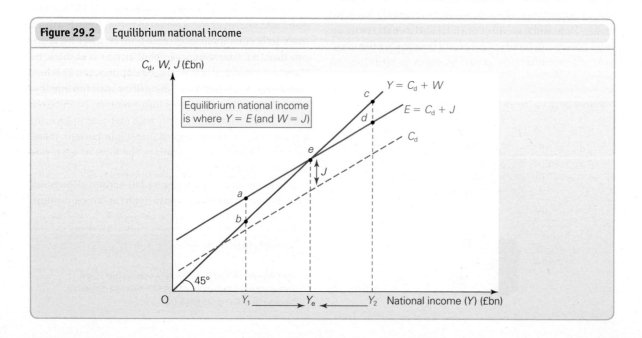

Figure 29.2 Equilibrium national income

Figure 29.3 The multiplier: a rise in aggregate expenditure

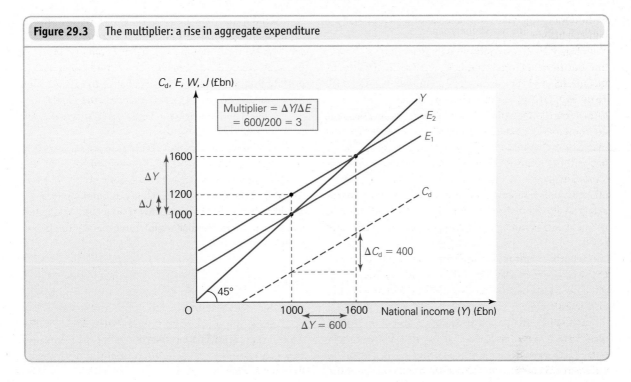

would be 3. Figure 29.3 is drawn on the assumption that the multiplier is 3.

Assume in Figure 29.3 that aggregate expenditure rises by £200 billion, from E_1 to E_2. This could be caused by a rise in injections, by a fall in withdrawals (and hence a rise in consumption of domestically produced goods) or by some combination of the two. Equilibrium GDP rises by £600 billion, from £1000 billion (£1 trillion) to £1600 billion (£1.6 trillion) (where the E_2 line crosses the *GDP* line).

What determines the size of the multiplier? The answer is that it depends on the **'marginal propensity to consume domestically produced goods and services'** (mpc_d). The mpc_d is the proportion of any rise in GDP that gets spent on domestically produced goods (in other words the proportion that is not withdrawn as saving, taxes or spending on imports).

$$mpc_d = \Delta C_d / \Delta Y$$

In Figure 29.3, $mpc_d = \Delta C_d / \Delta Y =$ £400bn/£600bn $= \frac{2}{3}$ (i.e. the slope of the C_d line). The higher the mpc_d the greater the proportion of income generated from GDP that recirculates around the circular flow of income and thus generates extra output.

The **multiplier formula** is given by:

$$k = \frac{1}{1 - mpc_d}$$

In our example, with $mpc_d = \frac{2}{3}$

$$k = \frac{1}{1 - \frac{2}{3}} = \frac{1}{\frac{1}{3}} = 3$$

If the mpc_d were $\frac{3}{4}$, the multiplier would be 4. Thus the higher the mpc_d, the higher the multiplier.

Pause for thought

Think of two reasons why a country might have a steep E line and hence a high value for the multiplier.

The multiplier and the full-employment level of national income

The simple Keynesian theory assumes that there is a maximum level of national income that can be obtained at any one time. If the equilibrium level of income is at this level, there will be no deficiency of aggregate demand. This level of income is referred to as the **full-employment level of national income** (or **full-employment level of GDP**).

Definitions

Marginal propensity to consume domestically produced goods and services The fraction of a rise in national income (Y) that is spent by consumers on domestic product (C_d) and hence is not withdrawn from the circular flow of income: $mpc_d = \Delta C_d / \Delta Y$.

Multiplier formula The formula for the multiplier is $k = 1/(1 - mpc_d)$.

Full-employment level of national income or **full-employment level of GDP** The level of GDP at which there is no deficiency of demand.

Figure 29.4 The recessionary gap

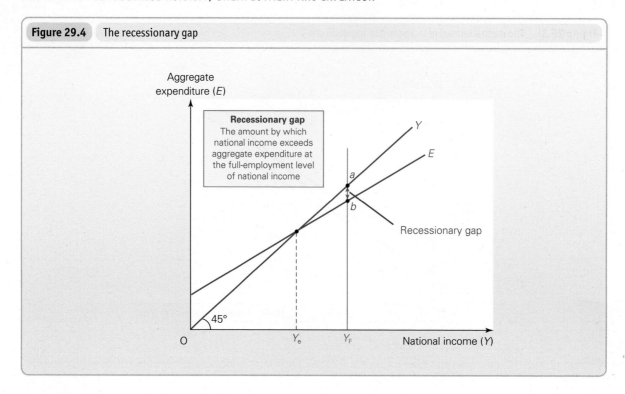

In practice, although at this level of national income there would be no cyclical unemployment, there would still be some unemployment for other reasons (see section 26.4). Hence, the concept is similar to that of *potential output* in that it reflects a normal-capacity output level.

Recessionary gap

Unfortunately, the equilibrium level of GDP (Y_e) could fall *below* the full-employment level (Y_F) resulting in a ***recessionary gap*** (also known as a ***deflationary gap***) and ***demand-deficient unemployment.*** (see page 518) This is illustrated in Figure 29.4.

The full-employment level of GDP (Y_F) is represented by the vertical line. The equilibrium level of national income is Y_e, where $Y = E$. The deflationary gap is $a - b$: namely, the amount that the E line is below the 45° line at the full-employment level of GDP (Y_F).

Note that the size of the recessionary gap is *less* than the amount by which Y_e falls short of Y_F. This provides another illustration of the multiplier. If aggregate demand was raised by $a - b$, income would rise by $Y_F - Y_e$. The multiplier is thus given by:

$$\frac{Y_F - Y_e}{c - d}$$

In this simple Keynesian model, then, the cure for demand-deficient unemployment is to close the deflationary gap. To close the deflationary gap, an increase in aggregate expenditure is needed. This could be achieved by an expansionary *fiscal* policy of increasing government expenditure and/or lowering taxes, or by an expansionary *monetary* policy of reducing interest rates and increasing the amount of money in the economy, thereby encouraging extra consumption and investment. (We examine demand-side policies in Chapter 30.)

Inflationary gap

The equilibrium level could lie *above* the full-employment level. This situation involves an ***inflationary gap***. This is the amount by which aggregate expenditure exceeds national income or injections exceed withdrawals at the full-employment level of national income. This is illustrated by the gap $c - d$ in Figure 29.5.

The problem is that Y_F represents a real ceiling to output. Hence, national output and the resulting *real* level of national income cannot expand beyond this point, other than for a very short time where the factors of production are used very intensively, for example with labour working overtime. This, however, is not sustainable and so results in *demand-pull inflation* (see page 523–5).[1]

Definitions

Recessionary or deflationary gap The shortfall of aggregate expenditure below GDP at the full-employment level of GDP.

Inflationary gap The excess of aggregate expenditure over GDP at the full-employment level of GDP.

---

[1] Note that the horizontal axis in the 45° line diagram represents *real* national income. If incomes were to rise by, say, 10 per cent but prices also rose by 10 per cent, real income would not have risen at all. People could not buy any more than before. In such a case, there will have been no rightward movement along the horizontal axis.

KI 43
p 575

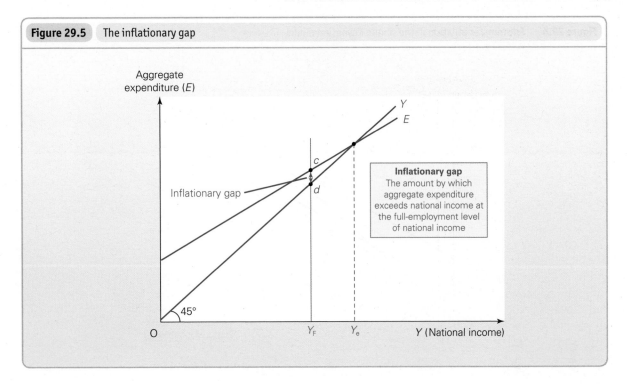

Figure 29.5 The inflationary gap

Inflationary gap

Inflationary gap
The amount by which aggregate expenditure exceeds national income at the full-employment level of national income

---

Pause for thought

Assume that full-employment GDP is £500 billion and that current GDP is £450 billion. Assume also that the mpc_d is $^4/_5$. (a) Is there an inflationary or deflationary gap? (b) What is the size of this gap?

To eliminate this inflation, the inflationary gap must be closed by reducing aggregate demand until Y_e equals Y_F. This could involve either a contractionary *fiscal* policy of lowering government expenditure and/or raising taxes or a contractionary *monetary* policy of raising interest rates and reducing the amount of money in the economy.

Even if the government does not actively pursue a deflationary policy, the inflationary gap may still close *automatically*. The mechanisms by which this could occur would move the E line down in the Keynesian cross diagram. These automatic mechanisms include the following:

- When prices rise, people's wages may not rise in line, at least not in the short run. Consumers could therefore see a cut in real incomes and thus spend less.
- Higher domestic prices will lead to fewer exports being sold (lower injections) and more imports being bought (higher withdrawals) in preference to the now more expensive home-produced goods.
- Higher prices reduce the real value of people's savings. They may, therefore, save more to compensate for this.
- Higher prices increase the demand for money (see section 28.4). The average amount of money that people and

firms would need to hold for spending purposes is greater. In the absence of an increase in the money supply, the shortage of money drives up interest rates. This reduces investment and encourages saving.

Pause for thought

How would each of these possible mechanisms affect the shape of the aggregate demand curve capturing the relationship between the economy's average price level and real national income?

The problem for policymakers is that these automatic effects may take some time to take effect and, even then, may be difficult to predict.

Inflation and the multiplier

The simple Keynesian model implies that up to the full-employment level of GDP (Y_F), output and employment can increase with no rise in prices at all. There is no inflation because the economy's deflationary gap is being closed. Hence, increases in aggregate expenditure set in motion the multiplier process and the result is a multiplied increase in real national income.

However, according to the model, beyond Y_F further rises in aggregate demand are entirely reflected in higher prices. An inflationary gap opens. Hence, the additional demand no longer generates an increase in national output. There is no increase in real national income because the real value of expenditure has not increased. Additional sums of spending

Figure 29.6   Allowing for inflation in the simple Keynesian model

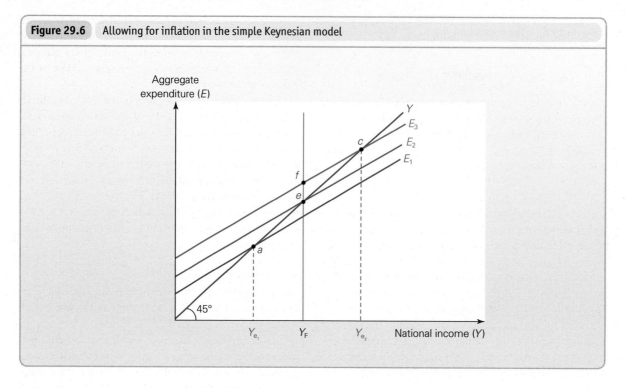

on domestically produced goods and services are purely *nominal*, reflecting only higher prices. The volume of purchases and, hence, the level of output is unchanged.

In this simple model, therefore, resource constraints become effective at the full-employment national income level. Any further increases in aggregate demand generate only inflation. The multiplier process ceases to operate. Figure 29.6 applies the 45° line diagram to illustrate these ideas.

Assume that the economy is initially at Y_{e1} where E_1 crosses the 45° line. Now let us assume that there is a rise in aggregate demand. The aggregate expenditure function shifts to E_2, resulting in a full multiplied rise in real income. Therefore, equilibrium national income rises to Y_F.

Consider now a further rise in aggregate demand which causes the aggregate expenditure function to shift to E_3. An inflationary gap opens up, illustrated by the gap $e - f$.

This time, the increase in demand will be reflected only in higher prices with no increase in output. Equilibrium *real* income will be unchanged. If there is no compensating increase in money supply, the E line will tend to fall back to E_2. The means by which this happen are the automatic mechanisms identified above. Alternatively, fiscal or money policy may be used to shift the E curve back to E_2.

The simple Keynesian model suggests, therefore, inflation only occurs when Y_F is reached and the E line rises above E_2 in Figure 29.6. In reality, inflation will begin to occur *before* the full-employment level of income is reached. For example, not all firms operate with the same degree of slack. Therefore, some firms may respond to a general rise in aggregate demand by taking up slack and hence increasing output, while other firms, having little or no slack, respond by raising prices.

29.2   ALTERNATIVE PERSPECTIVES ON AGGREGATE SUPPLY

In the previous section, we developed the simple Keynesian model to analyse the impact of fluctuations in aggregate demand on national output. It illustates how these fluctuations can have a multiplied effect on national income. However, it implies that aggregate demand can increase national output without impacting on prices up to the full-employment output level. In other words, aggregate supply is perfectly flexible in response to demand fluctuations. In reality, supply decisions, as well as being influenced by current levels of demand, are also influenced by prices and costs.

The flexibility of aggregate supply is important because it determines the balance between output and price changes in response to changes in aggregate demand. To be able to analyse the impact of changes in aggregate demand on national income *and* prices, we need to make use of the aggregate demand–aggregate supply (*AD/AS*) model.

In fact, the debate concerning the impact of changes in aggregate demand on prices and output can best be understood in terms of the nature of the aggregate supply (*AS*) curve. We will start with the short-run aggregate supply (*SRAS*) curve and then look at the long-run curve.

The short-run aggregate supply curve

Assume that there is a rise in aggregate demand. The short-run effect on national output and prices will depend on the shape of the *SRAS* curve. Let us examine the different analyses of the *SRAS* curve. The various approaches to analysing aggregate supply are illustrated in Figure 29.7.

The extreme Keynesian position

First consider the position that mirrors the assumptions about the flexibility of aggregate supply in the simple Keynesian model developed in the previous section. This is shown in Figure 29.7(a) and is sometimes referred to as the extreme Keynesian position. The *SRAS* curve is *horizontal* up to the full-employment level of GDP (Y_F). A rise in aggregate demand from AD_1 to AD_2, say, will raise output from Y_1 to Y_2, but there will be *no effect on prices* until full employment is reached. Once equilibrium national income has reached Y_F, any further rise in aggregate demand will lead merely to an increase in prices and no increase in real income.

In this extreme Keynesian model, aggregate supply up to the full-employment level is determined entirely by the level of aggregate demand. But there is no guarantee that aggregate demand will intersect aggregate supply at full employment. Therefore, governments should manage aggregate demand by appropriate fiscal and monetary policies to ensure production at Y_F (we examine such policies in the next chapter).

The mainstream position

Next, consider the mainstream view, i.e. the view generally thought to reflect the position of the majority of economists. This is shown in Figure 29.7(b) and shows the *SRAS* curve as upward sloping. This is because wages and many other input prices are thought to exhibit *some* 'stickiness' in the short term (as we saw in section 26.4). A rise in demand will not simply be absorbed in higher input prices: in other words, output will rise too.

Nevertheless, as more variable factors are used, firms will experience diminishing returns. Marginal costs will rise. The less the spare capacity in firms, the more rapidly marginal costs will rise for any given increase in output and hence the steeper will be the *SRAS* curve.

Therefore, the mainstream view is that an increase in *AD* will have some effect on prices and some effect on national output and employment (see Figure 29.7(b) and 26.10). The extent of these effects will depend on the economy's current level of output relative to its potential (normal capacity) output. The higher actual output is relative to potential output, the less slack in the economy and the steeper the *SRAS* becomes. Therefore, aggregate supply become less and less responsive to aggregate demand as cyclical unemployment continues to fall.

The new classical position

Finally, consider another 'extreme' position. Economists known as new classicists[2] argue that the *SRAS* curve may be *vertical* at potential output (Y_P), as in Figure 29.7(c). This rests on two important assumptions. First is the assumption of **continuous market clearing**. This means that all markets continuously adjust to their equilibrium. Second, is the assumption of **rational expectations**. This means that people use all

---

> ### Definitions
>
> **Continuous market clearing** The assumption that all markets in the economy continuously clear so that the economy is permanently in equilibrium.
>
> **Rational expectations** Expectations based on the *current* situation. These expectations are based on the information people have to hand. While this information may be imperfect and therefore people will make errors, these errors will be random.

---

[2]They are known as 'new classicists' because their analysis is similar to the pre-Keynesian or 'classical' theory that output is determined by the economy's capacity to produce, not by the level of demand.

Figure 29.7 Different short-run aggregate supply curves

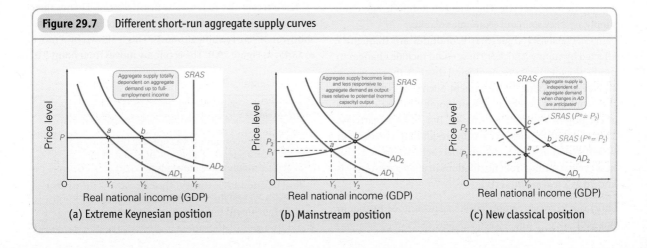

(a) Extreme Keynesian position

(b) Mainstream position

(c) New classical position

available information and predict inflation or any other macroeconomic variable as well as they can. The important point here is that forecasting errors are random so that, on average, people's expectations of inflation are correct.

Therefore, *anticipated* changes in aggregate demand will quickly work through both goods and factor markets into higher prices. There has been no increase in *real* aggregate demand. Real national income remains at its potential (normal capacity) level Y_P. Thus it is essential to keep (nominal) demand under control if *prices* are to be kept under control.

Unanticipated change in aggregate demand. An upward-sloping *SRAS* curve would be observable only if changes in aggregate demand were *unanticipated* and even then deviations in output from its potential level would be transitory. If, in Figure 29.7(c), aggregate demand were to rise unexpectedly, say from AD_1 to AD_2, people would not foresee the upward effect on general prices. Hence, workers and firms would have negotiated specific input prices, including wages, on the expectation that the general price level would be P_1. Therefore, the expected price level P^e is P_1 ($P^e = P_1$). As the general price level rises, firms (wrongly) believe it is profitable for businesses to expand output levels. This is equivalent to the move from *a* to *b* in Figure 29.7(c).

Once people recognise these errors, however, output adjusts back to its potential level Y_P. The economy moves from point *b* to *c*. In the presence of rational expectations and continuous market clearing, this adjustment is likely to happen relatively quickly.

If the government wants to expand aggregate supply and get more rapid economic growth, it is no good, they argue, concentrating on demand. Instead, governments should concentrate directly on supply by encouraging enterprise and competition and, generally, by encouraging markets to operate more freely. For this reason, this approach is often labelled **supply-side economics**. If successful, these will shift the vertical *SRAS* curve to the right.

Real business cycles. Since new classicists emphasise the speed with which the economy adjusts towards potential output following fluctuations in aggregate demand, they also emphasise the importance of fluctuations in aggregate supply in generating the business cycle. They argue that shifts in aggregate supply are a key source of economic volatility.

New classicists argue that economies are frequently affected by supply 'shocks'. These could include changes to production methods ('technological shocks'), the regulatory climate or the political environment. Such shocks then affect the economy's potential output. Some of these changes affect potential output positively, but some negatively. Therefore, the business cycle is the result of fluctuations in potential output, which, in turn, affect actual output. A business cycle resulting from fluctuations in aggregate supply is known as a **real business cycle**.

Short-run aggregate supply curves are examined further in Box 29.1.

> **Pause for thought**
>
> *If there was an unexpected decrease in aggregate demand, would new classicists expect output to fall below its potential level?*

The long-run aggregate supply curve

A vertical long-run AS curve

While some new classical economists argue that the short-run *AS* curve is vertical, most economists argue that it is only the *long-run AS* curve that is vertical at the potential level of output (Y_P): see Figure 29.8(b). In the long run, any rise in nominal aggregate demand would lead simply to a rise in prices and no long-term increase in output at all.

The mainstream view is that long-term increases in output could occur only through rightward shifts in this vertical long-run *AS* curve, in other words through increases in potential output. To achieve this, governments should focus largely on supply-side policy, such as policies that help foster technological progress (see Chapter 31).

But why do these economists argue that the long-run *AS* curve is vertical? They justify this by focusing on the *interdependence of markets*. Assume initially that the economy is operating at the potential level of output (Y_P). Now assume that there is an increase in demand, such as from an increase in government expenditure. The increase in aggregate demand initially will lead firms to raise both prices and output in accordance with the short-run *AS* curve. In other words, the short-run aggregate supply curve is upward sloping. There is a movement from point *a* to point *b* in Figure 29.9. Output rises to Y_2.

However, as raw material and intermediate goods producers raise their prices, so this will raise the costs of production of firms using these inputs. A rise in the price of steel will raise the costs of producing cars and washing machines. At the same time, workers, seeing the prices of goods rising, will demand higher wages. Firms will be relatively willing to grant these wage demands, given that they are experiencing a buoyant demand from their customers.

The effect of all this is to raise firms' *costs*, and hence their prices. As prices rise for any given level of output, so the short-run *AS* curve shifts upwards. This is shown by a move to $SRAS_2$ in Figure 29.9. The economy moves from point *b* to

> **Definitions**
>
> **Supply-side economics** An approach that focuses directly on aggregate supply and how to shift the aggregate supply curve outwards.
>
> **Real business cycle theory** The new classical theory that explains cyclical fluctuations in terms of shifts in aggregate supply, rather than aggregate demand.

KI 13
p 75

BOX 29.1 SHORT-RUN AGGREGATE SUPPLY

To understand the shape of the short-run *AS* curve, it is necessary to look at its microeconomic foundations. How will *individual* firms and industries respond to a rise in demand? What shape will their individual supply curves be?

In the short run, we assume that firms respond to the rise in demand for their product *without* considering the effects of a general rise in demand on their suppliers or on the economy as a whole. We also assume that the prices of inputs, including wage rates, are constant.

In the case of a profit-maximising firm under monopoly or monopolistic competition, there will be a rise in price and a rise in output. In diagram (a), profit-maximising output rises from where $MC = MR_1$ to where $MC = MR_2$. Just how much price changes compared with output depends on the slope of the marginal cost (MC) curve.

The nearer the firm is to full capacity, the steeper the MC curve is likely to be. Here the firm is likely to find diminishing returns setting in rapidly, and it is also likely to have to use more overtime with correspondingly higher unit labour costs.

(a) Short-run response of a profit-maximising firm to a rise in demand

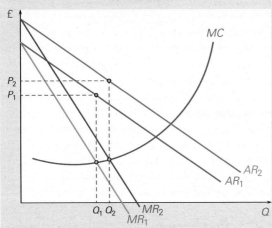

(b) The SRAS curve and the effect of an increase in AD

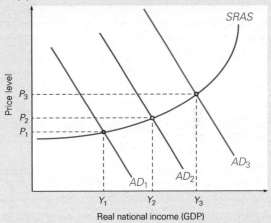

If, however, the firm is operating well below capacity, it can probably supply more with little or no increase in price. Its *MC* curve may thus be horizontal at lower levels of output.

When there is a general rise in demand in the economy, the *aggregate* supply response in the short run can be seen as simply the sum of the responses of all the individual firms. The short-run *AS* curve will look something like that in diagram (b).

If there is generally plenty of spare capacity, a rise in aggregate demand (e.g. from AD_1 to AD_2) will have a big effect on output and only a small effect on prices. However, as more and more firms find their costs rising as they get nearer to full capacity, so the *SRAS* curve becomes steeper. Further increases in aggregate demand (e.g. from AD_2 to AD_3) will have bigger effects on prices and smaller effects on output (GDP).

A general rise in prices, of course, means that individual firms were mistaken in assuming that a rise in price from P_1 to P_2 in diagram (b) was a *real* price rise (i.e. relative to prices elsewhere).

1. *What happens to real wage rates as we move up the SRAS curve?*
2. *If markets were to become dominated by oligopolies what effect might this have on the SRAS curve?*

Write a short briefing note contrasting the orthodox, extreme Keynesian and new classical views of the SRAS curve.

point *c*. Thus output can only rise temporarily above the potential level (Y_P). Although the process may take some time, the more flexible markets are, the more quickly higher costs are likely to be passed through into higher prices.

The long-run effect, therefore, of a rise in aggregate demand from AD_1 to AD_2 is a movement from point *a* to point *c*. The long-run aggregate supply curve passes through these two points. It is vertical at the potential level of output. A rise in aggregate demand therefore will have no long-run

effect on output. The entire effect will be felt in terms of higher prices.

An upward-sloping long-run AS curve

Some Keynesian economists, however, argue that the long-run *AS* curve is upward sloping, not vertical. Indeed, it may be even shallower than the short-run curve. For them, potential output is affected by changes in aggregate demand.

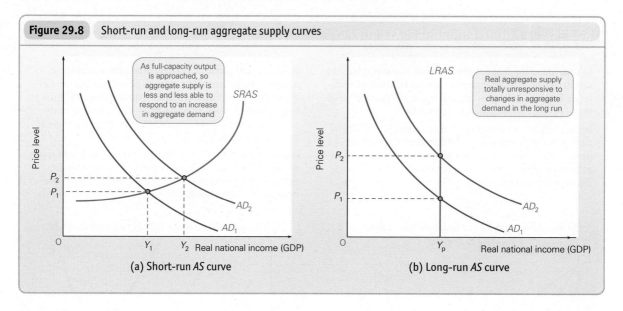

Figure 29.8 Short-run and long-run aggregate supply curves

(a) Short-run *AS* curve

(b) Long-run *AS* curve

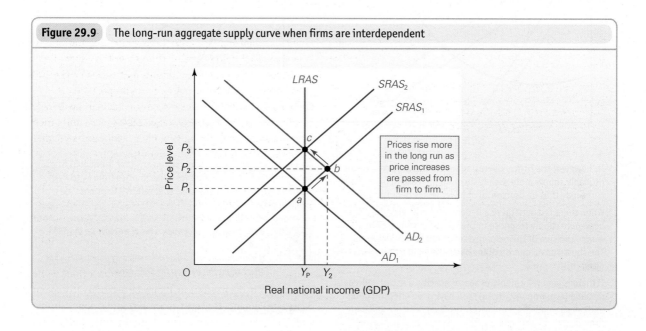

Figure 29.9 The long-run aggregate supply curve when firms are interdependent

The key here is investment. If the increase in aggregate demand includes an increase in investment (*I*), this can positively affect the economy's *capacity* to produce. Alternatively, in observing an increase in demand, firms may then be encouraged to invest in new plant and machinery. Either way, an increase in aggregate demand can increase potential output. The result is that firms may well be able to increase output significantly in the long run with little or no increase in their prices. Their long-run *MC* curves are much flatter than their short-run *MC* curves.

Again, assume initially that output is at the potential level. In Figure 29.10, this is shown as Y_{P1}. Aggregate demand then increases to AD_2. Equilibrium moves to point

KI 42
p 507

b with GDP at Y_2. The resulting increased investment shifts the short-run *AS* curve to the right. Equilibrium moves from point *b* to *d*. Point *d* is now at the new potential level of output, Y_{P2}. The long-run *AS* curve thus joins points *a* and *d*.

The way the diagram is drawn, the long-run *AS* curve is more elastic than the short-run curve. There is a relatively large increase in output and a relatively small increase in price. If the rise in costs had been more substantial, curve $SRAS_2$ could be above curve $SRAS_1$. In this case, although the long-run *AS* curve would still be upward sloping, it would be steeper than the short-run curves: point *d* would be above point *b*.

Figure 29.10 Effect of investment on the long-run aggregate supply curve

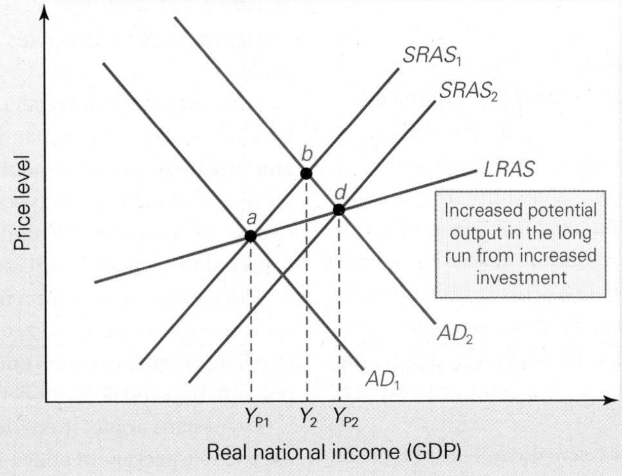

KI 36
p 376

Pause for thought

If a shift in the aggregate demand curve from AD_1 to AD_2 in Figure 29.10 causes a movement from point a to point d in the long run, will a shift in the aggregate demand curve from AD_2 to AD_1 cause a movement from point d back to point a in the long run?

The long-run *AS* curve will be steeper if the extra investment causes significant shortages of materials, machinery or labour. This is more likely when the economy is already operating near its full-capacity output. It will be flatter, and possibly even downward sloping, if the investment involves the introduction of new cost-reducing technology.

Areas of general agreement

Despite differences between economists on the nature of aggregate supply, there are two general points of agreement that have emerged, at least among the majority of economists.

■ In the short run, changes in aggregate demand can have a significant effect on output and employment. If there is a collapse in demand, as in 2008, governments and/or central banks should intervene through expansionary fiscal and/or monetary policies. Only a few extreme new classical economists would disagree with this proposition.

■ In the long run, changes in aggregate demand will have much less effect on output and employment and much more effect on prices. In fact, many economists say that there will be no effect at all on output and employment, and that the whole effect will be on prices. There is still a substantial body of Keynesians, however, especially 'post-Keynesians', who argue that changes in aggregate demand will have substantial effects on long-term output and employment via changes in investment and hence in potential output.

The mainstream view generally recognises that, if the economy is in deep recession, it may be necessary to expand aggregate demand. However, macroeconomic policy should not focus exclusively on the demand side. Long-term growth, it is argued, depends primarily on changes in supply (i.e. in potential output). It is important, therefore, for governments to develop an effective supply-side policy if they want to achieve faster long-term economic growth.

29.3 OUTPUT, UNEMPLOYMENT AND INFLATION

Fluctuations in aggregate demand and aggregate supply generate business cycles, with fluctuations in the level of output (real national income) and the rates of unemployment and inflation.

Our macroeconomic models allow us to analyse how these key macroeconomic variables fluctuate and the relationships between them. These models are, in effect, different windows looking out on to the economy.

We begin with the *AD/AS* model before considering the Phillips curve.

AD/AS model

Fluctuations in aggregate demand

In the previous section, we saw the importance of the flexibility of aggregate supply in determining the impact of fluctuations in aggregate demand on unemployment and inflation. The mainstream view is that a rise in aggregate demand can therefore lead to *both* a reduction in unemployment *and* a rise in prices at output levels *below* the full-employment level of GDP (Y_F). This is illustrated in Figure 29.11. An increase in aggregate demand leads to a rightward shift of the *AD* curve from AD_1 to AD_2. As a result, real national income rises from Y_1 to Y_2 and the general price level from Y_1 to Y_2.

Because inflation can occur *before* the full-employment level of real national income is reached, increases in (nominal) aggregate demand no longer increase real national income by the full extent of the multiplier process. In the absence of inflation, the increase in aggregate demand shown in Figure 29.11 would have meant real national income increasing from Y_1 to Y_3.

Since the progressively steeper *SRAS* curve means that inflationary pressures become more significant as national output rises, the size of the multiplier grows smaller, the closer the economy is to the full-employment national income level. At higher levels of national output, an increasingly large part of any increase in nominal aggregate demand is therefore reflected in higher prices and an increasingly small part in higher output.

Other types of inflation and unemployment

The mainstream *SRAS* curve helps to explain how fluctuations in aggregate demand affect national output, employment and prices. However, it is important to recognise other influences on economic activity and prices.

First, there are *other* types of unemployment not caused by a lack of aggregate demand. Examples include frictional and structural unemployment (see section 26.4).

Second, there are *other* types of inflation not caused by an excess of aggregate demand, such as cost-push and expectations-generated inflation (see section 26.5).

Thus, even if a government could manipulate national income so as to achieve a zero output gap, this would not eliminate all inflation and unemployment – only demand-pull inflation and demand-deficient unemployment.

Keynesians argue, therefore, that governments should use a whole package of policies, each tailored to the specific type of problem. But certainly, one of the most important of these policies will be the management of aggregate demand.

The Phillips curve

The relationship between inflation and unemployment was examined by A.W. Phillips in 1958. He showed the statistical relationship between wage inflation and unemployment in the UK from 1861 to 1957. With wage inflation on the vertical axis and the unemployment rate on the horizontal axis, a scatter of points was obtained. Each point represented the observation for a particular year. The curve that best fitted the scatter has become known as

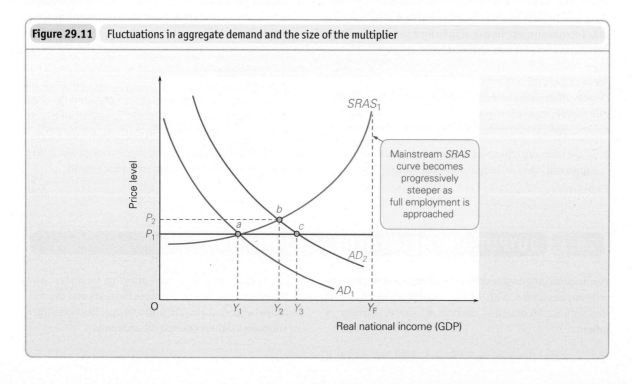

Figure 29.11 Fluctuations in aggregate demand and the size of the multiplier

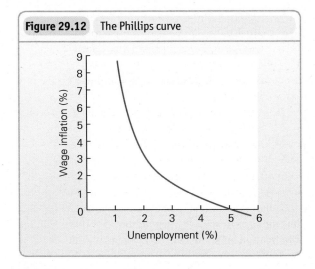

Figure 29.12 The Phillips curve

Wage inflation (%) / Unemployment (%)

the ***Phillips curve***. It is illustrated in Figure 29.12 and shows an inverse relationship between inflation and unemployment.

Given that wage increases over the period were approximately 2 per cent above price increases (made possible by increases in labour productivity), a similar-shaped, but lower curve could be plotted showing the relationship between *price* inflation and unemployment.

The curve has been used often to illustrate the short-run effects of changes in (real) aggregate demand. When aggregate demand rose (relative to potential output), inflation rose and unemployment fell: there was an upward movement along the curve. When aggregate demand fell, there was a downward movement along the curve.

The Phillips curve was bowed in to the origin. The usual explanation for this is that as aggregate demand expanded, at first there would be plenty of surplus labour, which could be employed to meet the extra demand without the need to raise wage rates very much. But as labour became increasingly scarce, firms would find that they had to offer increasingly higher wage rates to obtain the labour they required, and the position of trade unions would be increasingly strengthened.

The *position* of the Phillips curve depended on *non*-demand factors causing inflation and unemployment: frictional and structural unemployment; and cost-push and expectations-generated inflation. If any of these non-demand factors changed so as to raise inflation or unemployment, the curve would shift outward to the right.

Pause for thought

What would an alternative Phillips curve, drawn showing the relationship between inflation and output, look like?

KI 41
p 506 The Phillips curve seemed to present governments with a simple policy choice. They could trade off inflation against

unemployment. Lower unemployment could be bought at the cost of higher inflation and vice versa. Unfortunately, the experience since the late 1960s has suggested that no such simple relationship exists beyond the short run.

From about 1967, the Phillips curve relationship seemed to break down. The UK, along with many other countries in the Western world, began to experience growing unemployment and higher rates of inflation.

Figure 29.13 shows price inflation and unemployment in the UK from 1960. From 1960 to 1967, a curve similar to the Phillips curve can be fitted through the data. From 1968 to the early 1990s, however, no simple picture emerges. Certainly the original Phillips curve could no longer fit the data; but whether the curve shifted to the right and then back again somewhat (the broken lines), whether the relationship broke down completely or whether there was some quite different relationship between inflation and unemployment is not clear by simply looking at the data.

Since 1997, the Bank of England has been targeting consumer price inflation (see section 29.4). For much of this period, the 'curve' would seem to have become a virtually horizontal straight line at the targeted rate!

However, from the late 2000s, against a backdrop of marked economic volatility, the range of inflation rates increased despite inflation rate targeting. A contributory factor was the volatility of commodity prices as their demand fluctuated, exacerbated by the instability of the global economy

Nonetheless, despite difficulties in keeping inflation to target, many economists continue to argue that expectations concerning future inflation rates are an important influence on the inflation–unemployment relationship and that inflation has become much less volatile since inflation targeting was introduced.

The expectations-augmented Phillips curve

A major contribution to the theory of unemployment and inflation was made by Milton Friedman and others in the late 1960s. They incorporated people's expectations about the future level of prices into the Phillips curve. In its simplest form, the ***expectations-augmented Phillips curve*** is given by the following:

KI 13
p 75

$$\pi = f(^1/_U) + \pi^e + k$$

Definition

Phillips curve A curve showing the relationship between (price) inflation and unemployment. The original Phillips curve plotted *wage* inflation against unemployment for the years 1861–1957.

Expectations-augmented Phillips curve A (short-run) Phillips curve whose position depends on the expected rate of inflation.

Figure 29.13 The breakdown of the Phillips curve

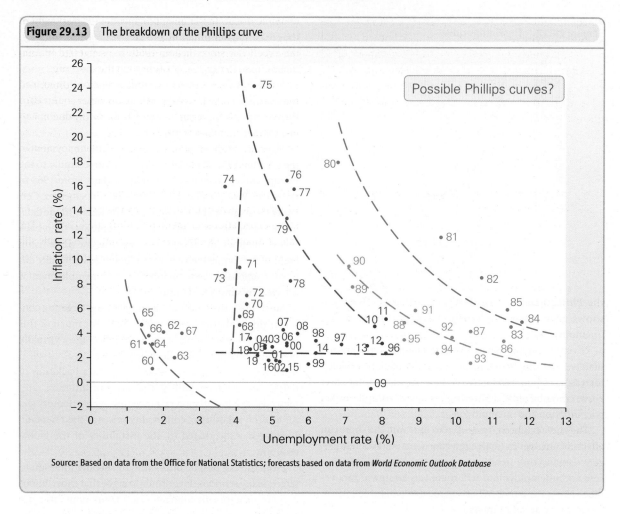

Source: Based on data from the Office for National Statistics; forecasts based on data from *World Economic Outlook Database*

This states that the rate of price inflation (π) depends on three things:

- First, it is a function (f) of the inverse of unemployment (1/U). This is simply the original Phillips curve relationship. A rise in aggregate demand will lead to a fall in unemployment (a rise in 1/U) and a rise in inflation – a move *along* the EAPC.

- **[KI 13]** **[p 75]** Second, the expected rate of inflation π^e must be added to the inflation that would result simply from the level of excess demand represented by (1/U).

- Third, if there are any exogenous cost pressures on inflation (k) (such as increases in international commodity prices), this must be added, too.

Thus, if people expected a 3 per cent inflation rate ($\pi^e = 3\%$) and if excess demand were causing demand-pull inflation of 2 per cent ($f(1/U) = 2\%$) and exogenous increases in costs were adding another 1 per cent to inflation ($k = 1\%$), actual inflation would be 3 + 2 + 1 = 6 per cent.

By augmenting the Phillips curve with expectations, we move from a single curve to a family of Phillips curves. The vertical position of each curve is determined by inflationary expectations (π^e) and any exogenous cost pressures (k). If we

assume that, on average, $k = 0$, then we simplify the *EAPC* framework so that each expectations-augmented Phillips curve is associated with a particular rate of inflationary expectations.

Natural rate hypothesis

A key conclusion of monetarists, such as Milton Friedman, was that, in the long run, the equilibrium rate of unemployment is determined independently of aggregate demand. Following fluctuations in aggregate demand, unemployment will return to its equilibrium rate and national output to its potential level. This is known as the *natural rate hypothesis* because Friedman and other monetarists refer to

Definition

Natural rate hypothesis The theory that, following fluctuations in aggregate demand, unemployment will return to a natural rate. This rate is determined by supply-side factors, such as labour mobility.

the equilibrium rate as the **natural rate** (U_n). The natural rate of unemployment is sometimes also known as the **non-accelerating-inflation rate of unemployment (NAIRU)**.

Under the natural rate hypothesis the long-run Phillips curve (*LRPC*) is vertical. In the long run, it is supply-side policies that affect levels of structural and frictional unemployment.

Pause for thought

How might fluctuations in the rate of unemployment affect potential output?

Short-run trade-off

However, in the short run, unemployment may deviate from its natural rate. To understand why we develop a simple monetarist model of the economy, sometimes known as the 'fooling model' for reasons that will become clear.

This model is based on two key assumptions. First, prices adjust relatively quickly to ensure equilibrium between demand and supply in both the goods and labour markets. Second, people form **adaptive expectations** of inflation. This occurs when people base their expectations of inflation on *past* inflation rates. If, for example, last year people under-predicted the rate of inflation, then this year they will adapt by revising, i.e. adapting, their expectations of inflation upwards.

Pause for thought

Can it ever be rational to form adaptive expectations?

We will assume that people adopt the simplest form of adaptive expectations: they use last year's actual inflation rate (π_{t-1}) as their prediction for the expected rate of inflation this year (π_t^e). We also assume that the economy's inflation rate last year was zero; no inflation is expected; and there are no exogenous cost pressures on inflation ($k = 0$).

In Figure 29.14, the economy is initially at point *a* with both actual and expected inflation of zero. The goods and labour markets are in equilibrium: $AD = AS$ and unemployment is at its natural rate, U_n.

Increase in aggregate demand. Assume that there is an increase in aggregate demand. The economy moves to, say, point *b* along expectations-augmented Phillips curve, $EAPC_0$. The rate of inflation rises from zero to π_1. But, with people still expecting zero inflation, the labour market experiences a fall in the average real wage rate, leading to a rise in the demand for labour. Assuming that workers are fooled into supplying the additional labour despite the fall in real wages, unemployment falls below its natural rate to U_1.

If we now move ahead a year, people will have revised their expectations of inflation upwards to π_1. The result is

Definitions

Natural rate of unemployment or **non-accelerating-inflation rate of unemployment (NAIRU)** The rate of unemployment consistent with a constant rate of inflation; the rate of unemployment at which the vertical long-run Phillips curve cuts the horizontal axis.

Adaptive expectations Where people adjust their expectations of inflation in the light of what has happened to inflation in the past.

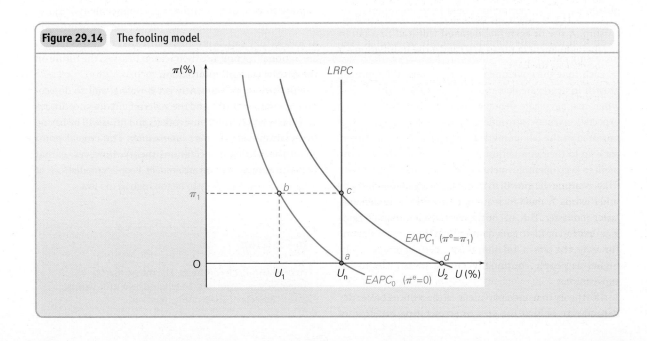

Figure 29.14 The fooling model

that the Phillips curve has shifted up vertically by π_1 to $EAPC_1$. If *nominal* aggregate demand (i.e. demand purely in monetary terms, irrespective of the level of prices) continues to rise at the same rate, the whole of the increase will now be absorbed in higher prices. *Real* aggregate demand will fall back to its previous level and the economy will move to point c on the long-run Phillips curve. Unemployment will return to its natural rate, U_n, consistent with the natural rate hypothesis. There is no *demand-pull* inflation now ($f(1/U) = 0$), but inflation is π_1 per cent due to inflationary expectations.

Decrease in aggregate demand. Assume that the economy is at point c in Figure 29.14, with expected inflation of π_1. It now experiences a decrease in the growth of nominal demand. Real aggregate demand falls. Let us assume that there is downward pressure on inflation such that the inflation rate falls to zero. The economy moves down $EAPC_1$ to point d. In the labour market, the expected average real wage rate increases because the expected inflation rate is π_1. The demand for labour falls and unemployment rises above its natural rate, U_n to U_2.

The following year, the expected rate of inflation will fall to zero. The $EAPC$ moves vertically down to $EAPC_0$. If the growth in nominal aggregate demand remains at its new lower rate, with inflation now at zero, the economy will again be at it point a on the long-run Phillips. Unemployment is again at its natural rate; the natural rate hypothesis again holds.

The accelerationist hypothesis

The preceding analysis shows how, when people form adaptive expectations of inflation, unemployment can deviate from its natural rate following changes in aggregate demand, even if markets clear fairly quickly. This raises the theoretical possibility that governments could keep unemployment below the natural rate. But, this would come at a cost, since to do so it must raise nominal aggregate demand at ever increasing rates.

Each time the government is able to raise the nominal growth in aggregate demand, there is a transitory period when real aggregate demand rises too. But, inflationary expectations then rise to reflect higher inflation rates. This is mirrored in the labour market by real wages being driven back up to their equilibrium level. Hence, for the government to keep unemployment below its natural rate, it needs to keep raising the growth in nominal aggregate demand – in other words, it must increase nominal aggregate demand faster and faster. This, of course, means that nominal aggregate demand needs to grow at more than the rate of inflation. However, the rate of inflation is itself getting progressively higher as people continually raising their inflationary expectations.

The theory that unemployment can be reduced below the natural rate only at the cost of accelerating inflation is known as the *accelerationist hypothesis*. Box 29.2 considers a numerical example of the hypothesis.

New classical perspective

New classical economists go further than the monetarist theory described above. They argue that, unless there are unexpected or 'surprise' events, there is no short-run trade-off between inflation and unemployment. The *EAPC* therefore represents a short-run trade-off between inflation and unemployment only in the presence of surprise events.

New classical assumptions

They base their arguments on two key assumptions (see section 29.2) – continuous market clearing and rational expectations.

Because prices and wage rates are flexible, markets clear very rapidly. This means that there will be no disequilibrium unemployment, even in the short run. All unemployment will be equilibrium unemployment or 'voluntary unemployment' as new classical economists prefer to call it.

In the monetarist model, expectations are adaptive. They are based on *past* information and thus take time to catch up with changes in aggregate demand. Such expectations are known as *adaptive expectations*. Thus for a short time a rise in nominal aggregate demand will raise output and reduce unemployment below the equilibrium rate, while prices and wages are still relatively low.

The new classical analysis, by contrast, is based on *rational expectations*. As we saw earlier, rational expectations are not based on past rates of inflation. Instead, they are based on the current state of the economy and the current policies being pursued by the government. Workers and firms look at the information available to them – at the various forecasts that are published, at various economic indicators and the assessments of them by various commentators, at government pronouncements, and so on. From this information, they predict the rate of inflation as well as they can. It is in this sense that the expectations are 'rational': people use their reason to assess the future on the basis of current -information.

But forecasters frequently get it wrong, and so do economic commentators! And the government does not always do what it says it will. Thus workers and firms will be basing expectations on *imperfect information*. The crucial point about the rational expectations theory, however, is that these errors in prediction are *random*. People's predictions of inflation are just as likely to be too high as too low.

> ### Definition
>
> **Accelerationist hypothesis** The theory that unemployment can only be reduced below the natural rate at the cost of accelerating inflation.

BOX 29.2   THE ACCELERATIONIST HYPOTHESIS

The race to outpace inflationary expectations

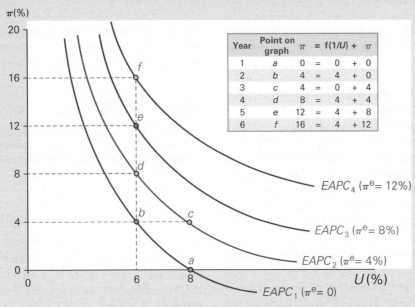

The accelerationist theory of inflation

Year	Point on graph	π	=	f(1/U)	+	π
1	a	0	=	0	+	0
2	b	4	=	4	+	0
3	c	4	=	0	+	4
4	d	8	=	4	+	4
5	e	12	=	4	+	8
6	f	16	=	4	+	12

Let us trace the course of inflation and expectations over a number of years in an imaginary economy. To keep the analysis simple, assume there is no growth in the economy and no exogenous cost pressures on inflation ($k = 0$ in the equation on page 603).

Year 1. Assume that, at the outset, in year 1, there is no inflation of any sort, that none is expected, that $AD = AS$, and that equilibrium unemployment is 8 per cent. The economy is at point *a* in the diagram.

Year 2. Now assume that the government expands aggregate demand in order to reduce unemployment. Unemployment falls to 6 per cent. The economy moves to point *b* along $EAPC_1$. Inflation has risen to 4 per cent, but people, basing their expectations of inflation on year 1, still expect zero inflation. There is therefore no shift as yet in the Phillips curve. $EAPC_1$ corresponds to an expected rate of inflation of zero.

Year 3. People now revise their expectations of inflation to the level of year 2. The Phillips curve shifts up by 4 percentage points to $EAPC_2$. If *nominal* aggregate demand (i.e. demand purely in monetary terms, irrespective of the level of prices) continues to rise at the same rate, the whole of the increase will now be absorbed in higher prices. *Real* aggregate demand will fall back to its previous level and the economy will move to point *c*. Unemployment will return to 8 per cent. There is no *demand-pull* inflation now ($f(1/U) = 0$), but inflation is still 4 per cent due to expectations ($\pi^e = 4$ per cent).

Year 4. Assume now that the government expands real aggregate demand again so as to reduce unemployment

once more to 6 per cent. This time it must expand nominal aggregate demand by more than it did in year 2, because this time, as well as reducing unemployment, it also has to validate the 4 per cent expected inflation. The economy moves to point *d* along $EAPC_2$. Inflation is now 8 per cent.

Year 5. Expected inflation is now 8 per cent (the level of actual inflation in year 4). The Phillips curve shifts up to $EAPC_3$. If, at the same time, the government tries to keep unemployment at 6 per cent, it must expand nominal aggregate demand 4 per cent faster in order to validate the 8 per cent expected inflation. The economy moves to point *e* along $EAPC_3$. Inflation is now 12 per cent.

Year 6 onwards. To keep unemployment at 6 per cent, the government must continue to increase nominal aggregate demand by 4 per cent more than the previous year. As the expected inflation rate goes on rising, the Phillips curve will go on shifting up each year.

 What determines how rapidly the short-run Phillips curves in the diagram shift upward?

 Construct a table like the one in the diagram, only this time assume that the government wishes to reduce unemployment to 5 per cent. Assume that every year from year 1 onwards the government is prepared to expand aggregate demand by whatever it takes to do this. If this expansion of demand gives $f(1/U) = 7$ per cent, fill in the table for the first six years. Do you think that after a couple of years people might begin to base their expectations differently?

Anticipating fluctuations in aggregate demand

Assume that the government raises aggregate demand and that the increase is expected. People will anticipate that this will lead to higher prices and wages. If both goods and labour markets clear continuously because of the flexibility of prices and wages, there will be *no* effect on output and employment. If their expectations of higher inflation are correct, this will thus *fully* absorb the increase in nominal aggregate demand such that there will have been no increase in *real* aggregate demand at all. Firms will not produce any more output or employ any more people: after all, why should they? If they anticipate that people will spend 10 per cent more money but that prices will rise by 10 per cent, their *volume* of sales will remain the same.

We can use Figure 29.15 to illustrate the adjustment of the economy under continuous market clearing, rational expectations and anticipated demand shocks. Assume that the economy is at point *a* with unemployment at its natural rate, U_n, and an actual and expected inflation rate of zero.

Now assume that government increases aggregate demand. With rational expectations and no surprises, people fully anticipate that the inflation rate will rise to π_1. $EAPC_0$ which is based on expectations of zero inflation cannot be moved along. The moment that aggregate demand rises people correctly anticipate an inflation rate of π_1. Thus the whole *EAPC* moves vertically upwards to $EAPC_1$. As a result, the economy moves *directly* from point *a* to point *c*.

Output and employment will only rise, therefore, if people make an error in their predictions (i.e. if they underpredict the rate of inflation and interpret an increase in money spent as an increase in *real* demand). But they are as likely to *over* predict the rate of inflation, in which case output and employment will fall! Thus there is no systematic trade-off between inflation and unemployment, even in the short run.

The vertical short-run Phillips curve is therefore comparable to the vertical short-run aggregate supply curve we examined in section 29.2. As we saw, this shows aggregate supply (output) being determined independently of aggregate demand.

Both the vertical short-run Phillips curve and the vertical *SRAS* curve can be used to illustrate how anticipated changes in economic policy, such as changes in government spending, have no effect on output and employment. Instead they remain at their equilibrium levels. This controversial conclusion is known as the *policy ineffectiveness proposition*.

> ### Pause for thought
>
> *For what reasons would a new classical economist support the policy of the Bank of England publishing its inflation forecasts and the minutes of the deliberations of the Monetary Policy Committee?*

Expectations of output and employment

Many economists, especially those who would describe themselves as 'Keynesian', criticise the approach of focusing exclusively on price expectations. Expectations, they argue, influence *output* and *employment* decisions, not just pricing decisions.

> ### Definition
>
> **Policy ineffectiveness proposition** The conclusion drawn from new classical models that, when economic agents anticipate changes in economic policy, output and employment remain at their equilibrium (or natural) levels.

Figure 29.15 Anticipated and unanticipated changes in aggregate demand

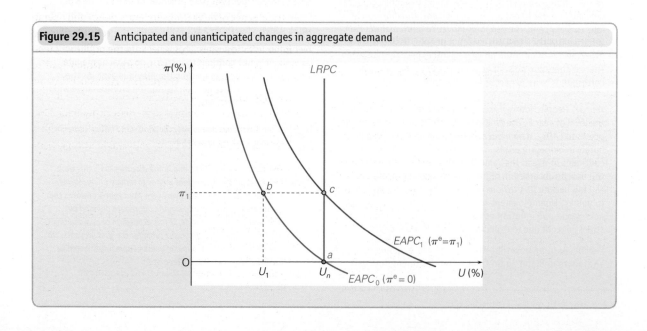

If there is a gradual but sustained expansion of aggregate demand, firms, seeing the economy expanding and seeing their orders growing, will start to invest more and make longer-term plans for expanding their labour force. Business and consumers will generally *expect* a higher level of output, and this optimism will cause businesses to produce more. In other words, expectations will affect output and employment as well as prices. Similarly, if businesses anticipate a recession, they are likely to cut back on production and investment.

Graphically, the increased output and employment from the recovery in investment will shift the Phillips curve to the left, offsetting (partially, wholly or more than wholly) the upward shift from higher inflationary expectations.

The lesson here for governments is that a sustained, but moderate, increase in aggregate demand can lead to a sustained growth in aggregate supply. What should be avoided is an excessive and unsustainable expansion of aggregate demand. In turn, this raises questions about the role that governments should play in managing aggregate demand in order to affect levels of business activity.

As the last two sections have helped to highlight, there are contrasting perspectives on the relationship between output, unemployment and inflation. These alternative perspectives are mirrored by debates among economists as to the role that governments should play in managing economic stability. Such debates were heightened by the financial crisis of the late 2000s, the subsequent global economic downturn and the fragility of the macroeconomic environment that then characterised much of the 2010s. Chapter 30 looks at government policy in more detail.

> ### Pause for thought
>
> *Why is it important in the Keynesian analysis for there to be a steady expansion of aggregate demand?*

29.4 INFLATION RATE TARGETING AND UNEMPLOYMENT

The period from the early 1990s up to the financial crisis of the late 2000s was to be known as the 'Great Moderation'. The period was characterised in many developed counties by low and stable inflation and continuous economic growth. In the UK, for example, between 1994 to 2007, annual UK growth averaged 3 per cent, while the annual rate of consumer price inflation averaged 1.75 per cent.

The period of the Great Moderation also saw the emergence of a new mainstream macroeconomic consensus. The consensus was a fusion of ideas drawn from different macroeconomic perspectives. It had two central elements:

■ First, there is no long-run trade-off between inflation and unemployment (the natural rate hypothesis). The natural rate of unemployment and potential output are argued to be principally determined by supply-side or structural factors.
■ Second, fluctuations in aggregate demand and supply can lead to short-term deviations of output from its potential level and unemployment from its natural rate. The extent of these deviations depends on market imperfections, including the inflexibility of goods prices and wage rates.

In the UK, as in many other industrialised countries, the Great Moderation was a period when policymakers emphasised the importance of maintaining stable economic environment and focused on raising long-term economic growth. This led policymakers to apply *constrained discretion*: a set of rules or principles providing a framework for economic policy.

Constrained discretion typically involves the use of targets, such as an inflation target or a public-sector deficit or debt ceiling. The key is to affect the *expectations* of the public, for example in relation to inflation.

Delegating monetary policy

In many countries, governments handed over the operation of monetary policy to central banks. This is known as the *delegation of monetary policy*. In the UK, in 1997, the Bank of England was granted independence to determine interest rates to meet an inflation rate target.

The natural rate hypothesis provides the theoretical grounds for central bank independence. If there is no long-run trade-off between inflation and unemployment, then, monetarists and new classical macroeconomists argue, it makes sense to remove the temptation for governments to use expansionary monetary policy unexpectedly and, perhaps, simply for their own political benefit.

In the absence of delegating monetary policy and operating a transparent inflation rate target, the result is likely to be higher inflation rates. This is because the public will tend to form higher expectations of inflation, which lead to higher actual inflation rates. The public do this since they are aware of governments' incentive to want to reduce unemployment (and increase output) by loosening monetary policy and creating additional, unexpected inflation. Higher expectations of inflation choke off increases in *real* aggregate

> ### Definitions
>
> **Constrained discretion** A set of principles or rules within which economic policy operates. These can be informal or enshrined in law.
>
> **Delegation of monetary policy** The handing over by government of the operation of monetary policy to central banks.

KI 38
p 500

demand, output and employment that the government might try to bring about.

The longer-term position, it is argued, is therefore one of higher rates of inflation, yet with output and unemployment at their natural levels. There is no additional output or employment, merely additional and hence excessive inflation. This excessive inflation is known as *inflation bias*.

Pause for thought

Why would delegating monetary policy reduce inflation bias?

The elimination of inflation bias is commonly identified as the key economic benefit of central bank independence. The delegation of monetary policy to the central bank with a clear mandate that it then sticks to is said to enhance the *credibility of monetary policy*.

By sticking to an inflation target, a central bank can create the stable environment necessary for the market to flourish: expectations will adjust to the target rate of inflation (assuming central banks are successful in achieving the target) and firms will be able to plan with more confidence. Investment

is thereby encouraged and this, in turn, encourages a growth in potential output. In other words, sticking to the targets creates the best environment for the expansion of aggregate *supply*.

Inflation targeting

For many countries, inflation targeting has become central to their macroeconomic policy. Table 29.1 gives the targets for a selection of countries (as of 2018).

Inflation targets have proved relatively easy to achieve. There may be problems at first if the actual rate of inflation is way above the target level. The high rates of interest

---

Definitions

Inflation bias Excessive inflation that results from people raising their expectations of the inflation rate following expansionary demand management policy, encouraging government to loosen policy even further.

Credibility of monetary policy The extent to which the public believes that the central bank will take the measures necessary to achieve the stated targets of monetary policy, for example an inflation rate target.

Table 29.1	Inflation rate targets of central banks (2018)

Country	Inflation target (%)	Details
Australia	2–3	Average over the medium term
Brazil	4.5	Tolerance band of ± 1.5 percentage points
Canada	2	Tolerance band of ± 1 percentage point
Chile	3	Tolerance band of ± 1 percentage point
Czech Republic	2	Tolerance band of ± 1 percentage point
Eurozone	<2 but close to it	Average for Eurozone as a whole; over medium term
Hungary	3	Tolerance band of ± 1 percentage point
Iceland	2.5	
Israel	1–3	
Japan	2	
Mexico	3	Tolerance band of ± 1 percentage point
New Zealand	2	Tolerance band of ± 1 percentage point
Norway	2.5	
Peru	2	Tolerance band of ± 1 percentage point
Poland	2.5	Tolerance band of ± 1 percentage point
South Africa	3–6	
South Korea	2	Target for 2016–18
Sweden	2	
Switzerland	<2	
Thailand	2.5	Tolerance band of ± 1.5 percentage points
UK	2	Forward-looking inflation target; tolerance band of ± 1 percentage point

Source: Various central bank websites

necessary to bring inflation down may cause a recession. But once inflation has been brought down and the objective is then simply to maintain it at the target level, most countries have been relatively successful. And the more successful they are, the more people will expect this success to be maintained, which in turn will help to ensure this success.

So, have there been any problems with inflation targeting?

The horizontal Phillips curve. Ironically, one of the main problems may lay in its success. With worldwide inflation having fallen, and with global trade and competition helping to keep prices down, there is now less of a link between inflation and the business cycle. The Phillips curve has become close to horizontal (see Figure 29.13). Thus, there will be movements left or right *along* this horizontal line from one year to the next, depending on the level of economic activity. Such fluctuations in unemployment had become consistent with a stable inflation rate.

Under inflation rate targeting, booms may no longer generate the inflation they once did. Therefore, gearing interest rate policy to maintaining low inflation could still see economies experiencing unsustainable booms, followed by recessions. Inflation may be controlled, but the business cycle may not be.

A further complication is that there may be movements left or right along the horizontal Phillips curve, depending on what happens to equilibrium unemployment. A reduction in equilibrium unemployment will result in a leftward movement, while an increase will lead to a rightward movement.

Financial cycles. Some argue that the low interest rates seen in many countries during the first half of the 2000s helped to fuel unsustainable flows of lending. Low interest rates were consistent with meeting the inflation rate target but, it is argued, were generating conditions that subsequently would see many sectors suffer from financial distress.

Low interest rates boosted asset prices, including housing, which generated even higher levels of confidence among borrowers and lenders alike. However, by encouraging further investments that increasingly stretched the financial well-being of economic agents, the point was reached when a significant retrenchment by banks, businesses and individuals became inevitable. This is the idea of a ***balance sheet recession*** (see page 582).

Cost-push inflation. When central banks use interest rates to manage demand-pull inflation, there is what economists call a ***divine coincidence***: the reduction or absence of a trade-off between stabilising inflation and stabilising output around potential output. If demand-pull inflation is increasing because the economy is nearing or exceeding its potential output, then raising interest rates is appropriate both to manage the output gap and to reduce demand-pull inflation. Equally, cutting interest rates is appropriate if the rate of inflation is falling and a negative output gap is emerging.

However, when cost-push inflation is the principal cause of inflation, then there becomes a trade-off between managing inflation and the output gap. This is because cost-push inflation raises prices but reduces output (see page 525). A rise in interest rates in such circumstances will help to reduce inflation, but will worsen the negative output gap.

An example of the dilemma from cost-push inflation is the periodic problem of rising world inflation resulting from rapidly developing economies, such as China, India and Brazil. The resulting rise in food and commodity prices pushes up inflation rates around the world. Too strict an adherence to an inflation target could see higher interest rates and slow economic growth.

This was a problem from 2010 to 2012 — just after the financial crisis. Several countries, including the UK, had only just emerged from recession but commodity prices were rising. Central banks faced a policy conundrum with the macroeconomic environment characterised on the one hand by increasing inflationary pressures but on the other by often sizeable negative output gaps. In fact, most central banks were to keep interest rates at historic lows.

> **Pause for thought**
>
> *What policy dilemma might cost-push deflation create for a central bank?*

29.5 THE VOLATILITY OF PRIVATE-SECTOR SPENDING

The composition of aggregate demand

We conclude Part J by looking in more detail at aggregate demand. This is important because most economists see it as a key determinant of economic activity, at least in the short term. Periods of rapid growth tend to be associated with periods of rapid expansion of aggregate demand. On the other hand, periods of recession are associated with a decline in aggregate demand. Understanding what drives changes in aggregate demand is therefore crucial for understanding the business cycle.

> **Definitions**
>
> **Balance sheet recession** An economic slowdown or recession caused by private-sector individuals and firms looking to improve their financial well-being by increasing their saving and/or paying down debt.
>
> **Divine coincidence (in monetary policy)** When the monetary authorities can choose a policy stance that is largely consistent with both stabilising inflation and stabilising output around potential output.

	Table 29.2	Composition of aggregate demand, % (average 1990–2016)				

	Household final consumption	Gross capital formation (public and private)	General government final consumption	Exports	Imports	Net exports (X – M)
Australia	52.4	23.5	17.7	21.4	15.8	5.6
Brazil	59.2	19.7	20.0	9.6	9.0	0.6
China	37.8	43.9	13.3	25.3	21.3	4.1
France	54.3	22.4	23.8	24.2	24.6	−0.4
Germany	57.3	20.8	18.7	33.8	30.3	3.6
India	57.2	33.6	11.2	18.9	21.4	−2.5
Ireland	44.4	23.1	20.0	91.4	79.1	12.3
Japan	56.7	26.5	18.2	11.9	12.7	−0.8
Netherlands	46.4	21.3	24.1	63.9	55.9	8.0
Singapore	38.7	27.5	9.9	182.4	159.7	22.7
Sweden	46.3	22.6	27.4	41.4	37.1	4.3
UK	63.6	17.2	20.5	25.7	27.5	−1.8
USA	66.8	20.2	16.6	10.9	14.3	−3.4

Note: Based on constant-price data.

Source: *National Accounts Main Aggregates Database* (United Nations Statistics Division)

Table 29.2 shows the composition of aggregate demand. It presents the average percentage composition of aggregate demand for a selection of countries over the period 1990 to 2016.

Although the composition of aggregate demand varies across countries, spending by consumers on goods and services (C) is, in most countries, the largest component of aggregate demand.

Pause for thought

There is a large difference between countries in their exports as a percentage of aggregate demand. Explain the reasons for this.

Consumption cycles

Spending by the household sector is the largest component by value of aggregate demand, even after subtracting the consumption of imported products. In the UK, household spending has averaged around 60 per cent of GDP over the past 50 years. Consequently, even relatively small changes in consumer behaviour can have a significant impact on the overall demand for firms' goods and services and so on the level of business activity.

Figure 29.16 shows annual rates of economic growth mirror closely those in household consumption. In comparison to consumption, investment levels fluctuate significantly more. We will return to this shortly. The key point though is that the business cycle tends to reflect the consumption cycle.

But what factors determine consumption? Which are most important? How do changes in consumption then affect output and other macroeconomic variables? Do these effects then feed back to influence further the level of consumption? Is the determination of consumption predictable?

The consumption function underpinning the simple Keynesian model (see section 29.1) suggests that current levels of national income determine aggregate consumption levels. But, clearly there are other factors influencing people's spending decisions.

Taxation. The higher the level of direct taxes (income tax and social insurance contributions), the less will people have left to spend out of their gross income: consumption depends on *disposable income*. Disposable income also rises when government increases cash benefits.

Expected future incomes. Many people take into account both current and expected future incomes when planning their current and future consumption. In other words, they are forward looking. You might have a relatively low income when you graduate, but can expect (you hope!) to earn much more in the future.

You are thus willing to take on more debts now in order to support your consumption, not only as a student but shortly afterwards as well, anticipating that you will be able to pay back these loans later. It is similar with people taking out a mortgage to buy a house. They might struggle to meet the repayments at first, but hope that this will become easier over time.

Figure 29.16 Annual growth of UK consumption, investment and output

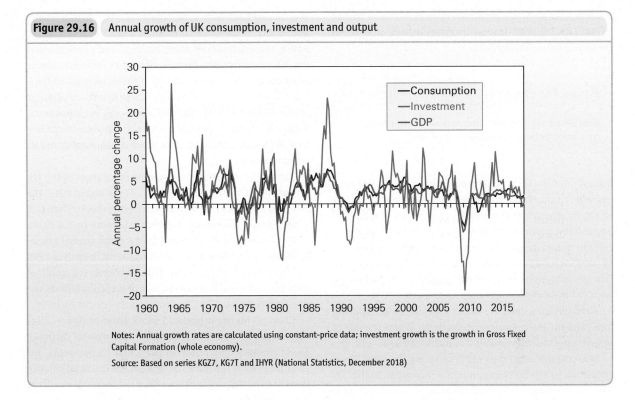

Notes: Annual growth rates are calculated using constant-price data; investment growth is the growth in Gross Fixed Capital Formation (whole economy).

Source: Based on series KGZ7, KG7T and IHYR (National Statistics, December 2018)

The financial system (such as banks and building societies) is fundamental to the *smoothing of consumption* by households. You can borrow when your income is low and pay back the loans later on when your income is higher. Therefore, the financial system provides households with greater flexibility as to when to spend their expected future incomes.

The smoothing of consumption can therefore play a role in reducing the peaks or troughs of the consumption and business cycles. However, expectations of futures incomes do get revised. Large revisions can have significant effects for current spending levels. If, for example, there is a general belief among people that future incomes will grow much less quickly than was previously expected, as was the case in many countries in the late 2000s following the financial crisis, then this can significantly dampen today's spending levels.

transactions to take place by bridging short-term gaps between income and expenditure flows. This helps to explain why short-term rates of change in household spending, such as those from one quarter of the year to the next, are generally less variable than those in disposable income.

However, the growth in consumption is affected if the ability and willingness of financial institutions to provide credit changes. The global financial crises of the second half of the 2000s saw credit criteria tighten dramatically. A tightening of credit practices, such as reducing overdraft facilities or reducing income multiples (the size of loans made available relative to household incomes), weakens consumption growth. This is because the growth of consumption becomes more dependent on the growth of current incomes. Consequently, there is a growth in the number of *credit-constrained households*.

In contrast, a relaxation of lending practices, as seen in many countries during the 1980s, can strengthen

Pause for thought

If a consumption-smoothing household expects a large payment to be made to their bank account later in a few months' time, what impact will this have on their spending now?

The financial system and the availability of credit. The financial sector provides households with both longer-term loans and also short-term credit. Short-term credit enables

Definitions

Consumption smoothing The act by households of smoothing their levels of consumption over time despite facing volatile incomes.

Credit-constrained households Households that are limited in their ability to borrow against expected future incomes.

consumption growth. This allows households more readily to borrow against future incomes: there are fewer credit-constrained households.

Pause for thought

What impact do credit constraints have on the short-term relationship between consumption and income?

Interest rates and cash flow effects. Changes in interest rates can affect household spending. They generate cash flow effects by affecting the interest receipts of savers (creditors) and interest payments by borrowers (debtors). With financialisation and the general increase seen in many countries in people's levels of indebtedness to financial institutions, changes in interest rates can have a significant impact on the costs to households of 'servicing' their loans.

Debt-servicing costs are the costs incurred in repaying loans and the interest payments on them. Where the rate of interest rate on debt is variable – a variable-rate loan – changes in interest rates affect the cost of servicing the debt. These effects can be especially important for mortgages. In the UK, where a large proportion of mortgage-payers are on a variable mortgage rate, changes in mortgage rates can have a sizeable impact on their debt-servicing costs. This then increases the proportion of current income that a household needs to set aside to paying the mortgage and reduces the proportion that could otherwise have been used for consumption.

Pause for thought

How might the marginal propensity to consume of debtors differ from that of creditors?

Wealth and household sector balance sheets. By borrowing and saving, households accumulate a stock of financial liabilities (debts), financial assets (savings) and physical assets (mainly property). The household sector's *financial* balance sheet details the sector's holding of financial assets and liabilities, while its *capital* balance sheet details its physical assets. The balance of financial assets over liabilities is the household sector's net financial wealth. The household sector's **net worth** is the sum of its net financial wealth and its physical wealth.

Table 29.3 shows the summary balance sheet of the UK household sector in 1995 and 2017. At the end of 2017, the sector had a stock of net worth estimated at £10.5 trillion (7.8 times annual household disposable income or 5.2 times GDP) compared with £2.6 trillion (4.5 times annual household disposable income or 3.1 times GDP) at the end of 1995 – an increase of 300 per cent. This, of course, is a nominal increase, not a real increase, as part of it merely reflects the rise in asset prices.

Changes on the household sector balance sheets affect the sector's financial well-being (or its financial distress). These changes may relate to particular components, for example certain categories of debt on the financial balance sheet or to broader aggregates such as net financial wealth or net worth.

The effects on spending from a sector's balance sheets are known as **balance sheet effects**. These effects apply not only

Definitions

Debt-servicing costs The costs incurred when repaying debt, including debt interest payments.

Net worth The market value of a sector's stock of financial and non-financial wealth.

Table 29.3 Summary balance sheet of household sector, 1995 and 2017

	1995			2017		
	£ billions	% of disposable income	% of GDP	£ billions	% of disposable income	% of GDP
Financial assets	2 063.3	352.5	243.7	6 553.5	482.4	320.5
Financial liabilities	533.7	91.2	63.0	1 803.6	132.8	88.2
Net financial wealth	**1 529.6**	**261.3**	**180.7**	**4 749.8**	**349.7**	**232.3**
Non-financial assets	1 107.5	189.2	130.8	5 781.0	425.6	282.8
Net worth	**2 637.1**	**450.5**	**311.5**	**10 530.8**	**775.2**	**515.1**

Source: Based on data from *National Balance Sheet, 2018 Estimates* and series *YBHA* and *QWND (National Statistics)*.

to households but to all sectors of the economy. In the context of households, a deterioration in financial well-being would be expected to dampen consumer spending. For example, a declining net worth-to-income ratio, perhaps caused by falling house prices or falling share prices, could lead to the household sector increasing its savings or repaying some of its outstanding debts. On the other hand, improvements to financial well-being can raise consumption levels.

Consumer confidence. Consumer confidence relates to the sentiment, emotion or anxiety of consumers. At its most simple, consumer (and business) confidence surveys (see Box 29.3) are trying to assess feelings of optimism or pessimism, particularly in relation to the economy or financial well-being. These surveys aim to shed light on spending intentions and hence the short-term prospects for consumption. A rise in confidence would be expected to lead to a rise in consumption, while a fall would lead to a fall in consumption.

Uncertainty. If people are uncertain about their future income prospects, or fear unemployment, they are likely to be cautious in their spending. Heightened uncertainty tends to erode confidence and hence increase saving. People become more prudent.

KI 14 **p 79** Saving undertaken by people (or businesses) to guard again uncertainty, such as in future income levels, is known as *precautionary* or *buffer-stock saving*. The resulting stock of savings acts as buffer that can, at some future point, be readily converted into a given amount of cash. This of course means foregoing an amount of consumption now.

An increase in economic uncertainly creates an incentive for people to increase their level of buffer-stock savings. **KI 9** **p 45** Consumption levels fall. On the other hand, with less uncertainty, people may feel more confident in holding a smaller buffer stock. The result is greater spending. They become less prudent.

Pause for thought

How does uncertainty affect the relative importance of 'prudence' and 'impatience' in determining people's current spending plans?

KI 13 **p 75** *Expectations of future prices.* If people expect prices to rise, they tend to buy durable goods such as furniture and cars before this happens. Conversely, if people expect prices to fall, they may wait. This has been a problem in Japan for many years, where periods of falling prices (deflation) led many consumers to hold back on spending, thereby weakening aggregate demand and hence economic growth.

The distribution of income. Poorer households will typically spend more than richer ones out of any additional income they receive. They have a higher marginal propensity to consume (*mpc*) than the rich, with very little left over to save. A

redistribution of national income from the poor to the rich will therefore tend to reduce the total level of consumption in the economy.

Tastes and attitudes. If people have a 'buy now, pay later' mentality or a craving for consumer goods, they are likely to have a higher level of consumption than if their tastes are more frugal. The more 'consumerist' and materialistic a nation becomes, facilitated by its financial system, the higher will its consumption be for any given level of income.

The age of durables. If people's car, carpets, clothes, etc. are getting old, they will tend to have a high level of 'replacement' consumption, particularly after a recession when they had cut back on their consumption of durables. Conversely, as the economy reaches the peak of the boom, people are likely to spend less on durables as they have probably already bought the items they want. This behaviour therefore amplifies the consumption cycle.

Instability of investment

Investment (*I*) is the most volatile expenditure component of aggregate demand. This is evident from Figure 29.16. But why is this the case? What drives this volatility?

The investment accelerator

When an economy begins to recover from a recession, investment can rise very rapidly. When the growth of the economy slows down, however, investment can fall dramatically and, during a recession, it can all but disappear. Since investment is an injection into the circular flow of income, these changes in investment will cause multiplied changes in income and thus heighten a boom or deepen a recession. **KI 43** **p 575**

The theory that relates investment to *changes* in national income is called the *accelerator theory*. The term 'accelerator' is used because a relatively modest rise in national income can cause a much larger percentage rise in investment.

When there is no change in income and hence no change in consumption, the only investment needed is a relatively small amount of replacement investment for machines that are wearing out or have become obsolete. When income and consumption increase, however, there will have to be *new*

Definitions

Balance sheet effects The effects on spending behaviour, such as consumer spending, that arise from changes in the composition or value of net worth.

Precautionary or buffer-stock saving Saving in response to uncertainty, for example uncertainty of future income.

Accelerator theory The *level* of investment depends on the *rate of change* of national income, and as a result tends to be subject to substantial fluctuations.

investment in order to increase production capacity. This is called *induced investment* (I_i). Once this has taken place, investment will fall back to mere replacement investment (I_r) unless there is a further rise in income and consumption.

Thus induced investment depends on *changes* in national income (ΔY):

$$I_i = \alpha \Delta Y$$

where α is the amount by which induced investment depends on changes in national income, and is known as the **accelerator coefficient**. Thus if a £1 billion *rise* in national income caused the *level* of induced investment to be £2 billion, the accelerator coefficient would be 2.

The size of α depends on the economy's **marginal capital-output ratio** ($\Delta K / \Delta Y$). If an increase in the country's capital stock of £2 million (i.e. an investment of £2 million) is required to produce £1 million extra national output, the marginal capital/output ratio would be 2. Other things being equal, the accelerator coefficient and the marginal capital/output ratio will therefore be the same.

In practice, the size of the accelerator effect is likely to be difficult to predict. Firms generally will have some spare capacity and/or carry stocks which means that they may be in a position to meet extra demand without having to invest. Machines do not, as a rule, suddenly wear out. A firm could thus delay replacing machines and keep the old ones for a bit longer if it was uncertain about its future level of demand.

Nevertheless, the accelerator effect still appears to exist with firms' investment spending responding to changes in aggregate demand (see web case J25 on the student website).

The interaction of the multiplier and accelerator

Once an accelerator effect takes place, it is then amplified by the multiplier. Similarly, an initial multiplier effect of, say, a rise in consumption can lead to an accelerator effect. The accelerator and multiplier interact. This amplifies the ups and downs of the business cycle.

For example, if there is a rise in government purchases (G), this will lead to a multiplied rise in national income. But this *rise* in national income will set off an accelerator effect: firms will respond to the rise in income and the resulting rise in consumer demand by investing more. But this rise in investment constitutes a further rise in injections and thus will lead to a second multiplied rise in income. If this rise in income is larger than the first, there will then be a second rise in investment (the accelerator), which in turn will cause a third rise in income (the multiplier). And so the process continues indefinitely.

But does this lead to an exploding rise in national income? Will a single rise in injections cause national income to go on rising for ever? The answer is no, for two reasons. The first is that national income, in real terms, cannot go on rising faster than the growth in potential output. It will bump up against the ceiling of full employment, whether of labour or of other resources.

A second reason is that, if investment is to go on rising, it is not enough that national income should merely go on *rising*: instead, national income must *rise faster and faster*. Once the growth in national income slows down, investment will begin to fall, and then the whole process will be reversed. A fall in investment will lead to a fall in national income, which will lead to a massive fall in investment. The multiplier/accelerator interaction is shown more formally in Case Study J.24 on the student website.

Other determinants of investment

There are other major determinants of investment. These too may contribute the volatility of investment spending.

Expectations of future market conditions. Since investment is made in order to produce output for the future, investment must depend on firms' expectations about future market conditions. But, this raises important questions about how people form their expectations. After all, the future cannot be predicted with accuracy. To what extent do firms, for instance, use current conditions or those of the recent past as a short-cut in their decision-making process?

If current economic growth helps determine firms' expectations of future growth, it increases the possibility of *bandwagon effects* affecting investment levels. Hence once the economy starts expanding, expectations become buoyant and firms increase investment which, through the multiplier and accelerator, boosts economic growth and further increases confidence. Likewise, in a recession, a mood of pessimism may set in and firms cut investment.

Uncertainty. Since future market conditions cannot be predicted with accuracy, investment is *risky*. Greater uncertainty about these conditions will make firms more cautious to invest. In the same way that households look to self-insure against uncertainty, firms are less likely to proceed with investment projects when uncertainty is high. Hence, greater uncertainty negatively affects levels of investment and aggregate demand. Uncertainty over the effects of Brexit led to a fall in investment following the referendum.

Business confidence. Confidence in the context of business relates to the sentiment, emotion or anxiety of firms about market conditions. Investment depends crucially on business confidence. The scale and cost of capital projects by firms can be very large indeed. Hence, increased pessimism

---

Definitions

Accelerator coefficient The level of induced investment as a proportion of a rise in national income: $\alpha = I_i / \Delta Y$.

Marginal capital-output ratio The amount of extra capital (in money terms) required to produce a £1 increase in national output. Since $I_i = \Delta K$, the marginal capital/output ratio $\Delta K / \Delta Y$ equals the accelerator coefficient (α).

among businesses may reduce investment quite significantly. This is examined further in Box 29.3.

The availability of finance. Investment often requires financing and this can involve very significant amounts of money. Firms may seek finance from banks or perhaps issue debt instruments, such as bonds or issue new shares. Therefore, difficulties in raising finance, such as seen in the late 2000s and into the early 2010s, can limit investment.

The rate of interest. The higher the rate of interest, the more expensive it will be for firms to finance investment, and hence the less profitable will the investment be. Economists keenly debate just how responsive total investment in the economy is to changes in interest rates.

The cost and efficiency of capital equipment. If the cost of capital equipment goes down or machines become more efficient, the return on investment will increase. Firms will invest more. Technological progress is an important determinant here.

> ### Pause for thought
>
> *To what extent are the 'other determinants' of investment also likely to be determinants of household consumption?*

The financial sector

We have already seen several ways in which the financial system can affect spending. Sometimes it can dampen expenditure cycles by helping people and businesses to smooth their spending through the provision of short-term credit. On other occasions, it appears to create volatility. This might be because of changes in the availability or cost of credit or through financial institutions' impact on the balance sheets of different sectors of the economy.

The financial sector as a source of volatility. Some economists argue that the financial sector is a major *source* of economic volatility. For example, the financial instability hypothesis (see Box 28.4), argues that the behaviour of financial institutions through their excessive lending and asset purchases generates unsustainable economic growth which inevitably ends with an economic downturn. People's financial well-being then deteriorates. Financial institutions respond by being much more cautious about lending and this then exacerbates the downturn.

The 2007–9 financial crisis is, for some economists, evidence of a *balance sheet recession*: an economic downturn caused by financially distressed sectors of the economy. The term is applied to sectors that become overly burdened by their debts. Policymakers are paying increasing attention as a result to various indicators of financial well-being across different sectors, including the household sector. Financial distress is seen as an early warning sign of a possible impending crisis and recession.

> ### Pause for thought
>
> *Can economies experience balance sheet booms?*

The financial sector as a magnifier of volatility. Other economists argue that the financial sector *amplifies* economic shocks. The argument here is not that financial institutions are the source of fluctuations in economic growth but rather that they magnify the shocks that affect the economy. They can do this by boosting lending when growth is strong or reducing lending when growth is weak. This generates a *financial accelerator effect* (see page 580).

Just as the investment accelerator interacts with the multiplier, so too does the financial accelerator. For example, an increase in aggregate demand, whether through a rise in injections (*J*) or a fall in withdrawals (*W*), leads to a multiplied rise in national income. But rising national income (GDP) may encourage banks to ease credit conditions and so provide more and/or cheaper credit, which itself increases aggregate demand.

In contrast, an economy experiencing a contraction of national income, might see banks tighten credit conditions. This, of course, weakens aggregate demand, further amplifying the contraction.

> ### Pause for thought
>
> *Can the financial and investment accelerators interact?*

Why do booms and recessions come to an end? What determines the turning points?

We have examined a variety of reasons why aggregate demand fluctuates. But why, once the economy is booming, does the boom come to an end? Why does a recession not go on for ever? What determines these turning points?

Ceilings and floors. Actual output can go on growing more rapidly than potential output only as long as there is slack in the economy. As full employment is approached and as more and more firms reach full capacity, so a ceiling to output is reached.

At the other extreme, there is a basic minimum level of consumption that people tend to maintain. During a recession, people may not buy much in the way of luxury and durable goods, but they will still continue to buy food and other basic goods. There is thus a floor to consumption.

Echo effects. Durable consumer goods and capital equipment may last several years, but eventually they will need replacing. The replacement of goods and capital purchased in a previous boom may help to bring a recession to an end.

| BOX 29.3 | SENTIMENT AND SPENDING |

Keynesian economists have frequently pointed to the importance of confidence or sentiment in influencing expenditure decisions. 'Confidence shocks' are often identified as a source of economic volatility. But what is confidence? Is it something tangible and can it be measured?

Measures of confidence

Each month, consumers and firms across the European Union are asked a series of questions, the answers to which are used to compile indicators of consumer and business confidence. For instance, consumers are asked about how they expect their financial position to change. They are offered various options such as 'get a lot better', 'get a lot worse' and balances are then calculated on the basis of positive and negative replies.[1]

The chart plots economic sentiment[2] in the Eurozone for consumers and different sectors of business since the mid-1990s.

The following chart captures the volatility of economic sentiment. This volatility is generally greater amongst businesses than consumers and especially so in the construction sector. However, confidence fell dramatically across all groups during the financial crisis of the late 2000s.

Confidence and expenditure

Now compare the volatility of economic sentiment in Chart (a) with the annual rates of growth in household consumption and gross capital formation (investment) in Chart (b). You can see that volatility in economic sentiment is reflected in patterns of both consumer and investment expenditure. However, capital formation is significantly more volatile than household spending.

[1] More information on EU business and consumer surveys can be found at http://ec.europa.eu/economy_finance/db_indicators/surveys/index_en.htm.
[2] https://ec.europa.eu/info/business-economy-euro/indicators-statistics/economic-databases/business-and-consumer-surveys_en.

(a) *Economic sentiment in the Eurozone*

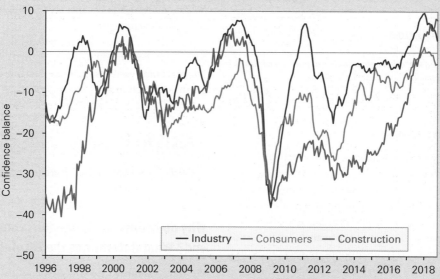

Notes: Eurozone figures are the weighted average of the 19 countries (as of Jan 2015) using the euro
Source: Based on data from *Business and Consumer Surveys* (European Commission, DGECFIN)

The accelerator. For investment to continue rising, consumer demand must rise at a faster and faster rate. If this does not happen, investment will fall back and the boom will break.

 Sentiment and expectations. Sentiment may change (see Box 29.3). People may start believing that a boom or recession will not last for ever.

Random shocks. National or international political, social or natural events can affect the mood and attitudes of firms, governments and consumers, and thus affect aggregate demand.

Changes in government policy. In a boom, a government may become most worried by inflation and balance of trade deficits and thus pursue contractionary policies. In a recession, it may become most worried by unemployment and lack of growth and thus pursue expansionary policies. These government policies, if successful, will bring about a turning point in the cycle. This was the hope for the expansionary policies pursued by many governments during the global recession of the late 2000s.

Pause for thought

Why is it difficult to predict precisely when a recession will come to an end and the economy will start growing rapidly?

What is less clear is the extent to which changes in sentiment *lead* to changes in spending In fact, a likely scenario is that spending and sentiment interact. High rates of spending growth may result in high confidence through economic growth, which, in turn, leads to more spending. The reverse is the case when economic growth is subdued: low spending growth leads to a lack of confidence, which results in low spending growth and so low rates of economic growth.

Therefore, while confidence may be a source of volatility it may also be part of the process by which shocks are transmitted through the economy. Consequently, it may be contributing to amplifying the peaks and troughs of the business cycle.

What makes measures of confidence particularly useful is that they are published monthly. By contrast, measures of GDP and spending are published annually or quarterly and with a considerable time delay. Therefore, measures of confidence are extremely timely for policy-makers and provide them with

very useful information about the likely path of spending and output growth.

1. *What factors are likely to influence the economic sentiment of (i) consumers and (ii) businesses?*
2. *Can consumers become more optimistic while businesses become more pessimistic, and vice versa?*

Using time series data from the European Commission based on business and consumer survey data (https://ec.europa.eu/ info/business-economy-euro/indicators-statistics/economic-databases/business-and-consumer-surveys_en), plot a line chart to show the path of consumer confidence for any two countries of your choice. Describe the patterns you observe noting any similarities or differences between the consumer confidence profile of the two countries.

(b) *Annual change in real consumption and investment in the Eurozone*

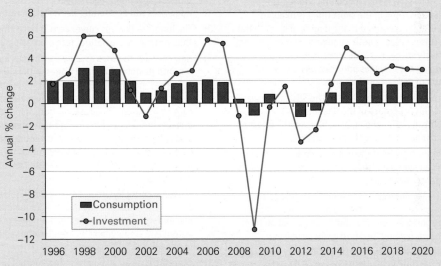

Notes: Figures from 2018 based on forecasts; Eurozone figures are the weighted average of the 19 countries (as of January 2015) using the euro.
Source: Based on data in *AMECO Database* (European Commission, DGECFIN)

SUMMARY

1a In the simple circular flow of income model, equilibrium national income (GDP) is where withdrawals equal injections: where $W = J$.

1b The simple Keynesian model can be illustrated through the Keynesian cross diagram. Prices are assumed constant. Equilibrium is where national income (Y) (i.e. GDP), shown by the 45° line, is equal to aggregate expenditure (E).

1c If there is an initial increase in aggregate expenditure (ΔE), which could result from an increase in injections or a reduction in withdrawals, there will be a multiplied rise

in national income (Y). The multiplier is defined as $\Delta Y / \Delta E$.

1d The size of the multiplier depends on the marginal propensity to consume domestically produced goods (mpc_d). The larger the mpc_d, the more will be spent each time incomes are generated around the circular flow, and thus the more will go round again as *additional* demand for domestic product. The multiplier formula is $1/1 - mpc_d$.

1e If equilibrium national income (Ye) is below the full-employment level of national income (Y_f), there will be a recessionary (deflationary) gap. This gap is equal to

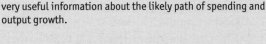

$Y - E$ at Y_f. If equilibrium national income exceeds the full-employment level of income, the inability of output to expand to meet this excess demand will lead to demand-pull inflation. This excess demand gives an inflationary gap, which is equal to $E - Y$ at Y_f.

1f The full-employment output level acts as a constraint on the multiplier process. Further increases in aggregate demand are inflationary and the multiplier process ceases to operate. In reality, inflationary effects may begin to occur before the full-employment level and so the impact on output from increases in aggregate demand may be less than implied by the simple Keynesian model.

2a The impact of changes in aggregate demand on prices (and output) is affected by the nature of aggregate supply (*AS*) curve.

2b In the extreme Keynesian model, increases in nominal aggregate demand have a full multiplied effect on real GDP up to the full-employment output level because prices are constant. Thereafter, further increases in aggregate demand are inflationary and increases in real GDP are only possible in the very short term. The *SRAS* curve is therefore a flat horizontal line.

2c The mainstream view is that if nominal aggregate demand changes, then in the short run it is likely to affect real GDP (*Y*) according to the degree of slack in the economy. This is because both wage rates and prices tend to be relatively sticky. The *SRAS* curve is, therefore, upward sloping but becomes progressively steeper at higher levels of real national income.

2d Some new classicists argue that that the *SRAS* curve may be vertical. This is because of the flexibility of markets and the ability of rational people to forecast the effect of expected changes in aggregate demand on prices.

2e New classicists argue that the business cycle is caused by fluctuations in aggregate supply. Such a business cycle is known as a 'real business cycle'.

2e The mainstream view is that the long-run aggregate supply (*LRAS*) curve is vertical because price increases from any rise in aggregate demand tend to be passed on from one firm to another and feed into wage increases.

2f Some argue, however, that the *LRAS* curve may be upward sloping. If a sustained increase in demand leads to increased investment, this can have the effect of shifting the short-run *AS* to the right and making the long-run *AS* curve upward sloping, not vertical.

3a With an upward sloping *SRAS* curve, increasing levels of aggregate demand will no longer increase real national income by the full extent of the multiplier process: increasingly, large parts of increases in aggregate demand are reflected in higher prices and a smaller part in higher output.

3b The Phillips curve showed the trade-off between inflation and unemployment. There seemed to be a simple inverse relationship between the two. After 1967, however, the relationship appeared to break down as inflation *and* unemployment rose.

3c Today, many central banks target inflation. The effect has been to make the Phillips curve appear more like an almost horizontal straight line.

3d Expectations can be incorporated into the analysis of the Phillips curve. The effect is to generate a series of expectations-augmented Phillips curves (*EAPCs*).

3e The natural rate hypothesis assumes that the natural, or equilibrium, rate of unemployment is determined independently of aggregate demand. The result is a vertical long-run curve at the equilibrium rate of unemployment.

3f Adaptive expectations are backward-looking expectations. The simplest form of adaptive expectations of inflation assumes that the expected rate of inflation this year is what it actually was last year: $\pi_t^e = \pi_{t-1}$.

3g The monetarist model assumes that markets are relatively flexible. But the assumption of adaptive expectations allows unemployment to deviate from the natural rate in the short term. People can be fooled, allowing unemployment and output to fluctuate.

3h If there is excess demand in the economy, producing upward pressure on wages and prices, initially unemployment will fall. The reason is that workers and firms will believe that wage and price increases represent *real* wage and price increases respectively. Thus workers are prepared to take jobs more readily and firms choose to produce more. But as people's expectations adapt upwards to these higher wages and prices, so ever-increasing rises in nominal aggregate demand will be necessary to maintain unemployment below the natural rate. Price and wage rises will accelerate, i.e. inflation will rise.

3i The long-run Phillips curve, according to this analysis, is thus vertical at the natural rate of unemployment.

3j New classical theories assume continuous market clearing with flexible prices and wages in the short run as well as in the long run. It also assumes that people base their expectations of inflation on a rational assessment of the *current* situation. These assumptions imply that only unexpected fluctuations in aggregate demand will cause unemployment to deviate from its natural rate. There can be no short-run trade-off between inflation and unemployment when changes in aggregate demand are anticipated.

3k If people correctly predict the rate of inflation, they will correctly predict that any increase in nominal aggregate demand will simply be reflected in higher prices. Total output and employment will remain the same: at the natural level.

3l Expectations can also impact upon output and employment. If business is confident that demand will expand and that order books will be healthy, then firms are likely to gear up production and take on extra labour.

4a The delegation by government of the operation of monetary policy to central banks and the adoption of inflation rate targeting is argued to reduce inflation bias. It enhances the credibility of monetary policy which provides the conditions for low and stable rate of inflation.

4b Inflation targeting in the UK has seen the rate of inflation typically very close to the target level. Inflation rate targeting helps to anchor inflationary expectations around the target rate. This has tended to make the time-path of the Phillips curve horizontal at the target rate of inflation.

4c Some economists argue that inflation rate targeting is not without issues. These include: the stages of the business cycle not being readily identifiable by rate of inflation; interest rates not taking into account sufficiently other macroeconomic concerns such as the sustainability of bank lending; and the policy dilemma for central banks when cost-push inflationary pressures develop.

5a The consumption cycle mirrors closely the economy's business cycle. Household consumption is thought to depend primarily on current and expected future disposable incomes. The financial system enables households to smooth their consumption by shifting incomes across their lifetimes through borrowing or saving.

5b Household consumption may be affected by a series of other determinants, which include: constraints on borrowing, confidence levels, economic uncertainty and a series of balance sheet effects.

5c Investment expenditure is highly volatile. The accelerator theory can help to explain this. It relates the level of investment to *changes* in national income and consumer demand. An initial increase in consumer demand can result in a very large percentage increase in investment; but as soon as the rise in consumer demand begins to level off, investment will fall; and even a slight fall in consumer demand can reduce investment to virtually zero. The accelerator interacts with the multiplier, each amplifying the other.

5d Investment, like consumption, is also affected by access to finance (borrowing constraints) and by expectations. The scale and cost of investment projects is likely to mean that expectations of the future market environment and business confidence are particularly important determinants.

5e The financial system is argued by some either to shape or to generate the business cycle. A balance sheet recession can arise from increased levels of indebtedness and financial distress. What is more, there may be a financial accelerator effect, whereby financial institutions lend more when growth is strong and less when growth is weak.

5f The interaction of the investment accelerator, the financial accelerator and the multiplier illustrate how the peaks and troughs of the business cycle can be amplified.

5g Booms and recessions do not last for ever. Turning points can be induced by various ceilings and floors, echo effects, the nature of the accelerator, changes in sentiment, random shocks and government policy measures.

REVIEW QUESTIONS

1 An economy is currently in equilibrium. The following figures refer to elements in its national income accounts.

	£bn
Consumption (total)	1200
Investment	100
Government expenditure	160
Imports	200
Exports	140

   a) What is the current equilibrium level of national income?
   b) What is the level of injections?
   c) What is the level of withdrawals?
   d) Assuming that tax revenues are £140 billion, how much is the level of saving?
   e) If national income now rises to £1600 billion and, as a result, the consumption of domestically produced goods rises to £1160 billion, what is the mpc_d?
   f) What is the value of the multiplier?
   g) Given an initial level of national income of £1600 billion, now assume that spending on exports rises by £80 billion, spending on investment rises by £20 billion and government expenditure falls by £40 billion. By how much will national income change?

2 Assume that the multiplier has a value of 3. Now assume that the government decides to increase aggregate demand in an attempt to reduce unemployment. It raises government expenditure by £100 million with no increase in taxes. Firms, anticipating a rise in their sales, increase investment by £200 million, of which £50 million consists of purchases of foreign machinery. How much will GDP rise? (Assume *ceteris paribus*.)

3 What factors could explain why some countries have a higher multiplier than others?

4 Why does the slope of the *E* line in a Keynesian diagram equal the mpc_d? (Clue: draw an mpc_d line.)

5 On a Keynesian diagram, draw two *E* lines of different slopes, both crossing the *Y* line at the same point. Now draw another two *E* lines, parallel with the first two and crossing each other vertically above the point where the first two crossed. Using this diagram, show how the size of the multiplier varies with the mpc_d.

6 In what way will the nature of aggregate supply influence the effect of a change in aggregate demand on prices and real national income?

7 What shape do you think the aggregate supply curve would be at the current output if the economy was in a deep recession?

8 What shape of aggregate supply curve is assumed by the simple Keynesian demand-driven model of the economy? Under what circumstances is this shape likely to be a true reflection of the aggregate supply curve?

9 What is the difference between adaptive explanations and rational expectations?

10 Assume that there is a trade-off between unemployment and inflation, traced out by a 'Phillips curve'. What could cause a leftward shift in this curve?

11 In the accelerationist model of the Phillips curve, if the government tries to maintain unemployment below the equilibrium rate, what will determine the speed at which inflation accelerates?

12 For what reasons might the equilibrium rate of unemployment increase?

13 How can adaptive expectations of inflation result in clockwise Phillips loops? Why would these loops not be completely regular?

14 What implications would a vertical short-run aggregate supply curve have for the effectiveness of demand management policy?

15 What is meant by inflation bias? What factors might affect the potential magnitude of inflation bias?

16 What is meant by the credibility of monetary policy? How could its credibility be assessed?

17 How can the interaction of the multiplier and accelerator explain cyclical fluctuations in GDP?

18 Does the financial system smooth or amplify the business cycle?

ADDITIONAL PART J CASE STUDIES ON THE *ECONOMICS FOR BUSINESS* STUDENT WEBSITE (www.pearsoned.co.uk/sloman)

J.1 **Theories of economic growth.** An overview of classical and more modern theories of growth.

J.2 **The costs of economic growth.** Why economic growth may not be an unmixed blessing.

J.3 **Technology and unemployment.** Does technological progress destroy jobs?

J.4 **The GDP deflator.** An examination of how GDP figures are corrected to take inflation into account.

J.5 **Comparing national income statistics.** The importance of taking the purchasing power of local currencies into account.

J.6 **The UK's current account deficit.** An examination of the UK's persistent trade and current account deficits.

J.7 **Making sense of the financial balances on the balance of payments.** An examination of the three main components of the financial account.

J.8 **A high exchange rate.** This case looks at whether a high exchange rate is necessarily bad news for exporters.

J.9 **Does PPP hold in the long run?** This considers the relationship between inflation rate differentials and movements in sterling.

J.10 **The Gold Standard.** A historical example of fixed exchange rates.

J.11 **The importance of international financial movements.** How a current account deficit can coincide with an appreciating exchange rate.

J.12 **Argentina in crisis.** An examination of the collapse of the Argentine economy in 2001/2.

J.13 **Currency turmoil in the 1990s.** Two examples of speculative attacks on currencies: first on the Mexican peso in 1995; then on the Thai baht in 1997.

J.14 **The attributes of money.** What makes something, such as metal, paper or electronic records, suitable as money?

J.15 **Secondary marketing.** This looks at one of the ways of increasing liquidity without sacrificing profitability. It involves selling an asset to someone else before the asset matures.

J.16 **Consolidated MFI balance sheet.** A look at the consolidated balance sheet of UK monetary financial institutions (banks, building societies and the Bank of England).

J.17 **Bailing out the banks.** An overview of the concerted efforts made to rescue the banking system in the crisis of 2007–9.

J.18 **John Maynard Keynes (1883–1946).** Profile of the great economist.

J.19 **The rational expectations revolution.** A profile of two of the most famous economists of the new classical rational expectations school.

J.20 **The phases of the business cycle.** A demand-side analysis of the factors contributing to each of the four phases.

J.21 **How does consumption behave?** The case looks at evidence on the relationship between consumption and disposable income.

J.22 **Trends in housing equity withdrawal (HEW).** An analysis of the patterns in HEW and consumer spending.

J.23 **UK monetary aggregates.** This case shows how UK money supply is measured using both UK measures and Eurozone measures.

J.24 **Credit and the business cycle.** This case traces cycles in the growth of credit and relates them to the business cycle. It also looks at some of the implications of the growth in credit.

J.25 **The multiplier/accelerator interaction.** Numerical example showing how the interaction of the multiplier and accelerator can cause cycles in economic activity.

J.26 **Has there been an accelerator effect since the 1960a?** This case examines GDP and investment data to see whether the evidence points to an accelerator effect.

J.27 **Modelling the financial accelerator.** This case looks at how we can incorporate the accelerator effect into the simple Keynesian model of the economy.

J.28 **The explosion of UK household debt.** The growth of household debt in the UK since the mid-1990s and its potential impact on consumption.

J.29 **An international comparison of household wealth and indebtedness.** An examination of households' financial assets and liabilities relative to disposable income in seven developed countries (the G7).

WEBSITES RELEVANT TO PART J

Numbers and sections refer to websites listed in the Web appendix and hotlinked from this text's website at
www.pearsoned.co.uk/sloman

- For news articles relevant to Part J, see the *Economics News Articles* link from the text's website.

- For general news on macroeconomic issues, both national and international, see websites in section A, and particularly A1–5, 7–9. For general news on money, banking and interest rates, see again A1–5, 7–9 and also 20–25, 31, 35, 36. For all of Part J, see links to newspapers worldwide in A38, 39, 43, 44, and the news search feature in Google at A41.

- For macroeconomic data, see links in B1, 2 and 3; also see B4 and 35. For UK data, see B2, 3, 5 and 6. For EU data, see B38 and 47. For US data, see B25 and the Data section of B17. For international data, see B15, 21, 24, 31, 33. For links to data sets, see B1, 4, 28, 35, 46; I14.

- For national income statistics for the UK (Appendix to Chapter 26), see B3 (search 'national accounts').

- For data on UK unemployment, see B3 (search 'unemployment'). For International data on unemployment, see B1, 21, 24, 31, 38, 47, 48; H3.

- For international data on balance of payments and exchange rates, see B1 > sites B.8 (*Statistical Annex of the European Economy*), B.9 (*OECD Economic Outlook: Statistical Annex Tables*), B.11 (*World Economic Outlook*). See also the Data Center in UNCTADStat in site 43.

- For details of individual countries' balance of payments, see B31.

- For UK data on balance of payments, see B3 (search 'Pink Book'). For EU data, see B38 and 47.

- For exchange rates, see A1, 3; B45; F2, 4, 5, 6, 8.

- For discussion papers on balance of payments and exchange rates, see H4 and 7.

- For monetary and financial data (including data for money supply and interest rates), see section F and particularly F2. Note that you can link to central banks worldwide from site F17. See also the links in B1.

- For information on the development of ideas, see C18.

- For student resources relevant to this chapter, see sites C1–7, 9, 10, 12, 19.

Macroeconomic policy

The FT Reports . . .

The Financial Times, 24 May 2018

ECB to maintain 'steady hand' in face of Eurozone growth slowdown

By Claire Jones

The Eurozone's central bankers want to maintain 'a steady hand' as they continue to plan for the removal of their crisis-era stimulus in the face of concern that the slowdown in growth may prove more than a blip.

The bank also warned that it needed to strengthen its message on government spending in the face of events in Italy.

After a bumper 2017, growth in the opening months of this year has been slower in the Eurozone. Most economists view the setback as temporary — though weak sentiment surveys for the second quarter have raised concern of a longer-lasting period of lower growth.

. . . The formation of an anti-establishment coalition government in Italy that has put increased spending at the core of its proposals has raised concern among officials in Frankfurt and Brussels.

The ECB said in the minutes: "There was broad agreement among members that it was warranted to reinforce calls for existing fiscal rules to be respected and for fiscal buffers to be rebuilt, in particular with regard to those member states with high levels of government debt."

The slowdown and political events have left policymakers in a bind. The council has signalled that it would like to stop buying new bonds under the €2.4tn quantitative easing programme by the end of the year and could begin to raise rates from their current record lows around the middle or during the second half of next year.

However, a spell of weak growth could force the council to delay its exit. While most expect QE to come to an end in December, markets are pushing back their expectations of when the bank will raise rates to later in 2019.

. . . The threat from protectionism and profligate governments had risen, meaning the bank would have to keep a close eye on incoming data in the months ahead.

"While risks surrounding the euro area growth outlook remained broadly balanced, it was acknowledged that the risks related to global factors, including the threat of increased protectionism, had become more prominent and warranted monitoring," the minutes said.

Weather conditions, strikes and an unusually severe wave of influenza have all been blamed for the slowdown by those who view it as temporary in nature. The closely-watched purchasing managers' index hit an 18-month low in May, leading some to suspect that the effects may be longer lasting.

> *When the world economy was plunged into deep crisis in the 1930s, the response, both nationally and internationally, was too little and too late. This failure to act turned a serious downturn into a prolonged depression. We will not repeat those mistakes again.*
>
> Alistair Darling, Chancellor of the Exchequer, Budget speech, 21 April 2009

The role of government and of central bankers in managing macroeconomic affairs has always been a contentious one. Economists keenly debate the extent to which policy makers should intervene in economies. Such debates concern not only regional and national economies, but also groups of economies such as the member states of the European Union (as the *Financial Times* article points out). Economists keenly debate the role that policy makers can play in reducing the inherent volatility of economies and in fostering more rapid long-term economic growth.

In this final part of the text, we consider the alternative policies open to policy makers in their attempts to manage or influence the macroeconomy. Chapter 30 focuses on fiscal and monetary policy in the context of affecting *aggregate demand*. We consider how such policies are supposed to work and how effective they are in practice.

Up to the financial crisis of the late 2000s, policy makers had taken a more passive approach towards policy, often advocating policy rules. The financial crisis saw fiscal rules relaxed, suspended or even abandoned. Many central banks continue to rely on policy rules: for example, the Bank of England sets interest rates so as to achieve a target rate of inflation of 2 per cent. Nonetheless, even here there is renewed interest in the merit of such rules.

Chapter 31, by contrast, focuses on *aggregate supply* and considers the role of government in attempting to improve economic performance by supply-side reforms: i.e. reforms designed to increase productivity and efficiency and achieve a growth in potential output. Both free-market and interventionist supply-side strategies will be considered.

Finally, Chapter 32 takes an international perspective. We shall see how, in a world of interdependent economies, national governments try to harmonise their policies so as to achieve international growth and stability. Unfortunately, there is frequently a conflict between the broader interests of the international community and the narrow interests of individual countries and, in these circumstances, national interests normally dictate policy.

Key terms

Fiscal policy
Sustainability of public finances
Fiscal stance
Automatic fiscal stabilisers and discretionary fiscal policy
Pure fiscal policy
Crowding out
Monetary policy
Open-market operations
Demand management
Inflation targeting
Market-orientated and interventionist supply-side policies
Regional and urban policy
Industrial policy
International business cycle
Policy co-ordination
International convergence
Economic and monetary union in Europe (EMU)
Single European currency
Currency union

30 Chapter

Demand-side policy

Business issues covered in this chapter

- What types of macroeconomic policy are there and in what ways might they affect business?
- What are the principal measures of a country's public finances?
- What is meant by the sustainability of the public finances?
- What will be the impact on the economy and business of various fiscal policy measures?
- What determines the effectiveness of fiscal policy in smoothing out fluctuations in the economy?
- What fiscal rules or frameworks are adopted by governments and what are the economic arguments for such constraints on government policy?
- How does monetary policy work in the UK and the Eurozone, and what are the roles of the Bank of England and the European Central Bank?
- How does targeting inflation influence interest rates and hence business activity?
- Are there better rules for determining interest rates than sticking to a simple inflation target?

There are two major types of demand-side policy: fiscal and monetary. In each case, we shall first describe how the policy operates and then examine its effectiveness. We shall also consider the more general question of whether the government and central bank ought to intervene actively to manage the level of aggregate demand or whether they ought merely to set targets or rules for various indicators – such as money supply, inflation or government budget deficits – and then stick to them.

30.1 FISCAL POLICY AND THE PUBLIC FINANCES

KI 43
p 575
Fiscal policy involves the government manipulating the level of government expenditure and/or rates of tax in order to affect the level of aggregate demand. An *expansionary* fiscal policy will involve raising government expenditure (an injection into the circular flow of income) or reducing taxes

Definition

Fiscal policy Policy to affect aggregate demand by altering government expenditure and/or taxation.

(a withdrawal from the circular flow). A *deflationary* (i.e. a contractionary) fiscal policy will involve cutting government expenditure and/or raising taxes.

Roles for fiscal policy

Fiscal policy may be used to affect the level of aggregate demand. There are two principal reasons for this.

Prevent the occurrence of fundamental disequilibrium in the economy. The government may wish to remove any severe deflationary or inflationary gaps. Hence, expansionary fiscal policy could be used to prevent an economy experiencing a severe or prolonged recession, such as that experienced in the Great Depression of the 1930s or, in 2008/9, when substantial tax cuts and increased government expenditure were used by many countries, including the UK and the USA, to combat the onset of recession. Likewise, deflationary fiscal policy could be used to prevent rampant inflation, such as that experienced in the 1970s.

Stabilisation policies. The government may wish to smooth out the fluctuations in the economy associated with the business cycle. This involves reducing government expenditure or raising taxes when the economy begins to boom. This will dampen down the expansion and prevent 'overheating' of the economy, with its attendant problems of rising inflation and a deteriorating current account balance of payments. Conversely, if a recession looms, the government should cut taxes or raise government expenditure in order to boost the economy.

Fiscal policy can also be used to influence *aggregate supply*. For example, government can increase its expenditure on training and infrastructure or give tax incentives for investment and research and development. Such initiatives would be intended to increase the rate of growth of the economy's potential output and reduce the natural rate of unemployment.

Public-sector finance

Government finances

The term 'government' is often used interchangeably with that of 'general government' when analysing government finances. General government includes both *central* and *local* government.

The terms **budget deficit** and **budget surplus** are frequently used in the context of government and especially *central* government. However, these terms can be applied to any organisation to assess its financial well-being by comparing expenditure with revenues.

If the total expenditure (including benefits) of both central and local government exceeds the revenue from taxation, council taxes, rates, etc., this is known as a **general government deficit**. Conversely, when general government's revenues exceed its expenditure, there is a **general government surplus**.

For most of the past 50 years, governments around the world have run deficits. In the late 1990s and early 2000s, however, many countries, the UK included, made substantial efforts to reduce the size of general government deficits and some achieved surpluses for periods of time. The position changed dramatically in 2008/9, however, as governments around the world increased their expenditure and cut taxes in an attempt to stave off recession. Government deficits in many countries soared.

Deficits, debt and borrowing. To finance their deficits, governments will have to borrow (e.g. through the issue of bonds (gilts) or Treasury bills). As we saw in section 28.3, this will lead to an increase in the money supply to the extent that the borrowing is from the banking sector. The purchase of bonds or Treasury bills by the (non-bank) private sector, however, will not lead to an increase in the money supply.

Deficits represent *annual* borrowing: a flow concept. The accumulated deficits over the years (minus any surpluses) gives total *debt*: a stock concept. It is the total amount owed by the government. Central and general government debt are known as **national debt** and **general government debt** respectively.

Note that the national debt is not the same thing as the country's overseas debt. In the case of the UK, only around 28 per cent of gilts are held overseas.[1] The remainder is held by UK financial institutions and some individual UK residents. In other words, the government finances its budget deficits largely by borrowing at home and not from abroad.

Table 30.1 shows general government deficits/surpluses and debt for selected countries. They are expressed as a proportion of GDP.

> ### Pause for thought
>
> *Why are historical and international comparisons of deficit and debt measures best presented as proportions of GDP?*

> ### Definitions
>
> **Budget deficit** The excess of an organisation's spending over its revenues. When applied to government, it is the excess of its spending over its tax receipts.
>
> **Budget surplus** The excess of an organisation's revenues over its expenditures. When applied to government, it is the excess of its tax receipts over its spending.
>
> **General government deficit** or **surplus** The combined deficit (or surplus) of central and local government.
>
> **National debt** The accumulated deficits of central government. It is the total amount owed by central government, both domestically and internationally.
>
> **General government debt** The accumulated deficits of central plus local government. It is the total amount owed by general government, both domestically and internationally.

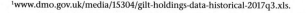

[1]www.dmo.gov.uk/media/15304/gilt-holdings-data-historical-2017q3.xls.

Table 30.1	General government deficits/surpluses and debt as a percentage of GDP			
	General government deficits (−) or surpluses (+)		General government debt	
	Average 1995–2007	Average 2008–2020	Average 1995–2007	Average 2008–2020
Belgium	−1.3	−2.6	108.1	102.1
France	−3.0	−4.0	61.8	91.6
Germany	−3.0	−0.1	60.9	69.4
Greece	−6.7	−5.8	102.4	163.5
Ireland	+1.2	−6.6	41.5	80.3
Italy	−3.6	−3.1	106.5	124.5
Japan	−5.7	−5.6	142.9	224.7
Netherlands	−1.5	−1.6	55.1	59.0
Portugal	−4.3	−4.7	58.6	114.5
Spain	−1.4	−6.0	52.9	83.7
Sweden	0.0	+0.2	55.3	39.5
UK	−2.0	−4.9	39.7	80.1
USA	−2.8	−7.1	62.0	100.6
Eurozone	−2.7	−2.7	69.1	86.7

Note: Data from 2018 are forecasts.

Source: Based on data from *AMECO database,* Tables 16.3 and 18.1 (European Commission, DG ECFIN)

As you can see, in the period from 1995 to 2007, all the countries, with the exception of Ireland and Sweden, ran an average deficit. In the period from 2008 to 2020, the average deficits increased for most countries. And the bigger the deficit, the faster debt increased.

Public sector

To get a more complete view of public finances, we would need to look at the spending and receipts of the entire public sector: namely, central government, local government and public corporations.

Current and capital expenditures. In presenting the public finances, it has become the custom to distinguish between **current** and **capital expenditures**. Current expenditures include items such as wages and salaries of public-sector staff, administration and the payments of welfare benefits. Capital expenditures give rise to a stream of benefits *over time*. Examples include expenditure on roads, hospitals and schools.

Figure 30.1 shows the scale and composition of public-sector expenditures in the UK since the 1960s. The figures are presented as shares of GDP. Over the period, total spending has averaged 40 per cent of GDP, current spending 34 per cent of GDP and capital spending just 6 per cent of GDP. However, a closer inspection of the chart shows that capital spending by the UK Government decreased consistently as a proportion of GDP from the late 1960s through to 2000. It then rose during the 2000s but has since declined again (but not as fast as current expenditure).

> ### Pause for thought
>
> *What could have driven the changes in the composition of UK public expenditure? Do such changes matter?*

Final expenditure and transfers. We can also distinguish between **final expenditure** on goods and services and **transfers**. This distinction recognises that the public sector directly adds to the economy's aggregate demand (an injection into the circular flow of income: see page 512–13) through its spending on goods and services, including the wages of public-sector workers, but also that it redistributes incomes between individuals and firms. Transfers include

> ### Definitions
>
> **Current expenditure** Recurrent spending on goods and factor payments.
>
> **Capital expenditure** Investment expenditure; expenditure on assets.
>
> **Final expenditure** Expenditure on goods and services. This is included in GDP and is part of aggregate demand.
>
> **Transfers** Transfers of money from taxpayers to recipients of benefits and subsidies. They are not an injection into the circular flow but are the equivalent of a negative tax (i.e. a negative withdrawal).

Figure 30.1   UK public-sector current and capital expenditures

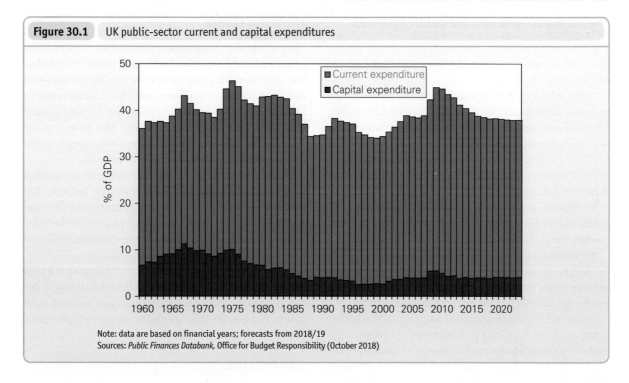

Note: data are based on financial years; forecasts from 2018/19
Sources: *Public Finances Databank,* Office for Budget Responsibility (October 2018)

---

subsidies and benefit payments, such as payments to the unemployed. These are not injections into the circular flow but count, instead, as negative taxes as they increase households' disposable income

Public-sector deficits.   If the public sector spends more than it earns, it will have to finance the deficit through borrowing: known as ***public-sector net borrowing (PSNB)***. The principal form of borrowing is through the sale of gilts (bonds). The precise amount of money the public sector requires to borrow in any one year is known as the ***public-sector net cash requirement (PSNCR)***. It differs slightly from the PSNB because of time lags in the flows of public-sector incomes and expenditure.

KI 27
p 341
As with central and general government debt, *public-sector debt* is the current stock of the accumulated deficits over the years. In assessing the sustainability of this stock of debt, it is usual to focus on ***public-sector net debt***. This is the sector's gross debt less its liquid assets, which comprise official reserves and deposits held with financial institutions.

Sustainability of public finances

KI 27
p 341
The sustainability of the public finances can be assessed by considering the ability of the public sector to maintain or reduce its debt-to-GDP ratio. Should the ratio continue rising, the public sector faces increasing financial pressure to meet its current debt obligations and divert more resources to these and away from other spending options.

Crucial to whether the public-sector debt-to-GDP ratio rises or falls are the current value of the ratio, the expected rate of interest on outstanding debts, the expected rate of economic growth and, finally, the public sector's ***primary surplus (or deficit)***. A primary surplus (deficit) occurs when public-sector receipts are greater (less) than public-sector expenditures *excluding* interest payments.

In fact, for the public sector to be able to run a primary deficit without the debt-to-GDP ratio rising, the rate of economic growth must be greater than the rate of interest. Therefore, the sustainability constraints on spending and/or the need to raise revenue from taxation are greater the higher the debt-to-GDP ratio and the lower the rate of economic growth.

Definitions

Public-sector net borrowing (PSNB) The difference between the expenditures of the public sector and its receipts from taxation, the revenues of public corporations and the sale of assets. If expenditures exceed receipts (a deficit), then the government has to borrow to make up the difference.

Public-sector net cash requirement (PSNCR) The (annual) deficit of the public sector (central government, local government and local corporations), and thus the amount that the public sector must borrow.

Public-sector net debt Gross public-sector debt minus liquid financial assets.

Primary surplus or **deficit** When public-sector receipts are greater (less) than public-sector expenditures *excluding* interest payments.

The business cycle and the public finances

The size of the deficit or surplus is not entirely due to deliberate government policy. It is influenced by the state of the economy.

If the economy is booming with people earning high incomes, the amount paid in taxes will be high. Also, in a booming economy, the level of unemployment will be low. Thus the amount paid out in unemployment benefits will be low. The combined effect of increased tax revenues and reduced benefits is to reduce the public-sector deficit (or increase the surplus).

By contrast, if the economy is depressed, tax revenues will be low and the amount paid in benefits will be high. This will increase the public-sector deficit (or reduce the surplus).

By 'cyclically adjusting' measures of public-sector deficits or surpluses we remove their cyclical component. In other words, we show just the direct effects of government policy, not the effects of the level of economic activity.

Figure 30.2 shows both actual and cyclically adjusted public-sector net borrowing as a percentage of GDP since the mid-1970s. Over the long run, the economy's output gap is zero (see Box 26.1). Hence, over the period shown, both net borrowing measures average the same (around 3 per cent of GDP).

The deficit or surplus that would arise if the economy were producing at the potential level of national income (see Box 26.1 on page 508) is termed the **structural deficit** or **surplus**. Remember that the potential level of national income is where there is no excess or deficiency of aggregate demand: where there is a zero output gap.

The fiscal stance

The government's *fiscal stance* refers to whether it is pursuing an expansionary or contractionary fiscal policy. Does the fact that countries such as the UK in most years run public-sector deficits mean that their government's fiscal stance is mainly expansionary? Would the mere existence of a surplus mean that the stance was contractionary? The answer is no. Whether the economy expands or contracts depends on the balance of *total* injections and *total* withdrawals.

What we need to focus on is *changes* in the size of the deficit or surplus. If the deficit this year is lower than last year, then (other things being equal) aggregate demand will be lower this year than last. The reason is that government expenditure (an injection) must have fallen, tax revenues (a withdrawal) must have increased or a combination of the two.

To conclude, the size of the deficit or surplus is a poor guide to the stance of fiscal policy. A large deficit *may* be due to a deliberate policy of increasing aggregate demand, but it may be due simply to the fact that the economy is depressed.

Definitions

Structural deficit or **surplus** The public-sector deficit (or surplus) that would occur if the economy were operating at the potential level of national income: i.e. one where there is a zero output gap.

Fiscal stance How expansionary or contractionary the Budget is.

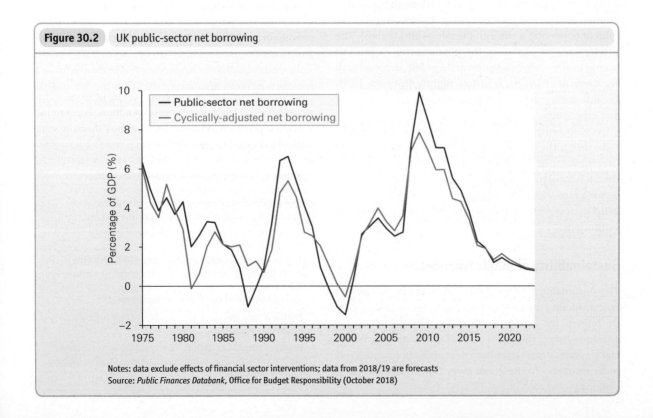

Figure 30.2 UK public-sector net borrowing

Notes: data exclude effects of financial sector interventions; data from 2018/19 are forecasts
Source: *Public Finances Databank*, Office for Budget Responsibility (October 2018)

30.2 THE USE OF FISCAL POLICY

In this section, we begin by considering how expenditure and taxation flows automatically change across the business cycle and, in so doing, help to stabilise the economy. We then move on to discuss why governments might make deliberate changes to taxation and government expenditures and how effective they may be in managing the economy.

Fiscal stabilisers and discretion

Automatic stabilisers

To some extent, government expenditure and taxation will have the effect of *automatically* stabilising the economy. For example, as national income rises, the amount of tax people pay automatically rises. This rise in withdrawals from the circular flow of income will help to damp down the rise in national income. This effect will be bigger if taxes are *progressive* (i.e. rise by a bigger percentage than national income). Some government transfers will have a similar effect. For example, the total paid in unemployment benefits will fall, if rises in national income cause a fall in unemployment. This again will have the effect of dampening the rise in national income.

Taxes whose revenues rise as national income rises and benefits that fall as national income rises are called *automatic stabilisers*.

Discretionary policy

Automatic stabilisers cannot *prevent* fluctuations; they merely reduce their magnitude. If there is a fundamental disequilibrium in the economy or substantial fluctuations in national income, these automatic stabilisers will not be enough. The government may thus choose to *alter* the level of government expenditure or the rates of taxation. This is known as *discretionary fiscal policy*.

Box 30.1 (and Case Studies K1, K2 and K14 on the student website) discusses the fiscal measures taken by the UK Government following the financial crisis. These measures initially focused on stimulating aggregate demand. Then, as the policy focus shifted to reducing the burgeoning public-sector deficit, fiscal policy was tightened.

If government expenditure on goods and services (roads, health care, education, etc.) is raised, this will create a full multiplied rise in national income. The reason is that all the money gets spent and thus all of it goes to boosting aggregate demand.

Cutting taxes (or increasing benefits), however, will have a smaller effect on national income than raising government expenditure on goods and services by the same amount. The reason is that cutting taxes increases people's *disposable* incomes, of which only part will be spent. Part will be withdrawn into extra saving, imports and other taxes. In other words, not all the tax cuts will be passed on round

the circular flow of income as extra expenditure. Thus, if one-fifth of a cut in taxes is withdrawn and only four-fifths is spent, the tax multiplier will be only four-fifths as big as the government expenditure multiplier.

> ### Pause for thought
>
> *Why will the multiplier effect of government transfer payments, such as child benefit, pensions and social security benefits, be less than the full multiplier effect from government expenditure on goods and services?*

The effectiveness of fiscal policy

How successful will fiscal policy be? Will it be able to 'fine-tune' aggregate demand? Will it be able to achieve the level of GDP that the government would like it to achieve?

There are various problems with using fiscal policy to manage the economy. These can be grouped under two broad headings: problems of magnitude and problems of timing.

Problems of magnitude

Before changing government expenditure or taxation, the government will need to calculate the effect of any such change on national income, employment and inflation. Predicting these effects, however, is often very unreliable for a number of reasons.

Predicting the effect of changes in government expenditure

A rise in government expenditure of £*x* may lead to a rise in total injections (relative to withdrawals) that is smaller than £*x*. This will occur if the rise in government expenditure *replaces* a certain amount of private expenditure. For example, a rise in expenditure on state education may dissuade some parents from sending their children to private schools. Similarly, an improvement in the National Health Service may lead to fewer people paying for private treatment.

Crowding out. Another reason for the total rise in injections being smaller than the rise in government expenditure is a

> ### Definitions
>
> **Automatic fiscal stabilisers** Tax revenues that rise and government expenditure that falls as national income rises. The more they change with income, the bigger the stabilising effect on national income.
>
> **Discretionary fiscal policy** Deliberate changes in tax rates or the level of government expenditure in order to influence the level of aggregate demand.

BOX 30.1 THE FINANCIAL CRISIS AND UK FISCAL POLICY

Fiscal rules prior to the financial crisis

On being elected in 1997, the UK's Labour government introduced two fiscal rules.

The golden rule

First, under its 'golden rule', it pledged over the cycle to achieve a **current budget balance**, where total receipts equal total current expenditures (i.e. excluding capital expenditures). This rule was designed not to unduly inhibit the automatic stabilisers from working and recognised both the current and future economic benefits of investment spending.

Sustainable investment rule

Second, under its 'sustainable investment rule', the government set itself the target of maintaining public-sector net debt at no more than 40 per cent of GDP, again averaged over the economic cycle. This rule, in conjunction with the golden rule, was designed to signal to the public the government's commitment to sustainable public finances.

The rules provided a framework within which discretionary policy choices would be made. They inevitably placed some constraints on these choices, but the economic benefits were thought to be worthwhile – until the financial crisis began to unfold.

What followed was an initial expansionary policy as attempts were made to mitigate the worst of the economic slowdown. But then, with a new government in place and with a burgeoning budget deficit, the UK turned rapidly to a policy of fiscal consolidation. Within a short space of time, the stance of fiscal policy changed markedly: a fiscal policy yo-yo.

Expansionary discretion

The impact of the financial crisis on economic growth in the UK was stark. The UK economy entered recession in the second quarter of 2008. After having expanded by an average of 2.8 per cent per year in the five-year period ending in 2007,

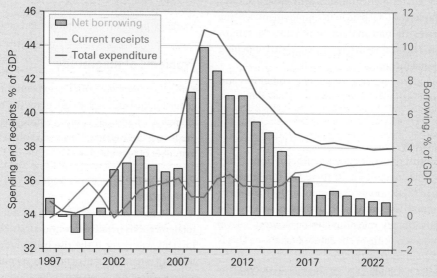

UK public-sector spending, receipts and borrowing (% of GDP)

Note: Data based on financial years; forecasts from 2018/19
Source: *Public Finances Databank,* Office for Budget Responsibility (October 2018)

phenomenon known as **crowding out**. If the government relies on **pure fiscal policy** – that is, if it does not finance an increase in the budget deficit by increasing the money supply – it will have to borrow the money from the non-bank private sector. It will thus be competing with the private sector for finance and will have to offer higher interest rates. This will force the private sector also to offer higher interest rates, which may discourage firms from investing and individuals from buying on credit. Thus government borrowing *crowds out* private borrowing. In the extreme case, the fall in

Definitions

Crowding out Where increased public expenditure diverts money or resources away from the private sector.

Pure fiscal policy Fiscal policy that does not involve any change in money supply.

Current budget balance The difference between public-sector receipts and those expenditures classified as current rather than capital expenditures.

the UK economy contracted in 2008 by 0.6 per cent and then by 4.3 per cent in 2009.

The severity of the economic downturn, the government argued, required more discretion than its fiscal policies allowed it. Consequently, its fiscal rules were lifted. The hope was that they could be reinstated in due course.

In the Pre-Budget Report of November 2008, among other measures, the Labour Government introduced a 13-month cut in VAT from 17.5 per cent to 15 per cent. It also brought forward from 2010/11 £3 billion of capital spending on projects such as motorways, new social housing, schools and energy efficiency.

The effect of the capital spending projects was to increase public-sector gross investment to 5.3 per cent and 5.5 per cent of GDP in 2008/9 and 2009/10 respectively (see Figure 30.1 on page 629). In the previous 10 years, the typical amount of public-sector gross investment spending had been just 3.1 per cent of GDP.

Meanwhile, as the chart shows, total government spending (excluding financial interventions) began to rise rapidly, fuelled by rising transfer payments on the back of the faltering economy, peaking at just over 45 per cent in 2009/10.

The UK came out of recession in the second quarter of 2009, after five consecutive quarters of declining output, which saw the economy shrink by 6.3 per cent. Meanwhile, the rate of unemployment, which had stood at 5.2 per cent at the start of 2008, peaked at 8 per cent in early 2010 and stood at 7.8 per cent in May when 13 years of Labour Government came to an end. Not only did this mark a change of government as a Conservative–Liberal coalition took charge, but it also a marked a change in the direction of fiscal policy.

Consolidation

In 2009/10, public-sector net borrowing hit 9.9 per cent of GDP, up from 2.6 per cent in 2007/8 (see the chart). Consequently, public-sector net debt grew rapidly: from £557 billion (35.5 per cent of GDP) in 2007/8 it rose to £1.0 trillion (64.8 per cent of GDP) by 2009/10.

The response of the new government was to begin a policy of consolidation. The framework for this was to be known as the 'fiscal mandate'. The initial mandate was for a balanced

current budget (after adjusting for the position in the economic cycle) five years ahead. Therefore, at the end of a rolling five-year forecast period public-sector receipts should at least equal public-sector current expenditures, after adjusting for the economy's output gap. This mandate was supplemented by a target for public-sector net debt as a percentage of GDP to be falling by 2015/16.

To achieve this, the government embarked on a series of spending cuts and tax rises. This started with a 'discretionary consolidation' of £8.9 billion in 2010/11 comprising spending cuts of £5.3 billion and tax increases worth £3.6 billion. It was announced that the consolidation would continue up to 2015/16. By the end of 2015/16, the government planned to have delivered a discretionary consolidation of £122 billion, with £99 billion coming from discretionary reductions in spending and £23 billion from tax increases. As it turned out, however, in real terms, total public-sector spending fell by just 1.5 per cent between 2010/11 and 2014/15.

The principal fiscal objectives were thus not met during the 2010–15 parliamentary period, although the government claimed that 'significant progress' had been made on its fiscal consolidation.

The new Conservative administration elected in 2015 loosened the fiscal mandate. This, ultimately, resulted in a looser set of rules, with targets (a) to reduce cyclically-adjusted public-sector net borrowing to below 2 per cent of GDP by 2020/21 and (b) for public-sector net debt as a percentage of GDP to be falling in 2020/21. The government believed that these rules struck a balance between ensuring the long-term sustainability of the public finances and providing government with sufficient discretion to provide further support for the economy, particularly given the UK's decision to leave the European Union.

Is it possible to design a fiscal framework that is sufficiently flexible to deal with all the shocks and events that economies face?

Download the Budget documents from HM Treasury from the last Budget and summarise the discretionary expenditure and taxation decisions taken by the UK Government.

consumption and investment may completely offset the rise in government expenditure, with the result that aggregate demand does not rise at all.

Predicting the effect of changes in taxes

A cut in taxes, by increasing people's real disposable income, increases not only the amount they spend, but also the amount they save. The problem is that it is not easy to predict the relative size of these two increases. In part, it will depend on whether people feel that the cut in tax is only

temporary, in which case they may simply save the extra disposable income, or permanent, in which case they may adjust their consumption upwards. More generally, it may depend on a broader set of variables, including confidence and financial well-being.

Predicting the resulting multiplied effect on national income

Even if the government *could* predict the net initial effect on injections and withdrawals, the extent to which national

BOX 30.2 THE EVOLVING FISCAL FRAMEWORKS IN THE EUROPEAN UNION

Constraining the fiscal discretion of national governments

Preparing for the euro

In signing the Maastricht Treaty in 1992, the EU countries agreed that to be eligible to join the single currency (i.e. the euro), they should have sustainable deficits and debts. This was interpreted as follows: the general government deficit should be no more than 3 per cent of GDP and general government debt should be no more than 60 per cent of GDP or should, at least, be falling towards that level at a satisfactory pace.

But, in the mid-1990s, several of the countries that were subsequently to join the euro had deficits and debts substantially above these levels (see chart). Getting them down proved a painful business. Government expenditure had to be cut and taxes increased. These fiscal measures, unfortunately, proved to be powerful! Unemployment rose and growth remained low.

The EU Stability and Growth Pact (SGP)

In June 1997, at the European Council meeting in Amsterdam, the EU countries agreed a Stability and Growth Pact (SGP).

This stated that member states should seek to balance their budgets (or even aim for a surplus) averaged over the course of the business cycle, and that deficits should not exceed 3 per cent of GDP in any one year. A country's deficit was permitted to exceed 3 per cent only if its GDP had declined by at least 2 per cent (or 0.75 per cent with special permission from the Council of Ministers). Otherwise, countries with deficits exceeding 3 per cent were required to make deposits of money with the European Central Bank. Under the Pact's Excessive Deficit Procedure, these would then become fines if the excessive budget deficit were not eliminated within two years.

There were two main aims of targeting a zero budget deficit over the business cycle. The first was to allow automatic stabilisers to work without 'bumping into' the 3 per cent deficit ceiling in years when economies were slowing. The second was to allow a reduction in government debts as a proportion of GDP (assuming that GDP grew, on average, at around 2–3 per cent per year).

From 2002, with slowing growth, Germany, France and Italy breached the 3 per cent ceiling (see chart). By 2007, however,

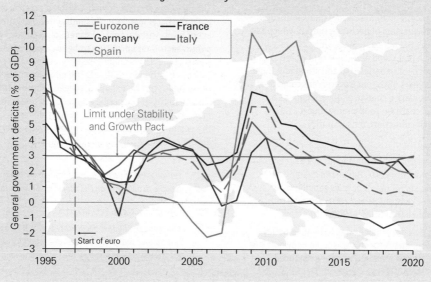

General government deficits in the Eurozone

Note: data from 2018 based on forecasts.
Source: Based on data in *AMECO Database* (European Commission, DGECFIN)

income will change is still hard to predict for the following reasons:

■ The size of the *multiplier* may be difficult to predict, since it is difficult to predict how much of any rise in income will be withdrawn. For example, the amount of a rise in income that households save or consume will depend on their expectations about future price and income changes.

■ Induced investment through the *accelerator* (see page 615–16) is also extremely difficult to predict. It may be that a relatively small fiscal stimulus will be all that is necessary to restore business confidence, and that induced investment will rise substantially. Similarly, rising confidence among financial institutions could see credit conditions relaxed with the *financial accelerator* (see page 580), resulting in rising levels of investment. In such situations, fiscal

after two years of relatively strong growth, deficits had been reduced well below the ceiling.

But then the credit crunch hit. As the EU economies slowed, so deficits rose. To combat the recession, in November 2008, the European Commission announced a €200 billion fiscal stimulus plan, mainly in the form of increased public expenditure. Of this sum, €170 billion would come from member governments and €30 billion from the EU, amounting to a total of 1.2 per cent of EU GDP. The money would be for a range of projects, such as job training, help to small businesses, developing green energy technologies and energy efficiency. Most member governments quickly followed by announcing how their specific plans would accord with the overall plan.

The combination of the recession and the fiscal measures pushed most EU countries' budget deficits well above the 3 per cent ceiling (see chart). The recession in EU countries deepened markedly in 2009, with GDP declining by 4.5 per cent in the Eurozone as a whole, and by 5.6 per cent in Germany, 5.5 per cent in Italy, 3.6 per cent in Spain and 2.9 per cent in France. Consequently, the deficits were not seen to breach SGP rules.

In some cases, countries' public finances deteriorated unsustainably. Following high-profile rescue packages to Greece, Ireland and Portugal involving the International Monetary Fund and EU, the EU established a funding mechanism for Eurozone countries in financial difficulties, known as the European Stability Mechanism[1] (ESM). The ESM can provide loans to such countries or purchase the countries' bonds in the primary market. It became operational in October 2012. As well as taking on the management of existing rescue packages, financial assistance was granted subsequently to Spain and Cyprus.

The Fiscal Compact

With many countries experiencing burgeoning deficits and some countries requiring financial assistance, the SGP was no longer seen as a credible vehicle for constraining deficits: it needed reform. The result was an intense period of

negotiation that culminated in early 2012 with a new intergovernmental treaty on limiting spending and borrowing.

The treaty, known as the Fiscal Compact, requires that, national governments not only abide by the excessive deficit procedure of the SGP but also keep structural deficits no higher than 0.5 per cent of GDP. As we have seen, structural deficits are that part of a deficit not directly related to the economic cycle and so would exist even if the economy were operating at its potential output.

In the cases of countries with a debt-to-GDP ratio significantly below 60 per cent, the structural deficit is permitted to reach 1 per cent of GDP. Finally, where the debt-to-GDP ratio exceeds 60 per cent, countries should, on average, reduce it by one-twentieth per year.

The average structural deficit across the Eurozone fell from 4.3 per cent of GDP in 2010 to 0.8 per cent in 2017. This improvement was mirrored in most individual Eurozone countries, with particularly large improvements in Greece (−9.4 to +4.6 per cent) and Ireland (−9.1 to −0.2 per cent), both of which had received financial assistance but with conditions attached that they cut spending and raise taxes. Nonetheless, most countries still had structural deficits in excess of the target levels of the Fiscal Compact.

Where a national government is found by the European Court of Justice not to comply with the Fiscal Compact, it has the power to fine that country up to 0.1 per cent of GDP, payable to the European Stability Mechanism.

What effects will an increase in government investment expenditure have on public-sector debt (a) in the short run and (b) in the long run?

From the AMECO database, download data on the actual and cyclically-adjusted budget balance, as a percentage of GDP, for general government (net lending). Then, for Germany and the UK, plot a time-series chart showing both balances across time. Finally, compose a short briefing note summarising the patterns in your chart.

---

[1] www.esm.europa.eu/.

---

policy can be seen as a 'pump primer'. It is used to *start* the process of recovery and then the *continuation* of the recovery is left to the market. But for pump priming to work, business people must *believe* that it will work. Business confidence can change very rapidly and in ways that could not have been foreseen a few months earlier.

■ Multiplier/accelerator interactions. If the initial multiplier and accelerator effects are difficult to estimate, their interaction will be virtually impossible to estimate. Small divergences in investment from what was initially predicted will become magnified as time progresses.

Random shocks

Forecasts cannot take into account the unpredictable, such as the attack on the World Trade Center in New York in September 2001. Even events that, with hindsight, should have been predicted, such as the banking crisis of 2007–9, often are not. Unfortunately, unpredictable or unpredicted events do occur and may seriously undermine the government's fiscal policy.

> **Pause for thought**
>
> *Give some other examples of 'random shocks' that could undermine the government's fiscal policy.*

Problems of timing

 Fiscal policy can involve considerable time lags. It may take time to recognise the nature of the problem before the government is willing to take action; tax or government expenditure changes take time to plan and implement – changes will have to wait until the next Budget to be announced and may come into effect some time later; the effects of such changes take time to work their way through the economy via the multiplier and accelerator.

If these time lags are long enough, fiscal policy could even be *de*stabilising. Expansionary policies taken to cure a recession may not come into effect until the economy has *already* recovered and is experiencing a boom. Under these circumstances, expansionary policies are quite inappropriate: they simply worsen the problems of overheating. Similarly, deflationary policies taken to prevent excessive expansion may not take effect until the economy has already peaked and is plunging into recession. The deflationary policies only deepen the recession.

This problem is illustrated in Figure 30.3. Path (a) shows the course of the business cycle without government intervention. Ideally, with no time lags, the economy should be dampened in stage 2 and stimulated in stage 4. This would make the resulting course of the business cycle more like path (b) or, even, if the policy were perfectly stabilising, a line that purely reflected the growth in potential output. With the presence of time lags, however, deflationary policies taken in stage 2 may not come into effect until stage 4, and reflationary policies taken in stage 4 may not come into effect until stage 2. In this case, the resulting course of the business cycle will be more like path (c). Quite obviously, in these circumstances, 'stabilising' fiscal policy actually makes the economy *less* stable.

If the fluctuations in aggregate demand can be forecast and if the lengths of the time lags are known, then all is not lost. At least the fiscal measures can be taken early and their delayed effects can be taken into account.

Fiscal rules

Given the problems of pursuing active fiscal policy, many governments today take a much more passive approach. Instead of changing the policy as the economy changes, countries apply a set of fiscal rules. These rules typically relate to measures of government deficits and to the stock of accumulated debt. Taxes and government expenditure can then be planned to meet these rules.

Following the severe disruption to the global economy that occurred with the credit crunch of 2008, countries around the world resorted to discretionary fiscal policy to boost aggregate demand. Many abandoned fiscal rules – at least temporarily. Rules were generally reinstated around the world, however, as the global economy pulled out of recession. In Boxes 30.1 and 30.2 we detail how the fiscal rules in the UK and the Eurozone, respectively, evolved following the events of the late 2000s.

In Section 30.4, we review the debate concerning constraints on a government's discretion over both its fiscal and monetary policies.

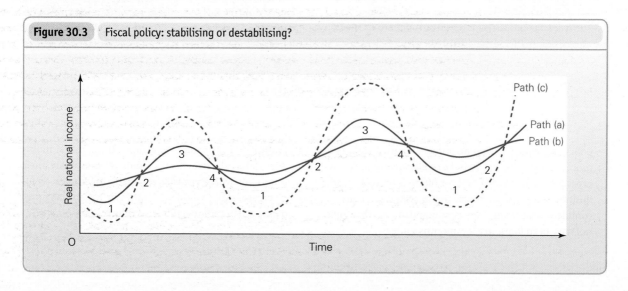

Figure 30.3   Fiscal policy: stabilising or destabilising?

30.3 MONETARY POLICY

The Bank of England's Monetary Policy Committee meets eight times per year to set Bank Rate. The event gets considerable media coverage. Pundits, for two or three days before the meeting, try to predict what the MPC will do and economists give their 'considered' opinions about what the MPC *ought* to do.

Changes in interest rates have gained a central significance in macroeconomic policy. And it is not just in the UK. Whether it is the European Central Bank setting interest rates for the Eurozone countries, the Federal Reserve Bank setting US interest rates or any other central bank around the world choosing what the level of interest rates should be, monetary policy is seen as having a major influence on a whole range of macroeconomic indicators.

But is monetary policy simply the setting of interest rates? In reality, it involves the central bank intervening in the money market to ensure that the interest rate that has been announced is also the *equilibrium* interest rate.

The policy setting

In framing its monetary policy, the government must decide on what the goals of the policy are. Is the aim simply to control inflation, does the government wish also to affect output and employment or does it want to control the exchange rate?

The government must also decide where monetary policy fits into the total package of macroeconomic policies. Is it seen as the major or even sole macroeconomic policy instrument or is it merely one of several?

A decision also has to be made about who is to carry out the policy. There are three possible approaches here.

In the first, the government both sets the policy and decides the measures necessary to achieve it. Here the government would set the interest rate, with the central bank simply influencing money markets to achieve this rate. This first approach was used in the UK before 1997.

The second approach is for the government to set the policy *targets,* but for the central bank to be given independence in deciding interest rates. This is the approach adopted in the UK today. The government has set a target rate of inflation of 2 per cent, but then the MPC is free to choose the rate of interest.

The third approach is for the central bank to be given independence not only in carrying out policy, but also in setting the policy targets itself. The ECB, within the statutory objective of maintaining price stability over the medium term, has decided on the target of keeping inflation below, but close to, 2 per cent over the medium term.

Finally, there is the question of whether the government or central bank should take a long-term or short-term perspective. Should it adopt a target for inflation or money supply growth and stick to it come what may? Or should it

adjust its policy as circumstances change and attempt to 'fine-tune' the economy?

We will be looking primarily at *short-term* monetary policy: that is, policy used to keep to a set target for inflation or money supply growth, or policy used to smooth out fluctuations in the business cycle.

It is important first, however, to take a longer-term perspective. Governments generally want to prevent an excessive growth in the money supply over the longer term. If money supply does grow rapidly, then inflation is likely to be high. Likewise, they want to ensure that money supply grows enough and that there is not a shortage of credit, such as that during the credit crunch. If money supply grows too rapidly, then inflation is likely to be high; if money supply grows too slowly, or even falls, then recession is likely to result.

Control of the money supply over the medium and long term

In section 28.3, we identified two major sources of monetary growth: (a) banks choosing to hold a lower liquidity ratio and; (b) public-sector borrowing financed by borrowing from the banking sector. If the government wishes to restrict monetary growth over the longer term, it could attempt to control either or both of these.

Liquidity of banks

The central bank could impose a statutory **minimum reserve ratio** on the banks, *above* the level that banks would otherwise choose to hold. Such ratios come in various forms. The simplest is where the banks are required to hold a given minimum percentage of deposits in the form of cash or deposits with the central bank.

The effect of a minimum reserve ratio is to prevent banks choosing to reduce their cash or liquidity ratio and creating more credit. This was a popular approach of governments in many countries in the past. Some countries imposed very high ratios indeed in their attempt to slow down the growth in the money supply.

A major problem with imposing restrictions of this kind is that banks may find ways of getting round them. After all, banks would like to lend and customers would like to borrow. It is very difficult to regulate and police every single part of countries' complex financial systems.

Definition

Minimum reserve ratio A minimum ratio of cash (or other specified liquid assets) to deposits (either total or selected) that the central bank requires banks to hold.

Nevertheless, attitudes changed substantially after the excessive lending of the mid-2000s. The expansion of credit had been based on 'liquidity' achieved through secondary marketing between financial institutions and the growth of securitised assets containing sub-prime debt (see Box 28.3). After the credit crunch and the need for central banks or governments to rescue ailing banks, such as Northern Rock and later the Royal Bank of Scotland in the UK and many other banks around the world, there were calls for greater regulation of banks to ensure that they had sufficient capital and operated with sufficient liquidity and that they were not exposed to excessive risk of default.

Public-sector deficits

Section 28.3 showed how government borrowing tends to lead to an increase in money supply. To prevent this, public-sector deficits must be financed by selling *bonds* (as opposed to bills, which could well be taken up by the banking sector, thereby increasing money supply). However, to sell extra bonds, the government will have to offer higher interest rates. This will have a knock-on effect on private-sector interest rates. The government borrowing will thus crowd out private-sector borrowing and investment. This is known as ***financial crowding out***.

If governments wish to reduce monetary growth and yet avoid financial crowding out, they must therefore reduce the size of public-sector deficits.

It is partly for this reason that many governments have constrained fiscal policy choices by applying fiscal rules or agreements, such as the 'fiscal mandate' in the UK (see Box 30.1) or the Fiscal Compact in the Eurozone (see Box 30.2).

Short-term monetary measures

Assume that inflation is above its target rate and that the central bank wishes to operate a tighter monetary policy in order to reduce aggregate demand and so the rate of inflation, what can it do?

When analysing spending decisions, it is typically *real* interest rates (r) that are important. Consumers and producers are interested in the additional future volumes of consumption and production respectively that their investment, borrowing or saving today will enable them to enjoy.

The *realised* ('*ex post*') real rate of interest (r) received on savings or paid on borrowing is the nominal (actual) interest rate (i) *less* the rate of inflation (π). However, for savers and borrowers it is the future rate of inflation that is relevant in their decision making. Of course, future inflation rates cannot be known with certainty and, instead, people must form *expectations* of inflation. Hence, the real interest rate when the decision is made ('*ex ante*') is the nominal interest rate (i) *less* the *expected* rate of inflation (π^e).

We will assume for ease of argument that, in the short term, the central bank is able to take the expected rate of inflation (π^e) as given. Consequently, any change in the nominal rate of interest (i) will be matched by an equivalent change in the real rate of interest (r).

For any given supply of money (M_s) there will be a particular equilibrium real rate of interest at any one time: where the supply of money (M_s) equals the demand for money (M_d). This is shown as r_1 in Figure 30.4.

Thus to operate a tighter monetary policy, the authorities can do one of the following:

- Reduce money supply and accept whatever equilibrium interest rate results. Thus if money supply is reduced to Q_2 in Figure 30.4, a new higher rate of interest, r_2, will result.
- Raise interest rates to r_2 and then manipulate the money supply to reduce it to Q_2. The more endogenous the money supply is, the more this will occur automatically through banks adjusting credit to match the lower demand at the higher rate of interest and the less the central bank will have to take deliberate action to reduce liquidity.
- Keep interest rates low (at r_1), but also reduce money supply to a level of Q_2. The trouble here is that the authorities cannot both control the money supply *and* keep interest rates down without running into the problem of disequilibrium. Since the demand for money now exceeds the supply by $Q_1 - Q_2$, some form of credit rationing would have to be applied.

Credit rationing was widely used in the past, especially during the 1960s. The aim was to keep interest rates low so as

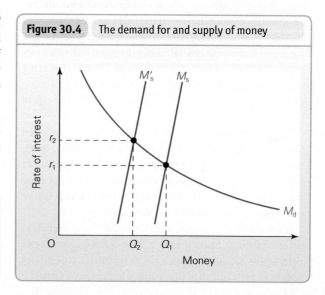

Figure 30.4   The demand for and supply of money

Definition

Financial crowding out Where an increase in government borrowing diverts money away from the private sector.

not to discourage investment, but to restrict credit to more risky business customers and/or to consumers. In the UK, the Bank of England could order banks to abide by such a policy, although, in practice, it always relied on persuasion. The government also, from time to time, imposed restrictions on hire-purchase credit, by specifying minimum deposits or maximum repayment periods.

Such policies were progressively abandoned around the world from the early 1980s. They were seen as stifling competition and preventing efficient banks from expanding. Hire-purchase controls may badly hit certain industries (e.g. cars and other consumer durables), whose products are bought largely on hire-purchase credit. What is more, with the deregulation and globalisation of financial markets up to 2007, it had become very difficult to ration credit. If one financial institution was controlled, borrowers could simply go elsewhere.

With the excessive lending in sub-prime markets that had triggered the credit crunch of 2007–9, there were calls around the world for tighter controls over bank lending. But this was different from credit rationing as we have defined it. In other words, tighter controls, such as applying counter-cyclical buffers of capital to all banks, would be used to prevent reckless behaviour by banks, rather than to achieve a particular level of money at a lower rate of interest.

We thus focus on techniques to alter the money supply and to change interest rates.

Techniques to control the money supply

There are four possible techniques that a central bank could use to alter money supply. They have one major feature in common: they involve manipulating the liquid assets of the banking system. The aim is to influence the total money supply by affecting the amount of credit that banks can create.

Open-market operations. **Open-market operations** are the most widely used of the four techniques around the world. They alter the monetary base. This then affects the amount

of credit banks can create and hence the level of broad money (M4 in the UK; M3 in the Eurozone).

Open-market operations involve the sale or purchase by the central bank of government securities (bonds or bills) in the open market. These sales (or purchases) are *not* in response to changes in the public-sector deficit and are thus best understood in the context of an unchanged deficit.

If the central bank wishes to *reduce* the money supply, it takes money from the banking system in return for securities. It can do this by borrowing from financial institutions against government securities (reverse repos on banks' balance sheets) or by selling securities outright. The borrowing or sale of these securities reduces banks' balances with the central bank. If this brings bank reserves below their prudent ratio, banks will reduce advances. There will be a multiple contraction of credit and hence of (broad) money supply. (Details of how open-market operations work in the UK are given in Box 30.3.)

Central bank lending to the banks. The central bank in most countries is prepared to provide extra money to banks (through gilt repos, rediscounting bills or straight loans). In some countries, it is the policy of the central bank to keep its interest rate to banks *below* market rates, thereby encouraging banks to borrow (or sell back securities) whenever such facilities are available. By cutting back the amount it is willing to provide, the central bank can reduce banks' liquid assets and hence the amount of credit they can create.

In other countries, such as the UK and the Eurozone countries, it is not so much the amount of money made available that is controlled, but rather the rate of interest (or discount). The higher this rate is relative to other market rates, the less willing to borrow will banks be, and the lower, therefore, will be the monetary base. Raising this rate, therefore, has the effect of reducing the money supply.

In response to the credit crunch of the late 2000s, central banks in several countries extended their willingness to lend to banks. The pressure on central banks to act as the 'liquidity backstop' grew as the inter-bank market ceased to function effectively in distributing reserves and, hence, liquidity between financial institutions. As a result, inter-bank rates rose sharply relative to the policy rate. Increasingly, the focus of central banks was on providing the necessary liquidity to ensure the stability of the financial system. Yet, at the same time, by providing more liquidity, central banks were ensuring monetary policy was not being compromised. The additional liquidity was needed to alleviate the upward pressure on market interest rates.

Funding. Rather than focusing on controlling the monetary base (as in the case of the above two techniques), an alternative is for the authorities (the Debt Management Office in the UK) to alter the overall liquidity position of the banks. An example of this approach is a change in the

---

> ### Pause for thought
>
> *Explain how open-market operations could be used to increase the money supply.*

> ### Definition
>
> **Open-market operations** The sale (or purchase) by the authorities of government securities in the open market in order to reduce (or increase) money supply and thereby affect interest rates.

balance of *funding* government debt. To reduce money supply, the authorities issue more bonds and fewer bills. Banks' balances with the central bank will be little affected, but to the extent that banks hold fewer bills, there will be a reduction in their liquidity and hence a reduction in the amount of credit created. Funding is thus the conversion of one type of government debt (liquid) into another (illiquid).

Variable minimum reserve ratios. In some countries (such as the USA), banks are required to hold a certain proportion of their assets in liquid form. The assets that count as liquid are known as 'reserve assets'. These include assets such as balances in the central bank, bills of exchange, certificates of deposit and money market loans. The ratio of such assets to total liabilities is known as the *minimum reserve ratio*. If the central bank raises this ratio (in other words, requires the banks to hold a higher proportion of liquid assets), then banks will have to reduce the amount of credit they grant. The money supply will fall.

Difficulties in controlling money supply

Targets for the growth in broad money were an important part of UK monetary policy from 1976 to 1985. Money targets were then abandoned and have not been used since. The European Central Bank targets the growth of M3 (see Box 30.5). This, however, is only a guideline and not a strict target. If, however, a central bank did choose to target money supply as its main monetary policy, how would the policy work?

Assume that money supply is above target and that the central bank wishes to reduce it. It would probably use open-market operations: i.e. it would sell more bonds or bills. The purchasers of the bonds or bills would draw liquidity from the banks. Banks would then supposedly be forced to cut down on the credit they create. But is it as simple as this?

The problem is that banks will normally be unwilling to cut down on loans if people want to borrow – after all, borrowing by customers earns profits for the banks. Banks can always 'top up' their liquidity by borrowing from the central bank and then carry on lending. True, they will have to pay the interest rate charged by the central bank, but they can pass on any rise in the rate to their customers.

The point is that, as long as people *want* to borrow, banks and other financial institutions will normally try to find ways of meeting the demand. In other words, in the short run at least, the supply of money is to a large extent demand determined. It is for this reason that central banks prefer to control the *demand* for money by controlling interest rates.

As we shall see in Box 30.4, there are similar difficulties in *expanding* broad money supply by a desired amount. Following the credit crunch, various central banks around the world engaged in a process of quantitative easing. The process results in an increase in the monetary base (narrow money); banks' liquidity increases. But just how much this results in an increase in broad money depends on the willingness of banks to lend and customers to borrow. In the recessionary climate after 2008, confidence was low. Much of the extra liquidity remained in banks and the money multiplier fell (see Figure 28.3 on page 576). The growth of M4 in the UK fell sharply during 2009, despite quantitative easing, and remained weak throughout the first half of the 2010s (see Figure 28.4 on page 576).

Techniques to control interest rates

The approach to monetary control today in most countries is to focus directly on interest rates. Normally, an interest rate change will be announced, and then open-market operations will be conducted by the central bank to ensure that the money supply is adjusted so as to make the announced interest rate the *equilibrium* one. Thus, in Figure 30.4, the central bank might announce a rise in interest rates from r_1 to r_2 and then conduct open-market operations to ensure that the money supply is reduced from Q_1 to Q_2.

Let us assume that the central bank decides to raise interest rates. What does it do? In general, it will seek to keep banks short of liquidity. This will happen automatically on any day when tax payments by banks' customers exceed the money they receive from government expenditure. This excess is effectively withdrawn from banks and ends up in the government's account at the central bank. Even when this does not occur, the issuing of government debt will, effectively, keep the banking system short of liquidity, at least in the short term.

This 'shortage' can then be used as a way of forcing through interest rate changes. Banks will obtain the necessary liquidity from the central bank through repos (see pages 561 and 570–2) or by selling it back bills. The central bank can *choose the rate of interest to charge*: i.e. the repo rate or the bill price. This will then have a knock-on effect on other interest rates throughout the banking system (see Figure 28.10 on page 584). Box 30.3 gives more details on just how the Bank of England manipulates interest rates on a day-to-day basis.

The effectiveness of changes in interest rates

Even though central bank adjustment of the repo rate is the current preferred method of monetary control in most

---

Definitions

Funding Where the authorities alter the balance of bills and bonds for any given level of government borrowing.

Minimum reserve ratio A minimum ratio of cash (or other specified liquid assets) to deposits (either total or selected) that the central bank requires banks to hold.

BOX 30.3 THE DAILY OPERATION OF MONETARY POLICY

What goes on at Threadneedle Street?

The Bank of England (the 'Bank') does not normally attempt to control money supply directly. Instead it seeks to control interest rates. The Monetary Policy Committee (MPC) of the Bank of England meets eight times per year to decide on Bank Rate. Changes in the Bank Rate are then intended to affect the whole structure of interest rates in the economy, from interbank rates to bank deposit rates and rates on mortgages and business loans. The framework designed to make this happen is known as the monetary framework and is outlined in the Bank of England's 'Red Book'.

Normal operation of the monetary framework

The monetary framework affects the economy's interest rates principally by affecting short-term *interbank rates*. Central to the process are the reserve accounts of financial institutions at the Bank of England (see section 28.2, pages 560 and 570). From the inception of the current system in May 2006, commercial banks have agreed with the Bank of England the average amount of reserve balances they would hold between MPC meetings. So long as the actual average over the period is kept within a small range of the agreed target, the reserves are remunerated at Bank Rate.

In order for individual banks to meet their reserve targets, the Bank of England needs to provide sufficient reserves. To do so, it uses OMOs. In normal circumstances, the Bank conducts short-term OMOs every week (on a Thursday) at Bank Rate. The size of the weekly OMO is adjusted to help banks maintain reserves at the target level and to reflect variations in the amount of cash withdrawn or deposited in banks.

To supply reserves, the Bank of England will either enter into short-term repo operations, lending against collateral ('high-quality' government securities), or buy securities outright. Although there is usually a shortage of liquidity in the banking system, in some weeks there may be a surplus. This ordinarily would drive market interest rates down. In such circumstances the Bank may look to reduce banks' reserves. To do this, it can sell government securities on a repo basis, invite bids for Bank of England 1-week sterling bills or sell outright some of its portfolio of securities.

At the end of the period between MPC interest rate decisions, the Bank of England conducts a 'fine-tuning' OMO. This is conducted on a Wednesday – the day before the MPC decision on interest rates. The idea is to ensure that banks meet their reserve targets as closely as possible. This OMO could expand or contract liquidity as appropriate.

Longer-term OMOs

Longer-term finance is available through longer-term open-market operations. Prior to the financial crisis of the late 2000s, longer-term OMOs normally would be conducted once per month. As well as the outright purchase of gilts, the Bank would conduct repo lending with 3-, 6-, 9- or 12-month maturities.

The rate of interest on the repos is market determined. Banks bid for the money and the funds are offered to the successful bidders. The bigger the demand for these funds by banks and the lower the supply by the Bank of England, the higher will be the interest rate that banks must pay. By adjusting the supply, therefore, the Bank of England can look to influence longer-term interest rates too.

With the aggregate amount of banks' reserves determined by the Bank of England's OMOs, the task now is for individual banks to meet their agreed reserve targets. This requires that they manage their balance sheets and, in particular, their level of liquidity. In doing so, commercial banks can make use either of the interbank market or the 'standing facilities' at the Bank of England. These standing facilities allow individual banks to borrow overnight (secured against high-quality collateral) at a rate above Bank Rate if they are short of liquidity or to deposit reserves with the Bank at a rate below Bank Rate if they have surplus liquidity. Consequently, banks will trade reserves with each other if interbank rates fall within the 'corridor' created by the interest rates of the standing facilities.

The financial crisis and open-market operations

The financial crisis meant that normal OMOs were no longer sufficient to maintain liquidity for purposes of monetary policy. There was a severe liquidity crisis – one that posed grave risks for financial stability.

In response, from January 2009, the Bank of England deliberately injected narrow money in a process known as 'quantitative easing' (see Box 30.4). This involved the Bank purchasing assets, largely gilts, from banks. It argued that its asset purchase programme was an important monetary policy tool in meeting its inflation rate target.

Between January 2009 and July 2012, the Bank of England injected £375 billion through the purchase of gilts. In August 2016, following the UK's vote to leave the European Union and concerns about deteriorating prospects for growth, the Bank of England decided to increase its gilt purchases by a further £60 billion and, in addition, to purchase up to £10 billion of UK corporate bonds.

As a result of this significant increase in aggregate reserves, banks were no longer required to set reserve targets. The supply of reserves was now being determined by MPC policy decisions. All reserves were to be remunerated at the Bank Rate.

Furthermore, short-term OMOs were temporarily suspended. Long-term repo operations continued but these were modified to allow financial institutions to sell a wider range of securities.

The Bank also adapted its means of providing liquidity insurance (see section 28.2, page 571). This included the introduction of the Discount Window Facility (DWF), which enables banks to borrow government bonds (gilts) against a wide range of collateral. Banks can then sell these bonds through repo operations and thereby secure liquidity.

Assume that the Bank of England wants to raise interest rates. Trace through the process by which it achieves this.

From the Bank of England Statistical Interactive database, download series IUMABEDR, the official Bank Rate. Construct a line chart of the Bank Rate from May 2006, when the current monetary framework in the UK began.

countries, it is not without its difficulties. The problems centre on the nature of the demand for loans. If this demand is (a) unresponsive to interest rate changes or (b) unstable because it is significantly affected by other determinants (such as anticipated income or foreign interest rates), then it will be very difficult to control by controlling the rate of interest.

 Problem of an inelastic demand for loans. If the demand for loans is inelastic (i.e. a relatively steep M_d curve in Figure 30.4), any attempt to reduce demand will involve large rises in interest rates. The problem will be compounded if the demand curve shifts to the right, due, say, to a consumer spending boom. High interest rates lead to the following problems:

■ They may discourage business investment and thereby reduce long-term growth.

■ They add to the costs of production, to the costs of house purchase and generally to the cost of living. They are thus cost inflationary.

■ They are politically unpopular, since people do not like paying higher interest rates on overdrafts, credit cards and mortgages.

■ The authorities may need to ensure a sufficient supply of longer-term securities so that liquidity can be constrained. This could commit the government to paying high rates on these bonds for some time.

■ High interest rates encourage inflows of money from abroad. This drives up the exchange rate. A higher exchange rate makes domestically produced goods expensive relative to goods made abroad. This can be very damaging for export industries and industries competing with imports. Many firms in the UK suffered badly between 1997 and 2007 from a high exchange rate, caused partly by higher interest rates in the UK than in the Eurozone and the USA.

Evidence suggests that the demand for loans may indeed be quite inelastic. Especially in the short run, many firms and individuals simply cannot reduce their borrowing commitments. What is more, although high interest rates may discourage many firms from taking out long-term fixed-interest loans, some firms may merely switch to shorter-term variable-interest loans.

 Problem of an unstable demand. Accurate monetary control requires the central bank to be able to predict the demand curve for money (in Figure 30.4). Only then can they set the appropriate level of interest rates. Unfortunately, the demand curve may shift unpredictably, making control very difficult. The major reason is *speculation*. For example, if people think interest rates will rise and bond prices fall, in the meantime, they will demand to hold their assets in liquid form. The demand for money will rise. Alternatively, if people think exchange rates will rise, they will demand the domestic currency while it is still relatively cheap. The demand for money will rise.

It is very difficult for the central bank to predict what people's expectations will be. Speculation depends so much on world political events, rumour and 'random shocks'.

If the demand curve shifts very much and, if it is inelastic, then monetary control will be very difficult. Furthermore, the central bank will have to make frequent and sizeable adjustments to interest rates. These fluctuations can be very damaging to business confidence and may discourage long-term investment.

> ### Pause for thought
>
> *Assume that the central bank announces a rise in interest rates and backs this up with open-market operations. What determines the size of the resulting fall in aggregate demand?*

The net result of an inelastic and unstable demand for money is that substantial interest rate changes may be necessary to bring about the required change in aggregate demand. For example, central banks had to cut interest rates to virtually zero in their attempt to tackle the global recession of the late 2000s. Indeed, as we see in Box 30.4, central banks took to other methods as the room for further interest rate cuts simply disappeared.

Using monetary policy

It is impossible to use monetary policy as a precise means of controlling aggregate demand. It is especially weak when it is pulling against the expectations of firms and consumers and when it is implemented too late. However, if the authorities operate a tight monetary policy firmly enough and long enough, they should eventually be able to reduce lending and aggregate demand. But there will, inevitably, be time lags and imprecision in the process.

An expansionary monetary policy is even less reliable. If the economy is in recession, no matter how low interest rates are driven, or however much the monetary base is expanded, people cannot be forced to borrow if they do not wish to. Firms will not borrow to invest if they predict a continuing recession.

A particular difficulty in using interest rate reductions to expand the economy arises if the repo rate is nearly zero, but this is still not enough to stimulate the economy. The problem is that (nominal) interest rates cannot be negative, for clearly nobody would be willing to lend in these circumstances. Japan was in such a situation in the early 2000s. It was caught in what is known as the *liquidity trap*. The UK and many Eurozone countries were in this position in the early 2010s. Despite record low interest rates and high levels of liquidity, borrowing and lending remained low, given worries about fiscal austerity and its dampening effects on economic growth.

Forward guidance. One way in which central banks, like the Federal Reserve, the Bank of England and the ECB, attempted to encourage spending following the financial crisis of the late 2000s was by publicly indicating the expected path of future interest rates. By stating that interest rates were likely to remain low for some time, central banks hoped that this *forward guidance* would give economic agents confidence to bring forward their spending.

Despite these problems, changing interest rates can often be quite effective in the medium term. After all, they can be changed very rapidly. There are not the time lags of implementation that there are with fiscal policy. Indeed, since the

early 1990s, most governments or central banks in OECD countries have used interest rate changes as the major means of keeping aggregate demand and inflation under control.

In the UK, the Eurozone and many other countries, a target is set for the rate of inflation. As we have seen, in the UK and the Eurozone the target is 2 per cent. If forecasts suggest that inflation is going to be above the target rate, the government or central bank raises interest rates. The advantage of this is that it sends a very clear messagew to people that inflation *will* be kept under control. People will, therefore, be more likely to adjust their expectations accordingly and keep their borrowing in check.

30.4 ATTITUDES TOWARDS DEMAND MANAGEMENT

Debates over the control of demand have shifted ground somewhat in recent years. There is now less debate over the relative effectiveness of fiscal and monetary policy in influencing aggregate demand. There is general agreement that a *combination* of fiscal and monetary policies will have a more powerful effect than either used separately.

Economists have become increasingly interested in the environment within which policy is made. In this section, we analyse debates around the extent to which governments ought to pursue active demand management policies or adhere to a set of policy rules.

 Those in the Keynesian tradition prefer discretionary policy – changing policy as circumstances change. Those in the monetarist and new classical tradition prefer to set firm rules (e.g. targets for inflation, public deficits or growth in the money supply) and then stick to them.

The case for rules and policy frameworks

Why should governments commit to rules or design policy frameworks that may involve their giving up control of economic instruments? There are two important arguments against discretionary policy.

Political behaviour. The first concerns the motivation of government. Politicians may attempt to manipulate the economy for their own political purposes – such as the desire to be re-elected. The government, if not constrained by rules, may overstimulate the economy some time before an election so that growth is strong at election time. After the election, the government strongly dampens the economy to deal with the higher inflation and rising public-sector debt, and to create enough slack for another boost in time for the next election.

If the effect of manipulating economic policy is to generate cycles in output, unemployment and inflation that mirror the political cycle, then the result is a *political business cycle*.

The theory of the political business cycle suggests that the discretionary policy choices of government can purposefully destabilise the economy. Therefore, it is argued, governments should be made to adopt policy rules.

The manipulation of policy instruments may not be necessarily as systematic or regular in the way that the political business cycle model implies. Nonetheless, the manipulation is intended to court short-term favour with the public and may store up problems for the economy and, in the case of fiscal policy, for the public finances.

It is argued that, when politicians behave in this way, fiscal policy may exhibit a *deficit bias*. Because governments are more willing to use their discretion to loosen fiscal policy than they are to tighten fiscal policy, persistent deficits and a rising debt-to-GDP ratio can result. Table 30.1 provides some support for this. Therefore, fiscal rules may be needed to ensure the long-term sustainability of public finances.

It is also argued that politically-motivated policymakers can lose *credibility* for sound economic management. This can lead to higher inflationary expectations, uncertainty and lower long-term investment. Trade unions are likely to bargain for increases in wages that protect their purchasing power should government loosen its policy stance to try to

> ### Definitions
>
> **Liquidity trap** When interest rates are at their floor and thus any further increases in money supply will not be spent but merely be held in idle balances as people wait for the economy to recover and/or interest rates to rise.
>
> **Political business cycle** The theory that governments will engineer an economic contraction, designed to squeeze out inflation, followed by a pre-election boom.
>
> **Deficit bias** The tendency for frequent fiscal deficits and rising debt-to-GDP ratios because of the reluctance of policymakers to tighten fiscal.

BOX 30.4   QUANTITATIVE EASING

Rethinking monetary policy in hard times

As the economies of the world slid into recession in 2008, central banks became more and more worried that the traditional instrument of monetary policy – controlling interest rates – was insufficient to ward off a slump in demand.

Running out of options?

Interest rates had been cut at an unprecedented rate and central banks were reaching the end of the road for further cuts. The Fed was the first to be in this position. By December 2008, the target federal funds rate (the overnight rate at which the Fed lends to banks) had been cut to a range between 0 and 0.25 per cent. Meanwhile, in the UK, Bank Rate had fallen to 0.5 per cent by March 2009. But you cannot, in most cases, cut nominal borrowing rates below zero – otherwise you would be paying people to borrow money, which would be like giving people free money!

The problem was that there was an acute lack of willingness of banks to lend and firms and consumers to borrow, as people saw the oncoming recession. Hence the cuts in interest rates were not having enough effect on aggregate demand.

Increasing the money supply

So what were central banks to do? The answer was to increase money supply directly, in a process known as *quantitative easing (QE)*. This involves an aggressive version of open-market operations, where the central bank buys up a range of assets, such as securitised mortgage debt and long-term government bonds. The effect is to pump large amounts of additional cash into the economy in the hope of stimulating demand and, through the process of credit creation, to boost broad money too.

QE in the USA

In the USA, in December 2008, at the same time as the federal funds rate was cut to a range of 0 to 0.25 per cent, the Fed embarked on large-scale quantitative easing. It began buying hundreds of billions of dollars' worth of mortgage-backed securities on the open market and planned also to buy large quantities of long-term government debt.

The Federal Open Market Committee (the interest rate setting body in the USA) said that, 'The focus of the committee's policy going forward will be to support the functioning of financial markets and stimulate the economy through open-market operations and other measures that sustain the size of the Federal Reserve's balance sheet at a high level.' The result was that considerable quantities of new money were injected into the system. At the conclusion of three rounds of QE in October 2014, the Fed had purchased assets of $2.5 trillion.

QE in the UK

A similar approach was adopted in the UK. In January 2009, the Bank of England was given powers by the Treasury to buy up to £50 billion of high-quality private-sector assets, such as corporate bonds and commercial paper. The purchases from non-bank financial institutions were with newly created electronic money. But this was only the start.

In March 2009, as the recession deepened, the Chancellor agreed to increase the scale of purchases, so beginning the second and much more significant phase of quantitative easing. These purchases, mainly government bonds (gilts), resulted in a substantial increase in banks' reserves at the Bank of England and hence in the Bank's balance sheet. By July 2012, asset purchases had been made totalling £375 billion.

In August 2016, with concerns about the prospects for the UK economy following the vote to leave the European Union, the Bank of England increased its gilt purchases by a further £60 billion to £435 billion. Additionally, it agreed to purchase up to £10 billion of UK corporate bonds.

---

boost its popularity. The result could be an *inflation bias,* with inflation typically higher than it would otherwise be, but with unemployment no lower.

As we saw in section 29.4, the possibility of inflation bias (see page 610) is one of the principal arguments behind the move in many countries for the delegation of monetary policy to central banks.

KI 35
p 376
Time lags with discretionary policy.   Both fiscal and monetary policies can involve long and variable time lags, which can make the policy at best ineffective and at worst destabilising. Taking the measures before the problem arises, and thus lessening the problem of lags, is no answer since forecasting tends to be unreliable.

In contrast, by setting and sticking to rules, and then not interfering further, the government can provide a sound monetary framework in which there is maximum freedom for individual initiative and enterprise, and in which firms are not cushioned from market forces and are therefore

Definition

Quantitative easing When the central bank increases the monetary base through an open market purchase of government bonds or other securities. It uses electronic money (reserve liabilities) created specifically for this purpose.

QE in the Eurozone

The ECB was more reticent about adopting quantitative easing. But, with the risk of deflation (falling prices) becoming established, it announced in September 2014 that a programme of quantitative easing would begin in March 2015. This would entail purchases of marketable debt instruments, including public-sector bonds and asset-backed private sector securities, such as securitised mortgages and commercial loans (see section 28.2).

It began at a rate of €60 billion of asset purchases per month. Initially, the scheme was to run to September 2016 with total purchases of up to €1.08 trillion. However, with the inflation rate now only around zero, the scheme was extended into 2017, with purchases rising in March 2016 to €80 billion (and including corporate bonds for the first time). With economic growth picking up, purchases fell back to €60 billion per month from April 2017 and then to €30 billion from January 2018 until the end of September 2018. In the final three months of 2018 purchases were to fall to €15 billion per month, taking the ECB's total asset purchases to over €2.5 trillion.

Transmission mechanisms

Quantitative easing involves directly increasing the amount of narrow money.[1] It can also, indirectly, increase broad money. There are two principal ways in which this can happen.

The first is through the effects on asset prices and yields. When non-bank financial companies, including insurance companies and pension funds, sell assets to the central bank, they can use the money to purchase other assets, such as shares. In doing so, this will drive up their prices. This, in turn, reduces the yields on these assets (at a higher price there is less dividend or interest per pound spent on them), which should help to reduce interest rates generally and make the cost of borrowing cheaper for households and firms, so boosting aggregate demand.

[1] www.bankofengland.co.uk/monetary-policy/quantitative-easing.

Also, for those holding these now more expensive assets, there is a positive wealth effect. For instance, households with longer-term saving plans involving securities will now have greater financial wealth. Again, this will boost spending.

The second mechanism is through bank lending. Commercial banks will find their reserve balances increase at the central bank as the sellers of assets to the central bank deposit the money in their bank accounts. This will increase the liquidity ratio of banks, which could encourage them to grant more credit.

However, it is all very well increasing the monetary base, but a central bank cannot force banks to lend or people to borrow. That requires confidence. As Figure 28.6 (page 579) shows, bank lending to the non-bank private sector was weak for some time in the early 2010s and significantly below pre-financial crisis levels.

This is not to say that quantitative easing failed in the UK and elsewhere: growth in broad money could have been weaker still. However, it does illustrate the potential danger of this approach if, in the short run, little credit creation takes place. In the equation $MV = PY$, the rise in (narrow) money supply (M) may be largely offset by a fall in the velocity of circulation (V) (see pages 586–7).

On the other hand, there is also the danger that, if this policy is conducted for too long, the growth in broad money supply could, ultimately, prove to be excessive, resulting in inflation rising above the target level. It is therefore important for central banks to foresee this and turn the monetary 'tap' off in time. This would involve 'quantitative tightening' – *selling* assets that the central bank had purchased, thereby driving down asset prices and driving up interest rates.

 Would it be appropriate to define the policy of quantitative easing as 'monetarist'?

 Undertake desktop research, including visiting the websites of major central banks such as the Bank of England, the ECB and the Federal Reserve. Search for materials explaining the process of the quantitative easing (QE), mechanisms by which it is expected to impact on inflation and economic activity and any assessment of its effects where QE has been employed. Briefly summarise your findings.

 encouraged to be efficient. By the government setting a target for a steady reduction in the growth of money supply, or a target for the rate of inflation, and then resolutely sticking to it, people's expectations of inflation will be reduced, thereby making the target easier to achieve.

 This sound and stable monetary environment, with no likelihood of sudden contractionary or expansionary fiscal or monetary policy, will encourage firms to take a longer-term perspective and to plan ahead. This could then lead to increased capital investment and raise long-term growth rates.

The optimum situation is for all the major countries to adhere to mutually consistent rules, so that their economies do not get out of line. This will create more stable exchange rates and provide the climate for world growth.

Advocates of this point of view in the 1970s and 1980s were the monetarists and new classical macroeconomists, but, in recent years, support for the setting of targets has become widespread. As we have seen, in both the UK and the Eurozone countries, targets are set for both inflation and public-sector deficits.

The case for discretion

Many economists, especially those in the Keynesian tradition, reject the argument that rules provide the environment for high and stable growth. Aggregate demand, they argue, is subject to many and sometimes violent shocks:

BOX 30.5 MONETARY POLICY IN THE EUROZONE

The role of the ECB

The European Central Bank (ECB) is based in Frankfurt and is charged with operating the monetary policy of those EU countries that have adopted the euro. Although the ECB has the overall responsibility for the Eurozone's monetary policy, the central banks of the individual countries, such as the Bank of France and Germany's Bundesbank, were not abolished. They are responsible for distributing euros and for carrying out the ECB's policy with respect to institutions in their own countries. The whole system of the ECB and the national central banks is known as the European System of Central Banks (ESCB).

In operating the monetary policy of a 'euro economy' roughly the size of the USA, and in being independent from national governments, the ECB's power is enormous and is equivalent to that of the Fed. So what is the structure of this giant on the European stage and how does it operate?

The structure of the ECB

The ECB has two major decision-making bodies: the Governing Council and the Executive Board.

The Governing Council consists of the members of the Executive Board and the governors of the central banks of each of the Eurozone countries. The Council's role is to set the main targets of monetary policy and to take an oversight of the success (or otherwise) of that policy. It also sets interest rates at six-weekly meetings. Decisions are by simple majority. In the event of a tie, the president has the casting vote.

The Executive Board consists of a president, a vice-president and four other members. Each serve for an eight-year, non-renewable term. The Executive Board is responsible for implementing the decisions of the Governing Council and for preparing policies for the Council's consideration. Each member of the Executive Board has a responsibility for some particular aspect of monetary policy.

ECB independence

The ECB is one of the most independent central banks in the world. It has very little formal accountability to elected politicians. Although its President can be called before the European Parliament, the Parliament has virtually no powers to influence the ECB's actions.

Until its January 2015 meeting, its deliberations were secret and no minutes of Council meetings were published. Subsequently, an account of meetings is published (usually with a lag of around two weeks) with an explanation of the policy stance. However, the minutes do not include details of how Council members voted or of future policy intentions, unlike the minutes published by the Bank of England which, from 2015, are available at the time of the policy announcement.

The targets of monetary policy

The overall responsibility of the ECB is to achieve price stability in the Eurozone. The target is a rate of inflation below, but close to, 2 per cent over the medium term. It is a weighted average rate for all the members of the Eurozone, not a rate that has to be met by every member individually.

Alongside its definition of price stability, the ECB's monetary policy strategy comprises what it calls 'a two-pillar approach to the analysis of the risks to price stability'. These two pillars are an analysis of (a) monetary developments and (b) economic developments. The former includes an analysis of monetary aggregates, including M3. The latter includes an analysis of economic activity, the labour market, cost indicators, fiscal policy and the balance of payments.

The ECB then attempts to 'steer' short-term interest rates to influence economic activity to maintain price stability in the euro area in the medium term. In May 2018, the rates were as follows: 0.00 per cent for the main 'refinancing operations' of the ESCB (i.e. the minimum rate of interest at which liquidity is offered once per week to 'monetary financial institutions' (MFIs) by the ESCB); a 'marginal lending' rate of 0.25 per cent (for providing overnight support to the MFIs); and a 'deposit rate' of −0.40 per cent (the rate paid to MFIs for depositing overnight surplus liquidity with the ESCB). The negative deposit rate meant that banks were being charged for 'parking' money with the ECB rather than lending it. The hope was that this would encourage banks to lend to each other or to households and businesses and, consequently, stimulate the economy.

The operation of monetary policy

The ECB sets a minimum reserve ratio for Eurozone banks. The ratio is designed primarily to prevent excessive lending and hence the need for excessive borrowing from the central bank or from other financial institutions. This, in turn, should help to reduce the volatility in interest rates.

The minimum reserve ratio was not designed, however, to be used to make changes in monetary policy. In other words, it was not used as a variable minimum reserves ratio and, for this reason, it was set at a low level. From 1 January 1999 to 17 January 2012, the ratio (also known as the reserve coefficient) was 2 per cent of key liquid and relatively liquid liabilities.

---

e.g. changes in expectations, domestic political events (such as an impending election), world economic factors (such as the world economic recession of 2008–9) or world political events (such as a war). The resulting shifts in injections or withdrawals cause the economy to deviate from a stable full-employment growth path.

Any change in injections or withdrawals will lead to a cumulative effect on national income via the multiplier and accelerator and via changing expectations. These effects take time and interact with each other, and so a process of expansion or contraction can last many months before a turning point is eventually reached.

However, as of 18 January 2012, the ratio was reduced to 1 per cent in an attempt to help stimulate bank lending. In other words, it was now being used for the first time as part of an active monetary policy.

The main instrument for keeping the ECB's desired interest rate as the equilibrium rate is open-market operations in government bonds and other recognised assets, mainly in the form of repos. These repo operations are conducted by the national central banks, which must ensure that the repo rate does not rise above the marginal overnight lending rate or fall below the deposit rate.

The ECB ordinarily uses two principal types of open-market operations

Main refinancing operations (MROs)

These are short-term repos with a maturity of one week. They take place weekly and are used to maintain liquidity consistent with the chosen ECB interest rate.

Longer-term refinancing operations (LTROs)

These take place monthly and normally have a maturity of three months. Longer maturities are available, but such operations are conducted more irregularly. They are to provide additional longer-term liquidity to banks as required at rates determined by the market, not the ECB.

Financial crisis and non-standard policy measures

The financial crisis of 2007–8 put incredible strains on commercial banks in the Eurozone and, hence, on the ECB's monetary framework. Consequently, monetary operations were gradually modified.

A Securities Market Programme (SMP) began in May 2010, designed to supply liquidity to the ailing banking system. It allowed for ECB purchases of central government debt in the secondary market (i.e. not directly from governments) as well as purchases both in primary and secondary markets of private-sector debt instruments. By June 2012, €214 billion of purchases had been made, largely of government bonds issued by countries experiencing financing difficulties, including Portugal, Ireland, Greece and Spain.

The SMP was supplemented in December 2011 by the introduction of three-year refinancing operations (LTROs) worth €529.5 billion and involving some 800 banks. These were cheap loans (repos) to the banks by the ECB. These were

followed in January 2012 by a fall in the minimum reserve ratio to 1 per cent (as we saw above).

By the end of February 2012, a further €489.2 billion of three-year loans to 523 banks took place, taking the ECB's repo operations to over €1 trillion. The hope was that the funds would help financially distressed banks pay off maturing debt and again increase their lending.

In June 2014, the ECB announced that it was adopting a negative deposit rate (see above) and that it was embarking on a series of targeted long-term refinancing operations (TLTROs). The TLROs were to provide long-term loans to commercial banks at cheap rates until September 2018. The amounts that banks could borrow were linked to the outstanding loans to households and non-financial corporations (excluding loans for house purchases). The aim was to stimulate bank lending to the non-financial private sector.

It also announced that that it would stop offsetting asset purchases under the Securities Market Programme by selling securities elsewhere. This offsetting process is known as *sterilisation* and is designed to leave the overall money supply unchanged. By ending sterilisation, the ECB would allow the money supply to expand.

A second series of four-year TLTROs was announced in March 2016, to run from June 2016 to March 2017. Amounts that could be borrowed through TLTRO-II, were again tied to the size of eligible outstanding loans, while the interest rate charged would depend on the credit provided by each bank over a two-year period from February 2016.

Finally, in September 2014, the ECB announced that it would be commencing quantitative easing by purchasing marketable debt instruments, including public-sector bonds and asset-backed private-sector securities, such as securitised mortgages and commercial loans (see section 28.2). For details, see Box 30.4.

 What are the arguments for and against publishing the minutes of the meetings of the ECB's Governing Council and Executive Board?

 Undertake a literature search on what is meant by central bank independence. How is independence defined or even measured? Write a short summary of your findings.

Since shocks to demand occur at irregular intervals and are of different magnitudes, the economy is likely to experience cycles of irregular duration and of varying intensity.

 Given that the economy is inherently unstable and is buffeted around by various shocks, Keynesians argue that the government needs actively to intervene to stabilise

Definition

Sterilisation Actions taken by a central bank to offset the effects of foreign exchange flows or its own bond transactions so as to leave money supply unchanged.

the economy. Otherwise, the uncertainty caused by unpredictable fluctuations will be very damaging to investment and hence to long-term economic growth (quite apart from the short-term effects of recessions on output and employment).

If demand fluctuates in the way Keynesians claim, and if the policy of having a money supply or inflation rule is adhered to, interest rates must fluctuate. But excessive fluctuations in interest rates will discourage long-term business planning and investment. What is more, the government may find it difficult to keep to its targets. This too may cause uncertainty and instability.

Difficulties with choice of target

Assume that the government or central bank sets an inflation target. Should it then stick to that rate, come what may? Might not an extended period of relatively low inflation warrant a lower inflation target? The government must at least have the discretion to *change* the rules, even if only occasionally.

Then there is the question of whether success in achieving the target will bring success in achieving other macroeconomic objectives, such as low unemployment and stable economic growth. The problem is that something called **Goodhart's Law** is likely to apply. The law, named after Charles Goodhart, formerly of the Bank of England, states that attempts to control an *indicator* of a problem may, as a result, make it cease to be a good indicator of the problem.

Targeting inflation may make it become a poor indicator of the state of the economy. If people believe that the central bank will be successful in achieving its inflation target, then those expectations will feed into their inflationary expectations and, not surprisingly, the target will be met. But that target rate of inflation may now be consistent with both a buoyant and a depressed economy. It is possible that the Phillips curve may become *horizontal* (as we saw for the UK in Figure 29.13).

The implication of Goodhart's Law is that, in achieving their inflation target, policymakers may not be tackling the much more serious problem of creating stable economic growth and an environment which will, therefore, encourage long-term investment.

Goodhart's Law. Controlling a symptom (i.e. an indicator) of a problem will not cure the problem. Instead, the indicator will merely cease to be a good indicator of the problem.

In extreme cases, as occurred in 2008, the economy may slow down rapidly and yet cost-push factors cause inflation to rise. Targeting inflation in these circumstances will demand *higher* interest rates, which will help to deepen the recession. A similar argument applied to the UK after the Brexit vote. The fall in the pound threatened to push up inflation and yet the Bank of England decided to cut Bank Rate. The aim was to ward off a downswing in the economy.

Central banks and a Taylor rule

Given the potential problems in adhering to simple inflation rate targets, many economists have advocated the use of a **Taylor rule**,[2] rather than a simple inflation target. A Taylor rule takes *two* objectives into account: (1) inflation and (2) either real national income or unemployment – and seeks to get the optimum degree of stability of the two. The degree of importance attached to each of the two objectives can be decided by the government or central bank. The central bank adjusts interest rates when either the rate of inflation diverges from its target or the rate of economic growth (or unemployment) diverges from its sustainable (or equilibrium) level.

Take the case where inflation is above its target level. The central bank following a Taylor rule will raise the rate of interest. It knows, however, that this will reduce real national income below the level at which it would otherwise have been. This, therefore, limits the amount that the central bank is prepared to raise the rate of interest. The more weight it attaches to stabilising inflation, the more it will raise the rate of interest. The more weight it attaches to achieving stable growth in real national income, the less it will raise the rate of interest.

Thus the central bank has to trade off inflation stability against stability in economic growth. This trade-off can be large when there are significant cost-push factors affecting the rate of inflation. In such circumstances, the weights attached to these two objectives become especially important.

Pause for thought

If people believe that the central bank will be successful in keeping inflation on target, does it matter whether a simple inflation rule or a Taylor rule is used? Explain.

Definitions

Goodhart's Law Controlling a symptom of a problem, or only part of the problem, will not cure the problem: it will simply mean that the part that is being controlled now becomes a poor indicator of the problem.

Taylor rule A rule adopted by a central bank for setting the rate of interest. It will raise the interest rate if (a) inflation is above target or (b) economic growth is above the sustainable level (or unemployment is below the equilibrium rate). The rule states how much interest rates will be changed in each case.

---

[2]Named after John Taylor, from Stanford University, who proposed that, for every 1 per cent that GDP rises above sustainable GDP, real interest rates should be raised by 0.5 percentage points and that, for every 1 per cent that inflation rises above its target level, real interest rates should be raised by 0.5 percentage points (i.e. nominal rates should be raised by 1.5 percentage points).

Conclusions

The following factors provide us with a framework to help analyse the relative merits of rules or discretion:

- The confidence of people in the effectiveness of either discretionary policies or rules: the greater the confidence, the more successful either policy is likely to be.
- The degree of self-stabilisation of the economy (in the case of rules) or, conversely, the degree of inherent instability of the economy (in the case of discretion).
- The size and frequency of exogenous shocks to demand: the greater they are, the greater the case for discretionary policy.

- In the case of rules, the ability and determination of governments to stick to the rules and the belief by the public that they will be effective.
- In the case of discretionary policy, the ability of governments to adopt and execute policies of the correct magnitude, the speed with which such policies can be effected and the accuracy of forecasting.

Case study K.14 on the student website looks at the history of fiscal and monetary policies in the UK from the 1950s to the current day. It illustrates the use of both rules and discretion and how the debates about policy shifted with historical events.

SUMMARY

1a The public sector comprises general government and public corporations. There exist a range of fiscal indicators that allow us to analyse the fiscal position and well-being of the public sector or its component sectors.

1b The sustainability of a country's public finances can be analysed by the fiscal arithmetic needed to maintain the current public-sector debt-to-GDP ratio. Countries with higher existing debt-to-GDP ratios, higher real interest costs and lower real rates of economic growth will need to operate larger primary surpluses (or smaller deficits) to prevent the ratio from rising further.

1c The government's fiscal policy influences the size of its budget deficit or surplus. Its size alone, however, is a poor guide to the government's fiscal stance. A large deficit, for example, may simply be due to the fact that the economy is in recession and therefore tax receipts are low. A better guide is whether the change in the deficit or surplus will be expansionary or contractionary.

2a Automatic fiscal stabilisers are tax revenues that rise and benefits that fall as national income rises. They have the effect of reducing the size of the multiplier and thus reducing cyclical upswings and downswings.

2b Discretionary fiscal policy is where the government deliberately changes taxes or government expenditure in order to alter the level of aggregate demand. Changes in government expenditure on goods and services will have a full multiplier effect. Changes in taxes and benefits will have a smaller multiplier effect as some of the tax/benefit changes will merely affect other withdrawals and thus have a smaller net effect on consumption of domestic product.

2d There are problems in predicting the magnitude of the effects of discretionary fiscal policy. Expansionary fiscal policy can act as a pump primer and stimulate increased private expenditure, or it can crowd out private expenditure. The extent to which it acts as a pump primer depends crucially on business confidence – something that is very difficult to predict beyond a few weeks or months. The extent of crowding out depends on monetary conditions and monetary policy.

2e There are various time lags involved with fiscal policy, which make it difficult to use fiscal policy to 'fine-tune' the economy.

2f In recent years, many governments around the world preferred a more passive approach towards fiscal policy. Targets were set for one or more measures of the public-sector finances and then taxes and government expenditure were adjusted so as to keep to the target.

2g Nevertheless, in extreme circumstances, as occurred in 2008/9, governments were prepared to abandon rules and give a fiscal stimulus to their economies.

3a Control of the growth of the money supply over the longer term will normally involve governments attempting to restrict the size of the budget deficit. This will be difficult to do, however, in a period of recession.

3b In the short term, the authorities can use monetary policy to restrict/increase the growth in aggregate demand in one of two major ways: (a) reducing/increasing money supply directly and (b) reducing/increasing the demand for money by raising/reducing interest rates.

3c The money supply can be reduced/increased directly by using open-market operations. This involves the central bank selling/buying more government securities and thereby reducing/increasing banks' reserves. Alternatively, the central bank can reduce/increase the amount it is prepared to lend to banks (other than as a last-resort measure).

2d The money supply is difficult to control precisely, however, and, even if it is successfully controlled, there then arises the problem of severe fluctuations in interest rates if the demand for money fluctuates and is relatively inelastic.

3e The current method of control in the UK and other countries involves the central bank influencing interest rates by its operations in the gilt repo and discount markets. The central bank keeps banks short of liquidity and then supplies them with liquidity, largely through gilt repos, at its chosen interest rate (gilt repo rate). This then has a knock-on effect on interest rates throughout the economy.

3f With an inelastic demand for loans, there may have to be substantial changes in interest rates in order to bring the

▶

required change in aggregate demand. What is more, controlling aggregate demand through interest rates is made even more difficult by fluctuations in the demand for money. These fluctuations are made more severe by speculation against changes in interest rates, exchange rates, the rate of inflation, etc.

3g Nevertheless, controlling interest rates is a way of responding rapidly to changing forecasts and can be an important signal to markets that inflation will be kept under control, especially when, as in the UK and the Eurozone, there is a firm target for the rate of inflation.

3h Faced with a deepening recession after the financial crisis of 2007–8, central banks embarked on programmes of quantitative easing, which involved their creating large amounts of new narrow money. This was used to purchase bonds and other assets from financial institutions, thereby increasing banks' reserves and allowing them to increase lending and hence increase broad money through the process of credit creation.

4a The case against discretionary policy is that it involves unpredictable time lags that can make the policy destabilising. Also, the government may *ignore* the long-run adverse consequences of policies designed for short-run political gain.

4b The case in favour of rules is that they help to reduce deficit bias and inflation bias and thus create a stable environment for investment and growth.

4c The case against sticking to money supply or inflation rules is that they may cause severe fluctuations in interest rates and thus create a less stable economic environment for business planning. Given the changing economic environment in which we live, rules adopted in the past may no longer be suitable for the present.

4d Although perfect fine-tuning may not be possible, Keynesians argue that the government must have the discretion to change its policy as circumstances demand.

REVIEW QUESTIONS

1 'The existence of a budget deficit or a budget surplus tells us very little about the stance of fiscal policy.' Explain and discuss.

2 Adam Smith remarked in *The Wealth of Nations* concerning the balancing of budgets, 'What is prudence in the conduct of every private family can scarce be folly in that of a great kingdom.' What problems might there be if the government decided to follow a balanced budget approach to its spending?

3 Of what significance are primary deficits or surpluses for the dynamics of a government's debt-to-GDP ratio?

4 What factors determine the effectiveness of discretionary fiscal policy?

5 Why is it difficult to use fiscal policy to 'fine-tune' the economy?

6 When the Bank of England announces that it is putting up interest rates, how will it achieve this, given that interest rates are determined by demand and supply?

7 How does the Bank of England attempt to achieve the target rate of inflation of 2 per cent? What determines its likelihood of success in meeting the target?

8 Imagine you were called in by the government to advise on whether it should adopt a policy of targeting the money supply. What advice would you give and how would you justify the advice?

9 Imagine you were called in by the government to advise on whether it should attempt to prevent cyclical fluctuations by the use of fiscal policy. What advice would you give and how would you justify the advice?

10 What do you understand by the term 'constrained discretion'? Illustrate your answer with reference to the UK and the Eurozone.

11 Is there a compromise between purely discretionary policy and adhering to strict targets?

12 Under what circumstances would adherence to an inflation target lead to (a) more stable interest rates and (b) less stable interest rates than pursuing discretionary demand management policy?

Supply-side policy

Business issues covered in this chapter

- What are the supply-side problems that countries face?
- How can supply-side policy influence business and the economy?
- How can supply-side policies affect labour productivity?
- What types of supply-side policy can be pursued and what is their effectiveness?
- What will be the impact on business of a policy of tax cuts?
- How can the government encourage increased competition?
- What is the best way of tackling regional problems and encouraging business investment in relatively deprived areas?

31.1 SUPPLY-SIDE PROBLEMS

Long-run growth and aggregate supply

In considering economic policy up to this point we have focused our attention on the demand side of the economy, where unemployment and slow growth are the result of a lack of aggregate demand, and where inflation and a balance of trade deficit are the result of excessive aggregate demand. Many of the causes of these problems, however, lie on the *supply side* and, as such, require an alternative policy approach.

KI 36
p 376

KI 42
p 507

  Supply-side policies aim to shift the aggregate supply curve to the right, thus increasing output for any given level of prices (or reducing the price level for any given level of output). In doing so, they increase an economy's level of *potential output*: the economy's output when firms are operating at normal levels of capacity utilisation.

  If successful, supply-side initiatives will not only increase the level of potential output but the rate at which

potential output grows over time. Thus they increase the rate at which the aggregate supply curve shifts rightwards. Figure 31.1 helps to illustrate this by applying the *AD/AS* model.

  Assume, initially, that the economy is at equilibrium with output (real national income) at the potential level (Y_{P_1}) and the economy's price level at P_1. Now assume that potential output rises from Y_{P_1} to Y_{P_2} as a result of supply-side policies.

  The short- and long-run *AS* curves move rightward – say to $SRAS_2$ and $LRAS_2$. The size of the shifts will reflect the

Definition

Supply-side policy Government policy that attempts to influence the level of aggregate supply directly, rather than through aggregate demand.

Figure 31.1 Supply-side policies and long-term growth

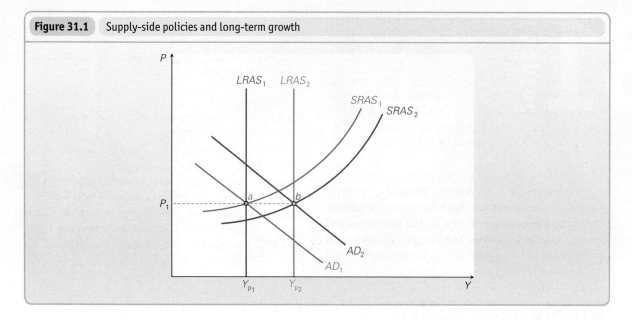

increase in the economy's productive capabilities. The more successful are supply-side policies, the greater the rightward move of the aggregate supply curve. If the economy's extra capacity is used, it has the effect of increasing the real national income of the country; people are now able to make more purchases.

There may also be a rightward shift in the AD curve. If the extra real income generated by the increase in potential output generates an equivalent amount of additional real spending, the AD curve will shift to AD_2. In such a case, actual output would increase by the same amount as potential output: i.e. $Y_{P_2} - Y_{P_1}$.

If, however, the rise in potential output did not translate into sufficient extra spending, the AD curve would not shift sufficiently to the right to give a new equilibrium at Y_{P_2} – a negative output gap would emerge. In such a case, discretionary rises in government spending and/or cuts in taxation (fiscal policy) or cuts in interest rates or increases in the money supply (monetary policy) may be required to shift the AD curve to AD_2.

Generally, however, over a time span of several years, periods of deficient demand are likely to be matched by periods of excess demand. In the long run, therefore, rightward shifts in the AS curves would be matched by equivalent rightward shifts in the AD curve. In other words, in the long run, economies tend towards equilibrium at the potential level of national income as markets and expectations adjust.

While supply-side policies can be evaluated on their ability to affect an economy's long-run growth rate, economic growth does not mean that everyone in the economy gains and so policymakers may also consider the distribution of costs and benefits of specific policies. Nonetheless, for overall living standards to increase, real national income *per capita* must increase.

The growth in labour productivity is crucial for raising national output per head of the population. Therefore supply-side policies may be designed to encourage capital accumulation, the development of human capital and foster technological progress and advance.

Box 31.1 discusses the concept of labour productivity further and compares its growth in the UK with that of other developed countries.

The quantity and productivity of factors of production

The growth of potential output is crucially dependent on an economy's factors of production (i.e. its resources, such as labour and capital). Supply-side policies are designed to influence both the *quantities* of factors employed and their *productivity*.

Physical capital

The rate at which economies accumulate capital, such as machinery and office space, is an important determinant of their long-term economic growth. The rate at which the stock of capital grows depends on the size of investment flows. The key here is for investment to enable *capital deepening* (see page 530). This occurs when there is a rise in an economy's capital intensity, i.e. in the amount of capital per worker.

In section 26.6, we saw that for capital deepening to occur, investment flows need to exceed the amount needed merely to offset diminishing returns to capital, to replace worn out or obsolete capital and to account for the growth in the size of the workforce. If successful, supply-side policies help to increase capital intensity and, in turn, increase output per head and overall living standards.

Box 31.2 considers the different types of physical capital as recorded in countries' national accounts. It also looks at the extent to which rates of capital accumulation vary across developed economies.

Of course, it is not just the *quantity* of investment that affects economic growth, but how *productive* that investment is. The greater the productivity of additional capital, the faster will national income and business profits rise and the greater the amount of additional investment that can be financed.

The productivity of capital depends crucially on technological progress and innovation. Therefore, effective supply-side policies are those that help to foster new inventions, their incorporation in new capital equipment and their adoption by businesses. These might be policies that encourage investment in 'cutting-edge' technologies or that raise the shares of national income devoted to education, training and research and development. A key question is what policies can encourage the effective propagation of innovation and technological progress.

The UK's record of low investment. Unfortunately, for the UK, for several decades it has experienced lower levels of investment relative to national income than other industrialised countries. This is illustrated in Table 31.1. In particular, investment by the private sector has been weak by international standards: a trend that seems to have persisted over five decades.

To some extent, the UK's poor investment performance has been offset by the fact that wage rates have been lower than in competing countries. This has at least made the UK

> ### Pause for thought
>
> *How can the UK's low level of investment relative to national income be explained?*

relatively attractive to inward investment, especially by US, Japanese, Korean and, more recently, Chinese and Indian companies seeking to set up production plants within the EU.

The poor performance of UK manufacturing firms has resulted in a growing import penetration of the UK market. Imports of manufactured products have grown more rapidly than UK manufactured exports and, since the early 1980s, the UK has been a net importer of manufactured products.

Some economists believe that the UK's low-investment economy highlights the need for more government intervention, especially in the fields of education and training, research and development and the provision of infrastructure. This has been the approach in many countries, including France, Germany and Japan.

Labour and human capital

The economy's potential output is also affected by both the quantity and quality of the labour input. In section 26.4, we introduced the concept of equilibrium unemployment: the difference between those who would like to work at the current wage rate and those willing and able to take a job. There can be a mismatch between the aggregate supply of labour and the aggregate demand for labour, which means that

Table 31.1	Gross fixed capital formation as a percentage of GDP: 1970–2020							
	1970–99		**2000–20**		**1970–2020**			
	General government	Private	General government	Private	General government	Private	Total	
Japan	5.7	26.2	4.0	20.0	5.0	23.7	28.7	
Norway	4.8	22.8	4.3	18.1	4.6	20.8	25.4	
Austria	4.9	21.6	2.9	20.4	4.1	21.1	25.2	
Spain	3.7	19.9	3.4	20.9	3.5	20.3	23.8	
Ireland	3.7	18.5	3.1	20.7	3.4	19.4	22.8	
Belgium	3.8	19.1	2.3	20.4	3.1	19.6	22.8	
France	4.4	18.5	3.8	18.3	4.1	18.5	22.6	
Netherlands	4.4	18.2	3.8	16.9	4.1	17.7	21.8	
USA	4.6	17.4	3.8	17.2	4.3	17.3	21.6	
Italy	3.6	19.1	2.6	16.8	3.2	18.2	21.3	
Germany	3.1	19.0	2.2	18.1	2.7	18.6	21.3	
Denmark	3.3	17.9	3.2	17.5	3.2	17.7	21.0	
UK	3.5	17.1	2.5	14.2	3.1	15.9	19.0	

Note: data from 2018 based on forecasts.

Source: *AMECO* database (European Commission, DGECFIN) Tables 3.2 and 6.1

BOX 31.1 | **MEASURING LABOUR PRODUCTIVITY**

Mind the UK productivity gap

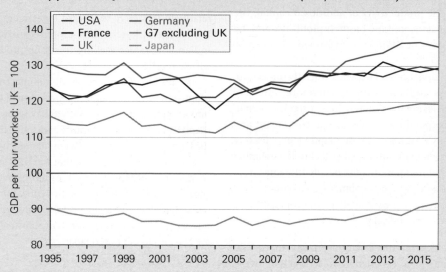

(a) Productivity in selected economies relative to the UK (GDP per hour worked)

Note: Figures are current-price GDP per hour worked
Source: Based on data in *International Comparisons of Productivity* (National Statistics, 2018)

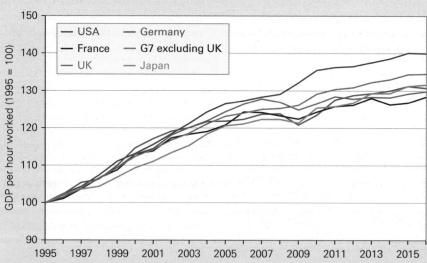

(b) Productivity in selected economies (GDP per hour worked, 1995 = 100)

Note: Figures are constant-price GDP per hour worked
Source: Based on data in *International Comparisons of Productivity* (National Statistics, 2018)

Long-term increases in real GDP per capita are fundamental to raising a country's living standards. The rate at which national output per head increases depends crucially on the growth in labour productivity. There are two common ways of measuring labour productivity. The first is *output per worker*. This is the most straightforward measure to calculate. All that is required is a measure of total output and employment.

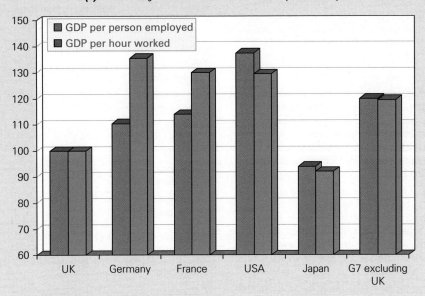

(c) *Productivity in selected economies, 2016 (UK = 100)*

Note: Figures are current-price GDP per hour worked/person employed.
Source: Based on data in *International Comparisons of Productivity* (National Statistics, 2018)

A second measure is *output per hour worked*. This has the advantage that it is not influenced by the *number* of hours worked. So, for an economy like the UK, with a very high percentage of part-time workers on the one hand, and long average hours worked by full-time employees on the other, such a measure would be more accurate in gauging worker efficiency.

International comparisons of labour productivity

Charts (a) and (b) show comparative productivity levels of various countries and the G7 (excluding the UK) using GDP per hour worked. Chart (a) shows countries' productivity relative to the UK. As you can see, GDP per hour worked is lower in the UK than the other countries with the exception of Japan. For example, in 2016, compared with the UK, output per hour was 35.5 per cent higher in Germany, 30 per cent higher in France and 29 per cent higher in the USA.

Compared with the rest of the G7 countries, UK output per hour was 19.5 per cent lower and, hence, essentially unchanged from the 19.6 per cent productivity gap recorded in 2015, which was an historic high.

A major explanation of lower productivity in the UK is the fact that for decades it has invested a smaller proportion of its national income than most other industrialised nations. Nevertheless, until 2006, the gap had been narrowing with

the rest of the G7. This was because UK productivity, although lower than in many other countries, was growing faster. This can be seen chart (b). Part of the reason for this was the inflow of investment from abroad.

Chart (c) compares labour productivity across both measures. Workers in the USA and the UK, on average, work longer hours than those in France and Germany. Thus, whereas output *per hour worked* in the USA is roughly on par with that in France and Germany, output *per person employed* in the USA is about 21 per cent higher than in France and 25 per cent higher than in Germany. As you can see, the evidence points to UK labour productivity being *lower* than that in the USA, France and Germany on both measures but higher than that in Japan.

In understanding the growth in labour productivity, we therefore need to focus on three factors: the accumulation of physical capital (see Box 31.2), human capital (see Box 26.4), and innovation and technological progress.

What could explain the differences in labour productivity between the five countries in chart (c), and why do the differences vary according to which of the two measures is used?

Do a search to find productivity levels and growth rates in two non-G7 developed countries. Explain your findings in comparison to the countries in the charts in this box.

BOX 31.2 GETTING INTENSIVE WITH CAPITAL

Capital intensity and labour productivity

KI 42
p 507

In this box, we take a look at two issues relating to physical capital. First, we consider what counts as capital in a country's national accounts. Second, we compare the growth of the physical capital stock per worker of a sample of developed economies and then see how this compares with their rates of growth in output per worker (labour productivity).

What is capital?

In a country's national accounts, physical capital consists of non-financial *fixed assets*. It does not include goods and services transformed or used up in the course of production; these are known as *intermediate goods and services*. Furthermore, it does not relate directly to the stock of human capital: the skills and attributes embodied in individuals that affect production (see Box 26.4).

A country's stock of fixed assets can be valued at its replacement cost, regardless of its age: this is its *gross* value. It can also be valued at its written-down value, known as its *net* value. The net value takes into account the *consumption of capital* which occurs through wear and tear (depreciation) or when capital becomes naturally obsolescent.

The table shows that the estimated value of the *net* capital stock of the UK in 2017 was £4.67 trillion, almost 2.3 times the value of GDP. This, however, is considerably less than the 2017 current-price (nominal) estimate of full human capital of £21.15 trillion, 10.3 times the value of GDP (see Box 26.4).

The table shows that there are six categories of fixed assets.

- The largest of these by value is *dwellings,* which includes houses, bungalows and flats. Residential housing yields rental incomes for landlords and, more generally, provides all of us with important consumption services, most notably shelter.
- The second largest component by value is *other buildings and structures*. This includes structures such as factories, schools and hospitals and the country's railway track.
- The third largest component by value is *ICT and other machinery, equipment and weapons systems*. It includes telecommunications equipment, computer hardware, office machinery and hardware as well as weapon systems equipment.

UK net capital stock, 2017

Type	£ billions	% of fixed assets	% of GDP
Dwellings	1 819.9	39.0	89.0
Other buildings and structures	1 799.7	38.5	88.0
ICT, other machinery, equipment & weapons systems	728.0	15.6	35.6
Intellectual property products	175.4	3.8	8.6
Transport equipment	139.0	3.0	6.8
Cultivated biological resources	9.3	0.2	0.5
All fixed assets	4 671.3	100.0	228.5

Sources: Based on data from *Capital Stocks, Consumption of Fixed Capital in the UK dataset* and series YBHA (National Statistics)

- The fourth largest is *intellectual property products*. This includes computer software, original works of literature or art and mineral exploration.
- Next by value is *transport equipment*. This includes equipment for moving people and objects, such as lorries for haulage, buses, railway rolling stock and civil aircraft.
- The smallest component by value is *cultivated biological resources*. This includes livestock for breeding, vineyards, orchards and forests.

How does capital grow? An international comparison

A key measure of the amount of capital being used in an economy is the amount of capital per worker (capital intensity). In the following chart, we plot the ratio of real GDP per worker in 2019 to that in 1960 (y-axis) against the ratio of capital per worker in 2019 to that in 1960 (x-axis) in a selection of developed countries. Therefore, the chart is plotting

---

vacancies are not filled, despite the existence of unemployment. Perhaps workers have the wrong qualifications, are poorly motivated, are living a long way away from the job, or simply are unaware of the jobs that are vacant.

Generally, the problem is that labour is not sufficiently mobile, either occupationally or geographically, to respond to changes in the job market. Labour supply for particular jobs is too inelastic. Supply-side policies might look to increase labour

KI 12
p 64

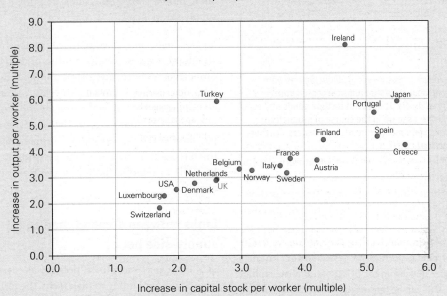

Growth in output and capital per worker: 1960–2019

Note: Figures from 2018 are forecasts.
Source: Based on data from *AMECO* database (European Commission)

the increase in labour productivity against the increase in capital intensity.

For each country, we observe an increase in capital intensity, although the rates of capital deepening differ quite significantly. The data show that the UK ranks relatively lowly in terms of capital deepening. In the UK, the capital stock per worker is 2.6 times higher in 2019 than in 1960. In Japan, by contrast, it is 5.5 times higher and in France it is 3.8 times higher.

We would expect that the higher the level of capital per worker, the greater will be the level of output per worker (labour productivity). This is largely borne out in the chart. However, while there is a strong statistical association between capital deepening and economic growth, there are other factors that impact on long-term growth. Three of these are technological

progress, *human* capital and the efficiency with which capital is deployed. We examine these later in this chapter.

1. *How does capital accumulation differ from capital deepening?*
2. *Could the composition, as well as the size, of a country's capital be important for its long-run economic growth?*

From the AMECO database, download data on the net capital stock at constant prices per person employed. Then, for a sample of up to five countries of your choice, plot a time series chart showing the year-to-year rates of growth across time. Finally, comprise a short briefing note summarising the patterns in your chart.

market flexibility, to provide better job information, to support retraining and to enhance the skills of the workforce.

As well as making workers more responsive to job opportunities, supply-side policies may aim to make employers

more adaptable and more effective in operating within existing labour constraints.

Successful supply-side policies that reduce equilibrium unemployment and increase employment also increase the economy's potential output. The benefits for potential output can be enduring too. A more flexible and skilful workforce increases the economy's stock of *human capital* (see page 530). The concept of human capital captures the knowledge, skills and attributes that are embodied within the workforce and that affect production activities.

> ### Pause for thought
>
> *How can increasing the effectiveness of labour improve both the productivity of labour and the productivity of capital?*

Human and physical capital

An increase in an economy's stock of human capital increases the effectiveness with which the economy's existing stock of physical capital can be employed. This therefore contributes to further accumulation of physical capital.

Greater levels of human capital also contribute to the development of new products, processes and techniques and, hence, in the development of higher quality capital. As we have seen, this can be important in increasing the rate of technological progress. There is also the potential that *knowledge spillovers* hasten progress. These spillovers are a form of externality with some of the benefits of new ideas captured or consumed by others. The point here is that these ideas can then be developed by others.

Supply-side policies may foster the development of new ideas and the subsequent benefits from knowledge spillovers. This can involve encouraging the clustering of businesses within particular sectors so as to enable the exchange of ideas. The development of business parks or enterprise zones (see page 668) are a means of doing this.

Some economists argue that it is competition that helps foster the development of ideas and technological progress. By seeking a competitive advantage over their rivals, firms may look to deliver products and services that provide consumers with greater satisfaction or develop processes which allow them to produce more cost-effectively. Whichever strategy businesses choose, it is argued, the benefits help to drive technological progress.

Types of supply-side policy

Supply-side policies are commonly grouped under two general types: *market-orientated* and *interventionist*.

Market-orientated policies focus on ways of 'freeing up' the market, such as encouraging private enterprise, risk-taking and competition: policies that provide incentives for innovation, hard work and productivity. These are considered in section 31.2.

Interventionist policies focus on means of counteracting the deficiencies of the free market and typically involve government expenditure on infrastructure and training and financial support for investment. These are considered in section 31.3.

However, some policies may draw on elements of both types: for instance, by providing financial support (interventionist) through the use of tax reliefs (market-orientated). Such policies are sometimes described as 'third-way' supply-side policies.

Regional imbalances. Supply-side policies and initiatives should not be seen solely in terms of delivering *national* objectives. There are often marked differences in incomes, unemployment rates and other measures of economic and social well-being *within* a country. Therefore, both national governments and international bodies, such as the EU, may adopt supply-side projects and initiatives that help to tackle regional inequalities. We look at regional policy in the final section of this chapter.

Links between demand-side and supply-side policy

While we may categorise policies as 'demand-side' or 'supply-side' according to their focus, the reality is that policies often have *both* demand-side and supply-side effects. For example, many supply-side policies involve increased government expenditure, whether on retraining schemes, on research and development projects or on industrial relocation. They will, therefore, cause a rise in aggregate demand (unless accompanied by a rise in taxes). Similarly, supply-side policies of tax cuts designed to increase incentives will increase aggregate demand (unless accompanied by a cut in government expenditure). It is thus important to consider the consequences for demand when planning various supply-side policies.

Likewise, demand management policies often have supply-side effects. If a cut in interest rates boosts investment, there will be a multiplied rise in national income: a demand-side effect.

> ### Pause for thought
>
> *Why might it take time for the benefits of supply-side policies to become evident?*

But that rise in investment will also create increased productive capacity: a supply-side effect.

> ### Definition
>
> **Knowledge spillover** The capture by third parties of benefits from the development by others of new ideas, for example new products, processes and technologies.

31.2 MARKET-ORIENTATED SUPPLY-SIDE POLICIES

Radical market-orientated supply-side policies were first adopted in the early 1980s by the Thatcher Government in the UK and the Reagan administration in the USA, but subsequently were copied by other right and centre-right governments around the world. The essence of these supply-side policies is to encourage and reward individual enterprise and initiative and to reduce the role of government; to put more reliance on market forces and competition and less on government intervention and regulation.

Reducing government expenditure

The desire of many governments to cut government expenditure is not just to reduce the size of the public-sector deficit; it is also an essential ingredient of their supply-side strategy.

The public sector is portrayed by some as more bureaucratic and less efficient than the private sector. What is more, it is claimed that a growing proportion of public money has been spent on administration and other 'non-productive' activities, rather than on the direct provision of goods and services.

Two things are needed, it is argued: (a) a more efficient use of resources within the public sector and (b) a reduction in the size of the public sector. This would allow private investment to increase with no overall rise in aggregate demand. Thus the supply-side benefits of higher investment could be achieved without the demand-side costs of higher inflation.

In practice, governments have found it very difficult to cut their expenditure relative to GDP. However, many countries were faced with trying to do this after the financial crisis and global economic slowdown of the late 2000s (see Figure 31.2). Governments found that this means making difficult choices, particularly concerning the levels of services and the provision of infrastructure.

Pause for thought

Why might a recovering economy (and hence a fall in government expenditure on social security benefits) make the government feel even more concerned to make discretionary cuts in government expenditure?

Tax cuts

The imposition of taxation can distort a variety of choices that individuals make. Changes to the rates of taxation can lead individuals to substitute one activity for another. Three examples that are commonly referred to in the context of aggregate supply are:

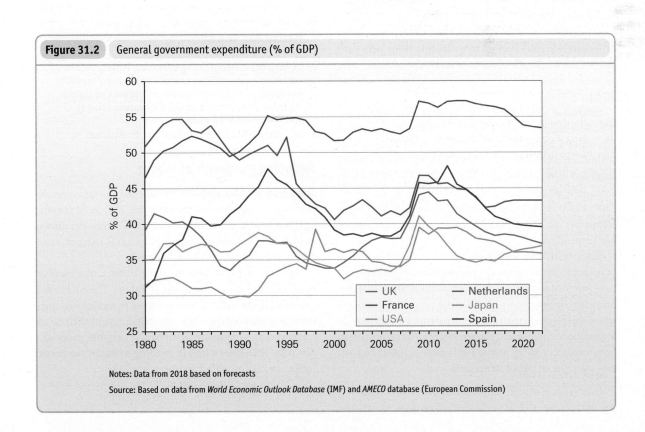

Figure 31.2 General government expenditure (% of GDP)

Notes: Data from 2018 based on forecasts

Source: Based on data from *World Economic Outlook Database* (IMF) and *AMECO* database (European Commission)

- taxation of labour income and its impact on labour supply (including hours worked and choice of occupation);
- taxation of interest income earned on financial products (savings) and its impact on the funds available for investment;
- taxation of firms' profits and its impact on capital expenditure by firms.

Over time, many countries have witnessed a decline in the marginal rates of taxation associated with each of these cases. Here we consider the case of the UK.

In 1979, the basic rate of income tax in the UK was 33 per cent, with higher rates rising to 83 per cent. By 2008, the standard rate was 20 per cent and the higher rate was 40 per cent. From 2010, an additional 50 per cent tax rate was implemented for those earning in excess of £150 000, largely as a means of plugging the deficit in the public finances. Subsequently, this was reduced to 45 per cent from 2013.

Similar reductions in rates of corporation tax (the tax on business profits) have increased after-tax profits, leaving more funds for ploughing back into investment, as well as increasing the after-tax return on investment. In 1983, the main rate of corporation tax in the UK stood at 52 per cent. A series of reductions have taken place since then. By 2011, the main rate had been halved to 26 per cent; by 2017, it had fallen to 19 per cent; by 2020, the rate is due to have fallen to 17 per cent.

Governments have also looked to increase investment allowances or R&D expenditure credits. Investment allowances enable firms to offset the cost of investment against pre-tax profit, thereby reducing their tax liability. R&D expenditure credits operate by providing firms with cash payments for a proportion of their R&D expenditure which, although subject to tax, nonetheless increase their net profit.

Successive governments have applied such R&D incentives. For example, small and medium-sized enterprises (SMEs) can offset a multiple of research and development costs against corporation tax. From April 2015, the rate of relief for small and medium-sized enterprises (SMEs) was 230 per cent – taxable profits being reduced by £230 for every £100 of R&D expenditure. Meanwhile, from April 2016, larger companies can claim a taxable credit worth 11 per cent of R&D expenditures.

Since April 2013, firms have been subject to a lower rate of corporation tax on profits earned from inventions they have patented and certain other innovations. The idea is that firms will be provided with financial support to innovate where this results in their acquiring patents. Patents provide protection for intellectual property rights. Firms are liable to corporation tax on the profits attributable to qualifying patents at a reduced rate of 10 per cent.

Substitution effects of tax cuts. The argument for reducing tax rates on incomes and profits is that it contributes to higher levels of economic output. Specifically, it encourages an increased supply of labour hours, more moneys invested with financial institutions and more capital expenditure by firms than would otherwise be the case. The reason is that tax cuts increase the return on such activities. In other words, there is a *substitution effect* inducing more of these beneficial activities. In the case of labour, people are encouraged to substitute work for leisure as their after-tax wage rate is now higher.

Income effects of tax cuts. However, in each case there is a counteracting incentive. This is the *income effect.* Tax cuts increase the returns to working, saving and undertaking capital expenditure. This means that less of each activity needs to be undertaken to generate the same income flow as before. Take the case of labour: if a tax cut increases your hourly take-home pay, you may feel that you can afford to work fewer hours.

Because economic theory offers no firm conclusions as to the benefit of tax cuts, economists and policy makers often look to empirical evidence for guidance. In the case of whether or not tax cuts encourage people to work longer hours, the evidence suggests that the substitution and income effects just about cancel each other out. Anyway, for many people there is no such choice in the short run. There is no chance of doing overtime or working a shorter week. In the long run, there may be some flexibility in that people can change jobs.

> ## Pause for thought
>
> *UK Government receipts as a proportion of national income were roughly around 37 per cent at both the end of the 1970s and 2010s. Does this mean that there have been no positive incentive effects from the various tax measures taken by governments since the 1970s?*

Reducing the power of labour

The argument here is that if labour costs to employers are reduced, their profits will probably rise. This could encourage and enable more investment and hence economic growth. If the monopoly power of labour is reduced, then cost-push inflation will also be reduced.

The Thatcher Government, in the 1980s, took a number of measures to curtail the power of unions. These included introducing the right of employees not to join unions, preventing workers taking action other than against their direct employers and enforcing secret ballots on strike proposals (see page 323). It set a lead in resisting strikes in the public sector.

As labour markets have become more flexible, with increased part-time working and short-term and zero-hour contracts, and as the process of globalisation has exposed more companies to international competition, so this has further eroded the power of labour in many sectors of the economy (see section 18.4).

Reducing welfare

New classical economists claim that a major cause of unemployment is the small difference between the welfare benefits of the unemployed and the take-home pay of the employed. This causes voluntary unemployment (i.e. frictional unemployment). People are caught in a 'poverty trap': if they take a job, they lose their benefits.

A dramatic solution to this problem would be to cut unemployment benefits. A major problem with this approach, however, is that, with changing requirements for labour skills, many of the redundant workers from the older industries are simply not qualified for new jobs that are created. What is more, the longer people are unemployed, the more demoralised they become. Employers would probably be prepared to pay only very low wages to such workers. To persuade these unemployed people to take low-paid jobs, the welfare benefits would have to be slashed. A 'market' solution to the problem, therefore, may be a very cruel solution. A fairer solution would be an interventionist policy: a policy of retraining labour.

Another alternative is to make the payment of unemployment benefits conditional on the recipient making a concerted effort to find a job. Recipients of Universal Credit have to make a 'Claimant Commitment' which is the record of the responsibilities the claimant has accepted in return for receiving Universal Credit, and the consequences of not meeting them. Payments may be cut if the responsibilities are not met.

Policies to encourage competition

If the government can encourage more competition, this should have the effect of increasing national output and reducing inflation. Five major types of policy have been pursued under this heading.

Privatisation. If privatisation simply involves the transfer of a natural monopoly to private hands (e.g. the water companies), the scope for increased competition is limited. However, where there is genuine scope for increased competition (e.g. in the supply of gas and electricity), privatisation can lead to increased efficiency, more consumer choice and lower prices. There may still be a problem of oligopolistic collusion, however, and thus privatised industries are

monitored and regulated with the aim of making them genuinely competitive.

Alternatively, privatisation can involve the introduction of private services into the public sector (e.g. private contractors providing cleaning services in hospitals or refuse collection for local authorities). Private contractors may compete against each other for the franchise. This may well lower the cost of provision of these services, but the quality of provision may suffer unless closely monitored. The effects on unemployment are uncertain. Private contractors may offer lower wages and thus may use more labour. But, if they are trying to supply the service at minimum cost, they are likely to employ less labour.

Deregulation. This involves the removal of monopoly rights: again, largely in the public sector. The deregulation of the bus industry, opening it up to private operators, is a good example of this initiative.

Introducing market relationships into the public sector. This is where the government tries to get different departments or elements within a particular part of the public sector to 'trade' with each other, so as to encourage competition and efficiency. The best-known examples are within health and education.

One example is in the National Health Service. In 2003, the UK Government introduced a system of 'foundation trusts'. Hospitals can apply for foundation trust status. If successful, they are given much greater financial autonomy in terms of purchasing, employment and investment decisions. NHS Improvement is responsible for overseeing foundation trusts and NHS trusts. By May 2018, there were 153 NHS foundation trusts.

Critics argue that funds were being diverted to foundation hospitals away from the less well-performing hospitals where greater funding could help that performance. In the 2012 Health and Social Care Act, the government proposed that, in due course, all NHS hospitals become foundation trusts.

As far as general practice is concerned, groups of GP practices are formed into Clinical Commissioning Groups (CCGs). These are responsible for arranging most of the NHS services within their boundaries. A key principle of the system is to give GPs a choice of 'providers' with the hope of reducing costs and driving up standards.

The Private Finance Initiative (PFI). Public–private partnerships (PPPs) are a way of funding public expenditure with private capital. In the UK, the *Private Finance Initiative* (PFI), as it was known, began in 1992. The PFI meant that a private company, after a competitive tender, would be contracted by a government department or local authority to finance and build a project, such as a new road or a prison. The government then pays the company to maintain and/or run it, or simply rents the assets from the company. The public sector thus becomes a purchaser of services rather than a direct provider itself.

Critics claim that PFI projects have resulted in low quality of provision and that cost control has often been poor, resulting in a higher burden for the taxpayer in the long term. What is more, many of the projects have turned out to be highly profitable for the private provider, suggesting that the terms of the original contracts were too lax.

Following these criticisms, in 2012, the UK Government introduced a revised form of PFI (PF2) where the public sector would take stakes of up to 49 per cent in new projects. These would no longer include 'soft services', such as cleaning and catering. However, following the collapse in January 2018 of Carillion, one of the major private-sector firms involved in PPPs, criticsms of PFI intensified. In response, the Chancellor, in his October 2018 Budget, announced that there would be no further private finance projects, although existing agreements under PFI and PF2 would be honoured. (The benefits and costs of PFI and PF2 are explored in Case K.18 on the student website.)

Free trade and capital movements. The opening up of international trade and investment is central to a market-orientated supply-side policy. One of the first measures of the Thatcher Government (in October 1979) was to remove all controls on the purchase and sale of foreign currencies, thereby permitting the free inflow and outflow of capital, both long term and short term. Most other industrialised countries also removed or relaxed exchange controls during the 1980s and early 1990s.

The Single European Act of 1987, which came into force in 1993, was another example of international liberalisation. It created a 'single market' in the EU: a market without barriers to the movement of goods, services, capital and labour (see section 25.3).

Critics have claimed that, in the short term, industries may be forced to close by the competition from cheaper imported products, which can have a major impact on employment in the areas affected. A major election promise of the Trump campaign was that 'putting America first' would involve a move away from free trade, giving specific protection to US industries, such as vehicles and steel. (We examined arguments for and against protection in sections 24.2 and 24.3.)

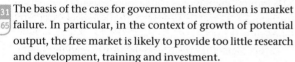

31.3 INTERVENTIONIST SUPPLY-SIDE POLICIES

KI 31
p 365
The basis of the case for government intervention is market failure. In particular, in the context of growth of potential output, the free market is likely to provide too little research and development, training and investment.

KI 33
p 367
There are, potentially, large external benefits from research and development. Firms investing in developing and improving products, and especially firms engaged in more general scientific research, may produce results that provide benefits to many other firms. Thus the *social* rate of return on investment may be much higher than the *private* rate of return. Investment that is privately unprofitable for a firm may therefore still be economically desirable for the nation.

Similarly, investment in training may continue yielding benefits to society that are lost to the firms providing the training when the workers leave.

KI 14
p 79
Investment often involves risks. Firms may be unwilling to take those risks, since the costs of possible failure may be too high. When looked at nationally, however, the benefits of investment might well have substantially outweighed the costs, and thus it would have been socially desirable for firms to have taken the risk. Successes would have outweighed failures.

Even when firms do wish to make such investments, they may find difficulties in raising finance. Banks may be unwilling to lend – a problem that increased after the credit crunch.

Alternatively, if firms rely on raising finance by the issue of new shares, this makes them very dependent on the stock market performance of their shares. This depends largely on current profitability and expected profitability in the near future, not on *long-term* profitability. Similarly, the fear of takeovers may make managers over-concerned to keep shareholders happy, further encouraging 'short-termism'.

Types of interventionist supply-side policy

Nationalisation. This is the most extreme form of intervention and one that most countries had tended to reject, given a worldwide trend for privatisation. Nevertheless, many countries had always stopped short of privatising certain key transport and power industries, such as the railways and electricity generation. One of the policies of the UK Labour Party is to renationalise the railways as franchises come up for renewal. One of the key arguments is that this will make the railways more affordable, more accountable and more efficient.

Nationalisation may also be a suitable solution for rescuing vital industries suffering extreme market turbulence. This was the case with the banks in the late 2000s (and beyond) as the financial crisis unfolded. With the credit crunch and the over-exposure to risky investments in securitised sub-prime debt, inadequate levels of capital,

| **Figure 31.3** | Gross expenditure on R&D (% of GDP) |

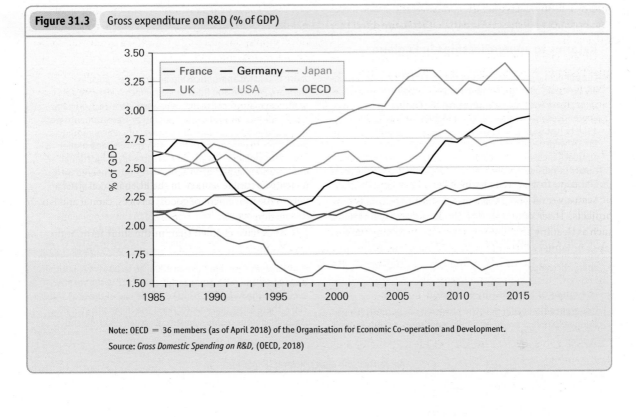

Note: OECD = 36 members (as of April 2018) of the Organisation for Economic Co-operation and Development.

Source: *Gross Domestic Spending on R&D,* (OECD, 2018)

declining confidence and plummeting share prices, several banks were taken into full or partial public ownership. In the UK, Northern Rock and Bradford & Bingley were fully nationalised, while the government took a majority share-holding in the Royal Bank of Scotland and Lloyds Banking Group, although later the government began selling its share of these banks.

Direct provision. Improvements in infrastructure, such as a better motorway system, can be of direct benefit to industry. Alternatively, the government could provide factories or equipment to specific firms. Following the financial crisis and the economic volatility that followed, the IMF, OECD and other international organisations began calling for greater international expenditure on infrastructure as a way of increasing not only potential output but also aggregate demand.

Funding research and development. Around about one-third of UK research and development (R&D) is financed by the government, but around half of this has been concentrated in the fields of defence, aerospace and the nuclear power indus-try. As a result, there has been little government sponsorship of research in the majority of industry. Since the mid-1970s, however, there have been several government initiatives in the field of information technology. Even so, the amount of government support in this field has been very small com-pared with Japan, France and the USA. What is more, the amount of support declined between the mid-1980s and the late 1990s.

Figure 31.3 shows that, despite encouraging R&D through the tax system, UK gross expenditure on research and devel-opment as a percentage of GDP has been lower than that of its main economic rivals.

Lower R&D has contributed to a productivity gap between the UK and other G7 countries (see Box 31.1). This produc-tivity gap is a drag on the UK's long-term economic growth. The UK's poor R&D record has occurred even though a size-able number of UK-based companies regularly make a list of the world's largest R&D spending companies. In part, this reflects the limited R&D expenditure by government. But, it also reflects the low R&D intensity across the private sector. In other words, total R&D expenditure by British firms has often been low *relative* to the income generated by sales.

Training and education. The government may set up train-ing schemes, encourage educational institutions to make their courses more vocationally relevant or introduce new vocational qualifications (such as GNVQs, NVQs and foun-dation degrees in the UK). Alternatively, the government can provide grants or tax relief to firms which themselves provide training schemes. (Alternative approaches to train-ing in the UK, Germany, France and the USA are examined in Case study K.19 on the student website.)

Assistance to small firms. UK governments in recent years have recognised the importance of small firms to the econ-omy and have introduced various forms of advisory services, grants and tax concessions. For example, as we saw above, they receive financial support for R&D expenditure through

BOX 31.3   PUBLIC FUNDING OF APPRENTICESHIPS

Reforms to apprenticeships in England

Current public policy in relation to apprenticeships can arguably be traced back to the launch in 1994 of *Modern apprenticeships*. These were aimed at reversing the decline in apprenticeship numbers which had fallen from 243 700 in 1966 to just 53 000 in 1990. Traditionally, apprenticeships in the UK were developed and run by employers. The new approach involved far greater levels of government intervention with subsidy payments available to help finance the costs of training that met certain criteria

Subsequent reviews of training policy carried by Lord Leitch (2006),[1] Professor Alison Wolf (2011)[2], Dolphin and Lanning (2011),[3] Doug Richard (2012)[4] and Lord Sainsbury (2016)[5] have all agreed on the need for further reform and, above all, to increase the number of publicly-funded apprenticeships.

The case for expanding provision

It is argued that expanding the provision of apprenticeships could help reduce youth unemployment rates. Countries with more extensive apprenticeship programmes, such as Germany, Austria and Norway, have much lower rates of youth unemployment than the UK (see Table 26.2 on page 516). Other benefits include a smoother transition into work for young people not attending university, encouraging employers to engage more fully with training and higher wages for employees who complete low-level vocational qualifications as part of an apprenticeship compared with people who complete the same qualifications outside of an apprenticeship.

Various governments have responded to this recommendation. The number of employees on apprenticeship schemes increased from 175 000 in 2005/6 to 912 200 in 2016/17. As the chart shows, the number of people starting on apprenticeship schemes rose rapidly from 2009/10 to 2011/12, but then levelled off and fell significantly in 2017/18 with the introduction of the Apprenticeship Levy (see end of the box). After 2009, there was a particularly rapid rise in people over 25 starting apprenticeship schemes. Between 2009/10 and

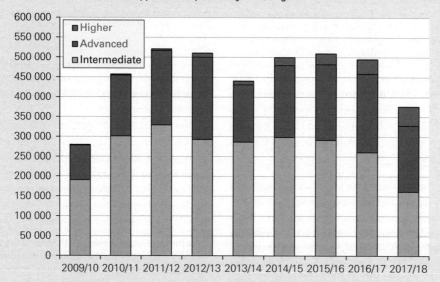

Apprenticeship starts by level, England

Source: Based on data from *DfE/EFSA FE data library: apprenticeships by geography and starts* (2018)

---

[1]Lord Leitch, *Prosperity for all in the global economy - world class skills: final report,* Leitch Review of Skills (HM Treasury, December 2006).

[2]Alison Wolf, *Review of vocational education: the Wolf report,* Department for Business, Education & Skills and Department for Education (March 2011).

[3]Tony Dolphin and Tess Lanning, *Rethinking Apprenticeships* (November 2011).

[4]Doug Richard, *The Richard Review of Apprenticeships* (November, 2012).

[5]David Sainsbury, *Report of the Independent Panel on Technical Education,* Crown Copyright (2016).

2011/12, their numbers rose from 49 100 to 229 300. Much of this increase was driven by the Government's decision to abolish the Train to Gain programme for adult workers in 2010 and redirect some of the funding into the apprenticeship scheme. In 2015, the Government set itself a target of increasing the number of apprenticeship starts to 3 million by 2020.

The case for reforming provision

There have been four main arguments for reforming the provision of apprenticeships.

The relevance of the training provided. In traditional apprenticeships, employers play a key role in the design of the schemes, which ensures the training is relevant and highly valued. However, publicly-funded apprenticeships have to meet external requirements, such as an Apprenticeship Framework. These set minimum standards detailing both the training and qualifications the employees should receive. The content, design and assessment of most Frameworks were determined by Sector Skills Councils, training providers and qualification bodies. Most employers played a very limited role in the whole process. This often led to the development of skills that were not highly valued by employers.

The level of the training provided. Apprenticeships can be taken at three different levels: *Intermediate* (Level 2, equivalent to 5 GCSEs), *Advanced* (Level 3, equivalent to 2 A Levels) and *Higher* (Levels 4–7, equivalent to undergraduate and postgraduate level). Because the level of government funding available to training providers was partly dependent on key measures of performance, including the proportion of trainees who passed and completed the courses, training providers have an incentive to focus on supplying lower level intermediate apprenticeships: i.e. the qualifications trainees were least likely to fail.

The chart supports this. For much of the period, approximately two thirds of apprenticeship starts were at Intermediate Level with less than 5 per cent at the Higher Level. The situation was to improve. In 2017/18, 43 per cent of starts were at Intermediate Level, 44 per cent at Advanced Level and 13 per cent at the Higher Level.

The short duration of many of the schemes. This was a particular issue during the 2010/12 period, when many were completed in less than a year. In some cases, Intermediate Level apprenticeships lasted less than 12 weeks. They typically last two years in most European countries.

The methods of assessment. Assessment under an Apprenticeship Framework involved the trainee completing numerous qualifications, of a short duration, on a continual basis throughout the programme. There was no end-point assessment to make sure the trainee could pull together all of the skills they had learned and demonstrate the competences required for a skilled job.

Recent reforms

The UK Government has introduced a number of reforms in response to these criticisms.

In October 2013, the 'Trailblazers' initiative was launched. Trailblazers are a self-selecting group of employers within a sector, who work together to determine the content and assessment of new apprenticeship standards. A Trailblazer group must include representatives from at least 10 different businesses with at least 2 that employ fewer than 50 people. Sector Skills Councils, training providers and qualification awarding bodies can be involved with the development of the standards but, unlike the Frameworks, they do not take the leading role.

Building on its Trailblazers initiative, the Government launched the Institute for Apprenticeships in April 2017, which replaced the National Apprenticeship Service as the main administrative body for the programme. It is responsible for supporting the development of new Apprenticeship Standards with Trailblazer groups. Apprenticeship Standards will gradually replace the existing system of Apprenticeship Frameworks by 2020.

Apprenticeships Standards will need to: (a) be in a skilled occupation; (b) require substantial and sustained training, lasting a minimum of 12 months, with at least 20 per cent of the training taking place off-the-job; (c) develop transferable skills, including those in maths and English; (d) lead to full competency in an occupation; and (e) provide training that allows employees to apply for professional recognition where it exists.

As part of the government's strategy to support apprenticeships, the Apprenticeship Levy was introduced from April 2017. This is a payment that large employers have to make into an online service account. It is calculated as 0.5 per cent of that part of the employer's annual wage bill that exceeds £3 million. Employers in England can then then use funds in their apprenticeship accounts to pay for apprenticeship training and assessment with the payment. The amount is aligned to the level of the apprenticeship and hence the equivalent educational level.

Despite the apparent incentive of being able to use the levy for training, many large firms saw it merely as a tax on labour. Smaller firms can claim 90 per cent of training costs from the government. However, they found the system too complex and argued that the government had provided too few courses that they could use for the required 20 per cent of 'off-the-job' training. The net effect was that apprenticeship starts fell sharply, from 494 900 in 2016/17 to 375 800 in 2017/18 (see chart).

The government subsidises course fees for qualifications taken by a trainee as part of an apprenticeship. However, course fees only represent one element of the costs of training a worker. What are the other economic costs?

Research how training taxes/levies operate in at least two other countries. Compare and contrast the schemes with the apprenticeship levy in England.

corporation tax relief. In addition, small firms are subject to fewer planning and other bureaucratic controls than large companies. (Support to small firms in the UK is examined in Case study K.18 on the student website.)

Advice, information and collaboration. The government may engage in discussions with private firms in order to find ways to improve efficiency and innovation. It may bring firms together to exchange information, so as to co-ordinate their decisions and create a climate of greater certainty. It may bring firms and unions together to try to create greater industrial harmony. It can provide various information services to firms: technical assistance, the results of public research, information on markets, etc.

Local Enterprise Partnerships (C) are an example of partnerships created between local government and businesses in England. LEPs began in 2011 and their aim is to promote local economic development. As well as facilitating the flow of information between public and private organisations, LEPs agree on local strategic economic objectives. They can seek funds from central government through 'Local Growth Deals' or co-ordinate the establishment of enterprise zones (see below) to meet these objectives.

31.4 REGIONAL POLICY

Within most countries, unemployment is not evenly distributed. Take the case of the UK. Northern Ireland and parts of the north and west of England, parts of Wales and parts of Scotland have unemployment rates substantially higher than in the south-east of England.

Similarly, countries experience regional disparities in average incomes, rates of growth and levels of prices, as well as in health, crime, housing, etc. In the UK, these disparities grew wider in the mid-1980s as the recession hit the north,

KI 32
p 365

with its traditional heavy industries, much harder than the south. In the recession of the early 1990s, however, it was the service sector that was hardest hit, a sector more concentrated in the south. Regional disparities therefore narrowed somewhat.

Figure 31.4 helps to illustrate more recent disparities in average incomes across the UK. It shows the levels of Gross Value Added (GVA) per head in 2016 for the English regions and the nations of the UK. The figures are known as

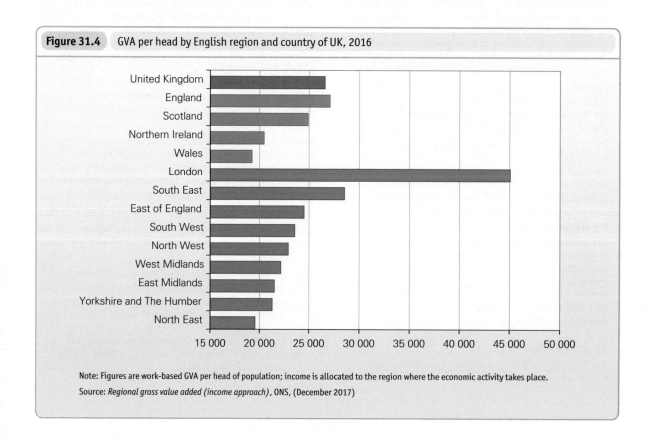

| **Figure 31.4** | GVA per head by English region and country of UK, 2016 |

Note: Figures are work-based GVA per head of population; income is allocated to the region where the economic activity takes place.

Source: *Regional gross value added (income approach)*, ONS, (December 2017)

work-based estimates because they attribute the income to the region or nation in which the income was generated. While the average GVA per head in Wales was only 72 per cent of the UK average, in London it was as high as 169 per cent of the UK average.

> ### Pause for thought
>
> *What potential problems might arise when using work-based estimates of GVA per head in evaluating living standards in a particular geographical area?*

Disparities are not only experienced at regional level. They are often more acutely felt in specific *areas*, especially inner cities and urban localities subject to industrial decline.

Within the European Union, differences exist not only within individual countries, but also between them. For example, in the EU, some countries are much less prosperous than others. Thus, especially with the opening up of the EU in 1993 to the free movement of factors of production, capital and labour may flow to the more prosperous regions of the Union, such as Germany, France and the Benelux countries, and away from the less prosperous regions, such as Portugal, Greece and southern Italy. With the enlargement of the EU since 2004 to include 13 new members, mainly from central and eastern Europe, regional disparities within the EU have widened further.

Causes of regional imbalance and the role of regional policy

If the market functioned perfectly, there would be no regional problem. If wages were lower and unemployment were higher in the north, people would simply move to the south. This would reduce unemployment in the north and help to fill vacancies in the south. It would drive up wage rates in the north and reduce wage rates in the south.

The process would continue until regional disparities were eliminated.

The capital market would function similarly. New investment would be located in the areas offering the highest rate of return. If land and labour were cheaper in the north, capital would be attracted there. This too would help to eliminate regional disparities.

A similar argument applies between countries. Take the case of the EU. Labour should move from the poorer countries, such as those of eastern Europe, to the richer ones and capital should flow in the opposite direction until disparities are eliminated.

In practice, the market does not always behave as just described. There are three major problems.

Labour and capital immobility. Labour may be geographically immobile. The regional pattern of industrial location may change more rapidly than the labour market can adjust to it. Thus jobs may be lost in the depressed areas more rapidly than people can migrate.

Similarly, the existing capital stock is highly immobile. Buildings and most machinery cannot be moved to where the unemployed are! *New* capital is much more mobile. But there may be insufficient new investment, especially during a recession, to halt regional decline, even if some investors are attracted into the depressed areas by low wages and cheap land.

Regional multiplier effects. The continuing shift in demand may, in part, be due to *regional multiplier effects*. In the prosperous regions, the new industries and the new workers attracted there create additional demand. This creates additional output and jobs and hence more migration. There is a multiplied rise in income. In the depressed regions, the decline in demand and loss of jobs causes a multiplied downward effect. Loss of jobs in manufacturing leads to less money spent in the local community; transport and other service industries lose custom. The whole region becomes more depressed.

Externalities. Labour migration imposes external costs on non-migrants. In the prosperous regions, the new arrivals compete for services with those already there. Services become overstretched; house prices rise; council house waiting lists lengthen; roads become more congested, etc. In the depressed regions, services decline or, alternatively, local taxes must rise for those who remain if local services are to be protected. Dereliction, depression and unemployment cause emotional stress for those who remain.

Approaches to regional policy

Market-orientated solutions

Supporters of market-based solutions argue that firms are the best judges of where they should locate. Government intervention would impede efficient decision taking by firms. It is better, they argue, to remove impediments to the market achieving regional and local balance. For example, they favour either or both of the following.

> ### Definition
>
> **Regional multiplier effects** When a change in injections into or withdrawals from a particular region causes a multiplied change in income in that region. The regional multiplier is given by $1/(1 - mpc_r)$, where mpc_r is the marginal propensity to consume products from the region.

Locally negotiated wage agreements. A problem with nationally negotiated wage rates is that that wages are not driven down in the less prosperous areas and up in the more prosperous ones. This discourages firms from locating in the less prosperous areas. At the same time, firms find it difficult to recruit labour in the more prosperous ones, where wages are not high enough to compensate for the higher cost of living there.

Reducing unemployment benefits. A general reduction in unemployment benefits and other welfare payments would encourage the unemployed in the areas of high unemployment to migrate to the more prosperous areas or enable firms to offer lower wages in the areas of high unemployment.

The problem with these policies is that they attempt initially to widen the economic divide between workers in the different areas in order to encourage capital and labour to move. Such policies would hardly be welcomed by workers in the poorer areas!

> ## Pause for thought
>
> 1. Think of some other 'pro-market' solutions to the regional problem.
> 2. Do people in the more prosperous areas benefit from pro-market solutions?

Interventionist solutions

Interventionist policies involve encouraging firms to move. Such policies include the following.

Subsidies and tax concessions in the depressed regions. Businesses could be given general subsidies, such as grants to move or reduced rates of corporation tax. Alternatively, grants or subsidies could be specifically targeted at increasing employment (e.g. reduced employer's National Insurance contributions) or at encouraging investment (e.g. investment grants or other measures to reduce the costs of capital).

The provision of facilities in depressed regions. The government or local authorities could provide facilities such as land and buildings at concessionary, or even zero, rents to incoming firms or spend money on improving the infrastructure of the area (roads and communications, technical colleges, etc.).

The siting of government offices in the depressed regions. The government could move some of its own departments out of the capital and locate them in areas of high unemployment. The siting of the vehicle licensing centre in Swansea is an example.

It is important to distinguish policies that merely seek to *modify* the market by altering market signals from policies that *replace* the market. *Regulation* replaces the market and, unless very carefully devised and monitored, may lead to ill-thought-out decisions being made. *Subsidies* and *taxes* merely modify the market, leaving it to individual firms to make their final location decisions.

Regional policy in England

The focus of the recent approach in England to regional policy has been the development of Enterprise Zones. First established in 2012, these zones are specific geographic locations where firms can benefit from reduced planning restrictions, tax breaks and improved infrastructure, including access to superfast broadband. The number of zones doubled from 24 in 2012 to 48 in 2017.

Many of the Enterprise Zones encourage clustering: businesses in the same sector grouping together. The hope is that they can mutually benefit from external economies of scale (see page 159) such as co-operation and/or the sorts of technological spillovers that we came across in section 31.1.

To benefit from clustering effects, the zones typically focus on specific sectors, such as automotive and transport (e.g. the MIRA technology park near Hinckley, Leicestershire), or renewable energy (e.g. the Humber Enterprise Zone) or science and innovation (e.g. Loughborough and Leicester Enterprise Zone).

The danger of such policies, particularly given the often small geographic area in question, is that they may merely divert investment away from other areas rather than resulting in *additional* investment.

> ## Pause for thought
>
> If you were the government, how would you set about deciding the rate of subsidy to pay a firm thinking of moving to a less prosperous area?

EU regional policy

For the period 2014–20, the EU allocated €352 billion to regional policy – around one-third of its total budget. Its regional policy should be seen in the context of economic and social disparities and its strategy for growth and jobs known as Europe 2020. Prior to the 2007–13 programme, about one-third of EU citizens had a GDP per head below the 'convergence level' of 75 per cent of the EU average. These disparities were to grow with the accession of 13 new members from 2004. Meanwhile, the EU's growth strategy emphasises the need to deliver high levels of employment, productivity and social cohesion.

The 2014–20 programme focuses primarily on the poorest member states and regions of the EU: i.e. those below the convergence level of GDP per head. The amount available for the less developed regions is €182 billion (52 per cent of the €352 billion budget).

In order to allocate its resources and meet its objectives, the EU operates a series of interrelated funds, collectively known as the Structural and Cohesion Funds.

Cohesion Fund (CF). This is aimed at member states whose national income per head is less than 90 per cent of the EU average. Its aim is to support the development of infrastructure projects, particularly trans-European transport networks, and enhance measures that help protect and improve the quality of the environment. For the 2014–20 period, a total of €63.4 billion was allocated to CF spending.

The European Regional Development Fund (ERDF). This fund allocates grants for projects designed to aid development in poorer regions of the EU and thereby correct for 'imbalances' and enhance economic, social and territorial cohesion. It focuses investment under the themes of innovation and research, the digital agenda, support for small and medium-sized enterprises (SMEs) and the low-carbon economy.

The European Social Fund (ESF). The fund is designed to improve education and employment opportunities and to help those people most at risk of poverty. Spending is focused on the themes of promoting employment and supporting labour mobility, promoting social inclusion and combating poverty, investing in education, skills and life-long learning and enhancing institutional capacity and efficient public administration. Over €80 billion was allocated for the 2014–20 period to improve human capital across the EU.

> ## Pause for thought
>
> *To what extent is the EU's regional policy consistent with those theories of long-term growth stressing the importance of innovation and technological progress?*

SUMMARY

1a Effective supply-side initiatives will raise the rate at which the level of potential output grows over time and therefore the rate at which the aggregate supply curve shifts rightwards.

1b Supply-side policies look to influence the quantity and productivity of factors of production. If successful, they will contribute to the growth of labour productivity, which is a key determinant of overall living standards.

1c The UK has had a lower rate of investment than most other industrialised countries. This has contributed to a historically low rate of economic growth and of labour productivity and a growing trade deficit in manufactures.

1c Supply-side policies often have demand-side effects and demand-side policies often have supply-side effects. It is important for governments to take these secondary effects into account when working out their economic strategy.

2a Market-orientated supply-side policies aim to increase the rate of growth of aggregate supply and reduce the rate of unemployment by encouraging private enterprise and the freer play of market forces.

2b Reducing government expenditure as a proportion of GDP is a major element of such policies.

2c Tax cuts can be used to encourage people to work more and more efficiently and to encourage investment. The effects of tax cuts will depend on how people respond to incentives. The substitution effect will result in greater output; the income effect in lower output.

2d Reducing the power of trade unions and a reduction in welfare benefits, especially those related to unemployment, may force workers to accept jobs at lower wages, thereby decreasing equilibrium unemployment.

2e Various policies can be introduced to increase competition. These include privatisation, deregulation, introducing market relationships into the public sector, the Private Finance Initiative and freer international trade and capital movements.

3 Interventionist supply-side policy can take the form of grants for investment and research and development, advice and persuasion, the direct provision of infrastructure and the provision, funding or encouragement of various training schemes.

4a Regional and local disparities arise from a changing pattern of industrial production. With many of the older industries concentrated in certain parts of the country and especially in the inner cities, and with an acceleration in the rate of industrial change, so the gap between rich and poor areas has widened.

4b Regional disparities can, in theory, be corrected by the market, with capital being attracted to areas of low wages and workers being attracted to areas of high wages. In practice, regional disparities persist because of capital and labour immobility and regional multiplier effects.

REVIEW QUESTIONS

1 Define demand-side and supply-side policies. Are there any ways in which such policies are incompatible?

2 What are the key influences on labour productivity? What sort of supply-side policies could be used to affect these in a positive way?

3 Outline the main supply-side policies that have been introduced in the UK since 1979. Does the evidence suggest that they have achieved what they set out to do?

4 What types of tax cuts are likely to create the greatest (a) incentives and (b) disincentives to effort?

5 Compare the relative merits of pro-market and interventionist solutions to regional imbalances.

6 Is the decline of older industries necessarily undesirable?

7 In what ways can interventionist supply-side policy work with the market, rather than against it? What are the arguments for and against such policy?

International economic policy

Business issues covered in this chapter

- How does the level of business activity in one country impact on that in other countries?
- How do international economic and financial interdependencies affect domestic economies?
- How do the major economies of the world seek to co-ordinate their policies and what difficulties arise in the process?
- How did the euro evolve and how effective was the system of exchange rates in Europe that preceded the birth of the euro?
- What are the advantages and disadvantages of the euro for members of the Eurozone and for businesses both inside and outside the Eurozone?
- What threats to the stability of the euro arise from the debt and deficit problems of some member states? What can be done to achieve economic growth while tackling these debt problems?
- How can greater currency stability be achieved, thereby creating a more certain global environment for business?

32.1 GLOBAL INTERDEPENDENCE

We live in an interdependent world. Countries are affected by the economic health of other countries and by their governments' policies. Problems in one part of the world can spread like a contagion to other parts, with perhaps no country immune. This was clearly illustrated by the credit crunch of 2007–8. A crisis that started in the sub-prime market in the USA soon snowballed into a worldwide recession.

There are two major ways in which this process of 'globalisation' affects individual economies. The first is through trade. The second is through financial markets.

Interdependence through trade

So long as nations trade with one another, the domestic economic actions of one nation will have implications for those that trade with it. For example, if the US administration feels that the US economy is growing too fast, it might adopt various contractionary fiscal and monetary measures, such as

higher tax rates or interest rates. US consumers will not only consume fewer domestically produced goods, but also reduce their consumption of imported products. But US imports are other countries' exports. A fall in these other countries' exports will lead to a multiplier effect in these countries. Output and employment will fall.

Changes in aggregate demand in one country thus send ripples throughout the global economy. The process whereby changes in imports into (or exports from) one country affect national income in other countries is known as the *international trade multiplier*.

KI 43 p 575

Definition

International trade multiplier The impact of changing levels of international demand on levels of production and output.

The more open an economy, the more vulnerable it will be to changes in the level of economic activity in the rest of the world. This problem will be particularly acute if a nation is heavily dependent on trade with one other nation (e.g. Canada on the USA) or one other region (e.g. Switzerland on the EU).

Pause for thought

Assume that the US economy expands. What will determine the size of the multiplier effect on other countries?

In Chapter 24, we saw how international trade had been growing as a proportion of countries' national income for many years (see Figure 24.1 on page 466). The ratio of the sum of global exports and imports of goods and services to global GDP, i.e. $(X + M)/Y$, doubled from around 30 per cent in the early 1970s to 60 per cent in 2008. Although, by 2016, the ratio had eased slightly to 56 per cent, this, nonetheless, pointed to a significant long-term increase in global trade flows.

Pause for thought

Are exports likely to continue growing faster than GDP indefinitely? What will determine the outcome?

The growth in the relative importance of trade has increased countries' interdependence and, in turn, their vulnerability to world trade fluctuations, such as the global recession of the late 2000s. World output fell by 2.1 per cent in 2009 (at market exchange rates), while worldwide exports fell by 12 per cent. This was the biggest contraction in global trade since the Second World War.

There is some doubt, however, over world attitudes towards free trade. With the growth in protectionist rhetoric and measures, especially by the Trump administration (see section 24.3), it is possible that world trade may have peaked as a proportion of GDP – at least for the time being.

Financial interdependence

International trade has grown rapidly, but international financial flows have grown much more rapidly. Trillions of dollars are traded daily across the foreign exchanges. Many of the transactions are short-term financial flows, moving to where interest rates are most favourable or to currencies where the exchange rate is likely to appreciate. This again makes countries interdependent.

Financial interdependency impacts not only on financial institutions around the world, but also on national economies. A stark example was the collapse of the sub-prime credit markets in the USA in the late 2000s, which spread like a contagion to cause a global recession. Household debt in many advanced economies, including the UK and USA, had grown markedly as a proportion of household disposable income. Between 1995 and 2007, the stock of debt held by UK households increased from around 100 per cent to 175 per cent of annual disposable income. In the USA, over the same period, the stock of household debt increased from 95 to 145 per cent of annual disposable income.

The growth of domestic credit has been facilitated both by financial deregulation, including the removal of capital controls, and the greater use by financial institutions of wholesale funding. The process of securitisation (see page 564 and Box 28.3), for instance, enabled financial institutions to raise capital from financial investors across the globe in order to provide domestic households with both mortgages and short-term credit. In other words, the aggressive expansion of domestic banks' balance sheets was funded by international financial flows.

Pause for thought

Are the balance sheets of individuals, businesses and governments affected by global interdependencies?

Financial deregulation and innovation have, therefore, created a complex chain of interdependencies between financial institutions, financial systems and economies. But this chain is only as strong as its weakest link. In the financial crisis of the late 2000s, overly aggressive lending practices by banks in one part of the world impacted on financial investors worldwide. As US interest rates rose from 2004 to 2007 (see Figure in Box 27.4), so many US households fell into arrears and, worse still, defaulted on their loans. Thus flows of money to banks (interest and loan repayments) declined. But these flows were the source of the return for global financial investors who had purchased collateralised debt obligations (see page 564). Hence, the new financial order meant the contagion went international.

Global policy response

As a consequence of both trade and financial interdependence, the world economy, like the economy of any individual country, tends to experience periodic fluctuations in economic activity – an *international* business cycle. The implication of this is that countries will tend to share common problems and concerns at the same time.

This can aid the process of international co-operation between countries. For instance, in response to the financial crisis of the late 2000s, world leaders were seriously worried that the whole world would plunge into recession. What was needed was a co-ordinated policy response from governments and central banks. This came in October 2008 when governments in Britain, Europe, North America and other parts of the world injected some $2 trillion of extra capital into banks.

Countries frequently meet in various groupings – from the narrow group of the world's seven richest countries (the G7, which includes the USA, Japan, Germany, the UK, France, Italy and Canada) to broader groups such as the G20, which, in addition to the G7 and other rich countries, also includes larger developing countries, such as China, India, Brazil, Indonesia, Mexico and South Africa.

Today, the G20 is considered to be the principal economic forum. This recognises two important developments. First, there has been a remarkable growth in emerging economies like Brazil, India, China and South Africa, which, along with Russia, are often collectively referred to as BRICS

(see section 24.1). Second, the increasing scale of interdependency through trade and finance typically requires a co-ordinated response from a larger representation of the international community.

Global interdependence also raises questions about the role that international organisations like the World Trade Organization (WTO) (see Chapter 24) and the International Monetary Fund (IMF) should play.

The IMF's remit is to promote global growth and stability to help countries through economic difficulty and to help developing economies achieve macroeconomic stability and reduce poverty. In response to the global economic and financial crisis of the late 2000s, the IMF's budget was substantially increased and it became more actively involved with what were previously defined as 'strong performing economies'.

32.2 INTERNATIONAL HARMONISATION OF ECONOMIC POLICIES

What is of crucial importance is to avoid major exchange rate movements between currencies. The five main underlying causes of exchange rate movements are divergences in *interest rates, growth rates, inflation rates, current account balance of payments and government deficits.* Such movements, which are often amplified by speculation, can play havoc with the profits of importers and exporters.

Table 32.1 shows the variation in these and other related indicators across a sample of advanced countries. These divergences remain considerable and some, such as indicators of the public finances (see section 31.1), were exacerbated by the financial crisis and the subsequent economic downturn.

In trying to generate world economic growth without major currency fluctuations, it is important that there is a **harmonisation** of economic policies between nations. In other words, it is important that all the major countries are pursuing consistent policies aiming at common international goals.

Pause for thought

Referring to Table 32.1, in what respects was there greater convergence between the countries in the period 2000–8 than in the period 2009–17?

But how can policy harmonisation be achieved? As long as there are significant domestic differences between the major economies, there is likely to be conflict, not harmony. For example, if one country, say the USA, is worried about the size of its budget deficit, it may be unwilling to respond to world demands for a stimulus to aggregate demand to pull the world economy out of recession. What is more, speculators, seeing differences between countries, are likely to

exaggerate them by their actions, causing large changes in exchange rates. The G7 countries have, therefore, sought to achieve greater **convergence** of their economies. But, while convergence may be a goal of policy, in practice it has proved elusive.

Because of a lack of convergence, there are serious difficulties in achieving international policy harmonisation:

- Countries' budget deficits and national debt differ substantially as a proportion of their national income. This puts very different pressures on the interest rates necessary to service these debts.
- Harmonising rates of monetary growth or inflation targets would involve letting interest rates fluctuate with the demand for money. Without convergence in the demand for money, interest rate fluctuations could be severe.
- Harmonising interest rates would involve abandoning money, inflation and exchange rate targets (unless interest rate 'harmonisation' meant adjusting interest rates so as to maintain money or inflation targets or a fixed exchange rate).
- Countries have different internal structural relationships. A lack of convergence here means that countries with higher endemic *cost* inflation would require higher

Definitions

International harmonisation of economic policies Where countries attempt to co-ordinate their macroeconomic policies so as to achieve common goals.

Convergence of economies When countries achieve similar levels of growth, inflation, budget deficits as a percentage of GDP, balance of payments, etc.

interest rates and higher unemployment if international inflation rates were to be harmonised, or higher inflation if interest rates were to be harmonised.

■ Countries have different rates of productivity increase (see Box 31.1), product development, investment and market penetration. A lack of convergence here means that the growth in exports (relative to imports) will differ for any given rate of inflation or growth.

■ Countries may be very unwilling to change their domestic policies to fall into line with other countries. They may prefer the other countries to fall into line with them!

If any one of the five – interest rates, growth rates, inflation rates, current account balance of payments or government deficits – could be harmonised across countries, it is likely that the other four would then not be harmonised.

Total convergence and thus total harmonisation may not be possible. Nevertheless, most governments favour some movement in that direction; some is better than none. To achieve this, co-operation is necessary.

Although co-operation is the ideal, in practice, discord often tends to dominate international economic relations. The reason is that governments are normally concerned with the economic interests of other countries only if they coincide with those of their own country. This, however, can create a prisoners' dilemma problem (see section 12.3). With each country looking solely after its own interests, the world economy suffers and everyone is worse off.

| BOX 32.1 | TRADE IMBALANCES IN THE USA AND CHINA |

An illustration of economic and financial interdependencies

In 2016, the USA had a current account deficit of $481 billion – the equivalent of 2.6 per cent of GDP (see the following chart). US current account deficits are not new. Over the 20-year period up to 2016, the US current account deficit has averaged 3.6 per cent of GDP, reaching as high as 5.9 per cent in 2006.

The current account deficit is offset by an equal and opposite capital-plus-financial account surplus, much of which consists of the purchase of US Government bonds and Treasury bills. These massive inflows to the USA are thought to represent some three-quarters of all the savings which the rest of the world invests abroad. These financial inflows have permitted the persistence of sizeable US current account deficits.

To attract such large inflows, it might be expected that US interest rates would have to be high. Yet, for much of the 2000s, they were at historically low levels. Nominal

interest rates from mid-2003 to mid-2004 were a mere 1 per cent and real rates were close to minus 1.5 per cent. Similarly, since the financial crisis of the late 2000s, interest rates have been very low by comparison with other countries. How is it, then, that with such low interest rates, the USA has managed to attract such vast inflows of finance and thereby maintain such a large financial account surplus?

China's appetite for dollars

Several Asian currencies, including the Chinese yuan (or 'renminbi'), were pegged to the dollar and had been running large current account surpluses. For instance, the Chinese current account surplus was running as high as 8 to 9 per cent of GDP during the 2000s (see chart). Instead of letting the yuan appreciate against the dollar, the Chinese Central Bank used the surpluses to buy dollars.

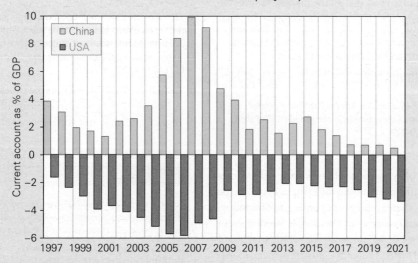

US and Chinese current account (% of GDP)

Note: Figures from 2018 are forecasts
Source: Based on data from *World Economic Outlook Database*, (IMF, October 2018)

32.3 EUROPEAN ECONOMIC AND MONETARY UNION

European economic and monetary union (EMU) involves the complete economic and financial integration of the EU countries. It is not just a common market, but a market with a single currency, a single central bank and a single monetary policy.

The ERM

The forerunner to EMU was the exchange rate mechanism (ERM). This came into existence in March 1979 and the majority of the EU countries were members. The UK, however, chose not to join. Spain joined in 1989, the UK joined in 1990 and Portugal in April 1992. Then, in September 1992, the UK and Italy indefinitely suspended their membership of the ERM, but Italy rejoined in November 1996 as part of its bid to join the single European currency. Austria joined in 1995, Finland in 1996 and Greece in 1998. By the time the ERM was replaced by the single currency in 1999, only Sweden and the UK were outside the ERM.

There were three perceived advantages in doing this:

- First, it allowed China to *build up reserves* and thereby bolster its ability to resist any future speculative attacks on its currency. Chinese foreign exchange reserves rose from around $170 billion in 2000 to $4 trillion in 2014 – a staggering 24-fold increase. The effect was a huge increase in global liquidity and hence money supply.
- Second, and more important, it *kept their exchange rates low* and thereby helped to keep their exports competitive. This helped to sustain their rapid rates of economic growth.
- Third, it helped to *keep US interest rates down* and therefore boost US spending on Asian exports.

In 2005, the Chinese, after much international pressure, agreed to revalue the yuan and would then peg it against a basket of currencies with subsequent further revaluations. Between July 2005 and July 2008, the yuan was allowed to appreciate by around 18 per cent against the US dollar while the exchange rate index rose by 7 per cent (the exchange rate index of the US dollar fell by 15 per cent).

But, with the global economic downturn biting in 2008 and concerns about slowing Chinese export growth, the Chinese authorities effectively fixed the yuan once again.

This remained the case until June 2010 when, again, the yuan was revalued. Between June 2010 and January 2014, the yuan appreciated a further 12 per cent against the US dollar. Therefore, over the period from July 2005 to January 2014, the yuan had appreciated by around 33 per cent against the US dollar.

China's economic slowdown

The managed appreciation of the yuan, coupled with the slowdown of the global economy, saw China's current account surplus begin to wane, falling from 9 per cent of GDP in 2008 to 1.5 per cent by 2013. Meanwhile, though still sizeable, the USA's current account deficit had shrunk. By 2013, the deficit had fallen to 2.1 per cent of GDP – less than half the level of the mid-2000s.

China's economic growth rate, which had been as high as 14 per cent in 2007, had fallen back to around 8 per cent in 2012 and 2013 and to around 7 per cent in 2014 to 2017. This weakening of growth reflected a sharp decline in the growth of China's exports of goods and services. While export volumes grew by 26 per cent per annum from 2002 to 2007, from 2014 to 2016, export growth averaged just 1 per cent per annum and the indication pointed to only a mild recovery (the IMF has forecast an annual export growth of 3.5 per cent from 2019 to 2023).

In late 2014, China's Central Bank began cutting interest rates in response to weaker growth. Then, in August 2015, it took the step to devalue the yuan by 2 per cent against the US dollar. However, this raised concerns of further devaluations and loosening of monetary policy. Hence, the yuan began falling more sharply.

The Central Bank responded by *selling* dollars to curb the depreciation. Despite this, the yuan depreciated by over 6 per cent against the now-rising dollar in 2016 on the back of rising US interest rates. Hence, private capital was now being attracted to the USA, while China was experiencing 'capital flight'. In its efforts to support the yuan, China's stock of foreign exchange reserves is estimated to have fallen by $830 billion during 2015 and 2016 to a little over $3 trillion (a fall of nearly 22 per cent).

The yuan subsequently appreciated against the dollar, rising by around 9 per cent in the 12 months to April 2018. In turn, foreign exchange reserves stabilised before then edging upwards once more.

 Examine the merits for the Chinese of (a) floating the yuan freely; (b) pegging it to a trade-weighted basket of currencies?

 Download from the IMF World Economic Outlook Database the annual percentage change in GDP at constant prices for China, the UK, the USA and Germany. Construct a line chart showing economic growth in these countries across time and then prepare a short note describing what your chart shows.

KI 13
p 75

Table 32.1 International macroeconomic indicators (averages over each period)

		Australia	Canada	France	Germany	Ireland	Japan	Norway	UK	USA
Nominal exchange rate index (annual % change)	2000–08	1.7	3.4	0.9	1.1	1.6	0.0	1.3	−0.8	−1.6
	2009–17	0.6	−1.1	−0.3	−0.3	−0.6	0.9	−1.7	−1.4	2.5
Short-term (3-month) nominal interest rates (%)	2000–08	5.7	3.6	3.4	3.4	3.4	0.3	4.8	5.0	3.5
	2009–17	3.3	1.0	0.4	0.4	0.4	0.2	2.3	0.7	0.5
Economic growth (% change in real GDP)	2000–08	3.3	2.6	1.9	1.6	4.9	1.2	2.2	2.4	2.3
	2009–17	2.6	1.8	0.8	1.2	5.4	0.7	1.2	1.3	1.6
Consumer price inflation (% change in CPI)	2000–08	3.3	2.3	2.1	1.8	3.5	−0.1	3.7	1.8	2.9
	2009–17	2.2	1.5	1.1	1.2	0.1	0.2	2.0	2.2	1.5
Current account balance (% of GDP)	2000–08	−5.0	1.5	1.1	3.1	−2.2	3.2	14.2	−2.7	−4.7
	2009–17	−3.6	−3.1	−1.0	7.1	2.3	2.5	9.3	−4.5	−2.5
Unemployment rate (% of labour force)	2000–08	5.5	6.9	8.5	9.0	4.9	4.6	3.7	5.2	5.1
	2009–17	5.6	7.3	9.8	5.4	12.1	4.0	3.7	3.7	7.1
General government gross debt (% of GDP)	2000–08	13.3	74.0	63.5	62.9	30.4	165.3	40.6	39.2	62.5
	2009–17	30.4	85.4	91.6	74.2	91.2	225.8	34.3	82.4	101.9
General government surplus (% of GDP)	2000–08	0.9	1.0	−2.7	−2.1	−2.1	−5.9	13.8	−2.2	−3.5
	2009–17	−3.4	−2.0	−4.6	−0.6	−8.8	−7.0	9.1	−6.1	−6.9
General government primary surplus (% of GDP)	2000–08	1.0	2.6	−0.2	0.4	1.5	−4.9	11.6	−0.7	−1.5
	2009–17	−2.8	−1.4	−2.5	1.0	−6.3	−6.1	6.9	−4.2	−4.9

Sources: *Stat Extracts*, OECD; *World Economic Outlook database*, IMF; *AMECO database*, European Commission

Features of the ERM

Under the system, each currency was given a central exchange rate with each of the other ERM currencies in a grid. However, fluctuations were allowed from the central rate within specified bands. For most countries, these bands were set at ±2.25 per cent. The central rates could be adjusted from time to time by agreement, thus making the ERM an *adjustable peg* system. All the currencies floated jointly with currencies outside the ERM.

If a currency approached the upper or lower limit against *any* other ERM currency, intervention would take place to maintain the currencies within the band. This would take the form of central banks in the ERM selling the strong currency and buying the weak one. It could also involve the weak currency countries raising interest rates and the strong currency countries lowering them.

The ERM in practice

In a system of pegged exchange rates, countries should harmonise their policies to avoid excessive currency misalignments and hence the need for large devaluations or revaluations. There should be a convergence of their economies: they should be at a similar point on the business cycle and have similar inflation rates and interest rates.

The ERM in the 1980s. In the early 1980s, however, French and Italian inflation rates were persistently higher than German rates. This meant that there had to be several realignments (devaluations and revaluations). After 1983, realignments became less frequent and then, from 1987 to 1992, they ceased altogether. This was due to a growing convergence of members' internal policies.

By the time the UK joined the ERM in 1990, it was generally seen by its existing members as being a great success. It had created a zone of currency stability in a world of highly unstable exchange rates and had provided the necessary environment for the establishment of a truly common market by the end of 1992.

Crisis in the ERM. Shortly after the UK joined the ERM, strains began to show. The reunification of Germany involved considerable reconstruction in the eastern part of the country.

Definition

Adjustable peg A system whereby exchange rates are fixed for a period of time, but may be devalued (or revalued) if a deficit (or surplus) becomes substantial.

Financing this reconstruction was causing a growing budget deficit. The Bundesbank (the German central bank) thus felt obliged to maintain high interest rates in order to keep inflation in check. At the same time, the UK was experiencing a massive current account deficit (partly the result of entering the ERM at what many commentators argued was too high an exchange rate). It was thus obliged to raise interest rates in order to protect the pound, despite the fact that the economy was sliding rapidly into recession. The French franc and Italian lira were also perceived to be overvalued, and there were the first signs of worries as to whether their exchange rates within the ERM could be retained.

At the same time, the US economy was moving into recession and, as a result, US interest rates were cut. This led to a large outflow of capital from the USA. With high German interest rates, much of this capital flowed to Germany. This pushed up the value of the German mark and with it the other ERM currencies.

In September 1992, things reached crisis point. First the lira was devalued. Then two days later, on 'Black Wednesday' (16 September), the UK and Italy were forced to suspend their membership of the ERM: the pound and the lira were floated. At the same time, the Spanish peseta was devalued by 5 per cent.

Turmoil returned in the summer of 1993. The French economy was moving into recession and there were calls for cuts in French interest rates. But this was only possible if Germany was prepared to cut its rates too, and it was not. Speculators began to sell francs and it became obvious that the existing franc/mark parity could not be maintained. In an attempt to rescue the ERM, the EU finance ministers agreed to adopt very wide ±15 per cent bands. The result was that the franc and the Danish krone depreciated against the mark.

Pause for thought

Under what circumstances may a currency bloc like the ERM (a) help to prevent speculation and (b) aggravate the problem of speculation?

A return of calm. The old ERM appeared to be at an end. The new ±15 per cent bands hardly seemed like a 'pegged' system at all. However, the ERM did not die. Within months, the members were again managing to keep fluctuations within a very narrow range (for most of the time, within ±2.25 per cent!). The scene was being set for the abandonment of separate currencies and the adoption of a single currency: the euro.

The Maastricht Treaty and the road to the single currency

Details of the path towards EMU were finalised in the Maastricht Treaty, which was signed in February 1992. The timetable for EMU involved adoption of a single currency by 1999 at the latest.

One of the first moves was to establish a European Monetary Institute (EMI) as a forerunner of the European Central Bank. Its role was to co-ordinate monetary policy and encourage greater co-operation between EU central banks. It also monitored the operation of the ERM and prepared the ground for the establishment of a European central bank in time for the launch of the single currency.

Before they could join the single currency, member states were obliged to achieve convergence of their economies. Each country had to meet five convergence criteria:

- Inflation: should be no more than 1.5 per cent above the average inflation rate of the three countries in the EU with the lowest inflation rates.
- Interest rates: the rate on long-term government bonds should be no more than 2 per cent above the average of the three countries with the lowest inflation rates.
- Budget deficit: should be no more than 3 per cent of GDP.
- General government debt: should be no more than 60 per cent of GDP.
- Exchange rates: the currency should have been within the normal ERM bands for at least two years with no realignments or excessive intervention.

Before the launch of the single currency, the Council of Ministers had to decide which countries had met the convergence criteria and would thus be eligible to form a *currency union* by fixing their currencies permanently to the euro. Their national currencies would effectively disappear.

At the same time, a European System of Central Banks (ESCB) would be created, consisting of a European Central Bank (ECB) and the central banks of the member states. The ECB would be independent, both from governments and from EU political institutions. It would operate the monetary policy on behalf of the countries that had adopted the single currency.

Birth of the euro

In March 1998, the European Commission ruled that 11 of the 15 member states were eligible to proceed to EMU in January 1999. The UK and Denmark were to exercise their opt-out, negotiated at Maastricht, and Sweden and Greece failed to meet one or more of the convergence criteria. (Greece joined the euro in 2001.)

All 11 countries unambiguously met the interest rate and inflation criteria, but doubts were expressed by many 'Eurosceptics' as to whether they all genuinely met the other three criteria.

The euro came into being on 1 January 1999, but euro banknotes and coins were not introduced until 1 January 2002.

Definition

Currency union A group of countries (or regions) using a common currency.

In the meantime, national currencies continued to exist alongside the euro, but at irrevocably fixed rates. The old notes and coins were withdrawn a few weeks after the introduction of euro notes and coins.

In May 2004, ten new members joined the EU, in January 2007 another two and in July 2013 another one. Under the Maastricht Treaty, they should all make preparations for joining the euro by meeting the convergence criteria and being in a new version of the exchange rate mechanism with a wide exchange rate band.

Under ERM II, euro candidate countries must keep their exchange rates within ± 15 per cent of a central rate against the euro. Estonia, Lithuania and Slovenia were the first to join ERM II in June 2004 with Latvia, Cyprus, Malta and Slovakia following in 2005. Slovenia adopted the euro in 2007, Malta and Cyprus in 2008, Slovakia in 2009, Estonia in 2011, Latvia in 2014 and Lithuania in 2015, making a total of 19 countries using the euro.

Advantages of the single currency

EMU has several major advantages for its members.

Elimination of the costs of converting currencies.   With separate currencies in each of the EU countries, costs were incurred each time one currency was exchanged into another. The elimination of these costs, however, was probably the least important benefit from the single currency. The European Commission estimated that the effect was to increase the GDP of the countries concerned by an average of only 0.4 per cent. The gains to countries like the UK, which have well-developed financial markets, would be even smaller.

Increased competition and efficiency.   Despite the advent of the single market, large price differences remained between member states. Not only has the single currency eliminated the need to convert one currency into another (a barrier to competition), but also it has brought more transparency in pricing and has put greater downward pressure on prices in high-cost firms and countries.

Elimination of exchange rate uncertainty (between the members).   Removal of exchange rate uncertainty has helped to encourage trade between the Eurozone countries. Perhaps more importantly, it has encouraged investment by firms that trade between these countries, given the greater certainty in calculating costs and revenues from such trade.

Increased inward investment.   Investment from the rest of the world is attracted to a Eurozone of around 340 million inhabitants, where there is no fear of internal currency movements. By contrast, the UK, by not joining, has found that inward investment has been diverted away to countries within the Eurozone.

Lower inflation and interest rates.   A single monetary policy forces convergence in inflation rates (just as inflation rates are very similar between the different regions within a country). With the ECB being independent from short-term political manipulation, this has resulted in a lower average inflation rate in the Eurozone countries. This, in turn, has helped to convince markets that the euro will be strong relative to other currencies. The result is lower long-term rates of interest. This, in turn, further encourages investment in the Eurozone countries, both by member states and by the rest of the world.

Opposition to EMU

European monetary union has, however, attracted considerable criticism. 'Eurosceptics' see within it a surrender of national political and economic sovereignty. Others, including those more sympathetic to monetary union in principle, raise concerns about the design of the monetary and financial systems within which monetary union operates – a design that, in principle, can be amended (see Boxes 30.3 and 30.5).

We begin with those arguments against EMU in principle.

Arguments against EMU in principle
The lack of national currencies.   This can be a serious problem if an economy is at all out of harmony with the rest of the Eurozone. For example, if countries such as Greece and Spain have lower productivity growth or higher endemic rates of inflation (due, say, to greater cost-push pressures), then how are they to make their goods competitive with the rest of the Eurozone? With separate currencies, these countries could allow their currencies to depreciate. With a single currency, however, they could become depressed 'regions' of Europe, with rising unemployment and all the other regional problems of depressed regions *within* a country.

> ### Pause for thought
>
> *Is greater factor mobility likely to increase or decrease the problem of cumulative causation associated with regional multipliers? (See page 667)*

Proponents of EMU argue that it is better to tackle the problem of high inflation or low productivity in such countries by the discipline of competition from other Eurozone countries, than merely to feed that inflation by keeping separate currencies and allowing periodic depreciations, with all the uncertainty that they bring.

What is more, the high-inflation countries tend to be the poorer ones with lower wage levels (albeit faster wage *increases*). With higher mobility of labour and capital as the single market develops, resources are likely to be attracted to such countries. This could help to narrow the gap between the richer and poorer member states.

The critics of EMU argue that labour is relatively immobile, given cultural and language barriers. Thus an unemployed worker in Cork or Kalamata could not easily move to a job in Turin or Helsinki. What the critics are arguing here is that the EU is not an *optimal currency area* (see Box 32.2).

Loss of separate monetary policies. The second problem identified is that the same central bank rate of interest must apply to all Eurozone countries: the 'one size fits all' criticism. The trouble is that, while some countries might require a lower rate of interest in order to ward off recession (such as Portugal, Ireland and Greece in 2010–11), others might require a higher one to prevent inflation.

The greater the divergence between economies within the Eurozone, the greater this problem becomes. It was hoped, however, that, with common fiscal rules and free trade, these divergences would diminish over time.

Asymmetric shocks. A third and related problem for members of a single currency occurs in adjusting to a shock when

---

Definition

Optimal currency area The optimal size of a currency area is one that maximises the benefits from having a single currency relative to the costs. If the area were to be increased or decreased in size, the costs would rise relative to the benefits.

BOX 32.2   OPTIMAL CURRENCY AREAS

When it pays to pay in the same currency

Imagine that each town and village used a different currency. Think how inconvenient it would be having to keep exchanging one currency into another, and how difficult it would be working out the relative value of items in different parts of the country.

Clearly there are benefits of using a common currency, not only within a country but also across different countries. The benefits include greater transparency in pricing, more open competition, greater certainty for investors and the avoidance of having to pay commission when you change one currency into another. There are also the benefits from having a single monetary policy if that is delivered in a more consistent and effective way than by individual countries.

So why not have a single currency for the whole world? The problem is that the bigger a single currency area gets, the more likely the conditions are to diverge in the different parts of the area. Some parts may have high unemployment and require expansionary policies. Others may have low unemployment and suffer from inflationary pressures. They may require contractionary policies.

What is more, different members of the currency area may experience quite different shocks to their economies, whether from outside the union (e.g. a fall in the price of one of their major exports) or from inside (e.g. a prolonged strike). These 'asymmetric shocks' would imply that different parts of the currency area should adopt different policies. But with a common monetary policy and hence common interest rates, and with no possibility of devaluation/revaluation of the currency of individual members, the scope for separate economic policies is reduced.

The costs of asymmetric shocks (and hence the costs of a single currency area) will be greater, the less the mobility of labour and capital, the less the flexibility of prices and wage rates, and the fewer the alternative policies there are that can be turned to (such as fiscal and regional policies).

So is the Eurozone an optimal currency area? Certainly strong doubts have been raised by many economists.

- Labour is relatively immobile.
- There are structural differences between the member states.
- The transmission effects of interest rate changes are different between the member countries, given that countries have different proportions of consumer debt relative to GDP and different proportions of debt at variable interest rates.
- Exports to countries outside the Eurozone account for different proportions of the members' GDP and thus their economies are affected differently by a change in the rate of exchange of the euro against other currencies.
- Wage rates are relatively inflexible.
- Under the Stability and Growth Pact and the Fiscal Compact (see Box 30.2), the scope for using discretionary fiscal policy is curtailed, except in times of severe economic difficulty (as in 2009).

This does not necessarily mean, however, that the costs of having a single European currency outweigh the benefits. Also, the problems outlined above should decline over time as the single market develops. Finally, the problem of asymmetric shocks can be exaggerated. European economies are highly diversified; there are often more differences within economies than between them. Thus shocks are more likely to affect different industries or localities, rather than whole countries. Changing the exchange rate, if that were still possible, would hardly be an appropriate policy in these circumstances.

Why is a single currency area likely to move towards becoming an optimal currency area over time?

Undertake a literature search on work looking at whether the Eurozone is an optimal currency area. Write a short review of the relevant literature you discover.

that shock affects members to different degrees. These are known as *asymmetric shocks*. For example, the banking crisis affected the UK more severely than other countries, given that London is a global financial centre. The less the factor mobility between member countries and the less the price flexibility within member countries the more serious is this problem.

Even when shocks are uniformly felt in the member states, however, there is still the problem that policies adopted centrally will have different impacts on each country. This is because the transmission mechanisms of economic policy (i.e. the way in which policy changes impact of economic variables like growth and inflation) vary across countries.

Criticisms of the current design of EMU

There are others who are critical of the design of EMU, but who argue that, with appropriate changes, the problems could be significantly reduced.

Monetary policy. In the case of monetary policy, it is argued that the ECB's remit makes it especially inflation-averse. Hence, it will tend to be more 'hawkish' and less proactive in response to economic downturns in the Eurozone, particularly if the downturn is accompanied by a persistence in inflation or by rising rates of inflation.

The hawkishness of the ECB is perhaps evident when comparing its monetary stance with other central banks in the aftermath of the financial crisis (see Box 30.5). Concerned by the above-target consumer price inflation rates that had resulted from the rising rates of global commodity inflation before the financial crisis, the ECB was cautious in relaxing monetary policy. In comparison, central banks such as the US Federal Reserve, the Bank of England and the Bank of Japan were more 'dovish' and aggressively relaxed monetary policy. It was not until late in 2014 that the ECB announced that it would be starting a programme of quantitative easing, around the very time that the Federal Reserve's programme was winding down.

Critics also point to the underlying weakness of a single currency operating alongside separate *national* government debt issues. The greater the divergence of the Eurozone countries, in terms of growth, inflation, deficits, debt and the proportions of debt securities maturing in the short term, the greater this problem becomes.

Fiscal policy. Under the Stability and Growth Pact (SGP) (which applies to the whole EU), countries were supposed to keep public-sector deficits below 3 per cent of GDP and their stocks of debt below 60 per cent of GDP (see Box 30.2). However, the Pact was not rigidly enforced. Furthermore, because the rules allowed for discretion in times of recession, deficits and debt rose sharply in the late 2000s (see Table 30.1 on page 628).

Subsequently, efforts have been made to change the framework within which national governments make their fiscal choices. The result is the Fiscal Compact, signed in March 2012 (see Box 30.2). This reaffirmed the SGP's excessive deficit rules, but added other requirements. For example, Eurozone countries would now be required to ensure that their *structural deficits* (i.e. budget deficits that would exist even if economies were operating at their potential output level) did not exceed 0.5 per cent of GDP and tougher penalties would be imposed on countries breaking the rules.

There are those who argue that for Eurozone members to benefit fully from monetary union tighter fiscal rules alone are insufficient. Instead, they advocate greater fiscal harmonisation. In other words, the problem, they say, is one of incomplete integration.

Future of the euro

When Lithuania adopted the euro on 1 January 2015, it became the nineteenth country to do so. Yet debates around the future of the euro intensified during 2015 as the Greek debt crisis raised the prospect of Greece's exit from the euro (Grexit).

The Greek crisis

The perilous state of Greece's public finances had already seen two international bailouts agreed. These involved the IMF, the European Commission and the ECB – the so-called 'Troika' – and were worth €240 billion. However, these loans were contingent on the Greek Government undertaking a series of economic measures, including significant fiscal tightening. However, the fiscal austerity measures contributed to a deterioration of the macroeconomic environment.

Matters came to a head at the end of 2014 when the final tranches of the Greek bailout programme were suspended by the Troika. This followed the formation in December 2014 of a Syriza-led Greek Government who had fought the election on an anti-austerity platform.

What followed was a drawn-out set of negotiations between Greece and its international creditors. With no agreement on further aid to Greece yet reached, Greece was unable to meet a €1.55 billion repayment to the IMF on 30 June 2015. This made Greece the first developed country to have defaulted on a loan from the IMF.

Definition

Asymmetric shocks Shocks (such as an oil price increase or a recession in another part of the world) that have different-sized effects on different industries, regions or countries.

Meanwhile, conditions for Greek citizens continued to deteriorate. In July, the ECB announced that it would maintain its emergency liquidity assurance for the Greek financial system at levels agreed at the end of June. Without further credit for an already financially-distressed banking system, capital controls were imposed with strict limits on withdrawals from bank accounts.

In August 2015, the Greek Government and its international creditors reached an agreement on the terms of a third bailout worth €85 billion over three years. Further austerity measures continued. These were required in order for the periodic release of funds, but they were to place further strains on an already weak economy.

Concerns continued to grow, however, that the fiscal arithmetic (see Box 30.2) to sustain Greece's current public-sector debt-to-GDP ratio simply did not add up. Larger and larger primary surpluses were needed merely to sustain the current national debt, thereby requiring further fiscal austerity and structural reform. Some, including the IMF, were arguing that only debt relief would ensure the long-term sustainability of Greece's public finances.

For the time being at least, Grexit had been avoided. Nonetheless, it raised important questions about the future of the euro and the conditions under which it would be beneficial for other EU member states to join or for existing members to exit.

The single currency and gains from trade

The benefits from a country being a member of a single currency are greater the more it leads to trade creation with other members of the single currency. Table 32.2 shows for a sample of member states of the European Union (including the UK) the proportion of their exports and imports to and from other member states. From the table, we can see that about two-thirds of trade in the European Union is between member states. However, there are considerable differences in the importance of intra-EU trade for member states.

On the basis of intra-industry trade, countries like Greece and Malta (and the UK, should it have chosen to join when a member of the EU) might appear to have least to gain from being part of a single currency with other EU nations. But, we need to consider other factors too. The theory of optimal currency areas (see Box 32.2) suggests, for example, that the degree of convergence between economies and the flexibility of labour markets are important considerations for countries considering the costs of relinquishing their national currency.

Convergence or divergence?

The more similar economies are, the more likely it is that they will face similar or symmetric shocks that can be accommodated by a common monetary policy. Furthermore, greater wage flexibility and mobility of labour provide mechanisms for countries within a single currency to remain internationally competitive.

Table 32.2	Intra-European Union exports and imports, % of total exports or imports			
	Exports		**Imports**	
	2002–8	2009–17	2002–8	2009–17
EU-28	68.4	64.0	64.9	62.6
Eurozone (19 countries)	68.8	64.0	65.3	62.7
Austria	74.5	70.9	81.0	77.3
Belgium	76.6	71.9	71.9	66.3
France	65.3	60.0	69.0	68.4
Germany	64.4	58.8	64.9	64.8
Greece	64.8	51.9	60.2	51.4
Ireland	63.6	55.9	67.3	66.0
Italy	61.8	55.8	60.1	57.0
Lithuania	64.9	59.8	60.7	62.8
Malta	47.8	44.2	72.4	68.3
Netherlands	79.6	76.2	51.2	46.6
Portugal	79.0	73.3	77.5	75.2
Slovakia	87.4	84.9	75.4	75.9
Spain	72.7	66.0	65.0	58.6
UK	58.9	48.8	55.3	50.6

Source: Based on data from *AMECO database,* (European Commission, DGECFIN)

However, there remain considerable differences in the macroeconomic performance of Eurozone countries, reflecting continuing differences in the structures of their economies. Some of these were exacerbated by the financial crisis of the late 2000s and the subsequent deterioration of the macroeconomic environment.

Among the differences is the contrasting trade positions of Eurozone economies. This is illustrated in Figure 32.1, which shows the current account balances of selected Eurozone economies since 2000. In the period 2000 to 2008 Greece, Spain and Portugal ran large current account deficits averaging 11, 6 and 4 per cent of GDP respectively. By contrast, Germany ran a current account surplus of around 3 per cent of its GDP. In more recent years, however, the divergences in current account balances has narrowed.

In the absence of nominal exchange rate adjustments, countries like Greece and Spain looking to a fall in the *real* exchange rate to boost competitiveness need to have relatively lower rates of price inflation. Therefore, in a single currency, productivity growth and wage inflation take on even greater importance in determining a country's competitiveness. The competitive position of countries will deteriorate if wage growth *exceeds* productivity growth. If this happens, unit labour costs (labour costs per unit of output) will increase.

Figure 32.2 shows how, in the period from 2000 to 2008, labour costs increased at an average of between 3 and 4 per cent per annum in Greece, Spain and Italy compared

Figure 32.1   Current account balance of selected Eurozone economies

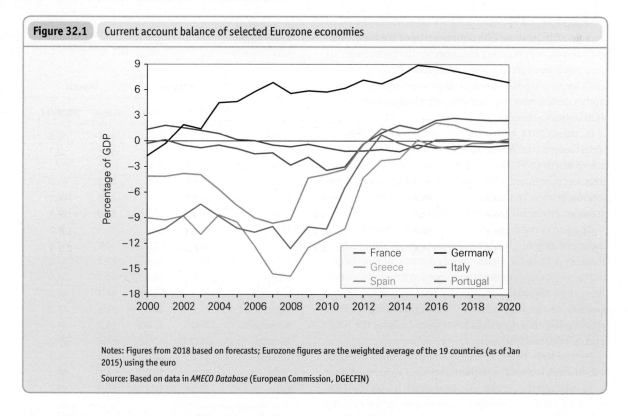

Notes: Figures from 2018 based on forecasts; Eurozone figures are the weighted average of the 19 countries (as of Jan 2015) using the euro

Source: Based on data in *AMECO Database* (European Commission, DGECFIN)

with close to zero in Germany. This, other things being equal, put these countries at a competitive disadvantage.

The fiscal framework

The discussion so far highlights the importance of economic convergence in affecting the benefits and costs of being a member of the euro. Fiscal policy can provide some buffer

against asymmetric shocks by enabling transfers of income to those areas experiencing lower rates of economic growth. Therefore, the fiscal framework within which the euro operates is important when considering the future of the euro.

To date, the Eurozone has resisted a centralisation of national budgets. In a more centralised (or federal) system, we would see automatic income transfers between different

Figure 32.2   Growth in unit labour costs of selected Eurozone economies

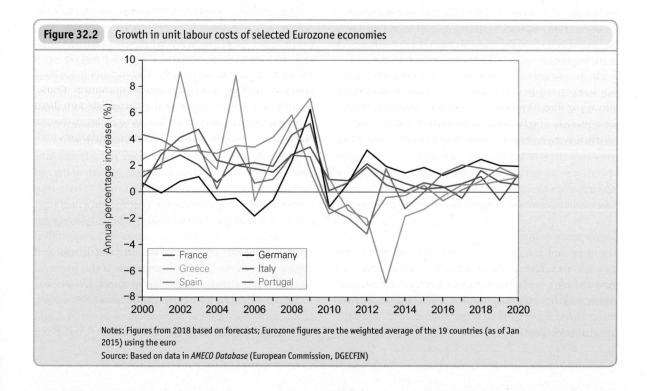

Notes: Figures from 2018 based on forecasts; Eurozone figures are the weighted average of the 19 countries (as of Jan 2015) using the euro

Source: Based on data in *AMECO Database* (European Commission, DGECFIN)

Table 32.3	Fiscal indicators in selected Eurozone economies				
	General government debt-to-GDP (%)		**2010–17 averages**		
	2010	**2017**	**Primary surplus-to-GDP (%)**	**Real short-term interest rates (%)**	**Economic growth (% p.a.)**
Eurozone	84.8	88.8	−1.0	−0.4	0.8
Belgium	99.7	103.1	−0.4	−1.1	1.1
France	85.1	97.0	−2.5	−0.4	1.0
Germany	80.9	64.1	1.4	−0.8	1.9
Greece	146.2	178.6	−4.0	1.3	−3.9
Ireland	86.1	68.0	−8.9	0.1	1.8
Italy	115.4	131.8	1.4	−0.4	−0.3
Lithuania	36.2	39.7	−2.7	−1.4	3.4
Malta	67.5	50.8	0.2	−1.7	3.0
Portugal	96.2	125.7	−2.3	0.0	−0.5
Spain	60.1	98.3	−5.6	0.5	0.0
UK	75.6	87.7	−2.9	−1.0	2.0

Source: *AMECO database* (European Commission, DGECFIN)

regions and countries. A country, say Greece, affected by a negative economic shock, would pay less tax revenues and receive more expenditures from a central Eurozone budget, while in a country, say Germany, experiencing a positive shock the opposite would be the case.

Since national budgets in the Eurozone remain largely decentralised, fiscal transfers principally take place *within* countries rather than between them. But this severely limits the use of fiscal policy to offset the effects of negative economic shocks in countries that already have large public-sector deficits and high debt-to-GDP ratios.

To provide maximum flexibility to use fiscal policy, it is important for countries to reduce the stock of public-sector debt as a percentage of annual GDP in times when the economy is growing. As we saw in Chapter 30 (page 629; see also Case Study K.1 on the student website), it will be easier to reduce this percentage if the economy runs a primary surplus. This is when public-sector receipts are greater than public-sector expenditures *excluding* interest payments: the bigger the surplus, the quicker the debt-to-GDP ratio can be reduced. Also, the faster the rate of economic growth and the lower the real rate of interest, the quicker the ratio can be reduced.[1]

Table 32.3 shows the public-sector debt-to-GDP ratios in a sample of Eurozone economies in 2010 and 2017 (and the UK) alongside the factors that affect the path of the ratio. The table illustrates considerable differences between countries in the state of their public finances. Therefore, where fiscal policy is left to individual countries, countries with an already high debt-to-GDP ratio, such as Greece, Italy and Portugal, will find it considerably more difficult to use fiscal policy to offset the effects of economic slowdowns. Consequently, the sustainability of the current decentralised approach to fiscal policy in the Eurozone is likely to be crucial in determining the future for the euro and those countries using the euro.

32.4 ALTERNATIVE POLICIES FOR ACHIEVING CURRENCY STABILITY

One important lesson of recent years is that concerted speculation has become virtually unstoppable. This was made clear by the expulsion of the UK and Italy from the ERM in 1992, the dramatic fall of the Mexican peso and rise of the yen in 1995, the collapse of various south-east Asian currencies and the Russian rouble in 1997–8, the collapse of the Argentine peso in 2002, the fall in the pound in 2008 and the fall in the euro in 2010 and 2014–5. In comparison with the vast amounts of short-term finance flowing across the foreign exchanges each day, the reserves of central banks seem trivial.

If there is a consensus in the markets that a currency will depreciate, there is little that central banks can do. For example,

---

[1]As a rule-of-thumb, the primary surplus-to-GDP ratio required to maintain a given public-sector debt to GDP ratio can be calculated by multiplying the existing debt-to-GDP ratio by the sum of the real rate of interest minus the rate of economic growth (see Box 30.1).

if there were a 50 per cent chance of a 10 per cent depreciation in the next week, then selling that currency now would yield an 'expected' return of just over 5 per cent for the week (i.e. 50 per cent of 10 per cent): equivalent to 1200 per cent at an annual rate!

For this reason, many commentators have argued that there are only two types of exchange rate system that can work over the long term. The first is a completely free-floating exchange rate, with no attempt by the central bank to support the exchange rate. With no intervention, there is no problem of a shortage of reserves!

The second is to share a common currency with other countries: to join a common currency area, such as the Eurozone, and let the common currency float freely. The country would give up independence in its monetary policy, but at least there would be no problem of exchange rate instability within the currency area. A similar alternative is to adopt a major currency of another country, such as the US dollar or the euro. Many smaller states have done this. For example, Kosovo and Montenegro have adopted the euro and Ecuador has adopted the US dollar.

An attempt by a country to peg its exchange rate is likely to have one of two unfortunate consequences. Either it will end in failure as the country succumbs to a speculative attack or the country's monetary policy will have to be totally dedicated to maintaining the exchange rate.

So is there any way of 'beating the speculators' and pursuing a policy of greater exchange rate rigidity without establishing a single currency? Or must countries be forced to accept freely floating exchange rates, with all the uncertainty for traders that such a regime brings?

We shall examine two possible solutions. The first is to reduce international financial mobility, by putting various types of restriction on foreign exchange transactions. The second is to move to a new type of exchange rate regime, which offers the benefits of a degree of rigidity without being susceptible to massive speculative attacks.

Controlling exchange transactions

Until the early 1990s, many countries retained restrictions of various kinds on financial flows. Such restrictions made it more expensive for speculators to gamble on possible exchange rate movements. It is not the case, as some commentators argue, that it is impossible to reimpose controls. Indeed, Malaysia did just that in 1998 when the ringgit was under speculative attack. Many countries in the developing world still retain controls, and the last ERM countries to give them up only did so in 1991. It is true that the complexity of modern financial markets provides the speculator with more opportunity to evade controls, but they will still have the effect of dampening speculation.

In September 1998, the IMF said that controls on inward movements of capital could be a useful tool, especially for countries that were more vulnerable to speculative attack. In its 1998 annual report, it argued that the Asian crisis of 1997–98 was the result not only of a weak banking system, but also of open capital accounts, allowing massive withdrawals of funds.

> **Pause for thought**
>
> *Before you read on, see if you can identify (a) the ways exchange transactions might be controlled; (b) the difficulties in using such policy.*

The aim of capital controls is not to prevent capital flows. After all, capital flows are an important source of financing investment. Also, if capital moves from countries with a lower marginal productivity of capital to countries where it is higher, this will lead to an efficient allocation of world savings. The aim of capital controls must therefore be to prevent *speculative* flows that are based on rumour or herd instinct rather than on economic fundamentals.

Types of control

In what ways can movements of short-term capital be controlled? There are various alternatives, each one with strengths and drawbacks.

Quantitative controls. Here the authorities would restrict the amount of foreign exchange dealing that could take place. Perhaps financial institutions would be allowed to exchange only a certain percentage of their assets. Developed countries and most developing countries have rejected this approach, however, since it is seen to be far too anti-market.

For example, the general principle of the free movement of capital is central to the Single Market of the European Union. The principle of the free movement of capital is defined in Article 63 of the Treaty on the Functioning of the European Union (TFEU). However, Article 66 allows 'safeguard measures' to be taken if 'in exceptional circumstances, movements of capital to or from third countries cause, or threaten to cause, serious difficulties for the operation of economic and monetary union'. Such measures could extend 'for a period not exceeding six months if such measures are strictly necessary'.

A Tobin tax. This is named after James Tobin, who, in 1972, advocated the imposition of a small tax of 0.1 to 0.5 per cent on all foreign exchange transactions or on just capital account transactions.[2] This would discourage destabilising speculation (by making it more expensive) and would thus impose some 'friction' in foreign exchange markets, making them less volatile. Such taxes (dubbed 'Robin Hood' taxes) have been advocated by a number of prominent people, such as Bill Gates and the Archbishop of Canterbury.

In November 2001. the French National Assembly became the first national legislature to incorporate into law

---

[2] Tobin, 'A proposal for international monetary reform', *Eastern Economic Journal*, Vol. 4, No. 3–4, 1978, pp. 153–9.

a Tobin tax of up to 0.1 per cent. Belgium followed in 2002. The EU finance ministers ordered the European Commission to undertake a feasibility study of such a tax. In late 2001, the charity War on Want declared that 13 March 2002 would be international 'Tobin tax day'. Ironically, Tobin died on 11 March 2002. Then, in October 2012, 11 of the then 17 Eurozone countries agreed to adopt a Tobin tax or 'financial transactions tax' (FTT) of 0.1 per cent on trading in bonds and shares and 0.01 per cent on trading in derivatives. However, the implementation of the tax was subsequently delayed as countries struggled to agree on the details of the tax, including the instruments that should be covered, the rates of the tax and the distribution of revenues.

Box 32.3 considers the arguments in more detail for and against Tobin taxes and the European financial transactions tax in particular.

Non-interest-bearing deposits. Here a certain percentage of inflows of finance would have to be deposited with the central bank in a non-interest-bearing account for a set period of time. Chile, in the late 1990s, used such a system. It required that 30 per cent of all inflows be deposited with Chile's central bank for a year. This clearly amounted to a considerable tax (i.e. in terms of interest sacrificed) and had the effect of discouraging short-term speculative flows. The problem was that it meant that interest rates in Chile had to be higher in order to attract finance.

One objection to all these measures is that they are likely only to dampen speculation, not eliminate it. If speculators believe that currencies are badly out of equilibrium and will be forced to realign, then no taxes on capital movements or artificial controls will be sufficient to stem the flood.

There are two replies to this objection. The first is that if currencies are badly out of line then exchange rates *should* be adjusted. The second is that *dampening* speculation is probably the ideal. Speculation *can* play the valuable role of bringing exchange rates to their long-term equilibrium more quickly. Controls are unlikely to prevent this aspect of speculation: adjustments to economic fundamentals. If they help to lessen the wilder forms of destabilising speculation, so much the better.

Exchange rate target zones

One type of exchange rate regime that has been much discussed in recent years is that proposed by John Williamson, of Washington's Peterson Institute for International Economics.[3] Williamson advocates a form of 'crawling peg' within broad bands. This system would involve a pegged central rate, where fluctuations around that rate would be allowed within bands (i.e. like the ERM). Unlike the ERM, however, the central value could be adjusted frequently, but only by small amounts: hence the term 'crawling'.

The system would have four major features:

- Wide bands. For example, currencies could be allowed to fluctuate by 10 per cent of their central parity.
- Central parity set in *real* terms, at the 'fundamental equilibrium exchange rate' (FEER): i.e. a rate that is consistent with long-run balance of payments equilibrium.
- Frequent realignments. In order to stay at the FEER, the central parity would be adjusted frequently (e.g. monthly) to take account of the country's rate of inflation. If its rate of inflation were 2 per cent per annum above the trade-weighted average of other countries, then the central parity would be devalued by 2 per cent per annum. Realignments would also reflect other changes in fundamentals, such as changes in the levels of protection or major political events, such as German reunification.
- 'Soft buffers'. Governments would not be forced to intervene at the 10 per cent mark or at some specified fraction of it. In fact, from time to time, the rate might be allowed to move outside the bands. The point is that the closer the rate approached the band limits, the greater would be the scale of intervention.

This system has two main advantages. First, the exchange rate would stay at roughly the equilibrium level and, therefore, the likelihood of large-scale devaluation or revaluation and, with it, the opportunities for large-scale speculative gains would be small. The reason why the narrow-banded ERM broke down in 1992 and 1993 was that the central parities were *not* equilibrium rates.

Second, the wider bands would leave countries freer to follow an independent monetary policy: one that could, therefore, respond to domestic needs.

The main problem with the system is that it may not allow an independent monetary policy. If the rate of exchange has to be maintained within the zone, then monetary policy may sometimes have to be used for that purpose rather than controlling inflation.

Nevertheless, crawling bands have been used relatively successfully by various countries, such as Chile and Israel over quite long periods of time. What is more, in 1999, Germany's finance minister at the time, Oskar Lafontaine, argued that they might be appropriate for the euro relative to the dollar and yen. A world with three major currencies, each changing gently against the other two in an orderly way, has a lot to commend it.

Pause for thought

Would the Williamson system allow countries to follow a totally independent monetary policy?

---

[3] See, for example, J. Williamson and M. Miller, 'Targets and indicators: a blueprint for the co-ordination of economic policy', *Policy Analyses in International Economics*, No. 22 (IIE, 1987).

BOX 32.3	THE TOBIN TAX

Adding a bit of friction

In the mid-1980s, the daily turnover in the world's foreign exchange markets was approximately $150 billion. By 2013, it had risen to a truly massive $5.3 trillion. But only some 5 per cent of this is used for trade in goods and services.

With the massive growth in speculative flows, it is hardly surprising that this can cause great currency instability and financial crises at times of economic uncertainty. Global financial markets have often been decisive in both triggering and intensifying economic crises. The ERM crisis in 1992, the Mexican peso crisis in 1994, the South East Asian crisis in 1997, the Russian rouble meltdown in 1998, the crisis in Argentina in 2001–2 and the currency instability of 2008–9 in the wake of the credit crunch are the most significant in a long list.

The main issue is one of volatility of exchange rates. If currency markets responded to shifts in economic fundamentals, then currency volatility would not be so bad. However, it is increasingly the case that vast quantities of money flow around the global economy purely speculatively, with the herd instinct often driving speculative waves. Invariably, given the volume of speculative flows, exchange rates overshoot their natural equilibrium, intensifying the distortions created. Such currency movements are a huge destabilising force, not just for individual economies, but for the global economy as a whole.

So is there anything countries can do to reduce destabilising speculation? One suggestion is the introduction of a Tobin tax.

The Tobin tax

Writing in 1972, James Tobin proposed a system for reducing exchange rate volatility without fundamentally impeding the operation of the market. This involved the imposition of an international tax of some 0.1 to 0.5 per cent payable on all spot or cash exchange rate transactions. He argued that this would make currency trading costlier and would, therefore, reduce the volume of destabilising short-term financial flows, which would, invariably, lead to greater exchange rate stability.

Tobin's original proposal suggested that the tax rate would need to be very low so as not to affect 'normal business'. Even if it was very low, speculators working on small margins would be dissuaded from regular movements of money, given that the tax would need to be paid per transaction. If a tax rate of 0.2 per cent was set, speculators who moved a sum of money once a day would face a yearly tax bill of approximately 50 per cent. An investor working on a weekly movement of money would pay tax of 10 per cent per annum, and a monthly movement of currency would represent a tax of 2.4 per cent for the year. Given that 40 per cent of currency transactions have only a two-day time horizon, and 80 per cent a time horizon of fewer than seven days, such a tax would clearly operate to dampen speculative currency movements.

In addition to moderating volatility and speculation, the Tobin tax might yield other benefits. It would, in the face of globalisation, restore to the nation state an element of control over monetary policy. In the face of declining governance over international forces, this might be seen as a positive advantage of the Tobin proposals.

The tax could also generate significant revenue. Estimates range from $150 to $300 billion annually. Many of the world's leading pressure groups, such as War on Want and Stamp out Poverty, have argued that the revenue from such an international tax could be used to tackle international problems, such as world poverty and environmental degradation. The World Bank estimates that some $225 billion is needed to eliminate the world's worst forms of poverty. The revenue from a Tobin tax would, in a relatively short period of time, easily exceed this amount. Even with a worldwide rate as low as 0.005 per cent (the rate recommended by Stamp out Poverty), the tax could still raise some $50 billion per year.

Problems with the Tobin tax

How far would a tax on currency transactions restrict speculative movements of money? The issue here concerns the rate of return investors might get from moving their money. If a currency was to devalue by as little as 3 to 4 per cent, a Tobin tax of 0.2 per cent would do little to deter a speculative transaction based upon such a potential return. Given devaluations of 50 per cent in Thailand and Indonesia following the 1997 crash and an 82 per cent appreciation of the euro against the dollar from 2002 to 2008, along with severe short-term-fluctuations, a 3 to 4 per cent movement in the currency appears rather modest. Raising the rate of the Tobin tax would be no solution, as it would begin to impinge upon 'normal business'.

One response to such a situation has been proposed by a German economist, Paul Bernd Spahn. He suggests that a two-tier system is used. On a day-to-day basis, a minimal tax rate, as originally envisaged by Tobin, is charged against each transaction conducted. However, during periods when exchange rates are highly unstable, a tax surcharge is levied. This would be at a far higher rate and would be triggered only once a currency moved beyond some predetermined band of exchange rate variation.

A further problem identified with the Tobin tax concerns the costs of its administration. However, given interlinked computer systems and the progressive centralisation of foreign exchange markets, in terms of marketplaces, traders and currencies, effective administration is becoming easier. Most foreign exchange markets are well monitored already and extending such monitoring to include overseeing tax collection would not be overly problematic.

Another problem is tax avoidance. For example, the Tobin tax is a tax payable on spot exchange rate transactions. This could encourage people to deal more in futures. Foreign exchange futures are a type of 'derivative' that allows people to trade currencies in the future at a price agreed today. These would be far more difficult to monitor, since no currency is exchanged today, and hence more difficult to tax. One solution would be to apply a tax on a notional value of a derivative contract. However, derivatives are an important way through which businesses hedge against future risk. Taxing them might seriously erode their use to a business and damage the derivatives market, making business riskier.

Even with avoidance, however, supporters of the Tobin tax argue that it is still likely to be successful. The main problem is one of political will. Several major economies, including the UK and USA, have consistently been opposed to it.

Financial transactions tax (FTT)

In 2009, Adair Turner, chairman of the Financial Services Authority, the UK's financial sector regulator at the time, proposed the possible use of Tobin taxes to curb destabilising financial transactions. This was met with criticism from many bankers that the tax would be unworkable at a global level and, if applied solely to the UK, would divert financial business away from London.

Despite international opinion on the imposition of a financial transactions tax remaining divided, the European Commission favours a FTT. In February 2013, the European Commission tabled a proposal for a Directive. The proposals were broadly supported by 11 countries – France, Germany, Austria, Belgium, Estonia, Greece, Italy, Portugal, Slovakia, Slovenia and Spain.

With a rate of 0.1 per cent on trading in bonds and shares and 0.01 per cent on trading in derivatives, the tax is designed to be too small to affect trading in shares or other financial products for purposes of long-term investment. It would, however, dampen speculative trades that take advantage of tiny potential gains from very short-term price movements.

Such trades account for huge financial flows between financial institutions around the world and tend to make markets more volatile. The short-term dealers are known as high-frequency traders (HFTs) and their activities now account for the majority of trading on exchanges. Most of these trades are by computers programmed to seek out minute gains and respond in milliseconds. And, while they add to short-term liquidity for much of the time, this liquidity can suddenly dry up if HFTs become pessimistic.

Supporters of the tax claim that, as well as bringing greater stability to the financial sector, it would make a major contribution to tackling the deficit problems of many Eurozone countries. The Commission estimated that revenues would be around €30 billion to €35 billion or 0.4 to 0.5 per cent of the GDP of the participating member states.

The implementation of the FTT was subsequently delayed. This was partly as a result of legal challenges instigated by the UK (before the country's vote to leave the European Union), but also because its proponents struggled to agree on the details of the tax. This led Estonia in December 2015 to declare that it would no longer be one of the countries introducing the tax. While there remained a general commitment to the FTT the timetable for its introduction continued to slip.

George Soros, multi-millionaire currency speculator, has referred to global capital markets as being like a wrecking ball rather than a pendulum, suggesting that such markets are becoming so volatile that they are damaging to all concerned, including speculators. What might lead Soros to such an observation?

Write a short report discussing the following motion: it would be in the interests of the UK to adopt a financial transactions tax if at least ten EU countries do.

SUMMARY

1a The more open the world economy, the more effect changes in economic conditions in one part of the world economy will have on world economic performance.

1b Changes in aggregate demand in one country will affect the amount of imports purchased and thus the amount of exports sold by other countries and hence their GDP. There is thus an international trade multiplier effect.

1c The world is also financially interdependent, with huge flows of finance flowing from one country to another. This makes all countries susceptible to financial shocks, such as the credit crunch of 2007–9.

1d To prevent problems in one country spilling over to other countries and to stabilise the international business cycle requires co-ordinated policies between nations and the intervention of various international agencies, such as the IMF.

2a Currency fluctuations can be lessened if countries harmonise their economic policies. Ideally, this will involve achieving common growth rates, inflation rates, balance of payments and government deficits (as a percentage of GDP) and interest rates. The attempt to harmonise one of these goals, however, may bring conflicts with one of the other goals.

2b Leaders of the G7 and G20 countries meet regularly to discuss ways of harmonising their policies. Usually, however, domestic issues are more important to the leaders than international ones and frequently they pursue policies that are not in the interests of the other countries.

3a One means of achieving greater currency stability is for a group of countries to peg their internal exchange rates and yet float jointly with the rest of the world. The exchange rate mechanism of the EU (ERM) was an example. Members' currencies were allowed to fluctuate against other member currencies within a band. The band was ± 2.25 per cent for the majority of the ERM countries until 1993.

3b The need for realignments seemed to have diminished in the late 1980s as greater convergence was achieved between the members' economies. Growing strains in the system, however, in the early 1990s, led to a crisis in September 1992. The UK and Italy left the ERM. There was a further crisis in July 1993 and the bands were widened to ± 15 per cent.

3c Thereafter, as convergence of the economies of ERM members increased, fluctuations decreased and remained largely within ± 2.25 per cent.

3d The ERM was seen as an important first stage on the road to complete economic and monetary union (EMU) in the EU.

3e The Maastricht Treaty set out a timetable for achieving EMU. This would culminate with the creation of a currency union: a single European currency with a common monetary policy operated by an independent European Central Bank.

3f The euro was born on 1 January 1999. Twelve countries adopted it, having at least nominally met the Maastricht convergence criteria. Euro notes and coins were introduced on 1 January 2002, with the notes and coins of the old currencies withdrawn a few weeks later.

3g The advantages claimed for EMU are that it eliminates the costs of converting currencies and the uncertainties associated with possible changes in former inter-EU exchange rates. This encourages more investment, both inward and by domestic firms. What is more, a common central bank, independent from domestic governments, will provide the stable monetary environment necessary for a convergence of the EU economies and the encouragement of investment and inter-Union trade.

3h Critics claim, however, that it might make adjustment to domestic economic problems more difficult. The loss of independence in policy making is seen by such people to be a major issue, not only because of the loss of political sovereignty, but also because domestic economic concerns may be at variance with those of the Union as a whole. A single monetary policy is claimed to be inappropriate for dealing with asymmetric shocks. What is more, countries and regions at the periphery of the Union may become depressed unless there is an effective regional policy.

3i The Greek sovereign debt crisis raised concerns about the future of the euro. Considerable differences remain in key macroeconomic indicators. These include differences in the growth of labour productivity and unit labour costs, which are especially significant in the absence of nominal exchange-rate adjustments between member countries.

3j There are also considerable differences in the financial health of the public finances of Eurozone governments. This is important because it affects the ability of national governments to use fiscal policy to absorb the adverse economic effects of negative shocks.

4a Many economists argue that, with the huge flows of short-term finance across the foreign exchanges, governments are forced to adopt one of two extreme forms of exchange rate regime: free floating or being a member of a currency union.

4b If financial flows could be constrained, however, exchange rates could be stabilised somewhat.

4c Forms of control include: quantitative controls, a tax on exchange transactions (a Tobin tax) and non-interest-bearing deposits of a certain percentage of capital inflows with the central bank. Such controls can dampen speculation, but may discourage capital flowing to where it has a higher marginal productivity.

4d An alternative means of stabilising exchange rates is to have exchange rate target zones. Here exchange rates are allowed to fluctuate within broad bands around a central parity which is adjusted to the fundamental equilibrium rate in a gradual fashion.

4e The advantage of this system is that, by keeping the exchange rate at roughly its equilibrium level, destabilising speculation is avoided and, yet, there is some freedom for governments to pursue an independent monetary policy. Monetary policy, however, may still, from time to time, have to be used to keep the exchange rate within the bands.

REVIEW QUESTIONS

1 What are the implications for a country attempting to manage its domestic economy if it is subject to an international business cycle? How might it attempt to overcome such problems?

2 What are the economic (as opposed to political) difficulties in achieving an international harmonisation of economic policies so as to avoid damaging currency fluctuations?

3 To what extent can international negotiations over economic policy be seen as a game of strategy? Are there any parallels between the behaviour of countries and the behaviour of oligopolies?

4 What are the causes of exchange rate volatility? Have these problems become greater or lesser in the last 10 years? Explain why.

5 Why did the ERM with narrow bands collapse in 1993? Could this have been avoided?

6 Did the exchange rate difficulties experienced by countries under the ERM strengthen or weaken the arguments for progressing to a single European currency?

7 By what means would a depressed country in an economic union with a single currency be able to recover? Would the market provide a satisfactory solution or would (union) government intervention be necessary? If so, what form would the intervention take?

8 Is the Eurozone likely to be an optimal currency area now? Is it more or less likely to be so over time? Explain your answer.

9 Assume that just some of the members of a common market like the EU adopt full economic and monetary union, including a common currency. What are the advantages and disadvantages to those members joining the full EMU and to those not joining?

10 Assess the difficulties in attempting to control exchange transactions. Might such a policy restrict the level of trade?

11 Would the Williamson system allow countries to follow a totally independent monetary policy?

12 If the euro were in a crawling peg system against the dollar, what implications would this have for the ECB in sticking to its inflation target of no more than 2 per cent?

ADDITIONAL PART K CASE STUDIES ON THE *ECONOMICS FOR BUSINESS* STUDENT WEBSITE (www.pearsoned.co.uk/sloman)

K.1 **Sustainable public finances.** This examines the necessary conditions for achieving a stable or declining public-sector debt to GDP ratio.

K.2 **Banks, taxes and the fiscal costs of the financial crisis.** A discussion of the government's financial interventions during the financial crisis and their impact on the public finances.

K.3 **The national debt.** This explores the question of whether it matters if a country has a high national debt.

K.4 **Trends in public expenditure.** This case examines attempts to control public expenditure in the UK and relates them to the crowding-out debate.

K.5 **The crowding-out effect.** The circumstances in which an increase in public expenditure can replace private expenditure.

K.6 **Any more G and T?** Did the Code for Fiscal Stability mean that the UK Government balanced its books? An examination of the evidence.

K.7 **Discretionary fiscal policy in Japan.** How the Japanese Government used fiscal policy on various occasions throughout the 1990s and early 2000s in an attempt to bring the economy out of recession.

K.8 **Central banking and monetary policy in the USA.** This case examines how the Fed conducts monetary policy.

K.9 **Goodhart's Law.** An examination of Key Idea 44.

K.10 **Should central banks be independent of government?** An examination of the arguments for and against independent central banks.

K.11 **Monetary targeting: its use around the world.** An expanded version of Box 30.4.

K.12 **Interest rate responses and the financial crisis of 2007/8.** A comparison of the policy responses of the Fed, the ECB and the Bank of England to the credit crunch.

K.13 **Using interest rates to control both aggregate demand and the exchange rate.** A problem of one instrument and two targets.

K.14 **Fiscal and monetary policy in the UK.** An historical overview of UK fiscal and monetary policy.

K.15 **Growth accounting.** This case study identifies factors that contribute to economic growth and shows how their contribution can be measured.

K.16 **The USA: is it a 'new economy'?** An examination of whether US productivity increases are likely to be sustained.

K.17 **Welfare to work.** An examination of the policy of the UK Labour Government (1997–2010) whereby welfare payments were designed to encourage people into employment.

K.18 **Assessing PFI.** Has this been the perfect solution to funding investment for the public sector without raising taxes?

K.19 **Alternative approaches to training and education.** This compares the approaches to training and education – a crucial element in supply-side policy – in the UK, France, Germany and the USA.

K.20 **Assistance to small firms in the UK.** An examination of current government measures to assist small firms.

K.21 **The modern approach to industrial policy.** An analysis of the changing role of government in industrial policy.

K.22 **Attempts at harmonisation.** A look at the meetings of the G7 economies where they attempt to come to agreement on means of achieving stable and sustained worldwide economic growth.

K.23 **The UK Labour Government's convergence criteria for euro membership.** An examination of the five tests

identified as needing to be passed before the question of euro membership would have been put to the electorate in a referendum.

K.24 **Balance of trade and the public finances.** An examination of countries' budget and balance of trade balances.

K.25 **2030 Agenda for Sustainable Development.** An overview of the UN's Agenda for Sustainable Development and its associated development goals and targets.

WEBSITES RELEVANT TO PART K

Numbers and sections refer to websites listed in the Web appendix and hotlinked from this book's website at www.pearsoned.co.uk/sloman

■ For news articles relevant to Part K, see the *Economics News Articles* link from the book's website.

■ For general news on macroeconomic policy, see websites in section A, and particularly A1–5, 7–13, 21, 35, 36. See also links to newspapers worldwide in A38, 39 and 43 and the news search feature in Google at A41.

■ For information on UK fiscal policy and government borrowing, see sites E18, 30, 36; F2. See also sites A1–8 at Budget time. For fiscal policy in the Eurozone, see sites G1 and 13.

■ For a model of the economy (based on the Treasury model), see *The Virtual Chancellor* (site D1).

■ For monetary policy in the UK, see F1 and E30. For monetary policy in the Eurozone, see F6 and 5. For monetary policy in the USA, see F8. For monetary policy in other countries, see the respective central bank site in section F and the links in F17.

■ For links to sites on money and monetary policy, see the *Financial Economics* sections in I8, 11, 14, 16.

■ For demand-side policy in the UK, see the latest Budget Report (e.g. section on maintaining macroeconomic stability) at site E30. See also site E18.

■ For inflation targeting in the UK and Eurozone, see sites F1 and 6.

■ For the current approach to UK supply-side policy, see the latest Budget Report (e.g. sections on productivity and training) at site E30. See also sites E5 and 9. For EU supply-side policy, see sites G5, 7, 9, 12, 14, 19.

■ For information on training in the UK and Europe, see sites E5, 10; G5, 14.

■ For support for a market-orientated approach to supply-side policy, see C17 and E34.

■ For European Union policies, see sites G1, 3, 6, 16, 17, 18.

■ For information on international harmonisation, see sites H4 and 5.

■ For student resources relevant to Part K, see sites C1–7, 9, 10, 12, 19.

Web appendix

All the following websites can be accessed from this book's own website (http://www.pearsoned.co.uk/sloman). When you enter the site, click on **Hot Links.** You will find all the following sites listed. Click on the one you want and the 'hot link' will take you straight to it.

The sections and numbers below refer to the ones used in the websites listed at the end of each Part. Thus, if the list contained the number A21, this would refer to the *Conversation* site.

A General news sources

As the title of this section implies, the websites here can be used for finding material on current news issues or tapping into news archives. Most archives are offered free of charge. However, some do require you to register. As well as key UK and US news sources, you will also notice some slightly different places from where you can get your news, such as *The Moscow Times* and *The Japan Times* . Check out site numbers 38. *Refdesk,* 43. *Guardian World News Guide* and 44. *Online newspapers* for links to newspapers across the world. Try searching for an article on a particular topic by using site number 41. *Google News Search.*

1. BBC News
2. The Economist
3. The Financial Times
4. The Guardian
5. The Independent
6. ITN
7. The Observer
8. The Telegraph
9. Aljazeera
10. The New York Times
11. Fortune
12. Time Magazine
13. The Washington Post
14. The Moscow Times (English)
15. Pravda (English)
16. Straits Times (Singapore)
17. New Straits Times (Malaysia)
18. The Scotsman
19. The Herald
20. Euromoney
21. The Conversation
22. Market News International
23. Bloomberg Businessweek
24. International Business Times
25. CNN Money
26. Vox (economic analysis and commentary)
27. Asia News Network
28. allAfrica.com
29. Greek News Sources (English)
30. France 24 (English)
31. Euronews
32. Australian Financial Review
33. Sydney Morning Herald
34. The Japan Times
35. Reuters
36. Bloomberg
37. David Smith's EconomicsUK.com
38. Refdesk (links to a whole range of news sources)
39. Newspapers and Magazines on World Wide Web
40. Yahoo News Search
41. Google News Search
42. ABYZ news links
43. Guardian World News Guide
44. Online newspapers

B Sources of economic and business data

Using websites to find up-to-date data is of immense value to the economist. The data sources below offer you a range of specialist and non-specialist data information. Universities have free access to the UK Data Service site (site 35 in this set), which is a huge database of statistics. The Economics Network's *Economic data freely available online* (site 1) gives links to various sections in over 40 UK and international sites.

1. Economics Network gateway to economic data
2. Office for Budget Responsibility
3. Office for National Statistics
4. Data Archive (Essex)
5. Bank of England Statistical Interactive Database
6. UK Official Statistics (GOV.UK)
7. Nationwide House Prices Site
8. House Web (data on housing market)
9. Economist global house price data
10. Halifax House Price Index
11. (House prices indices from ONS)
12. Penn World Table

13. Economist economic and financial indicators
14. FT market data
15. Economagic
16. Groningen Growth and Development Centre
17. AEAweb: Resources for economists on the Internet (RFE): data
18. Joseph Rowntree Foundation
19. OECD iLibrary statistics
20. Energy Information Administration
21. OECDStat
22. CIA world statistics site (World Factbook)
23. Millennium Development Goal Indicators Database
24. World Bank Data
25. Federal Reserve Bank of St Louis, US Economic Datasets (FRED)
26. Ministry of Economy, Trade and Industry (Japan)
27. Financial data from Yahoo
28. DataMarket
29. Index Mundi
30. Knoema: Economics
31. World Economic Outlook Database (IMF)
32. Telegraph shares and markets
33. Key Indicators (KI) for Asia and the Pacific Series (Asia Development Bank)
34. Open data from data.gov.uk (Business and Economy)
35. UK Data Service (incorporating ESDS)
36. BBC News, market data
37. NationMaster
38. Statistical Annex of the European Economy
39. Business and Consumer Surveys (all EU countries)
40. Gapminder
41. Trading Economics
42. WTO International Trade Statistics database
43. UNCTAD trade, investment and development statistics (UNCTADstat)
44. London Metal Exchange
45. Bank for International Settlements, global nominal and real effective exchange rate indices
46. Vizala (international data)
47. AMECO database
48. The Conference Board data
49. Institute for Fiscal Studies: tools and resources
50. European Central Bank (ECB): statistics

C Sites for students and teachers of economics

The following websites offer useful ideas and resources to those who are studying or teaching economics. It is worth browsing through some just to see what is on offer. Try out the first four sites, for starters. The *Internet for Economics* (site 8) is a very helpful tutorial for economics students on using the Internet.

1. The Economics Network
2. Teaching Resources for Undergraduate Economics (TRUE)
3. Timetric
4. Studying Economics
5. Economics and Business Education Association
6. Tutor2U
7. Council for Economic Education
8. Internet for Economics (tutorial on using the Web)
9. Econoclass: Resources for economics teachers
10. Teaching resources for economists (RFE)
11. METAL – Mathematics for Economics: enhancing Teaching And Learning
12. Federal Reserve Bank of San Francisco: Economics Education
13. Excel in Economics Teaching (from the Economics Network)
14. EcEdWeb resources
15. Dr. T's EconLinks: Teaching Resources
16. Online Opinion (Economics)
17. Free to Choose TV from the Idea Channel
18. History of Economic Thought
19. Resources For Economists on the Internet (RFE)
20. Games Economists Play (non-computerised classroom games)
21. Bank of England education resources
22. Why Study Economics?
23. Economic Classroom Experiments
24. Veconlab: Charles Holt's classroom experiments
25. Embedding Threshold Concepts
26. MIT Open Courseware in Economics
27. EconPort
28. ThoughtCo. – Economics

D Economic models, simulations and classroom experiments

Economic modelling is an important aspect of economic analysis. There are several sites that offer access to a model or simulation for you to use, e.g. *Virtual Chancellor* (where you can play being Chancellor of the Exchequer). Using such models can be a useful way of finding out how economic theory works within a specific environment. Other sites link to games and experiments, where you can play a particular role, perhaps competing with other students.

1. Virtual Chancellor
2. Virtual Factory
3. Interactive simulation models (Economics Web Institute)
4. Classroom Experiments in Economics (Pedagogy in Action)
5. MobLab
6. Economics Network Handbook, Chapter on Simulations, Games and Role-play
7. Experimental Economics Class Material (David J Cooper)
8. Simulations
9. Experimental economics: Wikipedia

10. Software available on the Economics Network site
11. RFE Software
12. Virtual Worlds
13. Veconlab: Charles Holt's classroom experiments
14. EconPort Experiments
15. Denise Hazlett's Classroom Experiments in Macroeconomics
16. Games Economists Play
17. Finance and Economics Experimental Laboratory at Exeter (FEELE)
18. Classroom Expernomics
19. The Economics Network's Guide to Classroom Experiments and Games
20. Economic Classroom Experiments (Wikiversity)

E UK Government and UK organisations' sites

If you want to see what a government department is up to, then look no further than the list below. Government departments' websites are an excellent source of information and data. They are particularly good at offering information on current legislation and policy initiatives.

1. Gateway site (GOV.UK)
2. Department for Communities and Local Government
3. Prime Minister's Office
4. Competition & Markets Authority
5. Department for Education
6. Department for International Development
7. Department for Transport
8. Department of Health
9. Department for Work and Pensions
10. Department for Business, Energy & Industrial Strategy
11. Environment Agency
12. Department of Energy and Climate Change
13. Low Pay Commission
14. Department for Environment, Food & Rural Affairs (Defra)
15. Office of Communications (Ofcom)
16. Office of Gas and Electricity Markets (Ofgem)
17. Official Documents OnLine
18. Office for Budget Responsibility
19. Office of Rail and Road (ORR)
20. The Takeover Panel
21. Sustainable Development Commission
22. Ofwat
23. National Statistics (ONS)
24. List of ONS releases from UK Data Explorer
25. HM Revenue & Customs
26. UK Intellectual Property Office
27. Parliament website
28. Scottish Government
29. Scottish Environment Protection Agency
30. HM Treasury
31. Equality and Human Rights Commission
32. Trades Union Congress (TUC)
33. Confederation of British Industry (CBI)
34. Adam Smith Institute
35. Chatham House
36. Institute for Fiscal Studies
37. Advertising Standards Authority
38. Businesses and Self-employed
39. Campaign for Better Transport
40. New Economics Foundation
41. Financial Conduct Authority
42. Prudential Regulation Authority

F Sources of monetary and financial data

As the title suggests, here are listed useful websites for finding information on financial matters. You will see that the list comprises mainly central banks, both within Europe and further afield. The links will take you to English language versions of non-English speaking countries' sites.

1. Bank of England
2. Bank of England Monetary and Financial Statistics
3. Banque de France (in English)
4. Bundesbank (German Central Bank)
5. Central Bank of Ireland
6. European Central Bank
7. Eurostat
8. US Federal Reserve Bank
9. Netherlands Central Bank (in English)
10. Bank of Japan (in English)
11. Reserve Bank of Australia
12. Bank Negara Malaysia (in English)
13. Monetary Authority of Singapore
14. Bank of Canada
15. National Bank of Denmark (in English)
16. Reserve Bank of India
17. Links to central bank websites from the Bank for International Settlements
18. The London Stock Exchange

G European Union and related sources

For information on European issues, the following is a wide range of useful sites. The sites maintained by the European Union are an excellent source of information.

1. Business, Economy, Euro (EC DG)
2. European Central Bank
3. EU official website
4. Eurostat
5. Employment, Social Affairs and Inclusion (EC DG)
6. Reports, Studies and Booklets on the EU
7. Internal Market, Industry, Entrepreneurship and SMEs (EC DG)
8. Competition (EC DG)
9. Agriculture and Rural Development (EC DG)

10. Energy (EC DG)
11. Environment (EC DG)
12. Regional Policy (EC DG)
13. Taxation and Customs Union (EC DG)
14. Education, Youth, Sport and Culture (EC DG)
15. European Patent Office
16. European Commission
17. European Parliament
18. European Council
19. Mobility and Transport (EC DG)
20. Trade (EC DG)
21. Maritime Affairs and Fisheries (EC DG)
22. International Co-operation and Development (EC DG)
23. Financial Stability, Financial Services and Capital Markets Union (EC DG)

H International organisations

This section casts its net beyond Europe and lists the Web addresses of the main international organisations in the global economy. You will notice that some sites are run by charities, such as Oxfam, while others represent organisations set up to manage international affairs, such as the International Monetary Fund and the United Nations.

1. UN Food and Agriculture Organization (FAO)
2. United Nations Conference on Trade and Development (UNCTAD)
3. International Labour Organization (ILO)
4. International Monetary Fund (IMF)
5. Organisation for Economic Co-operation and Development (OECD)
6. OPEC
7. World Bank
8. World Health Organization (WHO)
9. United Nations (UN)
10. United Nations Industrial Development Organization (UNIDO)
11. Friends of the Earth
12. Institute of International Finance
13. Oxfam
14. Christian Aid (reports on development issues)
15. European Bank for Reconstruction and Development (EBRD)
16. World Trade Organization (WTO)
17. United Nations Development Programme
18. UNICEF
19. EURODAD – European Network on Debt and Development
20. NAFTA
21. South American Free Trade Areas
22. ASEAN
23. APEC

I Economics search and link sites

If you are having difficulty finding what you want from the list of sites above, the following sites offer links to other sites and are a very useful resource when you are looking for something a little bit more specialist. Once again, it is worth having a look at what these sites have to offer in order to judge their usefulness.

1. Gateway for UK official sites
2. Alta Plana
3. Data Archive Search
4. Inomics (information on economics courses and jobs)
5. Ideas: RePEc bibliographic database
6. Wikidata
7. Portal site with links to other sites (Economics Network)
8. 50 Economics Resources for Students and Educators (Value Stock Guide)
9. Global goals 2030 (link to economic development resources)
10. Development Data Hub
11. DMOZ Open Directory: Economics (legacy site)
12. Web links for economists from the Economics Network
13. EconData.Net
14. Yale university: 75 Sources of Economic Data, Statistics, Reports, and Commentary
15. Excite Economics Links
16. Internet Resources for Economists
17. Trade Map (trade statistics)
18. Resources for Economists on the Internet
19. UK University Economics Departments
20. Economics education links
21. Development Gateway
22. Find the Data
23. Data on the Net
24. National Bureau of Economic Research links to data sources

J Internet search engines

The following search engines have been found to be useful.

1. Google
2. Bing
3. Whoosh UK
4. Excite
5. Zanran (search engine for data and statistics)
6. Search.com
7. MSN
8. Economics search engine (from RFE)
9. Yahoo
10. Ask
11. Lycos
12. Webcrawler
13. Metacrawler: searches several search engines

Key ideas

1. **The behaviour and performance of firms is affected by the business environment.** The business environment includes economic, political/legal, social/cultural and technological factors, as well as environmental, legal and ethical ones (page 11).

2. **Scarcity is the excess of human wants over what can actually be produced.** Because of scarcity, various choices have to be made between alternatives (page 17).

3. **The opportunity cost of something is what you give up to get it/do it.** In other words, it is cost measured in terms of the best alternative forgone (page 19).

4. **Rational decision making involves weighing up the marginal benefit and marginal cost of any activity.** If the marginal benefit exceeds the marginal cost, it is rational to do the activity (or to do more of it). If the marginal cost exceeds the marginal benefit, it is rational not to do it (or to do less of it) (page 19).

5. **Transaction costs.** The costs incurred when firms buy inputs or services from other firms as opposed to producing them themselves. They include the costs of searching for the best firm to do business with, the costs of drawing up, monitoring and enforcing contracts and the costs of transporting and handling products between the firms. These costs should be weighed against the benefits of outsourcing through the market (page 28).

6. **The nature of institutions and organisations is likely to influence behaviour.** There are various forces influencing people's decisions in complex organisations. Assumptions that an organisation will follow one simple objective (e.g. short-run profit maximisation) is thus too simplistic in many cases (page 29).

7. **The principal-agent problem.** Where people (principals), as a result of a lack of knowledge, cannot ensure that their best interests are served by their agents. Agents may take advantage of this situation to the disadvantage of the principals (page 30).

8. **Good decision making requires good information.** Where information is poor, or poorly used, decisions and their outcomes may be poor. This may be the result of bounded rationality (page 33).

9. **People respond to incentives.** It is important, therefore, that incentives are appropriate and have the desired effect (page 45).

10. **Changes in demand or supply cause markets to adjust.** Whenever such changes occur, the resulting 'disequilibrium' will bring an automatic change in prices, thereby restoring equilibrium (i.e. a balance of demand and supply) (page 46).

11. **Equilibrium is the point where conflicting interests are balanced.** Only at this point is the amount that demanders are willing to purchase the same as the amount that suppliers are willing to supply. It is a point that will be reached automatically in a free market through the operation of the price mechanism (page 53).

12. **Elasticity.** The responsiveness of one variable (e.g. demand) to a change in another (e.g. price). This concept is fundamental to understanding how markets work. The more elastic variables are, the more responsive is the market to changing circumstances (page 64).

13. **People's actions are influenced by their expectations.** People respond not just to what is happening now (such as a change in price), but to what they anticipate will happen in the future (page 75).

14. **People's actions are influenced by their attitudes towards risk.** Many decisions are taken under conditions of risk or uncertainty. Generally, the lower the probability of (or the more uncertain) the desired outcome of an action, the less likely will people be to undertake the action (page 79).

15. **The principle of diminishing marginal utility.** The more of a product a person consumes over a given period of time, the less will be the additional utility gained from one more unit (page 89).

16. **Adverse selection.** Where information is imperfect, high-risk groups will be attracted to profitable market opportunities to the disadvantage of the average buyer (or seller). In the context of insurance, it refers to those who are most likely to take out insurance posing the greatest risks to the insurer (page 98).

17. **Moral hazard.** Following a deal, the actions/behaviour of one party to a transaction may change in a way that reduces the pay-off to the other party. In the context of insurance, it refers to people taking more risks when they have insurance than they would have if they did not have insurance (page 99).

18. **The 'bygones' principle.** This states that sunk (fixed) costs should be ignored when deciding whether to

produce or sell more or less of a product. Only variable costs should be taken into account (page 147).

19. **Output depends on the amount of resources and how they are used.** Different amounts and combinations of inputs will lead to different amounts of output. If output is to be produced efficiently, then inputs should be combined in the optimum proportions (page 147).

20. **The law of diminishing marginal returns.** When increasing amounts of a variable factor are used with a given amount of a fixed factor, there will come a point when each extra unit of the variable factor will produce less extra output than the previous unit (page 149).

21. **Market power benefits the powerful at the expense of others.** When firms have market power over prices, they can use this to raise prices and profits above the perfectly competitive level. Other things being equal, the firm will gain at the expense of the consumer. Similarly, if consumers or workers have market power, they can use this to their own benefit (page 184).

22. **Economic efficiency.** This is achieved when each good is produced at the minimum cost and where consumers get maximum benefit from their income (page 191).

23. **People often think and behave strategically.** How you think others will respond to your actions is likely to influence your own behaviour. Firms, for example, when considering a price or product change will often take into account the likely reactions of their rivals (page 206).

24. **Nash equilibrium.** The position resulting from everyone making their optimal decision based on their assumptions about their rivals' decisions. Without collusion, there is no incentive for any firm to move from this position (page 217).

25. **Core competencies.** The key skills of a business that underpin its competitive advantage. A core competence is valuable, rare, costly to imitate and non-substitutable. Firms normally will gain from exploiting their core competencies (page 252).

26. **Flexible firm.** A firm that has the flexibility to respond to changing market conditions by changing the composition of its workforce and its working practices (page 334).

27. **Stocks and flows.** A stock is a quantity of something at a given point in time. A flow is an increase or decrease in something over a specified period of time. This is an important distinction and a common cause of confusion (page 341).

28. **The principle of discounting.** People generally prefer to have benefits today than in the future. Thus future benefits have to be reduced (discounted) to give them a present value (page 344).

29. **Efficient capital markets.** Capital markets are efficient when the prices of shares accurately reflect information about companies' current and expected future performance (page 357).

30. **Allocative efficiency in any activity is achieved where any reallocation would lead to a decline in net benefit.** It is achieved where marginal benefit equals marginal cost. Private efficiency is achieved where marginal private benefit equals marginal private cost ($MB = MC$). Social efficiency is achieved where marginal social benefit equals marginal social cost ($MSB = MSC$) (page 365).

31. **Markets generally fail to achieve social efficiency.** There are various types of market failure. Market failures provide one of the major justifications for government intervention in the economy (page 365).

32. **Equity is where income is distributed in a way that is considered to be fair or just.** Note that an equitable distribution is not the same as a totally equal distribution and that different people have different views on what is equitable (page 365).

33. **Externalities are spillover costs or benefits.** They are experienced by people not directly involved in the market transaction that created them. Where these exist, even an otherwise perfect market will fail to achieve social efficiency (page 367).

34. **The free-rider problem.** This occurs when people are able to enjoy the benefits from consuming a good that someone else has bought without having to pay anything towards the cost of providing it themselves. This problem can lead to a situation where a good or service is not produced, even though the benefits to society outweigh the costs of producing it (page 374).

35. **The problem of time lags.** Many economic actions can take a long time to take effect. This can cause problems of instability and an inability of the economy to achieve social efficiency (page 376).

36. **Government intervention may be able to rectify various failings of the market.** Government intervention in the market can be used to achieve various economic objectives, which may not be best achieved by the market. Governments, however, are not perfect and their actions may bring adverse, as well as beneficial, consequences (page 376).

37. **The law of comparative advantage.** Provided opportunity costs of various goods differ in two countries, both of them can gain from mutual trade if they specialise in producing (and exporting) those goods that have relatively low opportunity costs compared with the other country (page 470).

38. **The distinction between nominal and real figures.** Nominal figures are those using current prices, interest rates, etc. Real figures are figures corrected for inflation (page 500).

39. **Economies suffer from inherent instability.** As a result, economic growth and other macroeconomic indicators tend to fluctuate (page 500).

40. **Balance sheets affect peoples' behaviour.** The size and structure of governments', institutions' and individuals' liabilities (and assets too) affect economic well-being

and can have significant effects on behaviour and economic activity (page 505).

41. **Societies face trade-offs between economic objectives.** For example, the goal of faster growth may conflict with that of greater equality; the goal of lower unemployment may conflict with that of lower inflation (at least in the short run). This is an example of opportunity cost: the cost of achieving more of one objective may be achieving less of another. The existence of trade-offs means that policy-makers must make choices (page 506).

42. **Living standards are limited by a country's ability to produce.** Potential national output depends on the country's resources, technology and productivity (page 507).

43. **The principle of cumulative causation.** An initial event can cause an ultimate effect which is much larger (page 575).

44. **Goodhart's Law.** Controlling a symptom (i.e. an indicator) of a problem will not cure the problem. Instead, the indicator will merely cease to be a good indicator of the problem (page 648).

Glossary

Absolute advantage A country has an absolute advantage over another in the production of a good if it can produce it with fewer resources than the other country.

Absorptive capacity The ability of a country and its firms to incorporate and benefit from positive productivity spillovers.

Accelerationist hypothesis The theory that unemployment can only be reduced below the natural rate at the cost of accelerating inflation.

Accelerator coefficient The level of induced investment as a proportion of a rise in national income: $\alpha = I_i/\Delta Y$.

Accelerator theory The *level* of investment depends on the *rate of change* of national income, and the result tends to be subject to substantial fluctuations.

Actual growth The percentage annual increase in national output actually produced, usually measured over a 3-month or 12-month period.

***Ad valorem* tariffs** Tariffs levied as a percentage of the price of the import.

Adaptive expectations Where people adjust their expectations of inflation in the light of what has happened to inflation in the past.

Adjustable peg A system whereby exchange rates are fixed for a period of time, but may be devalued (or revalued) if a deficit (or surplus) becomes substantial.

Adverse selection Where information is imperfect, high risk groups will be attracted to profitable market opportunities to the disadvantage of the average buyer (or seller).

Adverse selection in the insurance market Where customers with the least desirable characteristics from the seller's point of view are more likely to purchase an insurance policy at a price based on the average risk of all the potential customers.

Advertising/sales ratio A ratio that reflects the intensity of advertising within a market.

Aggregate demand (*AD*) Total spending on goods and services made in the economy. It consists of four elements: consumer spending (*C*), investment (*I*), government spending (*G*) and the expenditure on exports (*X*), less any expenditure on foreign goods and services (*M*): $AD = C + I + G + X - M$.

Aggregate demand for labour curve A curve showing the total demand for labour in the economy at different average real wage rates.

Aggregate supply The total amount that firms plan to supply at any given level of prices.

Aggregate supply of labour curve A curve showing the total number of people willing and able to work at different average real wage rates.

Allocative efficiency A situation where the current combination of goods produced and sold gives the maximum satisfaction for each consumer at their current levels of income.

Altruism (in economics) Positively valuing the pay-offs to others.

Ambient-based standards Pollution control that requires firms to meet minimum standards for the environment (e.g. air or water quality).

Appreciation A rise in the free-market exchange rate of the domestic currency with foreign currencies.

Asset Possessions of an individual or institution, or claims held on others.

Assisted areas Areas of high unemployment qualifying for government regional selective assistance (RSA and SFI) and grants from the European Regional Development Fund (ERDF).

Asymmetric information A situation in which one party in an economic relationship knows more than another.

Asymmetric shocks Shocks (such as an oil price increase or a recession in another part of the world) that have different-sized effects on different industries, regions or countries.

Automatic fiscal stabilisers Tax revenues that rise and government expenditure that falls as national income rises. The more they change with income, the bigger the stabilising effect on national income.

Average (total) cost (*AC*) Total cost (fixed plus variable) per unit of output: $AC = TC/Q = AFC + AVC$.

Average cost pricing Where a firm sets its price by adding a certain percentage for (average) profit on top of average cost.

Average fixed cost (*AFC*) Total fixed cost per unit of output: $AFC = TFC/Q$.

Average physical product (*APP*) Total output (*TPP*) per unit of the variable factor in question: $APP = TPP/Qv$.

Average revenue Total revenue per unit of output. When all output is sold at the same price, average revenue will be the same as price: $AR = TR/Q = P$.

Average variable cost (*AVC*) Total variable cost per unit of output: $AVC = TVC/Q$.

Backwards induction A process by which firms consider the decision in the last round of the game and then work backwards through the game, thinking through the most likely outcomes in earlier rounds.

Balance of payments account A record of the country's transactions with the rest of the world. It shows the country's payments to or deposits in other countries (debits) and its receipts or deposits from other countries (credits). It also shows the balance between these debits and credits under various headings.

Balance of payments on current account The balance on trade in goods and services plus net incomes and current transfers.

Balance of trade Exports of goods and services minus imports of goods and services. If exports exceed imports, there is a 'balance of trade surplus' (a positive figure). If imports exceed exports, there is a 'balance of trade deficit' (a negative figure).

Balance on trade in goods and services or **balance of trade** Exports of goods and services minus imports of goods and services.

Balance on trade in goods or **balance of visible trade** or **merchandise balance** Exports of goods minus imports of goods.

Balance sheet A record of the stock of assets and liabilities of an individual or institution.

Balance sheet effects The effects on spending behaviour, such as consumer spending, that arise from changes in the composition or value of net worth.

Balance sheet recession An economic slowdown or recession caused by private-sector individuals and firms looking to improve their financial well-being by increasing their saving and/or paying down debt.

Bank (or bank deposits) multiplier The number of times greater the expansion of bank deposits is than the additional liquidity in banks that caused it: $1/L$ (the inverse of the liquidity ratio).

Barometric firm price leadership Where the price leader is the one whose prices are believed to reflect market conditions in the most satisfactory way.

Barometric forecasting A technique used to predict future economic trends based upon analysing patterns of time-series data.

Barter economy An economy where people exchange goods and services directly with one another without any payment of money. Workers would be paid with bundles of goods.

Base year (for index numbers) The year whose index number is set at 100.

Behavioural economics of the firm Attempts to explain why the behaviour of firms deviate from traditional profit maximisation because of (a) the managerial use of mental shortcuts to simplify complex decisions and (b) managerial preferences for fairness.

Bid rigging Where two or more firms secretly agree on the prices they will tender for a contract. These prices will be above those that would have been submitted under a genuinely competitive tendering process.

Bill of exchange A certificate promising to repay a stated amount on a certain date, typically three months from the issue of the bill. Bills pay no interest as such, but are sold at a discount and redeemed at face value, thereby earning a rate of discount for the purchaser.

Bounded rationality When individuals have limited abilities to find and process the relevant information required to make the best decision, i.e. purchase the goods that generate the most consumer surplus.

Broad money Cash in circulation plus retail and wholesale bank and building society deposits.

Budget deficit The excess of an organisation's spending over its revenues. When applied to government, it is the excess of its spending over its tax receipts.

Budget surplus The excess of an organisation's revenues over its expenditures. When applied to government, it is the excess of its tax receipts over its spending.

Business cycle or **trade cycle** The periodic fluctuations of national output round its long-term trend. Periods of rapid growth are followed by periods of low growth or even decline in national output.

By-product A good or service that is produced as a consequence of producing another good or service.

Capital All inputs into production that have themselves been produced, e.g. factories, machines and tools.

Capital account of the balance of payments The record of transfers of capital to and from abroad.

Capital accumulation An increase in the amount of capital that an economy has for production.

Capital adequacy ratio The ratio of a bank's capital (reserves and shares) to its risk-weighted assets.

Capital deepening An increase in the amount of capital per worker (K/L).

Capital expenditure Investment expenditure; expenditure on assets.

Capital intensity The amount of physical capital that workers have to operate with and that can be measured by the amount of capital per worker (K/L).

Cartel A formal collusive agreement.

CDOs See collateralised debt obligations.

Central bank A country's central bank is banker to the government and the banks as a whole. In most countries, the central bank operates monetary policy by setting interest rates and influencing the supply of money. The central bank in the UK is the Bank of England; in the Eurozone it is the European Central Bank (ECB) and in the USA it is the Federal Reserve Bank (the 'Fed').

Certainty equivalent The guaranteed amount of money that an individual would view as equally desirable as the expected value of a gamble. If a person is risk averse, the certainty equivalent is less than the expected value.

Certificates of deposit Certificates issued by banks for fixed-term interest-bearing deposits. They can be resold by the owner to another party.

Change in demand The term used for a shift in the demand curve. It occurs when a determinant of demand *other* than price changes.

Change in supply The term used for a shift in the supply curve. It occurs when a determinant other than price changes.

Change in the quantity demanded The term used for a movement along the demand curve to a new point. It occurs when there is a change in price.

Change in the quantity supplied The term used for a movement along the supply curve to a new point. It occurs when there is a change in price.

Characteristics (or attributes) theory The theory that demonstrates how consumer choice between different varieties of a product depends on the characteristics of these varieties, along with prices of the different varieties, the consumer's budget and the consumer's tastes.

Claimant unemployment Those in receipt of unemployment-related benefits.

Closed shop Where a firm agrees to employ only members of a recognised union.

Club good A good that has a low degree of rivalry but is easily excludable.

Cluster (business or industrial) A geographical concentration of related businesses and institutions.

Coase theorem When there are well-defined property rights and zero bargaining costs, then negotiations between the party creating the externality and the party affected by the externality can bring about the socially efficient market quantity.

Collateralised debt obligations (CDOs) These are a type of security consisting of a bundle of fixed-income assets, such as corporate bonds, mortgage debt and credit-card debt.

Collusive oligopoly When oligopolists agree (formally or informally) to limit competition between themselves. They may set output quotas, fix prices, limit product promotion or development, or agree not to 'poach' each other's markets.

Collusive tendering Where two or more firms secretly agree on the prices they will tender for a contract. These prices will be above those that would be put in under a genuinely competitive tendering process.

Command-and-control (CAC) systems The use of laws or regulations backed up by inspections and penalties (such as fines) for non-compliance.

Command or **planned economy** An economy where all economic decisions are taken by the central (or local) authorities.

Commercial bill A certificate issued by a firm promising to repay a stated amount on a certain date, typically three months from the issue of the bill. Bills pay no interest as such, but are sold at a discount and redeemed at their face value, thereby earning a rate of discount for the purchaser.

Common market A customs union where the member countries act as a single market with free movement of labour and capital, common taxes and common trade laws.

Comparative advantage A country has a comparative advantage over another in the production of a good if it can produce it at a lower opportunity cost, i.e. if it has to forgo less of other goods in order to produce it.

Competition for corporate control The competition for the control of companies through takeovers.

Complementary goods A pair of goods consumed together. As the price of one goes up, the demand for both goods will fall.

Compounding The process of adding interest each year to an initial capital sum.

Conglomerate merger Where two firms in different industries merge.

Conglomerate multinational A multinational that produces different products in different countries.

Constrained discretion A set of principles or rules within which economic policy operates. These can be informal or enshrined in law.

Consortium Where two or more firms work together on a specific project and create a separate company to run the project.

Consumer durable A consumer good that lasts a period of time, during which the consumer can continue gaining utility from it.

Consumer prices index (CPI) An index of the prices of goods bought by a typical household.

Consumer surplus The excess of what a person would have been prepared to pay for a good (i.e. the utility measured in money terms) over what that person actually pays. Total consumer surplus equals total utility minus total expenditure.

Consumption The act of using goods and services to satisfy wants. This will normally involve purchasing the goods and services.

Consumption externalities Spillover effects on other people of consumers' consumption.

Consumption of domestically produced goods and services (Cd) The direct flow of money payments from households to firms.

Consumption smoothing The act by households of smoothing their levels of consumption over time despite facing volatile incomes.

Continuous market clearing The assumption that all markets in the economy continuously clear so that the economy is permanently in equilibrium.

Convergence of economies When countries achieve similar levels of growth, inflation, budget deficits as a percentage of GDP, balance of payments, etc.

Co-ordination failure When a group of firms (e.g. banks) acting independently could have achieved a more desirable outcome if they had co-ordinated their decision making.

Core competence The key skills of a business that underpin its competitive advantage.

Corporate social responsibility Where a business integrates social, environmental, ethical and human rights concerns into its actions in close collaboration with its stakeholders.

Cost–benefit analysis The identification, measurement and weighing up of the costs and benefits of a project in order to decide whether or not it should go ahead.

Cost-push inflation Inflation caused by persistent rises in costs of production (independently of demand).

Countervailing power When the power of a monopolistic/oligopolistic seller is offset by powerful buyers who can prevent the price from being pushed up.

Cournot model A model of duopoly where each firm makes its price and output decisions on the assumption that its rival will produce a particular quantity.

Credibility of monetary policy The extent to which the public believes that the central bank will take the measures necessary to achieve the stated targets of monetary policy, for example an inflation rate target.

Credible threat (or promise) One that is believable to rivals because it is in the threatener's interests to carry it out.

Credit cycle The expansion and contraction of credit flows over time.

Cross-price elasticity of demand The responsiveness of demand for one good to a change in the price of another; the proportionate change in demand for one good divided by the proportionate change in price of the other.

Cross-section data Information showing how a variable (e.g. the consumption of eggs) differs between different groups or different individuals at a given time.

Crowding out Where increased public expenditure diverts money or resources away from the private sector.

Currency union A group of countries (or regions) using a common currency.

Current account of the balance of payments The record of a country's imports and exports of goods and services, plus incomes and transfers of money to and from abroad.

Current budget balance The difference between public-sector receipts and those expenditures classified as current rather than capital expenditures.

Current expenditure Recurrent spending on goods and factor payments.

Customs union A free trade area with common external tariffs and quotas.

Deadweight welfare loss The loss of consumer plus producer surplus in imperfect markets (when compared with perfect competition).

Debt/equity ratio The ratio of debt finance to equity finance.

Decision tree (or game tree) A diagram showing the sequence of possible decisions by competitor firms and the outcome of each combination of decisions.

Deficit bias The tendency for frequent fiscal deficits and rising debt-to-GDP ratios because of the reluctance of policymakers to tighten fiscal.

Deflation (definition 1) A period of falling prices: negative inflation.

Deflation (definition 2) A period of falling real aggregate demand. Note that 'deflation' is more commonly used nowadays to mean negative inflation.

Deflationary or recessionary gap The shortfall of aggregate expenditure below GDP at the full-employment level of GDP.

Deindustrialisation The decline in the contribution to production of the manufacturing sector of the economy.

Delegation of monetary policy The handing over by government of the operation of monetary policy to central banks.

Demand curve A graph showing the relationship between the price of a good and the quantity of the good demanded over a given time period. Price is measured on the vertical axis; quantity demanded is measured on the horizontal axis. A demand curve can be for an individual consumer or a group of consumers or, more usually, for the whole market.

Demand function An equation showing the relationship between the demand for a product and its principal determinants.

Demand schedule for an individual A table showing the different quantities of a good that a person is willing and able to buy at various prices over a given time period.

Demand: change in demand The term used for a shift in the demand curve. It occurs when a determinant of demand *other* than price changes.

Demand: change in the quantity demanded The term used for a movement along the demand curve to a new point. It occurs when there is a change in price.

Demand-deficient or cyclical unemployment Disequilibrium unemployment caused by a fall in aggregate demand with no corresponding fall in the real wage rate.

Demand-pull inflation Inflation caused by persistent rises in aggregate demand.

Demand-side policy Government policy designed to alter the level of aggregate demand, and thereby the level of output, employment and prices.

Dependent variable That variable whose outcome is determined by other variables within an equation.

Depreciation (capital) The decline in value of capital equipment due to age or to wear and tear.

Depreciation (currency) A fall in the free-market exchange rate of the domestic currency with foreign currencies.

Derived demand The demand for a factor of production depends on the demand for the good that uses it.

Destabilising speculation This is where the actions of speculators tend to make price movements larger.

Devaluation Where the government refixes the exchange rate at a lower level.

Diminishing marginal rate of substitution of characteristics The more a consumer gets of characteristic A and the less of characteristic B, the less and less of B the consumer will be willing to give up to get an extra unit of A.

Diminishing marginal utility of income Where each additional pound earned yields less additional utility.

Discount market An example of a money market in which new or existing bills are bought and sold.

Discounting The process of reducing the value of future flows to give them a present valuation.

Discretionary fiscal policy Deliberate changes in tax rates or the level of government expenditure in order to influence the level of aggregate demand.

Diseconomies of scale Where costs per unit of output increase as the scale of production increases.

Disequilibrium unemployment Unemployment resulting from real wages in the economy being above the equilibrium level.

Disposable income Income available for spending or saving after the deduction of direct taxes and the addition of benefits.

Diversification A business growth strategy in which a business expands into new markets outside of its current interests.

Divine coincidence (in monetary policy) When the monetary authorities can choose a policy stance that is largely consistent with both stabilising inflation and stabilising output around potential output.

Domestically systemically important banks (D-SIBs) Banks identified by national regulators as being significant banks in the domestic financial system.

Dominant firm price leadership When firms (the followers) choose the same price as that set by a dominant firm in the industry (the leader).

Dominant strategy game Where the *same* policy is suggested by different strategies.

Downsizing Where a business reorganises and reduces its size, especially in respect to levels of employment, in order to cut costs.

Dumping Where exports are sold at prices below marginal cost – often as a result of government subsidy.

Duopoly An oligopoly where there are just two firms in the market.

Econometrics The branch of economics that applies statistical techniques to economic data.

Economic agents The general term for individuals, firms, government and organisations when taking part in economic activities, such as buying, selling, saving, investing or in any other way interacting with other economic agents.

Economic globalisation (OECD definition) The process of closer economic integration of global markets: financial, product and labour.

Economies of scale When increasing the scale of production leads to a lower cost per unit of output.

Economies of scope When increasing the range of products produced by a firm reduces the cost of producing each one.

Efficiency (allocative) A situation where the current combination of goods produced and sold gives the maximum satisfaction for each consumer at their current levels of income.

Efficiency (productive) A situation where firms are producing the maximum output for a given amount of inputs, or producing a given output at the least cost.

Efficiency frontier A line showing the maximum attainable combinations of two characteristics for a given budget. These characteristics can be obtained by consuming one or a mixture of two brands or varieties of a product.

Efficiency wage hypothesis A hypothesis that states that a worker's productivity is linked to the wage he or she receives.

Efficiency wage rate The profit-maximising wage rate for the firm after taking into account the effects of wage rates on worker motivation, turnover and recruitment.

Efficient (capital) market hypothesis The hypothesis that new information about a company's current or future performance will be quickly and accurately reflected in its share price.

Elastic If demand is (price) elastic, then any change in price will cause the quantity demanded to change proportionately more. Ignoring the negative sign, it will have a value greater than 1.

Endogenous money supply Money supply that is determined (at least in part) by the demand for money.

Endowment effect (or **divestiture aversion**) The hypothesis that people ascribe more value to things when they own them than when they are merely considering purchasing or acquiring them – in other words, when the reference point is one of ownership rather than non-ownership

Enterprise culture One in which individuals are encouraged to become wealth creators through their own initiative and effort.

Envelope curve A long-run average cost curve drawn as the tangency points of a series of short-run average cost curves.

Environmental policy Initiatives by government to ensure a specified minimum level of environmental quality.

Environmental scanning Where a business surveys social and political trends in order to take account of changes in its decision-making process.

Envy (in economics) Negatively valuing the pay-offs to others.

Equation of exchange $MV = PY$. The total level of spending on GDP (MV) equals the total value of goods and services produced (PY) that go to make up GDP.

Equilibrium A position of balance. A position from which there is no inherent tendency to move away.

Equilibrium ('natural') unemployment The difference between those who would like employment at the current wage rate and those willing and able to take a job.

Equilibrium price The price where the quantity demanded equals the quantity supplied; the price where there is no shortage or surplus.

Equity The fair distribution of a society's resources.

ERM (exchange rate mechanism) A semi-fixed system whereby participating EU countries allowed fluctuations against each other's currencies only within agreed bands. Collectively, they floated freely against all other currencies.

Ethical consumerism Where consumers' decisions about what to buy are influenced by ethical concerns such as the producer's human rights record and care for the environment.

Excess burden (of a tax on a good) The amount by which the loss in consumer plus producer surplus exceeds the government surplus.

Excess capacity (under monopolistic competition) In the long run, firms under monopolistic competition will produce at an output below that which minimises average cost per unit.

Exchange equalisation account The gold and foreign exchange reserves account in the Bank of England.

Exchange rate The rate at which one national currency exchanges for another. The rate is expressed as the amount of one currency that is necessary to purchase one unit of another currency (e.g. £1 = €1.30).

Exchange rate index or **effective exchange rate** A weighted average exchange rate expressed as an index, where the value of the index is 100 in a given base year. The weights of the different currencies in the index add up to 1.

Exclusionary abuses Business practices that limit or prevent effective competition from either actual or potential rivals.

Exogenous money supply Money supply that does not depend on the demand for money but is set by the authorities (i.e. the central bank or the government).

Exogenous variable A variable whose value is determined independently of the model of which it is part.

Expectations-augmented Phillips curve A (short-run) Phillips curve whose position depends on the expected rate of inflation.

Expected value The average value of a variable after many repetitions: in other words, the sum of the value of a variable on each occasion divided by the number of occasions.

Explicit costs The payments to outside suppliers of inputs.

Exploitative abuse Business practices that directly harm the customer. Examples include high prices and poor quality.

External benefits Benefits from production (or consumption) experienced by people *other* than the producer (or consumer) directly involved in the transaction.

External costs Costs of production (or consumption) borne by people *other* than the producer (or consumer) directly involved in the transaction.

External diseconomies of scale Where a firm's costs per unit of output increase as the size of the whole industry increases.

External economies of scale Where a firm's costs per unit of output decrease as the size of the whole *industry* grows.

External expansion Where business growth is achieved by merger, takeover, joint venture or an agreement.

Externalities Costs or benefits of production or consumption experienced by people *other* than the producers and consumers directly involved in the transaction. They are sometimes referred to as 'spillover' or 'third-party' costs or benefits.

Factors of production (or resources) The inputs into the production of goods and services: labour, land and raw materials, and capital.

Final expenditure Expenditure on goods and services. This is included in GDP and is part of aggregate demand.

Financial accelerator When a change in national income is amplified by changes in the financial sector, such as changes in interest rate differentials or the willingness of banks to lend.

Financial account of the balance of payments The record of the flows of money into and out of the country for the purpose of investment or as deposits in banks and other financial institutions.

Financial crowding out Where an increase in government borrowing diverts money away from the private sector.

Financial deregulation The removal of or reduction in legal rules and regulations governing the activities of financial institutions.

Financial flexibility Where employers can vary their wage costs by changing the composition of their workforce or the terms on which workers are employed.

Financial instability hypothesis During periods of economic growth, economic agents (firms and individuals) tend to borrow more and MFIs are more willing to lend. This fuels the boom. In a period of recession, economic agents tend to cut spending in order to reduce debts and MFIs are less willing to lend. This deepens the recession. Behaviour in financial markets thus tends to amplify the business cycle.

Financial instruments Financial products resulting in a financial claim by one party over another.

Financial intermediaries The general name for financial institutions (banks, building societies, etc.) which act as a means of channelling funds from depositors to borrowers.

Financialisation A term used to describe the process by which financial markets, institutions and instruments become increasingly significant in economies.

Fine tuning The use of demand management policy (fiscal or monetary) to smooth out cyclical fluctuations in the economy.

Firm An economic organisation that co-ordinates the process of production and distribution.

First-degree price discrimination Where the seller of the product charges each consumer the maximum price they are prepared to pay for each unit of the good.

First-mover advantage When a firm gains from being the first one to take action.

Fiscal policy   Policy to affect aggregate demand by altering government expenditure and/or taxation.

Fiscal stance   How expansionary or contractionary the Budget is.

Fixed costs   Total costs that do not vary with the amount of output produced.

Fixed factor   An input that *cannot* be increased in supply within a given time period.

Flat organisation   One in which technology enables senior managers to communicate directly with those lower in the organisational structure. Middle managers are bypassed.

Flexible firm   A firm that has the flexibility to respond to changing market conditions by changing the composition of its workforce.

Floating exchange rate   When the government does not intervene in the foreign exchange markets, but simply allows the exchange rate to be freely determined by demand and supply.

Flow   An increase or decrease in quantity over a specified period.

Foreign exchange gap   The shortfall in foreign exchange that a country needs to purchase necessary imports such as raw materials and machinery.

Forward exchange market   Where contracts are made today for the price at which a currency will be exchanged at some specified future date.

Framing   Consumption decisions are influenced by the way that costs and benefits are presented.

Franchise   A formal contractual agreement whereby a company uses another company to produce or sell some or all of its product.

Franchising   Where a firm is granted the licence to operate a given part of an industry for a specified length of time.

Free market   One in which there is an absence of government intervention. Individual producers and consumers are free to make their own economic decisions.

Free-market or **laissez-faire economy**   An economy where all economic decisions are taken by individual households and firms, with no government intervention.

Free-rider problem   When people enjoy the benefits from consuming a good without paying anything towards the cost of providing it.

Free trade area   A group of countries with no trade barriers between themselves.

Frictional (search) unemployment   Unemployment that occurs as a result of imperfect information in the labour market. It often takes time for workers to find jobs (even though there are vacancies) and, in the meantime, they are unemployed.

Full-employment level of national income or **full-employment level of GDP**   The level of GDP at which there is no deficiency of demand.

Full-range pricing   A pricing strategy in which a business, seeking to improve its profit performance, assesses the pricing of its goods as a whole rather than individually.

Functional flexibility   Where employers can switch workers from job to job as requirements change.

Functional relationships   The mathematical relationships showing how one variable is affected by one or more others.

Functional separation of banks   The ringfencing by banks of core retail banking services, such as deposit-taking, from riskier investment banking activities.

Funding   Where the authorities alter the balance of bills and bonds for any given level of government borrowing.

Future price   A price agreed today at which an item (e.g. commodities) will be exchanged at some set date in the future.

Futures or forward market   A market in which contracts are made to buy or sell at some future date at a price agreed today.

Game theory (or the theory of games)   The study of alternative strategies that oligopolists may choose to adopt, depending on their assumptions about their rivals' behaviour.

GDP deflator   The price index of all final domestically produced goods and services: i.e. all items that contribute towards GDP.

Gearing or **leverage**   (US term) The ratio of debt capital to equity capital: in other words, the ratio of borrowed capital (e.g. bonds) to shares.

Gearing ratio   The ratio of debt finance to total finance.

General government debt   The accumulated deficits of central plus local government. It is the total amount owed by general government, both domestically and internationally.

General government deficit or **surplus**   The combined deficit (or surplus) of central and local government.

Global sourcing   Where a company uses production sites in different parts of the world to provide particular components for a final product.

Global systemically important banks (G-SIBs)   Banks identified by a series of indicators as being significant players in the global financial system.

Goodhart's Law   Controlling a symptom of a problem, or only part of the problem, will not cure the problem; it will simply mean that the part that is being controlled now becomes a poor indicator of the problem.

Goods in joint supply   These are two goods where the production of more of one leads to the production of more of the other.

Government surplus (from a tax on a good)   The total tax revenue earned by the government from sales of a good.

Grandfathering   Where the number of emission permits allocated to a firm is based on its *current* levels of emission (e.g. permitted levels for all firms could be 80 per cent of their current emission levels).

Green tax   A tax on output or consumption to charge for the adverse effect on the environment. The socially efficient level of a green tax is equal to the marginal environmental cost of production.

Grim trigger strategy   Once a player observes that its rival has broken some agreed behaviour, it will never again co-operate with them.

Gross domestic product (GDP)   The value of output produced within the country, typically over a 12-month period.

Gross domestic product (GDP) (at market prices)   The value of output produced within a country over a 12-month period in terms of the prices actually paid. GDP = GVA + taxes on products – subsidies on products.

Gross national income (GNY)   GDP plus net income from abroad.

Gross value added (GVA) at basic prices   The sum of all the values added by all industries in the economy over a year. The figures exclude taxes on products (such as VAT) and include subsidies on products.

Growth maximisation   An alternative theory that assumes that managers seek to maximise the growth in sales revenue (or the capital value of the firm) over time.

Growth vector matrix   A means by which a business might assess its product/market strategy.

Harrod–Domar model   A model that relates a country's rate of economic growth to the proportion of national income saved and the ratio of capital to output.

Heuristic   A mental short cut or rule of thumb that people use when trying to make complicated choices. They reduce the computational and/or research effort required but sometimes lead to systematic errors.

Historic costs   The original amount the firm paid for factors it now owns.

Holding company   A business organisation in which the present company holds interests in a number of other companies or subsidiaries.

Horizontal merger   Where two firms in the same industry at the same stage of the production process merge.

Horizontal product differentiation   Where a firm's product differs from its rivals' products, although the products are seen to be of a similar quality.

Horizontal strategic alliances   A formal or informal arrangement between firms to jointly provide a particular activity at a similar stage of the same technical process.

Horizontally integrated multinational   A multinational that produces the same product in many different countries.

Households' disposable income   The income available for households to spend, i.e. personal incomes after deducting taxes on incomes and adding benefits.

Human capital   The knowledge, skills, competencies and other attributes embodied in individuals or groups of individuals that are used to produce goods and services.

Hyper-globalisation   A term used to describe the rapid pace of globalisation seen in recent years.

Hysteresis   The persistence of an effect even when the initial cause has ceased to operate. In economics it refers to the persistence of unemployment even when the demand deficiency that caused it no longer exists.

Imperfect competition   The collective name for monopolistic competition and oligopoly.

Implicit costs   Costs that do not involve a direct payment of money to a third party, but that, nevertheless, involve a sacrifice of some alternative.

Import substitution   The replacement of imports by domestically produced goods or services.

Impure public good   A good that is partially non-rivalrous and non-excludable.

Income effect   The effect of a change in price on quantity demanded arising from the consumer becoming better or worse off as a result of the price change.

Income effect of a rise in wages   Workers get a higher income for a given number of hours worked and may thus feel they need to work fewer hours as wages rise.

Income elasticity of demand   The responsiveness of demand to a change in consumer incomes; the proportionate change in demand divided by the proportionate change in income.

Independence (of firms in a market)   When the decisions of one firm in a market will not have any significant effect on the demand curves of its rivals.

Independent risks   Where two risky events are unconnected. The occurrence of one will not affect the likelihood of the occurrence of the other.

Independent variables   Those variables that determine the dependent variable, but are themselves determined independently of the equation they are in.

Index number   The value of a variable expressed as 100 plus or minus its percentage deviation from a base year.

Indifference curve   A line showing all those combinations of two characteristics of a good between which a consumer is indifferent, i.e. those combinations that give a particular level of utility.

Indifference map   A diagram showing a whole set of indifference curves. The further away a particular curve is from the origin, the higher the level of utility it represents.

Indivisibilities   The impossibility of dividing a factor of production into smaller units.

Industrial concentration   The degree to which an industry is dominated by large business enterprises.

Industrial policies   Policies to encourage industrial investment and greater industrial efficiency.

Industrial sector   A grouping of industries producing similar products or services.

Industry   A group of firms producing a particular product or service.

Industry's infrastructure   The network of supply agents, communications, skills, training facilities, distribution channels, specialised financial services, etc. that support a particular industry.

Inelastic   If demand is (price) inelastic, then any change will cause the quantity demanded to change by a proportionately smaller amount. Ignoring the negative sign, it will have a value less than 1.

Infant industry An industry that has a potential comparative advantage, but that is, as yet, too underdeveloped to be able to realise this potential.

Inferior goods Goods whose demand falls as people's incomes rise.

Inflation bias Excessive inflation that results from people raising their expectations of the inflation rate following expansionary demand management policy, encouraging government to loosen policy even further.

Inflationary gap The excess of aggregate expenditure over GDP at the full-employment level of GDP.

Injections (J) Expenditure on the production of domestic firms coming from outside the inner flow of the circular flow of income. Injections equal investment (I_d) plus government expenditure (G_d) plus expenditure on exports (X_d) (less any imported components of these three elements).

Integrated international enterprise One in which an international company pursues a single business strategy. It co-ordinates the business activities of its subsidiaries across different countries.

Interdependence (under oligopoly) This is one of the two key features of oligopoly. Each firm is affected by its rivals' decisions and its decisions will affect its rivals. Firms recognise this interdependence and take it into account when making decisions.

Internal expansion Where a business adds to its productive capacity by adding to existing or by building new plant.

Internal funds Funds used for business expansion that come from ploughed-back profit.

Internal rate of return (IRR) The rate of return of an investment: the discount rate that makes the net present value of an investment equal to zero.

Internalisation advantages Where the benefits of extending the organisational structure of the MNC by setting up an overseas subsidiary are greater than the costs of arranging a contract with an external party.

International harmonisation of economic policies Where countries attempt to co-ordinate their macroeconomic policies so as to achieve common goals.

International liquidity The supply of currencies in the world acceptable for financing international trade and investment.

International trade multiplier The impact of changing levels of international demand on levels of production and output.

Inter-temporal pricing Where the price a firm charges for a product varies over time. It occurs where the price elasticity of demand for a product varies at different points in time.

Investment The purchase by the firm of equipment or materials that will add to its stock of capital.

Irrational exuberance Where banks and other economic agents are over confident about the economy and/or financial markets and expect economic growth to remain stronger and/or asset prices to rise further than warranted by evidence.

Joint-stock company A company where ownership is distributed between a large number of shareholders.

Joint venture Where two or more firms set up and jointly own a new independent firm.

Just-in-time methods Where a firm purchases supplies and produces both components and finished products as they are required. This minimises stock holding and its associated costs.

Kinked demand theory The theory that oligopolists face a demand curve that is kinked at the current price: demand being significantly more elastic above the current price than below. The effect of this is to create a situation of price stability.

Knowledge spillover The capture by third parties of benefits from the development by others of new ideas, for example, new products, processes and technologies.

Labour All forms of human input, both physical and mental, into current production.

Labour force The number employed plus the number unemployed.

Labour productivity Output per unit of labour: for example, output per worker or output per hour worked.

Laissez-faire economy A free-market economy where all economic decisions are taken by individual households and firms, with no government intervention.

Land (and raw materials) Inputs into production that are provided by nature, e.g. unimproved land and mineral deposits in the ground.

Law of comparative advantage Trade can benefit all countries if they specialise in the goods in which they have a comparative advantage.

Law of demand The quantity of a good demanded per period of time will fall as the price rises and rise as the price falls, other things being equal (*ceteris paribus*).

Law of diminishing (marginal) returns When one or more factors are held fixed, there will come a point beyond which the extra output from additional units of the variable factor will diminish.

Law of large numbers The larger the number of events of a particular type, the more predictable will be their average or expected outcome.

Leading indicators Indicators that help predict future trends in the economy.

Lender of last resort The role of the Bank of England as the guarantor of sufficient liquidity in the monetary system.

Leverage The extent to which a company relies upon debt finance as opposed to equity finance.

Liability Claims by others on an individual or institution; debts of that individual or institution.

Licensing Where the owner of a patented product allows another firm to produce it for a fee.

Limit pricing Where a business strategically sets its price below the level that would maximise its profits in the short run in an attempt to deter new rivals entering the market.

This enables the firm to make greater profits in the long run.

Liquidity The ease with which an asset can be converted into cash without loss.

Liquidity ratio The proportion of a bank's total assets held in liquid form.

Liquidity trap When interest rates are at their floor and thus any further increases in money supply will not be spent but merely be held in idle balances as people wait for the economy to recover and/or interest rates to rise.

Locational advantages Those features of a host economy that MNCs believe will lower costs, improve quality and/or facilitate greater sales.

Lock-outs Union members are temporarily laid off until they are prepared to agree to the firm's conditions.

Logistics The process of managing the supply of inputs to a firm and the outputs from a firm to its customers.

Long run The period of time long enough for *all* factors to be varied.

Long run under perfect competition The period of time that is long enough for new firms to enter the industry.

Long-run average cost (*LRAC*) curve A curve that shows how average cost varies with output on the assumption that *all* factors are variable. (It is assumed that the least-cost method of production will be chosen for each output.)

Long-run profit maximisation An alternative theory that assumes that managers aim to shift cost and revenue curves so as to maximise profits over some longer time period.

Long-run shut-down point This is where the *AR* curve is tangential to the *LRAC* curve. The firm can just make normal profits. Any fall in revenue below this level will cause a profit-maximising firm to shut down once all costs have become variable.

Loss aversion Where a loss is disliked far more than the pleasure associated from an equivalent sized gain. This dislike of losses is far greater than that predicted by standard economic theory.

Loss leader A product whose price is cut by the business in order to attract custom.

Macro-prudential regulation Regulation that focuses on the financial system as a whole and that monitors its impact on the wider economy and ensures that it is resilient to shocks.

Macroeconomics The branch of economics that studies economic aggregates (grand totals), for example the overall level of prices, output and employment in the economy.

Managed flexibility (dirty floating) A system of flexible exchange rates, but where the government intervenes to prevent excessive fluctuations or even to achieve an unofficial target exchange rate.

Managerial utility maximisation An alternative theory that assumes that managers are motivated by self-interest. They will adopt whatever policies are perceived to maximise their own utility.

Margin squeeze Where a vertically integrated firm with a dominant position in an upstream market deliberately charges high prices for an input required by firms in a downstream market to drive them out of business.

Marginal benefits The additional benefits of doing a little bit more (or *1 unit* more if a unit can be measured) of an activity.

Marginal capital-output ratio The amount of extra capital (in money terms) required to produce a £1 increase in national output. Since $I_i = \Delta K$, the marginal capital/output ratio $\Delta K/\Delta Y$ equals the accelerator coefficient (α).

Marginal consumer surplus The excess of utility from the consumption of one more unit of a good (MU) over the price paid: $MCS = MU - P$.

Marginal cost (*MC*) The cost of producing one more unit of output: $MC = \Delta TC/\Delta Q$.

Marginal cost of capital The cost of one additional unit of capital.

Marginal costs The additional cost of doing a little bit more (or *1 unit* more if a unit can be measured) of an activity.

Marginal disutility of work The extra sacrifice/hardship to a worker of working an extra unit of time in any given time period (e.g. an extra hour per day).

Marginal efficiency of capital (MEC) or internal rate of return (IRR) The rate of return of an investment: the discount rate that makes the net present value of an investment equal to zero.

Marginal physical product (*MPP*) The extra output gained by the employment of one more unit of the variable factor: $MPP = \Delta TPP/\Delta Qv$.

Marginal productivity theory The theory that the demand for a factor depends on its marginal revenue product.

Marginal propensity to consume The proportion of a rise in national income (Y) that is spent on goods and services by households and non-profit institutions serving households.

Marginal propensity to consume domestically produced goods and services The fraction of a rise in national income (Y) that is spent on domestic product (C_d) and hence is not withdrawn from the circular flow of income: $mpc_d = \Delta C_d/\Delta Y$.

Marginal propensity to consume from disposable income The proportion of a rise in disposable income that is spent on goods and services by households and non-profit institutions serving households.

Marginal revenue The extra revenue gained by selling one or more unit per time period: $MR = \Delta TR/\Delta Q$.

Marginal revenue product of capital The additional revenue earned from employing one additional unit of capital.

Marginal revenue product of labour The extra revenue a firm earns from employing one more unit of labour.

Marginal utility The extra satisfaction gained from consuming one extra unit of a good within a given time period.

Market The interaction between buyers and sellers.

Market clearing A market clears when supply matches demand, leaving no shortage or surplus. The market is in equilibrium.

Market demand schedule A table showing the different total quantities of a good that consumers are willing and able to buy at various prices over a given time period.

Market experiments Information gathered about consumers under artificial or simulated conditions. A method used widely in assessing the effects of advertising on consumers.

Market loans Loans made to other financial institutions.

Market niche A part of a market (or new market) that has not been filled by an existing brand or business.

Market segment A part of a market for a product where the demand is for a particular variety of that product.

Market surveys Information gathered about consumers, usually via a questionnaire, that attempts to enhance the business's understanding of consumer behaviour.

Marketing mix The mix of product, price, place (distribution) and promotion that will determine a business's marketing strategy.

Mark-up pricing A pricing strategy adopted by business in which a profit mark-up is added to average costs.

Maturity gap The difference in the average maturity of loans and deposits.

Maturity transformation The transformation of deposits into loans of a longer maturity.

Maximum price A price ceiling set by the government or some other agency. The price is not allowed to rise above this level (although it is allowed to fall below it).

Medium of exchange Something that is acceptable in exchange for goods and services.

Menu costs of inflation The costs associated with having to adjust price lists or labels.

Merger The outcome of a mutual agreement made by two firms to combine their business activities.

Merit goods Goods that the government feels that people will under-consume and therefore ought to be subsidised or provided free.

M-form business organisation One in which the business is organised into separate departments, such that responsibility for the day-to-day management enterprise is separated from the formulation of the business's strategic plan.

Microeconomics The branch of economics that studies individual units (e.g. households, firms and industries). It studies the interrelationships between these units in determining the pattern of production and distribution of goods and services.

Minimum efficient scale (MES) The size of the individual factory or of the whole firm, beyond which no significant additional economies of scale can be gained. For an individual factory the MES is known as the *minimum efficient plant size* (MEPS).

Minimum price A price floor set by the government or some other agency. The price is not allowed to fall below this level (although it is allowed to rise above it).

Minimum reserve ratio A minimum ratio of cash (or other specified liquid assets) to deposits (either total or selected) that the central bank requires banks to hold.

Minsky moment A turning point in a credit cycle, where a period of easy credit and rising debt is replaced by one of tight credit and debt consolidation.

Mixed economy An economy where economic decisions are made partly through the market and partly by the government.

Mobility of labour The ease with which labour can either shift between jobs (occupational mobility) or move to other parts of the country in search of work (geographical mobility).

Monetary base Notes and coin in circulation, i.e. outside the central bank.

Monetary financial institutions (MFIs) Deposit-taking financial institutions including banks, building societies and central banks.

Money market The market for short-term loans and deposits.

Money multiplier The number of times greater the expansion of money supply (M_s) is than the expansion of the monetary base (M_b) that caused it: $\Delta M_s / \Delta M_b$.

Monopolistic competition A market structure where, like perfect competition, there are many firms and freedom of entry into the industry, but where each firm produces a differentiated product and thus has some control over its price.

Monopoly A market structure where there is only one firm in the industry.

Monopsony A market with a single buyer or employer.

Moral hazard Where one party to a transaction has an incentive to behave in a way that reduces the pay-off to the other party. The temptation to take more risks when you know that someone else will cover the risks if you get into difficulties. In the case of banks taking risks, the 'someone else' may be another bank, the central bank or the government.

Multinational corporations Businesses that own or control foreign subsidiaries in more than one country.

Multiplier The number of times a rise in GDP (ΔY) is bigger than the initial rise in aggregate expenditure (ΔE) that caused it. Using the letter k to stand for the multiplier, the multiplier is defined as: $k = \Delta Y / \Delta E$.

Multiplier effect An initial increase in aggregate demand of £xm leads to an eventual rise in national income that is greater than £xm.

Multiplier formula The formula for the multiplier is: $k = 1/(1 - mpc_d)$.

Mutual recognition The EU principle that one country's rules and regulations must apply throughout the Union. If they conflict with those of another country, individuals and firms should be able to choose which to obey.

Nash equilibrium The position resulting from everyone making their optimal decision based on their assumptions about their rivals' decisions. Without collusion, there is no incentive for any firm to move from this position.

National debt The accumulated deficits of central government. It is the total amount owed by central government, both domestically and internationally.

Nationalised industries State-owned industries that produce goods or services that are sold in the market.

Natural monopoly A situation where long-run average costs would be lower if an industry were under monopoly than if it were shared between two or more competitors.

Natural rate hypothesis The theory that, following fluctuations in aggregate demand, unemployment will return to a natural rate. This rate is determined by supply-side factors, such as labour mobility.

Natural rate of unemployment or **non-accelerating-inflation rate of unemployment (NAIRU)** The rate of unemployment consistent with a constant rate of inflation; the rate of unemployment at which the vertical long-run Phillips curve cuts the horizontal axis.

Net errors and omissions A statistical adjustment to ensure that the two sides of the balance of payments account balance. It is necessary because of errors in compiling the statistics.

Net national income (NNY) GNY minus depreciation.

Net present value (NPV) of an investment The discounted benefits of an investment minus the cost of the investment.

Network The establishment of formal and informal multi-firm alliances across sectors.

Network economies The benefits to consumers of having a network of other people using the same product or service.

Net worth The market value of a sector's stock of financial and non-financial wealth.

Nominal GDP GDP measured in current prices. These figures take no account of the effect of inflation.

Non-bank private sector Household and non-bank firms. The category thus excludes the government and banks.

Non-collusive oligopoly When oligopolists have no agreement between themselves – formal, informal or tacit.

Non-excludability Where it is unfeasible or simply too costly to implement a system that would, effectively, prevent people who have not paid from enjoying the benefits from consuming a good.

Non-price competition Competition in terms of product promotion (advertising, packaging, etc.) or product development.

Non-rivalry Where the consumption of a good or service by one person will not prevent others from enjoying it.

Normal goods Goods whose demand rises as people's incomes rise.

Normal profit The opportunity cost of being in business. It consists of the interest that could be earned on a riskless asset, plus a return for risk taking in this particular industry. It is counted as a cost of production.

Number unemployed (economist's definition) Those of working age who are without work, but who are available for work at current wage rates.

Numerical flexibility Where employers can change the size of their workforce as their labour requirements change.

Observations of market behaviour Information gathered about consumers from the day-to-day activities of the business within the market.

Oligopoly A market structure where there are few enough firms to enable barriers to be erected against the entry of new firms.

Oligopsony A market with just a few buyers (or employers in the case of labour markets).

Open-market operations The sale (or purchase) by the authorities of government securities in the open market in order to reduce (or increase) money supply and thereby affect interest rates.

Opportunity cost The cost of any activity measured in terms of the best alternative forgone.

Optimal currency area The optimal size of a currency area is one that maximises the benefits from having a single currency relative to the costs. If the area were to be increased or decreased in size, the costs would rise relative to the benefits.

Organisational slack When managers allow spare capacity to exist, thereby enabling them to respond more easily to changed circumstances.

Output gap Actual output minus potential output.

Outsourcing or subcontracting Where a firm employs another firm to produce part of its output or some of its input(s).

Overheads Costs arising from the general running of an organisation and only indirectly related to the level of output.

Ownership-specific assets Assets owned by the firm, such as technology, product differentiation and managerial skills, which reflect its core competencies.

Paradox of debt (or paradox of deleveraging) The paradox that one individual can increase his or her net worth by selling assets, but, if this is undertaken by a large number of people, aggregate net worth declines because asset prices fall.

Peak-load pricing The practice of charging higher prices at times when demand is highest because the constraints on capacity lead to higher marginal cost.

Perfect competition A market structure in which there are many firms; where there is freedom of entry to the industry; where all firms produce an identical product; and where all firms are price takers.

Perfectly competitive market (preliminary definition) A market in which all producers and consumers of the product are price takers. There are other features of a perfectly competitive market (these are examined in Chapter 11).

Perfectly contestable market A market where there is free and costless entry and exit.

PEST analysis Where the political, economic, social and technological factors shaping a business environment are assessed by a business so as to devise future business strategy.

Phillips curve A curve showing the relationship between (price) inflation and unemployment. The original Phillips curve plotted *wage* inflation against unemployment for the years 1861–1957.

Picketing Where people on strike gather at the entrance to the firm and attempt to dissuade workers or delivery vehicles from entering.

Planned or **command economy** An economy where all economic decisions are taken by the central (or local) authorities.

Plant economies of scale Economies of scale that arise because of the large size of the factory.

Policy ineffectiveness proposition The conclusion drawn from new classical models that, when economic agents anticipate changes in economic policy, output and employment remain at their equilibrium (or natural) levels.

Political business cycle The theory that governments will engineer an economic contraction, designed to squeeze out inflation, followed by a pre-election boom.

Potential growth The percentage annual increase in the output that would be produced if all firms were operating at their normal level of capacity utilisation.

Potential output The output that could be produced in the economy if all firms were operating at their normal level of capacity utilisation.

Poverty trap Where poor people are discouraged from working or getting a better job because any extra income they earn will be largely or entirely taken away in taxes and lost benefits.

Precautionary or **buffer-stock saving** Saving in response to uncertainty, for example uncertainty of future income.

Predatory pricing Where a firm sets its average price below average cost in order to drive competitors out of business.

Preferential trading arrangement A trading arrangement whereby trade between the signatories is freer than trade with the rest of the world.

Present bias Where the relative weight people place on immediate costs and benefits versus those that occur in the future is far greater than predicted by standard economic theory. This leads to time inconsistent behaviour.

Present value approach to appraising investment This involves estimating the value *now* of a flow of future benefits (or costs).

Price benchmark This is a price that typically is used. Firms, when raising prices, usually will raise them from one benchmark to another.

Price-cap regulation Where the regulator puts a ceiling on the amount by which a firm can raise its price.

Price discrimination Where a firm sells the same product at different prices and the difference in price cannot be fully accounted for by any differences in the costs of supply.

Price elasticity of demand The responsiveness of quantity demanded to a change in price: the proportionate change in quantity demanded divided by the proportionate change in price.

Price elasticity of supply The responsiveness of quantity supplied to a change in price: the proportionate change in quantity supplied divided by the proportionate change in price.

Price maker (price chooser) A firm that has the ability to influence the price charged for its good or service.

Price mechanism The system in a market economy whereby changes in price in response to changes in demand and supply have the effect of making demand equal to supply.

Price taker A person or firm with no power to be able to influence the market price.

Price to book ratio or Valuation ratio The ratio of stock market value to book value. The stock market value is an assessment of the firm's past and anticipated future performance. The book value is a calculation of the current value of the firm's assets.

Price-cap regulation Where the regulator puts a ceiling on the amount by which a firm can raise its price.

Primary labour market The market for permanent full-time core workers.

Primary market in capital Where shares are sold by the issuer of the shares (i.e. the firm) and where, therefore, finance is channelled directly from the purchasers (i.e. the shareholders) to the firm.

Primary production The production and extraction of natural resources, plus agriculture.

Primary surplus or **deficit** When public-sector receipts are greater (less) than public-sector expenditures *excluding* interest payments.

Principal–agent problem One where people (principals), as a result of lack of knowledge, cannot ensure that their best interests are served by their agents.

Principle of diminishing marginal utility As more units of a good are consumed, additional units will provide less additional satisfaction than previous units.

Prisoners' dilemma Where two or more firms (or people), by attempting independently to choose the best strategy, based upon what other(s) are likely to do, end up in a worse position than if they had co-operated from the start.

Producer surplus The difference between the minimum price required for a firm to supply a good and the price that is actually paid. Total producer surplus is the excess of firms' total revenue over total (variable) costs..

Product differentiation When one firm's product is sufficiently different from its rivals', it can raise the price of the product without customers all switching to the rivals' products. This gives a firm a downward-sloping demand curve.

Production The transformation of inputs into outputs by firms in order to earn profit (or meet some other objective).

Production externalities   Spillover effects on other people of firms' production.

Production function   The mathematical relationship between the output of a good and the inputs used to produce it. It shows how output will be affected by changes in the quantity of one or more of the inputs.

Productive efficiency   A situation where firms are producing the maximum output for a given amount of inputs, or producing a given output at the least cost.

Productivity deal   Where, in return for a wage increase, a union agrees to changes in working practices that will increase output per worker.

Productivity externalities   Where the productivity of an individual is affected by the average productivity of other individuals.

Profit satisficing   Where decision makers in a firm aim for a target level of profit rather than the absolute maximum level. By not aiming for the maximum profit, this allows managers to pursue other objectives, such as sales maximisation or their own salary or prestige.

Profit-maximising rule   Profit is maximised where marginal revenue equals marginal cost.

Prudential control   The insistence by the monetary authorities (e.g. the Bank of England) that banks maintain adequate liquidity.

Public good   A good or service that has the features of non-rivalry and non-excludability and, as a result, would not be provided by the free market.

Public-sector net borrowing (PSNB)   The difference between the expenditures of the public sector and its receipts from taxation, the revenues of public corporations and the sale of assets. If expenditures exceed receipts (a deficit), then the government has to borrow to make up the difference.

Public-sector net cash requirement (PSNCR)   The (annual) deficit of the public sector (central government, local government and public corporations) and thus the amount that the public sector must borrow.

Public-sector net debt   Gross public-sector debt minus liquid financial assets.

Pure public good   A good or service that has the features of being perfectly non-rivalrous and completely non-excludable and, as a result, would not be provided by the free market.

Pure fiscal policy   Fiscal policy that does not involve any change in money supply.

Quantitative easing   When the central bank increases the monetary base through an open market purchase of government bonds or other securities. It uses electronic money (reserve liabilities) created specifically for this purpose.

Quantity demanded   The amount of a good that a consumer is willing and able to buy at a given price over a given period of time.

Quantity supplied   The amount of a good that a firm is willing and able to sell at a given price over a given period of time.

Quantity theory of money   The price level (P) is directly related to the quantity of money in the economy (M).

Quota (set by a cartel)   The output that a given member of a cartel is allowed to produce (production quota) or sell (sales quota).

Random walk   Where fluctuations in the value of a share away from its 'correct' value are random, i.e. have no systematic pattern. When charted over time, these share price movements would appear like a 'random walk' – like the path of someone staggering along drunk!

Rate of discount   The rate that is used to reduce future values to present values.

Rate of economic growth   The percentage increase in output, normally expressed over a 12-month period.

Rate of inflation (annual)   The percentage increase in the level of prices over a 12-month period.

Rate of return approach   The benefits from investment are calculated as a percentage of the costs of investment. This rate is then compared to the rate at which money has to be borrowed in order to see whether the investment should be undertaken.

Rational choices   Choices that involve weighing up the benefit of any activity against its opportunity cost.

Rational consumer behaviour   The attempt to maximise total consumer surplus.

Rational expectations   Expectations based on the *current* situation. These expectations are based on the information people have to hand. While this information may be imperfect and therefore people will make errors, these errors will be random.

Rationalisation   The reorganising of production (often after a merger) so as to cut out waste and duplication and generally to reduce costs.

Real business cycle theory   The new classical theory that explains cyclical fluctuations in terms of shifts in aggregate supply, rather than aggregate demand.

Real exchange rate index (RERI)   The nominal exchange rate index (NERI) adjusted for changes in the relative prices of exports and imports: $\text{RERI} = \text{NERI} \times P_X/P_M$.

Real GDP   GDP measured in constant prices that ruled in a chosen base year, such as 2000 or 2015. These figures *do* take account the effect of inflation. When inflation is positive, real GDP figures will grow more slowly than nominal GDP figures.

Real growth values   Values of the rate of growth of GDP or any other variable after taking inflation into account. The real value of the growth in a variable equals its growth in money (or 'nominal') value minus the rate of inflation.

Recession   A period where national output falls for a few months or more. The official definition is where real GDP declines for two or more consecutive quarters.

Recessionary or deflationary gap   The shortfall of aggregate expenditure below GDP at the full-employment level of GDP.

Reciprocity (in economics)   Where people's preferences depend on the kind or unkind behaviour of others.

Rediscounting bills of exchange Buying bills before they reach maturity.

Reference dependent preferences Where people value (or 'code') outcomes as either gains or losses in relation to a reference point.

Regional Development Agencies (RDAs) Nine agencies, based in English regions, which initiate and administer regional policy within their area.

Regional multiplier effects When a change in injections into or withdrawals from a particular region causes a multiplied change in income in that region. The regional multiplier is given by $1/(1 - mpc_r)$, where mpc_r is the marginal propensity to consume products from the region.

Regional unemployment Structural unemployment occurring in specific regions of the country.

Regression analysis A statistical technique that shows how one variable is related to one or more other variables.

Regulatory capture Where the regulator is persuaded to operate in the industry's interests rather than those of the consumer.

Replacement costs What the firm would have to pay to replace factors it currently owns.

Repo Short for 'sale and repurchase agreement'. An agreement between two financial institutions whereby one in effect borrows from another by selling it assets, agreeing to buy them back (repurchase them) at a fixed price and on a fixed date.

Resale price maintenance Where the manufacturer of a product (legally) insists that the product should be sold at a specified retail price.

Reserve capacity A range of output over which business costs will tend to remain relatively constant.

Restrictive practices Where two or more firms agree to engage in activities that restrict competition.

Retail banking Branch, telephone, postal and Internet banking for individuals and businesses at published rates of interest and charges. Retail banking involves the operation of extensive branch networks.

Reverse repos When gilts or other assets are *purchased* under a sale and repurchase agreement. They become an asset of the purchaser.

Risk This is when an outcome may or may not occur, but where its probability of occurring is known.

Risk premium The expected value of a gamble minus a person's certainty equivalent.

Risk transformation The process whereby banks can spread the risks of lending by having a large number of borrowers.

Sale and repurchase agreements (repos) An agreement between two financial institutions whereby one, in effect, borrows from another by selling its assets, agreeing to buy them back (repurchase them) at a fixed price and on a fixed date.

Sales revenue maximisation An alternative theory of the firm that assumes that managers aim to maximise the firm's short-run total revenue.

Savings gap The shortfall in savings to achieve a given rate of economic growth.

Scarcity The excess of human wants over what can actually be produced to fulfil these wants.

Seasonal unemployment Unemployment associated with industries or regions where the demand for labour is lower at certain times of the year.

Secondary action Industrial action taken against a firm not directly involved in the dispute.

Secondary labour market The market for peripheral workers, usually employed on a temporary or part-time basis or a less secure 'permanent' basis.

Secondary market in capital Where shareholders sell shares to others. This is thus a market in 'second-hand' shares.

Secondary marketing Where assets are sold before maturity to another institution or individual.

Secondary production The production from manufacturing and construction sectors of the economy.

Second-degree price discrimination Where a firm offers consumers a range of different pricing options for the same or similar product. Consumers are then free to choose whichever option they wish, but the lower prices are conditional on some other aspect of the sale such as the quantity or the exact version of the product purchased.

Securitisation Where future cash flows (e.g. from interest rate or mortgage payments) are turned into marketable securities, such as bonds.

Self-fulfilling speculation The actions of speculators tend to cause the very effect that they had anticipated.

Semi-strong efficiency (of share markets) Where share prices adjust quickly, fully and accurately to publicly available information.

Sensitivity analysis Assesses how sensitive an outcome is to different variables within an equation.

Services balance Exports of services minus imports of services.

Short run The period of time over which at least one factor is fixed.

Short run under perfect competition The period during which there is too little time for new firms to enter the industry.

Short-run shut-down point This is where the *AR* curve is tangential to the *AVC* curve. The firm can only just cover its variable costs. Any fall in revenue below this level will cause a profit-maximising firm to shut down immediately.

Short-termism Where firms and investors take decisions based on the likely short-term performance of a company, rather than on its long-term prospects. Thus, firms may sacrifice long-term profits and growth for the sake of quick return.

Sight deposits Deposits that can be withdrawn on demand without penalty.

Single-move or one-shot games Where each player (e.g. each firm) makes just one decision (or move) and then the 'game' is over.

Simultaneous game   Where each player (e.g. each firm) makes its decision at the same time and is therefore unable to respond to other players' moves.

Social benefit   Private benefit plus consumption externalities.

Social cost   Private cost plus production externalities.

Social efficiency   Production and consumption at the point where $MSB = MSC$.

Social responsibility   Where a firm takes into account the interests and concerns of a community rather than just its shareholders.

Social-impact standards   Pollution control that focuses on the effects on people (e.g. on health or happiness).

Special purpose vehicle (SPV)   Legal entities created by financial institutions for conducting specific financial functions, such as bundling assets together into fixed-interest bonds and selling them.

Specialisation and division of labour   Where production is broken down into a number of simpler, more specialised tasks, thus allowing workers to acquire a high degree of efficiency.

Speculation   This is where people make buying or selling decisions based on their anticipations of future prices.

Spot price   The current market price.

Spreading risks (for an insurance company)   The more policies an insurance company issues and the more independent the risks of claims from these policies are, the more predictable will be the number of claims.

Stabilising speculation   This is where the actions of speculators tend to reduce price fluctuations.

Stakeholders (in a company)   People who are affected by a company's activities and/or performance (customers, employees, owners, creditors, people living in the neighbourhood, etc.). They may or may not be in a position to take decisions, or influence decision taking, in the firm.

Standard Industrial Classification (SIC)   The name given to the formal classification of firms into industries used by the government in order to collect data on business and industry trends.

Standardised unemployment rate   The measure of the unemployment rate used by the ILO and OECD. The unemployed are defined as people of working age who are without work, available for work and actively seeking employment.

STEEPLE analysis   Where the social, technological, economic, environmental, political, legal and ethical factors shaping a business environment are assessed by a business so as to devise future business strategy.

Sterilisation   Actions taken by a central bank to offset the effects of foreign exchange flows or its own bond transactions so as to leave money supply unchanged.

Stock   The quantity of something held.

Strategic alliance   Where two or more firms work together, formally or informally, to achieve a mutually desirable goal.

Strategic management   The management of the strategic long-term activities of the business, which includes strategic analysis, strategic choice and strategic implementation.

Strategic trade theory   The theory that protecting/supporting certain industries can enable them to compete more effectively with large monopolistic rivals abroad. The effect of the protection is to increase long-run competition and may enable the protected firms to exploit a comparative advantage that they could not have done otherwise.

Strong efficiency (of share markets)   Where share prices adjust quickly, fully and accurately to all available information, both public and that available only to insiders.

Structural deficit or **surplus**   The public-sector deficit (or surplus) that would occur if the economy were operating at the potential level of national income: i.e. one where there is a zero output gap.

Structural unemployment   Unemployment that arises from changes in the pattern of demand or supply in the economy. People made redundant in one part of the economy cannot immediately take up jobs in other parts (even though there are vacancies).

Subcontracting   The business practice where various forms of labour (frequently specialist) are hired for a given period of time. Such workers are not directly employed by the hiring business, but either employed by a third party or self-employed.

Sub-prime debt   Debt where there is a high risk of default by the borrower (e.g. mortgage holders who are on low incomes facing higher interest rates and falling house prices).

Substitute goods   A pair of goods that are considered by consumers to be alternatives to each other. As the price of one goes up, the demand for the other rises.

Substitutes in supply   These are two goods where an increased production of one means diverting resources.

Substitution effect   The effect of a change in price on quantity demanded arising from the consumer switching to or from alternative (substitute) products.

Substitution effect of a rise in wages   Workers will tend to substitute income for leisure as leisure now has a higher opportunity cost. This effect leads to *more* hours being worked as wages rise.

Sunk costs   Costs that cannot be recouped (e.g. by transferring assets to other uses).

Supernormal profit (also known as **pure profit, economic profit, abnormal profit** or **simply profit**)   The excess of total profit above normal profit.

Supply curve   A graph showing the relationship between the price of a good and the quantity of the good supplied over a given time period.

Supply schedule   A table showing the different quantities of a good that producers are willing and able to supply at various prices over a given time period. A supply schedule can be for an individual producer or group of producers, or for all producers (the market supply schedule).

Supply: change in supply   The term used for a shift in the supply curve. It occurs when a determinant other than price changes.

Supply: change in the quantity supplied   The term used for a movement along the supply curve to a new point. It occurs when there is a change in price.

Supply-side economics   An approach that focuses directly on aggregate supply and how to shift the aggregate supply curve outwards.

Supply-side policy   Government policy that attempts to alter the level of aggregate supply directly rather than through aggregate demand.

Switching costs   The costs to a consumer of switching to an alternative supplier

Tacit collusion   When oligopolists follow unwritten 'rules' of collusive behaviour, such as price leadership. They will take care not to engage in price cutting, excessive advertising or other forms of competition.

Takeover   Where one business acquires another. A takeover may not necessarily involve mutual agreement between the two parties. In such cases, the takeover might be viewed as 'hostile'.

Takeover bid   Where one firm attempts to purchase another by offering to buy the shares of that company from its shareholders.

Takeover constraint   The effect that the fear of being taken over has on a firm's willingness to undertake projects that reduce distributed profits.

Tapered vertical integration   Where a firm is partially integrated with an earlier stage of production; where it produces *some* of an input itself and buys some from another firm.

Taylor rule   A rule adopted by a central bank for setting the rate of interest. It will raise the interest rate if (a) inflation is above target or (b) economic growth is above the sustainable level (or unemployment is below the equilibrium rate). The rule states how much interest rates will be changed in each case.

Technical or productive efficiency   The least-cost combination of factors for a given output.

Technological unemployment   Structural unemployment that occurs as a result of the introduction of labour-saving technology.

Technology policy   Involves government initiatives to affect the process and rate of technological change.

Technology transfer   Where a host state benefits from the new technology that an MNC brings with its investment.

Technology-based standards   Pollution control that requires firms' emissions to reflect the levels that could be achieved from using the best available pollution control technology.

Telecommuting   Working from home or locally and being linked to work via the Internet.

Terms of trade   The price index of exports divided by the price index of imports and then expressed as a percentage. This means that the terms of trade will be 100 in the base year.

Tertiary production   The production from the service sector of the economy.

Third-degree price discrimination   Where a firm divides consumers into different groups based on some characteristic that is relatively easy to observe, legal, informative about their willingness to pay and acceptable. The firm then charges a different price to consumers in different groups, but the same price to all the consumers within a group.

Tie-in-sales   Where a firm is only prepared to sell a first product on the condition that its customers buy a second product from it.

Time consistency   Where a person's preferences remain the same over time. If they plan to do something in the future, such as change energy supplier, they do so when the time arrives.

Time deposits   Deposits that require notice of withdrawal or where a penalty is charged for withdrawals on demand.

Time-series data   Information depicting how a variable (e.g. the price of eggs) changes over time.

Tit-for-tat strategy   Where a firm will cut prices, or make some other aggressive move, *only* if the rival does so first. If the rival knows this, it will be less likely to make an initial aggressive move.

Total (sales) revenue (*TR*)   The amount a firm earns from its sales of a product at a particular price: $TR = P * Q$. Note that we are referring to *gross* revenue; that is, revenue before the deduction of taxes or any other costs.

Total consumer surplus   The excess of a person's total utility from the consumption of a good (*TU*) over the amount that person spends on it (*TE*): $TCS = TU - TE$.

Total cost (*TC*)   The sum of total fixed costs (*TFC*) and total variable costs (*TVC*): $TC = TFC + TVC$.

Total physical product   The total output of a product per period of time that is obtained from a given amount of inputs.

Total revenue   A firm's total earnings from a specified level of sales within a specified period: $TR = P * Q$.

Total utility   The total satisfaction a consumer gets from the consumption of all the units of a good consumed within a given time period.

Tradable permits   Firms are issued or sold permits by the authorities that give them the right to produce a given level of pollutants. Firms that do not have permits to match their emission levels can purchase additional permits to cover the difference from firms that have spare permits, while those that reduce their emission levels can sell any surplus permits for a profit.

Trade creation   Where a customs union leads to greater specialisation according to comparative advantage and thus a shift in production from higher-cost to lower-cost sources.

Trade diversion   Where a customs union diverts consumption from goods produced at a lower cost outside the union to goods produced at a higher cost (but tariff free) within the union.

Tragedy of the commons   When resources are commonly available at no charge, people are likely to overexploit them.

Transactions costs The costs incurred when firms buy inputs or services from other firms as opposed to producing them themselves. They include the costs of searching for the best firm to do business with, the costs of drawing up, monitoring and enforcing contracts and the costs of transporting and handling products between the firms.

Transfer payments Moneys transferred from one person or group to another (e.g. from the government to individuals) without production taking place.

Transfer pricing The pricing system used within a business organisation to transfer intermediate products between the business's various divisions.

Transfers Transfers of money from taxpayers to recipients of benefits and subsidies. They are not an injection into the circular flow but are the equivalent of a negative tax (i.e. a negative withdrawal).

Transnational association A form of business organisation in which the subsidiaries of a company in different countries are contractually bound to the parent company to provide output to or receive inputs from other subsidiaries.

Transnational Index An index of the global presence of multinational corporations (MNCs) based on the ratios of foreign assets to total assets, foreign sales to total sales and foreign employment to total employment.

Two-part tariff A pricing system that requires customers to pay an access and a usage price for a product.

Tying Where a firm is prepared to sell a first product (the tying good) only on the condition that its consumers buy a second product from it (the tied good).

U-form business organisation One in which the central organisation of the firm (the chief executive or a managerial team) is responsible both for the firm's day-to-day administration and for formulating its business strategy.

Uncertainty This is when an outcome may or may not occur and where its probability of occurring is not known.

Underemployment When people work fewer hours than they would like at their current wage rate. *International Labour Organisation (ILO) definition*: a situation where people currently working less than 'full time' (40 hours in the UK) would like to work more hours (at current wage rates), either by working more hours in their current job, or by switching to an alternative job with more hours or by taking on an additional part-time job or any combination of the three. *Eurostat definition*: where people working less than 40 hours per week would like to work more hours in their current job at current wage rates.

Unemployed (number) (economist's definition) Those of working age who are without work, but who are available for work at current wage rates.

Unemployment The number of people who are actively looking for work but are currently without a job. (Note that there is much debate as to who should be counted as officially unemployed.)

Unemployment rate The number unemployed expressed as a percentage of the labour force.

Unit elasticity When the price elasticity of demand is unity, this is where quantity demanded changes by the same proportion as the price. Price elasticity is equal to 1.

Valuation ratio or **price to book ratio** The ratio of stock market value to book value. The stock market value is an assessment of the firm's past and anticipated future performance. The book value is a calculation of the current value of the firm's assets.

Value chain The stages or activities that help to create product value.

Variable costs Total costs that do vary with the amount of output produced.

Variable factor An input that *can* be increased in supply within a given time period.

Velocity of circulation The number of times annually that money on average is spent on goods and services that make up GDP.

Vertical integration A business growth strategy that involves expanding within an existing market, but at a different stage of production. Vertical integration can be 'forward', such as moving into distribution or retail, or 'backward', such as expanding into extracting raw materials or producing components.

Vertical merger Where two firms in the same industry at different stages in the production process merge.

Vertical product differentiation Where a firm's product differs from its rivals' products with respect to quality.

Vertical restraints Conditions imposed by one firm on another which is either its supplier or its customer.

Vertical strategic alliance A formal or informal arrangement between firms operating at different stages of an activity to jointly provide a product or service.

Vertically integrated multinational A multinational that undertakes the various stages of production for a given product in different countries.

Wage taker The wage rate is determined by market forces.

Weak efficiency (of share markets) Where share dealing prevents cyclical movements in shares.

Weighted average The average of several items where each item is ascribed a weight according to its importance. The weights must add up to 1.

Wholesale banking Where banks deal in large-scale deposits and loans, mainly with companies and other banks and financial institutions. Interest rates and charges may be negotiable.

Wholesale deposits and loans Large-scale deposits and loans made by and to firms at negotiated interest rates.

Withdrawals (*W*) (or leakages) Incomes of households or firms that are not passed on round the inner flow. Withdrawals equal net saving (*S*) plus net taxes (*T*) plus import expenditure (*M*): $W = S + T + M$.

Working to rule Workers do no more than they are supposed to, as set out in their job descriptions.

Yield on a share The dividend received per share expressed as a percentage of the current market price of the share.

Index